Ba

America
Reads

Edmund James Farrell *Assistant Executive Secretary, National Council of Teachers of English. Formerly Supervisor of Secondary English, University of California, Berkeley; formerly English Department Chairman, James Lick High School, San Jose, California.*

John Pfordresher *Assistant Professor of English, University of New Hampshire, Durham. Editor,* Variorum Edition of The Idylls of the King, *Columbia University Press.*

Thomas E. Gage *Consultant in English and Reading, Mt. Diablo Unified School District, Concord, California. Formerly Chairman of English Department, Concord High School, Concord, California; formerly Chairman of the Humanities Department, Fremont High School, Oakland, California.*

Raymond J. Rodrigues *Teacher of English, Robertson High School, Las Vegas, New Mexico. Formerly teacher of English, Edward W. Clark High School, Las Vegas, Nevada; formerly President, Southern Nevada Teachers of English.*

Exploring Life
through
Literature

Scott, Foresman and Company • Glenview, Illinois
Dallas, Tex. • Oakland, N.J. • Palo Alto, Cal. • Tucker, Ga. • Brighton, England

Edmund James Farrell
Thomas E. Gage
John Pfordresher
Raymond J. Rodrigues

ISBN: 0-673-10210-6

2345678910-VHJ-85848382818079787776

Two Plays 1

(1–73)

The
Short Story 2

(74–189)

 Poetry

(190–253)

4 Julius Caesar

(254 – 345)

(346-463)

Prose Forms 5

(464–569)

6

Medieval Tales and Legends

Three One-Act Plays 7

(570–603)

AUTHORS' CRAFTS

POETS' CRAFTS

SUPPLEMENTARY ARTICLES

Two Plays

TWELVE ANGRY MEN
AN ENEMY OF THE PEOPLE

Warren Linn

DESCRIPTIONS OF JURORS

FOREMAN
A small, petty man who is impressed with the authority he has and handles himself quite formally. Not overly bright, but dogged.

JUROR NUMBER TWO
A meek, hesitant man who finds it difficult to maintain any opinions of his own. Easily swayed and usually adopts the opinion of the last person to whom he has spoken.

JUROR NUMBER THREE
A very strong, very forceful, extremely opinionated man within whom can be detected a streak of sadism. A humorless man who is intolerant of opinions other than his own and accustomed to forcing his wishes and views upon others.

JUROR NUMBER FOUR
Seems to be a man of wealth and position. A practiced speaker who presents himself well at all times. Seems to feel a little bit above the rest of the jurors. His only concern is with the facts in this case, and he is appalled at the behavior of the others.

JUROR NUMBER FIVE
A naïve, very frightened young man who takes his obligations in this case very seriously, but who finds it difficult to speak up when his elders have the floor.

JUROR NUMBER SIX
An honest but dull-witted man who comes upon his decisions slowly and carefully. A man who finds it difficult to create positive opinions, but who must listen to and digest and accept those opinions offered by others which appeal to him most.

JUROR NUMBER SEVEN
A loud, flashy, glad-handed salesman type who has more important things to do than to sit on a jury. He is quick to show temper, quick to form opinions on things about which he knows nothing. Is a bully and, of course, a coward.

JUROR NUMBER EIGHT
A quiet, thoughtful, gentle man. A man who sees all sides of every question and constantly seeks the truth. A man of strength tempered with compassion. Above all, a man who wants justice to be done and will fight to see that it is.

JUROR NUMBER NINE
A mild, gentle old man, long since defeated by life and now merely waiting to die. A man who recognizes himself for what he is and mourns the days when it would have been possible to be courageous without shielding himself behind his many years.

JUROR NUMBER TEN
An angry, bitter man. A man who antagonizes almost at sight. A bigot who places no values on any human life save his own. A man who has been nowhere and is going nowhere and knows it deep within him.

JUROR NUMBER ELEVEN
A refugee from Europe who had come to this country in 1941. A man who speaks with an accent and who is ashamed, humble, almost subservient to the people around him, but who will honestly seek justice because he has suffered through so much injustice.

JUROR NUMBER TWELVE
A slick, bright advertising man who thinks of human beings in terms of percentages, graphs, and polls and has no real understanding of people. A superficial snob, but trying to be a good fellow.

Twelve Angry Men

Reginald Rose

Act One

Fade in[1] on a jury box. Twelve men are seated in it, listening intently to the voice of the JUDGE *as he charges them.[2] We do not see the* JUDGE. *He speaks in slow, measured tones and his voice is grave. The camera drifts over the faces of the* JURYMEN *as the* JUDGE *speaks and we see that most of their heads are turned to camera's left.* SEVEN *looks down at his hands.* THREE *looks off in another direction, the direction in which the defendant would be sitting.* TEN *keeps moving his head back and forth nervously. The* JUDGE *drones on.*

JUDGE. Murder in the first degree—premeditated homicide—is the most serious charge tried in our criminal courts. You've heard a long and complex case, gentlemen, and it is now your duty to sit down to try and separate the facts from the fancy. One man is dead. The life of another is at stake. If there is a reasonable doubt in your minds as to the guilt of the accused . . . then you must declare him not guilty. If, however, there is no reasonable doubt, then he must be found guilty. Whichever way you decide, the verdict must be unanimous. I urge you to deliberate honestly and thoughtfully. You are faced with a grave responsibility. Thank you, gentlemen.

(There is a long pause.)

CLERK *(droning).* The jury will retire.

(And now, slowly, almost hesitantly, the members of the jury begin to rise. Awkwardly, they file out of the jury box and off camera to the left. Camera holds on jury box, then fades out.)

(Fade in on a large, bare, unpleasant-looking room. This is the jury room in the county criminal court of a large Eastern city. It is about 4:00 P.M. The room is furnished with a long conference table and a dozen chairs. The walls are bare, drab, and badly in need of a fresh coat of paint. Along one wall is a row of windows which look out on the skyline of the city's financial district. High on another wall is an electric clock. A washroom opens off the jury room. In one corner of the room is a water fountain. On the table are pads, pencils, ashtrays. One of the windows is open. Papers blow across the table and onto the floor as the door opens. Lettered on the outside of the door are the words "Jury Room." A uniformed GUARD *holds the door open. Slowly, almost self-consciously, the twelve* JURORS *file in. The* GUARD *counts them as they enter the door, his lips moving, but no sound coming forth. Four or five of the* JURORS *light cigarettes as they enter the room.* FIVE *lights his pipe, which he smokes constantly throughout the play.* TWO *and* TWELVE *go to the water fountain,* NINE *goes into the washroom, the door of which is lettered "Men." Several of the* JURORS *take seats at the table. Others stand awkwardly around the room. Several look out the windows. These are men who are ill at ease, who do not really know each other to talk to, and who wish they were anywhere but here.* SEVEN, *standing at window, takes out a pack of gum, takes a piece, and offers it around. There are no takers. He mops his brow.)*

---

1. *Fade in.* This is one of several terms that indicate the way in which the television camera functions. When the camera "fades in," it gradually brings the picture into focus. When the camera "fades out," the picture disappears, leaving a blank screen.
2. *he charges them.* He tells them what their duties are as jurors.

Twelve Angry Men from SIX TELEVISION PLAYS by Reginald Rose. Reprinted by permission of International Famous Agency. Copyright © 1956 by Reginald Rose.

SEVEN (*to* SIX). Y'know something? It's hot. (SIX *nods.*) You'd think they'd at least air-condition the place. I almost dropped dead in court.

(SEVEN *opens the window a bit wider. The* GUARD *looks them over and checks his count. Then, satisfied, he makes ready to leave.*)

GUARD. Okay, gentlemen. Everybody's here. If there's anything you want, I'm right outside. Just knock. (*He exits, closing the door. Silently they all look at the door. We hear the lock clicking.*)

FIVE. I never knew they locked the door.

TEN (*blowing nose*). Sure, they lock the door. What did you think?

FIVE. I don't know. It just never occurred to me.

(*Some of the* JURORS *are taking off their jackets. Others are sitting down at the table. They still are reluctant to talk to each other.* FOREMAN *is at head of table, tearing slips of paper for ballots. Now we get a close shot of* EIGHT.[3] *He looks out the window. We hear* THREE *talking to* TWO.)

THREE. Six days. They should have finished it in two. Talk, talk, talk. Did you ever hear so much talk about nothing?

TWO (*nervously laughing*). Well . . . I guess . . . they're entitled.

THREE. Everybody gets a fair trial. (*He shakes his head.*) That's the system. Well, I suppose you can't say anything against it.

(TWO *looks at him nervously, nods, and goes over to water cooler. Cut to shot of* EIGHT *staring out window. Cut to table.[4]* SEVEN *stands at the table, putting out a cigarette.*)

SEVEN (*to* TEN). How did you like that business about the knife? Did you ever hear a phonier story?

TEN (*wisely*). Well, look, you've gotta expect that. You know what you're dealing with.

SEVEN. Yeah, I suppose. What's the matter, you got a cold?

TEN (*blowing*). A lulu. These hot-weather colds can kill you.

(SEVEN *nods sympathetically.*)

FOREMAN (*briskly*). All right, gentlemen. Let's take seats.

SEVEN. Right. This better be fast. I've got tickets to *The Seven Year Itch*[5] tonight. I must be the only

guy in the whole world who hasn't seen it yet. (*He laughs and sits down.*) Okay, your honor, start the show.

(*They all begin to sit down. The* FOREMAN *is seated at the head of the table.* EIGHT *continues to look out the window.*)

FOREMAN (*to* EIGHT). How about sitting down? (EIGHT *doesn't hear him.*) The gentleman at the window. (EIGHT *turns, startled.*)

FOREMAN. How about sitting down?

EIGHT. Oh, I'm sorry.

(*He heads for a seat.*)

TEN (*to* SIX). It's tough to figure, isn't it? A kid kills his father. Bing! Just like that. Well, it's the element. They let the kids run wild. Maybe it serves 'em right.

FOREMAN. Is everybody here?

TWELVE. The old man's inside.

(*The* FOREMAN *turns to the washroom just as the door opens.* NINE *comes out, embarrassed.*)

FOREMAN. We'd like to get started.

NINE. Forgive me, gentlemen. I didn't mean to keep you waiting.

FOREMAN. It's all right. Find a seat.

(NINE *heads for a seat and sits down. They look at the* FOREMAN *expectantly.*)

FOREMAN. All right. Now, you gentlemen can handle this any way you want to. I mean, I'm not going to make any rules. If we want to discuss it first and then vote, that's one way. Or we can vote right now to see how we stand.

SEVEN. Let's vote now. Who knows, maybe we can all go home.

TEN. Yeah. Let's see who's where.

THREE. Right. Let's vote now.

FOREMAN. Anybody doesn't want to vote?

(*He looks around the table. There is no answer.*) Okay, all those voting guilty raise your hands.

(*Seven or eight hands go up immediately. Several others go up more slowly. Everyone looks around the table. There are two hands not raised,* NINE's *and* EIGHT's. NINE's *hand goes up slowly now as the* FOREMAN *counts.*)

FOREMAN. . . . Nine . . . ten . . . eleven . . . That's eleven for guilty. Okay. Not guilty? (EIGHT's *hand is raised.*) One. Right. Okay. Eleven to one, guilty. Now we know where we are.

THREE. Somebody's in left field. (*To* EIGHT) You think he's not guilty?

EIGHT (*quietly*). I don't know.

---

3. *a close shot of Eight,* a head-and-shoulders view of *Eight.*
4. *Cut to shot of Eight. . . . Cut to table.* The word *cut* indicates an immediate switch from one camera to another camera in order to show what is happening on another part of the television stage.
5. *The Seven Year Itch,* a comedy that opened on Broadway in 1952.

THREE. I never saw a guiltier man in my life. You sat right in court and heard the same thing I did. The man's a dangerous killer. You could see it.

EIGHT. He's nineteen years old.

THREE. That's old enough. He knifed his own father. Four inches into the chest. An innocent little nineteen-year-old kid. They proved it a dozen different ways. Do you want me to list them?

EIGHT. No.

TEN (to EIGHT). Well, do you believe his story?

EIGHT. I don't know whether I believe it or not. Maybe I don't.

SEVEN. So what'd you vote not guilty for?

EIGHT. There were eleven votes for guilty. It's not so easy for me to raise my hand and send a boy off to die without talking about it first.

SEVEN. Who says it's easy for me?

EIGHT. No one.

SEVEN. What, just because I voted fast? I think the guy's guilty. You couldn't change my mind if you talked for a hundred years.

EIGHT. I don't want to change your mind. I just want to talk for a while. Look, this boy's been kicked around all his life. You know, living in a slum, his mother dead since he was nine. That's not a very good head start. He's a tough, angry kid. You know why slum kids get that way? Because we knock 'em on the head once a day, every day. I think maybe we owe him a few words. That's all. (He looks around the table. Some of them look back coldly. Some cannot look at him. Only NINE nods slowly. TWELVE doodles steadily. FOUR begins to comb his hair.)

TEN. I don't mind telling you this, mister. We don't owe him a thing. He got a fair trial, didn't he? You know what that trial cost? He's lucky he got it. Look, we're all grownups here. You're not going to tell us that we're supposed to believe him, knowing what he is I've lived among 'em all my life. You can't believe a word they say. You know that.

NINE (to TEN very slowly). I don't know that. What a terrible thing for a man to believe! Since when is dishonesty a group characteristic? You have no monopoly on the truth——

THREE (interrupting). All right. It's not Sunday. We don't need a sermon.

NINE. What this man says is very dangerous——
(EIGHT puts his hand on NINE's arm and stops him. Somehow his touch and his gentle expression calm the old man. He draws a deep breath and relaxes.)

FOUR. I don't see any need for arguing like this. I think we ought to be able to behave like gentlemen.

SEVEN. Right!

FOUR. If we're going to discuss this case, let's discuss the facts.

FOREMAN. I think that's a good point. We have a job to do. Let's do it.

ELEVEN (with accent). If you gentlemen don't mind, I'm going to close the window. (He gets up and does so.) (Apologetically) It was blowing on my neck. (TEN blows his nose fiercely.)

TWELVE. I may have an idea here. I'm just thinking out loud now, but it seems to me that it's up to us to convince this gentleman—(indicating EIGHT)—that we're right and he's wrong. Maybe if we each took a minute or two, you know, if we sort of try it on for size——

FOREMAN. That sounds fair enough. Supposing we go once around the table.

SEVEN. Okay, let's start it off.

FOREMAN. Right. (To TWO) I guess you're first.

TWO (timidly). Oh. Well . . . (Long pause) I just think he's guilty. I thought it was obvious. I mean nobody proved otherwise.

EIGHT (quietly). Nobody has to prove otherwise. The burden of proof is on the prosecution. The defendant doesn't have to open his mouth. That's in the Constitution. The Fifth Amendment.[6] You've heard of it.

TWO (flustered). Well, sure, I've heard of it. I know what it is. I . . . what I meant . . . well, anyway, I think he was guilty.

THREE. Okay, let's get to the facts. Number one, let's take the old man who lived on the second floor right underneath the room where the murder took place. At ten minutes after twelve on the night of the killing he heard loud noises in the upstairs apartment. He said it sounded like a fight. Then he heard the kid say to his father, "I'm gonna kill you." A second later he heard a body falling, and he ran to the door of his apartment, looked out, and saw the kid running down the stairs and out of the house. Then he called the police. They found the father with a knife in his chest.

FOREMAN. And the coroner fixed the time of death at around midnight.

---

6. *The Fifth Amendment,* the amendment that guarantees that a person on trial for a criminal offense cannot be forced to testify against himself.

THREE. Right. Now what else do you want?

FOUR. The boy's entire story is flimsy. He claimed he was at the movies. That's a little ridiculous, isn't it? He couldn't even remember what pictures he saw.

THREE. That's right. Did you hear that? *(To* FOUR*)* You're absolutely right.

TEN. Look, what about the woman across the street? If her testimony don't prove it, then nothing does.

TWELVE. That's right. She saw the killing, didn't she?

FOREMAN. Let's go in order.

TEN *(loud).* Just a minute. Here's a woman who's lying in bed and can't sleep. It's hot, you know. *(He gets up and begins to walk around, blowing his nose and talking.)* Anyway, she looks out the window, and right across the street she sees the kid stick the knife into his father. She's known the kid all his life. His window is right opposite hers, across the el tracks, and she swore she saw him do it.

EIGHT. Through the windows of a passing elevated train.

TEN. Okay. And they proved in court that you can look through the windows of a passing el train at night and see what's happening on the other side. They proved it.

EIGHT. I'd like to ask you something. How come you believed her? She's one of "them" too, isn't she?

(TEN walks over to EIGHT.)

TEN. You're a pretty smart fellow, aren't you?

FOREMAN *(rising).* Now take it easy.

(THREE gets up and goes to TEN.)

THREE. Come on. Sit down. *(He leads TEN back to his seat.)* What're you letting him get you all upset for? Relax.

(TEN and THREE sit down.)

FOREMAN. Let's calm down now. *(To FIVE)* It's your turn.

FIVE. I'll pass it.

FOREMAN. That's your privilege. *(To SIX)* How about you?

SIX *(slowly).* I don't know. I started to be convinced, you know, with the testimony from those people across the hall. Didn't they say something about an argument between the father and the boy around seven o'clock that night? I mean, I can be wrong.

ELEVEN. I think it was eight o'clock. Not seven.

EIGHT. That's right. Eight o'clock. They heard the father hit the boy twice and then saw the boy walk angrily out of the house. What does that prove?

SIX. Well, it doesn't exactly prove anything. It's just part of the picture. I didn't say it proved anything.

FOREMAN. Anything else?

SIX. No.

(SIX goes to the water fountain.)

FOREMAN *(to SEVEN).* All right. How about you?

SEVEN. I don't know, most of it's been said already. We can talk all day about this thing, but I think we're wasting our time. Look at the kid's record. At fifteen he was in reform school. He stole a car. He's been arrested for mugging. He was picked up for knife-fighting. I think they said he stabbed somebody in the arm. This is a very fine boy.

EIGHT. Ever since he was five years old his father beat him up regularly. He used his fists.

SEVEN. So would I! A kid like that.

THREE. You're right. It's the kids. The way they are— you know? They don't listen. *(Bitter)* I've got a kid. When he was eight years old he ran away from a fight. I saw him. I was so ashamed, I told him right out, "I'm gonna make a man out of you or I'm gonna bust you up into little pieces trying." When he was fifteen he hit me in the face. He's big, you know. I haven't seen him in three years. Rotten kid! You work your heart out. . . . *(Pause)* All right. Let's get on with it. *(Looks away embarrassed.)*

FOUR. We're missing the point here. This boy—let's say he's a product of a filthy neighborhood and a broken home. We can't help that. We're not here to go into the reasons why slums are breeding grounds for criminals. They are. I know it. So do you. The children who come out of slum backgrounds are potential menaces to society.

TEN. You said it there. I don't want any part of them, believe me.

(There is a dead silence for a moment, and then FIVE speaks haltingly.)

FIVE. I've lived in a slum all my life——

TEN. Oh, now wait a second!

FIVE. I used to play in a back yard that was filled with garbage. Maybe it still smells on me.

FOREMAN. Now let's be reasonable. There's nothing personal——*(FIVE stands up.)*

FIVE. There is something personal!

(Then he catches himself and, seeing everyone looking at him, sits down, fists clenched.)

THREE (*persuasively*). Come on, now. He didn't mean you, feller. Let's not be so sensitive. . . . (*There is a long pause.*)

ELEVEN. I can understand this sensitivity.

FOREMAN. Now let's stop the bickering. We're wasting time. (*To* EIGHT) It's your turn.

EIGHT. All right. I had a peculiar feeling about this trial. Somehow I felt that the defense counsel never really conducted a thorough cross-examination. I mean, he was appointed by the court to defend the boy. He hardly seemed interested. Too many questions were left unasked.

THREE (*annoyed*). What about the ones that were asked? For instance, let's talk about that cute little switch-knife. You know, the one that fine upright kid admitted buying.

EIGHT. All right. Let's talk about it. Let's get it in here and look at it. I'd like to see it again, Mr. Foreman. (*The* FOREMAN *looks at him questioningly and then gets up and goes to the door. During the following*

dialogue the FOREMAN *knocks, the* GUARD *comes in, the* FOREMAN *whispers to him, the* GUARD *nods and leaves, locking the door.*)

THREE. We all know what it looks like. I don't see why we have to look at it again. (*To* FOUR) What do you think?

FOUR. The gentleman has a right to see exhibits in evidence.

THREE (*shrugging*). Okay with me.

FOUR (*to* EIGHT). This knife is a pretty strong piece of evidence, don't you agree?

EIGHT. I do.

FOUR. The boy admits going out of his house at eight o'clock after being slapped by his father.

EIGHT. Or punched.

FOUR. Or punched. He went to a neighborhood store and bought a switch-knife. The storekeeper was arrested the following day when he admitted selling it to the boy. It's a very unusual knife. The storekeeper identified it and said it was the only

one of its kind he had in stock. Why did the boy get it? *(Sarcastically)* As a present for a friend of his, he says. Am I right so far?

EIGHT. Right.

THREE. You bet he's right. *(To all)* Now listen to this man. He knows what he's talking about.

FOUR. Next, the boy claims that on the way home the knife must have fallen through a hole in his coat pocket, that he never saw it again. Now there's a story, gentlemen. You know what actually happened. The boy took the knife home and a few hours later stabbed his father with it and even remembered to wipe off the fingerprints.

(The door opens and the GUARD walks in with an oddly designed knife with a tag on it. FOUR gets up and takes it from him. The GUARD exits.)

FOUR. Everyone connected with the case identified this knife. Now are you trying to tell me that someone picked it up off the street and went up to the boy's house and stabbed his father with it just to be amusing?

EIGHT. No, I'm saying that it's possible that the boy lost the knife and that someone else stabbed his father with a similar knife. It's possible.

(FOUR flips open the knife and jams it into the table.)

FOUR. Take a look at that knife. It's a very strange knife. I've never seen one like it before in my life. Neither had the storekeeper who sold it to him.

(EIGHT reaches casually into his pocket and withdraws an object. No one notices this. He stands up quietly.)

FOUR. Aren't you trying to make us accept a pretty incredible coincidence?

EIGHT. I'm not trying to make anyone accept it. I'm just saying it's possible.

THREE *(shouting)*. And I'm saying it's not possible.

(EIGHT swiftly flicks open the blade of a switch-knife and jams it into the table next to the first one. They are exactly alike. There are several gasps and everyone stares at the knife. There is a long silence.)

THREE *(slowly, amazed)*. What are you trying to do?

TEN *(loud)*. Yeah, what is this? Who do you think you are?

FIVE. Look at it! It's the same knife!

FOREMAN. Quiet! Let's be quiet.

(They quiet down.)

FOUR. Where did you get it?

EIGHT. I got it last night in a little junk shop around the corner from the boy's house. It cost two dollars.

THREE. Now listen to me! You pulled a real smart trick here, but you proved absolutely zero. Maybe there are ten knives like that, so what?

EIGHT. Maybe there are.

THREE. The boy lied and you know it.

EIGHT. He may have lied. *(To TEN)* Do you think he lied?

TEN *(violently)*. Now that's a stupid question. Sure he lied!

EIGHT *(to FOUR)*. Do you?

FOUR. You don't have to ask me that. You know my answer. He lied.

EIGHT *(to FIVE)*. Do you think he lied?

(FIVE can't answer immediately. He looks around nervously.)

FIVE. I . . . I don't know.

SEVEN. Now wait a second. What are you, the guy's lawyer? Listen, there are still eleven of us who think he's guilty. You're alone. What do you think you're gonna accomplish? If you want to be stubborn and hang this jury,[7] he'll be tried again and found guilty, sure as he's born.

EIGHT. You're probably right.

SEVEN. So what are you gonna do about it? We can be here all night.

NINE. It's only one night. A man may die.

(SEVEN glares at NINE for a long while, but has no answer. EIGHT looks closely at NINE and we can begin to sense a rapport[8] between them. There is a long silence. Then suddenly everyone begins to talk at once.)

THREE. Well, whose fault is that?

SIX. Do you think maybe if we went over it again? What I mean is——

TEN. Did anyone force him to kill his father? *(To THREE)* How do you like him? Like someone forced him!

ELEVEN. Perhaps this is not the point.

FIVE. No one forced anyone. But listen——

TWELVE. Look, gentlemen, we can spitball all night here.

TWO. Well, I was going to say——

SEVEN. Just a minute. Some of us've got better things to do than sit around a jury room.

FOUR. I can't understand a word in here. Why do we all have to talk at once?

---

7. **hang this jury**, keep this jury from reaching a verdict. A jury that fails to reach a verdict is called a "hung" jury.
8. **rapport** (ra pôrt´), agreement, harmony.

FOREMAN. He's right. I think we ought to get on with it.

(EIGHT *has been listening to this exchange closely.*)

THREE (*to* EIGHT). Well, what do you say? You're the one holding up the show.

EIGHT (*standing*). I've got a proposition to make.

(*We catch a close shot of* FIVE *looking steadily at him as he talks.* FIVE, *seemingly puzzled, listens closely.*)

EIGHT. I want to call for a vote. I want you eleven men to vote by secret ballot. I'll abstain. If there are still eleven votes for guilty, I won't stand alone. We'll take in a guilty verdict right now.

SEVEN. Okay. Let's do it.

FOREMAN. That sounds fair. Is everyone agreed?

(*They all nod their heads.* EIGHT *walks over to the window, looks out for a moment and then faces them.*)

FOREMAN. Pass these along.

(*The* FOREMAN *passes ballot slips to all of them, and now* EIGHT *watches them tensely as they begin to write.*) (*Fade out*)

DISCUSSION

1. As the play begins, the JUDGE is charging the twelve jurors. What are his specific instructions to them?

2. (a) How might the jury room itself, the time, and the weather affect the jurors? (b) Which juror is particularly anxious to reach a quick decision? Why is he in such a hurry?

3. Before the first vote is taken, what do you learn about (a) the nature of the crime, and (b) the defendant?

4. (a) What is the result of the first vote? (b) Which juror seems the least confident of his vote? (c) What reasons does EIGHT give to account for his vote? (d) How do the jurors react to EIGHT's statements?

5. In order to convince EIGHT of the defendant's guilt, the jurors decide to discuss the facts of the case. (a) How does TWO interpret the facts? How does EIGHT answer TWO's interpretation? (b) What is the testimony cited by THREE? How do the FOREMAN and FOUR support THREE's statement? (c) What is the testimony cited by TEN? By SIX? How does EIGHT counter their statements?

6. (a) What comments do SEVEN, THREE, and FOUR make about the defendant? (b) Do their comments pertain to the facts of the case? Explain. (c) Why does FIVE react as he does?

7. (a) How does EIGHT describe his reaction to the trial? (b) How does THREE react to EIGHT's comments?

8. (a) Why is the switch-knife an important exhibit in evidence? (b) What was the defendant's testimony about the switch-knife? (c) How do FOUR and EIGHT differ in their interpretation of this testimony?

9. (a) What is the dramatic climax of Act One? (b) How do the jurors react to this incident? (c) What does EIGHT prove by his action? (d) What does this incident reveal about EIGHT's motives?

10. (a) What proposition does EIGHT make to his fellow jurors? (b) How do you think FOUR, THREE, FIVE, and NINE will vote on the second ballot? Cite specific passages from the play to account for your answer.

11. (a) If you were one of the jurors, how would you vote on the second ballot? (b) On what grounds would you base your decision?

WORD STUDY

Words in the courtroom

If you were one of the twelve jurors who must decide the guilt or innocence of the accused, you would need to understand the meanings of many words as they are used in a court of law. Further, with a man's life in the balance, you would be obligated to use these words with absolute precision. You would need to understand, for example, the precise difference between *homicide* and *premeditated homicide*. Do you? If not, check with the Glossary and then explain the difference.

As one of the jurors, you would need to understand the meaning of the word *reasonable* in the phrase "reasonable doubt." Why is the meaning of this word significant? You may consult the Glossary.

Before voting guilty or not guilty, it would be necessary for you, the juror, to consider evidence that was given during the trial. What distinction does the Glossary make between the meanings of *evidence*, *testimony*, and *proof*?

List the following six words on a separate sheet of paper: (1) *acquittal*; (2) *defendant*; (3) *defense*; (4) *jury*; (5) *prosecution*; and (6) *verdict*. How many possible meanings does the Glossary cite for each word? Which meaning would be used in a court of law? Alongside each word on your list, write a sentence using the word as it would be used in a courtroom.

Act Two

Fade in on same scene, no time lapse. EIGHT *stands tensely watching as the* JURORS *write on their ballots. He stays perfectly still as one by one they fold the ballots and pass them along to the* FOREMAN. *The* FOREMAN *takes them, riffles through the folded ballots, counts eleven and now begins to open them. He reads each one out loud and lays it aside. They watch him quietly, and all we hear is his voice and the sound of* TWO *sucking on a cough drop.*

FOREMAN. Guilty. Guilty. Guilty. Guilty. Guilty. Guilty. Guilty. Guilty. Guilty.
  (He pauses at the tenth ballot and then reads it.) Not Guilty. (THREE *slams down hard on the table. The* FOREMAN *opens the last ballot.)* Guilty.

TEN *(angry).* How do you like that!

SEVEN. Who was it? I think we have a right to know.

ELEVEN. Excuse me. This was a secret ballot. We agreed on this point, no? If the gentleman wants it to remain secret——

THREE *(standing up angrily).* What do you mean? There are no secrets in here! I know who it was. *(He turns to* FIVE.*)* What's the matter with you? You come in here and you vote guilty and then this slick preacher starts to tear your heart out with stories about a poor little kid who just couldn't help becoming a murderer. So you change your vote. If that isn't the most sickening——
  *(*FIVE *stares at* THREE, *frightened at this outburst.)*

FOREMAN. Now hold it.

THREE. Hold it? We're trying to put a guilty man into the chair where he belongs—and all of a sudden we're paying attention to fairy tales.

FIVE. Now just a minute——

ELEVEN. Please. I would like to say something here. I have always thought that a man was entitled to have unpopular opinions in this country. This is the reason I came here. I wanted to have the right to disagree. In my own country, I am ashamed to say——

TEN. What do we have to listen to now—the whole history of your country?

SEVEN. Yeah, let's stick to the subject. *(To* FIVE*)* I want to ask you what made you change your vote. *(There is a long pause as* SEVEN *and* FIVE *eye each other angrily.)*

NINE *(quietly).* There's nothing for him to tell you.

He didn't change his vote. I did. *(There is a pause.)* Maybe you'd like to know why.

THREE. No, we wouldn't like to know why.

FOREMAN. The man wants to talk.

NINE. Thank you. *(Pointing at* EIGHT*)* This gentleman chose to stand alone against us. That's his right. It takes a great deal of courage to stand alone even if you believe in something very strongly. He left the verdict up to us. He gambled for support and I gave it to him. I want to hear more. The vote is ten to two.

TEN. That's fine. If the speech is over, let's go on.
  (FOREMAN *gets up, goes to door, knocks, hands* GUARD *the tagged switch-knife and sits down again.)*

THREE *(to* FIVE*).* Look, buddy, I was a little excited. Well, you know how it is. I . . . I didn't mean to get nasty. Nothing personal. (FIVE *looks at him.)*

SEVEN *(to* EIGHT*).* Look, supposing you answer me this. If the kid didn't kill him, who did?

EIGHT. As far as I know, we're supposed to decide whether or not the boy on trial is guilty. We're not concerned with anyone else's motives here.

NINE. Guilty beyond a reasonable doubt. This is an important thing to remember.

THREE *(to* TEN*).* Everyone's a lawyer. *(To* NINE*)* Supposing you explain what your reasonable doubts are.

NINE. This is not easy. So far, it's only a feeling I have. A feeling. Perhaps you don't understand.

TEN. A feeling! What are we gonna do, spend the night talking about your feelings? What about the facts?

THREE. You said a mouthful. *(To* NINE*)* Look, the old man heard the kid yell, "I'm gonna kill you." A second later he heard the father's body falling, and he saw the boy running out of the house fifteen seconds after that.

TWELVE. That's right. And let's not forget the woman across the street. She looked into the open window and saw the boy stab his father. She saw it. Now if that's not enough for you . . .

EIGHT. It's not enough for me.

SEVEN. How do you like him? It's like talking into a dead phone.

FOUR. The woman saw the killing through the windows of a moving elevated train. The train had five cars, and she saw it through the windows of the last two. She remembers the most insignificant details.

(*Cut to close shot of* TWELVE *who doodles a picture of an el train on a scrap of paper.*)

THREE. Well, what have you got to say about that?

EIGHT. I don't know. It doesn't sound right to me.

THREE. Well, supposing you think about it. (*To* TWELVE) Lend me your pencil.

(TWELVE *gives it to him. He draws a tick-tack-toe square on the same sheet of paper on which* TWELVE *has drawn the train. He fills in an X, hands the pencil to* TWELVE.)

THREE. Your turn. We might as well pass the time.

(TWELVE *takes the pencil.* EIGHT *stands up and snatches the paper away.* THREE *leaps up.*)

THREE. Wait a minute!

EIGHT (*hard*). This isn't a game.

THREE (*angry*). Who do you think you are?

SEVEN (*rising*). All right, let's take it easy.

THREE. I've got a good mind to walk around this table and belt him one!

FOREMAN. Now, please. I don't want any fights in here.

THREE. Did ya see him? The nerve! The absolute nerve!

TEN. All right. Forget it. It don't mean anything.

SIX. How about sitting down.

THREE. This isn't a game. Who does he think he is?

(*He lets them sit him down.* EIGHT *remains standing, holding the scrap of paper. He looks at it closely now and seems to be suddenly interested in it. Then he throws it back toward* THREE. *It lands in center of table.* THREE *is angered again at this, but* FOUR *puts his hand on his arm.* EIGHT *speaks now and his voice is more intense.*)

EIGHT (*to* FOUR). Take a look at that sketch. How long does it take an elevated train going at top speed to pass a given point?

FOUR. What has that got to do with anything?

EIGHT. How long? Guess.

FOUR. I wouldn't have the slightest idea.

EIGHT (*to* FIVE). What do you think?

FIVE. About ten or twelve seconds, maybe.

EIGHT. I'd say that was a fair guess. Anyone else?

ELEVEN. I would think about ten seconds, perhaps.

TWO. About ten seconds.

FOUR. All right. Say ten seconds. What are you getting at?

EIGHT. This. An el train passes a given point in ten seconds. That given point is the window of the room in which the killing took place. You can almost reach out of the window of that room and touch the el. Right? (*Several of them nod.*) All right. Now let me ask you this. Did anyone here ever live right next to the el tracks? I have. When your window is open and the train goes by, the noise is almost unbearable. You can't hear yourself think.

TEN. Okay. You can't hear yourself think. Will you get to the point?

EIGHT. The old man heard the boy say, "I'm going to kill you," and one second later he heard a body fall. One second. That's the testimony, right?

TWO. Right.

EIGHT. The woman across the street looked through the windows of the last two cars of the el and saw the body fall. Right? The *last two* cars.

TEN. What are you giving us here?

EIGHT. An el takes ten seconds to pass a given point or two seconds per car. That el had been going by the old man's window for at least six seconds, and maybe more, before the body fell, according to the woman. The old man would have had to hear the boy say, "I'm going to kill you," while the front of the el was roaring past his nose. It's not possible that he could have heard it.

THREE. What d'ya mean! Sure he could have heard it.

EIGHT. Could he?

THREE. He said the boy yelled it out. That's enough for me.

NINE. I don't think he could have heard it.

TWO. Maybe he didn't hear it. I mean with the el noise——

THREE. What are you people talking about? Are you calling the old man a liar?

FIVE. Well, it stands to reason.

THREE. You're crazy. Why would he lie? What's he got to gain?

NINE. Attention, maybe.

THREE. You keep coming up with these bright say-ings. Why don't you send one in to a newspaper? They pay two dollars.

(EIGHT *looks hard at* THREE *and then turns to* NINE.)

EIGHT (*softly*). Why might the old man have lied? You have a right to be heard.

NINE. It's just that I looked at him for a very long time. The seam of his jacket was split under the arm. Did you notice that? He was a very old man with a torn jacket, and he carried two canes. I think I know him better than anyone here. This is a quiet, frightened, insignificant man who has been nothing all his life, who has never had recognition—his name in the newspapers. Nobody knows him after seventy-five years. That's a very sad thing. A man like this needs to be recognized. To be questioned, and listened to, and quoted just once. This is very important.

TWELVE. And you're trying to tell us he lied about a thing like this just so that he could be important?

NINE. No, he wouldn't really lie. But perhaps he'd make himself believe that he heard those words and recognized the boy's face.

THREE (*loud*). Well, that's the most fantastic story I've ever heard. How can you make up a thing like that? What do you know about it?

NINE (*low*). I speak from experience. (*There is a long pause. Then the* FOREMAN *clears his throat.*)

FOREMAN (*to* EIGHT). All right. Is there anything else? (EIGHT *is looking at* NINE. TWO *offers the* FOREMAN *a box of cough drops. The* FOREMAN *pushes it away.*)

TWO (*hesitantly*). Anybody . . . want a cough . . . drop?

FOREMAN (*sharply*). Come on. Let's get on with it.

EIGHT. I'll take one. (TWO *almost gratefully slides him one along the table.*) Thanks. (TWO *nods and* EIGHT *puts the cough drop into his mouth.*)

EIGHT. Now. There's something else I'd like to point out here. I think we proved that the old man couldn't have heard the boy say, "I'm going to kill you," but supposing he really did hear it? This phrase: how many times has each of you used it? Probably hundreds. "If you do that once more, Junior, I'm going to murder you." "Come on, Rocky, kill him!" We say it every day. This doesn't mean that we're going to kill someone.

THREE. Wait a minute. The phrase was "I'm going to kill you," and the kid screamed it out at the top of his lungs. Don't try and tell me he didn't mean it. Anybody says a thing like that the way he said it—they mean it.

TEN. And how they mean it!

EIGHT. Well, let me ask you this. Do you really think the boy would shout out a thing like that so the whole neighborhood would hear it? I don't think so. He's much too bright for that.

TEN (exploding). Bright! He's a common, ignorant slob. He don't even speak good English!

ELEVEN (slowly). He doesn't even speak good English.
(TEN stares angrily at ELEVEN, and there is silence for a moment. Then FIVE looks around the table nervously.)

FIVE. I'd like to change my vote to not guilty.
(THREE gets up and walks to the window, furious, but trying to control himself.)

FOREMAN. Are you sure?

FIVE. Yes. I'm sure.

FOREMAN. The vote is nine to three in favor of guilty.

SEVEN. Well, if that isn't the end. (To FIVE) What are you basing it on? Stories this guy—(indicating EIGHT)—made up! He oughta write for Amazing Detective Monthly. He'd make a fortune. Listen, the kid had a lawyer, didn't he? Why didn't his lawyer bring up all these points?

FIVE. Lawyers can't think of everything.

SEVEN. Oh, brother! (To EIGHT) You sit in here and pull stories out of thin air. Now we're supposed to believe that the old man didn't get up out of bed, run to the door, and see the kid beat it downstairs fifteen seconds after the killing. He's only saying he did to be important.

FIVE. Did the old man say he ran to the door?

SEVEN. Ran. Walked. What's the difference? He got there.

FIVE. I don't remember what he said. But I don't see how he could run.

FOUR. He said he went from his bedroom to the front door. That's enough, isn't it?

EIGHT. Where was his bedroom again?

TEN. Down the hall somewhere. I thought you remembered everything. Don't you remember that?

EIGHT. No. Mr. Foreman, I'd like to take a look at the diagram of the apartment.

SEVEN. Why don't we have them run the trial over just so you can get everything straight?

EIGHT. Mr. Foreman——

FOREMAN (rising). I heard you.
(The FOREMAN gets up, goes to door during following dialogue. He knocks on door, GUARD opens it, he whispers to GUARD, GUARD nods and closes door.)

THREE (to EIGHT). All right. What's this for? How come you're the only one in the room who wants to see exhibits all the time?

FIVE. I want to see this one, too.

THREE. And I want to stop wasting time.

FOUR. If we're going to start wading through all that nonsense about where the body was found . . .

EIGHT. We're not. We're going to find out how a man who's had two strokes in the past three years, and who walks with a pair of canes, could get to his front door in fifteen seconds.

THREE. He said twenty seconds.

TWO. He said fifteen.

THREE. How does he know how long fifteen seconds is? You can't judge that kind of a thing.

NINE. He said fifteen. He was positive about it.

THREE (angry). He's an old man. You saw him. Half the time he was confused. How could he be positive about . . . anything?
(THREE looks around sheepishly, unable to cover up his blunder. The door opens and the GUARD walks in, carrying a large pen-and-ink diagram of the apartment. It is a railroad flat. A bedroom faces the el tracks. Behind it is a series of rooms off a long hall. In the front bedroom is a diagram of the spot where the body was found. At the back of the apartment we see the entrance into the apartment hall from the building hall. We see a flight of stairs in the building hall. The diagram is clearly labeled and included in the information on it are the dimensions of the various rooms. The GUARD gives the diagram to the FOREMAN.)

GUARD. This what you wanted?

FOREMAN. That's right. Thank you.
(The GUARD nods and exits. EIGHT goes to FOREMAN and reaches for it.)

EIGHT. May I?
(The FOREMAN nods. EIGHT takes the diagram and sets it up on a chair so that all can see it. EIGHT looks it over. Several of the JURORS get up to see it better. THREE, TEN, and SEVEN, however, barely bother to look at it.)

SEVEN (to TEN). Do me a favor. Wake me up when this is over.

EIGHT (ignoring him). All right. This is the apartment in which the killing took place. The old man's apartment is directly beneath it and exactly the same. (Pointing) Here are the el tracks. The bedroom. Another bedroom. Living room. Bathroom. Kitchen. And this is the hall. Here's the front door to the apartment. And here are the steps. *(Pointing to front bedroom and then front door)* Now the old man was in bed in this room. He says he got up, went out into the hall, down the hall to the front door, opened it, and looked out just in time to see the boy racing down the stairs. Am I right?

THREE. That's the story.

EIGHT. Fifteen seconds after he heard the body fall.

ELEVEN. Correct.

EIGHT. His bed was at the window. It's—*(looking closer)*—twelve feet from his bed to the bedroom door. The length of the hall is forty-three feet, six inches. He had to get up out of bed, get his canes, walk twelve feet, open the bedroom door, walk forty-three feet, and open the front door—all in fifteen seconds. Do you think this possible?

TEN. You know it's possible.

ELEVEN. He can only walk very slowly. They had to help him into the witness chair.

THREE. You make it sound like a long walk. It's not. *(EIGHT gets up, goes to the end of the room, and takes two chairs. He puts them together to indicate a bed.)*

NINE. For an old man who uses canes, it's a long walk.

THREE *(to EIGHT)*. What are you doing?

EIGHT. I want to try this thing. Let's see how long it took him. I'm going to pace off twelve feet—the length of the bedroom. *(He begins to do so.)*

THREE. You're crazy. You can't re-create a thing like that.

ELEVEN. Perhaps if we could see it . . . this is an important point.

THREE *(mad)*. It's a ridiculous waste of time.

SIX. Let him do it.

EIGHT. Hand me a chair. *(Someone pushes a chair to him.)* All right. This is the bedroom door. Now how far would you say it is from here to the door of this room?

SIX. I'd say it was twenty feet.

TWO. Just about.

EIGHT. Twenty feet is close enough. All right, from here to the door and back is about forty feet. It's shorter than the length of the hall, wouldn't you say that?

NINE. A few feet, maybe.

TEN. Look, this is absolutely insane. What makes you think you can——

EIGHT. Do you mind if I try it? According to you, it'll only take fifteen seconds. We can spare that. *(He walks over to the two chairs now and lies down on them.)* Who's got a watch with a second hand?

TWO. I have.

EIGHT. When you want me to start, stamp your foot. That'll be the body falling. Time me from there. *(He lies down on the chairs.)* Let's say he keeps his canes right at his bedside. Right?

TWO. Right!

EIGHT. Okay. I'm ready.

(They all watch carefully. TWO stares at his watch, waiting for the second hand to reach 60. Then, as it does, he stamps his foot loudly. EIGHT begins to get up. Slowly he swings his legs over the edges of the chairs, reaches for imaginary canes, and struggles to his feet. TWO stares at the watch. EIGHT walks as a crippled old man would walk, toward the chair which is serving as the bedroom door. He gets to it and pretends to open it.)

TEN *(shouting)*. Speed it up. He walked twice as fast as that.

(EIGHT, not having stopped for this outburst, begins to walk the simulated forty-foot hallway.)

ELEVEN. This is, I think, even more quickly than the old man walked in the courtroom.

EIGHT. If you think I should go faster, I will.

(He speeds up his pace slightly. He reaches the door and turns now, heading back, hobbling as an old man would hobble, bent over his imaginary canes. They watch him tensely. He hobbles back to the chair, which also serves as the front door. He stops there and pretends to unlock the door. Then he pretends to push it open.)

EIGHT *(loud)*. Stop.

TWO. Right.

EIGHT. What's the time?

TWO. Fifteen . . . twenty . . . thirty . . . thirty-one seconds exactly.

ELEVEN. Thirty-one seconds.

(Some of the JURORS adlib[1] their surprise to each other.)

EIGHT. It's my guess that the old man was trying to get to the door, heard someone racing down the stairs, and assumed that it was the boy.

SIX. I think that's possible.

THREE *(infuriated)*. Assumed? Now, listen to me, you people. I've seen all kinds of dishonesty in my day . . . but this little display takes the cake. *(To FOUR)* Tell him, will you?

---

1. *adlib*, to make up words or gestures that are not in the script.

(FOUR *sits silently.* THREE *looks at him and then he strides over to* EIGHT.)

THREE. You come in here with your heart bleeding all over the floor about slum kids and injustice and you make up these wild stories, and you've got some soft-hearted old ladies listening to you. Well I'm not. I'm getting real sick of it. *(To all)* What's the matter with you people? This kid is guilty! He's got to burn! We're letting him slip through our fingers here.

EIGHT *(calmly).* Our fingers. Are you his executioner?

THREE *(raging).* I'm one of 'em.

EIGHT. Perhaps you'd like to pull the switch.

THREE *(shouting).* For this kid? You bet I'd like to pull the switch!

EIGHT. I'm sorry for you.

THREE *(shouting).* Don't start with me.

EIGHT. What it must feel like to want to pull the switch!

THREE. Shut up!

EIGHT. You're a sadist.

THREE *(louder).* Shut up!

EIGHT *(strong).* You want to see this boy die because you personally want it—not because of the facts.

THREE *(shouting).* Shut up!

(*He lunges at* EIGHT, *but is caught by two of the* JURORS *and held. He struggles as* EIGHT *watches calmly.*)

THREE *(screaming).* Let me go! I'll kill him. I'll kill him!

EIGHT *(softly).* You don't really mean you'll kill me, do you?

(THREE *stops struggling now and stares at* EIGHT. *All the* JURORS *watch in silence as we fade out.*)

DISCUSSION

1. How does the result of the second vote create a conflict between juror THREE and jurors FIVE, ELEVEN, and NINE?

2. (a) What evidence does EIGHT offer first to discount the old man's testimony? (b) What is the connection between the el train's noise and the old man's testimony?

3. Reread on page 14, column 2 the comments NINE makes about the old man. Are NINE's comments based on fact or do they reflect his personal feelings? Explain.

4. (a) What is the significance of TEN's comment that the defendant "don't even speak good English"? (b) How does this comment affect ELEVEN? FIVE? (c) Is the comment consistent with TEN's previous behavior? Why or why not?

5. How does EIGHT interpret the result of his timed experiment?

6. (a) In Act Two THREE contradicts his earlier views. In what ways? (b) How do you think each juror would vote at the end of Act Two?

THE AUTHOR'S CRAFT

The dramatist and the camera As the camera fades out on Act Two, few viewers would be apt to flick their television dials to another station. Part of the impact of *Twelve Angry Men* lies in the way in which the author relies upon the camera to heighten his dramatic effects. His stage directions specify when the camera fades in and out, when it moves in for a close shot, and when one camera cuts to another. In Act One, it is the camera that makes the transition from the courtroom to the jury room:

"And now, slowly almost hesitantly, the members of the jury begin to rise. Awkwardly they file out of the jury box and off camera to the left. Camera holds on jury box, then fades out."

"Fade in on a large, bare, unpleasant-looking room . . ."

A *fade-out* followed by a *fade-in* is a device used by a television dramatist to indicate a change of scene or a lapse of time.

Act One also contains two examples of the *close shot.* Reread the stage direction in the middle of column 1 on page 6. Why does Mr. Rose specify a close shot of EIGHT so early in the play? Reread the stage direction on page 11, column 1. Why does Rose specify a close shot of FIVE at this point? The following stage direction appears in Act Two:

"Cut to close shot of TWELVE *who doodles a picture of an el train on a scrap of paper."*

Why is this close shot not only effective but necessary? The television dramatist may also specify when he wishes a change of cameras. Mr. Rose does this on page 6, column 1:

*"*TWO *looks at him nervously, nods, and goes over to the water cooler. Cut to shot of* EIGHT *staring out window. Cut to table.* SEVEN *stands at the table, putting out a cigarette.*

Although TWO, EIGHT, and SEVEN are at different parts of the room, the cuts from one camera to another emphasize that their actions are simultaneous. At what points in Act Two could you emphasize simultaneous action in this way?

Reginald Rose comments on his play

TWELVE ANGRY MEN is the only play I've written which has any relation at all to actual personal experience. A month or so before I began the play I sat on the jury of a manslaughter case in New York's General Sessions Court. This was my first experience on a jury, and it left quite an impression on me. The receipt of my jury notice activated many grumblings and mutterings, most of which began with lines like "Eight million people in New York and they have to call me!" All the prospective jurors I met in the waiting room the first day I appeared had the same grim, horribly persecuted attitude. But, strangely, the moment I walked into the courtroom to be empaneled and found myself facing a strange man whose fate was suddenly more or less in my hands, my entire attitude changed. I was hugely impressed with the almost frightening stillness of the courtroom, the impassive, masklike face of the judge, the brisk, purposeful scurrying of the various officials in the room, and the absolute finality of the decision I and my fellow jurors

would have to make at the end of the trial. I doubt whether I have ever been so impressed in my life with a role I had to play, and I suddenly became so earnest that, in thinking about it later, I probably was unbearable to the eleven other jurors.

It occurred to me during the trial that no one anywhere ever knows what goes on inside a jury room but the jurors, and I thought then that a play taking place entirely within a jury room might be an exciting and possibly moving experience for an audience.

Actually, the outline of *Twelve Angry Men*, which I began shortly after the trial ended, took longer to write than the script itself. The movements in the play were so intricate that I wanted to have them down on paper to the last detail before I began the construction of the dialogue. I worked on the idea and outline for a week and was stunned by the time I was finished to discover that the outline was twenty-seven typewritten pages long. The average outline is perhaps five pages long, and many are as short as one or two

pages. This detailed setting down of the moves of the play paid off, however. The script was written in five days and could have been done in four had I not written it approximately fifteen pages too long.

In writing *Twelve Angry Men* I attempted to blend four elements which I had seen at work in the jury room during my jury service. These elements are: (a) the evidence as remembered and interpreted by each individual juror (the disparities here were incredible); (b) the relationship of juror to juror in a life-and-death situation; (c) the emotional pattern of each individual juror; and (d) physical problems such as the weather, the time, the uncomfortable room, etc. All of these elements are of vital importance in any jury room, and all of them presented excellent dramatic possibilities.

From the Author's Commentary on *Twelve Angry Men* from SIX TELEVISION PLAYS by Reginald Rose. Reprinted by permission of International Famous Agency. Copyright © 1956 by Reginald Rose.

Act Three

Fade in on same scene. No time lapse. THREE *glares angrily at* EIGHT. *He is still held by two jurors. After a long pause, he shakes himself loose and turns away. He walks to the windows. The other* JURORS *stand around the room now, shocked by this display of anger. There is silence. Then the door opens and the* GUARD *enters. He looks around the room.*

GUARD. Is there anything wrong, gentlemen? I heard some noise.

FOREMAN. No. There's nothing wrong. *(He points to the large diagram of the apartment.)* You can take that back. We're finished with it.

(The GUARD *nods and takes the diagram. He looks curiously at some of the* JURORS *and exits. The* JURORS *still are silent. Some of them slowly begin to sit down.* THREE *still stands at the window. He turns around now. The* JURORS *look at him.)*

THREE *(loud)*. Well, what are you looking at?

(They turn away. He goes back to his seat now. Silently the rest of the JURORS *take their seats.* TWELVE *begins to doodle.* TEN *blows his nose, but no one speaks. Then, finally—)*

FOUR. I don't see why we have to behave like children here.

ELEVEN. Nor do I. We have a responsibility. This is a remarkable thing about democracy. That we are . . . what is the word? . . . Ah, notified! That we are notified by mail to come down to this place and decide on the guilt or innocence of a man we have not known before. We have nothing to gain or lose by our verdict. This is one of the reasons why we are strong. We should not make it a personal thing.

(There is a long, awkward pause.)

TWELVE. Well—we're still nowhere. Who's got an idea?

SIX. I think maybe we should try another vote. Mr. Foreman?

FOREMAN. It's all right with me. Anybody doesn't want to vote?

(He looks around the table.)

SEVEN. All right, let's do it.

THREE. I want an open ballot. Let's call out our votes. I want to know who stands where.

FOREMAN. That sounds fair. Anyone object? *(No one does.)* All right. I'll call off your jury numbers.

(He takes a pencil and paper and makes marks now in one of two columns after each vote.)

FOREMAN. I vote guilty. Number Two?

TWO. Not guilty.

FOREMAN. Number Three?

THREE. Guilty.

FOREMAN. Number Four?

FOUR. Guilty.

FOREMAN. Number Five?

FIVE. Not guilty.

FOREMAN. Number Six?

SIX. Not guilty.

FOREMAN. Number Seven?

SEVEN. Guilty.

FOREMAN. Number Eight?

EIGHT. Not guilty.

FOREMAN. Number Nine?

NINE. Not guilty.

FOREMAN. Number Ten?

TEN. Guilty.

FOREMAN. Number Eleven?

ELEVEN. Not guilty.

FOREMAN. Number Twelve?

TWELVE. Guilty.

FOUR. Six to six.

TEN *(mad)*. I'll tell you something. The crime is being committed right in this room.

FOREMAN. The vote is six to six.

THREE. I'm ready to walk into court right now and declare a hung jury. There's no point in this going on any more.

SEVEN. I go for that, too. Let's take it in to the judge and let the kid take his chances with twelve other guys.

FIVE *(to SEVEN)*. You mean you still don't think there's room for reasonable doubt?

SEVEN. No, I don't.

ELEVEN. I beg your pardon. Maybe you don't understand the term "reasonable doubt."

SEVEN *(angry)*. What do you mean I don't understand it? Who do you think you are to talk to me like that? *(To all)* How do you like this guy? He comes over here running for his life, and before he can even take a big breath he's telling us how to run the show. The arrogance of him!

FIVE *(to SEVEN)*. Wait a second. Nobody around here's asking where you came from.

SEVEN. I was born right here.

FIVE. Or where your father came from. . . . *(He looks at SEVEN, who doesn't answer but looks away.)*

Maybe it wouldn't hurt us to take a few tips from people who come running here! Maybe they learned something we don't know. We're not so perfect!

ELEVEN. Please—I am used to this. It's all right. Thank you.

FIVE. It's not all right!

SEVEN. Okay,. okay, I apologize. Is that what you want?

FIVE. That's what I want.

FOREMAN. All right. Let's stop the arguing. Who's got something constructive to say?

TWO (hesitantly). Well, something's been bothering me a little . . . this whole business about the stab wound and how it was made, the downward angle of it, you know?

THREE. Don't tell me we're gonna start that. They went over it and over it in court.

TWO. I know they did—but I don't go along with it. The boy is five feet eight inches tall. His father was six two. That's a difference of six inches. It's a very awkward thing to stab *down* into the chest of someone who's half a foot taller than you are.

(THREE *jumps up, holding the knife.*)

THREE. Look, you're not going to be satisfied till you see it again. I'm going to give you a demonstration. Somebody get up.

(He looks around the table. EIGHT *stands up and walks toward him.* THREE *closes the knife and puts it in his pocket. They stand face to face and look at each other for a moment.*)

THREE. Okay. (To TWO) Now watch this. I don't want to have to do it again. (He crouches down now until he is quite a bit shorter than EIGHT.) Is that six inches?

TWELVE. That's more than six inches.

THREE. Okay, let it be more.

(He reaches into his pocket and takes out the knife. He flicks it open, changes its position in his hand, and holds the knife aloft, ready to stab. He and EIGHT look steadily into each other's eyes. Then he stabs downward, hard.)

TWO (shouting). Look out!

(He stops short just as the blade reaches EIGHT's chest. THREE laughs.)

SIX. That's not funny.

FIVE. What's the matter with you?

THREE. Now just calm down. Nobody's hurt, are they?

EIGHT (low). No. Nobody's hurt.

THREE. All right. There's your angle. Take a look at it. Down and in. That's how I'd stab a taller man in the chest, and that's how it was done. Take a look at it and tell me I'm wrong.

(TWO *doesn't answer.* THREE *looks at him for a moment, then jams the knife into the table, and sits down. They all look at the knife.*)

SIX. Down and in. I guess there's no argument.

(EIGHT *picks the knife out of the table and closes it. He flicks it open and, changing its position in his hand, stabs downward with it.*)

EIGHT (to SIX). Did you ever stab a man?

SIX. Of course not.

EIGHT (to THREE). Did you?

THREE. All right, let's not be silly.

EIGHT. Did you?

THREE (loud). No, I didn't!

EIGHT. Where do you get all your information about how it's done?

THREE. What do you mean? It's just common sense.

EIGHT. Have you ever seen a man stabbed?

THREE (pauses and looks around the room nervously). No.

EIGHT. All right. I want to ask you something. The boy was an experienced knife fighter. He was even sent to reform school for knifing someone, isn't that so?

TWELVE. That's right.

EIGHT. Look at this. (EIGHT closes the knife, flicks it open, and changes the position of the knife so that he can stab overhanded.) Doesn't it seem like an awkward way to handle a knife?

THREE. What are you asking me for?

(EIGHT closes the blade and flicks it open, holds it ready to slash underhanded.)

FIVE. Wait a minute! What's the matter with me? Give me that. (He reaches out for the knife.)

EIGHT. Have you ever seen a knife fight?

FIVE. Yes, I have.

EIGHT. In the movies?

FIVE. In my back yard. On my stoop. In the vacant lot across the street. Too many of them. Switch-knives came with the neighborhood where I lived. Funny I didn't think of it before. I guess you try to forget those things. (Flicking the knife open) Anyone who's ever used a switch-knife would never have stabbed downward. You don't handle a switch-knife that way. You use it underhanded.

EIGHT. Then he couldn't have made the kind of wound which killed his father.

FIVE. No. He couldn't have. Not if he'd ever had any experience with switch-knives.

THREE. I don't believe it.

TEN. Neither do I. You're giving us a lot of mumbo jumbo.

EIGHT (*to* TWELVE). What do you think?

TWELVE (*hesitantly*). Well . . . I don't know.

EIGHT (*to* SEVEN). What about you?

SEVEN. Listen, I'll tell you something. I'm a little sick of this whole thing already. We're getting nowhere fast. Let's break it up and go home. I'm changing my vote to not guilty.

THREE. You're what?

SEVEN. You heard me. I've had enough.

THREE. What do you mean, you've had enough? That's no answer.

ELEVEN (*angry*). I think perhaps you're right. This is not an answer. (*To* SEVEN) What kind of a man are you? You have sat here and voted guilty with everyone else because there are some theater tickets burning a hole in your pocket. Now you have changed your vote for the same reason. I do not think you have the right to play like this with a man's life. This is an ugly and terrible thing to do.

SEVEN. Now wait a minute . . . you can't talk like that to me.

ELEVEN (*strong*). I can talk like that to you! If you want to vote not guilty, then do it because you are convinced the man is not guilty. If you believe he is guilty, then vote that way. Or don't you have the . . . the . . . guts—the guts to do what you think is right?

SEVEN. Now listen . . .

ELEVEN. Is it guilty or not guilty?

SEVEN (*hesitantly*). I told you. Not . . .guilty.

ELEVEN (*hard*). Why?

SEVEN. I don't have to——

ELEVEN. You have to! Say it! Why?

(*They stare at each other for a long while.*)

SEVEN (*low*). I . . . don't think . . . he's guilty.

EIGHT (*fast*). I want another vote.

FOREMAN. Okay, there's another vote called for. I guess the quickest way is a show of hands. Anybody object? (*No one does.*) All right. All those voting not guilty, raise your hands.

(TWO, FIVE, SIX, SEVEN, EIGHT, NINE, *and* ELEVEN *raise their hands immediately. Then, slowly,* TWELVE *raises his hand. The* FOREMAN *looks around the table carefully and then he too raises his hand. He looks around the table, counting silently.*)

FOREMAN. Nine. (*The hands go down.*) All those voting guilty.

(THREE, FOUR, *and* TEN *raise their hands.*)

FOREMAN. Three. (*They lower their hands.*) The vote is nine to three in favor of acquittal.

TEN. I don't understand you people. How can you believe this kid is innocent? Look, you know how those people lie. I don't have to tell you. They don't know what the truth is. And lemme tell you, they—(FIVE *gets up from table, turns his back to it, and goes to window.*)—don't need any real big reason to kill someone either. You know, they get drunk, and *bang*, someone's lying in the gutter. Nobody's blaming them. That's how they are. You know what I mean? Violent! (NINE *gets up and does the same. He is followed by* ELEVEN.)

TEN. Human life don't mean as much to them as it does to us. Hey, where are you going? Look, these people are drinking and fighting all the time, and if somebody gets killed, so somebody gets killed. They don't care. Oh, sure, there are some good things about them, too. Look, I'm the first to say that. (EIGHT *gets up, and then* TWO *and* SIX *follow him to the window.*)

TEN. I've known a few who were pretty decent, but that's the exception. Most of them, it's like they have no feelings. They can do anything. What's going on here?

(*The* FOREMAN *gets up and goes to the windows, followed by* SEVEN *and* TWELVE.)

TEN. I'm speaking my piece, and you—Listen to me! They're no good. There's not a one of 'em who's any good. We better watch out. Take it from me. This kid on trial . . .

(THREE *sits at table toying with the knife and* FOUR *gets up and starts for the window. All have their backs to* TEN.)

TEN. Well, don't you know about them? Listen to me! What are you doing? I'm trying to tell you something. . . .

(FOUR *stands over him as he trails off. There is a dead silence. Then* FOUR *speaks softly.*)

FOUR. I've had enough. If you open your mouth again, I'm going to split your skull.

(FOUR *stands there and looks at him. No one moves or speaks.* TEN *looks at him, then looks down at the table.*)

TEN (*softly*). I'm only trying to tell you . . .

(*There is a long pause as* FOUR *stares down at* TEN.)

FOUR (to all). All right. Sit down everybody.

(They all move back to their seats. When they are all seated, FOUR then sits down.)

FOUR (quietly). I still believe the boy is guilty of murder. I'll tell you why. To me, the most damning evidence was given by the woman across the street who claimed she actually saw the murder committed.

THREE. That's right. As far as I'm concerned, that's the most important testimony.

EIGHT. All right. Let's go over her testimony. What exactly did she say?

FOUR. I believe I can recount it accurately. She said that she went to bed at about eleven o'clock that night. Her bed was next to the open window, and she could look out of the window while lying down and see directly into the window across the street. She tossed and turned for over an hour, unable to fall asleep. Finally she turned toward the window at about twelve-ten and, as she looked out, she saw the boy stab his father. As far as I can see, this is unshakable testimony.

THREE. That's what I mean. That's the whole case.

(FOUR takes off his eyeglasses and begins to polish them, as they all sit silently watching him.)

FOUR (to the JURY). Frankly, I don't see how you can vote for acquittal. (To TWELVE) What do you think about it?

TWELVE. Well . . . maybe . . . there's so much evidence to sift.

THREE. What do you mean, maybe? He's absolutely right. You can throw out all the other evidence.

FOUR. That was my feeling.

(TWO, polishing his glasses, squints at clock, can't see it. SIX watches him closely.)

TWO. What time is it?

ELEVEN. Ten minutes of six.

TWO. It's late. You don't suppose they'd let us go home and finish it in the morning. I've got a kid with mumps.

FIVE. Not a chance.

SIX (to TWO). Pardon me. Can't you see the clock without your glasses?

TWO. Not clearly. Why?

SIX. Oh, I don't know. Look, this may be a dumb thought, but what do you do when you wake up at night and want to know what time it is?

TWO. What do you mean? I put on my glasses and look at the clock.

SIX. You don't wear them to bed.

TWO. Of course not. No one wears eyeglasses to bed.

TWELVE. What's all this for?

SIX. Well, I was thinking. You know the woman who testified that she saw the killing wears glasses.

THREE. So does my grandmother. So what?

EIGHT. Your grandmother isn't a murder witness.

SIX. Look, stop me if I'm wrong. This woman wouldn't wear her eyeglasses to bed, would she?

FOREMAN. Wait a minute! Did she wear glasses at all? I don't remember.

ELEVEN (excited). Of course she did. The woman wore bifocals. I remember this very clearly. They looked quite strong.

NINE. That's right. Bifocals. She never took them off.

FOUR. She did wear glasses. Funny. I never thought of it.

EIGHT. Listen, she wasn't wearing them in bed. That's for sure. She testified that in the midst of her tossing and turning she rolled over and looked casually out the window. The murder was taking place as she looked out, and the lights went out a split second later. She couldn't have had time to put on her glasses. Now maybe she honestly thought she saw the boy kill his father. I say that she saw only a blur.

THREE. How do you know what she saw? Maybe she's far-sighted.

(He looks around. No one answers.)

THREE (loud). How does he know all these things? (There is silence.)

EIGHT. Does anyone think there still is not a reasonable doubt?

(He looks around the room, then squarely at TEN. TEN looks down and shakes his head no.)

THREE (loud). I think he's guilty.

EIGHT (calmly). Does anyone else?

FOUR (quietly). No. I'm convinced.

EIGHT (to THREE). You're alone.

THREE. I don't care whether I'm alone or not! I have a right.

EIGHT. You have a right.

(There is a pause. They all look at THREE.)

THREE. Well, I told you I think the kid's guilty. What else do you want?

EIGHT. Your arguments. (They all look at THREE.)

THREE. I gave you my arguments.

EIGHT. We're not convinced. We're waiting to hear them again. We have time.

(THREE runs to FOUR and grabs his arm.)

THREE (*pleading*). Listen. What's the matter with you? You're the guy. You made all the arguments. You can't turn now. A guilty man's gonna be walking the streets. A murderer. He's got to die! Stay with me.

FOUR. I'm sorry. There's a reasonable doubt in my mind.

EIGHT. We're waiting.

(THREE *turns violently on him.*)

THREE (*shouting*). Well, you're not going to intimidate me! (*They all look at* THREE.) I'm entitled to my opinion! (*No one answers him.*) It's gonna be a hung jury! That's it!

EIGHT. There's nothing we can do about that, except hope that some night, maybe in a few months, you'll get some sleep.

FIVE. You're all alone.

NINE. It takes a great deal of courage to stand alone. (THREE *looks around at all of them for a long time. They sit silently, waiting for him to speak, and all of them despise him for his stubbornness. Then, suddenly, his face contorts as if he is about to cry, and he slams his fist down on the table.*)

THREE (*thundering*). All right!

(THREE *turns his back on them. There is silence for a moment and then the* FOREMAN *goes to the door and knocks on it. It opens. The* GUARD *looks in and sees them all standing. The* GUARD *holds the door for them as they begin slowly to file out.* EIGHT *waits at the door as the others file past him. Finally he and* THREE *are the only ones left.* THREE *turns around and sees that they are alone. Slowly he moves toward the door. Then he stops at the table. He pulls the switch-knife out of the table and walks over to* EIGHT *with it. He holds it in the approved knife-fighter fashion and looks long and hard at* EIGHT, *pointing the knife at his belly.* EIGHT *stares back. Then* THREE *turns the knife around.* EIGHT *takes it by the handle.* THREE *exits.* EIGHT *closes the knife, puts it away and, taking a last look around the room, exits, closing the door. The camera moves in close on the littered table in the empty room, and we clearly see a slip of crumpled paper on which are scribbled the words "Not guilty."*)

(*Fade out*)

DISCUSSION

1. In the beginning of Act Three the jurors vote for the third time. (a) What is the result of the third vote? (b) Which jurors have changed their votes?

2. FIVE provides information that discounts an important piece of testimony. (a) What information does FIVE provide? (b) Is he qualified to speak as an expert? Why or why not? (c) Is FIVE's ability to provide this information too coincidental to be believable? Account for your answer.

3. (a) In what way is SEVEN's willingness to change his vote consistent with his earlier behavior? (b) Why does ELEVEN question SEVEN so closely?

4. What is the result of the fourth vote?

5. How do the other jurors react to TEN's statements of his true feelings?

6. (a) Why does FOUR feel that he still cannot vote for acquittal? (b) What significant observation does SIX make at this point?

7. As the play draws to its close, THREE stands alone in his conviction that the boy is guilty. (a) Do you think THREE was pressured into agreeing with the majority? Explain your answer. (b) What does THREE reveal about himself in changing his vote?

8. Did the jury prove that the defendant was not guilty? Cite passages which will support your answer.

THE AUTHOR'S CRAFT

The jurors
When Reginald Rose began writing *Twelve Angry Men*, he knew that his play could not exceed fifty minutes. Faced with the time limits of television, many dramatists would present a limited number of characters. Rose, on the other hand, not only presents twelve jurors, but he keeps all twelve on the scene continuously.

It must have been obvious to Reginald Rose that he could not fully characterize twelve men in a fifty-minute play. He must have known that his jurors could be little more than *character types.* Early in Act One, for example, EIGHT (The Just Man) emerges as the hero; THREE (The Sadist) emerges as the villain. What single word would you use to describe SEVEN? TEN?

Character types are a device almost as old as English drama itself. In many medieval plays, *vices* (such as Ignorance and Shame) and *virtues* (such as Humility and Mercy) appear as real people. Mr. Rose borrows this device and then carries it one step further by assigning numbers instead of names to his characters.

A PLAY IN FIVE ACTS

Act One

SCENE: *Evening.* DOCTOR STOCKMANN'S *living room. It is decorated and furnished simply but neatly. In the side wall right are two doors, the upstage door leading to the hall and the one downstage to the doctor's study. In the opposite wall, facing the hall door, a door leading to the other rooms of the house. Against this wall, in the center of it, stands the stove: further downstage a sofa above which hangs a mirror, and in front of it an oval table: on this table is a lighted lamp with a shade. In the back wall, an open door leads to the dining room. The table is laid for supper and a lighted lamp stands on it.*

BILLING *is seated at the supper table; he has a napkin tucked under his chin.* MRS. STOCKMANN *stands by the table and places a dish of cold roast beef before him. The other seats round the table are empty; the table is in disorder, as though a meal had recently been finished.*

Henrik Ibsen

an ENEMY of the People

Characters

DR. TOMAS STOCKMANN, *physician at the Baths*[1]

MRS. KATRINE STOCKMANN, *his wife*

PETRA, *their daughter, a schoolteacher*

EJLIF
MORTEN } *their sons, aged thirteen and ten*

PETER STOCKMANN, *the doctor's elder brother; Mayor and Chief of Police; Chairman of the Board at the Baths*

MORTEN KIIL, *owner of a tannery;*[2] *Mrs. Stockmann's foster-father*

HOVSTAD, *editor of* The People's Monitor

BILLING, *his colleague on the paper*

CAPTAIN HORSTER

ASLAKSEN, *a printer*

Citizens of various types and standing; some women and a number of schoolboys

The action takes place in a town on the South Coast of Norway.

MRS. STOCKMANN. I'm afraid you'll have to put up with a cold meal, Mr. Billing; you were an hour late, you know.

BILLING (*Eating*). Never mind. It's delicious—absolutely delicious.

MRS. STOCKMANN. Stockmann is very strict about having his meals on time.

BILLING. It doesn't matter a bit. In fact I think food tastes even better when one's alone and undisturbed.

MRS. STOCKMANN. Well—as long as you enjoy it— (*Turns toward the hall door, listening*). That may be Mr. Hovstad—perhaps he's come to join you.

BILLING. Very likely.

(THE MAYOR, PETER STOCKMANN, *enters. He wears an overcoat, and the gold-braided cap of his office. He carries a cane.*)

THE MAYOR. Good evening, Sister-in-law.

MRS. STOCKMANN. Well! Good evening. (*She comes forward into the living room*) So, it's you! How nice of you to look in.

THE MAYOR. I happened to be passing by, and so— (*With a glance toward the dining room*). Oh—you have company, I see.

MRS. STOCKMANN (*Slightly embarrassed*). No, no— not really. Mr. Billing just happened to drop in. Won't you join him for a bite to eat?

THE MAYOR. No, thank you—nothing for me! I never eat hot food at night—not with my digestion.

MRS. STOCKMANN. Oh, just for once! It surely couldn't hurt you.

THE MAYOR. I'm much obliged—but, no! I stick to my

---

1. *the Baths,* Mineral Baths. Bathing in hot mineral waters has long been considered by some people to be healthful.
2. *tannery,* a factory where animal skins are processed for use as leather goods.

tea and bread and butter; it's much better for you —and it's more economical too.

MRS. STOCKMANN (*Smiling*). I hope you don't think Tomas and I are extravagant!

THE MAYOR. I know *you're* not, my dear; far be it from me to think that of *you*. (*Points to the doctor's study*) Is he home?

MRS. STOCKMANN. No. He went for a little walk after supper—with the boys.

THE MAYOR. Is that good for one's health, I wonder? (*Listens*) Here he comes now.

MRS. STOCKMANN. No, I don't think it can be he. (*A knock at the door*) Come in! (HOVSTAD *comes in from the hall*) Oh, it's Mr. Hovstad.

HOVSTAD. You must excuse me; I was held up at the printer's. Good evening, Mr. Mayor.

THE MAYOR (*Bowing rather stiffly*). Good evening. You're here on business, I presume?

HOVSTAD. Yes, partly. It's about an article for the paper.

THE MAYOR. I thought as much. I hear my brother has become quite a prolific contributor to *The People's Monitor*.

HOVSTAD. He's kind enough to write a piece for us now and then; whenever he has anything particular on his mind.

MRS. STOCKMANN (*To* HOVSTAD). But don't you want to—?

(*She points toward the dining room.*)

THE MAYOR. It's natural, I suppose, that he should want to reach the kind of people who understand his point-of-view. Not that I have any personal objection to your paper, Mr. Hovstad—you may rest assured of that.

HOVSTAD. No—of course not.

THE MAYOR. We have a fine spirit of mutual tolerance here in our town, I'm glad to say; a truly co-operative spirit; it comes, of course, from the great common interest we all share—an interest that naturally concerns all right-thinking citizens.

HOVSTAD. The Baths, of course.

THE MAYOR. Precisely. Those splendid Mineral Baths of ours! You mark my words, Mr. Hovstad; the whole life of our community will center more and more around the Baths—there can be no doubt of that!

MRS. STOCKMANN. That's just what Tomas says.

THE MAYOR. The way the town has grown in these past two years is quite extraordinary. People are prosperous; housing-developments are springing up; the value of property is soaring; there's life and activity everywhere!

HOVSTAD. And far less unemployment too.

THE MAYOR. That's true, of course; and that's a great load off the upper classes; taxes for home-relief have already been reduced—and they will be reduced still further if we have a really prosperous summer; a good rush of visitors—plenty of invalids to give the Baths a reputation—

HOVSTAD. I hear there's a good chance of that.

THE MAYOR. Every day inquiries about living quarters —apartments and so forth—keep pouring in. Things look highly promising.

HOVSTAD. Then the doctor's article will be most timely.

THE MAYOR. So he's been writing again, has he?

HOVSTAD. This is something he wrote during the winter. It's an article about the Baths—strongly recommending them, and laying particular stress on the excellence of sanitary conditions here. But I didn't use it at the time—I held it over.

THE MAYOR. Why? Was he indiscreet, as usual?

HOVSTAD. No, nothing like that; I only thought it would be better to hold it over till the spring, when people start thinking about summer plans.

THE MAYOR. Very sensible; highly sensible, Mr. Hovstad.

MRS. STOCKMANN. Tomas never spares himself where the Baths are concerned.

THE MAYOR. As one of the staff that's no more than his duty.

HOVSTAD. And, after all, it was his idea in the first place.

THE MAYOR. His idea? Was it indeed? I know some people are of that opinion. But it seems to me I too had at least a modest share in the enterprise.

MRS. STOCKMANN. That's what Tomas always says.

HOVSTAD. Of course, Mr. Mayor, that's undeniable; you put it all on a practical basis—you made the whole thing possible; we all know that. I simply meant that the initial idea was Dr. Stockmann's.

THE MAYOR. My brother has had plenty of ideas in his time—unfortunately; but it takes a very different type of man to work them out. I should have thought the members of this household would be among the first to—

MRS. STOCKMANN. My dear Peter—

HOVSTAD. You surely don't—?

MRS. STOCKMANN. Do go in and have some supper, Mr. Hovstad; my husband is sure to be home directly.

HOVSTAD. Thank you; I think I will have just a bite. (*He goes into the dining room.*)

THE MAYOR (*Lowering his voice*). It's amazing! These people who come from peasant stock never seem to lose their want of tact.

MRS. STOCKMANN. Now, why should you be upset? You and Tomas are brothers—isn't it natural that you should share the honor?

THE MAYOR. One would think so, yes; but a share is not enough for some people, it seems.

MRS. STOCKMANN. What nonsense! You and Tomas get on so well together. (*Listening*) I think I hear him now. (*She goes and opens the hall door.*)

DR. STOCKMANN (*Is heard laughing; he shouts in a loud voice, from the hall*). Here's another visitor for you, Katrine. Isn't this splendid, eh? Hang your coat up there on the peg, Captain Horster. But, I forgot—you don't wear an overcoat, do you? What do you think of this, Katrine? I met him on the street—I had a hard time persuading him; at first he wouldn't hear of coming up! (CAPTAIN HORSTER *enters and bows to* MRS. STOCKMANN) In with you, boys! They're starving again, Katrine! Come along, Captain Horster; you must try a piece of our roast-beef—

(*He forces* CAPTAIN HORSTER *into the dining room;* EJLIF *and* MORTEN *follow them.*)

MRS. STOCKMANN. But, Tomas, don't you see—!

DR. STOCKMANN (*Turns in the doorway*). Oh, it's you, Peter! (*Goes to him and holds out his hand*) Well, now this is really splendid!

THE MAYOR. I can only stay a minute—

DR. STOCKMANN. Nonsense! We'll have some hot toddy³ in a moment. You haven't forgotten the toddy, have you, Katrine?

MRS. STOCKMANN. Of course not! I've got the water boiling. (*She goes into the dining room.*)

THE MAYOR. Toddy, too—!

DR. STOCKMANN. Yes; let's sit down and be comfortable.

THE MAYOR. Thank you; I don't care for drinking parties.

DR. STOCKMANN. But this isn't a party!

THE MAYOR. It seems to me—(*He glances towards the*

---
3. *hot toddy*, a hot drink consisting of an alcoholic liquor, water, sugar, and spices.

dining room) It's incredible the amount of food they can get through!

DR. STOCKMANN (*Rubs his hands*). Yes—it does one good to see young people eat! They're always hungry! That's the way it should be—they must keep up their strength. They've got things to stir up—they have to build the future!

THE MAYOR. May I ask what there is that requires "stirring up"—as you call it?

DR. STOCKMANN. You'll have to ask the young people about that—when the time comes. Of course we shan't live to see it. A couple of old fogies like you and me—

THE MAYOR. A fine way to talk, I must say!

DR. STOCKMANN. You mustn't mind my nonsense, Peter. I'm in such high spirits today. It makes me so happy to be a part of all this fertile, teeming life. What a wonderful age we live in! A whole new world is springing up around us!

THE MAYOR. Do you really think so?

DR. STOCKMANN. Of course you can't appreciate it as well as I do. You've spent your whole life surrounded by all this—you take it all for granted. But after being stuck away for years in that dreadful little hole up North—never seeing a soul—never exchanging a stimulating word with anyone—I feel as though I'd suddenly been transported into the heart of some great metropolis!

THE MAYOR. I should hardly call it a metropolis—

DR. STOCKMANN. Oh, I know it may seem small compared to lots of other places; but there's life here—there's a future—there are innumerable things to work and strive for; that's what's important, after all. (*Calls out*) Katrine! Did the postman bring anything for me?

MRS. STOCKMANN (*From the dining room*). No—he didn't come today.

DR. STOCKMANN. And to be getting a good salary, Peter! That's something you appreciate when you've lived on starvation-wages as long as we have—

THE MAYOR. Oh, come now—

DR. STOCKMANN. Things were often very hard for us up there, let me tell you; but now we can live like princes! Today, for instance, we had roast beef for dinner; and then we had it for supper too. Don't you want to taste it? At least let me show it to you—do come and see it!

THE MAYOR. Certainly not!

DR. STOCKMANN. Well—come over here then. Look! Isn't our new table-cover handsome?

THE MAYOR. Yes—I noticed it.

DR. STOCKMANN. And we have a lamp-shade too; Katrine has been saving up for them. It makes the room look much more cozy. Don't you think so? Stand over here—no, no; not over there—here! That's right! You see how it concentrates the light? I think it's quite magnificent! What do you think?

THE MAYOR. Of course, if one can afford such luxuries—

DR. STOCKMANN. Oh, we can afford them now. Katrine says I earn almost as much as we spend.

THE MAYOR. Almost—!

DR. STOCKMANN. Besides, a man of science should live in a certain amount of style. I'll bet you a mere county commissioner spends more money a year than I do.

THE MAYOR. Well—I should hope so! A high-ranking government official—!

DR. STOCKMANN. Take an ordinary business man, then. I'll bet you a man like that spends ever so much more—

THE MAYOR. Such things are purely relative—

DR. STOCKMANN. As a matter of fact I don't squander money, Peter. But I do so enjoy inviting people to my home—I can't resist it; I was an exile for so long, you see. I feel the need of company—buoyant, active people—liberal-minded people—like those young fellows enjoying their food in there. To me, that makes life worth while. I wish you'd make a point of getting to know Hovstad—

THE MAYOR. That reminds me—Hovstad was telling me just now he plans to publish another article of yours.

DR. STOCKMANN. Of mine?

THE MAYOR. Yes—about the Baths. An article you wrote last winter.

DR. STOCKMANN. Oh, that one! I'd rather that didn't appear just now.

THE MAYOR. Why not? This seems to me to be the ideal time for it.

DR. STOCKMANN. Yes—under ordinary circumstances —(Paces across the room.)

THE MAYOR (Follows him with his eyes). What is there so unusual about circumstances now?

DR. STOCKMANN (Stands still). I'm afraid I can't tell you about it just now, Peter—not this evening, at any rate. The circumstances may turn out to be in the highest degree unusual, you see. On the other hand it may all amount to nothing—just an illusion on my part.

THE MAYOR. You sound very mysterious. Are you keeping something from me? Is anything the matter? As chairman of the Bath Committee I demand the right to—!

DR. STOCKMANN. And I demand the right to—! Oh, don't let's fly off the handle, Peter.

THE MAYOR. I am not in the habit of "flying off the handle," as you express it. But I must emphatically insist that all matters concerning the Baths be handled in a business-like manner, and through the proper channels. I shall not tolerate devious or underhanded methods.

DR. STOCKMANN. When have I ever used devious or underhanded methods?

THE MAYOR. You have an incorrigible tendency to take things into your own hands; in a well-ordered community that is equally reprehensible. The individual must subordinate himself to Society as a whole; or, more precisely, to those authorities responsible for the well-being of that Society.

DR. STOCKMANN. That may be so; but I can't see how the devil it concerns me!

THE MAYOR. That is where you are wrong, my dear Tomas; I can't seem to get that into your head! But be careful; sooner or later you'll have to pay for it. Now I've warned you. Goodbye.

DR. STOCKMANN. You're out of your mind, I tell you! You're on the wrong track entirely—!

THE MAYOR. I am seldom on the wrong track. Moreover—I take strong exception to—! (Bows in the direction of the dining room) Goodbye, Katrine. Good-day, Gentlemen. (He goes.)

MRS. STOCKMANN (Coming into the sitting room). Has he gone?

DR. STOCKMANN. Yes—and in a towering rage too!

MRS. STOCKMANN. Tomas, dear! What did you do to him this time?

DR. STOCKMANN. Nothing at all! He can't very well expect me to give him an account of things—before they happen.

MRS. STOCKMANN. An account of what things?

DR. STOCKMANN. Never mind about that now, Katrine —It's very odd that the postman didn't come.

(HOVSTAD, BILLING and HORSTER have risen from table and come into the sitting room; EJLIF and MORTEN follow presently.)

BILLING (Stretching himself). What a meal! Strike me dead if I don't feel like a new man!

HOVSTAD. His Honor didn't seem in a very sunny mood this evening.

DR. STOCKMANN. It's his stomach; his digestion's bad, you know.

HOVSTAD. I think he found it hard to digest us! He has no great love for *The People's Monitor*, I gather.

MRS. STOCKMANN. I thought you seemed to get on very well.

HOVSTAD. Only a temporary truce, I fear me!

BILLING. A truce, yes. That's the word for it.

DR. STOCKMANN. We mustn't forget poor Peter is a lonely bachelor. He has no home to be happy in. Business—nothing but business! And then that damned tea he's always filling himself up with. Now then, boys! Draw your chairs up to the table! Katrine—what about that toddy!

MRS. STOCKMANN (*Going towards the dining room*). I'm just getting it.

DR. STOCKMANN. You sit here on the sofa with me, Captain Horster. We don't often have the chance of seeing you!—Go on, boys! Sit down!

(*They sit down at the table.* MRS. STOCKMANN *brings in a tray with kettle, glasses, decanters, etc.*)

MRS. STOCKMANN. There you are! Now help yourselves. There's Arrak,[4] rum, and this is cognac.

DR. STOCKMANN (*Taking a glass*). We're ready for it! (*While the toddy is being mixed*) Now—the cigars. Ejlif, you know where the box is. And Morten can get my pipe. (*The boys go into the room right*) I have a suspicion Ejlif sneaks a cigar now and then —but I pretend not to notice. (*Calls*) And my smoking-cap,[5] Morten! Do you know where I left it, Katrine? Oh, he's found it. (*The boys bring in the various things*) Now, my friends, help your-·

---

4. *Arrak* (aʹrik), sometimes spelled *arrack*, a strong alcoholic drink made from rice or molasses.
5. *smoking-cap.* In the 19th century gentlemen often wore a soft lounge cap at home when they were relaxed and at ease.

selves! I stick to my pipe, you know; many's the long cold trip, up there in the North, that *this* has kept me company. (*They clink glasses*) Your health! It's a damn sight pleasanter to be sitting here in this warm comfortable room!

MRS. STOCKMANN (*Sits and starts to knit*). Are you sailing soon, Captain Horster?

HORSTER. I hope to be ready next week.

MRS. STOCKMANN. And you're going to America?

HORSTER. That's the intention.

BILLING. Then you won't be able to vote in the town election.

HORSTER. Oh, there's to be an election, is there?

BILLING. Didn't you know?

HORSTER. No—I don't bother about such things.

BILLING. You mean you have no interest in public affairs?

HORSTER. I don't know anything about them.

BILLING. Still—one ought at least to vote.

HORSTER. Even if you understand nothing about it?

BILLING. Not understand? How do you mean? Society is like a ship; it's up to every man to put his hand to the helm.

HORSTER. That may be all right on shore; but it would never do at sea.

HOVSTAD. Sailors rarely take an interest in public matters.

BILLING. Yes—it's amazing!

DR. STOCKMANN. Sailors are like birds of passage; North or South—every place is home to them! All the more reason for us to redouble our activities. Will there be anything of public interest in tomorrow's paper, Mr. Hovstad?

HOVSTAD. Nothing of local interest—no. But the day after tomorrow I thought I'd use your article.

DR. STOCKMANN. Oh, blast it, the article—of course! I'm afraid you'll have to hold it for a while.

HOVSTAD. Really? But we happen to have lots of space—and it seemed to me so timely.

DR. STOCKMANN. I dare say you're right—but you'll have to hold it all the same. I'll explain about it later—

(PETRA, *wearing a hat and cloak, enters from the hall; she carries a number of exercise books under her arm.*)

PETRA. Good evening.

DR. STOCKMANN. Oh, it's you, Petra. Good evening.

(*General greetings.* PETRA *takes off her hat and cloak and puts them, with the exercise books, on a chair by the door.*)

PETRA. So while I slave away at school—you sit here enjoying yourselves!

DR. STOCKMANN. Now you must come and enjoy yourself too.

BILLING. May I mix you a little drink?

PETRA (*Goes to the table*). Thanks, I'll do it myself; you always make it too strong. Oh—by the way, Father, I have a letter for you. (*Goes to the chair where she left her things.*)

DR. STOCKMANN. A letter! From whom?

PETRA (*Looking in the pocket of her cloak*). I met the postman on my way out—

DR. STOCKMANN (*Rises and goes towards her*). You might have given it to me before!

PETRA. I really didn't have time to run upstairs again. Here it is.

DR. STOCKMANN (*Seizing the letter*). Let me see—let me see, child. (*He reads the address*) Yes! This is it!

MRS. STOCKMANN. Is it the one you've been expecting, Tomas?

DR. STOCKMANN. Yes. I must go in and read it at once. What about a light, Katrine? I suppose there's no lamp in my study again!

MRS. STOCKMANN. Oh, yes there is! It's already lighted on the desk.

DR. STOCKMANN. Good. Excuse me a moment—(*He goes into his study, right.*)

PETRA. What's all that about, Mother?

MRS. STOCKMANN. I don't know; these last few days he's done nothing but ask for the postman.

BILLING. Perhaps it's from one of his patients out of town—

PETRA. Poor father! He's getting to be frightfully busy. (*Mixes her toddy*) Ah! This will be most welcome!

HOVSTAD. Have you been teaching at night school again this evening?

PETRA (*Sipping her drink*). Two hours, yes.

BILLING. And four hours this morning at the girls' school—?

PETRA (*Sitting down at the table*). Five.

MRS. STOCKMANN. And you have some exercises to correct this evening as well, I see.

PETRA. Quite a lot.

HORSTER. You seem to keep busy too!

PETRA. Yes—but I like it. It's good to feel thoroughly exhausted!

BILLING. Do you enjoy that?

PETRA. It makes one sleep so well.

MORTEN. You must be a great sinner, Petra.

PETRA. A sinner?

MORTEN. Yes—or you wouldn't have to work so hard. Work is a punishment for our sins—that's what Mr. Rörlund always says.

EJLIF. How can you be such a fool! Believing all that nonsense!

MRS. STOCKMANN. Now, now—Ejlif!

BILLING (*Laughing*). That's a good one!

HOVSTAD. Shouldn't you like to work hard, Morten?

MORTEN. No, I shouldn't.

HOVSTAD. What do you want to do when you grow up?

MORTEN. I want to be a Viking.

EJLIF. You'd have to be a heathen, then.

MORTEN. Well—so I'd *be* a heathen!

BILLING. Good for you, Morten! That's the spirit!

MRS. STOCKMANN (*Makes a sign to him*). I'm sure you don't really mean that, Mr. Billing!

BILLING. Strike me dead if I don't! I'm a heathen and I'm proud of it. You'll see—we'll all be heathens before long.

MORTEN. Then we could do anything we liked, couldn't we?

BILLING. Well—I don't know about that, Morten—

MRS. STOCKMANN. You'd better run along, boys; you must have home-work to do.

EJLIF. Couldn't I stay a little bit longer—?

MRS. STOCKMANN. No—you couldn't. Now, run along —both of you.

(*The boys say goodnight and go into the room, left.*)

HOVSTAD. Do you think it's bad for them to hear that sort of talk?

MRS. STOCKMANN. I don't know; but I know I don't like it.

PETRA. Don't be so stuffy, Mother!

MRS. STOCKMANN. That's all very well—but I don't. Not in one's own home at any rate.

PETRA. All this hypocrisy! At home we're taught to hold our tongues; and at school we have to teach the children lies!

HORSTER. Teach them lies?

PETRA. Yes, of course— We have to teach all kinds of things we don't believe a word of!

BILLING. That's true enough.

PETRA. If I had enough money, I'd start a school my-self—then I'd run things quite differently.

BILLING. Well—as far as the money goes—

HORSTER. If you're really serious about that, Miss Stockmann, I'd be glad to provide the necessary space; my father's old house is practically empty,

and there's a huge dining-room on the ground floor that would—

PETRA. Oh, I don't suppose anything will come of it —but, thanks, all the same!

HOVSTAD. I've a feeling Miss Petra is more likely to take up journalism. And, that reminds me—have you had a chance to read that English story you promised to translate for us?

PETRA. No, not yet. But I'll get it done for you in time—don't worry. (DR. STOCKMANN *comes in from his study with the letter open in his hand.*)

DR. STOCKMANN (*Flourishing the letter*). Well! Here's some news that will make the town sit up and take notice!

BILLING. News?

MRS. STOCKMANN. What sort of news, Tomas?

DR. STOCKMANN. A great discovery, Katrine!

HOVSTAD. Really?

MRS. STOCKMANN. A discovery of yours, you mean?

DR. STOCKMANN. Of mine—yes! (*Paces up and down*) And I defy them this time to call me a crack-pot, and laugh it off as nonsense. They won't dare! They simply won't dare!

PETRA. What is it, Father? Tell us!

DR. STOCKMANN. Just give me time, and I'll tell you all about it. I do wish Peter were here! It only goes to show how blind we are—just like a lot of moles!

HOVSTAD. What do you mean, Doctor?

DR. STOCKMANN. It's the general opinion that this town of ours is an exceedingly healthy place— isn't that true?

HOVSTAD. Of course.

DR. STOCKMANN. A quite exceptionally healthy place, as a matter of fact; a place to be highly recom-mended, not only to ordinary inhabitants, but to invalids as well—

MRS. STOCKMANN. My dear Tomas—

DR. STOCKMANN. And, as such, we have duly praised and recommended it; I myself have sung its praises innumerable times—not only in *The Peo-ple's Monitor*, but in many pamphlets too—

HOVSTAD. Well—what then?

DR. STOCKMANN. And these Mineral Baths that have been called "the pulse of the town"—its "nerve center"—and the devil only knows what else besides—

BILLING. "The throbbing heart of our city" I remem-ber I once called them—in a somewhat convivial mood—

DR. STOCKMANN. Yes—that too. Well—do you know

what these Baths are? These precious, magnificent Baths that have been established at such great expense—can you guess what they really are?

HOVSTAD. No—what?

MRS. STOCKMANN. Tell us, Tomas!

DR. STOCKMANN. They're nothing but a pest hole!

PETRA. The Baths, Father?

MRS. STOCKMANN (*At the same time*). Our Baths!

HOVSTAD (*Simultaneously*). But, Doctor—!

BILLING. This is incredible!

DR. STOCKMANN. I tell you the whole institution is a whited-sepulcher,[6] spreading poison; it's a menace to the Public Health! All that filth from the tanneries up at Milldale—and you know what a stench there is around there!—seeps into the feed-pipes of the pump-room; and, not only that, but this same poisonous offal seeps out onto the beach as well.

HOVSTAD. In the salt-water baths, you mean?

DR. STOCKMANN. Precisely.

HOVSTAD. How can you be sure of all this, Doctor?

DR. STOCKMANN. I've made the most painstaking investigations. I'd suspected something of the sort for quite some time, you see. I was struck by the curious amount of illness among the visitors at the Baths last year—there were several cases of typhoid and gastric fever[7]—.

MRS. STOCKMANN. Yes, I remember.

DR. STOCKMANN. At first we took it for granted that the visitors brought the infection with them; but later —this past winter—I began to think differently. I set to work to analyze the water, as best I could—

MRS. STOCKMANN. So that's what you've been working at!

DR. STOCKMANN. Yes—I've worked very hard at it, Katrine, but I didn't have the necessary equipment here; so I finally sent samples of the drinking-water and the sea-water by the beach to the laboratories at the university, and asked them to give me a full analysis.

HOVSTAD. And is that what you just received?

DR. STOCKMANN (*Showing the letter*). Yes—here it is! It proves beyond the shadow of a doubt the presence of decayed animal-matter in the water— millions of infusoria.[8] The use of this water, both internally and externally, is in the highest degree dangerous to health.

MRS. STOCKMANN. What a blessing you found it out in time!

DR. STOCKMANN. It is indeed, Katrine!

HOVSTAD. What do you propose to do about it, Doctor?

DR. STOCKMANN. Set things straight, of course.

HOVSTAD. You think that can be done?

DR. STOCKMANN. It *must* be done. Otherwise the Baths are entirely useless—ruined! But there's no need for that to happen; I'm quite clear as to how we should proceed.

MRS. STOCKMANN. To think of your keeping all this secret, Tomas, dear!

DR. STOCKMANN. You wouldn't have had me rushing all over town gabbing about it before I was absolutely certain, would you? I'm not as mad as all that, you know!

PETRA. But, surely, to us—

DR. STOCKMANN. I couldn't say a word to a living soul! But tomorrow you can run and tell that badger of yours all about it—

MRS. STOCKMANN. Oh, Tomas!

DR. STOCKMANN. Well—your grandfather, then. That'll give the old man something to gape at! He thinks I'm cracked in the head—and a lot of other people think so too, I've noticed. But I'll show them! Yes —this time I'll show them! (*Walks up and down rubbing his hands*) What a commotion there'll be in the town, Katrine! Think of it; they'll have to re-lay all the waterpipes.

HOVSTAD (*Rising*). All the waterpipes—?

DR. STOCKMANN. Well—naturally. The intake must be moved much higher up; I always said it was down too low.

PETRA. You were right after all, Father.

DR. STOCKMANN. Yes—you remember, Petra? I sent in a protest before they even started on the work; but, of course, at that time, no one listened to me. Well—I'll let them have it now! I've prepared a report for the Board of Directors; it's been ready for a week—I was only waiting for this. (*Points to the letter*) I'll send it off at once. (*Goes into his study and returns with a manuscript*) Look! Four closely written pages! And I'll enclose this letter too. A paper, Katrine! Something to wrap this up in. Good. And now give this to—to—what the devil is that girl's name! To the maid—*you* know! Tell her to deliver it to the Mayor immediately!

---

6. *whited-sepulcher* (sǝp′l kǝr), a tomb that has been painted white and therefore appears beautiful but within is "full of dead men's bones, and of all uncleanness" (Matt. 23:27). The Baths are beautiful but polluted.

7. *gastric fever*, a stomach disorder.

8. *infusoria* (in′fū sô′rē ǝ), microscopic animal life.

(MRS. STOCKMANN *takes the package and goes out through the dining room.*)

PETRA. What do you think Uncle Peter will say, Father?

DR. STOCKMANN. What *can* he say? He can't fail to be pleased that such an important fact has come to light.

HOVSTAD. May we announce this in *The People's Monitor?*

DR. STOCKMANN. I'd be most grateful if you would.

HOVSTAD. It's important that the public should know of this without delay.

DR. STOCKMANN. It is indeed!

MRS. STOCKMANN (*Returning*). She's gone with it.

BILLING. Strike me dead if you're not hailed as the leading citizen of our community, Dr. Stockmann!

DR. STOCKMANN (*Walks up and down in high glee*). Oh, nonsense! I only did my duty. I simply was lucky enough to spot it—that's all. But still—

BILLING. Hovstad, don't you think the town should get up some sort of a demonstration in Dr. Stockmann's honor?

HOVSTAD. I shall certainly propose it.

BILLING. I'll talk it over with Aslaksen.

DR. STOCKMANN. No, no—my dear friends! You mustn't bother with such nonsense; I won't hear of it! And, I warn you, Katrine—if the Board of Directors should think of offering me a raise in salary—I shall refuse it. I simply won't accept!

MRS. STOCKMANN. You're quite right, Tomas, dear.

PETRA (*Raising her glass*). Your health, Father!

HOVSTAD *and* BILLING. Your good health, Doctor!

HORSTER (*Clinks glasses with him*). I hope this brings you joy.

DR. STOCKMANN. Thank you, thank you—my dear, dear friends! I can't tell you how happy I am—! It's a wonderful thing to feel you've deserved well of your own hometown, and of your fellow-citizens. Hurrah, Katrine!

(*He puts his arms round her and whirls her round the room.* MRS. STOCKMANN *screams and struggles to free herself. Laughter, applause and cheers for the doctor. The two boys poke their heads in the door to see what is going on.*) CURTAIN

DISCUSSION

1. What is the general atmosphere of the Stockmann home? Cite passages that support your answer.

2. What business matter brings Billing and Hovstad to the Stockmann home?

3. (a) According to the Mayor, what is the one common interest that all of the townspeople share? (b) What are the reasons for this?

4. (a) How does the Mayor react to Hovstad's remark crediting Dr. Stockmann with the idea for the Baths? (b) What does this incident reveal about the Mayor's relationship to this brother?

5. When Dr. Stockmann refuses to discuss the unusual circumstances he is investigating at the Baths, what accusation does the Mayor make against the doctor?

6. (a) What is the Mayor's feeling about the relationship of the individual to society? (b) How does he apply this theory to Dr. Stockmann?

7. (a) What does Billing say about society, and how does he apply to Horster what he says? (b) Where do the Mayor and Billing differ in their evaluation of the individual's responsibility to society?

8. (a) What is the general reaction to Dr. Stockmann's disclosure regarding the Baths? (b) What does Billing propose? (c) How does Dr. Stockmann react to Billing's proposal? Do you believe Stockmann? Why or why not?

Act Two

SCENE: *The doctor's living room. The door to the dining room is closed. Morning.* MRS. STOCKMANN, *carrying a sealed letter in her hand, comes in from the dining room, goes to the door of the doctor's study and peeps in.*

MRS. STOCKMANN. Are you in there, Tomas?

DR. STOCKMANN (*From the study*). Yes, I just got back. (*Enters*) Do you want me?

MRS. STOCKMANN. Here's a letter from your brother. (*Hands it to him.*)

DR. STOCKMANN. Now—let's see. (*Opens the envelope and reads*) "The manuscript forwarded to me is returned herewith—" (*He reads on, mumbling to himself*) Hm.

MRS. STOCKMANN. Well? What does he say?

DR. STOCKMANN. Just that he'll be up to see me around noon.

MRS. STOCKMANN. You must be sure and be home, then.

DR. STOCKMANN. I can easily manage that; I've made all my morning calls.

MRS. STOCKMANN. I can't help wondering how he'll take it.

DR. STOCKMANN. He's sure to be annoyed that it was I, and not he, who discovered the whole business.

MRS. STOCKMANN. That's what I'm afraid of.

DR. STOCKMANN. He'll be glad at heart, of course. But still—; Peter's always so damnably resentful when anyone else does anything for the good of the town.

MRS. STOCKMANN. I know. I think it would be nice if you made a point of letting him share the honor; you might even imply that it was he who put you on the track—

DR. STOCKMANN. That's all right as far as I'm concerned. All I care about is getting the thing cleared up.

(*Old* MORTEN KIIL *sticks his head in at the hall door.*)

MORTEN KIIL (*Slyly*). Is—is all this true?

MRS. STOCKMANN (*Goes toward him*). Well! Here's Father.

DR. STOCKMANN. So it is! Good morning, Father-in-law!

MRS. STOCKMANN. Do come in.

MORTEN KIIL. If it's true, I will; otherwise I'll be off again.

DR. STOCKMANN. If what's true?

MORTEN KIIL. All this nonsense about the waterworks. Well? Is it?

DR. STOCKMANN. Of course it's true. But how did *you* find out about it?

MORTEN KIIL. From Petra. She ran in to see me on her way to school—

DR. STOCKMANN. Oh, did she?

MORTEN KIIL. Yes, indeed; and she told me—at first I thought she must be joking! But that's not like Petra, come to think of it.

DR. STOCKMANN. Of course not! She'd never joke about a thing like that.

MORTEN KIIL. You never know; and I don't like to be made a fool of. So it really is true, is it?

DR. STOCKMANN. Unquestionably. Do sit down, Father. (*Forces him down on the sofa*) Well—what do you think? It's a lucky thing for the town, isn't it?

MORTEN KIIL (*With suppressed laughter*). A lucky thing for the town?

DR. STOCKMANN. Yes, that I made this discovery in time—

MORTEN KIIL (*As before*). Oh, of course! Of course! —I must say I never thought you'd try your monkey-tricks on your own brother!

DR. STOCKMANN. Monkey-tricks—!

MRS. STOCKMANN. Father, dear—!

MORTEN KIIL (*Rests his hands and chin on the top of his cane and blinks slyly at the doctor*). Let me see —what was it now? Oh! yes—the waterpipes are full of little animals—isn't that it?

DR. STOCKMANN. Infusoria, yes.

MORTEN KIIL. And Petra said there were a lot of them—whole swarms of them.

DR. STOCKMANN. Certainly; hundreds of thousands of them.

MORTEN KIIL. And yet no one can see them—isn't that the story?

DR. STOCKMANN. Of course no one can see them.

MORTEN KIIL (*With quiet chuckling laughter*). I'll be damned if this isn't the best thing you've hit on yet!

DR. STOCKMANN. What do you mean?

MORTEN KIIL. You'll never get the Mayor to believe this nonsense!

DR. STOCKMANN. We shall see.

MORTEN KIIL. You think he's as crazy as all that?

DR. STOCKMANN. I'm confident that the whole town will be as crazy as all that.

MORTEN KIIL. The whole town! Yes—I wouldn't put it past them. And it'll serve them right, too—teach them a lesson. We old-timers aren't good enough for them—oh, no! They think themselves so clever! They hounded me out of the Town Council—hounded me out like a dog, that's what they did! But they'll get paid back now! Just you go on playing your monkey-tricks with them, Stockmann—

DR. STOCKMANN. But, Father—listen—!

MORTEN KIIL (*Rising*). Give 'em all the monkey-tricks you can think of, say I! If you can put this over on the Mayor and his cronies—so help me, I'll give a hundred crowns to charity!

DR. STOCKMANN. Very handsome of you.

MORTEN KIIL. Mind you, I've little enough to spare! But just you put this over, and next Christmas I'll give fifty crowns to charity!

(HOVSTAD *enters from the hall.*)

HOVSTAD. Good morning! (*Pausing*) Oh, excuse me—

DR. STOCKMANN. No—come in; come in.

MORTEN KIIL (*Chuckling again*). Is *he* in on this?

HOVSTAD. What do you mean?

DR. STOCKMANN. Yes, of course he is.

MORTEN KIIL. I might have known it! He's to put it in his paper. Ah! You're a good one, Stockmann! Well—I'm off. I'll leave you two together.

DR. STOCKMANN. No, Father; don't go yet.

MORTEN KIIL. Yes—I'll be off. Just you think up all the monkey-tricks you can. You can be damn sure you won't lose by it!

(*He goes;* MRS. STOCKMANN *goes with him.*)

DR. STOCKMANN (*Laughing*). What do you think—? The old man doesn't believe a word about the water-works!

HOVSTAD. Oh, was that what you were talking about?

DR. STOCKMANN. Yes. I suppose you've come about that, too?

HOVSTAD. Yes, I have. Have you a few moments, Doctor?

DR. STOCKMANN. As many as you like.

HOVSTAD. Have you heard anything from the Mayor yet?

DR. STOCKMANN. No, not yet. But he's to be here presently.

HOVSTAD. Since I left here last night I've thought a great deal about this matter.

DR. STOCKMANN. You have?

HOVSTAD. Yes. As a doctor and a man of science you naturally think of this business of the water-works as a thing apart. I mean by that—you probably haven't stopped to realize how many other things it may involve.

DR. STOCKMANN. In what way—? Let's sit down, my dear fellow. No—here on the sofa. (HOVSTAD *sits down on the sofa and* STOCKMANN *in an armchair on the other side of the table*) So—you think—?

HOVSTAD. You said last night that the water was polluted by decayed matter in the soil.

DR. STOCKMANN. The trouble comes from that poisonous swamp by the tanneries at Milldale. I'm convinced of that.

HOVSTAD. Forgive me, Doctor—but I think the trouble comes from poison of quite another sort.

DR. STOCKMANN. What poison do you mean?

HOVSTAD. I mean the poison that is polluting and contaminating our whole community.

DR. STOCKMANN. What the devil do you mean by that?

HOVSTAD. Little by little the whole town has come under the control of a pack of bureaucrats.

DR. STOCKMANN. Oh, come now—they're not all bureaucrats.

HOVSTAD. Perhaps not—but those of them who are not bureaucrats are the friends and hangers-on of those who are. We are under the thumb of a small clique of powerful men; it's the old established families, the men of wealth and position, who rule the town.

DR. STOCKMANN. But, remember—they are also men of ability and insight.

HOVSTAD. I suppose it was their ability and insight that controlled the installation of the water-system?

DR. STOCKMANN. That was a colossal piece of stupidity, I grant you. But it will be corrected now.

HOVSTAD. Do you think that will be such a simple matter?

DR. STOCKMANN. Simple or not, it must be done.

HOVSTAD. Yes; especially if the press exerts its influence.

DR. STOCKMANN. That won't be necessary, I assure you; I'm certain that my brother—

HOVSTAD. Excuse me, Doctor, but I want you to know that I intend to publicize the matter.

DR. STOCKMANN. In the newspaper?

HOVSTAD. Yes. When I took over *The People's Monitor*, it was with the thought of breaking up this ring of obstinate old reactionaries who now have full control.

DR. STOCKMANN. With the result that you nearly wrecked the paper—you told me that yourself.

HOVSTAD. We were obliged to draw in our horns for a while—that's true enough; if these particular men had been put out of office at that time, the Bath scheme might have fallen through entirely. But now that danger's over; the Baths are an accomplished fact—and we can afford to do without these high and mighty gentlemen.

DR. STOCKMANN. Do without them, yes; but still, we have a lot to thank them for.

HOVSTAD. Oh, we shall make a point of acknowledging the debt! But a journalist of my liberal turn of mind cannot be expected to let an opportunity like this go by. This myth of official infallibility must be exploded. That kind of superstition must be rooted out.

DR. STOCKMANN. There I agree with you entirely, Mr. Hovstad; if it's a superstition, we must get rid of it!

HOVSTAD. I hesitate to attack the Mayor—since he's your brother; on the other hand, I'm sure you feel as I do, that truth comes first.

DR. STOCKMANN. Undoubtedly—of course. (*Vehemently*) But, all the same!

HOVSTAD. I don't want you to think ill of me. I'm no more egotistical—no more ambitious—than the majority of men.

DR. STOCKMANN. My dear fellow—! No one says you are.

HOVSTAD. I come of a very humble family, Dr. Stockmann; and my knowledge of the common people has been gained through personal experience. I know their needs—I understand their aims. It's because they wish to develop their own ability, knowledge and self-respect, that they claim the right to share in the responsibilities of government—

DR. STOCKMANN. That's very understandable—

HOVSTAD. Yes. And it seems to me a journalist would incur a heavy responsibility by failing to seize the slightest chance of furthering the emancipation of the down-trodden masses. Oh! I know the powers-that-be will call this anarchy. But, let them! I shall at least have done my duty.

DR. STOCKMANN. Quite so—quite so, dear Mr. Hovstad. Still—damn it all—you must remember—! (A knock at the door) Come in!

(ASLAKSEN, the printer, appears at the hall door. He is shabbily but respectably dressed in a black suit with a slightly crumpled white necktie. He carries a silk hat and gloves.)

ASLAKSEN (Bowing). Excuse me, Doctor, if I intrude—

DR. STOCKMANN (Rising). Well—well! It's Mr. Aslaksen!

ASLAKSEN. Yes, it's me, Doctor—

HOVSTAD (Gets up). Do you want me, Aslaksen?

ASLAKSEN. No; I didn't even know you were here. It's the doctor I—

DR. STOCKMANN. What can I do for you?

ASLAKSEN. Is it true, what Mr. Billing tells me, that you're planning to improve our water-system?

DR. STOCKMANN. For the Baths, yes.

ASLAKSEN. Just as I thought; then I'd like you to know, Doctor, that I shall support this plan with all my might.

HOVSTAD (To the doctor). You see!

DR. STOCKMANN. I'm most grateful to you, I'm sure; but—

ASLAKSEN. You never know—we small middle-class men might be very useful to you. We form what you might call a solid majority in the town; if we really make up our minds to it, that is. And it's always a good thing to have the support of the majority, Dr. Stockmann.

DR. STOCKMANN. That's unquestionably true; but I can't conceive that any special measures will be necessary in this case. The matter is so simple— so straightforward—

ASLAKSEN. It might be helpful all the same. I know the local authorities very well. Suggestions from people outside their immediate circle are not looked upon too favorably by the powers-that-be. So I thought it might be a good idea if we arranged a demonstration of some sort.

HOVSTAD. I quite agree.

DR. STOCKMANN. A demonstration? But what form would this demonstration take?

ASLAKSEN. Oh, it would be conducted with the utmost moderation, Doctor; I strive for moderation in all things; moderation is a citizen's prime virtue—at least in my opinion.

DR. STOCKMANN. Your moderation is well-known, dear Mr. Aslaksen.

ASLAKSEN. I think I may safely say it is. And to us small middle-class men, this business of the water-works is of very great importance. Our Baths bid fair to become a small gold mine, as it were. Many of us count on them to provide us with a means of livelihood—the home-owners especially; so we naturally wish to support the Baths in every possible way. Now, since I happen to be chairman of the Home-owners Association—

DR. STOCKMANN. Yes—?

ASLAKSEN. —and also an active worker in the Temperance Society[9]—you know of course, Doctor, that I'm a temperance man—?

DR. STOCKMANN. That goes without saying—

ASLAKSEN. Then I need hardly tell you that I am in constant touch with a great number of my fellow-citizens. And since my reputation is that of a prudent, law-abiding man—as you yourself remarked—I have a certain influence in the town; a kind of modest authority—though I do say so myself.

DR. STOCKMANN. I'm well aware of that.

ASLAKSEN. So—should it be advisable—it would be a comparatively simple matter for me to get up some sort of a petition.

DR. STOCKMANN. A petition?

ASLAKSEN. Yes—a petition of thanks; of thanks to you, on behalf of the townspeople, for having taken up this all-important matter. It goes without saying that it must be worded with suitable moderation; it would never do to offend the authorities, or any of the men in power. But, if we keep this in mind, I see no reason for any possible objection.

HOVSTAD. Well—even if they did object—!

ASLAKSEN. No, no! There must be nothing in it to offend the powers-that-be, Mr. Hovstad. We can't afford to antagonize the men who control our destinies. I've seen plenty of that in my time—no good ever comes of it. But no one could object to a citizen expressing his opinion freely—provided it is couched in temperate terms.

---

9. *the Temperance Society*, an international organization which actively campaigns against the use of alcoholic beverages.

DR. STOCKMANN. I am delighted, my dear Mr. Aslaksen, to know I can count on the support of my fellow-townsmen; I can't tell you how happy this makes me! And now—how about a glass of sherry?

ASLAKSEN. No—many thanks; I never indulge in spirits.

DR. STOCKMANN. Well—you surely won't refuse a glass of beer?

ASLAKSEN. Thank you—but I never touch anything so early in the day. Now I'll be on my way; I must talk to some of the home-owners, and set about preparing public opinion.

DR. STOCKMANN. It's extremely kind of you, Mr. Aslaksen; but I can't conceive that all this preparation should be necessary. The issue is clear—I can't see any room for disagreement.

ASLAKSEN. The authorities have a way of functioning very slowly, Dr. Stockmann. Oh, far be it from me to blame them—!

HOVSTAD. We'll give them a good stirring up in the paper tomorrow—

ASLAKSEN. But I beg you, Mr. Hovstad—no violence! If you wish to get results, you must use moderation. Take my advice; I speak from experience. Well—now I'll say goodbye. Remember, Doctor, we—of the middle-class—stand behind you to a man. The solid majority is on your side.

DR. STOCKMANN. I'm most grateful to you, Mr. Aslaksen. (Holds out his hand) Goodbye, goodbye!

ASLAKSEN. Are you coming to the office, Mr. Hovstad?

HOVSTAD. I'll be there presently. There are still a couple of things I'd like to discuss.

ASLAKSEN. Very well. (He bows and goes out; DR. STOCKMANN shows him into the hall.)

HOVSTAD (As the doctor re-enters). Well—now what do you say, Doctor? Don't you agree it's high time we put a stop to all this half-hearted, cowardly, shilly-shallying?

DR. STOCKMANN. Are you referring to Aslaksen?

HOVSTAD. Yes, I am. He's been infected by the poison too, you see—though he's not a bad sort, in his way. He's typical of most people around here; always wavering, always on the fence. They never dare take a definite stand—they're too full of doubts, and scruples, and caution.

DR. STOCKMANN. He seems like a thoroughly well-intentioned man.

HOVSTAD. Intentions may be all very well—but give me a man with some self-confidence, some self-assurance.

DR. STOCKMANN. Yes—I agree with you there.

HOVSTAD. I'm going to use this opportunity to inject a little back-bone into their good intentions. This servile worship of the "Powers-that-be" must be wiped out. The inexcusable bungling about the water-works must be fully exposed. Every single voter must be made aware of it.

DR. STOCKMANN. Very well; as long as you think it's for the good of the Community. But I must speak to my brother first.

HOVSTAD. Meanwhile—I'll be writing my editorial. And if the Mayor refuses to take action—

DR. STOCKMANN. That's inconceivable.

HOVSTAD. Perhaps not so inconceivable as you might think. But suppose he does—

DR. STOCKMANN. Then, my dear Mr. Hovstad—if that should happen—you may print my full report, word for word—just as it is.

HOVSTAD. Is that a promise?

DR. STOCKMANN (Hands him the manuscript). Look —here it is; take it with you. There's no harm in your reading it; you can return it to me later on.

HOVSTAD. Very good; I shall do so. Goodbye for now, dear Doctor.

DR. STOCKMANN. Goodbye. But, you'll see, this whole thing will be cleared up quite simply, Mr. Hovstad; I'm confident of that.

HOVSTAD. Well—we shall see. (He bows and goes out through the hall.)

DR. STOCKMANN (Goes to the dining room and looks in). Katrine—! Oh! Are you back, Petra?

PETRA (Enters the sitting room). Yes; I just got back from school.

MRS. STOCKMANN (Enters). Hasn't he been here yet?

DR. STOCKMANN. Peter? No. But I had a long talk with Hovstad. He's quite excited about my discovery. He feels its implications are even more important than I thought. He's placed his newspaper at my disposal—in case I should require it.

MRS. STOCKMANN. But do you think you will?

DR. STOCKMANN. No! I'm sure I shan't. Still—it's very flattering to have the support of an enlightened, independent paper, such as his. I had a visit from the chairman of the Home-owners Association, too.

MRS. STOCKMANN. Really? What did he want?

DR. STOCKMANN. He, too, wanted to assure me of his support. They're all ready to stand by me, in case of need. Do you know what I have on my side, Katrine?

MRS. STOCKMANN. On your side? No—what?

DR. STOCKMANN. The solid majority.

MRS. STOCKMANN. And is that a good thing for you, Tomas, dear?

DR. STOCKMANN. A good thing! Well—I should hope so! (*He rubs his hands and paces up and down*) What a wonderful thing it is to feel in such close harmony with one's fellowmen!

PETRA. And to know one's doing good and valuable work!

DR. STOCKMANN. Especially when it's for your own home town, Petra.

MRS. STOCKMANN. There's the bell.

DR. STOCKMANN. That must be he. (*A knock at the door*) Come in!

THE MAYOR (*Enters from the hall*). Good morning.

DR. STOCKMANN. I'm glad to see you, Peter.

MRS. STOCKMANN. Good morning, Brother-in-law. And how are you today?

THE MAYOR. Thank you—only so-so. (*To the doctor*) Last night, after office-hours, I received a long dissertation from you on the subject of the Baths.

DR. STOCKMANN. Have you read it?

THE MAYOR. Yes—I have.

DR. STOCKMANN. Well—what do you think of it?

THE MAYOR (*With a side glance*). Hm—

MRS. STOCKMANN. Come along, Petra. (*She and* PETRA *go into the room left.*)

THE MAYOR. Why did you find it necessary to carry on these investigations behind my back?

DR. STOCKMANN. As long as I wasn't absolutely sure, I—

THE MAYOR. Then you think you're absolutely sure now?

DR. STOCKMANN. Didn't my report convince you of that?

THE MAYOR. Is it your intention to submit this report to the Board of Directors as an official document?

DR. STOCKMANN. Of course. Something must be done about it; and at once.

THE MAYOR. In your customary manner, you make use of some very strong expressions. You say among other things, that what we offer our visitors is nothing short of poison.

DR. STOCKMANN. But, Peter—what else can you call it? I tell you—whether you drink it or bathe in it —the water is poison! We can't do this to poor sick people who come here in good faith expecting to be cured!

THE MAYOR. You conclude your report by stating that a sewer must be built to carry off the alleged impurities at Milldale, and that the entire water-system must be redesigned and re-installed.

DR. STOCKMANN. Can you think of any other solution?

THE MAYOR. I found a pretext for calling on the town engineer this morning, and brought the matter up —in a joking way, of course—as something we should perhaps consider some time in the future.

DR. STOCKMAN. In the future!

THE MAYOR. He laughed at the extravagance of the suggestion—I naturally let him think it was my own idea. Have you taken the trouble to find out the cost of these proposed alterations? I gathered from the engineer it would amount to several hundred thousand crowns.

DR. STOCKMANN. As much as that?

THE MAYOR. Yes. But that's not the worst of it. The work would take at least two years.

DR. STOCKMANN. Two years? Two whole years?

THE MAYOR. At least. And what's to happen to the Baths in the meantime? Are we to close them? We'd have no alternative. You don't imagine people would go on coming here if it were rumored that the waters were injurious to the health?

DR. STOCKMANN. But, Peter —that's just what they are.

THE MAYOR. And that this should happen now—just when the Baths are beginning to gain a reputation. Other towns in this vicinity might qualify equally well as health resorts. They'd bend every effort to divert this stream of visitors from us, to them; why shouldn't they? And we should be left stranded. All the money that has been invested in this costly undertaking would be wasted; most likely the whole scheme would have to be abandoned. The town would be completely ruined—thanks to you!

DR. STOCKMANN. Ruined—!

THE MAYOR. The only future the town has is through the Baths—the only future worth mentioning, that is! You know that as well as I do.

DR. STOCKMANN. Well? What do you think should be done?

THE MAYOR. I find myself unconvinced by your report. I cannot fully persuade myself that conditions are as critical as your statement represents.

DR. STOCKMANN. If anything they're worse! At least they will be, during the summer, when the hot weather sets in.

THE MAYOR. I repeat that in my opinion you greatly exaggerate the situation. I am certain that a competent physician would find adequate steps to take

—would be able to counteract any harmful agents, should their presence be definitely established.

DR. STOCKMANN. I see. And then—?

THE MAYOR. The present water-system is an established fact and must, of course, be treated as such. At some future time the Directors might see their way clear—provided the cost was not too exorbitant—to inaugurate certain improvements.

DR. STOCKMANN. You don't imagine I could ever be party to such a swindle?

THE MAYOR. Swindle?

DR. STOCKMANN. Swindle, yes! It would be the worst kind of trickery—an out and out crime against Society!

THE MAYOR. I've already told you, I've not been able to persuade myself of the existence of any imminent danger.

DR. STOCKMANN. Yes, you have! You couldn't possibly have done otherwise. My report is so obviously clear and convincing. You understand the situation perfectly, Peter, but you simply refuse to face it. You were responsible for the placement of the Baths and the water-works—it was you who insisted on putting them where they are. It was a damnable mistake and now you refuse to admit it. Do you think I don't see through you?

THE MAYOR. And what if it were so? If I am concerned with protecting my reputation, it's only for the good of the town. I cannot possibly direct affairs in a manner conducive to the general welfare as I see it, unless my integrity and authority are unassailable. For this reason—among others—I consider it imperative that your report should not be brought to the notice of the Board of Directors. It must be withheld for the sake of the community. Later on I will bring the matter up for discussion and we will go to work quietly and see what can be done. Meanwhile not a word—not a breath —about this unfortunate business must be allowed to leak out.

DR. STOCKMANN. I'm afraid that can hardly be prevented, my dear Peter.

THE MAYOR. It must and shall be prevented.

DR. STOCKMANN. It's no use, I tell you; too many people know of it already.

THE MAYOR. Know of it! Whom? Surely not those fellows from *The People's Monitor*—?

DR. STOCKMANN. Yes—they know about it too. The free press will certainly see to it that you're made to do your duty.

THE MAYOR. You're an incredibly rash man, Tomas. Hasn't it occurred to you that all this might have serious consequences for you?

DR. STOCKMANN. Consequences—for me?

THE MAYOR. For you—and those dear to you, yes.

DR. STOCKMANN. What the devil do you mean by that?

THE MAYOR. As your brother, I've always been ready and willing to help you—I think I may say that?

DR. STOCKMANN. You have indeed—and I thank you for it.

THE MAYOR. I don't ask for thanks. In a way I was forced into it—for my own sake. By helping you to greater financial security I had hoped to keep you in check, to some extent.

DR. STOCKMANN. Do you mean to tell me you only did it for your own sake?

THE MAYOR. In a way, I said. It's extremely awkward for an official, when his closest relative is continuously compromising himself.

DR. STOCKMANN. You think I do that, do you?

THE MAYOR. Yes, you do—unfortunately; I daresay you're not even aware of it. You have a restless, violent, rebellious nature, and you can't resist going into print indiscriminately on any and all subjects. No sooner does a thought strike you than you dash off an article to the newspaper—or you write a whole pamphlet on the subject.

DR. STOCKMANN. Surely if one has new ideas, it's one's duty to share them with the public!

THE MAYOR. Believe me, the public has no need of new ideas; it's better off without them. The best way to serve the public is to give it what it's used to.

DR. STOCKMANN. That's a very bald statement!

THE MAYOR. For once I must be frank with you. I've tried to avoid it hitherto, because I know how irritable you are; but it's time I told you the truth, Tomas. You don't realize how you antagonize people by this intolerant attitude of yours. You criticize the authorities—you even criticize the Government; you do nothing but find fault. And then you complain of being slighted—of being persecuted. With your difficult nature, what can you expect?

DR. STOCKMANN. Oh—so I'm difficult too, am I?

THE MAYOR. Yes, Tomas; you are an extremely difficult man to get along with. I speak from experience. You seem to forget that you have me to thank for your present position as medical adviser to the Baths—

DR. STOCKMANN. I was entitled to that position—it belonged to me by right! It was I who first saw the possibility of creating a health resort here, and I was the only one at that time who believed in it. I fought for the idea single-handed for many years. I wrote about it—publicized it—

THE MAYOR. That is undeniable. But at that time the scheme was premature. Living as you did then, in that out-of-the-way corner of the world, you naturally couldn't be a judge of that. But later, when circumstances seemed more favorable, I—and the others—took the matter in hand—

DR. STOCKMANN. Yes. And a fine mess you made of it! You took my splendid plan and ruined it. And now the results of your cleverness and shrewdness are all too obvious.

THE MAYOR. Only one thing is obvious, in my opinion: you feel the need to be belligerent—to strike out at your superiors; that's an old habit of yours. You refuse to submit to the slightest authority; you regard anyone above you as a personal enemy, and are prepared to use every conceivable weapon against him. I have now pointed out to you what is at stake for the town as a whole—and consequently for me personally. I warn you, Tomas, I shall be completely ruthless unless you accept certain conditions.

DR. STOCKMANN. What conditions?

THE MAYOR. Since you have seen fit to go round gossiping about a subject, which should, of course, have been treated with the utmost discretion as an official secret, it is too late to hush the matter up. There are bound to be all sorts of rumors, and malicious-minded people will of course elaborate them. It will therefore be necessary for you publicly to refute them.

DR. STOCKMANN. I? But how? I don't understand.

THE MAYOR. We shall expect you, on further investigation, to come to the conclusion that the situation is not nearly as pressing or as dangerous as you had at first imagined.

DR. STOCKMANN. Oh! You expect that of me, do you?

THE MAYOR. Furthermore we will expect you to make a public statement expressing your faith in the management's integrity and in their intention to take thorough and conscientious steps to remedy any possible defects.

DR. STOCKMANN. But that's out of the question, Peter. No amount of patching or tinkering can put this matter right; I tell you I *know!* It is my firm and unalterable conviction—

THE MAYOR. As a member of the staff you have no right to personal convictions.

DR. STOCKMANN (*With a start*). No right to—?

THE MAYOR. Not as a member of the staff—no! As a private individual—that's of course another matter. But as a subordinate in the employ of the Baths you have no right openly to express convictions opposed to those of your superiors.

DR. STOCKMANN. This is too much! Do you mean to tell me that as a doctor—a scientific man—I have no right to—!

THE MAYOR. But this is not purely a scientific matter; there are other questions involved—technical and economic questions.

DR. STOCKMANN. To hell with all that! I insist that I am free to speak my mind on any and all questions!

THE MAYOR. You are free to do anything you please —as long as it doesn't concern the Baths. But we forbid you to touch on that subject.

DR. STOCKMANN (*Shouts*). Forbid it—you! A bunch of—!

THE MAYOR. *I* forbid it. I personally—your superior in chief. And when I give an order I expect to be obeyed.

DR. STOCKMANN (*Controlling himself*). By God! If you weren't my brother, Peter—!

PETRA (*Flings open the door*). Don't put up with this, Father!

MRS. STOCKMANN (*Following her*). Petra! Petra!

THE MAYOR. So! We've been listening at doors, have we?

MRS. STOCKMANN. You talked so loud—we couldn't very well help hearing—

PETRA. That's not true. I was listening on purpose.

THE MAYOR. Well—I can't say I'm sorry—

DR. STOCKMANN (*A step toward him*). You talked to me in terms of forbidding—of forcing me to obedience—

THE MAYOR. I had to; you gave me no choice.

DR. STOCKMANN. So you expect me to recant in public.

THE MAYOR. We consider it imperative that you issue a statement along the lines indicated.

DR. STOCKMANN. And what if I refuse?

THE MAYOR. Then—in order to reassure the public —we shall have to issue a statement ourselves.

DR. STOCKMANN. Very well. I shall attack you in the newspapers; I shall use every means to prove that

I am right and that you are wrong. What do you say to that?

THE MAYOR. In that case I shall not be able to prevent your dismissal.

DR. STOCKMANN. What—!

PETRA. Dismissal! Father!

MRS. STOCKMANN. Dismissal!

THE MAYOR. I shall be obliged to advise the Board to give you your notice and to see that you have no further connection with the Baths.

DR. STOCKMANN. You would dare do that!

THE MAYOR. It is you who force me to it.

PETRA. Uncle! This is a disgraceful way to treat a man like Father!

MRS. STOCKMANN. Do be quiet, Petra!

THE MAYOR (*Looking at* PETRA). So! We already presume to have opinions, do we? I suppose it's only natural. (*To* MRS. STOCKMANN) Sister-in-law, you seem to be the only sensible member of this household. I advise you to use what influence you have on your husband; try and make him realize what this will mean both for his family—

DR. STOCKMANN. My family is my own concern!

THE MAYOR. I repeat—both for his family, and for the town he lives in.

DR. STOCKMANN. I'm the one who has the good of the town at heart—you know that perfectly well! This is my home town and I love it. That's why I want to expose this dangerous situation that, sooner or later, must come to light.

THE MAYOR. And in order to prove your love for it you insist on destroying the town's one hope of prosperity?

DR. STOCKMANN. But it's a *false* hope, man! Are you mad? Do you want the town to grow rich by selling filth and poison? Must its prosperity be founded on a lie?

THE MAYOR. That's worse than nonsense—it's downright libelous! Only an enemy of Society could insinuate such things against his native town.

DR. STOCKMANN (*Steps towards him*). You dare to—!

MRS. STOCKMANN (*Throws herself between them*). Tomas!

PETRA (*Seizes her father's arm*). Steady, Father!

THE MAYOR. I refuse to expose myself to violence. You've been warned. I advise you to remember what you owe to yourself and to your family. Goodbye. (*He goes.*)

DR. STOCKMANN. They expect me to put up with that kind of treatment, do they? And in my own house too! What do you say to that, Katrine?

MRS. STOCKMANN. It's disgraceful, Tomas, I know—it's shameful—

PETRA. I wish I could have a talk with Uncle—!

DR. STOCKMANN. I suppose it's my own fault; I should have stood up to them long ago—held my own—defied them! An enemy of Society, am I? I'm damned if I'll put up with that!

MRS. STOCKMANN. Remember, Tomas—your brother has the power on his side—

DR. STOCKMANN. But I have the right on mine!

MRS. STOCKMANN. The right—yes, I daresay; but what good is right against might?

PETRA. Mother! How can you talk like that!

DR. STOCKMANN. Might, might! Don't talk nonsense, Katrine. In a free society to be *right* is what counts! I have the free press behind me, and the solid majority on my side—you heard what Aslaksen said. Isn't that might enough for you?

MRS. STOCKMANN. But, Tomas—you're surely not thinking of—?

DR. STOCKMANN. Of what?

MRS. STOCKMANN. Of going against your brother's wishes?

DR. STOCKMANN. What the devil do you expect me to do? What else *can* I do if I'm to stick up for what's honest and right?

PETRA. That's what I'd like to know!

MRS. STOCKMANN. But you know it won't be of any use! If they won't do it—they won't!

DR. STOCKMANN. Just give me time, Katrine. I'll succeed in the end—you'll see.

MRS. STOCKMANN. You'll succeed in getting dismissed—that's what it'll end with.

DR. STOCKMANN. In any case I shall have done my duty to Society—even though I am supposed to be its enemy!

MRS. STOCKMANN. But what about your family, Tomas? What about those dependent on you? Would you be doing your duty to us?

PETRA. Oh, do stop putting us first, Mother!

MRS. STOCKMANN. It's all very well for you to talk—you can manage alone, if need be. But what about the boys, Tomas? And yourself? And me?

DR. STOCKMANN. You must be stark, raving mad, Katrine! If I were such a coward as to kow-tow to Peter and his blasted crew—do you think I'd ever again have a moment's happiness?

MRS. STOCKMANN. I don't know about that; but God preserve us from the sort of happiness we'll have if you persist in defying them! We'll have nothing to live on; you'll be jobless, penniless—just as you were in the old days. We can't go through that again! Be sensible, Tomas; think of the consequences!

DR. STOCKMANN (*Struggling with himself and clenching his hands*). It's disgraceful that these damned bureaucrats should be able to do this to a free, honorable man! Don't you agree, Katrine?

MRS. STOCKMANN. They've treated you abominably —there's no doubt about that. But there's so much injustice in the world—one must just put up with it. Think of the boys, Tomas! Look at them! What's to become of them? You surely wouldn't have the heart to—

(EJLIF *and* MORTEN *have entered while she speaks; they carry their schoolbooks.*)

DR. STOCKMANN. The boys—! (*Firmly and decisively*) I don't care if the whole world crumbles, I refuse to be a slave to any man! (*He goes towards his study.*)

MRS. STOCKMANN (*Follows him*). Tomas! What are you going to do?

DR. STOCKMANN (*At the door*). When my boys grow up to be free men, I want to be able to look them in the face! (*He goes into his study.*)

MRS. STOCKMANN (*Bursting into tears*). God help us all!

PETRA. Father's wonderful, Mother! He'll never give in! CURTAIN

DISCUSSION

1. (a) Explain in what way Morten Kiil both understands and misunderstands what Dr. Stockmann is planning to do. (b) Why is Kiil so pleased with the doctor's "monkey-tricks"? (c) Do you think he would be pleased if he were fully aware of the situation? Explain.

2. Dr. Stockmann traces the source of the trouble at the Baths to the poisonous swamp by the tanneries. Hovstad talks about another kind of trouble. (a) What is it? (b) Where does it come from?

3. (a) In what way does Hovstad plan to take advantage of the situation which the doctor has uncovered? (b) How does Stockmann react?

4. (a) What political pressure group does Aslaksen represent? (b) Why does he think his support may be necessary? (c) What one condition does he impose?

5. What two reasons cause the Mayor to insist that Dr. Stockmann suppress his findings?

6. (a) According to the Mayor, what is the best way to serve the public? (b) Can you give an example (outside of the play) that shows this kind of attitude in practice?

7. (a) When the Mayor learns that it will be impossible to suppress the doctor's findings, what does he demand that Stockmann do? (b) What kind of threat does he use to enforce his demands?

8. Katrine pleads with her husband not to defy the Mayor, and, for a while, her arguments appear to convince him. (a) What finally persuades Stockmann not to give in to the Mayor's pressure? (b) In your opinion, has the doctor made a wise or unwise decision? Why?

THE AUTHOR'S CRAFT

Social drama

On June 21, 1882, Henrik Ibsen wrote to his publisher, Frederik Hegel, "Yesterday I completed my new dramatic work. It is entitled *An Enemy of the People,* and is in five acts. I am still a little uncertain whether to call it a comedy or simply a play; it has much of the character of a comedy, but there is also a serious basic theme."*

It is easy to understand Ibsen's reluctance to put a label on his play. It is not a comedy, though it contains many humorous elements. Nor is it a totally serious play, though it contains a serious basic theme. Today, the term which most satisfactorily describes *An Enemy of the People* is *social drama.*

Social drama addresses itself to the political, social, and environmental problems in life. It may contain humorous elements, but its subject is the serious examination of a social issue. It is this issue-oriented nature of social drama which distinguishes it from other types of modern plays.

As you continue reading *An Enemy of the People,* ask yourself these questions: What is humorous? What is serious? How do both elements contribute to the effectiveness of the play?

*From IBSEN by Michael Meyer. Copyright © 1967, 1971 by Michael Meyer. Reprinted by permission of Doubleday & Company, Inc. and David Higham Associates, Ltd. for the publisher, Hart-Davis.

Act Three

SCENE: *The editorial office of* The People's Monitor. *The entrance door is in the background to the left; in the same wall to the right another door with glass panes, through which can be seen the composing-room. A door in the wall right. A large table stands in the middle of the room covered with papers, newspapers and books. Down left a window and by it a desk with a high stool. A couple of armchairs by the table; other chairs along the walls. The room is dingy and cheerless, the furniture old and the armchairs dirty and torn. In the composing-room some printers can be seen at work; further back a hand-press is in operation.*

HOVSTAD *is seated at the desk writing. In a few moments* BILLING *enters from the door right, with the doctor's manuscript in his hand.*

BILLING. Well, I must say—!

HOVSTAD (*Still writing*). Have you read it?

BILLING (*Laying the ms. on the desk*). I have indeed!

HOVSTAD. The doctor has courage, hasn't he? It's a strong statement!

BILLING. Strong! Strike me dead—it's positively crushing! Every word has the impact of a sledge-hammer.

HOVSTAD. It'll take more than one blow to knock those fellows out.

BILLING. That's true enough; but we'll keep on pounding at them and one of these days they'll come crashing down. As I sat there reading that article I could almost hear the revolution thundering in the distance.

HOVSTAD (*Turning round*). Careful! Don't let Aslaksen hear that.

BILLING. Aslaksen is a chicken-hearted milksop—he hasn't an ounce of manly feeling in him! But you'll insist on having your own way this time, won't you? You'll definitely use the doctor's statement?

HOVSTAD. If the Mayor doesn't give in—yes.

BILLING. It'd be a damn nuisance if he did!

HOVSTAD. Well—fortunately we're bound to gain by the situation in any case. If the Mayor doesn't agree to the doctor's proposition he'll have all the little people on his neck—the Home-owners Association, and all the rest of them. And if he does agree to it, all the rich people will be up in arms; all the people who've hitherto been his chief supporters—including of course those who have the biggest investment in the Baths—

BILLING. Yes; I suppose it would cost them a pretty penny to make the alterations—

HOVSTAD. There's no doubt of that! And once the reactionary party is split up, we can continue to expose the Mayor's total inefficiency, and convince the public that the Liberals must be brought to power, for the general good of the community.

BILLING. Strike me dead if that isn't the truth! I feel it—I feel it—the revolution is approaching!

(*A knock at the door.*)

HOVSTAD. Hush! (*Calls out*) Come in!

(DR. STOCKMANN *enters from the door upper left.*)

HOVSTAD (*Going to meet him*). Ah, here's the doctor now. Well?

DR. STOCKMANN. You may go ahead and print it, Mr. Hovstad.

HOVSTAD. So it's really come to that, has it?

BILLING. Hurrah!

DR. STOCKMANN. Yes—it's come to that; so print away, I say! They've asked for war, now let them have it.

BILLING. War to the death, I hope; war to the death!

DR. STOCKMANN. This first article is only the beginning; I have four or five others in mind—my head's bursting with ideas. Where's Aslaksen?

BILLING (*Calling into the printing room*). Oh, Aslaksen! Come here a minute, will you!

HOVSTAD. Four or five others, you say? On the same subject?

DR. STOCKMANN. Oh, by no means; they'll deal with quite different matters. They all stem from the water-works and the sewerage-system, of course —one thing leads to another. It's exactly like trying to patch up an old building.

BILLING. Strike me dead—that's the truth! You do a bit here and a bit there, but the whole thing's so rotten, you end by tearing it down!

ASLAKSEN (*Enters from the printing room*). Tearing down! Surely, Doctor, you're not thinking of tearing down the Baths!

HOVSTAD. No, of course not; you needn't be alarmed.

DR. STOCKMANN. We were talking about something quite different. Well—what do you think of my article, Mr. Hovstad?

HOVSTAD. I think it's an absolute masterpiece—

DR. STOCKMANN. Yes, isn't it—? I'm so glad you agree!

HOVSTAD. It's clear and to the point—anyone could

follow it; there's no need to be a specialist. You'll have every intelligent man on your side.

ASLAKSEN. And the prudent ones as well, I hope.

BILLING. Prudent—and imprudent too! Pretty nearly the whole town in fact—

ASLAKSEN. In that case, I think we might safely venture to print it.

DR. STOCKMANN. Well—I should hope so!

HOVSTAD. It'll be in tomorrow morning.

DR. STOCKMANN. Splendid! There's no time to lose, you know. By the way, Mr. Aslaksen, there's one thing I'd like to ask you; you'll supervise the printing of the article yourself, won't you?

ASLAKSEN. Indeed I will.

DR. STOCKMANN. It's very precious, remember. We don't want any errors; every word is important: I'll drop in again presently—you might let me see a proof. I can't wait to have the thing in print—to get it launched.

BILLING. It'll be a bombshell!

DR. STOCKMANN. I want every enlightened citizen to read it and judge for himself. You've no idea what I've been through today. I've been exposed to every kind of pressure; my rights as an individual have been threatened—

BILLING. Your rights—!

DR. STOCKMANN. Yes! I was expected to crawl and humble myself. My deepest—my most sacred convictions were to be sacrificed for purely personal ends—

BILLING. Strike me dead! This is an outrage!

DR. STOCKMANN. But this time they've gone too far —and they shall be told so in no uncertain terms! I shall set up my headquarters here at *The People's Monitor*, and continue to attack them daily—

ASLAKSEN. But, just a minute—

BILLING. Hurrah! It's war—war!

DR. STOCKMANN. I'll run them into the ground; smash

them to pieces—wipe them out! I'll show the public what they really are—that's what I'll do!

ASLAKSEN. But you will use moderation, my dear Doctor; attack—but prudently.

BILLING. No! Don't spare the dynamite!

DR. STOCKMANN. It's no longer merely a question of sewers and water-works, you see; it's a question of cleaning up the whole community—

BILLING. That's the way to talk!

DR. STOCKMANN. All those old fogies must be kicked out of office, no matter what position they may hold. I have such a clear perspective on everything today; I don't see all the details yet, but I'll soon work them out. What we need, my friends, is young and vital leaders—new captains at the outposts.

BILLING. Hear, hear!

DR. STOCKMANN. If we stand together, we're bound to win. This whole revolution will be launched quite smoothly—like a new ship gliding down the ways. Don't you believe that?

HOVSTAD. I believe we have every hope of putting the right people into power at last.

ASLAKSEN. And if we proceed with caution, I see no reason why we should run into any danger.

DR. STOCKMANN. Who the hell cares about danger! This is a matter of truth and conscience!

HOVSTAD. You deserve every support, Doctor.

ASLAKSEN. Dr. Stockmann is a true friend of the town; a friend of Society—that's what he is.

BILLING. Strike me dead! He's a friend of the People, Aslaksen!

ASLAKSEN. I'm sure the Home-owners Association will use that as a slogan.

DR. STOCKMANN. My dear friends—I can't thank you enough for all your loyalty; it does me good to hear you. My sainted brother called me something very different; but he'll be repaid—with interest! I'll be off now—I have to see a poor devil of a patient—but I'll be back. Take good care of my article, won't you, Mr. Aslaksen? And don't cut out any exclamation-marks! You can even add a few if you like! Well—goodbye for now; I'll be back shortly. Goodbye.

(*General goodbyes as they accompany him to the door; he goes.*)

HOVSTAD. He can be exceedingly useful to us.

ASLAKSEN. Yes, providing he sticks to this matter of the Baths; if he goes beyond that, it might be unwise to follow him.

HOVSTAD. Hm; it all depends on—

BILLING. You're always so damned frightened, Aslaksen.

ASLAKSEN. Frightened? Yes, when it comes to attacking the local authorities I am frightened, Mr. Billing. I've learned in a hard school, you see. National politics however are another matter; in such things you wouldn't find me frightened, I assure you—even if you were to pit me against the Government itself.

BILLING. I dare say not; that's where you're so inconsistent.

ASLAKSEN. Where the good of the town is concerned, I am very conscientious. There's no harm in attacking the Government—what does the Government care? Those men at the top are unassailable. But the local authorities are different—they can be dismissed; and should their power fall into the hands of inexperienced men, not only the Home-owners but the entire community would suffer.

HOVSTAD. If the People are never allowed self-government how can they ever gain experience? Haven't you thought of that?

ASLAKSEN. When one has vested interests, Mr. Hovstad, one must protect them. A man can't think of everything.

HOVSTAD. Vested interests! Then I hope I never have any!

BILLING. Hear, hear!

ASLAKSEN (*With a smile*). Hm. (*Points to the desk*) There was a time when Commissioner Stensgaard sat in that editor's chair, if you remember.

BILLING (*Spitting*). Pooh! That turncoat!

HOVSTAD. Well—I'm no weathercock, and never will be!

ASLAKSEN. A politician should never say "never" about anything, Mr. Hovstad. And as for you, Mr. Billing—I understand you've applied for the post of secretary to the Town Council; hadn't you better use a little caution?

BILLING. I—!

HOVSTAD. Billing—is this true?

BILLING. As a matter of fact, it is. I'm only doing it to spite the Bigwigs, mind you!

ASLAKSEN. Well—it's no business of mine. I may be accused of cowardice and inconsistency, but my political record is an open book. I've never changed in anyway—except, possibly, to become more moderate. My heart is, and always has been, with the People; I must admit, however, that my common-sense inclines me towards the side of the authorities, to some extent; the local authorities, I mean. (*He goes into the printing office.*)

BILLING. Shouldn't we try to get rid of him, Hovstad?

HOVSTAD. Do you know of anybody else who'd be willing to pay our expenses?

BILLING. It's damnable to have no capital!

HOVSTAD (*Sits down at the desk*). Yes; we'd be all right if we had that!

BILLING. Why don't you talk to Dr. Stockmann?

HOVSTAD (*Looking through some papers*). What good would that do? He hasn't a penny.

BILLING. No—but he has connections; old Morten Kiil—"the badger" as they call him.

HOVSTAD (*Writing*). You really think he has money?

BILLING. Strike me dead—of course he has! And Stockmann's family is bound to get part of it. The old man's sure to provide for—for the children, at any rate.

HOVSTAD (*Half turning*). Are you counting on that?

BILLING. What do you mean—"counting?" You know I never count on anything.

HOVSTAD. You're wise. And you'd better not count on that job as secretary either; I assure you, you won't get it.

BILLING. Do you suppose I don't know that? That's the very reason I've applied for it. A slight of that sort fires the spirit of rebellion in one—gives one a fresh supply of vitriol,[10] as it were; and that's a very necessary thing in a God-forsaken hole like this where nothing really stimulating ever seems to happen.

HOVSTAD (*Still writing*). Yes, yes; I know, I know.

BILLING. But—one of these days they'll hear from me, I promise you! —Well—I'd better go in and write that appeal to the Home-owners Association. (*He goes into the room on the right.*)

HOVSTAD (*At the desk: he bites the end of his penholder[11] and says slowly*). Hm. —I see. —So that's it. (*A knock at the door*) Come in!

(PETRA *enters from the back, left.*)

HOVSTAD (*Rising*). Well! It's you, is it? What are you doing here?

PETRA. You must excuse me for—

HOVSTAD (*Pushes an armchair forward*). Do sit down.

PETRA. No thanks; I can only stay a minute.

HOVSTAD. Is it a message from your father—?

PETRA. No, I've come on my own account. (*Takes a book out of her coat pocket*) I've brought back that English story.

HOVSTAD. Brought it back—why?

PETRA. Because I don't want to translate it after all.

HOVSTAD. But you gave me a definite promise—

PETRA. I know; but I hadn't read it then. You haven't read it, have you?

HOVSTAD. No—I don't read English; but—

PETRA. That's what I thought; so I felt I should advise you to look around for something else. (*Putting the book on the table*) This would never do for *The People's Monitor*.

HOVSTAD. Why not?

PETRA. Because it's against everything you stand for.

HOVSTAD. Well, as far as that goes—

PETRA. No—you don't see my point; this story claims that there's a supernatural power looking after all the so-called good people in the world, so that everything turns out well for them in the end— whereas all the so-called bad people get punished.

HOVSTAD. Splendid! Just what the public wants.

PETRA. Yes; but you surely wouldn't want to be the one to give them such nonsense. You don't believe a word of it yourself; you know perfectly well that's not the way things really happen.

HOVSTAD. You're right, of course; but, you see, a publisher can't always do as he pleases—he often has to cater to the public in minor matters. Politics, after all, are the main thing—to a newspaper at any rate; if I want to steer people towards a more liberal way of thinking, I can't afford to scare them off. If they come across a nice moral tale like that tucked away somewhere in the back pages of the paper they feel safer, and they're more willing to accept what we give them on the front page.

PETRA. But that's disgusting! I'm sure you'd never play a trick like that. You're not a hypocrite!

HOVSTAD (*Smiling*). I'm glad you think so well of me. As a matter of fact it's Billing's idea, not mine.

PETRA. Billing's!

HOVSTAD. Yes; at least he was talking along those lines only the other day. It was Billing who wanted to print the story; I don't know anything about it.

PETRA. Mr. Billing! But that seems impossible; he has such a modern point of view!

HOVSTAD. Well, you see—Billing is a man of many parts. He's now decided he wants to become secretary to the Town Council—or so I hear.

---

10. *vitriol* (vit′rē əl), concentrated sulfuric acid, used here figuratively to suggest bitterness.
11. *penholder*, a straight pen in which a point is inserted.

PETRA. I don't believe that for a moment, Mr. Hovstad. He could never lower himself to that!

HOVSTAD. You'd better ask him about it.

PETRA. I never would have thought such a thing of Mr. Billing.

HOVSTAD (*Looks at her intently*). No? Is it really such a surprise to you?

PETRA. Yes, indeed it is. And yet—perhaps it isn't really. I don't know what to think—

HOVSTAD. We newspaper men are worthless fellows, Miss Petra.

PETRA. Do you really mean that?

HOVSTAD. Yes; at least, I sometimes think so.

PETRA. That may be true as far as ordinary petty everyday matters are concerned. But now that you're involved in a great cause—

HOVSTAD. You mean this business about your father?

PETRA. Yes, of course. It must give you a proud feeling; a sense of being worth more than just ordinary people.

HOVSTAD. You're right; I do feel a bit like that today.

PETRA. I'm sure you must. What a wonderful career you've chosen! To be a pioneer; to promote the truth; to fight for bold ideas—new ways of thinking! The mere fact of coming to the defense of someone who's been wronged—

HOVSTAD. Especially when that someone is—I don't quite know how to put it—

PETRA. When he's so true and honorable, you mean?

HOVSTAD (*In a low voice*). Yes; and especially when he happens to be your father.

PETRA (*Suddenly taken aback*). You mean—? Oh, no!

HOVSTAD. Yes, Petra—Miss Petra.

PETRA. Is that your reason—? Is that what matters most to you? Then, it isn't the thing itself; the truth means nothing to you—and my father's generosity of soul means nothing either!

HOVSTAD. Yes, of course it does, but—

PETRA. Thank you, Mr. Hovstad. You've said more than enough. I shall never trust you again in anything.

HOVSTAD. Come now—you mustn't be too hard on me! Even if it is mainly for your sake—

PETRA. What makes me angry is that you haven't been honest with my father. You let him think you were concerned with the truth, with the good of the community, when all the time—! You've made fools of us both, Mr. Hovstad. You're not at all the sort of man you pretended to be. I shall never forgive you for it—never!

HOVSTAD. I wouldn't be too caustic, Miss Petra; this is not the time for that.

PETRA. Not the time? Why not?

HOVSTAD. Because your father can't very well get on without my help.

PETRA. I see. So you're that sort of a person too.

HOVSTAD. No, no—really I'm not! I didn't think what I was saying; you must believe me!

PETRA. I know what to believe, I assure you. Goodbye.

ASLAKSEN (*Enters hurriedly and mysteriously from the printing office*). Hell and damnation, Mr. Hovstad—! (*Sees* PETRA) Oh, I beg your pardon—

PETRA. There's the book. Get someone else to do it for you. (*Goes towards the main entrance.*)

HOVSTAD (*Following her*). But, Miss Petra—

PETRA. Goodbye. (*She goes.*)

ASLAKSEN. Mr. Hovstad, listen!

HOVSTAD. Well—what is it? What's the matter?

ASLAKSEN. It's the Mayor! He's out in the printing office.

HOVSTAD. The Mayor?

ASLAKSEN. Yes; he says he wants to talk to you. He came in the back way—didn't want to be seen, I suppose.

HOVSTAD. What does this mean, I wonder? Wait a minute—I'll go myself— (*He goes toward the printing office, opens the door, bows and invites* THE MAYOR *to come in.*)

HOVSTAD. Be on the look-out, Aslaksen, and see that no one—

ASLAKSEN. I understand— (*He goes into the printing office.*)

THE MAYOR. I don't suppose you expected to see me here, Mr. Hovstad.

HOVSTAD. No, I can't say I did.

THE MAYOR (*Looking round*). A nice place you have here; most comfortable.

HOVSTAD. Well—

THE MAYOR. You must forgive me for dropping in like this, and taking up your time.

HOVSTAD. I'm only too delighted, Mr. Mayor; always at your service. Let me take your things— (*Takes* THE MAYOR's *hat and cane and puts them on a chair*) And now—won't you sit down?

THE MAYOR (*Sits by the table*). Thanks. (HOVSTAD *sits down at the table also*) I've been faced with—with a very troubling matter today, Mr. Hovstad.

HOVSTAD. Really? But, of course, you must have so many duties—

THE MAYOR. It concerns my brother, Mr. Hovstad.

HOVSTAD. Dr. Stockmann?

THE MAYOR. Yes. He's written a sort of memorandum to the directors of the Baths, alleging that there are certain defects in the establishment.

HOVSTAD. Really? Has he?

THE MAYOR. Hasn't he told you? I thought he said—

HOVSTAD. Now I come to think of it, I believe he did mention—

ASLAKSEN (*Enters from the printing office*): I'd better have that manuscript—

HOVSTAD (*With annoyance*): It's over on the desk.

ASLAKSEN. Ah, yes—here it is.

THE MAYOR. But surely—Isn't that—?

ASLAKSEN. It's Dr. Stockmann's article.

HOVSTAD. Oh—was that what you were referring to?

THE MAYOR. Precisely—What do you think of it?

HOVSTAD. I've only just glanced at it—and, of course, I'm not an expert—

THE MAYOR. And yet you intend to print it?

HOVSTAD. I can't very well refuse anything signed by—

ASLAKSEN. I've nothing to do with editing the paper, Mr. Mayor.

THE MAYOR. No, of course not.

ASLAKSEN. I just do the printing.

THE MAYOR. I understand.

ASLAKSEN. So—if you'll excuse me— (*Goes towards the pressroom.*)

THE MAYOR. Just one moment, Mr. Aslaksen. With your permission, Mr. Hovstad—?

HOVSTAD. Of course.

THE MAYOR. Mr. Aslaksen—you seem to me to be a discreet and sensible man.

ASLAKSEN. It's very kind of you to say so—

THE MAYOR. And a man of widespread influence too.

ASLAKSEN. Only among the little people, Your Honor.

THE MAYOR. It's the small taxpayers who form the majority—here, as everywhere.

ASLAKSEN. That's true enough.

THE MAYOR. And I've no doubt you are familiar with the general trend of sentiment among them. Are you not?

ASLAKSEN. I think I may say I am, Your Honor.

THE MAYOR. Well—since there appears to be such a fine feeling of self-sacrifice among the poorer classes—

ASLAKSEN. How do you mean?

HOVSTAD. Self-sacrifice?

THE MAYOR. It indicates an admirable sense of public-spirit. I find it a little surprising, I admit; but then I don't know the public sentiment as well as you do.

ASLAKSEN. But, Your Honor—

THE MAYOR. And it will entail no small sacrifice to the town, I can assure you.

HOVSTAD. To the town?

ASLAKSEN. I don't understand; surely, this concerns the Baths—

THE MAYOR. At a rough preliminary estimate, the alterations Dr. Stockmann has in mind will cost in the neighborhood of two hundred thousand crowns.

ASLAKSEN. That's a lot of money; but—

THE MAYOR. A municipal loan will naturally be necessary.

HOVSTAD (*Rising*). You surely can't mean that the town—?

ASLAKSEN. You mean the townspeople would have to pay for it out of their own pockets?

THE MAYOR. My dear Mr. Aslaksen, where else should the money come from?

ASLAKSEN. I should think the owners of the Baths would be responsible.

THE MAYOR. The owners are not prepared to increase their investment at this time.

ASLAKSEN. Are you quite sure of that?

THE MAYOR. I have positive information to that effect. So if these alterations are to be made, the town itself will have to pay for them.

ASLAKSEN. But then, damn it all, Mr. Hovstad—excuse me, Your Honor—this puts the matter in quite a different light!

HOVSTAD. It does indeed.

THE MAYOR. The worst part of it is we shall be obliged to close down the Baths for a couple of years.

HOVSTAD. Close them? Completely close them?

ASLAKSEN. For two years!

THE MAYOR. Yes; it will take at least two years to do the work.

ASLAKSEN. But, damn it! We could never survive that, Your Honor; we home-owners depend on these visitors—what are we to live on in the meantime?

THE MAYOR. That is a difficult question to answer, Mr. Aslaksen. But what's to be done? Once people get this notion into their heads that the waters are tainted, that the whole place is a pest-hole—we can hardly expect them to come here.

ASLAKSEN. Then you think it's no more than a notion?

THE MAYOR. Try as I will, I can't persuade myself to think otherwise.

ASLAKSEN. Then it's downright inexcusable of Dr. Stockmann—I beg pardon, Your Honor, but—

THE MAYOR. Unfortunately you're quite right, Mr. Aslaksen; my brother has always been an exceedingly rash man.

ASLAKSEN. And yet you are prepared to back him up in this, Mr. Hovstad!

HOVSTAD. But who would ever have thought that—!

THE MAYOR. I've drawn up a short statement on the matter, interpreting the facts from a more rational point of view; I've also indicated ways in which any small defects that might conceivably exist can be taken care of within the scope of the present financial budget.

HOVSTAD. Have you it with you?

THE MAYOR (*Feeling in his pocket*). Yes; I thought I'd better bring it in case you—

ASLAKSEN (*Quickly*). Damn it—there he is!

THE MAYOR. Who? My brother?

HOVSTAD. Where?

ASLAKSEN. Coming through the press-room.

THE MAYOR. This is unfortunate! I don't want to run into him here—yet there are several things I'd still like to talk to you about.

HOVSTAD (*Pointing to the door on the right*). Wait in there for a moment.

THE MAYOR. But—?

HOVSTAD. There's no one in there but Billing.

ASLAKSEN. Quick, Your Honor! Here he comes!

THE MAYOR. Very well; get rid of him as soon as you can, though. (*He goes out by the door right which* ASLAKSEN *opens, and closes after him.*)

HOVSTAD. Pretend to be busy, Aslaksen. (*He sits down and starts to write.* ASLAKSEN *goes through a pile of newspapers on a chair, right.*)

DR. STOCKMANN (*Enters from the composing-room*). Well—Here I am, back again. (*Puts down his hat and stick.*)

HOVSTAD (*Writing*). Already, Doctor? Get on with what we were just talking about, Aslaksen. We've no time to waste today.

DR. STOCKMANN (*To* ASLAKSEN). No proofs yet, I hear.

ASLAKSEN (*Without turning round*). You could hardly expect them yet, Doctor.

DR. STOCKMANN. No, of course not. It's just that I'm impatient—you can understand that; I can't wait to see the thing in print.

HOVSTAD. It'll be another hour at least; wouldn't you say so, Aslaksen?

ASLAKSEN. I'm afraid so, yes.

DR. STOCKMANN. Never mind; I'll come back. I don't mind coming back twice if need be. What's a little inconvenience compared to the welfare of the town—! (*Starts to go but stops and comes back*) By the way, there's something I must discuss with you.

HOVSTAD. I'm afraid, just now, you must excuse me, Doctor—

DR. STOCKMANN. It'll only take a moment. I was just thinking: when people read this article of mine tomorrow morning, and realize I devoted my whole winter to working for the good of the town—

HOVSTAD. But, after all, Doctor—

DR. STOCKMANN. Oh, I know what you're going to say—it was no more than my duty as a citizen—I know that as well as you do. But my fellow-townsmen—well, bless their hearts, they're so fond of me, you see—

ASLAKSEN. Yes—they've thought very highly of you up to now—

DR. STOCKMANN. I know; that's why I'm so afraid they might—what I mean is this: the people, especially the poorer classes, are bound to take this article of mine as a rousing call to action—as a summons to run things for themselves from now on—

HOVSTAD (*Rising*). As a matter of fact, Doctor, I think I ought to tell you—

DR. STOCKMANN. I knew it! I was sure they'd be up to something. But I won't hear of it, I tell you! So if they're planning anything like that—

HOVSTAD. Like what?

DR. STOCKMANN. Oh, I don't know—a parade, or a banquet, or a testimonial dinner of some sort—I count on you to put a stop to it. You, too, Mr. Aslaksen—remember now!

HOVSTAD. Excuse me, Doctor; I think you'd better know the truth once and for all—

(MRS. STOCKMANN *enters from the rear door, left.*)

MRS. STOCKMANN (*Seeing the doctor*). Just as I thought!

HOVSTAD (*Goes towards her*). You here too, Mrs. Stockmann?

DR. STOCKMANN. What the devil do you want here, Katrine?

MRS. STOCKMANN. You know very well what I want.

HOVSTAD. Won't you sit down? Or perhaps you'd rather—

MRS. STOCKMANN. Thanks—but please don't bother about me; and forgive my coming here to fetch my husband. I'm the mother of three children, let me tell you.

DR. STOCKMANN. Don't talk nonsense! As if we didn't all know that!

MRS. STOCKMANN. You don't seem to be giving much thought to it—otherwise you wouldn't be so anxious to ruin us all!

DR. STOCKMANN. You must be stark raving mad, Katrine! Just because he has a wife and children, can't a man stand up for the truth? Be a useful citizen? Serve the town he lives in?

MRS. STOCKMANN. If you'd only use a little moderation, Tomas!

ASLAKSEN. That's what I always say: everything in moderation!

MRS. STOCKMANN. It's very wrong of you, Mr. Hovstad, to lure my husband away from house and home; persuading him to get mixed up in all this—making a fool of him!

HOVSTAD. I don't make a fool of anyone—

DR. STOCKMANN. A fool! You think I let people make a fool of me!

MRS. STOCKMANN. Yes, Tomas—you do! Oh, I know you're the cleverest man in town, but you're easily fooled all the same. (To HOVSTAD) Don't you realize he'll lose his position if you print that article of his—

ASLAKSEN. What!

HOVSTAD. As a matter of fact, Dr. Stockmann—

DR. STOCKMANN (Laughing). They can't do a thing to me—they'd never dare! Don't forget, my dear, the solid majority is with me.

MRS. STOCKMANN. More's the pity. You'd be better off without it!

DR. STOCKMANN. Don't talk nonsense, Katrine; go home and tend to your house-work and leave Society to me. What is there to be afraid of! Can't you see how happy and confident I am? (Rubs his hands and walks up and down) The truth will conquer—I'm convinced of it. The people will band together in the cause of truth and freedom, and nothing can stop them—! (Stops suddenly by a chair) Why—what the devil's this doing here?

ASLAKSEN (Realizing). Oh, Lord.

HOVSTAD (The same). Hm—

DR. STOCKMANN (He picks up THE MAYOR's cap and holds it gingerly aloft). The crown of authority, is it not?

MRS. STOCKMANN. It's the Mayor's cap!

DR. STOCKMANN. And the staff of office, too! But what the devil are they doing here?

HOVSTAD. You might as well know—

DR. STOCKMANN. Ah, I see! He came to try and win you over. Well—he chose the wrong customer for once! I suppose he caught sight of me in the office and— (Bursts out laughing) Did he turn tail, Mr. Aslaksen?

ASLAKSEN (Hurriedly). Yes, Doctor, he—he turned tail.

DR. STOCKMANN. Ran off and left his stick and— But, wait a minute—that's not a bit like Peter. What have you done with him? Oh, of course—he's hiding in there. Now you're going to see something, Katrine!

MRS. STOCKMANN. Please, Tomas—!

ASLAKSEN. Be careful, Doctor!

(DR. STOCKMANN has put on THE MAYOR's cap and seized his stick; he goes to the door, flings it open and makes a military salute. THE MAYOR enters, flushed with anger, followed by BILLING.)

THE MAYOR. What is the meaning of these antics?

DR. STOCKMANN. Show some respect, Peter, if you please. (Struts up and down) I'm in authority now!

MRS. STOCKMANN (Almost in tears). Tomas—for heaven's sake!

THE MAYOR (Following him). Give me my cap and stick!

DR. STOCKMANN (As before). You may be chief of police, but I'm the Mayor—I'm king of the whole town!

THE MAYOR. Take off that cap, I tell you. Don't you realize it's a badge of office!

DR. STOCKMANN. Listen to him! We've roused the spirit of democracy—do you think a bit of gold braid can frighten me? Tomorrow the revolution starts, I'd have you know. You threatened to dismiss me, did you? Well now it's my turn to dismiss you—I'm going to kick you out of office! And if you don't think I can do it, you'll soon find out! The power is on my side—the power of an aroused public! Hovstad and Billing here will thunder away at you in the *Monitor*, and Aslaksen will lead the entire Home-owners Association into battle—!

ASLAKSEN. No, Doctor; I'll do nothing of the sort.

DR. STOCKMANN. Nonsense! Of course you will—

THE MAYOR. I see, so perhaps Mr. Hovstad will decide to join the rebels after all?

HOVSTAD. No, Your Honor.

ASLAKSEN. Mr. Hovstad's no fool; he's not likely to ruin both himself and the paper for the sake of a delusion.

DR. STOCKMANN (*Looks from one to the other*). What does this mean?

HOVSTAD. You've presented this whole matter in a false light, Doctor; that is why I cannot possibly give you my support.

BILLING. After what the Mayor so kindly explained to me just now—

DR. STOCKMANN. A false light, eh? Leave that part of it to me—you just print my article; I'll prove the truth of every word of it.

HOVSTAD. I shall not print it. I neither can, nor will, nor dare.

DR. STOCKMANN. Not *dare?* But that's absurd. You're the editor, aren't you? Don't you control your own paper?

ASLAKSEN. No—the subscribers do.

THE MAYOR. Fortunately—yes.

ASLAKSEN. Public opinion, majority interests, the Home-owners Association and other similar groups—they control the paper.

DR. STOCKMANN (*Calmly*). And they would all be against me, you think?

ASLAKSEN. Unquestionably. If your article were printed it would mean the ruin of the town.

DR. STOCKMANN. I see.

THE MAYOR. And now, my cap and stick!

(DR. STOCKMANN *takes off the cap and lays it on the table; he places the stick beside it.*)

THE MAYOR (*Picking them up*). Your term of office came to rather an abrupt end, didn't it?

DR. STOCKMANN. This is not the end, Peter—believe me. (*To* HOVSTAD) So you find it impossible to print my article in the *Monitor?*

HOVSTAD. Quite impossible; apart from anything else, consideration for your family would—

DR. STOCKMANN. Kindly leave my family to me, Mr. Hovstad.

THE MAYOR (*Takes a manuscript from his breast pocket*). This will put the necessary facts before the public. It is an official statement; I trust you to deal with it accordingly.

HOVSTAD (*Taking the manuscript*). Very good. We shall take care of it; it will appear without delay.

DR. STOCKMANN. But mine will be suppressed. Do you think you can suppress the truth? You'll find it's not so easy! Mr. Aslaksen, please take my manuscript and print it as a pamphlet—at my own expense—I'll publish it myself. I want four hundred copies; no, five—better make it six.

ASLAKSEN. I can't possibly use my printing-press for such a purpose, Doctor—not if you were to pay me its weight in gold. I dare not offend public opinion. No one in town will print it, I assure you.

DR. STOCKMANN. Then give it back to me.

HOVSTAD (*Hands it to him*). Gladly.

DR. STOCKMANN (*Takes up his hat and stick*). But you won't be able to suppress it all the same! I'll call a public meeting—I'll read it to the people myself; my fellow-townsmen are going to hear the truth!

THE MAYOR. It won't be any good; not a single hall will be available to you.

ASLAKSEN. Not one—I'll vouch for that.

BILLING. That's true—strike me dead if it isn't!

MRS. STOCKMANN. But this is disgraceful, Tomas! Why are they suddenly all against you?

DR. STOCKMANN. I'll tell you why. It's because all the men in this town are a lot of old women—just like you! They think of nothing but themselves; they don't care a damn about the general good!

MRS. STOCKMANN. Then I'll show them here's at least one old woman who knows how to be a man. I'll stand by you, Tomas!

DR. STOCKMANN. Well said, Katrine! Nothing can stop me; if I can't rent a hall, I'll hire a drum and march through the town with it. I'll read my statement at the corner of every street, of every square—the people are going to know the truth!

THE MAYOR. You can't do that! Are you a raving lunatic?

DR. STOCKMANN. Yes, I am!

ASLAKSEN. No one will go with you, Doctor Stockmann.

BILLING. Strike me dead—I'm sure of that!

MRS. STOCKMANN. Don't give in now, Tomas. I'll ask the boys—they'll go with you.

DR. STOCKMANN. That's a splendid thought!

MRS. STOCKMANN. Morten would be delighted—and I'm certain Ejlif would go too.

DR. STOCKMANN. Yes—and then there's Petra! And you, Katrine!

MRS. STOCKMANN. Oh, no; it wouldn't do for me to go. But I tell you what I'll do—I'll watch you from the window.

DR. STOCKMANN (*Throws his arms round her*). Thanks! Well—the fight is on, gentlemen! We'll see if you and your chicanery can prevent an honest citizen from cleaning up the town he lives in! Come, Katrine! (*He and* MRS. STOCKMANN *go out by the door upper left.*)

THE MAYOR (*Shakes his head thoughtfully*). He's managed to turn her head at last! Now she's as mad as he is.   CURTAIN

DISCUSSION

1. (a) According to Hovstad, what does the Mayor risk if he does not agree to Dr. Stockmann's proposal to rebuild the Baths? (b) If he does agree, what does he risk? (c) Either way, how do Hovstad and Billing plan to take advantage of the situation?

2. Why are Hovstad and Billing careful not to upset Aslaksen?

3. (a) What change in Dr. Stockmann's thinking is revealed by his telling Hovstad to go ahead and print his article? (b) What has caused this change?

4. Aslaksen expresses reluctance to support the doctor completely in his attack on the local officials. (a) What does he fear? (b) What distinction does he make between local and national government?

5. (a) What does Hovstad mean when he says "Well—I'm no weathercock, and never will be!" (b) What is later ironical about his statement?

6. (a) What reason does Billing give for having applied for the post of secretary to the Town Council? (b) Do you believe him? Why or why not?

7. What does Petra's visit to Hovstad reveal about *his* principles?

8. (a) What arguments does the Mayor use to convince Hovstad and Aslaksen not to print Dr. Stockmann's article? (b) Rather than telling them directly not to print the article, what does the Mayor do?

9. According to Aslaksen, who controls *The People's Monitor*? Do you agree? Explain.

AUTHOR

HENRIK JOHAN IBSEN was born on March 20, 1828, in Skien on the eastern coast of Norway. In 1835, financial ruin forced his father to move the family to a modest home in the country where young Ibsen spent eight unhappy years. At the age of fifteen, he left school to work as an apothecary's assistant. In his spare time he became involved in political agitation; dabbled in poetry, drama, and drama criticism; and studied, though unsuccessfully, to pass entrance examinations to the university in Christiania (now, Oslo).

In 1851, Ibsen accepted the position of playwright and stage manager for the Bergen Theater. Six years later he became director of the Norwegian Theater in Christiania. Though these experiences were marked by frustrations, setbacks, and finally defeat, he did gain invaluable stage knowledge and training. In 1862, the Norwegian Theater declared bankruptcy. Two years later Ibsen left Norway.

For the next twenty-seven years Ibsen lived abroad, devoting his energies fully to developing and refining his art. He divided his time between Germany and Italy, maintaining, nevertheless, close contact with the affairs of his homeland. During this period of self-imposed exile, Ibsen wrote most of his plays and achieved international recognition. In 1891, he returned to Norway permanently, where he wrote his last three works. Steadily declining health marked the last six years of his life. He died on May 23, 1906.

In his lifetime, Ibsen's popularity was based primarily on his early and middle plays (e.g., *Brand, The League of Youth*, and *The Pillars of Society*). His more mature work (e.g., *The Wild Duck, Hedda Gabler*, and *The Master Builder*) often confused and even angered his contemporaries. Today, Ibsen's reputation as a dramatist of the highest rank rests on these later plays.

Act Four

SCENE. *A large old-fashioned room in* CAPTAIN
HORSTER's *house. Open double doors in the back wall
lead to an anteroom. In the wall left are three windows; in the center of the opposite wall is a platform
on which stands a small table with two candles, a
carafe[12] of water, a glass and a bell placed on it.
Sconces[13] between the windows provide the general
lighting. Down left a small table with a candle, and
a chair beside it. Down right a door and near it a
couple of chairs.*

    *There is a large gathering of townspeople of var-
ious types. Among the crowd are seen a few women
and schoolboys. People continue to stream in from
the anteroom until the main room is quite full.*

FIRST MAN (*as he bumps into another one*). You're
here too, are you, Lamstad?

SECOND MAN. I never miss a public meeting.

ANOTHER MAN. I see you've brought your whistle.

SECOND MAN. Of course; haven't you?

THIRD MAN. I should hope so! Skipper Evensen said
he was going to bring his big horn!

SECOND MAN. That Evensen's a good one, he is!
(*Laughter in the group.*)

FOURTH MAN (*Joining them*). Tell me—what's going
on here this evening?

SECOND MAN. Doctor Stockmann and the Mayor are
holding a debate.

FOURTH MAN. But the Mayor's his brother, isn't he?

FIRST MAN. That makes no difference; Doctor Stockmann's not afraid of anyone.

THIRD MAN. But he's all wrong; it says so in the
Monitor.

SECOND MAN. He must be wrong this time; no one
would let him have a hall—not the Home-owners
Association, nor the Citizens' Club either.

FIRST MAN. Even the Baths refused him.

SECOND MAN. That's not surprising.

A MAN (*In another group*). Whom do we support in
this business?

ANOTHER MAN (*In the same group*). Just keep an eye
on Aslaksen and do as he does.

---

12. *carafe* (kə raf'), a bottle usually made of glass with a narrow
neck and spherical body.
13. *Sconces* (skon'sez), screened lanterns or candlesticks with
handles, often ornamental pieces secured to a wall.

BILLING (*With a portfolio under his arm pushes his
way through the crowd*). Excuse me, gentlemen.
May I get by please? I'm reporting for *The People's
Monitor.* Thanks—thank you! (*He sits at the table
left.*)

A WORKMAN. Who's he?

ANOTHER WORKMAN. Don't you know him? That's
Billing—he writes for Aslaksen's paper.
(CAPTAIN HORSTER *ushers in* MRS. STOCKMANN *and*
PETRA *through the door down right.* EJLIF *and* MOR-
TEN *follow them.*)

CAPTAIN HORSTER. I thought this would be a good
place for you to sit; it'll be easy for you to slip
away if anything should happen.

MRS. STOCKMANN. Will there be any disturbance, do
you think?

HORSTER. It's hard to say—with all these people. But
don't be anxious—just sit here quietly.

MRS. STOCKMANN (*Sitting down*). It was so kind of you
to let Stockmann have the room.

HORSTER. Since nobody else would, I thought I—

PETRA (*Who has also seated herself*). And it was brave
of you too, Captain Horster.

HORSTER. I don't see anything specially brave
about it. (HOVSTAD *and* ASLAKSEN *enter at the same
time, but separately, and make their way through
the crowd.*)

ASLAKSEN (*Going up to* HORSTER). Isn't Doctor Stockmann here yet?

HORSTER. He's waiting in there.
(*A movement in the crowd by the door at the back
of the room.*)

HOVSTAD (*To* BILLING). Here comes the Mayor! Look!

BILLING. Yes—strike me dead! So he's put in an
appearance after all!
(MAYOR STOCKMANN *advances graciously through
the crowd, bowing to right and left. He takes his
stand near the wall on the left. A moment later* DR.
STOCKMANN *enters from the door down right. He
wears a black frock coat and a white tie. There is
scattered applause countered by subdued hissing.
Then, silence.*)

DR. STOCKMANN (*In a low tone*). How do you feel,
Katrine?

MRS. STOCKMANN. I'm all right, thank you, dear.
(*Whispers to him*) Don't lose your temper, Tomas!

DR. STOCKMANN. Don't worry—I'll keep myself in
hand. (*Looks at his watch, mounts the platform
and bows*) It's a quarter past; I'm going to begin—
(*Takes out his manuscript.*)

ASLAKSEN. Wait! We must elect a chairman first.

DR. STOCKMANN. That won't be necessary.

SEVERAL GENTLEMEN (*Shouting*). Yes! Yes!

THE MAYOR. By all means; of course we must have a chairman.

DR. STOCKMANN. But I've called this meeting to read a paper, Peter.

THE MAYOR. All the same—your paper is likely to cause discussion.

SEVERAL VOICES IN THE CROWD. A chairman! We want a chairman!

HOVSTAD. The general voice seems to be in favor of a chairman.

DR. STOCKMANN (*Controlling himself*). Oh, very well —Let the "general voice" have its way.

ASLAKSEN. Perhaps the Mayor will honor us?

THREE GENTLEMEN (*Clapping*). Bravo! Bravo!

THE MAYOR. Many thanks. But for various obvious reasons, I must decline. However, we are fortunate in having in our midst a man who, I am certain, will be acceptable to all. I refer, of course, to the chairman of the Home-owners Association —Mr. Aslaksen!

MANY VOICES. Yes! Yes! Long live Aslaksen! Hurrah for Aslaksen! (DR. STOCKMANN *takes his manuscript and leaves the platform.*)

ASLAKSEN. Since my fellow-citizens are pleased to show me this signal mark of confidence—who am I to refuse? (*Applause and cheers.* ASLAKSEN *ascends the platform.*)

BILLING (*Making notes*). Mr. Aslaksen elected by acclamation—

ASLAKSEN. And now—since I stand here as your chairman—allow me to say a few brief words to you. I am a quiet peace-loving man, gentlemen; a man in favor of discreet moderation, and of—and of—moderate discretion. All those who know me are aware of that.

SEVERAL VOICES. Yes, yes! To be sure, Aslaksen!

ASLAKSEN. I have learned in the great common school of life and of experience, that moderation is the citizen's prime virtue—a virtue from which he reaps the highest benefits—

THE MAYOR. Hear! Hear!

ASLAKSEN. —and that discretion and moderation are also the best servants of Society. Allow me therefore to suggest to our respected fellow-citizen who has seen fit to call this meeting, that he take note; let us hope he will bend every effort to keep within the bounds of moderation.

A MAN (*By the door*). I propose a toast to the Temperance Society! Hurrah!

A VOICE. Shame! Shame!

VOICES. Sh! Quiet!

ASLAKSEN. No interruptions if you please, gentlemen! —Does anyone wish to offer any observations?

THE MAYOR. Mr. Chairman!

ASLAKSEN. The Mayor has the floor!

THE MAYOR. Because of my close relationship to the present medical adviser to the Baths—a relationship of which most of you are undoubtedly aware —I should have preferred not to speak here this evening. But my position as Chairman of the Board, as well as my deep concern for the welfare of the town, force me to make this motion. I think I may venture to assume that not a single soul here present would condone the spreading of exaggerated and irresponsible statements concerning the sanitary conditions of our Baths and of our town.

MANY VOICES. No, no! Never! Certainly not! We protest!

THE MAYOR. I therefore move that this meeting pass the following resolution: Dr. Stockmann cannot be allowed to read his paper or to address this assembly on this particular subject.

DR. STOCKMANN (*Flaring up*). Cannot be allowed—! What do you mean?

MRS. STOCKMANN (*Coughing*). Hm, hm!

DR. STOCKMANN (*Controlling himself*). So, I'm not to be allowed; I see.

THE MAYOR. I have acquainted the Public with the relevant facts through my statement in *The People's Monitor*, so that all right-thinking citizens may have no difficulty in forming their own judgment. It will be clearly seen that the doctor's report on the situation—apart from being a direct vote of censure against the leading men in the community—simply means saddling the taxpayers with a totally unnecessary outlay of at least one hundred thousand crowns.

(*Cries of protest and scattered whistles.*)

ASLAKSEN (*Rings the bell*). Order, order, gentlemen! I beg to second the Mayor's motion. I share the opinion that there are other motives behind the doctor's agitation; he may talk about the Baths, but his real aim is nothing short of revolution—the complete overthrow of the parties now in power. No one doubts the doctor's integrity of purpose —there can be no two opinions about that. I too am in favor of self-government by the People, provided it doesn't result in too great a burden on the tax-payer; in this case that is precisely what would occur. For this reason—well, damn it—excuse me, gentlemen!—on this occasion I cannot possibly side with Dr. Stockmann. You can pay too high a price—even for gold. At all events, that's my opinion. (*Loud applause from all sides.*)

HOVSTAD. I too should like to make my position clear in this matter. At first Dr. Stockmann's agitation met with considerable favor in many quarters and I did my best to give it my impartial support. It soon appeared however that we had been misled; that the facts had been presented in a false light—

DR. STOCKMANN. False—!

HOVSTAD. —an ambiguous light, if you prefer. The Mayor's report leaves no doubt on that score. I trust no one here questions my liberal principles; on the great political issues of the day, the views of *The People's Monitor* are well-known to you all. But I have learned from men of judgment and experience that when it comes to purely local matters, a newspaper should proceed with a certain amount of caution.

ASLAKSEN. I whole-heartedly endorse the speaker's views.

HOVSTAD. In the matter now under discussion public opinion is quite obviously against Dr. Stockmann. Now—what is a publisher's first and foremost duty, gentlemen? Is it not to work in harmony with his readers? Is he not obligated—by a tacit mandate, as it were—to serve indefatigably and tenaciously the interests of the majority? Or am I mistaken?

MANY VOICES. No, no! Hovstad is right!

HOVSTAD. It has not been easy, I assure you, to break with a man in whose home I have been a frequent guest of late. A man who up to this very day has enjoyed the unqualified goodwill of his fellow-citizens. A man whose only, or perhaps one should say whose chief fault, consists in following his heart rather than his head.

A FEW SCATTERED VOICES. That's true! Hurrah for Dr. Stockmann!

HOVSTAD. But my duty to Society has forced me, much against my will, to make this break. And there's another consideration that impels me to oppose him, and try, if I can, to stop him on the rash course on which he is embarked: consideration for his family, gentlemen—

DR. STOCKMANN. Stick to the sewers and water-works!

HOVSTAD. —consideration for his wife, and for his helpless children.

MORTEN. Does he mean us, Mother?

MRS. STOCKMANN. Hush!

ASLAKSEN. I shall now put the Mayor's resolution to a vote.

DR. STOCKMANN. That won't be necessary! I don't intend to speak about the filth and corruption of the Baths this evening. No! You're going to hear about something very different.

THE MAYOR (*Half to himself*). Now what's he up to?

A DRUNKEN MAN (*Near the main entrance*). I'm entitled to pay taxes—so I suppose I'm entitled to an opinion too. And it is my irrefutable and incomprehensible opinion that—

SEVERAL VOICES. Silence over there!

OTHERS. He's drunk! Throw him out!

(*The drunken man is put out.*)

DR. STOCKMANN. May I speak?

ASLAKSEN (*Ringing the bell*). Dr. Stockmann has the floor.

DR. STOCKMANN. I'd like to have seen anyone try —even a few days ago—to gag me as I've been gagged this evening. I should have fought like a lion for what I know to be my sacred rights. But that doesn't matter to me now. Now I have more important things to say.

(*The people crowd closer round him.* MORTEN KIIL *appears among the crowd.*)

DR. STOCKMANN (*Continuing*). I've done a lot of thinking these past days—turning things over in my mind, till my brain seemed all muddled and confused—

THE MAYOR (*Coughing*). Hm—!

DR. STOCKMANN. But gradually things straightened out, and I saw them in their true perspective. That's why I'm here this evening. I'm going to expose many things to you, my friends! The fact that our water-works are poisoned and that our health-resort is nothing but a pest-hole is comparatively unimportant compared to the discovery I'm about to reveal now.

MANY VOICES. No mention of the Baths! We won't listen! Leave them out of it!

DR. STOCKMANN. I've just told you—I'm going to speak about a great discovery I've made in these past days—and this is it: The very sources of our spiritual life are poisoned, and our whole community is founded on a pestilential lie!

A MURMUR OF AMAZED VOICES. What's he saying?

THE MAYOR. How dare he—!

ASLAKSEN (*His hand on the bell*). I call upon the speaker to moderate his language!

DR. STOCKMANN. No man could love his native town more than I've loved mine! I was very young when I left here, and distance, memory and homesickness combined to cast a kind of aura round the place and round its people. (*Scattered applause and expressions of approval*) I spent many years in the far North, in a God-forsaken hole of a place. I used to visit the few starving wretches scattered about in that rocky wilderness, and I often thought a horse-doctor would have served their purpose better than a man of science like myself.

(*Murmurs throughout the room.*)

BILLING (*Laying down his pen*). Strike me dead! I've never heard such—

HOVSTAD. An insult to honest country-folk!

DR. STOCKMANN. Just wait a minute! —All that time I don't think anyone could have accused me of forgetting my home town. I sat there brooding over an idea—like an eider-duck on her eggs—and what I finally hatched out was the plan for our Baths. (*Applause and protests*) And when at last fate was kind enough to make my return home possible—I felt as though my every wish had been fulfilled. I still had one wish, though; an ardent, unwavering, passionate desire to serve my home town and my fellow-citizens.

THE MAYOR (*Gazing into space*). A strange way to show it—!

DR. STOCKMANN. I was supremely happy—basking in joyous illusions. Then, yesterday morning—no, the preceding evening to be exact—I received a mental jolt; my eyes were suddenly wide open and the first thing I saw was the colossal stupidity of our reigning authorities—

(*Noise, cries and laughter. MRS. STOCKMANN coughs repeatedly.*)

THE MAYOR. Mr. Chairman!

ASLAKSEN (*Ringing his bell*). By virtue of my office—!

DR. STOCKMANN. Let the expression pass, Mr. Aslaksen—there's no need to be petty! I simply mean that the whole disgraceful situation at the Baths was suddenly revealed to me—a mess for which the so-called leading men of the town must take the blame. These leading men—I'm sick of them and all their works! They're like a lot of goats let loose in a young orchard—destroying everything; they stand in the way of free men and hamper them at every turn. For my part I'd like to see them exterminated together with all other predatory creatures—

(*Uproar in the room.*)

THE MAYOR. Mr. Chairman—can such things be allowed?

ASLAKSEN (*His hand on the bell*). Dr. Stockmann—!

DR. STOCKMANN. I can't conceive why it should have taken me so long to see through these gentlemen; every single day I've had a prime example before my very eyes—my brother Peter—empty of ideas and filled with prejudice—

(*Laughter, noise and catcalls. MRS. STOCKMANN coughs. ASLAKSEN violently rings his bell.*)

THE DRUNKEN MAN (*Who has returned*). Are you referring to me? My name's Pettersen all right—but I'll be damned if—

ANGRY VOICES. Throw him out! Throw that drunk out!

(*They throw him out again.*)

THE MAYOR. Who was that person?

A BYSTANDER. I don't know him, Your Honor.

ANOTHER MAN. He's not from around here.

A THIRD MAN. He must be that lumber-dealer from—

(*The rest is inaudible.*)

ASLAKSEN. The man was unquestionably intoxicated. Proceed, Dr. Stockmann; but with moderation, if you please!

DR. STOCKMANN. Well, fellow-citizens, I shall say no more about our leading men. And if anyone imagines, after what I have just said, that I'm here to attack these gentlemen this evening, he is quite wrong I assure you. You see, I cherish the comfortable conviction that these reactionaries, these relics of another age, are busily engaged in cutting their own throats—they don't need a doctor to help them. And besides, they are not the worst menace to Society; it is not primarily due to them that our spiritual well-being is endangered, and that the very ground we stand on reeks with corruption. They are not the most dangerous enemies to truth and freedom!

CRIES FROM ALL SIDES. Who then? Who do you mean? Name them! Name them!

DR. STOCKMANN. Oh, I shall name them—never fear! You see, that is my great discovery; I made it yesterday. (*Raising his voice*) In our Society, the worst enemy to truth and freedom is the majority. Yes! The damnable, solid, liberal majority—that's the great menace! There's your answer! (*Great commotion in the room. Most of the audience are shouting, stamping and whistling. A few old gentlemen exchange covert glances and seem to be enjoying the situation.* MRS. STOCKMANN *gets up anxiously;* EJLIF *and* MORTEN *advance threateningly towards the schoolboys who are making catcalls.* ASLAKSEN *rings his bell and calls for order.* HOVSTAD *and* BILLING *both try to speak but are drowned out. At last quiet is restored.*)

ASLAKSEN. The speaker is requested to withdraw this outrageous statement.

DR. STOCKMANN. Never, Mr. Aslaksen—never! This same great majority robs me of my freedom, and wishes to prevent me from stating the truth!

HOVSTAD. The majority is always right.

BILLING. Yes—but, strike me dead—truth is right too!

DR. STOCKMANN. The majority is never right—never, I tell you! That's one of those social lies against which every free, intelligent man ought to rebel. What does the majority consist of—of wise men or of fools? I think we must all of us agree that from one end of the world to the other the proportion is overwhelmingly in favor of the fools. And are wise men to be ruled by fools? What could be more senseless! (*Uproar and yells*) You can shout me down if you like, but you can't deny it! The majority has the power, unfortunately—but right is on the side of people like me—of the few—of the individual. It's the minority that's always right! (*Renewed commotion.*)

HOVSTAD. Ha, ha! Dr. Stockmann has turned aristocrat!

DR. STOCKMANN. I've said I won't waste any words on that little rear-guard of puny, narrow-chested, self-important men—the stream of life has already left them far behind. I'm thinking of the few—those rare spirits among us who have had the vision to recognize the truth in new ideas, new ways of thought—and have made those ways their own. These men are in the vanguard—so far ahead that the solid majority can't begin to reach them; and there they fight for new-born truths—too new and too daring to be accepted by that sacred majority of yours.

HOVSTAD. Now he's a revolutionist!

DR. STOCKMANN. Yes, by Heaven, I am, Mr. Hovstad! I intend to revolt against the lie that truth belongs exclusively to the majority. And what are these truths the majority worships? They're truths so old and worn—they're practically decrepit. And when

a truth reaches that age you can hardly tell it from a lie! (*Laughter and jeers*) You can believe me or not as you like; but truths are not such tough old Methuselahs[14] as most people imagine. A normal, ordinary truth is good for, say, seventeen or eighteen—at most twenty years; seldom more. And truths as venerable as that are nothing but skin and bones; yet it isn't until then that the great majority adopts them and prescribes them to Society as wholesome spiritual food. But there's not much nourishment in that kind of a diet, I assure you; as a doctor you can take my word for that. These tired old truths are as rancid and moldy as last year's bacon; they're the cause of all that moral scurvy[15] that plagues Society.

ASLAKSEN. Our honored speaker appears to have strayed somewhat from his subject.

THE MAYOR. I heartily endorse the chairman's observation.

DR. STOCKMANN. You must be mad, Peter! I'm doing my best to stick to my subject; I'm saying that it's the masses—that damnable solid majority—that poison the sources of our spiritual life and corrupt the very ground we walk on.

HOVSTAD. I see; in other words you condemn the great majority of liberal-minded men for having sense enough to rely on truths that are fundamental and conclusive.

DR. STOCKMANN. My dear Mr. Hovstad, don't speak about fundamental truths! The truths endorsed by the great majority of men today were considered fundamental by the vanguard in our grandfather's time; they are no longer endorsed by the vanguard of today. There's only one fundamental truth, in my opinion—and that is that Society cannot live a healthy life based on truths that have become old and spineless.

HOVSTAD. Can't you be more explicit? Instead of this vague talk, give us some examples of these so-called spineless truths you say we base our lives on.

(*Approval from several parts of the room.*)

DR. STOCKMANN. I could give you innumerable examples—but one will serve: the fundamental truth which, though basically a lie, you and your *Peo-*

---

14. *Methuselahs.* Methuselah was a man, in the Bible, represented as having lived 969 years, often used to suggest anything of great age.
15. *scurvy,* a disease caused by a dietary deficiency; moral sickness.

ple's Monitor and its adherents swear by all the same—

HOVSTAD. —which is?

DR. STOCKMANN. A doctrine inherited from your grandparents, and that you thoughtlessly go on proclaiming far and wide; the doctrine that the common herd, the crowd, the masses, are the very flower of the people—in fact *are* the people —and that the uncouth man, the vulgar man, the ignorant and unevolved, have the same right to condemn and sanction, to govern and counsel, as the intellectually and spiritually distinguished few.

BILLING. Well—strike me dead! I've never—!

HOVSTAD (*Shouting at the same time*). Take note of this, citizens!

ANGRY VOICES. Aren't we the people? Are we to have no say?

A WORKMAN. A man who talks like that deserves to be kicked out!

OTHERS. Throw him out!

A MAN (*Shouting*). Now's the time to blow your horn, Evensen!

(*The deep notes of a horn are heard; whistles, cat-calls and uproar.*)

DR. STOCKMANN (*As the noise subsides*). Be reasonable! Can't you endure the truth? I don't expect you all to agree with me—but I certainly thought Mr. Hovstad would calm down and back me up. Mr. Hovstad lays claim to being a free-thinker—

SEVERAL VOICES (*Subdued and astonished*). A free-thinker, did he say? What? Hovstad a free-thinker?

HOVSTAD. I dare you to prove it, Dr. Stockmann! Have I ever said so in black and white?

DR. STOCKMANN. No, damn it—you've never had the courage! Well, I don't want to get you into trouble; I'm the one who's the free-thinker, Mr. Hovstad. And now—let me prove to you all, scientifically, that *The People's Monitor* makes fools of you and leads you by the nose when it tells you that you, the masses, the crowd, are the flower of the people. That's just a journalistic lie! The masses are only the raw material from which a People can be made. (*Murmurs, laughter and general disturbance*) It's the same thing in all other forms of life. Fine animals are created by breeding and selection. Take an ordinary common hen, for instance —she's not much good for eating, and her eggs are not much better than a crow's eggs—or a raven's; she can't be compared with a really fine strain of poultry. But now take a Japanese or Spanish hen—a pheasant or a turkey—and you'll soon see the difference! Or in the case of dogs— so closely related to mankind; think first of a common ordinary cur—one of those filthy, ragged, plebeian[16] mongrels that haunt the gutters and dirty up the side-walks; and compare that mongrel with a pedigreed poodle, bred for generations from the finest stock, used to good food and accustomed to well-modulated voices and the sound of music. Don't you suppose the poodle's brain shows a marked superiority? Of course it does! A trainer can take a poodle pup like that and teach it the most fantastic tricks—things a common mongrel could never dream of learning!

(*Noise and laughter.*)

A MAN (*Shouting*). Are you comparing us with dogs?

ANOTHER. We're not animals, Doctor!

DR. STOCKMANN. Of course you are! We're all animals, my friend! What are we else? But there aren't many well-bred animals among us. There's a tremendous difference between poodle-men and mongrel-men. And it's so ridiculous—Mr. Hovstad agrees with me entirely as long as it's four-legged animals we're talking of—

HOVSTAD. An animal's an animal—and there's an end of it!

DR. STOCKMANN. Perhaps; but as soon as I apply the rule to two-legged animals, Mr. Hovstad rebels; he no longer has the courage of his convictions —he refuses to think things through to the end; so he turns the rule upside down and proclaims in the *Monitor* that the ordinary hen and the common cur are the prize specimens in the menagerie. And that's the way it'll always be, while we allow the cur in us to triumph, instead of working our way up to some sort of spiritual distinction.

HOVSTAD. I make no pretense of being distinguished in any way; I come from simple peasant stock and I'm proud of it. I'm proud to belong to those common people you're insulting!

SOME WORKMEN. Hurrah for Hovstad! Hurrah! Hurrah!

DR. STOCKMANN. The kind of common people I mean don't necessarily come from the lower classes; they're crawling and swarming all around us—you often find them in the very top ranks of Society. You've only to look at that smug, respectable

---

16. *plebeian* (pli bē′ən), a Latin word meaning the common people or common variety.

Mayor of yours! He's about as low as any man that ever walked on two feet—

THE MAYOR. I must protest against these personal remarks!

DR. STOCKMANN. —and that has nothing to do with the fact that one of our ancestors was a disgusting old pirate from somewhere in Pomerania[17]—

THE MAYOR. Pure invention! Utterly groundless!

DR. STOCKMANN. —no! It's because he thinks the thoughts of his superiors in office, and kow-tows to their opinions. And people who do that are common in spirit; that's why, in spite of his magnificence, my brother Peter is so fundamentally lacking in distinction, and is consequently so anti-liberal.

THE MAYOR. Mr. Chairman—!

HOVSTAD. So it seems you have to be a liberal to be distinguished! That's a new point of view if you like! (*Laughter.*)

DR. STOCKMANN. Yes, that's part of my new discovery too. And there's something else: I've discovered that morality and liberalism are almost precisely the same thing. That's why I consider it downright inexcusable of *The People's Monitor* to go on proclaiming day in and day out that morality and liberalism are the sole monopoly of the mob and the masses; and that culture automatically generates vice and spiritual depravity—just as the filth from the Milldale Tanneries generates the poison that pollutes our water-works. (*Noise and interruptions*) And yet this same *People's Monitor* prates about raising the masses to a higher level! Why, damn it—if the *Monitor's* premise were really sound, raising them to a higher level would be equivalent to hurling them straight to perdition!

17. *Pomerania,* a region of north central Europe along the Baltic coasts of Germany and Poland.

Fortunately the theory that culture demoralizes is just another of those lies handed down from the past. No! Stupidity, poverty and ugliness are the true evils—they're demoralizing if you like! And to live in a house that is never aired, and where the floors are never swept—my wife, incidentally, claims that floors should be *scrubbed* every day, but that's a debatable point—that's demoralizing too! Lack of oxygen weakens the moral fiber. And there must be precious little oxygen in the houses around here, if the moral fiber of our citizens is so feeble that the great majority of them are anxious and willing to build the future of our town on a foundation of hypocrisy and lies!

ASLAKSEN. This is an insult to the entire community —we shall not tolerate it!

A GENTLEMAN. I move that the speaker be called to order!

EAGER VOICES. Yes, yes! He's right! Sit down! Sit down!

DR. STOCKMANN (*Flaring up*). Then I shall shout it from the house-tops! I'll write to all the newspapers! I'll let the whole country know of the situation here!

HOVSTAD. Dr. Stockmann is evidently bent on ruining the town.

DR. STOCKMANN. I love my native town so much that I'd rather see it ruined than prosper on a lie!

ASLAKSEN. There's a statement for you!

(*Noise and catcalls.* MRS. STOCKMANN *coughs in vain; the doctor no longer hears her.*)

HOVSTAD (*Shouting above the tumult*). You're an enemy to this whole community, or you couldn't talk so lightly of the ruin of the town!

DR. STOCKMANN (*With growing excitement*). A community based on lies and corruption deserves to be destroyed! Men who live on lies should be wiped out like a lot of vermin. This poison will spread throughout the country, and eventually the whole country will deserve to be destroyed; and, should it ever come to that, I'd say from the bottom of my heart: let it be destroyed, and let all its people perish!

A MAN (*In the crowd*). He's the People's enemy— that's what he is!

BILLING. Strike me dead! Did you hear that? The Voice of the People!

THE WHOLE CROWD (*Shouting*). Yes, yes, yes! He's an enemy of the People! He's a traitor to his country! He's against the People!

ASLAKSEN. As a citizen of this town, and as a human being, I am deeply shocked by what I have heard here tonight. I must regretfully concur with the sentiments expressed by so many of my fellow-citizens, and I move that those sentiments be formulated in the following resolution: "This meeting hereby declares the former medical adviser to the Baths, Dr. Tomas Stockmann, to be an enemy of the People."

(*Thunders of applause and cheers. A number of people crowd around* DR. STOCKMANN, *jeering and booing.* MRS. STOCKMANN *and* PETRA *have risen.* MORTEN *and* EJLIF *exchange blows with some of the schoolboys who have joined in the jeering. Some grownups separate them.*)

DR. STOCKMANN (*To the jeering crowd*). Fools! You fools! I tell you that—

ASLAKSEN (*Ringing his bell*). Doctor Stockmann is out of order! A formal vote must now be taken. However, out of consideration for personal feelings, it will be by secret ballot. Have you any sheets of blank paper, Mr. Billing?

BILLING. Yes—I have some here; both blue and white.

ASLAKSEN. Splendid. That will expedite matters. We'll just cut it into slips—There! (*To the meeting*) Blue stands for no, and white for yes, I shall collect the votes myself.

(THE MAYOR *leaves the room.* ASLAKSEN *and a couple of others circulate about the room with the pieces of paper in hats.*)

A GENTLEMAN (*To* HOVSTAD). What can be the matter with the doctor? I don't know what to make of it!

HOVSTAD. He's a dreadfully impetuous man, you know!

ANOTHER GENTLEMAN (*To* BILLING). You've been a guest there; tell me—does the fellow drink?

BILLING. Strike me dead—I don't know how to answer that. I know there's always plenty of hot toddy in the house!

A THIRD GENTLEMAN. He strikes me as unbalanced.

FIRST GENTLEMAN. Is there any insanity in the family, I wonder?

BILLING. I don't know—I shouldn't be surprised.

A FOURTH GENTLEMAN. It's pure malice, if you ask me. He's got a chip on his shoulder about something.

BILLING. I remember one day he mentioned wanting a raise in salary—but I know he didn't get it.

ALL THE GENTLEMEN (*Together*). Then that must be it, of course!

THE DRUNKEN MAN (*In the crowd*). Give me a blue one! And I want a white one, too!

SEVERAL PEOPLE. There's that drunk again! Throw him out!

MORTEN KIIL (*Comes up to* STOCKMANN). Well, Stockmann! Look where your monkey-tricks have led to!

DR. STOCKMANN. I've simply done my duty.

MORTEN KIIL. What was that you said about the Milldale Tanneries?

DR. STOCKMANN. You heard; I said they generated filth.

MORTEN KIIL. You mean mine too?

DR. STOCKMANN. Yours is among the worst.

MORTEN KIIL. And are you going to print that in the papers?

DR. STOCKMANN. I shall keep nothing back.

MORTEN KIIL. It'll cost you dear—I warn you! (*He goes out.*)

A FAT GENTLEMAN (*Goes up to* HORSTER *without bowing to the ladies*). I see you lend your house to enemies of the People, Captain.

HORSTER. I've a right to use my property as I see fit, sir.

THE GENTLEMAN. Very good. Then I shall follow your example.

HORSTER. What do you mean by that?

THE GENTLEMAN. You'll hear from me tomorrow. (*Turns away and goes out.*)

PETRA. Captain Horster—wasn't that the owner of your ship?

HORSTER. Mr. Vik, yes.

ASLAKSEN (*His hands full of slips of paper, mounts the platform and rings*). Allow me to announce the result of the vote, gentlemen. All the voters, with one exception—

A YOUNG GENTLEMAN. That must have been the drunk!

ASLAKSEN. With the exception of one intoxicated person, this meeting unanimously declares Dr. Tomas Stockmann to be an enemy of the People. (*Cheers and applause*) Three cheers for our deeply loved and honorable community! (*Cheers*) And three cheers for our able and energetic Mayor who has so loyally set family prejudice aside! (*Cheers*) The meeting is adjourned. (*He steps down from the platform.*)

BILLING. Let's have three cheers for the chairman!

ALL. Three cheers for Aslaksen!

DR. STOCKMANN. Give me my hat and coat, Petra. Captain—have you room for any passengers on your trip to the New World?[18]

HORSTER. There'll always be room for you and yours, Dr. Stockmann.

DR. STOCKMANN (*As* PETRA *helps him with his coat*). Thanks. Come, Katrine! Come, boys! (*He gives his wife his arm.*)

MRS. STOCKMANN (*In a low voice*). Let's go out the back way, Tomas, dear.

DR. STOCKMANN. No back ways for us, Katrine. (*Raises his voice*) You'll hear more from the enemy of the People before he finally shakes the dust off his feet! I'm not as forbearing as a certain person I could mention; I can't bring myself to say "I forgive you, for you know not what you do."

ASLAKSEN. That comparison is blasphemous, Doctor Stockmann!

BILLING. Strike me—! If that isn't too much for a decent man to stand!

A COARSE VOICE. And he actually threatens us, too!

ANGRY SHOUTS. Let's smash in his windows! Duck him in the fjord![19]

A MAN (*In the crowd*). Blow your horn, Evensen! Go on, man! Blow!

(*Horn-blowing, whistles and catcalls; wild shouts.* DR. STOCKMANN *and his family go towards the door—*CAPTAIN HORSTER *clears the way for them.*)

ALL (*Yelling after them as they go out*). Enemy of the People! Enemy of the People! Enemy of the People!

BILLING. Strike me dead! I wouldn't want to drink toddy at the Stockmanns' house tonight!

(*The people throng towards the door; the shouting is taken up outside; from the street cries of "Enemy of the People! Enemy of the People!" are heard.*)

CURTAIN

---

18. *the New World*, the continental landmass of North and South America.
19. *fjord* (fyôrd), a narrow deep inlet of the sea.

DISCUSSION

1. Before the meeting begins, why does the crowd assume that Dr. Stockmann is in the wrong?

2. (a) Who suggests electing a chairman, and whom does he nominate? (b) Who is finally elected chairman, and who had nominated him? (c) Whom does the chairman first recognize to speak? For what purpose? (d) Review the above events. What appears to be happening here?

3. What reasons do Aslaksen and Hovstad give for supporting the Mayor's proposal?

4. (a) Dr. Stockmann is allowed to speak only after agreeing to what condition? (b) What oratorical trick does he use to get around this restriction?

5. (a) In what terms does Dr. Stockmann describe the leading men of the town? (b) What great discovery does he reveal that throws the crowd into an uproar? Do you agree with Dr. Stockmann completely? Partly? Not at all? Explain.

6. When Dr. Stockmann talks of the common herd, he emphasizes that he is *not* talking about people from the lower classes. What does he mean?

7. (a) Do you think that Dr. Stockmann's argument becomes unreasonable at any point? If so, when and why? (b) How do you explain his behavior at this point? (c) If you defend Dr. Stockmann's argument, give reasons for your position.

8. A drunken man interrupts the proceedings several times. What purpose does each interruption serve?

THE AUTHOR'S CRAFT

Foreshadowing
In Act One of this play the Mayor issues a prophetic warning. "But be careful"; he advises Dr. Stockmann, "sooner or later you'll have to pay for it." The warning, made in reference to Dr. Stockmann's secret investigations at the Baths, suggests that the doctor's tendency to take matters into his own hands will get him into trouble some day.

In Act One this warning appears meaningless. Dr. Stockmann does reveal his discovery and receives the support and admiration of his family and friends. All appears to

be well. By the end of Act Four, however, the significance of the Mayor's warning becomes obvious. For his efforts in behalf of the town, Dr. Stockmann is rewarded with insults, accusations, and the title "Enemy of the People."

The Mayor's warning in Act One anticipated Dr. Stockmann's predicament in Act Four. It *foreshadowed* the doctor's downfall. *Foreshadowing* is the implication by the author of events to come later in the narrative.

Reread the last page of Act Four, concentrating on Morten Kiil's conversation with Dr. Stockmann and Captain Horster's conversation with Mr. Vik, the ship-owner. What do you think Morten Kiil is planning? What do you suppose Mr. Vik is going to do? In each case, find the lines in the text which clearly *foreshadow* "something" to come later. As you read Act Five, watch for these events to unfold.

Act Five

SCENE: DR. STOCKMANN'S *study. The walls are lined with bookshelves and glass cabinets containing various medicines. In the back wall is the door to the living room. Two windows in the wall right, with all the panes smashed in. In the center of the room is the doctor's desk covered with books and papers. The room is in disorder. It is morning.* DR. STOCKMANN *in a dressing-gown and slippers and with a skull-cap[20] on his head is stooping down and raking under one of the cabinets with an umbrella; he succeeds in raking out a stone.*

DR. STOCKMANN (*Calling through the open door*). Here's another one, Katrine!

MRS. STOCKMANN (*From the living room*). You'll find a lot more, I expect.

DR. STOCKMANN (*Adds the stone to a pile on the table*). I'm going to keep these stones, Katrine; they're precious relics. I want Morten and Ejlif to have them constantly before their eyes—and I'll leave them as a heritage. (*Raking about under the bookcase*) By the way, hasn't—what the devil *is* that girl's name—hasn't she been to the glazier yet?

MRS. STOCKMANN (*Coming in*). Yes; but he wasn't sure he could come today.

DR. STOCKMANN. I suppose he doesn't dare.

MRS. STOCKMANN. That's what Randina thinks; she thinks he's afraid of the neighbors. (*Talks to someone in the living room*) What is it, Randina? Oh, thanks. (*Goes out and returns immediately*) A letter for you, dear.

DR. STOCKMANN. Let's see. (*Opens the letter and reads*) Well—it's not surprising!

MRS. STOCKMANN. Who is it from?

DR. STOCKMANN. The landlord. He's giving us notice.

MRS. STOCKMANN. Not really! He's such a nice man, too—!

DR. STOCKMANN (*Glancing at the letter*). He daren't do otherwise, he says. He's very sorry; but he daren't do otherwise—public opinion—he has to earn his living—he's afraid of offending certain influential men—and so on.

MRS. STOCKMANN. That just shows you, Tomas.

DR. STOCKMANN. Oh, yes; it shows me right enough. They're all cowards in this town; no one dares do anything for fear of offending someone else. (*Flings the letter on the table*) Well—what do we care, Katrine; we're off to the New World—

MRS. STOCKMANN. You really think that's a wise decision, Tomas?

DR. STOCKMANN. You don't expect me to stay here, do you? After being spat on? After being branded as an enemy of the People and having my windows smashed? And, look, Katrine! Somebody actually tore a hole in my black trousers!

MRS. STOCKMANN. Oh, Tomas! And they're your best ones too!

DR. STOCKMANN. Yes! Well—you should never wear your best trousers when you go out to fight for truth and freedom! But I don't care so much about the trousers—you can always patch them up for me. What I can't stomach is having that mob attack me as though they were my equals!

MRS. STOCKMANN. I know, Tomas; they've behaved abominably to you here. But does that necessarily mean we have to leave the country altogether?

DR. STOCKMANN. It'd be just as bad in all the other towns; the mob is just as insolent-minded there as here. Well—to Hell with it! Let the mongrels yap; that's not the worst of it. The worst of it is that all over the country men are nothing but abject slaves to the party-bosses. Not that the so-called Free West is apt to be much better; I daresay enlightened public opinion, the solid majority and all the rest of the trash is just as rampant there—but at least it's on a bigger scale; they may kill a man, but they don't put him to slow torture; they don't clamp a free soul into a strait jacket. And, at a pinch, there's room to get away. (*Walks up and down*) If only I knew of some primeval forest, some little South-Sea island that was going cheap—

MRS. STOCKMANN. But—what about the boys, Tomas?

DR. STOCKMANN (*Comes to a standstill*). What an amazing woman you are, Katrine! You wouldn't really want the boys to grow up in a society like ours, would you? You must have seen last night that half the population of this town is raving mad—and if the other half hasn't lost its wits, it's only because they're such block-heads that they have no wits to lose!

MRS. STOCKMANN. Dear Tomas—you say such reckless things!

DR. STOCKMANN. Well—isn't it true? They turn every

---

20. *skull-cap*, a sleeping cap.

idea upside-down; they make a hotch-potch out of right and wrong; they take lies for truth and truth for lies. But the craziest thing of all is to see a lot of grownup men calling themselves Liberals, parading about pretending to themselves and others that they're friends of freedom! You must admit that's pretty silly!

MRS. STOCKMANN. Yes; I suppose it is, but— (PETRA *enters from the living room*) Home from school already, Petra?

PETRA. I've been dismissed.

MRS. STOCKMANN. Dismissed!

DR. STOCKMANN. You too!

PETRA. Mrs. Busk gave me my notice—so I thought I'd better leave at once.

DR. STOCKMANN. You were quite right!

MRS. STOCKMANN. Fancy Mrs. Busk doing a thing like that! How disgraceful of her!

PETRA. It wasn't disgraceful of her, Mother. I could see how upset she was. But she didn't dare do otherwise, she said. So—I'm dismissed.

DR. STOCKMANN (*Laughs and rubs his hands*). She didn't dare do otherwise—just like the rest! This is delightful!

MRS. STOCKMANN. I suppose—after that dreadful scene last night—

PETRA. It wasn't only that. Father—listen to this!

DR. STOCKMANN. Well?

PETRA. Mrs. Busk showed me at least three letters she'd received this morning—

DR. STOCKMANN. Anonymous, of course?

PETRA. Yes.

DR. STOCKMANN. They never dare sign their names, Katrine!

PETRA. Two of them warned her that a certain gentleman—a frequent visitor at our house, so he said—had been talking at the club last night, and telling everyone that my views on certain subjects were decidedly advanced—

DR. STOCKMANN. I hope you didn't deny it!

PETRA. Of course not! Mrs. Busk has fairly advanced views too—that is, in private; but since I'd been publicly accused, she dared not keep me on.

MRS. STOCKMANN. A frequent visitor—just think of it! You see, Tomas—that's what comes of all your hospitality!

DR. STOCKMANN. We won't stay in this pig sty any longer. Get packed as soon as you can, Katrine. We'll leave this place at once—the sooner the better!

MRS. STOCKMANN. Be quiet a moment; I thought I heard someone in the hall. See who it is, Petra.

PETRA (*Opens the hall door*). Oh, it's you, Captain Horster! Do come in.

HORSTER (*From the hall*). Good morning. I thought I'd just come over and see how you were getting on.

DR. STOCKMANN (*Shaking his hand*). Thanks; that's very kind of you.

MRS. STOCKMANN. And thank you, Captain Horster, for helping us last night.

PETRA. How did you ever manage to get home?

HORSTER. It wasn't bad—I'm a pretty hefty man, you know. And, anyway—there was more noise than action!

DR. STOCKMANN. Isn't it amazing what cowards those people are? Come here—I want to show you something. Here are all the stones they threw in at us last night. Just look at them! There aren't more than two decent stones among the lot; most of them are pebbles—a lot of gravel! And yet they stood out there shouting and yelling that they were going to kill me! But as for really doing it— oh, no! Nothing as positive as that!

HORSTER. Well—for once—I should think you'd have been grateful, Doctor!

DR. STOCKMANN. Oh, I am—of course! But it's tragic all the same; I sometimes think—supposing a really serious struggle of national proportions were involved; you can be sure enlightened public opinion would instantly take to its heels and run away, and the great solid majority would scatter like a herd of frightened sheep; that's the depressing part of it—it makes me sick to think of. But, damn it—why should I care what they do! They've called me an enemy of the People, so I might as well *be* an enemy of the People!

MRS. STOCKMANN. You'll never be that, Tomas.

DR. STOCKMANN. I wouldn't be too sure, Katrine. One ugly word can act as an irritant sometimes— and that damned expression—! I can't get rid of it; it's dug its way into the pit of my stomach— I feel it gnawing away there like a bitter acid. All the magnesia tablets in the world won't make it stop!

PETRA. They're not worth taking seriously, Father.

HORSTER. Some day they'll change their minds, Doctor—you'll see.

MRS. STOCKMANN. Yes, Tomas; I'm sure of that.

DR. STOCKMANN. They may—when it's too late. Well

—serve them right! Let them wallow in their filth and cry their hearts out with remorse at having driven a patriot into exile. When do you sail, Captain?

HORSTER. Hm—that's really what I wanted to talk to you about—

DR. STOCKMANN. Oh? Is anything the matter with the ship?

HORSTER. No, nothing; except—I shan't be with her.

PETRA. You surely haven't been dismissed?

HORSTER (*With a smile*). But I have, you see.

PETRA. You, too.

MRS. STOCKMANN. That just shows you, Tomas.

DR. STOCKMANN. And all for the sake of truth! If I'd thought anything like this could happen—!

HORSTER. You mustn't be upset. Some other company will take me on.

DR. STOCKMANN. And to think that a man like Vik—! A man of means—who can afford to be completely independent—! How disgusting!

HORSTER. He's not such a bad man, really. He told me himself he'd like to keep me on—only he didn't dare—

DR. STOCKMANN. He didn't dare! Of course not!

HORSTER. He said it wasn't always easy—when you're a member of a party—

DR. STOCKMANN. He hit the nail on the head that time! A party—! A sausage-machine—that's what a party's like! All the brains are ground up together and reduced to hash; and that's why the world is filled with a lot of brainless, empty-headed numskulls!

MRS. STOCKMANN. Tomas! Please!

PETRA. (*To* HORSTER). If you hadn't seen us home, this mightn't have happened.

HORSTER. I don't regret it.

PETRA (*Holds out her hand to him*). Thank you!

HORSTER. But I wanted to tell you this: if you're really bent on going—there's another way it could be—

MRS. STOCKMANN. Hush! I thought I heard a knock.

PETRA. I believe it's Uncle.

DR. STOCKMANN. Aha! (*Calls*) Come in!

MRS. STOCKMANN. Now, Tomas—promise me, please—!

(THE MAYOR *enters from the hall.*)

THE MAYOR (*In the doorway*). Oh, you're busy. Then I'd better—

DR. STOCKMANN. No, no. Come in.

THE MAYOR. I wanted to speak to you alone.

MRS. STOCKMANN. We'll go into the living room.

HORSTER. I'll come back later, then.

DR. STOCKMANN. No, Captain Horster—don't go away. I'm anxious to hear more about—

HORSTER. Very well; I'll wait.

(*He follows* MRS. STOCKMANN *and* PETRA *into the living room.* THE MAYOR *says nothing, but glances at the windows.*)

DR. STOCKMANN. A bit draughty, isn't it? Better put on your hat.

THE MAYOR. Thanks—if I may. (*Does so*) I think I caught cold last night. I felt a sudden chill—

DR. STOCKMANN. Really? I thought it was a bit on the warm side!

THE MAYOR. I regret I was unable to prevent that most unfortunate business.

DR. STOCKMANN. Is there anything special you want to say to me?

THE MAYOR (*Producing a large envelope*). The management of the Baths sends you this document.

DR. STOCKMANN. My dismissal, I suppose.

THE MAYOR. Yes—as of today. We regret this decision but, frankly, we didn't dare do otherwise. Out of respect for public opinion, you understand.

DR. STOCKMANN. Didn't dare do otherwise. I seem to have heard those words before, today.

THE MAYOR. I think you should face the fact that from now on you won't be able to count on any practice here.

DR. STOCKMANN. To hell with my practice! But why are you so sure of that?

THE MAYOR. The Home-owners Association is circulating a petition urging all respectable citizens to refrain from calling on your services. Of course everyone will sign it—they wouldn't dare do otherwise.

DR. STOCKMANN. I don't doubt that. What else?

THE MAYOR. If you take my advice, you'll leave town for a while.

DR. STOCKMANN. Yes; I've already given serious thought to that.

THE MAYOR. You're wise. Then—after six months or so—when you've had time to think things over, you might perhaps feel ready to write us a few words of apology, admitting your mistake—

DR. STOCKMANN. And then I might be re-instated, do you think?

THE MAYOR. You might; it's by no means impossible.

DR. STOCKMANN. But what about public opinion? Aren't you forgetting that?

THE MAYOR. Public opinion has a way of changing; and, quite frankly, it would be greatly to our advantage to have a signed statement from you to that effect.

DR. STOCKMANN. Yes—I dare say it would be most convenient! I've already told you how I feel about that kind of crookedness.

THE MAYOR. You were in a very different position then. At that time you imagined you had the whole town at your back—

DR. STOCKMANN. And now, it seems, I have the whole town *on* my back! (*Flaring up*) But I don't care if the devil himself were on my back, I'll never consent to—! Never, I tell you; never!

THE MAYOR. As a family man you have no right to take this stand, Tomas. You simply have no right!

DR. STOCKMANN. I have no right, have I? There's only one thing in this world a free man has no right to do; you don't know what that is, do you?

THE MAYOR. No, I don't.

DR. STOCKMANN. Of course not; then I'll tell you. A free man has no right to wallow in filth. A free man has no right to debase himself to the point of wanting to spit in his own face!

THE MAYOR. That might sound quite convincing if there were no other explanation for your pig-headedness; but of course we know there is—

DR. STOCKMANN. What do you mean?

THE MAYOR. You know quite well what I mean. However as your brother, and as a man of some experience, I advise you not to put too much faith in certain hopes and prospects that may prove disappointing.

DR. STOCKMANN. What on earth are you getting at?

THE MAYOR. Don't try to tell me you're unaware of the terms of old Morten Kiil's will!

DR. STOCKMANN. I only know he's left what little he has to a home for indigent workmen. It's no business of mine.

THE MAYOR. To begin with, "what little he has" amounts to a considerable sum. Morten Kiil is a very wealthy man.

DR. STOCKMANN. I had no idea of that—

THE MAYOR. No? Are you sure? Perhaps you had no idea either that a large part of his fortune is to be placed in a trust fund for your children; and that during your lifetime you and your wife are to enjoy the income from this trust. Did he never tell you that?

DR. STOCKMANN. He never breathed a word of it! In fact he does nothing but complain how poor he is, and grumble about taxes. Peter—are you quite sure of this?

THE MAYOR. Quite sure. My information is most reliable.

DR. STOCKMANN. But—good heavens! Then the children are provided for—and Katrine too! I must tell her this at once—(*Calls*) Katrine, Katrine!

THE MAYOR (*Holding him back*). No, wait! Don't tell her yet.

MRS. STOCKMANN (*Opens the door*). What is it, dear?

DR. STOCKMANN. It's nothing; never mind.

(MRS. STOCKMANN *closes the door again.*)

DR. STOCKMANN (*Pacing up and down*). To think of it—provided for! All of them provided for—and for life too. How wonderful to feel one is provided for!

THE MAYOR. But that's just what you're not, you see. Morten Kiil can change his will whenever he sees fit.

DR. STOCKMANN. Oh, but he won't, Peter! The old badger's much too pleased with me for unmasking you and your precious friends.

THE MAYOR (*Starts and looks at him intently*). I see! That puts things in quite a different light.

DR. STOCKMANN. What things?

THE MAYOR. So it was all a put-up job! Those violent attacks you made on the leading men of the town—all in the name of truth, of course—were actually nothing but—!

DR. STOCKMANN. But what?

THE MAYOR. —nothing but a kind of sop to that vindictive old miser Morten Kiil. That was his reward for leaving all that money to you in his will!

DR. STOCKMANN. Peter—upon my word you are the lowest of the low!

THE MAYOR. I shall have no further dealings with you; your dismissal is irrevocable. We are well armed against you now.

(*He goes out.*)

DR. STOCKMANN. Of all the filthy—! (*Calls*) Katrine! Have this floor scrubbed at once! Tell the girl—what the devil's her—*you* know—the girl with the smutty nose—to bring her pail and scrub-brush!

MRS. STOCKMANN (*In the doorway*). Tomas, Tomas! Hush!

PETRA (*Also in the doorway*). Father; Grandfather's here. He wants to know if he can speak to you alone.

DR. STOCKMANN. Of course he can. (*By the door*) Come in, sir. (MORTEN KIIL *enters.* STOCKMANN *closes the door behind him.*)

DR. STOCKMANN. Well, what is it? Won't you sit down?

MORTEN KIIL. No thanks. (*He looks round*) Well, Stockmann—things look very cozy here.

DR. STOCKMANN. Yes, don't they?

MORTEN KIIL. Very cozy indeed; a nice lot of fresh air too; plenty of that oxygen you talked so much about. Your moral fiber must be flourishing.

DR. STOCKMANN. It is.

MORTEN KIIL. Yes, to be sure. (*Tapping his breast pocket*) But do you know what I have here?

DR. STOCKMANN. Plenty of moral fiber, too, I hope.

MORTEN KIIL. Something much better than that, I can assure you. (*Takes out a large wallet, opens it, and shows* STOCKMANN *a bundle of papers.*)

DR. STOCKMANN (*Looks at him in amazement*). Shares? Shares in the Baths?

MORTEN KIIL. They were easy enough to get today.

DR. STOCKMANN. Do you mean to say you've bought up—?

MORTEN KIIL. All I could lay my hands on!

DR. STOCKMANN. But, my dear sir—you know the present situation at the Baths—!

MORTEN KIIL. If you behave like a sensible man, you'll soon set that right again.

DR. STOCKMANN. You know I've tried to do everything I can—but these people are all lunatics!

MORTEN KIIL. You said last night that the worst filth came from my tannery. Now supposing that were true—it means that my father and my grandfather before me, and I myself for many years, have been poisoning the town—like three demons of destruction. You don't expect me to accept that accusation calmly, do you?

DR. STOCKMAN. I'm afraid you'll have to.

MORTEN KIIL. No thank you; my good name and reputation mean too much to me. People call me "the badger," so I'm told; and a badger's a kind of a pig, they tell me. But I intend to prove them wrong. While I live and after I die, my name shall be kept spotless.

DR. STOCKMANN. How are you going to manage that?

MORTEN KIIL. *You* are going to manage that for me, Stockmann. You are going to clear my name for me.

DR. STOCKMANN. I!

MORTEN KIIL. Do you know what money I used to buy these shares? No, of course you don't—but now I'm going to tell you. I used all the money Katrine, Petra and the boys were to inherit from me. For, in spite of everything, I have managed to save quite a bit, you see.

DR. STOCKMANN (*Flaring up*). Do you mean to say you used Katrine's money to do this!

MORTEN KIIL. Yes—I've invested every penny of it in the Baths. Now let's see how much of a madman you really are, Stockmann. Now if you keep on spreading this story that a lot of filthy animals seep into the water from my tannery, you'll just be flaying pieces of skin off Katrine, and off Petra too—to say nothing of the boys, of course. No decent father would dream of doing that—unless he were a madman.

DR. STOCKMANN (*Pacing up and down*). But I am a madman; I *am* a madman, don't you see?

MORTEN KIIL. Sacrifice your wife and children? You couldn't be as stark raving mad as that!

DR. STOCKMANN (*Stopping in front of him*). Why in God's name didn't you talk to me before buying all this rubbish?

MORTEN KIIL. What's done is done; it's too late now.

DR. STOCKMANN (*Walking about restlessly*). If only I weren't so absolutely certain—! But I'm absolutely positive I'm right.

MORTEN KIIL (*Weighing the wallet in his hand*). If you persist in this lunacy, these things won't be worth much, will they? (*Puts the wallet back in his pocket.*)

DR. STOCKMANN. Damn it! Surely there must be some scientific way of purifying the water—some sort of disinfectant—

MORTEN KIIL. To kill those animals, you mean?

DR. STOCKMANN. Yes—or at least to make them harmless.

MORTEN KIIL. You might try rat-poison.

DR. STOCKMANN. Oh! Don't talk nonsense! —And since everyone says it's merely an illusion on my part—why not let it be an illusion then! Let them have their way! Ignorant, damnable mongrels that they are! They've called me an enemy of the People—torn the clothes off my back—

MORTEN KIIL. And smashed in all your windows!

DR. STOCKMANN. And one has a duty toward one's family, after all. I must talk it over with Katrine. She's better at these things than I am.

MORTEN KIIL. A good idea; she'll give you sensible advice.

DR. STOCKMANN (*Turns on him angrily*). How could you behave in this fantastic manner? Gambling with Katrine's money; putting me through this agony—this torment! What kind of a devil are you!

MORTEN KIIL. If I'm a devil, perhaps I'd better go. But I want your decision—either yes or no—by two o'clock. If the answer's "no," I'll make these over to charity at once—this very day.

DR. STOCKMANN. And what will Katrine get?

MORTEN KIIL. Not a damn penny! (*The door to the hall opens;* HOVSTAD *and* ASLAKSEN *are seen outside*) I certainly never expected to meet them here!

DR. STOCKMANN (*Staring at them*). What does this mean? How dare you come to see me?

HOVSTAD. We have our reasons.

ASLAKSEN. We've something to discuss with you.

MORTEN KIIL (*In a whisper*). Yes or no—by two o'clock.

ASLAKSEN (*With a glance at* HOVSTAD). Aha!
(MORTEN KIIL *goes out.*)

DR. STOCKMANN. Well, what do you want? Be quick about it.

HOVSTAD. It's natural you should resent the attitude we were forced to take last night—

DR. STOCKMANN. So that's what you call an attitude, is it? A fine attitude! Behaving like a couple of cowards—a couple of old women—!

HOVSTAD. Call it what you like; but, you see, we have no alternative—

DR. STOCKMANN. You didn't dare do otherwise, I suppose!

HOVSTAD. If that's how you choose to put it.

ASLAKSEN. You should have given us some inkling, Dr. Stockmann. The slightest hint to Mr. Hovstad or to me—

DR. STOCKMANN. Hint? What about?

ASLAKSEN. About your real motive in this matter.

DR. STOCKMANN. I don't know what you mean.

ASLAKSEN (*Nods confidentially*). Of course you do, Dr. Stockmann.

HOVSTAD. Why make a mystery of it now?

DR. STOCKMANN (*Looks from one to the other*). What the devil's all this about—?

ASLAKSEN. You know your father-in-law's been all over town buying up shares in the Baths—isn't that so?

DR. STOCKMANN. Yes, he has—but what of that?

ASLAKSEN. It might have been wiser to choose some-body else to do it for you; the connection is a bit too obvious.

HOVSTAD. And wouldn't it have been more prudent if you hadn't mixed yourself up personally in this affair? The attack on the Baths should have been made by someone else. Why didn't you take me into your confidence, Dr. Stockmann?

DR. STOCKMANN (*Staring straight in front of him; a light seems to dawn on him, and he says as though thunderstruck*). This is incredible! Can such things be!

ASLAKSEN (*Smiling*). Well—obviously! But they should be handled with more delicacy, it seems to me.

HOVSTAD. And it was unwise to attempt it single-handed; it's always easier to avoid responsibility for a matter of this sort, if you have others working with you.

DR. STOCKMANN (*Calmly*). Come to the point, gentlemen. What is it you want?

ASLAKSEN. Perhaps Mr. Hovstad had better—

HOVSTAD. No, you explain it, Aslaksen.

ASLAKSEN. It's simply this: Now that we know how matters really stand, we feel safe in venturing to place *The People's Monitor* at your disposal.

DR. STOCKMANN. You feel safe, do you? What about public opinion? Aren't you afraid of raising a storm of protest?

HOVSTAD. We are prepared to weather it.

ASLAKSEN. And, before long, you can make a sudden change of tactics, Doctor. As soon as the charges made against the Baths have the desired effect—

DR. STOCKMANN. As soon as my father-in-law and I have bought up the shares at an attractive price, I suppose you mean—?

HOVSTAD. It's mainly for scientific reasons, I presume, that you wish to gain control of the establishment—?

DR. STOCKMANN. That goes without saying; and of course it was for scientific reasons too that I persuaded the old badger to become my partner in this plan. We'll patch up the pipes a bit, make a few little adjustments at the Beach—and it won't cost the town a penny. What do you think? That ought to do the trick!

HOVSTAD. I should think so—provided you have the *Monitor* to back you up.

ASLAKSEN. In a free community the Press is all-powerful, Doctor Stockmann.

DR. STOCKMANN. Unquestionably! And so is public

opinion too. I suppose you'll answer for the Home-owners Association, Mr. Aslaksen?

ASLAKSEN. The Home-owners Association, and the Temperance Society too; you may depend on that.

DR. STOCKMANN. Now, tell me, gentlemen—I'm almost ashamed to mention such a thing—what is your price?

HOVSTAD. I beg you to believe, Doctor, that we'd be only too happy to give you our support for nothing. But, unfortunately, the status of *The People's Monitor* is somewhat precarious; it's not as financially successful as it deserves to be. And it would seem a pity, just now when there's so much to be done in the field of general politics, to have to close our doors.

DR. STOCKMANN. I understand; I realize that would be very hard for a friend of the People, like yourself. (*Flaring up*) But *I'm* the People's enemy! An enemy of the People—have you forgotten that? (*Striding about the room*) Where's my stick? Where the devil is my stick?

HOVSTAD. What do you mean?

ASLAKSEN. You surely don't intend—?

DR. STOCKMANN (*Comes to a halt*). And what if I refuse to give you a penny of those shares? You must remember we rich people don't like parting with our money!

HOVSTAD. I advise *you* to remember that this business can be presented in a very ugly light.

DR. STOCKMANN. Yes; and you're just the man to do it! If I don't come to the rescue of your *Monitor,* I've no doubt you'll see to that. You'll hound me, won't you? You'll bait me—you'll slaughter me as a dog slaughters a hare!

HOVSTAD. That's the law of nature; every animal for himself, you know.

ASLAKSEN. We all have to take our food where we can find it.

DR. STOCKMANN. Then go out into the gutter, where you belong, and find it there! (*Striding about the room*) I'll show you who the strongest animal is here! (*Finds his umbrella and brandishes it at them*) Now—get out!

HOVSTAD. You wouldn't dare attack us—!

ASLAKSEN. Be careful with that umbrella—!

DR. STOCKMANN. Out of the window with you, Mr. Hovstad!

HOVSTAD (*By the hall door*). Have you gone raving mad?

DR. STOCKMANN. Out of the window, Mr. Aslaksen!

Jump, I tell you—and be quick about it!

ASLAKSEN (*Running round the desk*). Moderation, Doctor Stockmann—moderation! I'm not a strong man, you know; I can't stand things like this— (*Screams*) Help! Help!

(MRS. STOCKMANN, HORSTER *and* PETRA *enter from the living room.*)

MRS. STOCKMANN. Good gracious, Tomas! What are you doing?

DR. STOCKMANN (*Brandishing the umbrella*). Go on—jump, I tell you! Into the gutter where you belong!

HOVSTAD. You're a witness to this, Captain Horster! An unprovoked assault—!

(*Rushes out to the hall.*)

ASLAKSEN (*Bewildered*). I must look up the law on matters of this sort—! (*He escapes through the door to the living room.*)

MRS. STOCKMANN (*Clinging to the door*). Tomas—for heaven's sake control yourself!

DR. STOCKMANN (*Throws down the umbrella*). They both got away—damn them!

MRS. STOCKMANN. But what did they want, Tomas dear?

DR. STOCKMANN. I'll tell you presently; I've other things to attend to now. (*Goes to his desk and writes something on a visiting-card*) Look, Katrine! I want you to see what I've written here.

MRS. STOCKMANN. Three large "No's"—what can that mean?

DR. STOCKMANN. I'll tell you that presently too. (*Giving* PETRA *the card*) Here, Petra; tell Smudgy-face to run over to the badger and give him this. And hurry! (PETRA *goes out with the card*) I never expected to have so many visits from the devil's emissaries as I've had today! But I know how to deal with them; I'll sharpen my pen against them till it becomes a goad; I'll dip it in gall and venom; I'll hurl my entire ink-pot at their brazen heads!

MRS. STOCKMANN. But, Tomas—aren't we going away?

(PETRA *returns.*)

DR. STOCKMANN. Well?

PETRA. She's gone with it.

DR. STOCKMANN. Splendid!—Did you say going away? No, I'll be damned if we are, Katrine—we're going to stay right here!

MRS. STOCKMANN. Here in the town?

DR. STOCKMANN. Here in the town. The battle-field is here, and here the battle must be fought, and here I shall win the victory! As soon as you've patched my trousers I'll be off and try to find a place for us to live. We can't get through the winter without a roof over our heads!

HORSTER. Will my roof do?

DR. STOCKMANN. You really mean it?

HORSTER. Of course. I've such a lot of room, and I'm hardly ever home myself.

MRS. STOCKMANN. Oh, Captain Horster—that is kind of you!

PETRA. Thanks!

DR. STOCKMANN (*Shaking his hand*). Thanks—and thanks again! That's a great load off my mind. Now I can set to work in earnest. Oh, there's such a lot to do, Katrine! And I'll have all my time to myself—that's just as well; for, I forgot to tell you—I've been dismissed—

MRS. STOCKMANN (*Sighing*). Yes—I expected that!

DR. STOCKMANN. —and now they want to take away my practice, too! Well—let them! There are always the poor people—those that can't afford to pay; they're really the ones that need me most, you see. But, by God, they're going to hear from me! I'll harangue them every single day—"in season and out of season," as somebody or other put it.

MRS. STOCKMANN. Haven't you done enough talking, Tomas, dear?

DR. STOCKMANN. Don't be absurd, Katrine! Do you think I'd allow public opinion, and the solid majority, and all the rest of it to drive me from the field? No, thank you! Besides, my aim is perfectly simple and straightforward. I just want to din into the heads of these poor misguided mongrels, that these so-called Liberals are freedom's bitterest enemies—that party programs do nothing but stifle living truths—that justice and morality are being turned upside-down by expediency and greed—until eventually life itself will scarcely be worth living! Surely I ought to be able to make the people see that, Captain Horster? Don't you think so?

HORSTER. Perhaps, I don't know much about such things myself.

DR. STOCKMANN. It's all quite simple—let me explain it to you! First, the party-bosses have got to be wiped out; they're just like wolves, you see—like ravening wolves! They batten on the small-fry. In order to keep themselves alive they devour literally hundreds of them every single year. Take Hovstad and Aslaksen, for instance—think of the small-fry they devour! Or if they don't devour them, they debase them and corrupt them till all they're good for is to become Home-owners or subscribers to *The People's Monitor!* (*Sits on the edge of the table*) Come here, Katrine! Just look at that radiant, gallant sunshine! And doesn't the air smell fresh and clear this morning?

MRS. STOCKMANN. If only we could live on air and sunshine, Tomas, dear!

DR. STOCKMANN. Oh, but we can—with a little help from you! You'll scrimp and save away and we shall manage splendidly. That's the least of my worries. One thing does worry me though; where am I to find a decent freedom-loving man to carry on the work after I'm gone?

PETRA. Don't start worrying about that, Father; you've still got lots of time ahead of you!—Why, look; here are the boys!

(EJLIF and MORTEN *enter from the living room.*)

MRS. STOCKMANN. What's happened? It's not a holiday today!

MORTEN. We got into a fight with some of the other boys—

EJLIF. No, we didn't! They got into a fight with us!

MORTEN. And Mr. Rorlund said we'd better stay home for a few days.

DR. STOCKMANN (*Snapping his fingers and jumping down from the table*). That gives me an idea! Yes, by heaven, that gives me an idea! You shan't set foot in that blasted school again!

THE BOYS. Not go to school!

MRS. STOCKMANN. But, Tomas—

DR. STOCKMANN. Never again, I say! I'll start teaching you myself; or, better still—you shan't be taught a blessed thing—

MORTEN. Hurrah!

DR. STOCKMANN. The only thing I'll teach you, is to become decent freedom-loving men.—You'll help me, Petra, won't you?

PETRA. I'd love to, Father.

DR. STOCKMANN. We'll have the school in the very room where they branded me an enemy of the People. But we'll have to have more pupils—I want a dozen boys at least.

MRS. STOCKMANN. You'll never get them to come, Tomas; not in this town.

DR. STOCKMANN. Wait and see. (*To the boys*) You must know a few street-urchins—some regular guttersnipes—?

MORTEN. Oh, yes, Father! I know lots of them!

DR. STOCKMANN. Then find a few good specimens and bring them to me. I'm going to experiment with a few mongrels for a change; there's plenty of good raw-material there.

MORTEN. What are we to do, Father, when we grow up to be decent freedom-loving men?

DR. STOCKMANN. Drive the wolves away to the Far West, my boys!

MRS. STOCKMANN. But suppose it's the wolves who drive you away, Tomas, dear?

DR. STOCKMANN. Drive *me* away! Are you stark raving mad, Katrine? I'm the strongest man in the town! Don't you know that?

MRS. STOCKMANN. The strongest—? You mean, *now?*

DR. STOCKMANN. Yes! I'll even go so far as to say that I'm one of the strongest men in the whole world!

MORTEN. Are you really, Father?

DR. STOCKMANN (*Dropping his voice*). Hush! You mustn't say a word about it yet; I've made a great discovery, you see.

MRS. STOCKMANN. Not another, Tomas, dear!

DR. STOCKMANN. Another, yes—another! (*Gathers them round him and speaks in a confidential tone*) And I'll tell you what it is: the strongest man in the world is the man who stands alone.

MRS. STOCKMANN (*Smiles and shakes her head*). Oh, Tomas, dear—!

PETRA (*Grasps his hands and says with eyes full of faith*). Father!

CURTAIN

DISCUSSION

1. In how many different ways does "public opinion" express itself early in this act?

2. (a) According to Dr. Stockmann, how are political parties like sausage machines? (b) Do you agree with him? Why or why not?

3. (a) According to the doctor, what one thing does no man have a right to do? (b) In your own words, what does he mean?

4. (a) What does Morten Kiil propose to Stockmann? How does he make it difficult for the doctor to refuse his proposal? (b) At this point in the action, do you think Kiil has convinced Dr. Stockmann to comply with his wishes? Cite passages from the text to support your answer.

5. (a) What do Hovstad and Aslaksen offer Stockmann? (b) What is their price?

6. (a) At the beginning of this play, Dr. Stockmann has many friends. At the end who are his real friends?

7. Do you think that Dr. Stockmann's decision to stay in the town was a wise one? Practical? Explain.

8. What final discovery does Dr. Stockmann make?

COMPOSITION

Argument

An author has the enviable opportunity of using his writing as a forum for expressing his viewpoint on any subject and for any purpose. Whatever his intentions —debating the great issues of the day, airing publicly a personal grievance, or simply sounding off—an author recognizes that his writing enables him to get his ideas to the people. In *An Enemy of the People* Henrik Ibsen eagerly took advantage of this opportunity.

Ghosts, a play Ibsen had written one year earlier, created such a furor when it first appeared in print that for many years no major company in Norway would perform it. Though readers today would hardly consider it shocking, Ibsen's contemporaries were enraged.

Central to the plot of *Ghosts* was the subject of venereal disease. Ibsen used this subject symbolically to illustrate his theme: the potential consequences of blindly accepting convention. Public opinion, missing the point entirely, denounced Ibsen for writing a play *about* an "unmentionable" social disease. The press, both conservative and liberal, participated in attacking him as a corrupter of society. In part, *An Enemy of the People* was Ibsen's reply to his critics, particularly the hostile press.

The following excerpt is taken from a letter which Ibsen wrote to a friend eleven months before *An Enemy of the People* was published.

What is one to say of the attitude

taken by the so-called liberal press? These leaders who talk and write of freedom and progress, and at the same time allow themselves to be the slaves of the supposed opinions of their subscribers? . . . Under no circumstances will I ever link myself with any party which has the majority behind it. Bjornson says: 'The majority is always right.' As a practising politician I suppose he has to say that. But I say: 'The minority is always right.' . . . I believe that he is right who is most closely attuned to the future. . . . For me freedom is the first condition of life, and the highest. . . . In the course of their undeniably worthy efforts to turn our country into a democratic community, people have unwittingly gone a good way towards turning us into a mob community. The aristocracy of the intellect seems to be in short supply in Norway.*

The following statements represent ideas which Ibsen, through Dr. Stockmann, defends or attacks in the play:

1. The majority is always right.
2. The minority is always right.
3. He is right who is most closely attuned to the future.
4. Freedom is the first condition of life, and the highest.

Choose one of these statements and consider it carefully, weighing evidence, if any, for and against the idea it represents. Then write a brief composition (two or three paragraphs) in which you discuss the statement, noting the conclusions you have reached. Assume that your audience for the paper is a student who has taken a position opposite from yours.

UNIT 1 REVIEW

1. As a dramatist sets his major conflict in motion, he provides whatever background information his audience needs to understand the characters and their actions. Such explanatory information is called the *exposition* of the play, most of which occurs during the first act.

a. What information does Ibsen provide about Dr. Stockmann, the Mayor, and the present situation in the town? What one very important bit of information regarding the future financial security of the Stockmann family does Ibsen not reveal until well into the play? Why do you suppose he withheld this information?

b. In *Twelve Angry Men*, what information about the trial does Mr. Rose provide while the jurors are still in the courtroom? While they are assembling in the jury room? After they vote for the first time?

2. The main character involved in a dramatic conflict is called the

protagonist and the person (or forces) opposing him is called the *antagonist*.

a. Who is the protagonist in *An Enemy of the People?* In *Twelve Angry Men?* Who (or what) is the antagonist in each play?

b. Considering the identity of the protagonist in *An Enemy of the People*, do you think Ibsen has used the most appropriate title for his play? Suggest a substitute title for *Twelve Angry Men* that reflects the identity of the protagonist.

3. The conflict of a play creates several moments of *dramatic climax*—moments that excite the audience. What do you consider to be the most exciting moments in *An Enemy of the People?* In *Twelve Angry Men?* Explain.

4. The conflict of a play also builds toward a *technical climax*— a turning point in the action that determines whether or not the protagonist will succeed.

a. What is the protagonist's goal in *An Enemy of the People?* At what point in the play does it become obvious that he is not going to achieve this goal?

b. What is the protagonist's goal in *Twelve Angry Men?* What event in Act Three determines his success?

c. In your opinion, does the technical climax in each play coincide with a dramatic climax? Explain.

*From IBSEN by Michael Meyer. Copyright © 1967, 1971 by Michael Meyer. Reprinted by permission of Doubleday & Company, Inc. and David Higham Associates, Ltd. for the publisher, Hart-Davis.

2 The Short Story

CHALLENGE
RELATIONSHIPS
MYSTERY
SURVIVAL
PRINCIPLES

CHALLENGE

ENCOUNTER IN ILLINOIS

Robert M. Coates

"If he let them go farther, even a little farther, they could cut him off—run him right off the road or block him—"

As soon as the men—boys, really; none of them appeared to be much over eighteen—came into the café, Jerry Benedict knew, somehow, that there was going to be trouble. The café itself was a small, rather dingy roadside place, and it hadn't looked especially promising; low-roofed, conventionally clapboarded and neon-lighted, set down in a sea of gravel, it stood on the very outskirts of a town called Hazelton, in southern Illinois, and the only reason Jerry and Fran had stopped there at all was that it *was* on the outskirts, and so a sort of last chance for them. They had already driven through the rest of the town and had passed no doubt better eating places near its center. But by then it was getting late, and with that mile-by-mile consciousness the day-long motorist develops, they had no thought of turning back for even a short distance—and at the same time they knew that the next town on the map, a place called Newkirk, was a good forty miles away.

So, anyway, they stopped, heading in among the half-dozen cars parked haphazardly around the entrance, climbed out stiffly, and—Jerry remembered afterward, gratefully—debated about locking the car and decided against it. "We wouldn't lock it if we were near home, would we?" he argued. "I bet people are just as honest out here as they are around Yorktown."

It was a favorite thesis of his, and one that he'd voiced many times at dinner tables in the past: that one's confidence in the other man's honesty was somehow localized—a product of neighborliness, really—and diminished the farther one got away from his home grounds. But now he realized, even as he spoke, that this was no time to elaborate on it. Fran was already walking away. "OK, honey, do as you want," she said. "There's not much to steal anyway." So he just slammed the car door shut and followed.

As Jerry had expected, the place turned out to be more bar than restaurant, with the bar—at the rear, in the Midwestern fashion—well filled and noisy, and a cramped double row of booths, cheaply made of walnut-stained plywood and all unoccupied until Fran and he went in, leading up to it. The waitress, short and stocky, and offhand, though cheerful, looked as if she could handle anything. But the food was all right—they had martinis and a passable steak sandwich—and the place was clean and well lighted, and a rest from the endless trembling tension of motion. It was good, in a way, to be just sitting still for a while, and they were starting on a second cup of coffee when they heard an exhaust-roar outside and a skittering of gravel, another burst from an engine, and then silence, as if the ignition had been cut. "Is that the way they always arrive around here—in a shower of gravel?" Jerry asked. "But then," he added, "this is the hot-rod region, isn't it?"

He was still looking at Fran, and smiling, even as the boys came in, and he scarcely noticed them, as persons, until—just as they passed his and Fran's table, walking down toward the bar—they stopped.

"Hey, a dish!" he heard one of them say.

"Aw, come on, Ote!"[1] said another, and Jerry looked up to see the boys—there were three of them —in a kind of sudden jumble in the aisle just past his table. One was blond to the point, almost, of being towheaded; short and solidly built, pale-blue-eyed, pale-skinned, he had a broad, flat-featured face that looked vaguely Scandinavian, and he was obviously the one who had spoken first, for he was looking directly at Fran and Jerry—but more, Jerry noted a little uneasily, at Fran than at him—and grinning broadly. He had a crew cut, but the other two, one tall, one short, wore their dark hair fantastically long. All wore Levis and massively riveted leather jackets, and it was the tall one, Jerry realized, who had also spoken. He had a long, thin-featured, rather saturnine face and a long, lanky body, and he was looking at his friend the blond boy in a way that was at once complaisant and expectant. What's he up to now?, he seemed to be thinking, with relish as much as with anything (he hadn't yet even glanced at the Benedicts), but when he spoke it was, in a careless way, placatively. "Come on, Ote," he said again, and he gave the other's arm a tug. "Let's get up to the bar and have a quick one. We got things to do tonight." It came over Jerry, suddenly, that the blond boy might be more than a little drunk.

But he turned out to be—for the moment, anyway —amenable. "Oh, sure, sure," he said, and, still staring at Fran, he nodded with an air of ancient wisdom. "Only not at the bar. Back here," he said. "I like this, Eddie." And with that he planted him-

self suddenly in the booth opposite the Benedicts'. "A beer, Eddie. A beer," he said.

"Ah, Ote!" said the one called Eddie. But he said it again, with an air almost of delight, and for the first time he took a quick glance at Fran and Jerry. It was a look that was flat, hard, and curiously impersonal. "Come on, Hack," he said to the third boy, and together they went up to the bar. A moment later, they were back, Eddie carrying one beer and the smaller boy two, and they both squeezed onto the seat opposite the blond boy.

The blond boy was still staring at Fran, and Fran's face, Jerry noticed, was getting that slightly flushed, set look it always got when she was annoyed. Jerry was puzzled, mostly, and amused—after all, the whole thing was so blasted silly, really—but also troubled. He hated scenes, and he had a feeling that a scene might be developing. Fran apparently felt so, too, for she gave him the clear, direct look she frequently used as a signal between them. "Well, darling," she said, "don't you think it's time we were going?" and began picking up her purse and gloves.

Jerry, though, was stubborn. "No hurry," he told her. "Let's finish our coffee, at least." But, catching the waitress' eye as she stood near the bar, he did signal to her for the check.

There was silence all round while he paid. But when the waitress had gone, and the boys—all three now—still stared, Jerry felt a surge of real anger. It was time, after all, to call a halt to this, and he turned to face the group directly. "Do you have some idea that you know us, or something?" he demanded. In a way, he was still puzzled by their behavior. "Or you want to?" he went on, leaning a little toward them.

The blond boy paid no attention, but the dark one, Eddie, met his eye. He was holding his beer glass in both hands, upraised like a chalice, in an oddly graceful gesture, but his glance was so strange that Jerry, in spite of himself, was taken aback. Jerry Benedict was a normally personable, cheerful, friendly man, and he was accustomed to being liked. Certainly he was unused to encountering active hatred, and yet the glance he met from the fellow opposite was one of such sudden unyielding enmity —and from such a youth, too—that he was, for the moment, disconcerted. What the devil are they up to, anyway, he wondered. Is it just that we're East-erners? Are they practicing being tough guys? But

---

1. *Ote* (ō′tē), an abbreviation of Otis.

he kept his air of brisk amusement. "In any case, didn't anyone ever tell you it's impolite to stare?" he said.

"Whyn't you ditch him and come with us?" said the blond boy suddenly, speaking to Fran, and still with his blazing grin. "We'll give you a good time."

"What!" Jerry cried, and he found himself starting from his seat.

Fran was already in the aisle. "Jerry! Jerry! Come *on!*" she was saying, and after a moment to—well, catch his breath, really; compose himself—Jerry rose to follow her.

"Of course, darling," he said. "They're just kids, after all!" But he took the time to let his eye travel over them, one by one: the blond boy, grinning still, or with his teeth bared, anyway; the tall, dark one with his jaws tight, his eyes sparkling with resentment; the third one simply staring. "Sometime, though," Jerry couldn't help saying as he reached the door, "someone ought to teach them good manners."

And then Fran and Jerry were out in the cool prairie night, dark except for the spill of light from the café's neons and empty everywhere. Fran was in the car and Jerry was just going round to the driver's seat; he was saying "Well, wasn't *that* the weirdest thing!" when the door of the café opened and (Who else? Jerry was beginning to feel fatalistic about the whole venture) the three boys, obviously looking for trouble, came out.

Jerry didn't feel fear, exactly, and he didn't exactly hurry. He insisted to himself, even as he watched the boys, that he mustn't panic. But he was acutely conscious of the darkness and his and Fran's own isolation—not a light, not a house, nothing anywhere but the silent prairie—and he was glad, very glad, when he heard the engine churn once and then take hold, and realized that Fran had reached over and touched the starter. Except for one encounter with a drunk in a hotel bar, which had ended almost as soon as it began, Jerry hadn't had a fight with anyone since he and Wade Berry, his sophomore-year roommate at college, squared off against each other after an argument over some broken phonograph records, and when he saw the boys heading toward him, he did the only thing he could think of to do. "Maybe *you* need a lesson, Mister," one of them was saying, but Jerry didn't give him a chance to finish. They were coming bunched together, and with a lunge he leaped forward and shoved, simply shoved, the nearest one back on the

others. One—Jerry had the impression it was the blond one—fell, and falling, grabbed at the others, who stumbled until they were all in a tangle. They were on their feet again in a second or two, of course, swearing and plunging toward Jerry, but by that time he was in the car and away.

It was Fran who, a mile or so on down the road, noticed headlights approaching from behind. "I know," Jerry said when she called his attention to them. "But I swear I don't think it's they. I watched the place for quite a while in the rear-view mirror, and I didn't see anything start out."

And there wasn't a house, not a house—or none lighted—anywhere. And what good would it have done if there had been, either? Could they whirl into some strangers' driveway, dash in upon them and say they were being followed by a bunch of crazy youngsters, when there was a chance, still, that the car behind contained only a traveling salesman or some farmer and his family heading home after a day's marketing?

"What the devil was the name of that restaurant, anyway?" Jerry asked a moment later. Fran said nothing, and he answered for her. "Paul's Paradise, wasn't it? Some paradise!" And he went on, since she still said nothing, "And there we were, just before, talking"—as they had been earlier, driving doggedly through the flat sameness of the region— "about these kids that they have out here, and the wild things they do, and the reasons for it." He glanced at Fran and saw that she had her hands clasped tight between her knees, and her head bent down. She was shaking.

"Well, whoever it is, I'm not going to race them," he muttered. He'd been going at about fifty all along, and he was still going fifty when the car came slowly —in the sense that an extra five miles an hour is slow, no matter what the speed is—easily alongside. It was they, of course. Despite what he had said to Fran, he somehow had known it must be. It was an old black coupé the boys were in—a Pontiac or an Olds; he couldn't quite tell, for it had been cut down and altered in one way or another, and anyway he took only a quick look at it. The three boys were sitting crowded into the one seat—the blond boy, Ote, at the wheel, Eddie on the outside, nearest the Benedicts, and the smaller one in the middle. The odd—in a way, the almost eerie—thing was that none of the boys even looked at them. There they were, riding fender to fender with him, headlights bright on the road ahead, and Jerry, glancing over, could see the three youthful figures, lit ghostly by their dash lights; indeed, if the cars' windows had been down, he could almost have reached out and touched them. The dark boy, Eddie, had his back nearly turned to Jerry, revealing the soft, almost feminine look that the heavy growth of hair—a ducktail, he remembered they called it—gave to the back of his neck. But he never moved or turned. The blond boy, driving, looked straight ahead, and so did the other; it was as if they were in another world, and though both Jerry and Fran knew that two panes of glass, in addition to the sounds of the road, separated them from the boys, they spoke to each other in whispers.

"Let them pass, Jerry. Let them pass. It's dangerous this way," Fran said, and Jerry, glancing at her, saw that she was still trembling. He could feel his own hands clenching and unclenching in helpless rage on the wheel.

But he felt stubborn, somehow. "Why?" he asked. "They can pass, if they want to pass me. They seem to have plenty of power." And (how long was it later—a half mile, a mile, of this sullen careering?) when Fran said *"Please!"* so urgently that he did slack, he realized almost instantly that he had been right in the first place.

For, as he slowed, the black car, inching ahead of him, started to edge in toward him, too. Already its front fender was nosing in front of his, and in a sudden bright whirl of mixed knowledge, horror, and—this time—real fear, Jerry trod down heavily on the accelerator and forged determinedly ahead. If he let them go farther, even a little farther, they could cut him off—run him right off the road or block him—and then what would happen to him, against the three of them? What would happen to Fran? There was a thin scream of metal as the fenders touched, and Jerry felt his own car rock. Then the black car swung off and dropped back out of sight behind them; a few seconds later, its exhaust really blasting now, it shot past at full speed and dimmed away down the road. As it passed, the dark boy, Eddie, twisted about in his seat and thumbed his nose.

It was so silly, so inappropriate—above all, so youthful—a gesture that it made Jerry feel giddy, momentarily, in the letdown. It was what a kid did, from a distance, to a man who had reprimanded him or to another boy after a row over marbles, not after a deliberate near collision, and he felt his chest

shake in a gust of almost manic merriment. Then anger took hold of him, and he found himself pounding the wheel again. They were kids, sure enough, but they could wreck them all—they could kill him and Fran, too—with their infantile lack of responsibility. They might have killed them right then and there, he thought, if he'd held his course. And then, as something still too faint for thought stirred in his mind, he remembered Fran and turned to look at her. "I had to do it," he said. "I had to drive right at them."

"Oh, I know. I know," Fran said wanly. She still had her hands clenched between her knees, and her head bent down. She was still shivering.

"They could have driven us right off the road if I hadn't," Jerry went on. "They could have had us right where they wanted us." Then, suddenly, he stopped talking. They *still* could have us, he thought —if they really wanted to. And meantime the night flowed by, dark as ever and empty as ever—wide, immense, impersonal. Abruptly, Jerry found himself thinking beyond the night and the flat, dreary plain, and the small, identical towns it contained, to the life it fostered. Here the car was the one release, and it must be treasured. It would be worked on, too, as these boys' car obviously had been: the valves ground and the timing adjusted, the cylinders rebored and the body painted—and all done carefully, lovingly.

They must spend months working on their cars, he thought. And then to take them out on the road and risk wrecking them—against a stranger's, too. It didn't make sense, and Jerry was still puzzling over the craziness of it when he saw the boys' car coming up the road, heading toward him. He knew it now, or he was fairly sure he did. The beam from one head lamp was tilted a little, as he'd noticed it was before when he'd seen it in the rear-view mirror, and the car was holding the center of the road in a way that seemed slightly ominous.

It held so, even as it neared, and it was then that Jerry made his decision that there would have to be a showdown. If anyone was going to give way, the boys would have to do it. And he was somehow sure they would. "Get down, Fran," he told her. "Get as low as you can."

"No."

"Get down," he repeated, and this time she slid almost to the floor.

He wasn't going fast, perhaps about forty, and

the other car, he judged, was making about the same speed. He slowed, but even so their combined speeds must be sixty or seventy, and he was wondering what the impact would be when the time came for him to stop thinking (leaving them the time and the distance to make their own decisions). Then, shoving down as far as he could in the seat, he swung the wheel to head directly at them.

The next few instants were the emptiest Jerry had ever known. He saw the loom of the other car as it passed, and he heard a kind of skittering crash behind and to the left of him and felt his own car lurch onto gravel. Even while he was hauling himself up in the seat, he yanked the car onto the pavement again; then he stopped it and looked back. The other car was in the ditch, all right, at a slant that made the headlights shine off crazily, and there was a flutter of dust settling slowly around it. But beyond that it was clearly undamaged. It was just a car that had run off the road, that was all, and after a short while he saw first one boy and then the other two climb out of it.

They looked curiously spindly and doll-like, silhouetted against the glow of the headlights, and as far as he could make out, they never glanced even once in his direction. Jerry sat for a while watching them; he knew Fran was watching, too. "Well, there they are. The hot-rods," he said. "And right where they belong, I guess." He waited a moment. "I just figured," he went on, "I just figured that if they wouldn't ram me the first time, they wouldn't do it the second, either." But his head felt light, and the rest of him, even to his hands on the steering wheel, heavy. Just the effort of talking tired him, and after watching a few seconds more (they were all crouching in a bunch now, inspecting the car's rear end) he put his own car in gear and started slowly away toward (what was the town, anyway?) Newkirk. "I'll stop later and let us both catch our breath," he told Fran. "But first let's get out of here."

DISCUSSION

1. The opening scene in the café establishes Jerry Benedict's personality. (a) How does he initially regard the behavior of Ote, Eddie, and Hack? (b) Why is he later disconcerted by them? (c) When does Jerry first reveal his stubbornness? His anger?

2. (a) Trace the incidents that develop a conflict between Jerry and the boys. (b) How does Jerry meet each challenge?

3. (a) What insight into the boys' lives makes Jerry decide to have a showdown on the highway? (b) Would you agree or disagree that this decision marks the turning point, or climax, of the story? Explain. (c) Do you feel that this is the most suspenseful moment in the story? Why or why not?

4. Do you think it was difficult for Jerry to fight "active hatred"? Explain.

5. (a) What is the author's attitude toward the three boys? (b) Does he state this attitude directly or does he suggest it? Explain.

AUTHOR

ROBERT M. COATES (1897–1973), long associated with the *New Yorker* magazine as art critic and contributor of stories and articles, was born in New Haven, Connecticut. As a young man and a Yale graduate, he lived in Europe for five years, joining a famous group of American artists and writers who settled in the exciting postwar Paris of the 1920's. In his lifetime, Mr. Coates wrote a number of novels and several prize-winning short stories.

Concerning "Encounter in Illinois," Mr. Coates wrote: "The story was brought to fusion in my mind by an encounter I had with a bunch of young fellows while on a ski holiday in Vermont, in a restaurant." However, the central incident had been in Mr. Coates' mind ever since, two years earlier, he had had a slight brush with a carful of hot-rodders on an Illinois highway.

Mr. Coates believed that a writer should ponder on incidents which seem to have dramatic value "in the hope that they may eventually fuse with some other, apparently unrelated incident or incidents to form a story." An apt illustration of this process is "Encounter in Illinois."

CHALLENGE

Through the Tunnel

Doris Lessing

"He would do it if it killed him, he said defiantly to himself."

GOING to the shore on the first morning of the vacation, the young English boy stopped at a turning of the path and looked down at a wild and rocky bay, and then over to the crowded beach he knew so well from other years. His mother walked on in front of him, carrying a bright striped bag in one hand. Her other arm, swinging loose, was very white in the sun. The boy watched that white, naked arm, and turned his eyes, which had a frown behind them, toward the bay and back again to his mother. When she felt he was not with her, she swung around. "Oh, there you are, Jerry!" she said. She looked impatient, then smiled. "Why, darling, would you rather not come with me? Would you rather—" She frowned, conscientiously worrying over what amusements he might secretly be longing for, which she had been too busy or too careless to imagine. He was very familiar with that anxious, apologetic smile. Contrition sent him running after her. And yet, as he ran, he looked back over his shoulder at the wild bay; and all morning, as he played on the safe beach, he was thinking of it.

Next morning, when it was time for the routine of swimming and sunbathing, his mother said, "Are you tired of the usual beach, Jerry? Would you like to go somewhere else?"

"Oh, no!" he said quickly, smiling at her out of that unfailing impulse of contrition—a sort of chivalry. Yet, walking down the path with her, he blurted out, "I'd like to go and have a look at those rocks down there."

She gave the idea her attention. It was a wild-looking place, and there was no one there; but she said, "Of course, Jerry. When you've had enough, come to the big beach. Or just go straight

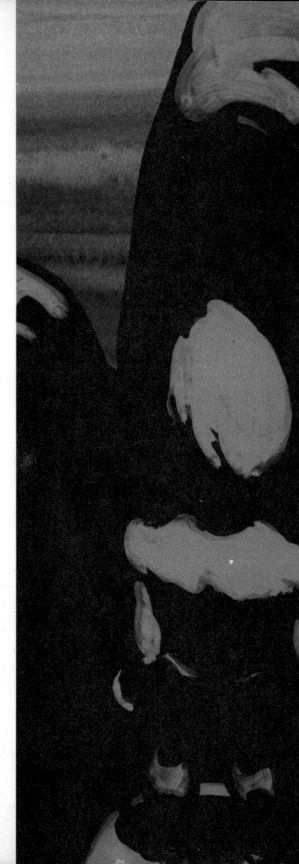

back to the villa, if you like." She walked away, that bare arm, now slightly reddened from yesterday's sun, swinging. And he almost ran after her again, feeling it unbearable that she should go by herself, but he did not.

She was thinking, Of course he's old enough to be safe without me. Have I been keeping him too close? He mustn't feel he ought to be with me. I must be careful.

He was an only child, eleven years old. She was a widow. She was determined to be neither possessive nor lacking in devotion. She went worrying off to her beach.

As for Jerry, once he saw that his mother had gained her beach, he began the steep descent to the bay. From where he was, high up among red-brown rocks, it was a scoop of moving bluish green fringed with white. As he went lower, he saw that it spread among small promontories and inlets of rough, sharp rock, and the crisping, lapping surface showed stains of purple and darker blue. Finally, as he ran sliding and scraping down the last few yards, he saw an edge of white surf and the shallow, luminous movement of water over white sand, and, beyond that, a solid, heavy blue.

He ran straight into the water and began swimming. He was a good swimmer. He went out fast over the gleaming sand, over a middle region where rocks lay like discolored monsters under the surface, and then he was in the real sea—a warm sea where irregular cold currents from the deep water shocked his limbs.

When he was so far out that he could look back not only on the little bay but past the promontory that was between it and the big beach, he floated on the buoyant surface and looked for his mother. There she was, a speck of yellow under an umbrella that looked like a slice of orange peel. He swam back to shore, relieved at being sure she was there, but all at once very lonely.

On the edge of a small cape that marked the side of the bay away from the promontory was a loose scatter of rocks. Above them, some boys were stripping off their clothes. They came running, naked, down to the rocks. The English boy swam toward them, but kept his distance at a stone's throw. They were of that coast; all of them were burned smooth dark brown and speaking a language he did not understand. To be with them, of them, was a craving that filled his whole body. He swam a little closer;

they turned and watched him with narrowed, alert dark eyes. Then one smiled and waved. It was enough. In a minute, he had swum in and was on the rocks beside them, smiling with a desperate, nervous supplication. They shouted cheerful greetings at him; and then, as he preserved his nervous, uncomprehending smile, they understood that he was a foreigner strayed from his own beach, and they proceeded to forget him. But he was happy. He was with them.

They began diving again and again from a high point into a well of blue sea between rough, pointed rocks. After they had dived and come up, they swam around, hauled themselves up, and waited their turn to dive again. They were big boys—men, to Jerry. He dived, and they watched him; and when he swam around to take his place, they made way for him. He felt he was accepted and he dived again, carefully, proud of himself.

Soon the biggest of the boys poised himself, shot down into the water, and did not come up. The others stood about, watching. Jerry, after waiting for the sleek brown head to appear, let out a yell of warning; they looked at him idly and turned their eyes back toward the water. After a long time, the boy came up on the other side of a big dark rock, letting the air out of his lungs in a sputtering gasp and a shout of triumph. Immediately the rest of them dived in. One moment, the morning seemed full of chattering boys; the next, the air and the surface of the water were empty. But through the heavy blue, dark shapes could be seen moving and groping.

Jerry dived, shot past the school of underwater swimmers, saw a black wall of rock looming at him, touched it, and bobbed up at once to the surface, where the wall was a low barrier he could see across. There was no one visible; under him, in the water, the dim shapes of the swimmers had disappeared. Then one, and then another of the boys came up on the far side of the barrier of rock, and he understood that they had swum through some gap or hole in it. He plunged down again. He could see nothing through the stinging salt water but the blank rock. When he came up the boys were all on the diving rock, preparing to attempt the feat again. And now, in a panic of failure, he yelled up, in English, "Look at me! Look!" and he began splashing and kicking in the water like a foolish dog.

They looked down gravely, frowning. He knew the frown. At moments of failure, when he clowned to claim his mother's attention, it was with just this grave, embarrassed inspection that she rewarded him. Through his hot shame, feeling the pleading grin on his face like a scar that he could never remove, he looked up at the group of big brown boys on the rock and shouted, "*Bonjour! Merci! Au revoir! Monsieur, monsieur!*" while he hooked his fingers round his ears and waggled them.

Water surged into his mouth; he choked, sank, came up. The rock, lately weighted with boys, seemed to rear up out of the water as their weight was removed. They were flying down past him, now, into the water; the air was full of falling bodies. Then the rock was empty in the hot sunlight. He counted one, two, three. . . .

At fifty, he was terrified. They must all be drowning beneath him, in the watery caves of the rock! At a hundred, he stared around him at the empty hillside, wondering if he should yell for help. He counted faster, faster, to hurry them up, to bring them to the surface quickly, to drown them quickly—anything rather than the terror of counting on and on into the blue emptiness of the morning. And then, at a hundred and sixty, the water beyond the rock was full of boys blowing like brown whales. They swam back to the shore without a look at him.

He climbed back to the diving rock and sat down, feeling the hot roughness of it under his thighs. The boys were gathering up their bits of clothing and running off along the shore to another promontory. They were leaving to get away from him. He cried openly, fists in his eyes. There was no one to see him, and he cried himself out.

It seemed to him that a long time had passed, and he swam out to where he could see his mother. Yes, she was still there, a yellow spot under an orange umbrella. He swam back to the big rock, climbed up, and dived into the blue pool among the fanged and angry boulders. Down he went, until he touched the wall of rock again. But the salt was so painful in his eyes that he could not see.

He came to the surface, swam to shore and went back to the villa to wait for his mother. Soon she walked slowly up the path, swinging her striped bag, the flushed, naked arm dangling beside her. "I want some swimming goggles," he panted, defiant and beseeching.

She gave him a patient inquisitive look as she said casually, "Well, of course, darling."

But now, now, now! He must have them this minute, and no other time. He nagged and pestered until she went with him to a shop. As soon as she had bought the goggles, he grabbed them from her hand as if she were going to claim them for herself, and was off, running down the steep path to the bay.

Jerry swam out to the big barrier rock, adjusted the goggles, and dived. The impact of the water broke the rubber-enclosed vacuum, and the goggles came loose. He understood that he must swim down to the base of the rock from the surface of the water. He fixed the goggles tight and firm, filled his lungs, and floated, face down, on the water. Now, he could see. It was as if he had eyes of a different kind—fish eyes that showed everything clear and delicate and wavering in the bright water.

Under him, six or seven feet down, was a floor of perfectly clean, shining white sand, rippled firm and hard by the tides. Two grayish shapes steered there, like long, rounded pieces of wood or slate. They were fish. He saw them nose toward each other, poise motionless, make a dart forward, swerve off, and come around again. It was like a water dance. A few inches above them the water sparkled as if sequins were dropping through it. Fish again—myriads of minute fish, the length of his fingernail, were drifting through the water, and in a moment he could feel the innumerable tiny touches of them against his limbs. It was like swimming in flaked silver. The great rock the big boys had swum through rose sheer out of the white sand—black, tufted lightly with greenish weed. He could see no gap in it. He swam down to its base.

Again and again he rose, took a big chestful of air, and went down. Again and again he groped over the surface of the rock, feeling it, almost hugging it in the desperate need to find the entrance. And then, once, while he was clinging to the black wall, his knees came up and he shot his feet out forward and they met no obstacle. He had found the hole.

He gained the surface, clambered about the stones that littered the barrier rock until he found a big one, and, with this in his arms, let himself down over the side of the rock. He dropped, with the weight, straight to the sandy floor. Clinging tight to the anchor of stone, he lay on his side and looked in under the dark shelf at the place where his feet had gone. He could see the hole. It was an irregular, dark gap; but he could not see deep into it. He let go of his anchor, clung with his hands to the edges of the hole, and tried to push himself in.

He got his head in, found his shoulders jammed, moved them in sidewise, and was inside as far as his waist. He could see nothing ahead. Something soft and clammy touched his mouth; he saw a dark frond moving against the grayish rock, and panic filled him. He thought of octopuses, of clinging weed. He pushed himself out backward and caught a glimpse, as he retreated, of a harmless tentacle of seaweed drifting in the mouth of the tunnel. But it was enough. He reached the sunlight, swam to shore, and lay on the diving rock. He looked down into the blue well of water. He knew he must find his way through that cave, or hole, or tunnel, and out the other side.

First, he thought, he must learn to control his breathing. He let himself down into the water with another big stone in his arms, so that he could lie effortlessly on the bottom of the sea. He counted. One, two, three. He counted steadily. He could hear the movement of blood in his chest. Fifty-one, fifty-two. . . . His chest was hurting. He let go of the rock and went up into the air. He saw that the sun was low. He rushed to the villa and found his mother at her supper. She said only "Did you enjoy yourself?" and he said "Yes."

All night the boy dreamed of the water-filled cave in the rock, and as soon as breakfast was over he went to the bay.

That night, his nose bled badly. For hours he had been underwater, learning to hold his breath, and now he felt weak and dizzy. His mother said, "I shouldn't overdo things, darling, if I were you."

That day and the next, Jerry exercised his lungs as if everything, the whole of his life, all that he would become, depended upon it. Again his nose bled at night, and his mother insisted on his coming with her the next day. It was a torment to him to waste a day of his careful self-training, but he stayed with her on that other beach, which now seemed a place for small children, a place where his mother might lie safe in the sun. It was not his beach.

He did not ask for permission, on the following day, to go to his beach. He went, before his mother could consider the complicated rights and wrongs of the matter. A day's rest, he discovered, had improved his count by ten. The big boys had made the passage while he counted a hundred and sixty. He had been counting fast, in his fright. Probably now, if he tried, he could get through that long tunnel, but he was not going to try yet. A curious, most unchildlike per-

sistence, a controlled impatience, made him wait. In the meantime, he lay underwater on the white sand, littered now by stones he had brought down from the upper air, and studied the entrance to the tunnel. He knew every jut and corner of it, as far as it was possible to see. It was as if he already felt its sharpness about his shoulders.

He sat by the clock in the villa, when his mother was not near, and checked his time. He was incredulous and then proud to find he could hold his breath without strain for two minutes. The words "two minutes," authorized by the clock, brought close the adventure that was so necessary to him.

In another four days, his mother said casually one morning, they must go home. On the day before they left, he would do it. He would do it if it killed him, he said defiantly to himself. But two days before they were to leave—a day of triumph when he increased his count by fifteen—his nose bled so badly that he turned dizzy and had to lie limply over the big rock like a bit of seaweed, watching the thick red blood flow on to the rock and trickle slowly down to the sea. He was frightened. Supposing he turned dizzy in the tunnel? Supposing he died there, trapped? Supposing—his head went around, in the hot sun, and he almost gave up. He thought he would return to the house and lie down, and next summer, perhaps, when he had another year's growth in him— *then* he would go through the hole.

But even after he had made the decision, or thought he had, he found himself sitting up on the rock and looking down into the water; and he knew that now, this moment, when his nose had only just stopped bleeding, when his head was still sore and throbbing —this was the moment when he would try. If he did not do it now, he never would. He was trembling with fear that he would not go; and he was trembling with horror at that long, long tunnel under the rock, under the sea. Even in the open sunlight, the barrier rock seemed very wide and very heavy; tons of rock pressed down on where he would go. If he died there, he would lie until one day—perhaps not before next year—those big boys would swim into it and find it blocked.

He put on his goggles, fitted them tight, tested the vacuum. His hands were shaking. Then he chose the biggest stone he could carry and slipped over the edge of the rock until half of him was in the cool, enclosing water and half in the hot sun. He looked up once at the empty sky, filled his lungs once, twice, and then sank fast to the bottom with the stone. He let it go and began to count. He took the edges of the hole in his hands and drew himself into it, wriggling his shoulders in sidewise as he remembered he must, kicking himself along with his feet.

Soon he was clear inside. He was in a small rock-bound hole filled with yellowish-gray water. The water was pushing him up against the roof. The roof was sharp and pained his back. He pulled himself along with his hands—fast, fast—and used his legs as levers. His head knocked against something; a sharp pain dizzied him. Fifty, fifty-one, fifty-two. . . . He was without light, and the water seemed to press upon him with the weight of rock. Seventy-one, seventy-two. . . . There was no strain on his lungs. He felt like an inflated balloon, his lungs were so light and easy, but his head was pulsing.

He was being continually pressed against the sharp roof, which felt slimy as well as sharp. Again he thought of octopuses, and wondered if the tunnel might be filled with weed that could tangle him. He gave himself a panicky, convulsive kick forward, ducked his head, and swam. His feet and hands moved freely, as if in open water. The hole must have widened out. He thought he must be swimming fast, and he was frightened of banging his head if the tunnel narrowed.

A hundred, a hundred and one. . . . The water paled. Victory filled him. His lungs were beginning to hurt. A few more strokes and he would be out. He was counting wildly; he said a hundred and fifteen, and then, a long time later, a hundred and fifteen again. The water was a clear jewel-green all around him. Then he saw, above his head, a crack running up through the rock. Sunlight was falling through it, showing the clean, dark rock of the tunnel, a single mussel shell, and darkness ahead.

He was at the end of what he could do. He looked up at the crack as if it were filled with air and not water, as if he could put his mouth to it to draw in air. A hundred and fifteen, he heard himself say inside his head—but he had said that long ago. He must go on into the blackness ahead, or he would drown. His head was swelling, his lungs cracking. A hundred and fifteen, a hundred and fifteen pounded through his head, and he feebly clutched at rocks in the dark, pulling himself forward, leaving the brief space of sunlit water behind. He felt he was dying. He was no longer quite conscious. He struggled on in the darkness between lapses into unconsciousness. An immense, swelling pain filled his head, and then the darkness cracked with an explosion of green light. His hands, groping forward, met nothing; and his feet, kicking back, propelled him out into the open sea.

He drifted to the surface, his face turned up to the air. He was gasping like a fish. He felt he would sink now and drown; he could not swim the few feet back to the rock. Then he was clutching it and pulling himself up on to it. He lay face down, gasping. He could see nothing but a red-veined, clotted dark. His eyes must have burst, he thought; they were full of blood. He tore off his goggles and a gout of blood went into the sea. His nose was bleeding, and the blood had filled the goggles.

He scooped up handfuls of water from the cool, salty sea, to splash on his face, and did not know whether it was blood or salt water he tasted. After a time, his heart quieted, his eyes cleared, and he sat up. He could see the local boys diving and playing half a mile away. He did not want them. He wanted nothing but to get back home and lie down.

In a short while, Jerry swam to shore and climbed slowly up the path to the villa. He flung himself on his bed and slept, waking at the sound of feet on the path outside. His mother was coming back. He rushed to the bathroom, thinking she must not see his face with bloodstains, or tearstains, on it. He came out of the bathroom and met her as she walked into the villa, smiling, her eyes lighting up.

"Have a nice morning?" she asked, laying her hand on his warm brown shoulder a moment.

"Oh, yes, thank you," he said.

"You look a bit pale." And then, sharp and anxious, "How did you bang your head?"

"Oh, just banged it," he told her.

She looked at him closely. He was strained; his eyes were glazed-looking. She was worried. And then she said to herself, Oh, don't fuss! Nothing can happen. He can swim like a fish.

They sat down to lunch together.

"Mummy," he said, "I can stay under water for two minutes—three minutes, at least." It came bursting out of him.

"Can you, darling?" she said. "Well, I shouldn't overdo it. I don't think you ought to swim any more today."

She was ready for a battle of wills, but he gave in at once. It was no longer of the least importance to go to the bay.

Weasles ripped my flesh

ZAPPA

DISCUSSION

1. (a) Describe the relationship between Jerry and his mother at the beginning of the story. (b) To what extent is the relationship a consequence of Jerry's being without a father? Explain.

2. (a) Under what circumstances does Jerry happen to encounter the group of older boys? (b) What seems to be their attitude toward the younger boy? Explain. (c) What signs of immaturity does Jerry display first in front of the boys and then immediately after they leave?

3. (a) Describe the preparations Jerry makes to conquer the underwater tunnel. (b) What risks to his health does the boy take in undergoing these preparations? (c) If Jerry had had numerous friends his own age, do you believe he would have taken the same risks? Explain.

4. (a) Describe Jerry's state of mind and his physical condition at the time he decides that he must immediately try swimming the tunnel. (b) What physical and mental experiences does he have while inside the tunnel?

5. How will Jerry's relationship to his mother and to others change as a consequence of his mastering the tunnel? Explain.

6. Describe situations in the story that indicate that each of the following adjectives might apply to Jerry at one time or another: (a) *immature,* (b) *impatient,* (c) *persistent,* (d) *foolhardy,* (e) *courageous,* (f) *mature.*

AUTHOR

DORIS LESSING is the daughter of an Army captain and was born in Kermanshah, Iran, in 1919. The family moved to Africa shortly afterwards, where she was educated at a convent and girls' school in Salisbury, Northern Rhodesia.

Her first novel, *The Grass Is Singing* (1950), was highly acclaimed. In 1952 she began a series of novels called *Children of Violence.* Her books deal with the problems of blacks and whites in the rapidly changing society of Africa. *African Stories* (1964), an anthology of short stories, contains some of her best portrayals of the problems of South Africa. In the introduction to that collection, she comments: "Writers brought up in Africa have many advantages—being at the centre of a modern battlefield; part of a society in rapid, dramatic change."

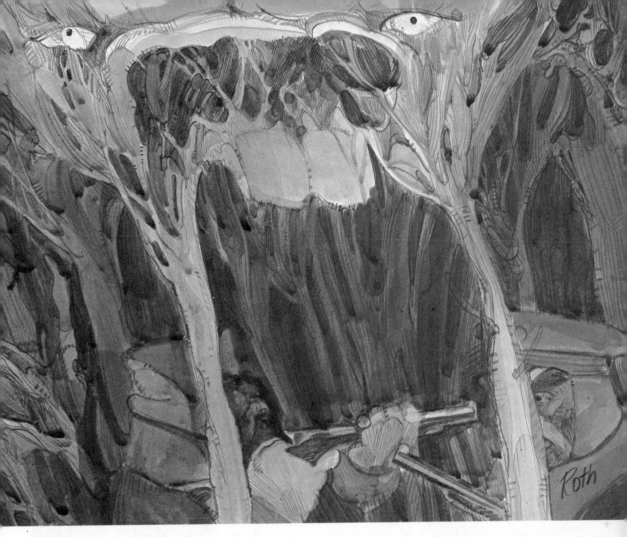

The Interlopers

Saki

*". . . as he stepped round the trunk of a huge
beech, he came face to face with the man he
sought."*

IN a forest of mixed growth somewhere on the
eastern spurs of the Carpathians,[1] a man stood one
winter night watching and listening, as though he
waited for some beast of the woods to come within
the range of his vision, and later, of his rifle. But
the game for whose presence he kept so keen an
outlook was none that figured in the sportsman's
calendar as lawful and proper for the chase; Ulrich
von Gradwitz patrolled the dark forest in quest of
a human enemy.

The forest lands of Gradwitz were of wide extent
and well stocked with game; the narrow strip of
precipitous woodland that lay on its outskirts was
not remarkable for the game it harbored or the shooting it afforded, but it was the most jealously guarded
of all its owner's territorial possessions. A famous
lawsuit, in the days of his grandfather, had wrested
it from the illegal possession of a neighboring family
of petty landowners; the dispossessed party had

---

1. *Carpathians* (kär pā'thē anz), mountain chain extending from
northern Rumania to Czechoslovakia.

From THE SHORT STORIES OF SAKI by H. H. Munro. Reprinted by
permission of The Viking Press, Inc., and The Bodley Head.

never acquiesced in the judgment of the courts, and a long series of poaching affrays[2] and similar scandals had embittered the relationships between the families for three generations. The neighbors' feud had grown into a personal one since Ulrich had come to be head of his family; if there was a man in the world whom he detested and wished ill to, it was Georg Znaeym, the inheritor of the quarrel and the tireless game snatcher and raider of the disputed border forest.

The feud might, perhaps, have died down or been compromised if the personal ill will of the two men had not stood in the way; as boys they had thirsted for one another's blood; as men each prayed that misfortune might fall on the other; and this wind-scourged winter night Ulrich had banded together his foresters to watch the dark forest, not in quest of four-footed quarry, but to keep a lookout for the prowling thieves whom he suspected of being afoot from across the land boundary. The roebuck, which usually kept in the sheltered hollows during a storm-wind, were running like driven things tonight; and there was movement and unrest among the creatures that were wont to sleep through the dark hours. Assuredly there was a disturbing element in the forest, and Ulrich could guess the quarter from whence it came.

He strayed away by himself from the watchers whom he had placed in ambush on the crest of the hill, and wandered far down the steep slopes amid the wild tangle of undergrowth, peering through the tree trunks and listening through the whistling and skirling of the wind and the restless beating of the branches for sight or sound of the marauders. If only on this wild night, in this dark, lone spot, he might come across Georg Znaeym, man to man, with none to witness—that was the wish that was uppermost in his thoughts. And as he stepped round the trunk of a huge beech, he came face to face with the man he sought.

The two enemies stood glaring at one another for a long, silent moment. Each had a rifle in his hand; each had hate in his heart and murder uppermost in his mind. The chance had come to give full play to the passions of a lifetime. But a man who has been brought up under the code of a restraining

civilization cannot easily nerve himself to shoot down his neighbor in cold blood and without a word spoken, except for an offense against his hearth and honor. And before the moment of hesitation had given way to action, a deed of nature's own violence overwhelmed them both. A fierce shriek of the storm had been answered by a splitting crash over their heads; and ere they could leap aside, a mass of falling beech tree had thundered down on them. Ulrich von Gradwitz found himself stretched on the ground, one arm numb beneath him and the other held almost as helpless in a tight tangle of forked branches, while both legs were pinned beneath the fallen mass. His heavy shooting boots had saved his feet from being crushed to pieces; but if his fractures were not so serious as they might have been, at least it was evident that he could not move from his present position till someone came to release him. The descending twigs had slashed the skin of his face, and he had to wink away some drops of blood from his eyelashes before he could take in a general view of the disaster. At his side, so near that under ordinary circumstances he could almost have touched him, lay Georg Znaeym, alive and struggling, but obviously as helplessly pinioned down as himself. All round them lay a thick-strewn wreckage of splintered branches and broken twigs.

Relief at being alive and exasperation at his captive plight brought a strange medley of pious thank offerings and sharp curses to Ulrich's lips. Georg, who was nearly blinded with the blood which trickled across his eyes, stopped his struggling for a moment to listen and then gave a short, snarling laugh.

"So you're not killed, as you ought to be; but you're caught, anyway," he cried; "caught fast. Ho, what a jest, Ulrich von Gradwitz snared in his stolen forest. There's real justice for you!"

And he laughed again, mockingly and savagely.

"I'm caught in my own forest land," retorted Ulrich. "When my men come to release us, you will wish, perhaps, that you were in a better plight than caught poaching on a neighbor's land. Shame on you!"

Georg was silent for a moment; then he answered quietly:

"Are you sure that your men will find much to release? I have men, too, in the forest tonight, close behind me; and *they* will be here first and do the releasing. When they drag me out from under these

---

2. *a long series of poaching affrays* (ə frāz'). The neighboring family did not accept the judgment of the courts. They retaliated by poaching (trespassing on the land to hunt game), which caused disturbances (affrays).

branches, it won't need much clumsiness on their part to roll this mass of trunk right over on the top of you. Your men will find you dead under a fallen beech tree. For form's sake I shall send my condolences to your family."

"It is a useful hint," said Ulrich fiercely. "My men had orders to follow in ten minutes' time, seven of which must have gone by already; and when they get me out—I will remember the hint. Only as you will have met your death poaching on my lands, I don't think I can decently send any message of condolence to your family."

"Good," snarled Georg, "good. We'll fight this quarrel out to the death—you and I and our foresters, with no cursed interlopers to come between us. Death and damnation to you, Ulrich von Gradwitz!"

"The same to you, Georg Znaeym, forest thief, game snatcher!"

Both men spoke with the bitterness of possible defeat before them, for each knew that it might be long before his men would seek him out or find him; it was a bare matter of chance which party would arrive first on the scene.

Both had now given up the useless struggle to free themselves from the mass of wood that held them down; Ulrich limited his endeavors to an effort to bring his one partially free arm near enough to his outer coat pocket to draw out his wine flask. Even when he had accomplished that operation, it was long before he could manage the unscrewing of the stopper or get any of the liquid down his throat. But what a Heaven-sent draft it seemed! It was an open winter, and little snow had fallen as yet, hence the captives suffered less from the cold than might have been the case at that season of the year; nevertheless, the wine was warming and reviving to the wounded man, and he looked across with something like a throb of pity to where his enemy lay, barely keeping the groans of pain and weariness from crossing his lips.

"Could you reach this flask if I threw it over to you?" asked Ulrich suddenly. "There is good wine in it, and one may as well be as comfortable as one can. Let us drink, even if tonight one of us dies."

"No, I can scarcely see anything, there is so much blood caked round my eyes," said Georg; "and in any case I don't drink wine with an enemy."

Ulrich was silent for a few minutes and lay listening to the weary screeching of the wind. An idea was slowly forming and growing in his brain, an idea that gained strength every time that he looked across at the man who was fighting so grimly against pain and exhaustion. In the pain and languor that Ulrich himself was feeling, the old fierce hatred seemed to be dying down.

"Neighbor," he said presently, "do as you please if your men come first. It was a fair compact. But as for me, I've changed my mind. If my men are the first to come, you shall be the first to be helped, as though you were my guest. We have quarreled like devils all our lives over this stupid strip of forest where the trees can't even stand upright in a breath of wind. Lying here tonight, thinking, I've come to think that we've been rather fools; there are better things in life than getting the better of a boundary dispute. Neighbor, if you will help me to bury the old quarrel I—I will ask you to be my friend."

Georg Znaeym was silent for so long that Ulrich thought, perhaps, he had fainted with the pain of his injuries. Then he spoke slowly and in jerks:

"How the whole region would stare and gabble if we rode into the market square together. No one living can remember seeing a Znaeym and a Von Gradwitz talking to one another in friendship. And what peace there would be among the forester folk if we ended our feud tonight. And if we choose to make peace among our people, there is none other to interfere, no interlopers from outside. . . . You would come and keep the Sylvester night[3] beneath my roof, and I would come and feast on some high day at your castle. . . . I would never fire a shot on your land, save when you invited me as a guest; and you should come and shoot with me down in the marshes where the wild fowl are. In all the countryside there are none that could hinder if we willed to make peace. I never thought to have wanted to do other than hate you all my life; but I think I have changed my mind about things, too, this last half-hour. And you offered me your wine flask. . . . Ulrich von Gradwitz, I will be your friend."

For a space both men were silent, turning over in their minds the wonderful changes that this dramatic reconciliation would bring about. In the cold, gloomy forest, with the wind tearing in fitful gusts through the naked branches and whistling around the tree trunks, they lay and waited for the help that

---

3. *the Sylvester night*, the night of December 31. On that day, festivals are held in many countries to honor St. Sylvester, bishop of Rome from A.D. 314 to 335.

would now bring release and succor to both parties. And each prayed a private prayer that his men might be the first to arrive, so that he might be the first to show honorable attention to the enemy that had become a friend.

Presently, as the wind dropped for a moment, Ulrich broke silence.

"Let's shout for help," he said; "in this lull our voices may carry a little way."

"They won't carry far through the trees and under-growth," said Georg; "but we can try. Together, then."

The two raised their voices in a prolonged hunting call.

"Together again," said Ulrich a few minutes later, after listening in vain for an answering halloo.

"I heard something that time, I think," said Ulrich.

"I heard nothing but the pestilential wind," said Georg hoarsely.

There was silence again for some minutes, and then Ulrich gave a joyful cry.

"I can see figures coming through the wood. They are following in the way I came down the hillside."

Both men raised their voices in as loud a shout as they could muster.

"They hear us! They've stopped. Now they see us. They're running down the hill toward us," cried Ulrich.

"How many of them are there?" asked Georg.

"I can't see distinctly," said Ulrich; "nine or ten."

"Then they are yours," said Georg; "I had only seven out with me."

"They are making all the speed they can, brave lads," said Ulrich gladly.

"Are they your men?" asked Georg. "Are they your men?" he repeated impatiently as Ulrich did not answer.

"No," said Ulrich with a laugh, the idiotic chattering laugh of a man unstrung with hideous fear.

"Who are they?" asked Georg quickly, straining his eyes to see what the other would gladly not have seen.

"*Wolves!*"

DISCUSSION

1. Recall some famous feuds you have read or heard about. (a) What characteristics do most feuds have in common? (b) In what ways was the feud between the Von Gradwitz and Znaeym families typical? (c) What attempts had been made to settle the feud? (d) Did the heads of the two families want the feud settled? Explain your answer.

2. Although feuding is an uncivilized way of handling a quarrel, were Georg and Ulrich essentially uncivilized men? Give reasons to support your opinion.

3. (a) What was the first friendly gesture made by either of the men? Who made it? (b) How was his kindness initially received? How later? (c) Why did the men change attitudes toward each other?

4. (a) What is implied by the single word "*Wolves!*" at the end of the story? (b) With what feeling does this conclusion leave you?

5. There are three conflicts in "The Interlopers." Which situation is an example of man against man? Of man against nature? Of man against himself?

AUTHOR

HECTOR HUGH MUNRO (1870-1916) was born in Burma, where his father was stationed with the British army. His mother died shortly before his second birthday and young Munro was sent to England to be reared by his aunts. He attended English grammar schools until 1885 when his father retired from the army to devote himself to his son's education; together they traveled widely in Europe. Munro began his literary career as a journalist, writing political sketches and short stories for the *Westminster Gazette;* later he became a foreign correspondent. His first collection of short stories, *Reginald* (1904), revealed Munro's talent for creating well-plotted tales of humor or horror.

A perfect hostess was once described as "one who puts a volume of Saki (sä′ki) by the guest-room bed." H. H. Munro borrowed his pen name from a twelfth-century Persian astronomer-poet who wrote four-line poems which were translated into English as *The Rubáiyât* (rü bī′yat′) *of Omar Khayyam* (o′mär kī yäm′). In *The Rubáiyât* there is a winebearer named Saki who goes "Among the Guests Star-scattered on the Grass."

RELATIONSHIPS

the ROCKING-HORSE WINNER

D. H. Lawrence

"And yet the voices in the house . . . simply trilled and screamed in a sort of ecstasy. 'There must be more money! Oh-h-h-; there must be more money! Oh, now, now-w!'"

THERE was a woman who was beautiful, who started with all the advantages, yet she had no luck. She married for love, and the love turned to dust. She had bonny children, yet she felt they had been thrust upon her, and she could not love them. They looked at her coldly, as if they were finding fault with her. And hurriedly she felt she must cover up some fault in herself. Yet what it was that she must cover up she never knew. Nevertheless, when her children were present, she always felt the centre of her heart go hard. This troubled her, and in her manner she was all the more gentle and anxious for her children, as if she loved them very much. Only she herself knew that at the centre of her heart was a hard little place that could not feel love, no, not for anybody. Everybody else said of her: "She is such a good mother. She adores her children." Only she herself, and her children themselves, knew it was not so. They read it in each other's eyes.

There was a boy and two little girls. They lived in a pleasant house, with a garden, and they had discreet servants, and felt themselves superior to anyone in the neighbourhood.

From THE COMPLETE SHORT STORIES OF D. H. LAWRENCE, Volume III. Copyright by the Estate of D. H. Lawrence, copyright © renewed 1961 by Angelo Ravagli and C. Montague Weekley, Executors of the Estate of Frieda Lawrence Ravagli. Reprinted by permission of The Viking Press, Inc., and Laurence Pollinger Ltd.

Although they lived in style, they felt always an anxiety in the house. There was never enough money. The mother had a small income, and the father had a small income, but not nearly enough for the social position which they had to keep up. The father went in to town to some office. But though he had good prospects, these prospects never materialized. There was always the grinding sense of the shortage of money, though the style was always kept up.

At last the mother said: "I will see if *I* can't make something." But she did not know where to begin. She racked her brains, and tried this thing and the other, but could not find anything successful. The failure made deep lines come into her face. Her children were growing up, they would have to go to school. There must be more money, there must be more money. The father, who was always very handsome and expensive in his tastes, seemed as if he never *would* be able to do anything worth doing. And the mother, who had a great belief in herself, did not succeed any better, and her tastes were just as expensive.

And so the house came to be haunted by the unspoken phrase: There *must* be more money! There *must* be more money! The children could hear it all the time, though nobody said it aloud. They heard it at Christmas, when the expensive and splendid toys filled the nursery. Behind the shining modern rocking horse, behind the smart doll's-house, a voice would start whispering: "There *must* be more money! There *must* be more money!" And the children would stop playing, to listen for a moment. They would look into each other's eyes, to see if they had all heard. And each one saw in the eyes of the other two that they too had heard. "There *must* be more money! There *must* be more money!"

It came whispering from the springs of the still-swaying rocking horse, and even the horse, bending his wooden, champing head, heard it. The big doll, sitting so pink and smirking in her new pram, could hear it quite plainly, and seemed to be smirking all the more self-consciously because of it. The foolish puppy, too, that took the place of the teddy-bear, he was looking so extraordinarily foolish for no other reason but that he heard the secret whisper all over the house: "There *must* be more money!"

Yet nobody ever said it aloud. The whisper was everywhere, and therefore no one spoke it. Just as no one ever says: "We are breathing!" in spite of the fact that breath is coming and going all the time.

"Mother," said the boy Paul one day, "why don't we keep a car of our own? Why do we always use uncle's, or else a taxi?"

"Because we're the poor members of the family," said the mother.

"But why *are* we, mother?"

"Well—I suppose," she said slowly and bitterly, "it's because your father has no luck."

The boy was silent for some time.

"Is luck money, mother?" he asked, rather timidly.

"No, Paul. Not quite. It's what causes you to have money."

"Oh!" said Paul vaguely. "I thought when Uncle Oscar said *filthy lucker*, it meant money."

"*Filthy lucre* does mean money," said the mother. "But it's lucre, not luck."

"Oh!" said the boy. "Then what is luck, mother?"

"It's what causes you to have money. If you're lucky you have money. That's why it's better to be born lucky than rich. If you're rich, you may lose your money. But if you're lucky, you will always get more money."

"Oh! Will you? And is father not lucky?"

"Very unlucky, I should say," she said bitterly.

The boy watched her with unsure eyes.

"Why?" he asked.

"I don't know. Nobody ever knows why one person is lucky and another unlucky."

"Don't they? Nobody at all? Does nobody know?"

"Perhaps God. But He never tells."

"He ought to, then. And aren't you lucky either, mother?"

"I can't be, if I married an unlucky husband."

"But by yourself, aren't you?"

"I used to think I was, before I married. Now I think I am very unlucky indeed."

"Why?"

"Well—never mind! Perhaps I'm not really," she said.

The child looked at her, to see if she meant it. But he saw, by the lines of her mouth, that she was only trying to hide something from him.

"Well, anyhow," he said stoutly, "I'm a lucky person."

"Why?" said his mother, with a sudden laugh.

He stared at her. He didn't even know why he had said it. "God told me," he asserted, brazening it out.

"I hope He did, dear!" she said, again with a laugh, but rather bitter.

"He did, mother!"

"Excellent!" said the mother, using one of her husband's exclamations.

The boy saw she did not believe him; or, rather, that she paid no attention to his assertion. This angered him somewhat, and made him want to compel her attention.

He went off by himself, vaguely, in a childish way, seeking for the clue to "luck." Absorbed, taking no heed of other people, he went about with a sort of stealth, seeking inwardly for luck. He wanted luck, he wanted it, he wanted it. When the two girls were playing dolls in the nursery, he would sit on his big rocking horse, charging madly into space, with a frenzy that made the little girls peer at him uneasily. Wildly the horse careered, the waving dark hair of the boy tossed, his eyes had a strange glare in them. The little girls dared not speak to him.

When he had ridden to the end of his mad little journey, he climbed down and stood in front of his rocking horse, staring fixedly into its lowered face. Its red mouth was slightly open, its big eye was wide and glassy-bright.

"Now!" he would silently command the snorting steed. "Now, take me to where there is luck! Now take me."

And he would slash the horse on the neck with the little whip he had asked Uncle Oscar for. He *knew* the horse could take him to where there was luck, if only he forced it. So he would mount again, and start on his furious ride, hoping at last to get there. He knew he could get there.

"You'll break your horse, Paul!" said the nurse.

"He's always riding like that! I wish he'd leave off!" said his elder sister Joan.

But he only glared down on them in silence. Nurse gave him up. She could make nothing of him. Anyhow he was growing beyond her.

One day his mother and his Uncle Oscar came in when he was on one of his furious rides. He did not speak to them.

"Hallo, you young jockey! Riding a winner?" said his uncle.

"Aren't you growing too big for a rocking horse? You're not a very little boy any longer, you know," said his mother.

But Paul only gave a blue glare from his big, rather close-set eyes. He would speak to nobody when he was in full tilt. His mother watched him with an anxious expression on her face.

At last he suddenly stopped forcing his horse into the mechanical gallop, and slid down. "Well, I got there!" he announced fiercely, his blue eyes still flaring, and his sturdy long legs straddling apart.

"Where did you get to?" asked his mother.

"Where I wanted to go," he flared back at her.

"That's right, son!" said Uncle Oscar. "Don't you stop till you get there. What's the horse's name?"

"He doesn't have a name," said the boy.

"Gets on without all right?" asked the uncle.

"Well, he has different names. He was called Sansovino last week."

"Sansovino, eh? Won the Ascot.[1] How did you know his name?"

"He always talks about horse races with Bassett," said Joan.

The uncle was delighted to find that his small nephew was posted with all the racing news. Bassett, the young gardener, who had been wounded in the left foot in the war and had got his present job through Oscar Cresswell, whose batman[2] he had been, was a perfect blade of the "turf." He lived in the racing events, and the small boy lived with him.

Oscar Cresswell got it all from Bassett.

"Master Paul comes and asks me, so I can't do more than tell him, sir," said Bassett, his face terribly serious, as if he were speaking of religious matters.

"And does he ever put anything on a horse he fancies?"

"Well—I don't want to give him away—he's a young sport, a fine sport, sir. Would you mind asking him himself? He sort of takes a pleasure in it, and perhaps he'd feel I was giving him away, sir, if you don't mind."

Bassett was serious as a church.

The uncle went back to his nephew, and took him off for a ride in the car.

"Say, Paul, old man, do you ever put anything on a horse?" the uncle asked.

The boy watched the handsome man closely.

"Why, do you think I oughtn't to?" he parried.

"Not a bit of it! I thought perhaps you might give me a tip for the Lincoln."

The car sped on into the country, going down to Uncle Oscar's place in Hampshire.

"Honour bright?" said the nephew.

"Honour bright, son!" said the uncle.

---

1. *Ascot*, a horse race. Other races mentioned are the Lincoln, Leger, and Derby.
2. *batman*. Bassett had been Cresswell's servant while the latter served in the army.

"Well, then. Daffodil."

"Daffodil! I doubt it, sonny. What about Mirza?"

"I only know the winner," said the boy. "That's Daffodil."

"Daffodil, eh?"

There was a pause. Daffodil was an obscure horse comparatively.

"Uncle!"

"Yes, son?"

"You won't let it go any further, will you? I promised Bassett."

"Bassett be . . ., old man! What's he got to do with it?"

"We're partners. We've been partners from the first. Uncle, he lent me my first five shillings, which I lost. I promised him, honour bright, it was only between me and him; only you gave me that ten-shilling note I started winning with, so I thought you were lucky. You won't let it go any further, will you?"

The boy gazed at his uncle from those big, hot, blue eyes, set rather close together. The uncle stirred and laughed uneasily.

"Right you are, son! I'll keep your tip private. Daffodil, eh! How much are you putting on him?"

"All except twenty pounds,"[3] said the boy. "I keep that in reserve."

The uncle thought it a good joke.

"You keep twenty pounds in reserve, do you, you young romancer? What are you betting, then?"

"I'm betting three hundred," said the boy gravely. "But it's between you and me, Uncle Oscar! Honour bright?"

The uncle burst into a roar of laughter.

"It's between you and me all right, you young Nat Gould,"[4] he said, laughing. "But where's your three hundred?"

"Bassett keeps it for me. We're partners."

"You are, are you! And what is Bassett putting on Daffodil?"

---

3. *twenty pounds.* At the time of this story, the English pound was worth nearly five dollars in United States currency.

4. *Nat Gould,* journalist, author, and highly respected racing authority.

"He won't go quite as high as I do, I expect. Perhaps he'll go a hundred and fifty."

"What, pennies?" laughed the uncle.

"Pounds," said the child, with a surprised look at his uncle. "Bassett keeps a bigger reserve than I do."

Between wonder and amusement Uncle Oscar was silent. He pursued the matter no further, but he determined to take his nephew with him to the Lincoln races.

"Now son," he said, "I'm putting twenty on Mirza, and I'll put five for you on any horse you fancy. What's your pick?"

"Daffodil, uncle."

"No, not the fiver on Daffodil!"

"I should if it was my own fiver," said the child.

"Good! Good! Right you are! A fiver for me and a fiver for you on Daffodil."

The child had never been to a race meeting before, and his eyes were blue fire. He pursed his mouth tight, and watched. A Frenchman just in front had put his money on Lancelot. Wild with excitement, he flayed his arms up and down, yelling *"Lancelot! Lancelot!"* in his French accent.

Daffodil came in first, Lancelot second, Mirza third. The child, flushed and with eyes blazing, was curiously serene. His uncle brought him four five-pound notes, four to one.

"What am I to do with these?" he cried, waving them before the boy's eyes.

"I suppose we'll talk to Bassett," said the boy. "I expect I have fifteen hundred now; and twenty in reserve; and this twenty."

His uncle studied him for some moments.

"Look here, son!" he said. "You're not serious about Bassett and that fifteen hundred, are you?"

"Yes, I am. But it's between you and me, uncle. Honour bright!"

"Honour bright all right, son! But I must talk to Bassett."

"If you'd like to be a partner, uncle, with Bassett and me, we could all be partners. Only, you'd have to promise, honour bright, uncle, not to let it go beyond us three. Bassett and I are lucky, and you must be lucky, because it was your ten shillings I started winning with. . . ."

Uncle Oscar took both Bassett and Paul into Richmond Park⁵ for an afternoon, and there they talked.

"It's like this, you see, sir," Bassett said. "Master Paul would get me talking about racing events, spinning yarns, you know, sir. And he was always keen on knowing if I'd made or if I'd lost. It's about a year since, now, that I put five shillings on Blush of Dawn for him—and we lost. Then the luck turned, with that ten shillings he had from you, that we put on Singhalese. And since that time it's been pretty steady, all things considering. What do you say, Master Paul?"

"We're all right when we're sure," said Paul. "It's when we're not quite sure that we go down."

"Oh, but we're careful then," said Bassett.

"But when are you *sure*?" smiled Uncle Oscar.

"It's Master Paul, sir," said Bassett, in a secret, religious voice. "It's as if he had it from heaven. Like Daffodil, now, for the Lincoln. That was as sure as eggs."

"Did you put anything on Daffodil?" asked Oscar Cresswell.

"Yes, sir. I made my bit."

"And my nephew?"

Bassett was obstinately silent, looking at Paul.

"I made twelve hundred, didn't I, Bassett? I told uncle I was putting three hundred on Daffodil."

"That's right," said Bassett, nodding.

"But where's the money?" asked the uncle.

"I keep it safe locked up, sir. Master Paul he can have it any minute he likes to ask for it."

"What, fifteen hundred pounds?"

"And twenty! And *forty*, that is, with the twenty he made on the course."

"It's amazing!" said the uncle.

"If Master Paul offers you to be partners, sir, I would if I were you; if you'll excuse me," said Bassett.

Oscar Cresswell thought about it.

"I'll see the money," he said.

They drove home again, and sure enough, Bassett came round to the garden-house with fifteen hundred pounds in notes. The twenty pounds reserve was left with Joe Glee, in the Turf Commission deposit.⁶

"You see, it's all right, uncle, when I'm *sure*! Then we go strong, for all we're worth. Don't we, Bassett?"

"We do that, Master Paul."

"And when are you sure?" said the uncle, laughing.

"Oh, well, sometimes I'm *absolutely* sure, like about Daffodil," said the boy; "and sometimes I have an idea; and sometimes I haven't even an idea, have

---

5. *Richmond Park*, a deer park just outside of London.

6. *Turf Commission deposit*, a type of bank in which English bettors deposit betting funds.

I, Bassett? Then we're careful, because we mostly go down."

"You do, do you! And when you're sure, like about Daffodil, what makes you sure, sonny?"

"Oh, well, I don't know," said the boy uneasily. "I'm sure, you know, uncle; that's all."

"It's as if he had it from heaven, sir," Bassett reiterated.

"I should say so!" said the uncle.

But he became a partner. And when the Leger was coming on, Paul was "sure" about Lively Spark, which was a quite inconsiderable horse. The boy insisted on putting a thousand on the horse, Bassett went for five hundred, and Oscar Cresswell two hundred. Lively Spark came in first, and the betting had been ten to one against him. Paul had made ten thousand.

"You see," he said, "I was absolutely sure of him." Even Oscar Cresswell had cleared two thousand.

"Look here, son," he said, "this sort of thing makes me nervous."

"It needn't, uncle! Perhaps I shan't be sure again for a long time."

"But what are you going to do with your money?" asked the uncle.

"Of course," said the boy, "I started it for mother. She said she had no luck, because father is unlucky, so I thought if I was lucky, it might stop whispering."

"What might stop whispering?"

"Our house. I hate our house for whispering."

"What does it whisper?"

"Why—why"—the boy fidgeted—"why, I don't know. But it's always short of money, you know, uncle."

"I know it, son, I know it."

"You know people send mother writs,[7] don't you, uncle?"

"I'm afraid I do," said the uncle.

"And then the house whispers, like people laughing at you behind your back. It's awful, that is! I thought if I was lucky . . ."

"You might stop it," added the uncle.

The boy watched him with big blue eyes, that had an uncanny cold fire in them, and he said never a word.

"Well, then!" said the uncle. "What are we doing?"

"I shouldn't like mother to know I was lucky," said the boy.

"Why not, son?"

"She'd stop me."

"I don't think she would."

"Oh!"—and the boy writhed in an odd way—"I don't want her to know, uncle."

"All right, son! We'll manage it without her knowing."

They managed it very easily. Paul, at the other's suggestion, handed over five thousand pounds to his uncle, who deposited it with the family lawyer, who was then to inform Paul's mother that a relative had put five thousand pounds into his hands, which sum was to be paid out a thousand pounds at a time, on the mother's birthday, for the next five years.

"So she'll have a birthday present of a thousand pounds for five successive years," said Uncle Oscar. "I hope it won't make it all the harder for her later."

Paul's mother had her birthday in November. The house had been "whispering" worse than ever lately, and, even in spite of his luck, Paul could not bear up against it. He was very anxious to see the effect of the birthday letter, telling his mother about the thousand pounds.

When there were no visitors, Paul now took his meals with his parents, as he was beyond the nursery control. His mother went into town nearly every day. She had discovered that she had an odd knack of sketching furs and dress materials, so she worked secretly in the studio of a friend who was the chief "artist" for the leading drapers. She drew the figures of ladies in furs and ladies in silk and sequins for the newspaper advertisements. This young woman artist earned several thousand pounds a year, but Paul's mother only made several hundreds, and she was again dissatisfied. She so wanted to be first in something, and she did not succeed, even in making sketches for drapery advertisements.

She was down to breakfast on the morning of her birthday. Paul watched her face as she read her letters. He knew the lawyer's letter. As his mother read it, her face hardened and became more expressionless. Then a cold, determined look came on her mouth. She hid the letter under the pile of others, and said not a word about it.

"Didn't you have anything nice in the post for your birthday, mother?" said Paul.

"Quite moderately nice," she said, her voice cold and absent.

---

7. *writs,* legal documents. Here the term is used to mean that legal action is about to be taken to collect unpaid bills.

She went away to town without saying more.

But in the afternoon Uncle Oscar appeared. He said Paul's mother had had a long interview with her lawyer, asking if the whole five thousand could not be advanced at once, as she was in debt.

"What do you think, uncle?" said the boy.

"I leave it to you, son."

"Oh, let her have it, then! We can get some more with the other," said the boy.

"A bird in the hand is worth two in the bush, laddie!" said Uncle Oscar.

"But I'm sure to *know* for the Grand National; or the Lincolnshire; or else the Derby. I'm sure to know for *one* of them," said Paul.

So Uncle Oscar signed the agreement, and Paul's mother touched the whole five thousand. Then something very curious happened. The voices in the house *more greedy* suddenly went mad, like a chorus of frogs on a spring evening. There were certain new furnishings, and Paul had a tutor. He was *really* going to Eton, his father's school, in the following autumn. There were flowers in the winter, and a blossoming of the luxury Paul's mother had been used to. And yet the voices in the house, behind the sprays of mimosa and almond blossom, and from under the piles of iridescent cushions, simply trilled and screamed in a sort of ecstasy. "There *must* be more money! Oh-h-h; there *must* be more money! Oh, now, now-w! Now-w-w —there *must* be more money!—more than ever! More than ever!"

It frightened Paul terribly. He studied away at his Latin and Greek with his tutors. But his intense hours were spent with Bassett. The Grand National had gone by: he had not "known," and had lost a hundred pounds. Summer was at hand. He was in agony for the Lincoln. But even for the Lincoln he didn't "know," and he lost fifty pounds. He became wild-eyed and strange, as if something were going to explode in him.

"Let it alone, son! Don't you bother about it!" urged Uncle Oscar. But it was as if the boy couldn't really hear what his uncle was saying.

"I've got to know for the Derby! I've got to know for the Derby!" the child reiterated, his big blue eyes blazing with a sort of madness.

His mother noticed how overwrought he was.

"You'd better go to the seaside. Wouldn't you like to go now to the seaside, instead of waiting? I think you'd better," she said, looking down at him anxiously, her heart curiously heavy because of him.

But the child lifted his uncanny blue eyes.

"I couldn't possibly go before the Derby, mother!" he said. "I couldn't possibly!"

"Why not?" she said, her voice becoming heavy when she was opposed. "Why not? You can still go from the seaside to see the Derby with your Uncle Oscar, if that's what you wish. No need for you to wait here. Besides, I think you care too much about these races. It's a bad sign. My family has been a gambling family, and you won't know till you grow up how much damage it has done. But it has done damage. I shall have to send Bassett away, and ask Uncle Oscar not to talk racing to you, unless you promise to be reasonable about it; go away to the seaside and forget it. You're all nerves!"

"I'll do what you like, mother, so long as you don't send me away till after the Derby," the boy said.

"Send you away from where? Just from this house?"

"Yes," he said, gazing at her.

"Why, you curious child, what makes you care about this house so much, suddenly? I never knew you loved it."

He gazed at her without speaking. He had a secret within a secret, something he had not divulged, even to Bassett or to his Uncle Oscar.

But his mother, after standing undecided and a little bit sullen for some moments, said:

"Very well, then! Don't go to the seaside till after the Derby, if you don't wish it. But promise me you won't let your nerves go to pieces. Promise you won't think so much about horse racing and *events*, as you call them!"

"Oh, no," said the boy casually. "I won't think much about them, mother. You needn't worry. I wouldn't worry, mother, if I were you."

"If you were me and I were you," said his mother, "I wonder what we *should* do!"

"But you know you needn't worry, mother, don't you?" the boy repeated.

"I should be awfully glad to know it," she said wearily.

"Oh, well, you *can*, you know. I mean, you *ought* to know you needn't worry," he insisted.

"Ought I? Then I'll see about it," she said.

Paul's secret of secrets was his wooden horse, that which had no name. Since he was emancipated from a nurse and a nursery-governess, he had had his rocking horse removed to his own bedroom at the top of the house.

"Surely, you're too big for a rocking horse!" his mother had remonstrated.

"Well, you see, mother, till I can have a *real* horse, I like to have *some* sort of animal about," had been his quaint answer.

"Do you feel he keeps you company?" she laughed.

"Oh, yes! He's very good, he always keeps me company, when I'm there," said Paul.

So the horse, rather shabby, stood in an arrested prance in the boy's bedroom.

The Derby was drawing near, and the boy grew more and more tense. He hardly heard what was spoken to him, he was very frail, and his eyes were really uncanny. His mother had sudden strange seizures of uneasiness about him. Sometimes, for half-an-hour, she would feel a sudden anxiety about him that was almost anguish. She wanted to rush to him at once, and know he was safe.

Two nights before the Derby, she was at a big party in town, when one of her rushes of anxiety about her boy, her first-born, gripped her heart till she could hardly speak. She fought with the feeling, might and main, for she believed in common sense. But it was too strong. She had to leave the dance and go downstairs to telephone to the country. The children's nursery-governess was terribly surprised and startled at being rung up in the night.

"Are the children all right, Miss Wilmot?"

"Oh, yes, they are quite all right."

"Master Paul? Is he all right?"

"He went to bed as right as a trivet. Shall I run up and look at him?"

"No," said Paul's mother reluctantly. "No! Don't trouble. It's all right. Don't sit up. We shall be home fairly soon." She did not want her son's privacy intruded upon.

"Very good," said the governess.

It was about one o'clock when Paul's mother and father drove up to their house. All was still. Paul's mother went to her room and slipped off her white fur cloak. She had told her maid not to wait up for her. She heard her husband downstairs, mixing a whiskey-and-soda.

And then, because of the strange anxiety at her heart, she stole upstairs to her son's room. Noiselessly she went along the upper corridor. Was there a faint noise? What was it?

She stood, with arrested muscles, outside his door, listening. There was a strange, heavy, and yet not loud noise. Her heart stood still. It was a soundless noise, yet rushing and powerful. Something huge, in violent, hushed motion. What was it? What in God's name was it? She ought to know. She felt that she knew the noise. She knew what it was.

Yet she could not place it. She couldn't say what it was. And on and on it went, like a madness.

Softly, frozen with anxiety and fear, she turned the door handle.

The room was dark. Yet in the space near the window, she heard and saw something plunging to and fro. She gazed in fear and amazement.

Then suddenly she switched on the light, and saw her son, in his green pajamas, madly surging on the rocking horse. The blaze of light suddenly lit him up, as he urged the wooden horse, and lit her up, as she stood, blonde, in her dress of pale green and crystal, in the doorway.

"Paul!" she cried. "Whatever are you doing?"

"It's Malabar!" he screamed, in a powerful, strange voice. "It's Malabar!"

His eyes blazed at her for one strange and senseless second, as he ceased urging his wooden horse. Then he fell with a crash to the ground, and she, all her tormented motherhood flooding upon her, rushed to gather him up.

But he was unconscious, and unconscious he remained, with some brain-fever. He talked and tossed, and his mother sat stonily by his side.

"Malabar! It's Malabar! Bassett, Bassett, I *know*! It's Malabar!"

So the child cried, trying to get up and urge the rocking horse that gave him his inspiration.

"What does he mean by Malabar?" asked the heart-frozen mother.

"I don't know," said the father stonily.

"What does he mean by Malabar?" she asked her brother Oscar.

"It's one of the horses running for the Derby," was the answer.

And, in spite of himself, Oscar Cresswell spoke to Bassett, and himself put a thousand on Malabar: at fourteen to one.

The third day of the illness was critical: they were waiting for a change. The boy, with his rather long, curly hair, was tossing ceaselessly on the pillow. He neither slept nor regained consciousness, and his eyes were like blue stones. His mother sat, feeling her heart had gone, turned actually into a stone.

In the evening, Oscar Cresswell did not come, but

Bassett sent a message, saying could he come up for one moment, just one moment? Paul's mother was very angry at the intrusion, but on second thought she agreed. The boy was the same. Perhaps Bassett might bring him to consciousness.

The gardener, a shortish fellow with a little brown moustache, and sharp little brown eyes, tiptoed into the room, touched his imaginary cap to Paul's mother, and stole to the bedside, staring with glittering, smallish eyes, at the tossing, dying child.

"Master Paul!" he whispered. "Master Paul! Malabar came in first all right, a clean win. I did as you told me. You've made over seventy thousand pounds, you have; you've got over eighty thousand. Malabar came in all right, Master Paul."

"Malabar! Malabar! Did I say Malabar, mother? Did I say Malabar? Do you think I'm lucky, mother? I knew Malabar, didn't I? Over eighty thousand

pounds! I call that lucky, don't you, mother? Over eighty thousand pounds! I knew, didn't I know I knew? Malabar came in all right. If I ride my horse till I'm sure, then I tell you, Bassett, you can go as high as you like. Did you go for all you were worth, Bassett?"

"I went a thousand on it, Master Paul."

"I never told you, mother, that if I can ride my horse, and *get* there, then I'm absolutely sure—oh, absolutely! Mother, did I ever tell you? I *am* lucky!"

"No, you never did," said the mother.

But the boy died in the night.

And even as he lay dead, his mother heard her brother's voice saying to her: "My God, Hester, you're eighty-odd thousand to the good, and a poor devil of a son to the bad. But, poor devil, poor devil, he's best gone out of a life where he rides his rocking horse to find a winner."

[handwritten annotations: "you are a loser"; "implies fit mother"]

DISCUSSION

1. (a) What causes the "hard little place" at the center of the mother's heart? (b) How does her attitude affect her children? (c) Although the children's father is mentioned in the story, he never actually appears. Why might Lawrence have excluded him from the story?

2. (a) What causes the whispering Paul and his sisters hear? (b) Why does it frighten them? (c) Why do the adults fail to hear the whispering?

3. (a) Why does Paul become so determined to have luck? (b) How does he go about getting it?

4. (a) What causes the whispering to grow louder after Paul gives his mother five thousand pounds? (b) How does Paul react to the increased whispering?

5. Shortly before Paul dies, his mother hears him on his rocking horse. What similarities exist between the effect of the noise made by the rocking horse on her and the effect of the house's whispering on Paul?

6. Reread the passages that deal with Paul's eyes, paying special attention to the adjectives used to describe them. How do the feelings reflected in his eyes show the changes he undergoes?

7. (a) What elements of fantasy does the story contain? (b) Do these fantastic elements strengthen or weaken the story? Justify your answer.

8. There are two important symbols in the story: the whispering and the rocking horse. Explain the symbolic significance of each.

9. Defend or criticize this statement: "Money is the root of all evil" is an adequate statement of the theme of "The Rocking-Horse Winner."

[handwritten annotation: "money is a catalyst"]

AUTHOR

DAVID HERBERT LAWRENCE (1885-1930) was born in the small provincial town of Eastwood, England. His father, a coal-miner, was uneducated, unrefined, and unambitious. His mother, a woman of some education and fierce ambitions, felt vastly superior to her husband. Mrs. Lawrence looked to David and an older brother to compensate for her bad marriage, and, when the brother died, she poured her affections and ambitions entirely upon David. This unhappy relationship was aggravated by poverty and the father's drinking; Lawrence's childhood was a wretched one.

After completing his education, Lawrence went to work in a local warehouse—a job that did not please his mother. After a few months, he left the warehouse to work as a teacher, a profession he followed for a number of years. During these years he wrote, and with the publication of his first work and his mother's death he left teaching to spend his time writing.

Lawrence was only forty-five when he died of the tuberculosis that had long been threatening him. He left behind him an exceptionally large body of work, among the largest in English literature. It is a varied and interesting collection.

[handwritten annotation, right margin: "Basset can't say last line becuz he's a servant (on lower level)"]

RELATIONSHIPS

Roy's Wound

James Baldwin

His house was filled with hatred. But what could he—or, for that matter, any of them—do to put an end to it?

As, in the late afternoon, John approached his home again, he saw little Sarah, her coat unbuttoned, come flying out of the house, and run the length of the street away from him, into the far drugstore. Instantly, he was frightened; he stopped a moment, wondering what could justify such hysterical haste. It was true that Sarah was full of self-importance and made any errand she was to run seem a matter of life or death; nevertheless, she had been sent on an errand, and with such speed that her mother had not had time to make her button up her coat.

Then he felt weary; if something had really happened it would be very unpleasant upstairs now, and he did not want to face it. Or perhaps it was simply that his mother had a headache and had sent Sarah to the store for aspirin. But if this were true, it meant that he would have to prepare supper, and take care of the children, and be naked under his father's eye all the evening long. And he began to walk more slowly.

There were some boys standing on the stoop. They watched him as he approached, and he tried not to look at them, and to approximate their swagger. One of them said, as John mounted the low stone steps and started into the hall, "Boy, your brother was hurt real bad today."

He looked at them in a kind of dread, not daring to ask for details; and he observed that they too might have been in a battle: something hangdog in their looks suggested they had been put to flight. Then he looked down, and saw that there was blood on the threshold, and blood spattered on the tile floor of the vestibule. He looked again at the boys, who had not ceased to watch him, and hurried up the stairs.

The door was half open—for Sarah's return, no doubt; and he walked in, making no sound, feeling a confused impulse to flee. There was no one in the kitchen, though the light was burning—the lights were on all through the house. On the kitchen table stood a shopping bag filled with groceries, and he knew that his Aunt Florence had arrived. The washtub, where his mother had been washing earlier, was open still, and filled the kitchen with a sour smell.

He had seen small, smudged coins of blood on the stairs on his way up, and there were drops of blood on the floor here too.

All this frightened him terribly. He stood in the middle of the kitchen, trying to imagine what had happened, and to prepare himself to walk into the living room, where he could hear his father's voice. Roy had been in trouble before, but this new trouble seemed the beginning of the fulfillment of a prophecy. He took off his coat, dropping it on a chair, and was about to go into the living room when he heard Sarah running up the steps.

He waited, and she burst through the door, carrying a clumsily shaped parcel.

"What happened?" he whispered.

She stared at him in astonishment, and a certain wild joy. He thought again that he really did not like his sister. Catching her breath, she said triumphantly, "Roy got stabbed with a knife!" and rushed into the living room.

Roy got stabbed with a knife. Whatever this meant, it meant that his father would be at his worst tonight. John walked slowly into the living room.

His father and mother, a small basin of water between them, knelt by the sofa where Roy lay, and his father was washing the blood from Roy's forehead. Apparently his mother, whose touch was so much more gentle, had been thrust aside by his father, who now could not bear to have anyone else touch his wounded son. And so she watched, one hand in the water, the other clenched in anguish at her waist, which was circled still by the improvised apron of the morning. Her face, as she watched, was tense with fear and pity. His father muttered sweet, delirious things to Roy, and his hands, when he dipped them again in the basin and wrung out the cloth, were trembling. Aunt Florence, still wearing her hat and carrying her handbag, stood a little removed, looking down at Roy with a troubled face.

His mother looked up as Sarah bounded into the room, reached out for the package, and saw him. She said nothing, but looked at him with a strange, quick intentness, almost as though there were a warning on her tongue which she did not at the moment dare to utter. His Aunt Florence said, "We been wondering where you was, boy. This bad brother of yours done gone out and got hisself hurt."

But John understood from her tone that the fuss was, possibly, a little greater than the danger. Roy was not, after all, going to die. And his heart lifted a little. Then his father turned and looked at him.

"Where you been, boy," he shouted, "all this time? Don't you know you's needed here at home?"

More than his words, his face made John stiffen instantly with fear and malice. His father's face was terrible in anger, but now there was more than anger in his face. John saw now what he had never seen there before, except in his own vindictive fantasies: a kind of wild, weeping terror that made the face seem younger, and yet, in another way, unutterably older, and more cruel. And John knew, in the moment his father's glance swept over him, that he hated John because John was not lying on the sofa, where Roy lay. John could scarcely meet his father's eyes, and yet, briefly, he did, saying nothing; feeling in his heart an odd sensation of triumph, and hoping in his heart that Roy, to bring his father low, would die.

His mother had unwrapped the package, and was opening a bottle of peroxide. "Here," she said, "you better wash it with this now." Her voice, was calm, and dry, her expression closed, as she handed the bottle and the cotton to his father.

"This going to hurt," his father said—in such a different voice, so sad and tender!—turning again to the sofa. "But you just be a little man, and hold still—it ain't going to take long."

John watched, and listened, hating him. Roy began to moan. Aunt Florence moved to the mantelpiece, and put her handbag down near the metal serpent. From the room behind him, John heard the baby begin to whimper.

"John," said his mother, "go and pick her up, like a good boy." Her hands, not trembling, were still busy: she had opened the bottle of iodine, and was cutting up strips of bandage.

John walked into his parents' bedroom, and picked up the squalling baby, who was wet. The moment Ruth felt him lift her up, she stopped crying, and stared at him, wide-eyed and pathetic, as though she knew there was trouble in the house. John laughed at her so-ancient seeming distress—he was very fond of his baby sister—and whispered in her ear, as he started back to the living room, "Now, you let your big brother tell you something, baby. Just as soon as you's able to stand on your feet, you run away from *this* house, run far away." He did not quite know why he said this, or where he wanted her to run, but it made him feel better instantly.

His father was saying, as John came back into the room, "I'm sure going to be having some questions to ask you in a minute, old lady. I'm going to be wanting to know just how come you let this boy go out and get half killed."

"Oh, no, you ain't," said Aunt Florence, "you ain't going to be starting none of that mess this evening. You know right doggone well that Roy don't never ask *nobody* if he can do *nothing*—he just go right ahead and do like he pleases. Elizabeth sure can't put no ball and chain on him. She got her hands full right here in this house, and it ain't her fault if Roy got a head just as hard as his father's."

"You got a awful lot to say, look like for once you could keep from putting your mouth in my business." He said this without looking at her.

"It ain't my fault," she said, "that you was born

a fool, and always been a fool, and ain't never going to change. I swear to my Father you'd try the patience of Job."

"I done told you before," he said—he had not ceased working over the moaning Roy, and was preparing now to dab the wound with iodine, "that I didn't want you coming in here and using that gutter language in front of my children."

"Don't you worry about my language, brother," she said, with spirit, "you better start worrying about your *life*. What these children hear ain't going to do them near as much harm as what they *see*."

"What they *see*," his father muttered, "is a poor man trying to serve the Lord. *That's* my life."

"Then I guarantee *you*," she said, "that they going to do their best to keep it from being *their* life. *You* mark my words."

He turned and looked at her; and intercepted the look that passed between the two women. John's mother, for reasons that were not at all his father's reasons, wanted Aunt Florence to keep still. He looked away, ironically. John watched his mother's mouth tighten bitterly. His father, in silence, began bandaging Roy's forehead.

"It's just the mercy of God," he said, at last, "that this boy didn't lose his eye. Look here."

His mother leaned over and looked into Roy's face with a sad, sympathetic murmur. Yet, John felt, she had seen instantly the extent of the danger to Roy's eye, and to his life, and was beyond that worry now; now she was merely marking time, as it were, and preparing herself for the moment when her husband's anger would turn, full force, against her.

His father now turned to John, who was standing near the French doors with Ruth in his arms.

"You come here, boy," he said, "and see what them white folks done to your brother."

John walked over to the sofa, holding himself as proudly beneath his father's furious eyes as a prince approaching the scaffold.

"Look here," said his father, grasping him roughly by one arm, "look at your brother."

John looked down at Roy; who gazed up at him with almost no expression in his dark eyes. But John knew, by the weary, impatient set of Roy's young mouth, that his brother was asking that none of this be held against him. It wasn't his fault, or John's, Roy's eyes said, that they had such a crazy father.

His father, with the air of one forcing the sinner to look down into the pit which is to be his portion, moved away slightly so that John could see Roy's wound.

Roy had been gashed by a knife, luckily not very sharp, but very jagged, from the center of his forehead where his hair began, downward to the bone just above his left eye: the wound described a kind of crazy half-moon, and ended in a violent fuzzy tail, which was the ruin of Roy's eyebrow. Time would darken the half-moon wound into Roy's dark skin, but nothing would bring together again the so violently divided hairs of his eyebrow. This crazy lift, this question, would remain with him forever, and emphasize forever something mocking and sinister in Roy's face. John felt a sudden impulse to smile, but his father's eyes were on him, and he fought the impulse back. Certainly the wound was now very ugly, and very red, and must, John felt, with a quickened sympathy toward Roy, who had not cried out, have been very painful. He could imagine the sensation caused when Roy staggered into the house, blinded with his blood; but, just the same, he wasn't dead, he wasn't changed, he would be in the streets again the moment he was better.

"You see," came now from his father. "It was white folks, some of them white folks *you* like so much, that tried to cut your brother's throat."

John thought, with immediate anger, and with a curious contempt for his father's inexactness, that only a blind man, however white, could possibly have been aiming at Roy's throat; and his mother said, with a calm insistence:

"And he was trying to cut theirs. Him and them bad boys."

"Yes," said Aunt Florence, "I ain't heard you ask that boy nary a question about how all this happened. Look like you just determined to raise cain any*how*—and make everybody in this house suffer because something done happened to the apple of your eye."

"I done ask you," cried his father, in exasperation, "to stop running your *mouth*. Don't none of this concern you—this is *my* family, and this is *my* house. You want me to slap you side of the head?"

"You slap me," she said placidly, "and I *do* guarantee you, you won't do no more slapping in a hurry."

"Hush now," said his mother, rising, "ain't no need for all this. What's done is done. We ought to be on our knees, thanking the Lord it weren't no worse."

"Amen to that," said Aunt Florence, "*tell* that foolish nigger something."

"You can tell that foolish *son* of yours something," he said to his wife, with venom, having decided, it seemed, to ignore his sister, "him standing there with them big, buck eyes. You can tell him to take this like a warning from the Lord. *This* is what white folks does to niggers, I been telling you, now you see."

"He better take it like a warning?" shrieked Aunt Florence, "*He* better take it? Why, Gabriel, it ain't *him* went halfway across this city to get in a fight with white boys. This boy on the sofa went—*deliberately*—with a whole lot of other boys, all the way to the west side, just *looking* for a fight. I declare, I *do* wonder what goes on in your head."

"You know right well," his mother said, looking directly at his father, "that Johnny don't travel with the same class of boys as Roy goes with. You done beat Roy too many times, here, in this very room, for going out with them bad boys. Roy got hisself hurt this afternoon because he was out doing something he didn't have no business doing, and that's the end of it. You ought to be thanking your Redeemer he ain't dead."

"And for all the care you take of him," he said, "he might as well be dead. Don't look like you much care whether he lives, or dies."

"*Lord*, have mercy," said Aunt Florence.

"He's my son, too," she said, with heat, "I carried him in my belly for nine months, and I know him just like I know his Daddy, and they's just *exactly* alike. Now. You ain't got no *right* in the world to talk to me like that."

"I reckon you *know*," he said, choked, and breathing hard, "all about a mother's love. I sure reckon on you telling me how a woman can sit in the house all day, and let her own flesh and blood go out and get half butchered. Don't you *tell* me you don't know no way to stop him—because I remember *my* mother, God rest her soul, and *she'd* have found a way."

"She was my mother, too," said Aunt Florence, "and I recollect, if you don't, you being brought home many a time more dead than alive. She didn't find no way to stop *you*. She wore herself *out*, beating on you, just like you been wearing yourself out, beating on this boy here."

"My, my, *my*," he said, "you got a lot to say."

"I ain't doing a thing," she said, "but trying to

talk some sense into your big, black, hard head. You better stop trying to blame everything on Elizabeth, and look to your own wrong doings."

"Never mind, Florence," his mother said, "it's all over, and done with now."

"I'm out of this house," he shouted, "every day the Lord sends, working to put the food in these children's mouths. Don't you think I got a right to ask the mother of these children to look after them, and see that they don't break their *necks* before I get back *home?*"

"You ain't got but one child," said his mother, "that's liable to go out and break his neck, and that's Roy, and you know it. And I don't know how in the world you expect me to run this house, and look after these children, and keep running around the block after Roy. *No,* I can't stop him, I done told you that, and you can't stop him neither. You don't know *what* to do with this boy, and that's why you all the time trying to fix the blame on somebody. Ain't nobody to *blame,* Gabriel. You just better pray God to stop him before somebody puts another knife in him, and puts him in his *grave.*"

They stared at each other a moment in an awful pause, a startled, pleading question in her eyes; then, with all his might, he reached out and slapped her across the face. She crumpled at once, hiding her face with one thin hand, and Aunt Florence moved to hold her up. Sarah watched all this with greedy eyes. Then Roy sat up, and said in a shaking voice:

"Don't you slap my mother. That's my *mother.* You slap her again, you black bastard, and I swear to God I'll kill you."

In the moment that these words filled the room, and hung in the air like the infinitesimal moment of hanging, jagged light which precedes an explosion, John and his father were staring into each other's eyes. John thought for that moment that his father believed that those words had come from him: his eyes were so wild, and depthlessly malevolent, and

his mouth was twisted into a snarl of pain. Then, in the absolute silence which followed Roy's words, John saw that his father was not seeing him, was not seeing anything, unless it were a vision. John wanted to turn and flee, as though he had encountered in the jungle some evil beast, crouching and ravenous, with eyes like hell unloosed; and exactly as though, on a road's turning, he found himself staring at certain destruction, he found that he could not move. Then his father turned away from him, and looked down at Roy.

"What did you say?" his father asked.

"I told you," said Roy, "not to touch my mother."

"You cursed me," said his father.

Roy said nothing; neither did he drop his eyes.

"Gabriel," said his mother, "Gabriel. Let us pray."

His father's hands were at his waist, and he took off his belt. Tears were in his eyes.

"Gabriel," cried Aunt Florence, "ain't you done playing the fool for tonight?"

Then his father raised his belt, and it fell with a whistling sound on Roy, who shivered and fell back, his face to the wall, but did not cry out. And the belt was raised again, and again; the air rang with the whistling, and the *crack!* against Roy's flesh. The baby, Ruth, began to scream.

"*My Lord, my Lord,*" his father whispered, "*my Lord, my Lord.*"

He raised the belt again, but Aunt Florence caught it from behind, and held it. His mother rushed over to the sofa, and caught Roy in her arms, crying as John had never seen a woman, or anybody, cry before. Roy caught his mother around the neck and held on to her as though he were drowning.

His Aunt Florence and his father faced each other.

"Yes, Lord," Aunt Florence said, "you was born wild, and you's going to die wild. But ain't no need to try to take the whole world with you. You can't change nothing, Gabriel. You ought to know that by now."

DISCUSSION

1. As he watched Sarah run out of the house and then to the drugstore, John "instantly was frightened" but soon after "felt weary." Then, after entering his home, he looked about and what he saw "frightened him terribly." What prompted each of these feelings in John?

2. (a) Gabriel, the father, interacts with every other character in the story. How does his wife respond to his behavior? John? Aunt Florence? Roy? (b) What evidence is there that Gabriel is a brutal man?

3. Roy's mother says that Roy is exactly like his father. What do you think she means?

4. If you could choose for each character in the story two words (for example, *angry, brutal*) to describe his or her personality, which two words would you choose for each. Why?

5. What are the possible meanings, literal and symbolic, of the title of the story?

6. Assume that you were a family counselor. In the light of what you know about the family from having read this story, what recommendations would you make to resolve as best as possible the family's problems?

THE AUTHOR'S CRAFT

Author's intent

If an author believes that one of his responsibilities is to depict life honestly, and if he chooses to write about persons living in an environment where, for example, violence, poverty, profanity, and racial tensions are commonplace, then it follows that the writer may describe situations and employ language potentially offensive to his readers.

Before choosing to take offense, careful readers attempt to infer an author's purposes in selecting his characters, his situations, and his language. They ask themselves such questions as these, which you should now ask about "Roy's Wound": Do, or might, persons like those the author describes exist in the world? Is their behavior credible, or is it beyond belief? Does the author appear to approve of, or glorify, violence; does he appear to be neutral; or does he seem to find violence distasteful, even though he describes it? Is the language of the characters appropriate to their personalities and to their environment? Or does the author seem to be endorsing the kind of life lived by his characters, making it so attractive that the reader might wish to participate in it or emulate it? Or would he appear to want for his characters something better than their present existence?

Such questions are not always easy to answer. But by attempting to answer them judiciously from internal evidence in what he reads, an individual can learn to separate realism from sensationalism, and artistic integrity from irresponsible writing.

AUTHOR

JAMES BALDWIN, a native New Yorker, was born in Harlem in 1924, one of nine children. His father was a minister. While a boy, James was attracted to the church and preaching; but after several years as a young minister, he turned to literature for expression of his views.

His first book, the novel *Go Tell It on the Mountain* (1953), was about growing up in Harlem. But real success came with his first collection of essays, *Notes of a Native Son* (1955). Though a well-known novelist, Baldwin is also considered an important essayist. *The Fire Next Time* (1963), an essay about his feelings on the problems of race, has already become a classic of black literature.

He has also written short stories and several plays, including *Blues for Mister Charlie* (1964). He now makes his home in France.

RELATIONSHIPS

Birds, Clouds, Frogs

R. C. Phelan

"The first day of his two weeks' vacation was gone already and he had not reached the comforting emptiness of the West. Instead he was walking toward a tenant farmhouse that he had never seen. . . ."

A hot breeze flapped at each window like a curtain, and yet a housefly cruised easily inside the bus. There were four passengers besides Zachary Calhoun —two country girls traveling together in identical hats, a soldier, and an old woman with bundles. The driver sat square in his seat, and beyond him the road flowed smoothly down the windshield. There was a sign that said: "Your driver is Orlando O. Sisler. Courteous—Competent—Careful."

Zachary closed the paperback collection of great short stories. The big spaces of west Texas would not open out around them before dark. He was on his first paid vacation and had forty-three dollars in his pocket. As a graduate of the University of Texas with a B.A. degree in English, he had not been offered the kind of salary that newly graduated engineers, business administration majors, or geologists expected and received. For more than a year he had been the junior half of a two-man, one-secretary public-relations firm in a town just barely big enough to *have* public-relations firms. He listened to complaints, drove people to the airport, and wrote speeches to be delivered before unimportant groups and letters of condolence for clients too busy to write their own. Now he was on his way to spend two weeks on his great-uncle's ranch south of San Angelo, in the driest, emptiest part of Texas. It was a land that Zachary loved but could find no way to make a living in. On his brief visits to the ranch he was a perennial tenderfoot, but his great-uncle and his various cousins liked him and he was welcome there.

Zachary wondered what the other *O* in the driver's name could stand for, that he should prefer Orlando to it.

"Hey, *stop that!*" the soldier roared suddenly, in a surprisingly big voice for a little man with glasses. The driver put his thumb on the horn button and kept it there. Zachary saw that the soldier had shouted at two tiny figures far ahead in the road—or, rather, at one of them. A woman lay on the pavement and a man stood over her, kicking her. Near them, on the shoulder of the road, was a pickup truck.

As the bus slowed the soldier got up and stood by the door, ready to leap out and save the woman in the road. Zachary, seeing that this was the alert, responsible thing to do and being the only other male passenger, got up and stood just behind him. But the driver's honking, probably,.had done what it was meant to do. By the time they stopped, the man was leaning against the back of the pickup truck with his elbows resting on the tailgate. His overalls were dirty and he was drunk.

The soldier walked up to him. With a hand in each hip pocket of his suntans and his elbows pointing back, he tilted his head to one side, looked up at the man in overalls and said, "Boy, just what do you *mean?*"

"That's my wife," the man answered.

Zachary and the driver knelt beside her. She had fresh bruises, but small ones, on her temple and upper arm. Her hair was unwashed and long uncombed, and her dress was very green and rather dirty. Lying on her back, she looked up at them sadly but not perceptively. She groaned, turned on her left side, made herself as comfortable as she could on the warm concrete, sighed, and closed her eyes as if to sleep.

Orlando Sisler touched one of her bruises lightly. "I believe she's drunker than he is," he said to Zachary.

"I think so," said Zachary.

It was only then that he heard the children crying in the pickup truck. He opened the door on the driver's side and there they were, three of them like a nestful of birds, their faces turned up, their mouths open, their tears round, fresh, and bright. Zachary took out his handkerchief and then decided there was more work than one handkerchief could do and put it back unused. The oldest and youngest were boys, in coveralls. The middle one was a girl.

"Mister," said the oldest, who seemed to be about ten, "are they going to put us in jay-ul?" Their faces still turned up, they stopped sobbing and waited for the answer.

Zachary leaned in across the seat and looked at them sternly, to give himself added authority."No, they are not going to put you in jail," he said. "Everything is going to be all right."

All three of them sniffed. They were beautiful children, yellow-haired, bare-footed, with perfect complexions under a lot of fresh dirt. Tools and wire and a coil of rope lay on the floor of the truck, and the seat was covered by an old quilt folded to size.

"Is that your daddy out there?" Zachary asked.

"Yes."

"And is that your mama?"

"Yes."

"Did you go to town?"

"Yes, and we had strawberry cones—dime ones," said the girl, smiling. The older boy wiped the younger children's faces and then his own with a corner of the quilt. "Stop crying, Ollie," he told his brother. "They're not going to put us in jail." The boy stopped crying.

"Daniel, let's get out," said the girl briskly.

"You'd better stay here," said Zachary, but Daniel had the other door open. Hooking one arm around his little brother's chest, he slid the boy quickly from the seat to the floorboards, the running board, and at last the ground, with Ollie grunting as he went. Then all three of them ran straight to the bus and entered it through its open door.

The children's mother was gone from the highway. "I carried her and put her in the bus," said Orlando Sisler. "She never woke up." He had joined the soldier, and both were staring at the children's father. Zachary walked over.

"Aw, we had a few, but we ain't drunk," the father said. The soldier still had his hands in his hip pockets, but he now was wearing sunglasses, with the case attached to his belt. He was one of those neat, ship-shape soldiers with carefully fitted uniforms. In his big, loud voice he now asked the father sternly, "You git your wife down in the road and kick her *ever'* time you had a few?"

"She needed it," the husband answered.

"My schedule is gonna be shot to little bitty pieces," said Orlando Sisler to Zachary. "I'll have to make out a report of this."

Since the bus had stopped no car had passed by. The wind was hot and the sky was clear, except for three buzzards wheeling against a string of white clouds along the south horizon. On the low, dry hills were pastures with cedar and black-jack oak, but there were no houses in sight.

Now a big truck came down the grade eastbound, backfiring gently, and stopped. Its driver lifted his cap by its visor and scratched his head, exchanging a look with the bus driver that was like a lodge handshake.

"Man just got drunk and was kickin' his wife down the road a ways," said Orlando Sisler comfortably. "I reckon he ought to be locked up awhile. You mind phonin' for the sheriff when you get to the junction?"

"Just be glad to," said the truck driver, and pulled away.

"Is the soldier getting off at the next town by any chance?" asked Zachary.

"I believe he is," said Orlando. "Why?"

"Well, if he would stay with *him* till the deputy sheriff gets here, we could take her and the children on home; I suppose they live just a few miles down the road. Then the deputy could take the soldier on into town."

"That don't sound like any deputy sheriff I ever heard of," said Orlando, "giving a man a ride. But we'll try it."

The soldier agreed almost eagerly, Zachary thought, to the arrangement. But then, he looked like a man who relished being in charge. Orlando explained matters to the children's father. "We're gonna take your wife and kids on home. This soldier's gonna stay here with you awhile. They gonna lock you up till you get sobered up good."

"I'd stay here all day if I just had a smoke," said the farmer. "I meant to get some in town and be derned if I didn't forget." Orlando gave the farmer his cigarettes. "Got a match, old buddy?" he said to the soldier, offering a cigarette.

The mother was asleep in the seat just behind the driver's. Zachary had expected to find the children playing tag in the aisle, but the three of them were sitting quietly together in a pair of seats, gazing out the window at some sunflowers and a clump of scrub oak. Ollie was standing up on the cushions.

"Daniel," said Zachary, "will you tell the bus driver when we get to your house?"

"Are we going to ride in the bus?" asked Daniel.

"Yes, if you'll tell us when we get to your house."

The children looked at each other and giggled. "We never was in a bus before," said the girl. "Just trucks."

"Edna," Daniel told her, "you get up in that seat and you can look out *that* window. I'll stay here and hold onto Ollie and we'll look out *this* window."

The old woman passenger came along the aisle, steadying herself on the backs of the seats, just as if the bus were moving. "I made this for my grandbabies," she said to the children, "but you'd better have it," and she held out three huge pieces of chocolate fudge on a fresh paper napkin.

Daniel handed the candy around, taking the third piece himself and leaving the napkin in the old woman's outstretched hand. "Thank ye kindly," he said.

"You're entirely welcome," she answered, and turned to Zachary. "Poor little heathens," she said,

shaking her head, and then changed the subject. "I shut all the windows, with that awful old drunkard outside, and then I couldn't figure out how to shut the door."

"I'll open them," said Zachary.

"Thank goodness!" one of the country girls said to the other, rolling her eyes to the ceiling, as Zachary began to struggle with windows. They had remained primly in their seats through everything.

Orlando Sisler counted his passengers, took his seat, and closed the door. "Wait," Daniel called. "I got to git the groceries." He left the bus, climbed into the back of his father's truck, and tugged at a cardboard carton. His father turned and watched him with interest.

"Lord," said Zachary, and he too got out of the bus. But by the time he reached the truck, the soldier had lifted the carton and set it on Daniel's shoulder.

The boy staggered with it toward the bus. "I got it, I got it," he grunted, refusing Zachary's help.

"You kids behave yourself, now, Son," the father called to Daniel, who didn't answer. The father then addressed himself to Zachary. "That oldest 'un's a good little old kid," he said, and exhaled smoke from one of Orlando's cigarettes.

Once more Zachary boarded the bus. As it moved away Edna looked down from her window at the two men beside the truck. "Good-by, Daddy and mister," she crooned, smiling at them affectionately.

Zachary sat beside the children's mother. She was asleep until Edna came from across the aisle and touched her arm. "Mama," she said, smiling, "I looked out the window and saw lots of houses and trees and things."

The mother turned her head and looked at Edna. "You sweet, darlin' thing," she said sadly. "Run off now and play nice with Ollie."

Edna returned to her window and the mother went back to sleep. Zachary opened his book and began reading.

It was six o'clock and the sun was low, visible through the windshield of the bus. Daniel came forward and stood by the driver for a while, watching the road. He pointed. "Right there," he said, indicating not a house but a dirt track that led off around a hill.

Orlando Sisler brought the bus to a stop. "All right, lady," he said, turning in his seat. "You're home now."

The woman woke up wearily, rose, and without a

word to anyone let herself carefully down the steps to the ground. Orlando set the box of groceries on the shoulder of the road. The children filed out: Ollie, Edna, and then Daniel, who silently held up to the bus driver on his open palm a nickel and three pennies. Orlando looked down at him and shook his head.

"Can you kids carry all that stuff?" he asked, and then added to Zachary, "The house is prob'ly a mile back in the brush."

"We'll hide some under the culvert and come back for it," said Daniel.

Zachary rose and got off the bus. "I'll carry the groceries for them," he told Orlando. "Maybe I'll get to San Angelo tomorrow sometime."

The driver was back in his seat now, with a foot on the accelerator and a hand ready to close the door. "You *might* catch a ride on in tonight," he said. "Anyways, I hope so." He and Zachary exchanged looks of good-humored commiseration—really a complete, miniature friendship of about a second's duration; then the driver closed the door and that particular friendship was over.

"Good-by," crooned Edna, waving, as the bus pulled away.

The children's mother had not waited; she was about to disappear around the hill now at a dogged, painful gait that suggested she was not so much drunk any longer as hungover and thinking of sleep. Zachary lifted the carton of groceries to his shoulder and set out with Daniel beside him and the younger children in front. They moved at Ollie's speed, which was slow; they would not overtake the mother.

The road ran gently downhill and entered a stand of scrub oak and cedar. It was nearly sunset. A crow called out a warning as they passed, and the dry wind brought an old skunk smell, faint and antiseptic and, to Zachary, pleasant. His shoulder began to ache. He saw that the printing on the box had rubbed off on his white shirt. His cousins would drive sixty miles to meet the bus in San Angelo, he reflected, and he would not be on it. He might not get to a telephone before tomorrow morning. His toothbrush was in his suitcase on the bus, and the paperback collection of great short stories, for which he had paid fifty cents that morning, was riding west unclaimed on the seat just behind Orlando Sisler. The first day of his two weeks' vacation was gone already and he had not reached the comforting emptiness of the West. Instead he was walking toward a tenant farmhouse that

he had never seen, where, at the inexperienced age of twenty-three, he might have to feed and bathe three children. He shifted the groceries and smiled. It was all amazingly irregular and agreeable.

Orlando Sisler had made a good guess; the house was at least a mile from the highway. It was unpainted and sagging, taking some shelter of its own from a big live oak. It had no television antenna and no wires or storage tank to indicate electric lights or running water. Behind the house was a small, weathered barn with a lean-to, and beyond that was a field in which the sunflowers grew taller than the corn. In the front yard were broken farm implements, a few worn-out tires, and a tree stump on which there rested an old dishpan planted with petunias. On the porch sat a little old woman rocking in a wicker chair.

"Grandma, we rode the bus," Edna called.

The old woman sat, rocking only a little, until they reached the porch.

Zachary set the carton down, smiled at her and said, "Here's your groceries."

She had an intricately wrinkled face, sharp blue eyes, and little teeth curved like bird claws. Her ankles seemed to narrow down to the very bones. She wore a black wool dress, hot though it was, and over it a blue cotton apron with a pocket.

"Thank ye kindly," she said. "I was worried when Ruby walked in here drunk a little while ago without the children. She never said a word, just went to bed. Did the truck break down?"

"They both got drunk," said Zachary. "I don't expect he'll be back until tomorrow sometime. I think the truck is all right, though."

The old woman lifted the sparse remains of her eyebrows and pursed her lips as if she were very slightly vexed. "Well," she said, "just sit down and I'll have supper in a little bit. Daniel, draw me a bucket of water, honey; I've been thirsty for an hour. Ollie and Edna, go look for eggs. I fed the chickens." She rose and picked a dead leaf from a geranium in a lard can at the edge of the porch. "I can't lift the bucket out of the well," she explained to Zachary. "I'm eighty-one years old and weigh eighty-seven pounds."

"My, you don't look it," he said.

She smiled. "Wasn't it a fine day?" she asked. "I set on the porch all day and nobody come to see me but a redbird."

Zachary was hungry; he did not take the trouble to

protest that he really ought to be going now. He merely followed the old woman to the kitchen, carrying the carton of groceries. Then he sat on the porch floor, leaned against a post and looked at the trees, the rocky ground and the empty sky. It was dusk. A breeze came and flapped about his legs and shoulders. He heard the sound of a well bucket, the complaint of a hen, the clank of stove lids from the kitchen. Daniel entered the kitchen by the back door and held a conversation with his grandmother. Zachary could hear their two light voices, the old one and the young, but he could not distinguish their words; he didn't try. Then the boy came to the porch and joined Zachary in looking at the trees and sky, waiting for supper. Daniel did not speak. Sitting cross-legged, he scratched one knee through a hole in his coveralls. His blue eyes, paler now than the sky, were fixed on something that Zachary could not see; Daniel was thinking.

They ate in the kitchen at a round table with a kerosene lamp in the center: pork chops, sliced tomatoes, black-eyed peas, hot corn bread, and glasses of buttermilk. The children ate busily.

"Grandma," said Ollie, "the little baby squirrel died and we won't get to play together." Ollie stared unhappily at his plate and began to sob. The others looked at him gravely and let him cry.

For dessert there were stewed apricots spread on more corn bread, and coffee for Zachary and the grandmother. Her name, she told Zachary, was Mrs. Sarah Shell; the children's father was her son.

"Do they get drunk every Saturday?" Zachary asked.

"No," said Mrs. Shell, "just when they have the money."

"They didn't get very drunk at all today," said Daniel. "Sometimes they go to sleep in the truck and we don't get back till way late."

"I'll say this for Son, and Ruby too—they buy the groceries the first thing when they get to town," said the grandmother. "If anything's left, they drink it up."

The children left the table, but Zachary and old Mrs. Shell sat on, finishing their coffee. He offered the old woman a cigarette. She looked at it thoughtfully before she refused.

"Have you lived here long?" he asked.

"No. We move to a different place every year. The furniture and the chickens and the six of us all can make it in one truckload. Son's not much of a farmer, though his daddy was. I don't reckon he'll ever have

anything." She did not appear to be either sorrowful or worried.

"That was a good supper," he said.

The old woman tried to look severe but managed only to look pleased. In spite of herself, she smiled. "I always say, if you're going to have corn bread, have it *hot*," she said.

"Look, ma'am," said Zachary, "I wish you'd take this. Don't tell your son and daughter-in-law. Just keep it in case you and the kids need it sometime." He put a ten-dollar bill on the table.

The old woman smiled, and her old face somehow looked as fresh and innocent as Edna's. She might have been a little girl with a secret. "Bless your heart, we don't need it," she said. "Daniel and me have got *twenty-three dollars* hid out down by the creek. If me and the kids ever need it, why, it's there. Just as long as Son and Ruby don't wreck the truck and hurt the children, why, we haven't got a worry on God's green earth. Daniel is eleven. It won't be long before he's big enough to take care of me and the babies, and Son and Ruby can go their way. They've run off before, stayed two months, but me and Daniel made out till they got back. I'll leave these dishes till tomorrow; it's too hot to build up the fire."

On their way to the front porch they passed through a bedroom. A strip of lamplight fell into it from the kitchen. Ollie lay flung out on the bed, face up, asleep in his coveralls. "Don't forget to undress him, Daniel," said old Mrs. Shell when they reached the porch. Edna was not there. Zachary wondered if she had gone into the other bedroom to sleep with her mother.

They simply sat—Daniel and Zachary on the porch floor, the old woman in her creaking wicker rocker—and looked at the magnificent night. After a while Daniel said apologetically, "We had a radio but the batteries ran down," and he took a harmonica from his pocket. He played two gentle, sad tunes that Zachary did not know, and then he stopped.

Zachary felt himself set free, gently, upon the earth. He had not known that people could be so tenuously attached to a place, so meagerly equipped with possessions. He thought of his own debts and duties and possessions. They lay a hundred miles to the east, weights that he had set down and did not have to pick up again. His stomach was comfortably filled with pork chops and corn bread and, just above it, his heart with love for the old woman and the children. He wanted to join them, take charge of them, protect them against the caprices of Son and Ruby. But he knew that he could not join them, any more than he could join a flock of birds. He was afraid of a freedom based on the possession of twenty-three dollars and the innocent feeling that the world was made to be lived in. It was an extension of the choice he had made when he decided to study English instead of geology, but he could not follow it that far. He would go on to the ranch, and then back to his job, debts, books, clothes, promises, phonograph, and camera. Even his collection of short stories would be returned to him, he knew; Orlando Sisler would put it with his luggage.

"I have to go," he said.

"Good night," they told him. "Thank ye kindly."

He walked up the dirt track, looking at the sky. The night was dark and perfect. Winter was somewhere far away and so was rain; it was a night, he thought sadly, that was safe even for him to wander in. He would walk the road and the highway, enjoying it, and in the morning someone would give him a lift.

From the dark trees on the left came Edna's voice, small, unemotional, and clear. "Good-by," she called, "good-by."

What was she doing out there? he wondered. Perhaps she chose to sleep there. Zachary answered, but only to himself, "Good-by, Edna."

DISCUSSION

1. From what you learn early in the story, what is Zachary's attitude toward his work?

2. (a) Why does Zachary get off the bus to help the woman? (b) Is the reason for his action in keeping with his character? (c) Why does he help the children get settled on the bus?

3. (a) Why does Zachary suggest the soldier stay with the father? (b) Why does he offer to carry the groceries? (c) Explain the meaning behind the look of "good-humored commiseration" he exchanges with Orlando.

4. (a) Once off the bus, what doubts does Zachary have? (b) Why, then, does he find the situation "amazingly irregular and agreeable"?

5. (a) What values does Zachary discover in the life of the migrants? (b) He would like to stay with them. Why doesn't he?

THE AUTHOR'S CRAFT

Imagery

Part of the charm of "Birds, Clouds, Frogs" lies in R. C. Phelan's descriptive power—his use of specific words and vivid details that enable you to create a mental picture, or image, of a sight or a sound, of a taste, smell, or sensation.

Phelan opens the story with a descriptive sentence: "A hot breeze flapped at each window like a curtain, and yet a housefly cruised easily inside the bus." To what senses does this description appeal? What feelings does it arouse in you? Does it help establish the overall atmosphere of the story? Explain.

Reread the first three paragraphs of the story, paying careful attention to the images they contain. To which sense do the images have their primary appeal? Which image, in your opinion, is most effective? Why?

How does the soldier's sudden roar in the fifth paragraph change the mood set by the opening passages? Show how this new atmosphere is reflected in the author's use of imagery.

Phelan also relies upon your image-making ability when he describes the children; obviously, he finds them appealing. Do you? Point out the images that affect your attitude toward them.

In the passages describing Zachary's trek to the house with the groceries, what image do you get of the setting in which the children live? Does visualizing Zachary's progress to the house help you to share more fully in his experience? Why?

Examine Zachary's desire to stay with the family he has discovered. Which images help you to share his emotions?

Imagery is a vital element in all imaginative writing, but its effectiveness is largely dependent upon the ability to read creatively.

AUTHOR

R. C. PHELAN (1921-   ), unlike the hero of "Birds, Clouds, Frogs," is unafraid to take chances and make changes. Since his college graduation, he has lived in widely scattered parts of the world and worked at an assortment of jobs. Phelan has been a student at the Sorbonne in Paris, a newspaper reporter in Houston, a magazine writer in New York, and an English teacher in Arkansas. Yet, despite his experiences in some of the world's most cosmopolitan cities, Phelan has not lost his love for the plains of Texas on which he grew up, and he often makes them the setting for his deceptively simple stories.

RELATIONSHIPS

A QUESTION OF BLOOD

Ernest Haycox

". . . she was a pretty woman with her black hair braided and her clothes neat and colorful under the sun. But he had forgotten her customs. . . ."

THAT fall of 1869 when Frank Isabel settled in the Yellow Hills the nearest town was a four-day ride to the north and his closest white neighbor lived at the newly established Hat ranch, seventy miles over in Two Dance Valley. The Indians were on reservation but it was still risky for a man to be alone in the country.

It made no difference to Isabel. He was young and self-willed and raised in that impoverished and faction-torn part of Missouri where manhood came to a male child almost as soon as he could lift a gun. He had a backwoodsman's lank loose height, his eyes were almost black and though he kept a smooth-shaven face there was always a clay-blue cast to the long sides of his jaw. The land was free, well grassed and watered and ideal for a poor man who had ambition. This was why he had come.

Yet self-sufficient as he was he had made no cal-culation for the imperious hungers that soon or late come to a lonely man. And presently, seeing no hope of a white woman in the land for many years, he went down to the reservation and took unto himself a Crow girl, the bargain being sealed by payment to her father of one horse and a quart of whisky.

She was quick and small and neat, with enormous eyes looking out of a round smooth face. The price paid was small and that hurt her pride for a little while, yet it was a white man who wanted her and the hurt died and she moved quietly into Frank Isabel's log house and settled down to the long, lonesome days without murmur.

She was more than he had expected in an Indian woman: quick to perceive the way his mind ran, showing him sudden streaks of mischief-making gaiety, and sometimes a flash of affection. Before the boy baby was born he drove her three hundred miles to Cheyenne and married her in the white way.

It was a sense of justice in him that impelled him to do this rather than any need in her eyes. For he was learning that the horse and bottle of whisky were as binding as any ceremony on earth; and he was also learning that though an Indian woman was a dutiful woman, immemorial customs guided her in a way he could not hope to touch or change. A man's work was a man's; a woman's work was hers and the line was hard and clear. In the beginning he had shocked her by cutting the firewood and by dressing down the game he brought in. It had shamed her for a while that he should descend to those things; and only by angry command had he established the habit of eating at table instead of crosslegged on a floor blanket. She was faithful to the discharge of the duty she owed him, but behind that girlish face was an adamant will. The ways of a thousand generations were ingrained in her.

Often at night, smoking before the fire and watching his boy crawl so awkwardly across the floor, he felt a strangeness at seeing her darkly crouched in a corner, lost in thoughts he could never reach. Sometimes the color and the sound of his early days in Missouri came strongly to him and he wished that she might know what was in his head. But he talked her tongue poorly and she would speak no English; and so silence lay between them.

Meanwhile Two Dance town was born on the empty prairie sixty miles away and the valley below him began to fill up with cattlemen long before he had thought they would come. Looking down from the ramparts of the Yellows he could see houses far off under the sun and dust spiral up along the Two Dance road, signals of a vanishing wildness. His own people had finally caught up with him. And then he knew he had become a squaw man.

One by one the few trappers who had pioneered the Yellows began to send their squaws and their half-breed children back to the reservation as a shamefaced gesture of a mistake that had to be righted. He said nothing of this to the Crow woman, yet when fear showed its luminous shadow in her eyes he knew she had heard. He said then: "Those men are fools. I am not ashamed of you." And was happy to see the fear die.

This was why he took her to Two Dance. It pleased him to have her be seen in that lively little cattle town for she was a pretty woman with her black hair braided and her clothes neat and colorful under the sun. But he had forgotten her customs and when they walked up the street she followed behind him as a squaw always did, obediently and with her head faintly lowered. He knew how Two Dance would see that and anger colored his talk to her on the way home. "A white man's wife walks beside him, not behind."

He saw that dark fear in her eyes again, and had no way of softening it. Never afterwards did she come to town.

He knew then how it was to be. At hay time when he went down to help out on Hat he could feel that faint line drawn between him and the others; at the roundup fire he sat apart, with the strangeness there —a white man who was yet not quite white. One fall night at town he stepped in to watch the weekly dance and felt all the loose bitterness of his position rise and grow to be a hard lump in his chest. Once he would have had a part in this, but the odor of the blanket was upon him now and those fair, pleasant girls went wheeling by and he saw their eyes touch him and pass on. Over the whisky bottle in Faro Charley's saloon later he understood how fatal his mistake had been; and how everlastingly long its penalty would be.

He went home late that night quite drunk. In the morning the Crow girl was gone with her boy.

He didn't follow, for he knew that either she would return or she wouldn't, and that nothing he did could change her mind. Late in the third day she came back without a word. When he went in to supper that night he sat down to a single plate on the table. Her own plate and the boy's were on a floor blanket in a corner of the room.

It was, he saw, her decision. He had told her nothing of the misery in his mind, but she knew it without need of speech and so had answered him. He was white and might eat at his table. But she was Indian and so was the boy, and the table was not for them.

There was a kindness in Frank Isabel that governed the strongest of his emotions and this was what held him still as the days went on. He was remembering back to the horse and bottle of whisky and to the time when her lips had been warm with humor. In those days the Yellows had been wild and his world had not caught up with him, but he could see the depth and the length of his mistake now. He had committed it and could stand it. Yet it passed beyond him and touched the Crow girl and the boy who was neither Crow nor white. For himself, Frank Isabel thought, there was no help. For the girl, none. It was the boy he kept weighing in his mind, so slowly and so painfully.

One winter night at meal time Jim Benbow of Hat dropped in for a cup of coffee. There was a little talk of cattle snowed into the timber and afterwards Benbow put on his hat and went to the door. As he left his glance crossed to the Crow woman and to the boy crouched in the corner and he said briefly: "Your youngster's growin' up, Frank," and left.

There was the rush of wind along the cabin eaves and deep silence inside. Isabel sat with his arms idle on the table remembering Benbow's words, which had contained a note of judgment. Presently he rose and brought another chair to the table and went over to where the Crow girl crouched mutely in the corner. He lifted the boy and put him in the chair at the table and stood there a moment, a long man throwing a thin shadow across the room. He said: "Hereafter he eats at the table."

She drew farther and farther back into the corner, like a shadow vanishing. And then, with his face turned suddenly away, he heard her stifled and terrible crying tremble the room's silence.

DISCUSSION

1. (a) Describe the Yellow Hills as Frank Isabel first knew them in 1869. (b) What had led him to settle in that area of the country? (c) What changes occurred in the country between the beginning and ending of the story?

2. (a) What evidence in the story suggests that Frank tried to be a just and devoted man to his wife? (b) What evidence indicates that the Crow girl was a capable and loyal wife and mother? (c) What, then, caused the strained relationship between them? Cite evidence to support your response.

3. (a) Twice in the story Frank thinks of his marriage as having been a mistake. Was the marriage a mistake before whites moved into the area? Explain. (b) Assume that whites had never come to Two Dance and the surrounding territory. Describe how you think Frank, the Crow girl, and their son would have gotten along over the years. (c) Was the marriage necessarily a mistake, then, or were the values of whites the "mistake"? Explain.

4. (a) What does Frank do that causes the Crow girl to break into "stifled and terrible crying"? (b) What do you think Frank's action symbolized to his wife? (c) Was his action self-motivated, or was it prompted by pressures from the white community? Explain.

COMPOSITION

Much of the impact of "A Question of Blood" derives from its ability to provoke intriguing speculation. Haycox encourages the reader to exercise his imagination and go beyond the bounds of the story. The following assignment asks you to do the same in writing.

Assume that five years have passed since the end of the story. You are a member of the community and have been asked to tell the story of the Isabel family to a newcomer. You begin your story where Ernest Haycox ends his. Using as many clues from the story as you can find, describe in several paragraphs what has happened to the Isabel family. Use the following questions as a guide:

1. What is the relationship of the Crow girl to her husband? To her son?

2. What is the relationship of the Isabel family to the growing community?

3. What is the personality of the boy?

AUTHOR

ERNEST HAYCOX· (1899-1950) was born in Portland, Oregon. Much of his childhood was spent in logging camps, on ranches, and in small towns. He attended Reed College for two years and graduated from the University of Oregon in 1923 with a degree in journalism.

In his lifetime, Haycox wrote more than twenty novels and hundreds of short stories. Four films, including the 1939 John Ford classic, *Stagecoach*, are based on his work.

FOOTFALLS

Wilbur Daniel Steele

He was willing to wait, years if need be, for the sound of that cachorra's steps.

THIS is not an easy story; not a road for tender or for casual feet. Better the meadows. Let me warn you, it is as hard as that old man's soul and as sunless as his eyes. It has its inception in catastrophe, and its end in an act of almost incredible violence; between them it tells barely how one long blind can become also deaf and dumb.

He lived in one of those old Puritan sea towns where the strain has come down austere and moribund, so that his act would not be quite unbelievable. Except that the town is no longer Puritan and Yankee. It has been betrayed; it has become an outpost of the Portuguese islands.

This man, this blind cobbler himself, was a Portuguese from St. Michael, in the Western Islands,[1] and his name was Boaz Negro.

He was happy. An unquenchable exuberance lived in him. When he arose in the morning he made

1. *St. Michael, in the Western Islands*, St. Michael or São Miguel (soun mi gel′), largest island of the Azores (ə zôrz′), a group of islands in the Atlantic Ocean west of and belonging to Portugal.

vast, as it were, uncontrollable, gestures with his stout arms. He came into his shop singing. His voice, strong and deep as the chest from which it emanated, rolled out through the doorway and along the street, and the fishermen, done with their morning work and lounging and smoking along the wharves, said, "Boaz is to work already." Then they came up to sit in the shop.

In that town a cobbler's shop is a club. One sees the interior always dimly thronged. They sit on the benches watching the artisan at his work for hours, and they talk about everything in the world. A cobbler is known by the company he keeps.

Boaz Negro kept young company. He would have nothing to do with the old. On his own head the gray hairs sat thickly.

He had a grown son. But the benches in his shop were for the lusty and valiant young, men who could spend the night drinking, and then at three o'clock in the morning turn out in the rain and dark to pull at the weirs, sing songs, buffet one another among the slippery fish in the boat's bottom, and make loud jokes about the fundamental things, love and birth and death. Hearkening to their boasts and strong prophecies, his breast heaved and his heart beat faster. He was a large, full-blooded fellow, fashioned for exploits; the flame in his darkness burned higher even to hear of them.

It is scarcely conceivable how Boaz Negro could have come through this much of his life still possessed of that unquenchable and priceless exuberance; how he would sing in the dawn; how, simply listening to the recital of deeds in gale or brawl, he could easily forget himself a blind man, tied to a shop and a last; easily make of himself a lusty young fellow breasting the sunlit and adventurous tide of life.

He had had a wife, whom he had loved. Fate, which had scourged him with the initial scourge of blindness, had seen fit to take his Angelina away. He had had four sons. Three, one after another, had been removed, leaving only Manuel, the youngest. Recovering slowly, with agony, from each of these recurrent blows, his unquenchable exuberance had lived. And there was another thing quite as extraordinary. He had never done anything but work, and that sort of thing may kill the flame where an abrupt catastrophe fails. Work in the dark. Work, work, work! And accompanied by privation, an almost miserly scale of personal economy. Yes, indeed, he

had "skinned his fingers," especially in the earlier years. When it tells most.

How he had worked! Not alone in the daytime, but also sometimes, when orders were heavy, far into the night. It was strange for one, passing along that deserted street at midnight, to hear issuing from the black shop of Boaz Negro the rhythmical tap-tap-tap of hammer on wooden peg.

Nor was that sound all: no man in town could get far past that shop in his nocturnal wandering unobserved. No more than a dozen footfalls, and from the darkness Boaz' voice rolled forth, fraternal, stentorian, "Good night, Antone!" "Good night to you, Caleb Snow!"

To Boaz Negro it was still broad day.

Now, because of this, he was what might be called a substantial man. He owned his place, his shop, opening on the sidewalk, and behind it the dwelling house with trellised galleries upstairs and down.

And there was always something for his son, a "piece for the pocket," a dollar, five, even a ten-dollar bill if he had "got to have it." Manuel was "a good boy." Boaz not only said this, he felt that he was assured of it in his understanding, to the infinite peace of his heart.

It was curious that he should be ignorant only of the one nearest to him. Not because he was physically blind. Be certain he knew more of other men and of other men's sons than they or their neighbors did. More, that is to say, of their hearts, their understandings, their idiosyncrasies, and their ultimate weight in the balance pan of eternity.

His simple explanation of Manuel was that Manuel "wasn't too stout." To others he said this, and to himself. Manuel was not indeed too robust. How should he be vigorous when he never did anything to make him so? He never worked. Why should he work, when existence was provided for, and when there was always that "piece for the pocket"? Even a ten-dollar bill on a Saturday night! No, Manuel "wasn't too stout."

In the shop they let it go at that. The missteps and frailties of everyone else in the world were canvassed there with the most shameless publicity. But Boaz Negro was a blind man, and in a sense their host. Those reckless, strong young fellows respected and loved him. It was allowed to stand at that. Manuel was "a good boy." Which did not prevent them, by the way, from joining later in the general condemnation of that father's laxity—"the ruination of the boy!"

"He should have put him to work, that's what."

"He should have said to Manuel, 'Look here, if you want a dollar, go earn it first.'"

As a matter of fact, only one man ever gave Boaz the advice direct. That was Campbell Wood. And Wood never sat in that shop.

In every small town there is one young man who is spoken of as "rising." As often as not he is not a native, but "from away."

In this town Campbell Wood was that man. He had come from another part of the state to take a place in the bank. He lived in the upper story of Boaz Negro's house, the ground floor now doing for Boaz and the meager remnant of his family. The old woman who came in to tidy up for the cobbler looked after Wood's rooms as well.

Dealing with Wood, one had first of all the sense of his incorruptibility. A little ruthless perhaps, as if one could imagine him, in defense of his integrity, cutting off his friend, cutting off his own hand, cutting off the very stream flowing out from the wellsprings of human kindness. An exaggeration, perhaps.

He was by long odds the most eligible young man in town, good-looking in a spare, ruddy, sandy-haired Scottish fashion, important, incorruptible, "rising." But he took good care of his heart. Precisely that; like a sharp-eyed duenna to his own heart. One felt that here was the man, if ever was the man, who held his destiny in his own hand. Failing, of course, some quite gratuitous and unforeseeable catastrophe.

Not that he was not human, or even incapable of laughter or passion. He was, in a way, immensely accessible. He never clapped one on the shoulder; on the other hand, he never failed to speak. Not even to Boaz.

Returning from the bank in the afternoon, he had always a word for the cobbler. Passing out again to supper at his boarding place, he had another, about the weather, the prospects of rain. And if Boaz were at work in the dark when he returned from an evening at the board of trade, there was a "Good night, Mr. Negro!"

On Boaz' part, his attitude toward his lodger was curious and paradoxical. He did not pretend to anything less than reverence for the young man's position; precisely on account of that position he was conscious toward Wood of a vague distrust. This was because he was an uneducated fellow.

To the uneducated the idea of large finance is as uncomfortable as the idea of the Law. It must be said for Boaz that, responsive to Wood's unfailing civility, he fought against this sensation of dim and somehow shameful distrust.

Nevertheless his whole parental soul was in arms that evening, when Wood, returning from the bank and finding the shop empty of loungers, paused a moment to propose the bit of advice already referred to.

"Haven't you ever thought of having Manuel learn the trade?"

A suspicion, a kind of premonition, lighted the fires of defense.

"Shoemaking," said Boaz, "is good enough for a blind man."

"Oh, I don't know, At least it's better than doing nothing at all."

Boaz' hammer was still. He sat silent, monumental. Outwardly. For once his unfailing response "Manuel ain't too stout, you know," had failed him. Perhaps it had become suddenly inadequate.

He hated Wood; he despised Wood; more than ever before, a hundredfold more, quite abruptly, he distrusted Wood.

How could a man say such things as Wood had said? And where Manuel himself might hear!

Where Manuel had heard! Boaz' other emotions—hatred and contempt and distrust—were overshadowed. Sitting in darkness, no sound had come to his ears, no footfall, no infinitesimal creaking of a floor plank. Yet by some sixth uncanny sense of the blind he was aware that Manuel was standing in the dusk of the entry joining the shop to the house.

Boaz made a Herculean effort. The voice came out of his throat, harsh, bitter, and loud enough to have carried ten times the distance to his son's ears.

"Manuel is a good boy!"

"Yes—h'm—yes—I suppose so."

Wood shifted his weight. He seemed uncomfortable.

"Well. I'll be running along, I—ugh! Heavens!"

Something was happening. Boaz heard exclamations, breathings, the rustle of sleeve cloth in large, frantic, and futile graspings—all without understanding. Immediately there was an impact on the floor, and with it the unmistakable clink of metal.

Boaz even heard that the metal was minted, and that the coins were gold. He understood. A coin sack, gripped not quite carefully enough for a moment under the other's overcoat, had shifted, slipped, escaped, and fallen.

And Manuel had heard!

It was a dreadful moment for Boaz, dreadful in its native sense, as full of dread. Why? It was a moment of horrid revelation, ruthless clarification. His son, his link with the departed Angelina, that "good boy" —Manuel, standing in the shadow of the entry, visible alone to the blind, had heard the clink of falling gold, and—*and Boaz wished that he had not!*

There, amazing, disconcerting, destroying, stood the sudden fact.

Sitting as impassive and monumental as ever, his strong, bleached hands at rest on his work, round drops of sweat came out on Boaz' forehead. He scarcely took the sense of what Wood was saying. Only fragments.

"Government money, understand—for the breakwater workings—huge—too many people know here, everywhere—don't trust the safe—tin safe— 'Noah's Ark'—give you my word—heavens, no!"

It boiled down to this—the money, more money than was good for that antiquated "Noah's Ark" at the bank, and whose contemplated sojourn there overnight was public to too many minds—in short, Wood was not only incorruptible, he was canny. To what one of those minds, now, would it occur that he should take away that money bodily, under casual cover of his coat, to his own lodgings behind the cobblershop of Boaz Negro? For this one, this important night!

He was sorry the coin sack had slipped, because he did not like to have the responsibility of secret sharer cast upon anyone, even upon Boaz, even by accident. On the other hand, how tremendously fortunate that it had been Boaz and not another. So far as that went, Wood had no more anxiety now than before. One incorruptible knows another.

"I'd trust you, Mr. Negro" (that was one of the fragments which came and stuck in the cobbler's brain), "as far as I would myself. As long as it's only you. I'm just going up here and throw it under the bed. Oh, yes, certainly."

Boaz ate no supper. For the first time in his life food was dry in his gullet. Even under those other successive crushing blows of fate the full and generous habit of his functionings had carried on unabated; he had always eaten what was set before him. Tonight, over his untouched plate, he watched Manuel with his sightless eyes, keeping track of his every mouthful, word, intonation, breath. What profit he expected to extract from this catlike surveillance it is impossible to say.

When they arose from the supper table, Boaz made another Herculean effort: "Manuel, you're a good boy!"

The formula had a quality of appeal, of despair, and of command.

"Manuel, you should be short of money, maybe. Look, what's this? A tenner?[2] Well, there's a piece for the pocket; go and enjoy yourself."

He would have been frightened had Manuel, upsetting tradition, declined the offering. With the morbid contrariness of the human imagination, the boy's avid grasping gave him no comfort.

He went out into the shop, where it was already dark, drew to him his last, his tools, mallets, cutters, pegs, leather. And having prepared to work, he remained idle. He found himself listening.

It has been observed that the large phenomena of sunlight and darkness were nothing to Boaz Negro. A busy night was broad day. Yet there was a difference; he knew it with the blind man's eyes, the ears.

Day was a vast confusion, or rather a wide fabric, of sounds; great and little sounds all woven together, voices, footfalls, wheels, far-off whistles and foghorns, flies buzzing in the sun. Night was another thing. Still there were voices and footfalls, but rarer, emerging from the large, pure body of silence as definite, surprising, and yet familiar entities.

Tonight there was an easterly wind, coming off the water and carrying the sound of waves. So far as other fugitive sounds were concerned it was the same as silence. The wind made little difference to the ears. It nullified, from one direction at least, the other two visual processes of the blind, the sense of touch and the sense of smell. It blew away from the shop, toward the living-house.

As had been said, Boaz found himself listening, scrutinizing with an extraordinary attention, this immense background of sound. He heard footfalls. The story of that night was written, for him, in footfalls.

He heard them moving about the house, the lower floor, prowling here, there, halting for long spaces, advancing, retreating softly on the planks. About this

---

2. *tenner*, ten-dollar bill. [Slang]

aimless, interminable perambulation there was something to twist the nerves, something led and at the same time driven like a succession of frail and indecisive charges.

Boaz lifted himself from his chair. All his impulse called him to make a stir, join battle, cast in the breach the reinforcement of his presence, authority, good will. He sank back again; his hands fell down. The curious impotence of the spectator held him.

He heard footfalls, too, on the upper floor, a little fainter, borne to the inner rather than the outer ear, along the solid causeway of partitions and floor, the legs of his chair, the bony framework of his body. Very faint indeed. Sinking back easily into the background of the wind. They, too, came and went, this room, that, to the passage, the stairhead, and away. About them, too, there was the same quality of being led and at the same time of being driven.

Time went by. In his darkness it seemed to Boaz that hours must have passed. He heard voices. Together with the footfalls, the abrupt, brief, and (in view of Wood's position) astounding interchange of sentences made up his history of the night. Wood must have opened the door at the head of the stair; by the sound of his voice he would be standing there, peering below perhaps, perhaps listening.

"What's wrong down there?" he called. "Why don't you go to bed?"

After a moment, came Manuel's voice, "Ain't sleepy."

"Neither am I. Look here, do you like to play cards?"

"What kind? Euchre! I like euchre all right. Or pitch."

"Well, what would you say to coming up and having a game of euchre then, Manuel? If you can't sleep?"

"That'd be all right."

The lower footfalls ascended to join the footfalls on the upper floor. There was the sound of a door closing.

Boaz sat still. In the gloom he might have been taken for a piece of furniture, of machinery, an extraordinary lay figure,[3] perhaps, for the trying on of the boots he made. He seemed scarcely to breathe, only the sweat starting from his brow giving him an aspect of life.

He ought to have run, and leaped up that inner stair and pounded with his fists on that door. He

seemed unable to move. At rare intervals feet passed on the sidewalk outside, just at his elbow, so to say, and yet somehow, tonight, immeasurably far away. Beyond the orbit of the moon. He heard Rugg, the policeman, noting the silence of the shop, muttering, "Boaz is to bed tonight," as he passed.

The wind increased. It poured against the shop with its deep, continuous sound of a river. Submerged in its body, Boaz caught the note of the town bell striking midnight.

Once more, after a long time, he heard footfalls. He heard them coming around the corner of the shop from the house, footfalls half swallowed by the wind, passing discreetly, without haste, retreating, merging step by step with the huge, incessant background of the wind.

Boaz' muscles tightened all over him. He had the impulse to start up, to fling open the door, shout into the night, "What are you doing? Stop there! Say! What are you doing and where are you going?"

And as before, the curious impotence of the spectator held him motionless. He had not stirred in his chair. And those footfalls, upon which hinged, as it were, that momentous decade of his life, were gone.

There was nothing to listen for now. Yet he continued to listen. Once or twice, half arousing himself, he drew toward him his unfinished work. And then relapsed into immobility.

As has been said, the wind, making little difference to the ears, made all the difference in the world with the sense of feeling and the sense of smell. From the one important direction of the house. That is how it could come about that Boaz Negro could sit, waiting and listening to nothing in the shop, and remain ignorant of disaster until the alarm had gone away and come back again, pounding, shouting, clanging.

"Fire!" he heard them bawling in the street. "Fire! Fire!"

Only slowly did he understand that the fire was in his own house.

There is nothing stiller in the world than the skeleton of a house in the dawn after a fire. It is as if everything living, positive, violent, had been completely drained in the one flaming act of violence, leaving nothing but negation till the end of time. It is worse than a tomb. A monstrous stillness! Even the footfalls of the searchers cannot disturb it, for they are separate and superficial. In its presence they are almost frivolous.

Half an hour after dawn the searchers found the

3. *lay figure*, jointed model of a human body.

body, if what was left from that consuming ordeal might be called a body. The discovery came as a shock. It seemed incredible that the occupant of that house, no cripple or invalid but an able man in the prime of youth, should not have awakened and made good his escape. It was the upper floor which had caught; the stairs had stood to the last. It was beyond calculation. Even if he had been asleep!

And he had not been asleep. This second and infinitely more appalling discovery began to be known. Slowly. By a hint, a breath of rumor here; there an allusion, half taken back. The man, whose incinerated body still lay curled in its bed of cinders, had been dressed at the moment of disaster; even to the watch, the cuff buttons, the studs, the very scarf pin. Fully clothed to the last detail, precisely as those who had dealings at the bank might have seen Campbell Wood any weekday morning for the past eight months. A man does not sleep with his clothes on. The skull of the man had been broken, as if with a blunt instrument of iron. On the charred lacework of the floor lay the leg of an old andiron with which Boaz Negro and his Angelina had set up housekeeping in that new house.

It needed only Mr. Asa Whitelaw, coming up the street from that gaping "Noah's Ark" at the bank, to round out the scandalous circle of circumstance.

"Where is Manuel?"

Boaz Negro still sat in his shop, impassive, monumental, his thick, hairy arms resting on the arms of his chair. The tools and materials of his work remained scattered about him, as his irresolute gathering of the night before had left them. Into his eyes no change could come. He had lost his house, the visible monument of all those years of "skinning his fingers." It would seem that he had lost his son. And he had lost something incalculably precious—that hitherto unquenchable exuberance of the man.

"Where is Manuel?"

When he spoke his voice was unaccented and stale, like the voice of a man already dead.

"Yes, where is Manuel?"

He had answered them with their own question.

"When did you last see him?"

Neither he nor they seemed to take note of that profound irony.

"At supper."

"Tell us, Boaz; you knew about this money?"

The cobbler nodded his head.

"And did Manuel?"

He might have taken sanctuary in a legal doubt. How did he know what Manuel knew? Precisely! As before, he nodded his head.

"After supper, Boaz, you were in the shop? But you heard something?"

He went on to tell them what he had heard: the footfalls, below and above, the extraordinary conversation which had broken for a moment the silence of the inner hall. The account was bare, the phrases monosyllabic. He reported only what had been registered on the sensitive tympanums of his ears, to the last whisper of footfalls stealing past the dark wall of the shop. Of all the formless tangle of thoughts, suspicions, interpretations, and the special and personal knowledge given to the blind which moved in his brain, he said nothing.

He shut his lips there. He felt himself on the defensive. Just as he distrusted the higher ramifications of finance (his house had gone down uninsured), so before the rites and processes of that inscrutable creature, the Law, he felt himself menaced by the invisible and the unknown, helpless, oppressed; in an abject sense, skeptical.

"Keep clear of the Law!" they had told him in his youth. The monster his imagination had summoned up then still stood beside him in his age.

Having exhausted his monosyllabic and superficial evidence, they could move him no further. He became deaf and dumb. He sat before them, an image cast in some immensely heavy stuff, inanimate. His lack of visible emotion impressed them. Remembering his exuberance, it was only the stranger to see him unmoving and unmoved. Only once did they catch sight of something beyond. As they were preparing to leave, he opened his mouth. What he said was like a swan song[4] to the years of his exuberant happiness. Even now there was no color of expression in his words, which sounded mechanical.

"Now I have lost everything. My house. My last son. Even my honor. You would not think I would like to live. But I go to live. I go to work. That *cachorra*,[5] one day he shall come back again, in the dark night, to have a look. I shall go to show you all. That *cachorra!*"

(And from that time on, it was noted, he never referred to the fugitive by any other name than *cachorra*, which is a kind of dog. "That *cachorra!*" As

---

4. *a swan song*, a farewell. This expression came into being because a swan is fabled to sing a song when it is dying.
5. *cachorra* (kä chôr′rä).

if he had forfeited the relationship not only of the family, but of the very genus, the very race! "That *cachorra!*")

He pronounced this resolution without passion. When they assured him that the culprit would come back again indeed, much sooner than he expected, "with a rope around his neck," he shook his head slowly.

"No, you shall not catch that *cachorra* now. But one day—"

There was something about its very colorlessness which made it sound oracular. It was at least prophetic. They searched, laid their traps, proceeded with all their placards, descriptions, rewards, clues, trails. But on Manuel Negro they never laid their hands.

Months passed and became years. Boaz Negro did not rebuild his house. He might have done so, out of his earnings, for upon himself he spent scarcely anything, reverting to his old habit of almost miserly economy. Yet perhaps it would have been harder after all. For his earnings were less and less. In that town a cobbler who sits in an empty shop is apt to want for trade. Folk take their boots to mend where they take their bodies to rest and their minds to be edified.

No longer did the walls of Boaz' shop resound to the boastful recollections of young men. Boaz had changed. He had become not only different, but opposite. A metaphor will do best. The spirit of Boaz Negro had been a meadowed hillside giving upon the open sea, the sun, the warm, wild winds from beyond the blue horizon. And covered with flowers, always hungry and thirsty for the sun and the fabulous wind and bright showers of rain. It had become an intrenched camp, lying silent, sullen, verdureless, under a gray sky. He stood solitary against the world. His approaches were closed. He was blind, and he was also deaf and dumb.

Against that what can young fellows do who wish for nothing but to rest themselves and talk about their friends and enemies? They had come and they had tried. They had raised their voices even higher than before. Their boasts had grown louder, more presumptuous, more preposterous, until, before the cold separation of that unmoving and as if contemptuous presence in the cobbler's chair, they burst of their own air, like toy balloons. And they went and left Boaz alone.

There was another thing which served, if not to keep them away, at least not to entice them back. That was the aspect of the place. It was not cheerful. It invited no one. In its way that fire-bitten ruin grew to be almost as great a scandal as the act itself had been. It was plainly an eyesore. A valuable property, on the town's main thoroughfare—and an eyesore! The neighboring owners protested.

Their protestations might as well have gone against a stone wall. That man was deaf and dumb. He had become, in a way, a kind of vegetable, for the quality of a vegetable is that, while it is endowed with life, it remains fixed in one spot. For years Boaz was scarcely seen to move foot out of that shop that was left him, a small, square, blistered promontory on the shores of ruin.

He must indeed have carried out some rudimentary sort of domestic program under the debris at the rear (he certainly did not sleep or eat in the shop). One or two lower rooms were left fairly intact. The outward aspect of the place was formless; it grew to be no more than a mound in time; the charred timbers, one or two still standing, lean and naked against the sky, lost their blackness and faded to a silvery gray. It would have seemed strange, had they not grown accustomed to the thought, to imagine that blind man, like a mole, or some slow slug, turning himself mysteriously in the bowels of that gray mound—that time-silvered "eyesore."

When they saw him, however, he was in the shop. They opened the door to take in their work (when other cobblers turned them off), and they saw him seated in his chair in the half-darkness, his whole person, legs, torso, neck, head, as motionless as the vegetable of which we have spoken—only his hands and his bare arms endowed with visible life. The gloom had bleached the skin to the color of damp ivory, and against the background of his immobility they moved with a certain amazing monstrousness, interminably. No, they were never still. One wondered what they could be at. Surely he could not have had enough work now to keep those insatiable hands so monstrously in motion. Even far into the night. Tap-tap-tap! Blows continuous and powerful. On what? On nothing? On the bare iron last? And for what purpose? To what conceivable end?

Well, one could imagine those arms, growing paler, also growing thicker and more formidable with that unceasing labor; the muscles feeding themselves, omnivorously on their own waste, the cords toughening, the bone tissues revitalizing themselves without end. One could imagine the whole aspiration of that mute and motionless man pouring itself out into those pallid arms, and the arms taking it up with a kind of blind greed. Storing it up. Against a day!

"That *cachorra!* One day—"

What were the thoughts of this man? What moved within that motionless cranium covered with long hair? Who can say? Behind everything, of course, stood that bitterness against the world—the blind world—blinder than he would ever be. And against "that *cachorra.*" But this was no longer a thought; it was the man.

Just as all muscular aspiration flowed into his arms, so all the energies of his senses turned to his ears. The man had become, you might say, two arms and two ears. Can you imagine a man listening, intently, through the waking hours of nine years?

Listening to footfalls. Marking with a special emphasis of concentration the beginning, rise, full passage, falling away, and dying of all footfalls. By day, by night, winter and summer and winter again. Unraveling the skein of footfalls passing up and down the street!

For three years he wondered when they would come. For the next three years he wondered if they would ever come. It was during the last three that a doubt began to trouble him. It gnawed at his huge moral strength. Like a hidden seepage of water, it undermined (in anticipation) his terrible resolution. It was a sign, perhaps of age, a slipping away of the reckless infallibility of youth.

Supposing, after all, that his ears should fail him. Supposing they were capable of being tricked, without his being able to know it. Supposing that that *cachorra* should come and go, and he, Boaz, living in some vast delusion, some unrealized distortion of memory, should let him pass unknown. Supposing precisely this thing had already happened!

Or the other way around. What if he should hear the footfalls coming, even into the very shop itself? What if he should be as sure of them as of his own soul? What, then, if he should strike? And what then, if it were not that *cachorra* after all? How many tens and hundreds of millions of people were there in the world? Was it possible for them all to have footfalls distinct and different?

Then they would take him and hang him. And that *cachorra* might then come and go at his own will, undisturbed.

As he sat there sometimes the sweat rolled down his nose, cold as rain.

Supposing!

Sometimes, quite suddenly, in broad day, in the booming silence of the night, he would start. Not outwardly. But beneath the pale integument of his skin all his muscles tightened and his nerves sang. His breathing stopped. It seemed almost as if his heart stopped.

Was that it? Were those the feet, there emerging faintly from the distance? Yes, there was something about them. Yes! Memory was in travail. Yes, yes, yes! No! How could he be sure? Ice ran down into his empty eyes. The footfalls were already passing. They were gone, swallowed up already by time and space. Had that been that *cachorra?*

Nothing in his life had been so hard to meet as this insidious drain of distrust in his own powers; this sense of a traitor within the walls. His iron-gray hair had turned white. It was always this now, from the beginning of the day to the end of the night: How was he to know? How was he to be inevitably, unshakably sure?

Curiously, after all this purgatory of doubts, he did know them. For a moment at least, when he had heard them, he was sure. It was on an evening of the winter holidays, the Portuguese festival of *Menin' Jesus.*[6] Christ was born again in a hundred mangers on a hundred tiny altars; there was cake and wine; songs went shouting by to the accompaniment of mandolins and tramping feet. The wind blew cold under a clear sky. In all the houses there were lights; even in Boaz Negro's shop a lamp was lit just now, for a man had been in for a pair of boots which Boaz had patched. The man had gone out again. Boaz was thinking of blowing out the light. It meant nothing to him.

He leaned forward, judging the position of the lamp chimney by the heat on his face, and puffed out his cheeks to blow. Then his cheeks collapsed suddenly, and he sat back again.

It was not odd that he had failed to hear the footfalls until they were actually within the door. A crowd of merrymakers was passing just then; their songs and tramping almost shook the shop.

Boaz sat back. Beneath his passive exterior his nerves thrummed; his muscles had grown as hard as wood. Yes! Yes! But no! He had heard nothing; no

---

6. *festival of "Menin'* (meˈnin) *Jesus,"* a Christmas festival brought to Massachusetts by early Portuguese settlers.

more than a single step, a single foot pressure on the planks within the door. Dear God! He could not tell!

Going through the pain of an enormous effort, he opened his lips.

"What can I do for you?"

"Well, I—I don't know. To tell the truth—"

The voice was unfamiliar, but it might be assumed. Boaz held himself. His face remained blank, interrogating, slightly helpless.

"I am a little deaf," he said. "Come nearer."

The footfalls came halfway across the intervening floor, and there appeared to hesitate. The voice, too, had a note of uncertainty.

"I was just looking around. I have a pair of—well, you mend shoes?"

Boaz nodded his head. It was not in response to the words, for they meant nothing. What he had heard was the footfalls on the floor.

Now he was sure. As has been said, for a moment at least after he had heard them he was unshakably sure. The congestion of his muscles had passed. He was at peace.

The voice became audible once more. Before the massive preoccupation of the blind man it became still less certain of itself.

"Well, I haven't got the shoes with me. I was—just looking around."

It was amazing to Boaz, this miraculous sensation of peace.

"Wait!" Then, bending his head as if listening to the winter wind, "It's cold tonight. You've left the door open. But wait!" Leaning down, his hand fell on a rope's end hanging by the chair. The gesture was one continuous, undeviating movement of the hand. No hesitation. No groping. How many hundreds, how many thousands of times, had his hand schooled itself in that gesture!

A single strong pull. With a little *bang* the front door had swung to and latched itself. Not only the front door. The other door, leading to the rear, had closed, too, and latched itself with a little *bang*. And leaning forward from his chair, Boaz blew out the light.

There was not a sound in the shop. Outside, feet continued to go by, ringing on the frozen road; voices were lifted; the wind hustled about the corners of the wooden shell with a continuous, shrill note of whistling. All of this outside, as on another planet. Within the blackness of the shop the complete silence persisted.

Boaz listened. Sitting on the edge of his chair, half

crouching, his head, with its long, unkempt, white hair, bent slightly to one side, he concentrated upon this chambered silence the full power of his senses. He hardly breathed. The other person in that room could not be breathing at all, it seemed.

No, there was not a breath, not the stirring of a sole on wood, not the infinitesimal rustle of any fabric. It was as if, in this utter stoppage of sound, even the blood had ceased to flow in the veins and arteries of that man, who was like a rat caught in a trap.

It was appalling even to Boaz; even to the cat. Listening became more than a labor. He began to have to fight against a growing impulse to shout out loud, to leap, sprawl forward without aim in that unstirred darkness—do something. Sweat rolled down from behind his ears, into his shirt collar. He gripped the chair arms. To keep quiet, he sank his teeth into his lower lip. He would not! He would not!

And of a sudden he heard before him, in the center of the room, an outburst of breath, an outrush from lungs in the extremity of pain, thick, laborious, fearful. A coughing up of dammed air.

Pushing himself from the arms of the chair, Boaz leaped.

His fingers, passing swiftly through the air, closed on something. It was a sheaf of hair, bristly and thick. It was a man's beard.

On the road outside, up and down the street for a hundred yards, merrymaking people turned to look at one another. With an abrupt cessation of laughter, of speech. Inquiringly. Even with an unconscious dilation of the pupils of their eyes.

"What was that?"

There had been a scream. There could be no doubt of that. A single, long-drawn note. Immensely high-pitched. Not as if it were human.

"God's sake! What was that? Where'd it come from?"

Those nearest said it came from the cobblershop of Boaz Negro.

They went and tried the door. It was closed, even locked, as if for the night. There was no light behind the window shade. But Boaz would not have a light. They beat on the door. No answer.

But from where, then, had that prolonged, as if animal, note come?

They ran about, penetrating into the side lanes, interrogating, prying. Coming back at last, inevitably, to the neighborhood of Boaz Negro's shop.

The body lay on the floor at Boaz' feet, where it had tumbled down slowly after a moment from the spasmodic embrace of his arms, those ivory-colored arms which had beaten so long upon the bare iron surface of a last. Blows continuous and powerful. It seemed incredible. They were so weak now. They could not have lifted the hammer now.

But that beard! That bristly, thick, square beard of a stranger!

His hands remembered it. Standing with his shoulders fallén forward and his weak arms hanging down, Boaz began to shiver. The whole thing was incredible. What was on the floor there, upheld in the vast gulf of darkness, he could not see. Neither could he hear it, smell it. Nor (if he did not move his foot) could he feel it. What he did not hear, smell, or touch did not exist. It was not there. Incredible!

But that beard! All the accumulated doubtings of those years fell down upon him. After all, the thing he had been so fearful of in his weak imaginings had happened. He had killed a stranger. He, Boaz Negro, had murdered an innocent man!

And all on account of that beard. His deep panic made him light-headed. He began to confuse cause and effect. If it were not for that beard, it would have been that *cachorra*.

On this basis he began to reason with a crazy directness. And to act. He went and pried open the door into the entry. From a shelf he took down his razor. A big, heavyheeled strop. His hands began to hurry. And the mug, half full of soap. And water. It would have to be cold water. But after all, he thought (light-headedly), at this time of night—

Outside, they were at the shop again. The crowd's habit is to forget a thing quickly, once it is out of sight and hearing. But there had been something about that solitary cry which continued to bother them, even in memory. Where had it been? Where had it come from? And those who stood nearest the cobblershop were heard again. They were certain now, dead certain. They could swear!

In the end they broke down the door.

If Boaz heard them, he gave no sign. An absorption as complete as it was monstrous wrapped him. Kneeling in the glare of the lantern they had brought, as impervious as his own shadow sprawling behind him, he continued to shave the dead man on the floor.

No one touched him. Their minds and imaginations were arrested by the gigantic proportions of the act. The unfathomable presumption of the act. As throwing murder in their faces to the tune of a jig in a

barbershop. It is a fact that none of them so much as thought of touching him. No less than all of them, together with all other men, shorn of their imaginations —that is to say, the expressionless and imperturbable creature of the Law—would be sufficient to touch that ghastly man.

On the other hand, they could not leave him alone. They could not go away. They watched. They saw the damp lather-soaked beard of that victimized stranger falling away, stroke by stroke of the flashing, heavy razor. The dead denuded by the blind!

It was seen that Boaz was about to speak. It was something important he was about to utter; something, one would say, fatal. The words would not come all at once. They swelled his cheeks out. His razor was arrested. Lifting his face, he encircled the watchers with a gaze at once of imploration and of command. As if he could see them. As if he could read his answer in the expressions of their faces.

"Tell me one thing now. Is it that *cachorra?*"

For the first time those men in the room made sounds. They shuffled their feet. It was as if an uncontrollable impulse to ejaculation, laughter, derision, forbidden by the presence of death, had gone down into their boot soles.

"Manuel?" one of them said. "You mean *Manuel?*"

Boaz laid the razor down on the floor beside its work. He got up from his knees slowly, as if his joints hurt. He sat down in his chair, rested his hands on the arms, and once more encircled the company with his sightless gaze.

"Not Manuel. Manuel was a good boy. But tell me now, is it that *cachorra?*"

Here was something out of their calculations; something for them, mentally, to chew on. Mystification is a good thing sometimes. It gives the brain a fillip, stirs memory, puts the gears of imagination in mesh. One man, an old, tobacco-chewing fellow, began to stare harder at the face on the floor. Something moved in his intellect.

"No, but look here now, by God—"

He had even stopped chewing. But he was forestalled by another.

"Say now, if it don't look like that fellow Wood, himself. The bank fellow—that was burned—remember? Himself."

"That *cachorra* was not burned. Not that Wood. You darned fool!"

Boaz spoke from his chair. They hardly knew his voice, emerging from its long silence: it was so didactic and arid.

"That *cachorra* was not burned. It was my boy that was burned. It was that *cachorra* called my boy upstairs. That *cachorra* killed my boy. That *cachorra* put his clothes on my boy, and he set my house on fire. I knew that all the time. Because when I heard those feet come out of my house and go away, I knew they were the feet of that *cachorra* from the bank. I did not know where he was going to. Something said to me —you better ask him where he is going to. But then I said, you are foolish. He had the money from the bank. I did not know. And then my house was on fire. No, it was not my boy that went away; it was that *cachorra* all the time. You darned fools! Did you think I was waiting for my own boy?

"Now I show you all," he said at the end. "And now I can get hanged."

No one ever touched Boaz Negro for that murder. For murder it was in the eye and letter of the Law. The Law in a small town is sometimes a curious creature; it is sometimes blind only in one eye.

Their minds and imaginations in that town were arrested by the romantic proportions of the act. Simply, no one took it up. I believe the man, Wood, was understood to have died of heart failure.

When they asked Boaz why he had not told what he knew as to the identity of that fugitive in the night, he seemed to find it hard to say exactly. How could a man of no education define for them his own but half-defined misgivings about the Law, his sense of oppression, constraint, and awe, of being on the defensive, even, in an abject way, his skepticism? About his wanting, come what might, to "keep clear of the Law"?

He did say this, "You would have laughed at me."

And this, "If I told folks it was Wood went away, then I say he would not dare come back again."

That was the last. Very shortly he began to refuse to talk about the thing at all. The act was completed. Like the creature of fable, it had consumed itself. Out of that old man's consciousness it had departed. Amazingly. Like a dream dreamed out.

Slowly at first, in a makeshift, piece-at-a-time, poor man's way, Boaz commenced to rebuild his house. That "eyesore" vanished.

And slowly at first, like the miracle of a green shoot pressing out from the dead earth, that priceless and unquenchable exuberance of the man was seen returning. Unquenchable, after all.

DISCUSSION

1. In the first paragraph of "Footfalls," the author briefly outlines the action of the story. It begins, he says, in "catastrophe"; it ends in "an act of almost incredible violence"; and it tells how a blind man "can become also deaf and dumb." Now that you have read the whole story, justify Steele's outline by citing the exact events he refers to in each quoted phrase.

2. (a) Describe Boaz' attitude toward Manuel as the story opens. (b) How do the townspeople react to this attitude? (c) Does Boaz ever cease to feel that "Manuel is a good boy"? Explain.

3. When Campbell Wood is introduced into the story, what is Boaz' opinion of him? Why?

4. (a) At the time of the fire, what evidence seemed to point to Manuel's guilt? (b) What secret knowledge did Boaz possess? (c) Why did he withhold it?

5. The emotional impact of "Footfalls" depends upon the reader's accepting Manuel's guilt just as the townspeople do. Explain how the following elements in the story lead you to this conclusion: (a) The author warns the reader in the first paragraph; (b) Boaz hears but does not see the murderer; (c) Wood's personality differs from Manuel's; (d) Boaz' spirit changes; and (e) Boaz uses the word *cachorra*.

6. Now that you have answered the previous question, do you feel the author deceived you or that you deceived yourself? In answering, consider the way the author uses the word *incorruptibility* (page 119, column 1, paragraph 6) when he describes Campbell Wood.

THE AUTHOR'S CRAFT

Characterization

A major task of the short-story writer is to develop the personality of his main character. Boaz Negro comes alive because Steele shows the *traits* of personality that make him act, think, and feel as he does.

Throughout the story, the author *labels* Boaz with the descriptive phrase "unquenchable exuberance." Why is this label an important one in guiding the reader to a sound appreciation of Boaz' character?

Steele also uses *direct comments* to develop a significant trait. He tells us Boaz is diligent: "How he had worked! Not alone in the daytime, but . . . far into the night."

In addition to a label and direct comments, Steele reveals the cobbler through *dialogue* and *action*. For example, what Boaz says— and what others say about him —reveal his devotion to Manuel. Boaz insists that Manuel isn't "too stout" and "is a good boy" while the townspeople criticize Boaz' indulgence: "He should have put him to work." To "hear" these remarks is to understand how Boaz could spend those long years waiting for the *cachorra*. After the fire, Boaz listens for the *cachorra*'s footfalls. What does this reveal about Boaz' character?

A writer may use one or several of these methods to develop a single trait. Explain which method or methods Steele uses to indicate Boaz' distrust of the Law.

A writer seldom develops secondary characters as fully as he does a main character. Compare the extent of the development of Wood and Manuel with that of Boaz Negro.

WORD STUDY

Meanings

Two good ways to discover the meaning of a word are to use: (1) *context clues*—hints which can be found in phrases, sentences, and paragraphs surrounding the unknown word; (2) the Glossary or a dictionary.

Sometimes the context will tell you directly what a word means. On page 122, column 2, paragraph 8, Mr. Steele explains that the word *cachorra* means "a kind of dog." Why, in this case, does the author give the meaning? Note the word *euchre* (page 121, column 1, paragraph 7). By reading the lines that precede and follow this word, you can easily guess that euchre is a card game.

There are times when no hints are given in the context. For instance, if you don't know the meaning of the word *andiron* (page 122, column 1, line 22) you will find little in the context to help you. You learn only that an andiron's leg was probably used as "a blunt instrument of iron" to kill a man and that an andiron serves some purpose in housekeeping.

Determine the meaning of each word below as it is used in "Footfalls." (1) Write the best definition you can by using context clues alone. (2) If there are no context clues, look up the word in the Glossary and write out its definition. If the Glossary offers a choice of definitions, select the one that best fits the context.

weirs	(p. 118, col. 1, par. 3)
duenna	(p. 119, col. 1, par. 7)
perambula-	
tion	(p. 121, col. 1, line 1)
inanimate	(p. 122, col. 2, par. 6)
strop	(p. 127, col. 2, line 3)

LAMB to the SLAUGHTER

Roald Dahl

It was going to be a Thursday night like all the others—first, the drinks, then quiet conversation, then out to dinner. Or so she thought.

THE room was warm and clean, the curtains drawn, the two table lamps alight—hers and the one by the empty chair opposite. On the sideboard behind her, two tall glasses, soda water, whiskey. Fresh ice cubes in the Thermos bucket.

Mary Maloney was waiting for her husband to come home from work.

Now and again she would glance up at the clock, but without anxiety, merely to please herself with the thought that each minute gone by made it nearer the time when he would come. There was a slow smiling air about her, and about everything she did. The drop of the head as she bent over her sewing was curiously tranquil. Her skin—for this was her sixth month with child—had acquired a wonderful translucent quality, the mouth was soft, and the eyes, with their new placid look, seemed larger, darker than before.

When the clock said ten minutes to five, she began to listen, and a few moments later, punctually as always, she heard the tires on the gravel outside, and the car door slamming, the footsteps passing the window, the key turning in the lock. She laid aside her sewing, stood up, and went forward to kiss him as he came in.

"Hullo darling," she said.

"Hullo," he answered.

She took his coat and hung it in the closet. Then she walked over and made the drinks, a strongish one for him, a weak one for herself; and soon she was back again in her chair with the sewing, and he in the other, opposite, holding the tall glass with both his hands, rocking it so the ice cubes tinkled against the side.

For her, this was always a blissful time of day. She knew he didn't want to speak much until the first drink was finished, and she, on her side, was content to sit quietly, enjoying his company after the long hours alone in the house. She loved to luxuriate in the presence of this man, and to feel—almost as a sunbather feels the sun—that warm male glow that came out of him to her when they were alone together. She loved him for the way he sat loosely in a chair, for the way he came in a door, or moved slowly across the room with long strides. She loved the intent, far look in his eyes when they rested on her, the funny shape of the mouth, and especially the way he remained silent about his tiredness, sitting still with himself until the whiskey had taken some of it away.

"Tired darling?"

"Yes," he said. "I'm tired." And as he spoke, he did an unusual thing. He lifted his glass and drained it in one swallow although there was still half of it, at least half of it left. She wasn't really watching him, but she knew what he had done because she heard the ice cubes falling back against the bottom of the empty glass when he lowered his arm. He paused a moment, leaning forward in the chair, then he got up and went slowly over to fetch himself another.

"I'll get it!" she cried, jumping up.

"Sit down," he said.

When he came back, she noticed that the new drink was dark amber with the quantity of whiskey in it.

"Darling, shall I get your slippers?"

"No."

She watched him as he began to sip the dark yellow drink, and she could see little oily swirls in the liquid because it was so strong.

"I think it's a shame," she said, "that when a policeman gets to be as senior as you, they keep him walking about on his feet all day long."

He didn't answer, so she bent her head again and went on with her sewing; but each time he lifted the drink to his lips, she heard the ice cubes clinking against the side of the glass.

"Darling," she said. "Would you like me to get you some cheese? I haven't made any supper because it's Thursday."

"No," he said.

"If you're too tired to eat out," she went on, "it's still not too late. There's plenty of meat and stuff in the freezer, and you can have it right here and not even move out of the chair."

Her eyes waited on him for an answer, a smile, a little nod, but he made no sign.

"Anyway," she went on, "I'll get you some cheese and crackers first."

"I don't want it," he said.

She moved uneasily in her chair, the large eyes still watching his face. "But you *must* have supper. I can easily do it here. I'd like to do it. We can have lamb chops. Or pork. Anything you want. Everything's in the freezer."

"Forget it," he said.

"But darling, you *must* eat! I'll fix it anyway, and then you can have it or not, as you like."

She stood up and placed her sewing on the table by the lamp.

"Sit down," he said. "Just for a minute, sit down."

It wasn't till then that she began to get frightened.

"Go on," he said. "Sit down."

She lowered herself back slowly into the chair, watching him all the time with those large, bewildered eyes. He had finished the second drink and was staring down into the glass, frowning.

"Listen," he said. "I've got something to tell you."

"What is it, darling? What's the matter?"

He had now become absolutely motionless, and he kept his head down so that the light from the lamp beside him fell across the upper part of his face, leaving the chin and mouth in shadow. She noticed there was a little muscle moving near the corner of his left eye.

"This is going to be a bit of a shock to you, I'm afraid," he said. "But I've thought about it a good deal and I've decided the only thing to do is tell you right away. I hope you won't blame me too much."

And he told her. It didn't take long, four or five

minutes at most, and she sat very still through it all, watching him with a kind of dazed horror as he went further and further away from her with each word.

no reason?

suspend judgement?

"So there it is," he added. "And I know it's kind of a bad time to be telling you, but there simply wasn't any other way. Of course I'll give you money and see you're looked after. But there needn't really be any fuss. I hope not anyway. It wouldn't be very good for my job."

Her first instinct was not to believe any of it, to reject it all. It occurred to her that perhaps he hadn't even spoken, that she herself had imagined the whole thing. Maybe, if she went about her business and acted as though she hadn't been listening, then later, when she sort of woke up again, she might find none of it had ever happened.

"I'll get the supper," she managed to whisper, and this time he didn't stop her.

When she walked across the room she couldn't feel her feet touching the floor. She couldn't feel anything at all—except a slight nausea and a desire to vomit. Everything was automatic now—down the steps to the cellar, the light switch, the deep freeze, the hand inside the cabinet taking hold of the first object it met. She lifted it out, and looked at it. It was wrapped in paper, so she took off the paper and looked at it again.

A leg of lamb.

All right then, they would have lamb for supper. She carried it upstairs, holding the thin bone-end of it with both her hands, and as she went through the living-room, she saw him standing over by the window with his back to her, and she stopped.

"For God's sake," he said, hearing her, but not turning round. "Don't make supper for me. I'm going out."

At that point, Mary Maloney simply walked up behind him and without any pause she swung the big frozen leg of lamb high in the air and brought it down as hard as she could on the back of his head.

She might just as well have hit him with a steel club.

She stepped back a pace, waiting, and the funny thing was that he remained standing there for at least four or five seconds, gently swaying. Then he crashed to the carpet.

The violence of the crash, the noise, the small table overturning, helped bring her out of the shock. She came out slowly, feeling cold and surprised,

and she stood for a while blinking at the body, still holding the ridiculous piece of meat tight with both hands.

All right, she told herself. So I've killed him.

It was extraordinary, now, how clear her mind became all of a sudden. She began thinking very fast. As the wife of a detective, she knew quite well what the penalty would be. That was fine. It made no difference to her. In fact, it would be a relief. On the other hand, what about the child? What were the laws about murderers with unborn children? Did they kill them both—mother and child? Or did they wait until the tenth month? What did they do?

Mary Maloney didn't know. And she certainly wasn't prepared to take a chance.

She carried the meat into the kitchen, placed it in a pan, turned the oven on high, and shoved it inside. Then she washed her hands and ran upstairs to the bedroom. She sat down before the mirror, tidied her hair, touched up her lips and face. She tried a smile. It came out rather peculiar. She tried again.

"Hullo Sam," she said brightly, aloud.

The voice sounded peculiar too.

"I want some potatoes please, Sam. Yes, and I think a can of peas."

That was better. Both the smile and the voice were coming out better now. She rehearsed it several times more. Then she ran downstairs, took her coat, went out the back door, down the garden, into the street.

It wasn't six o'clock yet and the lights were still on in the grocery shop.

"Hullo Sam," she said brightly, smiling at the man behind the counter.

"Why, good evening, Mrs. Maloney. How're *you?*"

"I want some potatoes please, Sam. Yes, and I think a can of peas."

The man turned and reached up behind him on the shelf for the peas.

"Patrick's decided he's tired and doesn't want to eat out tonight," she told him. "We usually go out Thursdays, you know, and now he's caught me without any vegetables in the house."

"Then how about meat, Mrs. Maloney?"

"No, I've got meat, thanks. I got a nice leg of lamb from the freezer."

"Oh."

"I don't much like cooking it frozen, Sam, but I'm taking a chance on it this time. You think it'll be all right?"

"Personally," the grocer said, "I don't believe it makes any difference. You want these Idaho potatoes?"

"Oh yes, that'll be fine. Two of those."

"Anything else?" The grocer cocked his head on one side, looking at her pleasantly. "How about afterwards? What you going to give him for afterwards?"

"Well—what would you suggest, Sam?"

The man glanced around his shop. "How about a nice big slice of cheesecake? I know he likes that."

"Perfect," she said. "He loves it."

And when it was all wrapped and she had paid, she put on her brightest smile and said, "Thank you, Sam. Goodnight."

"Goodnight, Mrs. Maloney. And thank *you*."

And now, she told herself as she hurried back, all she was doing now, she was returning home to her husband and he was waiting for his supper; and she must cook it good, and make it as tasty as possible because the poor man was tired, and if, when she entered the house, she happened to find anything unusual, or tragic, or terrible, then naturally it would be a shock and she'd become frantic with grief and horror. Mind you, she wasn't *expecting* to find anything. She was just going home with the vegetables. Mrs. Patrick Maloney going with the vegetables on Thursday evening to cook supper for her husband.

That's the way, she told herself. Do everything right and natural. Keep things absolutely natural and there'll be no need for any acting at all.

Therefore, when she entered the kitchen by the back door, she was humming a little tune to herself and smiling.

"Patrick!" she called. "How are you, darling?"

She put the parcel down on the table and went through into the living room; and when she saw him lying there on the floor with his legs doubled up and one arm twisted back underneath his body, it really was rather a shock. All the old love and longing for him welled up inside her, and she ran over to him, knelt down beside him, and began to cry her heart out. It was easy. No acting was necessary. *[finally realized what she did]*

A few minutes later she got up and went to the phone. She knew the number of the police station, and when the man at the other end answered, she cried to him, "Quick! Come quick! Patrick's dead!"

"Who's speaking?"

"Mrs. Maloney. Mrs. Patrick Maloney."

"You mean Patrick Maloney's dead?"

"I think so," she sobbed. "He's lying on the floor and I think he's dead."

"Be right over," the man said.

The car came very quickly, and when she opened the front door, two policemen walked in. She knew them both—she knew nearly all the men at that precinct—and she fell right into Jack Noonan's arms, weeping hysterically. He put her gently into a chair, then went over to join the other one, who was called O'Malley, kneeling by the body.

"Is he dead?" she cried.

"I'm afraid he is. What happened?"

Briefly, she told her story about going out to the grocer and coming back to find him on the floor. While she was talking, crying and talking, Noonan discovered a small patch of congealed blood on the dead man's head. He showed it to O'Malley who got up at once and hurried to the phone.

Soon, other men began to come into the house. First a doctor, then two detectives, one of whom she knew by name. Later, a police photographer arrived and took pictures, and a man who knew about fingerprints. There was a great deal of whispering and muttering beside the corpse, and the detectives kept asking her a lot of questions. But they always treated her kindly. She told her story again, this time right from the beginning, when Patrick had come in, and she was sewing, and he was tired, so tired he hadn't wanted to go out for supper. She told how she'd put the meat in the oven—"it's there now, cooking"—and how she'd slipped out to the grocer for vegetables, and come back to find him lying on the floor.

"Which grocer?" one of the detectives asked.

She told him, and he turned and whispered something to the other detective who immediately went outside into the street.

In fifteen minutes he was back with a page of notes, and there was more whispering, and through her sobbing she heard a few of the whispered phrases—". . . acted quite normal . . . very cheerful . . . wanted to give him a good supper . . . peas . . . cheesecake . . . impossible that she . . ."

After a while, the photographer and the doctor departed and two other men came in and took the corpse away on a stretcher. Then the fingerprint man went away. The two detectives remained, and so did the two policemen. They were exceptionally nice to her, and Jack Noonan asked if she wouldn't rather go somewhere else, to her sister's house perhaps, or to his own wife who would take care of her and put her up for the night.

No, she said. She didn't feel she could move even a yard at the moment. Would they mind awfully if she stayed just where she was until she felt better. She didn't feel too good at the moment, she really didn't.

Then hadn't she better lie down on the bed? Jack Noonan asked.

No, she said. She'd like to stay right where she was, in this chair. A little later perhaps, when she felt better, she would move.

So they left her there while they went about their business, searching the house. Occasionally one of the detectives asked her another question. Sometimes Jack Noonan spoke to her gently as he passed by. Her husband, he told her, had been killed by a blow on the back of the head administered with a heavy blunt instrument, almost certainly a large piece of metal. They were looking for the weapon. The murderer may have taken it with him, but on the other hand he may've thrown it away or hidden it somewhere on the premises.

"It's the old story," he said. "Get the weapon, and you've got the man."

Later, one of the detectives came up and sat beside her. Did she know, he asked, of anything in the house that could've been used as the weapon? Would she mind having a look around to see if anything was missing—a very big spanner, for example, or a heavy metal vase.

They didn't have any heavy metal vases, she said.

"Or a big spanner?"

She didn't think they had a big spanner. But there might be some things like that in the garage.

The search went on. She knew that there were other policemen in the garden all around the house. She could hear their footsteps on the gravel outside, and sometimes she saw the flash of a torch through a chink in the curtains. It began to get late, nearly nine she noticed by the clock on the mantel. The four men searching the rooms seemed to be growing weary, a trifle exasperated.

"Jack," she said, the next time Sergeant Noonan went by. "Would you mind giving me a drink?"

"Sure I'll give you a drink. You mean this whiskey?"

"Yes please. But just a small one. It might make me feel better."

He handed her the glass.

"Why don't you have one yourself," she said. "You must be awfully tired. Please do. You've been very good to me."

"Well," he answered. "It's not strictly allowed, but I might take just a drop to keep me going."

One by one the others came in and were persuaded to take a little nip of whiskey. They stood around rather awkwardly with the drinks in their hands, uncomfortable in her presence, trying to say consoling things to her. Sergeant Noonan wandered into the kitchen, came out quickly and said, "Look, Mrs. Maloney. You know that oven of yours is still on, and the meat still inside."

"Oh *dear* me!" she cried. "So it is!"

"I better turn it off for you, hadn't I?"

"Will you do that, Jack. Thank you so much."

When the sergeant returned the second time, she looked at him with her large, dark, tearful eyes. "Jack Noonan," she said.

"Yes?"

"Would you do me a small favour—you and these others?"

"We can try, Mrs. Maloney."

"Well," she said. "Here you all are, and good friends of dear Patrick's too, and helping to catch the man who killed him. You must be terrible hungry by now because it's long past your suppertime, and I know Patrick would never forgive me, God bless his soul, if I allowed you to remain in his house without offering you decent hospitality. Why don't you eat up that lamb that's in the oven. It'll be cooked just right by now."

"Wouldn't dream of it," Sergeant Noonan said.

"Please," she begged. "Please eat it. Personally I couldn't touch a thing, certainly not what's been in the house when he was here. But it's all right for you. It'd be a favour to me if you'd eat it up. Then you can go on with your work again afterwards."

There was a good deal of hesitating among the four policemen, but they were clearly hungry, and in the end they were persuaded to go into the kitchen and help themselves. The woman stayed where she was, listening to them through the open door, and she could hear them speaking among themselves, their voices thick and sloppy because their mouths were full of meat.

"Have some more, Charlie?"

"No. Better not finish it."

"She *wants* us to finish it. She said so. Be doing her a favour."

"Okay then. Give me some more."

"That's the hell of a big club the guy must've used to hit poor Patrick," one of them was saying. "The doc says his skull was smashed all to pieces just like from a sledgehammer."

"That's why it ought to be easy to find."

"Exactly what I say."

"Whoever done it, they're not going to be carrying a thing like that around with them longer than they need."

One of them belched.

"Personally, I think it's right here on the premises."

"Probably right under our very noses. What you think, Jack?"

And in the other room Mary Maloney began to giggle.

DISCUSSION

1. (a) What evidence is there early in the story that Mary Maloney loved her husband? (b) What motivates her to kill her spouse? (c) Was the slaying premeditated or spontaneous? Explain.

2. For what reason does she wish to cover up her crime?

3. Cite the evidence that indicates that Mary carefully planned her alibi.

4. Would this story have been strengthened or weakened (a) if Patrick Maloney had been a banker rather than a policeman? (b) if the author had told the reader what Patrick told Mary? (c) if the last line of the story had been eliminated?

5. (a) Before one has read the story, what meaning has the title? (b) After one has finished the story, what additional meaning does the title have? (c) Are both meanings appropriate to the story? Explain.

AUTHOR

ROALD DAHL is a Welshman born in Llandaff, South Wales, in 1916. The first part of Dahl's career was with Shell Oil in British East Africa from 1932–1939. After Hitler's invasion of Poland in 1939, Dahl joined the Royal Air Force, where he served six years.

A collection of short stories, *Someone Like You* (1953), plus regular appearances in The *New Yorker*, acquainted United States readers with him. *Kiss, Kiss* (1960) was another impressive story anthology that added to his reputation.

Dahl married the actress Patricia Neal in 1953 and they presently live in England with their four children. Dahl is also author of several books for children, including the original story for the film *Willie Wonka and the Chocolate Factory*.

MYSTERY

The Monkey's Paw

W. W. Jacobs

WITHOUT, the night was cold and wet, but in the small parlor of Lakesnam Villa the blinds were drawn and the fire burned brightly. Father and son were at chess, the former, who possessed ideas about the game involving radical changes, putting his king into such sharp and unnecessary perils that it even provoked comment from the white-haired old lady knitting placidly by the fire.

"Hark at the wind," said Mr. White, who, having seen a fatal mistake after it was too late, was amiably desirous of preventing his son from seeing it.

"I'm listening," said the latter, grimly surveying the board as he stretched out his hand. "Check."[1]

"I should hardly think that he'd come tonight," said his father, with his hand poised over the board.

"Mate," replied the son.

"That's the worst of living so far out," bawled Mr. White, with sudden and unlooked-for violence; "of all the beastly, slushy, out-of-the-way places to live in, this is the worst. Pathway's a bog, and the road's a torrent. I don't know what people are thinking about. I suppose because only two houses on the road are let, they think it doesn't matter."

"Never mind, dear," said his wife soothingly; "perhaps you'll win the next one."

Mr. White looked up sharply, just in time to intercept a knowing glance between mother and son. The words died away on his lips, and he had a guilty grin in his thin gray beard.

"There he is," said Herbert White, as the gate banged to loudly and heavy footsteps came toward the door.

The old man rose with hospitable haste, and opening the door, was heard condoling with the new arrival. The new arrival also condoled with himself, so that Mrs. White said "Tut, tut!" and coughed gently as her husband entered the room, followed by a tall burly man, beady of eye and rubicund of visage.

"Sergeant-Major Morris," he said, introducing him.

The sergeant-major shook hands, and, taking the proffered seat by the fire, watched contentedly while his host got out whiskey and tumblers and stood a small copper kettle on the fire.

At the third glass his eyes got brighter, and he began to talk, the little family circle regarding with eager interest this visitor from distant parts, as he squared his broad shoulders in the chair and spoke of strange scenes and doughty deeds, of wars and plagues and strange peoples.

"Twenty-one years of it," said Mr. White, nodding at his wife and son. "When he went away he was a slip of a youth in the warehouse. Now look at him."

"He don't look to have taken much harm," said Mrs. White politely.

"I'd like to go to India myself," said the old man, "just to look round a bit, you know."

From THE LADY OF THE BARGE by W. W. Jacobs. Reprinted by permission of Dodd, Mead & Company, Inc., and The Society of Authors as literary representative of the Estate of W. W. Jacobs.

1. "*Check*," a call made by a chess player to warn his opponent that the opponent's king piece is in danger and must be moved. When a chess player makes the winning move that will capture his opponent's king, he calls "Mate."

"Better where you are," said the sergeant-major, shaking his head. He put down the empty glass and, sighing softly, shook it again.

"I should like to see those old temples and fakirs and jugglers," said the old man. "What was that you started telling me the other day about a monkey's paw or something, Morris?"

"Nothing," said the soldier hastily. "Leastways, nothing worth hearing."

"Monkey's paw?" said Mrs. White curiously.

"Well, it's just a bit of what you might call magic, perhaps," said the sergeant-major offhandedly.

His three listeners leaned forward eagerly. The visitor absent-mindedly put his empty glass to his lips and then set it down again. His host filled it for him.

"To look at," said the sergeant-major, fumbling in his pocket, "it's just an ordinary little paw, dried to a mummy."

He took something out of his pocket and proffered it. Mrs. White drew back with a grimace, but her son, taking it, examined it curiously.

"And what is there special about it?" inquired Mr. White, as he took it from his son and, having examined it, placed it upon the table.

"It had a spell put on it by an old fakir," said the sergeant-major, "a very holy man. He wanted to show that fate ruled people's lives, and that those who interfered with it did so to their sorrow. He put a spell on it so that three separate men could each have three wishes from it."

His manner was so impressive that his hearers were conscious that their light laughter jarred somewhat.

"Well, why don't you have three, sir?" said Herbert White cleverly.

The soldier regarded him in the way that middle age is wont to regard presumptuous youth. "I have," he said quietly, and his blotchy face whitened.

"And did you really have the three wishes granted?" asked Mrs. White.

"I did," said the sergeant-major, and his glass tapped against his strong teeth.

"And has anybody else wished?" inquired the old lady.

"The first man had his three wishes, yes," was the reply. "I don't know what the first two were, but the third was for death. That's how I got the paw."

His tones were so grave that a hush fell upon the group.

"If you've had your three wishes, it's no good to you now, then, Morris," said the old man at last. "What do you keep it for?"

The soldier shook his head. "Fancy, I suppose," he said slowly. "I did have some idea of selling it, but I don't think I will. It has caused enough mischief already. Besides, people won't buy. They think it's a fairy tale, some of them, and those who do think anything of it want to try it first and pay me afterward."

"If you could have another three wishes," said the old man, eyeing him keenly, "would you have them?"

"I don't know," said the other. "I don't know."

He took the paw, and dangling it between his front finger and thumb, suddenly threw it upon the fire. White, with a slight cry, stooped down and snatched it off.

"Better let it burn," said the soldier solemnly.

"If you don't want it, Morris," said the old man, "give it to me."

"I won't," said his friend doggedly. "I threw it on the fire. If you keep it, don't blame me for what happens. Pitch it on the fire again, like a sensible man."

The other shook his head and examined his new possession closely. "How do you do it?" he inquired.

"Hold it up in your right hand and wish aloud," said the sergeant-major, "but I warn you of the consequences."

"Sounds like the *Arabian Nights*,"[2] said Mrs. White, as she rose and began to set the supper. "Don't you think you might wish for four pairs of hands for me?"

Her husband drew the talisman from his pocket and then all three burst into laughter as the sergeant-major, with a look of alarm on his face, caught him by the arm.

"If you must wish," he said gruffly, "wish for something sensible."

Mr. White dropped it back into his pocket, and placing chairs, motioned his friend to the table. In the business of supper the talisman was partly forgotten, and afterward the three sat listening in an enthralled fashion to a second installment of the soldier's adventures in India.

"If the tale about the monkey's paw is not more truthful than those he has been telling us," said Herbert, as the door closed behind their guest, just in

---

2. the "*Arabian Nights*," a collection of old tales from Arabia, Persia, and India, dating from the tenth century. Scheherazade (shə her′ ə zä′də) is said to have related these tales nightly to the Sultan of the Indies in order to save her life.

time for him to catch the last train, "we shan't make much out of it."

"Did you give him anything for it, Father?" inquired Mrs. White, regarding her husband closely.

"A trifle," said he, coloring slightly. "He didn't want it, but I made him take it. And he pressed me again to throw it away."

"Likely," said Herbert, with pretended horror. "Why, we're going to be rich, and famous, and happy. Wish to be an emperor, Father, to begin with; then you can't be henpecked."

He darted round the table, pursued by the maligned Mrs. White armed with an antimacassar.

Mr. White took the paw from his pocket and eyed it dubiously. "I don't know what to wish for, and that's a fact," he said slowly. "It seems to me I've got all I want."

"If you only cleared the house,[3] you'd be quite happy, wouldn't you?" said Herbert, with his hand on his shoulder. "Well, wish for two hundred pounds,[4] then; that'll just do it."

His father, smiling shamefacedly at his own credulity, held up the talisman, as his son, with a solemn face somewhat marred by a wink at his mother, sat down at the piano and struck a few impressive chords.

"I wish for two hundred pounds," said the old man distinctly.

A fine crash from the piano greeted the words, interrupted by a shuddering cry from the old man. His wife and son ran toward him.

"It moved," he cried, with a glance of disgust at the object as it lay on the floor. "As I wished it twisted in my hands like a snake."

"Well, I don't see the money," said his son, as he picked it up and placed it on the table, "and I bet I never shall."

"It must have been your fancy, Father," said his wife, regarding him anxiously.

He shook his head. "Never mind, though; there's no harm done, but it gave me a shock all the same."

They sat down by the fire again while the two men finished their pipes. Outside, the wind was higher than ever, and the old man started nervously at the sound of a door banging upstairs. A silence unusual and depressing settled upon all three, which lasted until the old couple rose to retire for the night.

---

3. *cleared the house,* paid the money that was still owing on the purchase of the house.
4. *two hundred pounds.* At the time of the story, this amount in English money was worth about a thousand dollars.

"I expect you'll find the cash tied up in a big bag in the middle of your bed," said Herbert, as he bade them good night, "and something horrible squatting up on top of the wardrobe watching you as you pocket your ill-gotten gains."

In the brightness of the wintry sun next morning as it streamed over the breakfast table Herbert laughed at his fears. There was an air of prosaic wholesomeness about the room which it had lacked on the previous night, and the dirty, shriveled little paw was pitched on the sideboard with a carelessness which betokened no great belief in its virtues.

"I suppose all old soldiers are the same," said Mrs. White. "The idea of our listening to such nonsense! How could wishes be granted in these days? And if they could, how could two hundred pounds hurt you, Father?"

"Might drop on his head from the sky," said the frivolous Herbert.

"Morris said the things happened so naturally," said his father, "that you might if you so wished attribute it to coincidence."

"Well, don't break into the money before I come back," said Herbert, as he rose from the table. "I'm afraid it'll turn you into a mean, avaricious man, and we shall have to disown you."

His mother laughed, and following him to the door, watched him down the road, and returning to the breakfast table, was very happy at the expense of her husband's credulity. All of which did not prevent her from scurrying to the door at the postman's knock, nor prevent her from referring somewhat shortly to retired sergeant-majors of bibulous habits when she found that the post brought a tailor's bill.

"Herbert will have some more of his funny remarks, I expect, when he comes home," she said as they sat at dinner.

"I dare say," said Mr. White, pouring himself out some beer; "but for all that, the thing moved in my hand; that I'll swear to."

"You thought it did," said the old lady soothingly.

"I say it did," replied the other. "There was no thought about it; I had just—What's the matter?"

His wife made no reply. She was watching the mysterious movements of a man outside, who, peering in an undecided fashion at the house, appeared to be trying to make up his mind to enter. In mental connection with the two hundred pounds, she noticed that the stranger was well dressed and wore a silk hat of glossy newness. Three times he paused at the gate and then walked on again. The fourth time he stood with his hand upon it, and then with sudden resolution flung it open and walked up the path. Mrs. White at the same moment placed her hands behind her and hurriedly unfastening the strings of her apron, put that useful article of apparel beneath the cushion of her chair.

She brought the stranger, who seemed ill at ease, into the room. He gazed furtively at Mrs. White, and listened in a preoccupied fashion as the old lady apologized for the appearance of the room, and her husband's coat, a garment which he usually reserved for the garden. She then waited as patiently as her sex would permit for him to broach his business, but he was at first strangely silent.

"I—was asked to call," he said at last, and stooped and picked a piece of cotton from his trousers. "I come from Maw and Meggins."

The old lady started. "Is anything the matter?" she asked breathlessly. "Has anything happened to Herbert? What is it? What is it?"

Her husband interposed. "There, there, Mother," he said hastily. "Sit down, and don't jump to conclusions. You've not brought bad news, I'm sure, sir," and he eyed the other wistfully.

"I'm sorry—" began the visitor.

"Is he hurt?" demanded the mother.

The visitor bowed in assent. "Badly hurt," he said quietly, "but he is not in any pain."

"Oh, thank God!" said the old woman, clasping her hands. "Thank God for that! Thank—"

She broke off suddenly as the sinister meaning of the assurance dawned upon her and she saw the awful confirmation of her fears in the other's averted face. She caught her breath, and turning to her slower-witted husband, laid her trembling old hand upon his. There was a long silence.

"He was caught in the machinery," said the visitor at length, in a low voice.

"Caught in the machinery," repeated Mr. White, in a dazed fashion, "yes."

He sat staring blankly out of the window, and taking his wife's hand between his own, pressed it as he had been wont to do in their old courting days nearly forty years before.

"He was the only one left to us," he said, turning gently to the visitor. "It is hard."

The other coughed, and rising, walked slowly to the window. "The firm wished me to convey their sincere sympathy with you in your great loss," he said, without looking round. "I beg that you will understand I am only their servant and merely obeying orders."

There was no reply; the old woman's face was white, her eyes staring, and her breath inaudible; on the husband's face was a look such as his friend the sergeant might have carried into his first action.

"I was to say that Maw and Meggins disclaim all responsibility," continued the other. "They admit no liability at all, but in consideration of your son's services they wish to present you with a certain sum as compensation."

Mr. White dropped his wife's hand, and rising to his feet, gazed with a look of horror at his visitor. His dry lips shaped the words, "How much?"

"Two hundred pounds," was the answer.

Unconscious of his wife's shriek, the old man smiled faintly, put out his hands like a sightless man, and dropped, a senseless heap, to the floor.

In the huge new cemetery, some two miles distant, the old people buried their dead, and came back to a house steeped in shadow and silence. It was all over so quickly that at first they could hardly realize it and remained in a state of expectation as though of something else to happen—something else which was to lighten this load, too heavy for old hearts to bear. But the days passed, and expectation gave place to resignation—the hopeless resignation of the old, sometimes miscalled apathy. Sometimes they hardly exchanged a word, for now they had nothing to talk about, and their days were long to weariness.

It was about a week after that that the old man, waking suddenly in the night, stretched out his hand and found himself alone. The room was in darkness, and the sound of subdued weeping came from the window. He raised himself in bed and listened.

"Come back," he said tenderly. "You will be cold."

"It is colder for my son," said the old woman and wept afresh.

The sound of her sobs died away on his ears. The bed was warm, and his eyes heavy with sleep. He dozed fitfully, and then slept until a sudden wild cry from his wife awoke him with a start.

"The monkey's paw!" she cried wildly. "The monkey's paw!"

He started up in alarm. "Where? Where is it? What's the matter?"

She came stumbling across the room toward him. "I want it," she said quietly. "You've not destroyed it?"

"It's in the parlor, on the bracket," he replied, marveling. "Why?"

She cried and laughed together, and bending over, kissed his cheek.

"I only just thought of it," she said hysterically. "Why didn't I think of it before? Why didn't you think of it?"

"Think of what?" he questioned.

"The other two wishes," she replied rapidly. "We've only had one."

"Was not that enough?" he demanded fiercely.

"No," she cried triumphantly; "we'll have one more. Go down and get it quickly, and wish our boy alive again."

The man sat up in bed and flung the bedclothes from his quaking limbs. "Good God, you are mad!" he cried, aghast.

"Get it," she panted; "get it quickly, and wish— Oh, my boy, my boy!"

Her husband struck a match and lit the candle. "Get back to bed," he said unsteadily. "You don't know what you are saying."

"We had the first wish granted," said the old woman feverishly; "why not the second?"

"A coincidence," stammered the old man.

"Go and get it and wish," cried the old woman, and dragged him toward the door.

He went down in the darkness, and felt his way to the parlor, and then to the mantelpiece. The talisman was in its place, and a horrible fear that the unspoken wish might bring his mutilated son before him ere he could escape from the room seized upon him, and he caught his breath as he found that he had lost the direction of the door. His brow cold with sweat, he felt his way round the table, and groped along the wall until he found himself in the small passage with the unwholesome thing in his hand.

Even his wife's face seemed changed as he entered the room. It was white and expectant, and to his fears seemed to have an unnatural look upon it. He was afraid of her.

"Wish!" she cried, in a strong voice.

"It is foolish and wicked," he faltered.

"Wish!" repeated his wife.

He raised his hand. "I wish my son alive again."

The talisman fell to the floor, and he regarded it shudderingly. Then he sank trembling into a chair as

the old woman, with burning eyes, walked to the window and raised the blind.

He sat until he was chilled with the cold, glancing occasionally at the figure of the old woman peering through the window. The candle end, which had burnt below the rim of the china candlestick, was throwing pulsating shadows on the ceiling and walls, until, with a flicker larger than the rest, it expired. The old man, with an unspeakable sense of relief at the failure of the talisman, crept back to his bed, and a minute or two afterward the old woman came silently and apathetically beside him.

Neither spoke, but both lay silently listening to the ticking of the clock. A stair creaked, and a squeaky mouse scurried noisily through the wall. The darkness was oppressive, and after lying for some time screwing up his courage, the husband took the box of matches and striking one went downstairs for a candle.

At the foot of the stairs the match went out, and he paused to strike another, and at the same moment a knock, so quiet and stealthy as to be scarcely audible, sounded on the front door.

The matches fell from his hand. He stood motionless, his breath suspended until the knock was repeated. Then he turned and fled swiftly back to his room and closed the door behind him. A third knock sounded through the house.

"What's that?" cried the old woman, starting up.

"A rat," said the old man, in shaking tones—"a rat. It passed me on the stairs."

His wife sat up in bed listening. A loud knock resounded through the house.

"It's Herbert!" she screamed. "It's Herbert!"

She ran to the door, but her husband was before her, and catching her by the arm, held her tightly.

"What are you going to do?" he whispered hoarsely.

"It's my boy; it's Herbert!" she cried, struggling mechanically. "I forgot it was two miles away. What are you holding me for? Let go. I must open the door."

"For God's sake don't let it in," cried the old man, trembling.

"You're afraid of your own son," she cried, struggling. "Let me go. I'm coming, Herbert; I'm coming."

There was another knock, and another. The old woman with a sudden wrench broke free and ran from the room. Her husband followed to the landing, and called after her appealingly as she hurried downstairs. He heard the chain rattle back and the bottom bolt drawn slowly and stiffly from the socket. Then the old woman's voice, strained and panting.

"The bolt," she cried loudly. "Come down. I can't reach it."

But her husband was on his hands and knees groping wildly on the floor in search of the paw. If he could only find it before the thing outside got in. A perfect fusillade of knocks reverberated through the house, and he heard the scraping of a chair as his wife put it down in the passage against the door. He heard the creaking of the bolt as it came slowly back, and at the same moment he found the monkey's paw and frantically breathed his third and last wish.

The knocking ceased suddenly, although the echoes of it were still in the house. He heard the chair drawn back and the door opened. A cold wind rushed up the staircase, and a long loud wail of disappointment and misery from his wife gave him courage to run down to her side, and then to the gate beyond. The street lamp flickering opposite shone on a quiet and deserted road.

DISCUSSION

1. (a) Contrast the scene outside the Whites' home with the scene within the living room as the Whites await the sergeant-major's arrival. (b) What does the author intend your attitude toward the White family to be?

2. (a) According to the sergeant-major, why did the fakir put a spell on the monkey's paw? (b) Do you agree with the fakir's belief? Why or why not?

3. The fact that "The Monkey's Paw" will end tragically is foreshadowed in several ways. Cite specific instances of foreshadowing that occur during the evening of the sergeant-major's visit.

4. (a) What seems to be the Whites' basic purpose in wanting to make a wish on the paw? (b) Does the making of the first wish change anyone's attitude toward the paw? Explain your answer.

5. (a) What is Mr. White's third wish? (b) Why does he make this third wish? (c) Can you think of a third wish which might have ended the story happily? (d) Why doesn't the author have Mr. White make such a wish?

THE AUTHOR'S CRAFT

Single effect
Many writers and critics have felt that the short story should produce only one dominant effect on the reader—it might amuse him, or shock him, or perhaps make him sad. In a horror story like "The Monkey's Paw," it is particularly important that each detail of the setting, each character trait, and each incident contribute to the author's chosen effect. Let's examine some of the elements in "The Monkey's Paw" that create its single effect of horror.

The action of the story takes place in the White home. How do the following details of the setting contribute to your sense of horror: (1) the isolation of the house; (2) the piano; and (3) the flickering candle in the final scene?

You will also notice that Mr. Jacobs develops only those traits of his characters that will contribute to his single effect. Which characters are shown to be superstitious? Why is it important that this trait be emphasized?

State one factor in the opening scene which contributes to the feeling of horror directly. Cite one factor that contributes to the sense of horror through contrast. Explain what is, to you, the most horrifying event in the story.

AUTHOR

W. W. JACOBS (1863–1943) was born in Wapping, near Tower Bridge, in the ship-docking section of London. There his father was employed as a wharfman, and there Jacobs gathered the raw material for many of his later stories. Educated privately, Jacobs accepted a Civil Service appointment in 1883 and during the next sixteen years served in a department of the General Post Office. In 1896, he published his first book, *Many Cargoes*, which was followed by numerous one-act plays, novels, and short stories. The influence of Jacobs' early life around the docks of London is reflected in many of his book titles, such as *Light Freights*, *Night Watches*, and *Deep Waters*, and in the plots of a number of his short stories.

SURVIVAL

The Lottery

Shirley Jackson

THE morning of June 27th was clear and sunny, with the fresh warmth of a full-summer day; the flowers were blossoming profusely and the grass was richly green. The people of the village began to gather in the square, between the post office and the bank, around ten o'clock; in some towns there were so many people that the lottery took two days and had to be started on June 26th, but in this village, where there were only about three hundred people, the whole lottery took less than two hours, so it could begin at ten o'clock in the morning and still be through in time to allow the villagers to get home for noon dinner.

The children assembled first, of course. School was recently over for the summer, and the feeling of liberty sat uneasily on most of them; they tended to gather together quietly for a while before they broke into boisterous play, and their talk was still of the classroom and the teacher, of books and reprimands. Bobby Martin had already stuffed his pockets full of stones, and the other boys soon followed his example, selecting the smoothest and roundest stones; Bobby and Harry Jones and Dickie Delacroix—the villagers pronounced this name "Dellacroy"—eventually made a great pile of stones in one corner of the square and guarded it against the raids of the other boys. The girls stood aside, talking among themselves, looking over their shoulders at the boys, and the very small children rolled in the dust or clung to the hands of their older brothers or sisters.

Reprinted with the permission of Farrar, Straus & Giroux, Inc. and Brandt & Brandt from THE LOTTERY by Shirley Jackson, copyright 1948, 1949 by Shirley Jackson.

Soon the men began to gather, surveying their own children, speaking of planting and rain, tractors and taxes. They stood together, away from the pile of stones in the corner, and their jokes were quiet and they smiled rather than laughed. The women, wearing faded house dresses and sweaters, came shortly after their menfolk. They greeted one another and exchanged bits of gossip as they went to join their husbands. Soon the women, standing by their husbands, began to call to their children, and the children came reluctantly, having to be called four or five times. Bobby Martin ducked under his mother's grasping hand and ran, laughing, back to the pile of stones. His father spoke up sharply, and Bobby came quickly and took his place between his father and his oldest brother.

The lottery was conducted—as were the square dances, the teen-age club, the Halloween program— by Mr. Summers, who had time and energy to devote to civic activities. He was a round-faced, jovial man and he ran the coal business, and people were sorry for him, because he had no children and his wife was a scold. When he arrived in the square, carrying the black wooden box, there was a murmur of conversation among the villagers, and he waved and called, "Little late today, folks." The postmaster, Mr. Graves, followed him, carrying a three-legged stool, and the stool was put in the center of the square and Mr. Summers set the black box down on it. The villagers kept their distance, leaving a space between themselves and the stool, and when Mr. Summers said, "Some of you fellows want to give me a hand?" there was a hesitation before two men, Mr. Martin and his oldest son, Baxter, came forward to hold the box steady on the stool while Mr. Summers stirred up the papers inside it.

The original paraphernalia for the lottery had been lost long ago, and the black box now resting on the stool had been put into use even before Old Man Warner, the oldest man in town, was born. Mr. Summers spoke frequently to the villagers about making a new box, but no one liked to upset even as much tradition as was represented by the black box. There was a story that the present box had been made with some pieces of the box that had preceded it, the one that had been constructed when the first people settled down to make a village here. Every year, after the lottery, Mr. Summers began talking again about a new box, but every year the subject was allowed to fade off without anything's being done. The black box grew shabbier each year; by now it was no longer completely black but splintered badly along one side to show the original wood color, and in some places faded or stained.

Mr. Martin and his oldest son, Baxter, held the black box securely on the stool until Mr. Summers had stirred the papers thoroughly with his hand. Because so much of the ritual had been forgotten or discarded, Mr. Summers had been successful in having slips of paper substituted for the chips of wood that had been used for generations. Chips of wood, Mr. Summers had argued, had been all very well when the village was tiny, but now that the population was more than three hundred and likely to keep on growing, it was necessary to use something that would fit more easily into the black box. The night before the lottery, Mr. Summers and Mr. Graves made up the slips of paper and put them in the box and it was then taken to the safe of Mr. Summers' coal company and locked up until Mr. Summers was ready to take it to the square next morning. The rest of the year, the box was put away, sometimes one place, sometimes another; it had spent one year in Mr. Graves' barn and another year underfoot in the post office, and sometimes it was set on a shelf in the Martin grocery and left there.

There was a great deal of fussing to be done before Mr. Summers declared the lottery open. There were the lists to make up—of heads of families, heads of households in each family, members of each household in each family. There was the proper swearing-in of Mr. Summers by the postmaster, as the official of the lottery; at one time, some people remembered, there had been a recital of some sort, performed by the official of the lottery, a perfunctory, tuneless chant that had been rattled off duly each year; some people believed that the official of the lottery used to stand just so when he said or sang it, others believed that he was supposed to walk among the people, but years and years ago this part of the ritual had been allowed to lapse. There had been, also, a ritual salute, which the official of the lottery had had to use in addressing each person who came up to draw from the box, but this also had changed with time, until now it was felt necessary only for the official to speak to each person approaching. Mr. Summers was very good at all this; in his clean white shirt and blue jeans, with one hand resting carelessly on the black box, he seemed very proper and important as he talked interminably to Mr. Graves and the Martins.

Just as Mr. Summers finally left off talking and turned to the assembled villagers, Mrs. Hutchinson came hurriedly along the path to the square, her sweater thrown over her shoulders, and slid into place in the back of the crowd. "Clean forgot what day it was," she said to Mrs. Delacroix, who stood next to her, and they both laughed softly. "Thought my old man was out back stacking wood," Mrs. Hutchinson went on, "and then I looked out the window and the kids were gone, and then I remembered it was the twenty-seventh and came a-running." She dried her hands on her apron, and Mrs. Delacroix said, "You're in time, though. They're still talking away up there."

Mrs. Hutchinson craned her neck to see through the crowd and found her husband and children standing near the front. She tapped Mrs. Delacroix on the arm as a farewell and began to make her way through the crowd. The people separated good-humoredly to let her through; two or three people said, in voices just loud enough to be heard across the crowd, "Here comes your Missus, Hutchinson," and "Bill, she made it after all." Mrs. Hutchinson reached her husband, and Mr. Summers, who had been waiting, said cheerfully, "Thought we were going to have to get on without you, Tessie." Mrs. Hutchinson said, grinning, "Wouldn't have me leave m'dishes in the sink, now, would you, Joe?" and soft laughter ran through the crowd as the people stirred back into position after Mrs. Hutchinson's arrival.

"Well, now," Mr. Summers said soberly, "guess we better get started, get this over with, so's we can go back to work. Anybody ain't here?"

"Dunbar," several people said. "Dunbar, Dunbar."

Mr. Summers consulted his list. "Clyde Dunbar," he said. "That's right. He's broke his leg, hasn't he? Who's drawing for him?"

"Me, I guess," a woman said, and Mr. Summers turned to look at her. "Wife draws for her husband," Mr. Summers said. "Don't you have a grown boy to do it for you, Janey?" Although Mr. Summers and everyone else in the village knew the answer perfectly well, it was the business of the official of the lottery to ask such questions formally. Mr. Summers waited with an expression of polite interest while Mrs. Dunbar answered.

"Horace's not but sixteen yet," Mrs. Dunbar said regretfully. "Guess I gotta fill in for the old man this year."

"Right," Mr. Summers said. He made a note on the list he was holding. Then he asked, "Watson boy drawing this year?"

A tall boy in the crowd raised his hand. "Here," he said. "I'm drawing for m' mother and me." He blinked his eyes nervously and ducked his head as several voices in the crowd said things like "Good fellow, Jack," and "Glad to see your mother's got a man to do it."

"Well," Mr. Summers said, "guess that's everyone. Old Man Warner make it?"

"Here," a voice said, and Mr. Summers nodded.

A sudden hush fell on the crowd as Mr. Summers cleared his throat and looked at the list. "All ready?" he called. "Now, I'll read the names—heads of families first—and the men come up and take a paper out of the box. Keep the paper folded in your hand without looking at it until everyone has had a turn. Everything clear?"

The people had done it so many times that they only half listened to the directions; most of them were quiet, wetting their lips, not looking around. Then Mr. Summers raised one hand high and said, "Adams." A man disengaged himself from the crowd and came forward. "Hi, Steve," Mr. Summers said, and Mr. Adams said, "Hi, Joe." They grinned at one another humorlessly and nervously. Then Mr. Adams reached into the black box and took out a folded paper. He held it firmly by one corner as he turned and went hastily back to his place in the crowd, where he stood a little apart from his family, not looking down at his hand.

"Allen," Mr. Summers said. "Andrews. . . . Bentham."

"Seems like there's no time at all between lotteries any more," Mrs. Delacroix said to Mrs. Graves in the back row. "Seems like we got through with the last one only last week."

"Time sure goes fast," Mrs. Graves said.

"Clark. . . . Delacroix."

"There goes my old man," Mrs. Delacroix said. She held her breath while her husband went forward.

"Dunbar," Mr. Summers said, and Mrs. Dunbar went steadily to the box while one of the women said, "Go on, Janey," and another said, "There she goes."

"We're next," Mrs. Graves said. She watched while Mr. Graves came around from the side of the box, greeted Mr. Summers gravely, and selected a slip of paper from the box. By now, all through the crowd there were men holding the small folded papers in their large hands, turning them over and over nervously. Mrs. Dunbar and her two sons stood together, Mrs. Dunbar holding the slip of paper.

"Harburt. . . . Hutchinson."

"Get up there, Bill," Mrs. Hutchinson said, and the people near her laughed.

"Jones."

"They do say," Mr. Adams said to Old Man Warner, who stood next to him, "that over in the north village they're talking of giving up the lottery."

Old Man Warner snorted. "Pack of crazy fools," he said. "Listening to the young folks, nothing's good enough for *them*. Next thing you know, they'll be wanting to go back to living in caves, nobody work any more, live *that* way for a while. Used to be a saying about 'Lottery in June, corn be heavy soon.' First thing you know, we'd all be eating stewed chickweed and acorns. There's *always* been a lottery," he added petulantly. "Bad enough to see young Joe Summers up there joking with everybody."

"Some places have already quit lotteries," Mrs. Adams said.

"Nothing but trouble in *that*," Old Man Warner said stoutly. "Pack of young fools."

"Martin." And Bobby Martin watched his father go forward. "Overdyke. . . . Percy."

"I wish they'd hurry," Mrs. Dunbar said to her older son. "I wish they'd hurry."

"They're almost through," her son said.

"You get ready to run tell Dad," Mrs. Dunbar said.

Mr. Summers called his own name and then stepped forward precisely and selected a slip from the box. Then he called, "Warner."

"Seventy-seventh year I been in the lottery," Old Man Warner said as he went through the crowd. "Seventy-seventh time."

"Watson." The tall boy came awkwardly through the crowd. Someone said, "Don't be nervous, Jack," and Mr. Summers said, "Take your time, son."

"Zanini."

After that, there was a long pause, a breathless pause, until Mr. Summers, holding his slip of paper in the air, said, "All right, fellows." For a minute, no one moved, and then all the slips of paper were opened. Suddenly, all the women began to speak at once, saying, "Who is it?" "Who's got it?" "Is it the Dunbars?" "Is it the Watsons?" Then the voices began to say, "It's Hutchinson. It's Bill." "Bill Hutchinson's got it."

"Go tell your father," Mrs. Dunbar said to her older son.

People began to look around to see the Hutchinsons. Bill Hutchinson was standing quiet, staring down at the paper in his hand. Suddenly, Tessie Hutchinson shouted to Mr. Summers, "You didn't give him time enough to take any paper he wanted. I saw you. It wasn't fair."

"Be a good sport, Tessie," Mrs. Delacroix called, and Mrs. Graves said, "All of us took the same chance."

"Shut up, Tessie," Bill Hutchinson said.

"Well, everyone," Mr. Summers said, "that was done pretty fast, and now we've got to be hurrying a little more to get done in time." He consulted his next list. "Bill," he said, "you draw for the Hutchinson family. You got any other households in the Hutchinsons?"

"There's Don and Eva," Mrs. Hutchinson yelled. "Make *them* take their chance!"

"Daughters draw with their husbands' families, Tessie," Mr. Summers said gently. "You know that as well as anyone else."

"It wasn't *fair*," Tessie said.

"I guess not, Joe," Bill Hutchinson said regretfully. "My daughter draws with her husband's family, that's only fair. And I've got no other family except the kids."

"Then, as far as drawing for families is concerned, it's you," Mr. Summers said in explanation, "and as far as drawing for households is concerned, that's you, too. Right?"

"Right," Bill Hutchinson said.

"How many kids, Bill?" Mr. Summers asked formally.

"Three," Bill Hutchinson said. "There's Bill, Jr., and Nancy, and little Dave. And Tessie and me."

"All right, then," Mr. Summers said. "Harry, you got their tickets back?"

Mr. Graves nodded and held up the slips of paper. "Put them in the box, then," Mr. Summers directed. "Take Bill's and put it in."

"I think we ought to start over," Mrs. Hutchinson said, as quietly as she could. "I tell you it wasn't *fair*. You didn't give him time enough to choose. *Everybody* saw that."

Mr. Graves had selected the five slips and put them in the box, and he dropped all the papers but those onto the ground, where the breeze caught them and lifted them off.

"Listen, everybody," Mrs. Hutchinson was saying to the people around her.

"Ready, Bill?" Mr. Summers asked, and Bill Hutchinson, with one quick glance around at his wife and children, nodded.

"Remember," Mr. Summers said, "take the slips and keep them folded until each person has taken one. Harry, you help little Dave." Mr. Graves took the hand of the little boy, who came willingly with him up to the box. "Take a paper out of the box, Davy," Mr. Summers said. Davy put his hand into the box and laughed. "Take just *one* paper," Mr. Summers said. "Harry, you hold it for him." Mr. Graves took the child's hand and removed the folded paper from the tight fist and held it while little Dave stood next to him and looked up at him wonderingly.

"Nancy next," Mr. Summers said. Nancy was twelve, and her school friends breathed heavily as she went forward, switching her skirt, and took a slip daintily from the box. "Bill, Jr.," Mr. Summers said, and Billy, his face red and his feet over-large, nearly knocked the box over as he got a paper out. "Tessie," Mr. Summers said. She hesitated for a minute, looking around defiantly, and then set her lips and went up to the box. She snatched a paper out and held it behind her.

"Bill," Mr. Summers said, and Bill Hutchinson reached into the box and felt around, bringing his hand out at last with the slip of paper in it.

The crowd was quiet. A girl whispered, "I hope it's not Nancy," and the sound of the whisper reached the edges of the crowd.

"It's not the way it used to be," Old Man Warner said clearly. "People ain't the way they used to be."

"All right," Mr. Summers said. "Open the papers. Harry, you open little Dave's."

Mr. Graves opened the slip of paper and there was a general sigh through the crowd as he held it up and everyone could see that it was blank. Nancy and Bill, Jr., opened theirs at the same time, and both beamed and laughed, turning around to the crowd and holding their slips of paper above their heads.

"Tessie," Mr. Summers said. There was a pause, and then Mr. Summers looked at Bill Hutchinson, and Bill unfolded his paper and showed it. It was blank.

"It's Tessie," Mr. Summers said, and his voice was hushed. "Show us her paper, Bill."

Bill Hutchinson went over to his wife and forced the slip of paper out of her hand. It had a black spot on it, the black spot Mr. Summers had made the night before with the heavy pencil in the coal-company office. Bill Hutchinson held it up, and there was a stir in the crowd.

"All right, folks," Mr. Summers said. "Let's finish quickly."

Although the villagers had forgotten the ritual and lost the original black box, they still remembered to use stones. The pile of stones the boys had made earlier was ready; there were stones on the ground with the blowing scraps of paper that had come out of the box. Mrs. Delacroix selected a stone so large she had to pick it up with both hands and turned to Mrs. Dunbar. "Come on," she said. "Hurry up."

Mrs. Dunbar had small stones in both hands, and she said, gasping for breath, "I can't run at all. You'll have to go ahead and I'll catch up with you."

The children had stones already, and someone gave little Davy Hutchinson a few pebbles.

Tessie Hutchinson was in the center of a cleared space by now, and she held her hands out desperately as the villagers moved in on her. "It isn't fair," she said. A stone hit her on the side of the head.

Old Man Warner was saying, "Come on, come on, everyone." Steve Adams was in the front of the crowd of villagers, with Mrs. Graves beside him.

"It isn't fair, it isn't right," Mrs. Hutchinson screamed, and then they were upon her.

DISCUSSION

1. (a) How are the village and its inhabitants typical of villages and villagers all over the world? (b) What value has this setting to the tone of the story and the intent of the author?

2. (a) In what ways is the lottery ritualistic? (b) What changes have occurred in the ritual over the years? (c) What aspects of the ritual are people reluctant to change? (d) Is there any irony underlying the entire ritual? Explain.

3. In ancient societies, innocent humans were often sacrificed to appease gods whom the primitives believed controlled nature and human destiny. What remark by Old Man Warner indicates the villagers might be making a sacrifice for similar reasons?

4. Some critics have said the story implies that contemporary man, despite his civilized exterior, is still superstitious and heartless, capable of scapegoating innocent victims to lessen his own fears. (a) Defend or criticize this interpretation. (b) Suggest other symbolic meanings for the story. (c) Form your own statement of the story's theme, or central idea.

5. Most readers are unprepared for the shock with which "The Lottery" ends. Has the author tricked her audience by not providing a stronger warning of impending horror, or is the shock ending justified? Explain.

AUTHOR

SHIRLEY JACKSON (1919–1965), student of black magic, often used the world of the supernatural as a basis for her savage comments on contemporary reality. Because of their shocking content, these macabre fantasies that curdle the blood and strip away all protective self-illusions are her most popular works. But Miss Jackson, seeming intimate of the ghoulish, was also Mrs. Stanley Hyman and the mother of four very funny children. Around her family life she wrote two memoirs noted for their lively humor.

Except for lectures to students, Miss Jackson did not like to talk about her work. She was, however, particularly proud that the Union of South Africa had banned "The Lottery." They, she felt, understood what it was about.

COMPOSITION

Shirley Jackson's "The Lottery" has immediate and potent shock value. The ritual of human sacrifice is an unfamiliar and repugnant practice to us. But, as shocking as Miss Jackson's story may seem, there are communities in other parts of the world where ritualistic human sacrifice is being practiced today. Such communities, as well as the fictitious one in "The Lottery," point out the power and influence of tradition on human behavior.

There are clues scattered throughout "The Lottery" to suggest that the townspeople's attitudes regarding the traditional sacrifice are slowly changing. Mrs. Adams even observes that some towns have abandoned the lottery. Perhaps, in the not too distant future, this community will be confronted with making the decision to maintain or abandon the lottery.

Choose one of the characters from Shirley Jackson's story and assume his or her identity. *From the point of view of the character whose identity you have assumed*, write a brief composition explaining which side you would take in a debate: Resolved that the annual lottery be abolished. Be sure to support your position with as many reasons as you can, either from clues in the story or from your imagination.

The Sea Devil

Arthur Gordon

*He had started out for a night of quiet fishing, not knowing
what awaited him in the dark.*

THE man came out of the house and stood quite
still, listening. Behind him, the lights glowed in the
cheerful room, the books were neat and orderly in
their cases, the radio talked importantly to itself.
In front of him, the bay stretched dark and silent, one
of the countless lagoons that border the coast where
Florida thrusts its great green thumb deep into the
tropics.

It was late in September. The night was breathless;
summer's dead hand still lay heavy on the land. The
man moved forward six paces and stood on the sea
wall. He dropped his cigarette and noted where the
tiny spark hissed and went out. The tide was beginning to ebb.

Somewhere out in the blackness a mullet jumped
and fell back with a sullen splash. Heavy with roe,
they were jumping less often, now. They would not
take a hook, but a practiced eye could see the swirls
they made in the glassy water. In the dark of the
moon, a skilled man with a cast net might take half
a dozen in an hour's work. And a big mullet makes
a meal for a family.

The man turned abruptly and went into the garage,
where his cast net hung. He was in his late twenties,
wide-shouldered and strong. He did not have to fish

for a living, or even for food. He was a man who worked with his head, not with his hands. But he liked to go casting alone at night.

He liked the loneliness and the labor of it. He liked the clean taste of salt when he gripped the edge of the net with his teeth as a cast netter must. He liked the arching flight of sixteen pounds of lead and linen against the starlight, and the weltering crash of the net into the unsuspecting water. He liked the harsh tug of the retrieving rope around his wrist, and the way the net came alive when the cast was true, and the thud of captured fish on the floor boards of the skiff.

He liked all that because he found in it a reality that seemed to be missing from his twentieth-century job and from his daily life. He liked being the hunter, skilled and solitary and elemental. There was no conscious cruelty in the way he felt. It was the way things had been in the beginning.

The man lifted the net down carefully and lowered it into a bucket. He put a paddle beside the bucket. Then he went into the house. When he came out, he was wearing swimming trunks and a pair of old tennis shoes. Nothing else.

The skiff, flat-bottomed, was moored off the sea wall. He would not go far, he told himself. Just to the tumbledown dock half a mile away. Mullet had a way of feeding around old pilings after dark. If he moved quietly, he might pick up two or three in one cast close to the dock. And maybe a couple of others on the way down or back.

He shoved off and stood motionless for a moment, letting his eyes grow accustomed to the dark. Somewhere out in the channel a porpoise blew with a sound like steam escaping. The man smiled a little; porpoises were his friends. Once, fishing in the Gulf he had seen the charter-boat captain reach overside and gaff a baby porpoise through the sinewy part of the tail. He had hoisted it aboard, had dropped it into the bait well, where it thrashed around, puzzled and unhappy. And the mother had swum alongside the boat and under the boat and around the boat, nudging the stout planking with her back, slapping it with her tail, until the man felt sorry for her and made the captain let the baby porpoise go.

He took the net from the bucket, slipped the noose in the retrieving rope over his wrist, pulled the slip-knot tight. It was an old net, but still serviceable; he had rewoven the rents made by underwater snags. He coiled the thirty-foot rope carefully, making sure there were no kinks. A tangled rope, he knew, would spoil any cast.

The basic design of the net had not changed in three thousand years. It was a mesh circle with a diameter of fourteen feet. It measured close to fifteen yards around the circumference and could, if thrown perfectly, blanket a hundred and fifty square feet of sea water. In the center of this radial trap was a small iron collar where the retrieving rope met the twenty-three separate drawstrings leading to the outer rim of the net. Along this rim, spaced an inch and a half apart, were the heavy lead sinkers.

The man raised the iron collar until it was a foot above his head. The net hung soft and pliant and deadly. He shook it gently, making sure that the drawstrings were not tangled, that the sinkers were hanging true. Then he eased it down and picked up the paddle.

The night was black as a witch's cat; the stars looked fuzzy and dim. Down to the southward, the lights of a causeway made a yellow necklace across the sky. To the man's left were the tangled roots of a mangrove swamp; to his right, the open waters of the bay. Most of it was fairly shallow, but there were channels eight feet deep. The man could not see the old dock, but he knew where it was. He pulled the paddle quietly through the water, and the phosphorescence glowed and died.

For five minutes he paddled. Then, twenty feet ahead of the skiff, a mullet jumped. A big fish, close to three pounds. For a moment it hung in the still air, gleaming dully. Then it vanished. But the ripples marked the spot, and where there was one there were often others.

The man stood up quickly. He picked up the coiled rope, and with the same hand grasped the net at a point four feet below the iron collar. He raised the skirt to his mouth, gripped it strongly with his teeth. He slid his free hand as far as it would go down the circumference of the net so that he had three points of contact with the mass of cordage and metal. He made sure his feet were planted solidly. Then he waited, feeling the tension that is older than the human race, the fierce exhilaration of the hunter at the moment of ambush, the atavistic desire to capture and kill and ultimately consume.

A mullet swirled, ahead and to the left. The man swung the heavy net back, twisting his body and bending his knees so as to get more upward thrust. He shot it forward, letting go simultaneously with rope hand and with teeth, holding a fraction of a second longer with the other hand so as to give the net the necessary spin, impart the centrifugal force that would make it flare into a circle. The skiff ducked sideways, but he kept his balance. The net fell with a splash.

The man waited for five seconds. Then he began to retrieve it, pulling in a series of sharp jerks so that the drawstrings would gather the net inward, like a giant fist closing on this segment of the teeming sea. He felt the net quiver, and knew it was not empty. He swung it, dripping, over the gunwhale, saw the broad silver side of the mullet quivering, saw too the gleam of a smaller fish. He looked closely to make sure no sting ray was hidden in the mesh, then raised the iron collar and shook the net out. The mullet fell with a thud and flapped wildly. The other victim was an angel fish, beautifully marked, but too small to keep. The man picked it up gently and dropped it overboard. He coiled the rope, took up the paddle. He would cast no more until he came to the dock.

The skiff moved on. At last, ten feet apart, a pair of stakes rose up gauntly out of the night. Barnacle encrusted, they once had marked the approach from the main channel. The man guided the skiff between them, then put the paddle down softly. He stood up, reached for the net, tightened the noose around his wrist. From here he could drift down upon the dock. He could see it now, a ruined skeleton in the starshine. Beyond it a mullet jumped and fell back with a flat, liquid sound. The man raised the edge of the net, put it between his teeth. He would not cast at a single swirl, he decided; he would wait until he saw two or three close together. The skiff was barely moving. He felt his muscles tense themselves, awaiting the signal from the brain.

Behind him in the channel he heard the porpoise blow again, nearer now. He frowned in the darkness. If the porpoise chose to fish this area, the mullet would scatter and vanish. There was no time to lose.

A school of sardines surfaced suddenly, skittering along like drops of mercury. Something, perhaps the shadow of the skiff, had frightened them. The old dock loomed very close. A mullet broke water just too far away; then another, nearer. The man marked the spreading ripples and decided to wait no longer.

He swung back the net, heavier now that it was wet. He had to turn his head, but out of the corner of his eye he saw two swirls in the back water just off the starboard bow. They were about eight feet apart, and they had the sluggish oily look that marks the presence of something big just below the surface. His conscious mind had no time to function, but instinct told him that the net was wide enough to cover both swirls if he could alter the direction of his cast. He could not halt the swing, but he shifted his feet slightly and made the cast off balance. He saw the net shoot forward, flare into an oval, and drop just where he wanted it.

Then the sea exploded in his face. In a frenzy of spray, a great horned thing shot like a huge bat out of the water. The man saw the mesh of his net etched against the mottled blackness of its body and he knew, in the split second in which thought was still possible, that those twin swirls had been made not by two mullet, but by the wing tips of the giant ray of the Gulf Coast, *Manta birostris*, also known as clam cracker, devil ray, sea devil.

The man gave a hoarse cry. He tried to claw the slipknot off his wrist, but there was no time. The quarter-inch line snapped taut. He shot over the side of the skiff as if he had roped a runaway locomotive. He hit the water head first and seemed to bounce once. He plowed a blinding furrow for perhaps ten yards. Then the line went slack as the sea devil jumped again. It was not the full-grown manta of the deep Gulf, but it was close to nine feet from tip to tip and it weighed over a thousand pounds. Up into the air it went, pearl-colored underbelly gleaming as it twisted in a frantic effort to dislodge the clinging thing that had fallen upon it. Up into the starlight, a monstrous survival from the dawn of time.

The water was less than four feet deep. Sobbing and choking, the man struggled for a foothold on the slimy bottom. Sucking in great gulps of air, he fought to free himself from the rope. But the slipknot was jammed deep into his wrist; he might as well have tried to loosen a circle of steel.

The ray came down with a thunderous splash and drove forward again. The flexible net followed every movement, impeding it hardly at all. The man weighed a hundred and seventy-five pounds, and he was braced for the shock, and he had the desperate strength that comes from looking into the blank eyes of death. It was useless. His arm straightened out with a jerk that seemed to dislocate his shoulder; his feet shot out from under him; his head went under again. Now at last he knew how the fish must feel when the line tightens and drags him toward the alien element that is his doom. Now he knew.

Desperately he dug the fingers of his free hand into the ooze, felt them dredge a futile channel through broken shells and the ribbonlike sea grasses. He tried to raise his head, but could not get it clear. Torrents of spray choked him as the ray plunged toward deep water.

His eyes were of no use to him in the foam-streaked blackness. He closed them tight, and at once an insane sequence of pictures flashed through his mind. He saw his wife sitting in their living room, reading, waiting calmly for his return. He saw the mullet he had just caught, gasping its life away on the floor boards of the skiff. He saw the cigarette he had flung from the sea wall touch the water and expire with a tiny hiss. He saw all these things and many others simultaneously in his mind as his body fought silently and tenaciously for its existence. His hand touched something hard and closed on it in a death grip, but it was only the sharp-edged helmet of a horseshoe crab, and after an instant he let it go.

He had been under the water perhaps fifteen seconds now, and something in his brain told him quite calmly that he could last another forty or fifty and then the red flashes behind his eyes would merge into darkness, and the water would pour into his lungs in one sharp painful shock, and he would be finished.

This thought spurred him to a desperate effort. He reached up and caught his pinioned wrist with his free hand. He doubled up his knees to create more drag. He thrashed his body madly, like a fighting fish, from side to side. This did not disturb the ray, but now one of the great wings tore through the mesh, and the net slipped lower over the fins projecting like horns from below the nightmare head, and the sea devil jumped again.

And once more the man was able to get his feet on the bottom and his head above water, and he saw ahead of him the pair of ancient stakes that marked the approach to the channel. He knew that if he was dragged much beyond those stakes he would be in eight feet of water, and the ray would go down to hug the bottom as rays always do, and then no power on earth could save him. So in the moment of respite that was granted him, he flung himself toward them. For a moment he thought his captor yielded a bit. Then the ray moved off again, but more slowly now, and for a few yards the man was able to keep his feet on the bottom. Twice he hurled himself back

against the rope with all his strength, hoping that something would break. But nothing broke. The mesh of the net was ripped and torn, but the draw lines were strong, and the stout perimeter cord threaded through the sinkers was even stronger.

The man could feel nothing now in his trapped hand, it was numb; but the ray could feel the powerful lunges of the unknown thing that was trying to restrain it. It drove its great wings against the un-yielding water and forged ahead, dragging the man and pushing a sullen wave in front of it.

The man had swung as far as he could toward the stakes. He plunged toward one and missed it by inches. His feet slipped and he went down on his knees. Then the ray swerved sharply and the second stake came right at him. He reached out with his free hand and caught it.

He caught it just above the surface, six or eight inches below high-water mark. He felt the razor-sharp barnacles bite into his hand, collapse under the pressure, drive their tiny slime-covered shell splinters deep into his flesh. He felt the pain, and he welcomed it, and he made his fingers into an iron claw that would hold until the tendons were severed or the skin was shredded from the bone. The ray felt the pressure increase with a jerk that stopped it dead in the water. For a moment all was still as the tremendous forces came into equilibrium.

Then the net slipped again, and the perimeter cord came down over the sea devil's eyes, blinding it momentarily. The great ray settled to the bottom and braced its wings against the mud and hurled itself forward and upward.

The stake was only a four-by-four of creosoted pine, and it was old. Ten thousand tides had swirled around it. Worms had bored; parasites had clung. Under the crust of barnacles it still had some heart left, but not enough. The man's grip was five feet above the floor of the bay; the leverage was too great. The stake snapped off at its base.

The ray lunged forward, dragging the man and the useless timber. The man had his lungs full of air, but when the stake snapped he thought of expelling the air and inhaling the water so as to have it finished quickly. He thought of this, but he did not do it. And then, just at the channel's edge, the ray met the porpoise coming in.

The porpoise had fed well this night and was in no hurry, but it was a methodical creature and it intended to make a sweep around the old dock before the tide dropped too low. It had no quarrel with any ray, but it feared no fish in the sea, and when the great black shadow came rushing blindly and unavoidably, it rolled fast and struck once with its massive horizontal tail.

The blow descended on the ray's flat body with a sound like a pistol shot. It would have broken a buffalo's back, and even the sea devil was half stunned. It veered wildly and turned back toward shallow water. It passed within ten feet of the man, face down in the water. It slowed and almost stopped, wing tips moving faintly, gathering strength for another rush.

The man had heard the tremendous slap of the great mammal's tail and the snorting gasp as it plunged away. He felt the line go slack again, and he raised his dripping face, and he reached for the bottom with his feet. He found it, but now the water was up to his neck. He plucked at the noose once more with his lacerated hand, but there was no strength in his fingers. He felt the tension come back into the line as the ray began to move again, and for half a second he was tempted to throw himself backward and fight as he had been doing, pitting his strength against the vastly superior strength of the brute.

But the acceptance of imminent death had done something to his brain. It had driven out the fear, and with the fear had gone the panic. He could think now, and he knew with absolute certainty that if he was to make any use of this last chance that had been given him, it would have to be based on the one faculty that had carried man to his pre-eminence above all beasts, the faculty of reason. Only by using his brain could he possibly survive, and he called on his brain for a solution, and his brain responded. It offered him one.

He did not know whether his body still had the strength to carry out the brain's commands, but he began to swim forward, toward the ray that was still moving hesitantly away from the channel. He swam forward, feeling the rope go slack as he gained on the creature.

Ahead of him he saw the one remaining stake, and he made himself swim faster until he was parallel with the ray and the rope trailed behind both of them in a deep U. He swam with a surge of desperate energy that came from nowhere so that he was slightly in the lead as they came to the stake. He passed on one side of it; the ray was on the other.

Then the man took one last deep breath, and he went down under the black water until he was sitting on the bottom of the bay. He put one foot over the line so that it passed under his bent knee. He drove both his heels into the mud, and he clutched the slimy grass with his bleeding hand, and he waited for the tension to come again.

The ray passed on the other side of the stake, moving faster now. The rope grew taut again, and it began to drag the man back toward the stake. He held his prisoned wrist close to the bottom, under his knee, and he prayed that the stake would not break. He felt the rope vibrate as the barnacles bit into it. He did not know whether the rope would crush the barnacles or whether the barnacles would cut the rope. All he knew was that in five seconds or less he would be dragged into the stake and cut to ribbons if he tried to hold on; or drowned if he didn't.

He felt himself sliding slowly, and then faster, and suddenly the ray made a great leap forward, and the rope burned around the base of the stake, and the man's foot hit it hard. He kicked himself backward with his remaining strength, and the rope parted and he was free.

He came slowly to the surface.

Thirty feet away the sea devil made one tremendous leap and disappeared into the darkness. The man raised his wrist and looked at the frayed length of rope dangling from it. Twenty inches, perhaps. He lifted his other hand and felt the hot blood start instantly, but he didn't care. He put this hand on the stake above the barnacles and held on to the good, rough, honest wood. He heard a strange noise, and realized that it was himself, sobbing.

High above, there was a droning sound, and looking up he saw the nightly plane from New Orleans inbound for Tampa. Calm and serene, it sailed, symbol of man's proud mastery over nature. Its lights winked red and green for a moment; then it was gone.

Slowly, painfully, the man began to move through the placid water. He came to the skiff at last and climbed into it. The mullet, still alive, slapped convulsively with its tail. The man reached down with his torn hand, picked up the mullet, let it go.

He began to work on the slip-knot doggedly with his teeth. His mind was almost a blank, but not quite. He knew one thing. He knew he would do no more casting alone at night. Not in the dark of the moon. No, not he.

DISCUSSION

1. This selection requires the reader to visualize a geographical setting. From descriptions in the story, try to sketch a map showing the location of the man's house and garage, the bay, the channel, the tumble-down dock, the sea wall, the mangrove swamp, the pair of stakes, and the spot where the ray and the porpoise meet.

2. What motivates the man to go fishing by himself at night?

3. The man casts his net twice. (a) What are the consequences of each cast? (b) What misjudgment does the man make in regard to the second cast?

4. Twice the man attempts to use one of the stakes to save himself. (a) Describe each attempt. (b) In what ways does the man's behavior change between the first and second attempts?

5. (a) What indications are there early in the story that the man is essentially kind? (b) By the end of the story, what has he learned from his experience with the ray? (c) How does this knowledge affect his behavior toward the mullet and his feelings about fishing?

6. (a) Would "The Sea Devil" be strengthened or weakened if the man were immediately given a full name? (b) If the reader knew at the outset of the story that the man had a wife?

WORD STUDY

Connotation

Words sometimes carry invisible meanings. One dictionary definition of the word *water* is: "liquid that constitutes rain, oceans, rivers, lakes, and ponds." To this definition each one of us adds his own special meaning to the word *water*. As a result, the word *water* does not mean exactly the same thing to one person as it does to another. A child at the beach, for instance, might think of water in terms of recreation. To a person stranded in the desert, however, water would mean survival. The man in Arthur Gordon's "Sea Devil" probably thought of water as a potential deathtrap.

The literal, or dictionary, meaning of a word is called its *denotation*. The interpretations we give words in addition to their denotations are called *connotations*. A word gets its connotative meanings from people's experiences with what the word suggests or represents. Since people's experiences differ, a word may have quite different connotations for different people. For example, the word *farm* denotes a "piece of land used to raise crops or animals." However, to a farm boy the word *farm* may connote home, security, serenity, and good times, while to a city boy the word *farm* may connote isolation, loneliness, or strangeness.

State the probable connotations of the word *policeman* when used by (a) a thief; (b) a lost child; (c) the victim of a robbery.

State the probable connotations of the word *work* when used by (a) a boy anxious to earn money for a date; (b) a family breadwinner; (c) a daydreamer.

State the probable connotations of the word *charity* when used by (a) a philanthropist; (b) a proud needy person; (c) a lazy beggar.

State the probable connotations of the word *lawn* when used by (a) its owner; (b) small children; (c) a nurseryman.

AUTHOR

ARTHUR GORDON was born July 27, 1912, in Savannah, Georgia. He graduated from Yale University in 1934 and Oxford University, as a Rhodes Scholar, in 1936. From 1942 to 1945 he served in the U.S. Army Air Forces, reaching the rank of lieutenant colonel. He was managing editor of *Good Housekeeping* from 1938 to 1941 and editor of *Cosmopolitan* from 1946 to 1948.

Mr. Gordon has written over two hundred stories and articles. At present, he works as an editor and is engaged in free-lance writing.

SURVIVAL

WAR

Luigi Pirandello

THE passengers who had left Rome by the night express had had to stop until dawn at the small station of Fabriano in order to continue their journey by the small old-fashioned local joining the main line with Sulmona.[1]

At dawn, in a stuffy and smoky second-class carriage[2] in which five people had already spent the night, a bulky woman in deep mourning was hoisted in—almost like a shapeless bundle. Behind her—puffing and moaning, followed her husband—a tiny man, thin and weakly, his face death-white, his eyes small and bright and looking shy and uneasy.

Having at last taken a seat, he politely thanked the passengers who had helped his wife and who had made room for her; then he turned around to the woman trying to pull down the collar of her coat, and politely inquired:

"Are you all right, dear?"

The wife, instead of answering, pulled up her collar again to her eyes, so as to hide her face.

"Nasty world," muttered the husband with a sad smile.

And he felt it his duty to explain to his traveling companions that the poor woman was to be pitied, for the war was taking away from her her only son, a

---

1. *Fabriano* (fä′brē ä′nō) . . . *Sulmona* (sül mō′nä), two towns in central Italy. Fabriano is northwest of Rome and Sulmona is southwest of Rome.
2. *second-class carriage,* a compartment in the moderately priced section of the train. Coach cars on many European trains are divided into compartments which have two long, facing seats.

boy of twenty to whom both had devoted their entire life, even breaking up their home at Sulmona to follow him to Rome, where he had to go as a student, then allowing him to volunteer for war with an assurance, however, that at least for six months he would not be sent to the front and now, all of a sudden, receiving a wire saying that he was due to leave in three days' time and asking them to go and see him off.

The woman under the big coat was twisting and wriggling, at times growling like a wild animal, feeling certain that all those explanations would not have aroused even a shadow of sympathy from those people who—most likely—were in the same plight as herself. One of them, who had been listening with particular attention, said:

"You should thank God that your son is only leaving now for the front. Mine has been sent there the first day of the war. He has already come back twice wounded and been sent back again to the front."

"What about me? I have two sons and three nephews at the front," said another passenger.

"Maybe, but in our case it is our *only* son," ventured the husband.

"What difference can it make? You may spoil your only son with excessive attention, but you cannot love him more than you would all your other children if you had any. Paternal love is not like bread that can be broken into pieces and split amongst the children in equal shares. A father gives *all* his love to each one of his children without discrimination, whether it be one or ten, and if I am suffering now for my two sons, I am not suffering half for each of them but double...."

"True ... true ...," sighed the embarrassed husband, "but suppose (of course we all hope it will never be your case) a father has two sons at the front and he loses one of them, there is still one left to console him ... while...."

"Yes," answered the other, getting cross, "a son left to console him but also a son left for whom he must survive, while in the case of the father of an only son if the son dies the father can die too and put an end to his distress. Which of the two positions is the worse? Don't you see how my case would be worse than yours?"

"Nonsense," interrupted another traveler, a fat, red-faced man with bloodshot eyes of the palest gray.

He was panting. From his bulging eyes seemed to

spurt inner violence of an uncontrolled vitality which his weakened body could hardly contain.

"Nonsense," he repeated, trying to cover his mouth with his hand so as to hide the two missing front teeth. "Nonsense. Do we give life to our children for our own benefit?"

The other travelers stared at him in distress. The one who had had his son at the front since the first day of the war sighed: "You are right. Our children do not belong to us; they belong to the Country...."

"Bosh," retorted the fat traveler. "Do we think of the Country when we give life to our children? Our sons are born because ... well, because they must be born, and when they come to life they take our own life with them. This is the truth. We belong to them but they never belong to us. And when they reach twenty they are exactly what we were at their age. We too had a father and a mother, but there were so many other things as well ... girls, cigarettes, illusions, new ties ... and the Country, of course, whose call we would have answered—when we were twenty—even if father and mother had said no. Now at our age, the love of our Country is still great, of course, but stronger than it is the love for our children. Is there any one of us here who wouldn't gladly take his son's place at the front if he could?"

There was a silence all round, everybody nodding as to approve.

"Why then," continued the fat man, "shouldn't we consider the feelings of our children when they are twenty? Isn't it natural that at their age they should consider the love for their Country (I am speaking of decent boys, of course) even greater than the love for us? Isn't it natural that it should be so, as after all they must look upon us as upon old boys who cannot move any more and must stay at home? If Country exists, if Country is a natural necessity, like bread, of which each of us must eat in order not to die of hunger, somebody must go to defend it. And our sons go, when they are twenty, and they don't want tears, because if they die, they die inflamed and happy (I am speaking, of course, of decent boys). Now, if one dies young and happy, without having the ugly sides of life, the boredom of it, the pettiness, the bitterness of disillusion ... what more can we ask for him? Everyone should stop crying; everyone should laugh, as I do ... or at least thank God—as I do—because my son, before dying, sent me a message saying that he was dying satisfied at having ended his life in the best way he could have wished. That is why, as you see, I do not even wear mourning. . . ."

He shook his light fawn coat so as to show it; his livid lip over his missing teeth was trembling, his eyes were watery and motionless, and soon after he ended with a shrill laugh which might well have been a sob.

"Quite so . . . quite so . . ." agreed the others.

The woman who, bundled in a corner under her coat, had been sitting and listening had—for the last three months—tried to find in the words of her husband and her friends something to console her in her deep sorrow, something that might show her how a mother should resign herself to send her son not even to death but to a probable danger of life. Yet not a word had she found amongst the many which had been said . . . and her grief had been greater in seeing that nobody—as she thought —could share her feelings.

But now the words of the traveler amazed and almost stunned her. She suddenly realized that it wasn't the others who were wrong and who could not understand her but herself who could not rise up to the same height of those fathers and mothers willing to resign themselves, without crying, not only to the departure of their sons but even to their death.

She lifted her head, she bent over from her corner trying to listen with great attention to the details which the fat man was giving to his companions about the way his son had fallen as a hero, for his King and his Country, happy and without regrets. It seemed to her that she had stumbled into a world she had never dreamed of, a world so far unknown to her, and she was so pleased to hear everyone joining in congratulating that brave father who could so stoically speak of his child's death.

Then suddenly, just as if she had heard nothing of what had been said and almost as if waking up from a dream, she turned to the old man, asking him: *[handwritten: finally personalize his son.]*

"Then . . . is your son really dead?"

Everybody stared at her. The old man, too, turned to look at her, fixing his great, bulging, horribly watery light-gray eyes, deep in her face. For some little time he tried to answer, but words failed him. He looked and looked at her, almost as if only then— at that silly, incongruous question—he had suddenly realized at last that his son was really dead—gone forever—forever. His face contracted, became horribly distorted; then he snatched in haste a handkerchief from his pocket and, to the amazement of everyone, broke into harrowing, heart-rending, uncontrollable sobs.

DISCUSSION

1. Writers frequently use a setting such as an ocean liner or a railroad train to bring their characters together. Is the "stuffy and smoky second-class carriage" an effective setting in this story? Explain.

2. (a) Why is the bulky woman wearing mourning? (b) Why does she not participate more in the conversation? (c) Why does she finally speak to the fat man?

[handwritten: conflict (PROBLEM) trying to accept personal loss]

3. Does the man who has two sons at the front feel more fortunate than the husband of the bulky woman? Explain his own reasons for feeling as he does.

4. (a) Why does the fat man, the only one who has actually lost a son in the war, not even wear mourning? (b) What suggestion does he have for the parents of "decent boys"? (c) How do his explanation and suggestion affect the other passengers? (d) What light does the ending of the story throw on the fat man's true feelings?

5. (a) What same internal conflict are both the fat man and the bulky woman trying to survive? (b) How do their methods of meeting it differ? (c) Which, if either, is successful in resolving this conflict? Explain your answer.

6. What are the "scarless wounds" that are sustained by the speakers in this story?

A Visit to Grandmother

William Melvin Kelley

CHIG knew something was wrong the instant his father kissed her. He had always known his father to be the warmest of men, a man so kind that when people ventured timidly into his office, it took only a few words from him to make them relax, and even laugh. Doctor Charles Dunford cared about people.

But when he had bent to kiss the old lady's black face, something new and almost ugly had come into his eyes: fear, uncertainty, sadness, and perhaps even hatred.

Ten days before in New York, Chig's father had decided suddenly he wanted to go to Nashville to attend his college class reunion, twenty years out. Both Chig's brother and sister, Peter and Connie, were packing for camp and besides were too young for such an affair. But Chig was seventeen, had nothing to do that summer, and his father asked if he would like to go along. His father had given him additional reasons: "All my running buddies got their diplomas and were snapped up by them crafty young gals, and had kids within a year—now all those kids, some of them gals, are your age."

The reunion had lasted a week. As they packed for home, his father, in a far too offhand way, had suggested they visit Chig's grandmother. "We this close. We might as well drop in on her and my brothers."

So, instead of going north, they had gone farther south, had just entered her house. And Chig had a suspicion now that the reunion had been only an excuse to drive south, that his father had been heading to this house all the time.

His father had never talked much about his family, with the exception of his brother, GL, who seemed part con man, part practical joker and part Don Juan; he had spoken of GL with the kind of indulgence he would have shown a cute, but ill-behaved and potentially dangerous, five-year-old.

Chig's father had left home when he was fifteen. When asked why, he would answer: "I wanted to go to school. They didn't have a Negro high school at home, so I went up to Knoxville and lived with a cousin and went to school."

They had been met at the door by Aunt Rose, GL's wife, and ushered into the living room. The old lady had looked up from her seat by the window. Aunt Rose stood between the visitors.

The old lady eyed his father. "Rose, who that? Rose?" She squinted. She looked like a doll, made of black straw, the wrinkles in her face running in one direction like the head of a broom. Her hair was white and coarse and grew out straight from her head. Her eyes were brown—the whites, too, seemed light brown—and were hidden behind thick glasses, which remained somehow on a tiny nose. "That Hiram?" That was another of his father's brothers. "No, it ain't Hiram; too big for Hiram." She turned then to Chig. "Now that man, he look like Eleanor, Charles' wife, but Charles wouldn't never send my grandson to see me. I never even hear from Charles." She stopped again.

"It Charles, Mama. That who it is." Aunt Rose, between them, led them closer. "It Charles come all the way from New York to see you, and brung little Charles with him."

The old lady stared up at them. "Charles? Rose, that really Charles?" She turned away, and reached for a handkerchief in the pocket of her clean, ironed, flowered housecoat, and wiped her eyes. "God have mercy, Charles." She spread her arms up to him, and he bent down and kissed her cheek. That was when Chig saw his face, grimacing. She hugged him; Chig watched the muscles in her arms as they tightened around his father's neck. She half rose out of her chair. "How are you, son?"

Chig could not hear his father's answer.

She let him go, and fell back into her chair, grabbing the arms. Her hands were as dark as the wood, and seemed to become part of it. "Now, who that standing there? Who that man?"

"That's one of your grandsons, Mama." His father's voice cracked. "Charles Dunford, junior. You saw him once, when he was a baby, in Chicago. He's grown now."

"I can see that, boy!" She looked at Chig squarely. "Come here, son, and kiss me once." He did. "What they call you? Charles too?"

"No, ma'am, they call me Chig."

She smiled. She had all her teeth, but they were too perfect to be her own. "That's good. Can't have two boys answering to Charles in the same house. Won't nobody at all come. So you that little boy. You don't remember me, do you. I used to take you to church in Chicago, and you'd get up and hop in time to the music. You studying to be a preacher?"

"No, ma'am. I don't think so. I might be a lawyer."

"You'll be an honest one, won't you?"

"I'll try."

"Trying ain't enough! You be honest, you hear? Promise me. You be honest like your daddy."

"All right. I promise."

"Good. Rose, where's GL at? Where's that thief? He gone again?"

"I don't know, Mama." Aunt Rose looked embarrassed. "He say he was going by his liquor store. He'll be back."

"Well, then where's Hiram? You call up those boys, and get them over here—now! You got enough to eat? Let me go see." She started to get up. Chig reached out his hand. She shook him off. "What they tell you about me, Chig? They tell you I'm all laid up? Don't believe it. They don't know nothing about old ladies. When I want help, I'll let you know. Only time I'll need help getting anywheres is when I dies and they lift me into the ground."

She was standing now, her back and shoulders straight. She came only to Chig's chest. She squinted up at him. "You eat much? Your daddy ate like two men."

"Yes, ma'am."

"That's good. That means you ain't nervous. Your mama, she ain't nervous. I remember that. In Chicago, she'd sit down by a window all afternoon and never say nothing, just knit." She smiled. "Let me see what we got to eat."

"I'll do that, Mama." Aunt Rose spoke softly. "You haven't seen Charles in a long time. You sit and talk."

The old lady squinted at her. "You can do the cooking if you promise it ain't because you think I can't."

Aunt Rose chuckled. "I know you can do it, Mama."

"All right. I'll just sit and talk a spell." She sat again and arranged her skirt around her short legs.

Chig did most of the talking, told all about himself before she asked. His father only spoke when he was spoken to, and then, only one word at a time, as if by coming back home, he had become a small boy again, sitting in the parlor while his mother spoke with her guests.

When Uncle Hiram and Mae, his wife, came they sat down to eat. Chig did not have to ask about Uncle GL's absence; Aunt Rose volunteered an explanation: "Can't never tell where the man is at. One Thursday morning he left here and next thing we knew, he was calling from Chicago, saying he went up to see Joe Louis fight. He'll be here though; he ain't as young and footloose as he used to be." Chig's father had mentioned driving down that GL was about five years older than he was, nearly fifty.

Uncle Hiram was somewhat smaller than Chig's father; his short-cropped kinky hair was half grey, half black. One spot, just off his forehead, was totally white. Later, Chig found out it had been that way since he was twenty. Mae (Chig could not bring himself to call her Aunt) was a good deal younger than Hiram, pretty enough so that Chig would have looked at her twice on the street. She was a honey-colored woman, with long eye lashes. She was wearing a white sheath.

At dinner, Chig and his father sat on one side, opposite Uncle Hiram and Mae; his grandmother and Aunt Rose sat at the ends. The food was good; there was a lot and Chig ate a lot. All through the meal, they talked about the family as it had been thirty years before, and particularly about the young GL. Mae and Chig asked questions; the old lady answered; Aunt Rose directed the discussion, steering the old lady onto the best stories; Chig's father laughed from time to time; Uncle Hiram ate.

"Why don't you tell them about the horse, Mama?" Aunt Rose, over Chig's weak protest, was spooning mashed potatoes onto his plate. "There now, Chig."

"I'm trying to think." The old lady was holding her fork halfway to her mouth, looking at them over her glasses. "Oh, you talking about that crazy horse GL brung home that time."

"That's right, Mama." Aunt Rose nodded and slid another slice of white meat on Chig's plate.

Mae started to giggle. "Oh, I've heard this. This is funny, Chig."

The old lady put down her fork and began: Well, GL went out of the house one day with an old, no-good chair I wanted him to take over to the church for a bazaar, and he met up with this man who'd just brung in some horses from out West. Now, I reckon you can expect one swindler to be in every town, but you don't rightly think there'll be two, and God forbid they should ever meet—but they did, GL and his chair, this man and his horses. Well, I wished I'd-a been there; there must-a been some mighty high-powered talking going on. That man with his horses, he told GL them horses was half-Arab, half-Indian, and GL told that man the chair was an antique he'd stole from some rich white folks. So they swapped. Well, I was a-looking out the window and seen GL dragging this animal to the house. It looked pretty gentle and its eyes was most closed and its feet was shuffling.

"GL, where'd you get that thing?" I says.

"I swapped him for that old chair, Mama," he says. "And made myself a bargain. This is even better than Papa's horse."

Well, I'm a-looking at this horse and noticing how he be looking more and more wide-awake every minute, sort of warming up like a teakettle until, I swears to you, that horse is blowing steam out its nose.

"Come on, Mama," GL says, "come on and I'll take you for a ride." Now George, my husband, God rest his tired soul, he'd brung home this white folks' buggy which had a busted wheel and fixed it and was to take it back that day and GL says: "Come on,

Mama, we'll use this fine buggy and take us a ride."

"GL," I says, "no, we ain't. Them white folks'll burn us alive if we use their buggy. You just take that horse right on back." You see, I was sure that boy'd come by that animal ungainly.

"Mama, I can't take him back," GL says.

"Why not?" I says.

"Because I don't rightly know where that man is at," GL says.

"Oh," I says. "Well, then I reckon we stuck with it." And I turned around to go back into the house because it was getting late, near dinner time, and I was cooking for ten.

"Mama," GL says to my back. "Mama, ain't you coming for a ride with me?"

"Go on, boy. You ain't getting me inside kicking range of that animal." I was eying that beast and it was boiling hotter all the time. I reckon maybe that man had drugged it. "That horse is wild, GL," I says.

"No, he ain't. He ain't. That man say he is buggy and saddle broke and as sweet as the inside of a apple."

My oldest girl, Essie, had-a come out on the porch and she says: "Go on, Mama. I'll cook. You ain't been out the house in weeks."

"Sure, come on, Mama," GL says. "There ain't nothing to be fidgety about. This horse is gentle as a rose petal." And just then that animal snorts so hard it sets up a little dust storm around its feet.

"Yes, Mama," Essie says, "you can see he gentle." Well, I looked at Essie and then at that horse because I didn't think we could be looking at the same animal. I should-a figured how Essie's eyes ain't never been so good.

"Come on, Mama," GL says.

"All right," I says. So I stood on the porch and watched GL hitching that horse up to the white folks' buggy. For a while there, the animal was pretty quiet, pawing a little, but not much. And I was feeling a little better about riding with GL behind that crazy-looking horse. I could see how GL was happy I was going with him. He was scurrying around that animal buckling buckles and strapping straps, all the time smiling, and that made me feel good.

Then he was finished, and I must say, that horse looked mighty fine hitched to that buggy and I knew anybody what climbed up there would look pretty good too. GL came around and stood at the bottom of the steps, and took off his hat and bowed and said: "Madam," and reached out his hand to me and I was feeling real elegant like a fine lady. He helped me up to the seat and then got up beside me and we moved out down our alley. And I remember how colored folks come out on their porches and shook their heads, saying: "Lord now, will you look at Eva Dunford, the fine lady! Don't she look good sitting up there!" And I pretended not to hear and sat up straight and proud.

We rode on through the center of town, up Market Street, and all the way out where Hiram is living now, which in them days was all woods, there not being even a farm in sight and that's when that horse must-a first realized he weren't at all broke or tame or maybe thought he was back out West again, and started to gallop.

"GL," I says, "now you ain't joking with your mama, is you? Because if you is, I'll strap you purple if I live through this."

Well, GL was pulling on the reins with all his meager strength, and yelling, "Whoa, you. Say now, whoa!" He turned to me just long enough to say, "I ain't fooling with you, Mama. Honest!"

I reckon that animal weren't too satisfied with the road, because it made a sharp right turn just then, down into a gulley and struck out across a hilly meadow. "Mama," GL yells. "Mama, do something!"

I didn't know what to do, but I figured I had to do something so I stood up, hopped down onto the horse's back and pulled it to a stop. Don't ask me how I did that; I reckon it was that I was a mother and my baby asked me to do something, is all.

"Well, we walked that animal all the way home; sometimes I had to club it over the nose with my fist to make it come, but we made it, GL and me. You remember how tired we was, Charles?"

"I wasn't here at the time." Chig turned to his father and found his face completely blank, without even a trace of a smile or a laugh.

"Well, of course you was, son. That happened in . . . in . . . it was a hot summer that year and—"

"I left here in June of that year. You wrote me about it."

The old lady stared past Chig at him. They all turned to him; Uncle Hiram looked up from his plate.

"Then you don't remember how we all laughed?"

"No, I don't, Mama. And I probably wouldn't have laughed. I don't think it was funny." They were staring into each other's eyes.

"Why not, Charles?"

"Because in the first place, the horse was gained by fraud. And in the second place, both of you might have been seriously injured or even killed." He broke off their stare and spoke to himself more than to any of them: "And if I'd done it, you would've beaten me good for it."

"Pardon?" The old lady had not heard him; only Chig had heard.

Chig's father sat up straight as if preparing to debate. "I said that if I had done it, if I had done just exactly what GL did, you would have beaten me good for it, Mama." He was looking at her again.

"Why you say that, son?" She was leaning toward him.

"Don't you know? Tell the truth. It can't hurt me now." His voice cracked, but only once. "If GL and I did something wrong, you'd beat me first and then be too tired to beat him. At dinner, he'd always get seconds and I wouldn't. You'd do things with him, like ride in that buggy, but if I wanted you to do something with me, you were always too busy." He paused and considered whether to say what he finally did say: "I cried when I left here. Nobody loved me, Mama. I cried all the way up to Knoxville. That was the last time I ever cried in my life."

"Oh, Charles." She started to get up, to come around the table to him.

He stopped her. "It's too late."

"But you don't understand."

"What don't I understand? I understood then; I understand now."

Tears now traveled down the lines in her face, but when she spoke, her voice was clear. "I thought you knew. I had ten children. I had to give all of them what they needed most." She nodded. "I paid more mind to GL. I had to. GL could-a ended up swinging if I hadn't. But you was smarter. You was more growed up than GL when you was five and he was ten, and I tried to show you that by letting you do what you wanted to do."

"That's not true, Mama. You know it. GL was light-skinned and had good hair and looked almost white and you loved him for that."

"Charles, no. No, son. I didn't love any one of you more than any other."

"That can't be true." His father was standing now, his fists clenched tight. "Admit it, Mama . . . please!" Chig looked at him, shocked; the man was actually crying.

"It may not-a been right what I done, but I ain't no liar." Chig knew she did not really understand what had happened, what he wanted of her. "I'm not lying to you, Charles."

Chig's father had gone pale. He spoke very softly. "You're about thirty years too late, Mama." He bolted from the table. Silverware and dishes rang and jumped. Chig heard him hurrying up to their room.

They sat in silence for awhile and then heard a key in the front door. A man with a new, lacquered straw hat came in. He was wearing brown and white two-tone shoes with very pointed toes and a white summer suit. "Say now! Man! I heard my brother was in town. Where he at? Where that rascal?"

He stood in the doorway, smiling broadly, an engaging, open, friendly smile, the innocent smile of a five-year-old.

DISCUSSION

1. List at least three functions served by the opening paragraph of "A Visit to Grandmother."

2. Chig sees "fear, uncertainty, sadness, and perhaps even hatred" in his father's eyes. Show how Dr. Dunford reveals these emotions.

3. In paragraphs four and five, it becomes clear that for Dr. Dunford the class reunion was just an excuse to go home. (a) What does Dunford want—or expect to get—from the visit? (b) What does he want Mama to admit to? (c) Dr. Dunford's last words are, "You're about thirty years too late, Mama." Thirty years too late for what?

4. (a) What do you learn about GL in the last sentence? (b) Did both GL and the doctor get what they needed from Mama? (c) Which man is better off? Why?

AUTHOR

WILLIAM MELVIN KELLEY (1937–   ) has this to say about "A Visit to Grandmother": "I think it is important for any reader to remember that fiction is *not* reality. Prose fiction is the attempt, preferably by one man ('committee' written fiction does not work) to put the real world into words. That very act separates fiction from fact. But at the same time a writer does this, he is also trying to create a world which reflects and comments on the real world. So, in a strange way, as a glass bottle is just as *real* as a human being, so fiction is as real in its way as reality. It is just another kind of reality. The reason I'm saying all this is to stop you at the start from reading 'A Visit to Grandmother' as fact. It is *based* on certain actual events from my life, and from my father's, but these events have been shaped in my writer's imagination, and by my personal view of the world, to make a definite point which the reader should be able to understand without my help. If you want some facts, here they are. When I was about fourteen, my father and I did drive South to see his relatives, and mine. But by that time, my father's mother was already dead. My idea of her comes from photographs I've seen of her. Long after I took the trip, I was told about my father's boyhood by some people who had known him when he was a boy. I took these various elements, bits and snatches of stories, and made them into a story about a man who had been living most of his adult life with misconceptions about his childhood and how his mother felt about him."

THE LANGUAGE OF MEN

Norman Mailer

*"He had suffered through all his army career
from an excess of eagerness. He had cared
too much. . . ."*

IN the beginning, Sanford Carter was ashamed of becoming an army cook. This was not from snobbery, at least not from snobbery of the most direct sort. During the two and a half years Carter had been in the army he had come to hate cooks more and more. They existed for him as a symbol of all that was corrupt, overbearing, stupid, and privileged in army life. The image which came to mind was a fat cook with an enormous sandwich in one hand, and a bottle of beer in the other, sweat pouring down a porcine face, foot on a flour barrel, shouting at the K.P. s, "Hurry up, you men, I ain't got all day." More than once in those two and a half years, driven to exasperation, Carter had been on the verge of throwing his food into a cook's face as he passed on the serving line. His anger often derived from nothing: the set of a pair of fat lips, the casual heavy thump of the serving spoon into his plate, or the resentful conviction that the cook was not serving him enough. Since life in the army was in most aspects a marriage, this rage over apparently harmless details was not a sign of unbalance. Every soldier found some particular habit of the army spouse impossible to support.

Yet Sanford Carter became a cook and, to elaborate the irony, did better as a cook than he had done as anything else. In a few months he rose from a private to a first cook with the rank of Sergeant, Technician. After the fact, it was easy to understand. He had suffered through all his army career from an excess of eagerness. He had cared too much, he had wanted to do well, and so he had often been tense at moments when he would better have been relaxed. He was very young, twenty-one, had lived the comparative gentle life of a middle-class boy, and needed some success in the army to prove to himself that he was not completely worthless.

In succession, he had failed as a surveyor in field artillery, a clerk in an infantry headquarters, a telephone wireman, and finally a rifleman. When the war ended, and his regiment went to Japan, Carter was still a rifleman; he had been a rifleman for eight months. What was more to the point, he had been in the platoon as long as any of its members; the skilled hard-bitten nucleus of veterans who had run

C. Mitchell

his squad had gone home one by one, and it seemed to him that through seniority he was entitled to at least a corporal's rating. Through seniority he was so entitled, but on no other ground. Whenever responsibility had been handed to him, he had discharged it miserably, tensely, overconscientiously. He had always asked too many questions, he had worried the task too severely, he had conveyed his nervousness to the men he was supposed to lead. Since he was also sensitive enough and proud enough never to curry favor with the noncoms in the platoon, he was in no position to sit in on their occasional discussions about who was to succeed them. In a vacuum of ignorance, he had allowed himself to dream that he would be given a squad to lead, and his hurt was sharp when the squad was given to a replacement who had joined the platoon months after him.

The war was over, Carter had a bride in the States (he had lived with her for only two months), he was lonely, he was obsessed with going home. As one week dragged into the next, and the regiment, the company, and his own platoon continued the same sort of training which they had been doing ever since he had entered the army, he thought he would snap. There were months to wait until he would be discharged and meanwhile it was intolerable to him to be taught for the fifth time the nomenclature of the machine gun, to stand a retreat parade three evenings a week. He wanted some niche where he could lick his wounds, some army job with so many hours of work and so many hours of complete freedom, where he could be alone by himself. He hated the army, the huge army which had proved to him that he was good at no work, and incapable of succeeding at anything. He wrote long, aching letters to his wife, he talked less and less to the men around him, and he was close to violent attacks of anger during the most casual phases of training—during close-order drill or cleaning his rifle for inspection. He knew that if he did not find his niche it was possible that he would crack.

So he took an opening in the kitchen. It promised him nothing except a day of work, and a day of leisure which would be completely at his disposal. He found that he liked it. He was given at first the job of baking the bread for the company, and every other night he worked till early in the morning, kneading and shaping his fifty-pound mix of dough.

At two or three he would be done, and for his work there would be the tangible reward of fifty loaves of bread, all fresh from the oven, all clean and smelling of fertile accomplished creativity. He had the rare and therefore intensely satisfying emotion of seeing at the end of an army chore the product of his labor.

A month after he became a cook the regiment was disbanded, and those men who did not have enough points to go home were sent to other outfits. Carter ended at an ordnance company in another Japanese city. He had by now given up all thought of getting a noncom's rating before he was discharged, and was merely content to work each alternate day. He took his work for granted and so he succeeded at it. He had begun as a baker in the new company kitchen; before long he was the first cook. It all happened quickly. One cook went home on points, another caught a skin disease, a third was transferred from the kitchen after contracting a venereal infection. On the shift which Carter worked there were left only himself and a man who was illiterate. Carter was put nominally in charge, and was soon actively in charge. He looked up each menu in an army recipe book, collected the items, combined them in the order indicated, and after the proper time had elapsed, took them from the stove. His product tasted neither better nor worse than the product of all other army cooks. But the mess sergeant was impressed. Carter had filled a gap. The next time ratings were given out Carter jumped at a bound from Private to Sergeant T/4.

On the surface he was happy; beneath the surface he was overjoyed. It took him several weeks to realize how grateful and delighted he felt. The promotion coincided with his assignment to a detachment working in a small seaport up the coast. Carter arrived there to discover that he was in charge of cooking for thirty men, and would act as mess sergeant. There was another cook, and there were four permanent Japanese K.P.s, all of them good workers. He still cooked every other day, but there was always time between meals to take a break of at least an hour and often two; he shared a room with the other cook and lived in comparative privacy for the first time in several years; the seaport was beautiful; there was only one officer, and he left the men alone; supplies were plentiful due to a clerical error which assigned rations for forty men rather than thirty; and in general everything was fine. The niche had become a sinecure.

This was the happiest period of Carter's life in the army. He came to like his Japanese K.P.s. He studied their language, he visited their homes, he gave them gifts of food from time to time. They worshipped him because he was kind to them and generous, because he never shouted, because his good humor bubbled over into games, and made the work in the kitchen seem pleasant. All the while he grew in confidence. He was not a big man, but his body filled out from the heavy work; he was likely to sing a great deal, he cracked jokes with the men on the chow line. The kitchen became his property, it became his domain, and since it was a warm room, filled with sunlight, he came to take pleasure in the very sight of it. Before long his good humor expanded into a series of efforts to improve the food. He began to take little pains and make little extra efforts which would have been impossible if he had been obliged to cook for more than thirty men. In the morning he would serve the men fresh eggs scrambled or fried to their desire in fresh butter. Instead of cooking sixty eggs in one large pot he cooked two eggs at a time in a frying pan, turning them to the taste of each soldier. He baked like a housewife satisfying her young husband; at lunch and dinner there was pie or cake, and often both. He went to great lengths. He taught the K.P.s how to make the toast come out right. He traded excess food for spices in Japanese stores. He rubbed paprika and garlic on the chickens. He even made pastries to cover such staples as corn beef hash and meat and vegetable stew.

It all seemed to be wasted. In the beginning the men might have noticed these improvements, but after a period they took them for granted. It did not matter how he worked to satisfy them; they trudged through the chow line with their heads down, nodding coolly at him, and they ate without comment. He would hang around the tables after the meal, noticing how much they consumed, and what they discarded; he would wait for compliments, but the soldiers seemed indifferent. They seemed to eat without tasting the food. In their faces he saw mirrored the distaste with which he had once stared at cooks.

The honeymoon was ended. The pleasure he took in the kitchen and himself curdled. He became aware again of his painful desire to please people, to discharge responsibility, to be a man. When he had been a child, tears had come into his eyes at a cross word, and he had lived in an atmosphere where his smallest accomplishment was warmly praised. He was the sort of young man, he often thought bitterly, who was accustomed to the attention and the protection of women. He would have thrown away all he possessed—the love of his wife, the love of his mother, the benefits of his education, the assured financial security of entering his father's business—if he had been able just once to dig a ditch as well as the most ignorant farmer.

Instead, he was back in the painful unprotected days of his first entrance into the army. Once again the most casual actions became the most painful, the events which were most to be taken for granted grew into the most significant, and the feeding of the men at each meal turned progressively more unbearable.

So Sanford Carter came full circle. If he had once hated the cooks, he now hated the troops. At mealtimes his face soured into the belligerent scowl with which he had once believed cooks to be born. And to himself he muttered the age-old laments of the housewife; how little they appreciated what he did.

Finally there was an explosion. He was approached one day by Corporal Taylor, and he had come to hate Taylor, because Taylor was the natural leader of the detachment and kept the other men endlessly amused with his jokes. Taylor had the ability to present himself as inefficient, shiftless, and incapable, in such a manner as to convey that really the opposite was true. He had the lightest touch, he had the greatest facility, he could charm a geisha in two minutes and obtain anything he wanted from a supply sergeant in five. Carter envied him, envied his grace, his charmed indifference; then grew to hate him.

Taylor teased Carter about the cooking, and he had the knack of knowing where to put the knife. "Hey, Carter," he would shout across the mess hall while breakfast was being served, "you turned my eggs twice, and I asked for them raw." The men would shout with laughter. Somehow Taylor had succeeded in conveying all of the situation, or so it seemed to Carter, insinuating everything, how Carter worked and how it meant nothing, how Carter

labored to gain their affection and earned their contempt. Carter would scowl, Carter would answer in a rough voice, "Next time I'll crack them over your head." "You crack 'em, I'll eat 'em," Taylor would pipe back, "but just don't put your fingers in 'em." And there would be another laugh. He hated the sight of Taylor.

It was Taylor who came to him to get the salad oil. About twenty of the soldiers were going to have a fish fry at the geisha house; they had bought the fish at the local market but they could not buy oil, so Taylor was sent as the deputy to Carter. He was charming to Carter, he complimented him on the meal, he clapped him on the back, he dissolved Carter to warmth, to private delight in the attention, and the thought that he had misjudged Taylor. Then Taylor asked for the oil.

Carter was sick with anger. Twenty men out of the thirty in the detachment were going on the fish fry. It meant only that Carter was considered one of the ten undesirables. It was something he had known, but the proof of knowledge is always more painful than the acquisition of it. If he had been alone his eyes would have clouded. And he was outraged at Taylor's deception. He could imagine Taylor saying ten minutes later, "You should have seen the grease job I gave to Carter. I'm dumb, but man, he's dumber."

Carter was close enough to giving him the oil. He had a sense of what it would mean to refuse Taylor, he was on the very edge of mild acquiescence. But he also had a sense of how he would despise himself afterward.

"No," he said abruptly, his teeth gritted, "you can't have it."

"What do you mean we can't have it?"

"I won't give it to you." Carter could almost feel the rage which Taylor generated at being refused.

"You won't give away a lousy five gallons of oil to a bunch of G.I.s having a party?"

"I'm sick and tired—" Carter began.

"So am I." Taylor walked away.

Carter knew he would pay for it. He left the K.P.s and went to change his sweat-soaked shirt, and as he passed the large dormitory in which most of the detachment slept he could hear Taylor's high-pitched voice.

Carter did not bother to take off his shirt. He returned instead to the kitchen, and listened to the sound of men going back and forth through the hall and of a man shouting with rage. That was Hobbs, a Southerner, a big man with a big bellowing voice.

There was a formal knock on the kitchen door. Taylor came in. His face was pale and his eyes showed a cold satisfaction. "Carter," he said, "the men want to see you in the big room."

Carter heard his voice answer huskily. "If they want to see me, they can come into the kitchen."

He knew he would conduct himself with more courage in his own kitchen than anywhere else. "I'll be here for a while."

Taylor closed the door, and Carter picked up a writing board to which was clamped the menu for the following day. Then he made a pretense of examining the food supplies in the pantry closet. It was his habit to check the stocks before deciding what to serve the next day, but on this night his eyes ranged thoughtlessly over the canned goods. In a corner were seven five-gallon tins of salad oil, easily enough cooking oil to last a month. Carter came out of the pantry and shut the door behind him.

He kept his head down and pretended to be writing the menu when the soldiers came in. Somehow there were even more of them than he had expected. Out of the twenty men who were going to the party, all but two or three had crowded through the door.

Carter took his time, looked up slowly. "You men want to see me?" he asked flatly.

They were angry. For the first time in his life he faced the hostile expressions of many men. It was the most painful and anxious moment he had ever known.

"Taylor says you won't give us the oil," someone burst out.

"That's right, I won't," said Carter. He tapped his pencil against the scratchboard, tapping it slowly and, he hoped, with an appearance of calm.

"What a stink deal," said Porfirio, a little Cuban whom Carter had always considered his friend.

Hobbs, the big Southerner, stared down at Carter. "Would you mind telling the men why you've decided not to give us the oil?" he asked quietly.

"'Cause I'm blowed if I'm going to cater to you men. I've catered enough," Carter said. His voice was close to cracking with the outrage he had suppressed for so long, and he knew that if he continued he might cry. "I'm the acting mess sergeant," he said as coldly as he could, "and I decide what goes out of this kitchen." He stared at each one in turn, trying to stare them down, feeling mired in the rut of his own failure. They would never have dared this approach to another mess sergeant.

"What crud," someone muttered.

"You won't give a lousy five-gallon can of oil for a G.I. party," Hobbs said more loudly.

"I won't. That's definite. You men can get out of here."

"Why, you lousy little snot," Hobbs burst out, "how many five-gallon cans of oil have you sold on the black market?"

"I've never sold any." Carter might have been slapped with the flat of a sword. He told himself bitterly, numbly, that this was the reward he received for being perhaps the single honest cook in the whole United States Army. And he even had time to wonder at the obscure prejudice which had kept him from selling food for his own profit.

"Man, I've seen you take it out," Hobbs exclaimed. "I've seen you take it to the market."

"I took food to trade for spices," Carter said hotly.

There was an ugly snicker from the men.

"I don't mind if a cook sells," Hobbs said, "every man has his own deal in this army. But a cook ought to give a little food to a G.I. if he wants it."

"Tell him," someone said.

"It's bull," Taylor screeched. "I've seen Carter take butter, eggs, every damn thing to the market."

Their faces were red, they circled him.

"I never sold a thing," Carter said doggedly.

"And I'm telling you," Hobbs said, "that you're a two-bit crook. You been raiding that kitchen, and that's why you don't give to us now."

Carter knew there was only one way he could possibly answer if he hoped to live among these men again. "That's a damn lie," Carter said to Hobbs. He laid down the scratchboard, he flipped his pencil slowly and deliberately to one corner of the room, and with his heart aching he lunged toward Hobbs. He had no hope of beating him. He merely intended to fight until he was pounded unconscious, advancing the pain and bruises he would collect as collateral for his self-respect.

To his indescribable relief Porfirio darted between them, held them apart, with the pleased ferocity of a small man breaking up a fight. "Now, stop this! Now, stop this!" he cried out.

Carter allowed himself to be pushed back, and he knew that he had gained a point. He even glimpsed a solution with some honor.

He shrugged violently to free himself from Por-

firio. He was in a rage, and yet it was a rage he could have ended at any instant. "All right, you men," he swore. "I'll give you the oil, but now that we're at it, I'm going to tell you a thing or two." His face red, his body perspiring, he was in the pantry and out again with a five-gallon tin. "Here," he said, "you better have a good fish fry, 'cause it's the last good meal you're going to have for quite a while. I'm sick of trying to please you. You think I have to work" —he was about to say, my fingers to the bone— "well, I don't. From now on, you'll see what chow in the army is supposed to be like." He was almost hysterical. "Take that oil. Have your fish fry." The fact that they wanted to cook for themselves was the greatest insult of all. "Tomorrow I'll give you real army cooking."

His voice was so intense that they backed away from him. "Get out of this kitchen," he said. "None of you has any business here."

They filed out quietly and they looked a little sheepish.

Carter felt weary, he felt ashamed of himself, he knew he had not meant what he said. But half an hour later, when he left the kitchen and passed the large dormitory, he heard shouts of raucous laughter, and he heard his name mentioned and then more laughter.

He slept badly that night, he was awake at four, he was in the kitchen by five, and he stood there white-faced and nervous, waiting for the K.P.s to arrive. Breakfast that morning landed on the men like a lead bomb. Carter rummaged in the back of the pantry and found a tin of dehydrated eggs covered with dust, memento of a time when fresh eggs were never on the ration list. The K.P.s looked at him in amazement as he stirred the lumpy powder into a pan of water. While it was still half-dissolved he put it on the fire. While it was still wet, he took it off. The coffee was cold, the toast was burned, the oatmeal stuck to the pot. The men dipped forks into their food, took cautious sips of their coffee, and spoke in whispers. Sullenness drifted like vapors through the kitchen.

At noontime Carter opened cans of meat-and-vegetable stew. He dumped them into a pan and heated them slightly. He served the stew with burned string beans and dehydrated potatoes which tasted like straw. For dessert the men had a single lukewarm canned peach and cold coffee.

So the meals continued. For three days Carter

cooked slop, and suffered even more than the men. When mealtime came he left the chow line to the K.P.s and sat in his room, perspiring with shame, determined not to yield and sick with the determination.

Carter won. On the fourth day a delegation of men came to see him. They told him that indeed they had appreciated his cooking in the past, they told him that they were sorry they had hurt his feelings, they listened to his remonstrances, they listened to his grievances, and with delight Carter forgave them. That night, for supper, the detachment celebrated. There was roast chicken with stuffing, lemon meringue pie and chocolate cake. The coffee burned their lips. More than half the men made it a point to compliment Carter on the meal.

In the weeks which followed the compliments diminished, but they never stopped completely. Carter became ashamed at last. He realized the men were trying to humor him, and he wished to tell them it was no longer necessary.

Harmony settled over the kitchen. Carter even became friends with Hobbs, the big Southerner. Hobbs approached him one day, and in the manner of a farmer talked obliquely for an hour. He spoke about his father, he spoke about his girl friends, he alluded indirectly to the night they had almost fought, and finally with the courtesy of a Southerner he said to Carter, "You know, I'm sorry about shooting off my mouth. You were right to want to fight me, and if you're still mad I'll fight you to give you satisfaction, although I just as soon would not."

"No, I don't want to fight with you now," Carter said warmly. They smiled at each other. They were friends.

Carter knew he had gained Hobbs' respect. Hobbs respected him because he had been willing to fight. That made sense to a man like Hobbs. Carter liked him so much at this moment that he wished the friendship to be more intimate.

"You know," he said to Hobbs, "it's a funny thing. You know I really never did sell anything on the black market. Not that I'm proud of it, but I just didn't."

Hobbs frowned. He seemed to be saying that Carter did not have to lie. "I don't hold it against a man," Hobbs said, "if he makes a little money in something that's his own proper work. Hell, I sell gas from the motor pool. It's just I also give gas if one of the G.I.s wants to take the jeep out for a joy ride, kind of."

"No, but I never did sell anything." Carter had to explain. "If I ever had sold on the black market, I would have given the salad oil without question."

Hobbs frowned again, and Carter realized he still did not believe him. Carter did not want to lose the friendship which was forming. He thought he could save it only by some further admission. "You know," he said again, "remember when Porfirio broke up our fight? I was awful glad when I didn't have to fight you." Carter laughed, expecting Hobbs to laugh with him, but a shadow passed across Hobbs' face.

"Funny way of putting it," Hobbs said.

He was always friendly thereafter, but Carter knew that Hobbs would never consider him a friend. Carter thought about it often, and began to wonder about the things which made him different. He was no longer so worried about becoming a man; he felt that to an extent he had become one. But in his heart he wondered if he would ever learn the language of men.

DISCUSSION

1. (a) What is Sanford Carter's feeling initially about becoming an army cook? (b) What had prompted this feeling?

2. (a) Prior to his becoming a cook, in what positions in the army had Carter failed? Why? (b) Immediately before he "took an opening in the kitchen," what is Carter's mental attitude and what are some of its causes? (c) What satisfaction does Carter quickly find in his new occupation?

3. Cite the sequence of events which enable Carter to advance from Private to Sergeant T/4 in one jump.

4. Carter finds that the happiest period of his life in the army follows his being assigned to a detachment working in a small seaport. (a) Describe the conditions which lead to his happiness. (b) Describe the physical, emotional, and behavioral changes in Carter that result from (and further contribute to) his happiness.

5. (a) How do the men respond to Carter's extra efforts on their behalf? (b) How does Carter respond in return? (c) What finally leads to "an explosion" between Carter and the men? (d) In what senses does Carter both lose and win the confrontation?

6. What incident at the end of the story suggests that Carter would never learn "the language of men"?

AUTHOR

NORMAN MAILER graduated from Harvard in 1943. During World War II, he served as an infantryman in the 112th Cavalry of the army. A number of his works, including "The Language of Men," are based on his wartime experiences.

Mr. Mailer's writings—fiction, journalism, essay, and poetry—have appeared in numerous prominent publications. *Armies of the Night,* a personal account of the events surrounding the antiwar demonstrations at the Pentagon, won him the Pulitzer Prize for general nonfiction in 1968. In addition to his writing, Mr. Mailer cofounded *The Village Voice* and served as an editor for *Dissent.*

Mr. Mailer's reputation as a public personality is well documented. He has directed and starred in several films and appears frequently on television. In 1969, he made an unsuccessful bid for the office of mayor of New York City. Jimmy Breslin, noted journalist and author, was his running mate.

Among Mr. Mailer's most popular and well-known writings are: *The Naked and the Dead, Advertisements for Myself, An American Dream, Why Are We in Vietnam?* and *Of a Fire on the Moon.*

The Beautiful Soul of Don Damián

Juan Bosch

He could see without being seen, hear without being heard, know others' motives without being known. And what he saw and heard and knew revolted him.

D ON Damián lapsed quickly into a coma as his temperature rose to over .104. His soul felt very uncomfortable, almost on the verge of being consumed by the heat, and for that reason it began to retire, gather itself into the heart. The soul had an infinite number of tentacles, like a squid with countless feet, each thrust into a vein and some of the slenderest into capillaries. Little by little it withdrew these feet, and as it did this Don Damián's body heat dropped and he grew pale. First his hands turned cold, then his legs and arms; his face began to grow dreadfully pale, as those gathered about his sumptuous bed noticed. The nurse herself became frightened and said it was time to send for the doctor. The soul heard her words and thought: I must hurry,

The Beautiful Soul of Don Damián by Juan Bosch

or that man will come and make me stay here until the fever consumes me.

It was growing light. Through the windowpanes came a wan light which announced the dawning day. Peering out of Don Damián's mouth—which was parted to let a little air in—the soul could see the light and told itself that if it did not act promptly it would not be able to do so later, inasmuch as people would see it leave and would prevent it from abandoning the body of its master. Don Damián's soul was ignorant of certain things; for example, it was unaware that once free it would be completely invisible.

There was a prolonged rustle of skirts around the rich bed where the sick man lay, and the sound of hurried words which the soul could not quite make out, engrossed as it was in escaping from its prison. The nurse came in with a hypodermic syringe in her hand.

"Please God it is not too late," clamored the voice of the old servant.

But it was too late. At the very moment the needle entered Don Damián's forearm, the soul withdrew the last of its tentacles from the dying man's mouth. It seemed to the soul that the injection had been an unnecessary expense. In a second, cries were heard and hurried footsteps, and while someone—undoubtedly the servant, for it could not possibly have been Don Damián's mother-in-law or wife—threw herself sobbing upon the bed, the soul took off into space, straight toward the superb chandelier of Bohemian crystal that hung from the middle of the ceiling. There it clung with all its strength and looked below: Don Damián was already a yellow shell, his features almost transparent and as brittle as the crystal; the bones of his face seemed to have become more prominent and the skin had taken on a repulsive luster. Around him his mother-in-law, his wife, and the nurse were milling; with her head buried in the bedclothes the old servant sobbed. The soul was completely cognizant of what each one was feeling and thinking, but it did not want to waste time watching them. The room was growing lighter by the minute, and it was afraid it might be noticed there where it hung, clinging to the lamp with a fear beyond words. Suddenly it saw Don Damián's mother-in-law take her daughter by the arm and lead her into the hall, where she spoke to her in an almost inaudible voice. These are the words the soul overheard: "You are not to behave as though you had no rearing. You must show grief."

"When the people get here, Mama," whispered the daughter.

"No, right now. Remember that the nurse may talk afterward."

Whereupon the newly minted widow ran toward the bed as though beside herself, screaming, "Damián, my Damián, oh, my Damián! How am I going to live without you, my beloved Damián?"

Another soul, less wise in the ways of the world, would have been astounded but Don Damián's, from its vantage point on the chandelier, was admiring the fine performance. Don Damián himself employed the same tactics on certain occasions, especially when it was a question of what he called "protecting his interests." The widow was fairly young, and attractive, whereas Don Damián was over sixty. She had had a sweetheart when Don Damián began courting her, and the soul had suffered unpleasant moments because of its ex-master's jealousy. It recalled one scene in particular which had taken place only a few months before in which the wife had said, "You can't forbid me to talk to him. You know perfectly well that I married you for your money."

To which Don Damián replied that with that money he had bought the right not to be made a fool of. The scene was extremely disagreeable, with the mother-in-law putting in her oar and threats of divorce. In a word, a bad moment, made even worse by the fact that the discussion was cut short because of the arrival of some very distinguished visitors whom both husband and wife received with charming smiles and delightful manners that only it, the soul of Don Damián, could assess at their real value.

The soul was still there, on the chandelier, recollecting these things, when a priest arrived in great haste. Nobody knew why he had showed up so opportunely, inasmuch as the sun wasn't quite up yet, and the priest had been with the patient during the night.

"I came because I had a foreboding; I came because I was afraid Don Damián might yield up his soul without making confession," he tried to explain.

To which the deceased's mother-in-law suspiciously replied, "Why didn't he confess last night, Father?"

She was referring to the fact that for nearly an hour the minister of the Lord had been alone behind closed doors with Don Damián, and everybody had believed that the sick man had made confession. But this had not been the case. Perched up on the chandelier the soul knew he had not, and it also knew why the priest had shown up. That long private interview had had as its subject a somewhat arid matter; for the priest had proposed to Don Damián that he leave in his will a considerable sum for the new church that was being built in the city, and Don Damián wanted to leave even more money than was requested, but to a hospital. They could not reach an agreement and when the priest got home he noticed that he did not have his watch. What was happening to the soul, once it was free, was nothing short of miraculous, this business of being able to know things that had not happened in its presence as well as to divine what people were thinking and going to do. The soul recalled that the priest had said to himself, "I remember that I took out my watch when I was at Don Damián's house to see what time it was; I must have left it there." So this visit at such an unusual hour had nothing to do with the kingdom of God.

"No, he did not confess," explained the priest, looking Don Damián's mother-in-law in the eye. "He did not get around to it last night, and we agreed that I would come first thing this morning to hear his confession and give him communion. I have come too late, and it is a great pity," he said, as he turned his head toward the different corners and the gilt tables, without doubt hoping to see his watch on one of them.

The old servant, who had been waiting on Don Damián for more than forty years, raised her face with its tear-reddened eyes. "After all, it was not necessary," she asseverated, "and may God forgive me. He did not need to confess because he had a beautiful soul, a very beautiful soul had Don Damián."

The devil, now this was interesting! Don Damián's soul had never envisaged itself as beautiful. Its master did certain strange things, and as he was an outstanding example of a rich man who dressed in the height of fashion, and managed his bank account with great dexterity, the soul had not had time to give thought to certain aspects that might bear upon its own beauty or possible ugliness. For instance, it recalled how its master had instructed it to feel good when after prolonged interviews with his lawyer Don Damián found a way of foreclosing his claim to the house of some debtor—who afterward often had no place to live—or when with the per-

suasion of jewels and cash in hand—for her studies, or because of her ailing mother's health—a pretty young thing from the working-class quarter agreed to visit a luxurious apartment Don Damián kept. Was it beautiful or ugly, the soul asked itself?

From the time it had managed to escape from the veins of its master until it became the object of this remark by the servant, very little time had elapsed by the soul's calculations, and probably even less than it thought. Everything was happening very quickly and, besides, with great confusion. It had felt as though it were boiling in the sick man's body and realized that it was the temperature that was going up. Before it had withdrawn, long before midnight, the doctor had warned that this might happen.

He had said, "Possibly the fever will rise toward morning; if that happens you must be on the alert. If he gets worse, call me."

Was the soul going to stand by and let itself be roasted? Its vital center, so to speak, was close to Don Damián's bowels, which gave off flames. It was going to die like an animal in an oven, and that did not appeal to it. But, as a matter of fact, how much time had elapsed since it left Don Damián's body? Very little, in view of the fact that it was still suffering from the heat in spite of the slight coolness the dawning day was spreading which reached the chandelier where it clung. It thought that the change of climate between the bowels of its sometime master and the glass of the chandelier had not been too sharp, thanks to which it had not caught cold. But with or without a sharp change, what about the servant's remark? "Beautiful" was the word the old woman had used, and she was a truthful person who had loved her master simply because she loved him, not because of his distinguished appearance or because of the gifts he gave her. In the words that followed, the soul did not feel the same ring of sincerity.

"Of course, his was a beautiful soul," agreed the priest.

"Beautiful is putting it mildly," affirmed the mother-in-law.

The soul took another look at her and observed how, as she spoke, she kept her eyes fixed on her daughter. Those eyes seemed to be ordering and pleading at one and the same time. It was as if they were saying: "Start crying this very minute, you imbecile, before the priest realizes that the death of this wretch has made you happy."

The daughter instantly understood that silent and angry language, for she at once broke into woeful lamentation. "Never, never was there a more beautiful soul than his. Oh, my Damián, my Damián, light of my life."

The soul could stand no more; it was torn between curiosity and disgust; it wanted to assure itself that it was beautiful and to get away from that place where everybody was trying to pull the wool over everybody else's eyes. So, curious and disgusted, it took off from the chandelier in the direction of the bathroom, whose walls were covered with huge mirrors. It calculated the distance carefully so as to fall on the carpet without making a noise. In addition to being unaware of the fact that people could not see it, it was equally unaware of the fact that it was weightless. It felt a great relief when it saw that it passed unnoticed and ran breathless to look at itself in the mirrors.

But, good Heavens, what was happening? In the first place, it had grown accustomed during more than sixty years to seeing through the eyes of Don Damián; and those eyes were high, almost five feet ten inches from the ground; it was, moreover, accustomed to the lively face of its master, his light eyes, his gleaming hair that was turning silver, to the proud bearing of his shoulders and head, to the fine clothes he wore. And what it now saw was nothing of all this, but instead a strange figure barely a foot tall, soft, colorless, without clear contours. In the first place, it resembled nothing it had ever seen before. For instead of what should have been two feet and legs as was always the case when it inhabited the body of Don Damián, there was a monstrous, and at the same time small, cluster of tentacles, like those of a squid, but devoid of any order, some shorter than the others, some thinner, and all as though made of dirty smoke, of some nondescript, intangible mud, seeming transparent without being so, flabby, limp, which buckled with repulsive ugliness. Don Damián's soul felt itself lost. Nevertheless it mustered courage enough to look up. It had no waistline. The fact is that it had neither body nor neck nor anything, except that where the tentacles came together a kind of drooping ear emerged on one side, something like a wrinkled, suppurating crust, and on the other a tuft of colorless hair, coarse, some twisted, others straight. But that was not the worst, nor even the strange grayish, yellowish light that enveloped it; the mouth was a formless hole, a cross between that of a mouse and

the gaping cavity in a rotten fruit, horrible, nauseating, truly revolting, and in the depth of this cavity glittered an eye, a single eye, holding dark reflections and an expression of terror and perfidiousness. How was it possible that those women and the priest could go on insisting in the adjacent room, beside the bed where Don Damián lay, that his had been a beautiful soul?

"Go out, me go out in the street looking like this, for people to see me?" it asked itself, in what it believed its loudest voice, still unaware of the fact that it was invisible and inaudible, lost in a black tunnel of confusion.

What was it to do, what future awaited it? The bell rang. In a moment the nurse was saying, "It is the doctor, madame. I'll go to the door."

On hearing this Don Damián's wife began to howl again, calling upon her dead husband and bemoaning the loneliness in which he had left her.

Paralyzed before its own image, the soul realized that it was lost. It had become accustomed to its refuge, to the tall body of Don Damián; it had even become accustomed to the unbearable smell of his bowels, to his heartburn, to the annoyance of his colds. Its thoughts were interrupted by the doctor's greeting and the voice of the mother-in-law declaiming, "Oh, doctor, what a misfortune, doctor, what a misfortune!"

"Calm yourself, madame, calm yourself," replied the doctor.

The soul peeped into the death chamber. There around the bed the women were gathered; standing at the foot, with an open book, the priest began to pray. The soul measured the distance and gave a leap. It was easier than it had believed, as though it were of air or were some strange animal that could move without being heard or seen. Don Damián's mouth was still slightly open. It was as cold as ice, but that did not matter. The soul slipped swiftly through it and instantly slid down the larynx and began to thrust its tentacles into the body, penetrating the inner walls without the least difficulty. It was settling itself in place when it heard the doctor speak.

"Just a moment, madame, if you please."

The soul could see the doctor, though very vaguely. He approached the body of Don Damián, picked up his wrist, seemed perplexed, laid his cheek against the dead man's chest and rested it there for a moment. Then, slowly, he opened his bag and took out a stethoscope; carefully he put the two discs in his ears and held the other end of the tube over the place where the heart must be. His expression once more became puzzled; he hunted about in his bag and took from it a hypodermic syringe. With the air of a sleight-of-hand artist making preparations for a sensational act, he told the nurse to fill the syringe while he began tying a slender rubber tube around Don Damián's elbow. Apparently, all these preparations alarmed the old servant.

"But why are you doing that to him when the poor thing is already dead?" she asked.

The doctor looked her in the eye with the air of a superior being, and this was what he said, though not so much for her to hear as for the wife and the mother-in-law of Don Damián, "Madame, science is science, and it is my duty to do everything in my power to bring Don Damián back to life. Souls as beautiful as his are not seen every day, and we cannot let him die without exploring every possibility."

This brief speech, spoken with august calm, alarmed the wife. It was easy to note a hard glitter in her eyes, and a strange tremor in her voice.

"But isn't he dead?" she asked.

The soul was now all back in place and only three tentacles were still feeling about for the old veins where they had been for years and years. The attention it was giving to getting those tentacles where they belonged did not, however, prevent it from noticing the puzzled accent in her question.

The doctor did not answer. He took Don Damián's forearm and began to rub it with his hand. It was at this point that the soul began to feel the warmth of life enveloping it, penetrating it, filling the old arteries which it had fled to avoid being consumed in the fire. Then, almost simultaneously with the beginning of this warmth, the doctor sank the needle into the vein of the arm, untied the ligature above the elbow and began to push down the plunger of the syringe. Little by little the warmth of life rose to Don Damián's skin.

DISCUSSION

"A miracle, Lord, a miracle," muttered the priest.

Suddenly, as he witnessed that resurrection, the priest turned pale and gave his imagination free rein. The donation for the church could be counted on, for how could Don Damián refuse his help once he told him, during the days of his convalescence, how he had seen him brought back to life seconds after he had prayed for such a miracle? "The Lord heeded my pleas and brought you back from the tomb, Don Damián," he would say.

Suddenly the wife, too, felt that her mind was a blank. She looked anxiously at her husband's face and turned toward her mother. Both of them were disconcerted, silent, almost terrified.

But the doctor smiled. He was pleased beyond words, though he tried to conceal it.

"Ah, but he has been saved, thanks to God and to you," the servant cried out, weeping tears of joy, and taking the doctor's hands in hers. "He has been saved, he is coming back to life. Ah, Don Damián will know how to repay you, sir," she assured him.

That was just what the doctor was thinking, that Don Damián had plenty with which to pay him. But he said something different. He said, "Even though he were unable to pay me, I would have done what I did, for it was my duty to save for society such a beautiful soul as his."

He was answering the servant, but he was really speaking for the others to hear; above all so they would repeat his words to the patient, some days later, when he was able to sign.

Wearied with all the lies it had heard, Don Damián's soul decided to go to sleep. A second later Don Damián moaned, though very weakly, and moved his head on the pillow.

"Now he will sleep for several hours," explained the doctor, "and nobody should disturb him."

Saying this he set the example and left the room on tiptoe.

1. (a) In what ways was Don Damián's soul like (a) a squid? (b) Like a human being? (c) Like a supranatural being?

2. (a) What did Don Damián's servant mean by the word *beautiful* used in reference to her master's soul? How did the soul interpret the word? (b) What prompted the soul to return to Don Damián's body?

3. (a) For what common reason were Don Damián's wife, doctor, and priest interested in his health? Why, on the other hand, was his servant concerned for his well-being? Explain. (b) If someone were to ask you, "What kind of person was Don Damián?" what would be your response? Explain.

4. Knowing what you now know as a result of having read the story, if you were Don Damián, what would you do with your life and money upon recuperating?

The Blood of the Martyrs

Stephen Vincent Benét

THE man who expected to be shot lay with his eyes open, staring at the upper lefthand corner of his cell. He was fairly well over his last beating, and they might come for him any time now. There was a yellow stain in the cell corner near the ceiling; he had liked it at first, then disliked it; now he was coming back to liking it again.

He could see it more clearly with his glasses on, but he put on his glasses only for special occasions now—the first thing in the morning, and when they brought the food in, and for interviews with the General. The lenses of the glasses had been cracked in a beating some months before, and it strained his eyes to wear them too long. Fortunately, in his present life he had very few occasions demanding clear vision. But, nevertheless, the accident to his glasses worried him, as it worries all near-sighted people. You put your glasses on the first thing in the morning, and the world leaps into proportion; if it does not do so, something is wrong with the world.

The man did not believe greatly in symbols, but his chief nightmare nowadays was an endless one in which, suddenly and without warning, a large piece of glass would drop out of one of the lenses and he would grope around the cell, trying to find it. He would grope very carefully and gingerly, for hours of darkness, but the end was always the same—the small, unmistakable crunch of irreplaceable glass beneath his heel or his knee. Then he would wake up sweating, with his hands cold. This dream alternated with the one of being shot, but he found no great benefit in the change.

As he lay there, you could see that he had an intellectual head—the head of a thinker or a scholar, old and bald, with the big, domed brow. It was, as a matter of fact, a well-known head; it had often appeared in the columns of newspapers and journals, sometimes when the surrounding text was in a language Professor Malzius could not read. The body, though stooped and worn, was still a strong peasant body and capable of surviving a good deal of ill-treatment, as his captors had found out. He had fewer teeth than when he came to prison, and both the ribs and the knee had been badly set, but these were minor matters. It also occurred to him that his blood count was probably poor. However, if he could ever get out and to a first-class hospital, he was probably good for at least ten years more of work. But, of course, he would not get out. They would shoot him before that, and it would be over.

Sometimes he wished passionately that it would be over—tonight—this moment; at other times he was shaken by the mere blind fear of death. The latter he tried to treat as he would have treated an attack of malaria, knowing that it was an attack, but not always with success. He should have been able to face it better than most—he was Gregor Malzius, the scientist—but that did not always help. The fear of death persisted, even when one had noted and classified it as a purely physical reaction. When he was out of here, he would be able to write a very instructive little paper on the fear of death. He

could even do it here, if he had writing materials, but there was no use asking for those. Once they had been given to him, and he had spent two days quite happily. But they had torn up the work and spat upon it in front of his face. It was a childish thing to do, but it discouraged a man from working.

It seemed odd that he had never seen anybody shot, but he never had. During the war, his reputation and his bad eyesight had exempted him from active service. He had been bombed a couple of times when his reserve battalion was guarding the railway bridge, but that was quite different. You were not tied to a stake, and the airplanes were not trying to kill you as an individual. He knew the place where it was done here, of course. But prisoners did not see the executions, they merely heard, if the wind was from the right quarter.

He had tried again and again to visualize how it would be, but it always kept mixing with an old steel engraving he had seen in boyhood—the execution of William Walker,[1] the American filibuster, in Honduras. William Walker was a small man with a white semi-Napoleonic face. He was standing, very correctly dressed, in front of an open grave, and before him a ragged line of picturesque natives were raising their muskets. When he was shot he would instantly and tidily fall into the grave, like a man dropping through a trap door; as a boy, the extreme neatness of the arrangement had greatly impressed Gregor Malzius. Behind the wall there were palm trees, and, somewhere off to the right, blue and warm, the Caribbean Sea. It would not be like that at all, for his own execution; and yet, whenever he thought of it, he thought of it as being like that.

Well, it was his own fault. He could have accepted the new regime; some respectable people had done that. He could have fled the country; many honorable people had. A scientist should be concerned with the eternal, not with transient political phenomena; and a scientist should be able to live anywhere. But thirty years at the university were thirty years and, after all, he was Malzius, one of the first biochemists in the world. To the last, he had not believed that they would touch him. Well, he had been wrong about that.

The truth, of course, was the truth. One taught it

1. *William Walker,* American adventurer who tried to make himself the ruler of two Central American countries, Nicaragua and Honduras. He was executed in Honduras in 1860.

or one did not teach it. If one did not teach it, it hardly mattered what one did. But he had no quarrel with any established government; he was willing to run up a flag every Tuesday, as long as they let him alone. Most people were fools, and one government was as good as another for them—it had taken them twenty years to accept his theory of cell mutation. Now, if he'd been like his friend Bonnard—a fellow who signed protests, attended meetings for the cause of world peace, and generally played the fool in public—they'd have had some reason to complain. An excellent man in his field, Bonnard—none better—but outside of it, how deplorably like an actor, with his short gray beard, his pink cheeks, and his impulsive enthusiasm! Any government could put a fellow like Bonnard in prison—though it would be an injury to science and, therefore, wrong. For that matter, he thought grimly, Bonnard would enjoy being a martyr. He'd walk gracefully to the execution post with a begged cigarette in his mouth, and some theatrical last quip. But Bonnard was safe in his own land— doubtless writing heated and generous articles on The Case of Professor Malzius—and he, Malzius, was the man who was going to be shot. He would like a cigarette, too, on his way to execution; he had not smoked in five months. But he certainly didn't intend to ask for one, and they wouldn't think of offering him any. That was the difference between him and Bonnard.

His mind went back with longing to the stuffy laboratory and stuffier lecture hall at the university; his feet yearned for the worn steps he had climbed ten thousand times, and his eyes for the long steady look through the truthful lens into worlds too tiny for the unaided eye. They had called him "The Bear" and "Old Prickly," but they had fought to work under him, the best of the young men. They said he would explain the Last Judgment in terms of cellular phenomena, but they had crowded to his lectures. It was Williams, the Englishman, who had made up the legend that he carried a chocolate éclair and a set of improper post cards in his battered brief case. Quite untrue, of course—chocolate always made him ill, and he never looked at an improper post card in his life. And Williams would never know that he knew the legend, too; for Williams had been killed long ago in the war. For a moment, Professor Malzius felt blind hate at the thought of an excellent scientific machine like

Williams being smashed in a war. But blind hate was an improper emotion for a scientist, and he put it aside.

He smiled grimly again; they hadn't been able to break up his classes—lucky he was The Bear! He'd seen one colleague hooted from his desk by a band of determined young hoodlums—too bad, but if a man couldn't keep order in his own classroom, he'd better get out. They'd wrecked his own laboratory, but not while he was there.

It was so senseless, so silly. "In God's name," he said reasonably, to no one, "what sort of conspirator do you think I would make? A man of my age and habits! I am interested in cellular phenomena!" And yet they were beating him because he would not tell about the boys. As if he had even paid attention to half the nonsense! There were certain passwords and greetings—a bar of music you whistled, entering a restaurant; the address of a firm that specialized, ostensibly, in vacuum cleaners. But they were not his own property. They belonged to the young men who had trusted The Bear. He did not know what half of them meant, and the one time he had gone to a meeting, he had felt like a fool. For they were fools and childish—playing the childish game of conspiracy that people like Bonnard enjoyed. Could they even make a better world than the present? He doubted it extremely. And yet, he could not betray them; they had come to him, looking over their shoulders, with darkness in their eyes.

A horrible, an appalling thing—to be trusted. He had no wish to be a guide and counselor of young men. He wanted to do his work. Suppose they were poor and ragged and oppressed; he had been a peasant himself, he had eaten black bread. It was by his own efforts that he was Professor Malzius. He did not wish the confidences of boys like Gregopolous and the others—for, after all, what was Gregopolous? An excellent and untiring laboratory assistant—and a laboratory assistant he would remain to the end of his days. He had pattered about the laboratory like a fox terrier, with a fox terrier's quick, bright eyes. Like a devoted dog, he had made a god of Professor Malzius. "I don't want your problems, man. I don't want to know what you are doing outside the laboratory." But Gregopolous had brought his problems and his terrible trust none the less, humbly and proudly, like a fox terrier with a bone. After that—well, what was a man to do?

He hoped they would get it over with, and quickly. The world should be like a chemical formula, full of reason and logic. Instead there were all these young men, and their eyes. They conspired, hopelessly and childishly, for what they called freedom against the new regime. They wore no overcoats in winter and were often hunted and killed. Even if they did not conspire, they had miserable little love affairs and ate the wrong food—yes, even before, at the university, they had been the same. Why the devil would they not accept? Then they could do their work. Of course, a great many of them would not be allowed to accept—they had the wrong ideas or the wrong politics—but then they could run away. If Malzius, at twenty, had had to run from his country, he would still have been a scientist. To talk of a free world was a delusion; men were not free in the world. Those who wished got a space of time to get their work done. That was all. And yet, he had not accepted—he did not know why.

Now he heard the sound of steps along the corridor. His body began to quiver, and the places where he had been beaten hurt him. He noted it as an interesting reflex. Sometimes they merely flashed the light in the cell and passed by. On the other hand, it might be death. It was a hard question to decide.

The lock creaked, the door opened. "Get up, Malzius!" said the hard, bright voice of the guard. Gregor Malzius got up. A little stiffly, but quickly.

"Put on your glasses, you old fool!" said the guard, with a laugh. "You are going to the General."

Professor Malzius found the stone floors of the corridor uneven, though he knew them well enough. Once or twice the guard struck him, lightly and without malice, as one strikes an old horse with a whip. The blows were familiar and did not register on Professor Malzius' consciousness; he merely felt proud of not stumbling. He was apt to stumble; once he had hurt his knee.

He noticed, it seemed to him, an unusual tenseness and officiousness about his guard. Once, even, in a brightly lighted corridor the guard moved to strike him, but refrained. However, that, too, happened occasionally, with one guard or another, and Professor Malzius merely noted the fact. It was a small fact, but an important one in the economy in which he lived.

But there could be no doubt that something unusual was going on in the castle. There were more guards than usual, many of them strangers. He tried to think, carefully, as he walked, if it could be one of the new national holidays. It was hard to keep track of them all. The General might be in a good humor. Then they would merely have a cat-and-mouse conversation for half an hour, and nothing really bad would happen. Once, even, there had been a cigar. Professor Malzius, the scientist, licked his lips at the thought.

Now he was being turned over to a squad of other guards, with salutings. This was really unusual; Professor Malzius bit his mouth inconspicuously. He had the poignant distrust of a monk or an old prisoner at any break in routine. Old prisoners are your true conservatives; they demand only that the order around them remain exactly the same.

It alarmed him as well that the new guards did not laugh at him. New guards almost always laughed when they saw him for the first time. He was used to the laughter and missed it—his throat felt dry. He would have liked, just once, to eat at the university restaurant before he died. It was bad food, ill-cooked and starchy, food good enough for poor students and professors, but he would have liked to be there, in the big smoky room that smelled of copper boilers and cabbage, with a small cup of bitter coffee before him and a cheap cigarette. He did not ask for his dog or his notebooks, the old photographs in his bedroom, his incomplete experiments or his freedom. Just to lunch once more at the university restaurant and have people point out The Bear. It seemed a small thing to ask, but of course it was quite impossible.

"Halt!" said a voice, and he halted. There were, for the third time, salutings. Then the door of the General's office opened, and he was told to go in.

He stood, just inside the door, in the posture of attention, as he had been taught. The crack in the left lens of his glasses made a crack across the room, and his eyes were paining him already, but he paid no attention to that. There was the familiar figure of the General, with his air of a well-fed and extremely healthy tomcat, and there was another man, seated at the General's desk. He could not see the other man very well—the crack made him bulge and waver—but he did not like his being there.

"Well, Professor," said the General, in an easy, purring voice. Malzius' entire body jerked. He had made a fearful, an unpardonable omission. He must remedy it at once. "Long live the state," he shouted in a loud thick voice, and saluted. He knew, bitterly, that his salute was ridiculous and that he looked ridiculous making it. But perhaps the General would laugh—he had done so before. Then everything would be all right, for it was not quite as easy to beat a man after you had laughed at him.

The General did not laugh. He made a half turn instead, toward the man at the desk. The gesture said, "You see, he is well trained." It was the gesture of a man of the world, accustomed to deal with unruly peasants and animals—the gesture of a man fitted to be General.

The man at the desk paid no attention to the General's gesture. He lifted his head, and Malzius saw him more clearly and with complete unbelief. It was not a man but a picture come alive. Professor Malzius had seen the picture a hundred times; they had made him salute and take off his hat in front of it, when he had had a hat. Indeed, the picture had presided over his beatings. The man himself was a little smaller, but the picture was a good picture. There were many dictators in the world, and this was one type. The face was white, beaky and semi-Napoleonic; the lean, military body sat squarely in its chair. The eyes dominated the face, and the mouth was rigid. I remember also a hypnotist, and a woman Charcot showed me, at his clinic in Paris, thought Professor Malzius. But there is also, obviously, an endocrine unbalance. Then his thoughts stopped.

"Tell the man to come closer," said the man at the desk. "Can he hear me? Is he deaf?"

"No, Your Excellency," said the General, with enormous, purring respect. "But he is a little old, though perfectly healthy. . . . Are you not, Professor Malzius?"

"Yes, I am perfectly healthy. I am very well treated here," said Professor Malzius, in his loud thick voice. They were not going to catch him with traps like that, not even by dressing up somebody as the Dictator. He fixed his eyes on the big old-fashioned inkwell on the General's desk—that, at least, was perfectly sane.

"Come closer," said the man at the desk to Professor Malzius, and the latter advanced till he could almost touch the inkwell with his fingers. Then he stopped with a jerk, hoping he had done right. The movement removed the man at the desk from the crack in his lenses, and Professor Malzius knew suddenly that it was true. This was indeed, the Dictator, this man with the rigid mouth. Professor Malzius began to talk.

"I have been very well treated here, and the General has acted with the greatest consideration," he said. "But I am Professor Gregor Malzius—professor of biochemistry. For thirty years I have lectured at the university; I am a fellow of the Royal Society, a corresponding member of the Academy of Sciences at Berlin, at Rome, at Boston, at Paris, and at Stockholm. I have received the Nottingham Medal, the Lamarck Medal, the Order of St. John of Portugal, and the Nobel Prize. I think my blood count is low, but I have received a great many degrees, and my experiments on the migratory cells are not finished. I do not wish to complain of my treatment, but I must continue my experiments."

He stopped, like a clock that has run down, surprised to hear the sound of his own voice. He noted, in one part of his mind, that the General had made a move to silence him, but had himself been silenced by the Dictator.

"Yes, Professor Malzius," said the man at the desk, in a harsh, toneless voice. "There has been a regrettable error." The rigid face stared at Professor Malzius. Professor Malzius stared back. He did not say anything.

"In these days," said the Dictator, his voice rising, "the nation demands the submission of every citizen. Encircled by jealous foes, our reborn land yet steps forward toward her magnificent destiny." The words continued for some time, the voice rose and fell. Professor Malzius listened respectfully; he had heard the words many times before, and they had ceased to have meaning to him. He was thinking of certain cells of the body that rebel against the intricate processes of Nature and set up their own bellicose state. Doubtless they, too, have a destiny, he thought, but in medicine it is called cancer.

"Jealous and spiteful tongues in other countries have declared that it is our purpose to wipe out learning and science," concluded the Dictator. "That is not our purpose. After the cleansing, the rebirth. We mean to move forward to the greatest science in the world—our own science, based on the enduring principles of our nationhood." He ceased abruptly, his eyes fell into their dream. Very like the girl Charcot showed me in my young days, thought Professor Malzius; there was first the ebullition, then the calm.

"I was part of the cleansing? You did not mean to hurt me?" he asked timidly.

"Yes, Professor Malzius," said the General, smiling, "you were part of the cleansing. Now that is over. His Excellency has spoken."

"I do not understand," said Professor Malzius, gazing at the fixed face of the man behind the desk.

"It is very simple," said the General. He spoke in a slow careful voice, as one speaks to a deaf man or a child. "You are a distinguished man of science—you have received the Nobel Prize. That was a service to the state. You became, however, infected by the wrong political ideas. That was treachery to the state. You had, therefore, as decreed by His Excellency, to pass through a certain period for probation and rehabilitation. But that, we believe, is finished."

"You do not wish to know the names of the young men any more?" said Professor Malzius. "You do not want the addresses?"

"That is no longer of importance," said the General patiently. "There is no longer opposition. The leaders were caught and executed three weeks ago."

"There is no longer opposition," repeated Professor Malzius.

"At the trial, you were not even involved."

"I was not even involved," said Professor Malzius. "Yes."

"Now," said the General, with a look at the Dictator, "we come to the future. I will be frank—the new state is frank with its citizens."

"It is so," said the Dictator, his eyes still sunk in his dream.

"There has been—let us say—a certain agitation in foreign countries regarding Professor Malzius," said the General, his eyes still fixed on the Dictator. "That means nothing, of course. Nevertheless, your acquaintance, Professor Bonnard, and others have meddled in matters that do not concern them."

"They asked after me?" said Professor Malzius, with surprise. "It is true, my experiments were reaching a point that——"

"No foreign influence could turn us from our firm purpose," said the Dictator. "But it is our firm purpose to show our nation first in science and culture as we have already shown her first in manliness and statehood. For that reason, you are here, Professor Malzius." He smiled.

Professor Malzius stared. His cheeks began to tremble.

"I do not understand," said Professor Malzius. "You will give me my laboratory back?"

"Yes," said the Dictator, and the General nodded as one nods to a stupid child.

Professor Malzius passed a hand across his brow. "My post at the university?" he said. "My experiments?"

"It is the purpose of our regime to offer the fullest encouragement to our loyal sons of science," said the Dictator.

"First of all," said Professor Malzius, "I must go to a hospital. My blood count is poor. But that will not take long." His voice had become impatient and his eyes glowed. "Then—my notebooks were burned, I suppose. I have a very good memory, an excellent memory. The theories are in my head, you know," and he tapped it. "I must have assistants, of course; little Gregopolous was my best one——"

"The man Gregopolous has been executed," said the General, in a stern voice. "You had best forget him."

"Oh," said Professor Malzius. "Well, then, I must have someone else. You see, these are important experiments. There must be some young men—clever ones—they cannot all be dead. I will know them." He laughed a little, nervously. "The Bear always got the pick of the crop," he said. "They used to call me The Bear, you know." He stopped and looked at them for a moment with ghastly eyes. "You are not fooling me?" he said. He burst into tears.

When he recovered he was alone in the room with the General. The General was looking at him as he himself had looked once at strange forms of life under the microscope, with neither disgust nor attraction, but with great interest.

"His Excellency forgives your unworthy suggestion," he said. "He knows you are overwrought."

"Yes," said Professor Malzius. He sobbed once and dried his glasses.

"Come, come," said the General, with a certain bluff heartiness. "We mustn't have our new president of the National Academy crying. It would look badly in the photographs."

"President of the Academy?" said Professor Malzius quickly. "Oh, no; I mustn't be that. They make speeches; they have administrative work. But I am a scientist, a teacher."

"I'm afraid you can't very well avoid it," said the General, still heartily, though he looked at Professor Malzius. "Your induction will be quite a ceremony. His Excellency himself will preside. And you will speak on the new glories of our science. It will be a magnificent answer to the petty and jealous criticisms of our neighbors. Oh, you needn't worry about the speech," he added quickly. "It will be prepared; you will only have to read it. His Excellency thinks of everything."

"Very well," said Professor Malzius, "and then may I go back to my work?"

"Oh, don't worry about that," said the General, smiling. "I'm only a simple soldier; I don't know about those things. But you'll have plenty of work."

"The more the better," said Malzius eagerly. "I still have ten good years."

He opened his mouth to smile, and a shade of dismay crossed the General's face.

"Yes," he said, as if to himself. "The teeth must be attended to. At once. And a rest, undoubtedly, before the photographs are taken. Milk. You are feeling sufficiently well, Professor Malzius?"

"I am very happy," said Professor Malzius. "I have been very well treated, and I come of peasant stock."

"Good," said the General. He paused for a moment and spoke in a more official voice.

"Of course, it is understood, Professor Malzius —" he said.

"Yes?" said Professor Malzius. "I beg your pardon. I was thinking of something else."

"It is understood, Professor Malzius," repeated the General, "that your—er—rehabilitation in the service of the state is a permanent matter. Naturally, you will be under observation, but, even so, there must be no mistake."

"I am a scientist," said Professor Malzius impatiently. "What have I to do with politics? If you wish me to take oaths of loyalty, I will take as many as you wish."

"I am glad you take that attitude," said the General, though he looked at Professor Malzius curiously. "I may say that I regret the unpleasant side of our interviews. I trust you bear no ill will."

"Why should I be angry?" said Professor Malzius. "You were told to do one thing. Now you are told to do another. That is all."

"It is not quite so simple as that," said the General rather stiffly. He looked at Professor Malzius for a third time. "And I'd have sworn you were one of the stiff-necked ones," he said. "Well, well, every man has his breaking point, I suppose. In a few moments you will receive the final commands of His Excellency. Tonight you will go to the capitol and speak over the radio. You will have no difficulty there—the speech is written. But it will put a quietus on the activities of our friend Bonnard and the question that has been raised in the British Parliament. Then a few weeks of rest by the sea and the dental work, and then, my dear president of the National Academy, you will be ready to undertake your new duties. I congratulate you and hope we shall meet often under pleasant auspices." He bowed from the waist to Malzius, the bow of a man of the world, though there was still something feline in his mustache. Then he stood to attention, and Malzius, too, for the Dictator had come into the room.

"It is settled?" said the Dictator. "Good. Gregor Malzius, I welcome you to the service of the new state. You have cast your errors aside and are part of our destiny."

"Yes," said Professor Malzius, "I will be able to do my work now."

The Dictator frowned a little.

"You will not only be able to continue your invaluable researches," he said, "but you will also be able—and it will be part of your duty—to further our national ideals. Our reborn nation must rule the world for the world's good. There is a fire within us that is not in other stocks. Our civilization must be extended everywhere. The future wills it. It will furnish the subject of your first discourse as president of the Academy."

"But," said Professor Malzius, in a low voice, "I am not a soldier. I am a biochemist. I have no experience in these matters you speak of."

The Dictator nodded. "You are a distinguished man of science," he said. "You will prove that our women must bear soldiers, our men abandon this nonsense of republics and democracies for trust in those born to rule them. You will prove by scientific law that certain races—our race in particular—are destined to rule the world. You will prove they are destined to rule by the virtues of war, and that war is part of our heritage."

"But," said Professor Malzius, "it is not like that. I mean," he said, "one looks and watches in the laboratory. One waits for a long time. It is a long process, very long. And then, if the theory is not proved, one discards the theory. That is the way it is done. I probably do not explain it well. But I am a biochemist; I do not know how to look for the virtues of one race against another, and I can prove nothing about war, except that it kills. If I said anything else, the whole world would laugh at me."

"Not one in this nation would laugh at you," said the Dictator.

"But if they do not laugh at me when I am wrong, there is no science," said Professor Malzius, knotting his brows. He paused. "Do not misunderstand me," he said earnestly. "I have ten years of good work left; I want to get back to my laboratory. But, you see, there are the young men—if I am to teach the young men."

He paused again, seeing their faces before him. There were many. There was Williams, the Englishman, who had died in the war, and little Gregopolous with the fox-terrier eyes. There were all who had passed through his classrooms, from the stupidest to the best. They had shot little Gregopolous for treason, but that did not alter the case. From all over the world they had come—he remembered the Indian student and the Chinese. They wore cheap overcoats, they were hungry for knowledge, they ate the bad, starchy food of the poor restaurants, they had miserable little love affairs and played childish games of politics, instead of doing their work. Nevertheless, a few were promising—all must be given the truth. It did not matter if they died, but they must be given the truth. Otherwise there could be no continuity and no science.

He looked at the Dictator before him—yes, it was a hysteric face. He would know how to deal with it in his classroom—but such faces should not rule countries or young men. One was willing to go through a great many meaningless ceremonies in order to do one's work—wear a uniform or salute or be president of the Academy. That did not matter; it was part of the due to Caesar.[2] But not to tell lies to young men on one's own subject. After all, they had called him The Bear and said he carried improper post cards in his brief case. They had given him their terrible confidence—not for love or kindness, but because they had found him honest. It was too late to change.

The Dictator looked sharply at the General.

---

2. *it was . . . due to Caesar*, it was part of the homage and obedience that must be given to civil authority. This is a reference to the passage in the New Testament which reads: "Render therefore unto Caesar the things which are Caesar's; and unto God the things that are God's." (Matthew 22:21)

"I thought this had been explained to Professor Malzius," he said.

"Why, yes," said Professor Malzius. "I will sign any papers. I assure you I am not interested in politics —a man like myself, imagine! One state is as good as another. And I miss my tobacco—I have not smoked in five months. But, you see, one cannot be a scientist and tell lies."

He looked at the two men.

"What happens if I do not?" he said, in a low voice. But, looking at the Dictator, he had his answer. It was a fanatic face.

"Why, we shall resume our conversations, Professor Malzius," said the General, with a simper.

"Then I shall be beaten again," said Professor Malzius. He stated what he knew to be a fact.

"The process of rehabilitation is obviously not quite complete," said the General, "but perhaps, in time—"

"It will not be necessary," said Professor Malzius. "I cannot be beaten again." He stared wearily around the room. His shoulders straightened— it was so he had looked in the classroom when they had called him The Bear. "Call your other officers in," he said in a clear voice. "There are papers for me to sign. I should like them all to witness."

"Why—" said the General. "Why—" He looked doubtfully at the Dictator.

An expression of gratification appeared on the lean, semi-Napoleonic face. A white hand, curiously limp, touched the hand of Professor Malzius.

"You will feel so much better, Gregor," said the hoarse, tense voice. "I am so very glad you have given in."

"Why, of course, I give in," said Gregor Malzius. "Are you not the Dictator? And besides, if I do not, I shall be beaten again. And I cannot—you understand?—I cannot be beaten again."

He paused, breathing a little. But already the room was full of other faces. He knew them well, the hard faces of the new regime. But youthful some of them too.

The Dictator was saying something with regard to receiving the distinguished scientist, Professor Gregor Malzius, into the service of the state.

"Take the pen," said the General in an undertone. "The inkwell is there, Professor Malzius. Now you may sign."

Professor Malzius stood, his fingers gripping the big, old-fashioned inkwell. It was full of ink—the

servants of the Dictator were very efficient. They could shoot small people with the eyes of fox terriers for treason, but their trains arrived on time and their inkwells did not run dry.

"The state," he said, breathing. "Yes. But science does not know about states. And you are a little man —a little, unimportant man."

Then, before the General could stop him, he had picked up the inkwell and thrown it in the Dictator's face. The next moment the General's fist caught him on the side of the head, and he fell behind the desk to the floor. But lying there, through his cracked glasses, he could still see the grotesque splashes of ink on the Dictator's face and uniform, and the small cut above his eye where the blood was gathering. They had not fired; he had thought he would be too close to the Dictator for them to fire in time.

"Take that man out and shoot him. At once," said the Dictator in a dry voice. He did not move to wipe the stains from his uniform—and for that Professor Malzius admired him. They rushed then, each anxious to be first. But Professor Malzius made no resistance.

As he was being hustled along the corridors, he fell now and then. On the second fall, his glasses were broken completely, but that did not matter to him. They were in a great hurry, he thought, but all the better—one did not have to think while one could not see.

Now and then he heard his voice make sounds of discomfort, but his voice was detached from himself. There was little Gregopolous—he could see him very plainly—and Williams, with his fresh English coloring—and all the men whom he had taught.

He had given them nothing but work and the truth; they had given him their terrible trust. If he had been beaten again, he might have betrayed them. But he had avoided that.

He felt a last weakness—a wish that someone might know. They would not, of course; he would have died of typhoid in the castle, and there would be regretful notices in the newspapers. And then he would be forgotten, except for his work, and that was as it should be. He had never thought much of martyrs—hysterical people in the main. Though he'd like Bonnard to have known about the ink; it was in the coarse vein of humor that Bonnard could not appreciate. But then, he was a peasant; Bonnard had often told him so.

They were coming out into an open courtyard now; he felt the fresh air of outdoors. "Gently," he said. "A little gently. What's the haste?" But already they were tying him to the post. Someone struck him in the face and his eyes watered. "A schoolboy covered with ink," he muttered through his lost teeth. "A hysterical schoolboy too. But you cannot kill truth."

They were not good last words, and he knew that they were not. He must try to think of better ones —not shame Bonnard. But now they had a gag in his mouth; just as well, it saved him the trouble.

His body ached, bound against the post, but his sight and his mind were clearer. He could make out the evening sky, gray with fog, the sky that belonged to no country, but to all the world.

He could make out the gray high buttress of the castle. They had made it a jail, but it would not always be a jail. Perhaps in time it would not even exist. But if a little bit of truth were gathered, that would always exist, while there were men to remember and rediscover it. It was only the liars and the cruel who always failed.

Sixty years ago, he had been a little boy, eating black bread and thin cabbage soup in a poor house. It had been a bitter life, but he could not complain of it. He had had some good teachers, and his students had called him The Bear.

The gag hurt his mouth—they were getting ready now. There had been a girl called Anna once; he had almost forgotten her. And his rooms had smelled a certain way and he had had a dog. It did not matter what they did with the medals. He raised his head and looked once more at the gray foggy sky. In a moment there would be no thought, but, while there was thought, one must remember and note. His pulse rate was lower than he would have expected and his breathing oddly even, but those were not the important things. The important thing was beyond, in the gray sky that had no country, in the stones of the earth and the feeble human spirit. The important thing was truth.

"Ready!" called the officer. "Aim! Fire!" But Professor Malzius did not hear the three commands of the officer. He was thinking about the young men.

DISCUSSION

1. Professor Malzius' glasses figure prominently in this story. (a) Explain their importance to the Professor. (b) What is their condition as the story opens? (c) At what point in the story are they completely broken? (d) The Professor feels that his glasses have a special significance as they appear in his recurring nightmare. What is this special significance?

2. (a) How did Professor Malzius' students regard him? (b) What was the Professor's reaction to their regard?

3. (a) In what ways does the author make clear the nature of the tyranny exercised by the state which has imprisoned Malzius? (b) Why has Malzius not fled to another country? (c) Why has he been imprisoned?

4. (a) What was Malzius' attitude toward the possibility of a free world? (b) Contrast Malzius' political behavior with that of his friend Bonnard. (c) To what degree, if any, was Malzius to blame for his own fate?

5. (a) In what ways has the state's treatment of Malzius affected him? (b) At what point does the state's attempt to "rehabilitate" Malzius fail completely? (c) In what ways has this failure been foreshadowed throughout the story?

6. (a) Do you find the tragic ending logical? Explain. (b) Would you prefer a different ending? Why, or why not?

THE AUTHOR'S CRAFT

Point of view

You can identify the point of view of any short story by determining *who* tells the story and the *extent* to which the narrator sees into the minds and hearts of the characters.

One way of presenting a story is to tell it in the *first person* from the *personal point of view* of a participant. In this case, the author assumes the identity of a character —usually the main one.

Stephen Vincent Benét chose to write ''The Blood of the Martyrs'' in the *third person*, taking the viewpoint of an observer-narrator. As observer-narrator, Benét describes, first of all, what anyone could have seen or heard by his looking on as Professor Malzius lived out his last days. In the opening paragraph of the story, for example, Benét observes that the Professor is lying in a cell staring at a yellow stain on a wall. Had Benét confined himself to that kind of observation alone, he would have been using the *dramatic point of view*, so called because it is commonly employed by dramatists. If the storyteller writes from this point of view, he can reveal his characters in one way only—by setting down their *audible* words and *observable* acts.

However, Benét does more than this. Again, consider the opening of the story. Benét not only tells us that the Professor is staring at a yellow stain; he also tells us the thoughts and emotions which accompany the Professor's

stare. Benét actually enters his character's mind as an observer of the inner man. When an author does this, he is using the *omniscient* (''all knowing'') *point of view*.

How important is the omniscient point of view in telling ''The Blood of the Martyrs''? In answering, consider how much—or how little—of the story could have been told if Mr. Benét had confined himself to using the dramatic point of view. If we did not know the Professor's thoughts and feelings, what kind of person would he appear to be?

AUTHOR

STEPHEN VINCENT BENÉT (1898–1943), the son of an army colonel, was reared at various army posts. Two early interests affected his later life: first, Stephen was an avid listener when his father, who loved poetry, read aloud to his children, as he often did; second, as a boy, Stephen pored over military records and

developed a strong interest in the Civil War period. After attending Yale, he studied at the Sorbonne in France. It was in Paris that he met his future wife, Rosemary Carr, who later collaborated with her husband in writing the well-known collection of poems, *A Book of Americans*.

Benét's first volume of verse was published when he was seventeen, and an early novel attracted some attention. In 1926 a fellowship enabled him to write *John Brown's Body*, a book-length narrative poem about the Civil War. The poem earned Benét a Pulitzer Prize and an enviable literary reputation.

Benét's love for his country and his pride in its achievements are apparent in everything he wrote. With the approach of World War II he dedicated himself to the task of awakening his fellow Americans to the dire threat of totalitarian forces to destroy all that the United States represented. Feverishly he turned out fiction (''The Blood of the Martyrs'' belongs to this period), radio scripts, and plays that made manifest his basic belief: the American democracy represents a far better way of life than any dictatorship could possibly offer. His efforts extended over three and a half years of World War II. On March 13, 1943, he died. Thus Benét did not live to see the final victory of the Allies over totalitarianism, but his writings had played an important rôle in encouraging America to hold fast to its ideals.

UNIT 2 REVIEW

There follow 20 statements about the short stories in the unit you have just completed. Number from 1 to 20 on a separate sheet of paper. After each number, write (a) if you *strongly agree* with the statement that corresponds in number; (b), if you *agree*; (c), if you have *no opinion*; (d), if you *disagree*; (e), if you *strongly disagree*.

Whenever possible, be prepared to support each of your opinions with evidence from the stories. Before beginning the Unit Review, you may find it helpful first to review in the articles on Author's Craft the following terms: *conflict, point of view, characterization, author's intent, single effect, imagery.*

1. "Encounter in Illinois" fails to be a realistic story in that the author exaggerates the behavior of the three boys.
2. Both "The Interlopers" and "Footfalls" achieve their strongest effects on the reader through surprise endings rather than through characterization.
3. Had Wilbur Daniel Steele written "Footfalls" in the first person, using the personal point of view, it could not have been as powerful a story as it is.
4. People who take seriously a story like "The Monkey's Paw" don't differ much in outlook from Old Man Warner in "The Lottery."

5. Without a foreign setting and an isolated home, "The Monkey's Paw" could not create its single effect of horror on the reader.
6. "War" is no longer a relevant story, since the attitude toward war of both children and parents has changed dramatically in recent years.
7. Had he had the opportunity to know him, Professor Malzius ("The Blood of the Martyrs") would have liked Boaz Negro ("Footfalls") as a friend.
8. The death of Professor Malzius indicates that a scientist must be as dedicated to preserving political freedom as he is to advancing his scientific field.
9. In the unit on the short story, it would have made better sense to place "A Visit to Grandmother" under the category *Relationships*, rather than *Principles*.
10. Hester, Paul's mother in "The Rocking-Horse Winner," would have been a happier woman had she been the wife of Don Damián.
11. In "The Rocking-Horse Winner" the word *luck* means the same as the word *fate* in "The Monkey's Paw."
12. Many readers are shocked by "The Lottery" because the imagery of the first paragraph

encourages them to hold false expectations for the plot.
13. The man in "The Sea Devil" behaves more courageously than does Jerry, the boy in "Through the Tunnel."
14. "The Language of Men" is as much about conflicts between cultures as is "A Question of Blood."
15. Because of its violence, a story like "Roy's Wound" should not be included in an anthology intended for high-school students.
16. Norman Mailer uses more complex methods to develop the character of Sanford Carter in "The Language of Men" than does Roald Dahl to develop the character of Mary Maloney in "Lamb to the Slaughter."
17. The experiences that the soul of Don Damián undergoes are similar in numerous respects to the experiences that the Indian wife undergoes in "A Question of Blood."
18. Because Roy's father in "Roy's Wound" and Son and Ruby in "Birds, Clouds, Frogs" are unfit parents, they should legally be deprived of their children.
19. "A Visit to Grandmother" achieves its principal effect through a reversal in the conflict.
20. Without terms like *point of view, imagery*, and *single effect*, one could understand short stories just as well, and perhaps appreciate them more.

Poetry

MONTAGES
PROFILES
TENDENCIES
LONGINGS
ISSUES
REFLECTIONS

Montages

Morning at the Window

T. S. Eliot

They are rattling breakfast plates in basement kitchens,
And along the trampled edges of the street
I am aware of the damp souls of housemaids
Sprouting despondently at area gates.

The brown waves of fog toss up to me
Twisted faces from the bottom of the street,
And tear from a passer-by with muddy skirts
An aimless smile that hovers in the air
And vanishes along the level of the roofs.

DISCUSSION

1. Where is the speaker of this poem?

2. How would you describe the total scene? The mood?

3. Have you ever had this kind of feeling as a result of looking at something? Explain.

4. *Personification* is a way of endowing non-human things with human characteristics or actions. Find an example of this poetic

device in "Morning at the Window."

5. In the last stanza, what do you think the speaker means by the fog tearing the aimless smile which "vanishes along the level of the roofs"?

AUTHOR

THOMAS STEARNS ELIOT (1888–1965), Nobel Prize-winning poet, critic, dramatist, and publisher, was born in St. Louis, Missouri. He received his Master's degree from Harvard in 1910 and then studied in France and England. Eliot moved to England in 1914, becoming a British subject thirteen years later.

Eliot was one of the most influential poets of his generation. His first volume of poetry, *Prufrock and Other Observations* (1917) displayed Eliot's recurring interest in themes of personal suffering. Disillusionment and despair figure largely in many of his poems, particularly in *The Waste Land* (1922). Eliot wrote much literary criticism and several plays, including *Murder in the Cathedral* (1935), *The Family Reunion* (1939), and *The Cocktail Party* (1950).

Vacation

William Stafford

One scene as I bow to pour her coffee:—

> Three Indians in the scouring drouth
> huddle at a grave scooped in the gravel,
> lean to the wind as our train goes by.
> Someone is gone.
> There is dust on everything in Nevada.

I pour the cream.

DISCUSSION

1. (a) Where is the speaker in this poem? (b) Does the title give you a clue? Explain.

2. Why are lines 2–6 indented?

3. What is the effect of the speaker mentioning dust being on everything in Nevada and then immediately following with the last line?

4. In light of the title and the scene, what feeling are you left with?

AUTHOR

WILLIAM STAFFORD, a native of Kansas was born in 1914. A graduate of the University of Kansas, he received his Ph.D. from the University of Iowa. Much of his time since then has been spent teaching literature at various colleges and universities. Stafford's first book of poetry was published in 1960, and three years later he won the National Book Award for his volume of poetry *Traveling Through the Dark.*

During World War II, Stafford did optional service as a conscientious objector and since that time has been active in pacifist organizations.

Now employed teaching literature at Lewis and Clark University in Oregon, Stafford recently had leave to serve as Consultant in Poetry at the Library of Congress.

Ohio: 1919

Peyton Houston

Milkweed feathers
On silken stalk
Explode at touch,
Blow and go.

5 And folded cows
In summer dust
Under shade
Chew their cud
By thinning creek.

10 In hot glare
Blond barley
Green corn
Sky and cloud
Shimmering noon
15 Birds' silence.

Fields go up
To sky's blue corners,
Fall away.

At the edges
20 Blackberry hedges.

Evening Scene

Diana Peterson

Cocooned fisher ships
rocked by lullabye waters,
creak to weathered wharfs.

Barnacle bitten
dock posts, ruled by monarch gulls,
uphold their sovereigns.

And the saintly sea
massages the weary beach
moaning, back and forth.

DISCUSSION

Ohio:1919

1. What is the predominant mood in this poem?
2. (a) What might the date in the title suggest about the content of the poem? (b) Could the title be "Ohio:1965"? Why or why not?
3. Which of the many images in this poem is most appealing to you? Why?

AUTHOR

PEYTON HOUSTON, Manhattan corporate executive by profession and poet by inclination, believes that poetry is the most precise and far reaching and fundamental act of the whole.mind.

Mr. Houston has published a collection of 106 poems entitled *Sonnet Variations* and more recently *Occasions in a World,* a collection of fifty-three poems including "Ohio:1919."

Evening Scene

1. How does the mood in this poem compare with "Morning at the Window"?
2. In which poem is the speaker's identity most evident?
3. What do the images "cocooned fisherships," "ruled by monarch gulls," and the "saintly sea" suggest about the scene?
4. What kind of music would you choose to accompany this scene?

A Trucker

Thom Gunn

Sometimes it is like a beast
barely controlled by a man.
But the cabin is lofty
as a skull, and all the rest
5 extends from his foot as an
enormous throbbing body:

if he left anything to
chance—see his great frame capsize,
and his rubber limbs explode
10 whirling! and see there follow
a bright fountain of red eyes
tinkling sightless to the road.

DISCUSSION

1. To what does the "it" in the first line refer?

2. (a) Why do you think the author called this poem "A Trucker" rather than "A Truck"? (b) Why do you think someone would want to write a poem about a trucker?

3. Describe the speaker's attitude toward the subject of the poem.

4. With what do you associate the phrase "a bright fountain of red eyes tinkling sightless"?

5. In what way are the hot rodders in "Encounter in Illinois" like the trucker in this poem?

AUTHOR

THOM GUNN, one of the "Angry Young Men" of the 1950's in England, titled his first book, *Fighting Terms*, which characterizes much of the mood of his early poetry.

Born Thomson William Gunn in 1929, at Gravesend, England, Thom Gunn has traveled widely and published a number of poetry books since the fifties. He has taught at the University of California, Berkeley, and presently free-lances while living in San Francisco, California.

The Thing

Theodore Roethke

Suddenly they came flying, like a long scarf of smoke,
Trailing a thing—what was it?—small as a lark
Above the blue air, in the slight haze beyond,
A thing in and out of sight,
5 Flashing between gold levels of the late sun,
Then throwing itself up and away from the implacable swift pursuers,
Confusing them once flying straight into the sun
So they circled aimlessly for almost a minute,
Only to find, with their long terrible eyes
10 The small thing diving down toward a hill,
Where they dropped again
In one streak of pursuit.

Then the first bird
Struck;
15 Then another, another,
Until there was nothing left,
Not even feathers from so far away.

And we turned to our picnic
Of veal soaked in marsala and little larks arranged on a long platter,
20 And we drank the dry harsh wine
While I poked with a stick at a stone near a four-pronged flower,
And a black bull nudged at a wall in the valley below,
And the blue air darkened.

DISCUSSION

1. (a) What does the image "a long scarf of smoke" suggest? (b) Who might wear a smoky or grey scarf?

2. Are we told what "the thing" is? What could it be?

3. (a) Why do you think the speaker mentions the lark again in the third stanza? (b) Were there really larks on the platter? Explain.

4. What do you think is the significance of the speaker's "poking with a stick at a stone"?

5. Study the references to color in this poem and then explain what you think the poet associates with each color.

AUTHOR

THEODORE ROETHKE was born in Saginaw, Michigan, in 1908. He received his education at the University of Michigan and Harvard. He served, at various times, on the faculties of Lafayette College, Pennsylvania State University and Bennington College.

Roethke received numerous honors in his lifetime, including the National Book Award, and the Pulitzer Prize for poetry in 1954 for his collection *The Waking.* He was a frequent contributor to the *Times Literary Supplement, The Observer, Poetry, Atlantic Monthly, Kenyon Review,* and numerous other literary publications.

Roethke's published works include *Open House, The Lost Son and Other Poems,* and *Works for the Wind.* At the time of his death, in 1963, he was professor of English and poet in residence at the University of Washington in Seattle.

THE POETS' CRAFT

An approach to poetry

Many readers think that a poet composes a poem very much as a chef tosses a salad. Their recipe for a poem might read like this: Combine a profound message with a pinch of inspiration. Add a dash of rhythm, sprinkle with rhyme, and garnish with elegant language. Toss well and serve as a stanza.

One difficulty with this approach to poetry is its false assumption that every poem contains a "message." Many poets, it is true, do present a situation and then comment upon it or draw a moral from it. Notice how the poet comments upon his images of spring in this brief poem:

The year's at the spring,
The day's at the morn;
Morning's at seven;
The hillside's dew-pearled;
The lark's on the wing;
The snail's on the thorn:
God's in His Heaven—
All's right with the world!

Robert Browning, "Song"
from *Pippa Passes*

But the reader who expects a message in every poem is at a loss when confronted with lines like these:

So much depends
upon

a red wheel
barrow

glazed with rain
water

beside the white
chickens.

William Carlos Williams
"The Red Wheelbarrow"

Here the poet writes about "So much depends." There is no message, no moral, no good advice. The reader who hunts for its message is apt to misread the poem entirely.

For every poem with a message there is another poem that conveys an attitude, or a feeling, or an impression. The one question a reader may ask of *all* poems is: What does the poet intend to express?

A second difficulty with the recipe approach to poetry is that it regards rhythm and rhyme as mere decoration. Suppose for a moment that Browning had cast his comment on spring in a prose statement, something like this:

At seven o'clock on a spring morning, a dewy hillside, a flying lark, and a snail on the thorn show the divine order of things. They assure us that all is right with the world.

Both the prose statement and the poem use thirty-five words, but the poem has a different effect. Reading both versions aloud, you will notice that the poem—in its rhythm and in its rhyme—makes an appeal to your ears. When the rhythm is altered and the rhyme is removed, the poet's expression undergoes a change.

The next two articles about the poets' craft (see page 212 and page 220) will show how rhythm and rhyme become part of a poet's meaning. Another article (see page 231) will discuss why some poets, like William Carlos Williams, dispense with rhyme in expressing themselves.

WORD STUDY

Poetic etymologies

Poetry is an ancient art and many of the words we use to discuss poetry have come down to us from earlier times. If you look up the word *verse* in the Glossary, you will find that it is derived from the Latin word *versus*, which means "rut" or "furrow." What is the modern meaning of *verse*? Does its modern meaning reflect its original meaning? Explain.

Copy each of the following words on a separate sheet of paper: (1) *stanza;* (2) *rhythm;* (3) *lyric;* (4) *ballad;* and (5) *ode.* Then alongside each word write down its etymology and its modern definition, which you will find in the Glossary. To what extent does the modern meaning of each of the five words reflect its original meaning? Judging from their etymologies, which of the five words indicate that in earliest times poems were composed to be sung?

Profiles

What She Did in the Morning, I Wouldn't Know, She Was Seated There in the Midst of Her Resilient Symptoms, Always

Merrill Moore

They were like sofa cushions.
She was constantly rearranging them
To form new patterns and support her frame.

Her attention was mainly directed toward herself
5 And some of it, a small part, I would say,
Was aimed at trying to bend others that way,
But few responded, few fulfilled her wish;
She was simply not their kind of dish,
So, she remained, unmarried and complaining.

10 She had a bird, a series of small pets—
A dog, a cat—but none of them ever thrived.
They were, in fact, unusually short-lived.
It almost seemed as if her infections spread.
I was always hearing one of them was dead.

DISCUSSION

1. To what does "they" in the first line refer?

2. (a) Have you ever known a person like this? (b) Were her symptoms real or imaginary or could you tell?

3. Does the woman in this poem have any idea of what others think of her? What lines explain her relationship with other people?

4. Do you think her pets were really "short-lived" as a result of her infections? Explain.

AUTHOR

MERRILL MOORE (1903–1957) achieved distinction both as a doctor of medicine and as a poet. He received his medical education at Vanderbilt University in Tennessee and in 1935 established his psychiatric practice in Boston. He served in the United States Army during World War II.

Dr. Moore began writing verse during his student days at Vanderbilt University and joined with some friends of similar literary interests to found the *Fugitive*, a magazine of poetry and criticism. In his several volumes of poetry, such as *The Noise that Time Makes* (1929) and *It is a Good Deal Later than You Think* (1934), Moore used only one poetic form—the sonnet, or fourteen-line stanza. One thousand of his sonnets were published in *M* in 1938.

Portrait

Carolyn M. Rodgers

mama spent pennies
in uh gallon milk jug
saved pennies
fuh four babies
5 college educashuns

and when the babies
got bigger they would
secretly "borrow" mama's
pennies to buy candy

10 and pop cause mama
saved extras
fuh college educashuns
and pop and candy

was uh non-credit in bad teeth
15 mama pooled pennies
in uh gallon milk jug

Borden's, by the way

and the babies went
to school cause mama saved
20 and spent and paid
fuh four babies

college educashuns
mama spent pennies
                    and nickels
25   and quarters
                    and dollars

and one life.
mama spent her life
in uh gallon milk jug
30 fuh four Black babies
college educashuns.

"Portrait" by Carolyn Rodgers from SONGS OF A BLACKBIRD published by Third World Press. Reprinted by permission of the author.

DISCUSSION

1. Describe mama.
2. How do you think the speaker feels about her mother?
3. (a) What does the speaker mean by "uh non-credit in bad teeth"? (b) What does she mean when she says "mama spent her life in a gallon milk jug"?
4. What is the significance of the spelling "educashun"?

AUTHOR

CAROLYN RODGERS describes her work as a love affair with words. She credits Gwendolyn Brooks, Pulitzer Prize-winning Chicago poet, with providing the encouragement she needed to quit her job as a counselor and language arts instructor for high school dropouts and pursue a writing career full time.

Miss Rodgers' first published poems appeared in *Black World* in 1967. She has since published two volumes of poetry, *Paper Soul* and *Songs of a Blackbird*. She is currently working on another volume of poetry to be titled *Blues Gittin' Up*.

Miss Rodgers is poet-in-residence and teaches creative writing at Malcolm X College.

The trouble was they left her too much alone,
feeding on books and dreaming of love
and watching willow tree shadows
sway across the polluted river.

5 Instead of running about and laughing
and talking of nothing with the other girls,
she grew wistful and wan and dangerously thin
and after hours of pondering such things as
frost on a window
10 or the frail filament fingers of an old nun on a bus,
she would look weaker than ever
and complain of a terrible pain in her chest.

Poemectomy

John W. Dickson

Until late one night when they rushed her to the hospital
and worked over her for hours in Emergency,
15 removing a huge tumorous verse
so horrible that even the nurses grew sick when they saw it.
For days afterwards
she was draining words where the stitches were
and then only a few letters now and then
20 until finally the wound was completely healed.

But there's still a large scar where they made the incision
and even now when she sees things
like a bird on a twig
or the shadow of leaves on the sand
25 or a butterfly wing washed up on the shore,
the scar turns pink or a livid red
and you almost wonder
if they succeeded in getting out all the infection.

DISCUSSION

1. What is the attitude of the speaker toward the girl in this poem?

2. (a) What caused the girl to become ill? (b) What particular experiences still cause her to become inflamed?

3. What do you think was the "extracted verse"?

AUTHOR

JOHN W. DICKSON, born in 1916 in Chicago, Illinois, began writing his first poetry in grammar school and continued through high school and college where he was a student at Furman University in Greensville, South Carolina.

During World War II, among his assignments was editing an army newspaper. After the war, although Mr. Dickson became a commodity merchant in grain, he continued to write poetry as well as short stories. For the latter, he has twice received honorable mention in *Best Short Stories of the Year,* edited by Martha Foley.

Dickson has published numerous poems in both popular and literary magazines, and anthologies, and in 1971, he won the highest honors in poetry in the English division of the International Poetry Competition sponsored by the Italian government. He is now planning to retire from the grain business to devote more of his time to writing.

The Boarder

Louis Simpson

The time is after dinner. Cigarettes
    Glow on the lawn;
Glasses begin to tinkle; TV sets
    Have been turned on.

5 The moon is brimming like a glass of beer
    Above the town,
And love keeps her appointments—"Harry's here!"
    "I'll be right down."

But the pale stranger in the furnished room
10   Lies on his back
Looking at paper roses, how they bloom,
    And ceilings crack.

DISCUSSION

1. (a) How long has the boarder lived in the furnished room? (b) How do you know?

2. Why do you think the poet uses the pronoun "her" rather than "his" to personify love in line 7?

3. What do the last two lines mean to you?

4. What particular things does the last stanza tell you about the boarder?

AUTHOR

LOUIS SIMPSON was born March 27, 1923, in Jamaica, British West Indies. He served in the United States Army from 1943 to 1946, distinguishing himself by earning the Bronze Star, the Purple Heart (twice), and a Presidential Unit Citation. Upon returning to civilian life, he entered Columbia University, where he received his B.S., M.A., and Ph.D. degrees, the last one in 1959.

Simpson began writing poems when he was thirteen. He has published a number of volumes including *Good News of Death* and *A Dream of Governors.* In 1964, he received the Pulitzer Prize for poetry for his collection *At the End of the Open Road.*

At present, Simpson is an associate professor of English at the University of California, Berkeley. He occasionally tours the country giving poetry readings and is a frequent contributor to the *New Yorker, New Statesman* and other literary magazines.

Aaron Stark

Edwin Arlington Robinson

Withal a meager man was Aaron Stark—
Cursed and unkempt, shrewd, shriveled, and morose.
A miser was he, with a miser's nose,
And eyes like little dollars in the dark.
5 His thin, pinched mouth was nothing but a mark;
And when he spoke there came like sullen blows
Through scattered fangs a few snarled words and close,
As if a cur were chary of its bark.

Glad for the murmur of his hard renown,
10 Year after year he shambled through the town—
A loveless exile moving with a staff;
And oftentimes there crept into his ears
A sound of alien pity, touched with tears—
And then (and only then) did Aaron laugh.

DISCUSSION

1. Which images do you think best portray the miserliness of Aaron?

2. (a) How do others feel about Aaron? (b) Does he know how they feel? (c) How does he react to their attitude?

3. In what way is Aaron like the woman in "What She Did in the Morning"?

AUTHOR

EDWIN ARLINGTON ROBINSON (1869–1935) was born near the Maine village of Head Tide and spent his youth in the village of Gardiner. He was a precocious child, reading the great classics at an early age and writing poetry before he was twelve. He went to Harvard University for two years, then moved to New York City. There he worked at whatever jobs he could find, living very simply and developing his poetic gift.

Robinson has been noted for his many verse portraits, like "Aaron Stark," which appeared in his *Children of the Night* (1897),

Karma

Edwin Arlington Robinson

Christmas was in the air and all was well
With him, but for a few confusing flaws
In divers of God's images. Because
A friend of his would neither buy nor sell,
5 Was he to answer for the axe that fell?
He pondered; and the reason for it was,
Partly, a slowly freezing Santa Claus
Upon the corner, with his beard and bell.

Acknowledging an improvident surprise,
10 He magnified a fancy that he wished
The friend whom he had wrecked were here again.
Not sure of that, he found a compromise;
And from the fulness of his heart he fished
A dime for Jesus who had died for men.

Captain Craig (1902), *Town Down the River* (1910), and *Man Against the Sky* (1916).

Robinson won his first Pulitzer Prize for his blank-verse narrative poem *Tristram* (1927); his second Pulitzer Prize for his *Collected Poems* (1921); his third award for his blank-verse narrative poem *The Man Who Died Twice* (1924).

DISCUSSION

1. Do you think the setting and time of year is particularly appropriate in revealing this character? Why or why not?

2. Explain the first three lines of the second stanza.

3. In line 13, would the word "found" be just as effective as the word "fished"? Explain.

4. (a) What do you think is the speaker's attitude toward his subject? (b) What words would you use to describe the person portrayed? (c) How is this man like Aaron Stark? How are they different?

5. Look up the meaning of the word "Karma" in the Glossary, and explain the relationship of the title to the poem.

Buffalo Bill

E. E. Cummings

Buffalo Bill's
defunct
           who used to
           ride a watersmooth-silver
                                   stallion
and break onetwothreefourfive pigeonsjustlikethat
                                                Jesus

he was a handsome man
                          and what i want to know is
how do you like your blueeyed boy
Mister Death

DISCUSSION

1. What does the physical shape, or form, of the poem suggest to you?

2. Do you think the word "dead" would be as appropriate as "defunct" (line 2)? Why or why not?

3. The sixth line is printed unconventionally. (a) How do you think Cummings would want the reader to read this line aloud? (b) Is this arrangement appropriate to the sound and sense of the poem? Explain.

4. What is the speaker's attitude toward Buffalo Bill? What particular words, phrases, or lines reveal this?

AUTHOR

EDWARD ESTLIN CUMMINGS (1894–1962), a painter and a poet, was born in Massachusetts. Following his graduation from Harvard in 1915, he served with the American Ambulance corps in France. During World War I he was mistakenly imprisoned by the French; his experiences as a prisoner were the basis of his novel, *The Enormous Room* (1922).

In the 1920's Cummings published several volumes of poetry. These poems were later included in *Poems 1922–1954*. Since then, two more volumes have been published: *95 Poems* (1958) *and 73 Poems* (1963).

Reading a free-verse poem by Cummings is a unique experience. His spacing and run-together words, his unusual capitalization, punctuation, and line lengths give the reader a new poetic experience.

Lee

Stephen Vincent Benét

The night had fallen on the narrow tent.
—Deep night of Virginia summer when the stars
Are burning wax in the near, languid sky
And the soft flowers hardly close all night
5 But bathe in darkness, as a woman bathes
In a warm, fragrant water and distill
Their perfume still, without the fire of the sun.

The army was asleep as armies sleep.
War lying on a casual sheaf of peace
10 For a brief moment, and yet with armor on,
And yet in the child's deep sleep, and yet so still.
Even the sentries seemed to walk their posts
With a ghost footfall that could match that night.

The aide-de-camp knew certain lines of Greek
15 And other such unnecessary things
As birds and music, that are good for peace
But are not deemed so serviceable for war.
He was a youth with an inquisitive mind
And doubtless had a failing for romance,
20 But then he was not twenty, and such faults
May sometimes be excused in younger men

Even when such creatures die, as they have done
At one time or another, for some cause
Which we are careful to point out to them
25 Much later, was no cause worth dying for,
But cannot reach them with our arguments
Because they are uneconomic dust.

So, when the aide-de-camp came toward the tent,
He knew that he was sleepy as a dog,
30 And yet the starlight and the gathered scents
Moved in his heart—like the unnecessary
Themes of a music fallen from a cloud
In light, upon a dark water.
                            And though he had
Some bitterness of mind to chew upon,
35 As well as messages that he must give
Before he slept, he halted in his tracks.

"Lee" reprinted by permission of Brandt & Brandt, New York, from JOHN BROWN'S BODY by Stephen Vincent Benét. Copyright 1927, 1928 by Stephen Vincent Benét. Copyright renewed 1955, 1956 by Rosemary Carr Benét. Published by Holt, Rinehart & Winston, Inc., New York.

He saw, imprinted on the yellow light
That made the tent a hollow jack-o'-lantern,
The sharp, black shadow of a seated man,
40 The profile like the profile in a bust.
Lee in his tent, alone.
He had some shadow-papers in his hand,
But you could see he was not reading them,
And, if he thought, you could not read his thoughts,
45 Even as shadows, by any light that shines.

"You'd know that face among a million faces,"
Thought the still watcher, "and yet, his hair and beard
Have quite turned white, white as the dogwood bloom
That blossomed on the way to Chancellorsville[1]
50 When Jackson[2] was alive and we were young
And we were winning and the end was near.
And now, I guess, the end is near enough
In spite of everything that we can do,
And he's alone tonight and Jackson's dead.

55 "I saw him in the Wilderness[3] that day
When he began to lead the charge himself
And the men wouldn't let him.
                                Gordon[4] spoke
And then the men themselves began to yell
'Lee to the rear—General Lee to the rear!'
60 I'll hear that all my life. I'll see those paws
Grabbing at Traveler[5] and the bridle rein
And forcing the calm image back from death.

"Reckon that's what we think of you, Marse Robert,
Reckon that's what we think, what's left of us,
65 The pool old devils that are left of us.
I wonder what he thinks about it all.
He isn't staring, he's just sitting there.
I never knew a man could look so still
And yet look so alive in his repose.

70 "It doesn't seem as if a cause could lose
When it's believed in by a man like that.
And yet we're losing.
                                And he knows it all.

No, he won't ever say it. But he knows.

"I'd feel more comfortable if he'd move.

75 "We had a chance at Spotsylvania,[6]
We had some chances in the Wilderness.
We always hurt them more than we were hurt
And yet we're here—and they keep coming on.

"What keeps us going on? I wish I knew.
80 Perhaps you see a man like that go on
And then you have to follow.
                                There can't be
So many men that men have followed so.

"And yet, what is it for? What is it for?
What does he think?
                                His hands are lying there
85 Quiet as stones or shadows in his lap.
His beard is whiter than the dogwood bloom,
But there is nothing ruined in his face,
And nothing beaten in those steady eyes.
If he's grown old, it isn't like a man,
90 It's more the way a river might grow old.

"My mother knew him at old dances once.
She said he liked to joke and he was dark then,
Dark and as straight as he can stand today.
If he would only move, I could go forward.

95 "You see the faces of spear-handling kings
In the old books they taught us from at school;
Big Agamemnon with his curly beard,
Achilles in the cruelty of his youth,
And Oedipus[7] before he tore his eyes.

100 "I'd like to see him in that chariot-rank,
With Traveler pulling at the leader pole.
I don't think when the winged claws come down
They'll get a groan from him.
                                So we go on.
Under the claws. And he goes on ahead."

105 The sharp-cut profile moved a fraction now.
The aide-de-camp went forward on his errand.

---

1. *Chancellorsville*, village in northeastern Virginia, the site of a Confederate victory in May, 1863.
2. *Jackson*, Thomas J. ("Stonewall") Jackson (1824–1863), a Confederate general who was killed at Chancellorsville.
3. *the Wilderness*, a wooded area in northeastern Virginia, the site of an indecisive battle between the armies of Grant and Lee on May 5–6, 1864.
4. *Gordon*, John Brown Gordon (1832–1904), a Confederate general.
5. *Traveler*, General Lee's horse.
6. *Spotsylvania*, village in northeastern Virginia, the scene of trench warfare between Grant and Lee on May 8–12, 1864.
7. *Agamemnon* (ag'ə mem'non) . . . *Achilles* (ə kil'ēz) . . . *Oedipus* (ed'ə pəs). According to Greek legend, Agamemnon and Achilles were Greek heroes of the Trojan War. Oedipus was the mythological Greek king who blinded himself.

DISCUSSION

1. The figure of Lee is revealed after several shifts in voice or in point of view. Between what lines do these shifts occur? What is the effect of moving the angle of vision in such a way?

2. Night has traditionally symbolized both death and adventure. Trace one idea or the other through the poem, listing the words or phrases that echo death or excitement.

3. Of the three battles mentioned, which appears to have made the greatest impact on Lee? Why?

4. Where is Lee and what is he doing while the aide-de-camp observes him?

5. What are the "winged claws" in line 102?

6. Do you think the last two abrupt lines are an appropriate conclusion to the poem? Why or why not?

7. After reading and discussing this poem, what adjectives would you use to describe your impression of General Lee?

THE POETS' CRAFT

Figurative language
The words the modern poet uses are the same words you use in your everyday speech. And like you, the poet uses words *figuratively* to be more brief or forceful, more vivid or precise.

Figurative statements convey information and also engage our emotions. Let us examine the effectiveness of figurative language by taking a single idea and casting it in a literal statement and then in various figures of speech.

Suppose that a poet wants to describe a young woman who is very frightened. Her fear could be expressed in a literal statement:

Her eyes revealed her terror.

Our imaginary poet can show us the woman's fear even more vividly by drawing a comparison between her eyes (which we have never seen) and something that is familiar to us—candles, for instance:

Her eyes *like* ghostly candles shone.

If the poet employs the word *like* or the word *as* to state the similarity between two things, he is using a *simile*. If he draws a similarity by implying that one thing *is* another, the poet is using a *metaphor*:

Her eyes were ghostly candles in the gloom.

When the poet uses these figurative comparisons, he ·relies upon us to transfer what we know about the way candles shine to the brightness in a frightened woman's eyes. The similarity, however, is limited. The poet does not intend for us to conclude that her eyes are like candles in other respects.

The poet can also speak of the woman's fear as if it were a living thing. When he speaks of a non-living thing or quality as if it were alive, the poet is using *personification*:

Fear lit flames of horror in her eyes.

A personification is a kind of metaphor because it, too, *implies* that one (nonliving) thing *is* another (living) thing.

The poet can also address the woman's fear as if it could understand his remarks:

O Fear, remove thy candles from my mistress' eyes!

When the poet addresses a thing or idea as if it could understand *or* when the poet addresses an absent person, he is using an *apostrophe*.

A single figurative statement may contain more than one figure of speech. If you will reread the example of an apostrophe, you will see that it also contains a personification. The following line contains a simile, a personification, and an apostrophe:

O Fear, remove thy horror from eyes that shine like ghostly candles.

Another example of figurative statements that contain more than one figure of speech may be found in a poem by Emily Dickinson. Identify the personifications and cite the lines that contain both personification and simile.

The clouds their backs together laid,
The north began to push,
The forests galloped till they fell,
The lightning skipped like mice;
The thunder crumbled like a stuff—
How good to be safe in tombs,
Where nature's temper cannot reach,
Nor vengeance ever comes!
                    Dickinson, "XVI"

Another figurative device the poet has at his disposal is the symbol. A *symbol* is something that stands for or represents something else. A symbol has both a literal and figurative meaning. This line, for example, is literal:

Judge not the play before the play be done.

When we read this line in the full context of the poem, "play" takes on a symbolic meaning:

My soul, sit thou a patient looker on;
Judge not the play before the play be done:
Her plot has many changes; every day
Speaks a new scene; the last act crowns the play.
                    Francis Quarles, from *Emblems*

What does "play" symbolize? How is the symbolism developed?

Tendencies

Before Dawn

Ann Darr

That practicing bird is sharpening his call
on my sleep. I shall wring him feather from feather
and string up his pimpled skin, and grind his beak
for sweep dust. I shall debird him. Hold.
       On what do I sharpen my cry?

The Peace of Wild Things

Wendell Berry

When despair for the world grows in me
and I wake in the night at the least sound
in fear of what my life and my children's lives may be,
I go and lie down where the wood drake
5 rests in his beauty on the water, and the great heron fe
I come into the peace of wild things
who do not tax their lives with forethought
of grief. I come into the presence of still water.
And I feel above me the day-blind stars
10 waiting with their light. For a time
I rest in the grace of the world, and am free.

The Elk

Hugh McNamar

In winter poachers had used the cabin.
Their empty beer and spaghetti
cans were in one corner,
and fence posts had been burned
5 in the old pot-bellied stove. Some
were left smoldering when,
hearing the truck turn up the road,
the three of them left by the
sun porch door. There,
10 not even gutted or bled,
we found him hanging
from the rafter beam,
hard and turning on the creaking rope.
Just that morning he had probably come

15 down to where the snow was blown
from the grass around the house.

We stayed one weekend in summer
to fish the stream.
Away from the city sounds
20 at night, we could only turn
in our sleeping bags on the floor
and listen: outside insects moved
against the screen; and in such
stillness, almost heard, was
25 the turning of a rope
and something large and restless.

DISCUSSION

Before Dawn

1. (a) About what is the speaker in this poem annoyed? (b) What suddenly makes her "Hold"?

2. If you were to italicize two words in the last line to make the speaker's meaning more clear, what would they be? Explain what this line implies.

"The Elk" by Hugh McNamar. Reprinted by permission of the author.

The Peace of Wild Things

1. What does the second line suggest about the speaker?

2. What does he mean when he states that wild things "do not tax their lives with forethought of grief"?

3. What figure of speech is the poet using in the phrase "day-blind stars"?

The Elk

1. What seasons of the year does the speaker refer to in this poem?

2. Do you think the "poachers" were hunters? Why or why not?

3. What do you think the phrase "something large and restless" symbolizes?

4. Why has the speaker left a line space between lines 16 and 17?

5. State in your own words what you think is the author's theme.

Part of the Darkness

Isabella Gardner

I had thought of the bear in his lair as fiercely free, feasting
      on honey and wildwood fruits;
I had imagined a forest lunge, regretting the circus shuffle and
      the zoo's proscribed pursuits.
Last summer I took books and children to Wisconsin's Great
      North woods. We drove
one night through miles of pines and rainy darkness to a garbage
      grove
5 that burgeoned broken crates and bulging paper bags and
      emptied cans of beer,
to watch for native bears, who local guides had told us,
      scavenged there.
After parking behind three other cars (leaving our headlights on
      but dim)
We stumbled over soggy moss to join the families blinking on
      the rim
of mounded refuse bounded east north and west by the forest.
10 The parents hushed and warned their pushing children each of
      whom struggled to stand nearest
the arena, and presently part of the darkness humped away
      from the foliage and lumbered bear-shaped
toward the heaping spoilage. It trundled into the litter while
      we gaped,
and for an instant it gaped too, bear-faced, but not a tooth was
      bared. It grovelled
carefully while tin cans clattered and tense tourists tittered.
      Painstakingly it nosed and ravelled
15 rinds and husks and parings, the used and the refused; bear-
      skinned and doggedly explored
the second-hand remains while headlights glared and flashlights
      stared and shamed bored
children booed, wishing aloud that it would trudge away so
      they might read its tracks.
They hoped to find an as yet unclassified spoor, certain that ño
      authentic bear would turn his back
upon the delicacies of his own domain to flounder where mere
      housewives' leavings rot.
20 I also was reluctant to concede that there is no wild honey in
      the forest and no forest in the bear.
Bereaved, we started home, leaving that animal there.

"Part of the Darkness" by Isabella Gardner from WEST OF CHILD-
HOOD: POEMS 1950–1965. Copyright © 1965 by Isabella
Gardner Tate. Reprinted by permission of Houghton Mifflin Com-
pany.

The Birth of a Shark

David Wevill

What had become of the young shark?
It was time for the ocean to move on.
Somehow, sheathed in the warm current
He'd lost his youthful bite, and fell
5 Shuddering among the feelers of kelp
And dragging weeds. His belly touched sand,
The shark ran aground on his shadow.

Shark-shape, he lay there.
But in the world above
10 Six white legs dangled, thrashing for the fun of it,
Fifty feet above the newborn shadow.

The shark nosed up to spy them out;
He rose slowly, a long grey feather
Slendering up through the dense air of the sea.
15 His eyes of bolted glass were fixed
On a roundness of sun and whetted flesh,.
Glittering like stars above his small brain—

The shark rose gradually. He was half-grown,
About four feet: strength of a man's thigh
20 Wrapped in emery, his mouth a watery
Ash of brambles. As he rose
His shadow paled and entered the sand,
Dissolved, in the twinkling shoals of driftsand
Which his thrusting tail spawned.

25 This was the shark's birth in our world.
His grey parents had left him
Mysteriously and rapidly—
How else is a shark born?
They had bequeathed him the odour of blood,
30 And a sense half of anguish at being
Perpetually the forerunner of blood:

A desire to sleep in the currents fought
Against the strong enchaining links of hunger,
In shoals, or alone,
35 Cruising the white haze off Africa,
Bucked Gibraltar, rode into the Atlantic—
Diet of squid, pulps, a few sea-perch.

But what fish-sense the shark had
Died with his shadow. This commonplace
40 Of kicking legs he had never seen:
He was attracted. High above him

The sunsoaked heads were unaware of the shark—
He was something rising under their minds
You could not have told them about: grey thought
45 Beneath the fortnight's seaside spell—
A jagged effort to get at something painful.

He knew the path up was direct:
But the young shark was curious.
He dawdled awhile, circling like a bee
50 Above stems, cutting this new smell
From the water in shapes of fresh razors.
He wasn't even aware he would strike;
That triggered last thrust was beyond his edgy
Power to choose or predict. This
55 Was carefully to be savoured first, as later
He'd get it, with expertise, and hit fast.

He knew he was alone.
He knew he could only snap off
A foot or a hand at a time—
60 And without fuss—for sharks and dogs
Do not like to share.
The taste for killing was not even pleasure to him.
And this was new:
This was not sea-flesh, but a kind
65 Of smoky scent of suntan oil and salt,
Hot blood and wet cloth. When he struck at it
He only grazed his snout,
And skulked away like a pickpocket—

Swerved, paused, turned on his side,
70 And cocked a round eye up at the dense
Thrashings of frightened spray his climb touched.

And the thrashing commotion moved
Fast as fire away, on the surface of sun.
The shark lay puzzling
75 In the calm water ten feet down,
As the top of his eye exploded above
Reef and sand, heading for the shallows.
Here was his time of choice—
Twisting, he thought himself round and round
80 In a slow circling of doubt,
Powerless to be a shark, a spawned insult.

But while he was thinking, the sea ahead of him
Suddenly reddened; and black

Shapes with snouts of blunted knives
85 Swarmed past him and struck
At the bladder of sunlight, snapping at it.
The shark was blinded—
His vision came to him,
Shred by piece, bone by bone
90 And fragments of bone. Instinctively
His jaws widened to take these crumbs

Of blood from the bigger, experienced jaws,
Whose aim lay in their twice-his-length
Trust in the body and shadow as one
95 Mouthful of mastery, speed, and blood—

He learned this, when they came for him;
The young shark found his shadow again.
He learned his place among the weeds.

DISCUSSION

Part of the Darkness

1. What was the purpose of the trip to "Wisconsin's Great North woods"?

2. (a) Why do the children boo the bear, preferring to "read its tracks"? (b) Why do they believe this bear cannot be "authentic"?

3. Which of the two following statements do you think more closely approximates the poet's theme: (a) Nature is tawdry and commonplace and only romantics think nature is nearly divine, superior to man. (b) Man in his curiosity or in his quest for progress has humbled the monarchs of nature. Defend your reasoning.

4. After reading and discussing the poem, what do you think the title symbolizes?

The Birth of a Shark

1. (a) What is the "newborn shadow" in line 11? (b) Do you think the metaphor of the feather (line 13) is appropriate? Why or why not?

2. Identify both the simile and the metaphor in lines 15–18.

3. In line 19, how does the phrase "strength of a man's thigh" affect you as you read through the rest of the poem?

4. Explain the sentence in lines 38–39, "But what fish-sense the shark had/Died with his shadow."

5. What occurs in lines 82–95?

6. What does the speaker mean by "struck/At the bladder of sunlight, snapping at it"? (Lines 85–86)

7. The word "shadow" frequently occurs. What does it symbolize?

8. Is this poem really about the birth of a shark? Explain.

AUTHOR

DAVID WEVILL, (1935–   ) although born in Yokohama, Japan, is a Canadian who has spent much of his life in England. He was educated at Cambridge University and spent two years teaching at Mandalay University. His first major book of poetry was *Birth of a Shark* in 1964.

THE POETS' CRAFT

Rhythm and meaning
Language has rhythm because we give words a certain stress, or accent, in pronouncing them. We say *beGIN* and *MERcy*, *interRUPT* and *BEAUtiful* when we meet these words in prose or when we meet these words in poetry. Both prose and poetry have rhythm, but in poetry the rhythm is regulated. What we call *meter* in English poetry is the arrangement of rhythm according to accented and unaccented syllables.

Meter alone does not make a poem, as these lines show:

> Birds GO rePAST the Ego YOU,
> Dull ROLLer SKATE sinCERE we
> DO.

In short, meter must echo sense. A poet who writes solemnly of death does not want his lines to bounce merrily along like a nursery jingle. Instead, he will use meter (in combination with other devices) to create a slow, solemn movement. The pace of a poem must be appropriate to the emotion.

The favorite meter in English poetry is the *iambic* (◡╱). The English language has many words that consist of two syllables. Because most of these two-syllabled words, like *beGIN*, take their accent on the final syllable, English speech has a natural iambic beat. As a result, the rhythm of an iambic line moves smoothly:

> Her deck,│once red│with he│roes'
>   blood.
> Oliver Wendell Holmes, "Old Ironsides"

The *trochaic* meter (╱◡), as in *MERcy*, reverses the natural iambic beat. As such, a trochaic line seems to move *roughly*:

> Thou, when │ thou re │ turnst, wilt │
>   tell me.   John Donne, "Song"

The *anapestic* meter (◡◡╱), as in *interRUPT*, lends itself effectively to the *leaping* action of Lord Byron's narrative poem, "The Destruction of Sennacherib":

The As syr | ian came down | like the
   wolf | on the fold.

Lord Tennyson found the *thrust*
of the *dactylic* meter (/ ˘ ˘), as in
BEAUtiful, well suited to his
"Charge of the Light Brigade":
Ó the wild | charge they made!

The poet can manipulate any
one of the basic meters so that it
moves quickly or slowly. He ad-
justs the motion of a poem (1) by
substituting a different meter in a
line, and (2) by using more accented monosyllables in a line.
The following four examples are
basically iambic. Identify the
substitute meter or any accented
monosyllables in each example.

1. The ship | was cheered, | the har |
      bor cleared,
      Mer ri | ly did | we drop.
      Samuel Taylor Coleridge, "The Rime
                  of the Ancient Mariner"

2. With a gol | den joy | in a sil | ver
      mirth:
      Thank God | for Life!
   James Thomson, "Let My Voice Ring Out"

3. How soon | hath Time | the sub |
      tle thief | of youth,
      Sto len on | his wing | my three |
      and twen|ti eth year!
      John Milton, "On His Having Arrived
               at the Age of Twenty-three"

4. An old, | mad, | blind, | de spised,
      | and dy | ing king.

      Percy Bysshe Shelley, "England in 1819"

You will observe in the examples from Coleridge, Thomson,
and Milton that (a) the iambic

pace quickens when the poet
increases the *unaccented* syllables;
that (b) the iambic pace slows
when the poet increases the *accented* syllables. This is *how* the
movement changes, but it is even
more important to recognize *why*
the movement changes. James
Thomson, for example, quickens
the iambic line so that its pace
echoes his joyous thanksgiving.
Shelley slows the iambic line so
that it echoes (and emphasizes)
his anger. Rhythm is part of a
poem's meaning.

WORD STUDY

Scansion vocabulary

When we *scan* a line of poetry,
we determine the kind of meter it
contains and then count the number of metrical units, or *feet*, in a
line.

Thus I,
Pass by,
And die
As one
Un known
And gone.
                        Robert Herrick,
            "Upon His Departure Hence"

Because each line of Herrick's
poem is written in the *iambic*
meter, and because each line contains *one* iambic foot, we say the
lines of the poem are *iambic monometer.*
   The English word *monometer* is
derived from the Greek prefix
mono- ("one") and the Greek
word *metron* ("measure"). Other
words which indicate the length
of lines are *dimeter* ("two feet"),
trimeter ("three feet"), *tetrameter*
("four feet"), and *pentameter*
("five feet").
   Scan each of the following four
examples. On a separate sheet of

paper, copy the defining sentence.
Then fill in the name of the meter
(*iambic, trochaic, anapestic,* or
dactylic), the number of feet in
the lines (*1, 2, 3, 4,* or *5*), and the
scansion pattern (the name of the
meter plus *monometer, dimeter,
trimeter, tetrameter,* or *pentameter*).
1. Mor tal | man and | wo man,
      Go up | on your | tra vel!
                  Elizabeth Barrett Browning,
                        "A Drama of Exile"

Each of Mrs. Browning's lines is
written in the _____ meter.
Beacuse each line contains _____
feet, the lines are _____ _____
meter.

2. How like | a win | ter hath | my
      ab | sence been
      From thee, | the plea | sure of |
      the fleet | ing year!
            William Shakespeare, "Sonnet 97"

Each of Shakespeare's lines is
written in the _____ meter.
Because each line contains _____
feet, the lines are _____ _____
meter.

3. Cold in hu | man i ty,
      Burn ing in | san i ty.
         Thomas Hood, "The Bridge of Sighs"

Each of Hood's lines is written in
the _____ meter. Because each
line contains _____ feet, the
lines are _____ _____ meter.

4. 'Twas Jones, | brave Jones | to
      bat | tle led
      As bold | a crew | as ev | er bled.
                        Philip Freneau,
            "On the Memorable Victory"

Each of Freneau's lines is written
in the _____ meter. Because
each line contains _____ feet, the
lines are _____ _____ meter.

Stone

Charles Simic

Go inside a stone
That would be my way.
Let somebody else become a dove
Or gnash with a tiger's tooth.
5 I am happy to be a stone.

From the outside the stone is a riddle:
No one knows how to answer it.
Yet within, it must be cool and quiet
Even though a cow steps on it full weight,
10 Even though a child throws it in a river;
The stone sinks, slow, unperturbed
To the river bottom
Where the fishes come to knock on it
And listen.

15 I have seen sparks fly out
When two stones are rubbed,
So perhaps it is not dark inside after all;
Perhaps there is a moon shining
From somewhere, as though behind a hill—
20 Just enough light to make out
The strange writings, the star-charts
On the inner walls.

DISCUSSION

1. What changes in feeling in this poem would result if the poet were to have used the word "rock" instead of "stone"?

2. What objects besides stones might be riddles which we can only know by imagining?

3. Think of getting inside a seed. What might this be like? Could the author possibly have had this in mind? Why or why not?

4. What word in line 11 personifies the stone? Explain.

5. What would your "way" (line 2) be if you had a chance to adventure in some unique place?

AUTHOR

CHARLES SIMIC was born May 9, 1938, and educated at New York University. He is married and has one child.

Mr. Simic served in the United States Army from 1961 to 1963. In 1966 he joined the editorial staff of the photography magazine, *Aperture*.

Mr. Simic's published works include the collections *What the Grass Says* and *Somewhere Among Us a Stone is Taking Notes*.

Mushrooms

Sylvia Plath

Overnight, very
Whitely, discreetly,
Very quietly

Our toes, our noses
5 Take hold on the loam,
Acquire the air.

Nobody sees us,
Stops us, betrays us;
The small grains make room.

10 Soft fists insist on
Heaving the needles,
The leafy bedding,

Even the paving.
Our hammers, our rams,
15 Earless and eyeless,

Perfectly voiceless,
Widen the crannies,
Shoulder through holes. We

Diet on water,
20 On crumbs of shadow,
Bland-mannered, asking

Little or nothing.
So many of us!
So many of us!

25 We are shelves, we are
Tables, we are meek,
We are edible,

Nudgers and shovers
In spite of ourselves.
30 Our kind multiplies:

We shall by morning
Inherit the earth.
Our foot's in the door.

DISCUSSION

1. In what line does the personification of mushrooms begin?
2. (a) What are the "soft fists" in line 10? (b) Do you think this is a good image? Explain.
3. How effective is the imagery in lines 25–26? Explain.
4. To which senses does Sylvia Plath's imagery mainly appeal?

AUTHOR

SYLVIA PLATH was born October 27, 1932, in Boston, Massachusetts. She received a B.A., from Smith College in 1955, studied briefly at Harvard, and received an M.A., from Newnham College, Cambridge, in 1957. For the next two years she taught English at Smith, and then, in 1959, she moved to England permanently, settling first in London and then Devon.

Miss Plath was a regular contributor to such magazines as *Seventeen, Harper's, Nation, Atlantic,* and *Poetry.* She published several volumes of poetry including *Colossus* and *Ariel.* Her only novel, *The Bell Jar,* was published in 1963 under the pseudonym Victoria Lucas. Republished in 1966 under her real name, it has enjoyed enormous success in the United States.

Miss Plath took her own life on February 11, 1963.

Donkeys

Edward Field

They are not silent like work-horses
Who are happy or indifferent about the plow and wagon;
Donkeys don't submit like that
For they are sensitive
5 And cry continually under their burdens;
Yes, they are animals of sensibility
Even if they aren't intelligent enough
To count money or discuss religion.

Laugh if you will when they hee-haw
10 But know that they are crying
When they make that noise that sounds like something
Between a squawking water-pump and a fog-horn.

And when I hear them sobbing
I suddenly notice their sweet eyes and ridiculous ears
15 And their naive bodies that look as though they never grew up
But stayed children, as in fact they are;
And being misunderstood as children often are
They are forced to walk up mountains
With men and bundles on their backs.

20 Somehow I am glad
That they do not submit without a protest;
But as their masters are of the deafest
The wails are never heard.

I am sure that donkeys know what life should be -
25 But alas, they do not own their bodies;
And if they had their own way, I am sure
That they would sit in a field of flowers
Kissing each other, and maybe
They would even invite us to join them.

30 For they never let us forget that they know
(As everyone knows who stays as sweet as children)
That there is a far better way to spend time;
You can be sure of that when they stop in their tracks
And honk and honk and honk.

35 And if I tried to explain to them
Why work is not only necessary but good,
I am afraid that they would never understand
And kick me with their back legs
As commentary on my wisdom.

40 So they remain unhappy and sob
And their masters who are equally convinced of being right
Beat them and hear nothing.

The Hippo

Theodore Roethke

A Head or Tail—which does he lack?
I think his Forward's coming back!
He lives on Carrots, Leeks and Hay;
He starts to yawn—it takes All Day—

Some time I think I'll live that way.

DISCUSSION

Donkeys

1. To what is Field comparing horses and donkeys in stanza one?

2. What is the tone of the last three lines of the first stanza?

3. How does the speaker feel about the donkeys' masters? Find and read the lines that tell you.

AUTHOR

EDWARD FIELD, born June 7, 1924, in New York City, has contributed regularly to the *Evergreen Review*. He received the Lamont Award in 1962 and was awarded a Guggenheim Fellowship in 1963. He has published two volumes of poetry: *Stand Up, Friend, With Me* and *Variety Photoplays*.

DISCUSSION

The Hippo

1. Explain the speaker's apparent confusion in line 2.

2. Why is the last line separate from the four preceding lines?

3. The poem has a very obvious rhythm. Do you think it is appropriate in communicating the sense of the poem? Explain.

4. In the first four lines there is balance within each line with a break near the middle that forms a kind of symmetry. How does this form agree with the subject of the poem?

Seagulls

John Updike

A gull, up close,
looks surprisingly stuffed.
His fluffy chest seems filled
with an inexpensive taxidermist's material
5 rather lumpily inserted. The legs,
unbent, are childish crayon strokes—
too simple to be workable. ·
And even the feather-markings,
whose intricate symmetry is the usual glory of birds,
10 are in the gull slovenly,
as if God makes too many
to make them very well.

Are they intelligent?
We imagine so, because they are ugly.
15 The sardonic one-eyed profile, slightly cross,
the narrow, ectomorphic head, badly combed,
the wide and nervous and well-muscled rump
all suggest deskwork: shipping rates
by day, Schopenhauer
20 by night, and endless coffee.

At that hour on the beach
when the flies begin biting in the renewed coolness
and the backsliding skin of the after-surf
reflects a pink shimmer before being blotted,
25 the gulls stand around in the dimpled sand
like those melancholy European crowds
that gather in cobbled public squares in the wake
of assassinations and invasions,
heads cocked to hear the latest radio reports.

30 It is also this hour when plump young couples
walk down to the water, bumping together,
and stand thigh deep in the rhythmic glass.
Then they walk back toward the car,
tugging as if at a secret between them,
35 but which neither quite knows;
walk capricious paths through the scattering gulls,
as in some mythologies
beautiful gods stroll unconcerned
among our mortal apprehensions.

Dreams of the Animals

Margaret Atwood

Mostly the animals dream
of other animals   each
according to its kind

5   (though certain mice and small rodents
       have nightmares of a huge pink
       shape with five claws descending)

: moles dream of darkness and delicate
mole smells

frogs dream of green and golden
10 frogs
sparkling like wet suns
among the lilies

red and black
striped fish, their eyes open
15 have red and black striped
dreams   defence, attack, meaningful
patterns

birds dream of territories
enclosed by singing.

20 Sometimes the animals dream of evil
in the form of soap and metal
but mostly the animals dream
of other animals.

There are exceptions:

25   the silver fox in the roadside zoo
        dreams of digging out
        and of baby foxes, their necks bitten

        the caged armadillo
        near the train
30   station, which runs
        all day in figure eights
        its piglet feet pattering,
        no longer dreams
        but is insane when waking;

35   the iguana
        in the petshop window on St. Catherine Street
        crested, royal-eyed, ruling
        its kingdom of water-dish and sawdust

        dreams of sawdust.

DISCUSSION

Seagulls

1. Do you think the speaker likes or dislikes seagulls? Give reasons for your answer.

2. What is the speaker's reasoning in stanza two?

3. Study the images Updike uses to describe seagulls. To which sense do most of them appeal? Cite examples.

4. In stanza three, to what does the speaker compare the gulls? Do you think this is a good comparison? Explain.

5. (a) In the last stanza, to what does the speaker shift his attention? (b) Who are the "beautiful gods" and "mortal apprehensions" in the last two lines?

AUTHOR

JOHN UPDIKE, born in 1932, in Shillington, Massachusetts, was educated at Harvard College and the Ruskin School of Drawing and Fine Arts. He is married and has four children.

From 1955 to 1957 Mr. Updike served as a staff reporter for *The New Yorker* magazine. He is a prolific writer in a variety of genres. He has published a number of volumes of poetry including *Telephone Poles* and *Midpoint and Other Poems*. Other published works include *Pigeon Feathers* and *The Music School* (short story collections), and *Rabbit, Run, The Centaur, Couples,* and *Rabbit Redux* (novels).

DISCUSSION

Dreams of the Animals

1. In what way and at what point does the tone of this poem change?

2. To what might the "soap and metal" in line 21 refer?

3. What kind of dream might the donkeys (page 216) have?

4. Compare the theme of this poem with that of McNamar's "The Elk" on page 209.

AUTHOR

MARGARET ATWOOD was born in 1939, in Ottawa, Ontario, Canada. She was educated at the University of Toronto, Radcliffe, and Harvard. She has written one novel, *The Edible Woman.* Her published verse includes *Double Persephone, The Circle Game,* and *The Animals in That Country.* Miss Atwood makes her home in Edmonton, Alberta, Canada.

THE POETS' CRAFT

Sound and meaning

You have seen how poets regulate the *stress* of words to create meter and how rhythm is part of a poem's meaning. A poet may also regulate the *sound* of his words. The sound effects in a poem, however, differ from the sound effects in a nonsense rhyme like this one:

Z was once a piece of zinc,
    Tinky,
    Winky,
    Blinky,

    Tinky,
    Tinky minky,
    Piece of zinc!
          Edward Lear, "Alphabet"

A poem differs from a nonsense rhyme because the sounds of a poem combine with its rhythm to reinforce its sense.

One way the poet regulates sound is to *repeat* identical or similar sounds. Alliteration, assonance, and rhyme unify the thought.

1. *Alliteration* repeats the sound of consonants, usually initial consonants:

The *d*eed and the *d*oer, the *s*eed
    and the *s*ower, the *d*ust
    which is God.
        Algernon Swinburne, "Hertha"

2. *Assonance* repeats the sound of accented vowels:

While in the *wild* wood *I* did *lie,*
A *child*—with a most knowing *eye.*
        Edgar Allan Poe, "Romance"

3. *Rhyme* repeats the *final* sound of two or more words. The most common kind of rhyme is *end rhyme,* in which the rhyming words come at the end of lines. Because end rhyme follows a fixed scheme, it is the most effec-

tive way of unifying the thought. When end rhyme is patterned into stanzas, it helps tie together the sense of several lines. A stanza is usually a sense unit like a paragraph:

I wander through each chartered
  street   *a*
Near where the chartered Thames
  does flow,   *b*
And mark in every face I meet   *a*
Marks of weakness, marks of
  woe.   *b*
         William Blake, "London"

Another kind of rhyme is *internal rhyme*, in which a word near the middle of a line rhymes with the last word in the line:

The ship drove *fast*, loud roared
  the *blast*.
         Coleridge, "The Rime
         of the Ancient Mariner"

Alliteration, assonance, and rhyme also affect the movement of a poem. Usually, they combine with meter to quicken the motion.

A second way of regulating sound may be shown in this line from Tennyson's "Lotus-Eaters":

The mild-eyed melancholy Lotus-
  eaters came,

In order to pronounce this line distinctly, you must pronounce it more slowly than you would pronounce the following line from the same poem:

And music in his ears his beating
  heart did make.

Poets, then, will *select* sounds for the way they affect motion:

True ease in writing comes from art,
  not chance,

As those move easiest who have
  learned to dance.
'T is not enough no harshness gives
  offense,
The sound must seem an echo to
  the sense:
5 Soft is the strain when Zephyr gently
  blows,
And the smooth stream in smoother
  numbers flows:
But when loud surges lash the
  sounding shore,
The hoarse, rough verse should like
  a torrent roar:
When Ajax strives some rock's vast
  weight to throw,
10 The line too labors, and the words
  move slow.
      Alexander Pope, "Essay on Criticism"

Each of Pope's ten lines is iambic pentameter, but lines 6 and 9 move more slowly than the others. The many vowels in line 6 and the groups of consonants in line 9 slow the pronunciation. Notice, also, that lines 5 and 6 have a melodic effect, while lines 7 and 8 have a clashing effect. In each case the sound effects reinforce the sense of the rhymed lines.

When the *sound* of words and the *stress* of words are regulated by the poet, they become part of his meaning. Rhyme and meter are thus said to be *functional*, rather than decorative. Some poets, however, abandon rhyme; other poets dispense with meter as well. The next article about the poets' craft will discuss how and why many poets drop these devices.

WORD STUDY

Stanza names
Stanza forms are usually classified according to the number of their lines. Some stanza names are derived from Latin words. The following examples illustrate three of

the many stanza forms in English poetry. The rhyme scheme is indicated by letters of the alphabet. Examine each example carefully.

1. This is a *couplet*:

Each purple peak, each flinty spire,
Was bathed in floods of living fire.
    Sir Walter Scott, "The Lady of the Lake"

The word *couplet*, like the word *couple*, is derived from the Latin word *copula* ("band" or "bond").

2. This is a *tercet*:

"The sap dries up: the plant
  declines.
A deeper tale my heart divines.
Know I not Death? The outward
  signs?"
        Tennyson, "The Two Voices"

The word *tercet* is derived from the Latin word *tertius* ("third").

3. This is a *quatrain*:

There lived a wife at Usher's Well,
  And a wealthy wife was she;
She had three stout and stalwart
  sons,
  And sent them o'er the sea.
    Anonymous, "The Wife of Usher's Well"

The word *quatrain* is derived from the Latin word *quattuor* ("four").

Using the Glossary, explain how many lines each of the following stanza forms contains: *quintain*, *sextain*, and *octave*.

Examine the rhyme schemes of the following two stanzas. State the *name* of the stanza in which line 2 rhymes with line 3.

There's a palace in Florence, the
  world knows well.
And a statue watches it from the
  square.
And this story of both do our townsmen tell.
     Browning, "The Statue and the Bust"

Ring out, wild bells, to the wild sky,
The flying cloud, the frosty light:
The year is dying in the night;
Ring out, wild bells, and let him die.
     Tennyson, "In Memoriam"

Longings

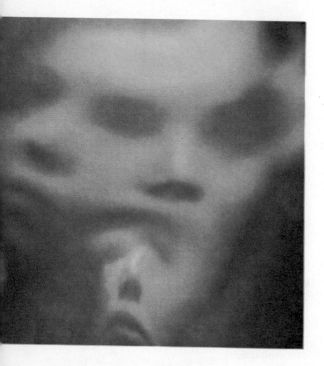

If There Be Sorrow

Mari Evans

If there be sorrow
let it be
for things undone . . .
undreamed
  unrealized
    unattained
to these add one:
Love withheld . . .
. . . restrained

DISCUSSION

1. (a) If, in the third line, "un-done" were to read "not done," would this affect the sound and/or sense of the poem? (b) What is the effect of the repetition of "un"?

2. How are things that are "undreamed," "unrealized," or "unattained" different from love being restrained?

3. State the theme of the poem.

"If There Be Sorrow" by Mari Evans from I AM A BLACK WOMAN, published by William Morrow and Company, Inc. Reprinted by permission of the author.

Those Winter Sundays

Robert Hayden

Sundays too my father got up early
and put his clothes on in the blueblack cold,
then with cracked hands that ached
from labor in the weekday weather made
5 banked fires blaze. No one ever thanked him.

I'd wake and hear the cold splintering, breaking.
When the rooms were warm, he'd call,
and slowly I would rise and dress,
fearing the chronic angers of that house,

10 Speaking indifferently to him,
who had driven out the cold
and polished my good shoes as well.
What did I know, what did I know
of love's austere and lonely offices?

DISCUSSION

1. What does the word "too" in the first line tell you?

2. Why do you think "No one ever thanked him"? (Line 5)

3. What type of figurative language is Robert Hayden using in line 6?

4. What are "chronic angers" of a house? Does your house have chronic angers? Explain.

5. (a) What is the meaning of the word "offices"? (b) Who performed "love's austere and lonely offices"? (c) What were these particular offices? (d) If the word "duties" were used in place of "offices" would it be just as effective? Why or why not?

6. What is the speaker saying about "longing"?

AUTHOR

ROBERT HAYDEN, born in Detroit, Michigan in 1913, is at present a Professor of English at the University of Michigan where he teaches courses in poetry and creative writing. For more than twenty years he was on the faculty at Fisk University in Nashville, Tennessee. He has published several books of poems and has received numerous awards for his poetry.

Robert Hayden's poetry frequently reflects his Negro heritage, but extends far beyond it. His poems reveal his love and compassion for humanity and his rage against what is mean and petty in man's nature. "Those Winter Sundays" is typical of much of Hayden's work: the language is simple, the images are clear and sharp, and the poem expresses intense emotion without sentimentality.

Among Hayden's published works are: *A Ballad of Remembrance* (1962), *Selected Poems* (1966), and *Words in the Mourning Time* (1970).

Eleven

Archibald MacLeish

And summer mornings the mute child, rebellious,
Stupid, hating the words, the meanings, hating
The Think now, Think, the O but Think! would leave
On tiptoe the three chairs on the verandah
5 And crossing tree by tree the empty lawn
Push back the shed door and upon the sill
Stand pressing out the sunlight from his eyes
And enter and with outstretched fingers feel
The grindstone and behind it the bare wall
10 And turn and in the corner on the cool
Hard earth sit listening. And one by one,
Out of the dazzled shadow in the room,
The shapes would gather, the brown plowshare, spades,
Mattocks, the polished helves of picks, a scythe
15 Hung from the rafters, shovels, slender tines
Glinting across the curve of sickles—shapes
Older than men were, the wise tools, the iron
Friendly with earth. And sit there, quiet, breathing
The harsh dry smell of withered bulbs, the faint
20 Odor of dung, the silence. And outside
Beyond the half-shut door the blind leaves
And the corn moving. And at noon would come,
Up from the garden, his hard crooked hands
Gentle with earth, his knees still earth-stained, smelling
25 Of sun, of summer, the old gardener, like
A priest, like an interpreter, and bend
Over his baskets.   And they would not speak:
They would say nothing. And the child would sit there
Happy as though he had no name, as though
30 He had been no one: like a leaf, a stem,
Like a root growing—

DISCUSSION

1. What is the probable setting of this poem? Find clues in the poem to support your answer.

2. In the first line, the speaker refers to the boy as "mute." From evidence in the poem, do you think the boy is physically unable to speak or that he is simply not speaking from choice? Quote words and phrases from the poem to defend your answer.

3. (a) What had the child been doing on the verandah before going to the shed? (b) Why did he leave?

4. Why do you think the author capitalized the word "Think"?

5. Why does the boy cross the lawn "tree by tree"?

6. What was it about the gardener that made the child feel happy?

7. To whom does "they" in line 28 refer?

8. From what does the boy's happiness (lines 29–31) come?

AUTHOR

ARCHIBALD MACLEISH, born in 1892, in Glencoe, Illinois, was educated at Yale and Harvard.

He worked on the editorial staff of *Fortune* magazine, was a Librarian of Congress, and in 1944-45 he served as Assistant Secretary of State. From 1949 to 1962 he taught poetry and creative writing at Harvard.

MacLeish has received three Pulitzer Prize awards: in 1933, for the poem *Conquistador;* in 1953 for *Collected Poems: 1917–1952;* and in 1959, for the successful drama *J.B.: A Play in Verse.*

Dream Variation

Langston Hughes

To fling my arms wide
In some place of the sun,
To whirl and to dance
Till the white day is done.
5 Then rest at cool evening
Beneath a tall tree
While night comes on gently,
      Dark like me—
That is my dream!

10 To fling my arms wide
In the face of the sun,
Dance! Whirl! Whirl!
Till the quick day is done.
Rest at pale evening . . .
15 A tall, slim tree . . .
Night coming tenderly
      Black like me.

Long Distance

Carole Gregory

That phone call, the one that you wait for
but never expect to come
was phoned today. And
that voice, the voice you ache for
but seldom expect to hear
spoke today. And that
loneliness, the loneliness you hurt from
but always held inside,
flies out like thin stones across water.

DISCUSSION

1. Note how each line in the first stanza nearly parallels each line in the second stanza. What are the differences and how do they relate to the title and the meaning of the poem?

2. What word or phrase would you use to describe the tone of this poem?

3. What figure of speech does the poet use in describing "night"?

AUTHOR

LANGSTON HUGHES was born in 1902, in Joplin Missouri. One of his most famous poems, "The Negro Speaks of Rivers," was written shortly after he graduated from high school. In 1921 Hughes attended Columbia University. During this period he became attached to Harlem which he called the "great dark city." Today, he is often referred to as the poet laureate of Harlem.

In 1922 Hughes quit school and devoted his time to writing poetry and traveling in Europe. Upon his return to America, while working as a bus boy in a Washington D.C., hotel, he met Vachel Lindsay, the poet. This chance meeting resulted in a scholarship to Lincoln University in Pennsylvania. While at Lincoln, Hughes published his first two books, launching a long and prolific literary career.

In his lifetime, Hughes published ten volumes of poetry, a two volume autobiography, two volumes of short stories, and a *Pictorial History of the Negro in America*. In addition, he edited two anthologies, *The Poetry of the Negro* and *The Book of Negro Folklore*. He is popularly remem-

Momentum

Tom Clark

I saw the busy street you crossed the last time I saw you
As the river of time, carrying you away forever.
Your pale coat swirled like a leaf in the current
In the crowd of anonymous bodies hurrying back to work.

I turned around and started to walk in the other direction
But because of the tears in my eyes I failed to see a dentist
Standing outside the entrance to his office and collided with him,
Knocking him down.

bered as the creator of the character Jesse B. Semple, ("Simple") who appeared in the columns he wrote for the *Chicago Defender* and the *New York Post*. Hughes died May 22, 1967, in New York City.

DISCUSSION

Long Distance
1. What ideas do you get from this poem as to who the caller and the person called might be?
2. Do you think the image of the word "stones" in the last line is a good one? What would the effect be if the word were changed to "leaves" for example?

Momentum
1. Who might be the "you" and "I" in this poem?
2. (a) With what does the speaker compare "the busy street"? (b) What is this figure of speech called?
3. Can you think of any reason why the poet chose a dentist to be the person with whom the speaker collides? If so, why?
4. What do you think is the relationship of the title to the poem?

AUTHOR

TOM CLARK, born in 1941, in Chicago, Illinois, has served as poetry editor for *The Paris Review* since 1963. He was educated at the University of Michigan, the University of Cambridge, and the University of Essex. He has published four volumes of verse: *Airplanes, The Sand Burg, Bun,* and *Stones.*

The Stone

Wilfrid Wilson Gibson

"And will you cut a stone for him,
To set above his head?
And will you cut a stone for him—
A stone for him?" she said.

5 Three days before, a splintered rock
Had struck her lover dead—
Had struck him in the quarry dead,
Where, careless of the warning call,
He loitered, while the shot was fired—
10 A lively stripling, brave and tall,
And sure of all his heart desired . . .
A flash, a shock,
A rumbling fall . . .
And, broken 'neath the broken rock,
15 A lifeless heap, with face of clay,
And still as any stone he lay,
With eyes that saw the end of all.

I went to break the news to her:
And I could hear my own heart beat
20 With dread of what my lips might say;
But some poor fool had sped before;
And, flinging wide her father's door,
Had blurted out the news to her,
Had struck her lover dead for her,
25 Had struck the girl's heart dead in her,
Had struck life, lifeless, at a word,
And dropped it at her feet:
Then hurried on his witless way,
Scarce knowing she had heard.
30 And when I came, she stood alone—

A woman, turned to stone:
And, though no word at all she said,
I knew that all was known.

Because her heart was dead,
35 She did not sigh nor moan.
His mother wept:
She could not weep.
Her lover slept:
She could not sleep.
40 Three days, three nights,
She did not stir:
Three days, three nights,
Were one to her,

Who never closed her eyes
45 From sunset to sunrise,
From dawn to evenfall—
Her tearless, staring eyes,
That, seeing naught, saw all.

The fourth night when I came from work,
50 I found her at my door.
"And will you cut a stone for him?"
She said: and spoke no more:
But followed me, as I went in,
And sank upon a chair;
55 And fixed her grey eyes on my face,
With still, unseeing stare.
And, as she waited patiently,
I could not bear to feel
Those still, grey eyes that followed me,
60 Those eyes that plucked the heart from me,
Those eyes that sucked the breath from me
And curdled the warm blood in me,
Those eyes that cut me to the bone,
And pierced my marrow like cold steel.

DISCUSSION

The Stone

1. (a) Who is the speaker in this poem? (b) How does the speaker relate to the girl?

2. Do you think this poem could be set to music effectively? Why or why not?

3. What words would you use to identify the tone of the poem?

One Perfect Rose

1. Identify "his messenger" that "he chose" so carefully.

2. (a) Where in the poem does the mood change? (b) How does it change?

3. Study the language of the first two stanzas. How would you describe it? Does it add to the humorous effect you experience at the end of the poem? Explain.

₆₅ And so I rose, and sought a stone;
And cut it, smooth and square:
And, as I worked, she sat and watched,
Beside me, in her chair.
Night after night, by candlelight,
₇₀ I cut her lover's name:
Night after night, so still and white,
And like a ghost she came;
And sat beside me, in her chair,
And watched with eyes aflame.
₇₅ She eyed each stroke,
And hardly stirred:
She never spoke
A single word:

And not a sound or murmur broke
₈₀ The quiet, save the mallet-stroke.

With still eyes ever on my hands,
With eyes that seemed to burn my hands,
My wincing, overwearied hands,
She watched, with bloodless lips apart,
₈₅ And silent, indrawn breath:
And every stroke my chisel cut,
Death cut still deeper in her heart:
The two of us were chiselling,
Together, I and death.

₉₀ And when at length the job was done,
And I had laid the mallet by,
As if, at last, her peace were won,
She breathed his name; and, with a sigh,
Passed slowly through the open door;
₉₅ And never crossed my threshold more.

Next night I laboured late, alone,
To cut her name upon the stone.

One Perfect Rose

Dorothy Parker

A single flow'r he sent me, since we met.
  All tenderly his messenger he chose;
Deep-hearted, pure, with scented dew still wet—
  One perfect rose.

₅ I knew the language of the floweret;
  "My fragile leaves," it said, "his heart enclose."
Love long has taken for his amulet
  One perfect rose.

Why is it no one ever sent me yet
₁₀ One perfect limousine, do you suppose?
Ah no, it's always just my luck to get
  One perfect rose.

AUTHOR

DOROTHY PARKER, (1893–1967) delighted the reading public with her witty, often cynical, verse for many years. Some of her book titles suggest the wry humor that she favored: *Enough Rope, Death and Taxes, Laments for the Living, Not So Deep as a Well,* and *Here Lies.* "One Perfect Rose" is typical of her stabbing wit. Dorothy Parker began her literary career as a drama and literary critic during the 1920's. She became known as a poet and short-story writer through her contributions of verse and prose sketches to *The New Yorker* magazine. She served as an American correspondent in Spain (1936–1939) at the time of the Spanish Civil War. In addition, Miss Parker wrote several plays and motion-picture scripts.

From THE PORTABLE DOROTHY PARKER. Copyright 1926, renewed 1954 by Dorothy Parker. Reprinted by permission of The Viking Press, Inc.

The Ballad of Sue Ellen Westerfield

(for Clyde)

Robert Hayden

She grew up in bedeviled southern wilderness,
but had not been a slave, she said,
because her father wept and set her mother free.
She hardened in perilous rivertowns
5 and after The Surrender,
went as maid upon the tarnished Floating Palaces.
Rivermen reviled her for the rankling cold
sardonic pride
that gave a knife-edge to her comeliness.

10 When she was old, her back still straight,
her hair still glossy black,
she'd talk sometimes
of dangers lived through on the rivers.
But never told of him,
15 whose name she'd vowed she would not speak again
till after Jordan.
Oh, he was nearer nearer now
than wearisome kith and kin.
His blue eyes followed her
20 as she moved about her tasks upon the *Memphis Rose.*
He smiled and joshed, his voice quickening her.
She cursed the circumstance. . . .

The crazing horrors of that summer night,
the swifting flames, he fought his way to her,
25 the savaging panic, and helped her swim to shore.
The steamer like besieged Atlanta blazing,
the cries, the smoke and bellowing flames,

the flamelit thrashing forms in hellmouth water,
and he swimming out to them,
30 leaving her dazed and lost.
A woman screaming under the raddled trees—
Sue Ellen felt it was herself who screamed.
The moaning of the hurt, the terrified—
she held off shuddering despair
35 and went to comfort whom she could.

Wagons torches bells
and whimpering dusk of morning
and blankness lostness nothingness for her
until his arms had lifted her
40 into wild and secret dark.

How long how long was it they wandered,
loving fearing loving,
fugitives whose dangerous only hidingplace
was love?
45 How long was it before she knew
she could not forfeit what she was,
even for him—could not, even for him,
forswear her pride?
They kissed and said farewell at last.
50 He wept as had her father once.
They kissed and said farewell.
Until her dying-bed,
she cursed the circumstance.

DISCUSSION

1. Where and when do the events in this ballad take place?
2. What were the "floating palaces"?
3. (a) What does line 19 tell you about "him"? (b) What circumstance did "she" curse?
4. What happens in lines 23–35?

5. Compare this ballad with "The Stone" on pages 228–229. In what ways are they alike? How are they different? Which did you enjoy more? Why?

THE POETS' CRAFT

Unrhymed poetry: blank verse and free verse

Over the years many poets have dispensed with rhyme and have developed two major unrhymed forms—*blank verse* and *free verse*. A blank-verse poem is a poem that consists of *any* number of *unrhymed iambic pentameter* lines. The first step in the development of blank verse was taken by sixteenth-century English lyric poets. They discovered that the English language has a natural *iambic* beat and that combinations of English words fall most naturally in lines of *five* feet each. Once these lyricists had recognized the *iambic pentameter* as the most natural English line, they used it extensively. They wrote *rhymed* iambic pentameter poems.

The second step in the development of blank verse was taken by the dramatists and narrative poets of the sixteenth century. They adopted the rhymed iambic pentameter line of the lyric poets. Unlike the lyricists, however, these poets were writing at great length. They found it difficult to sustain the rhyme for five acts of drama or for several hundred or more lines of narrative poetry. They were forced to recognize that, although there is a great variety of final sounds in English, comparatively few words end with the same sound. Consequently, the dramatists and narrative poets began to write *unrhymed* iambic pentameter lines, or *blank verse*. Although blank verse is unrhymed, its rhythm is regulated by the *iambic* meter in five-foot lines.

William Shakespeare, like his contemporaries, cast his dramas in blank-verse lines:

But, soft! | what light | through yon | der win | dow breaks?
It is | the east, | and Ju | liet is | the sun.
A rise, | fair sun, | and kill | the en | vious moon,
Who is | al read | y sick | and pale | with grief
That thou, | her maid, | art far | more fair | than she.

Romeo and Juliet

Free verse, the second form of unrhymed English poetry, was developed in the nineteenth century and has become a favorite form of many modern poets. Free verse is called "free" because the poet is not required to follow set patterns of rhyme, meter, or line length.

Free-verse poets believe rhyme is an inadequate poetic device. They point out that rhyme may restrict, perhaps dictate, the meaning of a poem. For example, imagine a poet who is composing a serious tercet about a dove he once held in his hand and had touched gently. The word *dove* suggests that his three lines will rhyme the *-ove* sound. He begins:

A gray, white-throated dove
Lay quivering in my glove.

In the next line, he wants to say, "I gave it a gentle touch." *Touch* does not rhyme with *dove* or *glove* so he casts about for a word that does, with this unfortunate result:

A gray, white-throated dove
Lay quivering in my glove;
I gave it a gentle *shove*.

The rhyme has drastically changed the poet's meaning. To avoid such a predicament, free-verse poets dispense with rhyme in all *poems*. If they regulate sound at all it will be mainly through alliteration and assonance.

Free-verse poets, unlike blank-verse poets, believe meter is an unnecessary poetic device since every word we use has a stress of accent—a natural rhythm of its own. Depending solely upon the natural rise and fall of words and phrases, free-verse lines such as these:

Beautiful evening
Calm, free

are just as rhythmical in their way as is this metrical version:

It is | a beau | teous eve | ning,
calm | and free.

William Wordsworth

Often the free-verse poet gives his reader a clue to the movement of his poem by beginning each rhythmical unit on a new line as Walt Whitman does in his free-verse poem "When I Heard the Learn'd Astronomer":

When I heard the learn'd astronomer,
When the proofs, the figures, were ranged in columns before me,
When I was shown the charts and diagrams, to add, divide, and measure them,
When I sitting heard the astronomer where he lectured with much applause in the lecture room,
How soon unaccountable I became tired and sick,
Till rising and gliding out I wandered off by myself,
In the mystical, moist night air, and from time to time,
Looked up in perfect silence at the stars.

Issues

Fair and Unfair

Robert Francis

The beautiful is fair, the just is fair.
Yet one is commonplace and one is rare,
One everywhere, one scarcely anywhere.

So fair unfair a world. Had we the wit
To use the surplus for the deficit,
We'd make a fairer fairer world of it.

DISCUSSION

1. The title suggests that the reader will find a paradox in the poem. Look up the term in a dictionary and then explain the paradoxical statement in the poem.

2. (a) According to the speaker, of what in life is there a surplus? (b) Of what is there a deficit? (c) What is the speaker's conclusion?

AUTHOR

ROBERT FRANCIS has contributed to such literary publications as the *Massachusetts Review, Virginia Quarterly Review, Poetry, New Yorker,* and *Commonweal.* He has published a number of volumes of poetry including *The Sound I Listened For, The Face Against the Glass,* and *The Orb Weaver.*

Born on August 12, 1901, Mr. Francis was educated at Harvard, has traveled extensively in Europe, and makes his home in Amherst, Massachusetts.

The Hand That Signed the Paper

Dylan Thomas

The hand that signed the paper felled a city;
Five sovereign fingers taxed the breath,
Doubled the globe of dead and halved a country;
These five kings did a king to death.

5 The mighty hand leads to a sloping shoulder,
The finger joints are cramped with chalk;
A goose's quill has put an end to murder
That put an end to talk.

The hand that signed the treaty bred a fever,
10 And famine grew, and locusts came;
Great is the hand that holds dominion over
Man by a scribbled name.

The five kings count the dead but do not soften
The crusted wound nor stroke the brow;
15 A hand rules pity as a hand rules heaven;
Hands have no tears to flow.

DISCUSSION

1. (a) To whom did the hand that signed the paper belong? (b) What kind of paper was signed?

2. Explain the line "These five kings did a king to death."

3. What do you think is the significance of "sloping shoulder" (line 5) and "The finger joints are cramped with chalk;" (line 6)?

4. Explain what the speaker means in the last two lines of the second stanza.

5. What do you think is the tone of voice behind the lines "Great is the hand that holds dominion over/Man by a scribbled name"?

6. State the author's theme in your own words.

AUTHOR

DYLAN THOMAS was born in Swansea, Wales, in 1914, the son of an English master. He published his first volume of verse, *Eighteen Poems*, in 1934. In 1936, he married Caitlin Macnamara.

During his lifetime, Thomas worked on Welsh newspapers, wrote scripts for documentary films and for radio, and, late in his career, toured England and America giving enormously successful poetry readings.

Collected Poems, published in 1953, contains the verse he considered to be his best from the various smaller volumes he had published. His voice play, *Under Milk Wood*, originally written for radio, was produced on Broadway in 1957.

Thomas died in New York City in November, 1953, while on a lecture tour of America.

Late Rising

Jacques Prévert
Translated by Selden Rodman

Terrible
is the soft sound of a hardboiled egg
cracking on a zinc counter
and terrible is that sound
5 when it moves in the memory
of a man who is hungry
Terrible also is the head of a man
the head of a man hungry
when he looks at six o'clock in the morning
10 in a smart shop window and sees
a head the color of dust
But it is not his head he sees
in the window of 'Chez Potin'
he doesn't give a damn
15 for the head of a man
he doesn't think at all
he dreams
imagining another head
calf's-head for instance
20 with vinegar sauce
head of anything edible
and slowly he moves his jaws
slowly slowly
grinds his teeth for the world
25 stands him on his head
without giving him any comeback
so he counts on his fingers one two three
one two three
that makes three days he has been empty
30 and it's stupid to go on saying It can't
go on It can't go on because
it does
Three days
three nights
35 without eating
and behind those windows

pâté de foie gras[1] wine preserves
dead fish protected by their boxes
boxes in turn protected by windows
40 these in turn watched by the police
police protected in turn by fear
How many guards for six sardines . . .
Then he comes to the lunch counter
coffee-with-cream buttered toast
45 and he begins to flounder
and in the middle of his head
blizzard of words
muddle of words
sardines fed
50 hardboiled eggs coffee-with-cream
coffee black rum food
coffee-with-cream
coffee-with-cream
coffee crime black blood
55 A respectable man in his own neighborhood
had his throat cut in broad daylight
the dastardly assassin stole from him
two bits that is to say
exactly the price of a black coffee
60 two slices of buttered toast
and a nickel left to tip the waiter

Terrible
is the sound of a hardboiled egg
cracking on a zinc counter
65 and terrible is that sound when it moves
in the memory
of a man who is hungry.

"Late Rising" by Jacques Prévert, translated by Selden Rodman, from PAROLES DE JACQUES PRÉVERT. © 1949 Editions Gallimard. Reprinted by permission.
1. *pâté de foie gras*, chopped goose livers.

Harlem

Langston Hughes

What happens to a dream deferred?

  Does it dry up
  like a raisin in the sun?
  Or fester like a sore—
  And then run?
  Does it stink like rotten meat?
  Or crust and sugar over—
  like a syrupy sweet?

  Maybe it just sags
  like a heavy load.

  Or does it explode?

DISCUSSION

Late Rising

1. Besides the fact that the sound of an egg being broken is no doubt terrible to a starving man, what in addition is effective about the sound and the sense of the lines ". . . the soft sound of a hardboiled egg / cracking on a zinc counter"?

2. (a) Explain what is meant in line 42. (b) How do you interpret lines 55-61?

3. The image of a head recurs throughout the poem. Reread the lines that use this image and explain why you think the poet has chosen to emphasize this part of the body.

4. After reading and discussing the poem, explain what the title means to you.

Harlem

1. What is the meaning of "deferred"?

2. What kind of a dream is the speaker talking about?

3. How does the spacing between stanzas influence the way the poem should be read?

4. How would you describe the tone of the poem?

pity the poor spiders

Don Marquis

i have just been reading
an advertisement of a certain
roach exterminator
the human race little knows
5 all the sadness it
causes in the insect world
i remember some weeks ago
meeting a middle aged spider
she was weeping
10 what is the trouble i asked
her it is these cursed
fly swatters she replied
they kill off all the flies
and my family and i are starving
15 to death it struck me as
so pathetic that i made
a little song about it
as follows to wit

twas an elderly mother spider
20 grown gaunt and fierce and gray
with her little ones crouched beside her
who wept as she sang this lay
curses on these here swatters
what kills off all the flies
25 for me and my little daughters
unless we eats we dies

swattin and swattin and swattin
tis little else you hear

and we ll soon be dead and forgotten
30 with the cost of living so dear

my husband he up and left me
lured off by a centipede
and he says as he bereft me
tis wrong but i ll get a feed

35 and me a working and working
scouring the streets for food
faithful and never shirking
doing the best i could

curses on these here swatters
40 what kills off all the flies
me and my poor little daughters
unless we eats we dies

only a withered spider
feeble and worn and old
45 and this is what
you do when you swat
you swatters cruel and cold

i will admit that some
of the insects do not lead
50 noble lives but is every
man s hand to be against them
yours for less justice
and more charity

                                    archy

DISCUSSION

1. (a) Who is the main speaker in this poem? (b) What caused him to write the poem?

2. How would you describe the tone of the second stanza?

3. What does the mother spider's song tell you about her?

4. Who is the speaker in the last stanza?

5. What do you think the "message" is in the last two lines.

AUTHOR

DON MARQUIS (1878–1937) received his education at Knox College, Galesburg, Illinois. He was a reporter for several newspapers and helped Joel Chandler Harris edit the *Uncle Remus* magazine. The popular duo of Archy the cockroach and Mehitabel the

cat first appeared in "The Sun Dial," a column that Marquis wrote for the *New York Sun* from 1912 to 1922.

DISCUSSION

Law Like Love

1. How would you define the gardener's philosophy of law as stated in the first stanza?

2. How different from the previous one are the notions of law as

Law Like Love

W. H. Auden

Law, say the gardeners, is the sun,
Law is the one
All gardeners obey
Tomorrow, yesterday, today.

5 Law is the wisdom of the old
The impotent grandfathers shrilly scold;
The grandchildren put out a treble tongue,
Law is the senses of the young.

Law, says the priest with a priestly look,
10 Expounding to an unpriestly people,
Law is the words in my priestly book,
Law is my pulpit and my steeple.

Law, says the judge as he looks down his nose,
Speaking clearly and most severely,
15 Law is as I've told you before,
Law is as you know I suppose,
Law is but let me explain it once more,
Law is The Law.

Yet law-abiding scholars write;
20 Law is neither wrong nor right,
Law is only crimes
Punished by places and by times,
Law is the clothes men wear
Anytime, anywhere,
25 Law is Good-morning and Good-night.

Others say, Law is our Fate;
Others say, Law is our State;
Others say, others say
Law is no more
30 Law has gone away.

And always the loud angry crowd
Very angry and very loud
Law is We,
And always the soft idiot softly Me.

35 If we, dear, know we know no more
Than they about the law,
If I no more than you
Know what we should and should not do
Except that all agree
40 Gladly or miserably
That the law is
And that all know this,
If therefore thinking it absurd
To identify Law with some other word,
45 Unlike so many men
I cannot say Law is again,
No more than they can we suppress
The universal wish to guess
Or slip out of our own position
50 Into an unconcerned condition.
Although I can at least confine
Your vanity and mine
To stating timidly
A timid similarity,
55 We shall boast anyway:
Like love I say.

Like love we don't know where or why
Like love we can't compel or fly
Like love we often weep
60 Like love we seldom keep.

discussed in the second stanza?

3. Does the speaker side with either end of the generation gap? Explain.

4. What is the speaker's attitude toward the two institutions focused on in stanzas three and four?

5. Find examples of Auden's use of alliteration in stanza three and assonance in stanza four. What do they contribute to the feeling of the lines?

6. (a) What is the speaker's attitude toward the law of the courts? (b) What word choice in this stanza (four) reveals his attitude?

7. How does the notion of law in stanza five compare with that in stanza one?

8. How would you interpret the last three lines in stanza five?

9. Who are the "others" in stanza six?

10. Explain stanza seven in your own words.

11. In the eighth stanza, the speaker poses three conditions beginning with "If"; what is his resolution and how does he further amend it in the concluding lines of the stanza?

12. In the last stanza Auden responds as a poet to the question Law is what? Interpret his final lines. Do you think these lines approach the truth of what is law as well as a lawyer or a judge might? How is love like law?

Homage

Kenneth Fearing

They said to him, "It is a very good thing that you have done,
　　yes, both good and great, proving this other passage to the
　　Indies. Marvelous," they said. "Very. But where, Señor,
　　is the gold?"
They said: "We like it, we admire it very much, don't mis-
　　understand us, in fact we think it's almost great. But isn't
　　there, well, a little too much of this Prince of Denmark?
　　After all, there is no one quite like you in your lighter
　　vein."
"Astonishing," they said. "Who would have thought you had
　　it in you, Orville?" They said, "Wilbur, this machine of
　　yours is amazing, if it works, and perhaps some day we
　　can use it to distribute eggs, or to advertise."

And they were good people, too. Decent people.
They did not beat their wives. They went to church. And they
　　kept the law.

---

grandad

Dave Russo

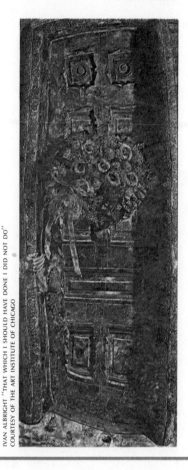

grandad is
      dead, sheath him safely away in tuxedo
(his furrowed chalk brow protrudes,
trowel make-up in its cracks)
fit him snugly in lidded coffin,
5 wedge him gently against billowed satin,
fold his hands in accepted anthem,
press a lily between them,
bury him,
he is dead and
10 of no further use

we can now fill in that patch of grass
we've been saving just for him,
right below aunt poinsetta and
to the left of uncle jim

15 grandad is
      dead, we shall have a garden party in
reverence (yes i know he hated garden parties
but he couldn't object just this once)

a garden party! yes indeed,
that is exactly what we need
20 to lift our hearts in time of dread
poor old gramps is finally dead

grandad is
      dead, straighten his tie,
touch powder to his nose
feather rouge on his cheek
25 brush your fingers from his eyes
good bye

DISCUSSION

Homage

1. To whom are "they" speaking in each stanza?

2. The language quoted in each stanza identifies the speakers just as their references identify the subject being addressed. What are some characteristics in the quote in the second stanza that would suggest that the speaker is British?

3. What dialect can you hear in the lines of the third stanza?

4. (a) Who are "they"? (b) Where can "they" be found?

5. How would you describe the tone in the last stanza?

6. What is the significance of the title?

7. What is the speaker of the poem saying about how contemporaries pay tribute to great achievements of their peers?

Grandad

1. Who is the speaker in this poem?

2. What is the attitude of the speaker toward grandad?

3. Who do we learn more about from the poem, grandad or the speaker?

4. What do you think is the theme of the poem?

"Grandad" by Dave Russo from *Typog,* Vol. I, No. 1 (Fall 1971). Published by Scott, Foresman and Company.

The Monument

Iosip Brodsky
Translated by W. S. Merwin

Let us set up a monument
in the city, at the end of the long avenue,
or at the center of the big square,
a monument
5 that will stand out against any background
because it will be
quite well built and very realistic.
Let us set up a monument
that will not disturb anybody.

10 We will plant flowers
around the pedestal
and with the permission of the city fathers
we will lay out a little garden
where our children
15 will blink
at the great orange sun
and take the figure perched above them
for a well-known thinker
a composer
20 or a general.

I guarantee that flowers will appear
every morning
on the pedestal.
Let us set up a monument
25 that will not disturb anybody.
Even taxi drivers
will admire its majestic silhouette.
The garden will be a place
for rendezvous.
30 Let us set up a monument,
we will pass under it
hurrying on our way to work,
foreigners will have their pictures taken
standing under it.
we will splash it at night with the glare
of floodlights.

Let us set up a monument to The Lie.

DISCUSSION

"The Monument" by Iosip Brodsky from SELECTED TRANSLATIONS by W. S. Merwin. Translated by W. S. Merwin with Vladimir Weidle. Copyright © 1968 by W. S. Merwin. Reprinted by permission of Atheneum Publishers and David Higham Associates, Ltd. Appeared originally in the *New York Review of Books*.

1. Study the three stanzas. How does the information in each differ?

2. (a) Why is the last line a kind of fourth stanza? (b) What was its effect on you when you first read it? After several readings, does its effect change? If so, how?

3. What is the speaker's tone throughout the poem?

4. What is a monument besides a piece of stone? For example, what is meant by the phrase "He was a monument to justice"?

5. What major issue is the speaker concerned with? What kinds of lies do you think he has in mind? Do you agree with him? Explain.

AUTHOR

IOSIP BRODSKY, born in 1940, is regarded by some liberal Russian intellectuals as the most talented living Russian poet. Mr. Brodsky's poetry is little known in Russia and virtually unknown outside. Much of his work, often printed on mimeographed sheets, is circulated by hand among his friends. Some of his poems have been published in underground Russian journals such as *Syntax*.

Mr. Brodsky's fondness for philosophically mystical and religious themes does not conform with the socialist realism which dominates contemporary Russian literature. His most recent poetry shows little interest in politics, though some of his earlier work, including "The Monument," does.

In 1964, Mr. Brodsky was brought to trial and sentenced to five years at forced labor for being an idler and a parasite. He was released in September, 1965, perhaps in part as a result of the public outcry on his behalf.

Mr. Brodsky is well read in a number of foreign languages and has done translations from Polish, Serbian, Spanish, and English sources. He recently translated John Donne into Russian.

In June, 1972, Mr. Brodsky, who is a Jew, was granted an exit visa to Israel. Although his immediate destination was Vienna, reliable sources believed that he eventually planned to settle in America. At the time of his departure from Russia, tentative arrangements were being made to establish him as a poet-in-residence at a major American university.

THE POETS' CRAFT

The Speaker and the Poet
In the previous essays you have seen how poets can use elements within a poem to reinforce the sense of the poem. Meter, rhyme, metaphor, or alliteration in themselves are not important; they are important only in the way they contribute to the meaning of the poem. In this essay we will consider one aspect of the poets' craft that might be thought of as being outside the poem and yet governing many of the elements within the poem: the speaking voice that the poet chooses to narrate his message or emotion.

We often make the mistake of thinking that the poem is autobiographical and that the poet is speaking directly to us. This mistake can frequently distort the meaning of the poem and cause us to respond insufficiently or inaccurately to the work.

In Don Marquis' poem the speaker of the work is clearly "archy," a character whose identity the poet assumes and from whose point of view he writes the poem. In Sylvia Plath's "Mushrooms" the speaker assumes the identity of a mushroom and speaks throughout the poem with that voice. Jacques Prévert's poem, "Late Rising," relies upon two voices: the first describes from a distance the squalid condition of the starving man; the second, a radio or TV broadcaster, reports the crime; and, finally, the first speaker reappears.

A poet will use different speakers in order to create humor, sadness, or irony, which is a type of figurative language in which the actual intent is expressed in a way that carries the opposite meaning.

The speaker in Dave Russo's poem "grandad" reveals more of himself than he does of his grandfather. In fact, we learn very little about grandad.

Frequently, the voice of the speaker is very subtle and disguised so that only with careful study can the reader identify the person the poet has chosen to speak. This speaker will have much to do with whether the poet will write in rhymed iambic pentameter, unrhymed iambic pentameter, or an unrhymed free verse. Also, the speaker will have much to do with the diction of the poem and with the type of figurative language used.

When you read poetry it is wise to read it several times. If possible, read it aloud and ask someone else to read it to you until you can hear the voice of the speaker of the poem. Then you will begin to see how the elements of poetry combine to make sense out of the sound of the language.

Reflections

Line Camp

Keith Wilson

It's abandoned now.

Once I rode by,
a boy, trying to make himself
believe he was a cowboy.
5 Two punchers there gave me
coffee, offered a bunk
for the night.

I rode on leaving
their lamp, the warmth
10 smell of frying bacon
& leather boots

young, very scared
but headed home
Now I am back
15 The roof has fallen in.
The floor is covered with dust.
The windmill, torn down.

No one stays there now.

—*Cambray, New Mexico, 1966*

DISCUSSION

Line Camp
1. The speaker begins his story in the first person "I." In the next line he changes to the third person "trying to make himself." What do you think is the purpose of this in the poem?
2. (a) What happens in stanza four? (b) Where is the time lapse?
3. How would you describe the tone and state the theme of this poem?

AUTHOR

KEITH WILSON was born in Clovis, New Mexico, in 1927. He was educated at the United States Naval Academy, Annapolis, Maryland and the University of New Mexico. Among his published collections of verse are *Sketches for a New Mexico Hill Town*, *Graves Registry and Other Poems*, and *Homestead*.

Mr. Wilson is married and has five children. He teaches English at New Mexico State University.

"Line Camp" from HOMESTEAD by Keith Wilson. Copyright © 1969 by Keith Wilson. Reprinted by permission of the author.

DISCUSSION

The Road Not Taken
1. Do you think the speaker in this poem is the poet, Robert Frost? Explain.
2. What might the "road" symbolize?
3. Explain lines 13-15.
4. Give some possible reasons why taking the less traveled road has "made all the difference" to the speaker.

The Road Not Taken

Robert Frost

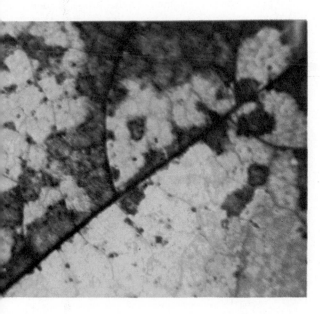

Two roads diverged in a yellow wood,
And sorry I could not travel both
And be one traveler, long I stood
And looked down one as far as I could
5 To where it bent in the undergrowth;

Then took the other, as just as fair,
And having perhaps the better claim,
Because it was grassy and wanted wear;
Though as for that, the passing there
10 Had worn them really about the same,

And both that morning equally lay
In leaves no step had trodden black.
Oh! I kept the first for another day!
Yet knowing how way leads on to way,
15 I doubted if I should ever come back.

I shall be telling this with a sigh
Somewhere ages and ages hence:
Two roads diverged in a wood, and I—
I took the one less traveled by,
20 And that has made all the difference.

AUTHOR

ROBERT FROST (1874–1963), the dean of American poets, was born in California and moved to Massachusetts at the age of ten. Thus New England, the home of his ancestors, became the emotional background of Frost's poetic life.

As a young man Frost attended Dartmouth College briefly and worked in a textile mill. He married at twenty. He studied at Harvard for two years and then supported himself at a number of odd jobs before settling down on a New Hampshire farm. After eleven years of farming and writing poetry, Frost had little success to show for his efforts: his farm was a failure and only the local newspaper would accept his poems for publication. In a discouraged mood he moved to England, where he offered his collected work to a publisher. The book came out as *A Boy's Will* in 1913 and was immediately recognized for its fresh, original poetry. Frost followed this with *North of Boston* (1914).

Frost, now famous, returned home in 1915. He became America's most honored poet: he received four Pulitzer Prizes and numerous other awards and honorary degrees. His eighty-eighth birthday in March, 1962, was another high point in Frost's long career. On that day he published his most recent volume of poetry, *In the Clearing,* and received a congressional medal in ceremonies at the White House.

From THE POETRY OF ROBERT FROST edited by Edward Connery Lathem. Copyright 1916, © 1969 by Holt, Rinehart and Winston, Inc. Copyright 1944 by Robert Frost. Reprinted by permission of Holt, Rinehart and Winston, Inc. and Jonathan Cape Ltd. for the Estate of Robert Frost.

This is a poem to my son Peter

Peter Meinke

whom I have hurt a thousand times
whose large and vulnerable eyes
have glazed in pain at my ragings
thin wrist and fingers hung
5 boneless in despair, pale freckled back
bent in defeat, pillow soaked
by my failure to understand.
I have scarred through weakness
and impatience your frail confidence forever
10 because when I needed to strike
you were there to be hurt and because
I thought you knew
you were beautiful and fair
your bright eyes and hair
15 but now I see that no one knows that
about himself, but must be told
and retold until it takes hold
because I think anything can be killed
after a while, especially beauty
20 so I write this for life, for love, for
you, my oldest son Peter, age 10,
going on 11.

"This is a poem to my son Peter" by Peter Meinke from *The New Republic* (December 25, 1971). Reprinted by permission of the author and *The New Republic*. © 1971, Harrison-Blaine of New Jersey, Inc.

If I Could Only Live at the Pitch That Is near Madness

Richard Eberhart

If I could only live at the pitch that is near madness
When everything is as it was in my childhood
Violent, vivid, and of infinite possibility:
That the sun and the moon broke over my head.

5 Then I cast time out of the trees and fields,
Then I stood immaculate in the Ego;
Then I eyed the world with all delight.
Reality was the perfection of my sight.

And time had big handles on the hands,
10 Fields and trees a way of being themselves.
I saw battalions of the race of mankind
Standing stolid, demanding a moral answer.

I gave the moral answer and I died
And into a realm of complexity came
15 Where nothing is possible but necessity
And the truth wailing there like a red babe.

"If I Could Only Live at the Pitch That Is near Madness" from COLLECTED POEMS 1930–1960 by Richard Eberhart. Copyright © 1960 by Richard Eberhart. Reprinted by permission of Oxford University Press, Inc., and Chatto and Windus Ltd.

DISCUSSION

This is a poem to my son Peter
1. What explanation does the speaker give for hurting his son? What lines tell you?
2. What important thing did the speaker fail to tell his son?
3. Explain lines 18-19. Do you agree?

If I Could Only Live . . . Madness
1. Explain the use of tenses in the line: "When everything *is* as it *was* in my childhood."
2. Have you ever "stood immaculate in the ego"? Explain.

3. In the first line of the second stanza the speaker "cast time out of the trees and fields" but in the first line of the third stanza he refers to time as having "big handles on the hands." What does he mean in each of these lines?
4. What has happened in the fourth stanza?
5. In the last stanza the speaker describes "truth" as a "wailing red babe." What do you think he means by this comparison?
6. Compare the tone and theme of this poem with "Line Camp" on page 242 and "Eleven" on page 225.

AUTHOR

RICHARD EBERHART was born in Austin, Minnesota, in 1904. He completed his college education at Dartmouth in 1926 and then studied at Cambridge University in England. In 1930 he was tutor to the son of the King of Siam.

Some of Eberhart's first poems appeared in a collection of modern poetry entitled *New Signatures*, which was published in England in 1932. In addition to writing his prize-winning poetry, Eberhart is vice president of a manufacturing company and regularly lectures at colleges and universities.

Exultation Is the Going

Emily Dickinson

Exultation is the going
Of an inland soul to sea,
Past the houses—past the headlands—
Into deep Eternity—

Bred as we, among the mountains,
Can the sailor understand
The divine intoxication
Of the first league out from land?

DISCUSSION

1. What can we tell about the speaker from what he or she is saying in the poem?

2. What question is the speaker asking in the second stanza?

3. After referring back to "Rhythm and Meaning" on page 212 and "Sound and Meaning" on pages 220–221, identify some of the elements of the Poets' Craft that Emily Dickinson uses to enhance the meaning of her poem.

AUTHOR

EMILY DICKINSON (1830–1886), one of the least-known poets in her lifetime, has now been acknowledged as a gifted lyricist. Born in the Massachusetts village of Amherst, she spent all her life there, seldom venturing outside her home. It is believed that an unhappy and hopeless love affair turned her away from the outside world.

Miss Dickinson wrote secretly on any available scrap of paper, caring nothing for recognition or publication. Only two of her poems were published during her lifetime, but these poems appeared without her consent. At her death, her sister discovered over one thousand lyric poems, which have since been collected and edited in several volumes.

Silence

Edgar Lee Masters

I have known the silence of the stars and of the sea,
And the silence of the city when it pauses,
And the silence of a man and a maid,
And the silence for which music alone finds the word,
5 And the silence of the woods before the winds of spring begin,
And the silence of the sick
When their eyes roam about the room.
And I ask: For the depths
Of what use is language?
10 A beast of the field moans a few times
When death takes its young:
And we are voiceless in the presence of realities—
We cannot speak.

A curious boy asks an old soldier
15 Sitting in front of the grocery store,
"How did you lose your leg?"
And the old soldier is struck with silence,
Or his mind flies away
Because he cannot concentrate it on Gettysburg.
20 It comes back jocosely
And he says, "A bear bit it off."
And the boy wonders, while the old soldier
Dumbly, feebly, lives over
The flashes of guns, the thunder of cannon,
25 The shrieks of the slain,
And himself lying on the ground,
And the hospital surgeons, the knives,
And the long days in bed.
But if he could describe it all
30 He would be an artist.
But if he were an artist there would be deeper wounds
Which he could not describe.

There is silence of a great hatred,
And the silence of a great love,
35 And the silence of a deep peace of mind,
And the silence of an embittered friendship.
There is the silence of a spiritual crisis,
Through which your soul, exquisitely tortured,
Comes with visions not to be uttered
40 Into a realm of higher life,
And the silence of the gods who understand each other without speech.
There is a silence of defeat.
There is the silence of those unjustly punished;
And the silence of the dying whose hand
45 Suddenly grips yours.
There is the silence between father and son,
When the father cannot explain his life,
Even though he be misunderstood for it.

There is the silence that comes between husband and wife,
50 There is the silence of those who have failed;
And the vast silence that covers
Broken nations and vanquished leaders.

There is the silence of Lincoln,
Thinking of the poverty of his youth.
55 And the silence of Napoleon
After Waterloo.
And the silence of Jeanne d'Arc
Saying amid the flames, "Blessed Jesus"—
Revealing in two words all sorrow, all hope.
60 And there is the silence of age,
Too full of wisdom for the tongue to utter it
In words intelligible to those who have not lived
The great range of life.

And there is the silence of the dead.
65 If we who are in life cannot speak
Of profound experiences,
Why do you marvel that the dead
Do not tell you of death?
Their silence shall be interpreted
70 As we approach them.

"Silence," reprinted by permission of Mrs. Ellen C. Masters, from SONGS AND SATIRES by Edgar Lee Masters. Copyright 1916, 1944 by Edgar Lee Masters. Published by the Macmillan Company, New York.

DISCUSSION

1. As the speaker talks about the many kinds of silences, he uses both concrete and abstract ideas. Give examples of each.

2. What do you think the poet is referring to in line 12? Give possible examples.

3. Which of the silences in this poem have you experienced? Explain.

4. How would you state the theme of this poem?

AUTHOR

EDGAR LEE MASTERS (1868–1950) was a Midwestern poet who, like Carl Sandburg, came into prominence in the early 1900's. Born in Kansas, Masters was reared in Illinois. He attended Knox College for a year and then studied law under his father's direction. Masters passed the bar examination in 1891 and went on to build a successful law practice in Chicago.

Masters wrote poetry for his own pleasure, publishing *A Book of Verses* in 1898 and *Maximilian* in 1902. In 1915 he published his *Spoon River Anthology*, a collection of epitaphs which the poet supposedly found in an Illinois cemetery. This volume of free-verse epitaphs is Masters' best-known work. He published several volumes of poetry, including *Domesday Book* (1920) and *Illinois Poems* (1941), as well as novels and biographies.

Epitaph on a Tyrant

W. H. Auden

Perfection, of a kind, was what he was after,
And the poetry he invented was easy to understand;
He knew human folly like the back of his hand,
And was greatly interested in armies and fleets;
When he laughed, respectable senators burst with laughter,
And when he cried the little children died in the streets.

DISCUSSION

1. What kind of "perfection" do you imagine the speaker is referring to in line 1?

2. What do you think is the meaning of "poetry" as used in line 2?

3. Why was his knowledge of "human folly" important to the tyrant?

4. In what sense of the word were the senators, line 5, "respectable"?

5. Explain what you think is meant in the last line.

AUTHOR

WYSTAN HUGH AUDEN (1907– --) has been described as the most consistently interesting and variously gifted poet writing in English in the twentieth century. In the past, critics of Auden have complained of the bewildering variety of his work and of the change in belief and attitude that his poetry has undergone during his career. Today, Auden, who was born in England and became a naturalized American citizen in 1946, is warmly praised for the multiplicity of his writing, and critics are now attempting to come to terms with the over-all unity in his work.

Recently, Auden undertook an extensive revision of his poetry. This task has resulted in the publication of two volumes—*Collected Shorter Poems 1927–1957* and *Collected Longer Poems*—which contain most of the verse which he wishes to preserve.

In addition to his verse, Auden has written three plays in collaboration with Christopher Isherwood, several opera libretti, and extensive literary criticism. His considerable achievement has convinced a growing number of critics to regard Auden as the greatest living poet.

Go Down, Death
A Funeral Sermon

James Weldon Johnson

Weep not, weep not,
She is not dead;
She's resting in the bosom of Jesus.
Heart-broken husband—weep no more;
5 Grief-stricken son—weep no more;
She's only just gone home.

Day before yesterday morning,
God was looking down from his great, high heaven,
Looking down on all his children,
10 And his eye fell on Sister Caroline,
Tossing on her bed of pain.
And God's big heart was touched with pity,
With the everlasting pity.

And God sat back on his throne,
15 And he commanded that tall, bright angel standing at his right hand:
Call me Death!
And that tall, bright angel cried in a voice
That broke like a clap of thunder:
Call Death!—Call Death!
20 And the echo sounded down the streets of heaven
Till it reached away back to that shadowy place,
Where Death waits with his pale, white horses.

And Death heard the summons,
And he leaped on his fastest horse,
25 Pale as a sheet in the moonlight.
Up the golden street Death galloped,
And the hoofs of his horse struck fire from the gold,
But they didn't make no sound.
Up Death rode to the Great White Throne,
30 And waited for God's command.

And God said: Go down, Death, go down,
Go down to Savannah, Georgia,
Down in Yamacraw,[1]
And find Sister Caroline.
35 She's borne the burden and heat of the day,
She's labored long in my vineyard,
And she's tired—
She's weary—
Go down, Death, and bring her to me.

From GOD'S TROMBONES by James Weldon Johnson. Copyright
1927 by The Viking Press, Inc., Copyright renewed 1955 by Grace
Nail Johnson. All rights reserved. Reprinted by permission of The
Viking Press, Inc.
1. *Yamacraw*, a section of Savannah, Georgia.

40 And Death didn't say a word,
But he loosed the reins on his pale, white horse,
And he clamped the spurs to his bloodless sides,
And out and down he rode,
Through heaven's pearly gates,
45 Past suns and moons and stars;
On Death rode,
And the foam from his horse was like a comet in the sky;
On Death rode,
Leaving the lightning's flash behind;
50 Straight on down he came.

While we were watching round her bed,
She turned her eyes and looked away,
She saw what we couldn't see;
She saw Old Death. She saw Old Death,
55 Coming like a falling star.
But Death didn't frighten Sister Caroline;
He looked to her like a welcome friend.
And she whispered to us: I'm going home,
And she smiled and closed her eyes.

60 And Death took her up like a baby,
And she lay in his icy arms,
But she didn't feel no chill.
And Death began to ride again—
Up beyond the evening star,
65 Out beyond the morning star,
Into the glittering light of glory,
On to the Great White Throne.
And there he laid Sister Caroline
On the loving breast of Jesus.

70 And Jesus took his own hand and wiped away her tears
And he smoothed the furrows from her face,
And the angels sang a little song,
And Jesus rocked her in his arms,
And kept a-saying: Take your rest,
75 Take your rest, take your rest.

Weep not—weep not,
She is not dead;
She's resting in the bosom of Jesus.

DISCUSSION

1. What is the main kind of figurative language used by the poet in "Go Down, Death"? Cite several examples.

2. How did the speaker feel about Sister Caroline's death?

3. How would you describe the mood of the poem. What particular poetic elements contribute to the mood?

AUTHOR

JAMES WELDON JOHNSON 1871–1938), one of America's best-known Negro poets, was born in Jacksonville, Florida, and was educated there until he entered Atlanta University. Upon graduation from the university in 1894, he taught school in Jacksonville and studied law in his free time. Johnson passed the Florida bar examination in 1897 and then worked with his brother composing songs and operas. Later, Johnson served as United States consul in Nicaragua and Venezuela.

Before he was killed in a train accident in Maine, Johnson had been successful not only as a teacher, a lawyer, and a diplomat, but had published several volumes of poetry, including *God's Trombones* (1927), and his autobiography *Along This Way* (1933).

The Dirty Hand
(after Carlos Drummond de Andrade)

Mark Strand

My hand is dirty.
I must cut it off.
To wash it is pointless.
The water is putrid.
5 The soap is bad.
It won't lather.
The hand is dirty.
It's been dirty for years.
I used to keep it
10 out of sight,
in my pants pocket.
No one suspected a thing.
People came up to me,
Wanting to shake hands.
15 I would refuse
and the hidden hand,
like a dark slug,
would leave its imprint
on my thigh.
20 And then I realized
it was the same
if I used it or not.
Disgust was the same.

Ah! How many nights
25 in the depths of the house
I washed that hand,
scrubbed it, polished it,
dreamed it would turn
to diamond or crystal
30 or even, at last,
into a plain white hand,
the clean hand of a man,
that you could shake,
or kiss, or hold
35 in one of those moments
when two people confess
without saying a word . . .
Only to have
the incurable hand,
40 lethargic and crablike,
open its dirty fingers.
And the dirt was vile.
It was not mud or soot
or the caked filth
45 of an old scab
or the sweat

of a laborer's shirt.
It was a sad dirt
made of sickness
50 and human anguish.
It was not black;
black is pure.
It was dull,
a dull grayish dirt.

55 It is impossible
to live with this
gross hand that lies
on the table.
Quick! Cut it off!

60 Chop it to pieces
and throw it
into the ocean.
With time, with hope
and its machinations,
65 another hand will come,
pure, transparent as glass,
and fasten itself to my arm.

DISCUSSION

1. Is the speaker's hand literally dirty? Explain.

2. (a) What does washing one's
hands often symbolize? (b) Who
in history or literature can you
think of that symbolically
"washed" his or her hands?

3. What might the speaker
previously have done that is causing his present anguish?

4. Compare and contrast the
theme of this poem with Dylan
Thomas' "The Hand that Signed
the Paper."

AUTHOR

MARK STRAND has published
two volumes of poems, *Sleeping
with One Eye Open* and *Reasons
for Moving.* In addition, he edited
the anthology *The Contemporary
American Poets.* His work has appeared in the *New Yorker* magazine, the *New York Review of
Books,* and *The New Republic.*

Mr. Strand was born in Summer-
side, Prince Edward Island, Canada, in 1934. He was educated at
Antioch College, Yale, and the
University of Iowa. He is married
and has one daughter.

A

Montages

1. In each of the poems in this section a montage or scene has been revealed to the reader through the eye of a speaker. In some poems the speaker is a kind of passive actor, in other poems he is entirely outside the world of the poem. List the poems in gradation starting with the one in which the speaker is most present, to the poem in which he is most distant.

2. Several of these montages suggest a brief glimpse of a scene and/or a kind of scene that can be revisited under certain conditions. Which of these poems suggest scenes that can be revisited? Which poems suggest a once only occurrence?

Profiles

1. A profile suggests an outline of a figure. The poems in this section outline characters in different ways. Some poems reveal more complete personalities than do others. Which poem do you think gives the most complete picture of a person? Which poem reveals the least about its subject? Defend your answers.

2. Poets use several techniques to reveal the characters they are portraying: (1) the character's own speech, (2) his actions, (3) his thoughts, (4) his description, (5)

the poet's attitude toward him, and (6) the other characters' attitudes toward him. Select one poem from this section and identify the way or ways in which the poet reveals the subject of his poem.

Tendencies

1. Which of the poems in this section had the most appeal for you? Why?

2. What non-literary art form do you think would most effectively interpret the mood and subject of each of the poems in this section: dance, music, animated film, painting, sculpture?

3. Do most of the speakers in these poems reveal their own feelings or do they simply describe a scene? Cite lines from the poems to support your answers.

Longings

1. Explain the kind of "longing" in each of four poems in this section.

2. Which of the poems in this section best lend themselves to be used as song lyrics? Explain.

3. How many of the poems are about love? Do these particular poems have anything in common besides the subject of love? Explain.

Issues

1. Issues result from conflict. In literature conflict is portrayed generally in one of three ways: man against man, man against nature, and man against himself. Reread the poems in this section and identify the type of conflict behind each issue.

2. Compare the issues revealed in "The Hand that Signed the Paper," "Late Rising," "Harlem," and "The Monument." (a) What do these poems have in common? (b) Which poem do you think most convincingly states its issue? (c) Which poem do you think discusses an issue most relevant to today's world?

Reflections

1. If you were to select one word to depict the dominant mood of the poems in this section, what word would you select? Beginning with this adjective in a topic sentence, expand by referring to two or more poems to support your judgment.

2. (a) Which of the poems in this section did you like best? (b) Which of all the poems in the unit did you like best? If your answer to (b) is different from your answer to (a) explain why you like the second poem more than the one you chose from "Reflections."

B

Beyond the low marsh-meadows and the beach,
Seen through the hoary trunks of windy pines,
The long blue level of the ocean shines.
The distant surf, with hoarse, complaining speech,
Out from its sandy barrier seems to reach;
And while the sun behind the woods declines,
The moaning sea with sighing boughs combines,
And waves and pines make answer, each to each.
O melancholy soul, whom far and near,
In life, faith, hope, the same sad undertone
Pursues from thought to thought! thou needs
　　must hear
An old refrain, too much, too long thine own:
'Tis thy mortality infects thine ear;
The mournful strain was in thyself alone.

Christopher Pearse Cranch,
''The Pines and the Sea''

It began with a splash.
The screams and noise of
the beach died away as the ripple
quietly moved out to sea, feeding
on other, smaller waves and growing fat.
Pushing onward, its determination
grew with its greed and size.
It roared now. Even gravity was helpless
in the force of its momentum.
And suddenly, there was
　　　　　a contender.
The gnarled rocks of a distant shore
looked as if they could withstand anything.
After all, they had been there,
　　　　　massive and unpenetrable,
　　　　　for centuries.
The wave did not falter.
It roared on, bellowing defiance.
The rocks sharpened their claws,
　　　　　waiting.

Leslie Smith

---

1. The two poems above describe the sea. Although the two poems have a similar subject, you will notice in reading them that they differ in their meaning and in their poetic technique.

　a. How does each poet view the sea?

　b. In which poem is the message more obvious, and in your own words explain what it is.

　c. Do you find any message in the other poem? Explain.

2. The rhythm of a poem may be regulated by *meter* (see page 212) or may derive from the natural rise and fall of words and phrases (see page 231).

　a. In which poem is the rhythm regulated by meter? What is the basic meter? How many *feet* are there in a line? What in the poem keeps it from being a *blank-verse* poem?

　b. Characterize the movement of the metrical poem. What is the relationship between rhythm and sense? How does the poet vary the basic meter? How does this variation affect the movement?

　c. Would you agree that one of the poems derives its rhythm from the natural rise and fall of words and phrases? If so, how would you characterize the movement? How does the movement echo the sense?

3. Poets may regulate the sound of words by repeating identical or similar sounds (see page 220).

''It began with a splash . . .'' by Leslie Smith from *Typog.* Vol. 1, No. 3 (Spring 1972). Published by Scott, Foresman and Company.

　a. What *rhyme* scheme, if any, do you find in the two poems? What does rhyme usually contribute to meaning?

　b. Is the nonmetrical poem a *free-verse* poem? If so, cite three reasons for your answer (see page 231).

4. Examine the *imagery* in the two poems (see page 113). Point out the images and the senses to which they appeal.

5. Poets use words *figuratively* to be more brief or forceful, more vivid or precise (see page 207).

　a. One of the poems contains an *apostrophe*. Identify it.

　b. Both poems contain *personification*. Cite the examples.

6. Now that you have examined the poetic elements of each poem, which of the two poems do you prefer? Why?

4 Julius Caesar

A TRAGEDY BY WILLIAM SHAKESPEARE

The physical features of Shakespeare's Globe Playhouse, as described in the text and as shown in the illustrations, are based upon the data assembled by Dr. John Cranford Adams in his *Globe Playhouse* (Barnes & Noble) and upon the model of the Globe constructed by Dr. Adams and Irwin Smith. The stage directions are given in terms of the actor's right and left.

I THE GLOBE ANNOUNCES SHAKESPEARE'S PLAY

LONDON in the last decade of the sixteenth century was the largest and most exciting city in England. Among its many attractions were the numerous playhouses and inn-theaters, where Elizabethans gathered for an afternoon's entertainment. Shakespeare's playhouse, the Globe, first opened in 1599. Here Londoners watched the greatest actors of the time perform the greatest English drama of all time—the plays of Shakespeare.

On one September morning in 1599, freshly mounted playbills appeared in London's crowded and twisted streets. They announced, in bold black letters, that the afternoon performance at the Globe would be "*The Tragedy of Julius Caesar* . . . a new play by William Shakespeare." The playbills would draw over two thousand people—noblemen and apprentices, merchants and housewives, law students and sailors—to the Globe Playhouse at two o'clock.

In order to obtain standing room in the playhouse yard, an Elizabethan apprentice made an especially early start. In his dark blue livery and jaunty flat cap, he hurried toward the Thames River while the city bells were tolling the noon hour. At the water's edge, one penny bought him a place in an already crowded boat that ferried playgoers to the opposite shore. Looking across the river, he could see the white silk flag floating above the playhouse turret. The flag continued to beckon as each stroke of the boatman's oars brought the apprentice closer; finally he stepped ashore. Dodging the other playgoers, he made his way down Maiden Lane to Globe Alley, across a footbridge, and then stood before the playhouse entrance.

The Globe Playhouse was a *three-storied octagon.* In between sturdy oak timbers, the exterior walls were coated with sparkling white plaster. From a previous visit, the apprentice knew that the eight sides of the playhouse frame enclosed a brick-paved *yard* that was open to the skies. It was fortunate, he thought, that the day was warm and sunny, for he would be standing in the unroofed yard during this afternoon's performance. Without further delay, he dropped a penny into the doorkeeper's box and stepped within the Globe Playhouse.

II THE INTERIOR OF THE GLOBE PLAYHOUSE

If you were to join an Elizabethan apprentice as he steps into the playhouse yard, you would face the performing area of the Globe. This performing area fills one-fourth of the octagon. It consists of a *platform stage* and, behind the platform, a three-storied structure which is called the *tiring house.*

The most important stage in the performing area is the *platform* (1), which juts into the yard. Its two ornate pillars support a *canopy* (2) which, in turn, supports the *huts* (3) and the playhouse *turret* (4). Elizabethans refer to the canopy, the huts, and the turret as the "Heavens." The area underneath the platform, where stage properties are stored, is known as "Hell" (5). In the center of the platform floor is the largest of five *trap doors* (6). The trap doors are not visible to the audience until they are opened from below.

The three-storied wall of the tiring house acts as a background for the platform. On its first level, the tiring house consists of a curtained *inner stage* (7), which is flanked at right and at left by *doors* (8). The inner stage has two trap doors—a floor trap and a ceiling trap. On its second level, the tiring house

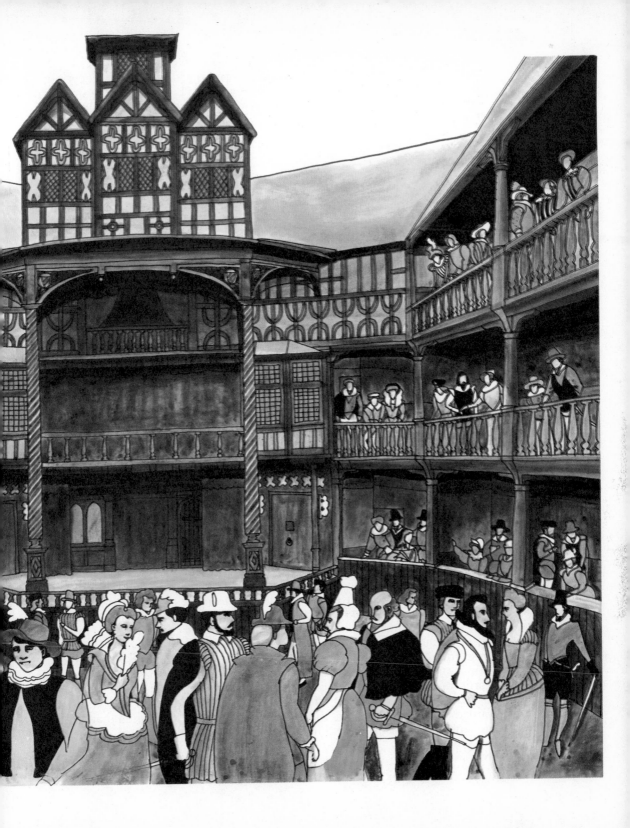

consists of a curtained *balcony stage* (9). The balcony stage projects slightly over the platform and is flanked at right and left by *bay-window stages* (10). The curtained *music gallery* (11), on the third level, may also function as a stage.

The inner stage and the balcony stage are almost identical. When the front curtains of either stage are drawn apart, you can see that the stage suggests the interior of a room. The side walls are made of tapestry hangings, which can be changed between scenes, and the rear wall has a door and a window with similar tapestry hangings in between. By replacing the tapestry with hangings made of plain or painted cloth, it is possible for the inner stage to represent the interior of a tent or the corner of a garden. When plain or painted hangings are used at the rear, they cover the entire wall.

The backstage area of the tiring house with its dressing rooms, storage rooms, and connecting stairways is not visible to the audience.

Since the Globe Playhouse has several stages on different levels, you may wonder how each stage will be used in this afternoon's play. The platform will always be used when a scene takes place *outdoors*. At various times in *Julius Caesar* the platform will represent a street, or a public place, or an army camp, or a battlefield. During these exterior scenes, the curtains of the inner and balcony stages are closed; actors enter and exit the platform through the doors at right and left or through the inner-stage curtains.

Scenes which take place *indoors* will use the inner stage or the balcony stage. Thus, the curtains of the inner stage will be drawn apart to reveal the interior of a tent or public building; the curtains of the balcony stage will be drawn apart to reveal the interior of a house. On one occasion, a bay-window stage will represent an interior. Actors enter and exit the inner and balcony stages through the rear door or through the side hangings.

In *Julius Caesar,* action on the inner stage is always combined with action on the platform. The platform, for example, will represent a garden and the inner stage a secluded corner of that garden. Or, the platform will represent an army camp and the inner stage a tent in that camp. Sometimes an outdoor scene on the platform requires the use of an elevated place, such as a raised pulpit or a hill. The narrow area between the closed balcony curtains and the balcony railing will represent these elevated places. In order to ascend the "pulpit" or "hill," an actor exits the platform and, by means of the backstage stairs, reappears at the balcony railing within twenty seconds.

While you have been examining the performing area of the Globe, many more spectators have entered the playhouse. Five hundred Elizabethans now jam the unroofed yard; fifteen hundred people have paid additional pennies to sit in the galleries that fill three-fourths of the Globe octagon. The crowd is boisterous and impatient for the play to begin. Vendors hawking apples and books elbow their way across the yard. Some people pass the time playing cards or reading; others speculate loudly about Shakespeare's play. From overhearing snatches of their conversation, it is obvious that Elizabethans already know a great deal about Julius Caesar and the events that led to the collapse of the Roman republic. If you are not as well informed, you will find it helpful to read the following sketch of Julius Caesar before Shakespeare's play begins.

III JULIUS CAESAR AND HIS TIMES

The short span of Caesar's life, 100–44 B.C., was an important period in the history of Rome. For centuries Romans had debated and even fought civil wars to decide whether a *monarchy,* a *republic,* or a *dictatorship* was the best form of government.

Before 509 B.C. Rome was a monarchy; but in that year a revolt, headed by the Brutus family, forced the cruel Tarquinius Superbus from the throne. The Romans established a republic, but the common people, or plebeians, soon found that they had merely exchanged the rule of a king for the rule of a group of wealthy, highborn citizens called patricians. The two consuls, chief magistrates of the republic, were patricians; the Senate, composed entirely of patricians, made the laws, while the popular assemblies, composed of plebeians, had no real power. Gradually the plebeians won the right to select tribunes—men who had the power to protect the lives and properties of plebeians and to intervene in any department of government. In time, the plebeians won the right to be elected as consuls or to hold seats in the Senate.

By Julius Caesar's time, Rome was a moderate democracy in form, but in practice was ruled by the Senate. The Senate, however, was disturbed by personal rivalries among its members. For the first time military leaders entered Rome with their legions to seize control of the government. Since it was possible to appoint a dictator during periods of emergency, an ambitious man could become an absolute ruler. Some Roman dictators championed the people's party; others belonged to the senatorial party.

Julius Caesar, a patrician, cast his lot with the people. Serving in various offices, he won their support by spending money for public entertainments and by establishing laws to free farmers and tradesmen from crushing taxes and debts. In 60 B.C. Caesar formed, with Crassus and Pompey, a triumvirate (a three-man rule) to govern Rome and its provinces. Two years later he was made governor of that part of Gaul (now southern France and northern Italy) which Rome then controlled. He conquered the rest of Gaul, and money from his conquests flowed into Rome. Much of it was used to provide bonuses for his soldiers and to relieve some of the burdens of the common people.

For a short time the triumvirate worked smoothly, but trouble was brewing. While conducting a campaign in Mesopotamia, Crassus was slain. Pompey, jealous of Caesar's popularity, turned more and more toward the senatorial party. The senators, alarmed by Caesar's advance toward unlimited power, issued a decree ordering him to disband his army or be considered an enemy of the state. Caesar accepted the challenge. He led his army across the Rubicon River, which separated his provinces in Gaul from Italy, invaded Rome, and gathered the reins of power into his own hands.

During the next four years Caesar made himself absolute ruler of the Roman world. After securing Spain and the West, Caesar followed Pompey to the East, where he had fled. In the decisive battle of Pharsalus Pompey's forces were routed; Pompey himself fled to Egypt and was later killed. Three years after this battle, Caesar made his final campaign against Pompey's faction and defeated Pompey's two sons at Munda, Spain. In the meantime he had been voted extraordinary honors: in 48 B.C. he was named dictator; in 46 B.C. he was made dictator for ten years; and in 45 B.C. the term was extended to life. Thus Caesar was the undisputed master of the Roman world when he returned in triumph from Spain. It is at this point that Shakespeare begins his play.

Cast of Characters

JULIUS CAESAR

OCTAVIUS CAESAR

MARCUS ANTONIUS

M. AEMILIUS LEPIDUS

*triumvirs after
the death of Julius Caesar*

CICERO

PUBLIUS

POPILIUS LENA,

senators

MARCUS BRUTUS

CASSIUS

CASCA

TREBONIUS

LIGARIUS

DECIUS BRUTUS

METELLUS CIMBER

CINNA

conspirators against Julius Caesar

FLAVIUS and MARULLUS   *tribunes*

ARTEMIDORUS of CNIDOS   *a teacher of Rhetoric*

A SOOTHSAYER   *a poet*

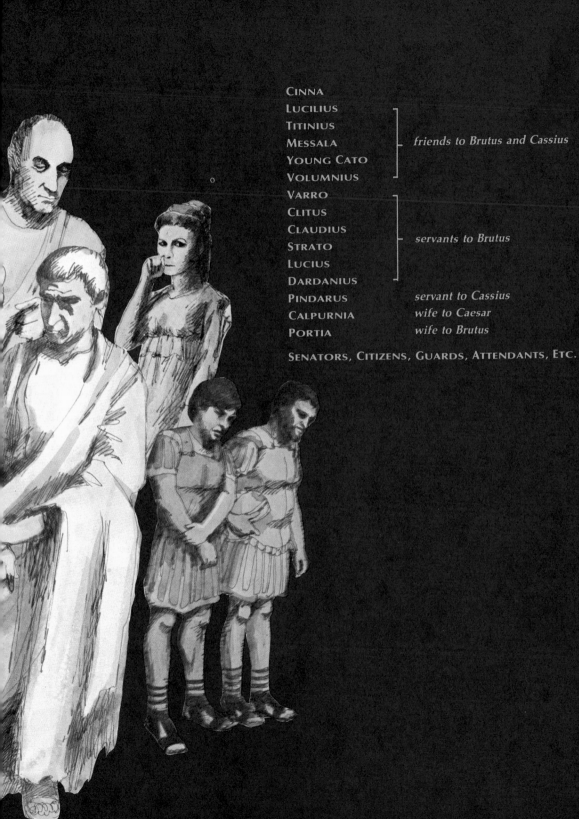

CINNA

LUCILIUS
TITINIUS
MESSALA   *friends to Brutus and Cassius*
YOUNG CATO
VOLUMNIUS

VARRO
CLITUS
CLAUDIUS
STRATO   *servants to Brutus*
LUCIUS
DARDANIUS

PINDARUS   *servant to Cassius*
CALPURNIA   *wife to Caesar*
PORTIA   *wife to Brutus*

SENATORS, CITIZENS, GUARDS, ATTENDANTS, ETC.

Act One

Scene 1: Rome. A street.

It is February fifteenth. The people of Rome are gathering to welcome CAESAR *whose triumphant return from Spain coincides with the festival of Lupercalia (lü /pər kā ꞁli ə). The* COMMONERS *are in a holiday mood, eager to celebrate* CAESAR'*s victory over Pompey's sons. There are other Romans, however, who fear* CAESAR'*s power and popularity. Like* FLAVIUS *and* MARULLUS, *they resent celebrating a victory over fellow Romans.*

A crowd of excited COMMONERS, *dressed in their holiday garments, rush onto the platform at left door. All talk at once and look expectantly toward the right, the direction in which* CAESAR'*s procession will appear. Offstage shouts and cheers, an indication that* CAESAR *draws much closer, send the* COMMONERS *scurrying for vantage points.*

Meanwhile, the tribunes FLAVIUS *and* MARULLUS *have entered at inner-stage curtains. As they stride briskly forward, it is apparent that the tribunes disapprove of the general holiday mood.* FLAVIUS *addresses the* COMMONERS *angrily.*

FLAVIUS. Hence! Home, you idle creatures, get you home!
  Is this a holiday? What! Know you not,
  Being mechanical,[1] you ought not walk
  Upon a laboring day without the sign
5 Of your profession?[2] *(Singing one out.)* Speak, what trade art thou?
FIRST COMMONER. Why, sir, a carpenter.
MARULLUS. Where is thy leather apron and thy rule?
  What dost thou with thy best apparel on?
  (To another.) You, sir, what trade are you?
10 SECOND COMMONER. Truly, sir, in respect of a fine workman, I am but, as you would say, a cobbler.[3]
MARULLUS *(impatiently)*. But what trade art thou? Answer me directly.
SECOND COMMONER. A trade, sir, that, I hope, I may use with a safe conscience; which is, indeed, sir, a mender of soles.
          (The COMMONERS *laugh at the pun.)*
15 FLAVIUS *(scowling)*. Thou art a cobbler, art thou?
SECOND COMMONER. Truly, sir, all that I live by is with the awl; I meddle with no tradesman's matters nor women's matters, but with awl.[4] I am, indeed, sir, a surgeon to old shoes; when they are in great danger, I re-cover them.
20 FLAVIUS. But wherefore art not in thy shop today?
  Why dost thou lead these men about the streets?
SECOND COMMONER *(grinning)*. Truly, sir, to wear out their shoes, to get myself into more work. But, indeed, sir, we make holiday, to see Caesar and to rejoice in his triumph.
          (The mob shouts its agreement.)
25 MARULLUS *(addressing the mob)*. Wherefore rejoice? What conquest brings he home?

1. *mechanical*, workingmen.

2. *you ought not . . . profession.* Shakespeare here refers to an English law of his own time, which required workingmen to wear their laboring clothes and carry the tools of their profession.

3. *cobbler.* In Shakespeare's time this word meant a clumsy workman and did not refer specifically to a mender of shoes. That explains Marullus' next question.

4. *I meddle . . . with awl.* How would spelling the last word *all* change the meaning? Elizabethan audiences delighted in such puns.

[handwritten: Ceaser didn't want to bring back his own people so he killed them]

What tributaries[5] follow him to Rome,
To grace in captive bonds his chariot wheels?

(*The shouting of the mob grows louder.*)

You blocks, you stones, you worse than senseless things!
O you hard hearts, you cruel men of Rome,
30 Knew you not Pompey?[6] Many a time and oft
Have you climbed up to walls and battlements,
To towers and windows, yea, to chimney tops,[7]
Your infants in your arms, and there have sat
The livelong day, with patient expectation,
35 To see great Pompey pass the streets of Rome:
And when you saw his chariot but appear,
Have you not made an universal shout,
That Tiber[8] trembled underneath her banks,
To hear the replication of your sounds
40 Made in her concave shores?
And do you now put on your best attire?
And do you now cull out a holiday? *[handwritten: select]*
And do you now strew flowers in his way
That comes in triumph over Pompey's blood?[9]

(*The mob, subdued by*
MARULLUS' *words, is silent now.*)

45 Be gone!
Run to your houses, fall upon your knees,
Pray to the gods to intermit the plague
That needs must light on this ingratitude.
FLAVIUS. Go, go good countrymen, and, for this fault,
50 Assemble all the poor men of your sort;
Draw them to Tiber banks, and weep your tears
Into the channel, till the lowest stream
Do kiss the most exalted shores of all.[10]

(*The* COMMONERS, *singly or in
pairs, file off the platform at left.*)

(*To* MARULLUS.) See, whether their basest metal be not moved;
55 They vanish tongue-tied in their guiltiness.

(*There is a loud flourish of trumpets offstage.*)

Go you down that way toward the Capitol;
This way will I: disrobe the images,[11]
If you do find them decked with ceremonies.
MARULLUS (*cautiously*). May we do so?
60 You know it is the feast of Lupercal.[12]
FLAVIUS. It is no matter; let no images
Be hung with Caesar's trophies. I'll about,
And drive away the vulgar[13] from the streets:
So do you, too, where you perceive them thick.
65 These growing feathers[14] plucked from Caesar's wing
Will make him fly an ordinary pitch,
Who else would soar above the view of men *[handwritten: otherwise]*
And keep us all in servile fearfulness.

(*The tribunes exit, going in different directions.*)

5. *tributaries*, captives who must pay tribute to Rome for their freedom.

6. *Knew you not Pompey?* Only a short time before, the fickle mob had been cheering Caesar's enemy Pompey, champion of Rome's conservative party.
7. *chimney tops*. There were no chimneys in ancient Rome. Such a slip on the part of an author is called an anachronism (ə nak′rə niz əm).

8. *Tiber* (tī′bər), a river flowing through Rome.

9. *Pompey's blood*. Caesar had slain Pompey's sons in Spain on March 17, 45 B.C. Marullus thinks Rome should have been horrified at the slaughter of two of its noblest sons.

10. *weep your tears . . . of all*, weep enough tears to bring the lowest water-line up to the highest. This type of exaggeration, used for effect, is called hyperbole (hī pèr′bl ē).
11. *disrobe the images*, take down the decorations and trophies that have been placed on Caesar's statues.
12. *the feast of Lupercal* (lü′pər kal). On February 15 of each year, the Romans celebrated in honor of Lupercus, god of fertility. The celebrants, young men who were priests of Lupercus, ran a specified course on the Palatine Hill, carrying thongs of goatskin with which they struck people who stood in their way. Women desiring children purposely sought to be struck by the runners, for they believed that the touch of the thongs would cure them of barrenness.

13. *the vulgar*, the common people.
14. *These growing feathers*, meaning Caesar's new followers. Falconers sometimes clip the wings of their birds to keep them from flying to too great a height, or pitch. So Caesar, without the help of the common people, would be checked in his ambition to rise to greater heights.

Scene 2: Rome. A public place.

Groups of COMMONERS *run onto the platform, looking offstage at* CAESAR's *approaching procession.* SOLDIERS *march on at right door and force the people back so that the procession can pass. There is a loud flourish of trumpets; and* CAESAR *appears at right, accompanied by* ANTONY, CAL-PURNIA, PORTIA, DECIUS, CICERO, BRUTUS, CASSIUS, *and* CASCA. *More* COM-MONERS *follow; among them is a* SOOTHSAYER. *Amid shouts and cheers,* CAESAR *leads the procession well onto the platform, then he stops. Everyone bows, rendering homage to* CAESAR.

CAESAR. Calpurnia!
CASCA.   Peace, ho! Caesar speaks.
CAESAR.   Calpurnia!
CALPURNIA *(stepping forward)*. Here, my lord.
CAESAR. Stand you directly in Antonius' way
   When he doth run his course.[1] Antonius!

> (ANTONY *hurries forward
>   and stands before* CAESAR.)

5 ANTONY. Caesar, my lord?
CAESAR. Forget not, in your speed, Antonius,
   To touch Calpurnia; for our elders say
   The barren, touchèd in this holy chase,
   Shake off their sterile curse.[2]
ANTONY.   I shall remember:
10   When Caesar says, "Do this," it is performed. *(He steps back.)*
CAESAR. Set on; and leave no ceremony out.

> *(The trumpets flourish;
>   the procession starts forward.)*

SOOTHSAYER *(in awesome tones)*. Caesar!
CAESAR *(stopping)*. Ha![3] Who calls?

> *(The crowd murmurs, wondering
>   who thus has accosted* CAESAR.)

CASCA. Bid every noise be still: peace yet again!
15 CAESAR. Who is it in the press that calls on me?
   I hear a tongue, shriller than all the music,
   Cry, "Caesar!" Speak; Caesar is turned to hear.[4]
SOOTHSAYER *(ominously)*. Beware the ides of March.[5]
CAESAR *(looking to right and left)*.   What man is that?
BRUTUS. A soothsayer bids you beware the ides of March.
20 CAESAR. Set him before me; let me see his face.
CASSIUS *(stepping forward)*. Fellow, come from the throng; look upon
      Caesar.

> (SOLDIERS *drag the* SOOTHSAYER *before* CAESAR.)

CAESAR. What sayest thou to me now? Speak once again.
SOOTHSAYER. Beware the ides of March.

> *(For a moment* CAESAR, *looking disturbed, stares at the*
>   SOOTHSAYER; *then he turns to* ANTONY, *who begins to
>   laugh. When others join in* ANTONY's *derisive laughter,*
>   CAESAR, *with a gesture, dismisses the* SOOTHSAYER.)

1. *When he doth run his course.* Antony, as head of the priests of Lupercus, is one of the young nobles who are to run through certain streets on the Palatine Hill, carrying goatskin thongs.

2. *Forget not . . . sterile curse.* This passage shows Caesar's desire for an heir. To Cassius this concern was indicative of Caesar's desire to be king.

3. *Ha!* This is an exclamation of surprise, rather than a word denoting laughter.

4. *Caesar is turned to hear.* In using his name when referring to himself, Caesar adopts a practice reserved only for royalty. The other patricians are quick to notice this assumption of undue authority on his part.

5. *the ides* (īdz) *of March*, the fifteenth day of the month of March.

CAESAR. He is a dreamer; let us leave him: pass.

> (*The trumpets flourish; the procession and the crowd go out at left,* BRUTUS *and* CASSIUS *remaining behind.* BRUTUS *stands at one side, lost in thought.* CASSIUS *approaches him.*)

25 CASSIUS. Will you go see the order of the course?

BRUTUS. Not I.

CASSIUS. I pray you, do.

BRUTUS. I am not gamesome; I do lack some part
Of that quick spirit[6] that is in Antony.
30 Let me not hinder, Cassius, your desires;
I'll leave you.

CASSIUS. Brutus, I do observe you now of late:
I have not from your eyes that gentleness
And show of love as I was wont to have:[7]
35 You bear too stubborn and too strange a hand
Over your friend that loves you.

BRUTUS.   Cassius,
Be not deceived: if I have veiled my look,
I turn the trouble of my countenance
Merely upon myself.[8] Vexed I am
40 Of late with passions of some difference,
Conceptions only proper to myself,
Which give some soil perhaps to my behaviors;
But let not therefore my good friends be grieved—
Among which number, Cassius, be you one—
45 Nor construe any further my neglect,
Than that poor Brutus, with himself at war,
Forgets the shows of love to other men.

CASSIUS. Then, Brutus, I have much mistook your passion;
By means whereof this breast of mine hath buried
50 Thoughts of great value, worthy cogitations.[9]
Tell me, good Brutus, can you see your face?

BRUTUS. No, Cassius; for the eye sees not itself, but by
reflection, by some other things. (*He moves toward front platform;* CASSIUS *follows.*)

CASSIUS. 'Tis just:
55 And it is very much lamented, Brutus,
That you have no such mirrors as will turn
Your hidden worthiness into your eye,
That you might see your shadow. I have heard,
Where many of the best respect in Rome,
60 Except immortal Caesar, speaking of Brutus
And groaning underneath this age's yoke,
Have wished that noble Brutus had his eyes.

BRUTUS (*facing* CASSIUS). Into what dangers would you lead me,
Cassius,
That you would have me seek into myself
65 For that which is not in me?

CASSIUS. Therefore, good Brutus, be prepared to hear:
And since you know you cannot see yourself

6. *quick spirit,* lively disposition.

7. *as I was wont to have,* that I customarily had.

8. *I turn . . . upon myself.* Brutus is troubled by his own thoughts, not by anything that Cassius has done to him.

9. *Then, Brutus . . . worthy cogitations.* Here Cassius hints of the thoughts (cogitations) that lie locked in his own breast and begins sounding out Brutus to see whether he will join forces with the conspirators. Brutus is an idealistic, impractical sort of man; and Cassius wishes to open his eyes to the dangers that lie in Caesar's rising ambition.

So well as by reflection, I, your glass,
Will modestly discover to yourself
That of yourself which you yet know not of.
And be not jealous on me, gentle Brutus;
Were I a common laugher,[10] or did use
To stale with ordinary oaths my love
To every new protester; if you know
That I do fawn on men and hug them hard
And after scandal them, or if you know
That I profess myself in banqueting
To all the rout,[11] then hold me dangerous.

10. *a common laugher*, a buffoon laughed
at or scorned by everybody.

11. *the rout*, the rabble; worthless people.

*(There is a flourish of trumpets offstage, then
loud cheers.* BRUTUS *and* CASSIUS *look up.)*

BRUTUS. What means this shouting? I do fear the people
  Choose Caesar for their king.

CASSIUS.   Aye, do you fear it?
  Then must I think you would not have it so.

BRUTUS. I would not, Cassius; yet I love him well.
  But wherefore do you hold me here so long?
  What is it that you would impart to me? →What info do you want to give to me?
  If it be aught toward the general good,
  Set honor in one eye and death in the other,
  And I will look on both indifferently,[12]
  For let the gods so speed me as I love
  The name of honor more than I fear death.

12. *If it be . . . indifferently*. If what
Cassius has in mind is for the public
welfare and is honorable, Brutus will do
it even though it means death.

CASSIUS. I know that virtue to be in you, Brutus,
  As well as I do know your outward favor.
  Well, honor *is* the subject of my story.
  I cannot tell what you and other men
  Think of this life; but, for my single self,
  I had as lief not be as live to be
  In awe of such a thing as I myself.
  I was born free as Caesar; so were you:
  We both have fed as well, and we can both
  Endure the winter's cold as well as he:
  For once, upon a raw and gusty day,
  The troubled Tiber chafing with her shores,
  Caesar said to me, "Darest thou, Cassius, now
  Leap in with me into this angry flood,
  And swim to yonder point?" Upon the word,
  Accoutered as I was,[13] I plungèd in
  And bade him follow; so indeed he did.
  The torrent roared, and we did buffet it,
  With lusty sinews, throwing it aside
  And stemming it with hearts of controversy.
  But ere we could arrive the point proposed,
  Caesar cried, "Help me, Cassius, or I sink!"
  I, as Aeneas, our great ancestor,
  Did from the flames of Troy upon his shoulder
  The old Anchises bear,[14] so from the waves of Tiber

13. *Accoutered* (ə kü′tərd) *as I was*.
Cassius was fully dressed.

14. *I, as Aeneas* (i nē′əs) *. . . Anchises*
(an kī′sēz) *bear*. Aeneas, carrying his
aged father Anchises and leading his
little son, escaped from burning Troy. For
years he wandered; then at last he reached
the banks of the Tiber, where his descendants founded Rome.

115   Did I the tired Caesar. (*Angrily.*) And this man
    Is now become a god, and Cassius is
    A wretched creature and must bend his body,
    If Caesar carelessly but nod on him. (*He pauses.*)
    He had a fever when he was in Spain,
120   And when the fit[15] was on him, I did mark
    How he did shake: 'tis true, this god did shake;
    His coward lips did from their color fly,[16]
    And that same eye whose bend doth awe the world
    Did lose his[17] luster: I did hear him groan:
125   Aye, and that tongue of his that bade the Romans
    Mark him and write his speeches in their books,
    Alas, it cried, "Give me some drink, Titinius,"
    As a sick girl. Ye gods, it doth amaze me
    A man of such a feeble temper[18] should
130   So get the start of the majestic world
    And bear the palm[19] alone.

            (*Loud shouts and the flourish of trumpets heard offstage.*)

BRUTUS (*crossing to right pillar*). Another general shout!
    I do believe that these applauses are
    For some new honors that are heaped on Caesar.
135 CASSIUS (*following*). Why, man, he doth bestride the narrow world
    Like a Colossus,[20] and we petty men
    Walk under his huge legs and peep about
    To find ourselves dishonorable graves.
    Men at some time are masters of their fates:
140   The fault, dear Brutus, is not in our stars,
    But in ourselves, that we are underlings.[21]
    Brutus and Caesar: what should be in that "Caesar"?
    Why should that name be sounded more than yours?
    Write them together, yours is as fair a name;
145   Sound them, it doth become the mouth as well;
    Weigh them, it is as heavy; conjure with 'em,
    "Brutus" will start a spirit[22] as soon as "Caesar."
    Now, in the names of all the gods at once,
    Upon what meat doth this our Caesar feed,
150   That he is grown so great?

            (*Loud shouts and the flourish of trumpets offstage.*)

BRUTUS (*thoughtfully*).   What you have said
    I will consider; what you have to say
    I will with patience hear, and find a time
    Both meet to hear and answer such high things.
    Till then, my noble friend, chew upon this:
155   Brutus had rather be a villager
    Than to repute himself a son of Rome
    Under these hard conditions as this time
    Is like to lay upon us.
CASSIUS. I am glad that my weak words
160   Have struck but thus much show of fire from Brutus.

        (*The sounds of approaching people are heard from offstage.*)

15. *the fit.* Caesar was subject to epileptic seizures, then termed "the falling sickness."

16. *His coward lips . . . fly.* His lips became white.

17. *his, its. Its* was just coming into use when the play was written.

18. *A man of such a feeble temper.* The Romans worshiped physical strength, and Cassius didn't see how a physical weakling could rule all the known world.
19. *the palm,* the symbol of victory and triumph.

20. *Like a Colossus* (kə los′ əs). The Colossus was a huge statue of Apollo at Rhodes. This wonder of the ancient world was so enormous that according to legend, it bestrode the entrance to the harbor, and ships passed between its legs.

21. *Men at some time . . . underlings.* Cassius believes that the star a man is born under is not so important in determining his destiny as is his own character.

22. *start a spirit,* call forth a ghost from the spirit world.

BRUTUS. The games are done and Caesar is returning.

CASSIUS. As they pass by, pluck Casca by the sleeve;
And he will, after his sour fashion, tell you
What hath proceeded worthy note today.

(CAESAR *and his followers reënter at left and
start across the platform.* ANTONY *is on* CAESAR's
left; CASCA *is at the rear of the procession.*)

165 BRUTUS. I will do so. But look you, Cassius,
The angry spot doth glow on Caesar's brow,
And all the rest look like a chidden train:[23]
Calpurnia's cheek is pale; and Cicero
Looks with such ferret and such fiery eyes[24]
170 As we have seen him in the Capitol,
Being crossed in conference by some senators.

CASSIUS. Casca will tell us what the matter is.

(CAESAR *stops before he reaches center platform and looks speculatively at* CASSIUS.)

CAESAR. Antonius!

ANTONY. Caesar?

175 CAESAR. Let me have men about me that are fat;
Sleek-headed men and such as sleep o' nights.
Yond Cassius has a lean and hungry look;
He thinks too much; such men are dangerous.

ANTONY. Fear him not, Caesar; he's not dangerous;
180 He is a noble Roman and well-given.

CAESAR. Would he were fatter! But I fear him not:
Yet if my name were liable to fear,
I do not know the man I should avoid
So soon as that spare Cassius. He reads much;
185 He is a great observer, and he looks
Quite through the deeds of men; he loves no plays,
As thou dost, Anthony; he hears no music;
Seldom he smiles, and smiles in such a sort
As if he mocked himself and scorned his spirit
190 That could be moved to smile at anything.
Such men as he be never at heart's ease
Whiles they behold a greater than themselves,
And therefore are they very dangerous.
I rather tell thee what is to be feared
195 Than what I fear; for always I am Caesar.
Come on my right hand, for this ear is deaf,
And tell me truly what thou think'st of him.

(ANTONY, *as bid, steps to* CAESAR's *right. The trumpets
sound again and the procession, with* CASCA *still at its rear,
moves slowly out at right door. When* CASCA *reaches center
platform he is detained by* BRUTUS *and* CASSIUS.)

CASCA. You pulled me by the cloak; would you speak with me?

BRUTUS. Aye, Casca; tell us what hath chanced today,
200 That Caesar looks so sad.

CASCA. Why, you were with him, were you not?

23. *like a chidden train,* like a group of
people who have been harshly scolded.

24. *such ferret and such fiery eyes,* eyes
that are red and angry looking, like the
eyes of a weasel.

BRUTUS. I should not then ask Casca what had chanced.

CASCA. Why, there was a crown offered him; and being offered him, he put it by with the back of his hand, thus; and then the people fell a-shouting.

205

BRUTUS. What was the second noise for?

CASCA. Why, for that, too.

CASSIUS. They shouted thrice; what was the last cry for?

CASCA. Why, for that, too.

210 BRUTUS (*incredulously*). Was the crown offered him thrice?

CASCA. Aye, marry,[25] was't, and he put it by thrice, every time gentler than other.

CASSIUS. Who offered him the crown?

CASCA. Why, Antony.

215 BRUTUS. Tell us the manner of it, gentle Casca.

CASCA. I can as well be hanged as tell the manner of it: it was mere foolery; I did not mark it. I saw Mark Antony offer him a crown—yet 'twas not a crown neither, 'twas one of these coronets—and, as I told you, he put it by once; but, for all that, to my thinking, he would

220 fain have had it. Then he offered it to him again; then he put it by again; but, to my thinking, he was very loath to lay his fingers off it. And then he offered it the third time; he put it the third time by; and still as he refused it, the rabblement hooted and clapped their chapped hands and threw up their sweaty nightcaps and uttered such

225 a deal of stinking breath because Caesar refused the crown that it had almost choked Caesar; for he swounded[26] and fell down at it; and for mine own part, I durst not laugh, for fear of opening my lips and receiving the bad air.

CASSIUS. But, soft, I pray you; what, did Caesar swound?

230 CASCA. He fell down in the market place, and foamed at mouth, and was speechless.

BRUTUS. 'Tis very like; he hath the falling sickness.

CASSIUS. No, Caesar hath it not; but you and I
And honest Casca, we have the falling sickness.

CASCA. I know not what you mean by that; but I am sure Caesar fell

235 down. If the tag-rag people did not clap him and hiss him, according as he pleased and displeased them, as they use to do the players in the theater, I am no true man.

BRUTUS. What said he when he came unto himself?

CASCA. When he came to himself again, he said if he had done or said

240 anything amiss, he desired their worships to think it was his infirmity. Three or four wenches, where I stood, cried, "Alas, good soul!" and forgave him with all their hearts. But there's no heed to be taken of them; if Caesar had stabbed their mothers, they would have done no less.

245 BRUTUS. And after that, he came, thus sad, away?

CASCA. Aye.

CASSIUS. Did Cicero say anything?

CASCA. Aye, he spoke Greek.

CASSIUS. To what effect?

250 CASCA. Nay, an [27] I tell you that, I'll ne'er look you i' th' face again; but

25. *marry*, a mild oath. Its original form was "by the Virgin Mary." (Why is Shakespeare's use of it here an anachronism?)

26. *swounded* (swound'əd), became faint.

27. *an, if.*

those that understood him smiled at one another and shook their heads. But, for mine own part, it was Greek to me.[28] I could tell you more news, too: Marullus and Flavius, for pulling scarfs off Caesar's images, are put to silence.[29] Fare you well. There was more foolery yet, if I could remember it.

CASSIUS. Will you sup with me tonight, Casca?

CASCA. No, I am promised forth.

CASSIUS. Will you dine with me tomorrow?

CASCA. Aye, if I be alive and your mind hold and your dinner worth the eating.

260 CASSIUS. Good; I will expect you.

CASCA. Do so. Farewell, both.

(He exits at inner-stage curtains.)

BRUTUS. What a blunt fellow is this grown to be!
He was quick mettle[30] when he went to school.

CASSIUS. So is he now in execution
265 Of any bold or noble enterprise,
However he puts on this tardy form.
This rudeness is a sauce to his good wit,
Which gives men stomach to digest his words
With better appetite.

270 BRUTUS. And so it is. For this time I will leave you;
Tomorrow, if you please to speak with me,
I will come home to you; or, if you will,
Come home to me, and I will wait for you.

CASSIUS. I will do so; till then, think of the world.

(BRUTUS exits at left.)

275 Well, Brutus, thou art noble;[31] yet, I see,
Thy honorable metal may be wrought
From that it is disposed. Therefore it is meet
That noble minds keep ever with their likes;
For who so firm that cannot be seduced? — everyone has their price
280 Caesar doth bear me hard;[32] but he loves Brutus.
If I were Brutus now and he were Cassius,
He should not humor me.[33] I will this night,
In several hands,[34] in at his windows throw,
As if they came from several citizens,
285 Writings all tending to the great opinion
That Rome holds of his name; wherein obscurely
Caesar's ambition shall be glancèd at[35]:
And after this let Caesar seat him sure;
For we will shake him, or worse days endure.

(He exits at inner-stage curtains.)

Scene 3: Rome. A street.

It is the night before the ides of March. A month has gone by since CASSIUS *first spoke to* BRUTUS *about the danger from* CAESAR. *Unperturbed*

---

28. *it was Greek to me.* People still quote this expression to signify that something is too difficult to be understood.
29. *put to silence,* deprived of their rank as tribunes and banished.

30. *quick mettle,* easily stirred to action.

31. *Well, Brutus, thou art noble.* Here Cassius begins the play's first soliloquy (sə lil′ə kwi), a speech made by an actor to himself. The speaker of a soliloquy is usually alone on the stage. If other characters are present, they do not hear the soliloquy.
32. *Caesar doth bear me hard.* Caesar hates me.
33. *humor me,* win me over to his opinions.
34. *In several hands,* in different handwritings.

35. *glancèd at,* hinted at.

by this wild and stormy night, CICERO *enters with a lantern at left.
There is a flash of lightning, then a violent clap of thunder just as*
CASCA, *his sword drawn, enters at right.*

CICERO (*calmly*). Good even,[1] Casca; brought you Caesar home?
  Why are you breathless? And why stare you so?

CASCA. Are not you moved, when all the sway of earth
  Shakes like a thing unfirm? O Cicero,
5 I have seen tempests, when the scolding winds
  Have rived the knotty oaks, and I have seen
  The ambitious ocean swell and rage and foam,
  To be exalted with the threatening clouds;
  But never till tonight, never till now,
10 Did I go through a tempest dropping fire.

                (*Another crash of thunder, followed by
                    a scream.* CASCA *darts to left pillar.*)

  Either there is a civil strife in heaven,
  Or else the world, too saucy with the gods,
  Incenses them to send destruction.

CICERO (*drawing closer*). Why, saw you anything more wonderful?

15 CASCA. A common slave—you know him well by sight—
  Held up his left hand, which did flame and burn
  Like twenty torches joined, and yet his hand,
  Not sensible of fire,[2] remained unscorched.
  And yesterday the bird of night did sit
20 Even at noon day upon the market place,
  Hooting and shrieking. When these prodigies
  Do so conjointly meet, let not men say,
  "These are their reasons; they are natural;"
  For, I believe, they are portentous things
25 Unto the climate that they point upon.[3]

CICERO. Indeed, it is a strange-disposèd time:
  But men may construe things after their fashion,
  Clean from the purpose of the things themselves.[4]
  Comes Caesar to the Capitol tomorrow?

30 CASCA. He doth; for he did bid Antonius
  Send word to you he would be there tomorrow.

CICERO. Good night then, Casca: this disturbèd sky
  Is not to walk in.

CASCA.   Farewell, Cicero.
      (*Leaving his lantern behind,* CICERO *exits at right. There is
      another flash of lightning and* CASCA *retreats to rear platform,
      where he takes shelter under the projecting balcony.* CASSIUS
      enters at left.)

CASSIUS. Who's there?

CASCA.   A Roman.

CASSIUS.   Casca, by your voice.
      (*He joins* CASCA *under the balcony.*)

35 CASCA. Your ear is good. Cassius, what night[5] is this!

CASSIUS. A very pleasing night to honest men.

CASCA. Who ever knew the heavens menace so?

CASSIUS. Those that have known the earth so full of faults.
    For my part, I have walked about the streets,
40   Submitting me unto the perilous night,
    And, thus unbracèd,[6] Casca, as you see,
    Have bared my bosom to the thunder-stone.
CASCA. But wherefore did you so much tempt the heavens?
    It is the part of men to fear and tremble
45   When the most mighty gods by tokens send
    Such dreadful heralds to astonish us.
CASSIUS. Now could I, Casca, name to thee a man
    Most like this dreadful night,
    That thunders, lightens, opens graves, and roars,
50   A man no mightier than thyself or me
    In personal action, yet prodigious grown
    And fearful, as these strange eruptions are.
CASCA. 'Tis Caesar that you mean; is it not, Cassius?
CASSIUS. Let it be who it is: for Romans now
55   Have thews and limbs like to their ancestors;
    But, woe the while! Our fathers' minds are dead,
    And we are governed with our mothers' spirits;
    Our yoke and sufferance show us womanish.
CASCA. Indeed, they say the senators tomorrow
60   Mean to establish Caesar as a king;
    And he shall wear his crown by sea and land,
    In every place, save here in Italy.
CASSIUS. I know where I will wear this dagger then;
    Cassius from bondage will deliver Cassius.[7]
65   That part of tyranny that I do bear
    I can shake off at pleasure.

              (The thunder rumbles menacingly; the
              two men gradually move forward.)

CASCA.   So can I;
    So every bondman in his own hand bears
    The power to cancel his captivity.
CASSIUS. And why should Caesar be a tyrant then?
70   Poor man! I know he would not be a wolf,
    But that he sees the Romans are but sheep:
    He were no lion, were not Romans hinds.[8]
    Where hast thou led me? I perhaps speak this
    Before a willing bondman; then I know
75   My answer must be made. But I am armed,
    And dangers are to me indifferent.
CASCA. You speak to Casca, and to such a man
    That is no fleering[9] tell-tale. *(Offering his hand.)* Hold, my hand;
    Be factious for redress of all these griefs,[10]
80   And I will set this foot of mine as far
    As who goes farthest.
CASSIUS.   There's a bargain made.
    Now know you, Casca, I have moved already
    Some certain of the noblest-minded Romans

6. *thus unbracèd.* Cassius opens his garment at the neck, exposing his chest to the thunderbolts.

7. *Cassius from bondage . . . Cassius.* Cassius will kill himself rather than live with Caesar as his acknowledged king.

8. *He were no lion . . . hinds.* Caesar's ambition would not be so great had he less chance of attaining it. The Romans are so weak that they make Caesar appear lionlike in contrast.

9. *fleering,* deceitful.

10. *Be factious . . . griefs,* be ready to join with Casca to right the grievances that the Romans have suffered at the hands of Caesar.

To undergo with me an enterprise
85 Of honorable-dangerous consequence;
And I do know, by this, they stay for me
In Pompey's porch;[11] for now, this fearful night,
There is no stir of walking in the streets;
And the complexion of the element
90 In favor's like the work we have in hand,
Most bloody, fiery, and most terrible.

(Hurrying footsteps are heard offstage at right.)

CASCA. Stand close awhile, for here comes one in haste.
CASSIUS. 'Tis Cinna; I do know him by his gait;
He is a friend.   *(CINNA enters in haste.)*
          Cinna, where haste you so?
95 CINNA. To find out you. *(Moving forward.)* Who's that? Metellus
          Cimber?
CASSIUS. No, it is Casca; one incorporate
To our attempts.[12] Am I not stayed for, Cinna?
CINNA. I am glad on't. What a fearful night is this!
There's two or three of us have seen strange sights.
100 CASSIUS. Am I not stayed for? Tell me.
CINNA.   Yes, you are.
O Cassius, if you could
But win the noble Brutus to our party—
CASSIUS. Be you content. Good Cinna, take this paper,
And look you lay it in the praetor's chair,[13]
105 Where Brutus may but find it; and throw this
In at his window; set this up with wax
Upon old Brutus' statue.[14] All this done,
Repair to Pompey's porch, where you shall find us.
Is Decius Brutus and Trebonius there?
110 CINNA *(stopping).* All but Metellus Cimber; and he's gone
To seek you at your house. Well, I will hie,
And so bestow these papers as you bade me.
CASSIUS. That done, repair to Pompey's theater.

(CINNA runs off at right as
CASSIUS turns to CASCA.)

Come, Casca, you and I will yet ere day
115 See Brutus at his house: three parts of him
Is ours already, and the man entire
Upon the next encounter yields him ours.[15]
CASCA. Oh, he sits high in all the people's hearts;
And that which would appear offense in us,
120 His countenance, like richest alchemy,
Will change to virtue and to worthiness.[16]
CASSIUS. Him and his worth and our great need of him
You have right well conceited.[17] Let us go,
For it is after midnight; and ere day
125 We will awake him and be sure of him.

(CASSIUS and CASCA collect the lan-
tern and then move off at right.)

11. *stay . . . porch,* wait for me in the porch of Pompey's theater.

12. *one incorporate . . . attempts,* one who knows of our plans and is in sympathy with us.

13. *in the praetor's chair.* Brutus, at this time, was praetor (prē′tər), Roman judge or magistrate.

14. *Upon old Brutus' statue,* upon the statue of Lucius Junius Brutus, ancestor of the present Brutus. He had acted as leader in expelling Tarquinius Superbus, the last of the seven Roman kings.

15. *three parts of him . . . ours.* Brutus is almost persuaded to join the conspirators; when they next meet with him, they will undoubtedly win him over completely.
16. *His countenance . . . worthiness.* The high regard with which the Romans hold Brutus and his honorable family name is a great asset. Linking him to the plan will give it sanction and worth.
17. *conceited,* estimated.

CONSIDERING
ACT ONE

Scene 1

1. (a) What quality of the mob does Marullus satirize in his speech beginning "Wherefore rejoice" (page 265, line 25)? (b) Do you think that his opinion is true of mobs in general?

2. (a) In talking with the tribunes do the commoners show: (1) a cringing fear; (2) a scornful contempt; or (3) a good-natured desire to annoy the officials? (b) With which group of people do you sympathize—the commoners or the tribunes? Why?

3. Would you say Shakespeare's main purpose in this scene was: (a) to provide a touch of humor for the beginning of the play; (b) to foreshadow a serious conflict; (c) to introduce the main characters? After making your choice, explain how Shakespeare achieves that purpose.

Scene 2

1. (a) As the scene begins, what attitude do various characters seem to take toward Caesar? (b) What are your own first impressions of the man?

2. (a) What physical weaknesses of Caesar are revealed later in the scene? How is each one brought out? (b) Does Caesar show any signs of being superstitious? (c) How good is he at sizing up individuals (Cassius, for example)? (d) Of the men around him, which could he safely trust? (e) How do we know the common people of Rome loved and idolized him?

3. (a) What is Cassius leading up to in his long talk with Brutus? (b) Why doesn't he come to the point at once? (c) What ideas does he develop in the conversation that would be most likely to influence Brutus?

4. Does Casca, later on, help or hinder Cassius in influencing Brutus? How?

5. (a) What fear does Brutus express to Cassius concerning Caesar? (b) Do you think Brutus is sincere in saying "yet I love him well"? (c) How are his feelings about Caesar related to his statement that lately he has been "at war" with himself?

6. (a) What is the conflict that was foreshadowed in Scene 1 and that is now taking more definite form? (b) On which side of that conflict do you think Brutus will decide to be?

Scene 3

1. (a) What subject is bothering Casca when he first encounters Cassius in the street? (b) How does Cassius cleverly turn the conversation to the subject that *he* considers most important?

2. (a) Why does Cassius think the Roman people themselves are largely responsible for Caesar's growing ambition? (b) Keeping in mind Casca's opinion of the "tag-rag people" as indicated in Scene 2, explain why Cassius' explanation of Caesar's tyranny would appeal to Casca. (c) What decision does Casca make regarding the conspirators?

3. (a) How does Cassius plan to use Cinna in advancing the conspirators' plan? (b) Why are he and the others so eager to have Brutus join them? (c) Quote at least three passages that show the conspirators' opinion of Brutus.

LOOKING BACK
—AND AHEAD

1. Make a brief outline indicating what has happened in Act One. Use as the first statement in your outline: Caesar returns to Rome after defeating the last of his opposition.

2. (a) Why do you think Elizabethans watching the play at the Globe Playhouse awaited Act Two with keen interest? (b) What questions would be uppermost in their minds?

THE
AUTHOR'S
CRAFT

". . . trippingly on the tongue"
Hamlet, III, iii

A modern playgoer will usually say that he is going to *see* a play, but an Elizabethan usually said that he was going to *hear* one. An Elizabethan playgoer was an attentive listener because the actors of his time had to speak their lines as rapidly as possible. In order to take advantage of the daylight, performances began at two o'clock and ended at about four. Thus the actors had but two short hours in which to enact their play. One of Shakespeare's problems as a dramatist was to create dialogue which could be delivered rapidly, yet clearly.

Shakespeare cast his plays in *blank verse*. In its rhythm and its flexibility, blank verse is ideal for dialogue. You will remember from "The Poets' Craft" article on page 231 that blank verse duplicates the natural rhythm of English speech. As such, it falls easily upon a playgoer's ears and an actor can speak it "trippingly on the tongue."

As natural as blank verse may be to listener and speaker alike, it can be very stiff when one *end-stopped* line follows another, like this:

O, Heaven be judge how I love Valentine,
Whose life's as tender to me as my soul!
And full as much, for more there cannot be,
I do detest false perjured Proteus.

Two Gentlemen of Verona

These four lines are end-stopped because sense suggests a pause at the end of each line. Shakespeare relied heavily upon end-stopped lines in his early plays; however, by the time he wrote *Julius Caesar*, he had mastered the more flexible *run-on* line:

Why, man, he doth bestride the narrow world
Like a Colossus, and we petty men
Walk under his huge legs and peep about
To find ourselves dishonorable graves.

Lines 1, 2, and 3 of this passage are run-on lines because the sense runs on from one line to another. The sense of line 1 is completed in line 2 with the word *Colossus*. The sense of lines 2 and 3 is completed in line 4. A series of run-on lines (a verse paragraph) gives Shakespeare's blank verse the flexibility to express the complicated thoughts and emotions of his characters.

Shakespeare departed from blank verse occasionally. He often used *prose* speeches, for example, for people of inferior birth. Where in Act One do you find people speaking in prose? He would also strike a note of finality by concluding some platform scenes with a *rhymed couplet*. Which of the scenes in Act One is ended with a rhymed couplet?

WORD STUDY

Diacritical marks
You have undoubtedly encountered words in which a mark has been placed over or under one of the letters. In such words as *rûle* and *façade*, the *diacritical mark* indicates the sound of a particular letter.

The grave accent(ˋ) and the dieresis (¨) may indicate an *extra syllable*. In reading lines of poetry, it is important to observe these marks carefully. The word *disposed*, for example, is usually pronounced as two syllables. This pronunciation, however, could affect the iambic flow of a blank-verse line:

Indeed, it is a strange-disposed time.

If *disposed* were pronounced as three syllables, the iambic flow would be maintained. The addition of a grave accent accomplishes this:

Indeed, it is a strange-disposèd time.

Assume for a moment that you are the actor who first created the rôle of Caesar on the Globe platform. Lines from five of your speeches are given below. Each passage contains an italicized word to which a diacritical mark has been added. Read each passage aloud, paying careful attention to the diacritical mark.

1. Forget not, in your speed, Antonius,
   To touch Calpurnia; for our elders say
   The barren *touchèd* in this holy chase
   Shakes off their sterile curse.

2. Caesar shall forth; the things that threatened me
   Ne'er looked but on my back; when they shall see
   The face of Caesar, they are *vanishèd*,

3. She dreamt tonight she saw my *statuë*
   Which, like a fountain with an hundred spouts,
   Did run pure blood. . . .

4. How foolish do your fears seem now, Calpurnia!
   I am *ashamèd* I did yield to them.

5. Thy brother by decree is *banishèd*;
   If thou dost bend and pray and fawn for him,
   I spurn thee like a cur out of my way. . . .

Henry V, 1, i

"within this wooden ❧O❧"

The Londoners who flocked to see *Julius Caesar* in September of 1599 were among the first to attend a performance at the new Globe Playhouse. The Globe was the newest theater in London, but its basic design was as old as England's first permanent playhouse.

James Burbage, who was both a carpenter and an actor, built the first public playhouse in London in 1576. In designing his building, he combined some features of an innyard with the shape of an arena. Like other Elizabethan actors, Burbage had usually performed in the courtyards of various London inns. Most inns were three-storied structures that enclosed a rectangular and unroofed yard. The innyard was converted into a theater by placing a temporary platform at one side of the yard. The spectators stood in the yard or filled the tiers of balconies that overlooked the yard. Like other Londoners, Burbage was also familiar with the circular arenas or "gardens," where bullbaiting and bearbaiting contests

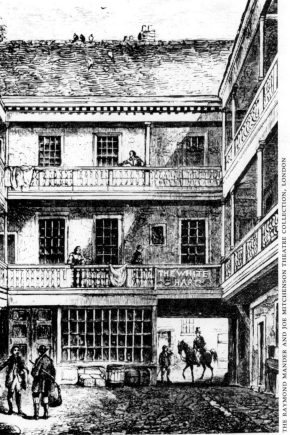

...ctangular courtyard of the White Hart, an Elizabethan inn.

THE RAYMOND MANDER AND JOE MITCHENSON THEATRE COLLECTION, LONDON

A picture-frame stage of the seventeenth century.

PHOTOGRAPH BY THE CLEVELAND
MUSEUM OF ART, CLEVELAND, OHIO

were held. In these arenas, spectators stood on wooden scaffolds that surrounded the baiting ring. They were protected from the animals by a fence.

Burbage adapted the circular shape of the "gardens" for his playhouse. Then, in the three-storied frame of his building, he constructed spectator galleries similar to inn balconies. Because of his example, Elizabethans came to think of a playhouse as an arena with galleries surrounding (or almost surrounding) an open yard. It could hardly have been a surprise to Elizabethan playgoers that the new eight-sided Globe was, in effect, a "wooden O."

It was the size of the Globe platform, not the shape of the playhouse, that astonished Shakespeare's audience. Measuring about 942 square feet, the Globe platform was the largest of its time. Why did the Elizabethan platform stage disappear in later theaters?

About the same time that

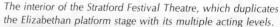

The interior of the Stratford Festival Theatre, which duplicates the Elizabethan platform stage with its multiple acting levels.

STRATFORD SHAKESPEAREAN FESTIVAL FOUNDATION OF CANADA

the Globe opened, playwrights began to write more and more scenes for the inner stage. As this stage became more important, it had to be enlarged. In theaters of the late seventeenth century, the inner stage was wider and deeper: all that remained of the Elizabethan platform was the narrow apron in front of the curtains. This is the stage you probably know the best—the picture-frame stage.

In a theater with a picture-frame stage, the audience sits in front at some distance from the actors. As a result, playgoers tend to be less actively involved in a performance than were the Elizabethans who had the platform thrust into their midst. Many modern theaters have recaptured the close relationship between actor and spectator by reviving the platform stage. In theaters such as these, it is more nearly possible to stage Shakespeare's plays as he intended them to be staged.

The platform stage of the Tyrone Guthrie Theatre in Minneapolis.

Act Two

Scene 1: Rome. Brutus' orchard.[1]

It is a few hours later. The scene opens as the curtains of the inner stage are drawn apart to reveal BRUTUS *in a secluded corner of his garden. He is seated, deep in thought, on a small bench which is flanked by a pair of trees.* BRUTUS *has spent a wakeful night, and now he begins to walk restlessly back and forth. Suddenly he strides forward, onto the platform, and calls to his serving boy, who lies asleep just inside the window at upper right.*

BRUTUS (*at the window*). What, Lucius, ho!
  (*To himself.*) I cannot by the progress of the stars,
  Give guess how near to day. (*Calling.*) Lucius, I say!
  I would it were my fault to sleep so soundly.
5 When, Lucius, when? Awake, I say! What, Lucius!
               (LUCIUS *appears in the window; he*
               opens the casement and leans out.)
LUCIUS (*sleepily*). Called you, my lord?
BRUTUS. Get me a taper in my study, Lucius;
  When it is lighted, come and call me here.
LUCIUS. I will, my lord.
          (*As* LUCIUS *withdraws,* BRUTUS *resumes*
          his restless pacing. He is alone with
          his thoughts, which he now speaks.)
10 BRUTUS. It must be by his[2] death; and for my part
  I know no personal cause to spurn at him,
  But for the general.[3] He would be crowned;
  How that might change his nature, there's the question.
  It is the bright day that brings forth the adder;
15 And that craves wary walking. Crown him?—that;—
  And then, I grant, we put a sting in him,
  That at his will he may do danger with.
  The abuse of greatness is, when it disjoins
  Remorse[4] from power: and, to speak truth of Caesar,
20 I have not known when his affections swayed
  More than his reason. But 'tis a common proof,
  That lowliness is young ambition's ladder,
  Whereto the climber-upward turns his face;
  But when he once attains the upmost round,
25 He then unto the ladder turns his back,
  Looks in the clouds, scorning the base degrees
  By which he did ascend. So Caesar may.
  Then, lest he may, prevent.[5] And, since the quarrel
  Will bear no color for the thing he is,
30 Fashion it thus; that what he is, augmented,

---

1. *orchard*, garden.

2. *his*, Caesar's.

3. *I know no personal . . . general.* Though Brutus has no personal reason for striking at Caesar, he nevertheless feels that he must do so for the public (general) good.

4. *Remorse*, pity.

5. *prevent*, he must be prevented.

Would run to these and these extremities:
And therefore think him as a serpent's egg
Which, hatched, would, as his kind, grow mischievous,
And kill him in the shell.

senate's agreement

(LUCIUS, *yawning, enters the platform at right door. He carries a letter—a small scroll.*)

35 LUCIUS. The taper burneth in your closet,[6] sir.
   Searching the window for a flint, I found
   This paper, thus sealed up; and I am sure
   It did not lie there when I went to bed. (*He gives* BRUTUS
      the letter.)
BRUTUS. Get you to bed again; it is not day.

(LUCIUS *starts to leave.*)

40 Is not tomorrow, boy, the ides of March?
LUCIUS. I know not, sir.
BRUTUS. Look in the calendar, and bring me word.
LUCIUS. I will, sir.

(*He exits at right.*)

BRUTUS. The exhalations whizzing in the air[7]
45 Give so much light that I may read by them. (*He opens
      the letter and reads.*)

—you're not aware   *—you're just as good as caesar*

Brutus, thou sleepest: awake, and see thyself.
Shall Rome, etc. Speak, strike, redress!

if written out, (they) Brutus will be killed

"Brutus, thou sleepest: awake!"
Such instigations have been often dropped
50 Where I have took them up.
"Shall Rome, etc." Thus must I piece it out:
Shall Rome stand under one man's awe? What, Rome?
My ancestors did from the streets of Rome
The Tarquin[8] drive, when he was called a king.
55 "Speak, strike, redress!" Am I entreated
   To speak and strike? (*He raises a clenched fist.*) O Rome,
      I make thee promise;
   If the redress will follow, thou receivest
   Thy full petition at the hand of Brutus!

if corrections are taken in Rome, he will do it. If only murder + another tyrant in — won't do it.

(LUCIUS *reënters.*)

LUCIUS. Sir, March is wasted fifteen days.

(*There is a knock at left.*)

60 BRUTUS. 'Tis good. Go to the gate; somebody knocks.

(LUCIUS *hurries to open the door at left.*)

Since Cassius first did whet me against Caesar,
I have not slept.
Between the acting of a dreadful thing
And the first motion, all the interim is
65 Like a phantasma, or a hideous dream:
The Genius and the mortal instruments[9]
Are then in council; and the state of man,
Like to a little kingdom, suffers then

he's felt physically bad about problems. His thoughts have been disturbed.

6. *closet,* study; room.

7. *The exhalations . . . air,* the falling stars.

8. *The Tarquin,* Tarquinius Superbus, the last Roman king.

9. *The Genius and the mortal instruments,* the soul and the body.

The nature of an insurrection.

70 LUCIUS (*rejoining* BRUTUS). Sir, 'tis your brother Cassius[10] at
    the door,
  Who doth desire to see you.
BRUTUS.   Is he alone?
LUCIUS. No, sir, there are moe[11] with him.
BRUTUS.   Do you know them?
LUCIUS. No, sir; their hats are plucked about their ears,
  And half their faces buried in their cloaks,
75 That by no means I may discover them
  By any mark of favor.[12]
BRUTUS.   Let 'em enter.
  They are the faction. O conspiracy,
  Sham'st thou to show thy dangerous brow by night,
  When evils are most free? Oh, then by day
80 Where wilt thou find a cavern dark enough
  To mask thy monstrous visage? Seek none, conspiracy;
  Hide it in smiles and affability;
  For if thou path, thy native semblance on,
  Not Erebus itself were dim enough
85 To hide thee from prevention.[13]

        (LUCIUS *ushers in the* CONSPIRATORS—CASSIUS,
       CASCA, DECIUS, CINNA, METELLUS CIMBER, LIGARIUS,
       and TREBONIUS. *While the* CONSPIRATORS *are*
       approaching BRUTUS, LUCIUS *exits at right.*)

CASSIUS (*stepping forward*). I think we are too bold upon your rest;
  Good morrow, Brutus; do we trouble you?
BRUTUS. I have been up this hour, awake all night.
  Know I these men that come along with you?
90 CASSIUS. Yes, every man of them, and no man here
  But honors you; and every one doth wish
  You had but that opinion of yourself
  Which every noble Roman bears of you.
  This is Trebonius.
BRUTUS (*extending his hand*). He is welcome hither.
CASSIUS. This, Decius Brutus.
95 BRUTUS.   He is welcome, too.
CASSIUS. This, Casca; this, Cinna; and this, Metellus Cimber.
BRUTUS. They are all welcome.
  What watchful cares do interpose themselves
  Betwixt your eyes and night?
100 CASSIUS. Shall I entreat a word?

        (BRUTUS *and* CASSIUS *step back a little to speak*
       privately. The other CONSPIRATORS *talk idly.*)

DECIUS. Here lies the east; doth not the day break here?
CASCA. No.
CINNA. Oh, pardon, sir, it doth; and yon gray lines
  That fret the clouds are messengers of day.
105 CASCA. You shall confess that you are both deceived.
  Here, as I point my sword, the sun arises.

10. *your brother Cassius.* We would say
brother-in-law. Cassius had married
Brutus' sister, Junia.

11. *moe,* more.

12. *any mark of favor,* any features by
which they can be recognized.

13. *For if thou path . . . prevention.* If
the conspirators walk about, plotting
openly, not even Erebus (er'ə bəs) would
be dim enough to hide them. Erebus,
according to Greek and Roman mythology,
was a dark, gloomy place through which
the dead passed en route to Hades.

(BRUTUS *and* CASSIUS *rejoin the group.*)

BRUTUS. Give me your hands all over, one by one.

CASSIUS. And let us swear our resolution.

BRUTUS. No, not an oath; if not the face of men,

110　The sufferance of our souls, the time's abuse—

If these be motives weak, break off betimes,

And every man hence to his idle bed;

So let high-sighted tyranny range on,

Till every man drop by lottery.[14] But if these,

115　As I am sure they do, bear fire enough

To kindle cowards and to steel with valor

The melting spirits of women, then, countrymen,

What need we any spur but our own cause? (*He clasps hands with all.*)

CASSIUS. But what of Cicero? Shall we sound him?

120　I think he will stand very strong with us.

CASCA. Let us not leave him out.

CINNA.　　　　　　　　　　No, by no means.

METELLUS CIMBER. Oh, let us have him, for his silver hairs

Will purchase us a good opinion

And buy men's voices to commend our deeds;

125　It shall be said, his judgment ruled our hands;

Our youths and wildness shall no whit appear,

But all be buried in his gravity.

BRUTUS. Oh, name him not; let us not break with him;[15]

For he will never follow anything

130　That other men begin.

CASSIUS.　　　　　　　Then leave him out.

CASCA. Indeed he is not fit.

DECIUS. Shall no man else be touched by only Caesar?

CASSIUS. Decius, well urged. I think it is not meet[16]

Mark Antony, so well beloved of Caesar,

135　Should outlive Caesar; we shall find of him

A shrewd contriver; and, you know, his means,[17]

If he improve them, may well stretch so far

As to annoy[18] us all—which to prevent,

Let Antony and Caesar fall together.

140　BRUTUS. Our course will seem too bloody, Caius Cassius,

To cut the head off and then hack the limbs,

Like wrath in death and envy afterwards;

For Antony is but a limb of Caesar;

Let us be sacrificers, but not butchers, Caius.

145　We all stand up against the spirit of Caesar;

And in the spirit of men there is no blood.

Oh, that we then could come by Caesar's spirit,

And not dismember Caesar! But, alas,

Caesar must bleed for it! And, gentle friends,

150　Let's kill him boldly, but not wrathfully;

Let's carve him as a dish fit for the gods,

Not hew him as a carcass fit for hounds.

And for Mark Antony, think not of him;

14. *if not the face . . . by lottery.* If the wrongs the conspirators see about them are not sufficient to bind them to firm purpose, then let each man go his own way, become a weakling, and die when it suits a tyrant's whims.

15. *break with him,* break the news of the conspiracy to him.

16. *meet,* fitting; suitable.

17. *his means,* Antony's influence.

18. *annoy,* harm.

For he can do no more than Caesar's arm
When Caesar's head is off.
CASSIUS *(still unconvinced).*   Yet I fear him;
For in the ingrafted love he bears to Caesar—
BRUTUS. Alas, good Cassius, do not think of him;
If he love Caesar, all that he can do
Is to himself, take thought and die for Caesar;
And that were much he should; for he is given
To sports, to wildness and much company.
TREBONIUS. There is no fear in him;[19] let him not die;
For he will live, and laugh at this hereafter.

(A clock offstage begins to strike.)

BRUTUS. Peace! Count the clock.[20]
CASSIUS.   The clock hath stricken three.
TREBONIUS. 'Tis time to part.
CASSIUS.   But it is doubtful yet,
Whether Caesar will come forth today, or no;
For he is superstitious grown of late,
Quite from the main opinion he held once
Of fantasy, of dreams, and ceremonies.
It may be, these apparent prodigies,
The unaccustomed terror of this night,
And the persuasion of his augurers[21]
May hold him from the Capitol today.
DECIUS. Never fear that: if he be so resolved,
I can o'ersway him; for he loves to hear
That unicorns may be betrayed with trees,
And bears with glasses, elephants with holes,
Lions with toils,[22] and men with flatterers;
But when I tell him he hates flatterers,
He says he does, being then most flattered.
Let me work;
For I can give his humor the true bent,[23]
And I will bring him to the Capitol.
CASSIUS. Nay, we will all of us be there to fetch him.
BRUTUS. By the eighth hour; is that the uttermost?
CINNA. Be that the uttermost, and fail not then.
CASSIUS. The morning comes upon 's; we'll leave you, Brutus.
And friends, disperse yourselves; but all remember
What you have said, and show yourselves true Romans.
BRUTUS. Good gentlemen, look fresh and merrily;
Let not our looks put on[24] our purposes,
But bear it as our Roman actors do,
With untired spirits and formal constancy;
And so good morrow to you every one.

(The CONSPIRATORS *move off at left. For a
moment* BRUTUS *stands lost in thought; then he
crosses to the window at upper right and calls.)*

Boy! Lucius! Fast asleep? It is no matter;
Enjoy the honey-heavy dew of slumber;

---

19. *There is no fear in him,* there is no reason to fear Antony.

20. *Count the clock.* This is a famous anachronism. There were, of course, no striking clocks in Caesar's day.

21. *his augurers* (ô'gər ərz), official interpreters who predicted the future by reading signs. They frequently were called *augurs.* In the next scene we hear of sacrificial animals being cut open; the way the inner parts (entrails) arranged themselves was considered significant in foretelling the future.
22. *That unicorns . . . toils,* methods thought effective for capturing wild beasts. The mythological unicorn was incited to charge; the hunter quickly stepped behind a nearby tree, and the unicorn, unable to stop, drove his horn firmly into the trunk. It was thought that a dangerous bear could be distracted by a mirror placed in its paws; it would be so fascinated by its reflection that a hunter could easily kill it. Elephants were captured in pits, and lions were sometimes rendered helpless by nets (toils).
23. *I can give his humor . . . bent.* Decius Brutus knows how to handle Caesar.

24. *put on,* betray.

Thou hast no figures nor no fantasies,
Which busy care draws in the brains of men.
Therefore thou sleepest so sound.

(PORTIA, *wearing a night robe, enters at*
right. Her face is pale and worried as
she follows BRUTUS *to the inner stage.)*

PORTIA.   Brutus, my lord!

200 BRUTUS. Portia, what mean you? Wherefore rise you now?
It is not for your health thus to commit
Your weak condition to the raw cold morning.
PORTIA. Nor for yours neither. You've ungently, Brutus,
Stole from my bed; and yesternight, at supper,
205 You suddenly arose, and walked about,
Musing and sighing, with your arms across,
And when I asked you what the matter was,
You stared upon me with ungentle looks;
I urged you further; then you scratched your head,
210 And too impatiently stamped with your foot;
Yet I insisted; yet you answered not,
But, with angry wafture of your hand,
Gave sign for me to leave you; so I did,
Fearing to strengthen that impatience
215 Which seemed too much enkindled, and withal[25]
Hoping it was but an effect of humor,[26]
Which sometime hath his hour with every man.
It will not let you eat, nor talk, nor sleep,
And could it work so much upon your shape
220 As it hath much prevailed on your condition,
I should not know you, Brutus. (*Pleadingly.*) Dear my lord,
Make me acquainted with your cause of grief.
BRUTUS. I am not well in health, and that is all.
PORTIA. Brutus is wise, and, were he not in health,
225 He would embrace the means to come by it.
BRUTUS. Why, so I do. (*He seats himself wearily on the*
nearby bench.) Good Portia, go to bed.
PORTIA (*drawing closer*). Is Brutus sick? And is it physical
To walk unbracèd and suck up the humors
Of the dank morning? What, is Brutus sick,
230 And will he steal out of his wholesome bed,
To dare the vile contagion of the night
And tempt the rheumy and unpurgèd air[27]
To add unto his sickness? No, my Brutus;
You have some sick offense within your mind,
235 Which, by the right and virtue of my place,
I ought to know of; and, upon my knees (*falling to her knees*)
I charm you, by my once commended beauty,
By all your vows of love and that great vow
Which did incorporate and make us one,
240 That you unfold to me, yourself, your half,
Why you are heavy, and what men tonight

25. *withal*, in addition to this.
26. *an effect of humor*, a whim.

27. *the rheumy* (rüm′i) . . . *air*, the air
that causes colds because it has not yet
been purified (purged) by the sun.

Have had resort to you; for here have been
Some six or seven, who did hide their faces
Even from darkness.
BRUTUS.   Kneel not, gentle Portia. *(He raises her.)*
245 PORTIA. I should not need, if you were gentle Brutus.
Within the bond of marriage, tell me, Brutus,
Is it excepted I should know no secrets
That appertain to you?[28]

BRUTUS. You are my true and honorable wife,
250   As dear to me as are the ruddy drops
That visit my sad heart.
PORTIA. If this were true, then should I know this secret.
I grant I am a woman, but withal
A woman that Lord Brutus took to wife;
255   I grant I am a woman, but withal
A woman well-reputed, Cato's daughter.
Think you I am no stronger than my sex,
Being so fathered[29] and so husbanded?
Tell me your counsels, I will not disclose 'em;
260   I have made strong proof of my constancy,
Giving myself a voluntary wound
Here, in the thigh: can I bear that with patience,
And not my husband's secrets?
BRUTUS *(to the heavens).*   O ye gods,
Render me worthy of this noble wife!
265   *(Turning to* PORTIA.) Portia, go in awhile:
And by and by thy bosom shall partake
The secrets of my heart.
All my engagements I will construe[30] to thee,
All the charactery[31] of my sad brows;
270   Leave me with haste.
                    (PORTIA hastens to right door and exits.
                 BRUTUS *remains seated on the bench as the*
               curtains of the inner stage are drawn closed.)

28. *Is it excepted . . . you?* Portia is asking if an exception was made in the marriage vows so that she would have no legal right to inquire into Brutus' affairs.

29. *Being so fathered.* Portia's father, Cato the Younger, had killed himself rather than submit to tyranny.

30. *construe,* explain.
31. *charactery,* lines of worry.

Scene 2: Rome. Caesar's house.

It is early morning on the ides of March. Several hours have elapsed since the CONSPIRATORS *met in* BRUTUS' *garden. The curtains of the balcony stage (above) are drawn open just as* CAESAR *enters at right. Speaking to himself, he crosses to the left, where his street robe is draped across a high-backed chair.*

CAESAR. Nor heaven nor earth have been at peace tonight;
Thrice hath Calpurnia in her sleep cried out,
"Help! Ho! They murder Caesar!" Who's within? *(He claps his hands.)*
                        (A SERVANT *enters at left.)*

SERVANT. My lord?

5 CAESAR. Go bid the priests do present sacrifice
And bring me their opinions of success.[1]

SERVANT. I will, my lord.

(He exits at the door in the rear wall of
the balcony stage as CALPURNIA, who is
clad in her night robe, enters at right.)

CALPURNIA. What mean you, Caesar? Think you to walk forth?
You shall not stir out of your house today.

10 CAESAR. Caesar shall forth; the things that threatened me
Ne'er looked but on my back; when they shall see
The face of Caesar, they are vanishèd.

CALPURNIA. Caesar, I never stood on ceremonies,[2]
Yet now they fright me. There is one within,[3]

15 Besides the things that we have heard and seen,
Recounts most horrid sights seen by the watch.
A lioness hath whelpèd in the streets;
And graves have yawned, and yielded up their dead;
Fierce fiery warriors fought upon the clouds,

20 In ranks and squadrons and right form of war,
Which drizzled blood upon the Capitol;
The noise of battle hurtled in the air,
Horses did neigh, and dying men did groan,
And ghosts did shriek and squeal about the streets.

25 O Caesar! These things are beyond all use,[4]
And I do fear them.

CAESAR.   What can be avoided
Whose end is purposed by the mighty gods?[5]
Yet Caesar shall go forth; for these predictions
Are to the world in general as to Caesar.

30 CALPURNIA. When beggars die, there are no comets seen;
The heavens themselves blaze forth the death of princes.

CAESAR. Cowards die many times before their deaths;
The valiant never taste of death but once.
Of all the wonders that I yet have heard,

35 It seems to me most strange that men should fear,
Seeing that death, a necessary end,
Will come when it will come.

(The SERVANT reënters.)
                    What say the augurers?

SERVANT. They would not have you to stir forth today.
Plucking the entrails of an offering forth,

40 They could not find a heart within the beast.

CAESAR. The gods do this in shame of cowardice;
Caesar should be a beast without a heart
If he should stay at home today for fear.
No, Caesar shall not; danger knows full well

45 That Caesar is more dangerous than he.
We[6] are two lions littered in one day,
And I the elder and more terrible;

1. *Go bid the priests . . . success.* Caesar wishes to consult the augurers.

2. *I never stood on ceremonies.* Calpurnia had never been one to believe greatly in signs and portents.

3. *one within,* a servant.

4. *beyond all use,* not customary; supernatural.

5. *What can be avoided . . . gods?* Note Caesar's belief in fatalism.

6. *We,* Caesar and danger.

And Caesar shall go forth.

CALPURNIA (*going to him*).   Alas, my lord;
  Your wisdom is consumed in confidence.
50 Do not go forth today; call it my fear
  That keeps you in the house, and not your own.
  We'll send Mark Antony to the Senate-house;
  And he shall say you are not well today. (*She kneels.*)
  Let me, upon my knee, prevail in this.
55 CAESAR (*raising her*). Mark Antony shall say I am not well;
  And, for thy humor, I will stay at home.
                          (DECIUS *enters at rear door.*)
  Here's Decius Brutus, he shall tell them so.
DECIUS (*bowing*). Caesar, all hail! Good morrow, worthy Caesar;
  I come to fetch you to the Senate-house.
60 CAESAR. And you are come in very happy time,
  To bear my greeting to the senators
  And tell them that I will not come today—
  Cannot is false, and that I *dare* not, falser;
  I *will* not come today. Tell them so, Decius.
65 CALPURNIA. Say he is sick.
CAESAR (*loudly*).   Shall Caesar send a lie?
  Have I in conquest stretched mine arm so far,
  To be afeard to tell graybeards the truth?
  Decius, go tell them Caesar will not come.
DECIUS. Most mighty Caesar, let me know some cause,
70 Lest I be laughed at when I tell them so.
CAESAR. The cause is in my will: I will not come;
  That is enough to satisfy the Senate.
  But for your private satisfaction,
  Because I love you, I will let you know:
75 Calpurnia here, my wife, stays me at home;
  She dreamt tonight she saw my statuë,[7]
  Which, like a fountain with an hundred spouts,
  Did run pure blood; and many lusty Romans
  Came smiling, and did bathe their hands in it;
80 And these does she apply for warnings, and portents,
  And evils imminent; and on her knee
  Hath begged that I will stay at home today.
DECIUS. This dream is all amiss interpreted;
  It was a vision fair and fortunate:
85 Your statue spouting blood in many pipes,
  In which so many smiling Romans bathed,
  Signifies that from you great Rome shall suck
  Reviving blood.
  This by Calpurnia's dream is signified.
90 CAESAR. And this way have you well expounded it.
DECIUS. I have, when you have heard what I can say;
  And know it now: the Senate have concluded
  To give this day a crown to mighty Caesar.
  If you shall send them word you will not come,

7. *statuë* (stach′ü ə), pronounced in three
syllables for the sake of the meter.

95   Their minds may change. Besides, it were a mock
      Apt to be rendered,[8] for someone to say,
      "Break up the Senate till another time,
      When Caesar's wife shall meet with better dreams."
      If Caesar hide himself, shall they not whisper,
100   "Lo, Caesar is afraid"?
      Pardon me, Caesar; for my dear, dear love
      To your proceeding bids me tell you this;
      And reason to my love is liable.
      CAESAR. How foolish do your fears seem now, Calpurnia!
105   I am ashamèd I did yield to them.
      Give me my robe, for I will go.

8. *it were a mock . . . rendered*, people would be likely to sneer at Caesar's excuse.

                    (While DECIUS *is assisting* CAESAR *with his robe*, PUBLIUS,
                BRUTUS, LIGARIUS, METELLUS, CASCA, TREBONIUS, *and* CINNA
                    enter at rear door. Each man, in turn, bows to CAESAR.)
      And look where Publius is come to fetch me.
      PUBLIUS. Good morrow, Caesar.
      CAESAR (*in a dignified manner*). Welcome, Publius.
      What, Brutus, are you stirred so early, too?
110   Good morrow, Casca. Caius Ligarius,
      Caesar was ne'er so much your enemy
      As that same ague which hath made you lean.
      What is 't o'clock?
      BRUTUS.   Caesar, 'tis strucken eight.
      CAESAR. I thank you for your pains and courtesy.

                              (ANTONY *enters at rear door.*)
115   See! Antony, that revels long o' nights,
      Is notwithstanding up. Good morrow, Antony.
      ANTONY (*bowing*). So to most noble Caesar.
      CAESAR.
                              Bid them prepare within;
      I am to blame to be thus waited for.
      Now, Cinna; now, Metellus; what, Trebonius!
120   I have an hour's talk in store for you.
      Remember that you call on me today;
      Be near me, that I may remember you.
      TREBONIUS. Caesar, I will. (*Aside.*) And so near will I be
      That your best friends shall wish I had been further.

                    (CAESAR, *followed by the others, leaves at rear door.*
                        CALPURNIA *lingers a moment, then exits as the*
                        curtains of the balcony stage are drawn closed.)

Scene 3: Rome. A street near the Capitol.

ARTEMIDORUS, *a teacher of rhetoric, enters at left. In his hands he carries
a paper which he intends to present to* CAESAR. *Moving slowly across
the platform, he begins to read to himself in a low tone.*

ARTEMIDORUS *(reading)*. "Caesar, beware of Brutus; take
   heed of Cassius; come not near Casca; have an eye to
   Cinna; trust not Trebonius; mark well Metellus Cimber;
   Decius Brutus loves thee not; thou hast wronged Caius
5 Ligarius. There is but one mind in all these men, and it
   is bent against Caesar. If thou beest not immortal, look
   about you; security gives way to conspiracy.[1] The mighty
   gods defend thee! Thy lover,[2]

                    ARTEMIDORUS."

10 Here will I stand till Caesar pass along,
   And as a suitor will I give him this.
   If thou read this, O Caesar, thou mayst live;
   If not, the Fates with traitors do contrive.

                                      (He exits.)

build suspense; will he get the letter in time

1. *security gives way to conspiracy.* False
confidence makes things easy for conspirators.
2. *lover.* Shakespeare often used this word
to mean "friend."

*Scene 4: Rome. Another part of the same street, before the house of
Brutus.*

*It is now nearly nine o'clock on the morning of the ides of March. Though
it is only a short time since* BRUTUS *left for the Capitol,* PORTIA's *anxiety
has become well-nigh unbearable. She enters the platform at inner-
stage curtains, followed by* LUCIUS, *the serving boy.*

PORTIA. I prithee, boy, run to the Senate-house;
                    (LUCIUS starts to speak, but PORTIA continues.)
   Stay not to answer me, but get thee gone.
                    (LUCIUS looks at her questioningly as she talks on.)
   Why dost thou stay?
LUCIUS *(in bewilderment)*. To know my errand, madam.
PORTIA. I would have had thee there, and here again,
5 Ere I can tell thee what thou shouldst do there.
   O constancy,[1] be strong upon my side;
   Set a huge mountain 'tween my heart and tongue!
   I have a man's mind, but a woman's might.
   How hard it is for women to keep counsel![2]
10 Art thou here yet?
LUCIUS.   Madam, what should I do?
   Run to the Capitol, and nothing else?
PORTIA. Yes, bring me word, boy, if thy lord look well,
   For he went sickly forth; and take good note
   What Caesar doth, what suitors press to him.
15 Hark, boy! What noise is that?[3]
LUCIUS. I hear none, madam.
PORTIA.   Prithee, listen well;
   I heard a bustling rumor, like a fray,[4]
   And the wind brings it from the Capitol.
LUCIUS. Sooth,[5] madam, I hear nothing.

                    (The SOOTHSAYER enters at left.)

1. *O constancy,* O self-control.

2. *to keep counsel,* to keep a secret.

3. *Hark, boy! What noise is that?* Note
Portia's extreme nervousness. What does
this tell you about her knowledge of
Brutus' plans?
4. *like a fray,* like fighting.

5. *Sooth,* short for *in sooth,* or *in truth.*

20 PORTIA (*eagerly*). Come hither, fellow; which way hast thou been?

SOOTHSAYER. At mine own house, good lady.

PORTIA. What is 't o'clock?

SOOTHSAYER.   About the ninth hour, lady.

PORTIA. Is Caesar yet gone to the Capitol?

SOOTHSAYER. Madam, not yet: I go to take my stand,

25 To see him pass on to the Capitol.

PORTIA. Thou hast some suit to Caesar, hast thou not?

SOOTHSAYER. That I have, lady; if it will please Caesar
   To be so good to Caesar as to hear me,
   I shall beseech him to befriend himself.

30 PORTIA. Why, know'st thou any harm's intended toward him?

SOOTHSAYER. None that I know will be, much that I fear may chance.
   Good morrow to you. Here the street is narrow;
   The throng that follows Caesar at the heels,
   Of senators, of praetors, common suitors,

35 Will crowd a feeble man almost to death.
   I'll get me to a place more void, and there
   Speak to great Caesar as he comes along.

(He crosses to right door and exits.)

PORTIA. I must go in. Aye me, how weak a thing
   The heart of woman is! O Brutus,

40 The heavens speed thee in thine enterprise!
   (Aside.) Sure the boy heard me.
   (Speaking breathlessly to LUCIUS.*)*   Brutus hath a suit
   That Caesar will not grant. Oh, I grow faint.
   Run, Lucius, and commend me to my lord;
   Say I am merry; come to me again,

45 And bring me word what he doth say to thee.

*(LUCIUS runs off at right; PORTIA
exits at inner-stage curtains.)*

CONSIDERING
ACT TWO

Scene 1

1. In this scene Brutus delivers several *soliloquies*; that is, he speaks aloud while on the stage alone. (a) What do you think is the purpose of his soliloquies? (b) Judging from them alone, would you say he has completely made up his mind regarding whether or not he will join the conspirators? (c) How does he justify the decision that he reaches?

2. (a) Why does Shakespeare have Brutus uncertain of the exact date? (b) What earlier incident has established this date as being of great importance?

3. The conspirators, while at Brutus' house, make various important decisions. (a) What is their decision concerning Cicero? (b) Concerning Mark Antony? (c) Explain the conspirators' final plan of action.

4. (a) How would you characterize Portia? (b) Do you consider her genuinely devoted to Brutus? Why or why not? (c) Do you blame Brutus for failing to confide in her? Explain your answer.

Scene 2

1. (a) What one question dominates this entire scene? (b) What traits does Caesar display as he wrestles with this problem?

2. (a) One of Caesar's speeches in this scene is very famous. Which one is it? (b) After explaining the meaning of the speech, comment on its truth.

3. (a) Keeping in mind what you learned in Act Two, Scene 1, explain why Decius is the first of the conspirators to arrive at Caesar's house. (b) In what way does Decius show his understanding of Caesar's personality during their conversation?

4. (a) How does Calpurnia compare with Portia as a "noble Roman matron"? (b) Trace her feelings as the argument with Caesar progresses. At what point does she realize that she has lost?

5. (a) Why would the audience be apprehensive about Caesar when, at the end of the scene, the famous Roman calls for his robe and plans to go to the Capitol? (b) What has the dramatist done to make the audience feel this way?

Scenes 3 and 4

1. How does Artemidorus' letter differ from the warnings in earlier scenes?

2. (a) How do you know that Portia now shares Brutus' secret? (b) Do you think she approves of the plot against Caesar? Give reasons for your answer.

3. (a) In what ways does Shakespeare bring out Portia's feverish anxiety? (b) How does she almost give away her secret thought to Lucius?

LOOKING BACK —AND AHEAD

1. Write a brief outline of the events in Act Two and add it to your outline of Act One.

2. What are the three most important things that have happened in this act? Explain.

3. (a) Why do you think Shakespeare introduces Portia and Calpurnia in Act Two? (b) How does each contribute to your interest in the play?

4. How does Shakespeare, in this act, build up an increasing sense of dread and foreboding?

5. Do you see any possible way left open for Caesar to escape death?

THE AUTHOR'S CRAFT

"Piece out our imperfections . . ."
Henry V, I, i

The Globe Playhouse did not have realistic scenery to represent the various localities in *Julius Caesar*. Nor was it customary to provide the playgoers with printed programs outlining the time and place of each scene. It was Shakespeare's task to set his scene in his dialogue.

Assume for a moment that you are attending a performance of *Julius Caesar* at the Globe. You cannot rely upon realistic scenery, a printed program, or the stage directions in your textbook to tell you where and when a scene takes place. What *dialogue clues* does Shakespeare provide in Act One, Scene 1 to tell you that the scene takes place on a street in Rome? Which lines indicate that the scene occurs during the day-time? Cite lines from Act Two, Scene 1 which indicate that this scene takes place early in the morning of the ides of March.

In addition to such verbal clues, Shakespeare employed two *visual devices* to indicate a change of locality. The first visual device is used when one platform scene follows another as they do in Act One. It consists of *emptying* the platform at the conclusion of a scene. How many platform scenes are there in Act One? What different localities do they represent? Do any characters remain on the platform at the conclusion of these scenes? Are there any dead bodies which must be carried off in order to empty the stage? It was unnecessary for Shakespeare to empty the inner and balcony stages in this way, because their front curtains could be drawn closed at the end of a scene.

The second visual device for indicating a change of locality is to use a *different* stage. A shift from the platform (Act One, Scene 3) to the inner stage (Act Two, Scene 1) indicates a change of place. What change of locality takes place when the action shifts to the balcony stage in Act Two?

Shakespeare must have been aware of how much he depended upon the imagination of his audience. In another of his plays, *Henry V*, he asks the playgoers to "piece out our imperfections with your thoughts."

"I will draw a bill of properties..."

Shakespeare does such a masterful job of setting his scenes in the dialogue of *Julius Caesar* that it would be possible to stage the play without special costumes or stage properties. The stage manager at the Globe, however, did have devices for heightening the illusion of reality. What kinds of stage properties did he have and how might they have been used in *Julius Caesar?*

Most of the properties used on the platform were light enough and small enough for the actors to carry on and off as part of their stage business. Backstage at the Globe could be found a large assortment of portable properties —swords and daggers, shields and scrolls, cushions, lutes, dishes, flagons. You have seen Cicero enter with a lantern and Casca with a sword in Act One, Scene 3. Both the sword and the lantern are carried off when Casca exits with Cassius.

Larger and heavier properties were stored in "Hell." Like the rock which will be used in Act Five, Scene 4, these properties were raised onto the platform through the large trap door.

It was possible to create greater scenic effects on the inner stage. Here the walls could be hung with cloth painted to suggest the garden of Act Two or with cloth drab enough to suggest the tent interior of Act Four. Several heavy properties could also be positioned on the inner stage before the curtains were drawn apart. Like the trees and bench of Act Two, Scene 1, these properties were stored backstage or in "Hell" until needed.

Any discussion of Elizabethan staging must take into consideration that Shakespeare's plays were performed in broad daylight. How, then, did the stage manager help Shakespeare create the illusion of night and darkness in *Julius Caesar?* This was done by indicating the need for light; that is, an actor would carry a torch or a lantern, or perhaps light a taper.

Act Three

Scene 1: Rome. Before the Capitol.

*Today—the ides of March—*CAESAR *is to meet with the Senators.* AR-
TEMIDORUS *and the* SOOTHSAYER *enter at left. They are among a crowd
of people who are gathering to honor* CAESAR *upon his arrival at the
Capitol. The crowd bursts into cheers as* CAESAR *enters at right, followed
by* ANTONY, POPILIUS, PUBLIUS, *and the* CONSPIRATORS. CAESAR *advances
until he faces the* SOOTHSAYER; *he speaks to him defiantly.*

CAESAR. The ides of March are come.
SOOTHSAYER. Aye, Caesar; but not gone.

> (CAESAR, *waving the* SOOTHSAYER *aside,
> is approached by* ARTEMIDORUS,
> *who presents his paper.)*

ARTEMIDORUS. Hail, Caesar! Read this schedule.

> (DECIUS *hurries forward and
> pushes* ARTEMIDORUS *aside.)*

DECIUS. Trebonius doth desire you to o'er-read,
5   At your best leisure, this his humble suit.
ARTEMIDORUS. O Caesar, read mine first; for mine's a suit
  That touches Caesar nearer: read it, great Caesar.
CAESAR. What touches us ourself shall be last served.
ARTEMIDORUS. Delay not, Caesar. *(He thrusts his paper in* CAESAR's
  face.) Read it instantly.
10 CAESAR. What, is the fellow mad?

> (PUBLIUS *and* CASSIUS *force* ARTEMIDORUS *aside.)*

PUBLIUS.   Sirrah, give place.
CASSIUS. What, urge you your petitions in the street?
  Come to the Capitol.

> (CASSIUS *points toward the inner stage, where the
> curtains are slowly being drawn apart to reveal the
> interior of the Senate-house. Some Senators are
> already seated on the stage; a statue of Pompey
> stands well forward at left.* CAESAR *moves onto the
> inner stage. He is followed by* ANTONY, PUBLIUS,
> METELLUS, TREBONIUS, *and* CAIUS LIGARIUS.)*

POPILIUS *(passing* CASSIUS). I wish your enterprise today may thrive.
CASSIUS *(innocently).* What enterprise, Popilius?
POPILIUS.   Fare you well. *(He joins* CAESAR.)*
15 BRUTUS *(fearfully).* What said Popilius Lena?
CASSIUS. He wished today our enterprise might thrive.
  I fear our purpose is discovered.
BRUTUS. Look, how he makes to Caesar;[1] mark him.
CASSIUS. Casca, be sudden, for we fear prevention.
20   Brutus, what shall be done? If this be known,
  Cassius or Caesar never shall turn back,
  For I will slay myself.

1. *makes to Caesar*, presses toward Caesar.

BRUTUS (with relief).   Cassius, be constant;
   Popilius Lena speaks not of our purposes;
   For, look, he smiles, and Caesar doth not change.
                         (ANTONY and TREBONIUS leave the inner
                              stage and move off the platform at right.)
25 CASSIUS. Trebonius knows his time; for, look you, Brutus,
   He draws Mark Antony out of the way.
DECIUS. Where is Metellus Cimber? Let him go,
   And presently prefer his suit² to Caesar.
BRUTUS. He is addressed;³ press near and second him.
30 CINNA. Casca, you are the first that rears your hand. —to stab Caesar
                         (BRUTUS, CASSIUS, CASCA, DECIUS, and
                              CINNA cross to the inner stage, where
                              CAESAR is calling the group to order.)
CAESAR. Are we all ready? What is now amiss
   That Caesar and his Senate must redress?
METELLUS. Most high, most mighty, and most puissant Caesar,
   Metellus Cimber throws before thy seat
35   An humble heart——(He falls on his knees.)
CAESAR.   I must prevent thee, Cimber.
   These couchings⁴ and these lowly courtesies
   Might fire the blood of ordinary men,
   And turn preordinance and first decree
   Into the law of children.⁵ Be not fond,⁶
40 To think that Caesar bears such rebel blood
   That will be thawed from the true quality
   With that which melteth fools; I mean, sweet words,
   Low-crooked court'sies and base spaniel-fawning.
· Thy brother⁷ by decree is banishèd;
45 If thou dost bend and pray and fawn for him,
   I spurn thee like a cur out of my way. (He pushes METELLUS aside.)
   Know, Caesar doth not wrong, nor without cause
   Will he be satisfied.
METELLUS. Is there no voice more worthy than my own,
50 To sound more sweetly in great Caesar's ear
   For the repealing of my banished brother?
BRUTUS (kneeling). I kiss thy hand, but not in flattery, Caesar;
   Desiring thee that Publius Cimber may
   Have an immediate freedom of repeal.
55 CAESAR (in surprise). What, Brutus!
CASSIUS (kneeling also).   Pardon, Caesar; Caesar, pardon.
   As low as to thy foot doth Cassius fall,
   To beg enfranchisement for Publius Cimber.⁸
                         (One by one, the other CONSPIRATORS kneel.)
CAESAR. I could be well moved, if I were as you.
   If I could pray to move, prayers would move me;
60 But I am constant as the northern star,
   Of whose true-fixed and resting quality given full rights to vote
   There is no fellow in the firmament.—earth + heavens
   The skies are painted with unnumbered sparks;

2. *prefer his suit*, present his petition.
3. *addressed*, ready.

4. *couchings*, kneelings.

5. *And turn preordinance . . . children*,
and turn established laws and procedures
into the whims of children. Note how
Caesar, as he continues this speech, talks
as if he were a crowned king.

6. *fond*, meaning here "foolish enough."
7. *Thy brother*, Publius Cimber, who had
incurred Caesar's wrath.

8. *To beg enfranchisement* (en fran'chiz-
mənt) . . . *Cimber*, to ask that Publius
Cimber be allowed to return to Rome and
be given again his full rights as a citizen.

They are all fire and every one doth shine;
65 But there's but one in all doth hold his place.
So in the world: 'tis furnished well with men,
And men are flesh and blood, and apprehensive;[9]
Yet in the number I do know but one
That unassailable holds on his rank,
70 Unshaked of motion; and that I am he,
Let me a little show it, even in this;
That I was constant Cimber should be banished,
And constant do remain to keep him so.

CINNA. O Caesar,——

CAESAR.   Hence! Wilt thou lift up Olympus?

75 DECIUS. Great Caesar,——

CAESAR.   Doth not Brutus bootless[10] kneel?

CASCA (leaping to his feet). Speak, hands, for me! (He stabs CAESAR.)

                    (The other CONSPIRATORS, daggers in hand,
                        spring to their feet. They surge forward,
                        and all but BRUTUS stab CAESAR. CAESAR,
                        crying out, tries to ward off the blows
                        until he sees BRUTUS' uplifted dagger; then he
                        covers his face with his cloak and submits.)

CAESAR. Et tu, Brute![11] Then fall, Caesar!

                    (CAESAR staggers forward and dies
                        at the foot of Pompey's statue.)

CINNA (shouting). Liberty! Freedom! Tyranny is dead!
Run hence, proclaim, cry it about the streets.

80 CASSIUS. Some to the common pulpits,[12] and cry out,
"Liberty, freedom, and enfranchisement."

                    (The CONSPIRATORS move onto the platform,
                        where the people stand stock still as if stunned
                        by the sudden attack on CAESAR. Then the
                        crowd, including ARTEMIDORUS and the
                        SOOTHSAYER, begins to flee in panic.)

BRUTUS (calling out). People and senators, be not affrighted;
Fly not; stand still; ambition's debt is paid.

CASCA. Go to the pulpit, Brutus.

DECIUS.   And Cassius, too.

85 BRUTUS. Where's Publius?

CINNA. Here, quite confounded with this mutiny.

METELLUS. Stand fast together, lest some friend of Caesar's
Should chance——

BRUTUS. Talk not of standing. (Extending his hand.) Publius, good cheer;
90 There is no harm intended to your person,
Nor to no Roman else; so tell them, Publius.

CASSIUS. And leave us, Publius; lest that the people,
Rushing on us, should do your age some mischief.

BRUTUS. Do so; and let no man abide this deed[13]
95 But we the doers.

                    (PUBLIUS, accompanied by POPILIUS, moves off
                        at left just as TREBONIUS reënters at right.)

9. *apprehensive*, aware of what is going on.

10. *bootless*, in vain.

11. *Et tu, Brute* (et tü, brü′te), "you, too, Brutus!" [*Latin*] The betrayal completely overwhelms Caesar.

12. *the common pulpits*, the elevated areas in the Forum where public debates were held.

no one else will take responsibility for Caesar's death except us

13. *abide this deed*, answer for this deed.

CASSIUS.   Where is Antony?

TREBONIUS. Fled to his house amazed;
Men, wives, and children stare, cry out, and run
As it were doomsday.

BRUTUS (*resignedly*).   Fates,[14] we will know your pleasures;
That we shall die, we know; 'tis but the time
100   And drawing days out, that men stand upon.[15]

CASSIUS. Why, he that cuts off twenty years of life
Cuts off so many years of fearing death.

BRUTUS. Grant that, and then is death a benefit;
So are we Caesar's friends, that have abridged
105   His time of fearing death. Stoop, Romans, stoop,
And let us bathe our hands in Caesar's blood
Up to the elbows, and besmear our swords;
Then walk we forth, even to the market place,
And, waving our red weapons o'er our heads,
110   Let's all cry, "Peace, freedom, and liberty!"

(*The* CONSPIRATORS *kneel and begin
to dip their hands in* CAESAR's *blood.*)

CASSIUS. Stoop, then, and wash. How many ages hence
Shall this our lofty scene be acted over
In states unborn and accents yet unknown!

BRUTUS. How many times shall Caesar bleed in sport,
115   That now on Pompey's basis[16] lies along
No worthier than the dust!

CASSIUS.   So oft as that shall be,
So often shall the knot of us be called
The men that gave their country liberty.

(*They rise.*)

DECIUS. What, shall we forth?

CASSIUS.   Aye, every man away;
120   Brutus shall lead; and we will grace his heels
With the most boldest and best hearts of Rome.

(*A* SERVANT *of* ANTONY *enters at right.*)

BRUTUS. Soft! Who comes here? A friend of Antony's?

SERVANT (*kneeling*). Thus, Brutus, did my master bid me kneel.
Thus did Mark Antony bid me fall down;
125   And, being prostrate, thus he bade me say:
Brutus is noble, wise, valiant, and honest;
Caesar was mighty, bold, royal, and loving.
Say I love Brutus, and I honor him;
Say I feared Caesar, honored him, and loved him.
130   If Brutus will vouchsafe that Antony
May safely come to him, and be resolved[17]
How Caesar hath deserved to lie in death,
Mark Antony shall not love Caesar dead
So well as Brutus living, but will follow
.135   The fortunes and affairs of noble Brutus
Through the hazards of this untrod state[18]   .
With all true faith. So says my master Antony.

14. *Fates*, the three goddesses who were thought to control human destinies.

15. *stand upon*, are concerned with.

16. *on Pompey's basis*, at the foot of Pompey's statue.

17. *be resolved*, have it explained to him.

18. *Through the hazards of this untrod state*, through all the uncertainties and dangers of this new and unfamiliar state of affairs.

BRUTUS. Thy master is a wise and valiant Roman;
I never thought him worse.
140 Tell him, so please him come unto this place,
He shall be satisfied; and by my honor,
Depart untouched.
SERVANT.   I'll fetch him presently. (SERVANT *exits.*)
BRUTUS. I know that we shall have him well to friend.
CASSIUS. I wish we may; but yet have I a mind
145 That fears him much; and my misgiving still
Falls shrewdly to the purpose.[19]

(ANTONY, *reëntering at right,
strides toward* CAESAR's *body.*)

BRUTUS. But here comes Antony. Welcome, Mark Antony.
ANTONY (*ignoring* BRUTUS). O mighty Caesar! Dost thou lie so low?
Are all thy conquests, glories, triumphs, spoils,
150 Shrunk to this little measure? Fare thee well.
(*To the* CONSPIRATORS.) I know not, gentlemen, what you intend,
Who else must be let blood, who else is rank;[20]
If I myself, there is no hour so fit
As Caesar's death hour, nor no instrument
155 Of half that worth as those your swords, made rich
With the most noble blood of all this world.
I do beseech ye, if you bear me hard,
Now, whilst your purpled hands do reek and smoke,
Fulfill your pleasure. Live a thousand years,
160 I shall not find myself so apt[21] to die;
No place will please me so, no mean[22] of death,
As here by Caesar, and by you cut off,
The choice and master spirits of this age.
BRUTUS (*disturbed*). O Antony, beg not your death of us.
165 Though now we must appear bloody and cruel,
As, by our hands and this our present act,
You see we do, yet see you but our hands
And this the bleeding business they have done;
Our hearts you see not; they are pitiful;
170 And pity to the general wrong of Rome—
As fire drives out fire, so pity pity—[23]
Hath done this deed on Caesar. For your part,
To you our swords have leaden points, Mark Antony;
Our arms in strength of malice, and our hearts
175 Of brothers' temper, do receive you in
With all kind love, good thoughts, and reverence.
CASSIUS. Your voice shall be as strong as any man's
In the disposing of new dignities.
BRUTUS. Only be patient till we have appeased
180 The multitude, beside themselves with fear,
And then we will deliver you the cause,
Why I, that did love Caesar when I struck him,
Have thus proceeded.
ANTONY (*extending his hand*). I doubt not of your wisdom.

19. *my misgiving . . . purpose.* Cassius'
suspicions usually are justified.

20. *Who else must . . . rank*, who else
must be destroyed.

21. *apt*, ready.
22. *mean*, method.

23. *so pity pity*, so pity for the wrongs
Rome has endured from Caesar over-
shadows pity for Caesar's death.

Let each man render me his bloody hand;
185 First, Marcus Brutus, will I shake with you;
Next, Caius Cassius, do I take your hand;
Now, Decius Brutus, yours; now, yours, Metellus;
Yours, Cinna; and, my valiant Casca, yours;
Though last, not least in love, yours, good Trebonius.
190 Gentlemen all—alas, what shall I say?
My credit now stands on such slippery ground
That one of two bad ways you must conceit[24] me,
Either a coward or a flatterer.
(*Addressing* CAESAR's *body.*) That I did love thee, Caesar,
Oh, 'tis true;
195 If then thy spirit look upon us now,
Shall it not grieve thee dearer than thy death,
To see thy Antony making his peace,
Shaking the bloody fingers of thy foes,
Most noble! in the presence of thy corse?[25]
200 Had I as many eyes as thou hast wounds,
Weeping as fast as they stream forth thy blood,
It would become me better than to close
In terms of friendship with thine enemies.
Pardon me, Julius! Here wast thou bayed, brave hart;
205 Here didst thou fall; and here thy hunters stand,
Signed in thy spoil, and crimsoned in thy lethe.[26]
O world, thou wast the forest to this hart;
And this, indeed, O world, the heart of thee.
How like a deer, strucken by many princes,
210 Dost thou here lie!
CASSIUS (*sharply*). Mark Antony——
ANTONY.   Pardon me, Caius Cassius;
The enemies of Caesar shall say this;
Then, in a friend, it is cold modesty.
CASSIUS. I blame you not for praising Caesar so;
215 But what compact mean you to have with us?
Will you be pricked in number of our friends;[27]
Or shall we on, and not depend on you?
ANTONY. Therefore I took your hands, but was, indeed,
Swayed from the point, by looking down on Caesar.
220 Friends am I with you all and love you all,
Upon this hope, that you shall give me reasons
Why and wherein Caesar was dangerous.
BRUTUS. Or else were this a savage spectacle;
Our reasons are so full of good regard[28]
225 That were you, Antony, the son of Caesar,
You should be satisfied.
ANTONY.   That's all I seek;
And am moreover suitor that I may
Produce his body to the market place;
And in the pulpit, as becomes a friend,
230 Speak in the order of his funeral.

24. *conceit*, consider.

25. *corse*, corpse.

26. *lethe* (lē′thi), death.

27. *pricked in number of our friends*, numbered among our friends.

28. *so full of good regard*, so full of merit.

BRUTUS. You shall, Mark Antony.

CASSIUS *(very much disturbed).*   Brutus, a word with you.
(Taking BRUTUS *aside.)* You know not what you do; do not consent
That Antony speak in his funeral.
Know you how much the people may be moved
35 By that which he will utter?

BRUTUS.   By your pardon;
I will myself into the pulpit first,
And show the reason of our Caesar's death;
What Antony shall speak, I will protest
He speaks by leave and by permission,
40 And that we are contented Caesar shall
Have all true rites and lawful ceremonies.
It shall advantage more than do us wrong.

CASSIUS *(dubiously).* I know not what may fall; I like it not.

                    (BRUTUS *and* CASSIUS *rejoin* ANTONY *and the others.)*

BRUTUS. Mark Antony, here, take you Caesar's body.
45 You shall not in your funeral speech blame us,
But speak all good you can devise of Caesar,
And say you do 't by our permission;
Else shall you not have any hand at all
About his funeral; and you shall speak
50 In the same pulpit whereto I am going,
After my speech is ended.

ANTONY.   Be it so;
I do desire no more.

BRUTUS. Prepare the body then, and follow us.

                    (The CONSPIRATORS *follow* BRUTUS *out at right.*
                    ANTONY *stands looking at* CAESAR; *then he slowly*
                        covers the body with the dead man's cloak.)

ANTONY. Oh, pardon me, thou bleeding piece of earth,
55 That I am meek and gentle with these butchers!
Thou are the ruins of the noblest man
That ever livèd in the tide of times.
Woe to the hand that shed this costly blood!
Over thy wounds now do I prophesy—
60 Which, like dumb mouths, do ope their ruby lips,
To beg the voice and utterance of my tongue—
A curse shall light upon the limbs of men;
Domestic fury and fierce civil strife
Shall cumber all the parts of Italy;
65 Blood and destruction shall be so in use
And dreadful objects so familiar
That mothers shall but smile when they behold
Their infants quartered with the hands of war;
All pity choked with custom of fell deeds;
70 And Caesar's spirit, ranging for revenge,
With Ate[29] by his side come hot from hell,
Shall in these confines with a monarch's voice
Cry "Havoc,"[30] and let slip the dogs of war,[31]

29. *Ate* (ā′ti), the Greek goddess of
vengeance.
30. *Cry "Havoc."* This cry, which could
be given only by a king, was a command
which meant "Kill all! Take no prisoners."
31. *let slip the dogs of war,* let loose the
dogs of war—fire, sword, and famine.

That this foul deed shall smell above the earth
275   With carrion men, groaning for burial.

                         (A SERVANT *enters at left.)*

    You serve Octavius Caesar, do you not?

SERVANT. I do, Mark Antony.

ANTONY. Caesar did write for him to come to Rome.

SERVANT. He did receive his letters, and is coming;
280   And bid me say to you by word of mouth——*(He sees the body.)*
    O Caesar!

ANTONY. Thy heart is big, get thee apart and weep.
    Passion, I see, is catching; for mine eyes,
    Seeing those beads of sorrow stand in thine,
285   Began to water. Is thy master coming?

SERVANT. He lies tonight within seven leagues[32] of Rome.

ANTONY. Post back with speed and tell him what hath chanced;
    Here is a mourning Rome, a dangerous Rome,
    No Rome of safety for Octavius yet;
290   Hie hence, and tell him so. *(The* SERVANT *starts to leave.)* Yet, stay
      awhile;
    Thou shalt not back till I have borne this corse
    Into the market place;[33] there shall I try,
    In my oration, how the people take
    The cruel issue of these bloody men;
295   According to the which, thou shalt discourse
    To young Octavius of the state of things.
    Lend me your hand.

                  (While ANTONY *and the* SERVANT *carry*
              CAESAR'*s body off at right door, the curtains*
                      of the inner stage are drawn closed.)

Scene 2: Rome. The Forum.

BRUTUS *and* CASSIUS, *with groups of indignant* CITIZENS *at their heels,
enter at left. The* CITIZENS *are clamoring for an explanation of* CAESAR'*s
assassination. It is apparent from their threatening gestures and shouts
that the people will become violent unless* BRUTUS *speaks to them. He
does so from the balcony, which represents a raised pulpit in this scene.*

CITIZENS *(angrily).* We will be satisfied; let us be satisfied.

BRUTUS. Then follow me, and give me audience, friends.
    Cassius, go you into the other street,
    And part the numbers.[1]
5   *(Loudly.)* Those that will hear me speak, let 'em stay here;
    Those that will follow Cassius, go with him;
    And public reasons shall be rendered
    Of Caesar's death.

                *(*BRUTUS *exits at inner-stage curtains*
                    in order to ascend the pulpit.)

32. *within seven leagues,* within twenty-one miles.

33. *the market place,* meaning here the Forum.

1. *part the numbers,* divide the crowd.

FIRST CITIZEN. I will hear Brutus speak.

SECOND CITIZEN. I will hear Cassius; and compare their reasons,

When severally[2] we hear them rendered.

2. *severally*, separately.

(CASSIUS *moves off at right, accompanied by various* CITIZENS *who clamor loudly.* BRUTUS *appears above at the balcony railing.*)

THIRD CITIZEN. The noble Brutus is ascended; silence!

BRUTUS (*speaking earnestly*). Be patient till the last. (*Pause.*) Romans, countrymen, and lovers!

(*There are shouts from the mob.*)

Hear me for my cause, and be silent, that you may hear; believe me for mine honor, and have respect to mine honor, that you may believe; censure me in your wisdom, and awake your senses, that you may the better judge. If there be any in this assembly, any dear friend of Caesar's, to him I say, that Brutus' love to Caesar was no less than his. If then that friend demand why Brutus rose against Caesar, this is my answer: Not that I loved Caesar less, but that I loved Rome more. Had you rather Caesar were living and die all slaves, than that Caesar were dead, to live all free men? As Caesar loved me, I weep for him; as he was fortunate, I rejoice at it; as he was valiant, I honor him; but, as he was ambitious, I slew him. There is tears for his love; joy for his fortune; honor for his valor; and death for his ambition. Who is here so base that would be a bondman? If any, speak; for him have I offended. Who is here so rude that would not be a Roman? If any, speak; for him I have offended. Who is here so vile that will not love his country? If any, speak; for him have I offended. I pause for a reply.

ALL (*shouting*). None, Brutus, none.

BRUTUS. Then none have I offended. I have done no more to Caesar than you shall do to Brutus. The question of his death is enrolled[3] in the Capitol; his glory not extenuated,[4] wherein he was worthy, nor his offenses enforced, for which he suffered death.

3. *The question of his death is enrolled*, the reason for Caesar's death is recorded.
4. *his glory not extenuated* (eks ten′ū ātəd), his fame has not been detracted from because of the manner of his dying.

(ANTONY *enters at left. Behind him come* ATTENDANTS *carrying* CAESAR's *bier.*)

Here comes his body, mourned by Mark Antony; who, though he had no hand in his death, shall receive the benefit of his dying, a place in the commonwealth; as which of you shall not? With this I depart—that, as I slew my best lover for the good of Rome, I have the same dagger for myself, when it shall please my country to need my death.

ALL (*shouting*). Live, Brutus! Live, live!

(BRUTUS *exits at balcony curtains in order to descend from the pulpit.*)

FIRST CITIZEN. Bring him with triumph home unto his house.

SECOND CITIZEN. Give him a statue with his ancestors.

THIRD CITIZEN. Let him be Caesar.

FOURTH CITIZEN. Caesar's better parts

Shall be crowned in Brutus.

FIRST CITIZEN. We'll bring him to his house

With shouts and clamors.

(The mob greets BRUTUS *with cheers as he reënters the platform at inner-stage curtains.)*

BRUTUS. My countrymen——

(The crowd cheers wildly.)

SECOND CITIZEN *(shouting)*. Peace, silence! Brutus speaks.

FIRST CITIZEN.   Peace, ho!

50 BRUTUS. Good countrymen, let me depart alone.
And, for my sake, stay here with Antony.
Do grace to Caesar's corpse, and grace his speech
Tending to Caesar's glories; which Mark Antony,
By our permission, is allowed to make.
55 I do entreat you, not a man depart
Save I alone, till Antony have spoke.

(He exits alone at right.)

FIRST CITIZEN. Stay, ho! And let us hear Mark Antony.
THIRD CITIZEN. Let him go up into the public chair;
We'll hear him. Noble Antony, go up.

(There are murmurs from the mob.)

60 ANTONY. For Brutus' sake, I am beholding to you.

*(*ANTONY *exits at inner-stage curtains in order to ascend the pulpit. His* ATTENDANTS, *meanwhile, have placed* CAESAR's *body well forward on platform.)*

FOURTH CITIZEN. What does he say of Brutus?
THIRD CITIZEN.   He says for Brutus' sake,
He finds himself beholding to us all.
FOURTH CITIZEN. 'Twere best he speak no harm of Brutus here.
FIRST CITIZEN. This Caesar was a tyrant.
THIRD CITIZEN.   Nay, that's certain;
65 We are blest that Rome is rid of him.

*(*ANTONY *appears above at the balcony railing.)*

SECOND CITIZEN. Peace! Let us hear what Antony can say.
ANTONY. You gentle Romans——

(The crowd is not yet quiet.)

CITIZENS.   Peace, ho! Let us hear him.
ANTONY. Friends, Romans, countrymen, lend me your ears;
I come to bury Caesar, not to praise him.
70 The evil that men do lives after them;
The good is oft interred with their bones;
So let it be with Caesar. The noble Brutus
Hath told you Caesar was ambitious;
If it were so, it was a grievous fault,
75 And grievously hath Caesar answered it.
Here, under leave of Brutus and the rest——

(The mob murmurs angrily.)

For Brutus is an honorable man;[5]
So are they all, all honorable men—
Come I to speak in Caesar's funeral.
80 He was my friend, faithful and just to me;
But Brutus says he was ambitious;

5. *Brutus is an honorable man.* The crowd's anger at words against Brutus makes Antony quick to express his admiration for the absent Roman—and for the other conspirators.

And Brutus is an honorable man.[6]
He[7] hath brought many captives home to Rome,
Whose ransoms did the general coffers fill;[8]
Did this in Caesar seem ambitious?
When that the poor have cried, Caesar hath wept.
Ambition should be made of sterner stuff; *a tyrant should be meaner*
Yet Brutus said he was ambitious,
And Brutus is an honorable man.[9]
You all did see that on the Lupercal
I thrice presented him a kingly crown,
Which he did thrice refuse; was this ambition?
Yet Brutus says he was ambitious;
And, sure, he is an honorable man.
I speak not to disprove what Brutus spoke,
But here I am to speak what I do know.
You all did love him once, not without cause;
What cause withholds you, then, to mourn for him?
O judgment! Thou art fled to brutish beasts,
And men have lost their reason.[10] *(He pauses.)* Bear with me;
My heart is in the coffin there[11] with Caesar,
And I must pause till it come back to me. *(He weeps openly.)*
FIRST CITIZEN *(soberly)*. Methinks there is much reason in his sayings.
SECOND CITIZEN. If thou consider rightly of the matter,
Caesar has had great wrong.
THIRD CITIZEN.   Has he, masters?
I fear there will a worse come in his place.
FOURTH CITIZEN. Marked ye his words? He would not take the crown;
Therefore 'tis certain he was not ambitious.
FIRST CITIZEN. If it be found so, some will dear abide[12] it.
SECOND CITIZEN. Poor soul! His eyes are red as fire with weeping.
THIRD CITIZEN. There's not a nobler man in Rome than Antony.
FOURTH CITIZEN *(pointing)*. Now mark him, he begins again to
     speak.
ANTONY. But yesterday the word of Caesar might
Have stood against the world; now lies he there,
And none so poor to do him reverence.
O masters, if I were disposed to stir
Your hearts and minds to mutiny and rage,
I should do Brutus wrong, and Cassius wrong,
Who, you all know, are honorable men:[13]
                    (There is derisive laughter from the mob.)
I will not do them wrong; I rather choose
To wrong the dead, to wrong myself and you,
Than I will wrong such honorable men. *(He pulls a scroll from his
     garment.)*
But here's a parchment with the seal of Caesar;
I found it in his closet, 'tis his will:
Let but the commons hear this testament—
Which, pardon me, I do not mean to read—
And they would go and kiss dead Caesar's wounds

6. *Brutus is an honorable man.* Note the tinge of irony. Remember Antony has promised to speak no harm of the conspirators. Is he really keeping his promise?
7. *He,* Caesar.
8. *the general coffers fill.* Caesar hadn't kept the ransom money for himself.

9. *Brutus is an honorable man.* Note how sarcasm begins to creep into the repetition of these words.

10. *And men have lost their reason.* Here Antony is overcome with grief and finds himself unable to go on. Do you think he realizes the effectiveness of this pause? Are his tears genuine?
11. *in the coffin there.* Here is another anachronism. The Romans did not use coffins; they cremated their dead.

12. *abide,* pay for.

13. *honorable men.* Note Antony's mounting sarcasm.

And dip their napkins[14] in his sacred blood,
Yea, beg a hair of him for memory,
130 And, dying, mention it within their wills,
Bequeathing it as a rich legacy
Unto their issue.
FOURTH CITIZEN. We'll hear the will; read it, Mark Antony.
ALL *(shouting)*. The will, the will! We will hear Caesar's will.
135 ANTONY. Have patience, gentle friends, I must not read it;
It is not meet you know how Caesar loved you. *(He puts the will away.)*
You are not wood, you are not stones, but men;
And, being men, hearing the will of Caesar,
It will inflame you, it will make you mad.
(There are cries of "No! No!")
140 'Tis good you know not that you are his heirs;
For, if you should, Oh, what would come of it!
FOURTH CITIZEN. Read the will; we'll hear it, Antony.
(There are cries of "Yes! Yes!")
You shall read us the will, Caesar's will.
ANTONY. Will you be patient? Will you stay awhile?
145 I have o'ershot myself[15] to tell you of it.
I fear I wrong the honorable men
Whose daggers have stabbed Caesar; I do fear it.
(There are angry shouts from the mob.)
FOURTH CITIZEN. They were traitors; *(sarcastically)* honorable men!
ALL *(clamoring)*. The will! The testament!
150 SECOND CITIZEN. They were villains, murderers; the will!
Read the will.
(There are cries of "Read! Read!")
ANTONY. You will compel me, then, to read the will?
Then make a ring about the corpse of Caesar,
And let me show you him that made the will.
155 Shall I descend? And will you give me leave?
SEVERAL CITIZENS. Come down.
SECOND CITIZEN. Descend.
THIRD CITIZEN. You shall have leave.
*(ANTONY exits at balcony curtains in order to descend
from the pulpit; the crowd circles CAESAR's body.)*
FOURTH CITIZEN. A ring; stand round.
160 FIRST CITIZEN. Stand from the hearse,[16] stand from the body.
*(The crowd moves back, opening the
ring, when ANTONY reënters the platform.)*
SECOND CITIZEN. Room for Antony, most noble Antony.
ANTONY. Nay, press not so upon me; stand far off.
SEVERAL CITIZENS. Stand back; room; bear back!
ANTONY. If you have tears, prepare to shed them now.
165 You all do know this mantle. *(Pointing to CAESAR's cloak.)* I remember
The first time Caesar ever put it on;
'Twas on a summer evening, in his tent,
That day he overcame the Nervii;[17]

14. *napkins,* handkerchiefs.

15. *I have o'ershot myself.* Antony has said more than he intended, or pretends he has.

16. *hearse,* bier.

17. *Nervii* (nèr′vi ī), the most warlike of the tribes of Gaul. Caesar led the decisive charge against them in person.

Look, in this place ran Cassius' dagger through;
170　See what a rent the envious Casca made;
Through this the well-beloved Brutus stabbed,[18]
And as he plucked his cursèd steel away,
Mark how the blood of Caesar followed it,
As rushing out of doors, to be resolved
175　If Brutus so unkindly knocked, or no;
For Brutus, as you know, was Caesar's angel;
Judge, O you gods, how dearly Caesar loved him!
This was the most unkindest cut of all;
For when the noble Caesar saw him stab,
180　Ingratitude, more strong than traitor's arms,
Quite vanquished him; then burst his mighty heart;
And, in his mantle muffling up his face,
Even at the base of Pompey's statuë,
Which all the while ran blood, great Caesar fell.
185　Oh, what a fall was there, my countrymen!
Then I, and you, and all of us fell down,
Whilst bloody treason flourished over us.
Oh, now you weep; and, I perceive, you feel
The dint[19] of pity; these are gracious drops.
190　Kind souls, what, weep you when you but behold
Our Caesar's vesture wounded?[20] (He flings CAESAR's cloak aside.)
　　Look you here!
Here is himself, marred as you see, with traitors.
　　　　　(The CITIZENS cry out in horror.)

FIRST CITIZEN. O piteous spectacle!
SECOND CITIZEN. O noble Caesar!
195　THIRD CITIZEN. O woeful day!
FOURTH CITIZEN. O traitors, villains!
FIRST CITIZEN. O most bloody sight!
SECOND CITIZEN. We will be revenged.
ALL (shouting). Revenge! About! Seek! Burn! Fire! Kill! Slay!
200　Let not a traitor live! (They start to leave.)
ANTONY (commandingly). Stay, countrymen.
FIRST CITIZEN. Peace there! Hear the noble Antony.
SECOND CITIZEN. We'll hear him, we'll follow him, we'll die with him.
　　　　　(The mob returns to ANTONY.)
ANTONY. Good friends, sweet friends, let me not stir you up
205　To such a sudden flood of mutiny.
They that have done this deed are honorable;
What private griefs[21] they have, alas, I know not,
That made them do it; they are wise and honorable,
And will, no doubt, with reasons answer you.
210　I come not, friends, to steal away your hearts;[22]
I am no orator, as Brutus is,
But, as you know me all, a plain, blunt man,
That love my friend; and that they know full well
That gave me public leave to speak of him;[23]
215　For I have neither wit, nor words, nor worth,

18. *Through this . . . Brutus stabbed.*
Could Antony possibly have known which
cut Brutus made?

19. *dint*, effect.

20. *Caesar's vesture wounded*, the rents
in Caesar's clothing.

21. *private griefs*, personal reasons.

22. *I come not . . . hearts.* Is Antony
sincere here?

23. *public leave to speak of him*, permission
to speak of him in public.

Action, nor utterance, nor the power of speech,
To stir men's blood; I only speak right on;[24]
I tell you that which you yourselves do know;
Show you sweet Caesar's wounds, poor, poor, dumb mouths,
220 And bid them speak for me. But were I Brutus,
And Brutus Antony, there were an Antony
Would ruffle up your spirits and put a tongue
In every wound of Caesar that should move
The stones of Rome to rise and mutiny.

         (The excitement of the mob is at fever pitch.
         They are nearly uncontrollable and shout wildly.)

225 ALL. We'll mutiny!
FIRST CITIZEN. We'll burn the house of Brutus!
THIRD CITIZEN. Away, then! Come, seek the conspirators!

         (Again the mob starts to leave.)

ANTONY. Yet hear me, countrymen; yet hear me speak.
ALL *(turning)*. Peace, ho! Hear Antony. Most noble Antony!
230 ANTONY. Why, friends, you go to do you know not what;
Wherein hath Caesar thus deserved your loves?
Alas, you know not; I must tell you then:
You have forgot the will I told you of. *(He takes the will from his*
    garment.)
ALL *(returning to him)*. Most true. The will! Let's stay and hear the will.
235 ANTONY *(showing it)*. Here is the will, and under Caesar's seal. *(He*
        breaks the seal, unrolls the scroll, and reads.)
To every Roman citizen he gives,
To every several[25] man, seventy-five drachmas.[26]

         (The mob murmurs its approval.)

SECOND CITIZEN. Most noble Caesar! We'll revenge his death.
THIRD CITIZEN. O royal Caesar!
240 ANTONY. Hear me with patience.
ALL. Peace, ho!
ANTONY. Moreover, he hath left you all his walks,
His private arbors and new-planted orchards,
On this side Tiber; he hath left them you,
245 And to your heirs forever, common pleasures,
To walk abroad, and recreate yourselves.
Here was a Caesar! When comes such another?
FIRST CITIZEN. Never, never! Come, away, away!
We'll burn his body in the holy place,
250 And with the brands fire the traitors' houses!
Take up the body!

         (A group of CITIZENS take up CAESAR's bier.)

SECOND CITIZEN. Go fetch fire!
THIRD CITIZEN. Pluck down benches!
FOURTH CITIZEN. Pluck down forms,[27] windows, anything!

         (The CITIZENS, bearing CAESAR's
        body aloft, exit at right door.)

255 ANTONY. Now let it work. Mischief, thou art afoot;
Take thou what course thou wilt!

24. *right on*, openly; frankly.

25. *several*, separate; individual.
26. *seventy-five drachmas* (drak′məz).
Authorities disagree in estimating this
amount; some say as little as $10 a per-
son; others, as much as $100. Whatever
the exact amount, we must remember
that the purchasing power of the money
was far greater in Caesar's time than
today.

27. *forms*, public benches.

(*A* SERVANT *of* OCTAVIUS CAESAR *enters at left.*)
How now, fellow!

SERVANT. Sir, Octavius is already come to Rome.

ANTONY. Where is he?

SERVANT. He and Lepidus are at Caesar's house.

260 ANTONY. And thither will I straight to visit him.
He comes upon a wish. Fortune is merry,—good turn of luck
And in this mood will give us anything.

SERVANT. I heard him say, Brutus and Cassius
Are rid[28] like madmen through the gates of Rome.

265 ANTONY. Belike they had some notice of the people,
How I had moved them. Bring me to Octavius.

(ANTONY *leads his* ATTENDANTS *and
the* SERVANT *out at left door.*)

28. *Are rid*, have ridden. Brutus and Cassius are fleeing before the wrath of the mob.

CONSIDERING ACT THREE

Scene 1

1. (a) After Caesar appears at the Capitol, what incidents cause the conspirators to fear that their plans may go wrong? (b) How do they show alertness in warding off these dangers?

2. (a) What is your final opinion of Caesar in this scene? (b) Why are his dying words especially dramatic? (c) Do you think that he was afraid to die?

3. (a) What urgent problem do the assassins face immediately after stabbing Caesar? (b) Which of them assumes the leadership in attacking that problem? (c) State briefly his argument of justification for Caesar's murder.

4. Which of the following statements best sums up the impression that Antony wishes to make on the conspirators? And which of them represents his true feelings?

(a) Although I loved Caesar, I admire Brutus greatly and will follow him unquestioningly.

(b) I intend to arouse the fury of the people against the butchers of Caesar.

(c) I loved Caesar; I admire Brutus; I am willing to be friendly with the conspirators once I understand why they considered Caesar dangerous.

5. (a) Why is Cassius worried by Brutus' promise to allow Mark Antony to speak at Caesar's funeral? (b) Why is Brutus willing for Antony to do so?

6. What does Shakespeare foreshadow in the final speeches of this scene?

Scene 2

1. Because the crowd is so great, Brutus asks some of the people to go into "the other street" and hear Cassius speak there. Why do you think Shakespeare does not include Cassius' speech in this play?

2. (a) In his speech, does Brutus appeal principally to the people's intellect or emotions? (b) Quote the parts of his speech that you think best explain why the conspirators killed Caesar. (c) How do the citizens' comments show that they have missed the entire point of Brutus' speech?

3. As Mark Antony ascends the pulpit, the citizens are still shouting. (a) From their remarks what do you learn about their present feelings toward Brutus? (b) Toward the dead Caesar? (c) If Antony is to change those feelings, he must choose his words carefully. Cite what you consider the best examples of his skill in using words that play on the emotions of his audience.

4. (a) Why is Antony's pause where he stops to look at Caesar's body (page 309, line 100) effective? (b) Why doesn't he read Caesar's will when he first mentions it? (c) How does he almost miss the chance to read it at all? (d) In what way does he appeal to the morbid curiosity of the crowd? (e) Do you think crowds of today sometimes exhibit a similar morbid curiosity? If so, cite some examples.

LOOKING BACK —AND AHEAD

1. Continue your outline of the play, listing the most important events that take place in Act Three.

2. In Act Three we see Brutus assuming leadership of the anti-Caesar forces. Keeping in mind what you have learned about him in this act, answer the following questions. Explain why you decided as you did.

(a) Does Brutus really regard Caesar as being a dangerous man as far as Roman liberties are concerned?

(b) Is Brutus respected by both the pro-Caesar and the anti-Caesar forces?

(c) Does Brutus show self-confidence in his acts?

(d) Is he aware of the dangers of trusting men less sincere than himself?

(e) Is he capable of judging the common people accurately?

3. (a) What qualities of leadership does Mark Antony possess? (b) Which of them do you consider most important?

4. (a) What is Mark Antony's attitude toward the future as Act Three comes to an end? (b) Do you think his expectations will be met? Explain your answer.

Macbeth, V, v

"his hour upon the stage"

Two great
tragedians
of the
Elizabethan
stage—
Edward Alleyn
(left) and
Richard Burbage
(right)

Shakespeare was an actor as well as a playwright. He must have been a competent performer, for in 1594 he was a member of the Lord Chamberlain's Company—one of the principal acting companies of the time.

The acting companies usually consisted of ten or twelve adult actors and six boy apprentices. All of the women's rôles in Elizabethan plays were performed by the apprentices. The patronage of an important nobleman, like the Lord Chamberlain of England, protected the actors from London authorities who wished to suppress the playhouses. What particular abilities did an actor possess to qualify for membership in an Elizabethan acting company?

The prime requisite must have been a resonant speaking voice. From his personal experience, Shakespeare undoubtedly learned to value dialogue that could be spoken rapidly, yet clearly. In addition, an actor had to be a singer and musician. Since most Elizabethan plays featured songs, an actor was frequently assigned a rôle, like the rôle of Lucius in *Julius Caesar*, which required him to sing and play a musical instrument.

Plays of the period also featured numerous duels and mock battles. The daggers, swords, and rapiers used in these scenes were sharp, not blunted weapons. To avoid injury, an actor had to be a competent swordsman. Some plays demanded that he be an acrobat as well!

An Elizabethan actor also possessed an astonishing memory. As many as forty plays were given during a single season, but an actor might memorize eighty rôles. The practice of *doubling*, that is, of performing two or more rôles in a single play, was typical of the Elizabethan stage. Most acting companies had only eighteen people to enact, for example, the thirty or more speaking parts in *Julius Caesar*. Extra actors could be hired, but the problem was largely solved through doubling. Thus the actor who portrayed Flavius in Act One of *Julius Caesar* might also have portrayed Artemidorus in Acts Two and Three and Octavius in Acts Four and Five.

If an actor performed well, the audience applauded; if not, they pelted him with apple cores. An actor who strutted "his hour upon the stage" was paid out of the penny admissions which were charged to enter the playhouse. If he was a part-owner of the playhouse, as Shakespeare was, he also shared in the gallery admissions.

Act Four

Scene 1: A house in Rome.

For many months after Caesar's death in March, 44 B.C., chaos has reigned in Rome. The leading conspirators have fled eastward to Greece and Asia Minor. Mark Antony has attempted to make himself virtual dictator of Rome, but has been opposed by young Octavius Caesar, the grandnephew and political heir of Julius Caesar; and a devastating civil war has broken out. In October, 43 B.C., Antony and Octavius agree to combine forces, and invite M. Aemilius Lepidus, one of Julius Caesar's former lieutenants, to join them in forming the second triumvirate. Together they will control Rome—and rule the world.

The scene begins as the curtains of the balcony stage are drawn apart to reveal ANTONY, OCTAVIUS, *and* LEPIDUS *seated around a table. They are scrutinizing a wax tablet which lists the names of those Romans who might oppose them. The three men are making plans to crush all opposition to their scheme.*

ANTONY. These many, then, shall die; their names are pricked.[1] —cold blooded, heartless

OCTAVIUS. Your brother, too, must die; consent you, Lepidus?

LEPIDUS. I do consent——

OCTAVIUS.   Prick him down, Antony.

LEPIDUS. Upon condition Publius shall not live,

5   Who is your sister's son, Mark Antony.

ANTONY (*picking up the stylus*). He shall not live; look, with a spot I
    damn him.[2]

    But, Lepidus, go you to Caesar's house;

    Fetch the will hither, and we shall determine

    How to cut off some charge in legacies.[3]

10 LEPIDUS. What, shall I find you here?

OCTAVIUS. Or here, or at the Capitol.

                        (LEPIDUS *leaves at the door in
                        the rear wall of the balcony stage.*)

ANTONY. This is a slight, unmeritable man,

    Meet to be sent on errands; is it fit,

    The threefold world divided, he should stand

15   One of the three to share it?

OCTAVIUS.   So you thought him;

    And took his voice who should be pricked to die,

    In our black sentence and proscription.[4]

ANTONY. Octavius, I have seen more days than you;

    And though we lay these honors on this man,

20   To ease ourselves of divers sland'rous loads,

    He shall but bear them as the ass bears gold,

    To groan and sweat under the business,

    Either led or driven, as we point the way;

    And having brought our treasure where we will,

1. *These many . . . pricked.* With a needle, knife, or stylus the list of the names of many men has been marked.

2. *with a spot I damn him.* The puncture condemns him to death.

3. *we shall determine . . . legacies.* Antony wishes to find a way to reduce the amount Caesar has bequeathed each Roman. Here Antony reveals himself as a grafter.

4. *our black sentence and proscription,* the list indicating those condemned to death.

25   Then take we down his load, and turn him off,
      Like to the empty ass, to shake his ears,
      And graze in commons.[5]
      OCTAVIUS.   You may do your will;
      But he's a tried and valiant soldier.
      ANTONY. So is my horse. And now, Octavius,
30   Listen great things: Brutus and Cassius
      Are levying powers; we must straight make head;[6]
      Therefore let our alliance be combined,
      Our best friends made, our means stretched,
      And let us presently go sit in council,
35   How covert matters may be best disclosed,
      And open perils surest answered.[7]
      OCTAVIUS. Let us do so; for we are at the stake,[8]
      And bayed about with many enemies;
      And some that smile have in their hearts, I fear,
40   Millions of mischiefs.

                    (As ANTONY and OCTAVIUS exit, the curtains
                      of the balcony stage are drawn closed.)

*Scene 2: Brutus' camp at Sardis, a city in Asia Minor. Before Brutus'
tent.*

*Several months have passed since the members of the second triumvirate
made their plans. Far from Rome,* BRUTUS *awaits the arrival of* CASSIUS,
whose actions have so troubled BRUTUS *that he has asked him here for
a conference.*

  The scene begins as LUCIUS *enters the platform at inner-stage curtains. He then draws the curtains aside, revealing the interior of* BRUTUS'
*tent. The interior is sparsely furnished with a table, some low stools,
and a few cushions.*

  While LUCIUS *busies himself within the tent,* BRUTUS *and a group of
his* SOLDIERS *enter the platform at left door.* LUCILIUS *and* TITINIUS, *friends
of* BRUTUS, *enter the platform at right. They have just returned from*
CASSIUS' *camp and are accompanied by his servant* PINDARUS.

BRUTUS (*raising his arm in salute*). Stand, ho![1]
LUCILIUS. Give the word, ho![2] And stand.
BRUTUS. What now, Lucilius! Is Cassius near?
LUCILIUS. He is at hand; and Pindarus is come
5   To do you salutation[3] from his master.
BRUTUS. He greets me well. Your master, Pindarus,
      In his own change, or by ill officers,[4]
      Hath given me some worthy cause to wish
      Things done, undone; but if he be at hand,
10   I shall be satisfied.[5]
PINDARUS.   I do not doubt
      But that my noble master will appear

5. *commons*, the public pasture lands.
Here again we have an anachronism: the
custom of having public pasture lands is
English, not Roman.

6. *Brutus and Cassius . . . head.* Brutus
and Cassius were in Greece and Asia
Minor, gathering forces and strengthening
themselves; Antony knew that the triumvirate must do so also.

7. *How covert matters . . . answered,*
how hidden (covert) dangers may be
discovered, and dangers already known
be met.
8. *we are at the stake*, an allusion to the
English custom of tying a bear to a
stake and setting dogs on it.

1. *Stand, ho!* Halt!
2. *Give the word, ho!* Pass the word *Halt*
along to the soldiers.

3. *To do you salutation*, to bring you
greeting.

4. *In his own change, or by ill officers*,
by a change of heart himself or by bad
advice from troublemakers.

5. *be satisfied*, find out.

Such as he is, full of regard and honor.

BRUTUS. He is not doubted. (*Motioning* LUCILIUS *aside.*) A word,
Lucilius,
How he received you; let me be resolved.[6]

15 LUCILIUS. With courtesy and with respect enough;
But not with such familiar instances,[7]
Nor with such free and friendly conference,
As he hath used of old.

BRUTUS.   Thou hast described
A hot friend cooling; ever note, Lucilius,
20 When love begins to sicken and decay,
It useth an enforcèd ceremony.[8]
There are no tricks in plain and simple faith.
Comes his army on?

LUCILIUS. They mean this night in Sardis to be quartered;
25 The greater part, the horse in general,[9]
Are come with Cassius.

(*Martial music is heard offstage,
followed by a sentry's ringing
challenge and the murmured answer.*)

BRUTUS.   Hark! He is arrived.

(CASSIUS, *accompanied by a group
of his* SOLDIERS, *enters at right.*)

CASSIUS (*saluting*). Stand, ho!

BRUTUS (*returning the salute*). Stand, ho! Speak the word along.

FIRST SOLDIER. Stand!

SECOND SOLDIER. Stand!

30 THIRD SOLDIER. Stand!

CASSIUS. Most noble brother, you have done me wrong.

BRUTUS. Judge me, you gods! Wrong I mine enemies?
And, if not so, how should I wrong a brother?

CASSIUS. Brutus, this sober form of yours hides wrongs;
35 And when you do them——

BRUTUS (*interrupting*). Cassius, be content;
Speak your griefs softly; I do know you well.
Before the eyes of both our armies here,
Which should perceive nothing but love from us,
Let us not wrangle. Bid them move away;
40 Then in my tent, Cassius, enlarge your griefs,
And I will give you audience.

CASSIUS (*to his servant*).   Pindarus,
Bid our commanders lead their charges off
A little from this ground.

(PINDARUS, *followed by the* SOLDIERS
of CASSIUS, *departs at right.*)

BRUTUS. Lucilius, do you the like; and let no man
45 Come to our tent till we have done our conference.
Let Lucius and Titinius guard our door.

(BRUTUS *watches as his* SOLDIERS *follow* LUCILIUS *off
at left. Then he and* CASSIUS *move to the inner stage.*)

6. *A word, Lucilius . . . resolved.* Not content with Pindarus' assurance of Cassius' loyalty, Brutus wishes further report from Lucilius.

7. *familiar instances,* marks of friendship.

8. *an enforcèd ceremony,* forced politeness.

9. *the horse in general,* the regular cavalry.

Scene 3: Sardis. Within Brutus' tent.

Only a few seconds have elapsed since the preceding scene. LUCIUS *and* TITINIUS *guard the entrance to* BRUTUS' *tent.* BRUTUS *and* CASSIUS *stand facing each other on the inner stage.* CASSIUS' *anger is very apparent.*

[handwritten annotation, top right: argument - Brutus made Cassius seem a fool by punishing his men. Cassius doesn't, Cassius mad]

CASSIUS. That you have wronged me doth appear in this:
  You have condemned and noted[1] Lucius Pella
  For taking bribes here of the Sardians;[2]
  Wherein my letters, praying on his side
5 Because I knew the man, were slighted off.
BRUTUS. You wronged yourself to write in such a case.
CASSIUS. In such a time as this it is not meet *—proper*
  That every nice offense should bear his comment.[3]
BRUTUS. Let me tell you, Cassius, you yourself
10 Are much condemned to have an itching palm;[4]
  To sell and mart[5] your offices for gold
  To undeservers.
CASSIUS (*hotly*).   I an itching palm!
  You know that you are Brutus that speaks this,
  Or, by the gods, this speech were else your last!

[handwritten: If you weren't Brutus, I would have killed you]
[handwritten: If you weren't Cassius, I would have killed you]

15 BRUTUS. The name of Cassius honors this corruption,
  And chastisement doth therefore hide his head.[6]
CASSIUS. Chastisement!
BRUTUS. Remember March, the ides of March remember;
  Did not great Julius bleed for justice' sake?
20 What villain touched his body, that did stab,
  And not for justice? What, shall one of us,
  That struck the foremost man of all this world
  But for supporting robbers,[7] shall we now
  Contaminate our fingers with base bribes,
25 And sell the mighty space of our large honors
  For so much trash as may be graspèd thus?
  I had rather be a dog, and bay the moon,
  Than such a Roman.

[handwritten: — I'd rather be a dog than be like you]
[handwritten: — don't push me Brutus]

CASSIUS.   Brutus, bait not me;
  I'll not endure it; you forget yourself,
30 To hedge me in;[8] I am a soldier, I,
  Older in practice, abler than yourself
  To make conditions.[9]
BRUTUS.   Go to; you are not, Cassius.
CASSIUS. I am.
BRUTUS (*firmly*). I say you are not.
35 CASSIUS. Urge me no more, I shall forget myself;
  Have mind upon your health, tempt me no further.
BRUTUS (*unconcernedly*). Away, slight man! *—whimp*
CASSIUS (*in amazement*). Is 't possible?
BRUTUS. Hear me, for I will speak.
  Must I give way and room to your rash choler?[10]

1. *noted*, disgraced.

2. *For taking bribes . . . Sardians* (sär'di-ənz). Brutus had, on the complaints of the Sardians, publicly accused Lucius Pella (pel'ə) of embezzling public money and, upon finding him guilty, had condemned him. Cassius, on the other hand, had acquitted two of his friends similarly accused.

3. *That every nice offense . . . comment,* that every minor offense should be criticized.

4. *to have an itching palm,* to be greedy for money.

5. *mart,* market.

6. *The name of Cassius . . . head.* If anyone but Cassius had been guilty of these deeds, he would have received severe punishment.

7. *That struck . . . robbers,* who killed Caesar for protecting grafters.

8. *hedge me in,* interfere with me.

9. *To make conditions,* to plan the campaign and tend to its details.

10. *your rash choler,* your violent temper.

40   Shall I be frighted when a madman stares?

CASSIUS. O ye gods, ye gods! Must I endure all this?

BRUTUS. All this! Aye, more. Fret till your proud heart break;
      Go show your slaves how choleric you are,
      And make your bondmen tremble. Must I budge?
45   Must I observe you? Must I stand and crouch
      Under your testy humor? By the gods,
      You shall digest the venom of your spleen,
      Though it do split you; for, from this day forth,
      I'll use you for my mirth, yea, for my laughter,
50   When you are waspish.

CASSIUS (in disbelief).   Is it come to this?

BRUTUS. You say you are a better soldier;
      Let it appear so; make your vaunting true,
      And it shall please me well; for mine own part,
      I shall be glad to learn of noble men.

55 CASSIUS (pleading). You wrong me every way; you wrong me, Brutus;
      I said an elder soldier, not a better;
      Did I say "better"?

BRUTUS (indifferently). If you did, I care not.

CASSIUS. When Caesar lived, he durst not thus have moved me.

BRUTUS. Peace, peace! You durst not so have tempted him.

60 CASSIUS. I durst not!

BRUTUS. No.

CASSIUS. What, durst not tempt him!

BRUTUS.   For your life you durst not.

CASSIUS (hand on dagger). Do not presume too much upon my love;
      I may do that I shall be sorry for.

65 BRUTUS. You have done that you should be sorry for.
      There is no terror, Cassius, in your threats,
      For I am armed so strong in honesty
      That they pass by me as the idle wind,
      Which I respect not. I did send to you
70   For certain sums of gold, which you denied me;
      For I can raise no money by vile means;
      By heaven, I had rather coin my heart,
      And drop my blood for drachmas than to wring
      From the hard hands of peasants their vile trash
75   By any indirection;[11] I did send
      To you for gold to pay my legions,
      Which you denied me; was that done like Cassius?
      Should I have answered Caius Cassius so?
      When Marcus Brutus grows so covetous,
80   To lock such rascal counters[12] from his friends,
      Be ready, gods, with all your thunderbolts;
      Dash him to pieces!

CASSIUS.   I denied you not.

BRUTUS. You did.

CASSIUS. I did not; he was but a fool that brought
85   My answer back. Brutus hath rived[13] my heart;

11. *I had rather . . . indirection.* Brutus seems rather unrealistic here. How was Cassius to get money except by taking from farmers their eggs and cattle and hoarded money? And wasn't Brutus as guilty as Cassius if he was willing to use the money thus secured?

12. *rascal counters,* worthless coins.

13. *rived,* broken.

A friend should bear his friend's infirmities, *weaknesses*
But Brutus makes mine greater than they are.
BRUTUS. I do not, till you practice them on me.
CASSIUS. You love me not.
BRUTUS (coldly).   I do not like your faults.
90 CASSIUS. A friendly eye could never see such faults.
BRUTUS. A flatterer's would not, though they do appear
    As huge as high Olympus.
CASSIUS (tragically). Come, Antony, and young Octavius, come,
    Revenge yourselves alone on Cassius,
95 For Cassius is aweary of the world;
    Hated by one he loves; braved by his brother;
    Checked like a bondman; all his faults observed,
    Set in a notebook, learned, and conned by rote,[14]
    To cast into my teeth. Oh, I could weep
100 My spirit from mine eyes! (He unsheathes his dagger.) There is my
        dagger,
    And here my naked breast; within, a heart
    Dearer than Plutus' mine,[15] richer than gold;
    If that thou be'st a Roman, take it forth,
    I, that denied thee gold, will give my heart;
105 Strike, as thou didst at Caesar; for, I know
    When thou didst hate him worst, thou lovedst him better
    Than ever thou lovedst Cassius.
BRUTUS (his good humor returning).   Sheathe your dagger.
    Be angry when you will, it shall have scope;
110 Do what you will, dishonor shall be humor.[16]
    O Cassius, you are yokèd with a lamb
    That carries anger as the flint bears fire;
    Who, much enforcèd, shows a hasty spark,
    And straight is cold again.
CASSIUS (misunderstanding). Hath Cassius lived
115 To be but mirth and laughter to his Brutus,
    When grief and blood ill-tempered vexeth him?
BRUTUS. When I spoke that, I was ill-tempered, too.
CASSIUS. Do you confess so much? Give me your hand.
BRUTUS. And my heart, too.
CASSIUS (overcome with emotion).   O Brutus!
BRUTUS.   What's the matter?
120 CASSIUS. Have not you love enough to bear with me,
    When that rash humor which my mother gave me
    Makes me forgetful?
BRUTUS.   Yes, Cassius; and, from henceforth,
    When you are over-earnest with your Brutus,
    He'll think your mother chides, and leave you so. (Stepping forward,
        he sees that LUCILIUS has rejoined TITINIUS.)
125 Lucilius and Titinius, bid the commanders
    Prepare to lodge their companies tonight.
CASSIUS. And come yourselves, and bring Messala with you
    Immediately to us.

14. *conned by rote*, memorized until letter-perfect.

15. *Plutus' mine.* Plutus (plü′təs), the Greek god of wealth, was believed to control all precious minerals.

Brutus stops him 'cause of guilt.

16. *dishonor shall be humor*, when you dishonor me by insults, I shall consider it merely your whim.

(LUCILIUS *and* TITINIUS *exit at left.*)

BRUTUS. Lucius, a bowl of wine!
(LUCIUS *follows* BRUTUS *to the inner stage.*
He crosses to the table, where he lights a
taper and pours a bowl of wine for BRUTUS.)

CASSIUS *(wryly).* I did not think you could have been so angry.

130 BRUTUS. O Cassius, I am sick of many griefs.

CASSIUS. Of your philosophy you make no use,[17]
If you give place to accidental evils.

BRUTUS. No man bears sorrow better. Portia is dead.

CASSIUS. Ha! Portia!

135 BRUTUS. She is dead.

CASSIUS. How 'scaped I killing when I crossed you so?
O insupportable and touching loss!
Upon what sickness?

BRUTUS. Impatient of my absence,
And grief that young Octavius with Mark Antony

140 Have made themselves so strong—for with her death *beside yourself*
That tidings came—with this she fell distract
And, her attendants absent, swallowed fire.[18]

CASSIUS. And died so?

BRUTUS *(nodding his head).* Even so.

CASSIUS. O ye immortal gods!

BRUTUS. Speak no more of her. Give me a bowl of wine.

145 In this I bury all unkindness, Cassius. *(He drinks.)*

CASSIUS. My heart is thirsty for that noble pledge.
Fill, Lucius, till the wine o'erswell the cup;
I cannot drink too much of Brutus' love.
(LUCIUS *pours a bowl of wine for* CASSIUS. *As*
he does so, BRUTUS *greets* TITINIUS, *who has*
reëntered the platform at left. TITINIUS *is*
accompanied by MESSALA, *a friend of* BRUTUS.)

BRUTUS. Come in, Titinius!
Welcome, good Messala.

150 Now sit we close about this taper here,
And call in question our necessities,[19]
Messala, I have here receivèd letters,
That young Octavius and Mark Antony
Come down upon us with a mighty power,

155 Bending their expedition toward Philippi.
(BRUTUS, CASSIUS, TITINIUS, *and* MESSALA *seat*
themselves at the table. BRUTUS *unrolls a scroll.*)

MESSALA. Myself have letters of the selfsame tenor.[20]

BRUTUS. With what addition?

MESSALA. That by proscription and bills of outlawry,[21]
Octavius, Antony, and Lepidus

160 Have put to death an hundred senators.

BRUTUS. Therein our letters do not well agree;
Mine speaks of seventy senators that died
By their proscriptions, Cicero being one.

17. *Of your philosophy . . . use.* Brutus was a Stoic (stō′ik). Believers in this philosophy thought that people should rise above emotional upsets and be unmoved by any of life's happenings.

18. *swallowed fire.* Portia reportedly snatched some burning charcoal from a fire, and holding it in her closed mouth, stifled herself and thus died.

19. *call in question our necessities,* discuss our problems.

20. *of the selfsame tenor,* bearing the same tidings.

21. *bills of outlawry,* public notices declaring certain persons no longer protected by Roman law. As enemies of the state they may be killed.

CASSIUS *(in disbelief).* Cicero one!

MESSALA. Cicero is dead,

165 And by that order of proscription.

BRUTUS. Well, to our work alive.[22] What do you think
Of marching to Philippi presently?[23]

CASSIUS. I do not think it good.

BRUTUS. Your reason?

CASSIUS. This it is:
'Tis better that the enemy seek us;

170 So shall he waste his means, weary his soldiers,
Doing himself offense; whilst we, lying still,
Are full of rest, defense, and nimbleness.

BRUTUS. Good reasons must, of force, give place to better.
The people 'twixt Philippi and this ground

175 Do stand but in a forced affection;
For they have grudged us contribution;
The enemy, marching along by them,
By them shall make a fuller number up,
Come on refreshed, new-added, and encouraged;

180 From which advantage shall we cut him off,
If at Philippi we do face him there,
These people at our back.

CASSIUS *(pleading).* Hear me, good brother.

BRUTUS. Under your pardon. You must note beside,
That we have tried the utmost of our friends,

185 Our legions are brimful, our cause is ripe;
The enemy increaseth every day;
We, at the height, are ready to decline.
There is a tide in the affairs of men,
Which, taken at the flood, leads on to fortune;

190 Omitted, all the voyage of their life
Is bound in shallows and in miseries.
On such a full sea are we now afloat;
And we must take the current when it serves,
Or lose our ventures.

CASSIUS *(resignedly).* Then, with your will, go on;

195 We'll along ourselves, and meet them at Philippi.

BRUTUS. The deep of night is crept upon our talk,
And nature must obey necessity;
Which we will niggard[24] with a little rest.
There is no more to say?

CASSIUS. No more. Good night.

200 Early tomorrow will we rise, and hence.

BRUTUS *(standing).* Lucius! My gown. *(To the three others.)* Farewell,
good Messala;
Good night, Titinius. Noble, noble Cassius,
Good night, and good repose.

CASSIUS. O my dear brother!
This was an ill beginning of the night;

205 Never come such division 'tween our souls!

22. *to our work alive,* to work that concerns the living.
23. *presently,* immediately.

24. *we will niggard,* we will satisfy somewhat.

rejects Cassius' advice again

Let it not, Brutus.

BRUTUS. Everything is well.

CASSIUS. Good night, my lord.

BRUTUS. Good night, good brother.

TITINIUS *and* MESSALA. Good night, Lord Brutus.

BRUTUS. Farewell, every one.

(CASSIUS, TITINIUS, *and* MESSALA *move from the
inner stage to the platform and exit at right.*
LUCIUS *unfolds his master's night robe.*)

Give me the gown. Where is thy instrument?[25]

210 LUCIUS. Here in the tent.

BRUTUS. What, thou speak'st drowsily?
Poor knave,[26] I blame thee not; thou art o'er-watched.[27]
Call Claudius and some other of my men;
I'll have them sleep on cushions in my tent.

LUCIUS (*moving onto platform*). Varro and Claudius!

(VARRO *and* CLAUDIUS, *entering the
platform at left, cross to the inner stage.*)

215 VARRO. Calls my lord?

BRUTUS. I pray you, sirs, lie in my tent and sleep;
It may be I shall raise you by and by
On business to my brother Cassius.

VARRO. So please you, we will stand and watch your pleasure.

220 BRUTUS. I will not have it so; lie down, good sirs;
It may be I shall otherwise bethink me.
Look, Lucius, here's the book I sought for so;
I put it in the pocket of my gown.

(VARRO *and* CLAUDIUS *lie down on the cushions.*)

LUCIUS. I was sure your lordship did not give it me.

225 BRUTUS. Bear with me, good boy, I am much forgetful.
Canst thou hold up thy heavy eyes awhile,
And touch thy instrument a strain or two?

LUCIUS. Aye, my lord, an't[28] please you.

BRUTUS. It does, my boy;
I trouble thee too much, but thou art willing.

230 LUCIUS. It is my duty, sir.

BRUTUS. I should not urge thy duty past thy might;
I know young bloods look for a time of rest. (*He seats himself at
the table.*)

LUCIUS. I have slept, my lord, already.

BRUTUS. It was well done; and thou shalt sleep again;
235 I will not hold thee long; if I do live,
I will be good to thee.

(LUCIUS *sits on some cushions near the table
and plays and sings, gradually falling asleep.*)

BRUTUS. This is a sleepy tune. O murderous slumber,
Lay'st thou thy leaden mace[29] upon my boy,
That plays thee music? Gentle knave, good night;
240 I will not do thee so much wrong to wake thee;
If thou dost nod, thou break'st thy instrument.

25. *thy instrument,* thy lute.

26. *knave,* lad.
27. *thou art o'er-watched.* Lucius has
been on sentry duty too long.

28. *an't,* if it.

29. *thy leaden mace.* Morpheus (môr'fi-
əs), the Greek god of dreams, carried a
leaden club with which he cast the spell
of slumber.

I'll take it from thee; and, good boy, good night.
Let me see, let me see; is not the leaf turned down[30]
Where I left reading? Here it is, I think. *(He begins to read.)*

(The GHOST OF CAESAR *slowly ascends through
the trap door in the floor of the inner stage.)*

245   How ill this taper burns![31] Ha! Who comes here?
I think it is the weakness of mine eyes
That shapes this monstrous apparition.
It comes upon me——Art thou anything?
Art thou some god, some angel, or some devil,
250   That mak'st my blood cold and my hair to stare?
Speak to me what thou art.
GHOST *(in sepulchral tones).* Thy evil spirit, Brutus.
BRUTUS. Why com'st thou?
GHOST. To tell thee thou shalt see me at Philippi.
BRUTUS. Well; then I shall see thee again?
255   GHOST. Aye, at Philippi.
BRUTUS. Why, I will see thee at Philippi, then.

(The GHOST *descends.)*

Now I have taken heart thou vanishest;
Ill spirit, I would hold more talk with thee.
Boy, Lucius! Varro! Claudius! Sirs, awake!
260   Claudius!
LUCIUS *(still half-asleep).* The strings, my lord, are false.
BRUTUS. He thinks he still is at his instrument.
Lucius, awake!
LUCIUS. My lord?
BRUTUS. Didst thou dream, Lucius, that thou so criedst out?
265   LUCIUS. My lord, I do not know that I did cry.
BRUTUS. Yes, that thou didst; didst thou see anything?
LUCIUS. Nothing, my lord.
BRUTUS. Sleep again, Lucius. Sirrah Claudius! *(To* VARRO.) Fellow thou,
     awake!
VARRO. My lord?
270   CLAUDIUS. My lord?
BRUTUS. Why did you so cry out, sirs, in your sleep?
VARRO *and* CLAUDIUS. Did we, my lord?
BRUTUS.   Aye, saw you anything?
VARRO. No, my lord, I saw nothing.
CLAUDIUS.   Nor I, my lord.
BRUTUS. Go and commend me to my brother Cassius;
275   Bid him set on his powers betimes before,[32]
And we will follow.
VARRO *and* CLAUDIUS.   It shall be done, my lord.

*(*VARRO *and* CLAUDIUS *move from the inner stage to the
platform and exit at right.* BRUTUS *and* LUCIUS *remain
on the inner stage as the curtains are drawn closed.)*

30. *the leaf turned down.* Here is another anachronism, Roman books were in the form of large scrolls.

31. *How ill this taper burns!* According to a popular superstition of the times, the presence of a ghost made lights burn blue.

32. *set on . . . before,* start his forces moving ahead.

CONSIDERING
ACT FOUR

Scene 1

1. (a) What is the significance of the marked names on Antony's list? (b) What does the plan for dealing with the suspected Romans show about the character of each man in the second triumvirate? (c) What would the plan be called in a modern dictatorship?

2. When Antony characterizes Lepidus for Octavius (see Act Four, Scene 1, lines 12–15, 18–27), he also betrays his own traits. What does he reveal about himself?

3. (a) How had Antony used Caesar's will to his advantage when he swayed the commoners during the funeral oration? (b) How does he propose to use it now?

Scenes 2 and 3

1. (a) What is the state of affairs between Brutus and Cassius when Brutus sends for Cassius at the army camp near Sardis? (b) Keeping in mind what you have learned in the play up to this point, explain why a quarrel between the two men was inevitable. (c) With which of them are your sympathies? Why?

2. (a) Upon what plan of action do Brutus and Cassius decide after their quarrel? (b) What is your opinion of this plan?

3. Over two years have elapsed since Julius Caesar was killed. (a) Do you think that Brutus often thinks of him? (b) How does the dead man again become an important character as the play nears its end?

LOOKING BACK—
AND AHEAD

1. Make a brief outline of the main events in Act Four, and add it to your outline for the first three acts.

2. As a dramatist advances the plot of his play, he must be very careful to keep the actions of each of his characters consistent with what has gone before. How have the actions of the leading characters in Act Four of *Julius Caesar* been consistent with their natures as portrayed earlier in the play?

THE
AUTHOR'S
CRAFT

". . . the noblest Roman . . ."
Julius Caesar, V, iv

In his thirty-seven plays, Shakespeare created a vast array of realistic characters who are as fascinating to modern playgoers as they were to the patrons of the Globe. Brutus—"the noblest Roman of them all"—is one of Shakespeare's most memorable creations.

Shakespeare develops the character of Marcus Brutus through *contrast*; that is, he endows Brutus with a personality that contrasts sharply with the personalities of Cassius and Antony. Early in the play Brutus emerges as an idealist willing to murder his friend only because he is convinced that Caesar's death will benefit the Roman people. Throughout the play, Brutus will act according to his ideals of what ought to be. In

Brutus, idealism is both a strength and a weakness, for it prevents him from seeing people and events as they really are.

Acting as a *foil* to Brutus, is Cassius. Practical as well as ambitious, Cassius is willing to murder Caesar because he envies Caesar's power. He will always be more concerned with action than theory. Cassius, moreover, is a shrewd judge of character. In persuading Brutus to join the conspiracy, for example, does Cassius appeal to Brutus' ambition or to his sense of honor?

During Act Two, Scene 1 (lines 107–161) and Act Three, Scene 1 (lines 231–243), Brutus' idealism overrides Cassius' practicality. Describe these two incidents. Does Cassius reveal a weakness in being too easily influenced by Brutus? Explain your answer. Brutus overrides Cassius for a third time in Act Four, Scene 3 (lines 166–195). What decision does Brutus make? Do his reasons seem to be practical? Judging from the two previous incidents, do

you think his decision will prove to be the right one? Why or why not?

Antony emerges as a *foil* to Brutus in Act Three, Scene 1. How does Antony's personality differ from Brutus'? What incident in this scene excites your admiration for Antony? How does Antony's funeral oration in Scene 2 show that he is a far more clever politician than Brutus could ever be? Would Brutus be capable of the actions that Antony takes in Act Four, Scene 1? Explain your answer.

A lesser dramatist than Shakespeare would have drawn a superficial contrast, for example, between Brutus (the paragon of virtue) and Antony (the dastardly villain). By contrasting both the strength and the weakness he saw in Brutus, Cassius, and Antony, Shakespeare achieves the realism that makes his characters so memorable.

A Latin root word
The word *salus* (or some form of it), meaning "health" was often used by Romans as a greeting. Many English words are formed from *salus* and carry the idea of "greeting" or "health." On a sheet of paper answer the following questions with *Yes* or *No* and explain why you decided as you did. You may use a dictionary for help, if necessary.

1. Are the words *Thy lover* in Artemidorus' letter to Caesar (Act II, Scene 3, line 8) the *salutation* of that letter?

2. If a Roman gentleman wished to send *salutations* to another Roman, would he have to send along something to improve that person's health?

3. Is the mild climate of a country like Italy *salubrious?*

4. When a *salutatorian* in a high school of today delivers his *salutatory*, must he use health as the subject of his address?

5. Do people often *salute* their relatives with a kiss?

"This dreadful night that thunders"

During a performance of *Julius Caesar*, the stagehands and musicians at the Globe were busy creating a variety of special effects.

Act One, Scene 3, for example, calls for a "dreadful night that thunders, lightens, opens graves, and roars." To simulate thunder, stagehands in the huts (above) rolled a cannon ball back and forth or down a few stairs. Elizabethan stagehands could create lightning with a squib (a ball of shiny cloth filled with sulfur powder), which they had attached to the top of a long wire. They lowered the wire through the opening in the canopy and then ignited the squib. This small firework rolled down the wire with a fine hissing sound and exploded with a resounding "crack."

Since Elizabethan audiences delighted in the sight of blood and gore, the assassination scene in Act Three must have pleased them mightily. The actor portraying Caesar probably wore (beneath his costume) a bladder filled with sheep's blood. When the moment for stabbing Caesar arrived, Casca punctured the bladder with his dagger. Later the conspirators "washed" their hands in this blood. It is likely that Antony delivered his funeral oration over a dummy corpse of Caesar. When Antony flung Caesar's cloak aside, the dummy's many gaping wounds undoubtedly horrified the Globe audience.

Stagehands operating the trap doors from "Hell" were responsible for the ghostly appearances. A ghost ascended through the floor traps in the platform or, like the Ghost of Caesar in Act Four, ascended through the floor trap in the inner stage.

If *Julius Caesar* had called for angels and spirits, the actors portraying these beings would have been lowered and raised (by means of a pulley) through the trap door in the canopy.

The battle scenes in Act Five call for sound effects, such as the clash of arms offstage. The musicians created the alarums with their trumpets, drums, and cymbals. Sometimes real cannons were discharged to increase the realism of a battle scene. However, the use of explosives in a building made of wood and thatch was ill-advised, for it was the discharge of a backstage cannon that destroyed the Globe Playhouse in June of 1613. An eyewitness account describes the fire in this way: ". . . and certain chambers being shot off some of the paper or other stuff wherewith one of them was stopped, did light on the thatch, where being thought at first but an idle smoke . . . it kindled inwardly and ran around like a train, consuming within less than an hour the whole house to the very ground. . . . Nothing did perish but wood and straw, and a few forsaken cloaks. Only one man had his breeches set on fire, that would perhaps have broiled him, if he had not by the benefit of a provident wit put it out with bottle ale."

Act Five

Scene 1: The plains of Philippi.

The combined armies of BRUTUS *and* CASSIUS *have engaged the combined forces of* ANTONY *and* OCTAVIUS. *Offstage can be heard occasional cries, the staccato clash of arms, and the sound of soldiers fleeing to more distant points. For a moment there is silence; then* BRUTUS *enters at left, followed by* CASSIUS.

CASSIUS.   Now, most noble Brutus,
   The gods today stand friendly, that we may,
   Lovers in peace, lead on our days to age![1]
   But since the affairs of men rest still incertain,
5   Let's reason with the worst that may befall.
   If we do lose this battle, then is this
   The very last time we shall speak together;
   What are you then determinèd to do?
BRUTUS. Even by the rule of that philosophy[2]
10   By which I did blame Cato[3] for the death
   Which he did give himself—I know not how,
   But I do find it cowardly and vile,
   For fear of what might fall, so to prevent
   The time of life[4]—arming myself with patience
15   To stay the providence of some high powers
   That govern us below.[5]
CASSIUS (*unbelievingly*).   Then if we lose this battle,
   You are contented to be led in triumph
   Through the streets of Rome?
BRUTUS. No, Cassius, no; think not, thou noble Roman,
20   That ever Brutus will go bound to Rome;
   He bears too great a mind. But this same day
   Must end that work the ides of March begun;
   And whether we shall meet again I know not.
   Therefore, our everlasting farewell take;
25   Forever, and forever, farewell, Cassius! (*He places his hand on*
      CASSIUS' *shoulder.*)
   If we do meet again, why, we shall smile;
   If not, why then, this parting was well made.
CASSIUS. Forever, and forever, farewell, Brutus!
   If we do meet again, we'll smile indeed;
30   If not, 'tis true this parting was well made.
BRUTUS. Why, then, lead on. Oh, that a man might know
   The end of this day's business ere it come!
   But it sufficeth that the day will end,
   And then the end is known. Come, ho! Away!
             (BRUTUS *and* CASSIUS *move off at right.*)

1. *Now . . . lead on our days to age!* Cassius hopes that the gods will be on their side so that the two men will end their days as friends in peaceful times.

2. *that philosophy,* Stoicism (stō′ə siz əm), which taught indifference to pleasure or pain. The Stoics did not believe in suicide.
3. *Cato,* Cato (kā′tō) the Younger, the father-in-law of Brutus. He had killed himself rather than submit to Julius Caesar's tyranny.
4. *to prevent the time of life,* to cut short one's own life by suicide.
5. *To stay . . . below.* As a Stoic, Brutus regards suicide as cowardly, and believes that a man should bear his troubles with patience and await (stay) a normal death to be sent when the gods so decree.

Scene 2: The field of battle.

The battle is well under way. BRUTUS *and his followers form the left flank of the combined army and face the forces of* OCTAVIUS; CASSIUS *and his men form the right flank and are opposed to* ANTONY. BRUTUS, *with* MESSALA *following, enters at left. He has been observing the battle and has prepared various dispatches which he must send to* CASSIUS *and his legions.*

BRUTUS. Ride, ride, Messala, ride and give these bills
  Unto the legions on the other side.

    (Loud alarums are heard offstage.)

  Let them set on at once; for I perceive
  But cold demeanor in Octavius' wing,

5 And sudden push gives them the overthrow.[1]
  Ride, ride, Messala; let them all come down.

    *(BRUTUS and MESSALA exit,
    going in different directions.)*

1. *I perceive . . . overthrow.* The signs of faltering (cold demeanor) that Brutus sees in Octavius' men lead him to hazard everything on one swift, punishing general attack.

Scene 3: A hill in another part of the battlefield.

It is now late afternoon. Several SOLDIERS, *disheveled and weary from the fighting, enter at right and group themselves near the left pillar. As offstage alarums sound,* CASSIUS *and* TITINIUS *enter at right.* CASSIUS *carries a broken standard in his left hand. He speaks with great anger.*

CASSIUS *(pointing to right).* Oh, look, Titinius, look, the villains fly!
  Myself have to mine own turned enemy;[1]
  This ensign here of mine was turning back;
  I slew the coward, and did take it[2] from him.

5 TITINIUS. O Cassius, Brutus gave the word too early;
  Who, having some advantage on Octavius,
  Took it too eagerly; his soldiers fell to spoil,
  Whilst we by Antony are all enclosed.[3]

    *(CASSIUS tosses the broken standard to the
    SOLDIERS. As they move off at left,* PINDARUS,
    the servant of CASSIUS, *runs on at right.)*

PINDARUS. Fly further off, my lord, fly further off;
10 Mark Antony is in your tents, my lord;
  Fly, therefore, noble Cassius, fly far off.
CASSIUS. This hill is far enough. Look, look, Titinius;
  Are those my tents where I perceive the fire?
TITINIUS. They are, my lord.
CASSIUS.   Titinius, if thou lovest me,
15 Mount thou my horse, and hide thy spurs in him,
  Till he have brought thee up to yonder troops,
  And here again; that I may rest assured
  Whether yon troops are friend or enemy.[4]

1. *Myself have to . . . enemy.* Cassius has had to turn on some of his own men who were deserting. Even a standard bearer (ensign) was in headlong flight.
2. *it,* the standard.

3. *his soldiers fell . . . enclosed.* Brutus' soldiers, thinking Cassius' men had attacked at the same time and had been as successful as they, were plundering Octavius' camp. Actually Cassius' forces had been encircled by Antony's men. Their plight seemed doubly tragic to them because they knew it could have been avoided.

4. *that I may rest . . . enemy.* Since so many of his men have deserted, Cassius wonders if the horsemen he sees approaching are deserters from his army or are Antony's men. In reality, they are messengers from Brutus. They are led by Messala and bear tidings of Brutus' victory over Octavius.

TITINIUS. I will be here again, even with a thought.[5]

(TITINIUS *hurries off at right.*)

20 CASSIUS (*pointing to the balcony*). Go, Pindarus, get higher on that hill;
My sight was ever thick; regard Titinius,
And tell me what thou not'st about the field.

(PINDARUS *exits at inner-stage curtains
in order to ascend the hill.*)

This day I breathèd first; time is come round,
And where I did begin, there shall I end;[6]
25 My life is run his compass. Sirrah, what news?
PINDARUS (*appearing above*). O my lord!
CASSIUS. What news?
PINDARUS. Titinius is enclosèd round about
With horsemen, that make to him on the spur;
30 Yet he spurs on. Now they are almost on him.
Now, Titinius! Now some light. Oh, he lights, too.
He's ta'en.

(*There are shouts offstage.*)

And, hark! They shout for joy.[7]
CASSIUS. Come down, behold no more.
Oh, coward that I am, to live so long,
35 To see my best friend ta'en before my face!

(PINDARUS *exits at balcony curtains in order to descend
from the hill. In a moment he rejoins* CASSIUS.)

Come hither, sirrah.
In Parthia[8] did I take thee prisoner;
And then I swore thee, saving of thy life,
That whatsoever I did bid thee do,
40 Thou shouldst attempt it.[9] Come now, keep thine oath;
Now be a freeman; and with this good sword,
That ran through Caesar's bowels, search this bosom.[10]
Stand not to answer; here, take thou the hilts;
And, when my face is covered, as 'tis now,
45 Guide thou the sword.

(PINDARUS *obeys and stabs* CASSIUS.)

Caesar, thou art revenged,
Even with the sword that killed thee. (CASSIUS *dies.*)
PINDARUS. So, I am free; yet would not so have been,
Durst I have done my will. O Cassius,
Far from this country Pindarus shall run,
50 Where never Roman shall take note of him.

(PINDARUS, *leaving* CASSIUS' *sword behind, hastens
to left door and exits. Then,* TITINIUS, *with*
MESSALA, *reënters at right. On his head* TITINIUS
wears a garland signifying victory.)

MESSALA. It is but change,[11] Titinius; for Octavius
Is overthrown by noble Brutus' power,
As Cassius' legions are by Antony.
TITINIUS. These tidings will well comfort Cassius.
55 MESSALA. Where did you leave him?

5. *even with a thought,* quick as a thought.

6. *This day I breathèd . . . end.* This is Cassius' birthday.

7. *He's ta'en . . . shout for joy.* Pindarus misinterprets this meeting. Brutus' messengers are telling Titinius of their victory over Octavius and are giving him a victor's wreath to carry to Cassius.

8. *Parthia* (pär'thi ə), an ancient country in Asia southeast of the Caspian Sea.

9. *And then I swore . . . attempt it.* Pindarus, in return for his life, had had to swear to do whatever Cassius ordered.
10. *Now be a freeman . . . bosom.* Cassius will give Pindarus liberty if he (Pindarus) will kill Cassius.

Why no funeral for Cassius — don't want funeral discouraging in middle of battle 'cause soldiers won't wanna fight

11. *but change,* a fair exchange.

TITINIUS.   All disconsolate,
    With Pindarus his bondman, on this hill.
MESSALA. Is not that he that lies upon the ground?
TITINIUS (*running forward*). He lies not like the living. O my heart!
MESSALA. Is not that he?
TITINIUS (*sadly*).   No, this was he, Messala,
60   But Cassius is no more. O setting sun,
    As in thy red rays thou dost sink tonight,
    So in his red blood Cassius' day is set;
    The sun of Rome is set! Our day is gone;
    Clouds, dews, and dangers come; our deeds are done!
65   Mistrust of my success hath done this deed.
MESSALA. Mistrust of good success hath done this deed.
    O hateful error, melancholy's child,
    Why dost thou show to the apt thoughts of men
    The things that are not?[12] O error, soon conceived,
70   Thou never com'st unto a happy birth,
    But kill'st the mother that engendered thee!
TITINIUS (*calling*). What, Pindarus! Where art thou, Pindarus?
MESSALA. Seek him, Titinius, whilst I go to meet
    The noble Brutus, thrusting this report
75   Into his ears; I may say thrusting it,
    For piercing steel and darts envenomed
    Shall be as welcome to the ears of Brutus
    As tidings of this sight.
TITINIUS.   Hie, you, Messala,
    And I will seek for Pindarus the while.

                    (As MESSALA *exits at left*, TITINIUS
                    falls to one knee beside CASSIUS.)

80   Why didst thou send me forth, brave Cassius?
    Did I not meet thy friends? And did not they
    Put on my brows this wreath of victory,
    And bid me give it thee? Didst thou not hear their shouts?
    Alas, thou hast misconstrued everything![13]
85   But, hold thee, take this garland on thy brow;
    Thy Brutus bid me give it thee, and I
    Will do his bidding. (*He rises.*) Brutus, come apace,
    And see how I regarded Caius Cassius. (*He picks up* CASSIUS' *sword.*)
    By your leave, gods—this is a Roman's part;[14]
90   Come, Cassius' sword, and find Titinius' heart. (*He kills himself.*)
              (*Alarums sound offstage.* MESSALA *reënters at left.*
              He is accompanied by BRUTUS, *young* CATO, STRATO,
                    VOLUMNIUS, LUCILIUS, *and several* SOLDIERS.)
BRUTUS. Where, where, Messala, doth his body lie?
MESSALA. Lo, yonder, and Titinius mourning it.
BRUTUS. Titinius' face is upward.
CATO (*going to* TITINIUS).   He is slain.
BRUTUS. O Julius Caesar, thou art mighty yet!
95   Thy spirit walks abroad, and turns our swords
    In our own proper entrails.

12. *Why dost thou . . . not,* why do men
so readily accept things as true when they
really are not.

13. *Alas, thou hast misconstrued everything!* Titinius is appalled by the fact that
Cassius' tragic death is due to a misin-
terpretation of the meeting between him
(Titinius) and Messala's men. Had Cassius
realized that the men were Brutus' and
that they bore news of a victory, he would
still be alive!
14. *this is a Roman's part.* The Romans
prided themselves on being freemen,
and traditionally preferred death at their
own hands to acknowledging another man
their master.

(There are low alarums offstage.)

CATO.   Brave Titinius!

Look, whether he have not crowned dead Cassius!

BRUTUS. Are yet two Romans living such as these?

The last of all the Romans, fare thee well!

100   It is impossible that ever Rome

Should breed thy fellow. Friends, I owe more tears

To this dead man that you shall see me pay.

I shall find time, Cassius, I shall find time.

(He motions to the SOLDIERS, who pick
up the bodies of CASSIUS and TITINIUS.)

Come, therefore, and to Thasos[15] send his body;

105   His funerals shall not be in our camp,

Lest it discomfort us. Lucilius, come;

And come, young Cato; let us to the field.

We shall try fortune in a second fight.

(All exit at left.)

15. *Thasos* (thä′sôs), an island in the Aegean Sea.

Scene 4: Another part of the battlefield.

As the scene begins, a large rock is raised through the trap door in the center of the platform. Then VOLUMNIUS, carrying a lighted torch, enters at left. He is followed by BRUTUS, CLITUS, DARDANIUS, and STRATO. All are overcome with fatigue and their sense of defeat.

BRUTUS. Come, poor remains of friends, rest on this rock.

CLITUS. Statilius showed the torchlight, but, my lord,

He came not back; he is or ta'en or slain.[1]

BRUTUS. Sit thee down, Clitus; slaying is the word;

5   It is a deed in fashion. Hark thee, Clitus. *(He whispers to CLITUS.)*

CLITUS. What, I, my lord? No, not for all the world.

BRUTUS. Peace, then! No words.

CLITUS *(with fervor).*   I'll rather kill myself.

BRUTUS. Hark thee, Dardanius. *(Again BRUTUS whispers his request.)*

DARDANIUS *(aghast).*   Shall I do such a deed?

(BRUTUS walks away from the men.)

CLITUS. O Dardanius!

10   DARDANIUS. O Clitus!

CLITUS. What ill request did Brutus make to thee?

DARDANIUS. To kill him, Clitus. Look, he meditates.

CLITUS. Now is that noble vessel full of grief,

That it runs over even at his eyes.

BRUTUS. Come hither, good Volumnius; list a word.

15   VOLUMNIUS *(going to him).* What says my lord?

BRUTUS.   Why, this, Volumnius:

The ghost of Caesar hath appeared to me

Two several times by night; at Sardis once,

And, this last night, here in Philippi fields;

20   I know my hour is come.

1. *Statilius* (stə til′i əs) . . . *slain.* Statilius had volunteered to slip through the enemy's lines and observe happenings in their camp; later—if all was well with him—he would signal with a torch. Although his signal was seen, Statilius did not return. It was thought he lost his life shortly after he flashed the signal.

VOLUMNIUS.   Not so, my lord.

BRUTUS. Nay, I am sure it is, Volumnius.
  Thou seest the world, Volumnius, how it goes;
  Our enemies have beat us to the pit;[2]

  *(Low alarums sound offstage signaling
  the approach of* ANTONY *and* OCTAVIUS.*)*

  It is more worthy to leap in ourselves
  Than tarry till they push us. Good Volumnius,
  Thou know'st that we two went to school together;
  Even for that our love of old, I prithee,[3]
  Hold thou my sword hilts, whilst I run on it.

VOLUMNIUS. That's not an office for a friend, my lord.

  (More alarums are sounded, this time louder.)

CLITUS. Fly, fly, my lord; there is no tarrying here.

BRUTUS *(going to each in turn).* Farewell to you; and you; and you,
  Volumnius.
  Strato, thou hast been all this while asleep;
  Farewell to thee, too, Strato. Countrymen,
  My heart doth joy that yet in all my life
  I found no man but he was true to me.
  I shall have glory by this losing day
  More than Octavius and Mark Antony
  By this vile conquest shall attain unto.
  So fare you well at once; for Brutus' tongue
  Hath almost ended his life's history;
  Night hangs upon mine eyes; my bones would rest,
  That hath but labored to attain this hour.

  *(The alarum grows urgent and is ac-
  companied by cries of "Fly, fly, fly!")*

CLITUS. Fly, my lord, fly!

BRUTUS.   Hence! I will follow.

  *(*CLITUS, DARDANIUS, *and* VOLUMNIUS *hurry off at
  right.* STRATO, *awake now, starts to follow them.)*

  I prithee, Strato, stay thou by thy lord.
  Thou art a fellow of a good respect;
  Thy life hath had some smatch[4] of honor in it;
  Hold then my sword, and turn away thy face,
  While I do run upon it. Wilt thou, Strato?

STRATO. Give me your hand first. Fare you well, my lord.

BRUTUS. Farewell, good Strato.

  *(*STRATO *takes the sword, and holds it firmly
  with the blade exposed. As* STRATO *turns his
  face aside,* BRUTUS *runs upon the naked blade.)*
  Caesar, now be still.
  I killed not thee with half so good a will. (*BRUTUS dies.*)

  *(Offstage trumpets sound retreat as two
  SOLDIERS, bearing torches, enter at left.
  They light the way for* ANTONY *and* OCTAVIUS.
  More SOLDIERS *follow, among them are* MESSALA
  and LUCILIUS *who have been taken prisoner.)*

2. *Our enemies have . . . pit,* an allusion
to the method of forming a large circle
around a wild animal (such as a tiger)
and beating on drums to drive it into a pit,
where it can be captured.

3. *prithee,* pray thee.

4. *smatch,* taste; touch.

[handwritten: Smart move for Brutus to kill himself? yes]

[handwritten: Strato holds sword. servant]

[handwritten: char. view Brutus to be: worthy of adoration respect him + his judgment]

All see STRATO *standing over the dead* BRUTUS.)

OCTAVIUS. What man is that?

MESSALA. My master's man. Strato, where is thy master?

STRATO. Free from the bondage you are in, Messala;

55   The conquerors can but make a fire of him;[5]
     For Brutus only overcame himself,
     And no man else hath honor by his death.[6]

LUCILIUS. So Brutus should be found.

OCTAVIUS. All that served Brutus, I will entertain them.[7]

60   Fellow, wilt thou bestow thy time with me?

STRATO. Aye, if Messala will prefer[8] me to you.

OCTAVIUS. Do so, good Messala.

MESSALA. How died my master, Strato?

STRATO. I held the sword, and he did run on it.

65 MESSALA. Octavius, then take him to follow thee,
     That did the latest service to my master.

ANTONY (*looking at the body*). This was the noblest Roman of them all.
     All the conspirators, save only he,
     Did that they did in envy of great Caesar;
70   He only, in a general honest thought
     And common good to all, made one of them.[9]
     His life was gentle, and the elements
     So mixed in him that nature might stand up
     And say to all the world, "This was a man!"

          (ANTONY *removes his cloak and covers* BRUTUS
               with it. He then signals to the SOLDIERS *who
                    lift* BRUTUS' *body onto their shields.*)

75 OCTAVIUS. According to his virtue let us use him,
     With all respect and rites of burial.
     Within my tent his bones tonight shall lie,
     Most like a soldier, ordered honorable.
     So call the field to rest; and let's away
     To part the glories[10] of this happy day.

          (*All exit at right to the solemn accompaniment
               of offstage drums beating a death march.*)

5. *The conquerors can but make . . . him,* a reference to the Roman custom of burning their dead.

6. *no man else . . . death.* No one can claim the honor of defeating Brutus in combat.

7. *I will entertain them.* Octavius means to take all of Brutus' servants and make them his own.

8. *prefer,* recommend.

9. *made one of them,* joined them.

10. *part the glories,* divide the honors.

THANKS!!! (notes?)

CONSIDERING ACT FIVE

Scenes 1 and 2

1. As a Stoic, Brutus has not believed in allowing the fortunes or misfortunes of life to affect him and he has frowned on the idea of suicide. Do any of his beliefs seem to be changing? Explain.

2. (a) What is the attitude of Brutus and Cassius toward each other as they part before the battle? (b) In what mood do Brutus and Cassius say farewell?

3. (a) What is the plan of attack that Brutus wishes to put into action? (b) For what purpose do you think Scene 2, which is so very short, is included in Act Five?

Scene 3

1. (a) What is Cassius' mood as this scene opens? (b) What reasons does he have for feeling as he does? (c) Who is the person responsible for the existing state of affairs?

2. (a) What mistake do Pindarus and Cassius make concerning Titinius? (b) What misleads them?

3. (a) How are Cassius' decision to die and the manner of his death in keeping with his character? (b) How does Pindarus help him? (c) Why does the servant flee afterwards?

4. (a) What effect does the death of Cassius have on Brutus? (b) Why does he exclaim, "O Julius Caesar, thou are mighty yet!"? (c) Do you consider Brutus a quitter? Why, or why not?

Scene 4

1. As Brutus bids his friends farewell, he says that in all his life he has found "no man but he was true to me." (a) Who did take unfair advantage of Brutus' trust? Under what circumstances? (b) What does the making of that remark—after all that has happened—show about Brutus' character?

2. What do you think is the significance of Brutus' words as he was about to die: "Caesar, now be still"?

3. (a) What was your reaction to Antony's estimate of Brutus? (b) Do you feel that Antony was sincere?

4. Decide what the word *tragedy* means to you. Then complete this sentence: The chief tragedy of Brutus' life was . . . .

5. As the play ends, Octavius and Antony speak of dividing the honors that have come from the victory. (a) What do you think Rome's future will be under these men? (b) From an encyclopedia or an ancient history book find out what actually did happen after the battle at Philippi and see how accurately you prophesied the future.

THE AUTHOR'S CRAFT

". . . the death of princes"
Julius Caesar, II, ii

Now that you have read *Julius Caesar*, you can see that a Shakespearean tragedy is more than "a serious play having an unhappy ending." What aspects of *Julius Caesar* are typical of a Shakespearean tragedy?

(1) Shakespeare always develops a *tragic hero* as a focal point of his tragedy. His tragic hero is a nobleman and a leader whose death affects the course of empire. Moreover, Shakespeare endows his tragic hero with a character weakness, or *flaw*, that ultimately causes him to make a fatal mistake. Both Caesar and Brutus qualify as the tragic hero of *Julius Caesar*. What is Caesar's fatal mistake? What weaknesses in his character cause him to make this mistake? What errors in judgment does Brutus commit? What do you consider his tragic flaw to be?

(2) Shakespeare builds a tragedy on external and internal *conflicts*. He uses the political controversy in Rome to create the external conflict in *Julius Caesar*. How does Shakespeare develop this external conflict in the play? What internal conflict does Caesar experience? What internal conflict does Brutus experience?

(3) Shakespeare uses *humor* to relieve the somber mood of a tragedy. Describe the two humorous incidents that occur in Act One of *Julius Caesar*. Why would comic relief be inappropriate to Act Three?

(4) Shakespeare often includes a *supernatural* incident in a tragedy. What do the supernatural incidents in *Julius Caesar* reveal about Caesar and Brutus?

(5) One of the major characters in Shakespeare's tragedy is often motivated by a desire for *revenge*. To what extent does revenge figure in *Julius Caesar*?

(6) Shakespeare introduces a *chance happening* that precipitates the catastrophe of a tragedy. In Act Five, Scene 3 of *Julius Caesar*, for example, Cassius and Pindarus misinterpret the meeting between Titinius and Brutus' men. How does this chance happening affect the fortunes of Cassius and Brutus?

A Shakespearean tragedy is "a serious blank-verse play having an unhappy ending. In his *Tragedy of Julius Caesar*, Shakespeare combines the following dramatic elements: a tragic hero with a tragic flaw; external and internal conflicts; humorous relief; supernatural incidents; a revenge motive; and a chance happening."

"...with silken coats and caps..."

Costuming on the Elizabethan stage was both lavish and colorful. Shakespeare's fellow actors—"with silken coats and caps and golden rings, with ruffs and cuffs and farthingales and things"—were a brilliant sight to behold.

The costumes worn by Elizabethan actors usually were so costly that it was necessary to protect them from soil or other damage during the course of a performance. For this reason, rushes were strewn on the inner stage, the rear platform, and the outer edges of the platform. When the moment came for an actor to fall down, for example, he would be careful to fall on one of these rush-strewn areas. If you will re-examine the assassination scene in Act Three of *Julius Caesar*, you will see that Caesar's costume is protected in this way.

Costuming has always been an important visual device to help playgoers distinguish one character from another. Appropriate costuming may also reinforce characterization. In staging their plays, Elizabethan acting companies usually did not attempt to duplicate historical dress. Some of the characters in *Julius Caesar* may have worn Roman robes and cloaks as they do in the illustrations in your textbook. It is more likely, however, that Roman characters wore sixteenth-century dress. The Globe audience did not think it strange to see Brutus and Antony in Elizabethan doublet and hose! When Shakespeare's plays are staged today, some productions will adopt historical dress, while others will adopt modern dress.

Although Elizabethans probably did not duplicate Roman dress in *Julius Caesar*, the chances are that their costumes combined fabric and color in a symbolic way. Englishmen of Shakespeare's time were extremely class-conscious. One indication of a person's "high" or "low" estate was the fabric of his clothing. This was true of stage costumes as well. On the Globe platform, aristocratic Romans would be distinguished by their costumes of satin or taffeta, damask or velvet. The commoners would be identified by their coarse linsey-woolsey; workingmen by their canvas aprons. If the Ghost of Caesar did not wear the same costume as the living Caesar, he would be clad in leather.

Color also symbolized social status to Elizabethans. It was customary in those days to see apprentices, for example, in their liveries of dark blue, and to see Queen Elizabeth I in her state robes of scarlet. On the stage, dark blue was also reserved for one who served, just as scarlet was reserved for one who ruled. In addition to symbolizing social status, color symbolized such abstract qualities as love or courage. A costume with many touches of yellow would indicate that a character was jealous. Similarly, orange would represent pride; azure blue would convey honor; and rose would symbolize gallantry.

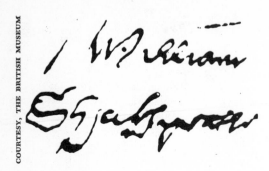

PLAYWRIGHT

The first reference to William Shakespeare is a baptismal record for April 26, 1564, at Holy Trinity Church in Stratford-on-Avon. Since in that time it was customary for infants to be baptized when three days old, it is generally assumed that Shakespeare was born on April 23. His father was John Shakespeare, a glove-maker and a dealer in farm products. During William's boyhood his father was elected to one civic office after another, becoming in time high bailiff, or mayor. There is little doubt that once young William had learned to read and write English he was admitted to the free grammar school which had been the pride of Stratford since the Middle Ages. In a sixteenth-century grammar school the boys studied the classical languages—first Latin and then Greek.

When Will Shakespeare was about thirteen, his father suffered business reverses. The boy probably left school and became an apprentice at some trade. At eighteen he married Anne Hathaway, and in 1583 his daughter Susanna was born. Two years later, twins, Hamnet and Judith, were born.

About 1584 Shakespeare left Stratford. No one knows exactly the reasons for his going. By 1592 he was in London and was well enough known as a playwright to excite the jealousy of a fellow playwright, Robert Greene, who wrote a vicious attack on him. How he had spent the eight missing years is not known. It is not possible to determine with which acting company Shakespeare was first associated; but by 1594 he was both actor and playwright with the Lord Chamberlain's Company. When James I became king in 1603, he took the members of the Lord Chamberlain's Company under his patronage and from that time on they were known as the King's Men.

For fifteen years Shakespeare was the principal playwright of this company and wrote an average of two plays a year. Among his first group of plays were light, gay comedies and historical plays about some of the past kings of England. The genius of Shakespeare began to show itself in his second group of plays—dramas like *A Midsummer-Night's Dream*, *Romeo and Juliet*, and *The Merchant of Venice*. The plays of the third group sparkle with Elizabethan humor and vigor. Here are the comedies, *As You Like It* and *Twelfth Night*, and the great chronicle plays, *Henry IV* and *Henry V*.

By 1597 Shakespeare was a successful man, prosperous enough to purchase the house and gardens of New Place, one of the largest homes in Stratford. Two years later he purchased an interest in the Globe Playhouse. Although he now probably spent some time each year in Stratford, London remained his headquarters. It was at this time that he wrote his fourth group of plays. Most of these plays, beginning with *Julius Caesar*, are tragedies; among them are *Hamlet*, *Othello*, *King Lear*, and *Macbeth*.

About 1610 Shakespeare seems to have left London for Stratford to live the life of a retired gentleman. Probably the last few of his plays, including *The Winter's Tale* and *The Tempest*, were written there. On April 23, 1616, he died and was buried in the chancel of Holy Trinity Church at Stratford.

UNIT 4 REVIEW

1. The physical conditions of an Elizabethan playhouse, like the Globe, made specific demands upon Shakespeare's stagecraft. Reread "The Author's Craft" articles on page 277 and page 296; then, answer the following questions.

a. Elizabethan actors usually spoke between twenty and twenty-five lines a minute. Why did they deliver their lines so rapidly? What problem did this situation create for Shakespeare?

b. Why is blank verse an excellent medium for dialogue? How does Shakespeare make his blank verse flexible enough to express the complicated thoughts and emotions of his characters? Where in *Julius Caesar* does Shakespeare use prose?

c. Part of Shakespeare's task was to set his own scenes in his dialogue. Why did he have to do this?

d. Shakespeare empties the platform at the end of a platform scene. He also shifts the action of the play from one stage to another. Why did Shakespeare use these two visual devices?

2. Shakespeare's insight into the behavior of human beings was profound; no dramatist has ever surpassed him in creating characters that are true to life. Reread "The Author's Craft" article on page 330 before answering the following questions.

a. What is a character foil? How does Shakespeare use character foils in *Julius Caesar*?

b. How does Shakespeare make his characters realistic? Cite the realistic qualities that you find in Caesar and Brutus, Antony and Cassius.

3. A *tragedy* may be defined as "a serious play having an unhappy ending." Why is this an inadequate definition of a Shakespearean tragedy? Rereading "The Author's Craft" article on page 342 will help you answer this question.

4. Some scholars believe that Shakespeare was correct in titling his play *The Tragedy of Julius Caesar*. Other scholars argue that he should have titled his play *The Tragedy of Marcus Brutus*. Read the following two quotations and then explain which title you prefer and why.

"It is the spirit of Caesar which is the dominant power of the tragedy; against this—the spirit of Caesar—Brutus fought; but Brutus, who forever errs in practical politics, succeeded only in striking down Caesar's body; he who had been weak now rises pure in spirit, strong and terrible, and avenges himself upon the conspirators."

Edward Dowden, *Shakespeare, A Critical Study of His Mind and Heart* (Routledge & Kegan Paul, Ltd., 1949). page 287

"The true hero of the piece is Brutus . . . Shakespeare, having so arranged his drama that Brutus should be its tragic hero, had to concentrate his art on placing him in the foreground, and making him fill the scene. . . . He had to be the center and pivot of everything, and therefore Caesar was diminished and belittled to such a degree, unfortunately, that this matchless genius in war and statesmanship has become a miserable caricature."

Georg M. C. Brandes, *William Shakespeare: A Critical Study* (Macmillan, 1936). page 306.

Prose Forms

EFFORTS
RECOLLECTIONS
COMMENTS
CULTURES

IN this unit you will encounter a number of different prose forms: autobiography, essay, letter, anecdotal record, personal remembrance, biographical sketch. (There is a clear distinction between the biographical sketch and biography. Biography as a type of literature is not included because the form itself demands a well developed thorough explication of the many complex facets of a personality in terms of the time and events during which he lived. Biography, per se, like the full length novel, exceeds the space limitations of this anthology. The author's craft article on page 363 explains the difference between autobiographical and general biographical writing.)

Francis Bacon wrote, "Some books are to be tasted, others to be swallowed, and some few to be chewed and digested." In such a way you should approach this unit. Remember that here are writers presenting ideas—some more objective and some more subjective. Ideas are inevitably personal. Do not accept everything you read, but question the ideas and values of the writers. Are they your ideas and values? And if they are not, should they be?

If you are a careful reader, you will try to determine the writer's attitude. Is he serious or joking? Did he write when he was angry? Happy? Sad? Is he rational or does he allow his emotions to control his point of view?

Some of the styles will be more appealing to you than others. A few of the writers are very formal. They follow a clear, step-by-step process, trying to lead you to the same conclusion they have arrived at. Others are informal. They ramble from point to point. Their main ideas often become obscure. They sometimes leave you wondering what they meant. But, taste all of the selections, swallow some, and you may want to chew and digest a few.

EFFORTS

The Letter "A"

Christy Brown

I was born in the Rotunda Hospital[1], on June 5th, 1932. There were nine children before me and twelve after me, so I myself belong to the middle group. Out of this total of twenty-two, seventeen lived, but four died in infancy, leaving thirteen still to hold the family fort.

Mine was a difficult birth, I am told. Both mother and son almost died. A whole army of relations queued up outside the hospital until the small hours of the morning, waiting for news and praying furiously that it would be good.

After my birth mother was sent to recuperate for some weeks and I was kept in the hospital while she was away. I remained there for some time, without name, for I wasn't baptized until my mother was well enough to bring me to church.

It was mother who first saw that there was something wrong with me. I was about four months old at the time. She noticed that my head had a habit of falling backward whenever she tried to feed me. She attempted to correct this by placing her hand on the back of my neck to keep it steady. But when she took it away, back it would drop again. That was the first warning sign. Then she became aware of other de-

fects as I got older. She saw that my hands were clenched nearly all of the time and were inclined to twine behind my back, my mouth couldn't grasp the teat of the bottle because even at that early age my jaws would either lock together tightly, so that it was impossible for her to open them, or they would suddenly become limp and fall loose, dragging my whole mouth to one side. At six months I could not sit up without having a mountain of pillows around me. At twelve months it was the same.

Very worried by this, mother told my father her fears, and they decided to seek medical advice without any further delay. I was a little over a year old when they began to take me to hospitals and clinics, convinced that there was something definitely wrong with me, something which they could not understand or name, but which was very real and disturbing.

Almost every doctor who saw and examined me, labeled me a very interesting but also a hopeless case. Many told mother very gently that I was mentally defective and would remain so. That was a hard blow to a young mother who had already reared five

---

1. *Rotunda Hospital,* a hospital in Dublin, Ireland.

healthy children. The doctors were so very sure of themselves that mother's faith in me seemed almost an impertinence. They assured her that nothing could be done for me.

She refused to accept this truth, the inevitable truth—as it then seemed—that I was beyond cure, beyond saving, even beyond hope. She could not and would not believe that I was an imbecile, as the doctors told her. She had nothing in the world to go by, not a scrap of evidence to support her conviction that, though my body was crippled, my mind was not. In spite of all the doctors and specialists told her, she would not agree. I don't believe she knew why— she just knew, without feeling the smallest shade of doubt.

Finding that the doctors could not help in any way beyond telling her not to place her trust in me, or, in other words, to forget I was a human creature, rather to regard me as just something to be fed and washed and then put away again, mother decided there and then to take matters into her own hands. I was *her* child, and therefore part of the family. No matter how dull and incapable I might grow up to be, she was determined to treat me on the same plane as the others, and not as the "queer one" in the back room who was never spoken of when there were visitors present.

That was a momentous decision as far as my future life was concerned. It meant that I would always have my mother on my side to help me fight all the battles that were to come, and to inspire me with new strength when I was almost beaten. But it wasn't easy for her because now the relatives and friends had decided otherwise. They contended that I should be taken kindly, sympathetically, but not seriously. That would be a mistake. "For your own sake," they told her, "don't look to this boy as you would to the others; it would only break your heart in the end." Luckily for me, mother and father held out against the lot of them. But mother wasn't content just to say that I was not an idiot: she set out to prove it, not because of any rigid sense of duty, but out of love. That is why she was so successful.

At this time she had the five other children to look after besides the "difficult one," though as yet it was not by any means a full house. They were my brothers, Jim, Tony, and Paddy, and my two sisters, Lily and Mona, all of them very young, just a year or so between each of them, so that they were almost exactly like steps of stairs.

Four years rolled by and I was now five, and still as helpless as a newly born baby. While my father was out at bricklaying, earning our bread and butter for us, mother was slowly, patiently pulling down the wall, brick by brick, that seemed to thrust itself between me and the other children, slowly, patiently penetrating beyond the thick curtain that hung over my mind, separating it from theirs. It was hard, heartbreaking work, for often all she got from me in return was a vague smile and perhaps a faint gurgle. I could not speak or even mumble, nor could I sit up without support on my own, let alone take steps. But I wasn't inert or motionless. I seemed, indeed, to be convulsed with movement, wild, stiff, snakelike movement that never left me, except in sleep. My fingers twisted and twitched continually, my arms twined backwards and would often shoot out suddenly this way and that, and my head lolled and sagged sideways. I was a queer, crooked little fellow.

Mother tells me how one day she had been sitting with me for hours in an upstairs room, showing me pictures out of a great big storybook that I had got from Santa Claus last Christmas and telling me the names of the different animals and flowers that were in them, trying without success to get me to repeat them. This had gone on for hours while she talked and laughed with me. Then at the end of it she leaned over me and said gently into my ear:

"Did you like it, Chris? Did you like the bears and the monkeys and all the lovely flowers? Nod your head for yes, like a good boy."

But I could make no sign that I had understood her. Her face was bent over mine hopefully. Suddenly, involuntarily, my queer hand reached up and grasped one of the dark curls that fell in a thick cluster about her neck. Gently she loosened the clenched fingers, though some dark strands were still clutched between them.

Then she turned away from my curious stare and left the room, crying. The door closed behind her. It all seemed hopeless. It looked as though there was some justification for my relatives' contention that I was an idiot and beyond help.

They now spoke of an institution.

"Never!" said my mother almost fiercely, when this was suggested to her. "I know my boy is not an idiot, it is his body that is shattered, not his mind. I'm sure of that."

Sure? Yet inwardly, she prayed God would give her some proof of her faith. She knew it was one thing to believe but quite another thing to prove.

I was now five, and still I showed no real sign of intelligence. I showed no apparent interest in things except with my toes—more especially those of my left foot. Although my natural habits were clean, I could not aid myself, but in this respect my father took care of me. I used to lie on my back all the time in the kitchen or, on bright warm days, out in the garden, a little bundle of crooked muscles and twisted nerves, surrounded by a family that loved me and hoped for me and that made me part of their own warmth and humanity. I was lonely, imprisoned in a world of my own, unable to communicate with others, cut off, separated from them as though a glass wall stood between my existence and theirs, thrusting me beyond the sphere of their lives and activities. I longed to run about and play with the rest, but I was unable to break loose from my bondage.

Then, suddenly, it happened! in a moment everything was changed, my future life molded into a definite shape, my mother's faith in me rewarded and her secret fear changed into open triumph.

It happened so quickly, so simply after all the years of waiting and uncertainty, that I can see and feel the whole scene as if it had happened last week. It was the afternoon of a cold, gray December day. The streets outside glistened with snow, the white sparkling flakes stuck and melted on the windowpanes and hung on the boughs of the trees like molten silver. The wind howled dismally, whipping up little whirling columns of snow that rose and fell at every fresh gust. And over all, the dull, murky sky stretched like a dark canopy, a vast infinity of grayness.

Inside, all the family were gathered round the big kitchen fire that lit up the little room with a warm glow and made giant shadows dance on the walls and ceiling.

In a corner Mona and Paddy were sitting, huddled together, a few torn school primers before them. They were writing down little sums on to an old chipped slate, using a bright piece of yellow chalk. I was close to them, propped up by a few pillows against the wall, watching.

It was the chalk that attracted me so much. It was a long, slender stick of vivid yellow. I had never seen anything like it before, and it showed up so well against the black surface of the slate that I was fascinated by it as much as if it had been a stick of gold.

Suddenly, I wanted desperately to do what my sister was doing. Then—without thinking or knowing exactly what I was doing, I reached out and took the stick of chalk out of my sister's hand—with my left foot.

I do not know why I used my left foot to do this. It is a puzzle to many people as well as to myself, for, although I had displayed a curious interest in my toes at an early age, I had never attempted before this to use either of my feet in any way. They could have been as useless to me as were my hands. That day, however, my left foot, apparently by its own volition, reached out and very impolitely took the chalk out of my sister's hand.

I held it tightly between my toes, and, acting on an impulse, made a wild sort of scribble with it on the slate. Next moment I stopped, a bit dazed, surprised, looking down at the stick of yellow chalk stuck between my toes, not knowing what to do with it next, hardly knowing how it got there. Then I looked up and became aware that everyone had stopped talking and was staring at me silently. Nobody stirred. Mona, her black curls framing her chubby little face, stared at me with great big eyes and open mouth. Across the open hearth, his face lit by flames, sat my father, leaning forward, hands outspread on his knees, his shoulders tense. I felt the sweat break out on my forehead.

My mother came in from the pantry with a steaming pot in her hand. She stopped midway between the table and the fire, feeling the tension flowing through the room. She followed their stare and saw me in the corner. Her eyes looked from my face down to my foot, with the chalk gripped between my toes. She put down the pot.

Then she crossed over to me and knelt down beside me, as she had done so many times before.

"I'll show you what to do with it, Chris," she said, very slowly and in a queer, choked way, her face flushed as if with some inner excitement.

Taking another piece of chalk from Mona, she hesitated, then very deliberately drew, on the floor in front of me, *the single letter "A."*

"Copy that," she said, looking steadily at me. "Copy it, Christy."

I couldn't.

I looked about me, looked around at the faces that were turned towards me, tense, excited faces that were at that moment frozen, immobile, eager, waiting for a miracle in their midst.

The stillness was profound. The room was full of

flame and shadow that danced before my eyes and lulled my taut nerves into a sort of waking sleep. I could hear the sound of the water tap dripping in the pantry, the loud ticking of the clock on the mantelshelf, and the soft hiss and crackle of the logs on the open hearth.

I tried again. I put out my foot and made a wild jerking stab with the chalk which produced a very crooked line and nothing more. Mother held the slate steady for me.

"Try again, Chris," she whispered in my ear. "Again."

I did. I stiffened my body and put my left foot out again, for the third time. I drew one side of the letter. I drew half the other side. Then the stick of chalk broke and I was left with a stump. I wanted to fling it away and give up. Then I felt my mother's hand on my shoulder. I tried once more. Out went my foot. I shook, I sweated and strained every muscle. My hands were so tightly clenched that my fingernails bit into the flesh. I set my teeth so hard that I nearly pierced my lower lip. Everything in the room swam till the faces around me were mere patches of white. But—I drew it—*the letter "A."* There it was on the floor before me. Shaky, with awkward, wobbly sides and a very uneven center line. But it *was* the letter "A." I looked up. I saw my mother's face for a moment, tears on her cheeks. Then my father stooped and hoisted me on to his shoulder.

I had done it! It had started—the thing that was to give my mind its chance of expressing itself. True, I couldn't speak with my lips. But now I would speak through something more lasting than spoken words —written words.

That one letter, scrawled on the floor with a broken bit of yellow chalk gripped between my toes, was my road to a new world, my key to mental freedom. It was to provide a source of relaxation to the tense, taut thing that was I, which panted for expression behind a twisted mouth.

DISCUSSION

1. The above selection is an autobiographical account. Is there any biography in it? Explain. (See Author's Craft article on page 363.)

2. What do you think prevented Mrs. Brown from accepting the "inevitable truth" about her son's condition?

3. Throughout this selection Christy Brown relies a great deal on his mother's memory. (a) At what point in the story does he rely on his own recollections? (b) Why do you suppose he has such a vivid memory of this event?

4. Explain what Christy Brown means in the last paragraph, where he says that the letter "A" was the key to his mental freedom.

COMPOSITION

If you are not already familiar with the term *euthanasia*, look up the word in a dictionary. In a composition of two or more paragraphs state your position, for or against, euthanasia.

AUTHOR

CHRISTY BROWN, as he writes in "The Letter 'A'", was born in Dublin, Ireland, on June 5, 1932. He was the tenth child of the twenty-two his mother would bear. Soon after his birth he was discovered to have cerebral palsy. But the steadfast faith of his mother encouraged him to struggle with this grave handicap and attempt to overcome it.

With the help of physical therapy, he enabled himself to write and type by using his feet. Through this arduous method, he wrote an autobiography, *My Left Foot* (1954). Then, in 1970, he finished a novel, *Down All the Days*, which brought him world fame.

His life in the Dublin slums supplied him with more than enough material for his books. Though handicapped in movement, he became a serious student of human nature. "I've had no choice but to be an observer," he has said, "Always on the outside looking in."

EFFORTS

OPEN LETTER TO A YOUNG NEGRO

Jesse Owens

"Tell them how the good times between us were."
—Luz Long

Aᴸᴸ black men are insane. . . . Almost any living thing would quickly go mad under the unrelenting exposure to the climate created and reserved for black men in a white racist society. . . . I am secretly pleased about the riots. Nothing would please the tortured man inside me more than seeing bigger and better riots every day."

Those words were spoken by Bob Teague to his young son in *Letters to a Black Boy*. He wrote these letters to "alert" his son to "reality" so that the boy wouldn't "be caught off guard—unprepared and undone."

Are his words true?

Does a black man have to be just about insane to exist in America?

Do all Negroes feel a deep twinge of pleasure every time we see a white man hurt and a part of white society destroyed?

Is reality something so stinking terrible that it'll grab your heart out of your chest with one hand and your manhood with the other if you don't meet it armed like a Nazi storm trooper?

Bob Teague is no "militant." He's a constructive, accomplished journalist with a wife and child. If he feels hate and fear, can *you* ever avoid feeling it?

Whether it's Uncle Tom or ranting rioter doing the talking today, you're told that you'll have to be afraid and angry. The only difference is that one tells you to hold it in and the other tells you to let it out. Life is going to be torture because you're a Negro, they all say. They only differ on whether you should grin and bear it or take it out on everyone else. But National Urban League official, Black Panther leader or any of the in-betweens all seem to agree on one thing today: "We must organize around our strongest bond—our blackness."

Is that really our strongest bond? Isn't there something deeper, richer, better in this world than the color of one's skin?

Let me tell you the answer to that. Let me prove it to you so strong and deep that you'll taste it for all the days to come. Let me throw my arm around your shoulder and walk you to where so much good is and where the only blackness worth fearing is the black they're trying to color your soul.

Even though you weren't born for ten, maybe twenty years after, you've probably heard the story—the story of the 1936 Olympics and how I managed to come out with four gold medals. A lot of words have been written about those medals and about the one for the broad jump in particular. Because it was during that event that Hitler walked out on me and where, in anger, I supposedly fouled on my first two jumps against his prize athlete, Luz Long. The whole Olympics for me and, symbolically, for my country, seemed to rest on that third jump.

Yes, a lot of words have been written about that day and the days that followed. And they've almost been true, just as it's almost true that sometimes every black man weakens a little and does hate the white man, just as it's almost true that reality is tough at times and does make you want to weaken.

Yet, just like *those* "truths," what was written about me was only a half-truth without some other more important words. I want to say them to you now.

I *was* up against it, but long before I came to the broad jump. Negroes had gone to the Olympics before, and Negroes had won before. But so much more was expected of me. Because this was the time of the most intense conflict between dictatorship and freedom the world had ever known. Adolf Hitler was arming his country against the entire world, and almost everyone sensed it. It was ironic that these last Olympic Games before World War II was to split the earth were scheduled for Berlin, where he would be the host. From the beginning, Hitler had perverted the games into a test between two forms of government, just as he perverted almost everything else he touched.

Almost everything else.

The broad jump preliminaries came before the finals of the other three events I was in—the hundred-meter and two-hundred-meter dashes and the relay. How I did in the broad jump would determine how I did in the entire Olympics. For here was where I held a world record that no one had ever approached before except one man: Luz Long, Hitler's best athlete.

Long, a tall, sandy-haired, perfectly built fellow (the ideal specimen of Hitler's "Aryan supremacy"[1] idea), had been known to jump over twenty-six feet in preparing for the Games. No one knew for sure what he could really do because Hitler kept him under wraps. But stories had filtered out that he had gone as far as I had, farther than anyone else in the world. I was used to hearing rumors like that and tried not to think too much about it. Yet the first time I laid eyes on Long, I sensed that the stories hadn't been exaggerated. After he took his first jump, I knew they hadn't. This man was something. I'd have to set an Olympic record and by no small margin to beat him.

It would be tough. August in Berlin was muggier than May in Ann Arbor or Columbus. Yet the air was cool, and it was hard getting warmed up. The ground on the runway to the broad jump pit wasn't the same consistency as that at home. Long was used to it. I wasn't.

His first jump broke the Olympic record. In the trials!

Did it worry me a little? More than a little. He was on his home ground and didn't seem susceptible to the pressure. In fact, he'd already done one thing I always tried to do in every jumping event and race I ran: discourage the competition by getting off to a better start.

Well, there was only one way to get back the psychological advantage. Right off the bat I'd have to make a better jump than he did. I didn't want to do it that way—it wasn't wise to use up your energy in preliminaries. Long could afford to showboat in the trials. This was his only event, the one he'd been groomed for under Hitler for years. I had to run three races besides, more than any other athlete on either team.

But I felt I had to make a showing right then. I measured off my steps from the takeoff board and got ready. Suddenly an American newspaperman came up to me. "Is it true, Jesse?" he said.

"Is what true?" I answered.

"That Hitler walked out on you? That he wouldn't watch you jump?"

I looked over at where the German ruler had been sitting. No one was in his box. A minute ago he

---

1. *"Aryan* (är′ yən) *supremacy"*, a theory that a so-called race of "Aryans", caucasian primitives, were superior to other races. It was adopted by the Nazis as their chief policy of conquest.

had been there. I could add two and two. Besides, he'd already snubbed me once by refusing the Olympic Committee's request to have me sit in that box.

This was too much. I was mad, hate-mad, and it made me feel wild. I was going to show him. He'd hear about this jump, even if he wouldn't see it!

I felt the energy surging into my legs and tingling in the muscles of my stomach as it never had before. I began my run, first almost in slow motion, then picking up speed, and finally faster and faster until I was moving almost as fast as I did during the hundred-yard dash. Suddenly the takeoff board was in front of me. I hit it, went up, up high—so high I

knew I was outdoing Long and every man who ever jumped.

But they didn't measure it. I heard the referee shout "Foul!" in my ears before I even came down. I had run too fast, been concentrating too much on a record and not enough on form. I'd gone half a foot over the takeoff board.

All the newspaper stories and books I've ever seen about that Olympic broad jump had me fouling on the next of my three tries, because the writers felt that made the story more dramatic. The truth is I didn't foul at all on my second jump.

I played it safe. Too safe. I was making absolutely sure I didn't foul. All right, I said to myself. Long had won his point. But who would remember the preliminaries tomorrow? It was the finals that counted. I had to make sure I got into those finals. I wasn't going to let him psyche me out of it. I wasn't going to let Hitler anger me into throwing away what I'd worked ten years for.

So I ran slower, didn't try to get up as high during my jump. Hell, I said to myself, if I can do twenty-six feet trying my best, I sure ought to be able to do a foot less without much effort. That would be enough to qualify for the finals, and there I'd have three fresh jumps again. That's where I'd take apart Luz Long.

It's funny how sometimes you can forget the most important things. I forgot that I wasn't the kind of guy who could ever go halfway at anything. More than that, no sprinter or jumper can really take just a little bit off the top. It's like taking a little bit off when you're working a mathematical equation or flying an airplane through a storm. You need the total concentration and total effort from beginning to end. One mistake and you're dead. More than that, my whole style was geared to giving everything I had, to using all my speed and energy every second of what I was doing. Once or twice I'd tried a distance race just for kicks. I was miserable at it. If I couldn't go all out all the time, I was no good.

So my second jump was no good.

I didn't foul. But I didn't go far enough to qualify, either. It wasn't just Long and Owens in the event anymore. There were dozens of other participants from other countries, and a bunch of them—too many—were now ahead of me.

I had one jump left.

It wasn't enough.

I looked around nervously, panic creeping into every cell of my body. On my right was Hitler's box. Empty. His way of saying I was a member of an inferior race who would give an inferior performance. In back of that box was a stadium containing more than a hundred thousand people, almost all Germans, all wanting to see me fail. On my right was the broad jump official. Was he fair? Yeah. But a Nazi. If it came to a close call, a hairline win-or-lose decision, deep down didn't he, too, want to see me lose? Worst of all, a few feet away was Luz Long, laughing with a German friend of his, unconcerned, confident, *Aryan.*

They were against me. Every one of them. I was back in Oakville again.[2] I was a nigger.

2. *Oakville,* Oakville, Alabama, where Jesse Owens was raised.

Did I find some hidden resource deep within me, rise to the occasion and qualify for the finals—as every account of those Olympics says?

The hell I did.

I found a hidden resource, but it wasn't inside of me. It was in the most unlikely and revealing place possible.

Time was growing short. One by one the other jumpers had been called and taken their turns. What must have been twenty minutes or half an hour suddenly seemed like only seconds. I was going to be called next. I wasn't ready. I wanted to shout it—*I wasn't ready!*

Then the panic was total. I had to walk in a little circle to keep my legs from shaking, hold my jaw closed tight to stop my teeth from chattering. I didn't know what to do. I was lost, with no Charles Riley to turn to. If I gave it everything I had, I'd foul again. If I played it safe, I wouldn't go far enough to qualify. *And this is what it all comes down to,* I thought to myself. *Ten years and 4,500 miles to make a nigger of myself and not even reach the finals!*

And then I couldn't even think anymore. I started to feel faint, began to gasp for breath. Instinctively, I turned away from everyone so they couldn't see me. But I couldn't help hearing them. The thousands of different noises of the stadium congealed into one droning hum—*ch-ch-ch-ch-ch-ch-ch-ch,* louder and louder in my ears. It was as though they were all chanting it. Hatefully, gleefully. *Ch-ch-ch-ch. Ch-ch-ch-ch. CH-CH-CH-CH.*

Suddenly I felt a firm hand on my arm. I turned and looked into the sky-blue eyes of my worst enemy.

"Hello, Jesse Owens," he said. "I am Luz Long."

I nodded. I couldn't speak.

"Look," he said. "There is no time to waste with manners. What has taken your goat?"

I had to smile a little in spite of myself—hearing his mixed-up American idiom.

"Aww, nothing," I said. "You know how it is."

He was silent for a few seconds. "Yes," he said finally, "I know how it is. But I also know you are a better jumper than this. Now, *what has taken your goat?*"

I laughed out loud this time. But I couldn't tell him, him above all. I glanced over at the broad jump pit. I was about to be called.

Luz didn't waste words, even if he wasn't sure of which ones to use.

"Is it what Reichskanzler[3] Hitler did?" he asked.

I was thunderstruck that he'd say it. "I—" I started to answer. But I didn't know what to say.

"I see," he said, "Look, we talk about that later. Now you must jump. And you must qualify."

"But how?" I shot back.

"I have thought," he said. "You are like I am. You must do it one hundred percent. Correct?" I nodded. "Yet you must be sure not to foul." I nodded again, this time in frustration. And as I did, I heard the loudspeaker call my name.

Luz talked quickly. "Then you do both things, Jesse. You remeasure your steps. You take off six inches behind the foul board. You jump as hard as you can. But you need not fear to foul."

All at once the panic emptied out of me like a cloudburst.

Of course!

I jogged over to the runway. I remeasured my steps again. Then I put a towel parallel to the place half a foot before the takeoff board from where I wanted to jump.

I walked back to the starting spot. I began my run, hit the place beside the towel, shot up into the air like a bird and qualified by more than a foot.

The next day I went into the finals of the broad jump and waged the most intense competition of my life with Luz Long. He broke his own personal record and the Olympic record, too, and then I— thanks to him—literally flew to top that. Hours before I had won the hundred meters in 10.3, and then afterward the 200 meters in 20.7 and helped our team to another gold medal and record in the relay.

During the evenings that framed those days, I would sit with Luz in his space or mine in the Olympic village, and we would form an even more intense friendship. We were sometimes as different inside as we looked on the outside. But the things that were the *same* were much more important to us.

Luz had a wife and a young child, too. His was a son. We talked about everything from athletics to art, but mostly we talked about the future. He didn't say it in so many words, but he seemed to know that war was coming and he would have to be in it. I

didn't know then whether the United States would be involved, but I did realize that this earth was getting to be a precarious place for a young man trying to make his way. And, like me, even if war didn't come, Luz wasn't quite sure how he would make the transformation from athletics to life once the Olympics were over.

We talked, of course, about Hitler and what he was doing. Luz was torn between two feelings. He didn't believe in Aryan supremacy any more than he believed the moon was made of German cheese, and he was disturbed at the direction in which Hitler was going. Yet he loved his country and felt a loyalty to fight for it if it came to that, if only for the sake of his wife and son. I couldn't understand how he could go along with Hitler under any circumstances, though, and I told him so.

He wasn't angry when I said it. He just held out his hands and nodded. He didn't explain because he didn't understand completely himself, just as I couldn't explain to him how the United States tolerated the race situation. So we sat talking about these things, some nights later than two Olympic performers should have. We didn't come up with any final answers then, only with a unique friendship. For we were simply two uncertain young men in an uncertain world. One day we would learn the truth, but in the meantime, we would make some mistakes. Luz's mistake would cost him too much.

Yet we didn't make the mistake of not seeing past each other's skin color to what was within. If we couldn't apply that principle to things on a world scale, we still could live it fully in our own way in the few days we had together, the only days together we would ever have.

We made them count. We crammed as much understanding and fun as we could into every hour. We didn't even stop when we got out on the track. Luz was at my side cheering me on for every event, except the broad jump, of course. There he tried to beat me for all he was worth, but nature had put just a little more spring into my body and I went a handful of inches farther.

After he failed in his last attempt to beat me, he leaped out of the pit and raced to my side. To congratulate me. Then he walked toward the stands pulling me with him while Hitler was glaring, held up my hand and shouted to the gigantic crowd, "Jesse Owens! Jesse Owens!"

The stadium picked it up. "Jesse Owens!" they

---

3. *Reichskanzler* (rīHs′ kän slr), Hitler's title as leader of Nazi Germany. It means "Imperial Chancellor".

responded—though it sounded more like "*Jaz-eee-ooh-wenz*. Each time I went for a gold medal and a record in the next three days, the crowd would greet me with "*Jaz-eee-ooh-wenz! Jaz-eee-ooh-wenz!*"

I'd had people cheering me before, but never like this. Many of those men would end up killing my countrymen, and mine theirs, but the truth was that they didn't want to, and would only do it because they "had" to. Thanks to Luz, I learned that the false leaders and sick movements of this earth must be stopped in the beginning, for they turn humanity against itself.

Luz and I vowed to write each other after the Games, and we did. For three years we corresponded regularly, though the letters weren't always as happy as our talks at the Olympics had been. Times were hard for me and harder for Luz. He had had to go into the German army, away from his wife and son. His letters began to bear strange postmarks. Each letter expressed more and more doubt about what he was doing. But he felt he had no other choice. He was afraid for his family if he left the army. And how could they leave Germany? It was Luz's world, just as the South had been the only world for so many Negroes.

The last letter I got from him was in 1939. "Things become more difficult," he said, "and I am afraid, Jesse. Not just the thought of dying. It is that I may die for the wrong thing. But whatever might become of me, I hope only that my wife and son will stay alive. I am asking you who are my only friend outside of Germany, to someday visit them if you are able, to tell them about why I had to do this, and how the good times between us were. Luz."

I answered right away, but my letter came back. So did the next, and the one after. I inquired about Luz through a dozen channels. Nothing. A war was on. Finally, when it was over, I was able to get in touch with Luz's wife and find out what had happened to him. He was buried somewhere in the African desert.

Luz Long had been my competition in the Olympics. He was a white man—a Nazi white man who fought to destroy my country.

I loved Luz Long, as much as my own brothers. I still love Luz Long.

I went back to Berlin a few years ago and met his son, another fine young man. And I told Karl about his father. I told him that, though fate may have thrown us against one another, Luz rose above it,

rose so high that I was left with not only four gold medals I would never have had, but with the priceless knowledge that the only bond worth anything between human beings is their humanness.

Today there are times when that bond doesn't seem to exist. I know. I felt the same way before my third jump at the 1936 Olympics, as well as a thousand other times. There've been many moments when I did feel like hating the white man, all white men, felt like giving in to fearful reality once and for all.

But I've learned those moments aren't the real me. And what's true of me is true of most men I've met. My favorite speech in a movie is the scene in *High Noon* when Gary Cooper, alone and hunted by the four sadistic killers, momentarily weakens and saddles a horse to get out of town. Like everyone else, his deputy wants him to do it and helps him. But Cooper finally won't get up on the horse.

"Go on!" his deputy shouts. "Do it!"

"I can't do it," Cooper says.

"You were going to a minute ago!"

"I was tired," Cooper tells him. "A man thinks a lotta things when he's tired. But I *can't* do it."

We all get tired. But know yourself, know your humanness, and you'll know why you can never finally throw in with the bigotry of blackthink. You must not be a Negro. You must be a human being first and last, if not always.

Reach back, Harry Edwards. Reach back inside yourself and grapple for that extra ounce of guts, that last cell of manhood even you didn't know you had, that something that let you stand the pain and beat the ghetto and go on to break the records. Use it now to be totally honest with yourself.

For when the chips are really down, you can either put your skin first or you can go with what's inside it.

Sure, there'll be times when others try to keep you from being human. But remember that prejudice isn't new. It goes way back, just as slavery goes way back, to before there ever was an America. Men have always had to meet insanity without losing their own minds.

That doesn't mean you should stand still for bigotry. Fight it. Fight it for all you're worth. But fight your own prejudice, too. Don't expect protection in your white brother until there's not an ounce of blackthink left in you. And remember that the hardest thing in all of us isn't to fight, but to stop and think. *Black, think . . .* is the opposite of *. . . blackthink.*

I'm not going to play any establishment games with you. My way isn't its own reward. Self-knowledge, getting rid of the bitterness, a better life, are the rewards.

So be a new kind of "militant," an *immoderate moderate,* one hundred percent involved but as a man, not a six-foot hunk of brown wrapping paper, be an extremist when it comes to your ideals, a moderate when it comes to the raising of your fist.

Live every day deep and strong. Don't pass up *your* Olympics and *your* Luz Long. Don't let the blackthinkers sell you out for a masquerade rumble where the real you can never take off the mask.

You see, black *isn't* beautiful.

White isn't beautiful.

Skin-deep is *never* beautiful.

DISCUSSION

1. (a) What caused Jesse Owens almost to foul out in qualifying for the broad jump? (b) In what way did Luz Long come to his aid?

2. (a) What could Owens not understand about Long? (b) What could Long not understand about Owens?

3. State in your own words what Owens learned from his experience with Long.

4. (a) Does Owens say that blacks should not fight for the rights of blacks? (b) Explain his use of the term "immoderate moderate."

5. (a) What do you think is the purpose of an open letter? (b) What might the writer achieve through an open letter that he could not achieve in a formal article or essay?

COMPOSITION

(1) Choose some aspect of life today which you feel is unjust. Write an open letter to someone you believe will understand your feelings about this issue. Include your own personal experiences relating to the situation and/or the experiences of friends.

(2) If the last sentence in Jesse Owens' letter "Skin-deep is *never* beautiful" suggests or recalls any experience of your own that reinforces this statement, recount the experience in a letter or essay.

THE MONSTER

Deems Taylor

H E was an undersized little man, with a head too big for his body—a sickly little man. His nerves were bad. He had skin trouble. It was agony for him to wear anything next to his skin coarser than silk. And he had delusions of grandeur.

He was a monster of conceit. Never for one minute did he look at the world or at people, except in relation to himself. He was not only the most important person in the world, to himself; in his own eyes he was the only person who existed. He believed himself to be one of the greatest dramatists in the world, one of the greatest thinkers, and one of the greatest composers. To hear him talk he was Shakespeare, and Beethoven, and Plato, rolled into one. And you would have had no difficulty in hearing him talk. He was one of the most exhausting conversationalists that ever lived. An evening with him was an evening spent in listening to a monologue. Sometimes he was brilliant; sometimes he was maddeningly tiresome. But whether he was being brilliant or dull, he had one sole topic of conversation: himself. What *he* thought and what *he* did.

He had a mania for being in the right. The slightest hint of disagreement, from anyone, on the most trivial point, was enough to set him off on a harangue that might last for hours, in which he proved himself right in so many ways, and with such exhausting volubility, that in the end his hearer, stunned and deafened, would agree with him, for the sake of peace.

It never occurred to him that he and his doing were not of the most intense and fascinating interest to anyone with whom he came in contact. He had theories about almost any subject under the sun, including vegetarianism, the drama, politics, and music; and in support of these theories he wrote pamphlets, letters, books . . . thousands upon thousands of words, hundreds and hundreds of pages. He not only wrote these things, and published them—usually at somebody else's expense—but he would sit and read them aloud, for hours, to his friends and his family.

He wrote operas; and no sooner did he have the synopsis of a story, but he would invite—or rather summon—a crowd of his friends to his house and read it aloud to them. Not for criticism. For applause. When the complete poem was written, the friends had to come again, and hear *that* read aloud. Then he would publish the poem, sometimes years before the music that went with it was written. He played the piano like a composer, in the worst sense of what that implies, and he would sit down at the piano before parties that included some of the finest pianists of his time, and play for them, by the hour, his own music, needless to say. He had a composer's voice. And he would invite eminent vocalists to his house, and sing them his operas, taking all the parts.

He had the emotional stability of a six-year-old child. When he felt out of sorts, he would rave and stamp, or sink into suicidal gloom and talk darkly of going to the East to end his days as a Buddhist monk. Ten minutes later, when something pleased him, he would rush out of doors and run around the garden, or jump up and down on the sofa, or stand on his head. He could be grief-stricken over the death of a pet dog, and he could be callous and heartless to a degree that would have made a Roman emperor shudder.

He was almost innocent of any sense of responsibility. Not only did he seem incapable of supporting himself, but it never occurred to him that he was under any obligation to do so. He was convinced that the world owed him a living. In support of this belief, he borrowed money from everybody who was good for a loan—men, women, friends, or strangers. He wrote begging letters by the score, sometimes groveling without shame, at others loftily offering his intended benefactor the privilege of contributing to his support, and being mortally offended if the recipient declined the honor. I have found no record of his ever paying or repaying money to anyone who did not have a legal claim upon it.

What money he could lay his hands on he spent like an Indian rajah.[1] The mere prospect of a performance of one of his operas was enough to set him running up bills amounting to ten times the amount of his prospective royalties. On an income that would

reduce a more scrupulous man to doing his own laundry, he would keep two servants. Without enough money in his pocket to pay his rent, he would have the walls and ceiling of his study lined with pink silk. No one will ever know—certainly he never knew—how much money he owed. We do know that his greatest benefactor gave him 6,000 dollars to pay the most pressing of his debts in one city, and a year later had to give him 16,000 dollars to enable him to live in another city without being thrown into jail for debt.

He was equally unscrupulous in other ways. An endless procession of women marches through his life. His first wife spent twenty years enduring and forgiving his infidelities. His second wife had been the wife of his most devoted friend and admirer, from whom he stole her. And even while he was trying to persuade her to leave her first husband he was writing to a friend to inquire whether he could suggest some wealthy woman—*any* wealthy woman —whom he could marry for her money.

He was completely selfish in his other personal relationships. His liking for his friends was measured solely by the completeness of their devotion to him, or by their usefulness to him, whether financial or artistic. The minute they failed him—even by so much as refusing a dinner invitation—or began to lessen in usefulness, he cast them off without a second thought. At the end of his life he had exactly one friend left whom he had known even in middle age.

He had a genius for making enemies. He would insult a man who disagreed with him about the weather. He would pull endless wires in order to meet some man who admired his work, and was able and anxious to be of use to him—and would proceed to make a mortal enemy of him with some idiotic and wholly uncalled-for exhibition of arrogance and bad manners. A character in one of his operas was a caricature of one of the most powerful music critics of his day. Not content with burlesquing him, he invited the critic to his house and read him the libretto aloud in front of his friends.

The name of this monster was Richard Wagner. Everything that I have said about him you can find on record—in newspapers, in police reports, in the testimony of people who knew him, in his own letters, between the lines of his autobiography. And the curious thing about this record is that it doesn't matter in the least.

---

1. *Indian rajah*, a ruling nobleman in India, usually quite wealthy.

Because this undersized, sickly, disagreeable, fascinating little man was right all the time. The joke was on us. He *was* one of the world's great dramatists; he *was* a great thinker; he *was* one of the most stupendous musical geniuses that, up to now, the world has ever seen. The world did owe him a living. People couldn't know those things at the time, I suppose; and yet to us, who know his music, it does seem as though they should have known. What if he did talk about himself all the time? If he talked about himself for twenty-four hours every day for the span of his life he would not have uttered half the number of words that other men have spoken and written about him since his death.

When you consider what he wrote—thirteen operas and music dramas, eleven of them still holding the stage, eight of them unquestionably worth ranking among the world's great musico-dramatic masterpieces—when you listen to what he wrote, the debts and heartaches that people had to endure from him don't seem much of a price. Eduard Hanslick, the critic whom he caricatured in *Die Meistersinger*[2] and who hated him ever after, now lives only because he was caricatured in *Die Meistersinger*. The women whose hearts he broke are long since dead; and the man who could never love anyone but himself has made them deathless atonement, I think, with *Tristan and Isolde*.[3] Think of the luxury with which for a time, at least, fate rewarded Napoleon, the man who ruined France and looted Europe; and then perhaps you will agree that a few thousand dollars' worth of debts were not too heavy a price to pay for the *Ring* trilogy.[4]

What if he was faithless to his friends and to his wives? He had one mistress to whom he was faithful to the day of his death: music. Not for a single moment did he ever compromise with what he believed, with what he dreamed. There is not a line of his music that could have been conceived by a little mind. Even when he is dull, or downright bad, he is dull in the grand manner. There is a greatness about his worst mistakes. Listening to his music, one does not forgive him for what he may or may not have been. It is not a matter of forgiveness. It is a matter of being dumb with wonder that his poor brain and body didn't burst under the torment of the demon of creative energy that lived inside him, struggling, clawing, scratching to be released; tearing, shrieking at him to write the music that was in him. The miracle is that what he did in the little space of seventy years could have been done at all, even by a great genius. Is it any wonder that he had no time to be a man?

2. *Die Meistersinger* (dē mīs′ tər sing′ r), an opera by Wagner first performed in 1868. It means in German 'The Master Singers.'
3. *Tristan and Isolde* (i sol′ də), another Wagnerian opera. First presented in Munich in 1865.
4. *the Ring Trilogy*, three operas, which tell the story of the fall of the old Teutonic gods, adapted by Wagner from legend.

DISCUSSION

1. This biographical sketch has a very clear organization. Explain how Deems Taylor treats his subject in the following paragraphs: paragraph 1, paragraphs 2 to 11, paragraph 12, paragraphs 13 to 15.

2. Can you find any defense for the disagreeable characteristics of Wagner that Taylor discusses? If so, explain.

3. Why do you think Taylor waits until almost the end of his essay before revealing the name of his subject?

4. Do you think a biographer has the right or the responsibility or both to reveal the bad characteristics of his subject? Defend your answer.

5. Rock poet Don McLean wrote a song "Vincent" about the famous artist Vincent Van Gogh, whose life was full of hardships and violent acts, and who eventually committed suicide. Yet McLean says in his song that "the world has never meant for one as beautiful as you." Could you in any way consider Wagner a "beautiful" person? Explain.

COMPOSITION

(1) Listen to any piece of music by Wagner and try to describe in writing what you hear.

(2) Write a brief autobiography in which you list and discuss all your bad traits. At the end of the autobiography, explain why you believe those bad traits should be ignored by others.

THE AUTHOR'S CRAFT

Objective vs. subjective

A. "Cardinals Wipe Out Oilers 5–2."
B. "Cardinals Defeat Oilers 5–2."
A. "Enemy Soldiers in Full Scale Retreat."
B. "Enemy Drops Back to Safer Positions."
A. "My teacher hates me."
B. "I failed a test."

Examine the above statements. Which of them would you be more likely to accept as an accurate statement of an event? If you are interested in facts and truths, you will have chosen the more *objective* example.

If an author is impersonal, unbiased, and unemotional, his writing is described as *objective*. Which would you expect to be more objective: an autobiographer, one who writes about himself, or a biographer, one who writes about someone else?

Christy Brown, in "The Letter 'A'," is writing about one of the most important events in his life: that moment when he was suddenly able to communicate with the world outside his own crippled body. Is it at all possible for a person to write about himself unemotionally? When a writer allows his feelings and personal biases to affect his choice of words, he is *subjective*.

A good biographer always relies upon facts to write his story. His sources are letters, official documents, eye-witness accounts, and often personal experience with his subject or people and places related to his subject.

Does Deems Taylor in "The Monster" indicate his sources of information? Has he relied completely on facts? Does he at any time bring in his own feelings about his subject? Find evidence in the selection to support your answers.

The line between subjectivity and objectivity is not always clear. As a reader, it is your responsibility to judge each work you read. To do so, you must be alert to the degree of subjectivity of an author.

AUTHOR

DEEMS TAYLOR (1885–1966) was born Joseph Deems Taylor in New York City. He began his career as a war correspondent for the old *New York Tribune* in 1916–17. He became a music critic after the war, and shortly thereafter, turned to composition. He wrote many popular books on classical music, including *Of Men and Music* (1937) and *Music to My Ears* (1949).

In his time, Mr. Taylor was a highly regarded composer, his best known works being *Through the Looking-Glass* (1923), after Lewis Carroll, and the opera *Peter Ibbetson* (1931).

Many recall him as the narrator in Walt Disney's film, *Fantasia*.

Lena Horne

Believing in Oneself

As rewarding as they sometimes are, books can teach you only so much. The best you can hope for is to strike some sympathetic note in somebody else when you write, or to see something a little clearer when you read because you're viewing things through another person's eyes. There are some things you just have to live through before you can understand them; books alone are not enough, although the vicarious experiences gained from them can certainly be helpful. This idea was in my mind when I "wrote" *In Person*, my first autobiography, which came out in 1950. (That is, I talked, and somebody else did the writing. People who call that the lazy man's way of writing a book don't realize how much talking you have to do.) I certainly don't feel like bragging about that book, but the fact is it *did* seem

to fill a need at the time. That book was not designed to give people a penetrating look at my mind and soul; I was far too unaware of myself and far too self-protective then to permit that. It was written for my fans, especially the young ones with anxious mothers, who wanted to know what it was like to be a Negro woman in show business. Frankly, it capitalized on my success in Hollywood; and it reinforced the new idea that Negroes were no longer restricted to bit parts in Tarzan movies, or to parts in which they rolled their eyes and spoke in fearful tones of ghosts and other superstitions, or to parts depicting them as servants. I was a new Hollywood "creation"—the Negro glamor girl. Although I was what I've called "pinned to a pillar" in most of my movie roles (I stood there looking as provocative as possible and sang), the point was that I didn't play any "mammy" roles full of patient suffering and good-heartedness; and in those days that was something of an achievement. The stereotype image had cracked, even if it hadn't completely broken.

Ironically enough, the stereotypes still persisted in my real life: I was walking a very narrow path most of the time. I had become one of the "first Negroes who . . ." people, and I was advised to be very careful. I had always to be on my best behavior so as not to spoil things for those who might follow. I had become a symbol, and symbols are not supposed to act like people: they are just molded to fit a pattern that everyone can find acceptable.

It still pleases me to think about my father's role in connection with my first big contract. I had called and asked him to help me, and he did. I still wish that that particular scene could be put into a real movie: my father, absolutely unimpressed and unmoved, telling the moguls that he didn't want his daughter to work anyway, that all the colored performers he'd seen in movies were waiting on white performers, and that he could hire somebody to wait on me if that was what I wanted. He was magnificent and gave me just the confidence I needed. And I'll bet that not many professional performers have pulled a stunt as effectively. It was just one of several times that my Dad crashed through on my behalf. I scarcely saw him during my childhood, but when I was touring at nineteen we were very satisfyingly reunited, and since then have had some memorable times together.

When I look back over my life, my sharpest impressions are of the many ways in which I have been segregated, the many kinds of prejudice I have experienced. It is hardly surprising that I have only within the past few years begun to consider myself as a whole person, as an individual rather than a segment. When I was little—in fact until well after I was sixteen and got my first job, at the Cotton Club—my life was one of extreme contrasts, conflicts, and constant moving. I was either in the home of my father's parents in Brooklyn, where I was a member of one of the "first families" and segregated not only from white people but from the majority of my own people; or I was on the road with my mother, an aspiring but

hardly very successful actress; or I was being taken care of by strangers in a succession of vastly different settings. Everywhere I went, with a few rare and happy exceptions, I was somewhat out of place. I lived in an adult world, although I was a child; I lived in the Southern world, although I was a Northerner; I lived with my father's family, although my mother was not welcome there. It was a life of dramatic upheavals and changes, and whatever stability I had was pretty much of my own creation. My vision of the house in Brooklyn sustained me on many occasions; and after I married and had two children, I went back there for what turned out to be an idyllic—but brief—period.

When I started to work, I was too young to be included in some social affairs. In others I was fiercely chaperoned by my mother. I was separated from friends of my own age by my work. And when we went on tour, I was not only segregated from the other performers by my mother and her second husband—a temperamental Cuban—but I learned the facts of life about segregation in America. These were about the only facts of life I knew anything of during those years. I had been so much removed from any kind of normal development, any kind of consistent upbringing, that I was really existing in a dream world. Perhaps that was why the unreal world of segregation didn't come as any great shock: it matched the unreality I lived with day by day. My stepfather once brutally pointed out to Noble Sissle, with whom I was touring, that his calling us "ladies" didn't mean that we could enter the building through the front door. Unconsciously we all knew it already; the shocking thing was to hear it said right out loud. My stepfather was just being honest, and furious—but that kind of honesty you had to learn to live without in those days, because nobody had the energy to work and fight at the same time. We had to make a living, and we did it according to the available terms, trusting that if we behaved well we'd be allowed to continue. Being on tour was a bleak enough business without being reminded continually of the conditions you had to face; you hoped to avoid patronizing kindness as well as stark ugliness, because anything that upset the balance destroyed the flat level of endurance and the forced poise you had achieved.

Young and naïve as I was, I inevitably married to escape what seemed to me an unbearable grind, and to attain the kind of happy domestic closeness I dreamed that marriage would bring—why, I don't know, since I had seen little enough of it in my own family. I met my first husband through my father. He was a minister's son, which in the Negro hierarchy of that time meant that he was just as spoiled and inexperienced as I was; we simply could do nothing for each other, because we had not yet done much for ourselves. I was married long enough to have two children; but we were existing side by side, not as a unit, and we were both painfully disillusioned.

The birth of my first child, my daughter Gail, presented me with the first really excruciating realization of the extent to which segregation dehumanizes us. I had a Negro doctor, whom I naturally trusted implicitly—I had to, knowing nothing myself and being really frightened of this new thing that was going to happen to me. When the time came and I was taken to the hospital, the doctor met me there; and then he said goodby, wished me the best of luck, and said he was sure I'd be all right! I was absolutely speechless with fright and shock—in fact, I was so paralyzed by my emotions that I could not give birth for two days—as it slowly dawned on me that he was not allowed to practice in that hospital because he was a Negro. The Negro maternity cases were clustered together in a special little place of their own; the doctors were white.

One other incident gave me the same kind of shock, but on this occasion it was at least followed by a cleansing kind of anger, and I was at least able to do something about it. During the second World War, I did a good deal of USO work, traveling to army camps around the country and entertaining troops. It always galled me that the officers got the front-row seats, and it further annoyed me that the Negro troops had to be entertained separately—this involved two kinds of segregation. On one occasion we were required to do two shows—one for white troops and one for Negro troops—which meant extending our tour an extra day. At the second show, presumably for the Negro soldiers, there were white men in the front rows. When I asked who they were, I was told "German POW's". I nearly exploded in anger. Imagine! The enemy we were supposed to be fighting had front-row seats at a show that was intended for our own men. I couldn't believe it! I went right out past those prisoners and sang to the soldiers, but the whole situation made me so sick that I just couldn't continue. As a result of that incident I quit the show, called a cab, and went to the nearest NAACP office. I introduced myself, and the lady behind the desk said, "I'm Daisy Bates. What's on your mind?" I didn't realize how close I was to history at that moment; but I sent off my telegram and made my public comment, and that was pretty much where the incident ended. It was certainly not the first public statement I had made, but it was probably the most heartfelt and necessary one from my own point of view.

I've been married to my second husband, Lennie Hayton, for twenty years now—a long enough time, it would seem to me, to prove that we get along well. Yet when we married we felt it was necessary to go to Europe to do it; and even at that we received mail which would make you sick to read (I was not allowed to read most of it), for the very simple reason that Lennie is white and I am not. Many Negroes are every bit as prejudiced about intermarriage as whites are; to them, a Negro woman who marries a white man is rejecting her own men and her own people. This attitude is the grand accomplishment of prejudice and segregation: of hypocrisy so powerful that it can destroy individual private lives as well as public reputations. It can mean that in some places a husband and wife cannot be seen together, much less share the same room; that they have to be concerned about a thousand trivial things which ordinarily would never be noticed. In some states they can't even be husband and wife legally. Yet you have to bear with this kind of arrogant interference and ignore it if you can. You have to realize that the people who attack you don't even think of you as a person: they see the symbol, the threat to their way of thinking, and they strike at it blindly because they have never learned to react to people instead of symbols.

For most of my life I have been a symbol. The role of Public Object has brought me many rewards, but none of them can take the place of self-knowledge. Knowing yourself is very difficult under these circumstances, and being yourself is probably even more difficult, but it seems to me the only worthwhile thing a person can achieve. In the past few years I have really begun to feel an awakening as an individual. An urge to be a person has taken hold of me, and I frequently think of what Paul Robeson said to me many years ago: "You are Negro, and that is the whole basis of what you are and what you will become," and he added, "when you live and learn some more, you will be Lena Horne, Negro." I must have known then that he was telling me the truth, because I remembered his words even though I wasn't sure what he meant; just as I said earlier, there are some things you have to live through before you can understand them. The Civil Rights movement, more than any other one thing, has given me the urge to find out who I am and what I'm doing here.

In 1963 I was invited by James Baldwin to take part in a meeting in New York, which had been called by Robert Kennedy. I was on the verge of committing myself to *something,* of identifying myself with my people if they would have me, but I was not interested in acting out the role of Public Symbol any more. I had come to the conclusion that all of us—the "first Negroes who . . . "—had outlived our usefulness, that all we had ever done was to make it possible for the whites to postpone any kind of real justice. We were tokens, that was all: concessions to the white conscience, concessions to the aspirations of Negroes.

That same summer I accepted an offer from *SHOW* magazine to write an article about myself and about being a Negro in America, because I thought it was about time I gave serious thought to such matters. I had scarcely ever "been" a Negro, although my skin makes clear that this is what I am. I hadn't lived as most Negroes live, and I had rarely thought as a Negro. I was beginning to be Lena Horne, Negro, at last. In that article I said that while I couldn't sing protest songs or suddenly take up the guitar, or describe Southern atrocities with any kind of integrity, I thought there was something I could do: I could stop singing about penthouses up in the sky, with rents to match, when we couldn't even afford them, and I could stop singing those old stereotypes from musicals; and, if someone would help me out by writing some new songs, I thought I could sing things that would still be true to me and yet be more realistic, more in keeping with this generation.

Much to my surprise, I got a very prompt reply to that article from Harold Arlen; the outcome was the song "Silent Spring," dedicated to the four children murdered in the bombing of the Birmingham church. I had my wish: I had a protest song that I felt was true to me and true to the times. And I felt that I had come home—to myself and to my people. The symbol had been useful in its day, but now it had helped me to create something much larger than a symbol, much larger than myself.

I'm mature now, and a grandmother, and I have to confess that I've written another autobiography. People have commented that it is very different from the first one. I'm glad it is, because it was meant to be. There comes a time in your life when you have to talk straight to yourself, and that's what I'm trying to do. I don't feel the need to protect myself any longer; instead, I feel the strength of *being* myself, let the chips fall where they may. If I were to give any advice to young persons beginning their careers, I would urge them to choose their goals carefully, to believe thoroughly in themselves, and to always remember that in reaching for that ultimate freedom —the freedom of the individual—one's inner self is strong enough to make the choice of being human (in its better sense) or of merely being a beast.

DISCUSSION

1. Reread the first three sentences of "Believing in Oneself." Do you agree that only through experience can one truly learn? Why or why not?

2. How does Lena Horne portray herself as a child and during her early career? What are some of the examples she gives to support this idea?

3. What examples of prejudice has Lena Horne experienced as an adult?

4. (a) Lena Horne indicates that her first book was not entirely truthful. Why? (b) Do you feel that she is being entirely truthful in this selection? Explain.

5. Reread the last paragraph. Do you agree with her advice? Explain.

6. Who do you think is more outspoken on the position of being a Black symbol, Jesse Owens or Lena Horne? Explain.

from Annapurna

The Summit

Maurice Herzog

When Maurice Herzog (her′tsōk) *and Louis Lachenal*
(lä shə′näl′) *stood atop Annapurna on June 3, 1950,
they were the first mountaineers to conquer so high a
summit. Annapurna is one of fourteen peaks over
8,000 meters (26,000 feet) in the Himalaya Mountains. Often called "the roof of the world," the Himalayas stretch for sixteen hundred miles along the
northern border of India, their major peaks being
in Nepal.*

*The French Himalayan Expedition, led by Herzog,
arrived in Nepal in April, 1950. The nine experienced
members of the Expedition hoped to be the first mountaineers to reach the summit of an "eight thou-
sander." Since the summer monsoon was predicted
for early June, they had only two months to accomplish their task. The Expedition first attempted to
surmount Dhaulagiri* (dou′lu gi′rē), *which is 26,795
feet high. After weeks of exploration, this peak
proved to be unclimbable, and the mountaineers
turned their efforts to Annapurna (26,493 feet).
They had to find Annapurna, for its approaches had
not been previously explored. By mid-May, they had
located the peak and had decided that the most
practical route to the summit lay along Annapurna's
northwest flank. Racing against time—the monsoon
was only three weeks away—the mountaineers began
their laborious assault. They worked in two-man
teams to establish a series of five camps between the
mountain base and the summit. The highest of these
camps, Camp V, was established by Herzog and
Lachenal on the second of June.*

*Maurice Herzog and Louis "Biscante" Lachenal
spent the night of June 2, 1950, at Camp V. Their
tent was perched on a dangerously steep slope of
Annapurna at 24,600 feet. The wind threatened to
blow them off the mountain and heavy snows nearly
crushed them where they lay.*

PHOTOGRAPHS FROM THE BOOK ANNAPURNA. DIAGRAM BASED UPON A MAP BY MARCEL ICHAC FROM THE BOOK ANNAPURNA BY
MAURICE HERZOG: COPYRIGHT, 1952, BY E. P. DUTTON & CO., INC., NEW YORK; REPRODUCED BY PERMISSION OF E. P. DUTTON & CO., INC., AND JONATHAN CAPE LTD., LONDON.

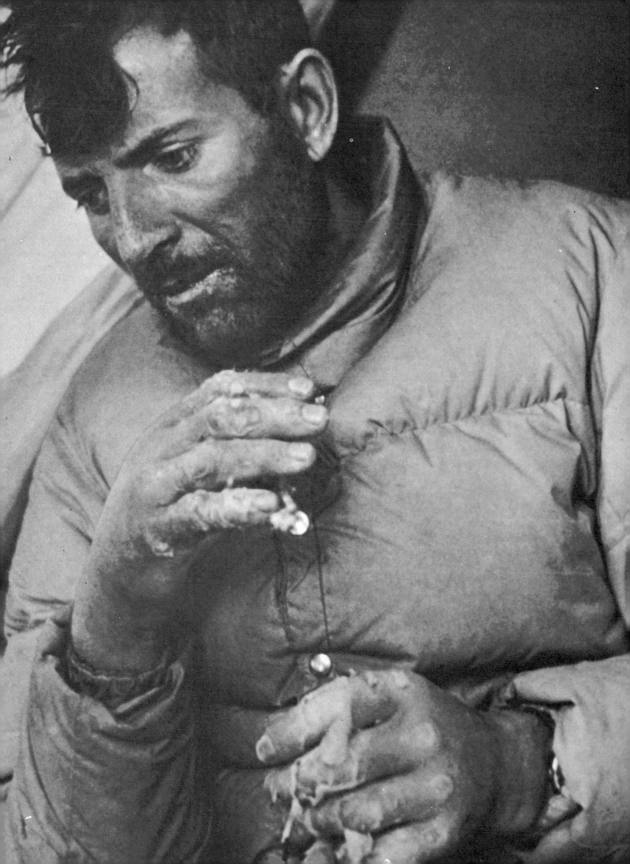

O N the third of June, 1950, the first light of dawn found us still clinging to the tent poles at Camp V. Gradually the wind abated and, with daylight, died away altogether. I made desperate attempts to push back the soft, icy stuff which stifled me, but every movement became an act of heroism. My mental powers were numbed: thinking was an effort, and we did not exchange a single word.

What a repellent place it was! To everyone who reached it, Camp V became one of the worst memories of their lives. We had only one thought—to get away. We should have waited for the first rays of the sun, but at half-past five we felt we couldn't stick it any longer.

"Let's go, Biscante," I muttered. "Can't stay here a minute longer."

"Yes, let's go," repeated Lachenal.

Which of us would have the energy to make tea? Although our minds worked slowly we were quite able to envisage all the movements that would be necessary—and neither of us could face up to it. It couldn't be helped—we would just have to go without. It was quite hard enough work to get ourselves and our boots out of our sleeping bags—and the boots were frozen stiff so that we got them on only with the greatest difficulty. Every movement made us terribly breathless. We felt as if we were being stifled. Our gaiters were stiff as a board, and I succeeded in lacing mine up; Lachenal couldn't manage his.

"No need for the rope, eh, Biscante?"

"No need," replied Lachenal laconically.

That was two pounds saved. I pushed a tube of condensed milk, some nougat, and a pair of socks into my sack; one never knew, the socks might come in useful—they might even do as balaclavas.[1] For the time being I stuffed them with first-aid equipment. The camera[2] was loaded with a black-and-white film; I had a color film in reserve. I pulled the movie camera out from the bottom of my sleeping bag, wound it up, and tried letting it run without film. There was a little click, then it stopped and jammed.

"Bad luck after bringing it so far," said Lachenal.

In spite of our photographer, Ichac's, precautions[3] taken to lubricate it with special grease, the intense cold, even inside the sleeping bag, had frozen it. I left it at the camp rather sadly: I had looked forward to taking it to the top. I had used it up to 24,600 feet.

We went outside and put on our crampons,[4] which we kept on all day. We wore as many clothes as possible; our sacks were very light. At six o'clock we started off. It was brilliantly fine, but also very cold. Our superlightweight crampons bit deep into the steep slopes of ice and hard snow up which lay the first stage of our climb.

Later the slope became slightly less steep and more uniform. Sometimes the hard crust bore our weight, but at others we broke through and sank into soft powder snow which made progress exhausting. We took turns in making the track and often stopped without any word having passed between us. Each of us lived in a closed and private world of his own. I was suspicious of my mental processes; my mind was working very slowly and I was perfectly aware of the low state of my intelligence. It was easiest just

From the book ANNAPURNA by Maurice Herzog. Translated by Nea Martin and Janet Adam Smith. Copyright, 1952, by E. P. Dutton & Co., Inc. Reprinted by permission of E. P. Dutton & Company and Jonathan Cape Ltd.

1. *they might even do as balaclavas.* A balaclava (bä′ lä klä′vä) is a knitted cap which covers the head, neck, and shoulders.
2. *The camera,* the still camera. Herzog had carried a still camera and a movie camera to Camp V.
3. *our photographer, Ichac's, precautions.* Marcel Ichac (ē chä′) was the Expedition's cameraman.
4. *our crampons* (kram′pənz), spiked iron plates which mountaineers fasten to their boots to prevent slipping.

to stick to one thought at a time—safest, too. The cold was penetrating; for all our special eiderdown clothing we felt as if we'd nothing on. Whenever we halted, we stamped our feet hard. Lachenal went as far as to take off one boot which was a bit tight; he was in terror of frostbite.

"I don't want to be like Lambert," he said. Raymond Lambert, a Geneva guide, had to have all his toes amputated after an eventful climb during which he got his feet frostbitten.[5] While Lachenal rubbed himself hard, I looked at the summits all around us; already we overtopped them all except the distant Dhaulagiri. The complicated structure of these mountains, with which our many laborious explorations had made us familiar, was now spread out plainly at our feet.

The going was incredibly exhausting, and every step was a struggle of mind over matter. We came out into the sunlight, and by way of marking the occasion made yet another halt. Lachenal continued to complain of his feet. "I can't feel anything. I think I'm beginning to get frostbite." And once again he undid his boot.

I began to be seriously worried. I realized very well the risk we were running; I knew from experience how insidiously and quickly frostbite can set in if one is not extremely careful. Nor was Lachenal under any illusions. "We're in danger of having frozen feet. Do you think it's worth it?"

This was most disturbing. It was my responsibility as leader to think of the others. There was no doubt about frostbite being a very real danger. Did Annapurna justify such risks? That was the question I asked myself; it continued to worry me.

Lachenal had laced his boots up again, and once more we continued to force our way through the exhausting snow. The whole of the Sickle Glacier[6] was now in view, bathed in light. We still had a long way to go to cross it, and then there was that rock band—would we find a gap in it?

My feet, like Lachenal's, were very cold and I continued to wriggle my toes, even when we were moving. I could not feel them, but that was nothing new in the mountains, and if I kept on moving them it would keep the circulation going.

Lachenal appeared to me as a sort of specter— he was alone in his world, I in mine. But—and this was odd enough—any effort was slightly *less* exhausting than lower down. Perhaps it was hope lending us wings. Even through dark glasses the snow was blinding—the sun beating straight down on the ice. We looked down upon precipitous ridges which dropped away into space, and upon tiny glaciers far, far below. Familiar peaks soared arrowlike into the sky. Suddenly Lachenal grabbed me:

"If I go back, what will you do?"

A whole sequence of pictures flashed through my head: the days of marching in sweltering heat, the hard pitches[7] we had overcome, the tremendous efforts we had all made to lay siege to the mountain, the daily heroism of all my friends in establishing the camps. Now we were nearing our goal. In an hour or two, perhaps, victory would be ours. Must we give up? Impossible! My whole being revolted against the idea. I had made up my mind, irrevocably. Today we were consecrating an ideal, and no sacrifice was too great. I heard my voice clearly:

"I should go on by myself."

I would go alone. If he wished to go down it was not for me to stop him. He must make his own choice freely.

"Then I'll follow you."

The die was cast. I was no longer anxious. Nothing could stop us now from getting to the top. The psychological atmosphere changed with these few words, and we went forward now as brothers.

I felt as though I were plunging into something new and quite abnormal. I had the strangest and most vivid impressions, such as I had never before known in the mountains. There was something unnatural in the way I saw Lachenal and everything around us.[8] I smiled to myself at the paltriness of our efforts, for I could stand apart and watch myself making these efforts. But all sense of exertion was gone, as though there were no longer any gravity. This diaphanous landscape, this quintessence of purity—these were not the mountains I knew: they were the mountains of my dreams.

The snow, sprinkled over every rock and gleaming in the sun, was of a radiant beauty that touched me to the heart. I had never seen such complete transparency, and I was living in a world of crystal. Sounds

---

5. *Raymond Lambert* (län'bär') . . . *feet frostbitten.* In May 1952, Lambert reached the highest point yet attained on Mount Everest.
6. *Sickle Glacier,* large mass of ice, shaped like a sickle, that lies near the summit of Annapurna.

7. *hard pitches,* difficult slopes.
8. *There was something unnatural . . . around us.* Herzog is feeling the effects of the altitude. At great heights, the low oxygen content of the air produces intense fatigue and grogginess.

were indistinct, the atmosphere like cotton wool.

An astonishing happiness welled up in me, but I could not define it. Everything was so new, so utterly unprecedented. It was not in the least like anything I had known in the Alps, where one feels buoyed up by the presence of others—by people of whom one is vaguely aware, or even by the dwellings one can see in the far distance.

This was quite different. An enormous gulf was between me and the world. This was a different universe—withered, desert,[9] lifeless; a fantastic universe where the presence of man was not foreseen, perhaps not desired. We were braving an interdict, overstepping a boundary, and yet we had no fear as we continued upward. I thought of the famous ladder of St. Teresa of Avila.[10] Something clutched at my heart.

Did Lachenal share these feelings? The summit ridge drew nearer, and we reached the foot of the ultimate rock band. The slope was very steep and the snow interspersed with rocks.

"Couloir!"[11]

A finger pointed. The whispered word from one to another indicated the key to the rocks—the last line of defense.

"What luck!"

The couloir up the rocks though steep was feasible.

The sky was a deep sapphire blue. With a great effort we edged over to the right, avoiding the rocks; we preferred to keep to the snow on account of our crampons and it was not long before we set foot in the couloir. It was fairly steep, and we had a minute's hesitation. Should we have enough strength left to overcome this final obstacle?

Fortunately the snow was hard, and by kicking steps we were able to manage, thanks to our crampons. A false move would have been fatal. There was no need to make handholds—our axes,[12] driven in as far as possible, served us for an anchor.

Lachenal went splendidly. What a wonderful contrast to the early days![13] It was a hard struggle here,

but he kept going. Lifting our eyes occasionally from the slope, we saw the couloir opening out on to . . . well, we didn't quite know, probably a ridge. But where was the top—left or right? Stopping at every step, leaning on our axes, we tried to recover our breath and to calm down our racing hearts, which were thumping as though they would burst. We knew we were there now—that nothing could stop us. No need to exchange looks—each of us would have read the same determination in the other's eyes. A slight detour to the left, a few more steps— the summit ridge came gradually nearer—a few rocks to avoid. We dragged ourselves up. Could we possibly be there?

Yes!

A fierce and savage wind tore at us.

We were on top of Annapurna! 8,075 meters, 26,493 feet.

Our hearts overflowed with an unspeakable happiness.

"If only the others could know. . . ."

If only everyone could know!

The summit was a corniced crest of ice, and the precipices on the far side which plunged vertically down beneath us, were terrifying, unfathomable. There could be few other mountains in the world like this. Clouds floated halfway down, concealing the gentle, fertile valley of Pokhara, 23,000 feet below. Above us there was nothing!

Our mission was accomplished. But at the same time we had accomplished something infinitely greater. How wonderful life would now become! What an inconceivable experience it is to attain one's ideal and, at the very same moment, to fulfill oneself. I was stirred to the depths of my being. Never had I felt happiness like this—so intense and yet so pure. That brown rock, the highest of them all, that ridge of ice—were these the goals of a lifetime? Or were they, rather, the limits of man's pride?

"Well, what about going down?"

Lachenal shook me. What were his own feelings? Did he simply think he had finished another climb, as in the Alps? Did he think one could just go down again like that, with nothing more to it?

"One minute, I must take some photographs."

"Hurry up!"

I fumbled feverishly in my sack, pulled out the camera, took out the little French flag which was right on the bottom, and the pennants. Useless gestures, no doubt, but something more than symbols—

9. *desert*, dry, barren.
10. *the famous ladder of St. Teresa* (tā rā′sä) *of Avila.* St. Teresa was a 16th-century nun who established convents in Spain. At one time she envisioned a ladder leading to heaven.
11. *"Couloir!"* A couloir (kü′lwar′) is a gorge on a mountainside. It is more common to find couloirs in the European Alps than in the Himalayas.
12. *our axes*, ice axes.
13. *the early days!* Herzog is referring to the first days of high-altitude climbing when the members of the Expedition were still unaccustomed to the low oxygen content of the air.

eloquent tokens of affection and good will. I tied the strips of material—stained by sweat and by the food in the sacks—to the shaft of my ice ax, the only flag-staff at hand. Then I focused my camera on Lachenal.

"Now, will you take me?"

"Hand it over—hurry up!" said Lachenal.

He took several pictures and then handed me back the camera. I loaded a color film and we repeated the process to be certain of bringing back records to be cherished in the future.

"Are you mad?" asked Lachenal. "We haven't a minute to lose: we must go down at once."

And in fact a glance round showed me that the weather was no longer gloriously fine as it had been in the morning. Lachenal was becoming impatient.

"We must go down!"

He was right. His was the reaction of the moun-taineer who knows his own domain. But I just could not accustom myself to the idea that we had won our victory. It seemed inconceivable that we should have trodden those summit snows.

It was impossible to build a cairn; there were no stones; everything was frozen. Lachenal stamped his feet; he felt them freezing. I felt mine freezing too, but paid little attention. The highest mountain to be climbed by man lay under our feet! The names of our predecessors on these heights raced through my mind: Mummery, Mallory and Irvine, Bauer, Wel-zenbach, Tilman, Shipton.[14] How many of them were dead—how many had found on these mountains what, to them, was the finest end of all?

My joy was touched with humility. It was not just one party that had climbed Annapurna today, but a whole expedition. I thought of all the others in the camps perched on the slopes at our feet, and I knew it was because of their efforts and their sacrifices that we had succeeded. There are times when the most complicated actions are suddenly summed up, distilled, and strike you with illuminating clarity: so it was with this irresistible upward surge which had landed us two here.

Pictures passed through my mind—the Chamonix Valley,[15] where I had spent the most marvelous mo-ments of my childhood; Mont Blanc, which so tremendously impressed me! I was a child when I first saw "the Mont Blanc people" coming home, and

14. *The names of our predecessors . . . Shipton.* Herzog names mountaineers who had previously assaulted Himalayan peaks.
15. *Chamonix* (shä′mō nē′) *Valley,* mountain valley in eastern France, north of Mont Blanc (môn blän′). Mont Blanc, long fa-miliar to Herzog, is the highest mountain in the Alps (15,781 feet).

to me there was a queer look about them; a strange light shone in their eyes.

"Come on, straight down," called Lachenal.

He had already done up his sack and started going down. I took out my pocket aneroid: 8,500 meters.[16] I smiled. I swallowed a little condensed milk and left the tube behind—the only trace of our passage. I did up my sack, put on my gloves and my glasses, seized my ice ax; one look around and I, too, hurried down the slope. Before disappearing into the couloir I gave one last look at the summit which would henceforth be all our joy and all our consolation.

Lachenal was already far below; he had reached the foot of the couloir. I hurried down in his tracks. I went as fast as I could, but it was dangerous going. At every step one had to take care that the snow did not break away beneath one's weight. Lachenal, going faster than I thought he was capable of, was now on the long traverse. It was my turn to cross the area of mixed rock and snow. At last I reached the

foot of the rock band. I had hurried and I was out of breath. I undid my sack. What had I been going to do? I couldn't say.

"My gloves!"

Before I had time to bend over, I saw them slide and roll. They went farther and farther straight down the slope. I remained where I was, quite stunned. I watched them rolling down slowly, with no appearance of stopping. The movement of those gloves was engraved in my sight as something irredeemable, against which I was powerless. The consequences might be most serious. What was I to do?

"Quickly, down to Camp V."

Rébuffat and Terray would be there.[17] My concern dissolved like magic. I now had a fixed objective again: to reach the camp. Never for a minute did it occur to me to use as gloves the socks which I always carry in reserve for just such a mishap as this.

On I went, trying to catch up with Lachenal. It had been two o'clock when we reached the summit; we

16. *pocket aneroid* (an'ər oid): *8,500 meters.* An aneroid barometer indicates altitude by the pressure of air on the elastic lid of a box containing no air.

17. *Rébuffat* (rā by'fä') *and Terray* (târ'ā') *would be there.* Gaston Rébuffat and Lionel Terray were scheduled to advance from Camp IV to Camp V this same day.

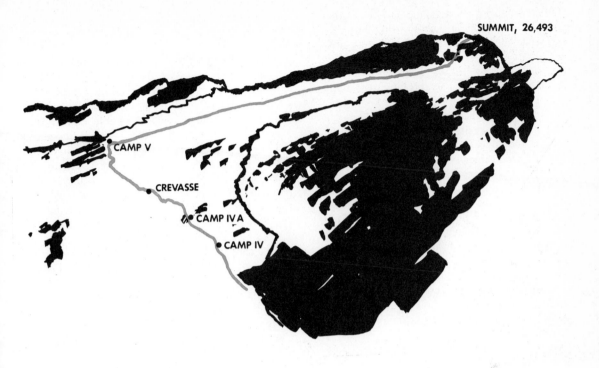

SUMMIT, 26,493

CAMP V

CREVASSE

CAMP IV A

CAMP IV

had started out at six in the morning, but I had to admit I had lost all sense of time. I felt as if I were running, whereas in actual fact I was walking normally, perhaps rather slowly, and I had to keep stopping to get my breath. The sky was now covered with clouds, everything had become gray and dirty-looking. An icy wind sprang up, boding no good. We must push on! But where was Lachenal? I spotted him a couple of hundred yards away, looking as if he was never going to stop. And I had thought he was in indifferent form!

The clouds grew thicker and came right down over us; the wind blew stronger, but I did not suffer from the cold. Perhaps the descent had restored my circulation. Should I be able to find the tents in the mist? I watched the rib[18] ending in the beaklike point which overlooked the camp. It was gradually swallowed up by the clouds, but I was able to make out the spearhead rib lower down. If the mist should thicken I would make straight for that rib and follow it down, and in this way I should be bound to come upon the tent.

Lachenal disappeared from time to time, and then the mist was so thick that I lost sight of him altogether. I kept going at the same speed, as fast as my breathing would allow.

The slope was now steeper; a few patches of bare ice followed the smooth stretches of snow. A good sign—I was nearing the camp. How difficult to find one's way in thick mist! I kept the course which I had set by the steepest angle of the slope. The ground was broken; with my crampons I went straight down walls of bare ice. There were some patches ahead—a few more steps. It was the camp all right, but there were *two tents!*

So Rébuffat and Terray had come up. What a mercy! I should be able to tell them that we had been successful, that we were returning from the top. How thrilled they would be!

I got there, dropping down from above. The platform had been extended, and the two tents were facing each other. I tripped over one of the guy ropes of the first tent; there was movement inside, they had heard me. Rébuffat and Terray put their heads out.

"We've made it. We're back from Annapurna!"

18. *the rib,* a ridge.

Rébuffat and Terray received the news with great excitement.

"But what about Biscante?" asked Terray anxiously.

"He won't be long. He was just in front of me! What a day—started out at six this morning—didn't stop . . . got up at last."

Words failed me. I had so much to say. The sight of familiar faces dispelled the strange feeling that I had experienced since morning, and I became, once more, just a mountaineer.

Terray, who was speechless with delight, wrung my hands. Then the smile vanished from his face: "Maurice—your hands!" There was an uneasy silence. I had forgotten that I had lost my gloves; my fingers were violet and white and hard as wood. The other two stared at them in dismay—they realized the full seriousness of the injury. But, still blissfully floating on a sea of joy remote from reality, I leaned over toward Terray and said confidentially, "You're in such splendid form, and you've done so marvelously, it's absolutely tragic you didn't come up there with us!"

"What I did was for the Expedition, my dear Maurice, and anyway you've got up, and that's a victory for the whole lot of us."

I nearly burst with happiness. How could I tell him all that his answer meant to me? The rapture I had felt on the summit, which might have seemed a purely personal, egotistical emotion, had been transformed by his words into a complete and perfect joy with no shadow upon it. His answer proved that this victory was not just one man's achievement, a matter for personal pride; no—and Terray was the first to understand this—it was a victory for us all, a victory for mankind itself.

"Hi! Help! Help!"

"Biscante!" exclaimed the others.

Still half-intoxicated and remote from reality, I had heard nothing. Terray felt a chill at his heart, and his thoughts flew to his partner on so many unforgettable climbs; together they had so often skirted death, and won so many splendid victories. Putting his head out, and seeing Lachenal clinging to the slope a hundred yards lower down, he dressed in frantic haste.

Out he went. But the slope was bare now; Lachenal had disappeared. Terray was horribly frightened, and he could only utter unintelligible cries. It was a ghastly moment for him. A violent wind sent the mist tearing by. Under the stress of emotion Terray had not realized how it falsified distances.

"Biscante! Biscante!"

He had spotted him, through a rift in the mist, lying on the slope much lower down than he had thought. Terray set his teeth and glissaded down like a madman.[19] How would he be able to brake without crampons, on the wind-hardened snow? But Terray was a first-class skier, and with a jump turn he stopped beside Lachenal, who was suffering from concussion after his tremendous fall. In a state of collapse, with no ice ax, balaclava, or gloves, and only one crampon, he gazed vacantly around him.

"My feet are frostbitten. Take me down . . . take me down, so that Oudot[20] can see to me."

"It can't be done," said Terray sorrowfully. "Can't you see we're in the middle of a storm? . . . It'll be dark soon."

But Lachenal was obsessed by the fear of amputation. With a gesture of despair he tore the ax out of Terray's hands and tried to force his way down, but soon saw the futility of his action and resolved to climb up to the camp. While Terray cut steps without stopping, Lachenal, ravaged and exhausted as he was, dragged himself along on all fours.

Meanwhile I had gone into Rébuffat's tent. He was appalled at the sight of my hands and, as rather incoherently I told him what we had done, he took a piece of rope and began flicking my fingers. Then he took off my boots with great difficulty, for my feet were swollen, and beat my feet and rubbed me. We soon heard Terray giving Lachenal the same treatment in the other tent.

For our comrades it was a tragic moment: Annapurna was conquered, and the first eight-thousander had been climbed. Every one of us had been ready to sacrifice everything for this. Yet, as they looked at our feet and hands, what can Terray and Rébuffat have felt?

Outside the storm howled and the snow was still falling. The mist grew thick and darkness came. As on the previous night we had to cling to the poles to prevent the tents being carried away by the wind. The only two air mattresses were given to Lachenal and myself while Terray and Rébuffat both sat on

19. *Terray . . . glissaded down like a madman.* Terray made a sliding descent of the snow slope while in a standing position. Such a maneuver requires a balance such as that needed on skis.
20. *Oudot* (ü′dō′), Jacques Oudot, the Expedition's doctor.

ropes, rucksacks, and provisions to keep themselves off the snow. They rubbed, slapped, and beat us with a rope. Sometimes the blows fell on living flesh, and howls arose from both tents. Rébuffat persevered; it was essential to continue, painful as it was. Gradually life returned to my feet as well as to my hands, and circulation started again. Lachenal, too, found that feeling was returning.

Now Terray summoned up the energy to prepare some hot drinks. He called to Rébuffat that he would pass him a mug, so two hands stretched out toward each other between the two tents and were instantly covered with snow. The liquid was boiling though scarcely more than 60 degrees centigrade[21] (140 degrees Fahrenheit). I swallowed it greedily and felt infinitely better.

The night was absolute hell. Frightful onslaughts of wind battered us incessantly, while the never-ceasing snow piled up on the tents.

Now and again I heard voices from next door—it was Terray massaging Lachenal with admirable perseverance, only stopping to ply him with hot drinks. In our tent Rébuffat was quite worn out, but satisfied that warmth was returning to my limbs.

Lying half-unconscious I was scarcely aware of the passage of time. There were moments when I was able to see our situation in its true dramatic light, but the rest of the time I was plunged in an inexplicable stupor with no thought for the consequences of our victory.

As the night wore on the snow lay heavier on the tent, and once again I had the frightful feeling of being slowly and silently asphyxiated. I tried, with all the strength of which I was capable, to push off with both forearms the mass that was crushing me. These fearful exertions left me gasping for breath and I fell back into the same exhausted state. It was much worse than the previous night.

"Rébuffat! Gaston! Gaston!"

I recognized Terray's voice.

"Time to be off!"

I heard the sounds without grasping their meaning. Was it light already? I was not in the least surprised that the other two had given up all thought of going to the top, and I did not at all grasp the measure of their sacrifice.

Outside the storm redoubled in violence. The tent shook and the fabric flapped alarmingly. It had usually been fine in the mornings: did this mean the monsoon was upon us? We knew it was not far off— could this be its first onslaught?

"Gaston! Are you ready?" Terray called again.

"One minute," answered Rébuffat. He did not have an easy job: he had to put my boots on and do everything to get me ready. I let myself be handled like a baby. In the other tent Terray finished dressing Lachenal whose feet were still swollen and would not fit into his boots. So Terray gave him his own, which were bigger. To get Lachenal's on to his own feet he had to make slits in them. As a precaution he put a sleeping bag and some food into his sack and shouted to us to do the same. Were his words lost in the storm? Or were we too intent on leaving this hellish place to listen to his instructions?

Lachenal and Terray were already outside.

"We're going down!" they shouted.

Then Rébuffat tied me on the rope and we went out. There were only two ice axes for the four of us, so Rébuffat and Terray took them as a matter of course. For a moment as we left the two tents of Camp V, I felt childishly ashamed at leaving all this good equipment behind.

Already the first rope seemed a long way down below us. We were blinded by the squalls of snow and we could not hear each other a yard away. We had both put on our *cagoules*,[22] for it was very cold. The snow was apt to slide and the rope often came in useful.

Ahead of us the other two were losing no time. Lachenal went first and, safeguarded by Terray, he forced the pace in his anxiety to get down. There were no tracks to show us the way, but it was engraved on all our minds—straight down the slope for four hundred yards then traverse to the left for one hundred fifty to two hundred yards to get to Camp IV. The snow was thinning and the wind less violent. Was it going to clear? We hardly dared to hope so. A wall of seracs[23] brought us up short.

"It's to the left," I said, "I remember perfectly."

Somebody else thought it was to the right. We started going down again. The wind had dropped completely, but the snow fell in big flakes. The mist was thick, and, not to lose each other, we walked in line: I was third and I could barely see Lachenal, who was first. It was impossible to recognize any of

---

21. *The liquid was boiling . . . centigrade.* At high altitudes the boiling point of liquids is lower than it is at sea level.

22. *cagoules* (kä gül'), hoods. [French]

23. *A wall of seracs.* A serac (sä'rak') is a pinnacle of ice among the crevices of a glacier.

the pitches. We were all experienced enough mountaineers to know that even on familiar ground it is easy to make mistakes in such weather. Distances are deceptive, one cannot tell whether one is going up or down. We kept colliding with hummocks which we had taken for hollows. The mist, the falling snowflakes, the carpet of snow, all merged into the same whitish tone and confused our vision. The towering outlines of the seracs took on fantastic shapes and seemed to move slowly around us.

Our situation was not desperate, we were certainly not lost. We would have to go lower down; the traverse must begin further on—I remembered the serac which served as a milestone. The snow stuck to our *cagoules*, and turned us into white phantoms noiselessly flitting against a background equally white. We began to sink in dreadfully, and there is nothing worse for bodies already on the edge of exhaustion.

Were we too high or too low? No one could tell. Perhaps we had better try slanting over to the left! The snow was in a dangerous condition, but we did not seem to realize it. We were forced to admit that we were not on the right route, so we retraced our steps and climbed up above the serac which overhung us. No doubt, we decided, we should be on the right level now. With Rébuffat leading, we went back over the way which had cost us such an effort. I followed him jerkily, saying nothing, and determined to go on to the end. If Rébuffat had fallen I could never have held him.

We went doggedly on from one serac to another. Each time we thought we had recognized the right route, and each time there was a fresh disappointment. If only the mist would lift, if only the snow would stop for a second! On the slope it seemed to be growing deeper every minute. Only Terray and Rébuffat were capable of breaking the trail, and they relieved each other at regular intervals without a word and without a second's hesitation.

I admired this determination of Rébuffat's for which he is so justly famed. He did not intend to die! With the strength of desperation and at the price of superhuman effort he forged ahead. The slowness of his progress would have dismayed even the most obstinate climber, but he would not give up, and in the end the mountain yielded in face of his perseverance.

Terray, when his turn came, charged madly ahead. He was like a force of nature: at all costs he would break down these prison walls that penned us in. His physical strength was exceptional, his will power no less remarkable. Lachenal gave him considerable trouble. Perhaps he was not quite in his right mind. He said it was no use going on; we must dig a hole in the snow and wait for fine weather. He swore at Terray and called him a madman. Nobody but Terray would have been capable of dealing with him—he just tugged sharply on the rope and Lachenal was forced to follow.

We were well and truly lost.

The weather did not seem likely to improve. A minute ago we had still had ideas about which way to go—now we had none. This way or that. . . . We went on at random to allow for the chance of a miracle which appeared increasingly unlikely. The instinct of self-preservation in the two fit members of the party alternated with a hopelessness which made them completely irresponsible. Each in turn did the maddest things: Terray traversed the steep and avalanchy slopes with one crampon badly adjusted. He and Rébuffat performed incredible feats of balance without the least slip.

Camp IV was certainly on the left, on the edge of the Sickle. On that point we were all agreed. But it was very hard to find. The wall of ice that gave it such magnificent protection was now ironical, for it hid the tents from us. In mist like this we should have to be right on top of them before we spotted them.

Perhaps if we called, someone would hear us? Lachenal gave the signal, but snow absorbs sound and his shout seemed to carry only a few yards. All four of us called out together: "One . . . two . . . three . . . *Help!*"

We got the impression that our united shout carried a long way, so we began again: "One . . . two . . . three . . . *Help!*" Not a sound in reply!

Now and again Terray took off his boots and rubbed his feet; the sight of our frostbitten limbs had made him aware of the danger and he had the strength of mind to do something about it. Like Lachenal, he was haunted by the idea of amputation. For me, it was too late: my feet and hands, already affected from yesterday, were beginning to freeze up again.

We had eaten nothing since the day before, and we had been on the go the whole time, but men's resources of energy in face of death are inexhaustible. When the end seems imminent, there still remain reserves, though it needs tremendous will power to call them up.

Time passed, but we had no idea how long. Night was approaching, and we were terrified, though none of us made any complaint. Rébuffat and I found a way that we thought we remembered, but were brought to a halt by the extreme steepness of the slope—the mist turned it into a vertical wall. We were to find next day that at that moment we had been only thirty yards from the camp, and that the wall was the very one that sheltered the tent which would have been our salvation.

"We must find a crevasse."[24]

"We can't stay here all night!"

"A hole—it's the only thing."

"We'll all die in it."

Night had suddenly fallen, and it was essential to come to a decision without wasting another minute; if we remained on the slope, we should be dead before morning. We would have to bivouac.[25] What the conditions would be like, we could guess, for we all knew what it meant to bivouac above 23,000 feet.

With his ax Terray began to dig a hole. Lachenal went over a snow-filled crevasse a few yards further on, then suddenly let out a yell and disappeared before our eyes. We stood helpless: should we, or rather would Terray and Rébuffat, have enough strength for all the maneuvers with the rope that would be needed to get him out? The crevasse was completely blocked up save for the one little hole which Lachenal had fallen through.

"Lachenal!" called Terray.

A voice, muffled by many thicknesses of ice and snow, came up to us. It was impossible to make out what it was saying.

"Lachenal!"

Terray jerked the rope violently; this time we could hear.

"I'm here!"

"Anything broken?"

"No! It'll do for the night! Come along."

This shelter was heaven-sent. None of us would have had the strength to dig a hole big enough to protect the lot of us from the wind. Without hesitation Terray let himself drop into the crevasse, and a loud "Come on!" told us he had arrived safely. In my turn I let myself go; it was a regular toboggan slide. I shot down a sort of twisting tunnel, very steep, and about thirty feet long. I came out at great

speed into the opening beyond and was literally hurled to the bottom of the crevasse. We let Rébuffat know he could come by giving a tug on the rope.

The intense cold of this minute grotto shriveled us up, the enclosing walls of ice were damp and the floor a carpet of fresh snow; by huddling together there was just room for the four of us. Icicles hung from the ceiling, and we broke some of them off to make more head room and kept little bits to suck—it was a long time since we had anything to drink.

That was our shelter for the night. At least we should be protected from the wind, and the temperature would remain fairly even, though the damp was extremely unpleasant. We settled ourselves in the dark as best we could. As always in a bivouac we took off our boots; without this precaution the constriction would cause immediate frostbite. Terray unrolled the sleeping bag which he had had the foresight to bring, and settled himself in relative comfort. We put on everything warm that we had, and to avoid contact with the snow I sat on the movie camera. We huddled close up to each other, in our search for a hypothetical position in which the warmth of our bodies could be combined without loss, but we couldn't keep still for a second.

We did not open our mouths—signs were less of an effort than words. Every man withdrew into himself and took refuge in his own inner world. Terray massaged Lachenal's feet; Rébuffat felt his feet freezing too, but he had sufficient strength to rub them himself. I remained motionless, unseeing. My feet and hands went on freezing, but what could be done? I attempted to forget suffering by withdrawing into myself; trying to forget the passing of time, trying not to feel the devouring and numbing cold which insidiously gained upon us.

Terray shared his sleeping bag with Lachenal, putting his feet and hands inside the precious eiderdown. At the same time he went on rubbing.

Anyhow the frostbite won't spread further, he was thinking.

None of us could make any movement without upsetting the others, and the positions we had taken up with such care were continually being altered so that we had to start all over again. This kept us busy. Rébuffat persevered with his rubbing and complained of his feet; like Terray he was thinking: We mustn't look beyond tomorrow—afterward we'll see. But he was not blind to the fact that "afterward" was one big question mark.

---

24. *crevasse* (krə vas′), deep crack or crevice in the ice of a glacier.

25. *to bivouac* (biv′ü ak), to camp outdoors without tents.

Terray generously tried to give me part of his sleeping bag. He had understood the seriousness of my condition, and knew why it was that I said nothing and remained quite passive; he realized that I had abandoned all hope for myself. He massaged me for nearly two hours; his feet, too, might have frozen, but he didn't appear to give the matter a thought. I found new courage simply in contemplating his unselfishness; he was doing so much to help me that it would have been ungrateful of me not to go on struggling to live. Though my heart was like a lump of ice itself, I was astonished to feel no pain. Everything material about me seemed to have dropped away. I seemed to be quite clear in my thoughts and yet I floated in a kind of peaceful happiness. There was still a breath of life in me, but it dwindled steadily as the hours went by. Terray's massage no longer had any effect upon me. All was over, I thought. Wasn't this cavern the most beautiful grave I could hope for? Death caused me no grief, no regret—I smiled at the thought.

After hours of torpor a voice mumbled "Daylight!"

This made some impression on the others. I only felt surprised—I had not thought that daylight would penetrate so far down.

"Too early to start," said Rébuffat.

A ghastly light spread through our grotto and we could just vaguely make out the shapes of each other's heads. A queer noise from a long way off came down to us—a sort of prolonged hiss. The noise increased. Suddenly I was buried, blinded, smothered beneath an avalanche of new snow. The icy snow spread over the cavern, finding its way through every gap in our clothing. I ducked my head between my knees and covered myself with both arms. The snow flowed on and on. There was a terrible silence. We were not completely buried, but there was snow everywhere. We got up, taking care not to bang our heads against the ceiling of ice, and tried to shake ourselves. We were all in our stockinged feet in the snow. The first thing to do was to find our boots.

Rébuffat and Terray began to search and realized at once that they were blind. Yesterday they had taken off their glasses to lead us down and now they were paying for it. Lachenal was the first to lay hands upon a pair of boots. He tried to put them on, but they were Rébuffat's. Rébuffat attempted to climb up the chute down which we had come yesterday, and which the avalanche had followed in its turn.

"Hi, Gaston! What's the weather like?" called up Terray.

"Can't see a thing. It's blowing hard."

We were still groping for our things. Terray found his boots and put them on awkwardly, unable to see what he was doing. Lachenal helped him, but he was all on edge and fearfully impatient, in striking contrast to my immobility. Terray then went up the icy channel, puffing and blowing, and at last reached the outer world. He was met by terrible gusts of wind that cut right through him and lashed his face.

Bad weather, he said to himself, this time it's the end. We're lost . . . we'll never come through.

At the bottom of the crevasse there were still two of us looking for our boots. Lachenal poked fiercely with an ice ax. I was calmer and tried to proceed more rationally. We extracted crampons and an ax in turn from the snow, but still no boots.

Well—so this cavern was to be our last resting place! There was very little room—we were bent double and got in each other's way. Lachenal decided to go out without his boots. He called frantically, hauled himself up on the rope, trying to get a hold or to wiggle his way up, digging his toes into the snow walls. Terray from outside pulled as hard as he could. I watched him go; he gathered speed and disappeared.

When he emerged from the opening he saw the sky was clear and blue, and he began to run like a madman, shrieking, "It's fine, it's fine!"

I set to work again to search the cave. The boots *had* to be found, or Lachenal and I were done for. On all fours, with nothing on my hands or feet I raked the snow, stirring it around this way and that, hoping every second to come upon something hard. I was no longer capable of thinking—I reacted like an animal fighting for its life.

I found one boot! The other was tied to it—a pair! Having ransacked the whole cave I at last found the other pair. But in spite of all my efforts I could not find the movie camera, and gave up in despair. There was no question of putting my boots on—my hands were like lumps of wood and I could hold nothing in my fingers; my feet were very swollen—I should never be able to get boots on them. I twisted the rope around the boots as well as I could and called up the chute:

"Lionel. . . . Boots!"

There was no answer, but he must have heard, for with a jerk the precious boots shot up. Soon after the rope came down again. My turn. I wound the rope around me. I could not pull it tight so I made a whole series of little knots. Their combined strength, I hoped, would be enough to hold me. I had no strength to shout again; I gave a great tug on the rope, and Terray understood.

At the first step I had to kick a notch in the hard snow for my toes. Further on I expected to be able to get up more easily by wedging myself across the tunnel. I wriggled up a few yards like this and then I tried to dig my hands and my feet into the wall. My hands were stiff and hard right up to the wrists and my feet had no feeling up to the ankles; the joints were inflexible, and this hampered me greatly.

Somehow or other I succeeded in working my way up, while Terray pulled so hard he nearly choked me. I began to see more distinctly and so knew I must be nearing the opening. Often I fell back, but I clung on and wedged myself in again as best I could. My heart was bursting and I was forced to rest. A fresh wave of energy enabled me to crawl to the top. I pulled myself out by clutching Terray's legs; he was just about all in and I was in the last stages of exhaustion. Terray was close to me and I whispered:

"Lionel . . . I'm dying!"

He supported me and helped me away from the crevasse. Lachenal and Rébuffat were sitting in the snow a few yards away. The instant Lionel let go of me I sank down and dragged myself along on all fours.

The weather was perfect. Quantities of snow had fallen the day before and the mountains were resplendent. Never had I seen them look so beautiful— our last day would be magnificent.

Rébuffat and Terray were completely blind; as he came along with me Terray knocked into things and I had to direct him. Rébuffat, too, could not move a step without guidance. It was terrifying to be blind when there was danger all around. Lachenal's frozen feet affected his nervous system. His behavior was disquieting—he was possessed by the most fantastic ideas:

"I tell you we must go down . . . down there. . . ."

"You've nothing on your feet!"

"Don't worry about that."

"You're off your head. The way's not there . . . it's to the left!"

He was already standing up; he wanted to go straight down to the bottom of the glacier. Terray held him back, made him sit down, and though he couldn't see, helped Lachenal put his boots on.

Behind them I was living in my own private dream. I knew the end was near, but it was the end that all mountaineers wish for—an end in keeping with their ruling passion. I was consciously grateful to the mountains for being so beautiful for me that day, and as awed by their silence as if I had been in church. I was in no pain, and had no worry. My utter calmness was alarming. Terray came staggering toward me, and I told him: "It's all over for me. Go on . . . you have a chance . . . you must take it . . . over to the left . . . that's the way."

I felt better after telling him that. But Terray would have none of it: "We'll help you. If we get away, so will you."

At this moment Lachenal shouted: "Help! Help!"

Obviously he didn't know what he was doing. . . . Or did he? He was the only one of the four of us who could see Camp II down below. Perhaps his calls would be heard. They were shrieks of despair, reminding me tragically of some climbers lost in the Mont Blanc massif[26] whom I had endeavored to save. Now it was our turn. The impression was vivid: we were lost.

I joined in with the others: "One . . . two . . . three . . . *Help!* One . . . two . . . three . . . *Help!*" We tried to shout together, but without much success; our voices could not have carried more than ten feet. The noise I made was more of a whisper than a shout. Terray insisted that I should put my boots on, but my hands were dead. Neither Rébuffat nor Terray, who were unable to see, could help much, so I said to Lachenal: "Come and help me to put my boots on."

"Don't be silly, we must go down!"

And off he went once again in the wrong direction, straight down. I was not in the least angry with him; he had been sorely tried by the altitude and by everything he had gone through.

Terray resolutely got out his knife, and with fumbling hands slit the uppers of my boots back and front. Split in two like this I could get them on, but it was not easy and I had to make several attempts. Soon I lost heart—what was the use of it all anyway since I was going to stay where I was? But Terray pulled violently and finally he succeeded. He laced up my now-gigantic boots, missing half the hooks. I was

---

26. *massif* (ma'sēf'), principal mountain mass.

ready now. But how was I going to walk with my stiff joints?

"To the left, Lionel!"

"You're crazy, Maurice," said Lachenal, "it's to the right, straight down."

Terray did not know what to think of these conflicting views. He had not given up like me, he was going to fight; but what, at the moment, could he do? The three of them discussed which way to go.

I remained sitting in the snow. Gradually my mind lost grip—why should I struggle? I would just let myself drift. I saw pictures of shady slopes, peaceful paths, there was a scent of resin. It was pleasant—I was going to die in my own mountains. My body had no feeling—everything was frozen.

"Aah . . . aah!"

Was it a groan or a call? I gathered my strength for one cry: "They're coming!" The others heard me and shouted for joy. What a miraculous apparition! "Schatz[27] . . . it's Schatz!"

Barely two hundred yards away Marcel Schatz, waist-deep in snow, was coming slowly toward us like a boat on the surface of the slope. I found this vision of a strong and invincible deliverer inexpressibly moving. I expected everything of him. The shock was violent, and quite shattered me. Death clutched at me, and I gave myself up.

When I came to again the wish to live returned and I experienced a violent revulsion of feeling. All was not lost! As Schatz came nearer my eyes never left him for a second—twenty yards—ten yards—he came straight toward me. Why? Without a word he leaned over me, held me close, hugged me, and his warm breath revived me.

I could not make the slightest movement—I was like marble. My heart was overwhelmed by such tremendous feelings and yet my eyes remained dry.

"It is wonderful—what you have done!"

---

27. *Schatz* (shätz). Marcel Schatz, who had moved from Camp III to Camp IV the day before. On the third of June he unexpectedly decided to make a track between Camp IV and Camp V, which would guide Herzog and Lachenal on their descent. Thus he happened to be on the right spot at the right moment to rescue the lost party.

DISCUSSION

1. Judging from this selection, explain what dangers mountaineers face in high-altitude climbing.

2. As Herzog and Lachenal move from Camp V toward the summit of Annapurna, Lachenal reveals his "terror of frostbite." What does this incident tell you about (a) Lachenal's character, and (b) Herzog's character?

3. In describing the ascent, Herzog comments: "I felt as though I were plunging into something new and quite abnormal" (page 371, column 2, paragraph 7). Why does he feel that Annapurna is a unique experience?

4. (a) What are Herzog's feelings when he stands on the summit? (b) Do you think Lachenal's impatience with Herzog is justified? Explain why or why not.

5. Terray tells Herzog that the conquest of Annapurna is "a victory for the whole lot of us" (page 376, column 1, paragraph 6). Why does Herzog react as he does to Terray's comment?

6. Cite at least four instances in which the behavior of Terray and Rébuffat illustrates the selfless teamwork of the Expedition.

7. (a) Trace the shifts in Herzog's state of mind during the descent from Camp V. (b) What physical conditions contributed to these shifts? (c) What emotional factors were involved?

8. (a) Explain why you would agree or disagree that Herzog regards the conquest of Annapurna as an act of heroism. (b) Do you think a more objective account would support this view? Why or why not?

AUTHOR

MAURICE HERZOG was born in Lyons, France, in 1919. As a boy he spent his holidays on the dizzy heights of the Alps, where he became a hardened mountaineer. His skill in rock, ice, and snow climbing earned him the leadership of the French Himalayan Expedition when he was thirty-one. An engineer by profession, Herzog also holds a law degree and a degree in business administration. He commanded mountain troops during World War II.

Herzog began writing *Annapurna* in 1951 while recovering from the severe injuries he incurred on the descent from the summit. The book had to be dictated, for Annapurna had cost Herzog his fingers and toes.

ALONE on a MOUNTAIN TOP

Jack Kerouac

ANYBODY who's been to Seattle and missed Alaskan Way, the old waterfront, has missed the point. Here the totem-pole stores, the waters of Puget Sound washing under old piers, the dark gloomy look of ancient warehouses and pier sheds, and the most antique locomotives in America switching boxcars up and down the waterfront, give a hint, under the pure cloud-mopped, sparkling skies of the Northwest, of great country to come. Driving north from Seattle on Highway 99 is an exciting experience because suddenly you see the Cascade Mountains rising on the northeast horizon, truly *Komo Kulshan* under their uncountable snows. The great peaks covered with trackless white, worlds of huge rock twisted and heaped and sometimes almost spiraled into fantastic, unbelievable shapes.

All this is seen far above the dreaming fields of the Stilaquamish and Skagit valleys, agricultural flats of peaceful green, the soil so rich and dark it is proudly referred to by inhabitants as second only to the Nile in fertility. At Milltown, Washington, your car rolls over the bridge across the Skagit River. To the left— seaward, westward—the Skagit flows into Skagit Bay and the Pacific Ocean. At Burlington you turn right and head for the heart of the mountains along a rural valley road through sleepy little towns and one bustling agricultural market center known as Sedro

Woolley with hundreds of cars parked aslant on a typical country-town Main Street of hardware stores, grain-and-feed stores and five-and-tens. On deeper into the deepening valley, cliffs rich with timber appearing by the side of the road, the narrowing river rushing more swiftly now, a pure translucent green like the green of the ocean on a cloudy day but a saltless rush of melted snow from the High Cascades . . . almost good enough to drink north of Marblemount. The road curves more and more till you reach Concrete, the last town in Skagit Valley with a bank and a five-and-ten; after that the mountains rising secretly behind foothills are so close that now you don't see them but begin to feel them more and more.

At Marblemount the river is a swift torrent, the work of the quiet mountains. Fallen logs beside the water provide good seats to enjoy a river wonderland. Leaves jiggling in the good clean northwest wind seem to rejoice. The topmost trees on nearby timbered peaks, swept and dimmed by low-flying clouds, seem contented. The clouds assume the faces of hermits or of nuns, or sometimes look like

---

sad dog acts hurrying off into the wings over the horizon. Snags struggle and gurgle in the heaving bulk of the river. Logs rush by at twenty miles an hour. The air smells of pine and sawdust and bark and mud and twigs; birds flash over the water looking for secretive fish.

As you drive north across the bridge at Marblemount and on to Newhalem the road narrows and twists until finally the Skagit is seen pouring over rocks, frothing, and small creeks come tumbling from steep hillsides and pile right in. The mountains rise on all sides, only their shoulders and ribs visible, their heads out of sight and now snowcapped.

At Newhalem extensive road construction raises a cloud of dust over shacks and cats and rigs; the dam there is the first in a series that create the Skagit watershed which provides all the power for Seattle.

The road ends at Diablo, a peaceful company settlement of neat cottages and green lawns surrounded by close-packed peaks named Pyramid and Colonial and Davis. Here a huge lift takes you one thousand feet up to the level of Diablo Lake and Diablo Dam. Over the dam pours a jet roar of water through which a stray log sometimes goes shooting out like a toothpick in a one-thousand-foot arc. Here for the first time you're high enough really to begin to see the Cascades. Dazzles of light to the north show where Ross Lake sweeps back all the way to Canada, opening a view of the Mt. Baker National Forest as spectacular as any vista in the Colorado Rockies.

The Seattle City Light and Power boat leaves on regular schedule from a little pier near Diablo Dam and heads north between steep timbered rocky cliffs toward Ross Dam, about half an hour's ride. The passengers are power employees, hunters and fishermen and forestry workers. Below Ross Dam the footwork begins; you must climb a rocky trail one thousand feet to the level of the dam. Here the vast lake opens out, disclosing small resort floats offering rooms and boats for vacationists, and just beyond, the floats of the U. S. Forestry Service. From this point on, if you're lucky enough to be a rich man or a forest-fire lookout, you can get packed into the North Cascade Primitive Area by horse and mule and spend a summer of complete solitude.

I was a fire lookout and after two nights of trying to sleep in the boom and slap of the Forest Service floats, they came for me one rainy morning—a powerful tugboat lashed to a large corral float bearing four mules and three horses, my own groceries,

feed, batteries and equipment. The muleskinner's name was Andy and he wore the same old floppy cowboy hat he'd worn in Wyoming twenty years ago. "Well, boy, now we're gonna put you away where we can't reach ya; you better get ready."

"It's just what I want, Andy, be alone for three solid months, nobody to bother me."

"It's what you're sayin' now, but you'll change your tune after a week."

I didn't believe him. I was looking forward to an experience men seldom earn in this modern world: complete and comfortable solitude in the wilderness, day and night, sixty-three days and nights to be exact. We had no idea how much snow had fallen on my mountain during the winter, and Andy said: "If there's not enough it means you gotta hike two miles down that hard trail every day or every other day with two buckets, boy. I ain't envyin' you. I been back there. And one day it's gonna be hot and you're about ready to broil, and bugs you can't even count 'em; and next day a li'l 'ole summer blizzard come hit you around the corner of Hozomeen—which sits right there near Canada in your back yard—and you won't be able to stick logs fast enough in that potbelly stove of yours." But I had a full rucksack loaded with turtleneck sweaters and warm shirts and pants and long wool socks bought on the Seattle waterfront, and gloves and an earmuff cap, and lots of instant soup and coffee in my grub list.

"Shoulda brought yourself a quart of brandy, boy," said Andy, shaking his head as the tug pushed our corral float up Ross Lake, through the log gate and around to the left dead north, underneath the immense rain shroud of Sourdough Mountain and Ruby Mountain.

"Where's Desolation Peak?" I asked, meaning my own mountain (*A mountain to be kept forever*, I'd dreamed all that spring).

"You ain't gonna see it today till we're practically on top of it," said Andy, "and by that time you'll be so soakin' wet you won't care."

Assistant Ranger Marty Gohlke of Marblemount Ranger Station was with us, too, also giving me tips and instructions. Nobody seemed to envy Desolation Peak except me. After two hours pushing through the storming waves of the long rainy lake with dreary, misty timber rising steeply on both sides and the mules and horses chomping on their feedbags, patient in the downpour, we arrived at the foot of Desolation Trail and the tugman (who'd been providing us with good hot coffee in the pilot cabin) eased her over and settled the float against a steep, muddy slope full of bushes and fallen trees. The muleskinner whacked the first mule and she lurched ahead with her double-sided pack of batteries and canned goods, hit the mud with forehoofs, scrambled, slipped, almost fell back in the lake and finally gave one mighty heave and went skittering out of sight in the fog to wait on the trail for the other mules and her master. We all got off, cut the barge loose, waved to the tugman, mounted our horses, and started up, sad and dripping, in the heavy rain.

At first the trail, always steeply rising, was so dense with shrubbery we kept getting shower after shower from overhead and from branches hit by our outjutting knees. The trail was deep, with round rocks that kept causing the animals to slip. At one point a great fallen tree made it impossible to go on until Old Andy and Marty went ahead with axes and cleared a shortcut around the tree, sweating and cursing and hacking, as I watched the animals. By and by they were ready, but the mules were afraid of the rough steepness of the shortcut and had to be prodded through with sticks. Soon the trail reached alpine meadows powdered with blue lupine everywhere in the drenching mists, and with little red poppies, tiny-budded flowers as delicate as designs on a tiny Japanese teacup. Now the trail zigzagged widely back and forth up the high meadow. Soon we saw the vast, foggy heap of a rock-cliff face above and Andy yelled, "Soon's we get up high as that we're almost there, but that's another two thousand feet, though you'd think you could reach up and touch it!"

I unfolded my nylon poncho and draped it over my head, and, drying a little, or, rather, ceasing to drip, I walked alongside the horse to warm my blood and began to feel better. But the other boys just rode along with their heads bowed in the rain. As for altitude all I could tell was from some occasional frightening spots on the trail where we could look down on distant treetops.

The alpine meadow reached to timber line, and suddenly a great wind blew shafts of sleet on us. "Gettin' near the top now!" yelled Andy. And now there was snow on the trail, the horses were chumping through a foot of slush and mud, and to the left and right everything was blinding white in the gray fog. "About five and a half thousand feet right now," said Andy, rolling a cigarette as he rode in the rain.

We went down, then up another spell, down again, a slow gradual climb, and then Andy yelled, "There she is!" and up ahead in the mountaintop gloom I saw a little shadowy peaked shack standing alone on the top of the world and I gulped with fear:

"This my home all summer? And *this* is summer?"

The inside of the shack was even more miserable, damp and dirty, leftover groceries and magazines torn to shreds by rats and mice, the floor muddy, the windows impenetrable. But hardy Old Andy, who'd been through this kind of thing all his life, got a roaring fire crackling in the pot-bellied stove and had me lay out a pot of water with almost half a can of coffee in it, saying, "Coffee ain't no good 'less it's *strong!*" and pretty soon the coffee was boiling a nice brown aromatic foam and we got our cups out and drank deep.

Meanwhile I'd gone out on the roof with Marty and removed the bucket from the chimney and put up the weather pole with the anemometer and done a few other chores; and when we came back in, Andy was frying Spam and eggs in a huge pan and it was almost like a party. Outside, the patient animals chomped on their supper bags and were glad to rest by the old corral fence built of logs by some Desolation lookout of the thirties.

Darkness came, incomprehensible.

In the gray morning after they'd slept in sleeping bags on the floor and I on the only bunk in my mummy bag, Andy and Marty left, laughing and saying, "Well, what a you think now, hey? We been here twelve hours already and you still haven't been able to see more than twelve feet!"

"By gosh that's right, what am I going to do for watching fires?"

"Don't worry, boy, these clouds'll roll away and you'll be able to see a hunnerd miles in every direction."

I didn't believe it and I felt miserable and spent the day trying to clean up the shack or pacing twenty careful feet each way in my "yard" (the ends of which appeared to be sheer drops into silent gorges), and I went to bed early. About bedtime I saw my first star, briefly, then giant phantom clouds billowed all around me and the star was gone. But in that instant I thought I'd seen a mile below me gray-black Ross Lake where Andy and Marty were back in the Forest Service boat which had met them at noon.

In the middle of the night I woke up suddenly and my hair was standing on end: I saw a huge black shadow in my window. Then I saw that it had a star above it, and realized that this was Mt. Hozomeen (8,080 feet) looking in my window from miles away near Canada. I got up from the forlorn bunk with the mice scattering underneath and went outside and gasped to see black mountain shapes gianting all around; and not only that but the billowing curtains of the northern lights shifting behind the clouds. It was a little too much for a city boy. The fear that the Abominable Snowman might be breathing behind me in the dark sent me back to bed where I buried my head inside my sleeping bag.

But in the morning—Sunday, July sixth—I was amazed and overjoyed to see a clear blue sunny sky, and down below, like a radiant pure snow sea, the clouds made a marshmallow cover for all the world and all the lake while I abided in warm sunshine among hundreds of miles of snow-white peaks. I brewed coffee and sang and drank a cup on my drowsy warm doorstep.

At noon the clouds vanished and the lake appeared below, beautiful beyond belief, a perfect blue pool twenty-five miles long and more, and the creeks like toy creeks and the timber green and fresh everywhere below and even the fishing boats of vacationists on the lake and in the lagoons. A perfect afternoon of sun, and behind the shack I discovered a snowfield big enough to provide me with buckets of cold water till late September.

I had taken this job so I could round up a little grubstake and take off for Mexico for a year, but also I wanted to be alone on the top of a mountain and see what it was like, and besides, all the mountain climbers and loggers I'd known on the West Coast had told me not to miss the High Cascades.

My job was to watch for fires. One night a terrific lightning storm made a dry run across the Mt. Baker National Forest without any rainfall. When I saw that ominous black cloud flashing wrathfully toward me I shut off the radio and laid the aerial on the ground and waited for the worst. Hiss! hiss! said the wind, bringing dust and lightning nearer. Tick! said the lightning rod, receiving a strand of electricity from a strike on nearby Skagit Peak. Hiss! Tick! and in my bed I felt the earth move. Fifteen miles to the south, just east of Ruby Peak and somewhere near Panther Creek, a large fire raged, a huge orange spot. At ten o'clock lightning hit it again and it flared up dangerously.

I was supposed to note the general area of lightning strikes. By midnight I'd been staring so intently

out the dark window I got hallucinations of fires everywhere, three of them right in Lightning Creek, phosphorescent orange verticals of ghost fire that seemed to come and go.

In the morning, there at 177°16' where I'd seen the big fire, was a strange brown patch in the snowy rock showing where the fire had raged and sputtered out in the all-night rain that followed the lightning. But the result of this storm was disastrous fifteen miles away at McAllister Creek, where a great blaze had outlasted the rain and exploded the following afternoon in a cloud that could be seen from Seattle. I felt sorry for the fellows who had to fight these fires, the smoke-jumpers who parachuted down on them out of planes and the trail crews who hiked to them, climbing and scrambling over slippery rocks and scree slopes, arriving sweaty and exhausted only to face the wall of heat when they got there. As a lookout I had it pretty easy and only had to concentrate on reporting the exact location (by instrument findings) of every blaze I detected.

Most days, though, it was the routine that occupied me. Up at seven or so every day, a pot of coffee brought to a boil over a handful of burning twigs, I'd go out in the alpine yard with a cup of coffee hooked in my thumb and leisurely make my wind speed and wind direction and temperature and moisture readings. Then, after chopping wood, I'd use the two-way radio and report to the relay station on Sourdough. At 10 A.M. I usually got hungry for breakfast, and I'd make delicious pancakes, eating them at my little table that was decorated with bouquets of mountain lupine and sprigs of fir.

Early in the afternoon was the usual time for my kick of the day, instant chocolate pudding with hot coffee. Around two or three, I'd lie on my back on the meadowside and watch the clouds float by, or pick blueberries and eat them right there. I had tuned the radio loud enough to hear any calls for Desolation.

Then at sunset I'd roust up my supper out of cans of yams and Spam and peas, or sometimes just pea soup with corn muffins baked on top of the wood stove in aluminum foil. Then I'd go out to that precipitous snow slope and shovel my two pails of snow for the water tub and gather an armful of fallen firewood from the hillside like the proverbial Old Woman of Japan. For the chipmunks and conies I put pans of leftovers under the shack; in the middle of the night I could hear them clanking around.

The rat would scramble down from the attic and eat some too.

Sometimes I'd yell questions at the rocks and trees, and across gorges, or yodel, "What is the meaning of the void?" The answer was perfect silence, so I knew.

Before bedtime I'd read by kerosene lamp whatever books were in the shack. It's amazing how people in solitary hunger after books. After poring over every word of a medical tome, and the synopsized versions of Shakespeare's plays by Charles and Mary Lamb, I climbed up in the little attic and put together torn cowboy pocket books and magazines the mice had ravaged. I also played stud poker with three imaginary players.

Around bedtime I'd bring a cup of milk almost to a boil with a tablespoon of honey in it, and drink that for my lamby nightcap; then I'd curl up in my sleeping bag.

No man should go through life without once experiencing healthy, even bored solitude in the wilderness, finding himself depending solely on himself and thereby learning his true and hidden strength. Learning for instance, to eat when he's hungry and sleep when he's sleepy.

Also around bedtime was my singing time. I'd pace up and down the well-worn path in the dust of my rock singing all the show tunes I could remember, at the top of my voice, too, with nobody to hear except the deer and the bear.

In the red dusk, the mountains were symphonies in pink snow . . . Jack Mountain, Three Fools Peak, Freezeout Peak, Golden Horn, Mt. Terror, Mt. Fury, Mt. Despair, Crooked Thumb Peak, Mt. Challenger and the incomparable Mt. Baker bigger than the world in the distance . . . and my own little Jackass Ridge that completed the Ridge of Desolation. Pink snow and the clouds all distant and frilly like ancient remote cities of Buddhaland splendor, and the wind working incessantly—whish, whish—booming, at times rattling my shack.

For supper I made chop suey and baked some biscuits and put the leftovers in a pan for deer that came in the moonlit night and nibbled like big strange cows of peace—long-antlered buck and does and babies too—as I meditated in the alpine grass facing the magic moon-laned lake. And I could see firs reflected in the moonlit lake five thousand feet below, upside down, pointing to infinity.

And all the insects ceased in honor of the moon.

Sixty-three sunsets I saw revolve on that perpendicular hill . . . mad raging sunsets pouring in sea foams of cloud through unimaginable crags like the crags you grayly drew in pencil as a child, with every rose tint of hope beyond, making you feel just like them, brilliant and bleak beyond words.

Cold mornings with clouds billowing out of Lightning Gorge like smoke from a giant fire but the lake cerulean as ever.

August comes in with a blast that shakes your house and augurs little Augusticity[1] . . . then that snowy-air and woodsmoke feeling . . . then the snow comes sweeping your way from Canada, and the wind rises and dark low clouds rush up as out of a forge. Suddenly a green-rose rainbow appears right on your ridge with steamy clouds all around and an orange sun turmoiling . . .

> What is a rainbow,
>   Lord?—a hoop
> For the lowly

. . . and you go out and suddenly your shadow is ringed by the rainbow as you walk on the hilltop, a lovely-haloed mystery making you want to pray.

A blade of grass jiggling in the winds of infinity, anchored to a rock, and for your own poor gentle flesh no answer.

Your oil lamp burning in infinity.

One morning I found bear stool and signs of where the monster had taken a can of frozen milk and squeezed it in his paws and bit into it with one sharp tooth, trying to suck out the paste. In the foggy dawn I looked down the mysterious Ridge of Starvation with its fog-lost firs and its hills humping into invisibility, and the wind blowing the fog by like a faint blizzard, and I realized that somewhere in the fog stalked the bear.

And it seemed, as I sat there, that this was the Primordial Bear, and that he owned all the Northwest and all the snow and commanded all the mountains. He was King Bear, who could crush my head in his paws and crack my spine like a stick, and this was his house, his yard, his domain. Though I looked all day, he would not show himself in the mystery of those silent foggy slopes. He prowled at night among unknown lakes, and in the early morning the pearl-pure light that shadowed mountainsides of fir made him blink with respect. He had mil-

---

1. *little Augusticity,* not much like true August.

lenniums of prowling here behind him. He had seen the Indians and Redcoats come and go, and would see much more. He continuously heard the reassuring rapturous rush of silence, except when near creeks; he was aware of the light material the world is made of, yet he never discoursed, nor communicated by signs, nor wasted a breath complaining; he just nibbled and pawed, and lumbered along snags paying no attention to things inanimate or animate. His big mouth chew-chewed in the night, I could hear it across the mountain in the starlight. Soon he would come out of the fog, huge, and come and stare in my window with big burning eyes. He was Avalokitesvara the Bear, and his sign was the gray wind of autumn.

I was waiting for him. He never came.

Finally the autumn rains, all-night gales of soaking rain as I lie warm as toast in my sleeping bag and the mornings open cold wild fall days with high wind, racing fogs, racing clouds, sudden bright sun, pristine light on hill patches and my fire crackling as I exult and sing at the top of my voice. Outside my window a windswept chipmunk sits up straight on a rock, hands clasped as he nibbles an oat between his paws—the little nutty lord of all he surveys.

Thinking of the stars night after night I begin to realize "the stars are words" and all the innumerable worlds in the Milky Way are words, and so is this world too. And I realize that no matter where I am, whether in a little room full of thought, or in this endless universe of stars and mountains, it's all in my mind. There's no need for solitude. So love life for what it is, and form no preconceptions whatever in your mind.

When I came down in September a cool old golden look had come into the forest, auguring cold snaps and frost and the eventual howling blizzard that would cover my shack completely, unless those winds at the top of the world would keep her bald. As I reached the bend where the shack would disappear and I would plunge down to the lake to meet the boat that would take me out and home, I turned and blessed Desolation Peak and the little pagoda on top and thanked them for the shelter and the lesson I'd been taught.

DISCUSSION

1. In the first few paragraphs of Kerouac's recollection, what is his intent?

2. As Kerouac describes the land, he mixes specific (facts, names) and concrete (sensory) description with subjective impression. Make two lists in which you list as many of each type of description or impression as you can find in the first six paragraphs. Which is more meaningful to you: the specific and concrete or the subjective impression?

3. (a) What was Kerouac looking forward to before beginning his experience? (b) What was the mule-skinner Andy's attitude toward Kerouac's anticipation? (c) By the end of Kerouac's experience, which attitude, if either, proved more accurate?

4. (a) What is the difference between a realistic and a romantic attitude? (b) How would you describe Kerouac's attitude?

5. (a) When does the imagination of Kerouac take control of his mind? (b) Does he lose his grip on reality? Explain.

6. What is the lesson Kerouac learns from his experience? Do you agree with this attitude?

COMPOSITION

Not everyone can spend a summer on a mountain top, but almost everyone at some time confronts an aspect of the out-of-doors that is memorable. If you have had a particular experience with nature that made a lasting impression on you, try writing about it. Describe the situation leading up to the incident, the details of the experience, and what you learned from it or in what way it affected your attitude toward life.

THE AUTHOR'S CRAFT

Structure

Without a skeleton, your body would be a mass of uncontrolled muscles, nerves, and organs. Without some form of suspension, a bridge would not stand. Without structure, the goal of a writer—development of a mood, communication of facts, statement of an opinion, defense of a theory—would never be achieved.

Structure is the basic organizational framework of a piece of literature. The structure of a particular work may be *formal*—containing a clear beginning, end, and middle. Or it may be *informal*—the organization developing as the writer proceeds, often rambling, sometimes digressing, occasionally losing the main direction of thought. More often than not, an essay is a combination of the two—the writer having a general organizational pattern in mind, yet breaking from that pattern at certain points because such a break "feels" right.

Consider Jack Kerouac's "Alone on a Mountain Top." What is the basis for its organization? His first paragraphs are arranged *geographically*—from Seattle through various towns to his mountain. But then Kerouac shifts and gives a *chronological* account from the beginning of his adventure to the end.

By contrast, in some essays, such as Wallace Stegner's "The Dump Ground" (page 409), there almost appears to be no real organization at all. He begins with the dump, moves to a camp site, is reminded of old Mrs. Gustafson, then the flume, back to the dump, with its broken dishes, volumes of Shakespeare, a dead colt, a goat's head, and on to the end. The connections have been made in the writer's mind, one item leading naturally to another. When a writer's thoughts seem to flow from idea to idea, impression to impression, without a clear pattern, his method is termed *stream-of-consciousness*.

Be aware of additional organizational structures: *order of importance, cause-effect,* and other logical patterns. Look for words and phrases such as *once, then, therefore, but, in addition, for me, for us,* and *at last* to give you clues to the organization.

The structure of an essay is like the framework of a house. Without doors, windows, siding, paint, or wiring, the framework is not much of a place to live in. But without a framework, the house would never be a house.

AUTHOR

JACK KEROUAC (1922–1969) was born Jean-Louis Lebridd Kerouac in Lowell, Massachusetts, of French-Canadian parents.

The "leader" of the so-called Beat Generation, Jack Kerouac first came to public eye with his novel, *On the Road* (1957), an ecstatic narration of the wandering life of the Beatniks of the Fifties.

He had traveled widely before writing this first novel, both as a sailor during World War II, and as a vagabond on his own. He was greatly influenced by Eastern religions, especially Buddhism.

On the Road was followed by many novels and nonfiction books. But with the passing of the Fifties, the public lost interest in Kerouac's work. His early death in 1969, however, came at a time when an ecologically-minded generation was rediscovering his work, and appreciating anew his love of nature and his belief in the human spirit's possibilities.

MY WAR WITH THE OSPREYS

John Steinbeck

MY war with the ospreys, like most wars, was largely accidental and had a tendency to spread in unforeseen directions. It is not over yet. The coming of winter caused an uneasy truce. I had to go into New York while the ospreys migrated to wherever they go in the winter. Spring may open new hostilities, although I can find it in my heart to wish for peace and even friendship. I hope the ospreys, wherever they may be, will read this.

I shall go back to the beginning and set down my side of the affair, trying to be as fair as I possibly can, placing truth above either propaganda or self-justification. I am confident that until near the end of the association, my motives were kind to the point of being sloppy.

Two years and a half ago I bought a little place near Sag Harbor, which is quite near to the tip of Long Island. The outer end of Long Island is like the open jaws of an alligator and, deep in the mouth, about where the soft palate would be, is Sag Harbor, a wonderful village inhabited by people who have been here for a long time. It is a fishing town, a local town which has resisted the inroads of tourists by building no motor courts and putting up no hotels.

Sag Harbor was once one of the two great whaling ports of the world and was, according to local accounts, not at all second to Nantucket Island. At that time no fewer than one hundred and fifty whaling bottoms roved the great seas and brought back their riches in oil. Sag Harbor and Nantucket lighted the lamps of the world until kerosene was developed and the whaling industry languished.

With the wealth brought back by the whalers, beautiful houses were built in the village during the early 1800's, houses of neo-Greek architecture with fluted columns, Greek key decorations, with fan-lights and Adam doors and mantels. Some of these magnificent old houses have widow's walks, those high balconies on which the women kept watch for the return of their men from their year-long voyages. Some of these old houses are being rediscovered and restored. Many of the streets of Sag Harbor are named after old whaling men. My own place is near Jesse Halsey Lane and he is still locally known as Old Cap'n Jesse. I have a picture of his rough and whiskered face.

The place I bought is not one of the great old houses but a beautiful little point of land on the inland waters, a place called Bluff Point, with its own little bay—incidentally a bay which is considered hurricane-proof. Ordinarily only two boats are moored there, mine and one other, but during hurricane warnings as many as thirty craft come in for anchorage until the all clear is broadcast.

My point, just under two acres, is shaded by great oak trees of four varieties, and there are many bushes and pines to edge it on the water side. I myself have planted a thousand Japanese black pines, furnished by the State of New York to edge my point, to hold the soil with their roots and even-

---

tually to curve beautifully inward, urged by the wind which blows every day of the year—sometimes a zephyr and sometimes a fierce and strident gale.

Greensward grows on my place. On the highest point I have a small, snug cottage and in front of it a pier going out to nine feet at low water so that a fairly large boat can dock. My own boat, the *Lilly-maid,* with Astolat as her port of registry, is named for my wife. She, the boat, is a utility craft twenty feet long, a clinker-built Jersey sea skiff.[1] Her eight-foot beam[2] makes her highly dependable and sea-worthy. Many of these specifications could also describe my wife. She is not clinker-built, however. The *Lillymaid* has a Navy top to put up when the weather gets too rough and she has a hundred-horsepower engine so that we can run for it if a storm approaches. She is a lovely, efficient and sea-worthy craft and all we need for the fishing and coastal exploring which is our pleasure.

Our house, while very small, is double-walled and winterized so that we can drive out during cold weather when the not-so-quiet desperation of New York gets us down.

My young sons, ten and twelve, but eight and ten when the osprey war began, adore the place and spend most of their summers here, exploring about in their skiffs or quarreling happily on the pier or on the lawn under the oak trees. My wife, who I believe was realistically skeptical when I bought the place, has become its stanchest defender.

Our association with the village people of Sag Harbor is, I think, pleasant to all of us. I come originally from a small town on the West Coast, a fishing town where my people have lived for a long time. And I find that what applies in my home country is equally acceptable in Sag Harbor. If you pay your bills, trade locally as much as possible, mind your own business and are reasonably pleas-ant, pretty soon they forget that you are an out-lander. I feel that I belong in Sag Harbor and I truly believe that the people of the village have accepted us as citizens. I do not sense the resentment from them which is reserved for tourists and summer people.

But I must get back to the ospreys, because with them I have not only failed to make friends but

have, on the contrary, been insulted, have thrown down the gauntlet and had it accepted.

On the West Coast, in California's Monterey County where I was born, I learned from childhood the grasses and flowers, the insects and the fishes, the animals from gopher and ground squirrel to bobcat and coyote, deer and mountain lion, and of course the birds, the common ones at least. These are things a child absorbs as he is growing up.

When I first came to Long Island I knew none of these things. Trees, grasses, animals and birds were all strange to me; they had to be learned. And some-times the natives could not help me much because they knew the things so well and deeply that they could not bring them to the surface.

Thus with books and by asking questions I have begun to learn the names of trees and bushes, of berries and flowers. With a telescope, a birthday present from my wife, I have watched muskrats and a pair of otters swimming in our bay. I have tried to identify the migrating ducks and geese when they sit down in our bay to rest from their journey.

The mallards mate and nest in the reeds along our waterline and bring their ducklings for the bread we throw to them from the pier. I have watched my boys sitting quietly on the lawn with the wild ducks crawling over their legs to get pieces of doughnut from their fingers.

The baby rabbits skitter through my vegetable garden and, since I like the rabbits better than my scrawny vegetables, I permit them not only to live but to pursue happiness on my land.

Our house has a glassed-in sun porch and outside its windows I have built a feeding station for birds. Sitting inside I do my best to identify the different visitors with the help of an Audubon, and I have not always, I confess, been successful. There is one common blackish bird which looks to be of the grackle persuasion but his bill is the wrong color and I don't know what he is.

In the upper branches of a half-dead oak tree on the very tip of our point, there was, when I took possession, a tattered lump of trash which looked like an unmade bed in a motor court. In my first early spring a native named Ray Bassenden, our contractor and builder, told me, "That's an osprey's nest. They come back every year. I remember that nest since I was a little boy."

"They build a messy nest," I said.

"Messy, yes," he said professionally, "but I

---

1. *clinker-built Jersey sea skiff,* a strong rowboat built with over-lapping boards on the hull.
2. *eight-foot beam,* that is, it measures eight feet from side to side.

doubt if I could design something the winds wouldn't blow out. It isn't pretty but it's darned good architecture from a staying point of view."

Toward the end of May, to my delight, the ospreys came back from wherever they had been, and from the beginning they fascinated me. They are about the best fishermen in the world and I am about the worst. I watched them by the hour. They would coast along hanging on the breeze perhaps fifty feet above the water, then suddenly their wings raised like the fins of a bomb and they arrowed down and nearly always came up with a fish. Then they would turn the fish in their talons so that its head was into the wind and fly to some high dead branch to eat their catch. I became a habitual osprey watcher.

In time, two of my ospreys were nudged by love and began to install new equipment in the great nest on my point. They brought unusual material—pieces of wood, rake handles, strips of cloth, reeds, swatches of seaweed. One of them, so help me, brought a piece of two-by-four pine three feet long to put into the structure. They weren't very careful builders. The ground under the tree was strewn with the excess stuff that fell out.

I mounted my telescope permanently on the sun porch and even trimmed some branches from intervening trees, and from then on, those lovedriven ospreys didn't have a moment of privacy.

Then June came and school was out and my boys trooped happily out to Sag Harbor. I warned them not to go too near the point for fear of offending the nest builders, and they promised they would not.

And then one morning the ospreys were gone and the nest abandoned. When it became apparent that they weren't coming back I walked out to the point and saw, sticking halfway out of the nest, the shaft and feathers of an arrow.

Now Catbird, my youngest son, is the archer of the family. I ran him down and gave him whatfor in spite of his plaintive protests that he had not shot at the nest.

For a week I waited for the birds to come back, but they did not. They were across the bay. I could see them through the telescope building an uneasy nest on top of a transformer on a telephone pole where they were definitely not wanted.

I got a ladder and climbed up to the nest on our point and when I came down I apologized to Cat-bird for my unjust suspicions. For in the nest I had found not only the arrow, but my bamboo garden rake, three T shirts belonging to my boys and a Plaza Hotel bath towel. Apparently nothing was too unusual for the ospreys to steal for their nest building. But our birds were definitely gone and showed no intention of returning. I went back to my Audubon and it told me the following:

"Osprey (fish hawk) *Pandion haliaëtus*, length 23 inches, wingspread about 6½ feet, weight 3½ pounds.

"Identification—in flight the wings appear long and the outer half has a characteristic backward sweep.

"Habits—(age 21 years) Provided they are not molested, ospreys will nest wherever there is a reasonably extensive body of clear water and some sort of elevated nest sites exist. The birds have little fear of man and are excellent watchdogs, cheeping loudly at intruders and driving off crows and other birds of prey. For this reason platforms on tall poles are often erected to encourage them to nest about homes and farmyards. Their food consists entirely of fish. These they spot from heights of thirty to one hundred feet, then, after hovering for a moment, they half close their wings and plunge into the water. The fish is seized in their talons, the toes of which are used in pairs, two to a side. This and the rough surface of the foot gives them a firm grip on the most slippery prey. After a catch, they rise quickly . . . and arrange the fish head first."

There followed a list of the kinds of fish they eat and their range and habits. Those were our boys, all right.

I must admit I had been pleased and a little proud to have my own osprey nest, apart from being able to watch them fish. I had planned to observe the nestlings when they arrived. The empty nest on the point was a matter of sorrow and perplexity to me. The summer was a little darkened by the empty nest, and later the winter winds ripped at its half-completed messiness.

It was in February of 1956 that the answer came to me. If people put up platforms on poles, why could I not build a nest so attractive as to be irresistible to any passing osprey with procreation on his mind? Why could I not win back my own birds from the uncomfortable nest which the power company had meanwhile torn off the transformer? I had been to Denmark and had seen what the country people there did for storks. And the storks loved them for it and had their young on the roof tops and year by year brought luck to their benefactors.

In the late winter I went to work. Climbing the oak tree on the point, I cleaned away the old debris of the nest. Then I mounted and firmly wired in place horizontally a large wagon wheel. I cut dry pampas grass stalks and bound them in long faggots. Then with the freezing blasts of winter tearing at my clothes, I reascended the tree and wove the reeds into the spokes of the wheel until I had a nest which, if I had any oviparous impulses, I should have found irresistible.

My wife, dressed in warm clothing, stood dutifully on the ground under the trees and hooked bundles of reeds on the line I threw down to her. She has a highly developed satiric sense which on other occasions I have found charming. She shouted up against the howling wind: "If anybody sees you, a middle-aged man, up a tree in midwinter, building a nest, I will have trouble explaining it to a sanity commission."

Misplaced humor can, under some circumstances, almost amount to bad taste. Silently and doggedly I completed what I believe was the handsomest nest in the Western Hemisphere. Then I went back to my sun porch to await eventualities.

I did have some difficulty explaining the project to my boys. To my oldest son Thom's question, "Why do you build nests for birds?" I could only jocularly reply, "Well, I can build a better nest than they can, but I can't lay eggs, so you see we have to get together."

The winter was long and cold and there was hardly any spring at all. Summer came without warning about June first. I had trouble with the novel I was writing since I had to rush constantly to the telescope to see whether the ospreys, my prospective tenants, had returned.

Then school was out and my boys moved to Sag Harbor and I put them on watch.

One morning Catbird charged into my study, which is a corner of the garage.

"Ospreys!" he shouted. "Come running—ospreys!"

"Sh!" I shouted back. "Keep your voice down. You'll disturb them."

I rushed for my telescope, bowling Catbird over in my rush and tripping over Thom's feet.

There were the ospreys all right. But they weren't settling into my beautiful nest. They were dismantling it, tearing it to pieces, lifting out the carefully bound reed pads and carrying them across the bay and propping them clumsily on top of the same transformer.

Of course my feelings were hurt. Why should I deny it? And on top of all my work. But on the heels of injury came anger. Those lousy, slipshod, larcenous birds, those ingrates, those—those ospreys. My eyes strayed to the shotgun that hangs over my fireplace, but before I could reach for it a Machiavellian thought came to me.

I wanted to hurt the ospreys, yes. I wanted revenge on them, but with number-four shot? No. I ached to hurt them as they had hurt me—in their feelings, psychologically.

I am an adept at psychological warfare. I know well how to sink the knife into sensibilities. I was coldly quiet, even deadly in my approach and manner, so that my boys walked about under a cloud and Thom asked, "What's the matter, Father, did you lose some money playing poker?"

"You stay out of the garage," I said quietly.

I had made my plan. I declared the garage off limits to everyone. My novel came to a dead stop. Daily I worked in the garage using pieces of chicken wire and a great deal of plaster of Paris.

Then I paid a call on my neighbor, Jack Ramsey, a very good painter, and asked him to come to my work shop and to bring his palette and brushes. At the end of two days we emerged with our product—a lifesize perfect replica of a nesting whooping crane. It is my belief that there are only thirty-seven of these rare and wonderful birds in the world. Well, this was the thirty-eighth.

Chuckling evilly I hoisted the plaster bird up in the tree and wired her firmly in the nest where her blinding white body, black tail and brilliant red mask stood out magnificently against the sky. I had even made her bill a little overlarge to take care of foreshortening.

Finally I went back to the sun porch and turned my telescope on the ospreys who pretended to go about their nest building on the transformer as though nothing had happened. But I knew what must be going on over there, although they kept up their façade of listlessness, and I must say they were building an even messier nest than usual.

Mrs. Osprey was saying, "Lord almighty, George! Look who has moved into the apartment *you* didn't want. Why did I listen to you?"

To which he was replying, "*I* didn't want—what do you mean *I* didn't want? It was you who said the neighborhood wasn't good enough. Don't you put words in my mouth, Mildred."

"Everybody knows you have no taste or background," she was replying. "Your Uncle Harry built his nest over a slaughterhouse."

And I laughed to myself. These are the wounds that never heal. This is psychological warfare as it should be fought.

Two days later, Thom came running into my study in the garage.

"The nest," he cried. "Look at the nest."

I bolted for the door. The ospreys in jealous rage were dive-bombing my whooping crane, but all they could accomplish was the breaking of their talons on the hard surface of the plaster. Finally they gave up and flew away, followed by my shouts of derision.

I did hear my oldest boy say to his brother, "Father has been working too hard. He has gone nuts."

Catbird replied, "His id has been ruptured. Sometimes one broods too much on a subject and throws the whole psychic pattern into an uproar."

That isn't quite where it rests.

It is true that the ospreys have not attacked any more, but we have had other visitors, human visitors.

One morning I looked out the window to see a rather stout lady in khaki trousers and a turtle neck sweater, creeping across my lawn on her hands and knees. Field glasses dangled from her neck and she held a camera in front of her. When I went out to question her, she angrily waved me away.

"Go back," she whispered hoarsely. "Do you want her to fly away?"

"But you don't understand—" I began.

"*Will* you keep your voice down," she said hoarsely. "Do you know what that is? The club will never believe me. If I don't get a picture of her I'll kill you."

Yes, we have had bird watchers—lots of them. You see, our whooping crane can be sighted from a long way off. After a time they discovered the nature of the thing, but they would not listen to my explanation of the ruse. In fact, they became angry; not at the ospreys, where the blame rests—but at me.

As I write, it is autumn of 1956 and from the coldness and the growing winds, an early winter and a cold one is indicated. I have taken my whooping crane down and restored the nest to its old beauty. When the spring comes again—we shall see what we shall see. No one can say that I am unforgiving. The nest is ready and waiting. Let us see whether the ospreys are big enough to let bygones be bygones.

My wife says that if she has to go through another year like this she will—no, I won't tell you what she says. Sometimes her sense of humor seems a little strained.

DISCUSSION

1. Steinbeck's essay is organized into very definite sections. Identify the sections and explain what he does in each.

2. Have Steinbeck's motives been "kind to the point of being sloppy"? Explain.

3. (a) How is Steinbeck insulted by the ospreys? (b) How does he plan to gain revenge? Is he successful?

4. At what point does Steinbeck look upon the ospreys as human?

5. From evidence in the selection, what is Steinbeck like as (a) a father? (b) a husband? (c) a neighbor?

COMPOSITION

Write a description of the "war" between John Steinbeck and the ospreys from the point of view of the ospreys. What are your "real reasons" for moving? How do you feel about the plaster whooping crane? What do you think of Mr. Steinbeck?

AUTHOR

JOHN STEINBECK (1902–1968), winner of both the Pulitzer and Nobel prizes, was one of the most sensitive and vital writers of our time. Born in the center of California's agricultural district, his intimate knowledge of the problems of the landless farm laborer, his concern for them, and his gifts as a storyteller combined to produce some of America's finest social-protest fiction.

Among these books were: *Tortilla Flat, Of Mice and Men, The Grapes of Wrath,* and *The Wayward Bus.* In recent years, Steinbeck's writings took a different direction. *The Pearl* and *East of Eden* reveal Steinbeck's faith in man's ability to triumph over private and social evils. *Travels with Charley* is a comprehensive view of American life as seen by Steinbeck on a trip through forty states.

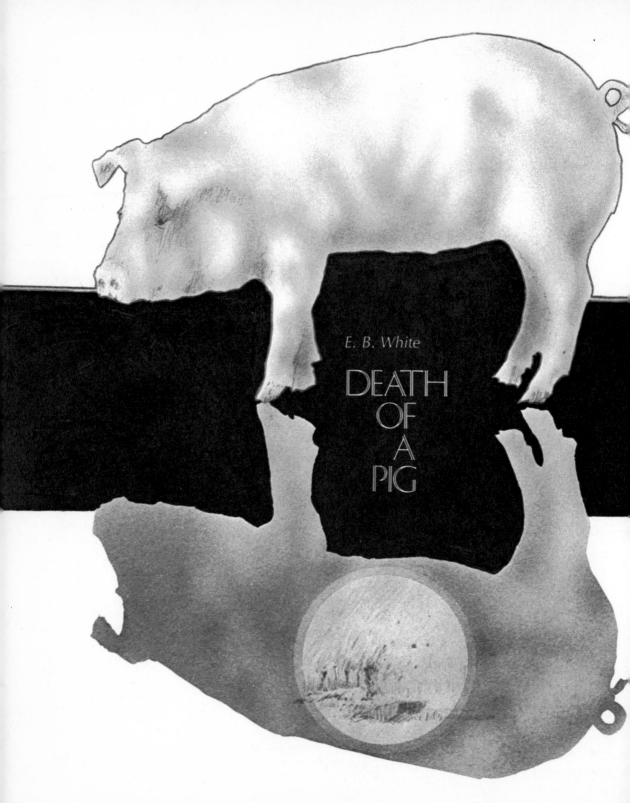

E. B. White

DEATH OF A PIG

I spent several days and nights in mid-September with an ailing pig, and I feel driven to account for this stretch of time, more particularly since the pig died at last, and I lived, and things might easily have gone the other way round and none left to do the accounting. Even now, so close to the event, I cannot recall the hours sharply and am not ready to say whether death came on the third night or the fourth night. This uncertainty afflicts me with a sense of personal deterioration; if I were in decent health I would know how many nights I had sat up with a pig.

The scheme of buying a spring pig in blossomtime, feeding it through summer and fall, and butchering it when the solid cold weather arrives is a familiar scheme to me and follows an antique pattern. It is a tragedy enacted on most farms with perfect fidelity to the original script. The murder, being premeditated, is in the first degree but is quick and skillful, and the smoked bacon and ham provide a ceremonial ending whose fitness is seldom questioned.

Once in a while something slips—one of the actors goes up in his lines and the whole performance stumbles and halts. My pig simply failed to show up for a meal. The alarm spread rapidly. The classic outline of the tragedy was lost. I found myself cast suddenly in the role of pig's friend and physician—a farcical character with an enema bag for a prop. I had a presentiment, the very first afternoon, that the play would never regain its balance and that my sympathies were now wholly with the pig. This was slapstick—the sort of dramatic treatment that instantly appealed to my old dachshund, Fred, who joined the vigil, held the bag, and, when all was

over, presided at the interment. When we slid the body into the grave, we both were shaken to the core. The loss we felt was not the loss of ham but the loss of pig. He had evidently become precious to me, not that he represented a distant nourishment in a hungry time, but that he had suffered in a suffering world. But I'm running ahead of my story and shall have to go back.

My pigpen is at the bottom of an old orchard below the house. The pigs I have raised have lived in a faded building that once was an icehouse. There is a pleasant yard to move about in, shaded by an apple tree that overhangs the low rail fence. A pig couldn't ask for anything better—or none has, at any rate. The sawdust in the icehouse makes a comfortable bottom in which to root, and a warm bed. This sawdust, however, came under suspicion when the pig took sick. One of my neighbors said he thought the pig would have done better on new ground—the same principle that applies in planting potatoes. He said there might be something unhealthy about that sawdust, that he never thought well of sawdust.

It was about four o'clock in the afternoon when I first noticed that there was something wrong with the pig. He failed to appear at the trough for his supper, and when a pig (or a child) refuses supper a chill wave of fear runs through any household, or ice-household. After examining my pig, who was stretched out in the sawdust inside the building, I went to the phone and cranked it four times. Mr. Dameron answered. "What's good for a sick pig?" I asked. (There is never any identification needed on a country phone; the person on the other end knows who is talking by the sound of the voice and by the character of the question.)

"I don't know, I never had a sick pig," said Mr. Dameron, "but I can find out quick enough. You hang up and I'll call Henry."

Mr. Dameron was back on the line again in five minutes. "Henry says roll him over on his back and give him two ounces of castor oil or sweet oil, and if that doesn't do the trick give him an injection of soapy water. He says he's almost sure the pig's plugged up, and even if he's wrong, it can't do any harm."

I thanked Mr. Dameron. I didn't go right down to the pig, though. I sank into a chair and sat still for a few minutes to think about my troubles, and then I got up and went to the barn, catching up on some odds and ends that needed tending to. Unconsciously I held off, for an hour, the deed by which I would officially recognize the collapse of the performance of raising a pig; I wanted no interruption in the regularity of feeding, the steadiness of growth, the even succession of days. I wanted no interruption, wanted no oil, no deviation. I just wanted to keep on raising a pig, full meal after full meal, spring into summer into fall. I didn't even know whether there were two ounces of castor oil on the place.

Shortly after five o'clock I remembered that we had been invited out to dinner that night and realized that if I were to dose a pig there was no time to lose. The dinner date seemed a familiar conflict: I move in a desultory society and often a week or two will roll by without my going to anybody's house to dinner or anyone's coming to mine, but when an occasion does arise, and I am summoned, something usually turns up (an hour or two in advance) to make all human intercourse seem vastly inappropriate. I have come to believe that there is in hostesses a special power of divination, and that they deliberately arrange dinners to coincide with pig failure or some other sort of failure. At any rate, it was after five o'clock and I knew I could put off no longer the evil hour.

When my son and I arrived at the pigyard, armed with a small bottle of castor oil and a length of clothesline, the pig had emerged from his house and was standing in the middle of his yard, listlessly. He gave us a slim greeting. I could see that he felt uncomfortable and uncertain. I had brought the clothesline thinking I'd have to tie him (the pig weighed more than a hundred pounds), but we never used it. My son reached down, grabbed both front legs, upset him quickly, and when he opened his mouth to scream I turned the oil into his throat—a pink, corrugated area I had never seen before. I had just time to read the label while the neck of the bottle was in his mouth. It said Puretest. The screams, slightly muffled by oil, were pitched in the hysterically high range of pig-sound, as though torture were being carried out, but they didn't last long: it was all over rather suddenly, and, his legs released, the pig righted himself.

In the upset position the corners of his mouth had been turned down, giving him a frowning expression. Back on his feet again, he regained the set smile that a pig wears even in sickness. He stood his ground, sucking slightly at the residue of oil; a few drops leaked out of his lips while his wicked eyes, shaded by their coy little lashes, turned on me in disgust and hatred. I scratched him gently with oily fingers and he remained quiet, as though trying to recall the satisfaction of being scratched when in health, and seeming to rehearse in his mind the indignity to which he had just been subjected. I noticed, as I stood there, four or five small dark spots on his back near the tail end, reddish brown in color, each about the size of a housefly. I could not make out what they were. They did not look troublesome but at the same time they did not look like mere surface bruises or chafe marks. Rather they seemed blemishes of internal origin. His stiff white bristles almost completely hid them and I had to part the bristles with my fingers to get a good look.

Several hours later, a few minutes before midnight, having dined well and at someone else's expense, I returned to the pighouse with a flashlight. The patient was asleep. Kneeling, I felt his ears (as you might put your hand on the forehead of a child) and they seemed cool, and then with the light made a careful examination of the yard and the house for sign that the oil had worked. I found none and went to bed.

We had been having an unseasonable spell of weather—hot, close days, with the fog shutting in every night, scaling for a few hours in midday, then creeping back again at dark, drifting in first over the trees on the point, then suddenly blowing across the fields, blotting out the world and taking possession of houses, men, and animals. Everyone kept hoping for a break, but the break failed to come. Next day was another hot one. I visited the pig before breakfast and tried to tempt him with a little milk in his trough. He just stared at it, while I made a sucking sound through my teeth to remind him of past pleasures of the feast. With very small, timid pigs, weanlings, this ruse is often quite successful and will encourage them to eat; but with a large, sick pig the ruse is senseless and the sound I made must have made him feel, if anything, more miserable. He not only did not crave food, he felt a positive revulsion to it. I found a place under the apple tree where he had vomited in the night.

At this point, although a depression had settled over me, I didn't suppose that I was going to lose my pig. From the lustiness of a healthy pig a man derives a feeling of personal lustiness; the stuff that goes into the trough and is received with such enthusiasm is an earnest of some later feast of his own, and when this suddenly comes to an end and the food lies stale and untouched, souring in the sun, the pig's imbalance becomes the man's, vicariously, and life seems insecure, displaced, transitory.

As my own spirits declined, along with the pig's, the spirits of my vile old dachshund rose. The frequency of our trips down the footpath through the orchard to the pigyard delighted him, although he suffers greatly from arthritis, moves with difficulty, and would be bedridden if he could find anyone willing to serve him meals on a tray.

He never missed a chance to visit the pig with me, and he made many professional calls on his own. You could see him down there at all hours, his white face parting the grass along the fence as he wobbled and stumbled about, his stethoscope dangling—a happy quack, writing his villainous prescriptions and grinning his corrosive grin. When the enema bag appeared, and the bucket of warm suds, his happiness was complete, and he managed to squeeze his enormous body between the two lowest rails of the yard and then assumed full charge of the irrigation. Once, when I lowered the bag to check the flow, he reached in and hurriedly drank a few mouthfuls of the suds to test their potency. I have noticed that Fred will feverishly consume any substance that is associated with trouble—the bitter flavor is to his liking. When the bag was above reach,

he concentrated on the pig and was everywhere at once, a tower of strength and inconvenience. The pig, curiously enough, stood rather quietly through this colonic carnival, and the enema, though ineffective, was not as difficult as I had anticipated.

I discovered, though, that once having given a pig an enema there is no turning back, no chance of resuming one of life's more stereotyped roles. The pig's lot and mine were inextricably bound now, as though the rubber tube were the silver cord. From then until the time of his death I held the pig steadily in the bowl of my mind; the task of trying to deliver him from his misery became a strong obsession. His suffering soon became the embodiment of all earthly wretchedness. Along toward the end of the afternoon, defeated in physicking, I phoned the veterinary twenty miles away and placed the case formally in his hands. He was full of questions, and when I casually mentioned the dark spots on the pig's back, his voice changed its tone.

"I don't want to scare you," he said, "but when there are spots, erysipelas has to be considered."

Together we considered erysipelas, with frequent interruptions from the telephone operator, who wasn't sure the connection had been established.

"If a pig has erysipelas can he give it to a person?" I asked.

"Yes, he can," replied the vet.

"Have they answered?" asked the operator.

"Yes, they have," I said. Then I addressed the vet again. "You better come over here and examine this pig right away."

"I can't come myself," said the vet, "but McFarland can come this evening if that's all right. Mac knows more about pigs than I do anyway. You needn't worry too much about the spots. To indicate erysipelas they would have to be deep hemorrhagic infarcts."[1]

"Deep hemorrhagic what?" I asked.

"Infarcts," said the vet.

"Have they answered?" asked the operator.

"Well," I said, "I don't know what you'd call these spots, except they're about the size of a housefly. If the pig has erysipelas I guess I have it, too, by this time, because we've been very close lately."

"McFarland will be over," said the vet.

I hung up. My throat felt dry and I went to the

---

1. *hemmorhagic infarcts,* dead or dying tissue caused by the bursting of blood vessels.

cupboard and got a bottle of whiskey. Deep hemorrhagic infarcts—the phrase began fastening its hooks in my head. I had assumed that there could be nothing much wrong with a pig during the months it was being groomed for murder; my confidence in the essential health and endurance of pigs had been strong and deep, particularly in the health of pigs that belonged to me and that were part of my proud scheme. The awakening had been violent, and I minded it all the more because I knew that what could be true of my pig could be true also of the rest of my tidy world. I tried to put this distasteful idea from me, but it kept recurring. I took a short drink of the whiskey and then, although I wanted to go down to the yard and look for fresh signs, I was scared to. I was certain I had erysipelas.

It was long after dark and the supper dishes had been put away when a car drove in and McFarland got out. He had a girl with him. I could just make her out in the darkness—she seemed young and pretty. "This is Miss Owen," he said. "We've been having a picnic supper on the shore, that's why I'm late."

McFarland stood in the driveway and stripped off his jacket, then his shirt. His stocky arms and capable hands showed up in my flashlight's gleam as I helped him find his coverall and get zipped up. The rear seat of his car contained an astonishing amount of paraphernalia, which he soon overhauled, selecting a chain, a syringe, a bottle of oil, a rubber tube, and some other things I couldn't identify. Miss Owen said she'd go along with us and see the pig. I led the way down the warm slope of the orchard, my light picking out the path for them, and we all three climbed the fence, entered the pighouse, and squatted by the pig while McFarland took a rectal reading. My flashlight picked up the glitter of an engagement ring on the girl's hand.

"No elevation," said McFarland, twisting the thermometer in the light. "You needn't worry about erysipelas." He ran his hand slowly over the pig's stomach and at one point the pig cried out in pain.

"Poor piggledy-wiggledy!" said Miss Owen.

The treatment I had been giving the pig for two days was then repeated, somewhat more expertly, by the doctor, Miss Owen and I handing him things as he needed them—holding the chain that he had looped around the pig's upper jaw, holding the syringe, holding the bottle stopper, the end of the tube, all of us working in darkness and in comfort, working with the instinctive teamwork induced by emergency conditions, the pig unprotesting, the house shadowy, protecting, intimate. I went to bed tired but with a feeling of relief that I had turned over part of the responsibility of the case to a licensed doctor. I was beginning to think, though, that the pig was not going to live.

He died twenty-four hours later, or it might have been forty-eight—there is a blur in time here, and I may have lost or picked up a day in the telling and the pig one in the dying. At intervals during the last day I took cool fresh water down to him, and at such times as he found the strength to get to his feet he would stand with head in the pail and snuffle his snout around. He drank a few sips but no more; yet it seemed to comfort him to dip his nose in water and bobble it about, sucking in and blowing out through his teeth. Much of the time, now, he lay indoors half buried in sawdust. Once, near the last, while I was attending him I saw him try to make a bed for himself but he lacked the strength, and when he set his snout into the dust he was unable to plow even the little furrow he needed to lie down in.

He came out of the house to die. When I went down, before going to bed, he lay stretched in the yard a few feet from the door. I knelt, saw that he was dead, and left him there: his face had a mild look, expressive neither of deep peace nor of deep suffering, although I think he had suffered a good deal. I went back up to the house and to bed, and cried internally—deep hemorrhagic intears. I didn't wake till nearly eight the next morning, and when I looked out the open window the grave was already being dug, down beyond the dump under a wild apple. I could hear the spade strike against the small rocks that blocked the way. Never send to know for whom the grave is dug, I said to myself, it's dug for thee. Fred, I well knew, was supervising the work of digging, so I ate breakfast slowly.

It was a Saturday morning. The thicket in which I found the gravediggers at work was dark and warm, the sky overcast. Here, among alders and young hackmatacks, at the foot of the apple tree, Lennie had dug a beautiful hole, five feet long, three feet wide, three feet deep. He was standing in it, removing the last spadefuls of earth while Fred patrolled the brink in simple but impressive circles, disturbing the loose earth of the mound so that it trickled back in. There had been no rain in weeks and the soil, even three feet down, was dry and powdery. As I stood and stared, an enormous earthworm which had been partially exposed by the spade at the bottom dug itself deeper and made a slow withdrawal, seeking even remoter moistures at even lonelier depths. And just as Lennie stepped out and rested his spade against the tree and lit a cigarette, a small green apple separated itself from a branch overhead and fell into the hole. Everything about this last scene seemed overwritten—the dismal sky, the shabby woods, the imminence of rain, the worm (legendary bedfellow of the dead), the apple (conventional garnish of a pig).

But even so, there was a directness and dispatch about animal burial, I thought, that made it a more decent affair than human burial: there was no stopover in the undertaker's foul parlor, no wreath nor spray; and when we hitched a line to the pig's hind legs and dragged him swiftly from his yard, throwing our weight into the harness and leaving a wake of crushed grass and smoothed rubble over the dump, ours was a businesslike procession, with Fred, the dishonorable pallbearer, staggering along in the rear, his perverse bereavement showing in every seam in his face; and the post mortem performed handily and swiftly right at the edge of the grave, so that the inwards that had caused the pig's death preceded him into the ground and he lay at last resting squarely on the cause of his own undoing.

I threw in the first shovelful, and then we worked rapidly and without talk, until the job was complete. I picked up the rope, made it fast to Fred's collar (he is a notorious ghoul), and we all three filed back up the path to the house, Fred bringing up the rear and holding back every inch of the way, feigning unusual stiffness. I noticed that although he weighed far less than the pig, he was harder to drag, being possessed of the vital spark.

The news of the death of my pig travelled fast and far, and I received many expressions of sympathy from friends and neighbors, for no one took the event lightly and the premature expiration of a pig is, I soon discovered, a departure which the community marks solemnly on its calendar, a sorrow in which it feels fully involved. I have written this account in penitence and in grief, as a man who failed to raise his pig, and to explain my deviation from the classic course of so many raised pigs. The grave in the woods is unmarked, but Fred can direct the mourner to it unerringly and with immense good will, and I know he and I shall often revisit it, singly and together, in seasons of reflection and despair, on flagless memorial days of our own choosing.

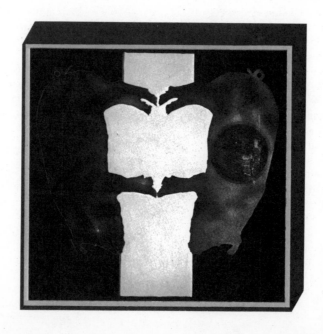

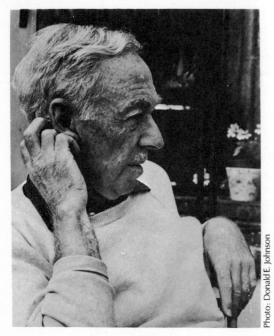

Photo: Donald E. Johnson

E.B. WHITE

DISCUSSION

1. E. B. White opens his essay by comparing the normal events in a pig's life to those of a play—more specifically a tragedy. Is this tragedy the same as Shakespearian tragedy (see Author's Craft, p. 342)? If not, what does he mean by tragedy?

2. "The loss we felt was not the loss of ham but the loss of pig." Explain.

3. Point out examples of humor in the essay. Does the humor detract from the seriousness of the essay subject?

4. (a) At what points does White seem to digress? (b) Is there a purpose to his digressions?

5. What fear begins to possess White as the pig's condition worsens?

6. (a) What was the burial of the pig like? (b) In what respect does White consider it better than a human burial? Do you agree? Why or why not?

7. What do you think was E. B. White's purpose in writing this essay?

COMPOSITION

Have you ever had a totally insignificant object suddenly become meaningful to you? If so, describe the events which led up to that realization. Looking back, how do you feel about it now?

diGGiNG foR piCTURES

William Golding

IF you examine a topographical map of England, you will see that the Southern part of the country is dominated by a huge starfish of high, chalk Downs,[1] with each arm reaching out to the sea. Once these Downs had the only roads in England—some of the oldest roads in the world. They are very little used now. They are simply wide tracks between hedges or wire fences, their surfaces turfs sometimes as perfect as the lawns of an Oxford college. A shepherd and his flock, a solitary walker smoking a pipe and glancing at his map, a man on horseback or a drover with his cows—this is the only traffic you will meet. Once the valleys below the Downs were full of forests and swamps, but the iron ax and the iron plow cleared them; and then the Romans briskly drove their military roads from one end of the country to the other and dictated the

future shape of English history. The old roads on the Downs were forgotten.

Where they meet, at the center of the starfish, was a prehistoric metropolis; and the cathedral of that metropolis was Stonehenge.[2] The whole of this area is sown thick with the remains of ancient peoples. To spend your life here in Wessex, as I have done, is to live where archaeology is as natural, or at least as usual, as gardening. Walk across a newly plowed field and you may pick up a stone spearhead which has not been touched by human hand for 20,000 years. As crops come up, you may be able to detect rows of plants which grow faster than the others—because they have more room for their roots in a forgotten and earth-filled ditch. That

---

1. *Downs*, the treeless, rolling highlands of Kent, England.

2. *Stonehenge*, a stone monument from prehistoric times.

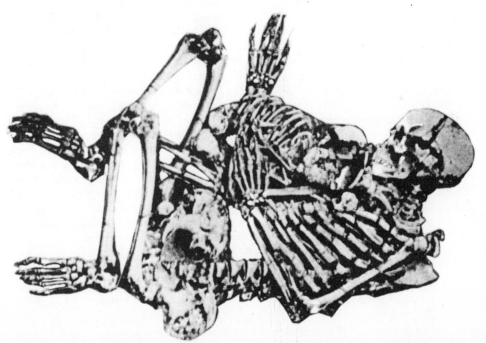

ditch is part of a camp lost 3,000 years ago, which thus emerges in shadowy outline until the rest of the crop catches up and the whole thing vanishes again. If you take your children for a walk, they may play 'king of the castle' on a grassy mound, without knowing that a king is already in residence below them, his calcined bones huddled in an earthen pot, the rest of his kingdom forgotten.

Of course our professional archaeologists are as brisk as the Romans were. You can see them often enough on the Downs. They dig and survey with infinite precision. They map and dissect, docket and assess. You see them using the delicate devices of their science—surveying instruments and mysterious boxes which do strange things with the earth's magnetism. They ponder, lost in thought over a map, while the west wind tumbles a mop of scholarly hair. They crouch in square holes, hour after hour, brushing the dust away from finds with camel's-hair brushes. They publish diagrams of digs, statistical analyses of pottery fragments and photographs of sections of the earth with each stratum labeled. They are very efficient. Their published minds never run away with them. They are austere proof against the perils of exercising an imagination which might assume too much.

We amateurs are allowed to help them sometimes —under strict supervision. But I have never had the courage to admit to a professional that, as far as I am concerned, archaeology is a game, and that I would not dig if I was unable to let my mind run riot.

For me, there is a glossy darkness under the turf, and against that background the people of the past play out their actions in technicolor. Sometimes I feel as though I have only to twitch aside the green coverlet of grass to find them there. Might I not come face to face with that most primitive of Europe's men—Neanderthal Man[3]—who once loped along the track where I used to take my Sunday walk? This sort of thinking is, of course, the rankest amateurism. It is to think like the Welsh, who say that King Arthur still sits inside Mount Snowdon, playing chess with his knights and waiting for the last battle.

For most of us, though, history is not diagrams—however accurate—but pictures; and in a place like this, the pictures lie under the grass, where our spades reach for them into the loaded soil. Do not the old men in the pub farther up my village talk of the golden boat that lies in the mound on top of the hill? Of course that must be a legend—but a golden boat *was* found under just such a mound in Sweden.

Of course our archaeologists have done a splendid piece of work, accurate and sober. They have established whole periods of prehistory in outline. But we amateurs are not like them. We are antiquarians.[4] We are akin to those nineteenth-century parsons and squires who would take the family, a wagon and a dozen bottles of port or sherry onto the Downs and make a picnic of digging. Awful was the damage they did, 150 years ago, digging, for the hell of it, into the burial mounds of kings. Yet year by year life lays down another layer of remains for tomorrow. We amateurs can even envy them their careless rapture. Our lawless hearts leap, not at a diagram, but at the luck of the villager who turns up a cache of golden ornaments with his plow— wonderful, barbaric ornaments which will go into a museum, but should gleam on some lovely throat or wrist. Gold dies in a museum despite all you can do. All the gold that Schliemann[5] dug up at Troy looks no better than tinsel, under glass.

Yet it was a local man who started the rot—or, as I suppose I had better say, who transformed the ancient game of the antiquarian into the modern science of the archaeologist. That man lived just over the hill outside my window, at an estate called Cranborne Chase. He was General Augustus Henry Pitt-Rivers, a character who contributed his own legend to the countryside. He was, in fact, one of the English eccentrics. We have had many such and they enliven our history, though they were an expensive way of getting results. General Pitt-Rivers stocked his park with rare animals, for instance, so that a poacher after a brace of pheasant might suddenly find himself surrounded by the mysterious shapes of kangaroos. He built a bandstand and gave concerts to which his tenants were obliged to come. He got interested in the mounds and ditches on his estate, and, at one stroke, paved the way for archaeology to become a science. He made it a military

3. *Neanderthal Man*, a Stone Age human whose skull was found in the Neander Valley in Germany.

4. *antiquarians* (an´ tə kwer´ ē əns), anyone who studies or collects anything old.

5. *Schliemann*, Heinrich Schliemann (shlē´ män) famous German archaeologist (1822–1890) who excavated the ancient city of Troy.

operation. He employed regiments of laborers, surveyors and young scholars. He measured and recorded everything he found—whether he understood what it implied or not—so that today, almost a century later, his results can be interpreted without fear of a mistake.

How strange the mind is! Pitt-Rivers tried to discover the history of his estate and all its petty kings; yet for me, at any rate, he has obscured it. Consider. In the early days of spring, General Pitt-Rivers would set out, in a vehicle drawn by two splendid horses, through the cuckoo-haunted woods. His coachman drove, in full livery, and two grooms sat with folded arms at the general's back. Behind them, pedaling madly through the white dust, came his squad of young scholars, whom we may now call archaeologists, and who each achieved eminence and fame as such in later life. They rode penny-farthings, bicycles so named because their front wheels were so much larger than their rear ones. They wore tweedy trousers, blazers or Norfolk jackets, and straw boaters[6] emblazoned with the general's colors.

Pitt-Rivers was a man of terrible authority. He had the body of the earth laid open for him as a surgeon might order an intern to make the first incision. No one has ever claimed that he was a likable man, and no one has ever doubted that he had some of the madness of genius. Yet his zoo and his band, his museum perched ridiculously on top of the Downs, near Farnham, his extravagant archaeology, his savage personality—these have obscured that same shadowy past he tried to illuminate. For if I walk over his estate I do not think of Stone, Bronze or Iron Age men. I find myself listening with my inward ear to the tramp of laborers in step. I hear the busy clatter of hoofs, and half-shrink into the hedge as I imagine the general bustling by; and behind him comes that learned covey of riders on penny-farthings—their solid tires bouncing over broken flint—each with a hand up to hold on his ridiculous, emblazoned hat.

But the land is aglow with every kind of picture. When our children were small, we used to take them to some woods which hang on the side of the Downs and seem as impenetrable as those which surrounded the Sleeping Beauty. They are deserted except for the fox and wood pigeon. But if you step aside from the country lane you find that a deep ditch leads up into them—not a dug ditch, but one of these smooth grooves, three yards deep and ten yards wide, which can be made by nothing but generations of feet.

Trees lean in and form, over the groove, a green tunnel. Nobody walks there now. Yet it is as visibly an ancient main road as is the Pilgrim's Way which Chaucer[7] followed across the green hills of Kent. Only when you have clambered along it for hundreds of yards do you see why it is there—and where it once led. The woods have grown up around and through an immense building. Its walls and roofs are down. There are blocks of masonry; there is a gable still standing; there are the stumps of pillars, outlines of rooms, corridors, halls. Beneath your feet is grass, but underneath it you feel the firmness of pavement. You stand in the plan of a hall and see that worn steps lead down from one end, and you have some sense of the myriad feet that scooped away their stone.

You wait, but nobody comes. At most you hear a distant shriek of laughter from the woodman's children, who are climbing trees far away in the forest. Meadowsweet and nettle, old-man's-beard and purple loosestrife[8] compete with the leaning oaks to shut away the world. The noisiest thing in the whole humpy, huddled ruin is the flight of bees. The worn steps will wait a long time for feet.

'My Palace of Clarendon,' said Henry the Second,[9] 'Clarendon, which I love best of all places in the world.'

The mind takes a sudden dive. Eight hundred years ago this place, tree-shattered and lost in the forest, was the center of our world. You could not have stood on this grassy pavement then, for the men-at-arms would have hustled you away. You might perhaps have sneaked to the door—there, where old-man's-beard has made a sunproof thicket —and watched the jugglers performing on a feast day before the high table. You could have begged for scraps over there, where a mountain ash has forced two blocks of stone from the lintel; and if you came for justice, you would have got it here, however long you had to wait your turn. For the

---

6. *Norfolk jackets and straw boaters*, a loose-fitting, belted jacket and a round hat.

7. *Chaucer*, Geoffrey Chaucer (1340?–1400), English poet who wrote the *Canterbury Tales*.

8. *Meadowsweet . . . purple loosestrife*, English wildflowers.

9. *Henry the Second*. The first English king (ruled 1154–1189) of the Plantagenet family. Clarendon was his palace.

Law was given here—the greatest gift a nation can hope to have. But to get that justice, no air has ever been torn as these few cubic feet of air were torn by mortal passion. For, on the pavement which still lies three inches below the grass, Henry the Second and Saint Thomas a Becket[10] stood face to face. When my daughter could just about walk, she found a piece of medieval glass here, a fragment iridescent as a soap bubble, and my mind fogged with the effort of realizing that the King or the Saint might have drunk from it.

The history of Clarendon is too crowded for the mind. You come up out of your imagination to an emptiness where the wood pigeons talk to each other and the steps wait, year in, year out, for feet. That is the trouble with what you might call official ruins. The mind needs a more personal stimulus than these acres of stone. Nor can we imagine a king or a saint. It is ordinary people to whom we reach out in imagination.

For this reason I prefer the humdrum in digging. I do not expect to dig up the Magna Charta[11]—do not need to, since it lies, at the moment, nine miles away from me in Salisbury Cathedral. I do not expect to find Arthur lying beside the sword Excalibur under Mount Badon. My pictures are more intimate and less important. I like to pick through the ashcans of the Iron Age[12] and guess how life went on. Digging, I lay my hand on things. I discover an immediacy which disappears when the find becomes official and is displayed behind glass. Just as the gold of Troy has lost gloss, so a bone or a stone dies a few moments after you lift it from the earth. But nevertheless, for those few moments, obscurely and indefinably, you feel a connection with the past.

This is where the specialty of our Downs comes in. Round any ancient settlement are hundreds of pits which have been filled in so completely that you can find them only when you can recognize the faint depression which is sometimes left. Those clever people of two or three thousand years ago used to scoop out a bottle-shaped pit in the chalk and line it with wickerwork and clay. This made a convenient silo for grain. But after a few years

the silo would be contaminated with fungus, so they would move off a few yards and dig another. Now when you consider that this went on for as much as 500 years, you can see that wherever the Downs were inhabited they must have been stippled like the skin of a trout.

But the old silos were not left empty. They became excellent rubbish pits, into which anything unwanted was dumped. Digging in them, you do not find inscriptions or careful burials; you find only the records of daily life. And, since the pits are multiplied by the thousands, you are unlikely to destroy anything which would be of value to the serious archaeologist. He may use them to work out the number of inhabitants and the duration of the settlement; but he need only excavate a pit here and there. The pits, in fact, provide the amateur archaeologist with an equivalent to the practice slopes for skiers.

First, after you have broken up and laid aside the hard earth, you will find bones of sheep or oxen, bones sometimes of deer or the tusks of a boar. They were good meals, and the marks of the knife are still on them. Time is kind to bones. It cleans them with an intimate care which cannot be duplicated even in the laboratory. Every delicate line, every ridge and pocket, lies there in your hand, so that the bones have a strange, functional beauty. And as you concentrate, leaning down, free of archaeological diagrams and statistics in your private world, it is strange if you cannot put the meat back on the bone and the whole joint, hissing and spluttering, on the dish which lies in fragments below you. For of course these pits are full of broken pottery. I do not know whether it is a failing of mine or a virtue that I am never able to see these fragments as clues in a dating series. My private world falls in fragments, like a pot, when the presiding archaeologist leans down into my pit and defines the pottery.

'Early Iron Age. I thought it would be.'

No. Crouched in my pit, I hold the fragment in my hand and enjoy it. Presently Dr. Stubbs will investigate it closely through his bifocal lenses; and then it will be presented in a plastic bag to Miss Wilson, who will record it in a ledger. But here and now, as I lift out the triangular fragment with the two sharp edges, I get a sort of warm domesticity from it. This is not very old pottery. It is very new. It was thrown in here five minutes ago. Holding the piece in my hand I can just make out voices.

---

10. *St Thomas à Becket* (1118?–1170), archbishop of Canterbury who opposed Henry II and was murdered by his agents on December 29, 1170.

11. *Magna Charta* (mag′nə kär′tə), or "great charter", Latin, signed in 1215 by King John giving the English people limited civil rights.

12. *Iron Age*, the period of history when iron first came into widespread use, about 1000 B.C.–100 A.D.

Owen, bach, look what you've done! Clear it up now—go on! Not another mouthful do you eat until the pieces are in the pit and the hearth as clean as a new leaf!

Those large lumps of chalk are loom weights.[13] They hung in a thumping, swinging row, to keep the warp straight; they must have been wonderful playthings for small children round their mother's feet— as attractive as a swallow to a cat, and providing a most mysterious place to hide in, behind them, as mother threw the shuttle and the length of unbleached cloth crept down toward the earthen floor.

Here is the flint scraper which she used for cleaning leather. Her mother used it before her, for the flint itself is worn away. This is the very bone needle she was using yesterday to sew leather. I know she used it to sew leather because there is that subtle shine you only get round a point that has pierced many times through oily skin. Of course that shine will dull in the museum. Indeed it dulls after only a few moments' exposure to the air, so that when I see the needle again under glass I shall wonder how I ever knew so much about it. But for the few seconds after I lift it out, I know it was used only last night. What was she sewing—Gwyneth, Olwen, Myfanwy[14]—at the door of the hut, when the Downs were mysterious with level rays of sun? Somehow it is more important to know that than to know about kings and priests and emperors.

Next to the needle is a spindle whorl cut out of chalk. Not many months ago, I saw women using just such spindle whorls in the wilder parts of Yugoslavia. You tuck the distaff, with its head of raw wool, between your left arm and breast. The spindle whorl turns, hanging on an end of thread; and as you mind the sheep you draw down the thread and spin it between finger and thumb. All day long you do that, when you are not rubbing down corn on a saddle stone or grinding it in a rotary quern. . . . It is possible to work very hard and be very happy.

These are innocent pictures. Yet I must remember, after what happened, that if we try in history to do nothing but escape from a corrupt present these pictures will be what we want them to be, rather than the truth. I must remember in particular the

time when excavation left me with something like a load of guilt.

We were doing a 'rescue dig'. The biggest airplane in the world—at that time—was coming to live on our Downs, and required a concrete runway several miles long. The runway, as it grew, pointed straight at the scene of an Iron Age settlement which had never been examined. We set to work, chased by cement-pouring machines. We dug feverishly, trying to wrench a few facts out of the earth before concrete buried them six feet deep. I was given an old silo to dig, because a quick look through their rubbish would confirm the picture we had built, from other sources, of this people's mixed farming and hunting. Pottery, too, would enable Miss Wilson to date the settlement. For others, there were the foundations of huts, with irregular post-holes; work which required the professional touch.

I dug with the tongue of concrete protruding toward me. The sense of hurry itself made me stubborn. I did not think the earth-shifting machines, the smoothing machines, the cement mixers and pourers would ignore me when they came to the lip of my pit. Moreover there was an indefinable sense of pathos in bringing this family to life for an hour or two, only to leave them and their innocent existence to be swallowed up forever. I found myself lingering. I paused to re-create, to enjoy myself in yet another tenuous contact. There was, I remember, a piece of chalk which might have been the head of a doll; but if ever there had been a rag or leather body, it had vanished. There was a spindle whorl only partly finished. You could see how the disc had been bored from both sides and how the maker had given up before the hole was complete. There was a mass of ashes and mortar, and a broken saddle quern. There was pottery too, of course, and piles of bones—the usual bones which I could have predicted, after these years of digging. But history must make certain.

Down in the dark and quiet pit, once more I made contact. Here they were again, another family from the days of innocence. Howsoever wicked they may have thought themselves, I gave them absolution. They could not match our wickedness. Above the roar of the advancing machines, I heard them speak.

The lump in the middle of the pit clearly covered something big and interesting. I attacked it with enthusiasm, as if it were going to bring me face to face with them. I was surprised, therefore, when

---

13. *loom weights,* in primitive weaving, the warp (vertical strands) of wool was held in place by loom weights of pebbles, while the shuttle moved the woof (horizontal strands) in and out of the warp.
14. *Gwyneth, Olwen, Myfanwy,* Welsh names of women.

the lump proved to be bone. There were two bones that were articulated. I traced a long bone up to a pelvic girdle, to vertebrae and ribs.

It lay sprawled. It was, I believe, an old woman. One arm was twisted behind her back, and her legs were splayed. Her beautiful skull was full of earth, and the pits that decay had made in her teeth had been cleaned out by time, to a gemlike perfection. Her jaws were wide open, grinning, perhaps, with cynicism at the fact that no one had troubled to close them.

I, and the phantom family, crouched over her. Only yesterday they had come here, laboring through the heather to the rubbish pit with their slack burden and flung it in. What kind of people were we, that we could go on living only a few yards away and fill the rest of the pit year by year with kitchen waste and broken pots?

'We've got to leave. Are you finished?'

I leaped up in a kind of terror. The machines were looming over us. I scrambled out, stood between Doctor Stubbs and the pit, and babbled at him.

'Yes, yes. It's all out. There it is—bones, pot, loom weights, quern. . . . No, there's nothing more to be done!'

Only when the approaching bulldozer had thrust the pile forward and the earth had fallen back into our pit with a long, silken swish did I feel a kind of easiness. The whole dreadful family was back underground. But even beneath six feet they have taken something of me with them. Now I confess, for the first time. Perhaps it is not so good an idea to try to penetrate temporal boundaries and identify yourself with people without first knowing what sort of people they are. There is a sense in which I share the guilt buried beneath the runway, a sense in which my imagination has locked me to them. I share in what was at the least a callous act—in what at the worst may very well have been a prehistoric murder.

DISCUSSION

1. Many archaeologists maintain that archaeology is not only a science but also an art which uses the tools of science. In what ways could this be true?

2. Explain the line "Gold dies in a museum. . . ."

3. Where does Golding prefer digging? Why?

4. Why does Golding feel he left a part of himself beneath the runway?

5. Do you share Golding's attitudes toward the relics of the past, or do you think he has allowed his imagination to take over? Explain your answer.

COMPOSITION

Put yourself in the position of someone from the past whose home or grave is being excavated. What would you say to the archeologist?

AUTHOR

WILLIAM GOLDING (1911–), prominent contemporary English novelist, submitted his first and most famous novel, *Lord of the Flies*, to twenty-one publishers before it was finally accepted. A short time after its publication, *Lord of the Flies* became required reading for many college and high-school literature courses. It was also made into a successful film.

Golding, born in Cornwall, England, began his college work in the field of science and two years later switched to literature. After receiving his Bachelor of Arts in 1935, he wrote, acted, and produced for a small London theater. He then taught school, spent five years in the Royal Navy after which he went back to teaching, and, in 1961, left this career to devote all of his time to writing.

Golding's non-fiction made its first American appearance in *Holiday* magazine in 1961. *The Hot Gates and Other Occasional Pieces*, a collection of many of his book reviews and essays, including "Digging for Pictures," was published in 1963.

William Golding's chief concern in much of his work is with the behavior of man in situations which remove surface civilization and reveal man's basic nature.

RECOLLECTIONS

the dump ground

Wallace Stegner

THE town dump of Whitemud, Saskatchewan, could only have been a few years old when I knew it, for the village was born in 1913 and I left there in 1919. But I remember the dump better than I remember most things in that town, better than I remember most of the people. I spent more time with it, for one thing; it had more poetry and excitement in it than people did.

It lay in the southeast corner of town, in a section that was always full of adventure to me. Just there the Whitemud River left the hills, bent a little south, and started its long traverse across the prairie and international boundary to join the Milk. For all I knew, it might have been on its way to join the Alph[1]: simply, before my eyes, it disappeared into strangeness and wonder.

Also, where it passed below the dumpground, it ran through willowed bottoms that were a favorite campsite for passing teamsters, gypsies, sometimes Indians. The very straw scattered around those camps, the ashes of those strangers' campfires, the manure of their teams and saddle horses, were hot with adventurous possibilities.

It was as an extension, a living suburb, as it were, of the dumpground that we most valued those camps. We scoured them for artifacts of their migrant tenants as if they had been archaeological sites full of the secrets of ancient civilizations. I remember toting around for weeks the broken cheek strap of a bridle. Somehow or other its buckle looked as if it had been fashioned in a far place, a place where they were accustomed to flatten the tongues of buckles for reasons that could only be exciting, and where they made a habit of plating the metal with some valuable alloy, probably silver. In places where the silver was worn away the buckle underneath shone dull yellow: probably gold.

It seemed that excitement liked that end of town better than our end. Once old Mrs. Gustafson, deeply religious and a little raddled in the head, went over there with a buckboard full of trash, and as she was driving home along the river she looked and saw a spent catfish, washed in from Cypress Lake or some other part of the watershed, floating on the yellow water. He was two feet long, his whiskers hung down, his fins and tail were limp. He was a kind of fish that no one had seen in the Whitemud in the three or four years of the town's life, and a kind that none of us children had ever seen anywhere. Mrs. Gustafson had never seen one like him either: she perceived at once that he was the devil, and she whipped up the team and reported him at Hoffman's elevator.

We could hear her screeching as we legged it for the river to see for ourselves. Sure enough, there he was. He looked very tired, and he made no great effort to get away as we pushed out a half-sunken rowboat from below the flume, submerged it under him, and brought him ashore. When he died three days later we experimentally fed him to two half-wild cats, but they seemed to suffer no ill effects.

At that same end of town the irrigation flume crossed the river. It always seemed to me giddily high when I hung my chin over its plank edge and looked down, but it probably walked no more than twenty feet above the water on its spidery legs. Ordinarily in summer it carried about six or eight inches of smooth water, and under the glassy hurrying of the little boxed stream the planks were coated with deep sun-warmed moss as slick as frogs' eggs. A boy could sit in the flume with the water walling up against his back, and grab a cross brace above him, and pull, shooting himself sledlike ahead until he could reach the next brace for another pull and another slide, and so on across the river in four scoots.

After ten minutes in the flume he would come out wearing a dozen or more limber black leeches, and could sit in the green shade where darning needles flashed blue, and dragonflies hummed and darted and stopped, and skaters dimpled slack and eddy with their delicate transitory footprints, and there stretch the leeches out one by one while their sucking ends clung and clung, until at last, stretched far out, they let go with a tiny wet *puk* and snapped together like rubber bands. The smell of the river and the flume and the clay cutbanks and the bars of that part of the river was the smell of wolf willow.

But nothing in that end of town was as good as the dump ground that scattered along a little runoff coulee dipping down toward the river from the south bench. Through a historical process that went back, probably, to the roots of community sanitation and distaste for eyesores, but that in law dated from the Unincorporated Towns Ordinance of the territorial

---

1. *Alph*, the river mentioned in Coleridge's poem, *Kublai Khan*.

government, passed in 1888, the dump was one of the very first community enterprises, almost our town's first institution.

More than that, it contained relics of every individual who had ever lived there, and of every phase of the town's history.

The bedsprings on which the town's first child was begotten might be there; the skeleton of a boy's pet colt; two or three volumes of Shakespeare bought in haste and error from a peddler, later loaned in carelessness, soaked with water and chemicals in a house fire, and finally thrown out to flap their stained eloquence in the prairie wind.

Broken dishes, rusty tinware, spoons that had been used to mix paint; once a box of percussion caps, sign and symbol of the carelessness that most of those people felt about all matters of personal or public safety. We put them on the railroad tracks and were anonymously denounced in the *Enterprise*. There were also old iron, old brass, for which we hunted assiduously, by night conning junkmen's catalogues and the pages of the *Enterprise* to find how much wartime value there might be in the geared insides of clocks or in a pound of tea lead carefully wrapped in a ball whose weight astonished and delighted us. Sometimes the unimaginable outside world reached in and laid a finger on us. I recall that, aged no more than seven, I wrote a St. Louis junk house asking if they preferred their tea lead and tinfoil wrapped in balls, or whether they would rather have it pressed flat in sheets, and I got back a typewritten letter in a window envelope instructing me that they would be happy to have it in any way that was convenient for me. They added that they valued my business and were mine very truly. Dazed, I carried that windowed grandeur around in my pocket until I wore it out, and for months I saved the letter as a souvenir of the wondering time when something strange and distinguished had singled me out.

We hunted old bottles in the dump, bottles caked with dirt and filth, half buried, full of cobwebs, and we washed them out at the horse trough by the elevator, putting in a handful of shot along with the water to knock the dirt loose; and when we had shaken them until our arms were tired, we hauled them off in somebody's coaster wagon and turned them in at Bill Anderson's pool hall, where the smell of lemon pop was so sweet on the dark pool-hall air that I am sometimes awakened by it in the night, even yet.

Smashed wheels of wagons and buggies, tangles of rusty barbed wire, the collapsed perambulator that the French wife of one of the town's doctors had once pushed proudly up the planked sidewalks and along the ditchbank paths. A welter of foul-smelling feathers and coyote-scattered carrion which was all that remained of somebody's dream of a chicken ranch. The chickens had all got some mysterious pip at the same time, and died as one, and the dream lay out there with the rest of the town's history to rustle to the empty sky on the border of the hills.

There was melted glass in curious forms, and the half-melted office safe from the burning of Bill Day's Hotel. On very lucky days we might find a piece of the lead casing that had enclosed the wires of the town's first telephone system. The casing was just the right size for rings, and so soft that it could be whittled with a jackknife. It was a material that might have made artists of us. If we had been Indians of fifty years before, that bright soft metal would have enlisted our maximum patience and craft and come out as ring and metal and amulet inscribed with the symbols of our observed world. Perhaps there were too many ready-made alternatives in the local drug, hardware, and general stores; perhaps our feeble artistic response was a measure of the insufficiency of the challenge we felt. In any case I do not remember that we did any more with the metal than to shape it into crude seal rings with our initials or pierced hearts carved in them; and these, though they served a purpose in juvenile courtship, stopped something short of art.

The dump held very little wood, for in that country anything burnable got burned. But it had plenty of old iron, furniture, papers, mattresses that were the delight of field mice, and jugs and demijohns that were sometimes their bane, for they crawled into the necks and drowned in the rain water or redeye that was inside.

If the history of our town was not exactly written, it was at least hinted, in the dump. I think I had a pretty sound notion even at eight or nine of how significant was that first institution of our forming Canadian civilization. For rummaging through its foul purlieus I had several times been surprised and shocked to find relics of my own life tossed out there to rot or blow away.

The volumes of Shakespeare belonged to a set that my father had bought before I was born. It had been carried through successive moves from town to town in the Dakotas, and from Dakota to Seattle, and from Seattle to Bellingham, and Bellingham to Redmond, and from Redmond back to Iowa, and from there to Saskatchewan. Then, stained in a stranger's house fire, these volumes had suffered from a house-cleaning impulse and been thrown away for me to stumble upon in the dump. One of the Cratchet girls had borrowed them, a hatchet-faced, thin, eager, transplanted Cockney girl with a frenzy, almost a hysteria, for reading. And yet somehow, through her hands, they found the dump, to become a symbol of how much was lost, how much thrown aside, how much carelessly or of necessity given up, in the making of a new country. We had so few books that I was familiar with them all, had handled them, looked at their pictures, perhaps even read them. They were the lares and penates,[2] part of the skimpy impedimenta of household gods we had brought with us into Latium.[3] Finding those three thrown away was a little like finding my own name on a gravestone.

And yet not the blow that something else was, something that impressed me even more with the dump's close reflection of the town's intimate life. The colt whose picked skeleton lay out there was mine. He had been incurably crippled when dogs chased our mare, Daisy, the morning after she foaled. I had labored for months to make him well; had fed him by hand, curried him, exercised him, adjusted the iron braces that I had talked my father into having made. And I had not known that he would have to be destroyed. One weekend I turned him over to the foreman of one of the ranches, presumably so that he could be cared for. A few days later I had found his skinned body, with the braces still on his crippled front legs, lying on the dump.

Not even that, I think, cured me of going there,

though our parents all forbade us on pain of cholera or worse to do so. The place fascinated us, as it should have. For this was the kitchen midden[4] of all the civilization we knew; it gave us the most tantalizing glimpses into our lives as well as into those of the neighbors. It gave us an aesthetic distance from which to know ourselves.

The dump was our poetry and our history. We took it home with us by the wagonload, bringing back into town the things the town had used and thrown away. Some little part of what we gathered, mainly bottles, we managed to bring back to usefulness, but most of our gleanings we left lying around barn or attic or cellar until in some renewed fury of spring cleanup our families carted them off to the dump again, to be rescued and briefly treasured by some other boy with schemes for making them useful. Occasionally something we really valued with a passion was snatched from us in horror and returned at once. That happened to the mounted head of a white mountain goat, somebody's trophy from old times and the far Rocky Mountains, that I brought home one day in transports of delight. My mother took one look and discovered that his beard was full of moths.

I remember that goat; I regret him yet. Poetry is seldom useful, but always memorable. I think I learned more from the town dump than I learned from school: more about people, more about how life is lived, not elsewhere but here, not in other times but now. If I were a sociologist anxious to study in detail the life of any community, I would go very early to its refuse piles. For a community may be as well judged by what it throws away—what it has to throw away and what it chooses to—as by any other evidence. For whole civilizations we have sometimes no more of the poetry and little more of the history than this.

---

2. *lares* (lãr' ēz) *and penates* (pə nā' tēz), the household gods of the Romans.
3. *Latium* (lā' shē əm), an ancient area of Italy, southeast of Rome.

4. *Kitchen midden*, the garbage heap. An archaeological term denoting ancient trash dumps, often the only source for discovering the private life of dead cultures.

DISCUSSION

1. In what respect was the dump ground both poetry and history?

2. In what way did Stegner learn more from the dump than he did from school?

3. What do you think of Stegner's statement that a community may be as well judged by what it throws away as anything else? Is this true of your community? Explain.

4. Choose examples of Stegner's experiences in the dump ground which illustrate: (a) creativity, (b) carelessness, (c) heartbreak, (d) enterprise, (e) living conditions of the town, (f) the generation gap.

5. Compare Golding's essay with Stegner's. In what respect are they alike?

The Law of Human Nature

C. S. Lewis

EVERY one has heard people quarrelling. Sometimes it sounds funny and sometimes it sounds merely unpleasant; but however it sounds, I believe we can learn something very important from listening to the kind of things they say. They say things like this: "How'd you like it if anyone did the same to you?"—"That's my seat, I was there first"—"Leave him alone, he isn't doing you any harm"—"Why should you shove in first?"—"Give me a bit of your orange, I gave you a bit of mine"—"Come on, you promised." People say things like that every day, educated people as well as uneducated, and children as well as grown-ups.

Now what interests me about all these remarks is that the man who makes them is not merely saying that the other man's behaviour does not happen to please him. He is appealing to some kind of standard of behaviour which he expects the other man to know about. And the other man very seldom replies: "To hell with your standard." Nearly always he tries to make out that what he has been doing does not really go against the standard, or that if it does there is some special excuse. He pretends there is some special reason in this particular case why the person who took the seat first should not keep it, or that things were quite different when he was given the bit of orange, or that something has turned up which lets him off keeping his promise. It looks, in fact, very much as if both parties had in mind some kind of Law or Rule of fair play or decent behaviour or morality or whatever you like to call it, about which they really agreed. And they have. If they had not, they might, of course, fight like animals, but they could not *quarrel* in the human sense of the word. Quarrelling means trying to show that the other man is in the wrong. And there would be no sense in trying to do that unless you and he had some sort of agreement as to what Right and Wrong are; just as there would be no sense in saying that a footballer had committed a foul unless there was some agreement about the rules of football.

Now this Law or Rule about Right and Wrong used to be called the Law of Nature. Nowadays, when we talk of the "laws of nature" we usually mean things like gravitation, or heredity, or the laws of chemistry. But when the older thinkers called the Law of Right and Wrong "the Law of Nature," they really meant the Law of *Human* Nature. The idea was that, just as all bodies are governed by the law of gravitation and organisms by biological laws, so the creature called man also had *his* law—with this great difference, that a body could not choose whether it obeyed the law of gravitation or not, but a man could choose either to obey the Law of Human Nature or to disobey it.

We may put this in another way. Each man is at every moment subjected to several different sets of law but there is only one of these which he is free to disobey. As a body, he is subjected to gravitation and cannot disobey it; if you leave him unsupported in mid-air, he has no more choice about falling than a stone has. As an organism, he is subjected to various biological laws which he cannot disobey any more than an animal can. That is, he cannot disobey those laws which he shares with other things; but the law which is peculiar to his human nature, the law he does not share with animals or vegetables or inorganic things, is the one he can disobey if he chooses.

This law was called the Law of Nature because people thought that every one knew it by nature and did not need to be taught it. They did not mean, of course, that you might not find an odd individual here and there who did not know it, just as you find a few people who are colour-blind or have no ear for a tune. But taking the race as a whole, they thought that the human idea of decent behaviour was obvious to every one. And I believe they were right. If they were not, then all the things we said about the war were nonsense. What was the sense in saying the enemy were in the wrong unless Right is a real thing which the Nazis at bottom knew as well as we did and ought to have practised? If they had had no notion of what we mean by right, then, though we might still have had to fight them, we could no more have blamed them for that than for the colour of their hair.

I know that some people say the idea of a Law of Nature or decent behaviour known to all men is unsound, because different civilisations and different ages have had quite different moralities.

But this is not true. There have been differences between their moralities, but these have never amounted to anything like a total difference. If anyone will take the trouble to compare the moral teaching of, say, the ancient Egyptians, Babylonians, Hindus, Chinese, Greeks and Romans, what will really strike him will be how very like they are to each other and to our own. Some of the evidence for this I have put together in the appendix of another book called *The Abolition of Man;* but for our present purpose I need only ask the reader to think what a totally different morality would mean. Think of a country where people were admired for running away in battle, or where a man felt proud of double-crossing all the people who had been kindest to him. You might just as well try to imagine a country where two and two made five. Men have differed as regards what people you ought to be unselfish to—whether it was only your own family, or your fellow countrymen, or everyone. But they have always agreed that you ought not to put yourself first. Selfishness has never been admired. Men have differed as to whether you should have one wife or four. But they have always agreed that you must not simply have any woman you liked.

But the most remarkable thing is this. Whenever you find a man who says he does not believe in a real Right and Wrong, you will find the same man going back on this a moment later. He may break his promise to you, but if you try breaking one to him he will be complaining "It's not fair" before you can say Jack Robinson. A nation may say treaties do not matter; but then, next minute, they spoil their case by saying that the particular treaty they want to break was an unfair one. But if treaties do not matter, and if there is no such thing as Right and Wrong—in other words, if there is no Law of Nature—what is the difference between a fair treaty and an unfair one? Have they not let the cat out of the bag and shown that, whatever they say, they really know the Law of Nature just like anyone else?

It seems, then, we are forced to believe in a real Right and Wrong. People may be sometimes mistaken about them, just as people sometimes get their sums wrong; but they are not a matter of mere taste and opinion any more than the multiplication table. Now if we are agreed about that, I go on to my next point, which is this. None of us are really keeping the Law of Nature. If there are any exceptions among you, I apologise to them. They had much better read some other work, for nothing I am going to say concerns them. And now, turning to the ordinary human beings who are left:

I hope you will not misunderstand what I am going to say. I am not preaching, and Heaven knows I do not pretend to be better than anyone else. I am only trying to call attention to a fact; the fact that this year, or this month, or, more likely, this very day, we have failed to practise ourselves the kind of behaviour we expect from other people. There may be all sorts of excuses for us. That time you were so unfair to the children was when you were very tired. That slightly shady business about the money—the one you have almost forgotten—came when you were very hard up. And what you promised to do for old So-and-so and have never done—well, you never would have promised if you had known how frightfully busy you were going to be. And as for your behaviour to your wife (or husband) or sister (or brother) if I knew how irritating they could be, I would not wonder at it— and who the dickens am I, anyway? I am just the same. That is to say, I do not succeed in keeping the Law of Nature very well, and the moment anyone tells me I am not keeping it, there starts up in my mind a string of excuses as long as your arm. The question at the moment is not whether they are good excuses. The point is that they are one more proof of how deeply, whether we like it or not, we believe in the Law of Nature. If we do not believe in decent behaviour, why should we be so anxious to make excuses for not having behaved decently? The truth is, we believe in decency so much—we feel the Rule or Law pressing on us so—that we cannot bear to face the fact that we are breaking it, and consequently we try to shift the responsibility. For you notice that it is only for our bad behaviour that we find all these explanations. It is only our bad temper that we put down to being tired or worried or hungry; we put our good temper down to ourselves.

These, then, are the two points I wanted to make. First, that human beings, all over the earth, have this curious idea that they ought to behave in a certain way, and cannot really get rid of it. Secondly, that they do not in fact behave in that way. They know the Law of Nature; they break it. These two facts are the foundation of all clear thinking about ourselves and the universe we live in.

DISCUSSION

1. What is the difference, according to C. S. Lewis, between the "Law of Nature" and the "Law of Human Nature"?

2. (a) Why was the "Law of Human Nature" called the "Law of Nature"? (b) Does C. S. Lewis agree with this attitude? Why or why not? (c) Do you agree with him?

3. (a) How does C. S. Lewis answer the charge that different cultures will have different "Laws of Nature"? (b) Do you know of any exceptions to Lewis' belief?

4. (a) Cite examples of people breaking the "Law of Nature." (b) What proof does Lewis offer of people knowing they are breaking the "Law of Nature"?

5. Summarize the two main points of C. S. Lewis' essay.

COMPOSITION

Write a "Law of Human Nature." What are its rewards and punishments? How is it enforced? Give examples of the "Law" in action.

AUTHOR

CLIVE STAPLES LEWIS is best known for two roles: as a Christian thinker and as a writer of allegorical fantasies. This would seem to qualify him as someone very much in harmony with the medieval world; and indeed he has spent much of his life teaching medieval literature. But his simple, direct style marks him as a man of the modern world dealing with ancient and unsolved problems: faith and morality.

Lewis was born in Belfast, Northern Ireland, in 1898. Privately tutored, he completed his education at Oxford. During World War I, he was wounded. Afterwards, he returned to his academic career.

First known as a poet, he attained real fame as a novelist in his fantasy *Out of the Silent Planet* (1938). Next, his satirical book, *The Screwtape Letters* (1942) was a very popular success and remains his most familiar work.

His life encompassed not only religion and writing, but scholarship in the field of medieval literature. He died in 1964, and his many-sided writings still appeal to old and young.

A FLAW in the GRAY FLANNEL

Mike Royko

I recently ran into a successful business executive in a bar. His hand shook so violently that his drink spilled on his impeccable suit. He explained that something terrible had happened.

"As you know," he said, "I am a successful business executive. Top-drawer.

"I have worked hard to become one. I have followed all of the advice of the experts.

"There has been nothing written in a financial page or a business section on the subject of how to be a successful executive that I have not read. And we receive more advice from experts than anyone else, even golfers, drunks, teenagers and other unfortunates.

"Look at my appearance. I am youthful—yet ma-

ture. Nobody can tell how old I am. Some people think I'm an elderly thirty. Others say I'm a youthful sixty. Perfect.

"Physical deterioration is a threat to the successful executive. I've read that fifty times.

"So I have fought it. I am now in better condition than I was when I was twenty-five years old. I have grown a foot since my thirtieth birthday. I walk like a panther.

"I am also perfectly groomed. This is important. Look at my haircut. I get it done at a stylist shop. Four times a week.

"Look at this suit. One of the experts said an executive must spend a certain amount of money every year on clothes. I have suits I have never worn, but I keep buying more.

"Another thing is my battery. As an executive, I must get it recharged when it wears down. I take regular vacations. Then I take sabbaticals. My battery is always charged.

"A long time ago, I read that I should be a good public speaker. I have worked at it. I now sound exactly like Hugh Downs.

"I read that it is important for me to appreciate good food, art, books, and sports—but not to become a cultural phony. I've done that, too.

"Someone else said business executives should avoid irrelevant reading. I've been so careful I haven't read a thing I've enjoyed for five years.

"I've kept a close watch on my career timetable. I've made the proper number of job changes for my age and industry. I even quit a job I loved because a chart in *Newsweek* magazine said it was time.

"I have battled anxiety, tension, worry, stress, just as the experts said I should. Some nights I haven't slept a wink figuring out ways to avoid worry.

"I read that executives must 'get involved.' So I got involved. I have a wide range of community in-

---

MUTT OF THE YEAR

Mike Royko

terests—politics, civic affairs, urban renewal, PTA, my church, government, charity, civil rights, schools. I take part in everything.

"I also have avoided letting my home become a jealous rival of my office. A successful executive must not be torn between the two. Yet I have not sacrificed family contacts for my career.

"That's where my wife comes in. She has grown with me, which is important, everyone says.

"She realizes that she, too, is a member of the management team.

"She is not too sexy but she is not drab or dowdy. She does not drink to excess but she is not a teetotaler. She isn't shy but she isn't aggressive. She not only is a good talker, but also a good listener.

"She is always prepared to entertain or to spend a quiet evening alone. She has social ease and a wide variety of interests in sports, civic affairs, cultural and current events.

"She has become so perfect that I can't stand to be around her.

"As you can see, I've done it all. Recently I even read an ad in one of the papers from a dance studio. It said: 'Every executive should know how to dance. Dancing is a social must and important to a business career.' I now can do everything from the tango to the American Indian.

"I think it was the dancing that did it. That plus the grooming, physical conditioning, civic interests, public speaking, vacations, sabbaticals, checkups, visits to the tailor, relevant reading, and watching my wife grow with me."

What happened?

"Some time ago, I forgot what my job is. I've been going to the office for weeks, not knowing what I should do. I'm afraid to ask. Indecision is bad for an executive."

That's terrible.

"That's not the worst of it. You see, today they called me in."

Fired?

"No. Promoted."

SOMEONE ought to sponsor a new kind of dog show. Maybe I'll do it myself. Better yet, the *Daily News* will do it. That ought to surprise some of the editors.

The obvious need for a new form of dog competition occurred to me after I read accounts of the International Dog Show held here over the weekend.

It sounded like a good show, but it was just like most of the others. The dogs were pure-bred aristocrats with names like Merry Rover of Valley Run, Molley Haven Sugar and Gala Cairns Redstar.

To get into the show, the dog owners must submit proof of ancestry. (The dog's ancestry, I mean. The owners don't have to prove anything about their own.)

These shows are fine and some of the dogs may even enjoy themselves, but my dog show would be just as interesting and even more exciting.

It would be open only to mixed-breed mutts, and the more mixed the better.

Instead of Merry Rover of Valley Run, we'd have Spot of Armitage Avenue.

Any dog that doesn't look like three different breeds couldn't get in. There even would be a special award for the dog who is so mixed that he looks like a goat or something.

Dogs would not be judged solely on the basis of their muttiness, although it would be of great importance in the winning of points. A dog whose legs were of uneven length and thus walked in a circle would naturally have a scoring advantage over a dog who walked sideways.

There would be obedience trials, work dog competition, sporting dog tests, and such things. But our competition would be more meaningful than that of the purebred dog shows. They have competition for sheepdogs, and how many people in Chicago keep sheep?

Our standards of obedience and performance would be up-to-date. Some of the possible categories follow:

Sporting Dogs: This would be open to the greatest modern sporting dog of them all—the dog that runs on the field during a football game.

Six judges, dressed like football officials, would chase each entry around the judging area. The dog that survived longest would be the champion. The judge who survived longest would get to kick the dog that survived longest.

Work Dogs: Entries in this field would be the noblest of all the modern work dogs—the tavern dog.

They would be judged for fierceness of gaze, loudness of bark, lightness of sleep, and quickness of bite.

Any tavern dog that did not try to bite a judge would be disqualified. Extra points would be given to tavern dogs that try to bite other tavern dogs. Bonus points would go to dogs that bite their owners.

Non-working Dogs: Eligible for this award would be all house or back-yard dogs.

They will be awarded points for their ability to withstand ear-pulling, tail-twisting and rib-tickling by children without biting them. The dog that takes the most without going mad would receive an award. Children who are bitten would receive first aid, a citation, and a good lesson.

Points also would be awarded to house dogs for their willingness to eat leftovers, including peanut-butter-and-jelly sandwich crusts, cold pizza, tuna-fish salad, cottage cheese, and Sugar Pops. What's good enough for me is good enough for them.

Obedience: All dogs will be expected to respond to the following commands:

Lie down, speak, shut up, get off the couch, get off the bed, get on the porch, get in the yard, get in the house, get in the kitchen, get in the basement, get out of here, and get.

Finally, there will be a special award, a trophy known as the Royko Cup.

It will go to the dog who demonstrates his ability to learn nothing.

He must prove that he barks only at passing airplanes, sleeps through burglaries, howls endlessly when left alone, prefers a new rug to an old fire plug, is affectionate to mice while trying to bite friends and relatives, snores, snarls, and snatches food from the table.

Of course, we might have to let in some of those tiny, fuzzy purebred dogs for that one.

DISCUSSION

A Flaw in the Gray Flannel

1. (a) What is your reaction to Royko's listing of some "experts": "golfers, drunks, teenagers and other unfortunates"? Is he serious? (b) If he had continued to list, what other "experts" and "other unfortunates" might he have listed?

2. Through the medium of laughter, a satirist attempts to point out flaws in society with the aim of encouraging people to change society so that the flaws no longer exist. He does not necessarily propose specific solutions to the problems he sees. (a) What executive behaviors is Royko satirizing? (b) What is the "flaw"?

3. What advice would you give Royko's executive?

Mutt of the Year

1. What does Royko think is wrong with the typical dog show?

2. What changes would Royko make in dog shows?

3. (a) Is Royko being unnecessarily cruel in any of his "rules"? (b) What is his purpose in suggesting such rules?

4. (a) What type of dog would win the Royko Cup? (b) What attitude of Royko's is revealed by this prize? (c) Do you agree with him? Why or why not?

COMPOSITION

Assume that you are a dog in charge of a "Human Show." What would be your rules and regulations? What categories would you devise? How would you award points?

AUTHOR

MIKE ROYKO is a native resident of the city he writes about: Chicago. Born in 1932, he was raised at the height of the Depression years. In 1952–56, he served in the U.S. Air Force. On returning, he worked as a reporter for neighborhood newspapers, and learned about the ins and outs of local politics. In 1959, he joined the *Chicago Daily News* as a reporter/columnist. Since then, he has written a column five days a week for the paper, covering local events and politics.

He reached national prominence with his book on Chicago's controversial mayor, Richard J. Daley, *Boss* (1971). In 1972, he won the Pulitzer Prize for journalism.

the decline of sport

(A PREPOSTEROUS PARABLE)

E. B. White

IN the third decade of the supersonic age, sport gripped the nation in an ever-tightening grip. The horse tracks, the ballparks, the fight rings, the gridirons, all drew crowds in steadily increasing numbers. Every time a game was played, an attendance record was broken. Usually some other sort of record was broken, too—such as the record for the number of consecutive doubles hit by left-handed batters in a Series game, or some such thing as that. Records fell like ripe apples on a windy day. Customs and manners changed, and the five-day business week was reduced to four days, then to three, to give everyone a better chance to memorize the scores.

Not only did sport proliferate but the demands it made on the spectator became greater. Nobody was content to take in one event at a time, and thanks to the magic of radio and television nobody had to. A Yale alumnus, class of 1962, returning to the Bowl with 197,000 others to see the Yale-Cornell football game would take along his pocket radio and pick

up the Yankee Stadium, so that while his eye might be following a fumble on the Cornell twenty-two-yard line, his ear would be following a man going down to second in the top of the fifth, seventy miles away. High in the blue sky above the Bowl, sky-writers would be at work writing the scores of other major and minor sporting contests, weaving an interminable record of victory and defeat, and using the new high-visibility pink news-smoke perfected by Pepsi-Cola engineers. And in the frames of the giant video sets, just behind the goal posts, this same alumnus could watch Dejected win the Futurity[1] before a record-breaking crowd of 349,872 at Belmont, each of whom was tuned to the Yale Bowl and following the World Series game in the video and searching the sky for further news of events either under way or just completed. The effect of this vast cyclorama of sport was to divide the spectator's attention, over-subtilize his appreciation, and deaden his passion. As the fourth supersonic decade was ushered in, the picture changed and sport began to wane.

A good many factors contributed to the decline of sport. Substitutions in football had increased to such an extent that there were very few fans in the United States capable of holding the players in mind during play. Each play that was called saw two entirely new elevens lined up, and the players whose names and faces you had familiarized yourself with in the first period were seldom seen or heard of again. The spectacle became as diffuse as the main concourse in Grand Central at the commuting hour.

Express motor highways leading to the parks and stadia had become so wide, so unobstructed, so devoid of all life except automobiles and trees that sport fans had got into the habit of travelling enormous distances to attend events. The normal driving speed had been stepped up to ninety-five miles an hour, and the distance between cars had been decreased to fifteen feet. This put an extraordinary strain on the sport lover's nervous system, and he arrived home from a Saturday game, after a road trip of three hundred and fifty miles, glassy-eyed, dazed, and spent. He hadn't really had any relaxation and he had failed to see Czlika (who had gone in for Trusky) take the pass from Bkeeo (who had gone in for Bjallo) in the third period, because at that moment a youngster named Lavagetto had been put

in to pinch-hit for Art Gurlack in the bottom of the ninth with the tying run on second, and the sky-writer who was attempting to write "Princeton 0 – Lafayette 43" had banked the wrong way, muffed the "3," and distracted everyone's attention from the fact that Lavagetto had been whiffed.

Cheering, of course, lost its stimulating effect on players, because cheers were no longer associated necessarily with the immediate scene but might as easily apply to something that was happening somewhere else. This was enough to infuriate even the steadiest performer. A football star, hearing the stands break into a roar before the ball was snapped, would realize that their minds were not on him, and would become dispirited and grumpy. Two or three of the big coaches worried so about this that they considered equipping all players with tiny ear sets, so that they, too, could keep abreast of other sporting events while playing, but the idea was abandoned as impractical, and the coaches put it aside in tickler files, to bring up again later.

I think the event that marked the turning point in sport and started it downhill was the Midwest's classic Dust Bowl game of 1975, when Eastern Reserve's great right end, Ed Pistachio, was shot by a spectator. This man, the one who did the shooting, was seated well down in the stands near the forty-yard line on a bleak October afternoon and was so saturated with sport and with the disappointments of sport that he had clearly become deranged. With a minute and fifteen seconds to play and the score tied, the Eastern Reserve quarterback had whipped a long pass over Army's heads into Pistachio's waiting arms. There was no other player anywhere near him, and all Pistachio had to do was catch the ball and run it across the line. He dropped it. At exactly this moment, the spectator—a man named Homer T. Parkinson, of 35 Edgemere Drive, Toledo, O.—suffered at least three other major disappointments in the realm of sport. His horse, Hiccough, on which he had a five-hundred-dollar bet, fell while getting away from the starting gate at Pimlico and broke its leg (clearly visible in the video); his favorite shortstop, Lucky Frimstitch, struck out and let three men die on base in the final game of the Series (to which Parkinson was tuned); and the Governor Dummer soccer team, on which Parkinson's youngest son played goalie, lost to Kent, 4–3, as recorded in the sky overhead. Before anyone could stop him, he drew a gun and drilled Pistachio, before 954,000 persons,

1. the Futurity, a horse race where the horses have been registered far in advance, some from birth.

the largest crowd that had ever attended a football game and the *second*-largest crowd that had ever assembled for any sporting event in any month except July.

This tragedy, by itself, wouldn't have caused sport to decline, I suppose, but it set in motion a chain of other tragedies, the cumulative effect of which was terrific. Almost as soon as the shot was fired, the news flash was picked up by one of the skywriters directly above the field. He glanced down to see whether he could spot the trouble below, and in doing so failed to see another skywriter approaching. The two planes collided and fell, wings locked, leaving a confusing trail of smoke, which some observers tried to interpret as a late sports score. The planes struck in the middle of the nearby eastbound coast-to-coast Sunlight Parkway, and a motorist driving a convertible coupé stopped so short, to avoid hitting them, that he was bumped from behind. The pileup of cars that ensued involved 1,482 ve-

hicles, a record for eastbound parkways. A total of more than three thousand persons lost their lives in the highway accident, including the two pilots, and when panic broke out in the stadium, it cost another 872 in dead and injured. News of the disaster spread quickly to other sports arenas, and started other panics among the crowds trying to get to the exits, where they could buy a paper and study a list of the dead. All in all, the afternoon of sport cost 20,003 lives, a record. And nobody had much to show for it except one small Midwestern boy who hung around the smoking wrecks of the planes, captured some aero news-smoke in a milk bottle, and took it home as a souvenir.

From that day on, sport waned. Through long, non-competitive Saturday afternoons, the stadia slumbered. Even the parkways fell into disuse as motorists rediscovered the charms of old, twisty roads that led through main streets and past barnyards, with their mild congestions and pleasant smells.

DISCUSSION

1. A parable is a story designed to develop a moral or lesson. What moral or lesson does E. B. White want to communicate?

2. He subtitles his essay "A Preposterous Parable." Does this change your answer to question 1? Is it really preposterous? Explain.

COMPOSITION

Do you believe that sports have too important a position in our society? Explain your opinion, giving examples as proof.

two letters, both open

E. B. White

New York, N. Y.
12 April 1951

The American Society for the Prevention of Cruelty to Animals
York Avenue and East 92nd Street
New York 28, N. Y.
Dear Sirs:

I have your letter, undated, saying that I am harboring an unlicensed dog in violation of the law. If by "harboring" you mean getting up two or three times every night to pull Minnie's blanket up over her, I am harboring a dog all right. The blanket keeps slipping off. I suppose you are wondering by now why I don't get her a sweater instead. That's a joke on you. She has a knitted sweater, but she doesn't like to wear it for sleeping: her legs are so short they work out of a sweater and her toenails get caught in the mesh, and this disturbs her rest. If Minnie doesn't get her rest, she feels it right away. I do myself, and of course with this night duty of mine, the way the blanket slips and all, I haven't had any real rest in years. Minnie is twelve.

In spite of what your inspector reported, she has a license. She is licensed in the State of Maine as an unspayed bitch, or what is more commonly called an "unspaded" bitch. She wears her metal license tag but I must say I don't particularly care for it, as it is in the shape of a hydrant, which seems to me a feeble gag, besides being pointless in the case of a female. It is hard to believe that any state in the Union would circulate a gag like that and make people pay money for it, but Maine is always thinking of something. Maine puts up roadside crosses along the highways to mark the spots where people have lost their lives in motor accidents, so the highways are beginning to take on the appearance of a cemetery, and motoring in Maine has become a solemn experience, when one thinks mostly about death. I was driving along a road near Kittery the other day thinking about death and all of a sudden I heard the spring peepers.[1] That changed me right away and I suddenly thought about life. It was the nicest feeling.

You asked about Minnie's name, sex, breed, and phone number. She doesn't answer the phone. She is a dachshund and can't reach it, but she wouldn't answer it even if she could, as she has no interest in outside calls. I did have a dachshund once, a male, who was interested in the telephone, and who got a great many calls, but Fred was an exceptional dog (his name was Fred) and I can't think of anything offhand that he *wasn't* interested in. The tele-

1. *spring peepers*, frogs that croak in the spring mating season.

phone was only one of a thousand things. He loved life—that is, he loved life if by "life" you mean "trouble," and of course the phone is almost synonymous with trouble. Minnie loves life, too, but her idea of life is a warm bed, preferably with an electric pad, and a friend in bed with her, and plenty of shut-eye, night and day. She's almost twelve. I guess I've already mentioned that. I got her from Dr. Clarence Little in 1939. He was using dachshunds in his cancer-research experiments (that was before Winchell was running the thing) and he had a couple of extra puppies, so I wheedled Minnie out of him. She later had puppies by her own father, at Dr. Little's request. What do you think about *that* for a scandal? I know what Fred thought about it. He was some put out.

Sincerely yours,
E. B. White

New York, N. Y.
12 April 1951

Collector of Internal Revenue
Divisional Office
Bangor, Maine
Dear Sir:

I have your notice about a payment of two hundred and some-odd dollars that you say is owing on my 1948 income tax. You say a warrant has been issued for the seizure and sale of my place in Maine, but I don't know as you realize how awkward that would be right at this time, because in the same mail I also received a notice from the Society for the Prevention of Cruelty to Animals here in New York taking me to task for harboring an unlicensed dog in my apartment, and I have written them saying that Minnie is licensed in Maine, but if you seize and sell my place, it is going to make me look pretty silly with the Society, isn't it? Why would I license a dog in Maine, they will say, if I don't live there? I think it is a fair question. I have written the Society, but purposely did not mention the warrant of seizure and sale. I didn't want to mix them up, and it might have sounded like just some sort of cock and bull story. I have always paid my taxes promptly, and the Society would think I was kidding, or something.

Anyway, the way the situation shapes up is this: I am being accused in New York State of dodging my dog tax, and accused in Maine of being behind in my federal tax, and I believe I'm going to have to rearrange my life somehow or other so that everything can be brought together, all in one state, maybe Delaware or some state like that, as it is too confusing for everybody this way. Minnie, who is very sensitive to my moods, knows there is something wrong and that I feel terrible. And now *she* feels terrible. The other day it was the funniest thing, I was packing a suitcase for a trip home to Maine, and the suitcase was lying open on the floor and when I wasn't looking she went and got in and lay down. Don't you think that was cute?

If you seize the place, there are a couple of things I ought to explain. At the head of the kitchen stairs you will find an awfully queer boxlike thing. I don't want you to get a false idea about it, as it looks like a coffin, only it has a partition inside, and two small doors on one side. I don't suppose there is another box like it in the entire world. I built it myself. I made it many years ago as a dormitory for two snug-haired dachshunds, both of whom suffered from night chill. Night chill is the most prevalent dachshund disorder, if you have never had one. Both these dogs, as a matter of fact, had rheumatoid tendencies, as well as a great many other tendencies, specially Fred. He's dead, damn it. I would feel a lot better this morning if I could just see Fred's face, as he would know instantly that I was in trouble with the authorities and would be all over the place, hamming it up. He was something.

About the tax money, it was an oversight, or mixup. Your notice says that the "first notice" was sent last summer. I think that is correct, but when it arrived I didn't know what it meant as I am no mind reader. It was cryptic. So I sent it to a lawyer, fool-fashion, and asked him if *he* knew what it meant. I asked him if it was a tax bill and shouldn't I pay it, and he wrote back and said, No, no, no, no, it isn't a tax bill. He advised me to wait till I got a bill, and then pay it. Well, that was all right, but I was building a small henhouse at the time, and when I get building something with my own hands I lose all sense of time and place. I don't even show up for meals. Give me some tools and some second-handed lumber and I get completely absorbed in what I am doing. The first thing I knew, the summer was gone, and the fall was gone, and it was winter. The lawyer must have been building something, too, because I never heard another word from him.

To make a long story short, I am sorry about this non-payment, but you've got to see the whole picture to understand it, got to see my side of it. Of course I will forward the money if you haven't seized and sold the place in the meantime. If you have, there are a couple of other things on my mind. In the barn, at the far end of the tieups, there is a goose sitting on eggs. She is a young goose and I hope you can manage everything so as not to disturb her until she has brought off her goslings. I'll give you one, if you want. Or would they belong to the federal government anyway, even though the eggs were laid before the notice was mailed? The cold frames are ready, and pretty soon you ought to transplant the young broccoli and tomato plants and my wife's petunias from the flats in the kitchen into the frames, to harden them. Fred's grave is down in the alder thicket beyond the dump. You have to go down there every once in a while and straighten the headstone, which is nothing but a couple of old bricks that came out of a chimney. Fred was restless, and his headstone is the same way— doesn't stay quiet. You have to keep at it.

I am sore about your note, which didn't seem friendly. I am a friendly taxpayer and do not think the government should take a threatening tone, at least until we have exchanged a couple of letters kicking the thing around. Then it might be all right to talk about selling the place, if I proved stubborn. I showed the lawyer your notice about the warrant of seizure and sale, and do you know what he said? He said, "Oh, that doesn't mean anything, it's just a form." What a crazy way to look at a piece of plain English. I honestly worry about lawyers. They never write plain English themselves, and when you give them a bit of plain English to read, they say, "Don't worry, it doesn't mean anything." They're hopeless, don't you think they are? To me a word is a word, and I wouldn't dream of writing anything like "I am going to get out a warrant to seize and sell your place" unless I meant it, and I can't believe that my government would either.

The best way to get into the house is through the woodshed, as there is an old crocus sack nailed on the bottom step and you can wipe the mud off on it. Also, when you go in through the woodshed, you land in the back kitchen right next to the cooky jar with Mrs. Freethy's cookies. Help yourself, they're wonderful.

Sincerely yours,
E. B. White

DISCUSSION

1. What led to E. B. White's writing his letter to the ASPCA?

2. (a) What is White's attitude toward the letter about his dog being unlicensed? (b) Is there a clear, formal plan to his letter? (c) In what way is his discussion of Maine, Minnie's sleeping habits, and Fred relevant to his purpose?

3. (a) What is White's purpose in his letter to the Collector of Internal Revenue? (b) What "human" concerns are revealed in his letter?

4. Based upon your reading of White's two letters, what type of man is E. B. White?

COMPOSITION

(1) Imagine that you are either a representative of the ASPCA or the Collector of Internal Revenue. Write a letter in response to either of White's letters. What kind of answer should he expect? Try writing a letter that uses a style similar to White's.

(2) Discuss an institution which you consider "inhuman." Describe your experiences with that institution. What could have made the institution more human?

THE AUTHOR'S CRAFT

Values

"He who knows a Why of living surmounts almost every How."

Nietzsche

"Yes, but are you willing to die for it?" "That's all very well for you to say, but. . . ." "If I were you. . . ." "Can you imagine what he did?" "Beautiful!" "The most disgusting thing I ever saw." "It'll never fly, Orville." "Now there is a man's man." "You male chauvinist, you!" "Now, now—no need for violence."

How often have you heard remarks such as the ones above? Have you been able to hear them without reacting in some way? Either you agree with the speaker or you disagree or you say to yourself, "Who cares?" But whichever way you respond, you are responding according to your values.

How does a person develop values? Every moment you live, you are *experiencing* life, and from these experiences, you are *learning*. So, when you have an experience similar to a previous one, you automatically make a *judgment* and *behave* accordingly. The way you behave is a reflection of your *values*.

So it is with an author. Whether he is writing an essay or biography or autobiography, he chooses his words and incidents carefully and then puts them together in a way that will communicate his values. When you read Jesse Owens' "Open Letter to a Young Negro," you cannot come away with the idea that he is in favor of violence.

A good author will not necessarily convince you that his values are the correct ones, but he should at least lead you to question yours. Do you agree with Deems Taylor about Richard Wagner? Do you think William Golding has the right attitude about archaeology? Has C. S. Lewis interpreted the law of human nature correctly?

These authors have learned from their experiences and made judgments based upon their values. Now you, as a reader, must judge their values based upon your own experiences and values. If an author has caused you to react in some way and perhaps given you some insight into yourself, then his effort has been successful.

from
PETER FREUCHEN's
BOOK OF THE ESKIMOS

EATING and VISITING

Peter Freuchen

THE Eskimos' extraordinary delight at visiting and eating together must be seen against the background of their basic loneliness and isolation. Any conglomeration of people over any extended length of time is impossible in their barren country, since the game of the area will quickly be exhausted or go away to safer places. Since the people are constantly en route to procure the various necessities of life, years might lapse between reunions of relatives or friends. During the summer, a family might be isolated for months, since the fragile kayaks cannot be used for long trips, and there are too many ice- and snow-free places for the sleds to traverse. If the family, moreover, goes on an extended journey, as for instance when a Polar Eskimo family goes to Ellesmereland[1] to get musk-ox skins, it may be a year or more before they see other human beings. No wonder, therefore, that they make the most of the occasion when it happens.

Under such conditions, there has naturally been no formation of societies. The only real social unit is the family, economically sufficient unto itself, and under the absolute rulership of the husband and provider. Most often, though, a few families—no more than four or five—will live together in a settlement. Rarely do they live in their houses for more than a few months of the winter, the rest of the time being spent on hunting trips. An Eskimo is not really regarded as "belonging" to any place until he is buried there.

Formally, the families in such a settlement have not given up any of their independence, since there is no chief. The men hunt together under the leadership of the hunter who is regarded as "the most successful." He is "the one who thinks for everybody"; he decides where and when the settlement is to go traveling, what game is to be hunted, etc. Very often, he is also endowed with the talents of an *angakok*, a conjurer with helping spirits at his command. This gives added weight to his words. You will never find two such strong-men at a settlement. If in the shuffling of families between settlements such a situation should arise, one of them will quickly move away with his family. If not, rivalry and open enmity will result.

Basically, the Eskimos regard the land and the game as belonging to everybody, inasmuch as they are all at the mercy of "the great woman who lies at the bottom of the sea and who sends out the game." Consequently, no hunter is ever spoken of as being good or bad, merely as being "successful" or "unsuccessful," and the unsuccessful hunter and his family have as much right to live as everybody else. The practical advantage of hunting in a group,

therefore, is that each man gets part of the proceeds even if he does not actually fell any animal.

I was first introduced to this custom when, after having survived our house-raising celebration at Thule,[2] we went walrus hunting on Saunders Island.[3] Knud and I were in our rowboat with a couple of the men, and we acted as mother ship to four or five kayaks. Even with this unusually large number of hunters present, each man knew exactly which part of each walrus was his, for the old tradition decided it according to his participation in the killing of the beast. The one who was "lucky to get first harpoon" got the best parts, "second harpoons" next best, and so on. The rules were automatically transferred to those with guns. Even the hunters who came up after the demise of an animal would throw their harpoons at it in a token gesture of their claims. Actually, we got plenty of walrus to go round during that excursion, but the Eskimos insisted upon upholding their rigorous code, and the flensing was done in the way that each man cut out his part. They turned out to be fine anatomists: every man knew exactly which joints to cut through and where they were. It was amazing to see them guide their knives down through meat and blood and hit exactly at the designated spot. If a man happened to be a little off, it was taken as a sign that he had lied the same day. Then everybody laughed and said that here was a man who had wasted his thoughts by failing to speak the truth, and so he had forgotten that animals are created with joints that serve to divide them.

Every single walrus we got gave gains to everyone in the party. Big heaps of meat became my property, and with tears in my eyes I would thank the hunter who first had thrust his harpoon in the animal. They laughed uproariously at that, but even the best joke can be repeated too often, and old Sorqaq—who had been a great angakok and chief hunter in his day—took it upon himself to put me straight:

"You must not thank for your meat; it is your right to get parts. In this country, nobody wishes to be dependent upon others. Therefore, there is nobody who gives or gets gifts, for thereby you become dependent. With gifts you make slaves just as with whips you make dogs!"

With these words, the old sage made me understand that we were all human beings helping each other under the hard conditions of the Arctic, and

---

1. *Ellesmereland*, a Canadian island, north of the Arctic Circle and northwest of Greenland.

2. *Thule*, a village on the northwest coast of Greenland.
3. *Saunders Island*, an island near Thule, just off Cape York.

nobody should suffer the indignity of charity.

To own dogs is the sign of manhood, and therefore the only condition for getting game parts is the presentation of dogs. This put the hunters who had half-grown sons at a distinct advantage. They would merely give a few dogs to their sons, who could then claim parts in the catch, and that particular household would get two or three parts. If any doubt was expressed as to the propriety of this practice, the hunter would immediately throw his own part to the complainer, shouting: "Here is something for you!" and then appeal to the rest of the party to do likewise, thus bringing dishonor on the dissatisfied fellow. Nevertheless, the hunters with sons did have an advantage.

It is important to the Polar Eskimo to have plenty of meat. It is a favorite form of bragging, when a visitor arrives, to feed his dogs so that they are too gorged to touch another bite. Shameful as it may seem, I often took advantage of this weakness by letting my dogs go off with me on a visit.

Even a man who was too lazy or too old to go hunting could claim a part in the catch by meeting it when it was hauled in and throwing some kind of weapon on it. Although such persons certainly did not enjoy a good reputation in the community, they were at least never hungry. The aforementioned Sorqaq eventually became too old to hunt, and was lame in both arms. Nevertheless, when a piece of game was hauled up to the beach, he would take some stones in his mouth and spit them out on the animal, thus claiming his part. The younger men would often tease him by placing the catch so far out on the ice that he couldn't get out there. Then they had their amusement listening to his impotent railing. I tried to shame them, but they merely answered me: "Why, we would rather die than to come to such humiliation." I often saw this same cruelty to older persons, but came to realize that it was a matter of necessity in a country where a useless hanger-on can be a hindrance to the maintenance of life. Often, an old father or mother would be left behind on the trek to starve and freeze to death, mostly upon his or her own insistence. And nobody thought the worse of the family for that.

There is yet another procedure established to see to it that riches are properly distributed, and that is another expression of the game being nobody's exclusive property. If, for instance, a hunter has been out alone and has caught a seal, and the other hunters in the settlement got no seal that day, parts of the animal must be given to the other families. This is called *payudarpok*, and responsibility for it rests completely on the women. No man debases himself to worry about the provisions, once the game is killed and brought in. But for the women it is an important matter to have payudarpok with honor—sufficiently to uphold the reputation of the house. It is a woman's pleasure, and her way of boasting a little, to run around to the other houses with her pieces of meat, saying: "My unworthy husband was lucky to get seal today. Please lower yourselves to taste a bite of his catch!"

At Thule, there once lived a man called Ivik. He was a good hunter, but the scarcity of women had forced him to marry a woman from southern Greenland, and she was burdened with the vice of avarice, and more intent upon keeping enough for herself than on giving her husband the esteem of being a great provider and a man who distributed generously. Navarana had several times mentioned to me that this woman, Puto, had come with some miserable pieces of meat, which gave cause for gossip among the women. Nobody understood how she could bring herself to do it, and they laughed much over her practice. The result was, of course, that when we had been lucky, and Ivik had caught nothing, we gave them that much more just to show them payudarpok.

One evening, I was at home; the hunt had been fruitless, but we had a few reserve provisions in the house. There was not much, for it was during the war, and there hadn't been a ship for a couple of years. We economized, but we still weren't destitute.

Then it was rumored that Ivik had caught a big seal, and there was great joy in the settlement. We were five families, all together, so we considered it a sure thing that we would have our fill of boiled meat that evening. After a while, we heard the dogs howl outside, reporting that somebody came visiting. It turned out to be Puto making her round and now bringing us our payudarpok. I quickly divined from Navarana's face that a veritable storm was coming up, for it was a wretched piece of three ribs and with the blubber carefully cut off. There were many people in our house, and it was such a ridiculous contribution that my wife broke out in righteous fury.

"Oh no," she said. "At long last, something has happened that we can tell about when we journey out to visit people. The great Ivik has had game, and his wife now takes leave of almost the entire seal without thinking of her own.''

There were some women visiting us, so Puto blushed from shame over these words.

''But please let me give you something in return,'' said Navarana. ''For it is impossible for me to accept all this without saying thank-you with a thing or two. Alas, I wish I had something better to give you, but I have only a little bread!''

And then she took the entire supply of the house, namely, one loaf of bread that she had kneaded and baked, watched with great reverence by the entire household, and put it in Puto's arm.

''Please, you shall have that, and it also turns out that I have a couple of cans of milk.''

Puto got two cans of milk, out of a store of only five!

''Yes, but please don't think that I would be so uncouth as to let you go away with so little, you who bring such masses of meat that you must have dragged yourself tired to come to our house. There you are, I have a little sugar here, and fortunately there is a pack of tea left; I give that to you who bring such huge gifts of meat!''

Puto was by now completely crushed, and the other women could barely retain their mirth. But Navarana wasn't finished.

''Oh, how lucky I am that I have a little tobacco,'' she said. ''Here is a pack for you!''

Everybody knew that we had only ten packs for the whole tribe, about a hundred smokers, until we could bring more up via a long journey across Melville Bay.

''Yes, but if only I had something to really show my gratitude!'' Navarana didn't leave the poor woman in peace. ''I see that in my misery I still have a couple of boxes of matches. Perhaps a bit of oats would please you, also. Now that you have given all your meat away, it is not impossible that your children need to have their mouths fed with a little porridge. There, I can give you just a little bit!''

And Puto was handed a large tin half full of oats, something precious and completely irreplaceable at that time. Puto reddened more and more from shame, and her eyes shifted helplessly from Navarana to the other women in the room. Then the tears began to trickle down her cheeks. She knew as well as anybody that this event would become a saga that would be told in the whole tribe from north to south. According to Eskimo thinking she had

deserved much punishment for her avarice, and now she got it. She couldn't budge for all the goods that were heaped upon her. But Navarana wanted to do a thorough job of it.

''But alas, whatever do I have to offer you? My presents are small and without value, but here are some sewing needles and a piece of linen that I can give you, I who am married to a bad husband, a poor provider, and certainly cannot give away such treasures as your payudarpok without any consideration of what you might be wanting yourself during the winter!''

This was the last straw, Puto broke out in loud sobs. She howled like a dog in clear frost weather, and since she had so much in her arms, she couldn't defend herself when Navarana stuck the needles in the piece of linen and tucked it all under her arm. Then she turned around and pushed the door open with her knee and tumbled out. She had broken the Eskimos' law, and Navarana was a lady who didn't permit that kind of thing to remain unpunished. She ran out after her, telling the other women to follow her. Everybody hurried outside where Navarana was standing, triumphantly raising in her hand the little piece of meat that Puto had payudarpok'd.

''Oh listen,'' she shouted after Puto, ''wait a moment! Wait, so that you can tell your husband something that I would wish him to know!''

Involuntarily, Puto turned about and stood still. She was still crying, but in her utter humiliation she was hoping for a little rehabilitation, I guess. Now she saw Navarana take the lump of meat that was our only share of the day's catch.

''Look, I have a poor dog that is utterly gluttonous. At last, I have the chance to give it something—if not a meal, then at least enough to make its mouth water!''

And then she heaved the notorious piece of meat into the mouth of the nearest dog, whereupon she turned and went inside, followed by her three lady friends. Inside, they collapsed holding their stomachs, cheering and laughing. They imitated the expressions in Puto's face and repeated Navarana's words so that they could correct each other if they had misunderstood anything, for this case had to be reported! Oh, how happy they were to have witnessed one of the great events of the winter!

I had been in the other room, and now I entered the scene, for in the lonely Polar winter one does not want to miss out on any amusement. Navarana told me the whole story, and I reminded her that now we had no bread that evening, and that we were short of all the other things, and all that for a miserable piece of meat.

"Oh yes," said Navarana. "When I think back on it, I really regret it, too, but I was born with a temper —I can't help it, and I got so angry that I thought she ought to be punished!"

The next day, it turned out that two of the women had lost no time in persuading their husbands to go on a journey visiting people so that they could tell what had happened. But we heard from the other houses that Puto had come home with all her gifts and had had to confess her guilt to Ivik, whose house now had been brought in disrepute.

Ivik went hunting and stayed away for a couple of days. He came home with three seals that he didn't flense. In the evening he brought them down to our meat rack and left them there. Then he returned home and beat his wife, the sinful Puto. They left the settlement the next day with their children and all their property and went up north, far, far away, so as not to be near people who had witnessed Ivik's loss of his honor as a hunter.

But for a long time we didn't have tea or sugar. We ran out of tobacco, and we lacked many other things. The result was that we often laughed and talked about the time Puto payudarpok'd. And Navarana said: "Oh, it is my misfortune that I was born with such a temper that I always want to punish people who do not behave right!"

Actually, I guess, she was justified in her behavior. It was not just that she was the first lady of Thule, and had been belittled, but that she had used her people's principal weapon against offenders: ridicule. In a land without police or government, who is nearer to mete out a sentence than the offended one? For a couple of years, Ivik and his family had to live almost in isolation; and what worse thing is there for a Polar Eskimo? In maintaining their code of human behavior, which is so very much based upon—and conditioned by—their merciless country, the Eskimos only rarely have to resort to violence.

DISCUSSION

1. Each culture has its own means of controlling its members. What are some examples of the social control of the Eskimo?

2. Do all of the Eskimos believe in the law of human nature? Do you think they live by it better than many other people? Explain.

3. Why does the Polar Eskimo seldom have to resort to violence?

4. "With gifts you make slaves just as with whips you make dogs." Explain what Sorqaq meant by that statement.

5. Explain the concept of *payudarpok*. What is the reason for this practice?

6. Do you think the behavior of the Eskimo toward the old or infirm is a form of cruelty? Explain your reasoning.

7. Explain why honor is so important among the Eskimos.

8. Navarana says she always wants to punish "people who do not behave right." (a) How do the Eskimos determine what is right behavior? (b) Why do they adhere to it so closely? (c) How does any society decide what is right or wrong?

9. Do you think it would be possible for us to adapt the practices of the Polar Eskimo to our own culture? Consider this in terms of our: welfare system, community responsibilities, methods of punishment, entertainment.

COMPOSITION

Imagine yourself in the position of Ivik and Puto after their exile. Take the place of one or the other and relate what happens to "you" in the next year.

AUTHOR

PETER FREUCHEN (1886–1957) explored the Arctic, lived with the Eskimos for many years, wrote books, and during World War II, as a citizen of Denmark, was part of the Danish underground. Towards the end of his long career, he won the "$64,000 Question" contest on American television, and became a frequent guest on television interview programs.

With his friend Knud Rasmus-

sen, Freuchen founded the first trading community in the Arctic, at Thule, in 1910. He married an Eskimo girl, Navarana, who was lost in an expedition in 1921. When he later lost a leg due to frostbite, he was forced to settle down. He then began his writing and lecturing career. His books translated into English include: *Vagrant Viking* (1953) and *Peter Freuchen's Book of the Eskimos* (1961).

CULTURE

"What a piece of work is man!"
Hamlet II, ii

Culture was once explained as something that humans have and other species do not. Each one of us belongs to a culture and is a reflection of that culture. The food we eat, the clothes we wear, the religion we practice, the language we speak, the tools we use, the ways we are educated, our concepts of right and wrong: all these and more are aspects of our culture.

Furthermore, it is impossible to say that one culture is more "right" than any other culture. For us, wearing clothes may appear to be obviously the socially acceptable thing to do. But for an Amazon Indian, to be burdened with damp cloth in a humid jungle might be a most impractical behavior. Who is to say that eating dog meat is worse than eating lobster? Yet, each culture does make such judgments, and, through various means of social control, sees to it that the beliefs and practices of that culture are carried out.

Why are the many cultures of man so diverse? One answer is environment. The world around us places demands upon us which we must meet in order to survive. In the relatively harsh environment of the Southwest, the Hopi Indians developed a form of communal living in which each member of the community was responsible for the other members of his community. When a Navajo speaks of his "family," he means not only his mother, father, sisters, and brothers, but also his uncles, aunts, cousins, grandparents, and various in-laws. Both Hopi and Navajo cultures are responses to an environment which would not allow every man to work for only himself.

Very often we tend to prejudge other cultures when we do not understand the reasons for their behavior. Laura Bohannan, in her novel *Return to Laughter*, tells of an experience she had when she first went to Nigeria.

A blind man was walking down a trail when a group of boys suddenly yelled, "Snake!" The blind man stopped in fear: he did not know whether the snake was in front of him or beside him. (In fact, there was no snake.) The boys said nothing more, and then laughed and laughed. To Laura Bohannan, this was the height of cruelty. Yet, she was later to realize that, in the severe living conditions of that area, the culture could not be burdened with the weak or sick, and the opportunity to laugh came seldom. She had to overcome her cultural prejudice.

We cannot hope to visit and live with all other cultures in order to learn their ways. But we can read about them, and perhaps, through the words of a gifted writer, begin to appreciate why other cultures are different from ours and to respect them for it.

CULTURES

Saturday Belongs to the Palomía

Daniel Garza

Every year, in the month of September, the cotton pickers come up from the Valley, and the braceros[1] come from Mexico itself. They come to the town in Texas where I live, all of them, the whole *palomía*.[2] "Palomía" is what we say: it is slang among my people, and I do not know how to translate it exactly. It means . . . the cotton pickers when they come. You call the whole bunch of them the *palomía*, but one by one they are cotton pickers, *pizcadores*.[3]

Not many of them have traveled so far north before, and for the ones who have not it is a great experience. And it is an opportunity to know other kinds of people, for the young ones. For the older ones it is only a chance to make some money picking cotton. Some years the cotton around my town is

1. *braceros* (brä ser′ ōs), farm laborers.
2. *palomía* (pä lō mē′ a).
3. *pizcadores* (pēs kä ᵺō′ res).

not so good, and then the *pizcadores* have to go farther north, and we see them less.

But when they come, they come in full force to my little town that is full of gringos. Only a few of us live there who speak Spanish among ourselves, and whose parents maybe came up like the *pizcadores* a long time ago. It is not like the border country where there are many of both kinds of people; it is gringo country mostly, and most of the time we and the gringos live there together without worrying much about such matters.

In September and October in my town, Saturdays belong to the *pizcadores*. During the week they are in the fields moving up and down the long cotton rows with big sacks and sweating frightfully, but making *centavitos*[4] to spend on Saturday at the movie, or on clothes, or on food. The gringos come to town during the week to buy their merchandise and groceries, but finally Saturday arrives, and the *pizcadores* climb aboard their trucks on the cotton farms, and the trucks all come to town. It is the day of the *palomía*, and most of the gringos stay home.

"*Ay, qué gringos!*"[5] the *pizcadores* say. "What a people to hide themselves like that. But such is life . . ."

For Saturday the *pizcadores* dress themselves in a special and classy style. The girls comb their black hair, put on new bright dresses and low-heeled shoes, and the color they wear on their lips is, the way we say it, enough. The boys dress up in black pants and shoes with taps on the heels and toes. They open their shirts two or three buttons to show their chests and their Saint Christophers; then at the last they put a great deal of grease on their long hair and comb it with care. The old men, the *viejos*,[6] shave and put on clean plain clothes, and the old women put on a tunic and comb their hair and make sure the little ones are clean, and all of them come to town.

They come early, and they arrive with a frightful hunger. The town, being small, has only a few restaurants. The *pizcadores*—the young ones and the ones who have not been up from Mexico before—go into one of the restaurants, and the owner looks at them.

One who speaks a little English says they want some *desayuno*,[7] some breakfast.

He looks at them still. He says: "Sorry. We don't serve Meskins."

Maybe then one of the *pachuco* types with the long hair and the Saint Christopher says something ugly to him in Spanish, maybe not. Anyhow, the others do not, but leave sadly, and outside the old men who did not go in nod among themselves, because they knew already. Then maybe, standing on the sidewalk, they see a gringo go into the restaurant. He needs a shave and is dirty and smells of sweat, and before the door closes they hear the owner say: "What say, Blacky? What'll it be this morning?"

The little ones who have understood nothing begin to holler about the way their stomachs feel, and the *papás* go to the market to buy some food there.

I am in the grocery store, me and a few gringos and many of the *palomía*. I have come to buy flour for my mother. I pass a *pizcador*, a father who is busy keeping his little ones from knocking cans down out of the big piles, and he smiles to me and says: "*¿Qué tal, amigo?*"[8]

"*Pues, así no más,*"[9] I answer.

He looks at me again. He asks in a quick voice, "You are a Chicano?"

"*Sí.*"

"How is it that you have missed the sun in your face, *muchacho?*"[10] he says. "A big hat, maybe?"

"No, señor," I answer. "I live here."

"You have luck."

And I think to myself, yes, I have luck; it is good to live in one place. And all of a sudden the *pizcador* and I have less to say to each other, and he says *adiós* and gathers up his flow of little ones and goes out to the square where the boys and girls of the *palomía* are walking together.

On the square too there is usually a little lady selling hot tamales. She is dressed simply, and her white hair is in a bun, and she has a table with a big can of tamales on it which the *palomía* buy while they are still hot from the stove at the little lady's home.

"*Mamacita, mamacita,*" the little ones shout at their mothers. "Doña Petra is here. Will you buy me some tamalitos?"

Doña Petra lives there in the town, and the mothers in the *palomía* are her friends because of her delicious tamales and because they go to her house to

---

4. *centavitos* (sen tä vē′ tos).
5. "*Ay, qué gringos!*" (ī′ kā grēng′ gōs), "Oh those Yankees!"
6. *viejos* (vyā′ Hōs)
7. *desayuno* (des ä yü′ nō).

8. "*Que tal, amigo?*" (kä täl′ ä mē′ gō), "How's it going?"
9. "*Pues, así no más,*" (pwäs ä sē′ nō mäs), "Not good, not bad,"
10. *muchacho* (mü chä′ chō) boy.

talk of the cotton picking, of children, and maybe of the fact that in the north of Texas it takes somebody like Doña Petra to find good *masa*[11] for tamales and tortillas. Away from home as the *pizcadores* are, it is good to find persons of the race in a gringo town.

On the street walk three *pachucos*, seventeen or eighteen years old. They talk *pachuco* talk. One says: "Listen, *chabos*,[12] let's go to the good movie."

"O. K.," another one answers. "Let's go flutter the good eyelids."

They go inside a movie house. Inside, on a Saturday, there are no gringos, only the *palomía*. The *pachucos* find three girls, and sit down with them. The movie is in English, and they do not understand much of it, but they laugh with the girls and make the *viejos* angry, and anyhow the cartoon—the *mono*, they call it—is funny by itself, without the need for English.

Other *pachucos* walk in gangs through the streets of the town, looking for something to do. One of them looks into the window of Mr. Jones' barber shop and tells the others that he thinks he will get a haircut. They laugh, because haircuts are something that *pachucos* do not get, but one of them dares him. "It will be like the restaurant," he says. "Gringo scissors do not cut Chicano hair."

So he has to go in, and Mr. Jones looks at him as the restaurant man looked at the others in the morning. But he is a nicer man, and what he says is that he has to go to lunch when he has finished with the customers who are waiting. "There is a Mexican barber across the square," he says. "On Walnut Street. You go there."

The *pachuco* tells him a very ugly thing to do and then combs his long hair in the mirror and then goes outside again, and on the sidewalk he and his friends say bad things about Mr. Jones for a while until they get tired of it, and move on. The gringo customers in the barber shop rattle the magazines they are holding in their laps, and one of them says a thing about cotton pickers, and later in the day it is something that the town talks about, gringos and *pizcadores* and those of my people who live there, all of them. I hear about it, but forget, because September in my town is full of such things, and in the afternoon I go to the barber shop for a haircut the way I do on Saturdays all year long.

Mr. Jones is embarrassed when he sees me. "You

hear about that?" he says. "That kid this morning?"

I remember then, and I say yes, I heard.

"I'm sorry, Johnny," he says. "Doggone it. You know I'm not . . . "

"I know," I say.

"The trouble is, if they start coming, they start bringing the whole damn family, and then your regular customers get mad," he says.

"I know," I say, and I do. There is no use in saying that I don't, because I live in the town for the other ten or eleven months of the year when the *palomía* is not here but in Mexico and the Valley. I know the gringos of the town and what they are like, and they are many different ways. So I tell Mr. Jones that I know what he means.

"Get in the chair," he says. "You want it short or medium this time?"

And I think about the *pizcador* in the grocery store and what he said about my having luck, and I think again it is good to live in one place and not to have to travel in trucks to where the cotton is.

At about six in the afternoon all the families begin to congregate at what they call the *campo*. *Campo* means camp or country, but this *campo* is an area with a big tin shed that the State Unemployment Commission puts up where the farmers who have cotton to be picked can come and find the *pizcadores* who have not yet found a place to work. But on Saturday nights in September the *campo* does not have anything to do with work. The families come, bringing tacos to eat and maybe a little beer if they have it. After it is dark, two or three of the men bring out guitars, and some others have concertinas. They play the fast, twisty *mariachi*[13] music of the places they come from, and someone always sings. The songs are about women and love and sometimes about a town that the song says is a fine town, even if there is no work there for *pizcadores*. All the young people begin to dance, and the old people sit around making certain that the *pachucos* do not get off into the dark with their daughters. They talk, and they eat, and they drink a little beer, and then at twelve o'clock it is all over.

The end of Saturday has come. The old men gather up their sons and daughters, and the mothers carry the sleeping little ones like small sacks of cotton to the trucks, and the whole *palomía* returns to the country to work for another week, and to earn more *centavitos* with which, the Saturday that comes

---

11. *masa* (mä′ sä), corn meal, flour.
12. *chabos* (chä′ bōs), slang for friends, pals.

13. *mariachi* (mä ryä′ chē).

after the week, to go to the movies, and buy groceries, and pay for tamalitos of Doña Petra and maybe a little beer for the dance at the *campo*. And the mothers will visit with Doña Petra, and the *pachucos* will walk the streets, and the other things will happen, all through September and October, each Saturday the same, until finally, early in November, the cotton harvest is over, and the *pizcadores* go back to their homes in the Valley or in Mexico.

The streets of my town are empty then, on Saturdays. It does not have many people, most of the year. On Saturday mornings you see a few gringo children waiting for the movie to open, and not much else. The streets are empty, and the gringos sit in the restaurant and the barber shop and talk about the money they made or lost on the cotton crop that fall.

DISCUSSION

1. Examine the title of this essay. Why is it that Saturday belongs to the *Palomía*? To whom does Monday through Friday belong?

2. (a) "Ay, que gringos! . . . What a people to hide themselves like that." Why do the *gringos* stay out of the streets on Saturday? (b) What are Saturdays like when the cotton season is over and the Palomía have moved on?

3. Though the speaker is Chicano, he is accepted by the businessmen of his community, while the *palomía,* also Chicano, are not. Why? Does this indicate anything about the nature of prejudice?

4. (a) The barber, Mr. Jones, tells the speaker, "I'm sorry, Johnny. . . . Doggone it. You know I'm not . . . ." Complete his sentence. (b) "I know," Johnny replies. What does he know? (c) Does the speaker excuse Mr. Jones or any other *gringos* for their behavior on Saturday? (d) Is Mr. Jones' reason for excluding the *pachuco* a good one?

5. A language reflects a culture. How one views life is revealed by the way he speaks of it. What is the difference between "You have luck" and "You are lucky"?; the difference between "How many years have you?" and "How old are you?"; the difference between "How do you call yourself?" and

"What is your name?" If you know a language other than English, what are some other examples of language differences?

6. As an essayist, Garza could have come out with a direct attack upon prejudice in his town. Would that have been more effective than his account of Saturday there?

COMPOSITION

Have you ever felt or experienced prejudice toward you? Have you ever witnessed prejudice against another? Write about that experience. How did you feel? What did you do, if anything?

AUTHOR

DANIEL GARZA is married, has two sons and is a publicist for the world's largest semiconductor maker. In addition, he does part-time free-lance writing. Some recent articles have been on Slippery Rock State College, foxhunting in Texas, and bilingual education in the Dallas public schools. He also has had published several short stories.

As for "Palomía," "It goes without saying," Mr. Garza writes, "that I identify with the Mexican-American cause quite strongly. I see a new era coming—one in which Chicanos in the Southwest will receive the many rights they've been denied for so long. It's ironic that my ancestors were in the Southwest long before the Anglos, but then in a turn of events in the last century, the Anglos took power and the Mexicans were put in a minority role.

"'Palomía' was born in the creative writing class of Mr. John Graves at Texas Christian University. My thoughts strayed away to another time a few years before to my home town in central Texas where each fall the palomía would come to harvest the cotton crop. The story gave me a chance to put down in writing some of the things that had been with me since childhood—the discrimination that Chicanos, especially migrants, suffered, for example. I experienced some of it as well, but thank goodness it was tempered by my having known some very fine Anglos during my early years, many of whom are still close friends. 'Palomía', incidentally, was written in Spanish and later translated into English."

MARRAKECH

George Orwell

As the corpse went past the flies left the restaurant table in a cloud and rushed after it, but they came back a few minutes later.

The little crowd of mourners—all men and boys, no women—threaded their way across the market-place between the piles of pomegranates and the taxis and the camels, wailing a short chant over and over again. What really appeals to the flies is that the corpses here are never put into coffins, they are merely wrapped in a piece of rag and carried on a rough wooden bier on the shoulders of four friends.

When the friends get to the burying-ground they hack an oblong hole a foot or two deep, dump the body in it and fling over it a little of the dried-up, lumpy earth, which is like broken brick. No grave-stone, no name, no identifying mark of any kind. The burying-ground is merely a huge waste of hummocky earth, like a derelict building-lot. After a month or two no one can even be certain where his own relatives are buried.

When you walk through a town like this—two hundred thousand inhabitants, of whom at least twenty thousand own literally nothing except the rags they stand up in—when you see how the people live, and still more how easily they die, it is always difficult to believe that you are walking among human beings. All colonial empires are in reality founded upon that fact. The people have brown faces—besides, there are so many of them! Are they really the same flesh as yourself? Do they even have names? Or are they merely a kind of undifferentiated brown stuff, about as individual as bees or coral insects? They rise out of the earth, they sweat and starve for a few years, and then they sink back into the nameless mounds of the graveyard and nobody notices that they are gone. And even the graves themselves soon fade back into the soil. Sometimes, out for a walk, as you break your way through the prickly pear, you notice that it is rather bumpy underfoot, and only a certain regularity in the bumps tells you that you are walking over skeletons.

I was feeding one of the gazelles in the public gardens.

Gazelles are almost the only animals that look good to eat when they are still alive, in fact, one can hardly look at their hindquarters without thinking of mint sauce. The gazelle I was feeding seemed to know that this thought was in my mind, for though it took the piece of bread I was holding out it obviously did not like me. It nibbled rapidly at the bread, then lowered its head and tried to butt me, then took another nibble and then butted again. Probably its idea was that if it could drive me away the bread would somehow remain hanging in mid-air.

An Arab navvy working on the path nearby lowered his heavy hoe and sidled towards us. He looked from the gazelle to the bread and from the bread to the gazelle, with a sort of quiet amazement, as though he had never seen anything quite like this before. Finally he said shyly in French:

"I could eat some of that bread."

I tore off a piece and he stowed it gratefully in some secret place under his rags. This man is an employee of the Municipality.

When you go through the Jewish quarters you gather some idea of what the medieval ghettoes were probably like. Under their Moorish rulers the Jews were only allowed to own land in certain restricted areas, and after centuries of this kind of treatment they have ceased to bother about overcrowding. Many of the streets are a good deal less than six feet wide, the houses are completely windowless, and sore-eyed children cluster everywhere in unbelievable numbers, like clouds of flies. Down the centre of the street there is generally running a little river of urine.

In the bazaar huge families of Jews, all dressed in the long black robe and little black skull-cap, are working in dark fly-infested booths that look like caves. A carpenter sits cross-legged at a prehistoric lathe, turning chair-legs at lightning speed. He works the lathe with a bow in his right hand and guides the chisel with his left foot, and thanks to a lifetime of sitting in this position his left leg is warped out of shape. At his side his grandson, aged six, is already starting on the simpler parts of the job.

I was just passing the coppersmiths' booths when somebody noticed that I was lighting a cigarette. Instantly, from the dark holes all round, there was a frenzied rush of Jews, many of them old grandfathers with flowing grey beards, all clamouring for a cigarette. Even a blind man somewhere at the back of one of the booths heard a rumour of cigarettes and came crawling out, groping in the air with his hand. In about a minute I had used up the whole packet. None of these people, I suppose, works less than twelve hours a day, and every one of them looks on a cigarette as a more or less impossible luxury.

As the Jews live in self-contained communities they follow the same trades as the Arabs, except for agriculture. Fruit-sellers, potters, silversmiths, blacksmiths, butchers, leather-workers, tailors, water-carriers, beggars, porters—whichever way you look you see nothing but Jews. As a matter of fact there are thirteen thousand of them, all living in the space of a few acres. A good job Hitler isn't here. Perhaps he is on his way, however. You hear the usual dark rumours about the Jews, not only from the Arabs but from the poorer Europeans.

"Yes, *mon vieux*,[1] they took my job away from me and gave it to a Jew. The Jews! They're the real rulers of this country, you know. They've got all the money. They control the banks, finance—everything."

---

1. *mon vieux* (mōN byœ′), French for 'old friend', 'old boy'.

"But," I said, "isn't it a fact that the average Jew is a labourer working for about a penny an hour?"

"Ah, that's only for show! They're all money-lenders really. They're cunning, the Jews."

In just the same way, a couple of hundred years ago, poor old women used to be burned for witchcraft when they could not even work enough magic to get themselves a square meal.

All people who work with their hands are partly invisible, and the more important the work they do, the less visible they are. Still, a white skin is always fairly conspicuous. In northern Europe, when you see a labourer ploughing a field, you probably give him a second glance. In a hot country, anywhere south of Gibraltar or east of Suez, the chances are that you don't even see him. I have noticed this again and again. In a tropical landscape one's eye takes in everything except the human beings. It takes in the dried-up soil, the prickly pear, the palm-tree and the distant mountain, but it always misses the peasant hoeing at his patch. He is the same colour as the earth, and a great deal less interesting to look at.

It is only because of this that the starved countries of Asia and Africa are accepted as tourist resorts. No one would think of running cheap trips to the Distressed Areas. But where the human beings have brown skins their poverty is simply not noticed. What does Morocco mean to a Frenchman? An orange-grove or a job in government service. Or to an Englishman? Camels, castles, palm-trees, Foreign Legionnaires, brass trays and bandits. One could probably live here for years without noticing that for nine-tenths of the people the reality of life is an endless, back-breaking struggle to wring a little food out of an eroded soil.

Most of Morocco is so desolate that no wild animal bigger than a hare can live on it. Huge areas which were once covered with forest have turned into a treeless waste where the soil is exactly like broken-up brick. Nevertheless a good deal of it is cultivated, with frightful labour. Everything is done by hand. Long lines of women, bent double like inverted capital Ls, work their way slowly across the fields, tearing up the prickly weeds with their hands, and the peasant gathering lucerne for fodder pulls it up stalk by stalk instead of reaping it, thus saving an inch or two on each stalk. The plough is a wretched wooden thing, so frail that one can easily carry it on one's shoulder, and fitted underneath with a rough iron spike which stirs the soil to a depth of about four inches. This is as much as the strength of the animals is equal to. It is usual to plough with a cow and a donkey yoked together. Two donkeys would not be quite strong enough, but on the other hand two cows would cost a little more to feed. The peasants possess no harrows, they merely plough the soil several times over in different directions, finally leaving it in rough furrows, after which the whole field has to be shaped with hoes into small oblong patches, to conserve water. Except for a day or two after the rare rainstorms there is never enough water. Along the edges of the fields channels are hacked out to a depth of thirty or forty feet to get at the tiny trickles which run through the subsoil.

Every afternoon a file of very old women passes down the road outside my house, each carrying a load of firewood. All of them are mummified with age and the sun, and all of them are tiny. It seems to be generally the case in primitive communities that the women, when they get beyond a certain age, shrink to the size of children. One day a poor old creature who could not have been more than four feet tall crept past me under a vast load of wood. I stopped her and put a five-sou piece (a little more than a farthing) into her hand. She answered with a shrill wail, almost a scream, which was partly gratitude but mainly surprise. I suppose that from her point of view, by taking any notice of her, I seemed almost to be violating a law of nature. She accepted her status as an old woman, that is to say as a beast of burden. When a family is travelling it is quite usual to see a father and a grown-up son riding ahead on donkeys, and an old woman following on foot, carrying the baggage.

But what is strange about these people is their invisibility. For several weeks, always at about the same time of day, the file of old women had hobbled past the house with their firewood, and though they had registered themselves on my eyeballs I cannot truly say that I had seen them. Firewood was passing—that was how I saw it. It was only that one day I happened to be walking behind them, and the curious up-and-down motion of a load of wood drew my attention to the human being underneath it. Then for the first time I noticed the poor old earth-coloured bodies, bodies reduced to bones and leathery skin, bent double under the crushing weight. Yet I suppose I had not been five minutes on Moroccan soil before I noticed the overloading of the donkeys and was infuriated by it. There is no question that the donkeys are damnably treated. The Moroccan donkey is hardly bigger than a St Bernard dog, it carries a load which in the British army would be considered too much for a fifteen-hands mule, and very often its pack-saddle is not taken off its back for weeks together. But what is peculiarly pitiful is that it is the most willing creature on earth, it follows its master like a dog and does not need either bridle or halter. After a dozen years of devoted work it suddenly drops dead, whereupon its master tips it into the ditch and the village dogs have torn its guts out before it is cold.

This kind of thing makes one's blood boil, whereas —on the whole—the plight of the human beings does not. I am not commenting, merely pointing to a fact. People with brown skins are next door to invisible. Anyone can be sorry for the donkey with its galled back, but it is generally owing to some kind of accident if one even notices the old woman under her load of sticks.

As the storks flew northward the Negroes were marching southward—a long, dusty column, infantry, screw-gun batteries and then more infantry, four or five thousand men in all, winding up the road with a clumping of boots and a clatter of iron wheels.

They were Senegalese, the blackest Negroes in Africa, so black that sometimes it is difficult to see whereabouts on their necks the hair begins. Their splendid bodies were hidden in reach-me-down khaki uniforms, their feet squashed into boots that looked like blocks of wood, and every tin hat seemed to be a couple of sizes too small. It was very hot and the men had marched a long way. They slumped under the weight of their packs and the curiously sensitive black faces were glistening with sweat.

As they went past a tall, very young Negro turned and caught my eye. But the look he gave me was not in the least the kind of look you might expect. Not hostile, not contemptuous, not sullen, not even inquisitive. It was the shy, wide-eyed Negro look, which actually is a look of profound respect. I saw how it was. This wretched boy, who is a French citizen and has therefore been dragged from the forest to scrub floors and catch syphilis in garrison towns, actually has feelings of reverence before a white skin. He has been taught that the white race are his masters, and he still believes it.

But there is one thought which every white man (and in this connection it doesn't matter twopence if he calls himself a Socialist) thinks when he sees a black army marching past. "How much longer can we go on kidding these people? How long before they turn their guns in the other direction?"

It was curious, really. Every white man there has this thought stowed somewhere or other in his mind. I had it, so had the other onlookers, so had the officers on their sweating chargers and the white NCOs marching in the ranks. It was a kind of secret which we all knew and were too clever to tell; only the Negroes didn't know it. And really it was almost like watching a flock of cattle to see the long column, a mile or two miles of armed men, flowing peacefully up the road, while the great white birds drifted over them in the opposite direction, glittering like scraps of paper.

Written [Spring] 1939

DISCUSSION

1. Orwell raises an interesting question about our attitudes toward other cultures. According to him, how do we view other cultures?

2. (a) What is the tone of the second paragraph? (b) Orwell is simply reporting what actually happens, but how do his opinions surface in the way he describes the event?

3. How does Orwell's matter-of-fact reporting at the end of the third paragraph heighten the reader's reaction?

4. In the incident at the zoo, Orwell again editorializes about the government. Explain his use of understatement to make his point.

5. (a) What contrast does Orwell draw between attitudes toward donkeys and old women, both burdened by wood? (b) Do you agree with his observation? Explain.

6. Orwell keeps mentioning the "invisibility" of these people. What does he mean?

7. Through a series of seemingly separate anecdotes (the flies, the gazelle, the Jewish quarter, the old woman and the donkeys, the black soldiers), Orwell has developed his essay into a single topic. What is that topic?

8. This essay was written in 1939, when colonial powers were still strong in Africa. In what respect is this essay prophetic?

COMPOSITION

(1) Describe your own community by employing anecdotes as Orwell does. Try to choose anecdotes which will clearly communicate your attitude toward some aspect of your community.

(2) Have you ever felt strongly for or against a person of another culture because he was of that other culture? Describe the circumstances.

AUTHOR

GEORGE ORWELL (1903–1950) was born Eric Arthur Blair in Motihari, Bengal, in India. His father was a British civil servant. After attending Eton public school in England (1917–21), he enlisted in the Burmese police force instead of going on to college. He returned to England after five years of service. Back in England, he chose to live as a tramp and write about the life of the poor. He moved to France where he wrote his first book, *Down and Out in Paris and London* (1933). He was forced by poverty back to England where he found odd jobs, and published three novels. In 1936 he was married, and both Orwells went off to Spain to fight in the civil war there. Orwell was seriously wounded.

Following this, he took up political journalism; but his health broke down and he had to retire.

During this retirement, however, he wrote his most memorable work, the two novels, *Animal Farm* (1945) and *Nineteen Eighty-Four* (1949). The strain of work worsened his health, and in 1950 he died of tuberculosis.

two eggs for the men

Jane Duncan

A friend of mine has told me that when, some years ago, he paid his first visit to the Highlands,[1] the thing that struck him most forcibly was that, in the hotel where he stayed, the men were automatically served with two eggs at breakfast while the women were given only one. Coming from the south, he found this an odd mark of favour.

He discovered quite a number of things which he found odd, in particular the fact that the bringing of fuel into the house, be it logs or peat, was regarded as a female task, as if it were beneath the dignity of the male, and he waxed positively indignant about the fact that, in the Highlands, no man took the trouble to see that a woman was seated before sitting down in comfort himself.

This reminded me of another friend of mine, an English girl, a graduate of Oxford who married a distinguished Highland scholar who was wont to spend his winters doing research in the British Museum while living in a London flat and his summers at his native croft[2] in Sutherland. It is well known that Highlanders are very adaptable, able to settle down in any odd corner of the earth and Donald, our Highland scholar, could adapt in the spring from research in Minoan[3] culture to the cultivation of his Sutherland croft and the management of the maternity ward among his flock of Blackface ewes.

Of Juliet's adaptability in this way I was less sure and when they spent a night with me last October on their way to London after her first crofting summer, I asked how things had gone. "Very well," she said, "after I caught on to the fact that Donald can't plug in the electric kettle at the croft." I asked if it was different from the London kettle and she said, "No, but Donald is different."

She looked thoughtful. "He can't milk the goats either. I asked why he kept a goat that he couldn't milk. After all, he wouldn't keep a book that he couldn't read." I asked who milked the goats. "I did," she replied and when I congratulated her on this acquired accomplishment, she went on, "All that is easy—the milking, the baking, and everything but there is one thing I haven't got used to yet."

I waited with bated breath and out it came. "When Donald's cronies came up in the evenings for a yarn, they would pull all four chairs round the fire and leave me with nothing to sit on except the floor or the table. The first time it happened, I went off to bed with a book because they didn't seem to want me around anyway, but the next morning, Donald was quite huffy and said he would have liked our neighbours to have a cup of tea."

And now she laughed. "I asked why *he* hadn't

---

1. *Highlands,* a mountainous region in northwest Scotland.
2. *croft,* small rented farm.
3. *Minoan,* Bronze Age culture in Crete.

"Two Eggs for the Men" by Jane Duncan, from *The Scots Magazine* (July 1967). Reprinted by permission of A. M. Heath & Company Ltd.

given them tea and he said he couldn't have done that, that if he had made tea his friends would have thought him a queer cove[4] who didn't give his wife her proper place. I was the mistress of the house, he said, so I said: With only the floor to sit on?

"And Donald got quite angry then and said there was the milking stool or the chair out of the bedroom. It was my place to see that our visitors were comfortable, he told me. So now I sit on the milking stool until it is time to make the tea," she ended. "But I am not quite used to it yet, although I see his point."

Juliet saw the point. She had reached the root of the matter in the old Highland male-female relationship which survives in Donald. The man was the provider who worked hard on the croft to see that his family and his animals were fed and he was given two eggs because his outdoor work created the appetite for them, but the woman was the mistress of the house. The husband and his friends might hog the fire and leave the wife without a chair, but he would not dream of invading her province by making a cup of tea.

Donald's "difference," when he arrives in Sutherland, is a survival of something that used to be much more marked than it is today, and so is the serving of two eggs to the men in a Highland hotel. To people who have no knowledge of the crofting background as it used to be, Donald's "difference" and and the two eggs for the men and only one for the women may seem to indicate that the latter are or were regarded as inferior beings in the Highlands.

Nothing could be further from the truth. The relationship between the crofter and his wife was the most balanced and dignified that I have ever known, a total partnership in the rearing of a family, in the cultivation of a small piece of land and in the getting of a plain but satisfactory living.

The father saw to the land and the animals, to the buying and selling, accepting any advice his wife might have to offer and, in the evenings, he sat in the most comfortable chair and position at the fire because he was bodily tired. The mother saw to the children until they were old enough to fend for themselves and she also saw to the household supplies including the carrying in of wood or peat. She saw to the milking and often gave a hand as well with the turnip-hoeing or the haymaking.

But, in most cases, she was the power that made the difference between stark poverty and plain

plenty. If a crofter's wife was clever with poultry, was a good baker, and had "a good hand with the butter," that croft prospered and its children were sturdy and well shod. The extra pennies earned by eggs, butter, crowdie,[5] and the occasional kebbock of cheese[6] made the difference between profit and loss, misery and contentment.

I remember that, when I was a child, a young crofter died in the district of the Black Isle where I spent my holidays, leaving a widow and five small children, and I was astounded when my grandmother said, "It is a terrible thing God knows, but it would have been worse if it had been Maggie." Maggie was the young man's wife. Down south, where I lived, it was regarded as a tragedy if the husband, the "breadwinner," died, but before my summer holiday was over, I saw the reason for the different attitude in the crofting community.

When my grandfather had the horses yoked to the mower, it was little trouble to drive through the gate from our hayfield to Maggie's and cut her crop before he came home—and my grandmother contributed by sending me down with his supper in a basket so that he could work until sunset. When another neighbour who had a small powered saw was cutting firewood, it was little trouble to cut an extra load and cart it down to Maggie. The men neighbours could do the work of Maggie's husband until her eldest son could take charge of the croft, but the women neighbours could not look after her children, her cow, her poultry, or her fireside, for they were all tied by children, cows, and poultry to their own firesides.

I was brought up not on a croft, but in an industrial area, but my parents were both of crofting stock and our city home was pervaded by the crofting culture. When I first went to England and experienced other customs and other manners, I was as startled as Juliet was during her first sojourn in Sutherland. I was taken to tea one Sunday afternoon to a fairly wealthy English middle-class home, and during this visit a remark which I have never forgotten was made by the rather pompous father of the household.

I do not remember the context but, at one point, he said patronisingly to his wife, "Don't you worry your pretty little head about money, my dear." I held my breath, awaiting the thunder, but nothing happened, because the lady behind the silver teapot

---

4. *cove*, a boy or man, chap.

5. *crowdie*, porridge, oatmeal.
6. *kebbock of cheese*, Scottish slang for cheese made of sheep's and cow's milk.

was neither my mother nor my grandmother, but a person of a different culture.

The relationship between the crofting man and woman was something far beyond mere manners. The two eggs for the man were a physical necessity, while the woman, working with food for the children, mash for the hens, butter for the market all day had little desire for even one egg. As I remember them, they ate sparingly, those women, but they were healthy and they liked above all else their cups of strong sweet tea, cooled with rich, coffee-coloured cream.

They sat down, it seems in my memory, for only a little while between four and five in the afternoon when, in reasonable weather, they paid calls on one another; and it was understood that, when a neighbour woman came in on a short visit, the man of the house would remember his place and keep out of the way. His place was out of doors, working, not sitting at the fire "clecking with the women," who had things to discuss too important and private for his hearing.

As to manners, I shall never forget the attitude of my grandmother to an undergraduate of an English university who came calling with his lady mother. My grandmother suggested that he should go out and join the menfolk who would show him round the stock and the place, but he did not want to do this and, instead, insisted on handing round plates of scones and seeing that the ladies were comfortably seated.

When he and his mother had gone, my grandmother said, "Mercy, I feel giddy in the head with that young dandy jumping up and down like a flea on a blanket. He seems to have no idea of a man's place, the poor cratur." I feel sure that she would not have offered him two eggs, but only one, beaten up in milk with a little sugar added, as befitted his invalid state of mind.

The most significant feature of crofting society, I think, was that there was no competition between the sexes, no thrust for superiority or authority, no patronage from man towards woman. It was a society which had recognised an obvious fact which many societies have overlooked: the fact that the sexes are not competitive, but complementary. The man had his "place," the woman had hers, and they respected and did not invade the provinces of one another.

The crofting society, like any other, had its cultural overtones and undertones, its subtle politenesses, its wily criticisms. I am certain that if my grandmother had been asked why men but not women were served with two eggs, she would have drawn herself up to say: "Mercy, no woman would *want* two eggs!" She would not say that only a brute would eat two eggs at a sitting, but, in the air, there would be the merest flicker of the idea that men, although necessary creatures with their place in the scheme of things, were of the coarser fibre of creation.

DISCUSSION

1. What type of audience is Jane Duncan writing for?
2. How does she feel about the relationship between the crofter and his wife? Give evidence to support your answer.
3. Why do crofting women derive so much pride and honor from a position that many modern women hold in such low regard?
4. (a) What is the most significant factor in a crofting society? (b) Do you believe that this factor would be an advantage or disadvantage in your own society? Explain. (c) Do you believe it would be possible for an industrial society to operate in the same way as a crofting society? Why or why not?

COMPOSITION

Do you think women are treated fairly in your own culture? Are they treated equal to or inferior to men? Explain your feelings and experiences in regard to this issue.

PURITANS FROM THE ORIENT

Jade Snow Wong

From the village of Fragrant Mountains in southern Canton,[1] my father had immigrated as a young man in 1903 to San Francisco. Many years later when I was a grown woman, he told me with sadness that when he had asked his mother, whom he adored, for permission to come to the United States, she had expressed her reluctance. When this only son had insisted that he must leave her, she had cursed him, "Go! Go! You will have the life to go, but not the life to return!"

Trained in his father's rice and lumber business, he had been offered a position as accountant for an importer of rice and other staples needed by the Chinese in San Francisco. The inhabitants of the new Chinatown clustered together for mutual protection and a degree of social life, even though most of them were employed outside the community, serving Westerners as laborers, laundrymen, waiters, cooks, or in other occupations not requiring much knowledge of the American language they hadn't mastered. It was a predominantly male group of bachelors and married men who had left their families behind while they sought fortunes in the new land, then and now dubbed in Chinese, "Old Golden Mountains," for the legend of the Forty-niner Gold Rush days had been grossly exaggerated in Canton to lure railroad workers to California.

The community lived toughly by its own code. Chinese ethics could not be honored by Western courts; they were implemented either peacefully or violently by Chinese organizations. Enterprises such as caring for the sick or providing burials for the dead were duties of "Benevolent Associations," whose members spoke a common dialect based on their various geographical Cantonese origins. Protection of property rights or from persecution was assumed by membership in a family name clan of greater power (such as all the Chans in their clan, and all the Wongs in theirs). Some clans embraced three or four names, their bearers descendants of historically friendly families. A man therefore thought twice before provoking another, depending on the relative family-name strength of his opponent.

It was the ambition of most of these men to work and save in the United States and return to China to marry or rejoin a waiting wife, buy property in their

FROM infancy to my sixteenth year, I was reared according to nineteenth century ideals of Chinese womanhood. I was never left alone, though it was not unusual for me to feel lonely, while surrounded by a family of seven others, and often by ten (including bachelor cousins) at meals.

My father (who enjoyed our calling him Daddy in English) was the vital, temperamental, dominating, and unquestioned head of our household. He was not talkative, being preoccupied with his business affairs and with reading constantly otherwise. My mother was mistress of domestic affairs. Seldom did these two converse before their children, but we knew them to be a united front, and suspected that privately she both informed and influenced him about each child.

"Puritans from the Orient" by Jade Snow Wong, from THE IMMIGRANT EXPERIENCE edited by Thomas C. Wheeler. Copyright © 1971 by The Dial Press. Reprinted by permission of the publisher.
1. *Canton* (kan′ ton), a city in southeastern China.

village, and enjoy rents for lifelong income. Many succeeded in doing so. But my father happened to combine free thinking with Chinese conservatism. While attending night classes at the Methodist Chinese Mission in San Francisco to learn English, he was exposed to Christian theory and the practical kindness of Christian Westerners. The Golden Rule did not conflict with the Confucian doctrines which he had carefully retained. The measure of human dignity accorded to Western women particularly impressed him. He was contemporary with Sun Yat Sen, founder of the new Chinese Republic in 1910, born in the same village district and a follower of the new Christianity in China. As part of his revolutionary demands in forging a new nation, Dr. Sun had advocated the elimination of the bound feet that had kept Chinese women crippled house slaves.

My father's motherland was in the grip of military and political upheaval. My father wrote to his family, "In America, I have learned how shamefully women in China have been treated. I will bleach the disgrace of my ancestors by bringing my wife and two daughters to San Francisco, where my wife can work without disgrace, and my daughters shall have the opportunity of education." He was beginning his own domestic revolution. For fifty-five years, my father was to remain in San Francisco. He retained a copy of every letter he wrote to China.

To support the family in America, Daddy tried various occupations—candy making, the ministry to which he was later ordained—but finally settled upon manufacturing men's and children's denim garments. He leased sewing equipment, installed machines in a basement where rent was cheapest, and there he and his family lived and worked. There was no thought that dim and airless quarters were terrible conditions for living and working, or that child labor was unhealthful. The only goal was for all in the family to work, to save, and to become educated. It was possible, so it would be done.

My father had had only a few years of formal Chinese schooling. He taught himself garment manufacturing, from cutting the yardage in five-dozen-layer lots to fixing the machines when they broke down. A Western jobber delivered the yardage to him and picked up finished garments for sales distribution to American retailers. My father figured his prices to include thread, machine use, labor, and his overhead-profit. He was a meticulous bookkeeper, using only an abacus, brush, ink, and

Chinese ledgers. Because of his newly learned ideals, he pioneered for the right of women to work. Concerned that they have economic independence, but not with the long hours of industrial home work, he went to shy housewives' apartments and taught them sewing.

Only the ambitious but poor gather their courage and tear up their roots to journey across the seas, in the hope of bettering their living abroad. In China, the winds of popular discontent were blowing, caused by the decaying old empire and the excessive concessions granted to various European powers. My father used to tell us of insults and injuries suffered by ordinary Chinese at the hands of East Indian mercenary police, employed by the British in Hong Kong.

My mother still talks of the poverty in Fragrant Mountains. If they had rice, they were fortunate. If there was salt, or oil, they were even more fortunate. Tea made the fourth absolute necessity; anything more was luxury. Meat and fish were rarities. Sometimes a relative would bring some fresh green vegetables. Sometimes they bought a penny's worth of salted olives or thick, red soy, to steam on the rice for a change of flavors. On a birthday or a feast day, there might be a chicken. For annual grave pilgrimages to pay respect to the dead, roast pig was first offered to the departed souls; later the meat was enjoyed by the worshippers.

My earliest memories of companionship with my father were as his passenger in his red wheelbarrow, sharing space with the piles of blue-jean materials he was delivering to a worker's home. He must have been forty. He was lean, tall, inevitably wearing blue overalls, rolled shirt sleeves, and high black kid shoes. In his pockets were numerous keys, tools, and pens. On such deliveries, I noticed that he always managed time to show a mother how to sew a difficult seam, or to help her repair a machine, or just to chat.

I observed from birth that living and working were inseparable. My mother was short, sturdy, young looking, and took pride in her appearance. She was at her machine the minute housework was done, and she was the hardest working seamstress, seldom pausing, working after I went to bed. The hum of sewing machines continued day and night, seven days a week. She knew that to have more than the four necessities, she must work and save. We knew that to overcome poverty, there were only two methods: working and education. It was our personal responsibility. Being poor did not entitle us to benefits. When welfare programs were created in the depression years of the thirties, my family would not make application.

Having provided the setup for family industry, my father turned his attention to our education. Ninety-five per cent of the population in China had been illiterate. He knew that American public schools would take care of our English, but he had to be the watchdog to nurture our Chinese knowledge. Only the Cantonese tongue was ever spoken by him or my mother. When the two oldest girls arrived from China, the schools of Chinatown received only boys. My father tutored his daughters each morning before breakfast. In the midst of a foreign environment, he clung to a combination of the familiar old standards and what was permissible in the newly learned Christian ideals.

My eldest brother was born in America, the only boy for fourteen years, and after him three daughters —another older sister, myself, and my younger sister. Then my younger brother, Paul, was born. That older brother, Lincoln, was cherished in the best Chinese tradition. He had his own room; he kept a German Shepherd as his pet; he was tutored by a Chinese scholar; he was sent to private school for American classes. As a male Wong, he would be responsible some day for the preservation of and pilgrimages to ancestral graves[2]—his privileges were his birthright. We girls were content with the unusual opportunities of working and attending two schools.

For by the time I was six, times in Chinatown were changing. The Hip Wo Chinese Christian Academy (in the same building as the Methodist Mission) had been founded on a coeducational basis, with nominal tuition. Financial support came from three Protestant church boards: the Congregational, Presbyterian, and Methodist churches contributed equal shares. My father was on the Hip Wo School Board for many years. By day, I attended American public school near our home. From 5:00 P.M. to 8:00 P.M. on five weekdays and from 9:00 A.M. to 12 noon on Saturdays, I attended the Chinese school. Classes numbered twenty to thirty students, and were taught by educated Chinese from China. We studied poetry, calligraphy, philosophy, literature, history, cor-

respondence, religion, all by exacting memorization. The Saturday morning chapel services carried out the purposes of the supporting churches.

Daddy emphasized memory development; he could still recite fluently many lengthy lessons of his youth. Every evening after both schools, I'd sit by my father, often as he worked at his sewing machine, sing-songing my lessons above its hum. Sometimes I would stop to hold a light for him as he threaded the difficult holes of a specialty machine, such as one for bias bindings. After my Chinese lessons passed his approval, I was allowed to attend to American homework. I was made to feel luckier than other Chinese girls who didn't study Chinese, and also luckier than Western girls without a dual heritage.

We lived on both levels of our factory, which had moved out of the basement to street level. The kitchen, bathroom, and sitting–dining room were at the rear of the street floor. Kitchen privileges were granted employee seamstresses, who might wish to heat lunch or wash hands; our family practically never had privacy. Floorboards ran the length of the factory; we were never permitted to play on them because of the danger of splinters. My mother carried each child on her back with a traditional Chinese support until he was able to walk firmly, to eliminate the necessity of crawling and the danger of injury by machine pulleys and motor belts. Only the living quarters were laid with what was known as "battleship linoleum," which was an uninspired brown, but unquestionably durable.

Bedrooms were upstairs, both in the front and the rear of the factory, to be where there were windows. Between front and rear bedrooms were more machines and the long cutting tables, which were partially lit by the skylights. I shared a room with my younger sister, and later with my baby brother, too. Windows were fitted with opaque glass to eliminate the necessity for curtains, and iron bars were installed by Daddy across the entire length of those upstairs windows to keep out intruders and keep in peeping children.

Both my older sisters married when I was a child, and my third older sister went to live with the oldest of them, for which my father paid room and board. Thus, congestion at our factory-home was relieved. There was little time for play and toys were unknown to me. In any spare time, I was supplied with embroidery and sewing for my mother.

The Chinese New Year, which by the old lunar

2. *ancestral graves*, in old China, the graves of ancestors were religiously worshipped.

chinese people do not swear a sho asho

calendar would fall sometime in late January or early February of the Western Christian calendar, was the most special time of the year, for then the machines stopped for three days. Mother would clean our living quarters very thoroughly, decorate the sitting room with flowering branches, fresh oranges, and arrange candied fruits or salty melon seeds for callers. All of us would be dressed in bright new clothes, and relatives or close friends, who came to call, would give each of us a red paper packet containing a good luck coin—usually a quarter. I remember how my classmates would gleefully talk of *their* receipts. But my mother made us give our money to her, for she said that she needed it to reciprocate to others.

Yet there was little reason for unhappiness. I was never hungry. Though we had no milk, there was all the rice we wanted. We had hot and cold running water—a rarity in Chinatown, as well as our own bathtub. Others in the community used the YWCA or YMCA facilities, where for twenty-five cents, a family could draw six baths. Our sheets were pieced from dishtowels, but we had sheets. I was never neglected, for my mother and father were always at home. During school vacation periods, I was taught to operate many types of machines—tacking (for pockets), overlocking (for the raw edges of seams), buttonhole, double seaming; and I learned all the stages in producing a pair of jeans to its final inspection, folding, and tying in bundles of a dozen pairs by size, ready for pickup. Denim jeans are heavy—my shoulders ached often. My father set up a modest nickel-and-dime piecework reward for me, which he recorded in my own notebook, and he paid me regularly.

On Sundays, we never failed to attend the Methodist Church, as my father's belief in the providence of God strengthened with the years, and his wife and family shared that faith. My father's faith in God was unwavering and unshakable. (Some day, we were to hear his will, which he wrote in Chinese, and which began, "I believe in God, Jehovah. . . .") I have no

statistics on the percentage of Christians in Chinatown at that time, but I am sure they were a minority. Our Methodist branch could not have had more than a hundred adult members, with less than fifty regular Sunday attendants. Many of Daddy's contemporaries scoffed at or ridiculed Christians as "do-gooders" who never gambled, when Mah-Jongg[3] games were Chinatown's favorite pastime. Father used to chase lottery peddlers away from his factory; cards were never allowed in our home. I suppose that for him, the Christian faith at first comforted him far from his loved ones. Secondly, it promised him individual worth and salvation, when all his life in China had been devoted only to his family's continuity and glorification. Third, to this practical man who was virtually self-taught in all his occupations, Christianity, suggested action on behalf of others in the community while Confucianism[4] was more concerned with regulating personal relationships. Daddy seldom hesitated to stick his neck out if he thought social action or justice were involved. For instance, he was on the founding board of the Chinese YMCA and fought for its present location, though he was criticized for its being on a hill, for being near the YWCA, for including a swimming pool.

Group singing and community worship in a church must have been dramatically different from the lonely worship of Chinese ancestral tablets at home. He listened to weekly sermons, expounding new ideas or reiterating old ones, and sometimes they were translated from the English spoken by visiting pastors. His daughters learned to sing in the choir and were permitted to join escorted church visits to Western churches—their only contact with a "safe" organization outside of Chinatown.

If my father had one addiction, it was to reading. He eagerly awaited the delivery of each evening's Chinese newspaper—for there had been none where he came from. His black leather-bound Testaments, translated into Chinese, were worn from constant reference. Before our Sunday morning departure for Sunday School, he conducted his own lessons at our dining table. No meal was tasted before we heard his thankful grace.

In a conservative, reactionary community, most members either peacefully avoided criticism, or if involved in controversial occupations (such as gambling, smuggling), joined the strength of the tongs[5] for self-defense. My father was neither type. He was genial, well known to the man on the street, liked to talk in public, but he had few intimate

---

3. *Mah-jongg* (mä′ jong′), a Chinese game played with domino-like pieces.

4. *Confucianism,* teachings of the Chinese philosopher Confucious (551?–478 B.C.).

5. *tongs,* in the United States, usually a Chinese-American association or club.

friends. Cousins and uncles sought his counsel; he never sought theirs. He contributed to causes or to individuals when he could scarcely provide for his own family, but he never asked another for help. During China's long years of conflict, first for the sake of the Revolution, and later against the Japanese, he worked tirelessly in the name of our church, to raise funds here for China war relief.

My mother dutifully followed my father's leadership. Because of his devotion to Christian principles, she was on the path to economic security. She was extremely thrifty, but the thrifty need pennies to manage, and the old world of Fragrant Mountains had denied her those. Upon arrival in the new world of San Francisco, she accepted the elements her mate had selected to shape her new life: domestic duties, seamstress work in the factory-home, mothering each child in turn, church once a week, and occasional movies. Daddy frowned upon the community Chinese operas because of their very late hours (they did not finish till past midnight) and their mixed audiences.

Very early in my life, the manners of a Chinese lady were taught to me. How to hold a pair of chopsticks (palm up, not down); how to hold a bowl of rice (one thumb on top, not resting in an open palm); how to pass something to elders (with both hands, never one); how to pour tea into the tiny, handleless porcelain cups (seven-eighths full so that the top edge would be cool enough to hold); how to eat from a center serving dish (only the piece in front of your place; never pick around); not to talk at table, not to show up outside of one's room without being fully dressed; not to be late, ever; not to be too playful—in a hundred and one ways, we were molded to be trouble-free, unobtrusive, quiescent, cooperative.

We were disciplined by first being told, and then by punishment if we didn't remember. Punishment was instant and unceremonious. At the table, it came as a sudden whack from Daddy's chopsticks. Away from the table, punishment could be the elimination of a privilege or the blow on our legs from a bundle of cane switches. My father used the switch, but mother favored a wooden clotheshanger. Now that I have four children myself, I can see that my parents' methods insured "domestic tranquility." Once, when I screamed from the sting of his switch, my father reminded me of my good fortune. In China, he had been hung by his thumbs before being whipped by an uncle or other older family member, called to do the job dispassionately.

Only Daddy and Oldest Brother were allowed individual idiosyncrasies. Daughters were all expected to be of one standard. To allow each one of many daughters to be different would have posed enormous problems of cost, energy, and attention. No one was shown physical affection. Such familiarity would have weakened my parents and endangered the one-answer authoritative system. One standard from past to present, whether in China or in San Francisco, was simpler to enforce. Still, am I not lucky that I am alive to tell this story? Mother used to point out to me one of the old women seamstresses, tiny of build, with bound feet. She came from another village which practiced the killing of unwanted newborn females, and admitted that she had done so herself in China. But a daughter was born here to her, and I remember her. She was constantly cowed by her mother's merciless tongue-lashings, the sounds of a bitter woman who had not been blessed by any son.

Thirty-five years later, I have four children, two sons and two daughters. In principle we remain true to my father's and mother's tradition, I believe. Our children respect my husband and me, but it is not a blind obedience enforced by punishment. It is a respect won from observing us and rounded by friendship. My parents never said "please" or "thank you" for any service or gift. In Chinese, both "please" and "thank you" can be literally translated as "I am not worthy" and naturally, no parent is going to say that about a service which should be their just due. There is no literal translation for "sorry" in Chinese. If someone dies, we can say, "It is truly regrettable." But if we regret an act, we say again, "I am not worthy." Now I say "thank you," "please," and "sorry" to my children, in English, and I do not think it lessens my dignity. The ultimate praise I ever remember from my parents was a single word, "good."

We do not abhor a show of affection. Each child looks forward to his goodnight kiss and tuck-in. Sometimes one or more of them will throw his arms around one of us and cry out, "I love you so."

My son, Mark, has completed more than eight years of night Chinese school, the same one I attended. I have also served on that school board, as my father before me. Unlike my well-attended Chinese classes—nearly every Chinese child in the community of my childhood was sent to night school for some years—Mark's last Chinese grade included only a handful of students. When I enrolled my youngest boy, Lance, in first grade this fall, the principal was distressed that the entering students were half the number entering in previous years. I saw parents and grandparents proudly shepherding the little ones who were to be his classmates—obviously, these were the parents who cared. The movement of second-generation Chinese Americans has been to the suburbs or to other parts of San Francisco, and it is no longer practical to send their children, the third generation, to Chinese school in Chinatown. My husband and I cherish our Chinese ties and knowledge, and waited many years to purchase a home which would be within walking distance of Chinatown. If a child has difficulty with homework, Chinese or American, he or she can come to see us at our office–studio, and we drop everything to help.

As in my own dual education, the children are learning Chinese history, culture, or what being a member of the Chinese race means. The six-year-old learns one new ideograph a day. After a week, he knew that one writes Chinese from top to bottom, from left to right. They do not lack time for playing, drawing, reading, or TV viewing. Sometimes they do complain, because Chinese is not taught as pleasurably as subjects at American school. When they ask why they must attend Chinese school, I say firmly, "This is our standard. If you lived in another home, you could do as they do." Our children chatter among themselves in English, but they can understand and speak Chinese when desired. It is a necessity when with their grandmothers. Even this simple ability contrasts with some children of Chinese ancestry. As my mother exclaimed in dismay when such a grandchild visited her, "We were as a duck and a chicken regarding each other without understanding."

As a wife and mother, I have naturally followed my Chinese training to wait on my husband and serve my children. While ceramics is my career, the members of my family know they come first, and they do not pay any penalty for my work. Chinese men expect to be family heads, and to receive loving service from wife and children, but they are also marvelously helpful as fathers, and nearly all Chinese men I know enjoy being creative cooks on occasion. If you visit the parks of Chinatown, you are likely to see more men than women overseeing the laughing children. If you shop in Chinatown, you find as many men as women choosing the groceries. My husband has given our children from birth more baths and shampoos than I have. He has also been their manicurist and ear cleaner, for once a week, when they were smaller, there were eight ears to swab clean and eighty nails to trim.

Selective self-expression, which was discouraged in my father's household, has been encouraged in our family. About two years ago, my husband established this tradition: every Sunday evening each child presents an original verbal or verbal-visual project, based on a news article, a school project, a drawing (since the youngest can't read yet), a film. We correct diction, posture, presentation, in the hope that each will be able to think aloud on his feet someday. Each of the three older children has one or more special friend. I have met these friends at our home, preferring that they be invited here rather than have our children leave home. Seldom do we plan children's parties, but when we entertain our adult friends, our children are included. How else would they learn correct etiquette and expect to fit into an adult world some day? At their age, I used to be uncertain to the point of being terrified of "foreigners." Thanks to the hospitality of our Western friends, we and our children have been guests at their homes, their pools, their country retreats. And when they come to our home, the whole family delights in helping to prepare Chinese treats to serve them.

Traditional Chinese parents pit their children against a standard of perfection without regard to personality, individual ambitions, tolerance for human error, or exposure to the changing social scene. It never occurred to that kind of parent to be friends with their children on common ground. Unlike our parents, we think we tolerate human error and human change. Our children are being encouraged to develop their individual abilities. They all draw and can use their hands in crafts, are all familiar with our office and love to experiment with the potter's wheel or enameling supplies at our studio. Sometimes I have been asked, "What would you like your children to be?" Let each choose his or her career. The education of our girls will be provided by us as well as that of our boys. My father used to say, "If no one educated girls, how can we have educated mothers for our sons?" I hope each

one will be a civilized, constructive, creative, conservative nonconformist.

During the Depression, my mother and father needed even more hours to work. Daddy had been shopping daily for groceries (we had no icebox) and my mother cooked. Now I was told to assume both those duties. The management of money, time, and cookery had to be mastered. My mother would give me fifty cents to buy enough fresh food for dinner and breakfast. In those years, twenty-five cents could buy a small chicken or three sand-dabs,[6] ten cents bought three bunches of green vegetables, and fifteen cents bought some meat to cook with these. After American school I rushed to the stores only a block or so away, returned and cleaned the foods, and cooked in a hurry in order to eat an early dinner and get to Chinese school on time. When I came home at 8:00 P.M., I took care of the dinner dishes before starting homework. Saturdays and Sundays were for housecleaning and the family laundry, which I scrubbed on a board, using big galvanized buckets in our bathtub.

Our children are all trained to assist in elementary housecleaning and bedmaking. Each is given an allowance commensurate with his necessary expenditures. But if anyone is occasionally loaded with homework or enchanted with a book or wishes to

see his favorite TV program following dinner, I never insist that chores come first.

I had no such sympathetic guidance as an eleven-year-old in my own reign in the kitchen, which lasted for four years. I finished junior high school, started high school, and continued studying Chinese. With the small earnings from summer work in my father's basement factory (we moved back to the basement during the Depression), I bought materials to sew my own clothes. But the routine of keeping house only to be dutiful, to avoid tongue or physical lashings, became exasperating. The tiny space which was the room for three sisters was confining. After I graduated from Chinese evening school, I began to look for part-time paying jobs as a mother's helper. Those jobs varied from cleaning house to baking a cake, amusing a naughty child to ironing shirts, but wearying, exhausting as they were, they meant money earned for myself.

As I advanced in American high school and worked at those jobs, I was gradually introduced to customs not of the Chinese world. My American teachers were mostly kind. I remember my third-grade teacher's skipping me half a year. I remember my fourth-grade teacher—with whom I am still friendly. She was the first person to hold me to her physically and affectionately—because a baseball bat had been accidentally flung against my hand. I also remember that I was confused by being held,

---

6. *sand-dabs,* flat fish found in the Pacific Ocean.

since physical comfort had not been offered by my parents. I remember my junior high school principal, who skipped me half a grade and commended me before the school assembly, to my great embarrassment.

In contrast, Chinese schoolteachers acted as extensions of Chinese parental discipline. There was a formal "disciplinarian dean" to apply the cane to wayward boys, and girls were not exempt either. A whisper during chapel was sufficient provocation to be called to the dean's office. No humor was exchanged; no praise or affection expressed by the teachers. They presented the lessons, and we had to learn to memorize all the words, orally, before the class. Then followed the written test, word for word. Without an alphabet, the Chinese language requires exact memorization. No originality or deviation was permitted and grading was severe. One word wrong during an examination could reduce a grade by 10 per cent. It was the principle of learning by punishment.

Interest and praise, physical or oral, were rewards peculiar to the American world. Even employers who were paying me thanked me for a service or complimented me on a meal well cooked, and sometimes helped me with extra dishes. Chinese often said that "foreigners" talked too much about too many personal things. My father used to tell me to think three times before saying anything, and if I said nothing, no one would say I was stupid. I perceived a difference between two worlds.

The difference was not always lovely. One day after junior high school classes (I was one of only two Chinese faces there), a tormentor chased me, taunting me with "Chinky, chinky, Chinaman . . ." and tacked on some insults. Suddenly, I wondered if by my difference, I was inferior. This question had to be resolved again and again later: when I looked for my first job, when I looked for an apartment, when I met with unexplained rejection. It was a problem I felt that I could not discuss with my parents.

It is a problem which has not diminished with the years. Only a few days ago, my two youngest children came home from their walk to the neighborhood library with the story that some boys had physically attacked them as they passed the schoolyard, insulting them because they were Chinese. Immediately I took them with me and looked for the schoolyard's director, who called the culprits. There were

defensive denials and looks of surprised guilt. But our children will not be wondering for years if being Chinese means being inferior.

By the time I was graduating from high school, my parents had done their best to produce an intelligent, obedient daughter, who would know more than the average Chinatown girl and should do better than average at a conventional job, her earnings brought home to them in repayment for their years of child support. Then, hopefully, she would marry a nice Chinese boy and make him a good wife, as well as an above-average mother for his children. Chinese custom used to decree that families should "introduce" chosen partners to each other's children—a custom which has some merits and which has not been abandoned. The groom's family should pay handsomely to the bride's family for rearing a well-bred daughter. They should also pay all bills for a glorious wedding banquet for several hundred guests. Then the bride's family could consider their job done. Their daughter belonged to the groom's family and must henceforth seek permission from all persons in his home before returning to her parents for a visit.

But having been set upon a new path, I did not oblige my parents with the expected conventional ending. At fifteen, I had moved away from home to work for room and board and a salary of twenty dollars per month. Having found that I could subsist independently, I thought it regretful to terminate my education. Upon graduating from high school at the age of sixteen, I asked my parents to assist me in college expenses. I pleaded with my father, for his years of encouraging me to be above mediocrity in both Chinese and American studies had made me wish for some undefined but hopefully brighter future.

My father was briefly adamant. He must conserve his resources for my oldest brother's medical training. Though I desired to continue on an above-average course, his material means were insufficient to support that ambition. He added that if I had the talent, I could provide for my own college education. When he had spoken, no discussion was expected. After his edict, no daughter questioned.

But this matter involved my whole future—it was not simply asking for permission to go to a night church meeting (forbidden also). Though for years I had accepted the authority of the one I honored most, his decision that night embittered me as nothing ever had. My oldest brother had so many privileges, had incurred unusual expenses for luxuries which were taken for granted as his birthright, yet these were part of a system I had accepted. Now I suddenly wondered at my father's interpretation of the Christian code: was it intended to discriminate against a girl after all, or was it simply convenient for my father's economics and cultural prejudice? Did a daughter have any right to expect more than a fate of obedience, according to the old Chinese standard? As long as I could remember, I had been told that a female followed three men during her lifetime: as a girl, her father; as a wife, her husband; as an old woman, her son.

My indignation mounted against that tradition and I decided then that my past could not determine my future. I knew that more education would prepare me for a different expectation than my other female schoolmates, few of whom were to complete a college degree. I, too, had my father's unshakable faith in the justice of God, and I shared his unconcern with popular opinion.

So I decided to enter junior college, now San Francisco's City College, because the fees were lowest. I lived at home and supported myself with an after-school job which required long hours of housework and cooking but paid me twenty dollars per month, of which I saved as much as possible. The thrills derived from reading and learning, in ways ranging from chemistry experiments to English compositions, from considering new ideas of sociology to the logic of Latin, convinced me that I had made a correct choice. I was kept in a state of perpetual mental excitement by new Western subjects and concepts and did not mind long hours of work and study. I also made new friends, which led to another painful incident with my parents, who had heretofore discouraged even girlhood friendships.

The college subject which had most jolted me was sociology. The instructor fired my mind with his interpretation of family relationships. As he explained to our class, it used to be an economic asset for American farming families to be large, since children were useful to perform agricultural chores. But this situation no longer applied and children should be regarded as individuals with their own rights. Unquestioning obedience should be replaced with parental understanding. So at sixteen, discontented as I was with my parents' apparent indifference to me, those words of my sociology professor gave voice to my sentiments. How old-fashioned was my parents' dead-end attitude! How ignorant they were of modern thought and progress! The family unit had been China's strength for centuries, but it had also been her weakness, for corruption, nepotism, and greed were all justified in the name of the family's welfare. If the system were so great, why could not China stand firm against Western violations? My new ideas festered; I longed to release them.

One afternoon on a Saturday, which was normally occupied with my housework job, I was unexpectedly released by my employer, who was departing for a country weekend. It was a rare joy to have free time and I wanted to enjoy myself for a change. There had been a Chinese-American boy who shared some classes with me. Sometimes we had found each other walking to the same 8:00 A.M. class. He was not a special boyfriend, but I had enjoyed talking to him and had confided in him some of my problems. Impulsively, I telephoned him. I knew I must be breaking rules, and I felt shy and scared. At the same time, I was excited at this newly found forwardness, with nothing more purposeful than to suggest another walk together.

He understood my awkwardness and shared my anticipation. He asked me to "dress up" for my first movie date. My clothes were limited but I changed to look more graceful in silk stockings and found a bright ribbon for my long black hair. Daddy watched, catching my mood, observing the dashing preparations. He asked me where I was going without his permission and with whom.

I refused to answer him. I thought of my rights! I thought he surely would not try to understand. Thereupon Daddy thundered his displeasure and forbade my departure.

I found a new courage as I heard my voice announce calmly that I was no longer a child, and if I could work my way through college, I would choose my own friends. It was my right as a person.

My mother heard the commotion and joined my father to face me; both appeared shocked and incredulous. Daddy at once demanded the source of this unfilial, non-Chinese theory. And when I quoted my college professor, reminding him that he had always felt teachers should be revered, my father denounced that professor as a foreigner who was disregarding the superiority of our Chinese culture, with its sound family strength. When Confucius had

already established his ethics for civilized behavior, the Westerners were bloodthirstily persecuting Christ. My father did not spare me; I was condemned as an ingrate for echoing dishonorable opinions which should only be temporary whims, yet nonetheless inexcusable.

The scene was not yet over. I completed my proclamation to my father, who had never allowed me to learn how to dance, by adding that I was attending a movie with a boy I had met at college, unchaperoned.

My startled father was sure that my reputation would be subject to whispered innuendos. I must be bent on disgracing the family name; I was ruining my entire future, for surely I would yield to temptation. My mother underscored him by saying that I hadn't any notion of the problems endured by parents of a young girl.

I would not give in. I reminded them that they and I were not in China, that I wasn't going out with just anybody but someone I trusted! Daddy gave a roar that no man could be trusted, but I devastated them in declaring that I wished the freedom to find my own answers.

Both parents were thoroughly angered, scolded me for being shameless, and predicted that I would some day tell them I was wrong. But I dimly perceived that they were conceding defeat and were perplexed at this breakdown of their training. I was too old to beat and too bold to intimidate.

That stormy disagreement climaxed my departure from total acceptance of my parents' ideas and authority. In the thirty years which have intervened, my receptiveness to Western ideas has not meant my unequivocal acceptance. Each situation which arises requires its own evaluation. Sometimes the Western assumption is rejected; sometimes Chinese caution is discarded.

My present standard of values was remarkably amplified at Mills College, which offered me a general scholarship because of a good junior college scholastic record. Mills is primarily a residence college for women, and I was given a chance to live on campus by working for room and board in the home of the dean. Additional duties at her office enabled me to earn money for books and necessities.

Many classes were small in number, with less than ten students. The professors' methods here were the opposite pole from the Chinese. No longer did I memorize wise echoes of the past. The emphasis was on originating, creating, articulating. I was awkwardly unsuccessful at first. But I groped, was made to express my thinking aloud, and had my ideas discussed, rejected, or commended by an audience. I learned too to make and fire pottery and copper enamels, an art that was to become my work. My two years there for completion of my B.A. degree convinced me that education in the liberal arts was a lifetime prize well worth my four years of struggle. It was a valuable concept to learn that academic excellence and skill with one's hands were compatible. The traditional Asian scholar from China to India, even today, refuses to get his hands dirty except with ink. I also learned to lay down forever the fear of prejudice, for I learned what educated Westerners thought of the Chinese culture.

Flanking the entrance to the Mills Art Gallery were two ancient Chinese marble "Fou Dogs," also called Temple Lions. Among the courses which thrilled me most was the one on the history of Chinese art. Those years of dull Chinese evening classes had not included this subject. My art professor at Mills, a European, spoke and read the Chinese language, which led us to fascinating discussions. The instructor for my pottery course emphasized that the greatest achievements in ceramics have been Chinese, with the Sung Dynasty (960 to 1279 A.D.) known as the Golden Age of pottery.

In the field of English at Mills, my work compared the Chinese novel with the English novel—the term paper was read at a conference. For English Club, my anecdotes on Chinatown delighted my classmates and advisor. Thus I concluded that my Chinese background could be accommodated in the widening knowledge of the Western world. Together with my parents' faith in the superiority of the Chinese culture, these exposures convinced me that my background was no liability.

This conclusion was strengthened by the personal friendliness of those whom I met in the new environment. Daily living with the dean was a calm and reassuring experience. I respected her, but she was my true friend and counselor. In her home, I met famous guests, such as visiting speakers and musicians, who were sincerely interested in me. In associating with the encouraging, exacting professors, mingling with students both Chinese and Western, none of whom cared that I alone in my circle of friends had to work my way, my restricted mental confines expanded. Even learning to laugh was an uncertain new sensation.

On occasional weekend home visits, I did not attempt to tell my family of my new life and slipped into the expected behavior forms. They were therefore most surprised when they came to the campus for my graduation ceremonies. They found an exhibit of my handicrafts at the art gallery. They were also astonished when Aurelia Henry Reinhardt, the president, came up to ask to meet my family and to be photographed with me.

Pearl Harbor's destruction had occurred six

months before that graduation day. It was patriotic to look for a job related constructively to the war effort. I decided that I would work for a while, to save money for graduate studies, which were necessary for a social service degree. At that time, I thought that this type of training would utilize my Chinese and Western educations for some type of effective work in Chinatown.

I moved back to my parents' home, which had been improved by a move from the basement to a second-floor location. The garment business was profiting from the war boom. My older brother did not complete his medical training, but was helping my father in his business. Moreover, we had a new baby brother, Jon.

I first worked for the Red Cross, then the shipyard, performing various secretarial duties. I thought it patriotic to work for organizations concerned with the war effort. When a San Francisco newspaper sponsored a contest to find a solution to absenteeism, I did research around our shipyard, interviewed medical authorities outside, and wrote a paper which took top prize. The reason for "absenteeism" was not complicated: human beings cannot work seven days a week to reap overtime pay, week after week, and not have to reckon with the physical inability to keep up the pace. My reward for finding this out was the honor of christening a liberty ship and a gift of a great round sterling platter. There was a good deal of newspaper fanfare, my paper was read into the Congressional Record, and the entire incident became the seven-day wonder of Chinatown and of my family.

After three years in the working world, I made some observations not in the realm of books. I was uncertain that helping people through a social service career would bring me the most rewarding work—many who needed help resented it. Traditionally, Chinese have distrusted investigators. In business and in civic work, I had no problem in getting along in a Caucasian world. If anything, people's interest and cordiality had been heightened by my difference. Yet I knew that secretarial work could never lead me to a great future.

How could I utilize my dual educations? I longed to be in some field which would someday bring me to see China. What work could I do in which I would find no prejudice as a woman? I went alone to the country, where I could think in quiet beauty, close to nature. Troubled, seeking, I had an idea. I liked making pottery and I liked writing. Could I not make a modest living for myself in this combination, which could utilize all I had learned? If I failed, I could return either to the conventional work world or to graduate studies. I was starting from nothing, so I had nothing to lose.

I was already working at my potter's wheel at home. A corner of the sewing factory was allocated for my equipment and cans of clays. At the age of twenty-four, I began a tiny business. I found a Grant Avenue shopkeeper in the heart of Chinatown who permitted me to install my wheel in one of his display windows and to sell my pottery in his store in return for a commission to him. Whenever I was throwing pottery in the window, day or night, great crowds gathered and automobiles caused traffic jams. I sold pottery, too, but not to the curious Chinese. When Chinatown's residents looked at my stoneware bowls made of California clays, they did not see the art in them. "Why, this is a rice bowl!" they would exclaim. "And not even a porcelain one. Only rough clay, suitable for coolies. How can she ask several dollars for something which would cost a few dimes in China? She will soon go out of business." I learned a peculiar human characteristic. People would talk about me as if my presence were not there, and they never thought to ask me for the explanation—that there were no porcelain clays in California and I made one-of-a-kind pieces, not sets of rice bowls. And when I went around Chinatown, I was jeered, "Here comes the girl who plays with mud." They must also have thought, "Here is a college graduate foolish enough to get her hands dirty."

Today, twenty-three years later, they do not jeer or patronize me. A Chinese artist friend tells me that when the popular crowd finds his calligraphy beautiful, he shudders. But when they cannot understand, then he knows that he has risen above the commonplace. By my occupation and my interests, I have become a minority in my own community.

I soon outgrew the store window and moved into a wooden frame building my father had purchased on the western edge of Chinatown, after carefully agreeing to pay my father the full normal rent. Daddy became a frequent visitor, not only to check on his property, but because he was genuinely concerned with my career. He had told me that his father had always stressed the importance of owning one's business, no matter how small, without partners.

Grandfather Wong also thought that anyone who knew how to use his hands would never starve. But the kindest remark Daddy made was that I had vindicated his promise to relatives that he "would bleach the disgrace of our ancestors" in respect to their treatment of women.

I discovered that it was impossible to work at pottery when I liked and write when I liked. "The work of one day is gazed upon a hundred days" is a familiar Chinese admonition to make that day's work worthy for gazing. Handwork should not be rushed, firing failures had to be remedied, and a host of other nonhandwork business details had to be handled. It took three long years before the ceramics business promised to survive.

In achieving new forms and colors not tried before, I retained principles of Chinese harmony, restraint, color tones. Through trial and error, a range of shapes, sizes, and stock colors was developed which could be sold wholesale to fine stores and retailed

to visitors at my studio. A number of exhibition prizes and museum purchase awards brought favorable recognition.

When I had been the most distracted over the success of my business, my mother had surprised me by a remark as I walked past her machine, "Jade Snow, it is fine to have a career when you are young, but it is not a complete life for a woman. When you grow older, you should have a husband to care for you in sickness, and children to relieve your loneliness."

I had assured her that I wasn't antimarriage (I had turned down several of their "introductions") but that I must marry someone right for me. As it happened, the man who was to be my husband, Woody, a childhood acquaintance, returned to Chinatown after fighting in World War II, to be amazed when he saw me working in that store window. We decided independently about our marriage and then told my father, who was pleased. Woody's mother had been one of his home seamstresses, and when I had been a

visitor to their home, riding that wheelbarrow, Woody had been sufficiently enchanted to buy me my first ice cream cone.

Woody studied handicrafts, especially silversmithing, at Mills during the summer before our marriage, preparatory to joining me in business. We planned a simple wedding and were married by the chaplain at Mills, who had been one of my professors. The dean and her husband were our matron-of-honor and best man. Our guests reflected my years of independence and growth from the Chinese community, for there were more Western faces than Chinese, although both our families were present.

Just about the time I had started the pottery business, I received letters of inquiry from Harper & Bros., signed by a woman editor who had read some magazine articles, expanded, actually, from college papers, which I had written about Chinatown. She asked me to think about writing an autobiography, and when I consulted with my junior college English

teacher, I received further encouragement on the project from her. The timing of our wedding was two months before the publication of my book, *Fifth Chinese Daughter*, in 1950. That book's rapid initial sales amazed us. It had been dedicated to my mother and father, and when the first royalty check came six months after publication, my reaction to its amount was to want to share it with my parents. Though my ways were different from those of their other children, I was no less filial and grateful. First, I asked my husband for permission. His reply was, "You don't have to ask me about anything which is right." He, too, is a Chinese son in a big family.

I telephoned my father to say we would come home to him for dinner. He wondered why. I replied, "I have something for you."

He was suspicious, "What is the something?"

I was secretive, "A surprise—you must wait."

Daddy and Mama were both in the kitchen, preparing the dinner. My gifts had been properly wrapped in red paper, as at New Year's, for presentation. My father opened his envelope at once, beamed in excitement, and gave his hundred-dollar bill an American kiss. My mother continued to cook, and ignoring her envelope on the stove top, murmured a rare "Thank you." Later, she left the kitchen with it, but made no additional comment.

Sometimes my father's grace was routine, sometimes it was a silent moment, sometimes it was to ask forgiveness for our sins. But tonight, it had a different tone. As my younger sister and two younger brothers, my husband, my mother, and I bowed together with him, he said, "We are gathered here because of a book about which fellow villagers, merchants, and friends on the street have been congratulating me. For this book was written in America by a Chinese, not only a Chinese, but a Chinese from San Francisco, not only a Chinese from San Francisco, but a Wong, not only a Wong, but a Wong from this house, not only a Wong from this house, but a daughter, Jade Snow. Heavenly Father, this accomplishment was not mine but yours. From your many blessings this girl, raised according to your commandments, was able to do this work."

My father, mentioning me in a prayer for the first time, had accepted me, and a part of him had accepted America. At the age of seventy plus, after years of attending night classes in citizenship, he became naturalized. He embraced this status wholeheartedly. One day when we were discussing plans for his birthday celebration, which was usually observed the tenth day of the fifth lunar month by the Chinese calendar, he announced, "Now that I have become a United States citizen, I am going to change my birthday. Henceforth, it will be on the Fourth of July."

My father's realistic adjustment was the more unusual because I knew that his emotional orientation was to China. As long as I could remember, I had seen hanging above his bed a pair of portraits of his mother and father, with photographs of their funeral processions and other pictures of their tombs. Annually, he sent to his village a generous amount to pay for grave pilgrimages and the necessary offerings. He had shown me the family manual, which carried maps of the sites and stipulated the quantity of food to be borne there, all by foot.

A few years later, he was increasingly weakened by the infirmities of old age and various physical problems and was bedridden for many months at home, with my mother nursing him. Finally, he asked me to arrange for an ambulance to take him to the Chinese hospital. I longed to spend more time with him, for I knew it was a terminal illness, but a four-year-old, a one-year-old, and another baby on the way prevented much absence from home. He died twelve days before my second daughter's birth. My father had chosen Chinese names for my two oldest children. For this second daughter I chose alone, Beautiful Wisdom.

Even though a daughter, I make the pilgrimage to his south San Francisco grave, for my oldest brother died and is buried not far from him. Can we be sorry that Daddy's bones do not rest near his adored mother? For he has given his own loved ones expectations of life which could not have been theirs in Fragrant Mountains.

DISCUSSION

1. (a) What were some of the "nineteenth-century ideals" under which Jade Snow Wong was raised? (b) What is your opinion of those ideals?

2. (a) Do you consider that Jade Snow was disrespectful to her parents? (b) As a parent, in what way is she different from her parents? (c) How is she similar to her parents?

3. (a) In what way was Jade Snow Wong's wanting to go to college a break with Chinese tradition? (b) In what ways did college change her? (c) Did she lose her respect for her own culture as a result of additional education? Explain.

4. Even though Jade Snow Wong's father did not favor her independence from his domination and from many Chinese traditions, in what respect did he bring about her attitudes?

5. Compare the treatment of women in "Marrakech," "Two Eggs for the Men," and "Puritans from the Orient." In what ways are they alike? Different? How do you explain both the differences and similarities of different cultures' treatment of women?

COMPOSITION

Try to recreate Jade Snow Wong's parents' view toward her "Americanization." Write a short dialogue that might have taken place between her mother and father when Jade Snow first decided to leave home and attend college.

UNIT 5 REVIEW

1. The sixteenth-century French author, Montaigne, was the first writer to describe his prose forms as *Essais,* or "attempts." In what way is this an accurate description of the prose forms which you have just read? What have these writers each "attempted" to do?

2. Reread "The Author's Craft" article on objective vs. subjective writing, page 363.

a. Of all the prose pieces you have read in this unit, which is the most objective? the most subjective? Why?

b. Comparing the two which you have chosen above, which is the more interesting? the more convincing?

c. What do you believe is more important for an author to attempt: to interest his reader or to convince him? Can an author successfully do both?

3. Which writer in this unit has given you the greatest insight into your own behavior? Why? Which writer's values seem to be most similar to yours? Which writer's values are most opposed to yours? Did the difference or similarity of values influence your appreciation of a particular work in this unit? In what way? Why?

4. Many of the writings in this unit are by or about people who are different from you. Which particular piece about someone with different cultural values has been the most worthwhile reading for you? Is this because of the subject matter itself or the way in which the author has organized and presented his ideas?

this
page
is
blank

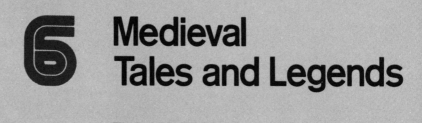

6 Medieval Tales and Legends

THE ARISTOCRAT
THE COMMONER

In many ways, life in the Middle Ages was completely different from the way we live now. Then kings, supported by the warriors, ruled the world. The common people had to obey all these rulers and carry on the work of keeping everyone fed and clothed from day to day. Rather than civil rights, every person had a set of duties which he owed to the other people of society and which he was expected to perform.

The land which we now know as crowded and tamed was then empty and frightening, because men had not learned to control it. People lived together in tiny bands—even the largest cities of medieval days would seem like small towns today.

All work was done by the power of muscle, either the muscles of men or of their animals. Daily life was simple and bare. Even the rich people owned few things.

And yet though there are these differences and many more between the people of medieval times and ourselves, the stories and poems which those people created still fascinate us today.

The reason for this is simple. While the ways of life may vary, people change little. The people of medieval times had much the same emotional life as we do today. They dreamed of themselves as more beautiful, stronger, better than they were. They loved stories of conflict and success, of love and danger, of triumph and despair, just as we do. They laughed at each other, envied each other, felt jealousy and rancor, comradeship and delight. Because they were human and we are human we can join with them through their literature and share the human bond which exists between us.

the aristocrat

Medieval readers who belonged to the aristocratic classes, who enjoyed power and wealth, liked to hear "romances." Such tales of adventure are populated with characters as rich and influential as the people who first read them. The heroes and heroines of medieval romances frequently conquer overwhelming obstacles—dragons, sorcerers, and wily outlaws.

Such romances are not just "fairy tales." They mirror for us, as they did for their first readers, the dreams and fantasies which we have about ourselves and the world in which we live. When through honesty and bravery, a medieval hero wins a victory over what seemed to be an invincible foe, we too share the delight that a medieval reader felt in the hope that men can still win impossible victories.

Sir Orfeo

Translated by Brian Stone

Sir Orfeo[1] was a king of might
In England and a noble lord,
Bold and valiant in the fight
A generous and a courteous knight.
5 His father came of Pluto's[2] line,
His mother of Juno's,[3] both divine
(Or so men called them for a time
For feats they did, much spoken of).
For Orfeo, above all things
10 The art of harping had his love:
And all good harpers were assured
Of honoured welcome from that lord.
He loved to play the harp himself,
And with devoted mind and grace
15 So studied that his harper's art
Was not surpassed in any place.
And never a man was born on earth
Who sat before Sir Orfeo,
Listening to the music's flow
20 But thought he was in Paradise,
Delighting in eternity,
His harping made such melody.
     This king held sway in Traciens,
A city nobly fortified;
25 That Winchester[4] then had the name
Of Traciens is not denied.

---

1. *Sir Orfeo*, medieval counterpart of Orpheus from the legend of Orpheus and Eurydice.
2. *Pluto's*. Pluto was the mythical lord of the Underworld.
3. *Juno's*. Juno, wife of Jupiter, was the goddess of marriage.
4. *Winchester*, town in southern England.

From "Sir Orfeo" from THE PENGUIN BOOK OF MEDIEVAL VERSE, translated by Brian Stone. © 1964. Reprinted by permission of Penguin Books, Ltd.

The king possessed a queen of fame,
The Lady Heurodis her name;
Of all the women of flesh and blood
30 Not one could be as fair and good,
And full of love: none could express
In words her perfect loveliness.

It so befell in early May,
When warm and merry is the day,
35 And gone are all the winter's showers,
And every field is full of flowers,
And glorious blossoms gay and fair
Put forth on branches everywhere,
That this same Lady Heurodis
40 And two fair maids one morning-tide
Went out to play in happiness
At a pretty orchard-side;
To see the flowers spread and spring
And to hear the song-birds sing.
45 There they sat them down all three
Beneath a lovely orchard-tree,
And straight away this comely queen
Fell asleep upon the green.
The maidens dared not break her sleep,
50 But let her lie in slumber deep,
And so she slept till afternoon,
When morning-tide was wholly gone.
As soon as she awoke, she cried,
And fearful clamour filled the place.
55 She wrung her hands and thrashed her feet,
And blood ran where she scratched her face.
Her sumptuous robe she tore in rents,
Deranged, distracted in her sense.
The maidens dared no longer stay
60 Beside the queen, but took their flight,
And at the palace straight away
They cried aloud to squire and knight
That Heurodis was mad or ill,
And told them they must hold her still.
65 Then out went knights, and ladies too,
Sixty maids in retinue,
And coming to the orchard found
The queen and raised her from the ground,
And brought her home to bed at last,
70 And there restrained her, held her fast.
But still she cried in great dismay,
And tried to rise and run away.

When Orfeo heard, it grieved him more
Than any other thing before.
75 To the chamber with ten knights he went,
And there he looked upon his wife,

And spoke in pitiful lament:
'What ails you, my beloved life,
That you, ever so calm and still,
80 Now cry aloud in accents shrill?
Your body, white and excellent,
Is by your nails all torn and rent.
Alas! Your hue of rosy red
Is wan, as if my queen were dead;
85 And then besides, your fingers small
Are pale and bloody one and all.
Alas! Your loving eyes now show
As those of one who sees his foe.
Ah Lady! Mercy, pity me,
90 And cease these cries of misery.
What ails you and whence came it? How
Can cure be found to help you now?'

And then all quiet she lay at last;
And as she wept, her tears fell fast,
95 And to the king she said these words:
'Alas! Sir Orfeo my lord,
Since we came together first
We never crossed each other in strife,
For I have loved you as my life
100 Always, just as you loved me.
But now our lives must separate be:
Fare you well, for I must go.'

'Alas!' said he. 'You seal my doom:
Where will you go, and then to whom?
105 Wherever you go, there I shall go,
And where I go, there you shall go.'

'No, no, sir, that cannot be so:
Now let me, leaving nothing out,
Tell you how it came about.
110 As I lay this morning-tide
Sleeping by our orchard side,
There came to me a troop of knights,
Fine to see and armed to rights,
Who told me to come hurrying
115 To audience with their lord the king.
To this I boldly answered no,
I neither dared nor wished to go.
So back they spurred with utmost speed,
And then their king came straight away
120 With a host on snow-white steeds,
At least a hundred knights, or more,
And damsels too, above five score.
Their lovely clothes were milky white,
And never yet there struck my sight
125 Beings so excellently bright.
A crown the king wore on his head,

Not silver, nor gold that glitters red,
But it was of a precious stone,
And brightly like the sun, it shone.
130 The moment that he came to me
He seized me irresistibly,
And force perforce he made me ride
Upon a palfrey[5] at his side,
And took me to his citadel,
135 A palace equipped and furnished well,
And showed me castles there, and towers,
Rivers, forests, woods with flowers,
And all the wealth of his domain.
And then he brought me home again,
140 And in our orchard said to me:
"See, Lady, that tomorrow you be
Here beneath this orchard-tree,
For then you must come back with me
And live with us eternally.
145 If you resist in any degree,
You shall be fetched, wherever you are,
And limb from limb be torn apart,
Till you are past all help and cure.
Though torn apart, yet still be sure
150 You shall be fetched away by us.'"
    When Orfeo heard this matter, thus
He cried: 'Alas! and woe, alas!
Better it were I lost my life
Than so to lose the queen my wife.'
155 He asked advice of every man,
But help King Orfeo, no man can.
The morrow morning being come,
Orfeo quickly grasped his arms
And took ten hundred knights with him,
160 Each stalwart stoutly armed and grim,
And with Queen Heurodis went he
Right to that same orchard-tree.
They made a wall of shields all round
And swore that they would hold that ground
165 And die to a man that very day
Before the queen were fetched away.
But all the same, from in their midst
The queen was spirited away
By magic; none could know or say
170 What became of her that day.
    Then they cried and wept their woes.
The king into his chamber goes,
And swoons upon the floor of stone,
Lamenting with such grief and moan

175 That in him life was almost spent;
But all this brought no betterment.
    He called his nobles to the hall,
Earls and barons, famous all,
And when they were assembled there,
180 'My lords,' he said, 'before you here,
My high steward I designate
To rule my kingdom from this date:
In my place he shall remain
To govern my entire domain.
185 For now that I have lost my queen,
The fairest lady ever seen,
I'll never look on woman more,
But to the wilderness I'll go,
And with the wild beasts evermore
190 I'll dwell in forests stark and hoar.
And when you hear my life is spent,
Summon together a parliament,
And then elect yourselves a king,
And do your best in everything.'
195   Then there was weeping in the hall
And mighty outcry from them all;
Scarcely could the old or young
For grief give utterance with tongue.
Then down upon their knees they fell
200 And begged him, if it were his will,
To stay with them, and not to go.
'Have done!' said he. 'It shall be so.'
    He left his kingdom and was gone,
With only a pilgrim's mantle on.
205 All other clothing he forsook;
No kirtle,[6] hood, or shirt he took.
But yet he had his harp, and straight
Barefoot left the city gate.
With him then no man might go.
210   Alas! What tears there were and woe,
When he that had been king with crown
Went so poorly out of town!
Through wood, and over heath and down,
Into the wilderness he went.
215 Nothing he found to bring content,
But ever lived in languishment.
Once, grey and varied furs he wore,
Had purple linen on his bed:
Now he lies on the rugged moor
220 With leaves and grass upon him spread.
He, once the lord of castles, towers,
Rivers, forests, woods with flowers,

---

5. *palfrey*, a saddle horse.

6. *kirtle*, a short coat.

Now, when come the snow and frost,
Must make his royal bed of moss.
25 He who had most noble knights
And ladies before him kneeling down,
Only looks on loathsome sights:
Vicious snakes writhe on the ground.
He who lived a life of plenty,
30 With meat and drink, and every dainty,
Must dig the earth and work all day
Before he find his fill of roots.
In summer he lives on wild fruits
And berries, little good to him.
35 In winter nothing can he find
But grasses, roots, bark, and rind.
These rigours were so cruel and hard,
His body was all thin and scarred.
Lord! Who could paint the suffering
40 Through ten long years of this poor king?
All black and shaggy his beard had grown,
And to his girdle-place hung down.
His harp, in which lay all his glee,

He hid within a hollow tree;
245 But when the sky was clear and bright,
He went and took it instantly
And harped on it for pure delight.
Throughout the woods the music thrilled,
And all the beasts of forest field
250 For very joy came round him there,
And all the birds that ever were
Came and sat on branches near
To hear his harping to the end,
The sound so sweetly filled the air:
255 But when his tuneful harping ceased,
Beside him stayed no bird or beast.
    On burning mornings often there
He saw the King of Fairyland
Hunting round him with his band
260 With dim crying and blowing sounds
Amid the baying of the hounds.
They caught no prey, nor could he tell
What afterwards to them befell.
At other times before his eye

265 A mighty multitude went by,
    Ten hundred well-accoutred knights
    Each equipped and armed to rights,
    Fierce of face and bold in manner,
    Displaying many a splendid banner;
270 And each his naked sword was showing.
    He never knew where they were going.
    At other times came other sights;
    Came dancing ladies, dancing knights,
    Elegant in poise and dress,
275 With skilful steps and quiet grace;
    To trumpet-sound and tabour-beat,
    All manner of music, moved their feet.
        And then he saw, one certain day,
    Sixty ladies riding by
280 As blithe and fair as birds on spray,
    With not a man in all their band.
    Each bore a falcon on her hand
    And hawking rode beside the river,
    Which many game-birds made their haunt—
285 Mallard, heron, cormorant.
    And when they from the water rise,
    The falcons mark them with their eyes,
    And each one strikes his victim dead.
        Orfeo watched and laughing said:
290 'By my faith, most pleasant game!
    I shall join them, in God's name!
    Such things I knew in former days.'
    He rises, thither makes his way,
    But then a lady meets his gaze:
295 He clearly understands and sees
    By every token, that she is
    His queen, the Lady Heurodis.
    He looks on her, and she on him
    In longing, but no word is said.
300 Then when she saw the wretched state
    Of him who had been rich and great,
    The tears came falling from her eyes.
    This the other ladies saw,
    And forced the queen to ride away,
305 And she could stay with him no more.
        'Alas, my sadness now!' he said.
    'Why will not death now strike me dead?
    Alas! How miserable am I
    To see this sight, and then not die!
310 Alas! Too long my wretched life
    When I dare not bid my wife
    To hasten to my side, or speak.
    Alas! Why does my heart not break?
    In faith,' said he, 'whatever betide,

315 Wheresoever these ladies ride,
    That self-same way I'll follow them,
    For life and death I do contemn.'
    He girded up his mantle then,
    And hung his harp upon his back,
320 And sternly followed on their track,
    Staying for neither stone nor stock.
    Then rode the ladies in at a rock,
    And Orfeo followed, pausing not.
    Three miles or more within the rock
325 He came upon a pleasant plain,
    As bright as sun on summer's day,
    Smooth and level and wholly green,
    Where neither hill nor dale was seen.
    And there upon the plain he saw
330 A castle of amazing height,
    A royal one whose outer wall,
    Like crystal, glittered clear and bright;
    And on it stood a hundred towers,
    Marvellous forts of mighty power.
335 Straight from the moat buttresses flew,
    Rich gold arches of splendid hue.
    The vaulting of the roofs was wrought
    With carved creatures of every sort.
    Within, the spacious presence-rooms
340 Were built throughout of precious stones.
    The poorest column one might behold
    Was wholly made of burnished gold.
    So all that land had endless light,
    For all the time of dark and night
345 The precious stones with lustre shone
    As brightly as the noonday sun.
    No man could tell or reach with thought
    The sumptuousness that there was wrought.
    By every sign one might surmise
350 It was the court of Paradise.
        Into this castle went the ladies:
    Wishing to follow if he might,
    King Orfeo knocked upon the gate.
    The ready porter came out straight
355 And asked what business brought him there.
    'I am a minstrel,' he declared.
    If it be to his accord,
    I come to please this castle's lord
    With music.' And the porter then
360 Unbarred the gate, and let him in.
        Once inside, he looked about
    And saw, disposed within the court,
    A host of people, thither brought
    As being dead, though they were not.

355 Some, though headless, stood erect,
From some of them the arms were hacked,
And some were pierced from front to back,
And some lay bound and raging mad.
And some on horse in armour sat,
370 And some were choked while at their food,
And some were drowning in a flood,
And some were withered up by fire;
Wives lay there in labour-bed,
Some raving mad, and others dead.
375 And also many others lay
As if asleep at height of day;
Like that they had been snatched away
And taken there by fairy riders.
There he saw his own dear life,
380 The Lady Heurodis his wife,
Asleep beneath an orchard-tree.
He knew by her clothes that it was she.
   And having seen these marvels all,
He went into the royal hall,
385 And there he saw a seemly sight:
Upon a dais serenely bright
There sat the king, the master there,
And the queen, most sweet and fair.
Their crowns, their clothing, shone so bright,
390 His eyes could hardly stand their light.
   When he had looked on everything,
He kneeled down before the king
And said, 'If, lord, your will it be,
You shall hear my minstrelsy.'
395 The king replied, 'What man are you
To come here now? For neither I
Nor any of my retinue
Have ever asked or sent for you.
And since the time my reign began,
400 If ever I found a reckless man
Who dared to visit us, I then
Promptly sent for him again.'
'My lord, believe me well,' said he,
'A poor minstrel is all you see;
405 And, sir, it is the way with us
To call at many a noble house,
And though unwelcome we may be,
Yet must we offer our minstrelsy.'
   Then down he sat before the king,
410 And took his tuneful harp in hand,
And skilfully he set the strings,
And plucked from them such heavenly airs,
That everybody who was there
About the palace came to hear,

415 And lay before the harpist's feet,
They thought his melody so sweet.
The king, attentive, sitting still,
Listened with his utmost will.
The music brought enjoyment keen
420 To him and to his gracious queen.
   Now when his harping reached its end,
Then to Orfeo said the king,
'Your playing, minstrel, I commend.
Now you may ask for anything,
425 And you shall have your whole request:
So speak, and put it to the test.'
Said he, 'Then give me of your grace
That lady there, of fairest face,
Who sleeps beneath the orchard-tree.'
430 'No,' said the king, 'that shall not be!
You'd make an ill-assorted pair,
For you are lank and beggarly,
And she is spotless, bright, and fair.
Therefore it would be villainy
435 To see her in your company.'
Said Orfeo, 'Most noble king,
Yet still more villainous a thing
To hear your mouth speak out a lie;
For since you did not specify
440 What I should ask, I must receive,
And to your promise you must cleave.'
Replied the king, 'Since that is so,
Then take her by the hand and go!
Have joy of her in everything.'
445   Orfeo knelt and thanked the king.
He took fair Heurodis by the hand
And with her swiftly left that land
By the self-same road that he had come.
   Long ways they journeyed from the place
450 And came to Winchester, his home.
There no man recognized his face,
But fearing that he might be known,
He did not dare to make his way
Beyond the outskirts of the town,
455 But in a narrow billet lay,
Took lodgings with a beggar-man
Both for himself and for his wife,
As minstrel folk of lowly life.
He asked what tidings in the land,
460 What ruler held it in his hand,
And that poor beggar in his cot
Gave all the news and stinted not:
How their queen, ten years before,
Was snatched away by fairy power,

465 And how their king went off alone,
An exile in a land unknown:
And how the steward ruled as king;
And told him many another thing.
    The morrow, at mid-morning-tide,
470 He made his wife remain behind
And, borrowing the beggar's rags,
He slung his harp upon his back
And went into the city's ways,
Showing himself to people's gaze.
475 Earls and barons bold and grim,
Townsmen and ladies looked on him.
'Look! What fellow is that?' they said.
'How long his hair hangs from his head!
His beard reaches to his knee:
480 He is as withered as a tree!'
And as he walked about the street,
His own high steward he chanced to meet,
To whom he called with piercing cry,
'Have mercy on me, Steward! I
485 Am a harper of a heathen nation;
Help me in my desolation!'
The steward said, 'Come with me, come:
Of what I have, you shall have some.
I welcome all good harpers here
490 For Orfeo's sake, who held them dear.'
    The steward sat at the castle board,
And round him many a noble lord.
Trumpeters and tabourers,
Many harpers, fiddlers were
495 Making music one and all
While Orfeo, motionless in hall,
Listened. When they all were still,
He loudly tuned his harp with skill,
And played on it the sweetest air
500 That ever mortal heard with ear:
The sound delighted each man there.
    The steward looked with searching eyes:
At once the harp he recognized.
'Minstrel, by your life, I vow,'
505 Said he, 'that you shall tell me now
Where you got this harp, and how.'
'My lord,' said he, 'in lands unknown
Wandering a waste alone,
I found there in a dip remains
510 Of one who had been rent by lions,
And torn by teeth wolfish and sharp.
Beside him there I found this harp;
And that is quite ten years ago.'
'Oh,' said the steward. 'What utter woe!

515 That was my lord Sir Orfeo.
Ah wretched me, what shall I do,
My lord being lost, and I forlorn?
Alas, that ever I was born!
That such hard fate should be ordained,
520 And such vile death should be his end!'
Then down he fell and lay as dead.
The barons raised him up and said
Such was the course of destiny;
For death there is no remedy.
525   King Orfeo could tell by then
His steward was a faithful man
Who loved him as he ought to do;
So standing up for all to view,
He said, 'Sir Steward, hear this thing!
530 If I were Orfeo the king,
And had endured great suffering
In barren wastes for many a day,
And had won my queen away
From Fairyland, and safe and sound
535 Had brought her to the city bounds,
And lodged that queen of noble grace
In a lowly beggar's place,
And come to court in guile and stealth,
Unmarked by royalty or wealth,
540 To put your fealty to the proof,
And found, as now I do, such truth,
No reason would you have to repent:
And certainly, in any event,
You should be king, my day being spent.
545 But had you hailed my death, no doubt
At once you would have been cast out.'
    Then all the company perceived
That he was Orfeo indeed.
The steward gazed at him and knew,
550 Leapt up and overthrew the board
And fell before his King and Lord.
So did every noble there,
And with one voice they all declared,
In gladness that his life was spared,
555 'You are our Lord, sir, and our King!'
They led him to a room with speed
And bathed him there and shaved his beard,
And robed him as a king indeed.
And afterwards they went and brought
560 The queen with lofty pomp to court,
With every kind of minstrelsy.
Lord! What mighty melody!
For very gladness wept they then
To see them come safe home again.

Now is Orfeo crowned anew,
And Heurodis, his own queen, too.
And when their long lives reached their end,
The steward was king, and ruled the land.
　　Later, Breton harpers heard
How this marvel had occurred,

And made of it a pleasing lay,
And gave to it the name of the king.
So 'Orfeo' it is called today;
Fine is the lay, and sweet to sing.
575　Thus did Orfeo quit his care:
God grant that all of us so fare!

DISCUSSION

1. (a) Where does Heurodis fall asleep? (b) Describe her dream. In what way are the people in her dream striking or unusual?

2. (a) What efforts does Orfeo make to protect Heurodis? (b) Why are his efforts unsuccessful?

3. (a) What does Orfeo vow when Heurodis disappears? (b) Does he have any hope of seeing her again? Explain.

4. (a) How long does Orfeo wander in the wild wood? (b) How has his appearance changed?

5. (a) What does Orfeo vow after seeing Heurodis in the wood? (b) What does he no longer fear? Why?

6. (a) Describe the castle of the fairy king. (b) Describe the inhabitants of the castle. (c) Where does Orfeo find Heurodis?

7. (a) Who is the fairy king? (b) Why is he surprised to see Orfeo in his castle? (c) Reread lines 400–402. What does the fairy king mean?

8. (a) What does the fairy king offer Orfeo, and what had prompted his rash offer? (b) What reason does he give for refusing Orfeo's request at first? (c) What argument does Orfeo use to answer the fairy king?

9. (a) Why does Orfeo hide his identity upon returning to his kingdom? (b) What results from his deception?

THE AUTHOR'S CRAFT

The origin of Sir Orfeo

The original source for the story of Sir Orfeo comes from ancient Greece, in the legend of Orpheus and Eurydice. The medieval writer of Sir Orfeo transforms the Greek myth, converting many elements of the original story into familiar medieval ideas.

In the original myth, Orpheus, who lived in Thrace, sang and played his harp so beautifully that beasts and trees as well as men were charmed by him. One day, Orpheus' wife Eurydice is bitten by a snake and dies. Orpheus, mourning her loss, goes to the Underworld, the land of the dead, and begs its lord, Pluto, to permit him to bring back Eurydice. Pluto imposes one condition: Orpheus must not turn to look back at Eurydice on the return trip. Orpheus agrees to the condition, but his love proves too strong. He looks

back only to see his wife disappear from him forever.

In comparing the legend of Orpheus and Eurydice to the tale of Sir Orfeo we find some basic similarities and a number of differences. In the Greek myth, little is made of Orpheus' rank in society. Sir Orfeo, however, is a king of considerable power and wealth. Both versions contain a ruler of the land of the dead, the former, a god of the Underworld; the latter, the king of an enchanted castle. In the original myth, Orpheus goes directly to the Underworld. Sir Orfeo, however, wanders for ten years in a wild wood before he discovers the enchanted castle. The Greek myth ends in tragedy; Orpheus loses Eurydice forever. Sir Orfeo, on the other hand, is successful in bringing back Heurodis. The episode of Sir Orfeo's return to his kingdom has no precedent in the legend of Orpheus and Eurydice and was simply added on by the medieval writer.

By comparing Sir Orfeo to the legend of Orpheus and Eurydice, especially noting the changes and additions, we can learn much about medieval tastes in literature. The Author's Craft article on page 495 discusses this subject further.

the arthurian world

The medieval tales that were written in the twelfth century about King Arthur were based upon an oral legend that was already centuries old. The legend of Arthur originated in Wales. There, as early as the sixth century, storytellers were celebrating his heroic deeds. It seems likely that their stories were inspired by Arturius, a British chieftain who helped to defend Britain against the Saxon invaders. During five centuries of telling and retelling, the Welsh embroidered Arthur's courageous exploits with fiction and fantasy and pagan belief.

By the twelfth century, Arthur's fame had spread from Wales to Brittany, and from Brittany throughout France and western Europe. Seeing the legendary Arthur as a perfect feudal and Christian king, the French endowed him with the principles of chivalry, attached to his court a number of colorful knights, and made him the hero of their metrical romances. In the fifteenth century, Sir Thomas Malory brought together the first complete English collection of King Arthur stories. In the nineteenth century, Alfred, Lord Tennyson used the Arthurian legends for the subject of his epic poem *Idylls of the King*. Recently, T. H. White retold the story of King Arthur in the novel *The Once and Future King*. Some of the principal characters who inhabit the Arthurian world, and whom you will encounter in the selections which follow, are introduced below.

Uther Pendragon, King of Britain and father of Arthur. He gives his infant son Arthur to Merlin and dies two years later without proclaiming his heir.

Merlin, also Merlyn, the magician. He arranges for Arthur to be reared by Sir Ector who promises not to reveal Arthur's identity. Merlin is Arthur's principal adviser during the early years of his reign.

Guinevere, also Guenever, Arthur's queen. She falls in love with Sir Launcelot.

King Lot of Lowthean and Orknay, husband of Queen Margawse. He is one of the rebel kings of Britain whom Arthur must subdue in order to unify his kingdom.

Queen Margawse, also Margause, Arthur's aunt. She is the mother of Sir Gawain, Sir Gareth, and Sir Modred.

Sir Launcelot, also Lancelot, the bravest of King Arthur's knights. His love for Queen Guinevere eventually destroys the fellowship of the Round Table.

Sir Kay, the son of Sir Ector. He and Arthur are reared as brothers. When Arthur becomes King of Britain, Sir Kay is appointed Royal Seneschal and becomes one of the knights of the Round Table.

Sir Gawain, eldest son of King Lot. He is fatally wounded by Sir Launcelot after attempting to avenge the death of his brother Sir Gareth.

Sir Gareth, youngest son of King Lot. He serves for a year in King Arthur's kitchen.

Sir Modred, also Mordred, one of the knights of the Round Table. He attempts to usurp the throne during Arthur's absence abroad. Arthur kills Sir Modred, but is fatally wounded by him.

THE story of King Arthur and his Knights of the Round Table has been so popular for the past nine-hundred years that it has been told again and again, in verse and prose, in English, German, and French. Though each writer has told the story a little differently, all accounts retain the basic outline of the tale: that Arthur lived a humble childhood, coming to power at a time of political confusion in England; that as a young king he conquered and ruled over great territories, his knights checking the savage outlaws of the day; and that as Arthur aged, his enemy Mordred plotted against him and in a last great battle destroyed Arthur's ideal kingdom.

The Legend of King Arthur

*The following ballad outlines the important events in
Arthur's life. We are to imagine that Arthur is speaking.*

Of Brutus' blood,[1] in Brittaine borne,
  King Arthur I am to name;
Through Christendome, and Heathynesse[2]
  Well knowne is my worthy fame.

In Jesus Christ I doe beleeve;
  I am a christyan bore.[3]
The Father, Sone, and Holy Gost
  One God, I doe adore.

In the four hundred ninetieth yeere,
10 Over Brittaine I did rayne,
After my savior Christ his byrth:
  What time I did maintaine

The fellowshipp of the table round,
  Soe famous in those dayes;
15 Whereatt a hundred noble knights,
  And thirty sat alwayes:

Who for their deeds and martiall feates,
  As bookes do yett record,
Amongst all other nations
20 Wer feared throwgh the world.

And in the castle off Tyntagill[4]
  King Uther mee begate
Of Agyana a bewtyous ladye,
  And come of "hie" estate.

25 And when I was fifteen yeere old,
  Then was I crowned kinge:
All Brittaine that was att an uprore,
  I did to quiett bringe.

And drove the Saxons from the realme,
30 Who had opprest this land;
All Scotland then throughe manly feats
  I conquered with my hand.

Ireland, Denmarke, Norway,
  These countryes wan I all;
35 Iseland, Gotheland, and Swethland;
  And made their kings my thrall.[5]

I conquered all Gallya,
  That now is called France;
And slew the hardye Froll[6] in feild
40 My honor to advance.

And the ugly gyant Dynabus
  Soe terrible to vewe,
That in Saint Barnards mount did lye,
  By force of armes I slew:

45 And Lucyus the emperour of Rome
  I brought to deadly wracke;
And a thousand more of noble knightes
  For feare did turne their backe:

---

1. *Brutus' blood.* Medieval Englishmen believed that their earliest ancestor was a Roman explorer named Brute.
2. *Christendom and Heatheness,* Christian and Pagan lands.
3. *bore,* born.
4. *Tyntagill,* village in Cornwall.

"The Legend of King Arthur" from RELIQUES OF ANCIENT ENGLISH POETRY, Vol. III, edited by Percy.
5. *thrall,* subjects.
6. *Froll,* from Frollo, a French knight of legend.

Five kinges of "paynims" I did kill
50 Amidst that bloody strife;
Besides the Grecian emperour
Who alsoe lost his liffe.

Whose carcasse I did send to Rome
Cladd poorlye on a beere;
55 And afterward I past Mount-Joye[7]
The next approaching yeere.

Then I came to Rome, where I was mett
Right as a conquerour,
And by all the cardinalls solempnelye
60 I was crowned an emperour.

One winter there I made abode:
Then word to mee was brought
How Mordred had oppressd the crowne:
What treason he had wrought

65 Att home in Brittaine with my queene;
Therfore I came with speede
To Brittaine backe, with all my power,
To quitt[8] that traiterous deede:

And soone at Sandwiche[9] I arrivde,
70 Where Mordred me withstoode:
But yett at last I landed there,
With effusion of much blood.

---

7. *Mount-Joye*, from Montjoie, a town in Germany, southeast of
Aachen, now called Monschau.
8. *quit*, punish through revenge.
9. *Sandwiche*, a town on the southeastern coast of England.

For there my nephew sir Gawaine dyed,
Being wounded in that sore,
75 The whiche sir Lancelot in fight
Had given him before.

Thence chased I Mordered away,
Who fledd to London right,
From London to Winchester, and
80 To Cornewalle tooke his flyght.

And still I him pursued with speed
Till at the last we mett:
Whereby an appointed day of fight
Was there agreed and sett.

85 Where we did fight, of mortal life
Eche other to deprive,
Till of a hundred thousand men
Scarce one was left a live.

There all the noble chivalrye
90 Of Brittaine tooke their end.
O see how fickle is their state
That doe on feates depend!

There all the traiterous men were slaine
Not one escapte away;
95 And there dyed all my vallyant knightes.
Alas! that woefull day!

Two and twenty yeere I ware the crowne
In honor and great fame;
And thus by death was suddenlye
100 Deprived of the same.

DISCUSSION

1. In this poem Arthur tells the story of his life. (a) What feats does he choose to talk most about? (b) What does this tell you about his concept of kingship?

2. (a) What are the attributes Arthur praises in his knights? (b) What does this tell you about his concept of knighthood?

3. Do you share the same ideals and values you find in this poem? Defend your answer.

4. Who is Arthur's final foe and what is the outcome of their struggle?

5. Do you think the ending of this poem is tragic? Defend your answer.

6. What elements of this poem contribute most to produce its sound? How would you describe the sound of this poem?

Wᴴɪʟᴇ Arthur is the most important figure of the Arthurian tales, many of these stories concentrate on the knights who swore allegiance to Arthur and who served him. To accommodate all these men without giving unfair precedent to any particular man, Arthur is said to have had his knights sit at a great round table, where no seat was of greater honor than another. Thus Arthur's knights were called, as a group, the Knights of the Round Table.

Of these legendary heroes a few are particularly famous. Launcelot, traditionally the most powerful knight of Arthur's realm, entered into a dangerous love for Arthur's wife, Queen Guinevere. Gawaine, a knight of handsome appearance, is sometimes described as loyal to his king, at other times as shiftless and lazy. Sir Kay, head of the kitchens, is usually represented as bitter and jealous.

The following tale, about the youthful Sir Gareth's first appearance at Arthur's court, comes from a version of the Arthurian tales written by Sir Thomas Malory in the 1460's. Living in a time of civil struggle in England, a time of great lawlessness and discord, Malory looks back on the days of Arthur as a time when, even in battle, men adhered to a code of conduct and lived noble lives.

The Tale of Sir Gareth

Sir Thomas Malory

translated by Keith Baines

IT happened one Pentecost when King Arthur and his knights of the Round Table had all assembled at the castle of Kynke Kenadonne and were waiting, as was customary, for some unusual event to occur before settling down to the feast, that Sir Gawain saw through the window three gentlemen riding toward the castle, accompanied by a dwarf. The gentlemen dismounted, and giving their horses into the care of the dwarf, started walking toward the castle gate.

"My lords," Sir Gawain shouted, "we can sit down to the feast, for here come three gentlemen and a dwarf who are certain to bring strange tidings."

The king and his knights sat down at the great Round Table, which provided seats for a hundred and fifty knights; but this year, as in most, several were vacant because their owners had either been killed in the course of their adventures, or else taken prisoner.

The three gentlemen entered the hall, and there was complete silence as they approached the king. All three were richly clothed; and the one who walked in the center was obviously young, but taller than his companions by eighteen inches, strongly built, of noble features, and with large and beautiful hands. He leaned heavily on his companions' shoulders and did not stand up to his full height until he was confronting the king. Then he spoke:

"Most noble king, may God bless you and your knights of the Round Table! I come to ask you for three gifts, and none of them is unreasonable or such as to give you cause to repent. The first of the gifts I will ask for now, the other two at the next Pentecost."

"The three gifts shall be yours for the asking," Arthur replied.

"Sire, today I ask that you shall give me food and drink for twelve months, until the next Pentecost, when I shall ask for the other two."

"My dear son, this is a simple thing to ask for. I have never denied food and drink either to my friends or to my enemies. Can you ask for no worthier gift? For you have the appearance of a man nobly born and bred."

"Sire, for the present I ask nothing more."

"Very well, then; but pray tell me your name."

"Sire, that I cannot tell you."

From Malory's LE MORTE D'ARTHUR as translated by Keith Baines. Copyright © 1962 by Keith Baines. Published by arrangement with The New American Library, Inc., New York, New York.

"It is strange indeed that you should not know your name."

King Arthur then commanded Sir Kay, his steward, to serve the young gentleman with the best fare available throughout the coming year, and to treat him with the courtesy due to a nobleman.

"Sire, that is unnecessary," Sir Kay answered sourly, "for were he of noble birth he would have asked for a horse and for armor. No! he is nothing but a great loafer born of a serving wench, you may be sure. However, I will keep him in the kitchen and feed him until he is as fat as any pig, and the kitchen shall be his sty. And since he has neither name nor purpose. I shall call him Beaumains."[1]

And so Beaumains' companions duly delivered him into the charge of Sir Kay, who lost no opportunity to gibe and jeer at him. Both Sir Gawain and Sir Launcelot were deeply ashamed of Sir Kay's cavalier behavior, and Sir Launcelot spoke his mind:

"Sir Kay, take warning! Beaumains may yet prove to be of noble birth, and win fame for himself and for our liege."

Throughout the next twelve months, while Sir Kay remained irate and contemptuous, both Sir Launcelot and Sir Gawain treated Beaumains with the greatest courtesy, inviting him frequently to their quarters to dine, and urging him to accept money for his needs. With Sir Launcelot this was due to his habitually gentle nature; but with Sir Gawain it was more, for he had an unexplained feeling of kinship with Beaumains. However, Beaumains always refused them, remaining in the kitchen to work and eat with the servants, and meekly obedient to Sir Kay. Only when the knights were jousting would he leave the kitchen to watch them, or when games were played, then he participated, and by virtue of his natural strength and skill, was always the champion; and only then would Sir Kay take pride in his charge, and say: "Well, what do you think of my kitchen lad now?"

Once more the feast of Pentecost came around, and once more King Arthur and his knights waited for an unusual occurrence before sitting down to the banquet. This time a squire came running into the hall, and straight up to Arthur:

"Sire, you may take your seats at the Round Table, for a lady is approaching the castle, with strange tidings to relate."

As soon as the king and his knights were seated at the table the lady entered the hall, and kneeling before Arthur, begged his aid.

"Lady, pray tell us your story," Arthur responded.

"Sire, I have a sister, of noble birth and wide dominion, who for two years has been held captive by a most audacious and tyrannical knight; so now I beseech Your Majesty, who is said to command the flower of the chivalry, to dispatch one of your knights to her rescue."

"My lady, pray tell me her name and where she lives, also the name of the knight who holds her prisoner."

"Sire, I may not reveal her name or where she lives; I can only plead that she is a lady of great worth. The knight who holds her prisoner while extorting wealth from her estates is known as the Red Knight of the Red Lands."

"Then I do not know him."

"Sire, I do!" cried Sir Gawain. "He is a knight who is said to have the strength of seven men, and I can believe it, because I fought him once and barely escaped with my life."

"My lady," said Arthur, "I can send a knight to rescue your sister only if I know her name and where she lives; otherwise you can have no help from this court."

"Alas! I thought you would not fail me; so now I must resume my search."

But then Beaumains spoke up: "Sire, for twelve months I have eaten in your kitchen; now the time has come for me to ask you for the other two gifts."

"You ask at your peril, Beaumains," said the king.

"The first is that I pursue the quest besought by this lady, for I believe that it is my appointed one. The second, that Sir Launcelot should follow us, and when I have proved myself worthy, make me a knight, for it is only by him, who is peerless among all knights, that I should wish to be sworn into the order."

"I grant you both gifts, Beaumains."

"Sire, you shame me! To send a kitchen boy on such a noble quest! I will have none of it," said the lady, and walked angrily from the hall.

Meanwhile Beaumains' two companions and the dwarf had arrived, leading a fine charger with gold trappings, and an excellent sword and suit of armor; only a spear and shield were lacking. Beaumains armed at once and mounted; and Arthur's knights were astonished to discover him the possessor of such fine equipment and to see how nobly he bore

1. *Beaumains* (bō mänz′), "Fair Hands."

himself, once clad in it. Beaumains returned to the hall, took his leave of Arthur and of Sir Gawain, and then set off after the lady, followed by Sir Launcelot.

Just as they were leaving the court, Sir Kay appeared, fully armed and mounted. "I too am going to follow this kitchen lout," he said grimly.

"Sir Kay, you would do better to remain here," said Sir Launcelot.

But Sir Kay was not to be dissuaded, and he galloped up to Beaumains and shouted: "Well, Beaumains, do you still recognize your master?"

"I know you for the most ungracious knight at the court, Sir Kay, so now beware!"

Sir Kay couched his spear and charged at him. Beaumains, having neither shield nor spear, drew his sword, and as Sir Kay bore down on him, made two rapid strokes. With the first he knocked the spear out of Sir Kay's grasp, and with the second lunged at Sir Kay and drove the sword into his side, wounding him deeply so that he fell to the ground as though dead.

Beaumains dismounted, took possession of Sir Kay's spear and shield, and then remounted and instructed his dwarf to take the spare horse. At this point Sir Launcelot rode up to him, and Beaumains asked if he would like to joust, to which Sir Launcelot agreed.

They drew apart and then galloped together, and the collision sent both men and horses tumbling to the ground. Recovering quickly, both drew their swords and attacked each other with the ferocity of wild boars. Sir Launcelot, who had hitherto been unmatched, was astonished at Beaumains' strength and skill, and felt as if he were fighting a giant rather than an ordinary man. Each succeeded in delivering blows that sent his opponent staggering to the ground, only to recover immediately. After a while, however, Sir Launcelot began to realize that his strength was not equal to that of Beaumains, and fearing an ignominious defeat, called a halt.

"My friend, pray hold off! for we have no quarrel," he said.

"That is true, Sir Launcelot, yet it does me good to feel your strength, though I have not yet fought to my uttermost."

"Then you are matchless: I called a halt just now for fear that I should be shamed into begging for mercy!"

"Sir Launcelot, will you make me a knight?"

"Certainly, but first you must reveal to me your true name, and of whom you were born."

"Sir, if you will pledge yourself to absolute secrecy, I will tell you."

"I shall not betray you."

"My name is Gareth of Orkney; I am Sir Gawain's brother, born of the same parents."

"Gareth, that gladdens my heart, for I guessed that you were of noble birth."

Sir Launcelot then knighted Gareth and left him. Sir Kay was still lying senseless, so he laid him on his shield and brought him to the court, where the other knights, especially Sir Gawain, taunted him without mercy.

Sir Gareth, meanwhile, had ridden after the lady, and as soon as he caught up with her she rounded on him:

"Why do you follow me, you wretched lackey? Your clothes still stink of tallow and grease; and I know from Sir Kay that you are nameless and have to be called Beaumains, and how treacherously you overcame that excellent knight! Now leave me, I command you; have done!"

"Madame, I have come to serve you, and your words shall not deter me."

"Lewd little knave! Well, before long we shall meet a knight who will frighten you back to your kitchen quickly enough."

At this moment a man came running frantically out of the forest.

"My good fellow, what is your trouble?" asked Sir Gareth.

"My lord, six thieves have attacked my master; they have him bound and at any moment will kill him."

"Pray lead me to them."

Sir Gareth killed three of the thieves as soon as they came upon them. The other three fled, and Sir Gareth chased them until they turned about and attacked him fiercely, but before long he had killed them all. Returning to the knight, he released him from his bonds, and the knight begged Sir Gareth to accompany him to his castle, where he would be able to reward him as he deserved.

"Sir, I need no reward for doing as a knight should; and today I have been knighted by the peerless Sir Launcelot, so I am content enough. Pray forgive me now if I return to my lady, whose quest I am pursuing."

Sir Gareth returned to the lady, and she turned on him again:

"Misshapen wretch! What pleasure do you expect me to take in your cumbrous deeds? Now leave me, get back to your kitchen, I say!"

The knight whom Sir Gareth had rescued now rode up to them both and offered them hospitality for the night. It was already dusk, and the lady accepted. At dinner she found herself sitting opposite to Sir Gareth, and protested at once: "Sir, forgive me, but I cannot possibly dine in company with this stinking kitchen knave; why he is fit only for sticking pigs."

Thereupon the knight set Sir Gareth at a side table, and excusing himself, removed his own place there as well.

In the morning, after thanking their host, Sir Gareth and the lady resumed their journey. Soon they came to a broad stream, and on the further bank were two knights.

"Now," said the lady, "I think you had better fly, and save your bacon."

"My lady, were there six knights, I should not fly."

The first of the knights and Sir Gareth galloped their horses into the stream, and both broke their spears as they collided. They drew their swords, and soon Sir Gareth stunned his opponent with a blow on the helmet, and he fell into the water and was drowned. Urging his horse through the stream, Sir Gareth met the second knight on the far bank, and again, both spears were broken, and again Sir Gareth struck his opponent on the helmet, this time with a blow that killed him outright.

"It is strange," said the lady when Sir Gareth had joined her once more, "that fortune should favor so vile a wretch as you. But do not suppose for one moment that it was either by skill or daring that you overcame those two excellent knights. No, I watched you closely. The first was thrown into the water by his horse stumbling, and so unhappily drowned. The second you won by a cowardly blow when he was not expecting it. However, had you not better turn back now? For the next knight we meet will certainly cut you down without mercy or remorse."

"My lady, I shall not turn back. So far I have fought with such ability as God gave me, and trusting in His protection. My only discouragement has been your own extraordinary abuse."

All day they rode together, and the lady's villainous tongue never ceased to wag. In the evening they came to the Black Land. By a black hawthorne on which was hung a black shield, and by the side of which was a black rock, stood a black standard.

Under the tree stood a knight in black armor, who was Knight of the Black Lands.

"Now fly," said the lady to Gareth, "for here is a knight before whom even the brave might tremble."

"I am not a coward, my lady."

"My lady!" shouted the Black Knight, "are you come with your champion from King Arthur's court?"

"Sir, unhappily not! This ill-gotten lout has pursued me from King Arthur's kitchen, and continues to force his odious presence upon me. Purely by mischance, and by treachery, he has overcome a few knights on the way; but I beg you to rid me of him."

"My lady, that I will happily do. I thought for a moment that since he was accompanying you, he must be of noble birth. Now let us see: it would be degrading to fight him, so I will just strip him of his armor and horse, and then he can run back to his kitchen."

"Sir, I shall pass through this country as it pleases me, and whether you will or no. It appears that you covet my horse and my armor. Very well, let us see if you can win them! Now—defend yourself!"

And with that, both knights, in a black rage, galloped thunderously at each other. Both broke their spears, but while Sir Gareth was unharmed, the point of his own spear was embedded deeply in the body of his opponent. They fought with their swords, and for an hour and a half the Black Knight held out, but then he fell dead from his horse.

Noticing the fine quality of the Black Knight's armor, Sir Gareth stripped him of it, and exchanged it for his own. He then remounted and joined his lady.

"Alas! the lackey still lives. Shall I never be rid of him? Tell me, cockroach, why do you not run off now? You could boast to everyone that you have overcome all these knights, who, entirely through misfortune, have fallen to you."

"My lady, I shall accompany you until I have accomplished my quest or died in the attempt. This, whether you will or no."

Next they came upon the Green Knight, clad in green armor, who, seeing Sir Gareth's black armor, inquired if it were not his brother, the Black Knight.

"Alas! no," the lady replied. "This is but a fat pauper from King Arthur's kitchen, who has treacherously murdered your noble brother. I pray you, avenge him!"

"My lady, this is most shameful; certainly I will avenge him."

"This is slander," said Sir Gareth. "I killed him in fair combat; so now defend yourself!"

The Green Knight blew three times on his horn, and two maids appeared, who handed him his green spear and green shield.

They jousted and both broke their spears, then continued the fight with swords, still on horseback, until Sir Gareth wounded his opponent's horse and it collapsed under him. They both leaped clear and resumed the fight on foot. The Green Knight was powerful, and both were soon liberally wounded. At last the lady spoke up:

"Why sir, for shame! Does it take so long to dispatch a mere scullery boy! Surely you can finish him off; this is the weed overshooting the corn!"

The Green Knight, deeply ashamed, redoubled his blows, and succeeded in splintering Sir Gareth's shield. Sir Gareth then exerted his full strength, and striking his opponent on the helmet, sent him reeling to the ground, where he unlaced his helmet in order to behead him; and the Green Knight cried for mercy.

"Mercy you shall not have, unless this lady pleads for you," Sir Gareth replied.

"And that I should be beholden to a servant? Never!" the lady replied.

"Very well, sweet lady, he shall die."

"Not so fast, knave!"

"Good knight, I pray you, do not kill me for want of a good word from the lady. Spare me, and not only shall I forgive you the death of my brother, but I will myself swear you allegiance, together with that of the thirty knights at my command."

"In the devil's name! The Green Knight and his thirty followers at the command of a scullery boy! For shame, I say!"

For answer, Sir Gareth raised his sword, and made as if to behead the Green Knight.

"Hold, you dog, or you will repent it!" said the lady.

"My lady's command is a pleasure, and I shall obey her in this as in all things; for surely I would do nothing to displease her."

With that Sir Gareth released the Green Knight, who at once swore him homage.

The two knights and the lady rode to the Green Knight's castle, and as ever, the lady unbridled her flow of invective against Sir Gareth, and once more refused to dine at the same table with him. The Green Knight removed both his own and Sir Gareth's places to a side table, and the two knights ate merrily together. Then the Green Knight addressed the lady:

"My lady, it astonishes me that you can behave in such unseemly fashion before this noble knight, who has proved himself worthier than I—and believe me, I have encountered the greatest knights of my time. He is surely rendering you an honorable service, and I warn you that whatever mystery he pretends concerning his birth, it will be proved in the end that he is of noble, if not royal, blood."

"My lord, you make me sick," the lady responded.

Before retiring to their chambers, the Green Knight commanded thirty of his retainers to watch over Sir Gareth while he slept, and to be on their guard against treachery.

In the morning, after Mass and breakfast, the Green Knight accompanied Sir Gareth and the lady through the forest, and when he came to take leave of them, spoke to Sir Gareth:

"Noble knight, please remember that I and my thirty knights are sworn to your service, to command when you will."

"Sir, I thank you; when the time comes, I shall request you to make your allegiance to King Arthur."

"Sir, we shall be ready at all times," said the Green Knight.

"For shame! For shame!" cried the lady.

They parted, and then the lady spoke to Sir Gareth:

"Now, you greasy knave, surely you have run to the end of your leash. Ahead of us lies the Passage Perelous, and it would take a true-born knight, and one of the quality of Sir Launcelot, Sir Tristram, or Sir Lamerok, to pass through this stage of the journey without losing courage. And so I advise you to run for it now!"

"Perhaps, my lady, I shall not run," Sir Gareth replied.

They were approaching a castle comprising a fine white tower, surrounded by machicolated walls[2] and double ditches. Leading up to the gate was a large jousting field, with a pavilion in process of erection for a coming tournament; and hung above the gate were fifty shields bearing different devices. The lord of the castle, seeing Sir Gareth approach with the lady and his dwarf, decided to challenge him, so he clad himself in puce[3] armor, for he was the Puce Knight, and then rode out to meet them.

---

2. *machicolated* (mə chik′ ə lāt′ id) *walls.* Fortified castles in the Middle Ages often had openings (machicolations) through which missiles and hot liquid could be dropped upon attackers.

3. *puce* (pyüs), dull red or purplish brown color.

"Sir, are you not my brother, the Black Knight?" he asked.

"Sir, indeed he is not. He is a nameless servant from King Arthur's kitchen, called Beaumains. Purely by treachery and mischance he has killed your brother the Black Knight, and obtained the allegiance of your excellent brother the Green Knight. I beg you to avenge them, and rid me of his odious presence once and for all."

"My lady, it shall be done," the Puce Knight replied.

They jousted and both horses collapsed, and they continued to fight on foot. After two hours the lady could contain herself no longer:

"Sir, for shame that you should dally so long with a mere scullery boy. Pray do me the goodness to finish him off."

The Puce Knight was duly ashamed, and redoubled his strokes, but to no avail; for Sir Gareth, using only a little more strength, struck him to the ground, then, straddling him, dragged off his helmet to behead him. The Puce Knight pleaded for mercy.

"Mercy you shall not have unless my lady pleads for you."

"Leave him be, Beaumains; he is a noble knight," said the lady.

"Then, my lady, he shall thank you for his life," said Sir Gareth.

The Puce Knight rose, and begged them to accept hospitality in his castle for the night. The lady accepted and that evening they dined well and then went to bed; but as ever she continued to abuse Sir Gareth. Distrusting her, the Puce Knight commanded his sixty knights to keep watch over him while he slept. In the morning, after hearing Mass and breakfasting, the lady and Sir Gareth took leave of their host; and before parting the Puce Knight swore his allegiance, and that of his sixty knights, to Sir Gareth, who, as before, said that in due course he would require him to make his allegiance to King Arthur.

They resumed their journey, and by noon had come in sight of a beautiful city. Before it stretched a plain, the grass was newly mown, and many splendid pavilions had been erected. But one in particular caught the eye, being the color of indigo, and arranged about it were armor and equipment of the same color; so also were the adornments of the ladies who passed to and fro.

"Yonder lies the pavilion of Sir Persaunte, the Indigo Knight, and lord of this city. But for one, he is the greatest knight living. He has at his command a hundred and fifty knights, and it is his custom to challenge every knight who passes through his terrain. And so now, filthy knave, had you not better think twice and flee, before Sir Persaunte chastises you with the ignominy that you deserve?"

"My lady, if he is noble, as you say he is, he will not dispatch his knights to murder me, but fight with me in single combat; and if he has won honor as you say he has, the greater glory will be mine if I overcome him. Before each combat you yourself chasten me with your abuse; and after each you deny flatly what I have truly accomplished, distorting the event so that it serves only to augment the hatred you bear me!"

"Sir, your courteous speech and brave deeds astound me. I have with my own eyes witnessed what you have already accomplished, and I am becoming convinced that you must indeed be of noble birth. But this time I would save you, so please offer no challenge to the Indigo Knight, for both you and your horse have already suffered much in your previous combats. Up to now we have come safely through this difficult journey, but here we are within seven miles of the castle where my sister is held captive; and to combat the knight who holds her, you will need all your strength, for his is seven times that of ordinary men."

"My lady, I should be ashamed to withdraw from combat with the Indigo Knight now; but with God's grace, we shall be able to continue our journey in two hours."

"Ah Jesu!" exclaimed the lady. "Worthy Knight, you must indeed be of noble blood to have borne for so long and with such courtesy the terrible way in which I have reviled you."

"My lady, it would be an unworthy knight indeed who was unable to bear the chastisement of a lady. The anger your insults inspired in me I turned against my opponents, and so overcame them more readily. Always have I been determined to prove my own worth: I served in King Arthur's kitchen in order to discover who were my true friends, and who my enemies. What my blood may be shall be revealed in due course; but at present I wish to prove myself by my deeds alone. And so, my lady, I shall continue to serve you as I have already."

"I beg you, gentle knight, can you forgive me my terrible words?"

"My lady, you are forgiven; and if formerly anger made me strong, may joy now make me invincible!"

Meanwhile, the Indigo Knight had seen Sir Gareth and the lady approach, and sent a messenger to inquire whether they came in war or in peace. Sir Gareth replied that he offered a challenge only if the Indigo Knight wished to receive one. The Indigo Knight decided to accept the challenge and fight to his uttermost, so he mounted and rode out to meet Sir Gareth.

They charged at each other with equal determination, and both broke their spears into three pieces, while their horses tumbled to the ground.

The sword fight lasted for two hours, and in the course of it Sir Gareth wounded the Indigo Knight deeply in the side; however, he continued to fight bravely. At last, though somewhat loath because of his opponent's bravery, Sir Gareth delivered his crushing blow on the helmet, and the Indigo Knight was sent spinning to the ground. Once more Sir Gareth straddled his opponent and unlaced his helmet to behead him, and the Indigo Knight yielded. The lady at once begged that Sir Gareth should spare his life.

"My lady, that I will gladly do, for he is a noble knight."

"May God reward you!" said the Indigo Knight. "Now I understand well enough how it was that you killed my brother Sir Perarde the Black Knight, and won the allegiance of my other two brothers, Sir Pertolope the Green Knight and Sir Perymones the Puce Knight."

Sir Persaunte then led Sir Gareth and the lady to his pavilion, where he refreshed them with wine and spices, and insisted that Sir Gareth should rest both before and after supper.

In the morning Sir Persaunte asked the lady where she was leading Sir Gareth.

"To the Castle Dangerous."

"Ah ha! that is where the Red Knight of the Red Lands lives, and holds the Lady Lyoness prisoner, is it not? But tell me, you are surely her sister, Lady Lynet?"

"Sir, that is my name," the lady replied.

"Well, sir, you must prepare yourself for an ordeal, for it is said that the Red Knight has the strength of seven ordinary men. But you will be fighting for a worthy cause, for this knight has held the Lady Lyoness prisoner for two years now. He has been waiting for a challenge from one of four knights from King Arthur's court: Sir Launcelot, the most powerful of all, Sir Tristram, Sir Gawain, or Sir Lamerok. And although many other knights have achieved much fame, it is one of these four he wishes to fight. So, now, let me wish you God's speed, and strength for the coming battle."

"Sir Persaunte, would you have the goodness of heart to make my companion a knight?"

"My lady, I will gladly, if he will accept the order from so simple a man as I."

"Sir, I thank you for your gracious offer, but I have already been knighted by Sir Launcelot, for I wished it to be from no other hands than his. And if you will both swear to keep the secret, I will now reveal to you my name, and of whom I was born."

"We swear," they said together.

"I am Sir Gareth, Sir Gawain's brother, and the youngest son of King Lot of Lowthean and Orkney; my mother is Margawse, King Arthur's sister. But neither King Arthur, Sir Gawain, nor any other at his court, with the exception of Sir Launcelot, knows who I am."

In the morning, after Mass and breakfast, Sir Gareth and the lady rode through the forest, and then across a wide plain, to the Castle Dangerous, which stood on the seashore. The Red Knight had pitched his pavilions beneath the walls of the castle, and to one side Sir Gareth noticed a copse of tall trees, and from the branches hung forty knights. They were in full armor, with their swords in their hands, shields, and spurs at their heels. Sir Gareth was horrified.

"Tell, my lady, what is the meaning of this?"

"Sir Gareth, those are the knights who hitherto have attempted to rescue my sister, so take heed! The Red Knight is a formidable warrior, and lord of many marches;[4] but once he has overcome a knight in battle, he always puts him to this murderous end; and that is one reason why no gentlewoman can love him."

"May Jesu preserve me from such a death! Certainly I should prefer to die fighting. But how strange that no knight from King Arthur's court has yet defeated him."

"My lord, take courage; he is a powerful knight."

The castle moats were formed by two dikes which

---

4. *marches,* border lands. .

ran around from the sea. Several ships were at anchor and everywhere were signs of activity. On board the ships, in the Red Knight's pavilions, and from within the castle could be heard the merry sounds of minstrelsy,[5] while lords and their ladies walked upon the castle walls. Just by the gate grew a large sycamore tree, and on this was hung an elephant's horn for those who wished to challenge the Red Knight. Sir Gareth was about to blow it when the lady cautioned him:

"Sir Gareth, do not sound your challenge yet. Until noon the Red Knight's strength increases, after then it wanes, so if you will wait for a little the advantage will be yours."

"My lady, I should be ashamed not to challenge him at his greatest strength." And with that Sir Gareth blew a tremendous blast on the horn.

Immediately knights and ladies came running from all directions, to the castle walls and windows, or out of their pavilions, in order to witness the coming battle. The Red Knight hastily armed, assisted by his earls and barons. One of them laced on his helmet while another buckled on his spurs and a third handed him his blood-red shield and spear. He then mounted, rode out to a small hollow which could be easily viewed from the castle, and awaited his challenger.

"My lord, here comes your mortal enemy, and at the tower window stands your lady."

"Pray, tell me where," asked Sir Gareth.

The lady pointed with her finger, and Sir Gareth looked up and saw a lady whose beauty filled him with awe. She curtsied to him, and then held out her hands in supplication.

"Truly, she is the most beautiful lady on earth. My quarrel could not be better chosen," he said.

"Sir, you may cease looking at the lady, and look to your arms instead. She is not for you, nor shall she be," said the Red Knight grimly.

"Sir, it would seem that although you hold the lady, she is not yours, and therefore your love for her is nothing but folly. Further, now that I have seen her and I know that I love her, by the grace of God, I shall win her for myself."

"Sir, are you not warned by the array of corpses hung from the trees—your predecessors, who spoke as you do?"

"No, I am not. Rather am I filled with anger and contempt, and understand well why the lady does

5. *sounds of minstrelsy,* sounds of minstrels, or musicians.

not love you. And for myself, I wish only to fight you to the death and put an end to your murderous ways. Nor shall I feel any of that remorse in overcoming you which I have felt in the past for more honorable opponents."

"Sir, make ready—enough of your words!"

They jousted, and both crashed to the ground with such violence, and lay stunned for so long, that the onlookers supposed that they had broken their necks. However, they recovered, and drawing their swords, chopped at each other with heavy, deliberate blows, beneath which one or the other would occasionally stagger. So they fought until well past noon, when they paused for a moment to recover their breath. Both were streaming with blood from their wounds, panting, and momentarily exhausted as they leaned on their shields.

Beneath the steady rain of blows their shields were chipped and their armor and mail had given way in many places; and Sir Gareth soon learned, to his cost, to defend them from the shrewd blows of his opponent. Several times one or the other fell to the ground, half stunned by a blow, whereon the other would leap on top of him; and more than once in the ensuing scuffle they exchanged swords.

At eventide they agreed to rest, and sat on two molehills while their pages unlaced their helmets so that they should be refreshed by the cool breeze. Sir Gareth looked up to the tower, and seeing the lady, was inspired with fresh courage:

"Sir, let us continue; to the death!"

"To the death!" the Red Knight responded.

Despite their many wounds, they continued the fight with fresh vigor, until with two skillful blows the Red Knight first knocked the sword from Sir Gareth's hand, and then sent him spinning to the ground. Leaping on top of him, the Red Knight started unlacing his helmet, when suddenly Lady Lynet cried out:

"Alas! Sir Gareth, your lady weeps with despair, and my own heart is heavy."

Sir Gareth responded with a tremendous thrust of his body and succeeded in overturning his opponent, then, reaching swiftly for his sword, confronted him once more. A new and desperate battle ensued, as each strained to the limits of his strength to overmatch the other. Then it was Sir Gareth who sent his opponent's sword flying from his hand, and following it up with a hail of blows on the helmet, knocked him senseless to the ground, where he sprang on top of him. He had just unlaced his helmet to behead him when the Red Knight cried aloud:

"Most noble knight, I beg you for mercy!"

"Sir, how can I honorably spare you, when you have murdered so many courageous knights who yielded to you?"

"Sir, there was a reason for that, if you will only allow me to tell you."

"Speak on."

"Once I loved a lady whose brethren had all been killed by Sir Launcelot or Sir Gawain; and it was at her bidding that I fought with every knight who passed this way from King Arthur's court, and hung by the neck those whom I overcame. And to this day I have been waiting for either Sir Launcelot or Sir Gawain to mete her final revenge. And to accomplish this purpose, I have been enchanted, so that each day my strength increases until noon, when it is seven times that of other men, after which it wanes again."

Meanwhile the Red Knight's earls and barons had gathered round, and now they threw themselves on their knees and begged Sir Gareth to spare him:

"Sir, surely nothing can be gained by his death, nor can the dead be brought to life again. But spare him and he shall pay you homage, and learn to atone for his misdeeds."

"My lords, for your asking I will spare the Red Knight; and in my heart I can find some room for forgiveness, since what he did was at his lady's bidding. But these are my conditions: that first he shall yield to Lady Lyoness, making full redress for the damage done to her, and then go to King Arthur's court and yield to Sir Launcelot and Sir Gawain, confessing his enmity toward them."

"Sir, I thank you, and will most certainly fulfill your conditions."

For the next ten days, the Red Knight entertained Sir Gareth and the lady in his pavilion, where the lady treated their wounds. Then, in accordance with his oath, he first yielded to Lady Lyoness and then rode to King Arthur's court, where, in the presence of all, he yielded to Sir Launcelot and Sir Gawain, recounting fully his own misdeeds and defeat at the hands of Sir Gareth, whose progress through the Passage Perelous he also described.

"I wonder," said Arthur, "of whose blood he was born, for certainly he has proved himself a noble knight since he ate in our kitchen."

"Sire, it is no marvel, for such courage and en-durance as his surely stem from noble blood," said Sir Launcelot.

"Sir Launcelot, it would seem that you already know the secret of his birth?"

"Sire, I must admit that I do. I demanded to know before making him a knight, but I have been sworn to secrecy."

Sir Gareth, meanwhile, had asked Lady Lynet if he could not see her sister.

"Sir, most certainly you shall," she replied.

Sir Gareth armed and mounted and rode toward the castle, but as he did so, he was astonished to see the gate being closed and the drawbridge raised. Then Lady Lyoness spoke to him from one of the castle windows:

"Go your way, good knight, for you shall not have my love until you have won further fame; therefore you must strive for another year. Return to me then, and I will tell you more."

"My lady, I had not expected such thanks from one for whom I have already striven so hard, and for whom, alas! I was willing to shed the last drop of my blood."

"Worthy knight, be assured that I love you for your brave deeds, and go forth with a glad heart. Soon the twelve months will pass, and, in the meantime, do not doubt that I shall be faithful to you."

Sir Gareth rode into the forest, bitterly unhappy and careless of direction, his dwarf following. That night he lodged in a humble cottage, but was unable to sleep. He continued his aimless journey all the next day, and that night came to a marsh where, feeling sleepy, he lay on his shield, while his dwarf watched over him.

As soon as Sir Gareth had ridden into the forest, the Lady Lyoness had summoned her brother, Sir Gryngamour.

"My dearest brother, I need your help. Would you ride after Sir Beaumains, and when you find an opportunity, kidnap his dwarf? I am in difficulties because I do not know whether or not Sir Beaumains is of noble birth, and until I know, naturally, I cannot love him. But I feel certain that we can frighten his dwarf into telling us."

Sir Gryngamour prepared to do as his sister asked, and cladding himself entirely in black armor, and mounting a black horse, followed them faithfully until they came to the marsh. Then, as soon as Sir Gareth was asleep, he crept up on the dwarf, seized him suddenly, and tucked him under his arm. However, the dwarf roared lustily, and Sir Gareth awoke in time to see him disappearing in the arms of a black knight.

Arming himself hastily, Sir Gareth mounted and pursued them as best he could, but with great difficulty, owing to his ignorance of the lay of the land. All night he rode across wild moors, over steep hills, and through dense forest, and frequently his horse stumbled, nearly throwing him. But at dawn he came to a woodland path, and seeing a forester, asked him if he had seen a black knight riding that way, with a dwarf behind him.

"Sir, I have. It was Sir Gryngamour, whose castle lies two miles further on. But I should beware of him, for once provoked he is a dangerous enemy."

Meanwhile Sir Gryngamour had taken the dwarf to his castle, where Lady Lyoness was cross-examining him.

"Dwarf, we wish to know the secret of your master's birth; and if you would prefer not to starve in the castle dungeon, you had better tell us. Who was his father, and who his mother, and whence does he come?"

"My lady, I am not ashamed to tell you that my master is Sir Gareth, the son of King Lot of Orkney and Queen Margawse, King Arthur's sister. Furthermore he is such a knight that he will soon destroy your lands and bring this castle tumbling about your ears if you do not release me."

"As for that, I think we need not trouble ourselves," said Lady Lyoness. "But let us go now and dine."

In honor of his sister's visit, Sir Gryngamour had ordered a splendid banquet, so they all sat down and dined merrily.

"My dear sister," said Lady Lynet, "you know I can well believe that your paramour is of noble birth, for throughout our journey through the Passage Perelous, in scorn of what I assumed to be his low birth, I taunted him unmercifully, and never once did he rebuke me. And certainly, as you yourself have witnessed, his feats at arms are unexampled."

At this moment Sir Gareth rode up to the castle gate with his sword drawn, and shouted in a tremendous voice:

"Sir Gryngamour, treacherous knight that you are, deliver my dwarf to me at once."

"Sir, that I shall not," Sir Gryngamour replied through the window.

"Coward! Come out and fight for him, then."

"Very well," Sir Gryngamour said.

"My dear brother, not so fast!" said Lady Lyoness. "I think Sir Gareth could have his dwarf. Now that I know who he is, I can love him, and certainly I am indebted to him for releasing me from the Red Knight. Therefore let us entertain him, but I shall disguise myself so that he will not know me."

"My dear sister, just as you wish," said Sir Gryngamour, and then to Sir Gareth: "Sir, I beg your pardon for taking your dwarf. Now we know that your name, as well as your deeds, commends you, we invite you to accept hospitality at the castle."

"And my dwarf?" Sir Gareth shouted.

"Most certainly you shall have him," Sir Gryngamour replied; and then, accompanied by the dwarf, he went to the castle gate and, taking Sir Gareth by the hand, led him into the hall, where his wife welcomed him.

"Ah, my good dwarf, what a hunt I have had for you!" said Sir Gareth.

Presently Lady Lynet appeared with her sister, who had dressed in all her finery, and disguised herself as a princess. Minstrels were summoned, and amid dancing and singing Lady Lyoness set out to win the love of Sir Gareth. She succeeded, and was herself enraptured by him, so that before long ardent looks and tender words passed between them. Sir Gareth was completely deceived by her disguise, and several times wished secretly to himself that his paramour at the Castle Dangerous were as beautiful and as gracious.

At supper neither of the young lovers could eat, both being hungry only for the looks and words of the other. Sir Gryngamour noticed this, and after supper took Lady Lyoness aside and spoke to her:

"Dear sister, it appears that you love the young Sir Gareth, and certainly his noble blood and valor commend him. If you wish to pledge yourself to him, and I could think of none worthier, I will persuade him to stay at my castle."

"Dear brother, not only is what you say true, but also I am beholden to him more than to any man living."

Then Sir Gryngamour went to Sir Gareth and spoke to him:

"Sir, I could not but observe the semblance of love between you and my sister; and if this should be founded on true feeling on your part, as it is on hers, I should like to welcome you to stay in my castle for as long as it please you."

"Sir, you make me the happiest man on earth; I thank you."

"Good! Then that is arranged; and I can promise you that my sister will be here to entertain you, both day and night."

"Sir, again I thank you. In fact I have sworn to remain in this country for twelve months, and your castle has the advantage that should King Arthur, my liege, wish to find me, he will be able to do so readily."

Sir Gareth returned to Lady Lyoness, and she now revealed to him her true identity, and admitted that it was at her instigation that his dwarf had been kidnapped, so that she could discover the secret of his birth before declaring herself. Sir Gareth was overjoyed, and there followed an exchange of vows.

At Pentecost, each of the knights whom Sir Gareth had overcome went to Caerleon to surrender to Arthur: Sir Pertolope, the Green Knight, with his fifty retainers; Sir Perymones, the Puce Knight, with his sixty retainers; Sir Persaunte, the Indigo Knight, with his hundred and fifty retainers; and Sir Ironside, the Red Knight, with his five hundred retainers.

Arthur's amazement grew as each of the brothers in turn related how he had been overcome by the knight called Beaumains; also Arthur was delighted, for the five brothers had been among his most implacable enemies. The death of the Black Knight was regretted by all, and Arthur promised to make the four remaining brothers fellows of the Round Table as soon as Sir Beaumains returned.

The whole company now sat down to enjoy the banquet, but no sooner were they seated than Queen Margawse of Orkney arrived, attended by her royal suite. Her sons—Sir Gawain, Sir Aggravayne, and Sir Gaheris—at once left their places and knelt down to receive her blessing, as none of them had seen her for twelve years.

When all were seated once more, Queen Margawse inquired after her youngest son, Sir Gareth, and told Arthur frankly that word had reached her that he had been kept in the kitchen for a year in the charge of Sir Kay, who had dubbed him Beaumains and treated him with the utmost disrespect.

It was now clear to Arthur that Beaumains was none other than Sir Gareth, and so he described to his sister how Sir Gareth had come without revealing his identity and asked for the three gifts: to eat in his kitchen, to pursue the quest of Lady Lyoness, and to be knighted by Sir Launcelot.

"Dear brother," said Queen Margawse, "I can well believe it of him, for even as a child he always displayed a remarkable wit, and was wont to go his own way. And perhaps Sir Kay's scornful name is not so inept after all, for certainly since he was knighted he has won great honor by the use of his hands. But now how shall we find him again?"

"I pray you, let me go in search of him," cried Sir Gawain, "for I too was in complete ignorance of the fact that he was my brother."

"I think that will not be necessary," said Sir Launcelot. "Surely our best plan would be to send for Lady Lyoness, who is certain to know his whereabouts."

On Michaelmas Day[6] the Archbishop of Canterbury married Sir Gareth to Lady Lyoness and, at Arthur's request, Sir Gaheris to Lady Lynet (or Lady Saveage), and Sir Aggravayne to their niece, Lady Lawrell. When the triple wedding was over, the knights whom Sir Gareth had overcome arrived with their followers to swear him allegiance.

---

6. *Michaelmas* (mik′ əl məs) *Day*, September 29, when a church festival is held to honor the archangel Michael.

DISCUSSION

1. Malory's tale is loosely unified by three successive feasts of Pentecost. Why is it customary for King Arthur and his knights to delay celebrating the feast of Pentecost?

2. (a) What unusual event occurs on the first Pentecost? (b) Describe Gareth's appearance. (c) What does he request? (d) What impression does he make upon King Arthur?

3. (a) What is Sir Kay's attitude toward Gareth and why does he adopt this attitude? (b) How do Sir Launcelot and Sir Gawain typify the chivalrous ideal of courtesy? (c) Is Sir Launcelot or is Sir Kay the more realistic character? Why?

4. (a) Does Malory describe the physical appearance of Arthur? Of Kay, Launcelot, or Gawain? (b) Does he describe the appearance of the castle? (c) What conclusion do you draw about Malory's use of descriptive detail?

5. (a) On the second Pentecost, why does Lynet come to Arthur's court? (b) Why is she refused? (c) Why does she leave the court in

anger? (d) What three purposes does the joust between Gareth and Sir Launcelot serve in the story?

6. During the next twelve months, Gareth fights seven battles. Describe his first and his second battle and tell the outcome of each.

7. Gareth next battles five brother-knights. Taking each knight in correct order, answer the following questions: (a) What is the knight's proper name and the color of his armor? (b) What motive does he have for fighting Gareth? (c) How many other knights does he command? (d) What is the outcome of his battle with Gareth?

8. (a) How does Lynet increase Gareth's difficulties? (b) When does her attitude toward Gareth change and why does it change?

9. (a) Why does the rescued Lady Lyoness tell Gareth to "strive for another year"? (b) What must she know before she can love him? (c) How does Gareth eventually win the Lady Lyoness? (d) Do you think she merits his love? Why or why not?

10. (a) What unusual event occurs on the third Pentocost? (b) Why does Queen Margawse think Gareth's nickname is appropriate? (c) How does Malory conclude his tale?

THE AUTHOR'S CRAFT

Medieval romance
Medieval romance is a whirlwind of action. The tales are set in an atmosphere of magic and make-believe and are populated with handsome knights and brave kings, with beautiful maidens and cruel captors. The knights pursue high adventure—a religious crusade, a conquest for their liege, or perhaps the rescue of a captive lady. Medieval romances, among them Malory's "Tale of Sir Gareth," have certain characteristics that are called *romantic*.

(1) Medieval romance usually idealizes chivalry; that is, it represents chivalry as being more nearly perfect than it actually was. Since chivalry was an aristocratic code, a romance deals mainly with one social class—the nobility. Does Malory describe the life of the kitchen scullions with whom Gareth serves? Name some of the difficulties Gareth might have avoided by revealing his noble birth.

(2) Medieval romance also idealizes the hero-knight and his noble deeds. Gareth is superhuman in the way he overcomes such heavy odds. Why are Sir Launcelot and the Red Knight formidable opponents? Does Gareth ever reveal unchivalrous traits? Which knight of the Round Table is less ideal than Gareth and hence more realistic?

(3) An important element of medieval romance is the knight's love for his lady. How does "love at first sight" figure in Malory's tale? How does he use romantic love to conclude his tale?

(4) The settings of medieval romance tend to be imaginary and vague. Are the Passage Perelous and the Castle Dangerous real or imaginary places? Which of the following settings does Malory describe in realistic detail: (a) Arthur's castle; (b) castle of the Puce Knight; (c) the city of the Indigo Knight; and (d) the Castle Dangerous?

(5) Medieval romance derives mystery and suspense from supernatural elements. Which of Gareth's foes is enchanted? What is the nature of his enchantment?

(6) Medieval romance uses concealed or disguised identity. Who, other than Gareth, conceals or disguises identity?

The romantic characteristics of medieval romance have exerted a lasting influence on literature. You will often read stories that idealize characters and situations and that emphasize the unusual and adventurous aspects of life.

AUTHOR

SIR THOMAS MALORY (c. 1400–1471) seems to have pursued a life as adventurous, but less chivalrous, than the lives he describes in his book of Arthurian tales, *Morte d'Arthur*. Born into an old, noble family, Malory served as a knight during a war with France, and in 1445 represented his shire in Parliament. But for reasons which are unclear he lived a life of violence, and was repeatedly imprisoned for assault, extortion, and theft. Twice King Edward IV, while granting a general pardon for all criminals, specifically refused to free Malory. During the later years of his life Malory appears to have been in prison continuously, charged with sedition. It is at this time that his book was probably written. He began with old French versions of the Arthurian stories, translating them into his own language, at times expanding them, at times rewriting them. When he died in 1471, he left a manuscript with eight long prose tales in it. This manuscript in time fell into the hands of the first English printer, William Caxton, who cut and altered Malory's book, and then published it as a single, continuous narrative in 1485.

Lancelot and Elaine

Alfred, Lord Tennyson

*The Arthurian legends tell many a love story, but
none so famous as the tale of illicit love between
the King's best friend, Lancelot, and the King's
wife, Queen Guinevere. Alfred, Lord Tennyson's
"Lancelot and Elaine" tells only part of this famous
tale. When Tennyson's poem begins, Lancelot
and Guinevere are already entangled in their love
for each other. By the end of the poem, however,
jealousy and remorse have undermined that love.
And the agent of this change is the innocent maiden,
Elaine.*

Elaine the fair, Elaine the lovable,
Elaine, the lily maid of Astolat,
High in her chamber up a tower to the east
Guarded the sacred shield of Lancelot;
5 Which first she placed where morning's earliest ray
Might strike it, and awake her with the gleam;
Then fearing rust or soilure fashion'd for it
A case of silk, and braided thereupon
All the devices blazon'd on the shield
10 In their own tinct, and added, of her wit,
A border fantasy of branch and flower,
And yellow-throated nestling in the nest.
Nor rested thus content, but day by day,
Leaving her household and good father, climb'd
15 That eastern tower, and entering barr'd the door,
Stript off the case, and read the naked shield,
Now guess'd a hidden meaning in his arms,
Now made a pretty history to herself
Of every dint a sword had beaten in it,
20 And every scratch a lance had made upon it,
Conjecturing when and where: this cut is fresh;

"Lancelot and Elaine" from IDYLLS OF THE KING by Alfred, Lord
Tennyson.

That ten years back; this dealt him at Caerlyle;
That at Caerleon; this at Camelot:
And ah God's mercy, what a stroke was there!
25 And here a thrust that might have kill'd, but God
Broke the strong lance, and roll'd his enemy down,
And saved him: so she lived in fantasy.

How came the lily maid by that good shield
Of Lancelot, she that knew not ev'n his name?
30 He left it with her, when he rode to tilt
For the great diamond in the diamond jousts,
Which Arthur had ordain'd, and by that name
Had named them, since a diamond was the prize.

For Arthur, long before they crown'd him King,
35 Roving the trackless realms of Lyonesse,
Had found a glen, gray boulder and black tarn.
A horror lived about the tarn, and clave
Like its own mists to all the mountain side:
For here two brothers, one a king, had met

40 And fought together; but their names were lost;
And each had slain his brother at a blow;
And down they fell and made the glen abhorr'd:
And there they lay till all their bones were bleach'd,
And lichen'd into color with the crags:
45 And he, that once was king, had on a crown
Of diamonds, one in front, and four aside.
And Arthur came, and laboring up the pass,
All in a misty moonshine, unawares
Had trodden that crown'd skeleton, and the skull
50 Brake from the nape, and from the skull the crown
Roll'd into light, and turning on its rims
Fled like a glittering rivulet to the tarn:
And down the shingly scaur[1] he plunged, and caught,
And set it on his head, and in his heart
55 Heard murmurs. 'Lo, thou likewise shalt be King.'

Thereafter, when a King, he had the gems
Pluck'd from the crown, and show'd them to his knights,
Saying, 'These jewels, whereupon I chanced
Divinely, are the kingdom's, not the King's—
60 For public use: henceforward let there be,
Once every year, a joust for one of these:
For so by nine years' proof we needs must learn
Which is our mightiest, and ourselves shall grow
In use of arms and manhood, till we drive
65 The heathen,[2] who, some say, shall rule the land
Hereafter, which God hinder.' Thus he spoke:
And eight years past, eight jousts had been, and still
Had Lancelot won the diamond of the year,
With purpose to present them to the Queen,
70 When all were won; but meaning all at once
To snare her royal fancy with a boon
Worth half her realm, had never spoken word.

Now for the central diamond and the last
And largest, Arthur, holding then his court
75 Hard on the river nigh the place which now
Is this world's hugest,[3] let proclaim a joust
At Camelot, and when the time drew nigh
Spake (for she had been sick) to Guinevere,
'Are you so sick, my Queen, you cannot move
80 To these fair jousts?' 'Yea, lord,' she said, 'ye know it.'
'Then will ye miss,' he answer'd, 'the great deeds
Of Lancelot, and his prowess in the lists,
A sight ye love to look on.' And the Queen

---

1. *scaur*, rock slope covered with pebbles.
2. *heathen*, Arthur's Christian kingdom was constantly threatened from without by pagan Germans and Norsemen.
3. *place . . . hugest*, London.

Lifted her eyes, and they dwelt languidly
85 On Lancelot, where he stood beside the King.
He thinking that he read her meaning there,
'Stay with me, I am sick; my love is more
Than many diamonds,' yielded; and a heart
Love-loyal to the least wish of the Queen
90 (However much he yearn'd to make complete
The tale of diamonds[4] for his destined boon)
Urged him to speak against the truth, and say,
'Sir King, mine ancient wound is hardly whole,
And lets[5] me from the saddle'; and the King
95 Glanced first at him, then her, and went his way.
No sooner gone than suddenly she began:

'To blame, my lord Sir Lancelot, much to blame!
Why go ye not to these fair jousts? the knights
Are half of them our enemies, and the crowd
100 Will murmur, "Lo the shameless ones, who take
Their pastime now the trustful King is gone!"'
Then Lancelot vext at having lied in vain:
'Are ye so wise? ye were not once so wise,
My Queen, that summer, when ye loved me first.
105 Then of the crowd ye took no more account
Than of the myriad cricket of the mead,
When its own voice clings to each blade of grass,
And every voice is nothing. As to knights,
Them surely can I silence with all ease.
110 But now my loyal worship is allow'd
Of all men: many a bard, without offence,
Has link'd our names together in his lay,
Lancelot, the flower of bravery, Guinevere,
The pearl of beauty: and our knights at feast
115 Have pledged us in this union, while the King
Would listen smiling. How then? is there more?
Has Arthur spoken aught? or would yourself,
Now weary of my service and devoir,[6]
Henceforth be truer to your faultless lord?'

120 She broke into a little scornful laugh:
'Arthur, my lord, Arthur, the faultless King,
That passionate perfection, my good lord—
But who can gaze upon the Sun in heaven?
He never spake word of reproach to me,
125 He never had a glimpse of mine untruth,
He cares not for me: only here to-day
There gleam'd a vague suspicion in his eyes:

---

4. *make complete . . . diamonds.* To his collection of eight diamonds Lancelot would like to add the ninth, and so complete the set
as a present ("boon") for Guinevere.
5. *lets,* keeps.
6. *devoir,* duty.

Some meddling rogue has tamper'd with him—else
Rapt in this fancy of his Table Round,
130 And swearing men to vows impossible,
To make them like himself: but, friend, to me
He is all fault who hath no fault at all:
For who loves me must have a touch of earth;
The low sun makes the color: I am yours,
135 Not Arthur's, as ye know, save by the bond.
And therefore hear my words: go to the jousts:
The tiny-trumpeting gnat can break our dream
When sweetest; and the vermin voices here
May buzz so loud—we scorn them, but they sting.'

140 Then answer'd Lancelot, the chief of knights:
'And with what face, after my pretext made,
Shall I appear, O Queen, at Camelot, I
Before a King who honors his own word,
As if it were his God's?'

                    'Yea,' said the Queen,
145 'A moral child without the craft to rule,
Else had he not lost me: but listen to me,
If I must find you wit: we hear it said
That men go down before your spear at a touch,
But knowing you are Lancelot; your great name,
150 This conquers: hide it therefore; go unknown:
Win! by this kiss you will: and our true King
Will then allow your pretext, O my knight,
As all for glory; for to speak him true,
Ye know right well, how meek soe'er he seem,
155 No keener hunter after glory breathes.
He loves it in his knights more than himself:
They prove to him his work: win and return.'

Then got Sir Lancelot suddenly to horse,
Wroth at himself. Not willing to be known,
160 He left the barren-beaten thoroughfare,
Chose the green path that show'd the rarer foot,
And there among the solitary downs,
Full often lost in fancy, lost his way;
Till as he traced a faintly-shadow'd track,
165 That all in loops and links among the dales
Ran to the Castle of Astolat, he saw
Fired from the west, far on a hill, the towers.
Thither he made, and blew the gateway horn.
Then came an old, dumb, myriad-wrinkled man,
170 Who let him into lodging and disarm'd.
And Lancelot marvell'd at the wordless man;
And issuing found the Lord of Astolat
With two strong sons, Sir Torre and Sir Lavaine,

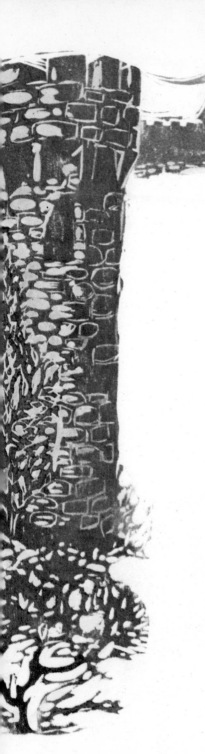

Moving to meet him in the castle court;
175 And close behind them stept the lily maid
Elaine, his daughter: mother of the house
There was not: some light jest among them rose
With laughter dying down as the great knight
Approach'd them: then the Lord of Astolat:
180 'Whence comest thou, my guest, and by what name
Livest between the lips? for by thy state
And presence I might guess thee chief of those,
After the King, who eat in Arthur's halls.
Him have I seen: the rest, his Table Round,
185 Known as they are, to me they are unknown.'

Then answer'd Lancelot, the chief of knights:
'Known am I, and of Arthur's hall, and known,
What I by mere mischance have brought, my shield.
But since I go to joust as one unknown
190 At Camelot for the diamond, ask me not,
Hereafter ye shall know me—and the shield—
I pray you lend me one, if such you have,
Blank, or at least with some device not mine.'

Then said the Lord of Astolat, 'Here is Torre's:
195 Hurt in his first tilt was my son, Sir Torre.
And so, God wot, his shield is blank enough.[7]
His ye can have.' Then added plain Sir Torre,
'Yea, since I cannot use it, ye may have it.'
Here laugh'd the father saying, 'Fie, Sir Churl,
200 Is that an answer for a noble knight?
Allow him! but Lavaine, my younger here,
He is so full of lustihood, he will ride,
Joust for it, and win, and bring it in an hour,
And set it in this damsel's golden hair,
205 To make her thrice as wilful as before.'

'Nay, father, nay, good father, shame me not
Before this noble knight,' said young Lavaine,

---

7. *his shield . . . enough.* Blank shields would be covered ("blazoned") with the symbols of a knight only after he achieved victory in battle.

'For nothing. Surely I but play'd on Torre:
He seem'd so sullen, vext he could not go:
210 A jest, no more! for, knight, the maiden dreamt
That some one put this diamond in her hand,
And that it was too slippery to be held,
And slipt and fell into some pool or stream,
The castle-well, belike; and then I said
215 That *if* I went and *if* I fought and won it
(But all was jest and joke among ourselves)
Then must she keep it safelier. All was jest.
But, father, give me leave, an if he will,
To ride to Camelot with this noble knight:
220 Win shall I not, but do my best to win:
Young as I am, yet would I do my best.'

     'So ye will grace me,' answer'd Lancelot,
Smiling a moment, 'with your fellowship
O'er these waste downs whereon I lost myself,
225 Then were I glad of you as guide and friend:
And you shall win this diamond,—as I hear
It is a fair large diamond,—if ye may,
And yield it to this maiden, if ye will.'
'A fair large diamond,' added plain Sir Torre,
230 'Such be for queens, and not for simple maids.'
Then she, who held her eyes upon the ground,
Elaine, and heard her name so tost about,
 . Flush'd slightly at the slight disparagement
Before the stranger knight, who, looking at her,
235 Full courtly, yet not falsely, thus return'd:
'If what is fair be but for what is fair,
And only queens are to be counted so,
Rash were my judgment then, who deem this maid
Might wear as fair a jewel as is on earth,
240 Not violating the bond of like to like.'

     He spoke and ceased: the lily maid Elaine,
Won by the mellow voice before she look'd,
Lifted her eyes, and read his lineaments.
The great and guilty love he bare the Queen,
245 In battle with the love he bare his lord,[8]
Had marr'd his face, and mark'd it ere his time.
Another sinning on such heights with one,
The flower of all the west and all the world,
Had been the sleeker for it: but in him
250 His mood was often like a fiend, and rose
And drove him into wastes and solitudes
For agony, who was yet a living soul.
Marr'd as he was, he seem'd the goodliest man

---

8. *his lord*, King Arthur.

That ever among ladies ate in hall,
255 And noblest, when she lifted up her eyes.
However marr'd, of more than twice her years,
Seam'd with an ancient swordcut on the cheek,
An bruised and bronzed, she lifted up her eyes
And loved him, with that love which was her doom.

260   Then the great knight, the darling of the court,
Loved of the loveliest, into that rude hall
Stept with all grace, and not with half disdain
Hid under grace, as in a smaller time,
But kindly man moving among his kind:
265 Whom they with meats and vintage of their best[9]
And talk and minstrel melody entertain'd.
And much they ask'd of court and Table Round,
And ever well and readily answer'd he:
But Lancelot, when they glanced at Guinevere,
270 Suddenly speaking of the wordless man,
Heard from the Baron that, ten years before,
The heathen caught and reft him of his tongue.
'He learnt and warn'd me of their fierce design
Against my house, and him they caught and maim'd;
275 But I, my sons, and little daughter fled
From bonds or death, and dwelt among the woods
By the great river in a boatman's hut.
Dull days were those, till our good Arthur broke
The Pagan yet once more on Badon hill.'

280   'O there, great lord, doubtless,' Lavaine said, rapt
By all the sweet and sudden passion of youth
Toward greatness in its elder, 'you have fought.
O tell us—for we live apart—you know
Of Arthur's glorious wars.' And Lancelot spoke
285 And answer'd him at full, as having been
With Arthur in the fight which all day long
Rang by the white mouth of the violent Glem;
And in the four loud battles by the shore
Of Duglas; that on Bassa; then the war
290 That thunder'd in and out the gloomy skirts
Of Celidon the forest; and again
By Castle Gurnion, where the glorious King
Had on his cuirass worn our Lady's Head,[10]
Carv'd of one emerald centr'd in a sun
295 Of silver rays, that lighten'd as he breathed;
And at Caerleon had he help'd his lord,
When the strong neighings of the wild white Horse[11]

9. *best*, wines.
10. *our Lady's Head*, an image of the Virgin Mary carved on a gem and set in Arthur's breastplate.
11. *wild white Horse*. One band of German invaders chose a white horse for their emblem.

Set every gilded parapet shuddering;
And up in Agned-Cathregonion too,
300 And down the waste sand-shores of Trath Treroit,
Where many a heathen fell; 'and on the mount
Of Badon I myself beheld the King
Charge at the head of all his Table Round,
And all his legions crying Christ and him,
305 And brake them; and I saw him, after, stand
High on a heap of slain, from spur to plume
Red as the rising sun with heathen blood,
And seeing me, with a great voice he cried,
"They are broken, they are broken!" for the King,
310 However mild he seems at home, nor cares
For triumph in our mimic wars, the jousts—
For if his own knight cast him down, he laughs
Saying, his knights are better men than he—
Yet in this heathen war the fire of God
315 Fills him: I never saw his like: there lives
No greater leader.'

                    While he utter'd this,
Low to her own heart said the lily maid,
'Save your great self, fair lord'; and when he fell
From talk of war to traits of pleasantry—
320 Being mirthful he, but in a stately kind—
She still took note that when the living smile
Died from his lips, across him came a cloud
Of melancholy severe, from which again,
Whenever in her hovering to and fro
325 The lily maid had striven to make him cheer,
There brake a sudden-beaming tenderness
Of manners and of nature: and she thought
That all was nature, all, perchance, for her.
And all night long his face before her lived,
330 As when a painter, poring on a face,
Divinely thro' all hindrance finds the man
Behind it, and so paints him that his face,
The shape and color of a mind and life,
Lives for his children, ever at its best
335 And fullest; so the face before her lived,
Dark-splendid, speaking in the silence, full
Of noble things, and held her from her sleep.
Till rathe[12] she rose, half-cheated in the thought
She needs must bid farewell to sweet Lavaine.
340 First as in fear, step after step, she stole
Down the long tower-stairs, hesitating:
Anon, she heard Sir Lancelot cry in the court,
'This shield, my friend, where is it?' and Lavaine

---

12. *rathe*, early.

Past inward, as she came from out the tower.
345 There to his proud horse Lancelot turn'd, and smooth'd
The glossy shoulder, humming to himself.
Half-envious of the flattering hand, she drew
Nearer and stood. He look'd, and more amazed
Than if seven men had set upon him, saw
350 The maiden standing in the dewy light.
He had not dream'd she was so beautiful.
Then came on him a sort of sacred fear,
For silent, tho' he greeted her, she stood
Rapt on his face as if it were a god's.
355 Suddenly flash'd on her a wild desire,
That he should wear her favor at the tilt.[13]
She braved a riotous heart in asking for it.
'Fair lord, whose name I know not—noble it is,
I well believe, the noblest—will you wear
360 My favor at this tourney?' 'Nay,' said he,
'Fair lady, since I never yet have worn
Favor of any lady in the lists.
Such is my wont, as those, who know me, know.'
'Yea, so,' she answer'd; 'then in wearing mine
365 Needs must be lesser likelihood, noble lord,
That those who know should know you.' And he turn'd
Her counsel up and down within his mind,
And found it true, and answer'd, 'True, my child.
Well, I will wear it: fetch it out to me:
370 What is it?' and she told him 'A red sleeve
Broider'd with pearls,' and brought it: then he bound
Her token on his helmet, with a smile
Saying, 'I never yet have done so much
For any maiden living,' and the blood
375 Sprang to her face and fill'd her with delight;
But left her all the paler, when Lavaine
Returning brought the yet-unblazon'd shield,[14]
His brother's; which he gave to Lancelot,
Who parted with his own to fair Elaine:
380 'Do me this grace, my child, to have my shield
In keeping till I come.' 'A grace to me,'
She answer'd, 'twice to-day. I am your squire!'
Whereat Lavaine said, laughing, 'Lily maid,
For fear our people call you lily maid
385 In earnest, let me bring your color back;
Once, twice, and thrice: now get you hence to bed':
So kiss'd her, and Sir Lancelot his own hand,
And thus they moved away: she stay'd a minute,
Then made a sudden step to the gate, and there—

---

13. *That he . . . tilt.* At medieval tournaments knights frequently
carried a symbolic garment ("favor") to indicate they fought for
the glory of a particular woman.
14. *yet unblazon'd shield,* that is, blank.

390 Her bright hair blown about the serious face
Yet rosy-kindled with her brother's kiss—
Paused by the gateway, standing near the shield
In silence, while she watch'd their arms far-off
Sparkle, until they dipt below the downs.
395 Then to her tower she climb'd, and took the shield,
There kept it, and so lived in fantasy.

Meanwhile the new companions past away
Far o'er the long backs of the bushless downs,
To where Sir Lancelot knew there lived a knight
400 Not far from Camelot, now for forty years
A hermit, who had pray'd, labor'd and pray'd,
And ever laboring had scoop'd himself
In the white rock a chapel and a hall
On massive columns, like a shorecliff cave,
405 And cells and chambers: all were fair and dry;
The green light from the meadows underneath
Struck up and lived along the milky roofs;
And in the meadows tremulous aspen-trees
And poplars made a noise of falling showers.
410 And thither wending there that night they bode.

But when the next day broke from underground,
And shot red fire and shadows thro' the cave,
They rose, heard mass, broke fast, and rode away:
Then Lancelot saying, 'Hear, but hold my name
415 Hidden, you ride with Lancelot of the Lake,'
Abash'd Lavaine, whose instant reverence,
Dearer to true young hearts than their own praise,
But left him leave to stammer, 'Is it indeed?'
And after muttering 'The great Lancelot,'
420 At last he got his breath and answer'd, 'One,
One have I seen—that other, our liege lord,
The dread Pendragon, Britain's King of kings,
Of whom the people talk mysteriously,
He will be there—then were I stricken blind
425 That minute, I might say that I had seen.'

So spake Lavaine, and when they reach'd the lists
By Camelot in the meadow, let his eyes
Run thro' the peopled gallery which half round
Lay like a rainbow fall'n upon the grass,
430 Until they found the clear-faced King, who sat
Robed in red samite,[15] easily to be known,
Since to his crown the golden dragon clung,[16]

---

15. *samite,* a heavy silk cloth.
16. *to his crown . . . clung.* Both Arthur and his father took the name "Pendragon" which literally means "dragon's head" but figuratively means "chief war leader." Thus the dragon is Arthur's symbol.

And down his robe the dragon writhed in gold,
And from the carven-work behind him crept
435 Two dragons gilded, sloping down to make
Arms for his chair, while all the rest of them
Thro' knots and loops and folds innumerable
Fled ever thro' the woodwork, till they found
The new design wherein they lost themselves,
440 Yet with all ease, so tender was the work:
And, in the costly canopy o'er him set,
Blazed the last diamond of the nameless king.[17]

    Then Lancelot answer'd young Lavaine and said,
'Me you call great: mine is the firmer seat,
445 The truer lance: but there is many a youth
Now crescent, who will come to all I am
And overcome it; and in me there dwells
No greatness, save it be some far-off touch
Of greatness to know well I am not great:
450 There is the man.' And Lavaine gaped upon him
As on a thing miraculous, and anon
The trumpets blew; and then did either side,
They that assail'd, and they that held the lists,
Set lance in rest, strike spur, suddenly move,
455 Meet in the midst, and there so furiously
Shock, that a man far-off might well perceive,
If any man that day were left afield,
The hard earth shake, and a low thunder of arms.
And Lancelot bode a little, till he saw
460 Which were the weaker; then he hurl'd into it
Against the stronger: little need to speak
Of Lancelot in his glory! King, duke, earl,
Count, baron—whom he smote, he overthrew.

    But in the field were Lancelot's kith and kin,
465 Ranged with the Table Round that held the lists,
Strong men, and wrathful that a stranger knight
Should do and almost overdo the deeds
Of Lancelot; and one said to the other, 'Lo!
What is he? I do not mean the force alone—
470 The grace and versatility of the man!
Is it not Lancelot?' 'When has Lancelot worn
Favor of any lady in the lists?
Not such his wont, as we, that know him, know.'
'How then? who then?' a fury seized them all,
475 A fiery family passion for the name
Of Lancelot, and a glory one with theirs.
They couch'd their spears and prick'd their steeds, and thus,
Their plumes driv'n backward by the wind they made

17. *Blazed . . . king.* Recall lines 34–66.

In moving, all together down upon him
480 Bare, as a wild wave in the wide North-sea,
Green-glimmering toward the summit, bears, with all
Its stormy crests that smoke against the skies,
Down on a bark, and overbears the bark,
And him that helms it, so they overbore
485 Sir Lancelot and his charger, and a spear
Down-glancing lamed the charger, and a spear
Prick'd sharply his own cuirass, and the head
Pierced thro' his side, and there snapt, and remain'd.

Then Sir Lavaine did well and worshipfully;
490 He bore a knight of old repute to the earth,
And brought his horse to Lancelot where he lay.
He up the side, sweating with agony, got,
But thought to do while he might yet endure,
And being lustily holpen by the rest,
495 His party,—tho' it seem'd half-miracle
To those he fought with,—drave his kith and kin,
And all the Table Round that held the lists,
Back to the barrier; then the trumpets blew
Proclaiming his the prize, who wore the sleeve
500 Of scarlet, and the pearls; and all the knights,
His party, cried, 'Advance and take thy prize
The diamond'; but he answer'd, 'Diamond me
No diamonds! for God's love, a little air!
Prize me no prizes, for my prize is death!
505 Hence will I, and I charge you, follow me not.'

He spoke, and vanish'd suddenly from the field
With young Lavaine into the poplar grove.
There from his charger down he slid, and sat,
Gasping to Sir Lavaine, 'Draw the lance-head':
510 'Ah my sweet lord Sir Lancelot,' said Lavaine,
'I dread me, if I draw it, you will die.'
But he, 'I die already with it: draw—
Draw,'—and Lavaine drew, and Sir Lancelot gave
A marvellous great shriek and ghastly groan,
515 And half his blood burst forth, and down he sank
For the pure pain, and wholly swoon'd away.
Then came the hermit out and bare him in,
There stanch'd his wound; and there, in daily doubt
Whether to live or die, for many a week
520 Hid from the wide world's rumor by the grove
Of poplars with their noise of falling showers,
And ever-tremulous aspen-trees, he lay.

But on that day when Lancelot fled the lists,
His party, knights of utmost North and West,
525 Lords of waste marches, kings of desolate isles,

Came round their great Pendragon, saying to him,
'Lo, Sire, our knight, thro' whom we won the day,
Hath gone sore wounded, and hath left his prize
Untaken, crying that his prize is death.'
530 'Heaven hinder,' said the King, 'that such an one,
So great a knight as we have seen to-day—
He seem'd to me another Lancelot—
Yea, twenty times I thought him Lancelot—
He must not pass uncared for. Wherefore, rise,
535 O Gawain, and ride forth and find the knight.
Wounded and wearied needs must he be near.
I charge you that you get at once to horse.
And, knights and kings, there breathes not one of you
Will deem this prize of ours is rashly given:
540 His prowess was too wondrous. We will do him
No customary honor: since the knight
Came not to us, of us to claim the prize,
Ourselves will send it after. Rise and take
This diamond, and deliver it, and return,
545 And bring us where he is, and how he fares,
And cease not from your quest until ye find.'

      So saying, from the carven flower above,
To which it made a restless heart, he took,
And gave, the diamond: then from where he sat
550 At Arthur's right, with smiling face arose,
With smiling face and frowning heart, a Prince
In the mid might and flourish of his May,
Gawain, surnamed The Courteous, fair and strong,
And after Lancelot, Tristram, and Geraint
555 And Gareth, a good knight, but therewithal
Sir Modred's brother, and the child of Lot,[18]
Nor often loyal to his word, and now
Wroth that the King's command to sally forth
In quest of whom he knew not, made him leave
560 The banquet, and concourse of knights and kings.

      So all in wrath he got to horse and went;
While Arthur to the banquet, dark in mood,
Past, thinking, 'Is it Lancelot who hath come
Despite the wound he spake of, all for gain
565 Of glory, and hath added wound to wound,
And ridd'n away to die?' So fear'd the King,
And, after two days' tarriance there, return'd.
Then when he saw the Queen, embracing ask'd,
'Love, are you yet so sick?' 'Nay, lord,' she said.

---

18. *Lot,* one of the old kings who fought Arthur's rise to power.
His son Modred, at the time of this tale, is already plotting to
overthrow Arthur's rule. Gawain comes from this family.

570 'And where is Lancelot?' Then the Queen amazed,
'Was he not with you? won he not your prize?'
'Nay, but one like him.' 'Why that like was he.'
And when the King demanded how she knew,
Said, 'Lord, no sooner had ye parted from us,
575 Than Lancelot told me of a common talk
That men went down before his spear at a touch,
But knowing he was Lancelot; his great name
Conquer'd; and therefore would he hide his name
From all men, ev'n the King, and to this end
580 Had made the pretext of a hindering wound,
That he might joust unknown of all, and learn
If his old prowess were in aught decay'd;
And added, "Our true Arthur, when he learns,
Will well allow my pretext, as for gain
585 Of purer glory."'

        Then replied the King:
'Far lovelier in our Lancelot had it been,
In lieu of idly dallying with the truth,
To have trusted me as he hath trusted thee.
Surely his King and most familiar friend
590 Might well have kept his secret. True, indeed,
Albeit I know my knights fantastical,
So fine a fear in our large Lancelot
Must needs have moved my laughter: now remains
But little cause for laughter: his own kin—
595 Ill news, my Queen, for all who love him, this!—
His kith and kin, not knowing, set upon him;
So that he went sore wounded from the field:
Yet good news too: for goodly hopes are mine
That Lancelot is no more a lonely heart.
600 He wore, against his wont, upon his helm
A sleeve of scarlet, broider'd with great pearls,
Some gentle maiden's gift.'

        'Yea, lord,' she said,
'Thy hopes are mine,' and saying that, she choked,
And sharply turn'd about to hide her face,
605 Past to her chamber, and there flung herself
Down on the great King's couch, and writhed upon it,
And clench'd her fingers till they bit the palm,
And shriek'd out 'Traitor' to the unhearing wall,
Then flash'd into wild tears, and rose again,
610 And moved about her palace, proud and pale.

    Gawain the while thro' all the region round
Rode with his diamond, wearied of the quest,
Touch'd at all points, except the poplar grove.
And came at last, tho' late, to Astolat:

615 Whom glittering in enamell'd arms the maid
Glanced at, and cried, 'What news from Camelot, lord?
What of the knight with the red sleeve?' 'He won.'
'I knew it,' she said. 'But parted from the jousts
Hurt in the side,' whereat she caught her breath;
620 Thro' her own side she felt the sharp lance go;
Thereon she smote her hand: wellnigh she swoon'd:
And, while he gazed wonderingly at her, came
The Lord of Astolat out, to whom the Prince
Reported who he was, and on what quest
625 Sent, that he bore the prize and could not find
The victor, but had ridd'n a random round
To seek him, and had wearied of the search.
To whom the Lord of Astolat, 'Bide with us,
And ride no more at random, noble Prince!
630 Here was the knight, and here he left a shield;
This will he send or come for: furthermore
Our son is with him; we shall hear anon,
Needs must we hear.' To this the courteous Prince
Accorded with his wonted courtesy,
635 Courtesy with a touch of traitor in it,
And stay'd; and cast his eyes on fair Elaine:
Where could be found face daintier? then her shape
From forehead down to foot, perfect—again
From foot to forehead exquisitely turn'd:
640 'Well—if I bide, lo! this wild flower for me!'
And oft they met among the garden yews,
And there he set himself to play upon her
With sallying wit, free flashes from a height
Above her, graces of the court, and songs,
645 Sighs, and slow smiles, and golden eloquence
And amorous adulation, till the maid
Rebell'd against it, saying to him, 'Prince,
O loyal nephew of our noble King,
Why ask you not to see the shield he left,
650 Whence you might learn his name? Why slight your King,
And lose the quest he sent you on, and prove
No surer than our falcon yesterday,
Who lost the hern we slipt her at, and went
To all the winds?'[19] 'Nay, by mine head,' said he,
655 'I lose it, as we lose the lark in heaven,
O damsel, in the light of your blue eyes;
But an ye will it let me see the shield.'
And when the shield was brought, and Gawain saw
Sir Lancelot's azure lions, crown'd with gold,
660 Ramp in the field,[20] he smote his thigh, and mock'd:

19. *No surer . . . winds?* Medieval aristocrats trained falcons to snatch other birds in their talons while in mid-flight, and bring them back to their masters. Gawain, in failing to find Lancelot, is like a falcon which misses its prey.
20. *azure lions . . . field,* the symbolic images on the shield.

'Right was the King! our Lancelot! that true man!'
'And right was I,' she answer'd merrily, 'I,
Who dream'd my knight the greatest knight of all.'
'And if I dream'd,' said Gawain, 'that you love
665 This greatest knight, your pardon! lo, ye know it!
Speak therefore: shall I waste myself in vain?'
Full simple was her answer, 'What know I?
My brethren have been all my fellowship;
And I, when often they have talk'd of love,
670 Wish'd it had been my mother, for they talk'd,
Meseem'd, of what they knew not; so myself—
I know not if I know what true love is,
But if I know, then, if I love not him,
I know there is none other I can love.'
675 'Yea, by God's death,' said he, 'ye love him well,
But would not, knew ye what all others know,
And whom he loves.' 'So be it,' cried Elaine,
And lifted her fair face and moved away:
But he pursued her, calling, 'Stay a little!
680 One golden minute's grace! he wore your sleeve:
Would he break faith with one I may not name?
Must our true man change like a leaf at last?
Nay—like enow: why then, far be it from me
To cross our mighty Lancelot in his loves!
685 And, damsel, for I deem you know full well
Where your great knight is hidden, let me leave
My quest with you; the diamond also; here!
For if you love, it will be sweet to give it;
And if he love, it will be sweet to have it
690 From your own hand; and whether he love or not,
A diamond is a diamond. Fare you well
A thousand times!—a thousand times farewell!
Yet, if he love, and his love hold, we two
May meet at court hereafter: there, I think,
695 So ye will learn the courtesies of the court,
We two shall know each other.'

                    Then he gave,
And slightly kiss'd the hand to which he gave,
The diamond, and all wearied of the quest
Leapt on his horse, and carolling as he went
700 A true-love ballad, lightly rode away.

    Thence to the court he past; there told the King
What the King knew, 'Sir Lancelot is the knight.'
And added, 'Sir, my liege, so much I learnt;
But fail'd to find him, tho' I rode all round
705 The region: but I lighted on the maid
Whose sleeve he wore; she loves him; and to her,
Deeming our courtesy is the truest law,

I gave the diamond: she will render it;
For by mine head she knows his hiding-place.'

710   The seldom-frowning King frown'd, and replied,
'Too courteous truly! ye shall go no more
On quest of mine, seeing that ye forget
Obedience is the courtesy due to kings.'

    He spake and parted. Wroth, but all in awe,
715 For twenty strokes of the blood, without a word,
Linger'd that other, staring after him;
Then shook his hair, strode off, and buzz'd abroad
About the maid of Astolat, and her love.
All ears were prick'd at once, all tongues were loosed:
720 'The maid of Astolat loves Sir Lancelot,
Sir Lancelot loves the maid of Astolat.'
Some read the King's face, some the Queen's, and all
Had marvel what the maid might be, but most
Predoom'd her as unworthy. One old dame
725 Came suddenly on the Queen with the sharp news.
She, that had heard the noise of it before,
But sorrowing Lancelot should have stoop'd so low,
Marr'd her friend's aim with pale tranquillity.
So ran the tale like fire about the court,
730 Fire in dry stubble a nine-days' wonder flared:
Till ev'n the knights at banquet twice or thrice
Forgot to drink to Lancelot and the Queen,
And pledging Lancelot and the lily maid
Smiled at each other, while the Queen, who sat
735 With lips severely placid, felt the knot
Climb in her throat, and with her feet unseen
Crush'd the wild passion out against the floor
Beneath the banquet, where the meats became
As wormwood, and she hated all who pledged.

740   But far away the maid in Astolat,
Her guiltless rival, she that ever kept
The one-day-seen Sir Lancelot in her heart,
Crept to her father, while he mused alone,
Sat on his knee, stroked his gray face and said,
745 'Father, you call me wilful, and the fault
Is yours who let me have my will, and now,
Sweet father, will you let me lose my wits?'
'Nay,' said he, 'surely.' 'Wherefore, let me hence,'
She answer'd, 'and find out our dear Lavaine.'
750 'Ye will not lose your wits for dear Lavaine:
Bide,' answer'd he: 'we needs must hear anon
Of him, and of that other.' 'Ay,' she said,
'And of that other, for I needs must hence
And find that other, wheresoe'er he be,

755 And with mine own hand give his diamond to him,
Lest I be found as faithless in the quest
As yon proud Prince who left the quest to me.
Sweet father, I behold him in my dreams
Gaunt as it were the skeleton of himself,
760 Death-pale, for lack of gentle maiden's aid.
The gentler-born the maiden, the more bound,
My father, to be sweet and serviceable
To noble knights in sickness, as ye know
When these have worn their tokens: let me hence
765 I pray you.' Then her father nodding said,
'Ay, ay, the diamond: wit ye well, my child,
Right fain were I to learn this knight were whole,
Being our greatest: yea, and you must give it—
And sure I think this fruit is hung too high
770 For any mouth to gape for save a queen's—
Nay, I mean nothing: so then, get you gone,
Being so very wilful you must go.'

Lightly, her suit allow'd, she slipt away,
And while she made her ready for her ride,
775 Her father's latest word humm'd in her ear,
'Being so very wilful you must go,'
And changed itself and echo'd in her heart,
'Being so very wilful you must die.'
But she was happy enough and shook it off,
780 As we shake off the bee that buzzes at us;
And in her heart she answer'd it and said,
'What matter, so I help him back to life?'
Then far away with good Sir Torre for guide
Rode o'er the long backs of the bushless downs
785 To Camelot, and before the city-gates
Came on her brother with a happy face
Making a roan horse caper and curvet
For pleasure all about a field of flowers:
Whom when she saw, 'Lavaine,' she cried, 'Lavaine,
790 How fares my lord Sir Lancelot?' He amazed,
'Torre and Elaine! why here? Sir Lancelot!
How know ye my lord's name is Lancelot?'
But when the maid had told him all her tale,
Then turn'd Sir Torre, and being in his moods
795 Left them, and under the strange-statued gate,
Where Arthur's wars were render'd mystically,
Past up the still rich city to his kin,
His own far blood,[21] which dwelt at Camelot;
And her, Lavaine across the poplar grove
800 Led to the caves: there first she saw the casque
Of Lancelot on the wall: her scarlet sleeve,

---

21. *far blood,* distant relations.

Tho' carved and cut, and half the pearls away,
Stream'd from it still; and in her heart she laugh'd,
Because he had not loosed it from his helm,
805 But meant once more perchance to tourney in it.
And when they gain'd the cell wherein he slept,
His battle-writhen arms and mighty hands
Lay naked on the wolfskin, and a dream
Of dragging down his enemy made them move.
810 Then she that saw him lying unsleek, unshorn,
Gaunt as it were the skeleton of himself,
Utter'd a little tender dolorous cry.
The sound not wonted in a place so still
Woke the sick knight, and while he roll'd his eyes
815 Yet blank from sleep, she started to him, saying,
'Your prize the diamond sent you by the King':
His eyes glisten'd: she fancied 'Is it for me?'
And when the maid had told him all the tale
Of King and Prince, the diamond sent, the quest
820 Assign'd to her not worthy of it, she knelt
Full lowly by the corners of his bed,
And laid the diamond in his open hand.
Her face was near, and as we kiss the child
That does the task assign'd, he kiss'd her face.
825 At once she slipt like water to the floor.
'Alas,' he said, 'your ride hath wearied you.
Rest must you have.' 'No rest for me,' she said;
'Nay, for near you, fair lord, I am at rest.'
What might she mean by that? his large black eyes,
830 Yet larger thro' his leanness, dwelt upon her,
Till all her heart's sad secret blazed itself
In the heart's colors on her simple face;
And Lancelot look'd and was perplext in mind,
And being weak in body said no more;
835 But did not love the color; woman's love,
Save one, he not regarded, and so turn'd
Sighing, and feign'd a sleep until he slept.

Then rose Elaine and glided thro' the fields,
And past beneath the weirdly-sculptured gates
840 Far up the dim rich city to her kin;
There bode the night: but woke with dawn, and past
Down thro' the dim rich city to the fields,
Thence to the cave: so day by day she past
In either twilight ghost-like to and fro
845 Gliding, and every day she tended him.
And likewise many a night: and Lancelot
Would, tho' he call'd his wound a little hurt
Whereof he should be quickly whole, at times
Brain-feverous in his heat and agony, seem
850 Uncourteous, even he: but the meek maid

Sweetly forbore him ever, being to him
Meeker than any child to a rough nurse,
Milder than any mother to a sick child,
And never woman yet, since man's first fall,
855 Did kindlier unto man, but her deep love
Upbore her; till the hermit, skill'd in all
The simples and the science of that time,
Told him that her fine care had saved his life.
And the sick man forgot her simple blush,
860 Would call her friend and sister, sweet Elaine,
Would listen for her coming and regret
Her parting step, and held her tenderly,
And loved her with all love except the love
Of man and woman when they love their best,
865 Closest and sweetest, and had died the death
In any knightly fashion for her sake.
And peradventure had he seen her first
She might have made this and that other world
Another world for the sick man; but now
870 The shackles of an old love straiten'd him,
His honor rooted in dishonor stood,
And faith unfaithful kept him falsely true.[22]

Yet the great knight in his mid-sickness made
Full many a holy vow and pure resolve.
875 These, as but born of sickness, could not live:
For when the blood ran lustier in him again,
Full often the bright image of one face,
Making a treacherous quiet in his heart,
Dispersed his resolution like a cloud.

---

22. *faith . . . true.* He must continue his immoral love for Guinevere.

880 Then if the maiden, while that ghostly grace
Beam'd on his fancy, spoke, he answer'd not,
Or short and coldly, and she knew right well
What the rough sickness meant, but what this meant
She knew not, and the sorrow dimm'd her sight,
885 And drave her ere her time across the fields
Far into the rich city, where alone
She murmur'd, 'Vain, in vain: it cannot be.
He will not love me: how then? must I die?'
Then as a little helpless innocent bird,
890 That has but one plain passage of few notes,
Will sing the simple passage o'er and o'er
For all an April morning, till the ear
Wearies to hear it, so the simple maid
Went half the night repeating, 'Must I die?'
895 And now to right she turn'd, and now to left,
And found no ease in turning or in rest;
And 'Him or death,' she mutter'd, 'death or him,'
Again and like a burthen,[23] 'Him or death.'

    But when Sir Lancelot's deadly hurt was whole,
900 To Astolat returning rode the three.
There morn by morn, arraying her sweet self
In that wherein she deem'd she look'd her best,
She came before Sir Lancelot, for she thought
'If I be loved, these are my festal robes,
905 If not, the victim's flowers before he fall.'
And Lancelot ever prest upon the maid
That she should ask some goodly gift of him
For her own self or hers; 'and do not shun
To speak the wish most near to your true heart;
910 Such service have ye done me, that I make
My will of yours, and Prince and Lord am I
In mine own land, and what I will I can.'
Then like a ghost she lifted up her face,
But like a ghost without the power to speak.
915 And Lancelot saw that she withheld her wish,
And bode among them yet a little space
Till he should learn it; and one morn it chanced
He found her in among the garden yews,
And said, 'Delay no longer, speak your wish,
920 Seeing I go to-day': then out she brake:
'Going? and we shall never see you more.
And I must die for want of one bold word.'
'Speak: that I live to hear,' he said, 'is yours.'
Then suddenly and passionately she spoke:
925 'I have gone mad. I love you: let me die.'
'Ah, sister,' answer'd Lancelot, 'what is this?'

---

23. *burthen,* chorus, or refrain, of a song.

And innocently extending her white arms,
'Your love,' she said, 'your love—to be your wife.'
And Lancelot answer'd, 'Had I chosen to wed,
930 I had been wedded earlier, sweet Elaine:
But now there never will be wife of mine.'
'No, no,' she cried, 'I care not to be wife,
But to be with you still, to see your face,
To serve you, and to follow you thro' the world.'
935 And Lancelot answer'd, 'Nay, the world, the world,
All ear and eye, with such a stupid heart
To interpret ear and eye, and such a tongue
To blare its own interpretation—nay,
Full ill then should I quit your brother's love,
940 And your good father's kindness.' And she said,
'Not to be with you, not to see your face—
Alas for me then, my good days are done.'
'Nay, noble maid,' he answer'd, 'ten times nay!
This is not love: but love's first flash in youth,
945 Most common: yea, I know it of mine own self:
And you yourself will smile at your own self
Hereafter, when you yield your flower of life
To one more fitly yours, not thrice your age:
And then will I, for true you are and sweet
950 Beyond mine old belief in womanhood,
More specially should your good knight be poor,
Endow you with broad land and territory
Even to the half my realm beyond the seas,
So that would make you happy: furthermore,
955 Ev'n to the death, as tho' ye were my blood,
In all your quarrels will I be your knight.
This will I do, dear damsel, for your sake,
And more than this I cannot.'

                              While he spoke
She neither blush'd nor shook, but deathly-pale
960 Stood grasping what was nearest, then replied:
'Of all this will I nothing'; and so fell,
And thus they bore her swooning to her tower.

      Then spake, to whom thro' those black walls of yew
Their talk had pierced, her father: 'Ay, a flash,
965 I fear me, that will strike my blossom dead.
Too courteous are ye, fair Lord Lancelot.
I pray you, use some rough discourtesy
To blunt or break her passion.'

                              Lancelot said,
'That were against me: what I can I will';
970 And there that day remain'd, and toward even
Sent for his shield: full meekly rose the maid,

Stript off the case, and gave the naked shield;
Then, when she heard his horse upon the stones,
Unclasping flung the casement back, and look'd
975 Down on his helm, from which her sleeve had gone.
And Lancelot knew the little clinking sound;
And she by tact of love was well aware
That Lancelot knew that she was looking at him.
And yet he glanced not up, nor waved his hand,
980 Nor bade farewell, but sadly rode away.
This was the one discourtesy that he used.

So in her tower alone the maiden sat:
His very shield was gone; only the case,
Her own poor work, her empty labor, left.
985 But still she heard him, still his picture form'd
And grew between her and the pictured wall.
Then came her father, saying in low tones,
'Have comfort,' whom she greeted quietly.
Then came her brethren saying, 'Peace to thee,
990 Sweet sister,' whom she answer'd with all calm.
But when they left her to herself again,
Death, like a friend's voice from a distant field
Approaching thro' the darkness, call'd; the owls
Wailing had power upon her, and she mixt
995 Her fancies with the sallow-rifted glooms
Of evening, and the moanings of the wind.

And in those days she made a little song,
And call'd her song 'The Song of Love and Death,'
And sang it: sweetly could she make and sing.

1000   'Sweet is true love tho' given in vain, in vain;
And sweet is death who puts an end to pain:
I know not which is sweeter, no, not I.

'Love, art thou sweet? then bitter death must be:
Love, thou art bitter; sweet is death to me.
1005 O Love, if death be sweeter, let me die.

'Sweet love, that seems not made to fade away,
Sweet death, that seems to make us loveless clay,
I know not which is sweeter, no, not I.

'I fain would follow love, if that could be;
1010 I needs must follow death, who calls for me;
Call and I follow, I follow! let me die.'

High with the last line scaled her voice, and this,
All in a fiery dawning wild with wind
That shook her tower, the brothers heard, and thought

1015 With shuddering, 'Hark the Phantom of the house
That ever shrieks before a death,' and call'd
The father, and all three in hurry and fear
Ran to her, and lo! the blood-red light of dawn
Flared on her face, she shrilling, 'Let me die!'

1020   And when we dwell upon a word we know,
Repeating, till the word we know so well
Becomes a wonder, and we know not why,
So dwelt the father on her face, and thought
'Is this Elaine?' till back the maiden fell,
1025 Then gave a languid hand to each, and lay,
Speaking a still good-morrow with her eyes.
At last she said, 'Sweet brothers, yesternight
I seem'd a curious little maid again,
As happy as when we dwelt among the woods,
1030 And when ye used to take me with the flood
Up the great river in the boatman's boat.
Only ye would not pass beyond the cape
That has the poplar on it: there ye fixt
Your limit, oft returning with the tide.
1035 And yet I cried because ye would not pass
Beyond it, and far up the shining flood
Until we found the palace of the King.
And yet ye would not; but this night I dream'd
That I was all alone upon the flood,
1040 And then I said, "Now shall I have my will":
And there I woke, but still the wish remain'd.
So let me hence that I may pass at last
Beyond the poplar and far up the flood,
Until I find the palace of the King.
1045 There will I enter in among them all,
And no man there will dare to mock at me;
But there the fine Gawain will wonder at me,
And there the great Sir Lancelot muse at me;
Gawain, who bade a thousand farewells to me,
1050 Lancelot, who coldly went, nor bade me one:
And there the King will know me and my love,
And there the Queen herself will pity me,
And all the gentle court will welcome me,
And after my long voyage I shall rest!'

1055   'Peace,' said her father, 'O my child, ye seem
Light-headed, for what force is yours to go
So far, being sick? and wherefore would ye look
On this proud fellow again, who scorns us all?'

Then the rough Torre began to heave and move,
1060 And bluster into stormy sobs and say,
'I never loved him: an I meet with him,

I care not howsoever great he be,
Then will I strike at him and strike him down,
Give me good fortune, I will strike him dead,
1065 For this discomfort he hath done the house.'

To whom the gentle sister made reply,
'Fret not yourself, dear brother, nor be wroth,
Seeing it is no more Sir Lancelot's fault
Not to love me, than it is mine to love
1070 Him of all men who seems to me the highest.'

'Highest?' the father answer'd, echoing 'highest?'
(He meant to break the passion in her) 'nay,
Daughter, I know not what you call the highest;
But this I know, for all the people know it,
1075 He loves the Queen, and in an open shame:
And she returns his love in open shame;
If this be high, what is it to be low?'

Then spake the lily maid of Astolat:
'Sweet father, all too faint and sick am I
1080 For anger: these are slanders: never yet
Was noble man but made ignoble talk.
He makes no friend who never made a foe.
But now it is my glory to have loved
One peerless, without stain: so let me pass,
1085 My father, howsoe'er I seem to you,
Not all unhappy, having loved God's best
And greatest, tho' my love had no return:
Yet, seeing you desire your child to live,
Thanks, but you work against your own desire;
1090 For if I could believe the things you say
I should but die the sooner; wherefore cease,
Sweet father, and bid call the ghostly man[24]
Hither, and let me shrive me clean,[25] and die.'

So when the ghostly man had come and gone,
1095 She with a face, bright as for sin forgiven,
Besought Lavaine to write as she devised
A letter, word for word; and when he ask'd
'Is it for Lancelot, is it for my dear lord?
Then will I bear it gladly'; she replied,
1100 'For Lancelot and the Queen and all the world,
But I myself must bear it.' Then he wrote
The letter she devised; which being writ
And folded, 'O sweet father, tender and true,
Deny me not,' she said—'ye never yet

---

24. *ghostly man,* a priest, one who has the divine spirit of the Holy Ghost.
25. *shrive me clean,* listen to her sins and absolve her through the ritual of Penance.

1105 Denied my fancies—this, however strange,
My latest: lay the letter in my hand
A little ere I die, and close the hand
Upon it; I shall guard it even in death.
And when the heat has gone from out my heart,
1110 Then take the little bed on which I died
For Lancelot's love, and deck it like the Queen's
For richness, and me also like the Queen
In all I have of rich, and lay me on it.
And let there be prepared a chariot-bier
1115 To take me to the river, and a barge
Be ready on the river, clothed in black.
I go in state to court, to meet the Queen.
There surely I shall speak for mine own self,
And none of you can speak for me so well.
1120 And therefore let our dumb old man alone
Go with me, he can steer and row, and he
Will guide me to that palace, to the doors.'

    She ceased: her father promised; whereupon
She grew so cheerful that they deem'd her death
1125 Was rather in the fantasy than the blood.
But ten slow mornings past, and on the eleventh
Her father laid the letter in her hand,
And closed the hand upon it, and she died.
So that day there was dole in Astolat.

1130   But when the next sun brake from underground,
Then, those two brethren slowly with bent brows,
Accompanying, the sad chariot-bier
Past like a shadow thro' the field, that shone
Full-summer, to that stream whereon the barge,
1135 Pall'd all its length in blackest samite, lay.
There sat the lifelong creature of the house,
Loyal, the dumb old servitor, on deck,
Winking his eyes, and twisted all his face.
So those two brethren from the chariot took
1140 And on the black decks laid her in her bed,
Set in her hand a lily, o'er her hung
The silken case with braided blazonings,
And kiss'd her quiet brows, and saying to her
'Sister, farewell for ever,' and again
1145 'Farewell, sweet sister,' parted all in tears.
Then rose the dumb old servitor, and the dead,
Oar'd by the dumb, went upward with the flood—
In her right hand the lily, in her left
The letter—all her bright hair streaming down—
1150 And all the coverlid was cloth of gold
Drawn to her waist, and she herself in white
All but her face, and that clear-featured face

Was lovely, for she did not seem as dead,
But fast asleep, and lay as tho' she smiled.

1155   That day Sir Lancelot at the palace craved
Audience of Guinevere, to give at last
The price of half a realm, his costly gift,
Hard-won and hardly won with bruise and blow,
With deaths of others, and almost his own,
1160 The nine-years-fought-for diamonds: for he saw
One of her house, and sent him to the Queen
Bearing his wish, whereto the Queen agreed
With such and so unmoved a majesty
She might have seem'd her statue, but that he,
1165 Low-drooping till he wellnigh kiss'd her feet
For loyal awe, saw with a sidelong eye
The shadow of some piece of pointed lace,
In the Queen's shadow, vibrate on the walls,
And parted, laughing in his courtly heart.

1170   All in an oriel[26] on the summer side,
Vine-clad, of Arthur's palace toward the stream,
They met, and Lancelot kneeling utter'd, 'Queen,
Lady, my liege, in whom I have my joy,
Take, what I had not won except for you,
1175 These jewels, and make me happy, making them
An armlet for the roundest arm on earth,
Or necklace for a neck to which the swan's
Is tawnier than her cygnet's: these are words:
Your beauty is your beauty, and I sin
1180 In speaking, yet O grant my worship of it
Words, as we grant grief tears. Such sin in words
Perchance, we both can pardon: but, my Queen,
I hear of rumors flying thro' your court.
Our bond, as not the bond of man and wife,
1185 Should have in it an absoluter trust
To make up that defect: let rumors be:
When did not rumors fly? these, as I trust
That you trust me in your own nobleness,
I may not well believe that you believe.'

1190   While thus he spoke, half-turn'd away, the Queen
Brake from the vast oriel-embowering vine
Leaf after leaf, and tore, and cast them off,
Till all the place whereon she stood was green;
Then, when he ceased, in one cold passive hand
1195 Received at once and laid aside the gems
There on a table near her, and replied:

      'It may be, I am quicker of belief

---

26. *oriel*, a projecting bay window.

Than you believe me, Lancelot of the Lake.
Our bond is not the bond of man and wife.
1200 This good is in it, whatsoe'er of ill,
It can be broken easier. I for you
This many a year have done despite and wrong
To one whom ever in my heart of hearts
I did acknowledge nobler. What are these?
1205 Diamonds for me! they had been thrice their worth
Being your gift, had you not lost your own.
To loyal hearts the value of all gifts
Must vary as the giver's. Not for me!
For her! for your new fancy. Only this
1210 Grant me, I pray you: have your joys apart.
I doubt not that however changed, you keep
So much of what is graceful: and myself
Would shun to break those bounds of courtesy
In which as Arthur's Queen I move and rule:
1215 So cannot speak my mind. An end to this!
A strange one! yet I take it with Amen.
So pray you, add my diamonds to her pearls;
Deck her with these; tell her she shines me down:
An armlet for an arm to which the Queen's
1220 Is haggard, or a necklace for a neck
O as much fairer—as a faith once fair
Was richer than these diamonds—hers not mine—
Nay, by the mother of our Lord himself,
Or hers or mine, mine now to work my will—
1225 She shall not have them.'

                          Saying which she seized,
And, thro' the casement standing wide for heat,
Flung them, and down they flash'd, and smote the stream.
Then from the smitten surface flash'd, as it were,
Diamonds to meet them, and they past away.
1230 Then while Sir Lancelot leant, in half disdain
At love, life, all things, on the window ledge,
Close underneath his eyes, and right across
Where these had fallen, slowly past the barge
Whereon the lily maid of Astolat
1235 Lay smiling, like a star in blackest night.

    But the wild Queen, who saw not, burst away
To weep and wail in secret; and the barge,
On to the palace-doorway sliding, paused.
There two stood arm'd, and kept the door; to whom,
1240 All up the marble stair, tier over tier,
Were added mouths that gaped, and eyes that ask'd
'What is it?' but that oarsman's haggard face,
As hard and still as is the face that men
Shape to their fancy's eye from broken rocks

1245 On some cliff-side, appall'd them, and they said,
     'He is enchanted, cannot speak—and she,
     Look how she sleeps—the Fairy Queen, so fair!
     Yea, but how pale! what are they? flesh and blood?
     Or come to take the King to Fairyland?
1250 For some do hold our Arthur cannot die,
     But that he passes into Fairyland.'

     While thus they babbled of the King, the King
     Came girt with knights: then turn'd the tongueless man
     From the half-face to the full eye, and rose
1255 And pointed to the damsel, and the doors.
     So Arthur bade the meek Sir Percivale
     And pure Sir Galahad to uplift the maid;
     And reverently they bore her into hall.
     Then came the fine Gawain and wonder'd at her,
1260 And Lancelot later came and mused at her,
     And last the Queen herself, and pitied her:
     But Arthur spied the letter in her hand,
     Stoopt, took, brake seal, and read it; this was all:

     'Most noble lord, Sir Lancelot of the Lake,
1265 I, sometime call'd the maid of Astolat,
     Come, for you left me taking no farewell,
     Hither, to take my last farewell of you.
     I loved you, and my love had no return,
     And therefore my true love has been my death.
1270 And therefore to our Lady Guinevere,
     And to all other ladies, I make moan:
     Pray for my soul, and yield me burial.
     Pray for my soul thou too, Sir Lancelot,
     As thou art a knight peerless.'

                              Thus he read;
1275 And ever in the reading, lords and dames
     Wept, looking often from his face who read
     To hers which lay so silent, and at times,
     So touch'd were they, half-thinking that her lips,
     Who had devised the letter, moved again.
1280 Then freely spoke Sir Lancelot to them all:
     'My lord liege Arthur, and all ye that hear,
     Know that for this most gentle maiden's death
     Right heavy am I; for good she was and true,
     But loved me with a love beyond all love
1285 In women, whomsoever I have known.
     Yet to be loved makes not to love again;
     Not at my years, however it hold in youth.
     I swear by truth and knighthood that I gave
     No cause, not willingly, for such a love:

1290 To this I call my friends in testimony,
Her brethren, and her father, who himself
Besought me to be plain and blunt, and use,
To break her passion, some discourtesy
Against my nature: what I could, I did.
1295 I left her and I bade her no farewell;
Tho', had I dreamt the damsel would have died,
I might have put my wits to some rough use,
And help'd her from herself.'

                            Then said the Queen
(Sea was her wrath, yet working after storm),
1300 'Ye might at least have done her so much grace,
Fair lord, as would have help'd her from her death.'
He raised his head, their eyes met and hers fell,
He adding,

                   'Queen, she would not be content
Save that I wedded her, which could not be.
1305 Then might she follow me thro' the world, she ask'd;
It could not be. I told her that her love
Was but the flash of youth, would darken down
To rise hereafter in a stiller flame
Toward one more worthy of her—then would I,
1310 More specially were he, she wedded, poor,
Estate them with large land and territory
In mine own realm beyond the narrow seas,
To keep them in all joyance: more than this
I could not; this she would not, and she died.'

1315   He pausing, Arthur answer'd, 'O my knight,
It will be to thy worship, as my knight,
And mine, as head of all our Table Round,
To see that she be buried worshipfully.'

        So toward that shrine[27] which then in all the realm
1320 Was richest, Arthur leading, slowly went
The marshall'd Order of their Table Round,
And Lancelot sad beyond his wont, to see
The maiden buried, not as one unknown,
Nor meanly, but with gorgeous obsequies,
1325 And mass, and rolling music, like a queen.
And when the knights had laid her comely head
Low in the dust of half-forgotten kings,
Then Arthur spake among them, 'Let her tomb
Be costly, and her image thereupon,
1330 And let the shield of Lancelot at her feet
Be carven, and her lily in her hand.

---

27. *that shrine*, Westminster Abbey in London.

And let the story of her dolorous voyage
For all true hearts be blazon'd on her tomb
In letters gold and azure!' which was wrought
1335 Thereafter; but when now the lords and dames
And people, from the high door streaming, brake
Disorderly, as homeward each, the Queen,
Who mark'd Sir Lancelot where he moved apart,
Drew near, and sigh'd in passing, 'Lancelot,
1340 Forgive me; mine was jealousy in love.'
He answer'd with his eyes upon the ground,
'That is love's curse; pass on, my Queen, forgiven.'
But Arthur, who beheld his cloudy brows,
Approach'd him, and with full affection said,

1345 'Lancelot, my Lancelot, thou in whom I have
Most joy and most affiance, for I know
What thou hast been in battle by my side,
And many a time have watch'd thee at the tilt
Strike down the lusty and long-practised knight,
1350 And let the younger and unskill'd go by
To win his honor and to make his name,
And loved thy courtesies and thee, a man
Made to be loved; but now I would to God,
Seeing the homeless trouble in thine eyes,
1355 Thou couldst have loved this maiden, shaped, it seems,
By God for thee alone, and from her face,
If one may judge the living by the dead,
Delicately pure and marvellously fair,
Who might have brought thee, now a lonely man
1360 Wifeless and heirless, noble issue, sons
Born to the glory of thy name and fame,
My knight, the great Sir Lancelot of the Lake.'

Then answer'd Lancelot, 'Fair she was, my King,
Pure, as you ever wish your knights to be.
1365 To doubt her fairness were to want an eye,
To doubt her pureness were to want a heart—
Yea, to be loved, if what is worthy love
Could bind him, but free love will not be bound.'

'Free love, so bound, were freëst,' said the King.
1370 'Let love be free; free love is for the best:
And, after heaven, on our dull side of death,
What should be best, if not so pure a love
Clothed in so pure a loveliness? yet thee
She fail'd to bind, tho' being, as I think,
1375 Unbound as yet, and gentle, as I know.'

And Lancelot answer'd nothing, but he went,
And at the inrunning of a little brook

Sat by the river in a cove, and watch'd
The high reed wave, and lifted up his eyes
1380 And saw the barge that brought her moving down,
Far-off, a blot upon the stream, and said
Low in himself, 'Ah, simple heart and sweet,
Ye loved me, damsel, surely with a love
Far tenderer than my Queen's. Pray for thy soul?
1385 Ay, that will I. Farewell too—now at last—
Farewell, fair lily. "Jealousy in love?"
Not rather dead love's harsh heir, jealous pride?
Queen, if I grant the jealousy as of love,
May not your crescent fear for name and fame
1390 Speak, as it waxes, of a love that wanes?
Why did the King dwell on my name to me?
Mine own name shames me, seeming a reproach,
Lancelot, whom the Lady of the Lake
Caught from his mother's arms—the wondrous one
1395 Who passes thro' the vision of the night—
She chanted snatches of mysterious hymns
Heard on the winding waters, eve and morn
She kiss'd me saying, "Thou art fair, my child,
As a king's son," and often in her arms
1400 She bare me, pacing on the dusky mere.[28]
Would she had drown'd me in it, where'er it be!
For what am I? what profits me my name
Of greatest knight? I fought for it, and have it:
Pleasure to have it, none; to lose it, pain;
1405 Now grown a part of me: but what use in it?
To make men worse by making my sin known?
Or sin seem less, the sinner seeming great?
Alas for Arthur's greatest knight, a man
Not after Arthur's heart! I needs must break
1410 These bonds that so defame me: not without
She[29] wills it: would I, if she will'd it? nay,
Who knows? but if I would not, then may God,
I pray him, send a sudden Angel down
To seize me by the hair and bear me far,
1415 And fling me deep in that forgotten mere,
Among the tumbled fragments of the hills.'

    So groan'd Sir Lancelot in remorseful pain,
Not knowing he should die a holy man.

---

28. *mere*, lake.
29. *She*, Guinevere.

DISCUSSION

1. (a) With whom is Tennyson concerned in the first 27 lines of the poem? (b) What does she do day after day? (c) Why does she embroider a cover for Lancelot's shield? (d) What does this indicate to you about her feelings for Lancelot?

2. In lines 34–72 Tennyson gives the background of the diamonds leading up to the present. (a) Where did Arthur discover the gems? (b) Who once owned them? (c) What plan did Arthur devise involving the diamonds? (d) What was the purpose of his plan and what has been the outcome so far?

3. (a) What excuse does Lancelot give for not participating in the joust for the central diamond? (b) What is his real reason?

4. Read lines 121–135. (a) In what terms does Guinevere describe her husband? (b) What is her attitude here?

5. What plan does Guinevere devise for Lancelot to save face and participate in the joust?

6. (a) Why does Lancelot go to the castle of Astolat on his way to the joust? (b) Who lives in the castle? (c) How do Sir Torre and Sir Lavaine differ? (d) What is significant about the old servant? How did he get this way?

7. (a) How is Lancelot described in lines 241–259? (b) How does Elaine react to him?

8. (a) What does Lancelot say about King Arthur in lines 305–316? (b) What is his attitude toward Arthur?

9. (a) What request does Elaine ask of Lancelot? (b) Why does he accept? (c) In return, what does Lancelot ask Elaine to do?

10. What is the relationship between lines 396–397 and the first 27 lines of the poem?

11. (a) To whom does Lancelot reveal his identity? (b) Why does the fighting in the tournament intensify as Lancelot begins to win? (c) What happens to him and who comes to his aid? (d) How does the tournament end?

12. (a) What does King Arthur do after Lancelot leaves the tournament? (b) How does Gawain feel about his assignment? (c) Read lines 550–560. What does Tennyson suggest about Gawain's personality?

13. (a) How does Guinevere react to Arthur's news of Lancelot? (b) How does Elaine react when Gawain brings her the same news?

14. (a) What does Gawain do with the diamond? (b) Why does Arthur become upset when Gawain reports back to him? (c) How does Queen Guinevere react to the gossip going around the court?

15. Read lines 859–872. (a) What are Lancelot's feelings for Elaine? (b) What prevents him from loving her? (c) Does Elaine know what his true feelings are?

16. (a) What does Elaine finally ask of Lancelot? (b) Why does he refuse, and what does he tell her? (c) What one discourtesy does he show her?

17. (a) What does Elaine's father say to try to break the passion in her heart? (b) What kills Elaine? (c) Did you anticipate her death? Explain.

18. (a) What does Guinevere do with Lancelot's gift of diamonds? (b) What happens immediately after this act? (c) What do you think Tennyson is suggesting by this coincidence?

19. (a) What does Arthur say to Lancelot after Elaine's funeral? (b) What is Lancelot's reply? (c) Do you think Arthur understands Lancelot? Explain.

20. Read Lancelot's last speech by the river. What do you think will happen to the relationship between Lancelot and Guinevere?

THE AUTHOR'S CRAFT

Analyzing Tennyson

Alfred, Lord Tennyson's "Lancelot and Elaine" is rich in its complexities of meaning, expression, and feeling. The following six considerations, all of which contribute to the beauty of the poem, will help to increase your understanding and appreciation of Tennyson's poetic achievement in "Lancelot and Elaine."

FORM. "Lancelot and Elaine" is written in verse. What kind of verse form does Tennyson employ? Why do you think Tennyson chose to ignore rhyme? Reread Elaine's song of death in lines 1000–1011. Why do you think Tennyson varied the verse form here? In Malory's "The Tale of Sir Gareth" you encountered an Arthurian story told in prose. Compare Malory's prose to Tennyson's verse. Which form allows the writer more freedom of expression? Why?

ORGANIZATION. "Lancelot and Elaine" begins in the middle of the story, with Elaine admiring Lancelot's shield. Then Tennyson goes back to the beginning of the story, to the time when Arthur first found the diamonds. Why do you think Tennyson used this unusual time sequence? Tennyson organizes his poem around two distinct locations: the world of Arthur and his court, and the world of Elaine and her family. Describe these two worlds. In terms of organization, what significance do you see in separating these two worlds from each other?

DESCRIPTION. "Lancelot and Elaine" is rich in descriptive detail. Recall the location and appearance of the cave in which Lancelot recovers from his wound. How many details can you remember? Recall the description of Arthur's throne at the tournament. What is Tennyson trying to suggest in this description? Reconstruct the scene in which Lancelot gives the diamonds to Guinevere. Where do Lancelot and Guinevere stand? What does Guinevere do with her hands while Lancelot talks? Tennyson uses descriptive detail abundantly to provide us with a clearer and deeper understanding of the story.

CHARACTERS. The eight major characters in "Lancelot and Elaine" are: King Arthur, Elaine's father, Lancelot, Lavaine, Torre, Gawain, Queen Guinevere, and Elaine. Describe each one. In what ways do the four young knights differ from each other?

Compare Guinevere's love for Lancelot to Elaine's love for him. What do you learn about the two women from this comparison?

MEANING. At one time Tennyson considered calling his book of Arthurian poems *The True and the False*. Using this title as a key to the meaning of the poem compare Lancelot and Gawain. Which one of them is a true knight? Which one is true to only part of the knightly code? Compare Guinevere and Elaine. Which one is true to Lancelot? Of all the characters in "Lancelot and Elaine" who alone seems true to the medieval ideals presented in the poem? Would you call this character a tragic hero? Defend your answer.

ATTITUDE. At the time Tennyson was writing "Lancelot and Elaine" England was experiencing growing pains brought on by the Industrial Revolution. Railroads and factories covered the landscape. Sprawling cities competed with over-worked farms for what land was left. Shortly before Tennyson began writing his poem there had been a real danger of a working-class revolt, and many Englishmen worried about law and order in their country. Yet, Tennyson chose to write a poem about medieval England. Why do you think he did this? Do you think "Lancelot and Elaine" is relevant to our own day and age? Explain.

AUTHOR

ALFRED, LORD TENNYSON (1809–1892) wrote poetry from childhood, training himself for the vocation of poet as another boy might train himself to be a doctor

or an engineer. At nineteen Tennyson entered Cambridge University, where he became the friend of Arthur Hallam. Hallam, more than anyone else, believed in Tennyson's future as a poet and constantly encouraged his efforts. In 1830 Tennyson's first independent volume, *Poems, Chiefly Lyrical*, appeared. In spite of its faults, it was a remarkable volume for a young man of twenty-one. In 1833 the publication of *Poems* convinced the critics that this young poet had genuine talents. In the midst of Tennyson's happiness, his friend Hallam died.

Tennyson's period of success and triumph began in 1842 with the two-volume edition of *Poems by Alfred Tennyson*. He immediately took his place as the leading English poet of the Victorian age. In 1850 he published *In Memoriam*, the moving series of poems about the death of Arthur Hallam, and shortly after he was made poet laureate of England.

It was 1859 before the first four poems of *The Idylls of the King* were published. For most of the remainder of his long life Tennyson worked on the *Idylls*, gradually rounding out the epic of the Round Table in its days of glory and in its fall. The *Idylls* had much to do with making Tennyson the most popular poet England has ever known.

FROM

The Once and Future King

T. H. White

The following selection, taken from the last chapter of T. H. White's modern re-telling of the Arthurian legend, brings Arthur's story to a close. It is the night before the last great confrontation. Arthur knows that he is destined to die in the forthcoming battle. He meditates on his unsuccessful efforts to transform the violence of men into virtue, and tries to comprehend the meaning of war.

ARTHUR was tired out. He had been broken by the two battles which he had fought already, the one at Dover, the other at Barham Down. His wife was a prisoner. His oldest friend was banished. His son[1] was trying to kill him. Gawaine was buried. His Table was dispersed. His country was at war. Yet he could have breasted all these things in some way, if the central tenet of his heart had not been ravaged. Long ago, when his mind had been a nimble boy's called Wart[2]—long ago he had been taught by an aged benevolence, wagging a white beard. He had been taught by Merlyn[3] to believe that man was perfectible: that he was on the whole more decent than beastly: that good was worth trying: that there was no such thing as original sin. He had been forged as a weapon for the aid of man, on the assumption that men were good. He had been forged, by that deluded old teacher, into a sort of Pasteur or Curie or patient discoverer of insulin.[4] The service for which he had

Reprinted by permission of G. P. Putnam's Sons and David Higham Associates, Ltd. from THE ONCE AND FUTURE KING by T. H. White. Copyright 1939, 1940 by T. H. White. Copyright © 1958 by T. H. White.

1. *His son*, Mordred; in this version, Arthur's illegitimate son by Morgause.
2. *Wart*, Arthur's youthful name.
3. *Merlyn*, a magician who, in this version, raised Arthur.
4. *Pasteur . . . insulin.* Pasteur (1822–1895) made discoveries in biology and medicine. Marie Curie (1867–1934) discovered and isolated radium. Insulin is a substance used to treat diabetics.

been destined had been against Force, the mental illness of humanity. His Table, his idea of Chivalry, his Holy Grail, his devotion to Justice: these had been progressive steps in the effort for which he had been bred. He was like a scientist who had pursued the root of cancer all his life. Might—to have ended it—to have made men happier. But the whole structure depended on the first premise: that man was decent.

Looking back at his life, it seemed to him that he had been struggling all the time to dam a flood, which, whenever he had checked it, had broken through at a new place, setting him his work to do again. It was the flood of Force Majeur.[5] During the earliest days before his marriage he had tried to match its strength with strength—in his battles against the Gaelic confederation—only to find that two wrongs did not make a right. But he had crushed the feudal dream of war successfully. Then, with his Round Table, he had tried to harness Tyranny in lesser forms, so that its power might be used for useful ends. He had sent out the men of might to rescue the oppressed and to straighten evil—to put down the individual might of barons, just as he had put down the might of kings. They had done so—until, in the course of time, the ends had been achieved, but the force had remained upon his hands unchastened. So he had sought for a new channel, had sent them out on God's business, searching for the Holy Grail.[6] That too had been a failure, because those who had achieved the Quest had become perfect and been lost to the world, while those who had failed in it had soon returned no better. At last he had sought to make a map of force, as it were, to bind it down by laws. He had tried to codify the evil uses of might by individuals, so that he might set bounds to them by the impersonal justice of the state. He had been prepared to sacrifice his wife and his best friend,[7] to the impersonality of Justice. And then, even as the might of the individual seemed to have been curbed, the Principle of Might had sprung up behind him in another shape—in the shape of collective might, of banded ferocity, of numerous armies insusceptible to individual laws.[8] He had bound the might of units, only to find that it was assumed by pluralities. He had conquered murder, to be faced with war. There were no Laws for that.

5. *Force Majeur*, primal energy or violent force.
6. *Holy Grail*, the cup used by Jesus at the Last Supper. Medieval knights sought to find this miraculous object.
7. *wife . . . friend*, Guinevere and Lancelot.
8. *in the shape . . . laws*, Mordred's rebellion.

The wars of his early days, those against Lot and the Dictator of Rome, had been battles to upset the feudal convention of warfare as foxhunting or as gambling for ransom. To upset it, he had introduced the idea of total war. In his old age this same total warfare had come back to roost as total hatred, as the most modern of hostilities.

Now, with his forehead resting on the papers and his eyes closed, the King was trying not to realize. For if there was such a thing as original sin, if man was on the whole a villain, if the Bible was right in saying that the heart of men was deceitful above all things and desperately wicked, then the purpose of his life had been a vain one. Chivalry and justice became a child's illusions, if the stock on which he had tried to graft them was to be the Thrasher, was to be *Homo ferox* instead of *Homo sapiens*.[9]

Behind this thought there was a worse one, with which he dared not grapple. Perhaps man was neither good nor bad, was only a machine in an insensate universe—his courage no more than a reflex to danger, like the automatic jump at the pin-prick. Perhaps there were no virtues, unless jumping at pin-pricks was a virtue, and humanity only a mechanical donkey led on by the iron carrot of love, through the pointless treadmill of reproduction. Perhaps Might was a law of Nature, needed to keep the survivors fit. Perhaps he himself . . .

But he could challenge it no further. He felt as if there was something atrophied between his eyes, where the base of the nose grew into the skull. He could not sleep. He had bad dreams. Tomorrow was the final battle. Meanwhile there were all these papers to read and sign. But he could neither read nor sign them. He could not lift his head from the desk.

Why did men fight?

The old man had always been a dutiful thinker, never an inspired one. Now his exhausted brain slipped into its accustomed circles: the withered paths, like those of the donkey in the treadmill, round which he had plodded many thousand times in vain.

Was it the wicked leaders who led innocent populations to slaughter, or was it wicked populations who chose leaders after their own hearts? On the face of it, it seemed unlikely that one Leader could force a million Englishmen against their will. If, for instance, Mordred had been anxious to make the English wear

9. *Homo ferox . . . sapiens*, savage man instead of intelligent man.

petticoats, or stand on their heads, they would surely not have joined his party—however clever or persuasive or deceitful or even terrible his inducements? A leader was surely forced to offer something which appealed to those he led? He might give the impetus to the falling building, but surely it had to be toppling on its own account before it fell? If this were true, then wars were not calamities into which amiable innocents were led by evil men. They were national movements, deeper, more subtle in origin. And, indeed, it did not feel to him as if he or Mordred had led their country to its misery. If it was so easy to lead one's country in various directions, as if she was a pig on a string, why had he failed to lead her into chivalry, into justice and into peace? He had been trying.

Then again—this was the second circle—it was like the Inferno[10]—if neither he nor Mordred had really set the misery in motion, who had been the cause? How did the fact of war begin in general? For any one war seemed so rooted in its antecedents. Mordred went back to Morgause, Morgause to Uther Pendragon, Uther to his ancestors. It seemed as if Cain[11] had slain Abel, seizing his country, after which the men of Abel had sought to win their patrimony again for ever. Man had gone on, through age after age, avenging wrong with wrong, slaughter with slaughter. Nobody was the better for it, since both sides always suffered, yet everybody was inextricable. The present war might be attributed to Mordred, or to himself. But also it was due to a million Thrashers, to Lancelot, Guenever, Gawaine, everybody. Those who lived by the sword were forced to die by it. It was as if everything would lead to sorrow, so long as man refused to forget the past. The wrongs of Uther and of Cain were wrongs which could have been righted only by the blessing of forgetting them.

Sisters, mothers, grandmothers: everything was rooted in the past! Actions of any sort in one generation might have incalculable consequences in another, so that merely to sneeze was a pebble thrown into a pond, whose circles might lap the furthest shores. It seemed as if the only hope was not to act at all, to draw no swords for anything, to hold oneself still, like a pebble not thrown. But that would be hateful.

What was Right, what was Wrong? What distinguished Doing from Not Doing? If I were to have my time again, the old King thought, I would bury myself in a monastery, for fear of a Doing which might lead to woe.

The blessing of forgetfulness: that was the first essential. If everything one did, or which one's fathers had done, was an endless sequence of Doings doomed to break forth bloodily, then the past must be obliterated and a new start made. Man must be ready to say: Yes, since Cain there has been injustice, but we can only set the misery right if we accept a *status quo*. Lands have been robbed, men slain, nations humiliated. Let us now start fresh without remembrance, rather than live forward and backward at the same time. We cannot build the future by avenging the past. Let us sit down as brothers, and accept the Peace of God.

Unfortunately men did say this, in each successive war. They were always saying that the present one was to be the last, and afterwards there was to be a heaven. They were always to rebuild such a new world as never was seen. When the time came, however, they were too stupid. They were like children crying out that they would build a house—but, when it came to building, they had not the practical ability. They did not know the way to choose the right materials.

The old man's thoughts went laboriously. They were leading him nowhere; they doubled back on themselves and ran the same course twice: yet he was so accustomed to them that he could not stop. He entered another circle.

Perhaps the great cause of war was possession, as John Ball[12] the communist had said. "The matters gothe nat well to passe in Englonde," he had stated, "nor shall nat do tyll every thyng be common, and that there be no villayns nor gentylmen."[13] Perhaps wars were fought because people said *my* kingdom, *my* wife, *my* lover, *my* possessions. This was what he and Lancelot and all of them had always held behind their thoughts. Perhaps, so long as people tried to possess things separately from each other, even honour and souls, there would be wars for ever. The hungry wolf would always attack the fat reindeer, the poor man would rob the banker, the

---

10. *Inferno*. The poet Dante, in his *Inferno*, describes the geography of Hell as a series of concentric circles.
11. *Cain*, was, according to the Bible, the first murderer.

12. *John Ball,* English priest and political agitator involved in the Peasant's Rebellion. He died in 1381.
13. *"The matters . . . gentylmen."* "Events are not going well in England and will not until everything is owned in common, and there are neither poor nor rich men."

serf would make revolutions against the higher class, and the lack-penny nation would fight the rich. Perhaps wars only happened between those who had and those who had not. As against this, you were forced to place the fact that nobody could define the state of "having." A knight with a silver suit of armour would immediately call himself a have-not, if he met a knight with a golden one.

But, he thought, assume for a moment that "having," however it is defined, might be the crux of the problem.

I have, and Mordred has not. He protested to himself in contradiction: it is not fair to put it like that, as if Mordred or I were the movers of the storm. For indeed, we are nothing but figureheads to complex forces which seem to be under a kind of impulse. It is as if there was an impulse in the fabric of society. Mordred is urged along almost helplessly now, by numbers of people too many to count: people who believe in John Ball, hoping to gain power over their fellow men by asserting that all are equal, or people who see in any upheaval a chance to advance their own might. It seems to come from underneath. Ball's men and Mordred's are the under-dogs seeking to rise, or the knights who were not leaders of the Round Table and therefore hated it, or the poor who would be rich, or the powerless seeking to gain power. And my men, for whom I am no more than a standard or a talisman, are the knights who were leaders—the rich defending their possessions, the powerful unready to let it slip. It is a meeting of the Haves and Have-Nots in force, an insane clash between bodies of men, not between leaders. But let that pass. Assume the vague idea that war is due to "having" in general. In that case the proper thing would be to refuse to have at all. Such, as Rochester had sometimes pointed out, was the advice of God. There had been the rich man who was threatened with the needle's eye, and there had been the money changers. That was why the Church could not interfere too much in the sad affairs of the world, so Rochester said, because the nations and the classes and the individuals were always crying out "Mine, mine," where the Church was instructed to say "Ours."

If this were true, then it would not be a question only of sharing property, as such. It would be a question of sharing everything—even thoughts, feelings, lives. God had told people that they would have to cease to live as individuals. They would have to go into the force of life, like a drop falling into a river.

God has said that it was only the men who could give up their jealous selves, their futile individualities of happiness and sorrow, who would die peacefully and enter the ring. He that would save his life was asked to lose it.

Yet there was something in the old white head which could not accept the godly view. Obviously you might cure a cancer of the womb by not having a womb in the first place. Sweeping and drastic remedies could cut out anything—and life with the cut. Ideal advice, which nobody was built to follow, was no advice at all. Advising heaven to earth was useless.

Another worn-out circle spun before him. Perhaps war was due to fear: to fear of reliability. Unless there was truth, and unless people told the truth, there was always danger in everything outside the individual. You told the truth to yourself, but you had no surety for your neighbour. This uncertainty must end by making the neighbour a menace. Such, at any rate, would have been Lancelot's explanation of the war. He had been used to say that man's most vital possession was his Word. Poor Lance, he had broken his own word: all the same, there had been few men with such a good one.

Perhaps wars happened because nations had no confidence in the Word. They were frightened, and so they fought. Nations were like people—they had feelings of inferiority, or of superiority, or of revenge, or of fear. It was right to personify nations.

Suspicion and fear: possessiveness and greed: resentment for ancestral wrong: all these seemed to be a part of it. Yet they were not the solution. He could not see the real solution. He was too old and tired and miserable to think constructively. He was only a man who had meant well, who had been spurred along that course of thinking by an eccentric necromancer[14] with a weakness for humanity. Justice had been his last attempt—to do nothing which was not just. But it had ended in failure. To do at all had proved too difficult. He was done himself.

Arthur proved that he was not quite done, by lifting his head. There was something invincible in his heart, a tincture of grandness in simplicity. He sat upright and reached for the iron bell.

"Page," he said, as the small boy trotted in, knuckling his eyes.

"My lord."

---

14. *necromancer,* magician.

The King looked at him. Even in his own extremity he was able to notice others, especially if they were fresh or decent. When he had comforted the broken Gawaine in his tent, he had been the one who was more in need of comfort.

"My poor child," he said. "You ought to be in bed."

He observed the boy with a strained, thread-bare attention. It was long since he had seen youth's innocence and certainty.

"Look," he said, "will you take this note to the bishop? Don't wake him if he is asleep."

"My lord."

"Thank you."

As the live creature went, he called it back.

"Oh, page?"

"My lord?"

"What is your name?"

"Tom, my lord," it said politely.

"Where do you live?"

"Near Warwick, my lord."

"Near Warwick."

The old man seemed to be trying to imagine the place, as if it were Paradise Terrestre, or a country described by Mandeville.[15]

"At a place called Newbold Revell. It is a pretty one."

"How old are you?"

"I shall be thirteen in November, my lord."

"And I have kept you up all night."

"No, my lord. I slept a lot on one of the saddles."

"Tom of Newbold Revell,"[16] he said with wonder. "We seem to have involved a lot of people. Tell me, Tom, what do you intend to do tomorrow?"

"I shall fight, sir. I have a good bow."

"And you will kill people with this bow?"

"Yes, my lord. A great many, I hope."

"Suppose they were to kill you?"

"Then I should be dead, my lord."

"I see."

"Shall I take the letter now?"

"No. Wait a minute. I want to talk to somebody, only my head is muddled."

"Shall I fetch a glass of wine?"

"No, Tom. Sit down and try to listen. Lift those chessmen off the stool. Can you understand things

15. Mandeville (man' də vil), fictional fourteenth-century traveler who went to fantastic places such as Paradise Terrestre, which means heaven on earth.
16. *Tom of Newbold Revell*, Sir Thomas Malory, author of *Morte d'Arthur*. White chooses to make Malory a page in Arthur's court.

when they are said?"

"Yes, my lord. I am good at understanding."

"Could you understand if I asked you not to fight tomorrow?"

"I should want to fight," it said stoutly.

"Everybody wants to fight, Tom, but nobody knows why. Suppose I were to ask you not to fight, as a special favour to the King? Would you do that?"

"I should do what I was told."

"Listen, then. Sit for a minute and I will tell you a story. I am a very old man, Tom, and you are young. When you are old, you will be able to tell what I have told tonight, and I want you to do that. Do you understand this want?"

"Yes, sir. I think so."

"Put it like this. There was a king once, called King Arthur. That is me. When he came to the throne of England, he found that all the kings and barons were fighting against each other like madmen, and, as they could afford to fight in expensive suits of armour, there was practically nothing which could stop them from doing what they pleased. They did a lot of bad things, because they lived by force. Now this king had an idea, and the idea was that force ought to be used, if it were used at all, on behalf of justice, not on its own account. Follow this, young boy. He thought that if he could get his barons fighting for truth, and to help weak people, and to redress wrongs, then their fighting might not be such a bad thing as once it used to be. So he gathered together all the true and kindly people that he knew, and he dressed them in armour, and he made them knights, and taught them his idea, and set them down, at a Round Table. There were a hundred and fifty of them in the happy days, and King Arthur loved his Table with all his heart. He was prouder of it than he was of his own dear wife, and for many years his new knights went about killing ogres, and rescuing damsels and saving poor prisoners, and trying to set the world to rights. That was the King's idea."

"I think it was a good idea, my lord."

"It was, and it was not. God knows."

"What happened to the King in the end?" asked the child, when the story seemed to have dried up.

"For some reason, things went wrong. The Table split into factions, a bitter war began, and all were killed."

The boy interrupted confidently.

"No," he said, "not all. The King won. We shall win."

Arthur smiled vaguely and shook his head. He would have nothing but the truth.

"Everybody was killed," he repeated, "except a certain page. I know what I am talking about."

"My lord?"

"This page was called young Tom of Newbold Revell near Warwick, and the old King sent him off before the battle, upon pain of dire disgrace. You see, the King wanted there to be somebody left, who would remember their famous idea. He wanted badly that Tom should go back to Newbold Revell, where he could grow into a man and live his life in Warwickshire peace—and he wanted him to tell everybody who would listen about this ancient idea, which both of them had once thought good. Do you think you could do that, Thomas, to please the King?"

The child said, with the pure eyes of absolute truth: "I would do anything for King Arthur."

"That's a brave fellow. Now listen, man. Don't get these legendary people muddled up. It is I who tell you about my idea. It is I who am going to command you to take horse to Warwickshire at once, and not to fight with your bow tomorrow at all. Do you understand all this?"

"Yes, King Arthur."

"Will you promise to be careful of yourself afterward? Will you try to remember that you are a kind of vessel to carry on the idea, when things go wrong, and that the whole hope depends on you alive?"

"I will."

"It seems selfish of me to use you for it."

"It is an honour for your poor page, good my lord."

"Thomas, my idea of those knights was a sort of candle, like these ones here. I have carried it for many years with a hand to shield it from the wind. It has flickered often. I am giving you the candle now—you won't let it out?"

"It will burn."

"Good Tom. The light-bringer. How old did you say you were?"

"Nearly thirteen."

"Sixty more years then, perhaps. Half a century."

"I will give it to other people, King. English people."

"You will say to them in Warwickshire: Eh, he wor a wonderly fine candle?"[17]

"Aye, lad, that I will."

"Then 'tis: Na, Tom, for thee must go right quickly. Thou'lt take the best son of a mare that thee kinst

find, and thou wilt ride post into Warwickshire, lad, wi' nowt but the curlew?"

"I will ride post, mate, so that the candle burn."

"Good Tom, then, God bless 'ee. Doant thee ferget thick Bishop of Rochester, afore thou goest."

The little boy kneeled down to kiss his master's hand—his surcoat, with the Malory bearings, looking absurdly new.

"My lord of England," he said.

Arthur raised him gently, to kiss him on the shoulder.

"Sir Thomas of Warwick," he said—and the boy was gone.

The tent was empty, tawny and magnificent. The wind wailed and the candles guttered. Waiting for the Bishop, the old, old man sat down at his reading desk. Presently his head drooped forward on the papers. The greyhound's eyes, catching the candles as she watched him, burned spectrally, two amber cups of feral light. Mordred's cannonade, which he was to keep up through the darkness until the morning's battle, began to thud and bump outside. The King, drained of his last effort, gave way to sorrow. Even when his visitor's hand lifted the tent flap, the silent drops coursed down his nose and fell on the parchment with regular ticks, like an ancient clock. He turned his head aside, unwilling to be seen, unable to do better. The flap fell, as the strange figure in cloak and hat came softly in.

"Merlyn?"

But there was nobody there: he had dreamed him in a catnap of old age.

Merlyn?

He began to think again, but now it was as clearly as it had ever been. He remembered the aged necromancer who had educated him—who had educated him with animals. There were, he remembered, something like half a million different species of animal, of which mankind was only one. Of course man was an animal—he was not a vegetable or a mineral, was he? And Merlyn had taught him about animals so that the single species might learn by looking at the problems of the thousands. He remembered the belligerent ants, who claimed their boundaries, and the pacific geese, who did not. He remembered his lesson from the badger. He remembered Lyo-lyok and the island which they had seen on their migration, where all those puffins, razorbills, guillemots and kittiwakes[18] had lived together peacefully,

---

17. *Eh . . . candle.* Here Arthur falls into an imitation of Warwichshire dialect.

18. *puffins . . . kittiwakes,* different kinds of birds.

preserving their own kinds of civilization without war—because they claimed no boundaries. He saw the problem before him as plain as a map. The fantastic thing about war was that it was fought about nothing—literally nothing. Frontiers were imaginary lines. There was no visible line between Scotland and England, although Flodden and Bannockburn[19] had been fought about it. It was geography which was the cause—political geography. It was nothing else. Nations did not need to have the same kind of civilization, nor the same kind of leader, any more than the puffins and the guillemots did. They could keep their own civilizations, like Esquimaux and Hottentots, if they would give each other freedom of trade and free passage and access to the world. Countries would have to become counties—but counties which could keep their own culture and local laws. The imaginary lines on the earth's surface only needed to be unimagined. The airborne birds skipped them by nature. How mad the frontiers had seemed to Lyo-lyok, and would to Man if he could learn to fly.

The old King felt refreshed, clear-headed, almost ready to begin again.

There would be a day—there must be a day—when he would come back to Gramarye with a new Round Table which had no corners, just as the world had none—a table without boundaries between the nations who would sit to feast there. The hope of making it would lie in culture. If people could be persuaded to read and write, not just to eat and make love, there was still a chance that they might come to reason.

But it was too late for another effort then. For that time it was his destiny to die, or, as some say, to be carried off to Avilion, where he could wait for better days. For that time it was Lancelot's fate and Guenever's to take the tonsure and the veil,[20] while Mordred must be slain. The fate of this man or that man was less than a drop, although it was a sparkling one, in the great blue motion of the sunlit sea.

The cannons of his adversary were thundering in the tattered morning when the Majesty of England drew himself up to meet the future with a peaceful heart.

EXPLICIT LIBER REGIS QUONDAM
REGISQUE FUTURI[21]

THE BEGINNING

19. *Flodden and Bannockburn*, battles. Flodden, in 1513, was the site of an English victory over the Scots. Bannockburn, in 1314, was the site of a Scottish victory over the English.
20. *tonsure . . . veil.* Lancelot became a monk, Guinevere a nun.
21. *Explicit . . . futuri.* Here ends the book of *The Once and Future King.*

DISCUSSION

1. (a) What was Arthur's goal when he first became King? (b) What did he assume to be true about the nature of man when he chose this goal?

2. Arthur muses that the "blessing of forgetfulness" is the first essential requirement for bringing an end to war. (a) Explain what he means. (b) According to Arthur, how successfully have men used the "blessing of forgetfulness" to end war? Why?

3. Arthur wonders if "having" causes war. (a) What does he mean? (b) How could this potential cause of war be eliminated? (c) Why does Arthur reject such a solution?

4. Lancelot had believed that man's most vital possession was his Word, his ability consistently to tell the truth. According to Arthur, how might a lack of confidence in the Word lead to war?

5. (a) What "story" does Arthur tell his page? (b) With what responsibility does Arthur entrust the page?

6. What does Arthur conclude is the reason for war? Explain.

7. Why do you think this selection ends with the words "The Beginning"?

AUTHOR

TERENCE HANBURY WHITE (1909–1964) was born the son of an English army officer in Bombay, India. He filled his days with a frenzy of activity, arguing that the only thing he found in life which seemed to survive most disasters of living was learning about things. He lived in a large house on an island off England and indulged his interests in underwater photography, sailing, falcony, gardening, and writing.

White produced nineteen books, all of them filled with delightful wit and fantasy and continuously reaffirming his conviction that mankind, on the whole, is more decent than beastly. *The Once and Future King* was White's greatest literary success. The broadway musical, *Camelot*, and the film of the same name are based on this novel.

the commoner

Medieval literature is not always about the lives of the aristocrats who lived in castles and never worked. There is also a literature of the common people.

This literature is set in the chilly fields where shepherds gathered, in the small villages of the farmers, and sometimes in the wilderness of the forest, where outlaws from society could roam freely.

The characters in this literature rarely dress well. Their speech is blunt, their actions frequently violent. But they face life without illusions, and their literature tells us of a hardy people on whose shoulders medieval society rested, a people of simple courage, strength, and monumental endurance.

FROM THE WAKEFIELD MYSTERY CYCLE

THE SECOND SHEPHERDS' PLAY

The commoner of medieval England viewed all aspects of life, including religion, in simple terms. The Second Shepherds' Play confronts us with medieval peasants, cold and hunger-bitten, stealing and squabbling through their dreary lives. Into this bleak world comes a divinity, as simple and poor as they are, to save them.

Dramatis Personae

FIRST SHEPHERD *(Coll)*
SECOND SHEPHERD *(Gib)*
THIRD SHEPHERD *(Daw), a youth*
MAK
JILL
ANGEL
MARY

The Second Shepherds' Play from REPRESENTATIVE MEDIEVAL AND TUDOR PLAYS, translated and edited by Henry W. Wells and Roger S. Loomis, Copyright 1942 Sheed & Ward Inc., New York. Reprinted by permission.

Scene I

[*Scene a moor. Enter* FIRST SHEPHERD, *stamping his feet and blowing on his nails.*]

FIRST SHEPHERD:

> Lord, but it's cold and wretchedly I'm wrapped;
> My wits are frozen, so long it is I've napped;
> My legs are cramped, and every finger chapped.
> All goes awry; in misery I'm trapped.
> By storms and gales distressed,
> Now in the east, now west,
> Woe's him who gets no rest!
> We simple shepherds walking on the moor,
> We're like, in faith, to be put out of door,
> And it's no wonder if we are so poor.
> Our fields they lie as fallow as a floor;
> We're driven till we're bowed;
> We're taxed until we're cowed
> By gentry, rich and proud.
> They take our rest; them may our Lady blast!
> For their own lords they make our plows stick fast.
> Some say it's for the best, but at the last
> We know that's false. We tenants are downcast,
> And always we're kept under.
> If we don't thrive, no wonder
> When they so rob and plunder.
> A man with broidered sleeve or brooch, these days,
> Can ruin anyone who him gainsays.
> There's not a soul believes one word he says,
> Or dares rebuke him for his bumptious ways.
> He makes his pride and boast,
> He gets his very post
> From those who have the most.
> There comes a fellow, proud as a peacock, now,
> He'd carry off my wagon and my plow.
> Before he'd leave, I must seem glad and bow.
> A wretched life we lead, you must allow.
> Whatever he has willed
> Must be at once fulfilled,
> Or surely I'd be killed.
> It does me good, when I walk round alone,
> About this world to grumble and to groan.
> Now to my sheep I'll slowly walk, and moan,
> And rest awhile on some old balk or stone.
> Some other men I'll see;
> Before it's noon I'll be
> In true men's company.

[*Enter* SECOND SHEPHERD, *not noticing*
FIRST SHEPHERD.]

SECOND SHEPHERD:

> Good Lord, good Lord, what does this misery mean?
> What ails the world? The like has seldom been.
> The weather's spiteful cold and bitter keen;
> My eyes they weep, such hideous frosts they've seen.
> Now in the snow and sleet
> My shoes freeze to my feet;
> No easy life I meet.
> So far as I can see, where'er I go,
> The griefs of married men increase and grow.
> We're always out of luck; I tell you so.
> Capul our hen goes cackling to and fro,
> But if she starts to croak,
> Our cock suffers a stroke;
> For him it is no joke.
> These wedded men have never once their will;
> When they're hard pressed, they sigh and just keep still,
> Groan to themselves and take the bitter pill.
> God knows they've got a nasty part to fill!
> And as for me I've found—
> I know the lesson's sound—
> Woe to the man who's bound![1]
> Late in my life it still amazes me,
> And my heart stops such miracles to see;
> But yet when destiny drives, such things can be:
> Some men have two wives, some have even three!
> But if his lot is sore
> Who has one wife in store,
> It's hell for him with more!
> Young men who'd woo, before you're fairly caught,
> Beware of wedding! Give the matter thought.
> To moan, "Had I but known!" will help you nought.
> Much misery has wedding often brought,
> And many a stormy shower.
> You catch in one short hour
> A lifelong taste of sour.
> I've one for mate, if ever I read the Epistle,
> Who's rough as is a briar and sharp as thistle.
> Her looks are sour; her eyebrows, like hog's bristle.
> She'd sing "Our Father" if once she wet her whistle.
> And like a whale she's fat,
> Full of gall as a vat.
> I don't know where I'm at.

FIRST SHEPHERD:

> Gib, look over the hedge! Are you deaf or no?

SECOND SHEPHERD:

> The devil take you! Was ever man so slow?
> Have you seen Daw?

---

1. *bound,* bound in marriage.

FIRST SHEPHERD:

      Just now I heard him blow

His horn. I see him on the lea below.

Be quiet!

SECOND SHEPHERD:

      Tell me why.

FIRST SHEPHERD:

     I think he's coming by.

SECOND SHEPHERD:

     He'll trick us with some lie.

                    [FIRST *and* SECOND SHEPHERDS *hide*.

                         Enter THIRD SHEPHERD.]

THIRD SHEPHERD:

     May Christ's cross help me, and St. Nicholas!

I've need of it; life's harder than it was.

Let men beware and let the false world pass.

It slips and slides, more brittle far than glass.

Never did it change so,

For now it's weal, now woe.

It's all a passing show.

Since Noah's flood, such floods were never seen,

Such dreadful winds and rains, and storms so keen.

Folk stammer or stand dumb with fear, I ween.

God turn it all to good! That's what I mean.

Just think how these floods drown

Us out in field and town;

No wonder that we're down.

We that walk at night, our herds to keep,

We see queer sights when others are asleep.

                    [*He spies the other shepherds*.]

My heart jumps. There I see two fellows peep,

Tall rascals both. I'll turn back to my sheep.

It was a bad mistake

This lonely path to take;

My toes I'll stub and break.

              [FIRST *and* SECOND SHEPHERDS *come forward*.]

May God save you, and you, O master sweet!

I want a drink and then a bite to eat.

FIRST SHEPHERD:

     Christ's curse, my boy, but you're a lazy cheat!

SECOND SHEPHERD:

     Does the boy rave? Let him wait for his meat!

Bad luck now on your pate!

The wretch, though he comes late,

Would eat, so starved his state.

THIRD SHEPHERD:

     Servants like me, who always sweat and swink,[2]

We eat our bread too dry, that's what I think.

---

2. *swink*, labor.

We're wet and weary while our masters blink.
It's late before we get to eat or drink.
Grand dame and noble sire
Delay and dock our hire,
Though we have run through mire.
But hear a truth, my master, for God's sake!
A fuss about my appetite you make!
But never supper gave me stomach-ache.
Henceforth I'll work as little as I take;
Or I can run away.
What one buys cheap, they say,
Won't in the long run pay.

FIRST SHEPHERD:

A fool you'd be if you yourself should bring
To serve a man who'd not spend anything.

SECOND SHEPHERD:

Peace, boy! I want no more rude chattering.
Or I will make you smart, by Heaven's King!
Our sheep are they left lorn?

THIRD SHEPHERD:

This very day at morn
I left them in the corn.
They have good pasture, so they can't go wrong.

FIRST SHEPHERD:

That's right. Oh, by the Rood,[3] these nights are long!
Before we go, I wish we'd have a song.

SECOND SHEPHERD:

I thought myself 'twould cheer us all along.

THIRD SHEPHERD:

I'm set.

FIRST SHEPHERD:

Tenor I'll try.

SECOND SHEPHERD:

And I the treble high.

THIRD SHEPHERD:

Then the middle am I.

[*Then* MAK *enters with a cloak drawn
over his tunic.*]

MAK:

Lord, of seven names, who made the moon that sails
And more stars than I know, Thy good will fails.
My brain is in a whirl; it's that which ails.
I wish I were in heaven where no child wails.

FIRST SHEPHERD:

Who is it pipes so poor?

MAK:

God knows what I endure,
A-walking on the moor!

---

3. *Rood,* the cross of Christ.

SECOND SHEPHERD [*stepping forward*]:
　Where do you come from, Mak? What news d'you bring?

THIRD SHEPHERD:
　Is he come? Keep close watch on everything!
　　　　　　　　　[*He snatches the cloak from him.*]

MAK [*with a southern accent*]:
　I tell you I'm a yeoman of the King.
　Make way for me! Lord's messages I bring.
　Fie on you! Get ye hence!
　This is no mere pretense.
　I must have reverence!

FIRST SHEPHERD:
　Why put on airs, Mak? It's no good to try.

SECOND SHEPHERD:
　Or play the actor, for I know you lie.

THIRD SHEPHERD:
　The scamp talks well, the Devil hang him high!

MAK:
　I'll make complaint; I'll make you sizzle and fry!
　I'll tell on you, in sooth.

FIRST SHEPHERD:
　O Mak, ere you speak truth,
　Take out your Southron tooth!

SECOND SHEPHERD:
　The Devil's in your eye. You need a whack!

　　　　　　　　　　　　　　　[*Strikes* MAK.]

THIRD SHEPHERD:
　So you don't know me? I'll teach you better, Mak!

MAK [*changing his tune*]:
　God keep all three! What I said I take back.
　You're all good fellows.

FIRST SHEPHERD:
　　　　Now you've changed your tack.

SECOND SHEPHERD:
　Why out so late, pray tell?
　Everyone knows right well
　You love roast-mutton smell.

MAK:
　I'm true as steel, as anyone will say,
　But I've a sickness takes my health away.
　My belly's in a parlous state today.

THIRD SHEPHERD:
　"The Devil seldom lies dead by the way."

MAK:
　As still as stone I'll lie,
　If this whole month have I
　Eat even a needle's eye.

FIRST SHEPHERD:
　How is your wife? how is she? tell us true.

MAK:

>She's sprawling by the fire; that's nothing new.
>The house is full of brats. She drinks ale, too.
>Come good or ill, that she will always do.
>She eats fast as she can,
>And each year gives a man
>A babe or two to scan.
>Though I had much more money in my purse,
>She'd eat and drink us to the Devil, sirs.
>Just look at her near by, the ugly curse!
>Will no one rid me of her?
>I'd give all in my coffer
>Mass for her soul to offer.[4]

SECOND SHEPHERD:

>I swear there's no one so tired in this shire.
>I must get sleep though I take less for hire.

THIRD SHEPHERD:

>I'm cold and nearly naked; I'd like a fire.

FIRST SHEPHERD:

>And I'm worn out with running in the mire.
>Keep watch.

[Lies down.]

SECOND SHEPHERD:

>   Not so, for I
>Must sleep. I'll put me by.

[Lies down.]

THIRD SHEPHERD:

>Equal with you I'll lie.

[Lies down.]

>Here, Mak, come here! Between us you must be.

MAK:

>You're sure you don't want to talk privately?

[Lies down, crosses himself and prays.]

>And now from head to toe
>*Manus tuas commendo,*
>*Pontio Pilato.*[5]

MAK [*while the* SHEPHERDS *sleep, rises and says*]:

>Now is the time for one who's short of gold
>To enter stealthily into a fold
>And nimbly work and yet be not too bold,
>For he might rue the bargain if 'twere told.
>He must be shrewd and wise
>Who likes his victuals nice,
>Yet hasn't got the price.

[Pretends to be a magician.]

>A circle round the moon I here fulfill.

---

4. *I'd give . . . offer.* He wishes she were dead.
5. *Manus . . . Pilato.* Mak is not very good at Latin. He has altered the conventional prayer "I put myself into your hands, God" to "I put myself into your hands, Pontius Pilate." Pilate permitted the execution of Jesus.

Until it's noon or I have done my will,
You must each one lie there and be stone still.
To make it sure some good strong words I'll spill.
Over you my hands I lift;
Your eyes go out and drift
Till I make better shift.
Lord, but they're sleeping sound! All men can hear!
I never was a shepherd, but now I'll learn their gear,
And though the flock be scared, I'll creep right near.
This fat sheep with its fleece improves my cheer.
And now goodbye to sorrow!

[*Seizes sheep.*]

Though I pay not tomorrow,
I'll in the meantime borrow.

[*Exit* MAK.]

Scene II

[*Interior of* MAK'S *cottage.* JILL *sits spinning.*]
MAK [*outside*]:
   Jill, are you in? Hello, get us some light!
JILL:
   Who makes this racket at this time of night?
   I'm busy spinning; I'll not stir a mite
   To get a day's pay. Curses on you light!
   It's thus a housewife fares.
   She's always rushed with cares,
   And all for nothing bears!
MAK [*outside*]:
   Open the latch, good wife! See what I bring!
JILL:
   I'll let you pull.

[*Opens door.* MAK *enters.*]

JILL:
            Come in, my own sweet thing!
MAK:
   Not much you care how long I stand and sing!
JILL:
   By your bare neck, for this[6] you're like to swing!
MAK:
   I'm good for something yet;
   For at a pinch I get
   More than the fools who sweat.
   I had a lucky lot and God's own grace.
JILL:
   To hang for it would be a foul disgrace!

---

6. *for this.* She points to the stolen sheep.

MAK:
> I've dodged before, my Jill, as hard a case.

JILL:
> Folk say that just so long a pot or vase
> To water it can come,
> Then broken it's brought home.

MAK:
> On that old saw be dumb!
> I wish that he were skinned; I want to eat.
> For twelve months I've not hankered so for meat.

JILL:
> Suppose they come here first and hear him bleat!

MAK:
> They'd catch me then. That puts me in a heat.
> Go bolt the door at back!
> I'd get from that whole pack
> The devil of a whack!

JILL:
> A good trick I have spied since you have none:
> We'll hide him in the crib till they have done.
> I'll lie and groan and say that he's my son.
> Let me alone to do what I've begun.

MAK:
> And I will say, tonight
> Of this boy you are light.

JILL:
> It's luck I was born bright.
> For cleverness this trick can't be surpassed.
> A woman's wit helps always at the last.
> Before they get suspicious, hurry fast.

MAK:
> If I don't get there soon, they'll blow a blast!

Scene III

[*The moor.* SHEPHERDS *sleeping. Enter* MAK.]
MAK:
> These men are still asleep.
> Their company I'll keep
> As if I'd stolen no sheep.

> > > [*Lies down between them.*]
> > [SHEPHERDS *wake one by one, and cross themselves.*]

FIRST SHEPHERD:
> *Resurrex a mortruis!* Here, take my hand!
> *Judas carnas Dominus!*[7] I can't well stand.
> My foot's asleep and I'm as dry as sand.

---

7. *Resurrex . . . Dominus,* nonsense Latin. The First Shepherd has picked up a few Latin phrases which he doesn't understand.

I dreamt we lay down near the English land!

SECOND SHEPHERD:
    I slept so well, I feel
As fresh as any eel,
And light upon my heel!

THIRD SHEPHERD:
    Lord bless us all! My body's all a-quake!
My heart jumps from my skin, and that's no fake.
Who's making all this din and my headache?
I'll teach him something! hear, you fellows, wake!
Where's Mak?

FIRST SHEPHERD:
        I vow he's near.
He went nowhere, that's clear.

THIRD SHEPHERD:
    I dreamt he was dressed up in a wolf's skin.

FIRST SHEPHERD:
    That's what too many rogues are wrapped up in!

THIRD SHEPHERD:
    While we were snoozing, seemed he did begin
To catch a sheep, without the slightest din.

SECOND SHEPHERD:
    Your dream has made you brood
On phantoms, by the Rood.
May God turn all to good!

                                [Shakes MAK.*]*

    Rise, Mak, for shame! You're sleeping far too long.

MAK:
    Now may Christ's holy name keep us from wrong!
What's this? St. James! I can hardly move along.
I'm just the same, and yet my neck's all wrong.

                    *[*SHEPHERDS *help him to his feet.]*

    Thank you! It's still uneven
For I've been plagued since even
With nightmares, by St. Stephen!
I thought that Jill she groaned in travail bad;
At the first cockcrow she had borne a lad
To increase our flock. Guess whether I am glad!
That's more wool on my distaff than I had!
Woe's him who has no bread
For young ones to be fed.
The Devil crack each head!
I must go home to Jill; she's in my thought.
Just look into my sleeve that I steal nought.
I wouldn't grieve you or take from you aught.

THIRD SHEPHERD:
    Go on, bad cess[8] to you!

                                      [Exit MAK.*]*

---

8. *bad cess,* bad luck.

I think we ought
To count our sheep this morn.
FIRST SHEPHERD:
I'll see if any's gone.
THIRD SHEPHERD:
We'll meet at the Crooked Thorn.

[*Exeunt* SHEPHERDS.]

Scene IV

[*Interior of* MAK'S *cottage.* JILL *at work.*]
MAK [*outside*]:
Undo this door! How long shall I stand here?
JILL:
Go walk in the waning moon! Who's shouting there?
MAK [*outside*]:
It's me, your husband, Mak. Hey, Jill, what cheer?
JILL:
Now we shall see the Devil hanged, that's clear.
I seem to hear a sound
As if a rope were round
His throat, and tightly bound.
MAK [*outside*]:
Just hear the fuss she makes for an excuse;
She doesn't do a stroke but to amuse.
JILL:
Who sits up late? Who comes and goes? Who brews?
Who bakes? Whose hand knits stockings, tell me, whose?
[*Opens the door.* MAK *enters.*]
It's a pity to behold,
Whether in hot or cold,
A womanless household!
But tell me how you left the herdsmen, Mak.
MAK:
The last word that they said when I turned back
Was that they'd count the sheep, the cursed pack!
They'll not be pleased to find a sheep they lack!
And so, however it goes,
They surely will suppose
From me the trouble rose.
You'll keep your promise?
JILL:
Why, of course, I will.
I'll put him in the cradle, and with skill
I'll swaddle him. Trust in a pinch to Jill!
[*She wraps sheep and puts it in cradle.*
Goes to bed.]
Come tuck me up. I'll lie here very still.

It may be a narrow squeak.

MAK:

Yes, if too close they peek,
Or if the sheep should speak!

JILL:

Hark, when they call, for they'll be here anon.
Let everything be ready. Sing alone
A lullaby, for I must lie and groan
And cry out by the wall on Mary and John.
You sing the lullaby,
And never doubt that I
Will pull wool over their eye.

Scene V

[*The moor. Enter three* SHEPHERDS.]

THIRD SHEPHERD:

Good morrow, Coll. What's wrong? Why not asleep?

FIRST SHEPHERD:

Alas that I was born! For this we'll keep
A villain's name. We've lost a good fat sheep!

SECOND SHEPHERD:

God save us! Who on us such wrong would heap?

FIRST SHEPHERD:

Some rascal. With my dogs
I've searched through Horbury Shrogs,
Found one ewe of fifteen hogs.

THIRD SHEPHERD:

Trust me, by Thomas, holy saint of Kent,
'Twas Mak or Jill who on that theft was bent.

FIRST SHEPHERD:

Peace, man, be quiet. I saw when he went.
You slander him unjustly and should repent.

SECOND SHEPHERD:

Though I may never succeed,
I'd say it though I bleed,
'Twas he who did the deed.

THIRD SHEPHERD:

Then let's go thither at a running trot.
I won't eat bread till at the truth I've got.

FIRST SHEPHERD:

And I won't drink until I've solved the plot.

SECOND SHEPHERD:

Until I find him, I won't rest one jot.
I make this vow aright:
Till I have him in sight
I will not sleep one night
In the same spot.   [*Exeunt.*]

Scene VI

[MAK's *cottage. Within* MAK *sings*, JILL *groans*. SHEPHERDS *approach the door.*]

THIRD SHEPHERD:

    D'you hear them sing? Mak thinks that he can croon!

FIRST SHEPHERD:

    I never heard a voice so out of tune!

SECOND SHEPHERD:

    Hey, Mak, open your door, and do it soon.

MAK:

    Who is it shouts as if it were high noon?

THIRD SHEPHERD:

    Good men, if it were day—

MAK [*opening door*]:

    As much as ever you may,

    Speak very soft, I pray.

    Here is a woman sick and ill at ease;

    I'd rather die than she had more misease.

JILL:

    Go to some other place, I beg you, please,

    Each footfall knocks my nose and makes me sneeze.

FIRST SHEPHERD:

    How are you, Mak, I say?

MAK:

    And how are you today,

    And what brings you this way?

    You're wet all through; you've run so in the mire,

    If you'll sit down, I'll light you here a fire.

    I've got what's coming to me. I'm no liar;

    My dream's come true; a nurse I've got to hire.

    I've more babes than you knew.

    Surely the saying's true:

    "We must drink what we brew."

    Stay eat before you go; I see you sweat.

SECOND SHEPHERD:

    Nothing will cheer us, neither drink nor meat.

MAK:

    What ails you, sir?

THIRD SHEPHERD:

        We've had a loss that's great;

    We found a sheep was stolen, when we met.

MAK:

    Alas! Had I been there,

    Someone had paid full dear.

FIRST SHEPHERD:

    Marry, some think you were!

SECOND SHEPHERD:

    Yes, Mak, just tell us who else could it be?

THIRD SHEPHERD:
> 'Twas either you or else your wife, say we.

MAK:
> If you suspect us, either Jill or me,
> Come rip our house apart, and then you'll see
> That here within this spot
> No sheep or cow I've got;
> And Jill's not stirred a jot.
> As I am true and leal, to God I pray,
> This is the first meal that I've had today.

FIRST SHEPHERD:
> Upon my soul, Mak, have a care, I say;
> He's early learned to steal who can't say nay.

> [SHEPHERDS *begin to search.*]

JILL:
> Out, thieves, get out from here!

MAK:
> When her great groans you hear,
> Your hearts should melt for fear.

JILL:
> Out, thieves; don't touch my child! Get out the door!

MAK:
> Knew you her pangs, your conscience would be sore.
> You're wrong, I warn you, thus to come before
> A woman in her pain. I say no more.

JILL:
> O God, who art so mild,
> If you I e'er beguiled,
> Let me eat up this child!

MAK:
> Peace, woman, for God's passion, speak more low!
> You spoil your brains and terrify me so.

SECOND SHEPHERD:
> I think our sheep is slain. Think you not so?

THIRD SHEPHERD:
> We search here all in vain. We may well go.
> There's nothing I can find,
> No bone or scrap or rind,
> But empty plates behind.
> Here's no tame cattle, and no wild there is
> That smells like our old ram, I'll swear to this.

JILL:
> You're right; and of this child God give me bliss!

FIRST SHEPHERD:
> I think we've failed and that we've done amiss.

SECOND SHEPHERD:
> Dame, is't a boy you have?
> Him may Our Lady save!

MAK:
> A son a lord might crave.

He grabs so when he wakes, it's a joy to see.

THIRD SHEPHERD:

Luck on his buttocks! Happy may they be!
But who god-fathered him so hurriedly?

MAK [*hesitating*]:

Blest be their lips!

FIRST SHEPHERD:

A lie it's going to be!

MAK:

Gibbon Waller was one,
And Perkin's mother's son;
John Horn supplied the fun.

SECOND SHEPHERD:

Mak, let us all be friends again, I say.

MAK [*haughtily*]:

It's little friendship you've shown me today.
Goodbye, and glad to see you go away.

THIRD SHEPHERD:

Fair words, no warmth—that's just as plain as day.

[SHEPHERDS *turn to go out.*]

FIRST SHEPHERD:

Gave you the child a thing?

SECOND SHEPHERD:

Not even one farthing!

THIRD SHEPHERD:

Wait here; fast back I'll fling.

[THIRD SHEPHERD *returns.* SECOND *and*
FIRST SHEPHERDS *follow.*]

THIRD SHEPHERD:

To see your baby, Mak, I ask your leave.

MAK:

No. Only insults from you I receive.

THIRD SHEPHERD:

Well, it won't make that little daystar grieve
If you let me give sixpence, I believe.

MAK:

Go way; I say he sleeps.

[*Approaches cradle.*]

THIRD SHEPHERD:

I think instead he peeps.

MAK:

When he wakes up, he weeps.

THIRD SHEPHERD:

Just let me kiss him once and lift the clout.
What in the devil! What a monstrous snout!

FIRST SHEPHERD:

He's birth-marked maybe. Let's not wait about!
The ill-spun cloth in truth comes foully out.
He looks like our own sheep!

THIRD SHEPHERD:

What, Gib! give me a peep.

FIRST SHEPHERD:
Where Truth can't walk 'twill creep.

SECOND SHEPHERD:
That was a clever trick, a shabby fraud!
The bare-faced swindle should be noised abroad.

THIRD SHEPHERD:
Yes, sirs, let's bind her fast and burn the bawd.
If she should hang, everyone would applaud.
Tucked in a cradle so,
I never saw, I vow,
A boy with horns till now!

MAK:
Peace, peace I ask! You'll give the child a scare.
For I'm his father and that's his mother there.

FIRST SHEPHERD:
What devil is he named for? Look, Mak's heir!

SECOND SHEPHERD:
Let be all that! I say, God give him care!

JILL:
A pretty child is he
To sit on woman's knee,
And make his father glee!

THIRD SHEPHERD:
I know him by his earmark, a good token.

MAK:
I tell you, sirs, his nose in truth was broken.
He was bewitched; so has a wise clerk spoken.

FIRST SHEPHERD:
Liar! you deserve to have your noddle broken!

JILL:
An elf took him away;
I saw him changed for aye
At stroke of twelve today.

SECOND SHEPHERD:
You two are fit to lie in the same bed!

THIRD SHEPHERD:
Since they maintain their theft, let's leave them dead.

MAK:
If I do wrong again, cut off my head!
I'm at your will.

THIRD SHEPHERD:
Men, take my plan instead.
We'll neither curse nor fight,
But here in canvas tight
We'll toss him good and right.

[SHEPHERDS *exeunt, carrying* MAK *in a blanket.*]

Scene VII

[*Moor. Enter* SHEPHERDS.]

FIRST SHEPHERD:

    Lord, I'm about to burst, I am so sore!

    Until I rest, in faith I can't do more.

SECOND SHEPHERD:

    He's hefty as a sheep of seven score.

    And now I'll lay me down to snooze and snore.

THIRD SHEPHERD:

    Let's lie down on this green.

FIRST SHEPHERD:

    These thieves are rascals mean!

THIRD SHEPHERD:

    We'd best forget what's been.

[SHEPHERDS *lie down.*]

[*An angel sings "Gloria in excelsis";*[9] *then
let him say:*]

ANGEL:

    Rise, herdsmen, rise, for now the Child is born

    Who frees mankind, for Adam's sin forlorn.

    To thwart the wicked fiend this night he's born.

    High God is made your friend. This very morn,

    To Bethlehem go ye;

    The new-born Deity

    In manger laid ye'll see.

[*The* ANGEL *withdraws.*]

FIRST SHEPHERD:

    That was as queer a voice as ever I heard;

    Wonder enough to make a man be scared.

SECOND SHEPHERD:

    To speak of God's own Son of Heaven he dared,

    And all the wood I thought with lightning glared.

THIRD SHEPHERD:

    He said the baby lay

    In Bethlehem today.

FIRST SHEPHERD:

    That star points out the way.

[*Points to star.*]

    Let's seek him there!

SECOND SHEPHERD:

        Did you hear how he cracked it?

    Three breves, one long.[10]

THIRD SHEPHERD:

        Yes, and he surely smacked it.

    There was no crotchet wrong, and nothing lacked it.

---

9. *"Gloria in excelsis,"* the song of the angels on Christ's birthday,
"Glory be to God on high."

10. *Three . . . long,* musical tones.

FIRST SHEPHERD:
> I'd like us three to sing, just as he knacked it.

SECOND SHEPHERD:
> Let's harken how you croon.
> Can you bark at the moon?

THIRD SHEPHERD:
> Shut up and hark, you loon!

[SHEPHERDS *sing off tune.*]

SECOND SHEPHERD:
> To Bethlehem he ordered us to go.
> I'm much afraid that we have been too slow.

THIRD SHEPHERD:
> Be merry, fellow, and don't croak like a crow.
> This news means endless joy to men below.

FIRST SHEPHERD:
> Though we are tired and wet,
> We'll hurry now and get
> Where Mother and Child are set.

[*They start to walk.*]

SECOND SHEPHERD:
> We find by ancient prophets—stop your din!—
> David, Isaiah, others of their kin,
> That God's own Son would someday light within
> A virgin's womb, to cleanse away our sin.
> Isaiah, don't forget,
> Foretold that one day yet
> "*Virgo concipiet.*"[11]

THIRD SHEPHERD:
> Right merry should we be that now's the day
> The lovely Lord is come who rules for aye.
> I'd be the happiest man if I could say
> That I had knelt before that Child to pray.
> But still the angel said
> The Babe was poorly arrayed
> And in a manger laid!

FIRST SHEPHERD:
> Prophets and patriarchs of old were torn
> With yearning to behold this Child now born.
> Without that sight they never ceased to mourn.
> But we shall see Him, now this very morn.
> When I see Him, I'll know
> The prophets' words were so.
> No liars were they, no!
> To men as poor as we He will appear.
> We'll find Him first, His messenger said clear.

SECOND SHEPHERD:
> Then let us hurry, for the place is near.

THIRD SHEPHERD:
> Ready am I and glad; let's go with cheer.

---

11. "*Virgo concipiet.*" A virgin will conceive a child.

Lord, if Thy will it be,
Allow poor yokels three
This happy sight to see.

Scene VIII

[*Bethlehem, a stable. The* VIRGIN *seated, the* CHILD *on her knee. The* SHEPHERDS *enter and kneel.*]

FIRST SHEPHERD:

Hail, pure and sweet one; hail, thou holy Child!
Maker of all, born of a maiden mild.
Thou hast o'ercome the Devil, fierce and wild.
That wily Trickster now has been beguiled.
Look, how He laughs, sweet thing!
As my poor offering
A cherry bunch I bring.

SECOND SHEPHERD:

Hail, Savior King, our ransom Thou hast bought!
Hail, mighty Babe, Thou madest all of naught.
Hail, God of mercy, Thou the Fiend hast fought.
I kneel and bow before Thee. Look, I've brought
A bird, my tiny one!
Other faith we have none,
Our day-star and God's Son.

THIRD SHEPHERD:

Hail, pretty darling, Thou art God indeed.
I pray to Thee, be near when I have need.
Sweet is Thy look, although my heart does bleed
To see Thee here, and dressed in such poor weed.
Hail, Babe, on Thee I call.
I bring a tennis ball.
Take it and play withal.

MARY:

The Lord of Heaven, God omnipotent,
Who made all things aright, His Son has sent.
My name He named and blessed me ere He went.
Him I conceived through grace, as God had meant.
And now I pray Him so
To keep you from all woe!
Tell this where'er you go.

FIRST SHEPHERD:

Farewell, Lady, thou fairest to behold,
With Christ-child on thy knee!

SECOND SHEPHERD:

             He lies full cold,
But well it is for me that Him you hold.

THIRD SHEPHERD:

Already this does seem a thing oft told.

FIRST SHEPHERD:
  Let's spread the tidings round!
SECOND SHEPHERD:
  Come; our salvation's found!
THIRD SHEPHERD:
  To sing it we are bound!

[*Exeunt* SHEPHERDS *singing*.]
Here ends the Pageant of the SHEPHERDS.

DISCUSSION

1. (a) What does the First Shepherd complain about? (b) Whom does he blame? (c) How does he console himself?

2. (a) What does the Second Shepherd complain about? (b) the Third? (c) What kind of picture emerges from the dialogue of the shepherds' lives?

3. (a) What does Mak try to do when he first enters the scene? (b) What does this indicate to you about his character?

4. (a) What do Mak and Jill decide to do with the stolen sheep? (b) Who thought of this idea?

5. (a) Describe Jill. (b) What seems to be her opinion of Mak? (c) What is her opinion of herself?

6. (a) Which shepherd dreams of Mak's theft? (b) Who is the first to accuse Mak?

7. Mak and Jill almost succeed in their scheme. (a) Under what circumstances are they finally exposed? (b) When does Mak confess his guilt? (c) How do the shepherds punish Mak?

8. (a) Who wakes the shepherds in scene VII? (b) What is his message? (c) What do the shepherds talk about as they walk to Bethlehem?

9. (a) What gifts do the shepherds bring? (b) In what ways are these gifts typical of the bearers.

THE AUTHOR'S CRAFT

Medieval drama

The playrights of Greece and Rome developed a highly sophisticated dramatic tradition that lasted hundreds of years. But with the decline of Roman power this theatrical tradition slowly died, and by the beginning of the Middle Ages there existed no theater at all in Europe.

The second birth of Western drama began in the churches. Religious festivals of Christianity were frequently based on highly dramatic events, such as the resurrection of Jesus. In the medieval church such feasts were first celebrated by choirs of monks singing the story. As time went on the monks began to dramatize the events. With time, these short dramatic versions of biblical events became so elaborate that they no longer fit into a religious service. So, for a while, they were performed separately on the broad front porch of the church.

These religious plays began to acquire a special significance of their own. Though a single play was relatively short, there were so many plays that to do all of them would sometimes take several days. When performed together, these plays told the history of the world as the medieval man saw it, beginning with the creation of the earth and ending with the ultimate destruction of the world.

Such a variety of short plays provided a complex problem in staging, and the medieval mind perfected a unique solution. Each play was mounted on a cart which was built much like a modern parade float. Each cart carried all the scenery and stage props for its short drama. For example, the cart carrying *The Second Shepherds' Play* probably was divided into three parts. Mak's cottage was at one end, the fields in the center, and the stable of Bethlehem at the other end. Such carts moved in procession through a town, stopping at specific points to perform their plays. An observer could sit in one place and, as the carts rolled by, see performed in succession all the significant events of history.

The scripts for these dramas were usually written by learned clergymen. But the productions were handled strictly by amateurs. Groups of townspeople would produce an entire play—building the sets, making the costumes, and playing the parts. Often, men who had a specific trade chose to produce plays that related to their own occupations. Thus, boat builders performed the play of Noah and the Flood; wine makers, the miracle of Christ's changing water into wine; and bakers, scenes of Hell depicting the fiery cooking of lost souls.

Robin Hood and Little John

The common people had their own heroes, and none is more famous than the legendary Robin Hood. Living in the wilds of Sherwood Forest, where no king could safely venture, Robin and his merry band of outlaws defended the peasants from the many injustices of their rulers. The selection which follows illustrates a truth which the commoner of medieval times treasured—that one can win even in losing.

"Robin Hood and Little John" from CHILD'S BALLADS, Vol. III.

WHEN Robin Hood was about twenty years old,
    With a hey down down and a down
He happend to meet Little John,
A jolly brisk blade, right fit for the trade,
5   For he was a lusty young man.

Tho he was calld Little, his limbs they were large,
    And his stature was seven foot high;
Where-ever he came, they quak'd at his name,
    For soon he would make them to fly.

10 How they came acquainted, I'll tell you in brief,
    If you will but listen a while;
For this very jest, amongst all the rest,
    I think it may cause you to smile.

Bold Robin Hood said to his jolly bowmen,
15   'Pray tarry you here in this grove;
And see that you all observe well my call,
    While thorough the forest I rove.

We have had no sport for these fourteen long days,
    Therefore now abroad will I go;
20 Now should I be beat, and cannot retreat,
    My horn I will presently blow.'

Then did he shake hands with his merry men all,
    And bid them at present good b'w'ye;[1]
Then, as near a brook his journey he took,
25   A stranger he chancd to espy.

They happend to meet on a long narrow bridge,
    And neither of them would give way;
Quoth bold Robin Hood, and sturdily stood,
    'I'll show you right Nottingham play.'

30 With that from his quiver an arrow he drew,
    A broad arrow with a goose-wing:
The stranger reply'd, 'I'll liquor[2] thy hide,
    If thou offerst to touch the string.'

Quoth bold Robin Hood, 'Thou dost prate like an ass,
35   For were I to bend but my bow,
I could send a dart quite thro thy proud heart,
    Before thou couldst strike me one blow.'

'Thou talkst like a coward,' the stranger reply'd;
    'Well armd with a long bow you stand,

40 To shoot at my breast, while I, I protest,
    Have nought but a staff in my hand.'

'The name of a coward,' quoth Robin, 'I scorn,
    Wherefore my long bow I'll lay by;
And now, for thy sake, a staff will I take,
45   The truth of thy manhood to try.'

Then Robin Hood stept to a thicket of trees,
    And chose him a staff of ground-oak;
Now this being done, away he did run
    To the stranger, and merrily spoke:

50 'Lo! see my staff, it is lusty and tough,
    Now here on the bridge we will play;
Whoever falls in, the other shall win
    The battel, and so we'll away.'

'With all my whole heart,' the stranger reply'd;
55   'I scorn in the least to give out';
This said, they fell to 't without more dispute,
    And their staffs they did flourish about.

And first Robin he gave the stranger a bang,
    So hard that it made his bones ring:
60 The stranger he said,' This must be repaid,
    I'll give you as good as you bring.

'So long as I'm able to handle my staff,
    To die in your debt, friend, I scorn.'
Then to it each goes and followd their blows,
65   As if they had been threshing of corn.

The stranger gave Robin a crack on the crown,
    Which caused the blood to appear;
Then Robin, enrag'd, more fiercely engag'd,
    And followd his blows more severe.

70 So thick and so fast did he lay it on him,
    With a passionate fury and ire,
At every stroke, he made him to smoke,
    As if he had been all on fire.

O then into fury the stranger he grew,
75   And gave him a damnable look,
And with it a blow that laid him full low,
    And tumbld him into the brook.

'I prithee, good fellow, O where art thou now?'
    The stranger, in laughter, he cry'd;

---

1. *good b'w'ye*, shortened form of "God be with you."
2. *liquor*, beat.

80 Quoth bold Robin Hood,' Good faith, in the flood,
      And floating along with the tide.

    'I needs must acknowledge thou art a brave soul;
      With thee I'll no longer contend;
    For needs must I say, thou hast got the day,
85   Our battel shall be at an end.'

    Then unto the bank he did presently wade,
      And pulld himself out by a thorn;
    Which done, at the last, he blowd a loud blast
      Straitway on his fine bugle-horn.

90 The eccho of which through the vallies did fly,
      At which his stout bowmen appeard,
    All cloathed in green, most gay to be seen;
      So up to their master they steerd.

    'O what's the matter?' quoth William Stutely;
95   'Good master, you are wet to the skin':
    'No matter,' quoth he; 'the lad which you see,
      In fighting, hath tumbld me in.'

    'He shall not go scot-free,' the others reply'd;
      So-strait they were seizing him there,
100 To duck him likewise; but Robin Hood cries,
      'He is a stout fellow, forbear.

    'There's no one shall wrong thee, friend, be not afraid;
      These bowmen upon me do wait;
    There's threescore and nine; if thou wilt be mine,
105   Thou shalt have my livery strait.

    'And other accourtrements fit for a man;
      Speak up, jolly blade, never fear;
    I'll teach you also the use of the bow,
      To shoot at the fat fallow-deer.'

110 'O here is my hand,' the stranger reply'd,
      'I'll serve you with all my whole heart;
    My name is John Little, a man of good mettle;
      Nere doubt me, for I'll play my part.'

    'His name shall be alterd,' quoth William Stutely,
115   'And I will his godfather be;
    Prepare then a feast, and none of the least,
      For we will be merry,' quoth he.

    They presently fetchd in a brace of fat does,
      With humming strong liquor likewise;

120 They lovd what was good; so, in the greenwood,
      This pretty sweet babe they baptize.

    He was, I must tell you, but seven foot high,
      And, may be, an ell[3] in the waste;
    A pretty sweet lad; much feasting they had;
125   Bold Robin the christning grac'd.

    With all his bowmen, which stood in a ring,
      And were of the Notti[n]gham breed;
    Brave Stutely comes then, with seven yeomen,
      And did in this manner proceed.

130 'This infant was called John Little,' quoth he,
      'Which name shall be changed anon;
    The words we'll transpose, so where-ever he goes,
      His name shall be calld Little John.'

    They all with a shout made the elements ring,
135   So soon as the office was ore;
    To feasting they went, with true merriment,
      And tippld strong liquor gillore.

    Then Robin he took the pretty sweet babe,
      And cloathd him from top to the toe
140 In garments of green, most gay to be seen,
      And gave him a curious long bow.

    'Thou shalt be an archer as well as the best,
      And range in the greenwood with us;
    Where we'll not want gold nor silver, behold,
145   While bishops have ought in their purse.

    'We live here like squires, or lords of renown,
      Without ere a foot of free land;
    We feast on good cheer, with wine, ale, and beer,
      And evry thing at our command.'

150 Then musick and dancing did finish the day;
      At length, when the sun waxed low,
    Then all the whole train the grove did refrain,
      And unto their caves they did go.

    And so ever after, as long as he livd,
155   Altho he was proper and tall,
    Yet nevertheless, the truth to express,
      Still Little John they did him call.
    (See page 567 for DISCUSSION)

---

3. an ell, about 45 inches.

Brainy Teacher

Brainy teacher, is it your
Desire to beat us daily more,
   Like a blooming lord?
We'd rather leave your school for good,
And learn another livelihood
   Than jump to your bossy word.

But if we caught you, with God's will,
At the stones beside the mill,
   Or by the crab-apple tree,
We'd scar you once upon your skin
For every swishing:[1] then your kin
   Would give you sympathy.

And if the Devil—he's your Puck[2]—
Waved his claw to bring you luck,

You'd get it then worse still.
If he prayed one word for you,
We'd knock him down and belt him too,
   Not spare you at his will.

For many times we groan and sigh
When signals from his glinting eye
   Make you beat our backs;
For you and he are of one mind,
And daily you are close combined
   To give us mighty whacks.

Poem #60: "Brainy Teacher" from THE PENGUIN BOOK OF MEDIEVAL VERSE, translated by Brian Stone. © 1964. Reprinted by permission of Penguin Books, Ltd.
1. *swishing.* It was customary to whip slow students with a flexible birch rod.
2. *Puck,* hobgoblin; a mythical figure of mischief.

The Song of the University of Paris

Much argument is heard of late,
The subject I'll attempt to state,
A question for dispute, I fear,
That will hang on for many a year.
The student-folk of Paris town
(I speak of those in cap and gown,
Students of art, philosophy,—
In short, "the University,"
And not our old-time learned men)
Have stirred up trouble here again.
Nothing they'll gain, it seems to me,
Except more bitter enmity,
Till there is no peace, day or night.
Does such a state of things seem right?

To give his son a chance to stay
In Paris, growing wise each day,
Is some old peasant's one ambition.
To pay his bills and his tuition
The poor hard-working father slaves;
Sends him each farthing that he saves,
While he in misery will stay
On his scant plot of land to pray
That his hard toil may help to raise
His son to honor and to praise.

But once the son is safe in town
The story then reads upside down.
Forgetting all his pledges now,
The earnings of his father's plow
He spends for weapons, not for books.
Dawdling through city streets, he looks
To find some pretty, loitering wench,
Or idle brawl by tavern bench;
Wanders at will and pries about,
Till money fails and gown wears out.—
Then he starts fresh on the old round;
Why sow good seed on barren ground?
Even in Lent[1] when men should do
Something pleasing in God's view,
Your students then elect to wear
For penitence, no shirts of hair,[2]
But swaggering hauberks,[3] as they sit

"The Song of the University of Paris" from LEGENDS AND SATIRES FROM MEDIEVAL LITERATURE, translated by Marion E. Markley. © 1913 by Ginn and Company, the publishers.
1. *Lent,* a time of fasting and penance in Christian churches.
2. *shirts of hair.* Hair shirts, worn next to the skin, were intolerably itchy. Medieval people wore them as a means of voluntary suffering for their sins.
3. *hauberks,* armor; a tunic of chain mail.

Drowning in drink their feeble wit;
While three or four of them excite
Four hundred students to a fight,
And close the University.
(Not such a great calamity!)

Yet, heavens, for one of serious mind
What life more pleasing can you find
Than earnest scholar's life may be?
More pains than precious gems has he,
And while he's struggling to grow wise,

Amusements he must sacrifice,—
Give up his feasting and his drinking,
And spend his time in sober thinking.
His life is just about as merry
As is a monk's in a monastery.
Why send a boy away to school
There to become an arrant fool?
When he should be acquiring sense,
He wastes his time and all his pence,
And to his friends brings only shame,
While they suppose him winning fame.

DISCUSSION

Robin Hood and Little John

1. What kind of story does the poet tell us to expect, and how does he want us to respond?

2. (a) What does Robin Hood go seeking in the forest? (b) Why? (c) What instructions does he leave with his men?

3. (a) Where do Robin and John Little meet? (b) What precipitates their fight? (c) Why does Robin put aside his bow and fight with a staff?

4. What is the outcome of the fight? (b) What does Robin do?

5. What does Robin propose when his men arrive?

6. (a) What is ironic about John Little's new name? (b) What does his mock "baptism" signify?

7. Explain how an apparent defeat becomes a victory in this poem.

Brainy Teacher

1. (a) What is the teacher doing to his students? (b) How do the students respond?

2. Whom do the students think is their teacher's ally?

3. Do you think the students are directly addressing the teacher or talking behind the teacher's back? Why?

4. What is the tone of this poem?

The Song of the University of Paris

1. According to the poem, how does the typical university student spend his time?

2. What are the "benefits" of the earnest scholar's life?

3. What does this poem conclude about sending a boy away to school?

4. What is the tone of this poem?

5. Compare "The Song of the University of Paris" to "Brainy Teacher." In what way does exaggeration in both poems contribute to the over-all effect?

THE AUTHOR'S CRAFT

The ballad

"Robin Hood and Little John" is a folk ballad, a form of verse story which seems to have been perfected toward ·the end of the Middle Ages. The ballad form, created by common folk and spread with the assistance of wandering minstrels, derives from a blend of popular songs and dances. Most ballads were sung to a simple, repetitious tune. Because the people who sang ballads were unable to read, the stories had to be uncomplicated so that they could be easily memorized.

With the passage of time ballads changed as singers forgot words and lines and substituted their own. Today, we have many versions of the same ballad story, often widely varying from one to another.

Ballads are characteristically simple and direct in their plot. Because they are straightforward and unadorned, ballads frequently make an immediate and memorable impact on the reader.

Barbara Allen's Cruelty

All in the merry month of May,
    When green buds they were swelling
Young Jemmy Grove on his death-bed lay
    For love of Barbara Allen.

He sent his man unto her then,
    To the town where she was dwelling:
"O haste and come to my master dear,
    If your name be Barbara Allen."

Slowly, slowly she rose up,
    And she came where he was lying;
And when she drew the curtain by,
    Says, "Young man, I think you're dying."

"O it's I am sick, and very, very sick,
    And it's all for Barbara Allen."
"O the better for me you'll never be,
    Tho' your heart's blood were a-spilling!

"O do not mind, young man," she says,
    "When the red wine you were filling,
That you made the healths go round and round,
    And slighted Barbara Allen?"

He turned his face unto the wall,
    And death with him was dealing:
"Adieu, adieu, my dear friends all;
    Be kind to Barbara Allen."

As she was walking o'er the fields,
    She heard the dead-bell knelling;
And every toll the dead-bell struck,
    Cried, "Woe to Barbara Allen!"

"O mother, mother, make my bed,
    To lay me down in sorrow.
My love has died for me today,
    I'll die for him tomorrow."

UNIT 6 REVIEW

1. The main themes of medieval romance were set by the chivalric code, and the main action of the stories deals with knights who attempt to live by this code.

a. Cite some of the rules and customs governing knightly behavior during the Middle Ages.

b. Recall the various knights who appear in "The Tale of Sir Gareth" and in "Lancelot and Elaine." Which knights best typify the ideals of chivalry? Which violate the chivalric code?

c. Look up the word *gentleman* in your dictionary. Would you agree or disagree that this definition was influenced by medieval ideals? Explain your answer.

2. Sharing the popularity of the medieval, or chivalric, romance was the medieval, or folk, ballad, the most common type of narrative poetry during the Middle Ages. While the chivalric romances were favorites with the upper classes, the folk ballads were created and sung by the common people. The ballad, "Barbara Allen's Cruelty," has more versions than any other ballad in existence. After you have read the ballad, discuss these questions:

a. What is the theme of "Barbara Allen's Cruelty"?

b. Explain the plot of this ballad.

c. Which two lines reveal a supernatural quality?

d. How many incidents does the ballad relate?

e. Is the story told through exposition or dialogue or both?

f. What clues can you find as to the class of people portrayed in this ballad?

g. Is the imagery in "Barbara Allen's Cruelty" simple and conventional or elaborate and unusual? Find examples to support your answer.

h. Some of the common characteristics of medieval ballads are: (1) simplicity of plot, theme, and language; (2) appeal to common folk; (3) use of the supernatural; (4) inclusion of only one incident; (5) conventional imagery; (6) musical and dramatic quality; (7) repetition and, or, a refrain. Which of these characteristics are also common to the medieval romance? In which characteristics do the medieval romance and the medieval ballad differ?

7 Three One-Act Plays

THE LICENSE
A MARRIAGE PROPOSAL
CHARLIE

ONE-ACT PLAYS

The one-act play has been a recent development in the history of the theater. Previously used only as a "curtain raiser" before a major production or in vaudeville, the one-act has now become a popular length. Perhaps responsible for its popularity has been the growth of the "small" theater with limited budgets and the experimental theater where beginning actors and playwrights can experiment and gain experience.

The requirements for a good one-act play are strict. More important than any other requirement is the author's need to achieve a clear effect upon his audience. In order to do so, he must not confuse his play by introducing unnecessary characters, overly complex plots, or excess dialogue. If the distinction between a one-act play and a three- or five-act play strikes you as similar to the distinction between a short story and a novel, then you are close to an understanding of the one-act play.

The three plays which follow have been chosen to give you a broad view of the one-act. You will find that they range from the serious to the farcical and that the authors' techniques vary from the traditional to the experimental.

The License

(La patente, 1919)

Luigi Pirandello

The Cast

JUDGE D'ANDREA	THIRD JUDGE
MARRANCA	ROSINELLA
FIRST JUDGE	ROSARIO CHIÀRCHIARO
SECOND JUDGE	(Rō sä′ rē ō Kē är′ kēä rō)

The chambers of JUDGE D'ANDREA, *an examining magistrate in a small provincial town of southern Italy. The rear wall consists almost entirely of shelves full of green letter-files, which, one imagines, are crammed with documents. Right rear, a desk covered with papers; next to it, against the wall, more crowded shelves. The* JUDGE'S *leather armchair is in front of the desk and there are other old chairs scattered about. The main entrance is at right. At left, a broad, high casement window framed by large shutters. In front of the window, a tall stand supporting a big bird cage. Also at left, a small secret doorway. The over-all impression is one of shabby disorder.*

At curtain, JUDGE D'ANDREA, *in hat and overcoat, enters through the main door, carrying a cage not much larger than his fist. He goes up to the stand, opens the door of the large cage, and transfers a goldfinch into it from the small cage.*

D'ANDREA. Go on, get in there! In with you, you lazy thing! Oh, at last . . . Now, you keep quiet, as usual, and let me dispense justice to these poor, ferocious little human beings.
(He removes his hat and coat and hangs them up on a rack, then he sits down at his desk, picks up a sheaf of documents pertaining to a case he is supposed to try, waves it impatiently about, and snorts.)
The fool!
(He pauses, lost in thought for a moment, then he rings a bell and the porter, MARRANCA, *enters through the main door.)*
MARRANCA. You rang for me, Your Honor?
D'ANDREA. Look, Marranca: I want you to run down the street—it's not far—to Chiàrchiaro's house—
MARRANCA *(leaping backward and making the sign against the Evil Eye, a downward thrusting of a closed fist with index and little fingers extended in the shape of horns).* For the love of God, don't even mention that name, Your Honor!
D'ANDREA *(very annoyed, pounding on his desk).* That's enough, by God! I forbid you to behave like an animal in my presence! And at the ex-

pense of a poor innocent man! Don't let this happen again!
MARRANCA. I'm sorry, Your Honor. I—I did it for your own good, too, you know.
D'ANDREA. Oh, so you insist—
MARRANCA. Not another word, Your Honor. What—what do you want me to do at this—this gentleman's house?
D'ANDREA. You'll tell him the public prosecutor wants to talk to him and you'll bring him here at once.
MARRANCA. At once, Your Honor. Yes, of course. Anything else?
D'ANDREA. That's all. You may go.
(MARRANCA exits, holding the door open as he leaves to admit three other magistrates, all dressed in their judicial robes and hats. They exchange greetings with D'ANDREA, then cluster about the goldfinch's cage.)
FIRST JUDGE. Well, and what does Mr. Goldfinch have to say for himself, eh?
SECOND JUDGE. You know, D'Andrea, you're becoming something of a joke, carrying this bird around with you everywhere.
THIRD JUDGE. You're known all over town as Judge Goldfinch.
FIRST JUDGE. Where is it? Where's that little cage you keep him in?
SECOND JUDGE *(picking it up from the desk).* Here it is! Gentlemen, look: a child's toy! And you a grown man!
D'ANDREA. I'm a child, am I? Just because of this little cage? And what about the rest of you, then, all dressed up like that?
THIRD JUDGE. Now, now, a little respect for the toga!
D'ANDREA. Go on, don't make me laugh! Nobody can hear us in here. As a boy, I used to make a game of this with my friends. One of us would play the defendant, somebody else would be the judge, the rest of us would be lawyers or members of the jury. . . . You must have played that game or something very much like it. . . . Well, I can tell you we took it much more seriously then than we do now.
FIRST JUDGE. Oh, you're right about that!
SECOND JUDGE. It always ended in a fight, I remember!
THIRD JUDGE *(displaying an old scar on his forehead).* Look at this: I still have a scar from a rock one of the defense lawyers threw at me while I was prosecuting his client!

D'ANDREA. The best part of the game was the robes we used to wear. They made us feel big and important, and under them we were still children. Now it's just the opposite: we're grown up and the robes belong to the game we played when we were little. You have to have a lot of nerve to be able to take it seriously. (*He picks up the documents pertaining to* CHIÀRCHIARO'S *case.*) For example, my friends, I'm supposed to try this case. Nothing could be more iniquitous than this trial. Iniquitous because here a poor wretch is trying desperately to rebel against the cruelest injustice, with no possibility of winning. A victim with no way of fighting back. By going to court he's doing his best to fight back: he's demanding justice from the first two people who happened to come along. And justice—justice, my friends— is the one thing he'll never, never have. The court is bound to rule mercilessly against him, thus confirming, and ferociously, too, the very wrong by which this poor man has been victimized.

FIRST JUDGE. What case is it?

D'ANDREA. The suit brought by Rosario Chiàrchiaro. (*At the mention of that name the three* JUDGES *behave exactly like* MARRANCA: *they leap backward, making signs against the Evil Eye.*)

ALL THREE (*shouting*). Holy Mother of God!—Touch iron, touch iron!—Don't mention that name!

D'ANDREA. There, you see? And you're the very people who are expected to make certain that this poor fellow receives justice.

FIRST JUDGE. Justice has nothing to do with it! The man's gone crazy!

D'ANDREA. He's a poor unfortunate wretch, that's all.

SECOND JUDGE. Unfortunate, yes, but you'll have to admit he's also more than a little mad! He's actually dared to bring a libel suit against the mayor's son, no less, as well as against that other fellow, what's his name. . . .

D'ANDREA. Fazio. Alderman Fazio.

THIRD JUDGE. A libel suit?

FIRST JUDGE. Yes, and you know why? He says he caught them making signs against the Evil Eye as he walked by.

SECOND JUDGE. How can it be libel when for two years now the whole town knows he has the Evil Eye and brings everybody bad luck?

D'ANDREA. And countless witnesses can appear in court to swear that many and many a time he's shown that he was well aware of his reputation by protesting violently against it.

FIRST JUDGE. Ah, you see? You admit it yourself.

SECOND JUDGE. Honestly, how can you condemn the mayor's boy and Fazio as slanderers for having done what everybody else has been doing openly for months now?

D'ANDREA. And you three along with the rest.

ALL THREE. Of course!—He's really terrible, you know!—God help us!

D'ANDREA. And then you wonder, my friends, why I carry this little goldfinch around with me. I've had him, you know, ever since last year, when my mother died. He used to be hers, and to me he's a living remembrance of her. I wouldn't know what to do without him. I talk to him, imitating his song, like this, and he answers me. I don't know what I'm saying to him, but if he answers, it means he probably gets something out of the sounds I make. Exactly like us, my friends. We think nature speaks to us, in the beauty of her flowers or in the stars above us, while in reality nature probably isn't even aware of our existence.

FIRST JUDGE. Keep on, keep on with that line of reasoning, my friend, and you'll see how happy it will make you!

(*Someone knocks at the main door. After a moment, it opens and* MARRANCA *thrusts his head in.*)

MARRANCA. Excuse me.

D'ANDREA. Come in, Marranca.

MARRANCA. *He* wasn't there, Your Honor. I told one of his daughters to send him over as soon as he comes home. Meanwhile, the youngest one, Rosinella, she came along with me. If Your Honor wants to see her—

D'ANDREA. No, no. I want to talk to him.

MARRANCA. She says she has something very important to ask you, Your Honor. She's very upset.

FIRST JUDGE. We'll be going along now. See you later, D'Andrea.

(*An exchange of good-bys and the three* JUDGES *leave.*)

D'ANDREA (*to* MARRANCA). Show her in.

MARRANCA. Right away, Your Honor.

(MARRANCA *exits.* ROSINELLA *now appears in the doorway. She is about sixteen, poorly but neatly dressed, her face half hidden by a black woolen shawl.*)

ROSINELLA. May I come in?

D'ANDREA. Come in, come in.

ROSINELLA. Your servant, Excellency . . . Oh, please, sir! Oh, my sweet Jesus! Your Excellency sent for my father? What's happened? Why? We're scared to death, Your Honor!

D'ANDREA. Calm yourself. What are you afraid of?

ROSINELLA. It's just that we've never had anything to do with the law before, Excellency.

D'ANDREA. The law terrifies you?

ROSINELLA. Yes, sir. I tell you, we're scared to death! Only wicked people, Excellency, have anything to do with the law. We're not wicked, sir, just unlucky. And now if the law turns against us, too . . .

D'ANDREA. What gave you that idea? There's nothing to worry about. Nothing at all. The law is not turning against you.

ROSINELLA. Then why did Your Excellency send for my father?

D'ANDREA. Because your father wishes to set himself up against the law.

ROSINELLA. My father? What do you mean?

D'ANDREA. Don't be frightened. Can't you see I'm smiling? . . . Do you mean to say you don't know that your father is bringing a libel suit against the mayor's son and Alderman Fazio?

ROSINELLA. My father? Oh, no, sir! We don't know anything about it! My father is suing somebody?

D'ANDREA. Here are all the documents.

ROSINELLA. My God, my God! Don't pay any attention to him, Your Honor! For more than a month now he's been like a crazy man! He hasn't worked for over a year, did you know that? Because they sent him away, they threw him out in the street! He's been kicked around by everybody, shunned like the plague by the whole town! He's suing somebody? The mayor's son, you said? He's gone crazy! Crazy! This horrible way they're all treating him, the things they say about him, it's no wonder he's out of his mind! Please, Your Honor, make him drop this suit! Make him drop it!

D'ANDREA. Of course, my child. That's exactly what I want him to do. And that's why I sent for him. I hope I can convince him. Still, you know, it's so much easier to do evil than good in this world.

ROSINELLA. Really, Your Excellency? For you, too?

D'ANDREA. Yes, for me, too. Because evil, my dear child, can be done to anyone and by everyone, but good can only be done to those who need it.

ROSINELLA. And you don't think my father needs it?

D'ANDREA. I do, I do. But it's this very need that makes it so difficult. The people who need help, my child, are very often those who have been so embittered by life that it becomes almost impossible to give it to them. Do you understand?

ROSINELLA. No, sir, I don't understand. But please do everything you can, Excellency. There isn't any good or any peace for us in this town any more.

D'ANDREA. Couldn't you go somewhere else?

ROSINELLA. Where? Your Honor doesn't know what it's like. Anywhere we'd run to people would find out about us and talk about us. We can't get rid of this thing, even if we tried to cut it out with a knife. If you could see my father, what he's become! He's grown a beard, a great big horrible beard that makes him look like an owl . . . and—and he's made himself a kind of suit, Excellency, that when he puts it on, he'll scare people, even dogs will run from him!

D'ANDREA. Why did he do that?

ROSINELLA. I don't know why. He knows. Ask him. He's like a crazy man, I tell you! Make him do it, make him drop this case, please! (*There's a knocking at the door.*)

D'ANDREA. Who is it? Come in. (MARRANCA *looks in, trembling.*)

MARRANCA. He's—he's here, Your Honor! What—what shall I do?

ROSINELLA. My father? (*Leaping to her feet.*) Oh, my God! Don't let him find me here, Your Honor! Please!

D'ANDREA. Why not? What's wrong? Would he eat you up if he found you here?

ROSINELLA. No, sir. But he doesn't want us to leave the house. Where can I hide?

D'ANDREA. Over here. Don't worry. (*He opens the secret door.*) Go out this way, then down the corridor, and you'll find an exit.

ROSINELLA. Yes, sir. Thank you, thank you. And don't forget, Excellency. Your servant.

(*She exits quickly.* D'ANDREA *shuts the door behind her.*)

D'ANDREA. Show him in.

(MARRANCA *opens the main door as wide as possible and hides behind it.*)

MARRANCA. Come in, come in. . . . His Honor's waiting. . . .

(*As soon as* CHIÀRCHIARO *enters,* MARRANCA *rushes out, shutting the door behind him.* ROSARIO CHIÀRCHIARO *has made himself up to look as much like a man with the Evil Eye as possible; his face alone is a miracle to behold. On his gaunt, yellow cheeks grows a rough tangled beard; a pair of huge, bone-rimmed spectacles perches on his nose, giving him the look of a marauding owl. He is wearing a glossy, mouse-colored suit that bulges out in every direction, and he carries a bamboo cane with a handle made of horn. His pace is funereal and at every heavy step he strikes the cane on the ground. He comes to a halt in front of* D'ANDREA's *desk.*)

D'ANDREA (*irritated, violently shoving the documents to one side*). Just what do you think you're doing? What is all this nonsense? You ought to be ashamed of yourself!

CHIÀRCHIARO (*not at all ruffled by* D'ANDREA's *outburst, speaking in a low, menacing voice through clenched teeth*). So you don't believe in my power?

D'ANDREA. I say it's all a lot of nonsense! Come now, this is no time for jokes, my dear Chiàrchiaro. Sit down. Sit down. Sit down over here.

(*He goes up to him and is about to put a hand on his shoulder.*)

CHIÀRCHIARO (*quickly drawing back and trembling*). Don't touch me! Be careful! Do you want to go blind?

D'ANDREA (*after a pause, staring at him coldly*). Keep it up as long as you like. I'm in no hurry. . . . I sent for you for your own good. There's a chair over there. Sit down whenever you're ready.

(CHIÀRCHIARO *takes the chair, sits down, looks at* D'ANDREA, *then begins to roll the cane back and forth on his lap, nodding heavily.*)

CHIÀRCHIARO (*muttering*). For my own good . . . For my own good, you said. . . . You dare to say it's for my own good, Your Honor, when you tell me you don't believe in the Evil Eye?

D'ANDREA (*also sitting down*). You want me to say I do believe in it? Then I'll say I believe in it. All right?

CHIÀRCHIARO (*firmly, very seriously*). No, sir, it's not all right. I want you to believe in it absolutely. Ab-so-lute-ly. Not only that, but I want you to prove it by the way you handle the case.

D'ANDREA. Now that, you see . . . Ah, that's going to be a little more difficult.

CHIÀRCHIARO (*rising and starting for the door*). Very well, then I'll be going.

D'ANDREA. Oh, come on! Sit down! I told you this is no time for jokes!

CHIÀRCHIARO. Jokes? You think I'm joking? Don't trifle with me or you'll find out. . . . I warn you! I warn you!

D'ANDREA. Do you expect me to jump up and down and make an idiot of myself? You're wasting your time.

CHIÀRCHIARO. I said I'm warning you! I can be very terrible, you know!

D'ANDREA (*severely*). That's enough, Chiàrchiaro! I'm bored with this. Sit down and let's see if we can talk sensibly. I sent for you because I want you to realize that the course you've taken is not one calculated to bring you safely into port.

CHIÀRCHIARO. Your Honor, I'm standing in a blind alley with my back against the wall. What port, what course are you talking about?

D'ANDREA. The one I see you embarked on in that costume and the other one you've taken with your libel suit. I'm sorry, but you seem to be headed in two different directions at once. Opposite directions, in fact.

(*He brings the tips of his index fingers together to drive home his point.*)

CHIÀRCHIARO. No sir. It just seems that way to you, Your Honor.

D'ANDREA. How can you say that? In your charges here you accuse two people of libel because they believe you have the Evil Eye. Then you come here, dressed in that ridiculous costume and made up to look the part, and you even announce that you expect *me* to believe in your Evil Eye.

CHIÀRCHIARO. Yes, sir. Exactly.

D'ANDREA. And you don't see any inconsistency in these two attitudes?

CHIÀRCHIARO. I see something else, Your Honor. That you've understood nothing.

D'ANDREA. Well, speak up, speak up, my dear Chiàrchiaro! What you've just said may be a gospel truth, but at least you'll be good enough to explain why I don't understand anything.

CHIÀRCHIARO. Gladly. I'll not only show you that you've missed the whole point, but I'll prove to you that you're my enemy.

D'ANDREA. I? Your enemy?

CHIÀRCHIARO. Yes, you. You. But first, tell me: do you or don't you know that the mayor's son has hired Lorecchio, the best lawyer in town, to defend him?

D'ANDREA. I'm quite aware of it.

CHIÀRCHIARO. And are you aware that I—I, Rosario

Chiàrchiaro—that I myself went to see Lorecchio to make sure that he has all the evidence he needs to win? In other words, I not only told him that I've known for more than a year about everyone making signs against the Evil Eye, and other more or less insulting gestures, whenever I go by, but I also gave him proofs, Your Honor, documented proofs—irrefutable evidence, you know, ir-re-fu-ta-ble—concerning the terrible events on which my reputation as a bearer of the Evil Eye is unshakably founded. Un-sha-ka-bly, Your Honor!

D'ANDREA. What? You what? . . . You mean to say you went and gave this testimony to the opposing lawyer?

CHIÀRCHIARO. To Lorecchio himself. Yes, sir.

D'ANDREA (*more nonplused than ever*). Well . . . I must admit I understand even less than I did before.

CHIÀRCHIARO. Less? You've never understood anything!

D'ANDREA. Forgive me, but . . . You went and testified against yourself to the lawyer for the other side. . . . Why? To make certain you'd lose the case? Then why did you sue these two men in the first place?

CHIÀRCHIARO. That very question, Your Honor, proves you've understood nothing. I brought the case into court because I want official recognition of my power. Now do you understand? I want this terrible power of mine to be officially recognized, to be legally established. It's the only capital I have left, Your Honor.

D'ANDREA (*as if to embrace him, deeply moved*). Oh, Chiàrchiaro! My poor Chiàrchiaro! Now I understand! A fine capital! My poor man, what good is it?

CHIÀRCHIARO. What good is it? What do you mean, what good is it? You, my dear sir, when you set out to be a judge—even allowing for the fact that you're a poor one—now tell me, didn't you have to have a diploma, some sort of license?

D'ANDREA. Oh, yes, certainly. A diploma . . .

CHIÀRCHIARO. Well, that's it! I want *my* diploma! I want *my* license to practice! My license to be a full-fledged menace! Signed, sealed, and delivered by this court!

D'ANDREA. And so? What will you do with it?

CHIÀRCHIARO. What will I do with it? Can you really be so simple-minded? I'll stamp it on my visiting

cards, I'll print it on my stationery! You think it's so unimportant? My whole life is at stake! I'm a ruined man, Your Honor! The poor father of an innocent family. For years I worked hard and honestly. They threw me out, kicked me into the gutter because they said I had the Evil Eye! In the gutter, with my wife a paralytic, bedridden for the past three years, and with two young daughters who, if you could just see them, Your Honor, it would break your heart, they're so pretty, both of them. But no one will have anything to do with them because they're mine, you understand? And do you know what we live on now, all four of us? On the bread my son takes out of his own mouth, and he a family man with three children of his own to feed! How much longer do you think the poor boy can go on sacrificing himself for me? Your Honor, there's nothing left for me to do but go into business with this Evil Eye of mine. I'm forced to practice the only profession I have.

D'ANDREA. What will you get out of it?

CHIÀRCHIARO. What will I get? I'll show you. Here, look at me: you see what sort of an impression I make. I frighten everyone. This beard . . . these glasses . . . As soon as you give me my license, I'm in business! You ask me how? That's because —and I'll say it again—that's because you're my enemy!

D'ANDREA. Your enemy? Is that what you really think?

CHIÀRCHIARO. Yes, sir. You are. Because you refuse to believe in my power. Everyone else believes in it, you know. All of them, they all believe in it. And it's lucky for me they do! For instance, there are quite a few gambling casinos in town. All I have to do, Your Honor, is put in an appearance. I won't have to open my mouth. The proprietor, the players, everyone will pay me to go away. I'll buzz around this town like a huge fly. I'll stand in front of one shop window after another . . . (*acting out his program*). Is that a jewelry store over there? Well, I plant myself in front of the window and I start eyeing everybody who goes by, like this! Who's going to enter that store, or even stop long enough to glance in that window? So the owner comes out and slips me a few lire to go away. A few more lire and I go and do guard duty in front of his competitor's place down the street. Now do you see? It's a new kind of tax I'm going to make people pay.

D'ANDREA. A tax on ignorance!

CHIÀRCHIARO. On ignorance? Oh, no, my dear sir! A tax on the public safety! Because I've accumulated so much spite and so much hatred against the whole of this disgusting humanity of ours that I really do believe, Your Honor, that here, in these eyes of mine, I have the power to reduce an entire city to rubble! Look out for me! Don't say I didn't warn you! You see? Look at you, standing there, frozen . . . like a pillar of salt! (D'ANDREA, *overcome by deep pity, has indeed remained motionless, struck dumb in the man's presence.*) Come now, let's get on with it! Let's get on with this case of mine! It's sure to be a famous one. Of course you'll acquit both these defendants, since they've obviously committed no crime. The decision of the court will be an official recognition of my professional standing.

D'ANDREA (*rising*). Your license?

CHIÀRCHIARO (*striking a grotesque pose and pounding his cane on the floor*). My license! Yes, sir! (*The words are barely out of his mouth when a shutter opens, as if blown by the wind, and strikes against the stand, toppling both stand and bird cage to the floor with a great crash.*)

D'ANDREA (*with a cry, running to the spot*). Oh, God! The goldfinch! My little goldfinch! Oh, my God! He's dead . . . dead. . . . The only thing my mother left me. . . . Dead . . . dead . . . (*At his cries,* MARRANCA *and the three* JUDGES *come running in. At the sight of* CHIÀRCHIARO, *they go pale and freeze in their tracks.*)

ALL. What is it? What is it?

D'ANDREA. The wind . . . that shutter . . . my little goldfinch . . .

CHIÀRCHIARO (*triumphantly*). What wind? What shutter? I did it! He wouldn't believe in my power and I proved it to him! I did it! No one else! That's how the bird died! (*The others back away from him in terror.*) And that's how you'll all die, one by one!

ALL (*protesting, imploring in chorus*). No! God help us! I hope you choke to death! I have a family to support! For the love of God!

CHIÀRCHIARO (*imperiously, holding out his hand*). All right, then come over here! Pay your taxes! All of you!

ALL (*giving him money*). Yes, yes, of course! Right away! Here! just get out! Leave us alone! Go away!

CHIÀRCHIARO (*turning triumphantly to* D'ANDREA *and holding out his hand to show him the money*). You see? And I don't even have my license yet! Get on with the trial!——I'm rich!——I'm rich!

Curtain

DISCUSSION

1. When the three judges enter Judge D'Andrea's chambers, the four men talk about being childish. (a) What do the judges think is childish about D'Andrea? (b) What does D'Andrea describe as childish? (c) Does this discussion have anything to do with the rest of the play? Explain.

2. (a) Does D'Andrea believe that Chiàrchiaro will receive justice? Explain. (b) What does D'Andrea intend to do about Chiàrchiaro?

3. What do the following people think about Chiàrchiaro's libel suit: (a) D'Andrea? (b) the three judges? (c) Rosinella? (d) Chiàrchiaro?

4. (a) What kind of license does Chiàrchiaro want? (b) What are his reasons for wanting that license?

5. (a) In your opinion is Chiàrchiaro sane or insane? Explain. (b) Do you think he really believes that he has some particular power or gift? Find lines in the play to defend your answer.

6. (a) How does the goldfinch die? (b) How does Chiàrchiaro use this incident to further his cause?

7. If you were Judge D'Andrea, would you give Chiàrchiaro his license? Why or why not?

THE AUTHOR'S CRAFT

Theme

In your classroom discussion of literature, you probably have been asked many times to state the *theme* of a poem, story, or play. So the idea of theme is not new to you. But, often, readers still tend to confuse the *subject* and the *theme* of a literary work. Assume that you have read a love story and someone asks you, "What is the story about?" What do you answer? "Love"? But what about love? Love is wonderful? Love is the most unfortunate experience one has?

To say that the story is about love is to say that its *subject* is love. But if you ask yourself,

"What is the author saying about love?" then you are asking, "What is the theme?" Does the author present *a specific statement about his subject?* That is his *theme.*

To determine the theme of a literary work, whether drama or prose or poetry, you must take into account all the elements of the work: setting, characterization, plot, dialogue, time, conflict. Look at the title. Perhaps it will state a theme: *You Can't Take It with You, My Heart's in the Highlands, Much Ado About Nothing.* Or, perhaps it only mentions the subject: *Death of a Salesman, Tom Thumb, Antigone.*

A play, or poem, or story may have more than one theme. The author may feel that love is wonderful, but at the same time, his main character may suffer before he finally wins the girl. In this case, what might the author be saying about love? After the two lovers are married for a short period of time, the wife may die from tuberculosis. Does this now change the theme? Or does it reinforce the theme? Or, does it add a new element to the theme?

Only after you have considered the entire work can you begin to state the theme or themes. Ultimately, your statement of the theme will say something about life. Now, state in your own words the theme of *The License.*

THE CREATIVE READER

You probably often wish that you could *see* the plays which are in your book rather than read them. Unfortunately, this is not always possible. Here, then, is where the creative reader enters. The creative reader must recreate the play in his mind. In essence, he builds a mental theater. A playwright has a particular environment in mind when he writes his play—sometimes detailed, sometimes not. The more sparse the playwright's directions, the more imagination the reader must use. What kind of setting would you use for a jury room, as in *Twelve Angry Men?* What do you picture as the "shabby disorder" Pirandello desires for *The License?*

How is a character to speak a particular line? Notice the author's directions on some lines: *(in even greater disbelief), (less definitely), (dreamily).* How would you read those lines? And what about the lines which have no instructions from the author?

In order to answer the preceding questions, the creative reader must consider the characters' motivations. What were the characters like before the play began? What is their relationship to other characters? What does each character want out of life and what is he willing to do to get what he wants? The creative reader must be alert for clues which help to answer those questions.

Consider the actions of a character on stage even when he is not speaking. Is he listening to someone? Attending to some business? How does he move?

A play *appears* easier to read than a novel or short story because there are fewer descriptions and the content is mostly dialogue. But because of that, the creative reader must bring much more to his reading of the play. He must be actor, director, set designer, and costume designer all rolled into one. Only in that way can his enjoyment of the play be increased and the words on the page come alive.

AUTHOR

LUIGI PIRANDELLO (1867–1936), poet, dramatist, novelist, and short-story writer was born at Girgenti, Sicily. He obtained his doctor's degree in letters and philosophy from the university at Bonn, Germany.

Pirandello returned to Rome in 1891 where he taught at a college for women and wrote his first novel. In 1904, his most famous novel, *The Late Mattia Pascal* was published. Married in 1894, Pirandello was later confronted with the serious illness of his wife and the subsequent financial problems. This tragedy plus the onset of World War I affected his work. "My art is full of bitter sympathy for those who deceive themselves. . . ." he once wrote.

His wife's death in 1918 freed him from debt to some extent and he began to write plays. *The License* was first published that year. Drama became his passion and brought him the financial security he needed. In the next years, he wrote his most renowned plays, *Henry IV* and *Six Characters in Search of an Author.* He was awarded the Nobel Prize in 1934. About his craft, he wrote: "As, above everything, the artist must be moved, from his being moved art will be born."

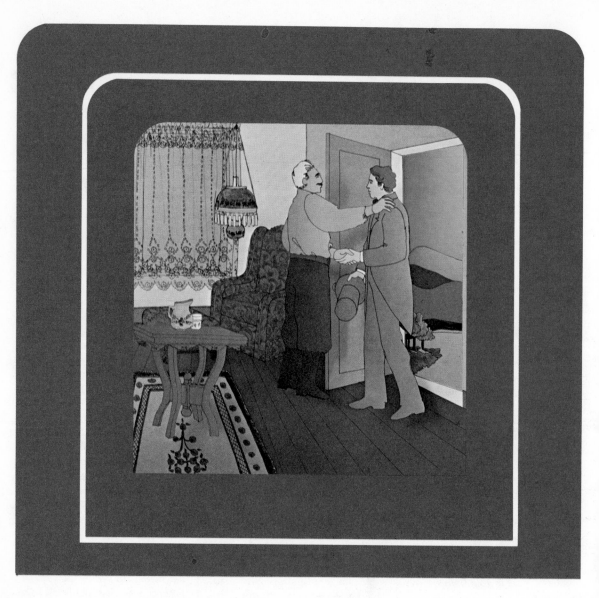

A Marriage Proposal

Anton Chekhov

*English Version by
Hilmar Baukhage and
Barrett H. Clark*

Characters

STEPAN STEPANOVITCH TSCHUBUKOV, *a country farmer*
(Stye pän' Stye pän' ō vich Chü bü'kôf)

NATALIA STEPANOVNA, *his daughter (aged 25)*
(Nä täl' yä Stye pän' ōv nä)

IVAN VASSILIYITCH LOMOV, *Tschubukov's neighbor*
(ē vän' vä sē' lē yich Lô môf')

SCENE: *Reception-room in* TSCHUBUKOV's *country home, Russia.*
TIME: *The present.*

TSCHUBUKOV *discovered as the curtain rises. Enter* LOMOV, *wearing a dress-suit.*

TSCHUB (*going toward him and greeting him*). Who is this I see? My dear fellow! Ivan Vassiliyitch! I'm so glad to see you! (*Shakes hands.*) But this is a surprise! How are you?

LOMOV. Thank you! And how are you?

TSCHUB. Oh, so-so, my friend. Please sit down. It isn't right to forget one's neighbor. But tell me, why all this ceremony? Dress clothes, white gloves and all? Are you on your way to some engagement, my good fellow?

LOMOV. No, I have no engagement except with you, Stepan Stepanovitch.

TSCHUB. But why in evening clothes, my friend? This isn't New Year's!

A Marriage Proposal (A Comedy in One Act) by Anton Chekhov: English version by Hilmar Baukhage and Barrett H. Clark. Copyright, 1914, by Barrett H. Clark. Copyright 1942 (in renewal) by Barrett H. Clark. Reprinted by permission of Samuel French, Inc.

LOMOV. You see, it's simply this, that—(*Composing himself.*) I have come to you, Stepan Stepanovitch, to trouble you with a request. It is not the first time I have had the honor of turning to you for assistance, and you have always, that is—I beg your pardon, I am a bit excited! I'll take a drink of water first, dear Stepan Stepanovitch. (*He drinks.*)

TSCHUB (*aside*). He's come to borrow money! I won't give him any! (*To* LOMOV.) What is it, then, dear Lomov?

LOMOV. You see—dear—Stepanovitch, pardon me, Stepan—Stepan—dearvitch—I mean—I am terribly nervous, as you will be so good as to see—! What I mean to say—you are the only one who can help me, though I don't deserve it, and—and I have no right whatever to make this request of you.

TSCHUB. Oh, don't beat about the bush, my dear fellow. Tell me!

LOMOV. Immediately—in a moment. Here it is, then: I have come to ask for the hand of your daughter, Natalia Stepanovna.

TSCHUB (*joyfully*). Angel! Ivan Vassiliyitch! Say that once again! I didn't quite hear it!

LOMOV. I have the honor to beg—

TSCHUB (*interrupting*). My dear, dear man! I am so happy that everything is so—everything! (*Embraces and kisses him.*) I have wanted this to happen for so long. It has been my dearest wish! (*He represses a tear.*) And I have always loved you, my dear fellow, as my own son! May God give you His blessings and His grace and—I always wanted it to happen. But why am I standing here like a blockhead? I am completely dumbfounded with pleasure, completely dumbfounded. My whole being—I'll call Natalia—

LOMOV. Dear Stepan Stepanovitch, what do you think? May I hope for Natalia Stepanovna's acceptance?

TSCHUB. Really! A fine boy like you—and you think she won't accept on the minute? Lovesick as a cat and all that—! (*He goes out, right.*)

LOMOV. I'm cold. My whole body is trembling as though I was going to take my examination! But the chief thing is to settle matters! If a person meditates too much, or hesitates, or talks about it, waits for an ideal or for true love, he never gets it. Brrr! It's cold! Natalia is an excellent housekeeper, not at all bad-looking, well educated—what more could I ask? I'm so excited my ears are roaring! (*He drinks water.*) And not to marry, that won't do! In the first place, I'm thirty-five—a critical age, you might say. In the second place, I must live a well-regulated life. I have a weak heart, continual palpitation, and I am very sensitive and always getting excited. My lips begin to tremble and the pulse in my right temple throbs terribly. But the worst of all is sleep! I hardly lie down and begin to doze before something in my left side begins to pull and tug, and something begins to hammer in my left shoulder—and in my head, too! I jump up like a madman, walk about a little, lie down again, but the moment I fall asleep I have a terrible cramp in the side. And so it is all night long!

(*Enter* NATALIA STEPANOVNA.)

NATALIA. Ah! It's you. Papa said to go in: there was a dealer in there who'd come to buy something. Good afternoon, Ivan Vassiliyitch.

LOMOV. Good day, my dear Natalia Stepanovna.

NATALIA. You must pardon me for wearing my apron and this old dress: we are working to-day. Why haven't you come to see us oftener? You've not been here for so long! Sit down. (*They sit down.*) Won't you have something to eat?

LOMOV. Thank you, I have just had lunch.

NATALIA. Smoke, do, there are the matches. To-day it is beautiful and only yesterday it rained so hard that the workmen couldn't do a stroke of work. How many bricks have you cut? Think of it! I was so anxious that I had the whole field mowed, and now I'm sorry I did it, because I'm afraid the hay will rot. It would have been better if I had waited. But what on earth is this? You are in evening clothes! The latest cut! Are you on your way to a ball? And you seem to be looking better, too—really. Why are you dressed up so gorgeously?

LOMOV (*excited*). You see, my dear Natalia Stepanovna—it's simply this: I have decided to ask you to listen to me—of course it will be a surprise, and indeed you'll be angry, but I—(*Aside.*) How fearfully cold it is!

NATALIA. What is it? (*A pause.*) Well?

LOMOV. I'll try to be brief. My dear Natalia Stepanovna, as you know, for many years, since my childhood, I have had the honor to know your family. My poor aunt and her husband, from whom, as you know, I inherited the estate, always had the greatest respect for your father and your poor mother. The Lomovs and the Tschubukovs have been for decades on the friendliest, indeed the closest, terms with each other, and furthermore my property, as you know, adjoins your own. If you will be so good as to remember, my meadows touch your birch woods.

NATALIA. Pardon the interruption. You said "my meadows"—but are they yours?

LOMOV. Yes, they belong to me.

NATALIA. What nonsense! The meadows belong to us—not to you!

LOMOV. No, to me! Now, my dear Natalia Stepanovna!

NATALIA. Well, that is certainly news to me. How do they belong to you?

LOMOV. How? I am speaking of the meadows lying between your birch woods and my brick-earth.

NATALIA. Yes, exactly. They belong to us.

LOMOV. No, you are mistaken, my dear Natalia Stepanovna, they belong to me.

NATALIA. Try to remember exactly, Ivan Vassiliyitch. Is it so long ago that you inherited them?

LOMOV. Long ago! As far back as I can remember they have always belonged to us.

NATALIA. But that isn't true! You'll pardon my saying so.

LOMOV. It is all a matter of record, my dear Natalia Stepanovna. It is true that at one time the title to the meadows was disputed, but now everyone knows they belong to me. There is no room for discussion. Be so good as to listen: my aunt's grandmother put these meadows, free from all costs, into the hands of your father's grandfather's peasants for a certain time while they were making bricks for my grandmother. These people used the meadows free of cost for about forty years, living there as they would on their own property. Later, however, when—

NATALIA. There's not a word of truth in that! My grandfather, and my great-grandfather, too, knew that their estate reached back to the swamp, so that the meadows belong to us. What further discussion can there be? I can't understand it. It is really most annoying.

LOMOV. I'll show you the papers, Natalia Stepanovna.

NATALIA. No, either you are joking, or trying to lead me into a discussion. That's not at all nice! We have owned this property for nearly three hundred years, and now all at once we hear that it doesn't belong to us. Ivan Vassiliyitch, you will pardon me, but I really can't believe my ears. So far as I am concerned, the meadows are worth very little. In all they don't contain more than five acres and they are worth only a few hundred roubles, say three hundred, but the injustice of the thing is what affects me. Say what you will, I can't bear injustice.

LOMOV. Only listen until I have finished, please! The peasants of your respected father's grandfather, as I have already had the honor to tell you, baked bricks for my grandmother. My aunt's grandmother wished to do them a favor—

NATALIA. Grandfather! Grandmother! Aunt! I know nothing about them. All I know is that the meadows belong to us, and that ends the matter.

LOMOV. No, they belong to me!

NATALIA. And if you keep on explaining it for two days, and put on five suits of evening clothes, the meadows are still ours, ours, ours! I don't want to take your property, but I refuse to give up what belongs to us!

LOMOV. Natalia Stepanovna, I don't need the meadows, I am only concerned with the principle. If you are agreeable, I beg of you, accept them as a gift from me!

NATALIA. But I can give them to you, because they belong to me! That is very peculiar, Ivan Vassiliyitch! Until now we have considered you as a good neighbor and a good friend; only last year we lent you our threshing machine so that we couldn't thresh until November, and now you treat us like thieves! You offer to give me my own land. Excuse me, but neighbors don't treat each other that way. In my opinion, it's a very low trick—to speak frankly—

LOMOV. According to you I'm a usurper, then, am I? My dear lady, I have never appropriated other people's property, and I shall permit no one to accuse me of such a thing! (He goes quickly to the bottle and drinks water.) The meadows are mine!

NATALIA. That's not the truth! They are mine!

LOMOV. Mine!

NATALIA. Eh? I'll prove it to you! This afternoon I'll send my reapers into the meadows.

LOMOV. W—h—a—t?

NATALIA. My reapers will be there to-day!

LOMOV. And I'll chase them off!

NATALIA. If you dare!

LOMOV. The meadows are mine, you understand? Mine!

NATALIA. Really, you needn't scream so! If you want to scream and snort and rage you may do it at home, but here please keep yourself within the limits of common decency.

LOMOV. My dear lady, if it weren't that I were suffering from palpitation of the heart and hammering of the arteries in my temples, I would deal with you very differently! (In a loud voice.) The meadows belong to me!

NATALIA. Us!

LOMOV. Me!

(Enter TSCHUBUKOV, right.)

TSCHUB. What's going on here? What is he yelling about?

NATALIA. Papa, please tell this gentleman to whom the meadows belong, to us or to him?

TSCHUB. (to LOMOV). My dear fellow, the meadows are ours.

LOMOV. But, merciful heavens, Stepan Stepanovitch, how do you make that out? You at least might be reasonable. My aunt's grandmother gave the use of the meadows free of cost to your grandfather's peasants; the peasants lived on the land for forty years and used it as their own, but later when—

TSCHUB. Permit me, my dear friend. You forget that your grandmother's peasants never paid, because there had been a lawsuit over the meadows, and everyone knows that the meadows belong to us. You haven't looked at the map.

LOMOV. I'll prove to you that they belong to me!

TSCHUB. Don't try to prove it, my dear fellow.

LOMOV. I will!

TSCHUB. My good fellow, what are you shrieking about? You can't prove anything by yelling, you know. I don't ask for anything that belongs to you, nor do I intend to give up anything of my own. Why should I? If it has gone so far, my dear man, that you really intend to claim the meadows, I'd rather give them to the peasants than you, and I certainly shall!

LOMOV. I can't believe it! By what right can you give away property that doesn't belong to you?

TSCHUB. Really, you must allow me to decide what I am to do with my own land! I'm not accustomed, young man, to have people address me in that tone of voice. I, young man, am twice your age, and I beg you to address me respectfully.

LOMOV. No! No! You think I'm a fool! You're making fun of me! You call my property yours and then expect me to stand quietly by and talk to you like a human being. That isn't the way a good neighbor behaves, Stepan Stepanovitch! You are no neighbor, you're no better than a landgrabber. That's what you are!

TSCHUB. Wh—at? What did he say?

NATALIA. Papa, send the reapers into the meadows this minute!

TSCHUB (to LOMOV). What was that you said, sir?

NATALIA. The meadows belong to us and I won't give them up! I won't give them up! I won't give them up!

LOMOV. We'll see about that! I'll prove in court that they belong to me.

TSCHUB. In court! You may sue in court, sir, if you like! Oh, I know you, you are only waiting to find an excuse to go to law! You're an intriguer, that's what you are! Your whole family were always looking for quarrels. The whole lot!

LOMOV. Kindly refrain from insulting my family. The entire race of Lomov has always been honorable! And never has one been brought to trial for embezzlement, as your dear uncle was!

TSCHUB. And the whole Lomov family were insane!

NATALIA. Every one of them!

TSCHUB. Your grandmother was a dipsomaniac, and the younger aunt, Nastasia Michailovna, ran off with an architect.

LOMOV. And your mother limped. (He puts his hand over his heart.) Oh, my side pains! My temples are bursting! Lord in Heaven! Water!

TSCHUB. And your dear father was a gambler—and a glutton!

NATALIA. And your aunt was a gossip like few others!

LOMOV. And you are an intriguer. Oh, my heart! And it's an open secret that you cheated at the elections—my eyes are blurred! Where is my hat?

NATALIA. Oh, how low! Liar! Disgusting thing!

LOMOV. Where's the hat—? My heart! Where shall I go? Where is the door—? Oh—it seems—as though I were dying! I can't—my legs won't hold me—

(Goes to the door.)

TSCHUB (following him). May you never darken my door again!

NATALIA. Bring your suit to court! We'll see!

(LOMOV staggers out, center.)

TSCHUB (angrily). The devil!

NATALIA. Such a good-for-nothing! And then they talk about being good neighbors!

TSCHUB. Loafer! Scarecrow! Monster!

NATALIA. A swindler like that takes over a piece of property that doesn't belong to him and then dares to argue about it!

TSCHUB. And to think that this fool dares to make a proposal of marriage!

NATALIA. What? A proposal of marriage?

TSCHUB. Why, yes! He came here to make you a proposal of marriage.

NATALIA. Why didn't you tell me that before?

TSCHUB. That's why he had on his evening clothes! The poor fool!

NATALIA. Proposal for me? Oh! (Falls into an armchair and groans.) Bring him back! Bring him back!

TSCHUB. Bring whom back?

NATALIA. Faster, faster, I'm sinking! Bring him back! (She becomes hysterical.)

TSCHUB. What is it? What's wrong with you? (His hands to his head.) I'm cursed with bad luck! I'll shoot myself! I'll hang myself!

NATALIA. I'm dying! Bring him back!

TSCHUB. Bah! In a minute! Don't bawl! (He rushes out, center.)

NATALIA (groaning). What have they done to me? Bring him back! Bring him back!

TSCHUB (comes running in). He's coming at once! The devil take him! Ugh! Talk to him yourself, I can't.

NATALIA (groaning). Bring him back!

TSCHUB. He's coming, I tell you! "Oh, Lord! What a task it is to be the father of a grown daughter!" I'll cut my throat! I really will cut my throat! We've argued with the fellow, insulted him, and

now we've thrown him out!—and you did it all, you!

NATALIA. No, you! You haven't any manners, you are brutal! If it weren't for you, he wouldn't have gone!

TSCHUB. Oh, yes, I'm to blame! If I shoot or hang myself, remember *you'll* be to blame. You forced me to it! You! (LOMOV *appears in the doorway.*) There, talk to him yourself!
(*He goes out.*)

LOMOV. Terrible palpitation!— My leg is lamed! My side hurts me—

NATALIA. Pardon us, we were angry, Ivan Vassiliyitch. I remember now—the meadows really belong to you.

LOMOV. My heart is beating terribly! My meadows— my eyelids tremble—(*They sit down.*) We were wrong. It was only the principle of the thing—the property isn't worth much to me, but the principle is worth a great deal.

NATALIA. Exactly, the principle! Let us talk about something else.

LOMOV. Because I have proofs that my aunt's grandmother had, with the peasants of your good father—

NATALIA. Enough, enough. *(Aside.)* I don't know how to begin. *(To* LOMOV.*)* Are you going hunting soon?

LOMOV. Yes, heath-cock shooting, respected Natalia Stepanovna. I expect to begin after the harvest. Oh, did you hear? My dog, Ugadi, you know him —limps!

NATALIA. What a shame! How did that happen?

LOMOV. I don't know. Perhaps it's a dislocation, or maybe he was bitten by some other dog. *(He sighs.)* The best dog I ever had—to say nothing of his price! I paid Mironov a hundred and twenty-five roubles for him.

NATALIA. That was too much to pay, Ivan Vassiliyitch.

LOMOV. In my opinion it was very cheap. A wonderful dog!

NATALIA. Papa paid eighty-five roubles for his Otkatai, and Otkatai is much better than your Ugadi.

LOMOV. Really? Otkatai is better than Ugadi? What an idea! *(He laughs.)* Otkatai better than Ugadi!

NATALIA. Of course he is better. It is true Otkatai is still young; he isn't full-grown yet, but in the pack or on the leash with two or three, there is no better than he, even—

LOMOV. I really beg your pardon, Natalia Stepanovna, but you quite overlooked the fact that he has a short lower jaw, and a dog with a short lower jaw can't snap.

NATALIA. Short lower jaw? That's the first time I ever heard that!

LOMOV. I assure you, his lower jaw is shorter than the upper.

NATALIA. Have you measured it?

LOMOV. I have measured it. He is good at running, though.

NATALIA. In the first place, our Otkatai is pure-bred, a full-blooded son of Sapragavas and Stameskis, and as for your mongrel, nobody could ever figure out his pedigree; he's old and ugly, and as skinny as an old hag.

LOMOV. Old, certainly! I wouldn't take five of your Otkatais for him! Ugadi is a dog and Otkatai is— it is laughable to argue about it! Dogs like your Otkatai can be found by the dozens at any dog dealer's, a whole pound-full!

NATALIA. Ivan Vassiliyitch, you are very contrary to-day. First our meadows belong to you and then Ugadi is better than Otkatai. I don't like it when a person doesn't say what he really thinks. You know perfectly well that Otkatai is a hundred times better than your silly Ugadi. What makes you keep on saying he isn't?

LOMOV. I can see, Natalia Stepanovna, that you consider me either a blindman or a fool. But at least you may as well admit that Otkatai has a short lower jaw!

NATALIA. It isn't so!

LOMOV. Yes, a short lower jaw!

NATALIA *(loudly)*. It's not so!

LOMOV. What makes you scream, my dear lady?

NATALIA. What makes you talk such nonsense? It's disgusting! It is high time that Ugadi was shot, and yet you compare him with Otkatai!

LOMOV. Pardon me, but I can't carry on this argument any longer. I have palpitation of the heart!

NATALIA. I have always noticed that the hunters who do the most talking know the least about hunting.

LOMOV. My dear lady, I beg of you to be still. My heart is bursting! *(He shouts.)* Be still!

NATALIA. I won't be still until you admit that Otkatai is better! *(Enter* TSCHUBUKOV.*)*

TSCHUB. Well, has it begun again?

NATALIA. Papa, say frankly, on your honor, which dog is better: Otkatai or Ugadi?

LOMOV. Stepan Stepanovitch, I beg of you, just answer this: has your dog a short lower jaw or not? Yes or no?

TSCHUB. And what if he has? Is it of such importance? There is no better dog in the whole country.

LOMOV. My Ugadi is better. Tell the truth, now!

TSCHUB. Don't get so excited, my dear fellow! Permit me. Your Ugadi certainly has his good points. He is from a good breed, has a good stride, strong haunches, and so forth. But the dog, if you really want to know it, has two faults; he is old and he has a short lower jaw.

LOMOV. Pardon me, I have palpitation of the heart!— Let us keep to facts—just remember in Maruskins's meadows, my Ugadi kept ear to ear with the Count Rasvachai and your dog.

TSCHUB. He was behind, because the Count struck him with his whip.

LOMOV. Quite right. All the other dogs were on the fox's scent, but Otkatai found it necessary to bite a sheep.

TSCHUB. That isn't so!—I am sensitive about that and

beg you to stop this argument. He struck him because everybody looks on a strange dog of good blood with envy. Even you, sir, aren't free from the sin. No sooner do you find a dog better than Ugadi than you begin to—this, that—his, mine—and so forth! I remember distinctly.

LOMOV. I remember something, too!

TSCHUB (*mimicking him*). I remember something, too! What do you remember?

LOMOV. Palpitation! My leg is lame—I can't—

NATALIA. Palpitation! What kind of hunter are you? You ought to stay in the kitchen by the stove and wrestle with the potato peelings, and not go fox-hunting! Palpitation!

TSCHUB. And what kind of hunter are you? A man with your diseases ought to stay at home and not jolt around in the saddle. If you were a hunter—! But you only ride round in order to find out about other people's dogs, and make trouble for everyone. I am sensitive! Let's drop the subject. Besides, you're no hunter.

LOMOV. You only ride around to flatter the Count!—My heart! You intriguer! Swindler!

TSCHUB. And what of it? (*Shouting.*) Be still!

LOMOV. Intriguer!

TSCHUB. Baby! Puppy! Walking drug-store!

LOMOV. Old rat! Jesuit! Oh, I know you!

TSCHUB. Be still! Or I'll shoot you—with my worst gun, like a partridge! Fool! Loafer!

LOMOV. Everyone knows that—oh, my heart!—that your poor late wife beat you. My leg—my temples —Heavens—I'm dying—I—

TSCHUB. And your housekeeper wears the trousers in your house!

LOMOV. Here—here—there—there—my heart has burst! My shoulder is torn apart. Where is my shoulder? I'm dying! (*He falls into a chair.*) The doctor! (*Faints.*)

TSCHUB. Baby! Half-baked clam! Fool!

NATALIA. Nice sort of hunter you are! You can't even sit on a horse. (*To* TSCHUB.) Papa, what's the matter with him? (*She screams.*) Ivan Vassiliyitch! He is dead!

LOMOV. I'm ill! I can't breathe! Air!

NATALIA. He is dead! (*She shakes* LOMOV *in the chair.*) Ivan Vassiliyitch! What have we done! He is dead! (*She sinks into a chair.*) The doctor—the doctor! (*She goes into hysterics.*)

TSCHUB. Ahh! What is it? What's the matter with you?

NATALIA (*groaning*). He's dead!—Dead!

TSCHUB. Who is dead? Who? (*Looking at* LOMOV.) Yes, he is dead! Good God! Water! The doctor! (*Holding the glass to* LOMOV's *lips.*) Drink! No, he won't drink! He's dead! What a terrible situation! Why didn't I shoot myself! Why have I never cut my throat? What am I waiting for now? Only give me a knife! Give me a pistol! (LOMOV *moves.*) He's coming to! Drink some water—there!

LOMOV. Sparks! Mists! Where am I?

TSCHUB. Get married! Quick, and then go to the devil! She's willing! (*He joins the hands of* LOMOV *and* NATALIA.) She's agreed! Only leave me in peace!

LOMOV. Wh—what? (*Getting up.*) Whom?

TSCHUB. She's willing! Well? Kiss each other and—the devil take you both!

NATALIA (*groans*). He lives! Yes, yes, I'm willing!

TSCHUB. Kiss each other!

LOMOV. Eh? Whom? (NATALIA *and* LOMOV *kiss.*) Very nice—! Pardon me, but what is this for? Oh, yes, I understand! My heart—sparks—I am happy, Natalia Stepanovna. (*He kisses her hand.*) My leg is lame!

NATALIA. I'm happy, too!

TSCHUB. Ahh! A load off my shoulders! Ahh!

NATALIA. And now at least you'll admit that Ugadi is worse than Otkatai!

LOMOV. Better!

NATALIA. Worse!

TSCHUB. Now the domestic joys have begun.—Champagne!

LOMOV. Better!

NATALIA. Worse, worse, worse!

TSCHUB (*trying to drown them out*). Champagne, champagne!

CURTAIN

DISCUSSION

1. (a) What is Tschubukov's attitude toward Lomov before Tschubukov is aware of Lomov's intentions? (b) How does Natalia receive Lomov?

2. (a) What is Lomov's physical condition? (b) His mental condition?

3. In the midst of proposing to Natalia, Lomov tries to impress her with the fact that their families have been friends for decades. (a) What does he say which antagonizes her? (b) Explain the logic each uses in claiming ownership of the meadows. (c) What is Natalia's response when Lomov offers to give her the meadows? (d) Do you think she is justified? Why or why not?

4. (a) How does Tschubukov respond to Natalia's and Lomov's argument? (b) Do you think Tschubukov understands his daughter? Explain.

5. What causes the second argument between Natalia and Lomov? Who starts it?

6. (a) When Lomov faints, what is Tschubukov's reaction? (b) Natalia's? (c) Which, if either, is more justified?

7. (a) At the end of the play, is Lomov happy? Natalia? Tschubukov? (b) If you were to continue the play, what would happen?

8. Are the characters in this play realistic? Explain.

THE AUTHOR'S CRAFT

Comic techniques
Have you ever thought something was extremely funny and then looked around to find that no one else was laughing? Often, what is humorous to one person is not humorous to another. Because not everyone views life from the same perspective, humor is one of the most difficult results for a dramatist to achieve. However, there are some characteristics of comedy which we can note.

One characteristic is exaggeration. Comic characters often act in extremes. The innocent girl is too innocent. The weakling is incapable of any strong actions. The bumbler destroys all he contacts. The very posture and facial expressions of these characters reveal their traits. The limitations of these characters are clear, and we can laugh at and identify with their faults.

Typically, the characters in comedy have inescapable strong feelings, or *obsessions*, which are obvious to the audience. In *A Marriage Proposal*, Lomov and Natalia are overly concerned with their land rights and dogs, almost to the point of throwing away their love for each other.

The characters are often *stereotypes*, that is, they act completely according to a fixed type or predesigned image. Thus, Lomov is a typical bumbling hypochondriac. Natalia is desperate for a husband. Tschubukov is the exasperated parent who longs to please his daughter, but cannot understand her actions.

Few comedies would be complete without an *absurd complication*. Lomov simply wants to ask Natalia to marry him. Yet the issue of land suddenly takes precedence and almost destroys his purpose.

The complications are usually resolved by a *sudden twist to the plot*, or a gimmick. Would Natalia ever have agreed to marry Lomov if he hadn't fainted?

Finally, a comedy moves toward a *happy ending*. At its conclusion, the hero or heroes are satisfied. What will happen after the play ends is *predictable*. Lomov and Natalia will marry and live happily (more or less) ever after.

At any rate, we, the audience, will go home with a pleasant feeling. Comedy likes people despite their faults and we wish that the real world were always that way.

AUTHOR

ANTON PAVLOVITCH CHEKHOV (1850–1904) was born in Taganrog, Russia. He developed a taste for the theater at a young age, attending local productions whenever possible and entertaining his family with his own impromptu performances. In 1876, his father went bankrupt and moved the family to Moscow. Anton remained in Taganrog to finish his secondary schooling. In 1879, Chekhov received a scholarship to study medicine at Moscow University. He graduated in 1884 and began a medical practice.

While in school Chekhov regularly contributed to the best humor magazines and published a collection of short stories under the pseudonym "Antosha Chekhonte." As the years went on, he devoted more and more time to his writing.

Chekhov was fond of traveling. During the summer of 1890, he journeyed to the island of Sakhalin where he devoted three months to studying life in a penal colony. In 1892, he made his first visit abroad, traveling extensively in Italy and France. Upon returning to Russia he bought a small farm in Melikhovo, where he lived with his parents and sister. He sold the farm in 1898 and settled in Yalta.

In 1901, Chekhov married Olga Knipper, an actress associated with the Moscow Art Theatre. In the next three years his health deteriorated drastically. He died of tuberculosis at Badenweiler, a health resort in the German Black Forest, in July 1904.

Chekhov wrote over three hundred short stories. *Tales of Melpomene* was his first published volume. *Motley Stories* brought him serious critical recognition in 1886. He received the Pushkin Prize in 1888 for the long short story "The Steppe."

Chekhov's early plays include *Ivanov, The Swan Song, The Bear,* and *A Marriage Proposal.* His most famous plays, all written after 1896, are *The Seagull, Uncle Vanya, The Three Sisters,* and *The Cherry Orchard.*

EXPERIMENTAL THEATER

In a sense, the history of the theater has been a history of experimentation. (See "Within This Wooden O" page 279.) Shakespeare wrote for the platform stage. Moliere wrote for the picture frame stage. In this century, the theater-in-the-round has placed the stage in the middle of the audience. Characters act in the aisles, and behind as well as in front of the audience. Some playwrights are now staging their plays at the very locations where they supposedly take place.

The modern playwright is confronted with a major problem: how can he possibly hope to present a stage drama which is as realistic as a motion picture, which can be filmed anywhere in the world, or as the 6 o'clock news, which constantly presents the viewer with the "real" world of warfare, riots, and sports events?

Some modern playwrights have decided not to try. Instead, they create plays in which the stage never pretends to be anything but a stage. On that stage, actors, or people, meet and attempt to work out real problems in real situations. The playwrights feel that if the audience is convinced then the play is real.

Recently "the theater of the absurd" has developed. In it, the characters *talk* to one another, but they never *communicate.* Is this realistic or not? "The theater of the absurd" attempts to explore the inner space of the mind, not to try to imitate the external appearances of the world around us. Initially, it often appears ridiculous. For example, the title of Luigi Pirandello's *Six Characters in Search of an Author* summarizes a plot which shows those six characters rehearsing another Pirandello play and meeting difficulties which involve everyone around them. In Samuel Beckett's *Endgame,* two of the characters are on stage in garbage pails—they never leave them. In Beckett's *Waiting for Godot,* two tramps sit along a roadside and philosophize about life while they wait for a third character named Godot. Godot never arrives. In *Charlie,* a stage dummy is "killed."

Many playwrights attempt to involve the audience so that the audience actually feels it is witnessing reality. Peter Weiss' *The Investigation* is often staged so that the audience is seemingly witnessing the trial of Nazi war criminals. Many of the characters actually talk to the audience and try to make it believe their points of view. Today, the "now" theater, often created out of improvisations, presents social and political issues in a manner that is designed to confront and even assault the audience.

Ultimately the live theater becomes more important because experimentation takes place. Experimentation is aimed at making the audience become involved and identify with the characters. In that way, the "experimental" theater truly becomes the "real" theater.

CHARLIE

Slawomir Mrozek

Characters

GRANDPA

GRANDSON

OCULIST

On stage there are two chairs, a cupboard and a telephone. On the wall there is a white sheet of paper with printed lines of letters and numbers of different sizes as used in eye tests. The OCULIST, *a middle-aged man in glasses, is lying on a sofa reading a book. There is a knock at the door and the* OCULIST *rises.*

OCULIST. Come in!

(*Enter* GRANDSON *and* GRANDPA. GRANDSON, *a man of thirty, strong and angular, comes in first, followed by* GRANDPA, *a slight little old man with a white beard. He is carrying a double-barrelled shotgun over his shoulder.*)

GRANDSON. Good morning, Doctor. May I present my grandfather?

OCULIST. Come in, please. Your grandfather? He looks remarkably young for his age.

GRANDSON. I've brought him to see you, specially.

OCULIST. Why, what's happened? A shooting accident? Somebody shot in the eye?

GRANDSON. Oh no! Grandpa hasn't started shooting yet.

OCULIST. Ah! You mean the accident will happen later. You've come as a precautionary measure.

GRANDSON. There won't be any accident. Grandpa is going to shoot, and that's the end of it.

OCULIST. Is that really necessary?

GRANDSON. Doctor, Grandpa has to shoot.

OCULIST. If he observes the safety rules of shooting, I see no reason to object. Old age has its rights.

GRANDSON. Exactly. But the problem is—glasses.

OCULIST. Trouble with his sight?

Charlie by Slawomir Mrozek from SIX PLAYS BY SLAWOMIR MROZEK, translated by Nicholas Bethell. Copyright © 1967 by Nicholas Bethell. Reprinted by permission of Grove Press, Inc. and Jonathan Cape Ltd.

GRANDSON. Grandpa can't see very well. When he gets some glasses, he'll shoot.

OCULIST. I see, I see. You mean he's going to shoot at a target?

GRANDSON. Exactly. Look, Doctor, he's searching for one now.

(GRANDPA, *who has up to now been standing quietly, begins to search the room, yard by yard, bent double, with his face almost on the floor, like a man suffering from terrible short-sightedness.*)

OCULIST. What's he looking for?

GRANDSON (*without answering the* OCULIST). Grandpa! Calm down! He's not here.

OCULIST. Precisely, there's nobody here except us.

GRANDSON. Grandpa's very vindictive. I know him.

OCULIST. A patriot?

GRANDSON. Amongst other things. But this time it's Charlie.

OCULIST. What Charlie?

GRANDSON. We'll soon see what Charlie.

OCULIST. Is he a friend of yours?

GRANDSON. That's what we've got to find out.

OCULIST. How?

GRANDSON. Grandpa has got to get some glasses. Then he'll recognize him.

OCULIST. And when he recognizes him?

GRANDSON. Then he'll shoot him. He needs glasses first so as to recognize him and then so as to shoot him. That's why we've come to you, Doctor.

(*Meanwhile* GRANDPA *looks under the sofa and under the chairs; searches everywhere but at no time takes his shotgun off his shoulder.*)

OCULIST. Has—er—Mr. Charlie done anything wrong?

GRANDSON. How are we supposed to know? Grandpa hasn't got any glasses and he can't recognize him.

OCULIST. So you don't know him at all?

GRANDSON. I've been trying to explain; we're looking for him.

OCULIST. Your grandpa doesn't know him either?

GRANDSON. Without glasses? You're joking!

OCULIST. Why do you want to meet somebody you don't know?

GRANDSON. Because we can't know him until we meet him. It's quite simple.

OCULIST. But why a man called Charlie?

GRANDSON. Do you want us to shoot the first person who comes along? Sadist! You've got to have some sort of justice.

OCULIST. In that case why shoot anybody?

GRANDSON. Doctor, you said yourself, Grandpa's got to shoot. Old age has its rights.

OCULIST. But he could shoot targets, into the air, birds, maybe . . .

GRANDSON. What?

OCULIST. Birds, targets . . .

GRANDSON. Who?

OCULIST. What do you mean, who?

GRANDSON. I said, who's supposed to shoot at targets?

OCULIST. Well, your grandpa.

GRANDSON (unbelievingly). Grandpa?

OCULIST. Yes, Grandpa.

GRANDSON. You don't know him.

OCULIST. In that case, you'd better take his gun away.

GRANDSON (in even greater disbelief). Whose?

OCULIST (less definitely). Grandpa's.

GRANDSON (in amazement). Grandpa's?

OCULIST. Well yes, I thought . . .

GRANDSON. Did you hear, Grandpa?

GRANDPA (for a moment interrupting his search, puts his hand to his ear). Eh?

GRANDSON. He says, take away your gun.

GRANDPA (taking his gun off his shoulder). Where is he?

GRANDSON. There he is, by the chair. Shall I get him for you?

OCULIST (hastily crossing over to the side of the stage). Well, anyway it's your private affair; I'm not interfering.

GRANDSON. Now you're talking sense. The gun's been loaded for twenty years; it just can't go on.

OCULIST. Why can't it?

GRANDSON. Ask Grandpa. Grandpa, this chap . . .

OCULIST (interrupting). No, no . . . If it can't it can't. Of course it can't.

GRANDSON. I'll ask him why not. Grandpa, this man . . .

OCULIST (interrupting again). No, I believe you. After all, if you've got a gun . . .

GRANDSON. Exactly. You've got to shoot. Before Grandpa's day his father, my great-grandpa, used to shoot, and before him his father's father. All of them shot, all the time.

OCULIST. Hm . . . yes . . . In that case perhaps we can start examining your grandfather.

GRANDSON. Now you're talking. Grandpa, come on, Grandpa, a little closer.

OCULIST. Would you be so good as to take a seat. (GRANDPA sits down in the chair offered to him, throwing his shotgun across his shoulder.)

GRANDSON. Now, Grandpa, listen to the doctor. Pif-paf later.

OCULIST. Perhaps we could put the gun down there for the moment. (Uncertainly he touches the gun. GRANDPA objects violently.)

OCULIST. No? All right, all right, just as you like.

GRANDSON. Grandpa never parts with his gun. He cleans it every day. We and our family—we know what our duty is.

OCULIST (going up to the sheet of paper with the eye-tests, points to the smallest row of signs). Can you read this?

GRANDPA (dreamily). Ah! I remember my old father—he let him have it, half a pound of shot right in the middle of the belly. From sixty yards, I tell you.

OCULIST. Please try and concentrate. Now then, does reading these letters cause you any difficulty?

GRANDPA (after long hesitation). Ah! Maybe it wasn't quite sixty. Fifty.

GRANDSON. Later, Grandpa, later. Now you must listen to what the doctor's saying.

OCULIST. Let's try again. Can you read this?

GRANDPA. Errr, no.

OCULIST. And this?

GRANDPA. No, not a thing. Where's Charlie?

GRANDSON. Be patient, Grandpa. You must listen to the doctor, otherwise there won't be any bum-bum at Charlie.

GRANDPA. I'll show him.

OCULIST. Can you read this?

GRANDPA. Er, no.

OCULIST (consolingly). The situation is still not hopeless. We'll carry on testing. Can you read this?

GRANDPA. You know, I'd rather put a bullet in it.

OCULIST. Or this?

GRANDPA. Oh! Doctor you really . . . No, I can't.

OCULIST. Hm. The weakness of vision is really considerable. Now let's try again. Can you read this?

GRANDPA. I haven't got my glasses.

OCULIST (to GRANDSON). That we shall try to remedy. May I know in what circumstances your grandpa lost his keenness of vision?

GRANDSON. Through being on guard. Grandpa was always watching to see if the enemy was walking about. And, you see, our windows are dirty.

OCULIST. Yes, that strains the eyes.

GRANDSON. More than once we've told him. If only, Grandpa, you'll put off watching until Easter the windows will be cleaned. But he was in too much of a hurry. He was on watch even in his sleep. That's the sort of man he is.

OCULIST. Let's get back to the patient. (Pointing to the largest row of letters.) What about this?

GRANDPA. What?

OCULIST. Can you read it?

GRANDPA. Read it?

OCULIST. Yes.

GRANDPA. No.

OCULIST. One moment. (Pulls out from behind the sofa a roll of white paper, unrolls it and fastens it to the wall. On it one single, huge letter 'A' is printed in black ink, almost as large as a man.) Now can you?

GRANDPA. I'm hungry.

OCULIST. Stick to the point. Can you read it now?

GRANDPA. Oh, what the hell!

OCULIST (takes from the cupboard a box full of pairs of glasses, puts a pair on GRANDPA. The following questions are spoken at high speed). And now?

GRANDPA. No.

OCULIST (changes them for another pair). Now?

GRANDPA. No.

OCULIST (as above). Now?

GRANDPA. No.

OCULIST (as above). Now?

GRANDPA (chuckling). No.

OCULIST (as above). Now?

GRANDPA (chuckling even more). No.

OCULIST (losing his patience, takes GRANDPA by the back of the neck and takes him right up to the sheet with the large letter 'A'). Now?

GRANDPA (doubling up with laughter). Oh dear!

OCULIST. What the devil are you laughing at?

GRANDPA. It tickles.

OCULIST (takes off the last pair of glasses and crosses his arms. To GRANDSON). Unfortunately, there is nothing I can do.

GRANDSON. Why?

OCULIST. This is an extraordinary case.

GRANDSON. You're taking the wrong approach. Grandpa can't read.

OCULIST. You mean he's illiterate?

GRANDSON. That's right. Any objections? You're literate, and so what? Are we afraid of you? No, it's you that's afraid of us.

OCULIST. But . . . it never entered my head.

GRANDSON. What?

OCULIST. I simply wanted to find out whether . . . whether reading lies among the sphere of activities practised by your progenitor and . . .

GRANDSON. Doctor, you're forgetting yourself! Maybe your grandpa was a progenitor but not mine! There has never been any venereal disease in our family! We're shooting men—exclusively!

OCULIST. You're missing the point! I quite simply wanted to find out whether your grandpa reads, reads, is in the habit of reading.

GRANDSON (with pride). My dear sir, neither my grandpa nor I have ever read anything. Is that clear? (Pointing to the huge letter 'A'.) And you wanted to force a poor old man, and exhaust him mentally, and give him a pain in the head, eh?

OCULIST (explaining). No, I was simply thinking of all our plans for universal education.

(Meanwhile GRANDPA resumes his search.)

GRANDSON. I've got an idea.

OCULIST. Oh, I'm sure you have.

GRANDSON. Let me see that.

OCULIST. Let you see what?

GRANDSON. Don't play the fool. (Taking a step towards the OCULIST.) Give them to me.

OCULIST (stepping back). I don't understand.

GRANDSON. Let me see your glasses.

OCULIST (trying to turn it all into a joke). Ha ha ha! You're a funny one! I remember we used to make jokes like that at school. I remember once we put a drawing-pin under the maths teacher's . . .

GRANDSON. Stop fooling about! Take your glasses off. Come on!

OCULIST (stiffening). I won't put up with this sort of behaviour. My glasses are my private property.

GRANDSON. We'll give you private property. Grandpa!

OCULIST (terrified). No, don't!

GRANDSON. Well?

OCULIST. There's no need to upset an old man. In

his excitement he might forget himself, get carried away. I understand that.

GRANDSON. I hope I make myself clear.

OCULIST. Maybe after all I can lend you them just for a moment. But just for a moment. Without my glasses I am almost blind. I can hardly see anything.

GRANDSON. All right, all right, that's unimportant. (OCULIST *takes off his glasses and hands them to* GRANDSON. *He turns them round for a moment in his hand and looks at them.*) Beautiful.

OCULIST. Zeiss lenses.

GRANDSON. Shall we try them?

OCULIST (*after taking off his glasses he becomes defenceless. His movements are uncertain. Every now and then he takes a step or two in some direction, but uncertainly, as if after every step he was sure he had taken the wrong direction*). My glasses!

GRANDSON. Grandpa! Here! Come here!

GRANDPA (*has already resumed his search and taken his gun off his shoulder, and is holding it at the ready and peering into the corners. He gets up and, with the haste typical of an old man, trots over to his* GRANDSON). Where? Where is he? Is he there?

GRANDSON. Calm down, Grandpa. Let's put these glasses on.

GRANDPA. Oh, I'm getting so excited!

GRANDSON. Stand up straight, Grandpa. That's it, you put them on your ears, like the doctor. (*Stepping back a pace.*) Now, what do you say?

GRANDPA (*loses his trembling fever and becomes motionless and more important-looking. He looks about himself with deliberation and surprise*). Good! Good!

GRANDSON (*excited*). What? Good, did you say?

GRANDPA (*has found just what the* OCULIST *has lost: confidence in his movements and keenness of vision. With growing satisfaction in his voice*). Good!

OCULIST. Can you really see better?

GRANDPA (*looking at him carefully*). Who's that?

GRANDSON. That's the doctor.

GRANDPA (*without taking his eyes off the* OCULIST). Doctor?

OCULIST. Doctor . . . of medicine.

GRANDSON. A doctor, and he didn't know how to give an old man a pair of glasses.

OCULIST (*justifying himself*). This is an extraordinary case, I could never have imagined . . .

GRANDPA (*still not taking his eyes off the* OCULIST, *approaches him more closely*). Do you know, it looks to me as if . . .

GRANDSON. I suppose it's just bad breeding . . .

OCULIST (*nervously smoothing back his hair, adjusting his dress*). I am delighted, sir, that you have recovered your keenness of vision. Delighted.

GRANDSON. What is it, Grandpa? (*Pause.*)

GRANDPA (*takes a step backwards. All the time gazing intently at the* OCULIST *he signs to* GRANDSON *to come nearer*). You know what I rather think?

GRANDSON (*running up*). What can you see?

OCULIST (*gets up violently from his place. Walks about the room, gesticulating nervously*). For the true man of science there is no greater joy than to witness the triumph of one's own methods. To organize the blind forces of nature, to set some harmony to the free play of the elements, such achievements produce their own true reward. May I ask you to return my glasses? I am short-sighted, and my head is beginning to ache . . . Furthermore, wearing somebody else's glasses may turn out harmful for you in the long run. (*Stops walking and tries to listen in on* GRANDPA *and* GRANDSON's *conversation.*)

GRANDPA. Something tells me . . . (*Whispers.*)

GRANDSON (*astounded*). Good lord! Really?

(GRANDPA *points his finger at the* OCULIST *listening in. The latter realizes he has been caught in the act and starts walking again, pretending that he is occupied in expounding his opinions.*)

OCULIST. Only in the society of today have men of science received the recognition due to them. I ask you not to forget that our power has grown immeasurably since the time of Paracelsus. We are now hacking out new paths for the human race. Please return my glasses immediately.

(GRANDPA *leans over and whispers something in* GRANDSON's *ear.*)

GRANDSON. Impossible! (GRANDPA *whispers something else.*) Are you absolutely sure?

GRANDPA. Ho, ho!

OCULIST. Who can foretell what future discoveries may transform our life, in what direction particular branches of science may extend? Thought, that property which places even an uneducated man on so infinitely higher a level than that of the beasts, lies at the root of these achievements. And at the head of this great progress of humanity, this procession marching in state through the history of nature, this crusade of reason to the

land of chaos and accident, go the priests of science, go we, true leaders of an army in the service of mankind. Excuse me, I must go outside for a moment.

(*During this speech the* OCULIST *has been maneuvering himself as near as possible to the door. Meanwhile* GRANDSON *has cut him off from the way out.*)

GRANDSON. Why have you gone so pale?

(*For a moment they stand opposite each other in silence.*)

OCULIST. I've gone pale? Extraordinary.

GRANDSON. White as a sheet. Or maybe we'd better say—ha! ha!—white as a corpse!

OCULIST. Metaphorical.

GRANDSON. Could be. We're uneducated. We shoot.

OCULIST. Where's the door? I can't see properly . . . There's such a mist in front of my eyes. I want to go outside. You admitted I was pale.

GRANDSON. That doesn't matter to us. I'd like to ask you a few questions.

OCULIST. I am not ready for them. Anyway, what about?

GRANDSON. Who about, you mean!

OCULIST. I know nobody, I've done nothing. I don't know any addresses. I won't tell you anything.

GRANDSON. And if I ask you nicely?

OCULIST. What do you want to know?

GRANDSON. Why did you want Grandpa to shoot at targets and birds?

OCULIST. In the name of humanity and of the preservation of moral laws of coexistence among men.

GRANDSON. And why did you want to take Grandpa's gun away?

OCULIST. I thought . . . I thought it might become dangerous and therefore . . .

GRANDSON. Dangerous? Who for?

OCULIST. Whatever you say he's an old man. Very honest, I'm sure, but tired by life. Weakened sense of responsibility. Still, I could be wrong.

GRANDSON. I said, dangerous for who?

OCULIST. Well, in general, for everybody.

GRANDSON. For everybody? You look at me. Am I afraid of this danger? No, and shall I tell you why?

OCULIST. How should I know? . . . Maybe, lack of imagination . . .

GRANDSON. I'm not afraid because I am not . . . Do you know who I'm not? Well? Oh . . . Oh . . . Come on!

OCULIST (*stammering*). Ch . . . Ch . . .

GRANDSON. Well, Cha, Cha, Char . . .

OCULIST. Char . . .

GRANDSON. Charlie . . . lie . . .

OCULIST. Charlie.

GRANDSON. You see. (*Pause.*)

OCULIST (*as if to himself*). You must be joking.

GRANDSON. No man on earth who's honest and straightforward has any objection to Grandpa shooting. Those who have clear consciences can sleep in peace. But Charlie, oh he's trembling with fear, and rightly because he knows that we shall recognize him anywhere, and especially now that Grandpa's got these glasses.

OCULIST (*hysterically*). Why won't you let me go outside? It's not democratic.

GRANDSON. So much the better. At this moment millions of simple, quiet people in the world are coming in and going out whenever they want. If it was an ordinary door, on hinges, with bolts, or a swing door, or even a bead curtain, the creak and rustle of these doors would resound uninterruptedly, freely and joyfully. Only you, you do not belong to these happy kingdoms. Is that our fault?

OCULIST. What have you got against me?

GRANDSON. You are Charlie.

OCULIST. No!

GRANDSON. Who protested when I said his gun had been loaded for twenty years and that something had to be done about it? Who wanted to force Grandpa to read?

OCULIST. Nonsense!

GRANDSON. Who didn't want to give glasses to a poor old man? You are Charlie!

OCULIST. No! I swear I'm not. (*Feverishly searching in his pockets.*) I've got my identity card, I'll show you my identity card.

GRANDSON. Your identity card doesn't mean a thing. Grandpa recognized you, Charlie!

OCULIST. Grandpa may be mistaken!

GRANDSON. Grandpa! Let's start!

(GRANDPA *takes off the safety-catch.*)

OCULIST. Gentlemen, wait, there must be a mistake, a tragic misunderstanding. I do not claim that Charlie is innocent. On the contrary, he is probably an exceptionally disgusting type, but why me? Grandpa, take a look around. There's always time for me. I take surgery every other day between two and six. You've got me, gentlemen, as it were, in the bank. Meanwhile you'd do well to have a look round; really, you would. And all this time the real Charlie is sitting cosily somewhere, drinking his milk and laughing in your face, gentlemen, the rotten swine! Hasn't this occurred to you?

GRANDSON. It has indeed. Perhaps you aren't the only Charlie in the world. There may be two, or three. Grandpa, when we've done this one, we'll carry straight on looking for the others.

OCULIST. Two? Three? Ten, a hundred, maybe they're all Charlies, all of them, but not me. And you're wasting all this time on that one person who is not Charlie, and meanwhile all the others are running around, free!

GRANDSON. That's an idea, Grandpa. Who said there was only one of them? Have you got the ammunition?

GRANDPA. Ho ho! There's enough, enough for them all.

GRANDSON (*rubbing his hands*). Fine, fine. (*Runs up to* GRANDPA *and kisses him in joy.*) What a grand idea, Grandpa. We'll have a real shooting match.

OCULIST. Yes, shoot, shoot, but not at me!

GRANDSON. I think we'll do him with buckshot first, and then with a bullet.

GRANDPA. Good idea.

OCULIST. No, no. (*Throws himself on to the floor, runs on all fours to the sofa and crawls under it. His voice now comes out from under the sofa.* GRANDSON *and* GRANDPA *bend down to try and spot him there*). There's no need to bother about me. I am not against shooting at all. Shooting is very good for the lungs, it's a fine sport. Not at targets or birds or anything, a true man doesn't shoot at nonsense like that. I understand, I'm on your side. I am simply surprised that the older gentleman has only got one shotgun, and that that only has two barrels. If he had eight guns, and each one had three barrels, that would still not be excessive. It's not a question of too many, he's got to have them. Wait, listen to me!

GRANDPA (*going down on to all fours with his gun pointing under the sofa*). It's dark, damn it.

GRANDSON. Shall I move the sofa?

OCULIST. I don't want anything. I don't even want the glasses. Grandpa can keep them for himself. But I want justice, I demand it! Not me but Charlie!

GRANDPA. Light a match for me, and I'll get him.

(GRANDSON *lights a match and brings it close to the sofa. The* OCULIST'*s head appears; he blows,* puts out the match and vanishes again under the sofa.)

OCULIST. Gentlemen, allow me to raise the cry, 'Hurrah for shooting!' But I cannot agree that the beautiful and noble idea of shooting should be defiled by a fatal shooting accident. Gentlemen, I'm not the one who should be shot at.

GRANDPA. It's no good, I'll shoot blind.

GRANDSON (*leaning to one side*). Aim more in the middle, Grandpa.

GRANDPA. I had him there. (*Prepares and takes aim —a pause. The* OCULIST'*s hand appears from under the sofa, waving a white handkerchief.*)

GRANDSON. That's good. It means he'll come out now.

GRANDPA. Ah, today's youth!

OCULIST (*crawls out from under the sofa and stands up in front of* GRANDPA *and* GRANDSON). All right, I'll tell you everything.

GRANDSON. Well?

OCULIST. He's coming here.

GRANDSON. Who?

OCULIST. Charlie. The real Charlie.

GRANDPA. When? When?

OCULIST. Any moment. He should be here now.

GRANDPA. Shall I shoot?

GRANDSON. In a minute, Grandpa. (*To the* OCULIST.) How can you prove to us that the man that's coming is a greater Charlie than you?

OCULIST. Because of various things he said about you.

GRANDSON. What things?

OCULIST. Various things.

GRANDSON. What does that mean?

OCULIST. Shall I repeat them?

GRANDSON. Yes.

OCULIST. He said that you are murderers.

GRANDSON. Oh, he said that, and what else?

OCULIST. That your grandpa is a blood-sucking old idiot . . .

GRANDSON. What?

OCULIST. I'm just repeating what I heard. As for you, he said you're an unbelievable fool and a pervert and a typical product of your nauseating family. Shall I go on?

GRANDSON. Everything.

OCULIST. He said that the very fact of your existence is sufficient proof of the senselessness and rottenness of the world, to such an extent that to be murdered, even by you, would be a merciful relief, and a splendid way of ceasing to share with you what is common to humanity.

GRANDSON. Did you hear that, Grandpa?

GRANDPA. Charlie! As if I heard his very words! That's Charlie.

GRANDSON. And what else?

OCULIST. And he also said, I don't know whether it's true, that you . . . I can't say it . . .

GRANDSON. I tell you, don't conceal anything.

OCULIST. No, I really can't.

GRANDSON. Tell me at once!

OCULIST. He said that you belch. (*Pause.*)

GRANDSON. The swine! Why didn't you tell me this before?

OCULIST. Because I've only just realized. I must admit that before you came here the idea of Charlie was quite new to me. But this discussion has opened my eyes. I am not Charlie; you don't believe me —too bad. But I cannot bear the idea that I will die and that the real Charlie will be walking about and laughing in your face. For what guarantee have I that, having once made a mistake about me and taken me for Charlie, you won't in turn make a mistake about Charlie and take him for me, for an innocent person. It's not so much a question of my life as of justice. You said yourself that there must be some justice, that one can't just shoot at anybody in the street. So, when I was lying under the sofa I thought to myself: my God, how tragic that these two gentlemen, instead of just resting, are spending their time chasing this Charlie, little knowing that their efforts will be quite wasted. So, I decided to rebel. I rejected the rest of my former pseudo-morality and resolved to tell all.

GRANDSON. Listen. The fact that you're Charlie is another matter. Grandpa recognized you, and he doesn't make mistakes. But it's true that there may be more than one Charlie. We shall wait here. If he doesn't come, we'll do you in and go. If he does come, we'll do him in and then think about it. It's quite possible that you know the whole organization. Why is he coming here, anyway?

OCULIST. He's my patient. Like you.

GRANDSON. Let's ambush him, Grandpa.

(GRANDSON *puts the chair opposite the door.* GRANDPA *kneels behind the chair with the gun pointing at the door.* GRANDSON *stands well back in the stage behind the cupboard.* OCULIST, *completely exhausted, sits on the sofa and wipes his forehead with a handkerchief. He covers his face with his hands.* GRANDPA *and* GRANDSON, *having*

taken up their positions, begin to wait. The stage grows slightly darker.)

GRANDSON. I can't see him.

OCULIST. He's not a young man. He walks slowly. (*Pause. Silence.*)

GRANDSON. He ought to be here now.

OCULIST. He'll come. He's sure to come. He's always punctual, and so well-mannered. (*Pause. Silence.*)

GRANDSON. There's something I don't like about this.

OCULIST. Why? The weather's nice . . . a beautiful sunset.

GRANDPA. I'm bored.

OCULIST. Shall I read something? (*Without waiting for an answer he opens a book and reads, holding it very close to his eyes.*) '. . . the traveller who attains the valley from the direction of the southeast will be greeted by a most impressive landscape. The vine-covered slopes promise that not only the marvellous vistas, purity of the air and colourfulness of the different flowers comprise the feast with which the surrounding district regales the newcomer. In truth, both spiritual and other advantages await in abundance all those who do not recoil before what is good and beautiful. The local inhabitants, though generally of moderate height, are attractively built . . .'

GRANDSON. Enough!

OCULIST. Just as you say. (*Closes the book.*)

GRANDSON. How much longer do we wait?

QCULIST. The whole fun of the hunt is waiting. (*Changing the subject.*) Shall I make you some coffee?

GRANDSON. No need. We don't drink coffee. (*Pause. Silence.* OCULIST *remains motionless. Suddenly he gets up again and begins to creep about the room. It continues to get just perceptibly darker.*)

GRANDSON. What is it?

OCULIST. A fly. (OCULIST *performs the usual waves of the hand, closing his fist, preceded by a quiet creeping noise. The fly keeps getting away.*)

GRANDSON (*with interest*). Got it?

OCULIST. Missed it. Ah, there it is! (*Pause.* GRANDPA *stops looking at the door; in spite of himself he is drawn into the fly-hunt.*)

GRANDSON. Now! Left hand!

(*A longer pause in which the* OCULIST *carries on his pantomime. He is enthralled, rapt, his mind completely concentrated on the chase. He alter-*

nately creeps along and then hurls himself forward. Being deprived of his glasses he guides himself more by ear. At a certain moment the fly settles on the gun of GRANDPA who has been kneeling down all this time and following the hunt simply by the motion of his head. GRANDSON, leaning out from behind the cupboard, watches the scene intently. OCULIST approaches the gun, and hovers menacingly over it. This is the moment of sharpest tension. Then suddenly he performs a lightning sweep of the hand along the barrel and stays motionless with closed fist. He looks first at GRANDPA and then at GRANDSON then very slowly opens his hand.)

OCULIST. Missed!

(Footsteps are heard on the other side of the door coming nearer and nearer. It is getting darker and darker.)

GRANDSON (exclaims triumphantly). He's coming!

GRANDPA (lets out something that resembles a joyful yodelling noise). Halla—lii . . . !

(OCULIST throws himself desperately on to the sofa and covers his head with a cushion.)

GRANDSON (blissfully). Now's your chance!

GRANDPA. Like my father!

GRANDSON. And your grandfather!

GRANDPA. Forward! Charge! (A knock at the door. GRANDPA questioningly to GRANDSON.) Now?

GRANDSON. Just a minute. (Draws from his bosom a bugle and plays a few notes of a rousing song. Renewed knocking.) Now!

(The door opens slowly. GRANDPA fires both barrels. Silence.)

GRANDSON (runs out from the corner behind the cupboard and gazes at the door which is still open). Got him!

GRANDPA (slowly puts down his gun and stretches his limbs). Well, that's a relief.

GRANDSON (yawning). A tense moment.

GRANDPA (pointing at the OCULIST who is still lying motionless covered with a cushion). And what about him?

OCULIST. My glasses!

GRANDPA. That's a great load off my mind.

GRANDSON. You see, Grandpa, the world is not so wicked.

OCULIST (slowly sitting up on the sofa). Is it all over?

GRANDSON (clapping him on the shoulder). It looks like you were telling the truth. He's lying there, on the floor.

OCULIST (lethargically). Yes, yes . . . And how is Grandpa feeling now?

GRANDSON. Grandpa? Grandpa has never felt better in his life. You've cured him, Doctor. Charlie was what he needed.

OCULIST (all the time as in a dream). I am very happy, very happy.

GRANDSON. And we must be off now. Grandpa has got to load both barrels.

OCULIST. Again?

GRANDSON. Then we'll be back. (Pause.)

OCULIST. Then . . . then you're going to go to all this trouble again.

GRANDSON. I'm afraid so. It could be that some Charlie is going to come here again, and even if he doesn't . . .

OCULIST. But I thought . . .

GRANDSON. You thought we weren't coming back, did you? Well, you needn't worry. There's enough ammunition. He's got his glasses. All he needs is his good health.

OCULIST. So when can I expect you?

GRANDSON (threatening him jokingly with his finger). Eh, eh! Don't you be so curious. We could be here tomorrow, in two days or maybe in ten minutes. Any time's a good time to shoot Charlie, as our saying goes.

OCULIST (resignedly sitting on the sofa with his head in his hands). So I'll have to . . .

GRANDSON. Come on, Grandpa. Slope arms and forward march. How much do we owe you?

OCULIST. Oh, nothing. We'll put it down to national insurance.

GRANDSON (giving him his card). This is our telephone number. If ever anything . . .

GRANDPA. Straight between the eyes, my friend. And remember an old man's advice: tea should be hot, an 'i' should have a dot, and Charlie should be . . .

GRANDSON (impatiently). Come on, Grandpa, let's go. (They leave the room. GRANDSON lets GRANDPA pass through and moves back from the door towards the OCULIST.) And if you know anybody else . . .

OCULIST. Yes? (Pause. They look at each other.)

GRANDSON. Because we'll be back. (Leaves the room. He stops in the doorway and says to himself, looking down at what is lying on the floor outside—)

GRANDSON. So he said I belch . . . (Really goes out this time.)

(The OCULIST *sits still for some time as before. It has got much darker but now stops darkening. Then he gets up slowly, goes out and drags into the room an inert figure. It is a dummy, of course. The corpse is not played by a live actor. He places the dummy on the sofa, lays its hands on its chest, then examines its eyes, turns back the eyelids and looks at the eyes according to the rules of eyetests.)*

OCULIST. Incurable separation of the cornea. Of course, the shock of the blast may have hastened the onset of the disease, but who can guarantee that tomorrow he wouldn't have fallen down the stairs, and then his cornea would have become separated completely? In any case there was nothing I could do for him. *(Pause.)* He didn't have to come either. His appointment wasn't for today. I was taking a chance. *(Pause.)* I'm short-sighted too and I'm still alive. *(The telephone rings. The* OCULIST *lifts the receiver.)* Hello! . . . Yes, can I help you? . . . Yes, speaking . . . Between two and six . . . Whenever it's convenient . . . Four o'clock? All right, tomorrow at four. Don't you worry, we'll soon fix you up. Can I have your name? *(Pulls a notebook and pencil out of his pocket. Begins to write.)* I must write it down in the appointments book . . . Hello! Yes. Now then . . . name—Charlie. Till tomorrow then. Goodbye. *(Replaces the receiver. Walks away from the telephone, looks at his watch, glances at the door, listens through the keyhole, then suddenly opens the door to check that nobody's listening. Reflects for a moment. Suddenly he runs to the telephone and hurriedly dials a number.)* Hello, hello! Who's speaking? Grandpa? Grandpa, this is the doctor. Yes, the doctor. What do you mean, what doctor? *(Ingratiatingly.)* Don't you recognize my voice? Don't you recognize your own doctor? . . . Well then, Grandpa, tomorrow at four. Yes, tomorrow at four. He'll be here. Who? What do you mean who? Charlie, of course. Well, cheerio! Till tomorrow! Goodbye! *(Pause. The* OCULIST *replaces the receiver, walks up to the sofa, lifts the dummy off it and pushes it underneath. He himself lies down on the sofa, opens his book and begins to read it just like at the beginning of the play.)*

Curtain

DISCUSSION

1. (a) Why do the Grandson and Grandpa visit an oculist? (b) What transformation of the oculist and Grandpa takes place when Grandpa gets the correct glasses? (c) What might the glasses represent other than eyeglasses?

2. (a) At what point in the play did you begin to suspect that the oculist was Charlie? (b) Was he really Charlie?

3. How does the oculist react when he realizes the Grandson and his Grandpa think he is Charlie?

4. How does the oculist keep Grandpa from killing him?

5. Why does the author direct that the dead man be a dummy, "of course"?

6. How does the oculist rationalize his taking part in the murder of Charlie?

7. (a) What facts about Charlie do you learn in the play? (b) What or who might Charlie represent?

THE AUTHOR'S CRAFT

Dramatic conventions In *A Marriage Proposal*, Tschubukov says of Lomov, "He's come to borrow money! I won't give him any!" Lomov is the only other person on stage, but he does not hear Tschubukov. No one in the audience shouts out, "Lomov, are you deaf? Can't you hear him?" We recognize that Tschubukov is speaking his thoughts out loud for our benefit.

When a character exits from the stage we do not think of him as standing behind a cardboard wall, even though we know that he is. When a character dies in a play we accept his "death" in order to appreciate the play, even though we know that the actor is not *really* dead.

How many other stage devices do we accept without question? The final curtain that signals the end? Shakespeare's characters speaking in blank verse? The dimming and raising of artificial lights? The passage of years within a very brief time? Historical characters? Indeed what about the very act of sitting to watch a play?

When, over the course of many years, the author of a play employs and the audience willingly agrees to accept certain techniques and situations which would be impossible in real life, then we have a *dramatic convention.*

AUTHOR

SLAWOMIR MROZEK, born on June 26, 1930, in Borzecin, Poland, has studied architecture, oriental culture, and painting. He has worked as a caricaturist and journalist for several newspapers and magazines in Cracow, Poland, and is fluent in English, French, Italian, and Russian.

Mrozek's work has only recently become widely known and appreciated in the United States. An English-language production of his play *The Police* has been presented several times on American television. He has written short stories, satires, novels, and a number of plays including: *Out at Sea, Striptease, The Party, Tango,* and *The Prophets.*

Mrozek, who has been described as a quiet, modest, and withdrawn man, had his passport cancelled for having spoken out against Poland's participation in the Russian invasion of Czechoslovakia. He lives in Paris as a stateless person.

UNIT 7 REVIEW

1. By having his characters speak and perform in a specific time, place, and manner, a dramatist develops his *theme,* or his statement about his *subject.* A play may have more than one theme.

a. In *The License,* all of the characters are concerned with justice. They want to be sure that each person is treated correctly and receives what he deserves. Does this happen? What do Chià- chiaro's last speeches reveal about the theme or themes?

b. In *The Marriage Proposal,* we see characters who are filled with pride and yet who exhibit great weaknesses. What do you think Chekhov is trying to say about human beings?

c. Determining what happens in *Charlie* is not difficult. The difficulty arises when we try to understand why it happens, and, more specifically, what it all means. There are many possible answers to the question "Who is Charlie?" What is Mrozek saying about the Charlies in the world and those who hunt them?

2. *Comedy* involves exaggeration, happy endings, predictability, characters with obsessions, stereotyped characters, absurd complications, and sudden twists to the plot.

a. Considering the above characteristics, which of the three one-act plays best fits the designation "comedy"?

b. Of the play or plays which are not comedies, does one have any of the characteristics of comedy? Why is that play not, then, a comedy?

3. A *convention* is a technique of drama, either as it is written or as it is staged, which has been accepted by both author and audience.

a. Make a list with three columns, one for each of the plays. In each column list as many conventions as you can that have been followed by each author.

b. Is there one play which seems to have fewer conventions than the other two? Which one? Why do you suppose this play is so different?

4. In your opinion, which of the three one-act plays is the most original? Consider as many aspects of the drama as you can: the convention used or not used, theme, setting, characterization, plot, conflict, dramatic license, dialogue, traditional versus experimental techniques.

Glossary

COMPLETE PRONUNCIATION KEY

The pronunciation of each word is shown just after the word, in this way: **ab bre vi ate** (ə brē′vē āt). The letters and signs used are pronounced as in the words below. The·mark ′ is placed after a syllable with primary or strong accent, as in the example above. The mark ′ after a syllable shows a secondary or lighter accent, as in **ab bre vi a tion** (ə brē′vē ā′shən).

Some words, taken from foreign languages, are spoken with sounds that otherwise do not occur in English. Symbols for these sounds are given at the end of the table as "Foreign Sounds."

a	hat, cap	j	jam, enjoy	th	thin, both
ā	age, face	k	kind, seek	ᴛʜ	then, smooth
ä	father, far	l	land, coal		
		m	me, am		
		n	no, in	u	cup, butter
b	bad, rob	ng	long, bring	u̇	full, put
ch	child, much			ü	rule, move
d	did, red				
				v	very, save
e	let, best	o	hot, rock	w	will, woman
ē	equal, see	ō	open, go	y	young, yet
ėr	term, learn	ô	order, all	z	zero, breeze
		oi	oil, voice	zh	measure, seizure
		ou	house, out		
f	fat, if				
g	go, bag			ə represents:
h	he, how	p	paper, cup	a in about
		r	run, try	e in taken
		s	say, yes	i in April
		sh	she, rush	o in lemon
i	it, pin	t	tell, it	u in circus
ī	ice, five			

foreign sounds

Y as in French *du*. Pronounce ē with the lips rounded as for English ü in **rule**.

œ as in French *peu*. Pronounce ā with the lips rounded as for ō.

N as in French *bon*. The N is not pronounced, but shows that the vowel before it is nasal.

H as in German *ach*. Pronounce k without closing the breath passage.

PARTS OF SPEECH

n.	noun	*adj.*	adjective	*prep.*	preposition
v.	verb	*adv.*	adverb	*conj.*	conjunction
pron.	pronoun			*interj.*	interjection

ETYMOLOGY KEY

<	from, derived from, taken from	**gen.**	genitive
?	possibly	**lang.**	language
abl.	ablative	**masc.**	masculine
accus.	accusative	**neut.**	neuter
cf.	compare	**pp.**	past participle
dial.	dialect	**ppr.**	present participle
dim.	diminutive	**pt.**	past tense
fem.	feminine	**ult.**	ultimately
		var.	variant

LANGUAGE ABBREVIATIONS

AF — Anglo-French (=Anglo-Norman, the dialect of French spoken by the Normans in England, esp. 1066-c.1164)

Am.E — American English (originating in U.S.)

Am.Ind. — American Indian

Am.Sp. — American Spanish

E — English

F — French

G — German

Gk. — Greek (from Homer to 300 A.D.)

Gmc. — Germanic (parent language of Gothic, Scandinavian, English, Dutch, German)

HG — High German (speech of Central and Southern Germany)

Hindu. — Hindustani (the commonest language of India)

Ital. — Italian

L — Latin (Classical Latin 200 B.C.-300 A.D.)

LG — Low German (speech of Northern Germany)

LGk. — Late Greek (300-700)

LL — Late Latin (300-700)

M — Middle

ME — Middle English (1100-1500)

Med. — Medieval

Med.Gk. — Medieval Greek (700-1500)

Med.L — Medieval Latin (700-1500)

MF — Middle French (1400-1600)

MHG — Middle High German (1100-1450)

MLG — Middle Low German (1100-1450)

NL — New Latin (after 1500)

O — Old

OE — Old English (before 1100)

OF — Old French (before 1400)

OHG — Old High German (before 1100)

Pg. — Portuguese

Scand. — Scandinavian (one of the Germanic languages of Northern Europe before Middle English times; Old Norse unless otherwise specified)

Skt. — Sanskrit (the ancient literary language of India, from the same parent language as Persian, Greek, Latin, Germanic, Slavonic, and Celtic)

Sp. — Spanish

VL — Vulgar Latin (a popular form of Latin, the main source of French, Spanish, Italian, Portuguese, and Romanian)

ab a cus (ab′ə kəs), *n., pl.* **-cus es, -ci** (-si). frame with rows of counters or beads that slide back and forth in grooves or on wires, used in calculating. [< L < Gk. *abax*]

a bash (ə bash′), *v.* embarrass and confuse; make uneasy and somewhat ashamed.

a bate (ə bāt′), *v.,* **a bat ed, a bat ing.** 1. make less in amount, intensity, etc.: *The medicine abated his pain.* 2. become less violent, intense, etc. [< OF *abatre* beat down < *a-* to (< L *ad-*) + *batre* beat < L *batuere*]

ab hor (ab hôr′), *v.* shrink away from with horror; feel disgust or hate for; detest.

ab ject (ab′jekt or ab jekt′), *adj.* wretched; miserable: *abject poverty.*

a bode (ə bōd′), *n.* place to live in; dwelling; residence.

ab so lu tion (ab′sə lü′shən), *n.* a freeing or freedom from guilt and punishment for sin; forgiveness.

ac cou ter (ə kü′tər), *v.* equip; array: *Knights were accoutered in armor.*

ac cou ter ments (ə kü′tər mənts), *n. pl.* 1. a soldier's equipment with the exception of his weapons and clothing. 2. personal equipment; outfit.

ac qui esce (ak′wē es′), *v.,* **-esced, -esc ing.** give consent by keeping silent; submit quietly: *We acquiesced in their plan because we could not suggest a better one.*

ac quit tal (ə kwit′l), *n.* 1. a setting free by declaring not guilty; discharge; release. 2. performance (of a duty, obligation, etc.).

ad a mant (ad′ə mant), *n.* substance too hard to be cut or broken. —*adj.* 1. too hard to be cut or broken. 2. unyielding; firm.

ad ept (*n.* ad′ept or ə dept′; *adj.* ə dept′), *n.* a thoroughly skilled or expert person. —*adj.* thoroughly skilled; expert.

ad u la tion (aj′ə lā′shən), *n.* too much praise; slavish flattery.

ad ver sar y (ad′vər ser′ē), *n., pl.* **-sar ies.** 1. person opposing or resisting another person; enemy. 2. person or group on the other side in a contest.

aes thet ic (es thet′ik), *adj.* 1. having to do with the beautiful, as distinguished from the useful, scientific, etc. 2. (of persons) sensitive to beauty.

af fi ance (ə fī′əns), *v.* promise in marriage; betroth. [< OF *afiancer* to promise < *afiance,* n., trust] *n.* 1. the pledging of faith; betrothal. 2. trust.

a ghast (ə gast′ or ə gäst′), *adj.* filled with horror; frightened; terrified. [pp. of obsolete *agast* terrify < OE *on-* on + *gæstan* frighten. Related to *ghost.*]

a gue (ā′gyü), *n.* 1. a malarial fever with chills and sweating that occur at regular intervals. 2. a fit of shivering; chill.

aide-de-camp (ād′də kamp′), *n., pl.* **aides-de-camp.** an army or navy officer who acts as an assistant to a superior officer.

al che my (al′kə mē), *n.* medieval chemistry, especially the search for a process by which cheaper metals could be turned into gold.

al der (ôl′dər), *n.* any of several trees and shrubs that usually grow in wet land and have clusters of catkins which develop into small woody cones. [OE *alor*]

al lege (ə lej′), *v.,* **-leged, -leg ing.** 1. assert without proof. 2. state positively; assert; declare: *This man alleges that his watch has been stolen.*

al lu sion (ə lü′zhən), *n.* indirect reference; slight mention.

am big u ous (am big′yü əs), *adj.* 1. having more than one possible meaning. 2. doubtful; not clear; uncertain. [< L *ambiguus < ambigere < ambi-* in two ways + *agere* drive]

a me na ble (ə mē′nə bl or ə men′ə bl), *adj.* open to suggestion or advice; responsive; submissive.

and i ron (and′ī′ərn), *n.* one of a pair of metal supports for wood burned in a fireplace.

an e mom e ter (an′ə mom′ə tər), *n.* instrument for measuring the velocity or pressure of the wind.

an i mate (*v.* an′ə māt; *adj.* an′ə mit), *v.,* **-mat ed, -mat ing,** *adj.* —*v.* 1. give life to; make alive. 2. make lively, gay, or vigorous. —*adj.* 1. living; having life. 2. lively; gay; vigorous.

a non (ə non′), *adv.* 1. in a little while; soon. 2. at another time; again.

an te ced ent (an′tə sēd′nt), *n.* 1. a previous thing or event; something happening before and leading up to another. 2. **antecedents,** *pl.* past life or history: *No one knew the antecedents of the mysterious stranger.*

an ti ma cas sar (an′tē mə kas′ər), *n.* a small covering to protect the back or arms of a chair, sofa, etc. [< *anti-* against + *macassar* a hair oil from Macassar]

an ti quate (an′tə kwāt), *v.,* **-quat ed, -quat ing.** make old-fashioned; make out-of-date.

ap a thet ic (ap′ə thet′ik), *adj.* with little interest or desire for action; indifferent. —**ap′a thet′i cal ly,** *adv.*

ap a thy (ap′ə thē), *n.* 1. lack of interest or desire for activity; indifference. 2. lack of feeling. [< L < Gk. *apatheia < a-* without + *pathos* feeling]

ap pall or **ap pal** (ə pôl′), *v.,* **-palled, -pall ing.** fill with horror; dismay; terrify.

ap pa ri tion (ap′ə rish′ən), *n.* 1. ghost; phantom. 2. something strange, remarkable, or unexpected which comes into view.

ap pease (ə pēz′), *v.* 1. satisfy (an appetite or desire): *A good dinner will appease your hunger.* 2. make calm; quiet. 3. give in to the demands of (especially those of a potential enemy).

ap pre hen sion (ap′ri hen′shən), *n.* 1. expectation of evil; fear; dread. 2. a seizing; being seized; arrest. 3. understanding; grasp by the mind.

ar id (ar′id), *adj.* 1. dry; barren. 2. dull; uninteresting: *an arid, tiresome speech.*

ar rant (ar′ənt), *adj.* thoroughgoing; downright: *He was such an arrant liar that nobody believed him.*

ar tic u late (*adj.* är tik′yə lit; *v.* är tik′yə-lāt), *adj., v.,* **-lat ed, -lat ing.** —*adj.* 1. uttered in distinct syllables of words.

2. able to put one's thoughts into words: *Julia is the most articulate of the sisters.* 3. made up of distinct parts; distinct. 4. jointed; segmented.

ar ti san (är′tə zən), *n.* workman skilled in some industry or trade; craftsman.

Ar y an (er′ē ən, ar′ē ən, or är′yən), *adj.* of or having to do with a family of languages from which most European languages are descended; Indo-European. —*n.* in Nazi use, a non-Jew.

as phyx i ate (as fik′sē āt), *v.,* **-at ed, -at ing.** suffocate because of lack of oxygen and excess of carbon dioxide in the blood.

as pi ra tion (as′pə rā′shən), *n.* earnest desire; longing.

as sail (ə sāl′), *v.* 1. set upon with violence; attack: *assail a fortress.* 2. set upon vigorously with arguments, abuse, etc.

as sess (ə ses′), *v.* 1. estimate the value of (property or income) for taxation. 2. fix the amount of (a tax, fine, damages, etc.). 3. figuratively, to appraise; evaluate.

as sid u ous (ə sij′ü əs), *adj.* careful and attentive; diligent. —**as sid′u ous ly,** *adv.*

at a vism (at′ə viz əm), *n.* 1. resemblance to a remote ancestor. 2. reversion to a primitive type.

a troc i ty (ə tros′ə tē), *n., pl.* **-ties.** 1. very great wickedness or cruelty. 2. very cruel or brutal act.

at ro phy (at′rə fē), *n., v.,* **-phied, -phy ing.** —*n.* wasting away; wasting away of a part or parts of the body. —*v.* waste away. [< LL < Gk. *atrophia < a-* without + *trophe* nourishment]

au da cious (ô dā′shəs), *adj.* bold; daring.

aught (ôt), *n.* anything: *You may go for aught I care.* —*adv.* in any way; to any degree; at all.

aug ment (ôg ment′), *v.* increase; enlarge.

au gur (ô′gər), *v.* 1. predict; foretell. 2. be a sign or promise.

au gust (ô gust′), *adj.* inspiring reverence and admiration; majestic; venerable. .

au ra (ô′rə), *n., pl.* **au ras, au rae** (ô′rē). something supposed to come from a person or thing and surround him or it as an atmosphere: *An aura of holiness surrounded the saint.*

aus pice (ôs′pis), *n., pl.* **aus pic es** (ôs′pə sēz). 1. favorable circumstance; indication of success. 2. omen; sign.

aus tere (ôs tir′), *adj.* 1. harsh; stern. 2. strict in morals. 3. severely simple.

av a rice (av′ə ris), *n.* greedy desire for money or property.

a vert (ə vėrt′), *v.* 1. prevent; avoid: *He averted the accident by a quick turn of his car.* 2. turn away; turn aside: *She averted her eyes from the wreck.* [< OF < L *avertere < ab-* from + *vertere* turn]

awe (ô), *n., v.,* **awed, aw ing.** —*n.* great fear and wonder; fear and reverence.

a wry (ə rī′), *adv., adj.* 1. with a twist or turn to one side: *Her hat was blown awry by the wind.* 2. wrong: *Our plans have gone awry.*

az ure (azh′ər or ā′zhər), *n.* 1. blue; sky blue. 2. the clear blue color of the unclouded sky. —*adj.* blue; sky blue.

bal lad (bal′əd), *n.* **1.** a simple song. **2.** a poem that tells a story in with one verse form, especially one that tells a popular legend and is passed from one generation to another orally. Ballads are often sung. [< OF *balade* < Provençal *balada* dancing song]

bane (bān), *n.* **1.** cause of death, ruin, or harm: *Wild animals were the bane of the mountain village.* **2.** ruin; harm.

bard (bärd), *n.* **1.** a poet and singer of long ago. Bards sang their own poems to the music of their harps. **2.** poet. [< Scotch Gaelic and Irish]

bark (bärk), *n.* **1.** ship with three masts, square-rigged on the first two masts and fore-and-aft-rigged on the other. **2.** *Poetic.* boat; ship. Also, **barque.**

bar na cle (bär′nə kl), *n.* animal with a shell that attaches itself to rocks, the bottoms of ships, the timbers of wharves, etc.

base (bās), *adj.*, **bas er, bas est,** *n.* —*adj.* **1.** morally low; mean; selfish; cowardly: *To betray a friend is a base action.* **2.** fit for an inferior person or thing; menial; unworthy: *No needful service is to be looked at as base.* **3.** *Archaic.* of humble birth or origin.

bate (bāt), *v.*, **bat ed, bat ing.** **1.** abate; lessen; hold back. **2. with bated breath,** holding the breath in great fear, awe, interest, etc.

bay (bā), *n.* **1.** the long, deep bark of a dog: *The hunters heard the distant bay of the hounds.* **2.** stand made by a hunted animal to face pursuers when escape is impossible: *The stag stood at bay on the edge of the cliff.* **3. bring to bay,** put in a position from which escape is impossible.

be gat (bi gat′), *v. Archaic.* a pt. of **beget.**

be get (bi get′), *v.*, **be got** or *(Archaic)* **be gat, be got ten** or **be got, be get ting.** **1.** become the father of. **2.** cause to be; produce: *Hate begets hate.*

be guile (bi gīl′), *v.* **1.** deceive; cheat. **2.** take away from deceitfully or cunningly. **3.** entertain; amuse.

be hold en (bi hōld′n), *adj.* under obligations; in debt: *I am much beholden to you for your help.*

be lit tle (bi lit′l), *v.*, **-tled, -tling. 1.** cause to seem little, unimportant, or less important; speak slightingly of: *Jealous people belittled the explorer's great discoveries.* **2.** make small.

bel li cose (bel′ə kōs), *adj.* warlike; fond of fighting. [< L *bellicosus* < *bellum* war]

ben e fac tor (ben′ə fak′tər or ben′ə-fak′tər), *n.* person who has given money or kindly help. [< L *benefactor* < *benefacere* < *bene* well + *facere* do]

be nev o lence (bə nev′ə ləns), *n.* **1.** good will; kindly feeling. **2.** act of kindness; something good that is done; generous gift.

be queath (bi kwēŦH′ or bi kwēth′), *v.* **1.** give or leave (property, etc.) by a will: *The father bequeathed the farm to his son.* **2.** hand down to posterity.

be reaved (bi rēvd′), *adj.* **1.** deprived *(of)* by death. **2.** left desolate.

be siege (bi sēj′), *v.* **1.** surround and try to capture: *For ten years the Greeks besieged the city of Troy.* **2.** crowd around. **3.** overwhelm with requests, questions, etc.

be stride (bi strīd′), *v.* get on or sit on (something) with one leg on each side.

be tide (bi tīd′), *v.* **1.** happen to: *Woe betide you if you betray us.* **2.** happen: *No matter what betides, the family will hold together.*

be to ken (bi tō′kən), *v.* be a sign or token of; indicate; show: *His smile betokens his satisfaction.*

bib u lous (bib′yə ləs), *adj.* **1.** fond of drinking alcoholic liquor. **2.** absorbent. [< L *bibulus* < *bibere* drink]

bier (bir), *n.* a movable stand on which a coffin or dead body is placed.

big ot (big′ət), *n.* a bigoted person; intolerant, prejudiced person.

bil let (bil′it), *n.* **1.** a written order to provide board and lodging for a soldier. **2.** place where a soldier is lodged. **3.** job; position.

blas phe mous (blas′fə məs), *adj.* speaking about God or sacred things with abuse or contempt.

blithe (blīŦH or blīth), *adj.* gay; happy; cheerful.

bog (bog or bôg), *n.* soft, wet, spongy ground; marsh; swamp.

bond man (bond′mən), *n.* **1.** slave. **2.** serf in the Middle Ages.

bon ny or **bon nie** (bon′ē), *adj.* **1.** pretty; handsome. **2.** fine; excellent.

bot tom (bot′əm), *n.* the low land along a river.

brace (brās), *n.* pair; couple: *a brace of ducks.*

bra zen (brā′zn), *adj.* **1.** made of brass. **2.** like brass in color or strength. **3.** loud and harsh. **4.** shameless; impudent. —*v.* **1.** make shameless or impudent. **2. brazen a thing out** or **through,** act as if unashamed of it.

breach (brēch), *n.* **1.** an opening made by breaking down something solid; gap. **2.** a breaking (of a law, promise, duty, etc.).

break wa ter (brāk′wô′tər or brāk′-wot′ər), wall or barrier to break the force of waves.

broach (brōch), *v.* **1.** open by making a hole: *broach a barrel of cider.* **2.** begin to talk about: *broach a subject.*

bump tious (bump′shəs), *adj.* unpleasantly assertive or conceited.

buoy (boi or bü′i), *n.* **1.** a floating object anchored in a certain place on the water to warn or guide. **2.** a cork belt, ring, or jacket to keep a person fron sinking.

bu reau crat (byúr′ə krat), *n.* **1.** official in a bureaucracy. **2.** a formal, pretentious government official.

bur geon (bėr′jən), *v., n.* bud; sprout.

bur lesque (bėr lesk′), *v.* imitate so as to ridicule.

bur ly (bėr′lē), *adj.*, **-li er, -li est. 1.** strong; sturdy; big. **2.** bluff; rough.

bur nish (bėr′nish), *v.,n.* polish; shine.

but tress (but′ris), *n.* support built against a wall or building to strengthen it.

cache (kash), *n.* a hidden store of food or supplies.

cairn (kern), *n.* pile of stones heaped up as a memorial, tomb, or landmark.

hat, āge, fär; let, ēqual, tėrm;
it, īce; hot, ōpen, ôrder;
oil, out; cup, pùt, rüle;
ch, child; ng, long; sh, she;
th, thin; ŦH, then; zh, measure;

ə represents *a* in about, *e* in taken, *i* in pencil, *o* in lemon, *u* in circus.

< = from, derived from, taken from.

cal cine (kal′sɪn or kal′sin), *v.*, **-cined, -cin ing. 1.** change to lime by heating. **2.** burn to ashes or powder.

cal lig ra phy (kə lig′rə fē), *n.* **1.** handwriting. **2.** beautiful handwriting. [< Gk. *kalligraphia* < *kallos* beauty + *graphein* write]

can ny (kan′ē), *adj. Scottish.* **1.** shrewd; cautious. **2.** thrifty.

ca pri cious (kə prish′əs or kə prē′shəs), *adj.* guided by one's fancy; full of unreasonable notions; changeable; fickle: *A spoiled child is often capricious.*

ca reer (kə rir′), *n.* **1.** a general course of action or progress through life. **2.** way of living; occupation; profession. **3.** speed; full speed: *We were in full career when we struck the post.*

car i ca ture (kar′ə kə chùr or kar′ə kə-chər), *n.* picture, cartoon, description, etc., that ridiculously exaggerates the peculiarities or defects of a person or thing.

car ri on (kar′ē ən), *n.* **1.** dead and decaying flesh. **2.** rottenness; filth.

casque (kask), *n.* helmet.

cause way (kôz′wā′), *n.* **1.** a raised road or path, usually built across wet ground, shallow water, etc. **2.** a paved road; highway.

cav a lier (kav′ə lir′), *n.* **1.** horseman; mounted soldier; knight. **2.** a courteous gentleman. **3.** a courteous escort for a lady. —*adj.* **1.** free and easy; offhand. **2.** proud and scornful; haughty; arrogant.

cen sure (sen′shər), *n.* act of blaming; expression of disapproval; criticism. —*v.* express disapproval of; find fault with; blame; criticize.

chal ice (chal′is), *n.* **1.** cup. **2.** cup that holds the wine used in the Communion service.

chan cel (chan′sl or chän′sl), *n.* space around the altar of a church, used by the clergy and the choir.

char y (char′ē), *adj.* **1.** careful: *A cat is chary of wetting its paws.* **2.** shy. **3.** sparing; stingy.

chas ten (chas′n), *v.* **1.** punish to improve. **2.** restrain from excess or crudeness. [< obsolete v. *chaste* < F < L *castigare* make pure < *castus* pure]

chas tise (chas tīz′), *v.* punish; beat.

chi can er y (shi kān′ər ē), *n.* low trickery; unfair practice; quibbling.

chol er ic (kol′ər ik), *adj.* easily made angry; irritable.

chron ic (kron′ik), *adj.* **1.** of a disease, lasting a long time. **2.** constant; habitual: *a chronic liar.*

citadel

cit a del (sit′ə dl or sit′ə del), *n.* 1. fortress commanding a city. 2. a strongly fortified place; stronghold.

ci vil i ty (sə vil′ə tē), *n.* 1. politeness; courtesy. 2. act of politeness or courtesy.

cleave (klēv), *v.,* **cleaved** or *(Archaic)* **clave, cleaved, cleav ing.** hold fast *(to)*; cling; be faithful *(to)*: cleave to an idea.

clique (klēk, klik), *n., v.,* **cliqued, cli quing.** —*n.* a small, exclusive group of people within a larger group. —*v.i.* INFORMAL. form or associate in a clique. [< F]

clout (klout), *n.* 1. *Informal.* a hit with the hand; rap; knock; cuff. 2. a white cloth target used in archery. 3. *Archaic.* cloth.

cof fer (kôf′ər or kof′ər), *n.* box, chest, or trunk, especially one used to hold money or other valuable things.

cog ni zant (kog′nə zənt or kon′ə zənt), *adj.* aware: *The general was cognizant of the movements of the enemy.*

come li ness (kum′lē nis), *n.* 1. pleasant appearance. 2. fitness; suitableness.

com men su rate (kə men′shə rit or kə men′sə rit), *adj.* 1. in the proper proportion; proportionate: *The pay should be commensurate with the work.* 2. of the same size, extent, etc.; equal.

com mis er a tion (kə miz′ər ā′shən), *n.* pity; sympathy.

com pat i ble (kəm pat′ə bl), *adj.* able to exist together; that can get on well together; agreeing; in harmony: *Health and hard work are compatible.*

com pel (kəm pel′), *v.* 1. force: *Rain compelled them to stop.* 2. cause or get by force: *A policeman can compel obedience.*

com pen sa tion (kom′pən sā′shən), *n.* something given as an equivalent; something given to make up for a loss, injury, etc.

com plai sant (kəm plā′znt or kom′plə zant), *adj.* obliging; gracious; courteous.

com pro mise (kom′prə mīz), *v.* 1. settle (a dispute) by agreeing that each contestant will give up a part of what he demands. 2. put under suspicion; put in danger: *You will compromise your good name if you go around with thieves and liars.*

con ces sion (kən sesh′ən), *n.* a conceding; granting; yielding: *As a concession, Mother let me stay up an hour longer.*

con course (kon′kôrs, kong′kôrs, kon′kōrs, or kong′kōrs), *n.* 1. a running, flowing, or coming together: *The fort was built at the concourse of two rivers.* 2. crowd. 3. place where crowds come. 4. an open space in a railroad station. 5. driveway; boulevard.

con dole (kən dōl′), *v.,* **-doled, -dol ing.** express sympathy; sympathize.

con done (kən dōn′), *v.* forgive; overlook.

con du cive (kən dü′siv or kən dyü′siv), *adj.* helpful; favorable.

con glom er a tion (kən glom′ər ā′shən), *n.* a mixed-up mass of various things or persons; mixture.

con jec ture (kən jek′chər), *n., v.,* **-tured, -tur ing.** —*n.* 1. formation of an opinion admittedly without sufficient evidence for proof; guessing. 2. a guess.

con jure (kun′jər or kon′jər), *v.,* 1. **conjure up, a.** cause to appear in a magic way. **b.** cause to appear in the mind. 2. compel (a spirit, devil, etc.) to appear or disappear by magic words. 3. make a solemn appeal to; request earnestly; entreat: *I conjure you not to betray your country.*

con no ta tion (kon′ə tā′shən), *n.* 1. a connoting. 2. what is suggested in addition to the simple meaning.

con se crate (kon′sə krāt), *v.* 1. set apart as sacred; make holy. 2. devote to a purpose: *A doctor's life is consecrated to curing sick people.*

con sole (kən sōl′), *v.* comfort. [< L *consolari* < *com-* + *solari* soothe]

con spire (kən spīr′), *v.* 1. plan secretly with others to do something wrong; plot. 2. act together: *All things conspired to make her birthday a happy one.*

con straint (kən strānt′), *n.* 1. confinement. 2. restraint. 3. a holding back of natural feelings.

con stric tion (kən strik′shən), *n.* 1. act of drawing together; contraction; compression. 2. feeling of tightness: *He coughed and complained of a constriction in his chest.*

con strue (kən strü′), *v.* 1. show the meaning of; explain; interpret: *Different lawyers may construe the same law differently.* 2. translate.

con trive (kən trīv′), *v.* 1. invent; design: *contrive a new kind of engine.* 2. plan; scheme; plot: *contrive a robbery.*

con vic tion (kən vik′shən), *n.* 1. act of proving or declaring guilty. 2. state of being proved or declared guilty. 3. act of convincing (a person). 4. being convinced. 5. firm belief.

con viv i al (kən viv′ē əl), *adj.* fond of eating and drinking with friends; jovial.

co ny (kō′nē), *n., pl.* **-nies.** 1. rabbit fur. Cony is used to make or trim coats. 2. rabbit. 3. a small rabbitlike rodent; pika.

coo lie (kü′lē), *n.* 1. an unskilled, native laborer in China, India, etc. 2. laborer who does hard work for very little pay. [probably < Tamil *kuli* hire, hired servant]

copse (kops), *n.* a thicket of small trees, bushes, shrubs, etc.

cor mo rant (kôr′mə rənt), *n.* 1. a very large, greedy sea bird that has a pouch under the beak for holding captured fish. 2. a greedy person.

cor nice (kôr′nis), *n., v.,* **-niced, -nic ing.** —*n.* 1. an ornamental molding that projects along the top of a wall, pillar, building, etc. 2. molding around the walls of a room just below the ceiling.

cor o net (kôr′ə net or kor′ə net), *n.* 1. a small crown worn as a mark of high rank. A king wears a crown; princes and nobles wear coronets. 2. circle of gold, jewels, or flowers worn around the head as an ornament.

cor ro sive (kə rō′siv), *adj.* producing corrosion; corroding; eating away.

cor ru gat ed (kôr′ə gāt′id or kor′ə gāt′id), *adj.* bent or shaped into a row of wavelike ridges.

cou lee (kü′lē), *n.* in the western United States, a deep ravine or gulch that is usually dry in summer.

cov ert (kuv′ərt), *adj.* secret; hidden; disguised: *covert glances.*

cov et ous (kuv′ə təs), *adj.* desiring things that belong to others.

cov ey (kuv′ē), *n., pl.* **-eys.** 1. brood of partridges, quail, etc. 2. a small flock.

cre du li ty (krə dü′lə tē or krə dū′lə tē), *n.* a too great readiness to believe.

cre o sote (krē′ə sōt), *n., v.,* **-sot ed, -sot ing.** —*n.* an oily liquid with a penetrating odor, obtained by distilling wood tar, used to preserve wood and in cough medicine.

cres cent (kres′nt), *n.* 1. shape of the moon in its first or last quarter. 2. anything having this or a similar shape. —*adj.* 1. shaped like the moon in its first or last quarter. 2. growing; increasing.

crotch et (kroch′it), *n.* 1. an odd notion; unreasonable whim. 2. a small hook or hooklike part. 3. *Esp. Brit.* a quarter note in music.

crux (kruks), *n.* the essential part; the most important point.

cryp tic (krip′tik), *adj.* having a hidden meaning; secret; mysterious: *a cryptic message.* [< LL *crypticus* < Gk. *kryptikos* < *kryptos* hidden]

cui rass (kwi ras′), *n.* 1. piece of armor for the body made of a breastplate and a plate for the back fastened together. 2. the breastplate alone.

cull (kul), *v.* pick out; select.

cu mu la tive (kyü′myə lā′tiv or kyü′ myələ tiv), *adj.* heaped up; accumulated; increasing or growing in amount, force, etc., by additions.

cur lew (kėr′lü), *n.* a wading bird with a long, thin bill.

cur ry (kėr′ē), *v.,* **-ried, -ry ing.** 1. rub and clean (a horse, etc.) with a brush or currycomb. 2. prepare (tanned leather) for use by soaking, scraping, beating, coloring, etc. 3. **curry favor,** seek a person's favor by insincere flattery, constant attentions.

cur vet (kėr′vit), *n.* leap in the air made by a horse. The forelegs are first raised and then the hind legs, so that all legs are off the ground for a second.

cy clo ram a (sī′klə ram′ə or sī′klə rä′mə), *n.* a large picture of a landscape, battle, etc., on the wall of a circular room.

cyg net (sig′nit), *n.* a young swan.

da is (dā′is; *esp. Brit.* dās), *n.* a raised platform at one end of a hall or large room.

das tard ly (das′tərd lē), *adj.* like a dastard; mean and cowardly; sneaking.

de base (di bās′), *v.* make low or lower; lessen the value of.

de crep it (di krep′it), *adj.* broken down or weakened by old age; old and feeble. [< L *decrepitus* broken down < *de-* + *crepare* creak]

deem (dēm), *v.* think; believe; consider.

de fame (di fām′), *v.* attack the good name of; harm the reputation of; speak evil of.

de fend ant (di fen′dənt), *n.* person accused or sued in a law court.

de fense (di fens′), *n.* 1. act of defending or protecting; a guarding against attack or harm. 2. thing that defends or protects; thing used to guard against attack or harm. 3. act of defending oneself in boxing or fencing. 4. team or players defending a goal in a game. 5. action, speech, or writing in favor of something. 6. answer of a defendant to an accusation or lawsuit against him. 7. a defendant and his lawyers. Also, *esp. Brit.* **defence.** [< OF < L *defensa* < *defendere* ward off]

def i cit (def′ə sit), *n.* amount by which a sum of money falls short; shortage: *Since the club owed $15, and had only $10 in the treasury, there was a deficit of $5.*

de file (di fīl′), *v.,* **-filed, -fil ing.** 1. make filthy or dirty; make disgusting in any way. 2. destroy the purity or cleanness of.

de funct (di fungkt′), *adj.* dead; extinct.

de hy drate (dē hī′drāt), *v.,* **-drat ed, -drat ing.** 1. deprive (a chemical compound) of water or the elements of water. 2. take moisture from; dry.

de lude (di lüd′), *v.,* **-lud ed, -lud ing.** mislead; deceive.

de lu sion (di lü′zhən), *n.* a false notion or belief: *The insane man had a delusion that he was the king.*

de mise (di mīz′), *n.* death.

de mor al ize (di môr′əl īz or di mor′əl īz), *v.* 1. corrupt the morals of: *The drug habit demoralizes people.* 2. weaken the spirit, courage, or discipline of; dishearten.

de no ta tion (dē′nō tā′shən), *n.* 1. meaning, especially the exact, literal meaning. The denotation of *home* is "place where one lives," but it has many connotations. 2. indication; a denoting or marking out. 3. mark; sign; symbol.
➜ The **denotation** of a word is the exact, literal meaning of that word as contrasted with its *connotation,* the added meaning the word suggests or implies. The denotation of *slender* and *skinny* is this, but *slender* connotes approval and *skinny,* disapproval.

de nounce (di nouns′), *v.,* **-nounced, -nounc ing.** 1. condemn publicly; express strong disapproval of. 2. inform against; accuse.

de nude (di nüd′ or di nyüd′), *v.* make bare; strip of clothing, covering, etc.: *Most trees are denuded of their leaves in winter.*

de plor a ble (di plôr′ə bl or di plōr′ə bl), *adj.* 1. to be deplored; regrettable; lamentable: *a deplorable accident.* 2. wretched; miserable. **—de plor′a bly,** *adv.*

de prav i ty (di prav′ə tē), *n.* 1. wickedness; corruption. 2. a corrupt act; bad practice.

de range (di rānj′), *v.,* **-ranged, -rang ing.** 1. disturb the order or arrangement of; throw into confusion. 2. make insane.

der e lict (der′ə likt), *adj.* abandoned; deserted; forsaken: *a derelict ship.*

de ri sion (di rizh′ən), *n.* 1. scornful laughter; ridicule; contempt. 2. an object of ridicule.

des ul to ry (des′əl tô′rē or des′əl tō′rē), *adj.* jumping from one thing to another: *The careful study of a few books is better than the desultory reading of many.*

de vi a tion (dē′vē ā′shən), *n.* a turning aside from a way, course, rule, truth, etc.

de vi ous (dē′vē əs), *adj.* winding; twisting; roundabout.

de void (di void′), *adj.* lacking (*of*): *devoid of sense.*

dex ter i ty (deks ter′ə tē), *n.* 1. skill in using the hands. 2. skill in using the mind.

di aph a nous (dī af′ə nəs), *adj.* transparent: *Gauze is a diaphanous fabric.* [< Med.L *diaphanus* < Gk. *diaphanes* < *dia-* through + *phainein* show]

dif fuse (di fūs′), *adj.* 1. not concentrated together at a single point; spread out: *diffuse light.* 2. using many words where a few would do: *a diffuse writer.* [< L *diffusus,* pp. of *diffundere* < *dis-* in every direction + *fundere* pour]

di la tion (dī lā′shən or də lā′shən), *n.* act of dilating; enlargement; widening.

din (din), *n.* a loud, confused noise that lasts.

dint (dint), *n.* 1. force: *By dint of hard work the man became successful.* 2. dent.

dip so ma ni a (dip′sə mā′nē ə), *n.* an abnormal, uncontrollable craving for alcoholic liquor.

dis con cert (dis′kən sėrt′), *v.* 1. disturb the self-possession of; embarrass greatly; confuse: *His arrest of the wrong man disconcerted the policeman.* 2. upset.

dis con so late (dis kon′sl it), *adj.* without hope; forlorn; unhappy; cheerless.

dis course (*n.* dis′kôrs or dis′kōrs; *v.* dis kôrs′ or dis kōrs′), *n.* 1. a formal speech or writing: *Lectures and sermons are discourses.* 2. conversation; a talk. *—v.* 1. speak or write formally. 2. converse; talk.

dis creet (dis krēt′), *adj.* careful and sensible in speech and action; wisely cautious; showing good sense. **—Syn.** prudent, wary.

di shev eled (də shev′ld), *adj.* rumpled; mussed; disordered; untidy.

dis il lu sion (dis′i lü′zhən), *v.* free from illusion: *People are apt to become disillusioned as they grow old.*

dis mem ber (dis mem′bər), *v.* 1. pull apart; cut to pieces; separate or divide into parts: *The defeated country was dismembered.* 2. cut or tear the limbs from.

dis par age ment (dis par′ij mənt), *n.* something that lowers a thing or person in worth or importance.

dis par i ty (dis par′ə tē), *n., pl.* **-ties.** inequality; difference.

dis pas sion ate (dis pash′ən it), *adj.* free from emotion or prejudice; calm.

dis pel (dis pel′), *v.,* **-pelled, -pel ling.** drive away and scatter; disperse: *The captain's cheerful laugh dispelled our fears.*

dis re pute (dis′ri pyüt′), *n.* disgrace; discredit; disfavor: *Many remedies formerly used are now in disrepute.*

dis taff (dis′taf or dis′täf), *n.* a stick, cleft at the tip, to hold wool, flax, etc., for spinning into thread.

dis tract (dis trakt′), *v.* 1. draw away (the mind, attention, etc.): *Noise distracts my attention from studying.* 2. confuse.

di vers (dī′vərz), *adj.* several different; various.

div i na tion (div′ə nā′shən), *n.* 1. act of foreseeing the future or foretelling the unknown. 2. a skillful guess or prediction.

dock (dok), *v.* 1. cut short; cut the end off. Horses' and dogs' tails are sometimes docked. 2. cut down; cut some off of.

dock et (dok′it), *v.* 1. enter on a docket. 2. make a summary or list of.

dog ged (dôg′id or dog′id), *adj.* stubborn; persistent; not giving up: *In spite of failures he kept on with dogged determination to succeed.* **—dog′ged ly,** *adv.* **—Syn.** obstinate, headstrong.

dol or ous (dol′ər əs or dō′lər əs), *adj.* 1. mournful; sorrowful. 2. grievous.

do min ion (də min′yən), *n.* supreme authority; rule; control.

dough ty (dou′tē), *adj.* brave; valiant; strong. [OE *dohtig* < *dugan* be good]

dow dy (dou′dē), *adj.* poorly dressed; not neat; not stylish; shabby.

down (doun), *n.* Usually, **downs,** *pl.* rolling, grassy land.

drave (drāv), *v.,* *Archaic.* a pt. of **drive.**

dredge (drej), *v.* 1. clean out or deepen (a channel, harbor, etc.) with a dredge. 2. bring up or gather with a dredge.

du bi ous (dü′bē əs or dyü′bē əs), *adj.* doubtful; uncertain.

du en na (dü en′ə or dyü en′ə), *n.* 1. an elderly woman who is the governess and chaperon of young girls in a Spanish or Portuguese family. 2. governess; chaperon. [< Sp. < L *domina* mistress]

eb ul li tion (eb′ə lish′ən), *n.* 1. a boiling; a bubbling up. 2. outburst (of feeling, etc.).

ec cen tric (ek sen′trik), *adj.* out of the ordinary; odd; peculiar.

ed dy (ed′ē), *n.* water, air, etc., moving against the main current, especially when having a whirling motion. *—v.* 1. move against the main current in a whirling motion; whirl. 2. move in circles.

e dict (ē′dikt), *n.* a public order or command by some authority; decree.

ed i fy (ed′ə fī), *v.,* **-fied, -fy ing.** improve morally; benefit spiritually; instruct.

ef fu sion (i fyü′zhən), *n.* 1. a pouring out: *the effusion of blood.* 2. unrestrained expression of feeling in talking or writing.

e go (ē′gō or eg′ō), *n.* 1. the individual as a whole in his capacity to think, feel, and act; self. 2. *Informal.* conceit. [< L *ego* I]

e go tis tic (ē′gə tis′tik or eg′ə tis′tik), *adj.* 1. characterized by egotism; conceited. 2. selfish.

e jac u la tion (i jak′yə lā′shən), *n.*
1. something said suddenly and briefly; exclamation. 2. ejection; discharge.

em a nate (em′ə nāt), *v.,* **-nat ed, -nat ing.** come forth: *Fragrance emanated from the flowers. The rumor emanated from Chicago.* [< L *emanare* < *ex-* out + *manare* flow]

em bez zle ment (em bez′l mənt), *n.* theft of money, securities, etc., entrusted to one's care.

em bow er (em bou′ər), *v.* enclose in a shelter of leafy branches.

em er y (em′ər ē or em′rē), *n.* a hard, dark mineral, an impure corundum, used for grinding, smoothing, and polishing.

en do crine (en′dō krin or en′dō krin), *adj.* 1. producing secretions that pass directly into the blood or lymph instead of into a duct. The thyroid is an endocrine gland. 2. of or having to do with the endocrine glands.

en fran chise (en fran′chīz), *v.* 1. give the right to vote: *The 19th amendment to the Constitution enfranchised American women.* 2. set free; release from slavery or restraint.

en gen der (en jen′dər), *v.* bring into existence; produce; cause: *Filth engenders disease.* [< OF *engendrer* < L *ingenerare* < *in-* in + *generare* create]

en mi ty (en′mə tē), *n.* the feeling that enemies have for each other; hate. —**Syn.** hostility, hatred, animosity, ill will.

en thrall or **en thral** (en thrôl′), *v.,* **-thralled, -thrall ing.** captivate; fascinate; charm: *The explorer enthralled the audience with the story of his exciting adventures.*

en ti ty (en′tə tē), *n., pl.* **-ties.** 1. something that has a real and separate existence either actually or in the mind; anything real in itself: *Persons, mountains, languages, and beliefs are distinct entities.* 2. being; existence.

en trails (en′trālz or en′trəlz), *n.pl.* 1. the inner parts of a man or animal. 2. intestines; bowels. 3. any inner parts. [< OF *entrailles* < LL *intralia* < L *interanea* < *inter* within]

en trench (en trench′), *v.* 1. surround with a trench. 2. establish firmly. 3. trespass; infringe. Also, **intrench.**

en ven om (en ven′əm), *v.* 1. make poisonous. 2. fill with bitterness, hate, etc.

en vis age (en viz′ij), *v.,* **-aged, -ag ing.** form a mental picture of.

ere (er), *prep.* before. —*conj.* 1. before. 2. sooner than; rather than. [OE *ǣr*]

er y sip e las (er′ə sip′l əs or ir′ə sip′l-əs), *n.* an acute infectious disease characterized by a fever and a deep-red inflammation of the skin. [< Gk.]

eu chre (yü′kər), *n.* a simple card game for two, three, or four players, using the 32 (or 28, or 24) highest cards in the pack.

e ven tu al i ty (i ven′chü al′ə tē), *n., pl.* **-ties.** a possible occurrence or condition; possibility: *We hope for peace, but are ready for all the eventualities of war.*

ev i dence (ev′ə dəns), *n., v.,* **-denced, -denc ing.** —*n.* 1. whatever makes clear the truth or falsehood of something: *The evidence showed that he had not been near the place.* 2. facts established and accepted in a court of law. Before deciding a case, the judge or jury hears all the evidence given by both sides. 3. indication; sign: *A smile gives evidence of pleasure.* 4. **in evidence,** easily seen or noticed. —*v.* make easy to see or understand; show clearly; prove: *His smiles evidenced his pleasure.*

ewe (yü) *n.* a female sheep. [OE *ēowu*]

ex cru ci at ing (eks krü′shē āt′ing), *adj.* very painful; torturing; causing great suffering. [< *excruciate* crucify, torture < L *excruciare* < *ex-* utterly + *cruciare* torture, crucify < *crux* cross]

ex pe di en cy (eks pē′dē ən sē), *n.* 1. usefulness; suitability for bringing about a desired result; desirability or fitness under the circumstances. 2. personal advantage; self-interest: *The crafty lawyer was influenced more by expediency than by the love of justice.*

ex plic it (eks plis′it), *adj.* 1. clearly expressed; distinctly stated; definite: *He gave such explicit directions that everyone understood them.* 2. not reserved; frank.

ex ploit (n. eks′ploit or eks ploit′; v. eks-ploit′), *n.* a bold, unusual act; daring deed.

ex po si tion (eks′pə zish′ən), *n.* 1. a public show or exhibition. A world's fair is an exposition. 2. a detailed explanation. 3. speech or writing explaining a process or idea. —**Syn.** 1. display, fair.

ex ul ta tion (eg′zul tā′shən or ek′sul tā′shən), *n.* act of exulting; great rejoicing; triumph: *There was exultation over the army's victory.*

fa çade (fə säd′), *n.* 1. the front part of a building. 2. any side of a building that faces a street or other open space. 3. the face or front of anything.

fag got (fag′ət), *n., v. Esp. Brit.* fagot.

fag ot (fag′ət), *n.* bundle of sticks or twigs tied together: *He built the fire with fagots.*

fain (fān), *Archaic and Poetic.* —*adv.* by choice; gladly. —*adj.* 1. willing, but not eager; forced by circumstances. 2. glad; willing. 3. eager; desirous. [OE *fægen*]

fa kir (fə kir′ or fā′kər), *n.* 1. a Moslem holy man who lives by begging. 2. a Hindu ascetic. Some fakirs lie on nails.

far ci cal (fär′sə kl), *adj.* of or like a farce; ridiculous; absurd; improbable.

far thing (fär′ᵺing), *n.* a former British coin worth a fourth of a British penny.

far thin gale (fär′ᵺing gāl), *n.* a hoop skirt or framework for expanding a woman's skirt, worn in England from about 1550 to about 1650.

fa tal is tic (fā′tə lis′tik), *adj.* 1. of or having to do with fatalism. 2. believing that fate controls everything.

fa vor (fā′vər), *n.* 1. act of kindness. 2. liking; approval. 3. more than fair treatment. 4. **a.** gift; token: *The knight wore his lady's favor on his arm.* **b.** a small token given to every guest at a party, dinner, etc.

fawn (fôn), *v.* 1. cringe and bow; act slavishly: *Many flattering relatives fawned on the rich old man.* 2. of dogs, etc., show fondness by crouching, wagging the tail, licking the hand, etc.

fe al ty (fē′əl tē), *n.* loyalty and duty owed by a vassal to his feudal lord.

fea si ble (fē′zə bl), *adj.* capable of being done or carried out easily; practicable.

fe line (fē′līn), *adj.* 1. of or belonging to the cat family. 2. catlike; stealthy; sly.

fell (fel), *adj.* 1. cruel; fierce; terrible: *a fell blow.* 2. deadly; destructive: *a fell disease.*

fe ral (fir′əl), *adj.* 1. wild; untamed. 2. brutal; savage. [< L *fera* beast]

fi del i ty (fi del′ə tē or fə del′ə tē), *n.* 1. faithfulness to a trust or vow; steadfast faithfulness; loyalty. 2. accuracy; exactness as in a copy.

fil a ment (fil′ə mənt), *n.* a very fine thread; very slender, threadlike part.

fil i al (fil′ē əl), *adj.* of a son or daughter; due from a son or daughter: *The children treated their parents with filial respect.*

fir ma ment (fèr′mə mənt), *n.* arch of the heavens; sky.

flume (flüm), *n.* a deep, narrow valley with a stream running through it.

foal (fōl), *v.* give birth to (a foal).

fod der (fod′ər), *n.* coarse food for horses, cattle, etc. [OE *fōdor* < *fōda* food]

foil (foil), *n.* 1. metal beaten, hammered, or rolled into a very thin sheet. 2. anything that makes something else look or seem better by contrast.

fold (fōld), *n.* pen to keep sheep in.

fore bod ing (fôr bōd′ing or fōr bōd′ing), *n.* 1. prediction; warning. 2. a feeling that something bad is going to happen.

fore shad ow (fôr shad′ō or fōr shad′ō), *v.* indicate beforehand; be a warning of: *Black clouds foreshadow a storm.*

fort night (fôrt′nīt or fôrt′nit), *n.* two weeks. [ME *fourtenight*, contraction of OE *fēowertiene niht* fourteen nights]

fos ter (fôs′tər or fos′tər), *v.* 1. help the growth or development of; encourage: *Ignorance fosters superstition.* 2. care for fondly; cherish. 3. bring up; rear. —**Syn.** *v.* 1. promote, further.

fra ter nal (frə tèr′nl), *adj.* 1. brotherly. 2. having to do with a fraternal order.

frat ri cide (frat′rə sīd or frā′trə sīd), *n.* act of killing one's own brother or sister.

friv o lous (friv′l es), *adj.* 1. lacking in seriousness or sense; silly. 2. of little worth or importance; trivial.

frond (frond), *n.* 1. a divided leaf of a fern, palm, etc. 2. a leaflike part of a seaweed, lichen, etc. [< L *frons, frondis* leaf]

fur tive (fèr′tiv), *adj.* 1. done stealthily; secret: *a furtive glance into the forbidden room.* 2. sly; stealthy; shifty.

fu tile (fyü′tl), *adj.* 1. not successful; useless. 2. not important; trifling.

gain say (gān′sā′), *v.* deny; contradict; dispute. [< *gain-* against + *say*]

gai ter (gā′tər), *n.* 1. a covering for the lower leg or ankle, made of cloth, leather, etc. 2. shoe with an elastic strip in each side. [< F *guêtre*]

gall (gôl), *n.* **1.** a bitter yellow, brown, or greenish liquid secreted by the liver and stored in the gall bladder; bile of animals. **2.** gall bladder. **3.** anything very bitter or harsh. **4.** bitterness; hate. **5.** *U.S. Slang.* too great boldness; impudence. [OE *galla*]

gar ri son (gar′ə sn), *n.* **1.** soldiers stationed in a fort, town, etc., to defend it. **2.** place that has a garrison.

gaunt (gônt or gänt), *adj.* **1.** very thin and bony; with hollow eyes and a starved look: *Hunger and suffering make people gaunt.* **2.** looking bare and gloomy; desolate.

gaunt let (gônt′lit or gänt′lit), *n.* **1.** a stout, heavy glove, usually of leather covered with plates of iron or steel, that was part of a knight's armor. **2. throw down the gauntlet,** challenge.

gei sha (gā′shə or gē′shə), *n.* a Japanese singing and dancing girl. [< Japanese]

ge nus (jē′nəs), *n., pl.* **gen er a** or **ge nus es. 1.** kind; sort; class. **2.** group of related animals or plants ranking below a family and above a species.

ger mi cide (jėr′mə sīd), *n.* any substance that kills germs, especially disease germs.

ghoul (gül), *n.* person who enjoys what is revolting, brutal, and horrible.

gird (gėrd), *v.* **1.** put a belt or girdle around. **2.** fasten with a belt or girdle. **3.** surround.

girt (gėrt), *v.* **1.** a pt. and a pp. of **gird. 2.** put a belt, girdle, or girt around; gird.

gla zier (glā′zhər), *n.* person whose work is putting glass in windows, picture frames.

glean (glēn), *v.* **1.** gather (grain) left on a field by reapers. **2.** gather little by little.

gra tu i tous (grə tü′ə təs or grə tyü′ ə təs), *adj.* **1.** freely given or obtained; free. **2.** without reason or cause; unnecessary.

gri mace (grə mās′ or grim′is), *n., v.,* **-maced, -mac ing.** —*n.* a twisting of the face; ugly or funny smile.

grin go (gring′gō), *n., pl.* **-gos.** among Spanish-Americans, an unfriendly term for an American or Englishman. [Am.E: < Mexican Sp. < Sp. *gringo* gibberish]

grot to (grot′ō), *n.* **1.** cave. **2.** an artificial cave made for coolness or pleasure.

grov el (gruv′l or grov′l), *v.,* **-eled, -el ing** or *esp. Brit.* **-elled, -el ling. 1.** lie face downward, crawl at someone's feet; humble oneself.

guile (gīl), *n.* crafty deceit; craftiness; sly tricks.

gul let (gul′it), *n.* passage for food from the mouth to the stomach; esophagus.

hack ma tack (hak′mə tak′), *n.* the American larch or tamarack tree.

hang dog (hang′dôg′ or hang′dog′), *adj.* ashamed; sneaking; degraded.

ha rangue (hə rang′), *n.* **1.** a noisy speech. **2.** a long, pompous speech.

har row (har′ō), *n.* a heavy frame with iron teeth or upright disks. Harrows are drawn over plowed land to break up clods, cover seeds, etc. —*v.* **1.** hurt; wound. **2.** arouse uncomfortable feelings in; distress; torment.

hart (härt), *n., pl.* **harts** or (*esp. collectively*) **hart.** a male deer; stag. A hart is usually a male red deer after its fifth year.

helm (helm), *n.* **1.** handle or wheel by which a ship is steered. **2.** position of control or guidance.

helve (helv), *n. Esp.Brit.* handle of an ax, hammer, etc. [OE *hielfe*]

hew (hyü), *v.,* **hewed, hewed** or **hewn, hew ing. 1.** cut with an ax, sword, etc. **2.** cut into shape.

hie (hī), *v.,* **hied, hie ing** or **hy ing.** hasten; go quickly.

hi er ar chy (hī′ər är′kē), *n.* organization of persons or things that has higher and lower ranks.

hoar y (hôr′ē or hōr′ē), *adj.* **1.** white or gray. **2.** old; ancient.

hom age (hom′ij or om′ij), *n.* respect; reverence; honor.

hom i cide[1] (hom′ə sīd) or hō′mə sīd), *n.* a killing of one human being by another. Intentional homicide is murder. [< OF < L *homicidium* < *homo* man + *-cidium* act of killing]

hom i cide[2] (hom′ə sīd or hō′mə sīd), *n.* person who kills a human being. [< OF < L *homicida* < *homo* man + *-cida* killer]

hum mock (hum′ək), *n.* **1.** a very small, rounded hill; knoll; hillock. **2.** bump or ridge in a field of ice. [origin unknown]

hu mor (hyü′mər or yü′mər), *n.* **1.** funny or amusing quality. **2.** ability to see or show the funny or amusing side of things. **3.** state of mind; mood. **4.** fancy; whim. —*v.* **1.** give in to the fancies or whims of (a person); indulge. **2.** adapt oneself to; act so as to agree with.

hy poc ri sy (hi pok′rə sē), *n.* **1.** act or fact of putting on a false appearance of goodness or religion. **2.** pretending to be what one is not; pretense.

hy po thet i cal (hī′pə thet′ə kl), *adj.* **1.** of or based on a hypothesis; assumed; supposed. **2.** fond of making hypotheses.

id e o graph (id′ē ə graf′, id′ē ə gräf′, ī′dē ə graf′, or ī′dē ə gräf′), *n.* a graphic symbol that represents a thing or an idea without indicating a word for the thing or idea. Most Egyptian hieroglyphics and Chinese characters are ideographs.

id i o syn cra sy (id′ē ō sing′krə sē), *n., pl.* **-sies.** a personal peculiarity.

ig no min i ous (ig′nə min′ē əs), *adj.* **1.** shameful; disgraceful; dishonorable; humiliating. **2.** contemptible.

ig no min y (ig′nə min′ē), *n.* **1.** loss of one's good name; public shame and disgrace; dishonor. **2.** shameful action or conduct.

il lit er ate (i lit′ər it), *adj.* **1.** unable to read or write. **2.** not cultured.

il lu sion (i lü′zhən), *n.* **1.** appearance which is not real; misleading appearance. **2.** a false impression or perception. **3.** a false idea, notion, or belief.

im mo bil i ty (im′ō bil′ə ti), *n.* state of not moving.

im pec ca ble (im pek′ə bl), *adj.* **1.** faultless. **2.** sinless. [< LL *impeccabilis* < *in-* not + *peccare* sin]

im ped (im pēd′), *v.,* **-ped ed, -ped ing.** hinder; obstruct. [< L *impedire* < *in-* on + *pes* foot] —**Syn.** hamper, retard.

hat, āge, fär; let, ēqual, tėrm;
it, īce; hot, ōpen, ôrder;
oil, out; cup, pùt, rüle;
ch, child; ng, long; sh, she;
th, thin; ŦH, then; zh, measure;

ə represents *a* in about, *e* in taken,
i in pencil, *o* in lemon, *u* in circus.

< = from, derived from, taken from.

im ped i men ta (im ped′ə men′tə), *n.pl.* traveling equipment; baggage.

im per a tive (im per′ə tiv), *adj.* not to be avoided; urgent; necessary.

im pe ri ous (im pir′ē əs), *adj.* **1.** haughty; arrogant; domineering; overbearing. **2.** imperative; necessary; urgent.

im per turb a ble (im′pər tėr′bə bl), *adj.* **1.** not capable of being excited or disturbed. **2.** not easily excited; calm.

im pet u ous (im pech′ù əs), *adj.* **1.** moving with great force or speed: *the impetuous rush of water over Niagara Falls.* **2.** acting hastily, rashly, or with sudden feeling: *Boys are more impetuous than old men.*

im pe tus (im′pə təs), *n.* a driving force; incentive.

im pla ca ble (im plä′kə bl or im plak′ə bl), *adj.* that cannot be placated, pacified, or appeased; relentless. —**im pla′ca bly,** *adv.* —**Syn.** unforgiving.

im plore (im plôr′ or im plōr′), *v.,* **-plored, -plor ing. 1.** beg earnestly for. **2.** beg (a person to do some act). [< L *implorare,* originally, invoke with weeping < *in-* toward + *plorare* cry] —**Syn. 1.** beseech, entreat.

im po tent (im′pə tənt), *adj.* not having power; helpless: *The cripple fell back in an impotent rage.* —**Syn.** weak, feeble.

im pov er ished (im pov′ər isht or im pov′risht), *adj.* very poor.

in an i mate (in an′ə mit), *adj.* **1.** lifeless: *inanimate stones.* **2.** dull: *an inanimate face.*

in ces sant (in ses′nt), *adj.* never stopping; continued or repeated without interruption.

in cin er ate (in sin′ər āt), *v.* burn to ashes. [< Med.L *incinerare* < L *in-* into + *cinis* ashes]

in co her ent (in′kō hir′ənt), *adj.* **1.** not sticking together; disconnected; confused. —**in′co her′ent ly,** *adv.*

in com pre hen si ble (in′kom pri hen′sə bl), *adj.* impossible to understand.

in con ceiv a ble (in′kən sēv′ə bl), *adj.* impossible to imagine; unthinkable.

in con gru ous (in kong′grù əs), *adj.* out of keeping; not appropriate; out of place: *Heavy walking shoes would be incongruous with a party dress.*

in cor ri gi ble (in kôr′ə jə bl or in kor′ə jə bl), *adj.* **1.** so firmly fixed (in bad ways, a bad habit, etc.) that nothing else can be expected: *an incorrigible liar.* **2.** so fixed that it cannot be changed or cured: *an incorrigible habit of wrinkling one's nose.*

incorruptible

in cor rupt i ble (in′kə rup′tə bl), *adj.*
1. not to be corrupted; honest: *The incorruptible man could not be bribed.* 2. not capable of decay.

in cred u lous (in krej′ə ləs), *adj.* not ready to believe; not credulous; doubting.

in de fat i ga ble (in′di fat′ə gə bl), *adj.* never getting tired or giving up; tireless. —**in′de fat′i ga bly,** *adv.* —**Syn.** untiring, persistent.

in di gent (in′də jənt), *adj.* poor; needy.

in di go (in′də gō), *n.* a deep violet-blue.

in dis creet (in′dis krēt′), *adj.* not discreet; not wise and judicious; imprudent: *The indiscreet girl often talked with strangers.* —**Syn.** unwise, foolish, rash.

in dis crim i nate (in′dis krim′ə nit), *adj.* 1. confused. 2. not discriminating; with no feeling for differences: *He is an indiscriminate reader and likes both good books and bad ones.*

in duce ment (in düs′mənt or in dyüs′mənt), *n.* something that influences or persuades; incentive: *Prizes are inducements to work.*

in ert (in ėrt′), *adj.* 1. having no power to move or act; lifeless. 2. inactive; slow.

in ev i ta ble (in ev′ə tə bl), *adj.* not avoidable; sure to happen; certain to come.

in ex pli ca ble (in eks′plə kə bl or in′eks plik′ə bl), *adj.* impossible to explain or understand; mysterious.

in ex tri ca ble (in eks′trə kə bl), *adj.* 1. that one cannot get out of. 2. that cannot be disentangled or solved.

in fal li bil i ty (in fal′ə bil′ə tē), *n.* absolute freedom from error.

in fi del i ty (in′fə del′ə tē), *n., pl.* **-ties.** 1. lack of religious faith. 2. unbelief in Christianity. 3. unfaithfulness, especially of husband or wife; disloyalty.

in fi ni tes i mal (in′fi nə tes′ə ml), *adj.* so small as to be almost nothing.

in fin i ty (in fin′ə ti), *n.* state of being infinite; unlimited extent of time, space, or quantity; eternity; boundlessness.

in fir mi ty (in fėr′mə tē), *n., pl.* **-ties.** 1. weakness; feebleness. 2. sickness; illness. 3. a moral weakness or failing.

in grate (in′grāt), *n.* an ungrateful person.

in gra ti ate (in grā′shē āt), *v.* bring (oneself) into favor: *He tried to ingratiate himself with the teacher by giving her presents.*

in iq ui tous (in ik′wə təs), *adj.* very unjust; wicked.

in nu en do (in′yü en′dō), *n., pl.* **-does.** 1. an indirect hint or reference. 2. an indirect suggestion against somebody.

in or gan ic (in′ôr gan′ik), *adj.* not having the organized physical structure of animals and plants. Minerals are inorganic.

in sa tia ble (in sā′shə bl), *adj.* that cannot be satisfied; extremely greedy.

in scru ta ble (in skrü′tə bl), *adj.* that cannot be understood; so mysterious or obscure that one cannot make out its meaning; incomprehensible.

in sen sate (in sen′sāt or in sen′sit), *adj.* 1. without sensation. 2. unfeeling: *insensate cruelty.* 3. senseless; stupid.

in sid i ous (in sid′ē əs), *adj.* 1. wily; sly; crafty; tricky; treacherous. 2. working secretly or subtly: *an insidious disease* —**in sid′i ous ly,** *adv.* —**Syn.** 1. cunning.

in sin u ate (in sin′yü āt), *v.,* **-at ed, -at ing.** 1. suggest indirectly; hint: *To say "Fred can't do it; no coward can" is to insinuate that Fred is a coward.* 2. push in or get in by an indirect, twisting way: *The spy insinuated himself into the confidence of important army officers.* [< L *insinuare* < *in-* + *sinus* a curve, winding]

in so lent (in′sə lənt), *adj.* boldly rude; insulting. —**Syn.** arrogant, impudent.

in sti gate (in′stə gāt), *v.* urge on; stir up.

in sus cep ti ble (in′sə sep′tə bl), *adj.* not susceptible; not easily influenced.

in tan gi ble (in tan′jə bl), *adj.* 1. not capable of being touched: *Sound and light are intangible.* 2. not easily grasped by the mind; vague.

in teg ri ty (in teg′rə tē), *n.* 1. honesty; sincerity; uprightness: *A man of integrity is respected.* 2. wholeness; completeness. 3. perfect condition; soundness. [< L *integritas* < *integer* whole]

in teg u ment (in teg′yə mənt), *n.* a natural outer covering. The skin or shell of an animal is its integument.

in ter dict (*v.* in′tər dikt′; *n.* in′tər dikt), *v.* 1. prohibit; forbid. 2. restrain. —*n.* prohibition based on authority; formal order forbidding something.

in ter im (in′tər im), *n.* meantime; between. —*adj.* for the meantime.

in ter lop er (in′tər lōp′ər), *n.* intruder. [probably < Dutch *enterlooper* < *entre-* between (< L *inter-*) + *looper* runner < *loopen* run]

in ter ment (in tėr′mənt), *n.* act of putting a dead body into a grave or tomb; burial.

in ter mi na ble (in tėr′mə nə bl), *adj.* endless; so long as to seem endless. [< LL *interminabilis,* ult. < L *in-* not + *terminare* to end] —**Syn.** endless, limitless.

in ter mit (in′tər mit′), *v.* stop for a time.

in ter pose (in′tər pōz′), *v.* 1. put between; insert. 2. come between other things; be between other things. 3. interrupt.

in ter sperse (in′tər spėrs′), *v.* vary with something put here and there.

in ter vene (in′tər vēn′), *v.* 1. come between; be between. 2. come in to help settle a dispute.

in tim i date (in tim′ə dāt), *v.* 1. frighten; make afraid. 2. influence or force by fear.

in trench (in trench′), *v.* entrench.

in vec tive (in vek′tiv), *n.* violent attack in words; abusive language.

in vin ci ble (in vin′sə bl), *adj.* not to be overcome; unconquerable.

i ron i cal (ī ron′ə kl), *adj.* 1. expressing one thing and meaning the opposite: *"Speedy" would be an ironical name for a snail.* 2. contrary to what would naturally be expected: *It was ironical that the man was run over by his own automobile.* —**i ron′i cal ly,** *adv.*

ir re deem a ble (ir′i dēm′ə bl), *adj.* 1. that cannot be bought back. 2. that cannot be exchanged for coin: *irredeemable paper money.* 3. beyond remedy; hopeless.

ir ref u ta ble (ir′i fyüt′ə bl or i ref′yə tə bl), *adj.* that cannot be refuted or disproved. —**Syn.** undeniable, unanswerable.

ir rel e vant (i rel′ə vənt), *adj.* not to the point; off the subject.

ir res o lute (i rez′ə lüt), *adj.* not resolute; unable to make up one's mind; not sure of what one wants; hesitating: *Irresolute persons make poor leaders.* —**Syn.** doubtful.

ir rev o ca ble (i rev′ə kə bl), *adj.* not to be recalled, withdrawn, or annulled: *an irrevocable decision.*

jo cose (jō kōs′), *adj.* jesting; humorous; playful. [< L *jocosus* < *jocus* jest] —**jo cose′ly,** *adv.*

joc u lar (jok′yə lər), *adj.* funny; joking. [< L *jocularis* < *joculus,* dim. of *jocus* jest]

joust (just, joust, or jüst), *n.* 1. combat between two knights on horseback, armed with lances. 2. **jousts,** *pl.* a tournament. [< OF *jouste* < *jouster.* See JOUST, *v.*] —*v.* fight with lances on horseback. Knights used to joust with each other for sport.

ju ry[1] (jür′ē), *n., pl.* **ju ries.** 1. group of persons selected to hear evidence in a law court and sworn to give a decision in accordance with the evidence presented to them. See also **grand jury** and **petty jury.** 2. group of persons chosen to give a judgment or to decide a contest and award prizes. [< AF *jurie* < *jurer* swear < L *jurare*]

ju ry[2] (jür′ē), *adj.* for temporary use on a ship; makeshift. [probably ult. < OF *ajurie* help < L *adjutare* < *ad-* to + *juvare* aid]

kar ma (kär′mə), *n.* the actions which are said by Hindu and Buddhist religions to determine one's destiny. [Skt. a deed, act]

kelp (kelp), *n.* 1. a large, tough, brown seaweed. 2. ashes of seaweed.

kith and kin (kith′ ənd kin′), friends and relatives.

kow tow (kou′tou′), *v.* 1. kneel and touch the ground with the forehead to show deep respect, submission, or worship. 2. show slavish respect or obedience. [< Chinese *k'o-t'ou,* literally, knock (the) head]

lack ey (lak′ē), *n.* 1. a male servant; footman. 2. a slavish follower.

la con i cal ly (lə kon′ik lē), *adv.* in few words; briefly; concisely.

lan guid (lang′gwid), *adj.* 1. drooping; weak; weary; without energy: *A hot, sticky day makes a person feel languid.* 2. without interest or enthusiasm; indifferent. 3. sluggish; dull; not brisk or lively. [< L *languidus* < *languere* be faint] —**lan′guid ly,** *adv.* —**Syn.** 1. feeble, fatigued, exhausted. 2. apathetic, listless.

lank (langk), *adj.* long and thin; slender; lean: *a lank boy.*

lar ce nous (lär′sə nəs), *adj.* thievish; guilty of larceny.

last (last or läst), *n.* block shaped like a person's foot, on which shoes and boots are formed or repaired.

lathe (lāᴛн), *n.* machine for holding ar-

pe rim e ter (pə rim′ə tər), *n.* 1. the outer boundary of a surface or figure. 2. distance around such a boundary.

per ju ry (pèr′jər ē), *n.* act of swearing that something is true which one knows to be false.

per plex i ty (pər plek′sə tē), *n.* 1. perplexed condition; confusion; being puzzled; not knowing what to do or how to act. 2. something that perplexes. —**Syn.** 1. bewilderment.

per se ver ance (pèr′sə vir′əns), *n.* a sticking to a purpose or an aim; never giving up what one has set out to do.

per sist ence (pər sis′təns or pər zis′-təns), *n.* 1. being persistent. 2. continuing existence: *the persistence of a cough.* **Syn.** 1. **Persistence, perseverance** mean a holding fast to a purpose or course of action. **Persistence,** having a good or bad sense according to one's attitude toward what is done, emphasizes holding stubbornly or obstinately to one's purpose and continuing firmly and often annoyingly against disapproval, opposition, advice, etc.: *By persistence many people won religious freedom.* **Perseverance,** always in a good sense, emphasizes refusing to be discouraged by obstacles or difficulties, but continuing steadily with courage and patience: *Perseverance leads to success.*

per son a ble (pèr′sn ə bl), *adj.* having a pleasing appearance; good-looking; attractive.

per vade (pər vād′), *v.,* **-vad ed, -vad ing.** go or spread throughout; be throughout: *The odor of pines pervades the air.* [< L *pervadere* < *per-* through + *vadere* go]

per verse (pər vèrs′), *adj.* 1. contrary and willful; stubborn: *The perverse child did just what we told him not to do.* 2. persistent in wrong. 3. wicked. 4. not correct; wrong: *perverse reasoning.*

per vert (*v.* pər vèrt′; *n.* pèr′vèrt), *v.* 1. lead or turn from the right way or from the truth: *Reading silly stories perverts our taste for good books.* 2. give a wrong meaning to: *His enemies perverted his friendly remark and made it into an insult.* 3. use for wrong purposes or in a wrong way: *A clever criminal perverts his talents.* [< L *pervertere* < *per-* to destruction + *vertere* to turn]

pes ti len tial (pes′tə len′shəl), *adj.* 1. carrying infection. 2. harmful; dangerous.

phan tom (fan′təm), *n.* 1. image of the mind: *phantoms of a dream.* 2. a vague, dim, or shadowy appearance; ghost. —*adj.* like a ghost; unreal: *a phantom ship.*

phos pho res cence (fos′fə res′ns), *n.* 1. a giving out light without burning or by very slow burning that seems not to give out heat. 2. such light.

phys ic (fiz′ik), *n., v.,* **-icked, -ick ing.** —*n.* 1. medicine, especially one that moves the bowels. 2. art of healing; science and practice of medicine.

pin ion (pin′yən), *v.* 1. cut off or tie the pinions of (a bird) to prevent flying. 2. bind; bind the arms of; bind (to something): *pinion a man's arms.*

pip (pip), *n.* 1. a contagious disease of birds, characterized by the secretion of thick mucus in the mouth and throat. 2. *Informal.* a slight illness. [< MDutch < VL *pippita* < L *pituita* phlegm]

pla cate (plā′kāt or plak′āt), *v.* soothe or satisfy the anger of; make peaceful: *placate a person one has offended.* [< L *placatus* < *placare* please]

plac id (plas′id), *adj.* calm; peaceful; quiet: *a placid lake.* [< L *placidus* < *placere* please]

plain tive (plān′tiv), *adj.* mournful; sad.

pli ant (plī′ənt), *adj.* 1. bending easily; flexible; supple. 2. easily influenced; yielding.

plight (plīt), *n.* condition or state, usually bad. —**Syn.** dilemma, scrape, fix.

plu ral i ty (plù ral′ə tē), *n., pl.* **-ties.** 1. difference between the largest number of votes and the next largest in an election. 2. the greater number; the majority.

poign ant (poin′ənt or poin′yənt), *adj.* 1. very painful; piercing: *poignant suffering.* 2. keen; intense: *a subject of poignant interest.* 3. sharp to the taste or smell.

poise (poiz), *n., v.,* **poised, pois ing.** —*n.* mental balance, composure, or self-possession: *She has perfect poise and never seems embarrassed.*

por cine (pôr′sīn or pôr′sən), *adj.* 1. of pigs or hogs. 2. like or characteristic of pigs or hogs. [< L *porcinus* < *porcus* pig]

por tent (pôr′tent or por′tent), *n.* a warning of coming evil; sign; omen. —**Syn.** token, presage.

por ten tous (pôr ten′təs or pōr ten′təs), *adj.* 1. indicating evil to come; ominous; threatening. 2. amazing; extraordinary. —**por ten′tous ly,** *adv.* —**por ten′tous-ness,** *n.* —**Syn.** 1. foreboding. 2. wonderful, marvelous.

po ten cy (pōt′n sē), *n.* 1. power; strength: *the potency of an argument, the potency of a drug.* 2. power to develop.

prate (prāt), *v.* talk a great deal in a foolish way. —*n.* empty or foolish talk.

pre car i ous (pri kar′ē əs), *adj.* 1. dependent on the will or pleasure of another. 2. not safe or secure; uncertain; dangerous; risky: *A soldier leads a precarious life.* —**Syn.** 2. perilous, hazardous. —**Ant.** 2. certain, secure, safe, sure.

prec i pice (pres′ə pis), *n.* a very steep cliff; almost vertical slope. [< F < L *praecipitium* < *praeceps* steep, literally, headlong < *prae-* first + *caput* head]

pre cip i tous (pri sip′ə təs), *adj.* 1. like a precipice; very steep: *precipitous cliffs.* 2. hasty; rash.

pre con cep tion (prē′kən sep′shən), *n.* idea or opinion formed beforehand.

pred a to ry (pred′ə tô′rē or pred′ə-tō′rē), *adj.* 1. of or inclined to plundering or robbery: *Predatory tramps infested the highways.* 2. preying upon other animals. Hawks and owls are predatory birds.

pre med i tate (prē med′ə tāt), *v.,* **-tat ed, -tat ing.** consider or plan beforehand: *The murder was premeditated.* [< L *praemeditari* < *prae-* before + *meditari* meditate]

prem ise (*n.* prem′is; *v.* pri mīz′), *n.* in logic, a statement assumed to be true and

hat, āge, fär; let, ēqual, tèrm; it, īce; hot, ōpen, ôrder; oil, out; cup, pùt, rüle; ch, child; ng, long; sh, she; th, thin; ᴛʜ, then; zh, measure;

ə represents *a* in about, *e* in taken, *i* in pencil, *o* in lemon, *u* in circus.

< = from, derived from, taken from.

used to draw a conclusion. *Example:* Major premise: Children should go to school. Minor premise: He is a child. Conclusion: He should go to school.

pre mo ni tion (prē′mə nish′ən or prem′ə nish′ən), *n.* a forewarning. [< earlier F < L *praemonitio, -onis,* ult. < *prae-* before + *monere* warn]

pre pos ter ous (pri pos′tər əs or pri pos′trəs), *adj.* contrary to nature, reason, or common sense; absurd; senseless: *It would be preposterous to shovel coal with a teaspoon.*

pre sen ti ment (pri zen′tə mənt), *n.* a feeling or impression that something is about to happen; vague sense of approaching misfortune; foreboding. [< MF *presentiment,* ult. < L *prae-* before + *sentire* to sense]

pre sump tion (pri zump′shən), *n.* 1. act of presuming. 2. thing taken for granted: *Since he had the stolen jewels, the presumption was that he was the thief.*

pre sump tu ous (pri zump′chù əs), *adj.* acting without permission or right; too bold; forward.

pre text (prē′tekst), *n.* a false reason concealing the real reason; pretense; excuse: *He used his sore finger as a pretext for not going to school.* [< L *praetextus,* ult. < *prae-* in front + *texere* to weave]

pri me val (prī mē′vl), *adj.* 1. of or having to do with the first age or ages, especially of the world: *In its primeval state the earth was a fiery glowing ball.* 2. ancient: *primeval forests untouched by the ax.* [< L *primaevus* early in life < *primus* first + *aevum* age]

pri mor di al (prī môr′dē əl), *adj.* 1. existing at the very beginning; primitive. 2. original; elementary. [< L *primordialis* < *primordium* beginning]

pris tine (pris′tēn, pris′tən, or pris′tīn), *adj.* as it was in its earliest time or state; original; primitive: *The colors of the paintings inside the pyramid had kept their pristine freshness.*

pri va tion (prī vā′shən), *n.* 1. lack of the comforts or of the necessities of life: *Many children died because of privation during the war.* 2. loss; absence; being deprived.

pro cre a tion (prō′krē ā′shən), *n.* 1. a begetting; becoming a father. 2. production.

pro di gious (prə dij′əs), *adj.* 1. very great; huge; vast: *The ocean contains a prodigious amount of water.* 2. wonderful; marvelous.

prod i gy (prod′ə jē), *n.*, *pl.* **-gies.**
1. marvel; wonder. An infant prodigy is a child remarkably brilliant in some respect. 2. a marvelous example.

prof fer (prof′ər), *v.* offer; offer for acceptance: *We proffered regrets at having to leave so early.*

pro gen i tor (prō jen′ə tər), *n.* ancestor in the direct line; forefather. [< L *progenitor* < *pro-* + *gignere* beget]

pro lif ic (prə lif′ik), *adj.* 1. producing offspring abundantly: *prolific animals.* 2. producing much: *a prolific tree, garden, imagination, or writer.*

prom on to ry (prom′ən tô′rē or prom′ən tō′rē), *n.*, *pl.* **-ries.** a high point of land extending from the coast into the water; headland. [< Med.L *promontorium*, var. of L *promunturium* < *pro-* forward + *mons* mountain]

proof (prüf), *n.* 1. way or means of showing beyond doubt the truth of something. 2. establishment of the truth of anything. 3. act of testing; trial. 4. condition of having been tested and approved. 5. a trial impression from type. A book is first printed in proof so that errors can be corrected. 6. a trial print of an etching, photographic negative, etc. 7. **a.** the standard strength of alcoholic liquors. **b.** strength with reference to this standard: *brandy of 90% proof.* —*adj.* 1. of tested value against something: *proof against being taken by surprise.* 2. (of an alcoholic liquor) of standard strength. [< OF *prueve* < LL *proba* < L *probare* prove. Doublet of PROBE.] —**Syn.** *n.* 1. See **evidence.** 2. confirmation, corroboration. 3. experiment.

pro pri e ty (prə prī′ə tē), *n.*, *pl.* **-ties.** 1. quality of being proper; fitness. 2. proper behavior: *Propriety demands that a boy tip his hat to a lady whom he knows.* —**Syn.** 1. aptness, suitability. 2. etiquette, decorum, decency.

pro sa ic (prō zā′ik), *adj.* like prose; matter-of-fact; ordinary; not exciting.

pro scribe (prō skrīb′), *v.*, **-scribed, -scrib ing.** 1. prohibit as wrong or dangerous; condemn: *In earlier days, the church proscribed dancing and card playing.* 2. put outside of the protection of the law; outlaw. 3. forbid to come into a certain place; banish.

pros e cu tion (pros′ə kyü′shən), *n.* 1. the carrying on of a lawsuit: *The prosecution will be abandoned if the stolen money is returned.* 2. side that starts action against another in a law court. The prosecution makes certain charges against the defense. 3. a carrying out; following up: *In prosecution of his plan, he stored away a supply of food.*

pro trude (prō trüd′), *v.* 1. thrust forth; stick out: *The saucy child protruded her tongue.* 2. be thrust forth; project: *Her teeth protrude too far.* [< L *protrudere* < *pro-* forward + *trudere* to thrust]

prov i dence (prov′ə dəns), *n.* 1. God's care and help. 2. instance of God's care

and help. 3. care for the future; good management.

pro vin cial (prə vin′shəl), *adj.* 1. of a province. 2. local. 3. having the manners, speech, dress, point of view, etc., of people living in a province. 4. lacking refinement or polish; narrow: *a provincial point of view.*

pro voc a tive (prə vok′ə tiv), *adj.* 1. irritating; vexing. 2. tending or serving to call forth action, thought, laughter, anger, etc.: *a remark provocative of mirth.*

prow ess (prou′is), *n.* 1. bravery; daring. 2. brave or daring acts. 3. unusual skill or ability. —**Syn.** 1. courage, valor. —**Ant.** 1. cowardice, timidity.

pru dent (prüd′nt), *adj.* planning carefully ahead of time; sensible; discreet: *A prudent man saves part of his wages.*

pseu do (sü′dō), *adj.* 1. false; sham; pretended. 2. having only the appearance of. [< Gk. *pseudes* false]

psy chic (sī′kik), *adj.* 1. of the soul or mind; mental: *illness due to psychic causes.* 2. outside the known laws of physics; supernatural.

Puck (puk), *n.* 1. a mischievous fairy in English folklore, who appears in Shakespeare's play *A Midsummer Night's Dream.* 2. **puck, a.** a mischievous spirit; goblin. **b.** a rubber disk used in the game of ice hockey. [OE *pūca* goblin]

pu is sant (pyü′ə snt, pyü is′nt, or pwis′nt), *adj.* powerful; mighty; strong. [< OF *puissant* being powerful, ult. < var. of L *posse* be able]

pulp (pulp), *n.* 1. the soft part of any fruit or vegetable. 2. the soft inner part of a tooth, containing blood vessels and nerves. 3. any soft, wet mass. Paper is made from wood pulp.

pur ga to ry (pėr′gə tô′rē or pėr′gə tō′rē), *n.*, *pl.* **-ries.** 1. in the belief of the Roman Catholics, a temporary condition or place in which the souls of those who have died penitent are purified from venial sin or the effects of sin by punishment. 2. any condition or place of temporary suffering or punishment. [< Med.L *purgatorium*, originally neut. adj., purging < L *purgare*]

pur lieu (pėr′lü), *n.* 1. piece of land on the border of a forest. 2. one's haunt or resort; one's bounds. 3. any bordering, neighboring, or outlying region or district.

queue (kyü), *n.*, *v.*, **queued, queu ing.** —*n.* 1. braid of hair hanging down from the back of the head. 2. *Esp. Brit.* a long line of people, automobiles, etc. —*v. Esp. Brit.* form or stand in a long line.

qui es cent (kwī es′nt), *adj.* inactive; quiet; still; motionless. [< L *quiescens, -entis*, ppr. of *quiescere* to rest < *quies, n., rest*]

qui e tus (kwī ē′təs), *n.* a final getting rid of anything; finishing stroke; anything that ends or settles: *The arrival of the militia gave the riot its quietus.* [< Med.L *quietus est* he is discharged < L *quietus est* he is at rest.]

quin tain (kwin′tān), *n. Obs.* a five-line stanza. [L *quintus* fifth]

quin tes sence (kwin tes′ns), *n.* 1. pure essence; purest form. 2. the most perfect example of something. [< Med.L *quinta essentia* fifth essence, translation of Gk. *pempte ousia*]

quip (kwip), *n.*, *v.*, **quipped, quip ping.** —*n.* 1. a clever or witty saying. 2. a sharp, cutting remark. 3. quibble. 4. something odd or strange. —*v.* make quips. [for earlier *quippy* < L *quippe* indeed!, I dare say]

rad i cal (rad′ə kl), *adj.* 1. going to the root; fundamental; *Cruelty is a radical fault. If she wants to reduce, she must make a radical change in her diet.* 2. favoring extreme changes or reforms; extreme.

rail (rāl), *v.* complain bitterly; use violent and reproachful language: *He railed at his hard luck.* [< F *railler*, ult. < LL *ragere* to scream.] —**Syn.** scold, revile, upbraid.

ra jah or **ra ja** (rä′jə), *n.* ruler or chief in India, Java, Borneo, etc.

ram i fi ca tion (ram′ə fə kā′shən), *n.* 1. dividing or spreading out into branches or parts. 2. branch; part.

ram part (ram′pärt), *n.* 1. a wide bank of earth, often with a wall on top, built around a fort to help defend it. 2. anything that defends; defense; protection. [< F *rempart* < *remparer* fortify, ult. < L *re-* back + *ante* before + *parare* prepare]

ran cid (ran′sid), *adj.* 1. stale; spoiled: *rancid fat.* 2. tasting or smelling like stale fat or butter. [< L *rancidus* < *rancere* be rank]

rank (rangk), *adj.* 1. strongly marked; extreme: *rank ingratitude, rank nonsense.* 2. coarse; not decent.

ran kle (rang′kl), *v.*, **-kled, -kling.** be sore; cause soreness; continue to give pain: *The memory of the insult rankled in his mind.*

rapt (rapt), *adj.* lost in delight.

rap ture (rap′chər), *n.* a strong feeling that absorbs the mind; very great joy.

rau cous (rô′kəs), *adj.* hoarse; harsh-sounding: *the raucous caw of a crow.*

rav age (rav′ij), *v.*, **-aged, -ag ing**, *n.*, —*v.* lay waste; damage greatly; destroy: *The forest fire ravaged many miles of country.*

rav en ous (rav′ən əs), *adj.* 1. very hungry. 2. greedy.

rea son a ble (rē′zn ə bl or rēz′nə bl), *adj.* 1. according to reason; sensible; not foolish. 2. not asking too much; fair; just. 3. not high in price; inexpensive. 4. able to reason. —**rea′son a ble ness,** *n.*
Syn. 1. **Reasonable, rational** mean according to reason. **Reasonable,** describing people or their actions, words, plans, or procedures, emphasizes showing good judgment and being governed by reason in deciding and choosing: *He took a reasonable view of the dispute and offered a solution that was fair, sensible, and practical.* **Rational** emphasizes having or showing the power to think logically and to draw conclusions that guide in doing or saying what is wise, sensible, or reasonable: *His approach to the problem was rational.*

re buke (ri byük′), *v.* express disapproval of; reprove.

re cip ro cate (ri sip′rə kāt), *v.* give, do, feel, or show in return: *She likes me, and I reciprocate her liking.*

re coil (*v.* ri koil′; *n.* ri koil′ or rē′koil), *v.* 1. draw back; shrink back: *Most people would recoil at seeing a snake in the path.* 2. spring back: *The gun recoiled after I fired.* 3. react: *Revenge often recoils on the avenger.*

re dress (*v.* ri dres′; *n.* rē′dres or ri dres′), *v.* set right; repair; remedy. —*n.* a setting right; relief: *Any man deserves redress if he has been injured unfairly.* [< F *redresser* < *re-* again + *dresser* straighten, arrange]

reft (reft), *v.* pt. and pp. of **reave**. deprived by force.

re gale (ri gāl′), *v.* 1. entertain agreeably; delight with something pleasing: *The old sailor regaled the boys with sea stories.* 2. entertain with a choice repast; feast. [< F *régaler*, ult. < MDutch *wale* wealth]

reg i cide[1] (rej′ə sīd), *n.* crime of killing a king. [< L *rex, regis* + E *-cide*[1]]

reg i cide[2] (rej′ə sīd), *n.* person who kills a king. [< L *rex, regis* + E *-cide*[2]]

re ha bil i tate (rē′hə bil′ə tāt), *v.,* **-tat ed, -tat ing.** 1. restore to a good condition; make over in a new form: *The old house is to be rehabilitated.* 2. restore to former standing, rank, rights, privileges, reputation, etc.: *The former criminal completely rehabilitated himself and was trusted and respected by all.* [< Med.L *rehabilitare*, ult. < L *re-* again + *habilis* fit]

rem nant (rem′nənt), *n.* a small part left. —**Syn.** rest, fragment.

re mon strance (ri mon′strəns), *n.* protest; complaint. [< Med.L *remonstrantia* < *remonstrare*. See REMONSTRATE.]

re mon strate (ri mon′strāt), *v.,* **-strat ed, -strat ing.** object; protest: *The teacher remonstrated with the boy about his low marks.*

rend (rend), *v.,* **rent, rend ing.** 1. pull apart violently; tear: *Wolves will rend a lamb.* 2. split: *Lightning rent the tree.* 3. disturb violently: *His mind was rent by doubt.* 4. remove with force or violence.

rent (rent), *n.* a torn place; tear; split. —*adj.* torn; split.

re pel lent (ri pel′ənt), *adj.* 1. unattractive; disagreeable. 2. repelling; driving back.

rep re hen si ble (rep′ri hen′sə bl), *adj.* deserving reproof, rebuke, or blame.

re press (ri pres′), *v.* 1. prevent from acting; check: *She repressed an impulse to cough.* 2. keep down; put down: *The dictator repressed the revolt.* [< L *repressus,* pp. of *reprimere* < *re-* back + *premere* press] —**Syn.** 1. curb, restrain. 2. suppress.

re pute (ri pyüt′), *n.* 1. reputation. 2. good reputation. [< v.] —*v.* suppose to be; consider; suppose: *He is reputed the richest man in the State.* [< L *reputare* < *re-* over + *putare* think]

re sil i ent (ri zil′ē ənt or ri zil′yənt), *adj.* 1. springing back; returning to the original form or position after being bent, compressed, or stretched: *resilient steel.* 2. buoyant; cheerful.

res in (rez′n), *n.* a sticky yellow or brown substance that flows from certain plants and trees, especially the pine and fir.

res o lute (rez′ə lüt), *adj.* determined; firm; bold: *He was resolute in his attempt to climb to the top of the mountain.* —**res′o lute ly,** *adv.*

res o lu tion (rez′ə lü′shən), *n.* 1. thing decided on; thing determined: *He made a resolution to get up early.* 2. act of resolving or determining.

res pite (res′pit), *n.* 1. time of relief and rest; lull: *A thick cloud brought a respite from the glare of the sun.* 2. a putting off; delay, especially, in carrying out a sentence of death; reprieve.

re splend ent (ri splen′dənt), *adj.* very bright; shining; splendid: *The queen was resplendent with jewels.* [< L *resplendens, -entis,* ppr. of *resplendere* glitter < *re-* back + *splendere* to shine]

re strain (ri strān′), *v.* 1. hold back; keep down; keep in check; keep within limits: *She could not restrain her curiosity.* 2. keep in prison; confine.

re tain er (ri tān′ər), *n.* person who serves a person of rank; vassal; attendant; follower. [< *retain*]

ret i nue (ret′n ü or ret′n yü), *n.* group of attendants or retainers; following: *The king's retinue accompanied him on the journey.*

re vere (ri vir′), *v.* love and respect deeply; honor greatly; show reverence for. [< L *revereri* < *re-* back + *vereri* stand in awe of, fear]

re vile (ri vīl′), *v.,* **-viled, -vil ing.** call bad names; abuse with words: *The tramp reviled the man who drove him off.* [< OF *reviler* despise < *re-* again + *vil* vile < L *vilis* cheap]

re vul sion (ri vul′shən), *n.* a sudden, violent change or reaction.

rhet o ric (ret′ə rik), *n.* 1. art of using words in speaking or writing. 2. book about this art. 3. mere display in language. [< L *rhetorica* < Gk. *rhetorike (techne)* art of an orator < *rhetor* orator]

rhythm (riтн′əm), *n.* 1. movement with a regular repetition of a beat, accent, rise and fall, or the like: *the rhythm of dancing, skating, swimming, the rhythm of the tides, the rhythm of one's heartbeats.* 2. repetition of an accent; arrangement of beats in a line of poetry: *The rhythms of "The Lord's Prayer," "The Night Before Christmas," and "America" are different.* 3. grouping by accents or beats: *triple rhythm.* [< L < Gk. *rhythmos* < *rheein* to flow. Doublet of RHYME.]

rib ald (rib′ld), *adj.* offensive in speech; coarsely mocking; irreverent; indecent; obscene. [< OF *ribauld,* ult. < MDutch *ribe* prostitute] —**Syn.** *adj.* indelicate, gross.

rive (rīv), *v.,* **rived, rived** or **riv en, riv ing.** tear apart; split; cleave. [< Scand. *rifa*]

roan (rōn), *adj.* yellowish- or reddish-brown sprinkled with gray or white. —*n.* a roan horse.

roe (rō), *n.* fish eggs.

roe buck (rō′buk′), *n.* a male roe deer.

rood (rüd), *n.* 1. 40 square rods; one fourth

of an acre. 2. *Archaic.* the cross on which Christ died.

roy al ty (roi′əl tē), *n., pl.* **-ties.** share of the receipts or profits paid to an owner of a patent or copyright; payment for the use of any of various rights.

ru bi cund (rü′bə kund), *adj.* reddish; ruddy. [< L *rubicundus* < *rubere* be red]

rud dy (rud′ē), *adj.* 1. red. 2. healthy red: *ruddy cheeks.*

ru di men ta ry (rü′də men′tə rē or rü′də men′trē), *adj.* 1. to be learned or studied first; elementary. 2. in an early stage of development; undeveloped.

ruse (rüz or rüs), *n.* trick; stratagem. [< F *ruse* < *ruser* dodge]

sab bat i cal (sa bat′ə kl), *adj.* 1. of or suitable for the Sabbath. 2. of or for a rest from work.

sa dism (sā′diz əm or sad′iz əm), *n.* 1. kind of insanity in which a person enjoys hurting someone else. 2. an unnatural love of cruelty. [< F; from the Count (or Marquis) de *Sade,* who wrote of it]

sa dist (sā′dist or sad′ist), *n.* one affected with sadism.

sa lu bri ous (sə lü′brē əs), *adj.* healthful. [< L *salubris* < *salus* good health]

sal u ta tion (sal′yə tā′shən), *n.* 1. a greeting; saluting: *The man raised his hat in salutation.* 2. something uttered, written, or done to salute. You begin a letter with a salutation, such as "Dear Sir" or "My Dear Mrs. Jones."

sa lu ta to ri an (sə lü′tə tô′rē ən or sə lü′tə tō′rē ən), *n.* in American colleges and schools, the student who delivers the address of welcome at the graduation of a class. [Am.E]

sa lu ta to ry (sə lü′tə tô′rē or sə lü′tə tō′rē), *adj., n., pl.* **-ries.** —*adj.* expressing greeting; welcome. —*n.* an opening address welcoming guests at the graduation of a class. [Am.E]

sa lute (sə lüt′), *v.,* **-lut ed, -lut ing,** *n.* —*v.* 1. honor in a formal manner by raising the hand to the head, by firing guns, or by dipping flags: *We salute the flag every day at school. The soldier saluted the officer.* 2. meet with kind words, a bow, a kiss, etc.; greet. 3. make a bow, gesture, or the like to. 4. come to; meet: *Shouts of welcome saluted their ears.* 5. make a salute. —*n.* 1. act of saluting; sign of welcome, farewell, or honor. 2. position of the hand, gun, etc., in saluting. [< L *salutare* greet < *salus* good health] —**Syn.** *v.* 2. welcome.

salute

hat, āge, fär; let, ēqual, tėrm; it, īce; hot, ōpen, ôrder; oil, out; cup, pút, rüle; ch, child; ng, long; sh, she; th, thin; ₮H, then; zh, measure;

ə represents *a* in about, *e* in taken, *i* in pencil, *o* in lemon, *u* in circus.

< = from, derived from, taken from.

617

sam ite (sam′īt or sā′mīt), *n.* a heavy, rich silk fabric, sometimes interwoven with gold, worn in the Middle Ages.

sar don ic (sär don′ik), *adj.* bitter; sarcastic; scornful; mocking: *a fiend's sardonic laugh.* [< F < L < Gk. *Sardonios,* a supposed Sardinian plant that produced hysterical convulsions]

sat ur nine (sat′ər nīn), *adj.* gloomy; grave; taciturn. [< *Saturn;* those born under the planet's sign are supposed to be morose]

scape goat (skāp′gōt′), *n.* person or thing made to bear the blame for the mistakes or sins of others. The ancient Jewish high priests used to lay the sins of the people upon a goat (called the scapegoat) which was then driven out into the wilderness. [< *scape,* var. of *escape* + *goat*]

scourge (skėrj), *n., v.,* **scourged, scourg ing.** —*n.* 1. a whip. 2. any means of punishment. —*v.* 1. whip; punish. 2. trouble very much; afflict.

scru ple (skrü′pl), *n.* 1. a feeling of doubt about what one ought to do: *No scruple ever holds him back from prompt action.* 2. a feeling of uneasiness that keeps a person from doing something: *She has scruples about playing cards for money.*

scru pu lous (skrü′pyə ləs), *adj.* 1. having or showing a strict regard for what is right. 2. attending thoroughly to details; very careful: *A soldier must pay scrupulous attention to orders.*

scru ti nize (skrüt′n īz), *v.,* **-nized, -niz ing.** examine closely; inspect carefully: *The jeweler scrutinized the diamond for flaws.*

scul ler y (skul′ər ē or skul′rē), *n. Esp. Brit.* a small room where the dirty, rough work of a kitchen is done. [ult. < L *scutella,* dim. of *scutra* platter]

se pul chral (sə pul′krəl), *adj.* 1. of sepulchers or tombs. 2. of burial. 3. deep and gloomy; dismal; suggesting a tomb.

ser vile (sėr′vl), *adj.* 1. like that of slaves; mean; base: *servile flattery.* 2. of slaves; having to do with slaves: *a servile revolt, servile work.* 3. fit for a slave. 4. yielding through fear, lack of spirit, etc.: *An honest judge cannot be servile to public opinion.*

sex tain (seks′tān), *n.* a stanza having six lines. [< L *sextus* sixth < **sex** six]

sheathe (shēᴛн), *v.,* **sheathed, sheathing.** 1. put (a sword, etc.) into a sheath. 2. enclose in a case or covering: *mummy sheathed in linen, doors sheathed in metal.*

shoal (shōl), *n.* 1. place where the water is shallow. 2. sandbank or sand bar that makes the water shallow: *The ship was wrecked on the shoals.* —*adj.* shallow. —*v.* become shallow. [OE *sceald* shallow]

shut tle (shut′l), *n.* 1. instrument that carries the thread from one side of the web to the other in weaving. 2. instrument on which thread is wound. Shuttles are used in tatting (a kind of lacemaking).

sick le (sik′l), *n.* tool consisting of a short, curved blade on a short handle, used for cutting grass, etc.

sim per (sim′pər), *v.* smile in a silly, affected way. —*n.* a silly, affected smile. [cf. G *zimper* affected, coy]

si ne cure (sī′nə kyủr or sin′ə kyủr), *n.* an extremely easy job; position requiring little or no work and usually paying well.

sin ew y (sin′yə wē), *adj.* 1. having strong sinews; strong; powerful: *A blacksmith has sinewy arms.* 2. vigorous; forcible.

skein (skān), *n.* 1. a small, coiled bundle of yarn or thread. There are 120 yards in a skein of cotton yarn. 2. a confused tangle.

skep ti cal (skep′tə kl), *adj.* 1. of or like a skeptic; inclined to doubt; not believing easily. 2. questioning the truth of theories or apparent facts. —**Syn.** 1. doubting, incredulous, disbelieving, distrustful.

skirl (skėrl), *Scottish* and *British Dialect.* —*v.* of bagpipes, sound loudly and shrilly. —*n.* sound of a bagpipe. [< Scand. (dialectal Norwegian) *skrylla*]

slan der (slan′dər or slän′dər), *v.* talk falsely about.

slug (slug), *n.* a slow-moving animal like a snail, without a shell or with only a very small shell.

snag (snag), *n.* 1. tree or branch held fast in a river or lake. Snags are dangerous to boats. 2. any sharp or rough projecting point, such as the broken end of a branch.

sop (sop), *n.* 1. piece of food dipped or soaked in milk, broth, etc. 2. something given to soothe or quiet; bribe.

sou (sü), *n.* 1. a former French coin, worth 5 centimes or $^1/_{20}$ of a franc. 2. anything of little value.

sov er eign (sov′rən), *n.* king or queen; supreme ruler; monarch. —*adj.* 1. above all others; supreme; greatest: *Character is of sovereign importance.* 2. very excellent or powerful: *a sovereign cure for colds.* [< OF *soverain,* ult. < L *super* over]

spas mod ic (spaz mod′ik), *adj.* 1. having to do with spasms; resembling a spasm: *a spasmodic cough.* 2. sudden and violent, but brief; occurring very irregularly. 3. having or showing bursts of excitement. —**Syn.** 2. jerky, fitful, intermittent.

spawn (spôn), *v.* 1. produce eggs. 2. bring forth; give birth to.

spec ter (spek′tər), *n.* 1. ghost. 2. thing causing terror or dread.

spec tral (spek′trəl), *adj.* 1. of or like a specter; ghostly: *He saw the spectral form of the headless horseman.* 2. of or produced by the spectrum: *spectral colors.*

spin dling (spin′dling), *adj.* very long and slender; too tall and thin.

spoor (spủr), *n.* trail of a wild animal; track. —*v.* track by or follow a spoor. [< Dutch]

squall (skwôl), *n.* 1. a sudden, violent gust of wind, often with rain, snow, or sleet. 2. *Informal.* trouble. [cf. Swedish *skal-regn* sudden downpour of rain]

stac ca to (stə kä′tō), in music: —*adj.* with breaks between the successive tones; disconnected; abrupt. —*adv.* in a staccato manner. [< Ital. *staccato,* literally, detached]

stanch¹ (stänch or stanch), *v.* 1. stop or check the flow of (blood, etc.). 2. stop the flow of blood from (a wound).

stanch² (stänch or stanch), *adj.* 1. firm; strong: *stanch walls, a stanch defense.* 2. loyal; steadfast: *a stanch friend, a stanch supporter of the law.*

stand ard (stan′dərd), *n.* 1. anything taken as a basis of comparison; model: *Your work is not up to standard.* 2. flag, emblem, or symbol: *The dragon was the standard of China.* 3. an upright support: *The floor lamp has a long standard.*

stan za (stan′zə), *n.* group of lines of poetry, commonly four or more, arranged according to a fixed plan; verse of a poem. [< Ital. *stanza,* originally stopping place, ult. < L *stare* stand]

sten to ri an (sten tô′rē ən or sten tō′rē-ən), *adj.* very loud or powerful in sound.

ster e o type (ster′ē ə tīp′ or stir′ē ə -ling), *n.* a fixed form; something that never changes; convention.

stew ard (stü′ərd or styü′ərd), *n.* 1. man who manages another's property: *He is the steward of that great estate.* 2. man who takes charge of the food and table service for a club, ship, railroad train, etc. [OE *stigweard* < *stig* hall + *weard* keeper, ward]

stint (stint) *v.* 1. keep on short allowance; be saving or careful in using or spending; limit: *The parents stinted themselves of food to give it to their children.* 2. be saving; get along on very little. 3. *Archaic.* stop.

stip u late (stip′yə lāt), *v.,* **-lat ed, -lating.** arrange definitely; demand as a condition of agreement: *He stipulated that he should receive a month's vacation every year if he took the job.*

sto i cal (stō′ə kl), *adj.* like a stoic; self-controlled; indifferent to pleasure and pain. —*sto′i cal ly, adv.*

stra tum (strā′təm or strat′əm), *n., pl.* **stra ta** or **stra tums.** layer of material; especially, one of several parallel layers placed one upon another: *In digging the well, the men struck first a stratum of sand, then several strata of rock.*

stri dent (strī′dnt), *adj.* making or having a harsh sound; creaking; grating; shrill. [< L *stridens, -entis,* ppr. of *stridere* sound harshly]

strip ling (strip′ling), *n.* boy just coming into manhood; youth; lad. [< *strip* + *-ling*]

strop (strop), *n., v.,* **stropped, stropping.** —*n.* a leather strap used for sharpening razors. —*v.* sharpen on a strop. [ult. < L *stroppus* band < Gk. *strophos*]

sub ser vi ent (səb sėr′vē ənt), *adj.* 1. tamely submissive; slavishly polite and obedient; servile. 2. useful as a means to help a purpose or end; serviceable. [< L *subserviens, -entis,* ppr. of *subservire* < *sub-* under + *servire* serve]

suc cor (suk′ər), *n., v.* help; aid. [< OF *sucurs,* ult. < L *succurrere* run to help < *sub-* up (to) + *currere* run]

sump tu ous (sump′chủ əs), *adj.* costly; magnificent; rich: *The king gave a sumptuous banquet.* [< L *sumptuosus* < *sumptus* expense < *sumere* spend] —**Syn.** luxurious, lavish.

su per fi cial (sü′pər fish′əl), *adj.* 1. of the surface: *superficial measurement.* 2. on the surface; at the surface: *His burns were superficial and soon healed.* 3. concerned with or understanding only what is on the surface; not thorough; shallow: *Girls used to receive only a superficial education.* [< L *superficialis* < *superficies* surface < *super-* above + *facies* form]

sup pli ca tion (sup′lə kā′shən), *n.* 1. a supplicating. 2. a humble and earnest request or prayer.

sup pu rate (sup′yə rāt), *v.,* **-rat ed, -rat ing.** form pus; discharge pus; fester.

sur coat (sėr′kōt), *n.* an outer coat; especially, such a garment worn by knights over their armor.

sur e ty (shùr′ə tē), *n., pl.* **-ties.** 1. security against loss, damage, or failure to do something: *An insurance company gives surety against loss by fire.* 2. person who agrees to be responsible for another: *He was surety for his brother's appearance in court on the day set.* 3. Archaic. a sure thing; certainty.

sur mise (*v.* sər mīz′) guess: *We surmised that the delay was caused by some accident.*

sus cep ti ble (sə sep′tə bl), *adj.* 1. easily influenced by feelings or emotions; very sensitive: *Poetry appealed to his susceptible nature.* 2. **susceptible of, a.** capable of receiving, undergoing, or being affected by: *Oak is susceptible of a high polish.* **b.** sensitive to. 3. **susceptible to,** easily affected by; liable to; open to: *Vain people are susceptible to flattery.*

swad dle (swod′l), *v.* bind (a baby) with long, narrow strips of cloth; wrap tightly with clothes, bandages, etc.

ta bor (tā′bər), *n.* a small drum, used especially to accompany a pipe or fife. [< OF *tabour,* ult. < Persian *tabīr* drum]

tac it (tas′it), *adj.* 1. unspoken, silent: *a tacit prayer.* 2. implied or understood without being openly expressed: *His eating the food was a tacit confession that he liked it.* [< L *tacitus,* pp. of *tacere* be silent]

tack (tak), *n.* course of action or conduct: *He took the wrong tack to get what he wanted.*

taint (tānt), *n.* stain or spot; trace of decay, corruption, or disgrace.

tal is man (tal′is mən or tal′iz mən), *n.* 1. a stone, ring, etc., engraved with figures or characters supposed to have magic power; charm. 2. anything that acts as a charm.

tan gi ble (tan′jə bl), *adj.* 1. capable of being touched or felt by touch: *A chair is a tangible object.* 2. real; actual; definite: *The good will of a business is not so tangible as its buildings and stock.* [< LL *tangibilis* < *tangere* touch]

ta per (tā′pər), a very slender candle.

tarn (tärn), *n.* Brit. a small lake or pool in the mountains. [< Scand. *tjörn*]

taw dry (tô′drē), *adj.,* **-dri er, -dri est.** showy and cheap; gaudy. [ult. alteration of *St. Audrey,* from cheap laces sold at St. Audrey's fair in Ely, England] —**taw′dri ly,** *adv.* —**taw′dri ness,** *n.*

taw ny (tô′nē), *adj.,* **-ni er, -ni est.** brownish yellow: *A lion has a tawny skin.* [< OF *tané,* pp. of *taner* tan]

tem per ate (tem′pər it or tem′prit), *adj.* 1. not very hot and not very cold: *a temperate climate.* 2. self-restrained; moderate: *He spoke in a temperate manner, not favoring either side especially.* —**Syn.** 2. calm, dispassionate.

tem po ral (tem′pə rəl or tem′prəl), *adj.* 1. of time. 2. lasting for a time only. 3. of this life only. 4. not religious or sacred; worldly. [< L *temporalis* < *tempus* time] —**Syn.** 2. temporary, transient. 3. earthly, terrestrial.

te na cious (ti nā′shəs), *adj.* 1. holding fast: *the tenacious jaws of a bulldog, a person tenacious of his rights.* 2. stubborn; persistent: *a tenacious salesman.* 3. able to remember: *a tenacious memory.* 4. holding fast together; not easily pulled apart. —**te na′cious ly,** *adv.* —**Syn.** 2. obstinate. 3. retentive.

ten et (ten′it; *esp. Brit.* tē′nit), *n.* doctrine, principle, belief, or opinion held as true. [< L *tenet* he holds]

ten u ous (ten′yü əs), *adj.* 1. thin; slender. 2. not dense: *Air ten miles above the earth is very tenuous.* 3. having slight importance; not substantial. [< L *tenuis* thin] —**ten′u ous ly,** *adv.* —**ten′u ous ness,** *n.*

tes ti mo ny (tes′tə mō′nē), *n., pl.* **-nies.** 1. statement used for evidence or proof: *A witness gave testimony that Mr. Doe was at home at 9 p.m.* 2. evidence: *The pupils presented their teacher with a watch in testimony of their respect and affection.* 3. an open declaration or profession of one's faith. 4. Archaic. the Ten Commandments. 5. **testimonies,** *pl.* the laws of God; the Scriptures. [< L *testimonium* < *testis* witness] —**Syn.** 1,2. proof. See **evidence.**

thews (thüz), *n.pl.* 1. muscles. 2. sinews.

thrall (thrôl), *n.* 1. person in bondage; slave. 2. thralldom; bondage; slavery.

thwart (thwôrt), *v.* oppose and defeat; keep from doing something.

tilt (tilt), *v.* 1. slope; slant; lean; tip: *You tilt your head forward when you bow. This table tilts.* 2. rush, charge, or fight with lances. Knights used to tilt on horseback. 3. point or thrust (a lance).

tinct (tingkt), *Poetic.* —*adj.* tinged. —*n.* tint; tinge. [< L *tinctus,* pp.of *tingere* tinge]

tinc ture (tingk′chər), *n.* 1. solution of medicine in alcohol: *tincture of iodine.* 2. trace; tinge. 3. color; tint.

tip ple (tip′l), *v.,* **-pled, -pling,** *n.* —*v.* drink (alcoholic liquor) often. —*n.* an alcoholic liquor. [origin uncertain. Cf. Norwegian *tipla* drip, tipple]

to ga (tō′gə), *n.* 1. a loose outer garment worn by men of ancient Rome. 2. robe of office.

top o graph i cal (top′ə graf′ə kl), *adj.* of or having to do with topography. A topographical map shows mountains, rivers, etc.

tran si to ry (tran′sə tô′rē or tran′sə tō′rē), *adj.* passing soon or quickly; lasting only a short time.

hat, āge, fär; let, ēqual, tėrm;
it, īce; hot, ōpen, ôrder;
oil, out; cup, pùt, rüle;
ch, child; ng, long; sh, she;
th, thin; ᵺ, then; zh, measure;

ə represents *a* in about, *e* in taken,
i in pencil, *o* in lemon, *u* in circus.

< = from, derived from, taken from.

trans pose (trans pōz′), *v.* change the position or order of; interchange.

trav ail (trav′āl), *n.* 1. toil; labor. 2. trouble; hardship. 3. the pains of childbirth.

trel lis (trel′is), *n.* frame of light strips of wood or metal crossing one another with open spaces in between.

trem u lous (trem′yə ləs), *adj.* 1. trembling; quivering. 2. timid; fearful. —**Syn.** 1. shaking, vibrating.

trib une (trib′yün), *n.* 1. official in ancient Rome chosen by the plebeians to protect their rights and interests. 2. defender of the people. [< L *tribunus* < *tribus* tribe]

tri um vi rate (trī um′və rit or trī um′və rāt), *n.* 1. position or term of office of a triumvir. 2. government by three men together. 3. any association of three in office or authority. 4. any group of three.

triv et (triv′it), *n.* a stand or support with three legs or feet. Trivets are used over fires and under platters. [< L *tri-* three + OE *-fēte* footed]

trow el (trou′əl), *n.* 1. tool for spreading or smoothing plaster or mortar. 2. tool for taking up plants, loosening dirt, etc.

tym pa num (tim′pə nəm), *n., pl.* **-nums, -na** (-nə). 1. the eardrum. 2. the middle ear.

un can ny (un kan′ē), *adj.* strange and mysterious; weird: *The trees took uncanny shapes in the half darkness.* —**un can′ni ly,** *adv.* —**un can′ni ness,** *n.*

un couth (un küth′), *adj.* 1. awkward; clumsy; crude: *uncouth manners.* 2. unusual and unpleasant; strange: *The poor idiot made uncouth noises.* [OE *uncūth* < *un-*[1] + *cūth,* pp. of *cunnan* known] —**uncouth′ness,** *n.*

un e quiv o cal (un′i kwiv′ə kl), *adj.* clear; plain.

un kempt (un kempt′), *adj.* 1. not combed. 2. neglected; untidy. [< *un-* + OE *cembed* combed, pp. of *cemban* < *camb* comb]

un prec e dent ed (un pres′ə den′tid), *adj.* having no precedent; never done before; never known before. —**Syn.** unexampled, new.

un re lent ing (un′ri len′ting), *adj.* 1. not yielding to feelings of kindness or compassion; merciless. 2. not slackening or relaxing in severity or determination. —**un′re lent′ing ly,** *adv.* —**Syn.** 1. unyielding, obdurate, relentless.

unscrupulous

un scru pu lous (un skrü′pyə ləs), *adj.* not careful about right or wrong; without principles or conscience: *The unscrupulous boy cheated.* —**un scru′pu lous ly,** *adv.* —**un scru′pu lous ness,** *n.*

un seem ly (un sēm′lē), *adj.* not seemly; not suitable; improper. —*adv.* improperly; unsuitably. —**un seem′li ness,** *n.*

u surp (yü zėrp′ or yü sėrp′), *v.* seize and hold (power, position, authority, etc.) by force or without right: *The king's brother tried to usurp the throne.* [< L *usurpare,* ult. < *usu,* abl., through use + *rapere* seize]

van guard (van′gärd′), *n.* 1. soldiers marching ahead of the main part of an army to clear the way and guard against surprise. 2. the foremost or leading position. 3. leaders of a movement. [< OF *avant-garde* < *avant* before (< L *ab* from + *ante* before) + *garde* guard < Gmc.]

van quish (vang′kwish), *v.* conquer; defeat; overcome. [< OF *vencus,* pp. of *veintre* or < OF *vainquiss-,* stem of *vainquir,* both < L *vincere* conquer]

vaunt (vônt or vänt), *v., n.* boast. [< F < LL *vanitare* < *vanus* vain]

ven er a ble (ven′ər ə bl), *adj.* worthy of reverence; deserving respect because of age, character, or associations: *a venerable priest, venerable customs.* [< L *venerabilis* < *venerari* venerate]

ver dict (vėr′dikt), *n.* 1. the decision of a jury: *The jury returned a verdict of "Not guilty."* 2. decision; judgment. [< AF *verdit* < *ver* true (< L *verus*) + *dit,* pp. of *dire* speak < L *dicere*]

ver dure (vėr′jər), *n.* 1. fresh greenness. 2. a fresh growth of green grass, plants, or leaves. [< OF *verdure,* ult. < L *viridis* green]

ver min (vėr′mən), *n. pl. or sing.* 1. small animals that are troublesome or destructive. Fleas, lice, bedbugs, rats, and mice are vermin. 2. *Brit.* animals or birds that destroy game, poultry, etc. 3. a vile, worthless person or persons. [< OF *vermin,* ult. < L *vermis* worm]

verse (vėrs), *n.* 1. poetry; lines of words usually with a regularly repeated accent. 2. a single line of poetry. 3. a group of lines or short portion in poetry: *Sing the first verse of "America."* 4. type of poetry; meter: *blank verse, iambic verse.* 5. a short division of a chapter in the Bible. [late OE *vers* (replacing earlier *fers*) < L *versus,* originally, row, furrow < *vertere* turn around]

➤ **verse.** A full line or more of verse quoted in a paper should be lined off and written exactly as it is in the original. It should be indented from the left margin and, if very short, far enough not to leave a conspicuous blank at its right. No quotation marks are used.

vi car i ous (vī kar′ē əs or vi kar′ē əs), *adj.* 1. done or suffered for others: *vicarious work.* 2. felt by sharing in others' experience: *The invalid received vicarious*

pleasure from reading travel stories. 3. taking the place of another; doing the work of another: *a vicarious agent.* —**vi car′i ous ly,** *adv.*

vict ual (vit′l), *n., v.,* -**ualed, -ual ing** or *esp. Brit.* -**ualled, -ual ling.** —*n.* Usually, **victuals,** *pl. Informal* or *Dialect.* food.

vile (vīl), *adj.,* **vil er, vil est.** 1. very bad: *vile weather.* 2. foul; disgusting; obnoxious: *a vile smell.* 3. evil; low; immoral: *vile language.* 4. poor; mean; lowly: *the vile tasks of the kitchen.* [< OF < L *vilis* cheap]

vin di cate (vin′də kāt), *v.,* -**cat ed, -cat ing.** 1. clear from suspicion, dishonor, hint, or charge of wrongdoing, etc.: *The verdict of "Not guilty" vindicated him.* 2. defend successfully against opposition; uphold; justify: *The heir vindicated his claim to the fortune.* [< L *vindicare* < *vindex* defender] —**vin′di ca′tor,** *n.*

vin dic tive (vin dik′tiv), *adj.* 1. feeling a strong tendency toward revenge; bearing a grudge: *He is so vindictive that he never forgives anybody.* 2. showing a strong tendency toward revenge: *Vindictive acts rarely do much good.* [< L *vindicta* revenge] —**Syn.** 1, 2. revengeful, spiteful.

vis age (viz′ij), *n.* 1. face. 2. appearance. [< OF *visage* < *vis* face < L *visus* a look < *videre* see]

vis ta (vis′tə), *n.* 1. view seen through a narrow opening or passage: *The opening between the two rows of trees afforded a vista of the lake.* 2. such an opening or passage itself: *a shady vista of elms.* 3. a mental view: *Education should open up new vistas.* [< Ital. *vista,* ult. < L *videre* see]

vo li tion (vō lish′ən), *n.* 1. act of willing: *The man went away of his own volition.* 2. power of willing: *The use of drugs has weakened his volition.* [< Med.L *volitio, -onis* < L *volo* I wish] —**Syn.** 1. choice, decision.

vol u bil i ty (vol′yə bil′ə tē), *n.* 1. readiness to talk much; the habit of talking much. 2. great flow of words.

vouch safe (vouch sāf′), *v.,* -**safed, -saf ing.** be willing to grant òr give; deign (to do or give): *The proud man vouchsafed no reply when we spoke to him.* [original meaning "guarantee" to *vouch* for as *safe*]

waft (waft or wäft), *v.* 1. carry over water or through air: *The waves wafted the boat to shore.* 2. float. —*n.* 1. a breath or puff of air, wind, etc. 2. a waving movement.

wan (won), *adj.,* **wan ner, wan nest.** 1. pale; lacking natural color: *Her face looked wan after her long illness.* 2. looking worn or tired; faint; weak: *The sick boy gave the doctor a wan smile.* [OE *wann* dark]

wasp ish (wos′pish or wôs′pish), *adj.* 1. like a wasp; like that of a wasp. 2. bad-tempered; irritable. —**wasp′ish ly,** *adv.* —**wasp′ish ness,** *n.*

weal (wēl), *n. Archaic.* well-being; prosperity; happiness: *Good citizens act for the public weal.*

ween (wēn), *v. Archaic.* think; suppose; believe; expect. [OE *wēnan*]

weir (wir), *n.* 1. dam in a river. 2. fence of stakes or broken branches put in a stream or channel to catch fish. [OE *wer*]

wel ter (wel′tər), *v.* 1. roll or toss about; wallow. 2. lie soaked; be drenched. —*n.* 1. a rolling and tossing. 2. confusion; commotion.

wend (wend), *v.* **wend ed** or *(Archaic)* **went, wend ing.** 1. direct (one's way): *We wended our way home.* 2. go.

whelp (hwelp), *n.* 1. puppy or cub; young dog, wolf, bear, lion, tiger, etc. 2. a good-for-nothing boy or young man. —*v.* give birth to (whelps).

whet (hwet), *v.,* **whet ted, whet ting,** *n.* —*v.* 1. sharpen by rubbing: *whet a knife.* 2. make keen or eager; stimulate: *The smell of food whetted my appetite.* —*n.* 1. act of whetting. 2. something that whets. 3. appetizer.

wil y (wī′lē), *adj.* using subtle tricks to deceive; crafty; cunning; sly. —**Syn.** artful, subtle, designing, insidious.

wince (wins), *v.,* **winced, winc ing,** *n.* —*v.* draw back suddenly; flinch slightly: *The boy winced at the sight of the dentist's drill.* —*n.* act of wincing.

wist ful (wist′fəl), *adj.* 1. longing; yearning: *A child stood looking with wistful eyes at the toys in the window.* 2. pensive; melancholy. [< obsolete *wist* attentive (< *wistly* intently, of uncertain origin) + *-ful*]

with al (wiᴛн ôl′ or with ôl′), *Archaic.* —*adv.* with it all; as well; besides; also: *The lady is rich and fair and wise withal.*

wont (wunt or wōnt), *adj.* accustomed: *He was wont to read the paper at breakfast.* —*n.* custom; habit: *He rose early, as was his wont.* [originally pp., ult. < OE *wunian* be accustomed]

wrack (rak), *n.* 1. wreckage. 2. ruin; destruction. 3. seaweed cast ashore.

wrath ful (rath′fəl or räth′fəl), *adj.* feeling or showing wrath; very angry. —**Syn.** irate, furious, raging, incensed.

wrest (rest), *v.* 1. twist, pull, or tear away with force; wrench away: *The nurse bravely wrested the knife from the insane patient.* 2. take by force: *The usurper wrested the power from the king.* 3. twist or turn from the proper meaning, use, etc.

writhe (rīᴛн), *v.,* **writhed, writhed** or *(Obs. except Poetic)* **writh en** (riᴛн′ən), **writh ing.** 1. twist and turn; twist: *The snake writhed along the branch. The wounded man writhed in agony.* 2. suffer mentally; be very uncomfortable.

wroth (rôth or roth), *adj.* angry. [OE *wrāth*]

wrought (rôt), *v.* a pt. and a pp. of **work.** —*adj.* 1. made: *The gate was wrought with great skill.* 2. formed with care; not rough or crude. 3. manufactured or treated; not in a raw state. 4. of metals, formed by hammering.

zeph yr (zef′ər), *n.* 1. the west wind. 2. any soft, gentle wind; mild breeze. 3. a fine, soft yarn or worsted. [< L < Gk. *zephyros*]

zinc (zingk), *n.* a bluish-white metal very little affected by air and moisture.

Glossary of Literary Terms

Absurd, a term frequently used to describe the meaninglessness of life in today's world.

Alliteration, repetition of consonant sounds at the beginning of words or accented syllables.

Allusion, a brief, often indirect reference to a familiar person, place, event or work of art.

Anachronism, placing something at a time or place contrary to historical fact.

Anapest, three-syllable metrical *foot,* consisting of two unaccented syllables followed by an accented syllable.

Antagonist, a character or other force opposing the *protagonist.*

Aphorism, a short, pithy saying.

Apostrophe, a *figure of speech* in which an absent person, an abstract concept, or an inanimate object is addressed directly.

Assonance, repetition of vowel sounds.

Atmosphere, a prevading emotional quality developed largely through the handling of *setting.*

Autobiography, a biographical account of the writer's own life, or part of his life.

Ballad, a *narrative* song handed down in oral tradition, or a written poem which imitates the traditional ballad.

Biography, an account of a man's life and character written by another person.

Blank verse, unrhymed *iambic pentameter,* often written in sections of varying length, without regular *stanzaic* form.

Caricature, exaggeration of prominent features of appearance or character.

Characterization, techniques used by the writer in creating a character.

Classical, specifically, any part of the culture of the Greeks and Romans; generally, anything resembling that culture.

Cliché, an expression or phrase that has been so overused as to become trite.

Climax, dramatically, the decisive action, or turning point, in the plot.

Conceit, an elaborate and surprising *figure of speech* comparing two very dissimilar things.

Conflict, the interplay between opposing forces, a central element in most *plots.*

Connotation, the feeling or attitude associated with a word above and beyond its literal meaning, or *denotation.*

Convention, any artful *technique* widely accepted as appropriate to a given type of literature.

Couplet, verse form of two rhyming lines.

Dactyl, three-syllable metrical *foot,* consisting of one accented syllable followed by two unaccented syllables.

Denotation, the literal meaning of a word.

Dialect, the imitation of regional speech in writing, using altered, phonetic spelling.

Diacritical mark, an accent or other mark that indicates a change in pronunciation.

Diction, the particular choice of words made in a literary work. This choice considers both the *connotative* and the *denotative* meanings of a word and the level or type of usage.

Dimeter, line of verse containing two accented syllables.

Drama, a literary form designed for presentation in a theater by actors representing the characters.

Dramatic, a term used to describe any action presented directly, rather than told about, and often implying conflict and excitement.

Dramatic climax, the point of most intense excitement in a narrative. (See *climax.*)

Dramatic conventions, various devices in a play, impossible in real life, used by the dramatist and accepted by the audience.

Dramatic license, a dramatist's recognized freedom to change and adapt factual material.

Dramatic monologue, a poem in which the speaker addresses one or more persons who are present but whose replies are not recorded.

Dramatic point of view, *point of view* in which the author does not presume to know the thoughts and feelings of the characters; he simply reports what can be seen and heard. (Also known as the objective point of view.)

End rhyme, the rhyming of words at the ends of lines of verse. (Compare *internal rhyme.*)

End-stopped, a term applied to a line or couplet which contains a complete thought, thus necessitating the use of a semicolon or period at the end.

Epigram, a very short, highly polished verse or saying, usually ending with a witty turn.

Essay, a brief piece of nonfiction which presents a personal point of view either through informal discourse or formal analysis and argument.

Exposition, that part of a narrative, usually at the beginning, that sketches in the background of the characters and the action.

Farce, a type of *comedy* which depends for its effect on outlandish situations rather than on witty dialogue, plot and character.

Figurative language, language used in such a way as to force words out of their literal meanings and, by emphasizing their *connotations,* to bring new insight and feeling to the subject described.

Figures of speech, specific devices, such as *similes, metaphors, personifications,* for achieving the effects of *figurative language.*

Foil, a *character* in a narrative that sheds light on another, more important, character by a clearly implied comparison or contrast.

Foot, a metrical division consisting of one accented syllable and all unaccented syllables associated with it.

Foreshadowing, implication by the author of events to come later in the narrative.

Free verse, poetry written with *rhythm* and other poetic devices, but without *meter* or regular *rhyme scheme.*

Functional, a term applied to the elements in a work which are effectively related to other elements or to the unity of the work as a whole.

Hero, the *protagonist,* or central character of a narrative.

Heroine, the chief female *protagonist* of a narrative.

Hexameter, a verse line of six feet.

Iamb, two-syllable metrical *foot* consisting of one unaccented syllable followed by one accented syllable.

Imagery, vivid, concrete, sensory details.

Internal rhyme, rhyming of words within, rather than at the ends of, lines of verse.

Irony, a term used to describe a situation where two meanings are at odds. In verbal irony the actual meaning of a statement is opposite from what the statement says. Irony of situation is an occurrence which is contrary to what is expected.

Legend, a traditional story about a particular person, place, or deity, often popularly accepted as history.

Lyric, any short poem, or passage in a poem, intended mainly to express a state of mind or feeling.

Metaphor, a *figure of speech* involving an implied comparison.

Meter, any regular pattern of *rhythm.*

Monometer, a metrical line of one *foot.*

Mood, the prevailing emotional aura of a literary work.

Myth, a traditional tale of unknown authorship involving gods or other supernatural beings; often attempts to express some interpretation of an aspect of phenomenon of the natural world.

Narrative, any writing which concerns a series of happenings.

Narrator, the teller of a story, usually either a character or an anonymous voice used by the author.

Novelette, a piece of narrative prose fiction lying between the short story and the novel in both length and complexity; it contains from 20,000 to 50,000 words.

Octave, in its most general sense, an eight-line *stanza.*

Ode, a long *lyric* poem, formal in style and complex in form, often written for a special occasion.

Omniscient point of view, a *point of view* in which the author tells anything he wishes about the characters' thoughts and feelings.

Paradox, a statement that seems to be self-contradictory but which turns out to have valid meaning.

Parallel, a likeness, usually in pattern or structure (of a sentence, character, situation, etc.).

Parody, a kind of mimicking aimed particularly at making the style of an author ridiculous.

Pathos, the quality of literature which evokes pity.

Pentameter, metrical line of five *feet.*

Personal point of view, a *point of view* in which the person telling the story is one of the characters.

Personification, a *figure of speech* in which a thing or an abstraction is treated as a person.

Plot, the pattern of events in a narrative.

Poetry, the communication of feeling and thought through the carefully organized arrangement of words for their sounds, rhythm, and connotation, as well as their meaning.

Point of view, the relation assumed between the author and the characters in a narrative. This includes specifically the extent to which the narrator shows himself to be aware of what each character thinks and feels.

Properties, any kind of movable pieces used in staging a play.

Protagonist, the hero, or central character in a narrative.

Quatrain, verse *stanza* of four lines.

Quintain, verse *stanza* of five lines.

Realism, the tendency to emphasize the limitations that real life imposes on humanity through the use of very ordinary details, common, unheroic characters, and so forth.

Reversal, a point in a *plot* at which a force which had been dominant yields to another force.

Rhyme, exact repetition of sounds in at least the final accented syllables of two or more words.

Rhyme scheme, any pattern of *rhymes* in a stanza which is a conventional pattern or which is repeated in another stanza.

Rhythm, a series of stresses or emphases in a group of words, arranged so that the reader expects a similar series to follow.

Romance, a type of long narrative in verse or prose that originated in the Middle Ages. Its main elements are adventure, love, and magic.

Romanticism, a broad, often vague, term that may be applied to any work that tends to be unconventional, subjective, exotic, or idealistic.

Satire, the technique which employs wit to ridicule a subject, usually some social institution or human foible, with the intention to inspire reform.

Scansion, the marking off of a line of verse into *feet,* indicating the stressed and unstressed syllables.

Scene, the setting of an event in a narrative; or, the shortest major division of a play.

Setting, the represented place and time of an event in a literary work.

Sextain, verse *stanza* of six lines.

Short story, a brief, concentrated piece of narrative prose fiction.

Simile, a *figure of speech* involving a comparison made explicit by the use of the word *like* or *as.*

Single effect, the view that a short story should produce only one dominant emotional effect.

Sonnet, a *lyric* poem with a traditional form of fourteen *iambic pentameter* lines.

Stage directions, a dramatist's written directions as to how scenes are to be set and how the play is to be produced.

Staging, the method used in lighting the stage, designing the sets, and placing the actors in producing a play.

Stanza, the smallest division of a poem having a *rhyme scheme.*

Style, the distinctive handling of language by a given author.

Substitute meter or **substitute foot,** a metrical *foot* different from the one prevailing in a line or stanza.

Symbol, something relatively concrete, such as an object, action, character, or scene, which signifies something relatively abstract, such as a concept or an idea.

Symbolism, the use of symbols.

Technical climax, the main turning point in a narrative. (Compare *dramatic climax.*)

Tercet, a verse *stanza* of three lines.

Tetrameter, metrical line of four *feet.*

Theme, the main idea of a literary work.

Tragedy, in its most general sense, a term referring to any narrative writing in which the *protagonist* suffers disaster after a serious and significant struggle, but faces his downfall in such a way as to attain heroic stature.

Tragic flaw, a flaw of character in a tragic hero which precipitates his downfall.

Trilogy, three large, independent literary works, which, taken together, form a closely related sequence.

Trimeter, metrical line of three *feet.*

Trochee, metrical *foot* of one accented syllable followed by one unaccented syllable.

Type character, an uncomplicated, "flat" character having only a single, predictable motivation.

Verse. In its most general sense *verse* is a synonym for *poetry. Verse* may also be used to refer to poetry carefully composed as to rhythm and rhyme scheme, but of inferior literary value. Finally, *verse* may mean a single line of poetry.

Index of Authors and Titles